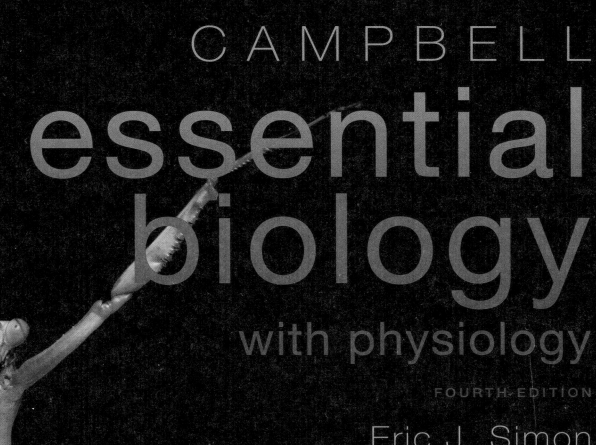

CAMPBELL

essential biology

with physiology

FOURTH EDITION

Eric J. Simon
New England College

Jean L. Dickey
Clemson University

Jane B. Reece
Berkeley, California

PEARSON

Boston Columbus Indianapolis New York San Francisco Upper Saddle River
Amsterdam Cape Town Dubai London Madrid Milan Munich Paris Montreal Toronto
Delhi Mexico City São Paulo Sydney Hong Kong Seoul Singapore Taipei Tokyo

Editorial Director: *Michael Young*
Editor-in-Chief: *Beth Wilbur*
Executive Director of Development: *Deborah Gale*
Executive Editor: *Chalon Bridges*
Senior Editorial Manager: *Ginnie Simione Jutson*
Development Editors: *Evelyn Dahlgren, Debbie Hardin,*
    Kim Krummel
Senior Supplements Project Editor: *Susan Berge*
Associate Editor: *Logan Triglia*
Editorial Assistant: *Rachel Brickner*
Director of Production: *Erin Gregg*
Managing Editor: *Michael Early*
Assistant Managing Editor: *Shannon Tozier*
Supplements Production Project Manager: *Jane Brundage*
Production Management and Composition:
    S4Carlisle Publishing Services
Illustrations: *Precision Graphics*
Design Manager and Interior Designer: *Marilyn Perry*
Cover Designer: *Riezebos Holzbaur Design Group*

Senior Photo Editor: *Donna Kalal*
Photo Researcher: *Kristin Piljay*
Manager, Rights and Permissions: *Beth Wollar*
Manufacturing Buyer: *Michael Penne*
Director of Media Development: *Lauren Fogel*
Senior Media Producer: *Jonathan Ballard*
Associate Media Project Manager (IRDVD): *Shannon Kong*
Associate Web Developer: *Pete Ratkevich*
Director of Editorial Content, MasteringBiology®: *Natania Mlawer*
Development Editor, MasteringBiology®: *Sarah Jensen*
Project Editor, Mastering Biology®: *Juliana Tringali*
Senior Mastering Media Producer: *Katie Foley*
Director of Marketing: *Christy Lesko*
Executive Marketing Manager: *Lauren Harp*
Executive Marketing Manager, Mastering: *Scott Dustan*
Marketing Manager: *Lauren Rodgers*
Text Printer: *Manufactured in the United States by RR Donnelley*
Cover Printer: *Lehigh-Phoenix Color/Hagerstown*

Cover Photo Credit: Igor Siwanowicz/Fame Pictures, Inc.; African Mega Mantis, *Plistospilota guineensis* male

Credits and acknowledgments borrowed from other sources and reproduced, with permission, in this textbook appear on page A-5.

Library of Congress Cataloging-in-Publication Data
Simon, Eric J. (Eric Jeffrey), 1967-
    Campbell essential biology with physiology / Eric J. Simon, Jane B. Reece, Jean L.
Dickey.--4th ed.
        p. cm.
    Includes index.
    ISBN-13: 978-0-321-77260-2
    ISBN-10: 0-321-77260-1
  1. Biology--Textbooks.   2. Physiology--Textbooks.   3. Plant physiology--Textbooks.
I. Reece, Jane B.   II. Dickey, Jean.   III. Title.
    QH308.2.C344 2013
    570--dc23

                                                                    2011038831

5 6 7 8 9 10—V011— 17 16 15

ISBN 13: 978-0-13-287906-4 (High School Binding)
ISBN 10: 0-13-287906-9 (High School Binding)

PEARSON

PearsonSchool.com/Advanced

Dorling Kindersley Limited,
80 Strand,
London WC2R ORL.

About the Authors

ERIC J. SIMON

is an associate professor in the Department of Biology and Health Science at New England College, in Henniker, New Hampshire. He teaches introductory biology to science majors and nonscience majors, as well as upper-level courses in genetics, microbiology, tropical marine biology, and careers in science. Dr. Simon received a B.A. in biology and computer science and an M.A. in biology from Wesleyan University and a Ph.D. in biochemistry from Harvard University. His research focuses on innovative ways to use technology to improve teaching and learning in the science classroom, particularly for nonscience majors. Dr. Simon is also a coauthor of *Campbell Biology: Concepts & Connections*, 7th Edition.

To Marshall, an intellectual role model, a source of data and wisdom, an organizational tour de force, a hardcore bicyclist, a bona fide Deadhead, a great father, and one cool dude

JANE B. REECE

has worked in biology publishing since 1978, when she joined the editorial staff of Benjamin Cummings. Her education includes an A.B. in biology from Harvard University (where she was initially a philosophy major), an M.S. in microbiology from Rutgers University, and a Ph.D. in bacteriology from the University of California, Berkeley. At UC Berkeley, and later as a postdoctoral fellow in genetics at Stanford University, her research focused on genetic recombination in bacteria. Dr. Reece taught biology at Middlesex County College (New Jersey) and Queensborough Community College (New York). During her 12 years as an editor at Benjamin Cummings, she played a major role in a number of successful textbooks. She is the lead author of *Campbell Biology*, 9th Edition, and *Campbell Biology: Concepts & Connections*, 7th Edition.

To my wonderful coauthors, who have made working on our books a pleasure

JEAN L. DICKEY

is a professor of biology at Clemson University in South Carolina. She had no idea that science was interesting until her senior year in high school, when a scheduling problem landed her in an advanced biology course. Abandoning plans to study English or foreign languages, she enrolled in Kent State University as a biology major. After receiving her B.S. in biology, she went on to earn a Ph.D. in ecology and evolution from Purdue University. Since joining the faculty at Clemson in 1984, Dr. Dickey has specialized in teaching nonscience majors, including a course designed for pre-service elementary teachers and workshops for in-service teachers. She also developed an investigative laboratory curriculum for general biology. Dr. Dickey is the author of *Laboratory Investigations for Biology*, 2nd Edition, and is a coauthor of *Campbell Biology: Concepts & Connections*, 7th Edition.

To my mother, who taught me to love learning, and to my daughters Katherine and Jessie, the twin delights of my life

NEIL A. CAMPBELL

(1946–2004) combined the inquiring nature of a research scientist with the soul of a caring teacher. Over his 30 years of teaching introductory biology to both science majors and nonscience majors, many thousands of students had the opportunity to learn from him and be stimulated by his enthusiasm for the study of life. While he is greatly missed by his many friends in the biology community, his coauthors remain inspired by his visionary dedication to education and are committed to searching for ever-better ways to engage students in the wonders of biology.

Detailed Contents

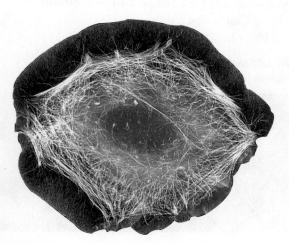

UNIT 2: Genetics

11 How Genes Are Controlled 198
CHAPTER THREAD: CANCER

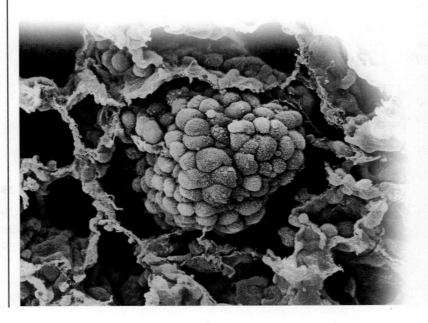

12 DNA Technology 218
CHAPTER THREAD: DNA PROFILING

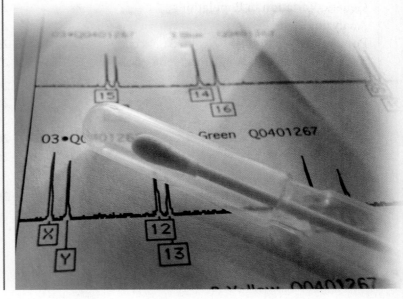

16 Plants, Fungi, and the Move onto Land 314

CHAPTER THREAD: PLANT-FUNGUS SYMBIOSIS

17 The Evolution of Animals 336

CHAPTER THREAD: HUMAN EVOLUTION

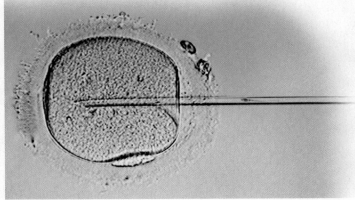

Each chapter is built around three
features connected by a unifying thread.

7 Photosynthesis: Using Light to Make Food

Grown for Biofuel

Capturing solar energy. Sunlight drives the process of photosynthesis, which plants use to produce sugars. We can then convert these sugars to other substances, such as ethanol, that can power our vehicles.

Other Exciting Chapter Thread Topics:

- Global Climate Change
- Athletic Endurance
- Steroid Abuse
- Controlling Your Weight
- Cancer
- DNA Profiling
- The Deadliest Virus
- Antibiotic-Resistant Bacteria

Chapter Thread

The chapter thread weaves a single compelling topic throughout the chapter. For example, here the thread is Green Energy, and you'll find this thread consistently at the beginning, middle, and end of each chapter.

 Green Energy BIOLOGY AND SOCIETY

Biofuels

What's old is sometimes new again. Throughout our early history, people relied on plants as our primary source of energy, burning wood to produce heat and light. Then, as societies became industrialized, wood was largely displaced as an energy source by fossil fuels such as coal, gas, and oil. But now, as fossil fuel supplies dwindle and concerns are raised about global climate change, spiking oil prices, and the need for a domestic energy source, scientists are researching better ways to harness energy from biomass (living material). Some researchers focus on burning plant matter directly (for example, wood pellet boilers), while others focus on using plant material to produce biofuels that can be burned.

There are several types of biofuels. Bioethanol is a type of alcohol (the same type found in alcoholic drinks) that is made from wheat, corn, sugar beets, sugarcane, and other food crops. Starch made naturally by plants is converted to glucose and then fermented to ethanol by microorganisms (such as single-celled algae). Bioethanol can be used directly as a fuel source in specially designed vehicles, but it is more commonly used as a gasoline additive that can increase fuel efficiency while decreasing vehicle emissions. You may have noticed a sticker on the gas pump that declares the percentage of ethanol in the gas you are pumping; most cars today run on a blend of 85% gasoline and 15% ethanol. Many car manufacturers are producing flexible-fuel vehicles that can run on any combination of gasoline and bioethanol.

Cellulosic ethanol is a form of bioethanol made through the same fermentation process as bioethanol, but its primary ingredient is cellulose from nonedible plant material such as wood or grass. Biodiesel, the most common biofuel in Europe, is made from plant oils such as recycled frying oil. Like bioethanol, it can be used on its own or as an additive to standard diesel.

Whatever its form, when we derive energy from biomass or biofuels, we are actually tapping into the energy of the sun, which drives the process of photosynthesis in plants. Biofuels are just one way that people take advantage of plants' ability to capture solar energy. The topic of this chapter is photosynthesis, the process whereby plants use light to make sugars from carbon dioxide—sugars that are food for the plant and the starting point for most of our own food. First, we'll examine some basic concepts of photosynthesis; then we'll look at the specific mechanisms involved.

 Green Energy BIOLOGY AND SOCIETY

BIOLOGY AND SOCIETY relates biology to your life and interests. For example, in this chapter, you'll learn about the types of biofuels, their sources, and their everyday uses.

 Green Energy THE PROCESS OF SCIENCE

THE PROCESS OF SCIENCE gives you real-world examples of how the scientific method is applied. For example, in this chapter, you'll learn how a researcher discovered which wavelengths of light are primarily responsible for photosynthesis.

 Green Energy EVOLUTION CONNECTION

EVOLUTION CONNECTION concludes the chapter by demonstrating how the theme of evolution runs throughout all of biology. For example, in this chapter, you'll learn how plants have adapted in different environments.

Orient yourself and find content

Find the chapter you want
Use the tabs on the left-hand page and quickly locate units by the color of the tabs.

CHAPTER 7
PHOTOSYNTHESIS: USING LIGHT TO MAKE FOOD

Locate study questions
Checkpoint questions in the margins help you assess your understanding of the content you just read.

☑ **CHECKPOINT**

Photosynthesis takes place within organelles called _____ using gases that are exchanged via pores called _____.

Answer: chloroplasts; stomata

Visual organizers
See important categories at a glance.

Identify the subject of the figure by glancing at the heading.

Spot the categories at once by looking at the subheadings.

The Basics of Photosynthesis

Photosynthesis is a process whereby plants, algae (which are protists), and certain bacteria transform light energy into chemical energy, using carbon dioxide and water as starting materials. The chemical energy produced via photosynthesis is stored in the bonds of sugar molecules. Organisms that generate their own organic matter from inorganic ingredients are called autotrophs (see Chapter 6). Plants and other organisms that do this by photosynthesis—photosynthetic autotrophs—are the producers for most ecosystems (**Figure 7.1**). This section presents an overview of photosynthesis, focusing on plants. Later, we'll take a closer look at some details of this process.

Chloroplasts: Sites of Photosynthesis

You have already learned that photosynthesis in plants and algae occurs within light-absorbing organelles called **chloroplasts** (see Chapter 4). All green parts of a plant have chloroplasts and can carry out photosynthesis. In most plants, however, the leaves have the most chloroplasts (about 500,000 per square millimeter of leaf surface) and are therefore the major locations of photosynthesis. Their green color is from **chlorophyll**, a light-absorbing molecule (a pigment) in the chloroplasts that plays a central role in converting solar energy to chemical energy.

Chloroplasts are concentrated in the interior cells of leaves (**Figure 7.2**), with a typical cell containing 30–40 chloroplasts. Carbon dioxide (CO_2) enters a leaf, and oxygen (O_2) exits, by way of tiny pores called **stomata** (singular, *stoma*, meaning "mouth"). In addition to carbon dioxide, photosynthesis requires water, which is absorbed by the plant's roots and transported to the leaves, where veins carry it to the photosynthetic cells.

Membranes within the chloroplast form the framework where many of the reactions of photosynthesis occur. Like a mitochondrion, a chloroplast has a double-membrane envelope. The chloroplast's inner membrane encloses a compartment filled with **stroma**, a thick fluid. Suspended in the stroma are interconnected membranous sacs called **thylakoids**. The thylakoids are concentrated in stacks called **grana** (singular, *granum*). The chlorophyll molecules that capture light energy are built into the thylakoid membranes. The structure of a chloroplast—with its stacks of disks—aids its function by providing a large surface area for the reactions of photosynthesis. ☑

▼ Figure 7.1 **A diversity of photosynthetic autotrophs.**

PHOTOSYNTHETIC AUTOTROPHS		
Plants (mostly on land)	**Photosynthetic Protists** (aquatic)	**Photosynthetic Bacteria** (aquatic)
Forest plants	Kelp, a large, multicellular alga	Micrograph of cyanobacteria

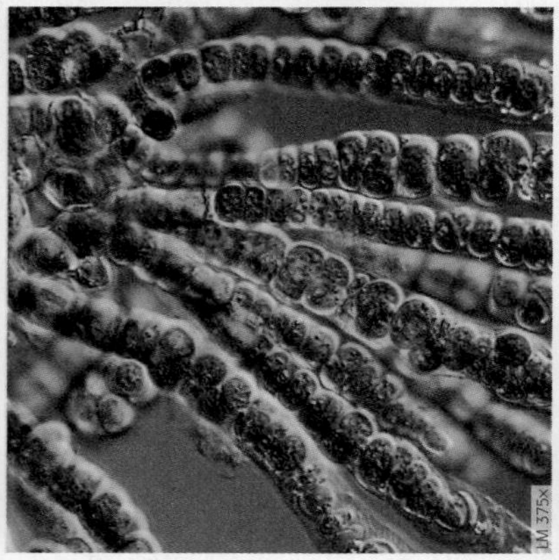

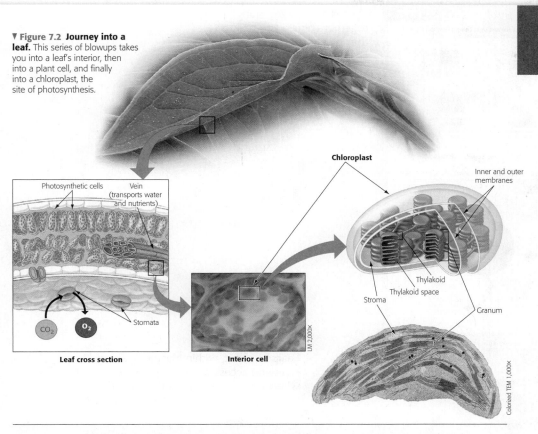

▼ **Figure 7.2 Journey into a leaf.** This series of blowups takes you into a leaf's interior, then into a plant cell, and finally into a chloroplast, the site of photosynthesis.

Photosynthetic cells
Vein (transports water and nutrients)

Chloroplast

Inner and outer membranes

Thylakoid

Thylakoid space

Stroma

Granum

CO₂   O₂

Stomata

Leaf cross section

Interior cell

LM 2,000×

Colorized TEM 1,000×

THE BASICS
OF PHOTOSYNTHESIS

Remember the main topic
Colored tabs at the top corner of each right-hand page help you to remember what you're studying.

The Simplified Equation for Photosynthesis

The following chemical equation, simplified to highlight the relationship between photosynthesis and cellular respiration, provides a summary of the reactants and products of photosynthesis:

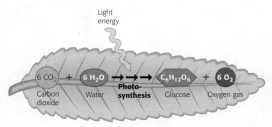

Light energy

6 CO₂ + 6 H₂O → → → C₆H₁₂O₆ + 6 O₂
Carbon dioxide   Water   **Photo-synthesis**   Glucose   Oxygen gas

Notice that the reactants of photosynthesis—carbon dioxide (CO_2) and water (H_2O)—are the same as the waste products of cellular respiration (see Figure 6.2). Also notice that photosynthesis produces what respiration uses—glucose ($C_6H_{12}O_6$) and oxygen (O_2). In other words, photosynthesis recycles the "exhaust" of cellular respiration and rearranges its atoms to produce food and oxygen. Photosynthesis is a chemical transformation that requires a lot of energy, and sunlight absorbed by chlorophyll provides that energy.

You learned in Chapter 6 that cellular respiration is a process of electron transfer. A "fall" of electrons from food molecules to oxygen to form water releases the energy that mitochondria can use to make ATP (see Figure 6.5). The opposite occurs in photosynthesis: Electrons are boosted "uphill" and added to carbon dioxide to produce sugar. Hydrogen is moved along with the electrons being transferred from water to carbon dioxide. This transfer of hydrogen requires the chloroplast to split water molecules into hydrogen and oxygen. The hydrogen is transferred along with electrons to carbon dioxide to form sugar. The oxygen escapes through stomata in leaves into the atmosphere as O_2, a waste product of photosynthesis. ☑

In what sense do photosynthesis and cellular respiration form a complementary cycle?

Intriguing questions
These questions help you relate core content to topics that pique your interest.

☑ **CHECKPOINT**
What molecules are the inputs of photosynthesis? What molecules are the outputs?

Answer: CO₂ and H₂O; glucose and O₂

109

Tools to help you study

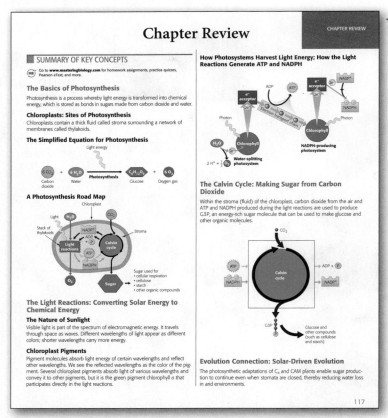

◀ **Chapter Review**

Words and images work together to help you review the key concepts of the chapter.

▼ **Pearson eText**

Pearson eText, within MasteringBiology™, gives you access to the text whenever and wherever you can access the Internet.

Highlight Function lets you highlight what you want to remember.

Annotation Function allows you to take notes.

Google®-based search function.

Zoom lets you zoom in and out for better viewing.

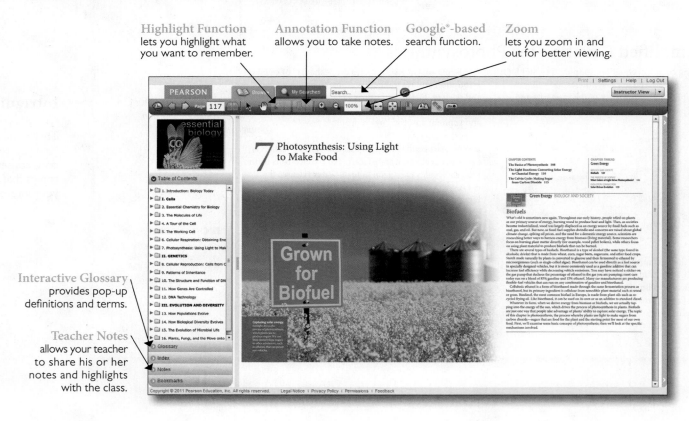

Interactive Glossary provides pop-up definitions and terms.

Teacher Notes allows your teacher to share his or her notes and highlights with the class.

MasteringBiology®

www.masteringbiology.com

The MasteringBiology online homework and tutoring system delivers self-paced tutorials that provide you with individualized coaching set to your teacher's class objectives. MasteringBiology helps you arrive prepared for class and offers additional study tools for you to use wherever you are!

BioFlix

BioFlix® Animation ▶

Dynamic 3-D animations help you to visualize and learn the toughest topics in biology covered in the coaching activity tutorial.

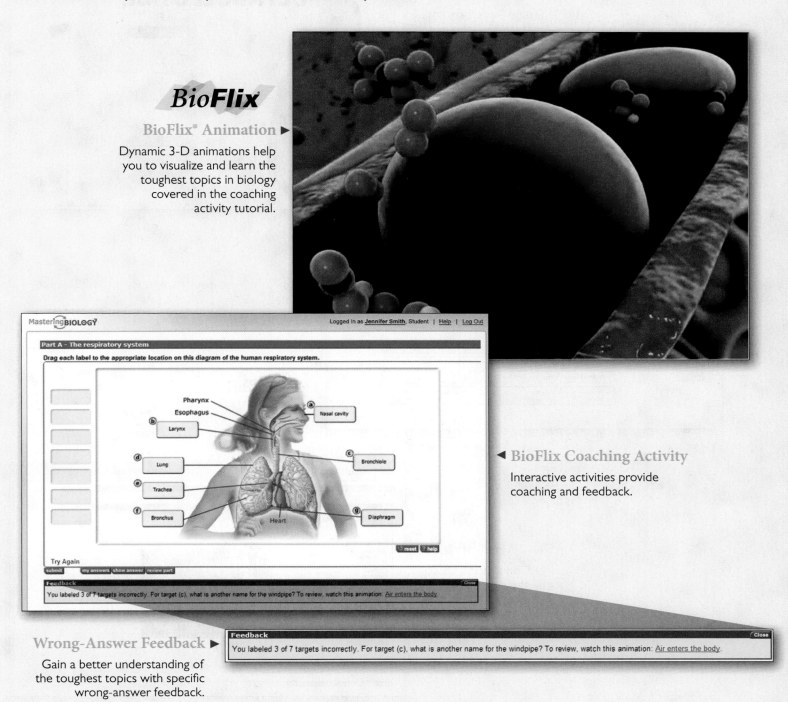

◀ **BioFlix Coaching Activity**

Interactive activities provide coaching and feedback.

Wrong-Answer Feedback ▶

Gain a better understanding of the toughest topics with specific wrong-answer feedback.

Feedback   Close

You labeled 3 of 7 targets incorrectly. For target (c), what is another name for the windpipe? To review, watch this animation: Air enters the body.

Author-Created Assignments

More than 100 new MasteringBiology® activities written
by the author team help you arrive prepared for class
and provide you with feedback and coaching.

**Video Tutor Sessions and ▶
MP3 Tutor Sessions**

Get help with key
concepts and vocabulary
with on-the-go tutorials
hosted by co-author
Eric Simon.

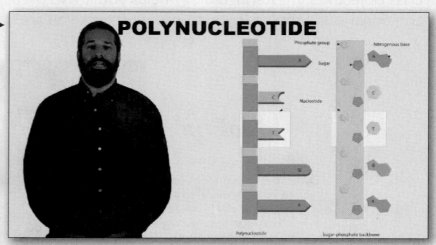

◀ **Building
Vocabulary
Activities**

Practice the new
vocabulary you are
learning in class.

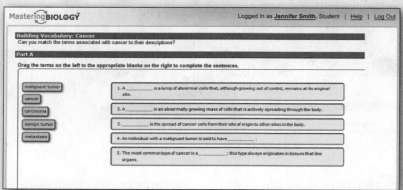

**Learning Through ▶
Art Activities**

Connect the art to
the concepts using
activities that enhance
the text's visual approach
to learning biology.

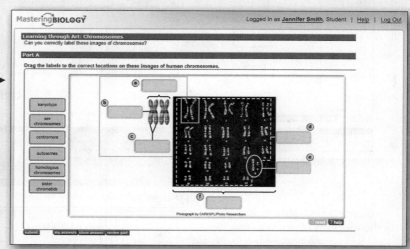

MasteringBiology®

www.masteringbiology.com

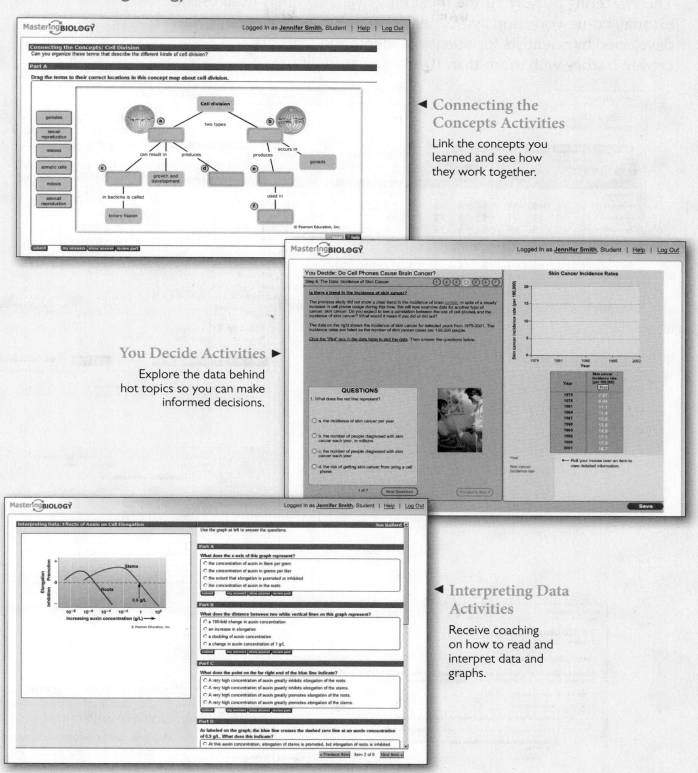

Connecting the Concepts Activities

Link the concepts you learned and see how they work together.

◄ You Decide Activities ►

Explore the data behind hot topics so you can make informed decisions.

Interpreting Data Activities

Receive coaching on how to read and interpret data and graphs.

How to Access MasteringBiology

Access to MasteringBiology is provided with textbook purchases. Students, ask your teachers for access. Teachers, see page xxvii for more information.

To the Teacher: MasteringBiology®

The Mastering platform is the most effective and widely used online tutorial, homework, and assessment system for the sciences. It was developed by scientists for science students and teachers and has a proven history with more than 10 years of student use.

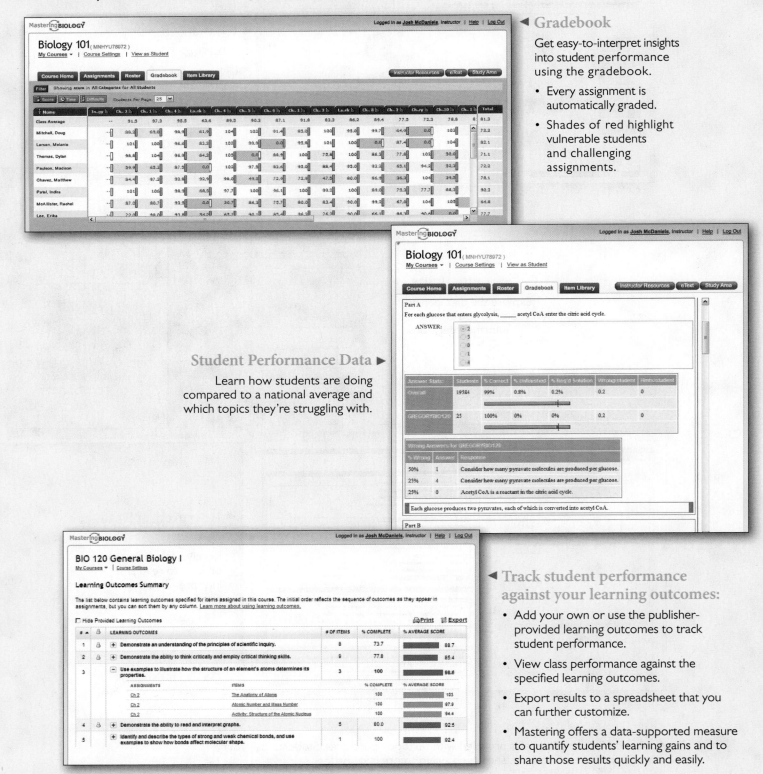

Gradebook

Get easy-to-interpret insights into student performance using the gradebook.

- Every assignment is automatically graded.

- Shades of red highlight vulnerable students and challenging assignments.

Student Performance Data ▶

Learn how students are doing compared to a national average and which topics they're struggling with.

◀ Track student performance against your learning outcomes:

- Add your own or use the publisher-provided learning outcomes to track student performance.

- View class performance against the specified learning outcomes.

- Export results to a spreadsheet that you can further customize.

- Mastering offers a data-supported measure to quantify students' learning gains and to share those results quickly and easily.

One-click Diagnostics ▶

Show where students are struggling or progressing.

Upon textbook purchase, students and teachers are granted access to MasteringBiology. High school teachers can obtain preview or adoption access for MasteringBiology in one of the following ways:

Preview Access

• Teachers can request preview access online by visiting PearsonSchool.com/Access_Request, using Option 2. Preview access information will be sent to the teacher via email.

Adoption Access

• With the purchase of this program a Pearson Adoption Access Card, with codes and complete instructions, will be delivered with your textbook purchase. (ISBN: 0-13-034391-9)

• Ask your sales representative for a Pearson Adoption Access Code Card. (ISBN: 0-13-034391-9)

OR

• By visiting PearsonSchool.com/Access_Request, using Option 3. Adoption access information will be sent to the teacher via email.

Preface

This is a wonderful time to teach and learn biology. Opportunities to marvel at the natural world and the life within it abound. It's difficult to peruse a news website without finding stories that touch on biology and its intersection with society. In addition, the world of pop culture is rich with books, movies, TV shows, comic strips, and video games that feature biological wonders and challenge us to think about important biological concepts and their implications. Although some people *say* that they don't like biology (or, more often, science in general), nearly everyone will admit to an inborn biophilia. After all, most of us keep pets, tend a garden, enjoy zoos and aquariums, or appreciate time spent outdoors. Furthermore, nearly everyone realizes that the subject of biology has a significant impact on his or her own life through its connections to medicine, biotechnology, agriculture, environmental issues, forensics, and myriad other areas. But despite the inborn affinity that nearly everyone has for biology, it can be a struggle for nonscientists to delve into the subject. Our primary goal in writing *Campbell Essential Biology with Physiology* is to help teachers motivate and educate the next generation of citizens by tapping into the inherent curiosity about life that we all share.

Goals of the Book

Although our world is rich with "teachable moments" and learning opportunities, the explosion of knowledge threatens to bury a curious person under an avalanche of information. "So much biology, so little time" is the universal lament of biology educators. Neil Campbell conceived of *Campbell Essential Biology with Physiology* as a tool to help teachers and students focus on the most important areas of biology. To that end, the book is organized into six core areas: cells, genes, evolution, ecology, animals, and plants. His vision, which we carry on and extend in this edition, has enabled us to keep *Campbell Essential Biology with Physiology* manageable in size without being superficial in developing the concepts that are most fundamental to understanding life. We take the "less is more" mantra in education today to mean fewer topics and more focused explanations, not content that is more diluted.

In countless conversations with teachers and students, we have noticed some important trends in how biology is taught. In particular, many teachers voice a desire to achieve three goals: (1) to engage students by relating the core content to their lives and the greater society; (2) to clarify the process of science by showing how it is applied in the real world; and (3) to demonstrate how evolution serves as biology's unifying theme. To help achieve these goals, every chapter of this book includes three important features. First, a chapter-opening section called Biology and Society highlights a connection between the chapter's core content and students' lives. Second, a section called The Process of Science describes how the scientific process has illuminated the topic at hand, using a classic or modern experiment as an example. Third, a chapter-closing Evolution Connection section relates the chapter to biology's unifying theme of evolution. To maintain a cohesive narrative for each topic, the content of each chapter is tied together with a unifying chapter thread, a relevant high-interest topic that is woven throughout the three chapter essays and throughout the entire chapter. In this way, the unifying chapter thread ties together the three pedagogical goals of the course using a topic that is compelling and relevant to students.

New to This Edition

We hope that this latest edition of *Campbell Essential Biology with Physiology* goes even further to help students relate the material to their lives, understand the process of science, and appreciate how evolution is the unifying theme of biology. To this end, we've added significant new features and content to this edition:

- **New high-interest topics** Every chapter in *Campbell Essential Biology with Physiology* has its own unifying chapter thread—a high-interest topic that helps to demonstrate the relevance of the chapter content. The chapter thread is incorporated into the three main essays of each chapter (Biology and Society, The Process of Science, and Evolution Connection) as well as throughout the chapter text. In this edition, we significantly updated many of these topics and essays. For example, Chapter 2 (Essential Chemistry for Biology) includes a new chapter-opening essay on the causes and impacts of droughts. Chapter 7 (Photosynthesis: Using Light to Make Food, a potentially difficult-to-relate-to topic for many students) has the new unifying chapter thread "Green Energy" and includes a new chapter-opening essay on biofuels. Chapter 23 (Circulation and Respiration) has the new unifying chapter thread "Athletic Endurance," along with three new essays in the chapter that emphasize the role of training on athletic performance, a topic of great interest to many students.

- **Updated content** As with every edition, we introduce timely, high-interest topics into the chapter content. For example, Chapter 6 (Cellular Respiration: Obtaining Energy from Food) mentions ethanol biofuels; Chapter 15 (The Evolution of Microbial Life) discusses the recent success that Craig Venter's team has had in "rebooting" one bacterial species with the lab-synthesized genome of another; Chapter 18 (An Introduction to Ecology and the Biosphere) notes the Deepwater Horizon oil spill; and Chapter 29 (The Working Plant) discusses the use of sunflowers to detoxify soil around the Fukushima nuclear disaster site.

- **Intriguing questions** Most people have questions about the subject of biology that are both relevant and highly illuminating. New to this edition, we have tapped into this innate curiosity by including a series of intriguing questions in large-type font within every chapter. Each chapter has from three to seven of these attention-grabbing questions, always placed alongside the text that answers them. We hope that as students read the chapter, they will be drawn in by such questions and motivated to read the surrounding content to discover the answers. For example, Chapter 3 (The Molecules of Life) asks, "Why does chocolate melt in your mouth but not in the package?" as a hook to discuss the different properties of saturated and unsaturated fats. In Chapter 11 (How Genes Are Controlled), the question "Can cloning reverse extinction?" relates the process of nuclear transplantation to a discussion of ethical questions that surround it. Chapter 13 (How Populations Evolve), poses the question "If your parents spend a lot of money on orthodontia for you, will your children inherit nice, straight teeth?" to make students consider the heritability of phenotypic traits. Chapter 18 (An Introduction to Ecology and the Biosphere) asks, "Are vampire devices consuming electricity while you sleep?" to draw students' attention to actions they can take to reduce their carbon footprints. We expect these questions to pique students' curiosity and deepen their engagement with the content.

- **MasteringBiology™ updates** Many teachers wish to encourage and assess student learning outside the classroom. To this end, we have created a new version of MasteringBiology that features more than 100 new interactive activities: Building Vocabulary exercises that ask students to place key terms within sentences and paragraphs, Learning Through Art activities that help students learn through labeling of important illustrations, Interpreting Graphs and YouDecide exercises that challenge students to assess quantitative information in ways that promote critical thinking, and Connecting the Concepts activities that help students see the relationship between different content areas. To make it easier for teachers to incorporate MasteringBiology into their classes, we have included a prebuilt course (SimonBiology: Bio-1010) that includes multiple assignments for each chapter. Each assignment is a mix of multimedia, interactive, and multiple-choice questions, which take between 20 and 40 minutes to complete. For each chapter, at least one assignment is written as pre-class preparation, and at least one more is intended as an applications-oriented summative assessment. Teachers can copy the entire course (and then simply change due dates to very quickly deploy the course) or pick and choose individual assignments. In addition, there are several new ways of assessing student achievement in key content areas in MasteringBiology,

including an Evolution Quiz that enables the teacher to track assumptions and measure learning gains and remedial exercises that can help students who struggle with the chemistry or math.

- **Teaching the issues** Many educators, including the authors, like to use current events to demonstrate the relevance of core content to students' lives. For this edition of *Campbell Essential Biology with Physiology,* we have created a series of PowerPoint presentations that focus on important issues such as cancer, HIV, and global climate change. Each PowerPoint presentation topic has an associated MasteringBiology homework assignment that can be used to demonstrate learning gains, check comprehension, and root out misconceptions.

- **Instructor Exchange** We know that educators often struggle to find new ways to engage and excite students, but many lack opportunities for interaction with like-minded colleagues. To tap into the tremendous wealth of talent that exists among biology educators, we have created an Instructor Exchange blog and website (available through the Instructor Resources area within MasteringBiology) as a means of discussing and distributing proven strategies from the classroom. We invite teachers to view the site, search for activities that can help their students, and contribute their own ideas.

- **Demonstrating learning outcomes** Teachers are often asked to demonstrate fulfillment of the learning outcomes that have been established for their class. The latest version of MasteringBiology greatly simplifies this process by keying individual questions and activities to one or more prewritten chapter-specific learning outcomes. In addition, teachers can add their own learning outcomes and associate them with specific tasks. Teachers can use the learning outcomes feature to generate a report that shows how student participation in MasteringBiology has fulfilled the goals established by these learning outcomes, allowing each teacher to assess student completion of the designated outcomes with greater ease.

Attitudes about science and scientists are often shaped by a single required science class—*this* class. We hope to tap into the innate appreciation of nature we all share and nurture this affection into a genuine love of biology. In this spirit, we hope that this textbook and its supplements will encourage all readers to make biological perspectives a part of their personal worldviews. Please let us know how we are doing and how we can improve the next edition of *Campbell Essential Biology with Physiology*.

ERIC SIMON
Department of Biology and Health Science
New England College
Henniker, NH 03242
esimon@nec.edu

JEAN DICKEY
Department of Biology
Clemson University
Clemson, SC 29634
dickeyj@clemson.edu

JANE REECE
C/O Pearson Education
1301 Sansome Street
San Francisco, CA 94111
JaneReece@cal.berkeley.edu

Acknowledgments

Throughout our time writing *Campbell Essential Biology with Physiology*, the author team has had the great fortune of collaborating with an extremely talented group of publishing professionals and educators. Although the responsibility for any shortcomings lies solely with us, the merits of the book and its supplements reflect the contributions of a great many dedicated colleagues.

First and foremost, we must acknowledge our huge debt to Neil Campbell, the original author of this book and a source of ongoing inspiration for each of us. Although this edition has been carefully and thoroughly revised—to update its science, its connections to students' lives, its pedagogy, and its currency—it remains infused with Neil's founding vision and his commitment to share biology with introductory students.

This book could not have been completed without the efforts of the *Campbell Essential Biology with Physiology* team at Pearson Science. The leading visionary of that team remains executive editor Chalon Bridges. All of us are continually inspired by Chalon's limitless positive energy, clear vision, and unwavering dedication to the nonmajors course, its students, and its instructors. The book team is lucky to be supported by the entire Pearson Science executive team. We are grateful to Linda Davis, president of Pearson Math and Science, and Paul Corey, president of Pearson Science, for the leadership they provide to the entire company. Further guidance was provided by editorial director Michael Young, editor-in-chief Beth Wilbur, executive director of development Deborah Gale, director of production Erin Gregg, and director of media development Lauren Fogel. All Pearson Science authors benefit from such supportive leadership.

It is no exaggeration to say that the fingerprints of the best editorial team in the industry appear on every page of this book. In dealing with the complexities of creating this book, the authors were masterfully and kindly guided by senior editorial manager Ginnie Simione Jutson. Our three development editors—Evelyn Dahlgren, Debbie Hardin, and Kim Krummel—worked tirelessly to hone the words that convey our love of biology. We owe this editorial team—including the wonderfully capable and friendly editorial assistant Rachel Brickner—a deep debt of gratitude for their talents, hard work, and seemingly limitless patience.

Once we formulated our words and images, the production and manufacturing teams transformed them into the book you hold in your hands. Assistant managing editor Shannon Tozier and managing editor Mike Early oversaw the production process and kept everyone and everything on track (a task that is much more daunting than it may sound). We hope you will agree that every edition of *Campbell Essential Biology with Physiology* is distinguished by unique and beautiful photography. For that we thank senior photo editor Donna Kalal and photo researcher Kristin Piljay, who constantly dazzle us with their keen ability to locate stunning images.

For the production and composition of the book, we thank senior project editor Emily Bush of S4Carlisle Publishing Services, whose professionalism and commitment to the quality of the finished product is visible throughout. The authors owe much to copyeditor Janet Greenblatt and proofreader Pete Shanks for polishing our words and making us seem like better writers. We thank design manager Marilyn Perry and the artists at Precision Graphics for developing the beautiful interior design and illustrations. The striking cover on this book can be credited to the cover designers at Riezebos Holzbaur Design Group. We also thank permissions editors Sue Ewing and Beth Keister and permissions manager Beth Wollar for keeping us on the straight and narrow. In the final stages of production, the talents of manufacturing buyer Michael Penne shone.

Most instructors view the textbook as just one piece of the learning puzzle. Filling in the gaps are this book's supplements and media. We are lucky to have a *Campbell Essential Biology with Physiology* supplements team that is fully committed to the core goals of accuracy and readability. Senior supplements project editor Susan Berge, with assistance from associate editor Logan Triglia, expertly coordinated the supplements, a difficult task given their number and variety; and production supervisor Jane Brundage handled the production of these materials (no small feat!). We also thank associate media project manager Shannon Kong for her work on the excellent Instructor Resources DVD set that accompanies the text.

We owe particular gratitude to the supplements authors, especially the indefatigable and eagle-eyed Ed Zalisko, of Blackburn College, who wrote the Instructor Guide and the PowerPoint® Lectures; the highly skilled and multitalented Tom Kennedy, of Central New Mexico Community College, who revised the Quiz Shows and Clicker questions and contributed to the Instructor Guide; Cindy Klevickis, of James Madison University, who worked on the Quizzes; and Jennifer Yeh, who helped with the exhaustive revision of the Test Bank. Kelly Hogan, of the University of North Carolina Chapel Hill, created the Instructor Exchange and brought her creativity and tremendous teaching talent to every aspect of the site. Jean DeSaix, of the University of North Carolina Chapel Hill; Jennifer Katcher, of Pima College; Calvin Young, of Fullerton College; and Lisa Urry, of Mills College, carefully crafted the Evolution Quiz. The author team is grateful for the hard work, talent, and teaching experience of these contributors. Thank you, all!

We wish to thank the talented group of publishing professionals who worked on the comprehensive media program that accompanies *Campbell Essential Biology with Physiology*, starting with director of media strategy Stacy Treco. The team members dedicated to MasteringBiology™ are true "game changers" in the field of biology education and are led by director of editorial content Natania Mlawer and developmental editor Sarah Jensen. We thank senior media producer Jonathan Ballard for exhibiting the Zen-like patience necessary to bring our collective vision to fruition. Vital contributions were also made by project editor Juliana Tringali, senior media producer Katie Foley, and associate Web developer Pete Ratkevich.

As educators and writers, we are very lucky to have a crack marketing team. Director of marketing Christy Lesko, executive marketing manager Lauren Harp, and marketing manager Lauren Rodgers seemed to be everywhere at once as they helped us achieve our authorial goals by keeping us constantly focused on the needs of students and instructors. For their amazing efforts, we also thank executive marketing manager Scott Dustan, creative director Lillian Carr, copywriter supervisor Jane Campbell, copywriter Jessica Perry, and designer Jessica Tree.

We also thank the Pearson Science sales reps, district/regional managers, and product specialists for representing *Campbell Essential Biology with Physiology* on campuses. These representatives are our lifeline to the greater educational community, telling us what you like (and don't like) about this book and the accompanying supplements and media. Their enthusiasm for helping students makes them not only ideal ambassadors but also our partners in education.

Eric Simon would like to thank his colleagues at New England College for their support and for providing a model of excellence in education. Eric would also like to acknowledge the contributions of Jim Newcomb for lending his keen eye for accuracy; Elyse Carter Vosen for providing much-needed social context; Jamey Barone for her sage sensitivity; and Amanda Marsh for her expert eye, sharp attention to detail, tireless commitment, constant support, compassion, and wisdom.

At the end of these acknowledgments, you'll find a list of the many instructors who provided valuable information about their courses, reviewed chapters, and/or conducted class tests of *Campbell Essential Biology with Physiology* with their students. All of our best ideas spring from the classroom, so we thank them for their efforts and support.

Most of all, we thank our families, friends, and colleagues, who continue to tolerate our obsession with doing our best for science education.

ERIC SIMON, JEAN DICKEY, JANE REECE

REVIEWERS OF THIS EDITION

Megan E. Anduri
California State University, Fullerton

Maitreyee Chandra
Diablo Valley College

Renee L. Engle-Goodner
Merritt College

Angela M. Foster
Wake Technical Community College

Brandon Lee Foster
Wake Technical Community College

Wendy Jean Garrison
University of Mississippi

Tamar L. Goulet
University of Mississippi

Robert A. Holmes
Hutchinson Community College

Scott Johnson
Wake Technical Community College

Lisa Maranto
Prince George's Community College

Maryanne Menvielle
California State University, Fullerton

Andrew Miller
Thomas University

Dawn Michelle Rogers
Austin Peay State University

Pamela Sandstrom
University of Nevada, Reno

Susmita Sengupta
City College of San Francisco

Michael Anthony Thornton
Florida Agriculture and Mechanical University

Leonard Vincent
Fullerton College

Daryle Waechter-Brulla
University of Wisconsin, Whitewater

Sean E. Walker
California State University, Fullerton

Arthur C. Washington
Florida Agriculture and Mechanical University

Bethany Williams
California State University, Fullerton

Jo Wen Wu
Fullerton College

Calvin Young
Fullerton College

REVIEWERS OF PREVIOUS EDITIONS

Marilyn Abbott
Lindenwood College

Tammy Adair
Baylor University

Felix O. Akojie
Paducah Community College

Shireen Alemadi
Minnesota State University, Moorhead

William Sylvester Allred, Jr.
Northern Arizona University

Estrella Z. Ang
University of Pittsburgh

David Arieti
Oakton Community College

C. Warren Arnold
Allan Hancock Community College

Mohammad Ashraf
Olive-Harvey College

Heather Ashworth
Utah Valley University

Bert Atsma
Union County College

Yael Avissar
Rhode Island College

Barbara J. Backley
Elgin Community College

Gail F. Baker
LaGuardia Community College

Neil Baker
Ohio State University

Kristel K. Bakker
Dakota State University

Andrew Baldwin
Mesa Community College

Linda Barham
Meridian Community College

Charlotte Barker
Angelina College

Verona Barr
Heartland Community College

S. Rose Bast
Mount Mary College

Sam Beattie
California State University, Chico

Rudi Berkelhamer
University of California, Irvine

Penny Bernstein
Kent State University, Stark Campus

Suchi Bhardwaj
Winthrop University

Donna H. Bivans
East Carolina University

Andrea Bixler
Clarke College

Brian Black
Bay de Noc Community College

Allan Blake
Seton Hall University

Karyn Bledsoe
Western Oregon University

Judy Bluemer
Morton College

Sonal Blumenthal
University of Texas at Austin

Lisa Boggs
Southwestern Oklahoma State University

Dennis Bogyo
Valdosta State University

David Boose
Gonzaga University

Virginia M. Borden
University of Minnesota, Duluth

James Botsford
New Mexico State University

Cynthia Bottrell
Scott Community College

Richard Bounds
Mount Olive College

Cynthia Boyd
Hawkeye Community College

Robert Boyd
Auburn University

B. J. Boyer
Suffolk County Community College

Mimi Bres
Prince George's Community College

Patricia Brewer
University of Texas at San Antonio

Jerald S. Bricker
Cameron University

Carol A. Britson
University of Mississippi

George M. Brooks
Ohio University, Zanesville

Janie Sue Brooks
Brevard College

Steve Browder
Franklin College

Evert Brown
Casper College

Mary H. Brown
Lansing Community College

Richard D. Brown
Brunswick Community College

Steven Brumbaugh
Green River Community College

Joseph C. Bundy
University of North Carolina at Greensboro

Carol T. Burton
Bellevue Community College

Rebecca Burton
Alverno College

Warren R. Buss
University of Northern Colorado

Wilbert Butler
Tallahassee Community College

Miguel Cervantes-Cervantes
Lehman College, City University of New York

Bane Cheek
Polk Community College

Thomas F. Chubb
Villanova University

Reggie Cobb
Nash Community College

Pamela Cole
Shelton State Community College

William H. Coleman
University of Hartford

Jay L. Comeaux
McNeese State University

James Conkey
Truckee Meadows Community College

Karen A. Conzelman
Glendale Community College

Ann Coopersmith
Maui Community College

Erica Corbett
Southeastern Oklahoma State University

James T. Costa
Western Carolina University

Pat Cox
University of Tennessee, Knoxville

Laurie-Ann Crawford
Hawkeye Community College

Pradeep M. Dass
Appalachian State University

Paul Decelles
Johnson County Community College

Galen DeHay
Tri County Technical College

Cynthia L. Delaney
University of South Alabama

Jean DeSaix
University of North Carolina at Chapel Hill

Elizabeth Desy
Southwest State University

Edward Devine
Moraine Valley Community College

Dwight Dimaculangan
Winthrop University

Deborah Dodson
Vincennes Community College

Diane Doidge
Grand View College

Don Dorfman
Monmouth University

Richard Driskill
Delaware State University

Lianne Drysdale
Ozarks Technical Community College

Terese Dudek
Kishawaukee College

Shannon Dullea
North Dakota State College of Science

David A. Eakin
Eastern Kentucky University

Brian Earle
Cedar Valley College

Ade Ejire
Johnston Community College

Dennis G. Emery
Iowa State University

Virginia Erickson
Highline Community College

Carl Estrella
Merced College

Marirose T. Ethington
Genesee Community College

Paul R. Evans
Brigham Young University

Zenephia E. Evans
Purdue University

Jean Everett
College of Charleston

Dianne M. Fair
Florida Community College at Jacksonville

Joseph Faryniarz
Naugatuck Valley Community College

Phillip Fawley
Westminster College

Lynn Fireston
Ricks College

Jennifer Floyd
Leeward Community College

Dennis M. Forsythe
The Citadel

Brandon Foster
Wake Technical Community College

Carl F. Friese
University of Dayton

Suzanne S. Frucht
Northwest Missouri State University

Edward G. Gabriel
Lycoming College

Anne M. Galbraith
University of Wisconsin, La Crosse

Kathleen Gallucci
Elon University

Gregory R. Garman
Centralia College

Gail Gasparich
Towson University

Kathy Gifford
Butler County Community College

Sharon L. Gilman
Coastal Carolina University

Mac Given
Neumann College

Patricia Glas
The Citadel

Ralph C. Goff
Mansfield University

Marian R. Goldsmith
University of Rhode Island

Andrew Goliszek
North Carolina Agricultural and Technical State University

Tamar Liberman Goulet
University of Mississippi

Curt Gravis
Western State College of Colorado

Larry Gray
Utah Valley State College

Tom Green
West Valley College

Robert S. Greene
Niagara University

Ken Griffin
Tarrant County Junior College

Denise Guerin
Santa Fe Community College

Paul Gurn
Naugatuck Valley Community College

Peggy J. Guthrie
University of Central Oklahoma

Henry H. Hagedorn
University of Arizona

Blanche C. Haning
Vance-Granville Community College

Laszlo Hanzely
Northern Illinois University

Reba Harrell
Hinds Community College

Sherry Harrel
Eastern Kentucky University

Frankie Harris
Independence Community College

Lysa Marie Hartley
Methodist College

Janet Haynes
Long Island University

Michael Held
St. Peter's College

Consetta Helmick
University of Idaho

J. L. Henriksen
Bellevue University

Michael Henry
Contra Costa College

Linda Hensel
Mercer University

Jana Henson
Georgetown College

James Hewlett
Finger Lakes Community College

Richard Hilton
Towson University

Juliana Hinton
McNeese State University

Phyllis C. Hirsch
East Los Angeles College

W. Wyatt Hoback
University of Nebraska at Kearney

Elizabeth Hodgson
York College of Pennsylvania

A. Scott Holaday
Texas Tech University

R. Dwain Horrocks
Brigham Young University

Howard L. Hosick
Washington State University

Carl Huether
University of Cincinnati

Celene Jackson
Western Michigan University

John Jahoda
Bridgewater State College

Dianne Jennings
Virginia Commonwealth University

Richard J. Jensen
Saint Mary's College

Tari Johnson
Normandale Community College

Tia Johnson
Mitchell Community College

Greg Jones
Santa Fe Community College

John Jorstad
Kirkwood Community College

Tracy L. Kahn
University of California, Riverside

Robert Kalbach
Finger Lakes Community College

Mary K. Kananen
Pennsylvania State University, Altoona

Thomas C. Kane
University of Cincinnati

Arnold J. Karpoff
University of Louisville

John M. Kasmer
Northeastern Illinois University

Valentine Kefeli
Slippery Rock University

Dawn Keller
Hawkeye College

John Kelly
Northeastern University

Cheryl Kerfeld
University of California, Los Angeles

Henrik Kibak
California State University, Monterey Bay

Kerry Kilburn
Old Dominion University

Joyce Kille-Marino
College of Charleston

Peter King
Francis Marion University

Peter Kish
Oklahoma School of Science and Mathematics

Robert Kitchin
University of Wyoming

Cindy Klevickis
James Madison University

Richard Koblin
Oakland Community College

H. Roberta Koepfer
Queens College

Michael E. Kovach
Baldwin-Wallace College

Jocelyn E. Krebs
University of Alaska, Anchorage

Ruhul H. Kuddus
Utah Valley State College

Nuran Kumbaraci
Stevens Institute of Technology

Holly Kupfer
Central Piedmont Community College

Gary Kwiecinski
The University of Scranton

Roya Lahijani
Palomar College

James V. Landrum
Washburn University

Lynn Larsen
Portland Community College

Brenda Leady
University of Toledo

Siu-Lam Lee
University of Massachusetts, Lowell

Thomas P. Lehman
Morgan Community College

William Leonard
Central Alabama Community College

Shawn Lester
Montgomery College

Leslie Lichtenstein
Massasoit Community College

Barbara Liedl
Central College

Harvey Liftin
Broward Community College

David Loring
Johnson County Community College

Eric Lovely
Arkansas Tech University

Lewis M. Lutton
Mercyhurst College

Maria P. MacWilliams
Seton Hall University

Mark Manteuffel
St. Louis Community College

Lisa Maranto
Prince George's Community College

Michael Howard Marcovitz
Midland Lutheran College

Angela M. Mason
Beaufort County Community College

Roy B. Mason
Mt. San Jacinto College

John Mathwig
College of Lake County

Lance D. McBrayer
Georgia Southern University

Bonnie McCormick
University of the Incarnate Word

Katrina McCrae
Abraham Baldwin Agricultural College

Tonya McKinley
Concord College

Mary Anne McMurray
Henderson Community College

Ed Mercurio
Hartnell College

Timothy D. Metz
Campbell University

David Mirman
Mt. San Antonio College

Nancy Garnett Morris
Volunteer State Community College

Angela C. Morrow
University of Northern Colorado

Patricia S. Muir
Oregon State University

James Newcomb
New England College

Jon R. Nickles
University of Alaska, Anchorage

Jane Noble-Harvey
University of Delaware

Michael Nosek
Fitchburg State College

Jeanette C. Oliver
Flathead Valley Community College

David O'Neill
Community College of Baltimore County

Sandra M. Pace
Rappahannock Community College

Lois H. Peck
University of the Sciences, Philadelphia

Kathleen E. Pelkki
Saginaw Valley State University

Jennifer Penrod
Lincoln University

Rhoda E. Perozzi
Virginia Commonwealth University

John S. Peters
College of Charleston

Pamela Petrequin
Mount Mary College

Paula A. Piehl
Potomac State College of West Virginia University

Bill Pietraface
State University of New York Oneonta

Gregory Podgorski
Utah State University

Rosamond V. Potter
University of Chicago

Karen Powell
Western Kentucky University

Martha Powell
University of Alabama

Elena Pravosudova
Sierra College

Hallie Ray
Rappahannock Community College

Jill Raymond
Rock Valley College

Dorothy Read
University of Massachusetts, Dartmouth

Nathan S. Reyna
Howard Payne University

Philip Ricker
South Plains College

Todd Rimkus
Marymount University

Lynn Rivers
Henry Ford Community College

Jennifer Roberts
Lewis University

Laurel Roberts
University of Pittsburgh

April Rottman
Rock Valley College

Maxine Losoff Rusche
Northern Arizona University

Michael L. Rutledge
Middle Tennessee State University

Mike Runyan
Lander University

Travis Ryan
Furman University

Tyson Sacco
Cornell University

Sarmad Saman
Quinsigamond Community College

Leba Sarkis
Aims Community College

Walter Saviuk
Daytona Beach Community College

Neil Schanker
College of the Siskiyous

Robert Schoch
Boston University

John Richard Schrock
Emporia State University

Julie Schroer
Bismarck State College

Karen Schuster
Florida Community College at Jacksonville

Brian W. Schwartz
Columbus State University

Michael Scott
Lincoln University

Eric Scully
Towson State University

Lois Sealy
Valencia Community College

Sandra S. Seidel
Elon University

Wayne Seifert
Brookhaven College

Patty Shields
George Mason University

Cara Shillington
Eastern Michigan University

Brian Shmaefsky
Kingwood College

Rainy Inman Shorey
Ferris State University

Cahleen Shrier
Azusa Pacific University

Jed Shumsky
Drexel University

Greg Sievert
Emporia State University

Jeffrey Simmons
West Virginia Wesleyan College

Frederick D. Singer
Radford University

Anu Singh-Cundy
Western Washington University

Kerri Skinner
University of Nebraska at Kearney

Sandra Slivka
Miramar College

Margaret W. Smith
Butler University

Thomas Smith
Armstrong Atlantic State University

Deena K. Spielman
Rock Valley College

Minou D. Spradley
San Diego City College

Robert Stamatis
Daytona Beach Community College

Joyce Stamm
University of Evansville

Eric Stavney
Highline Community College

Bethany Stone
University of Missouri, Columbia

Mark T. Sugalski
New England College

Marshall D. Sundberg
Emporia State University

Adelaide Svoboda
Nazareth College

Sharon Thoma
Edgewood College

Kenneth Thomas
Hillsborough Community College

Sumesh Thomas
Baltimore City Community College

Betty Thompson
Baptist University

Paula Thompson
Florida Community College

Linda Tichenor
University of Arkansas,
Fort Smith

John Tjepkema
University of Maine, Orono

Bruce L. Tomlinson
State University of New York, Fredonia

Leslie R. Towill
Arizona State University

Bert Tribbey
California State University, Fresno

Nathan Trueblood
California State University, Sacramento

Robert Turner
Western Oregon University

Michael Twaddle
University of Toledo

Virginia Vandergon
California State University, Northridge

William A. Velhagen, Jr.
Longwood College

Jonathan Visick
North Central College

Michael Vitale
Daytona Beach Community College

Lisa Volk

Fayetteville Technical Community
College

Stephen M. Wagener
Western Connecticut State University

James A. Wallis
St. Petersburg Community College

Helen Walter
Diablo Valley College

Kristen Walton
Missouri Western State University

Jennifer Warner
University of North Carolina at Charlotte

Dave Webb
St. Clair County Community College

Harold Webster
Pennsylvania State University, DuBois

Ted Weinheimer
California State University, Bakersfield

Lisa A. Werner
Pima Community College

Joanne Westin
Case Western Reserve University

Wayne Whaley
Utah Valley State College

Joseph D. White
Baylor University

Quinton White
Jacksonville University

Leslie Y. Whiteman
Virginia Union University

Rick Wiedenmann
New Mexico State University at Carlsbad

Peter J. Wilkin
Purdue University North Central

Daniel Williams
Winston-Salem University

Judy A. Williams
Southeastern Oklahoma State University

Dwina Willis
Freed Hardeman University

David Wilson
University of Miami

Mala S. Wingerd
San Diego State University

E. William Wischusen
Louisiana State University

Darla J. Wise
Concord College

Michael Womack
Macon State College

Bonnie Wood
University of Maine at Presque Isle

Mark L. Wygoda
McNeese State University

Shirley Zajdel
Housatonic Community College

Samuel J. Zeakes
Radford University

Uko Zylstra
Calvin College

1 Introduction: Biology Today

Biology is all around us. Like this student in New York City's Central Park, we are all surrounded by biology.

Biology in Our Everyday Lives BIOLOGY AND SOCIETY

Biology All Around Us

We are living in a golden age of biology. A large and diverse community of scientists is studying a myriad of questions that are as relevant to our lives as they are interesting: How can errors in cell growth lead to cancer? How do plants trap solar energy, and what might this teach us about global climate? How do living creatures form ecological networks, and how do human activities disrupt them? How did the great diversity of life on Earth evolve from the first microbes, and how does such evolution have an impact on human health? How do mutations in genes lead to disease? How can DNA—the molecular basis of heredity—be used in forensic investigations? These are just a few examples of how biology is woven into the fabric of society as never before. If you try, you can easily think of a dozen ways that biology affects your life each day. Welcome to the big adventure of the 21st century!

We wrote this book to help you—a student with little or no college-level science experience—develop an appreciation for biology and apply that understanding to your own life and to the society in which you live. We believe that such a biological perspective is essential for any educated person, which is why we named our book *Essential Biology*. So, whatever your reasons for taking this course, even if only to fulfill your school's science requirement, you'll soon discover that exploring life has never been more important or exhilarating.

To help you get started, this first chapter of *Essential Biology* defines biology and then expands on important concepts within this definition. First, we'll survey the properties of life and the scope of life. Next, we'll introduce evolution as the theme that unifies all of biology. Finally, we'll set the study of life in the broader context of science as a process of inquiry. Throughout this chapter (and, indeed, throughout all of *Essential Biology*), we'll provide examples of how biology intersects your everyday life, highlighting the relevance of this subject to society and everyone in it.

The Scope of Life

Biology is the scientific study of life. It's a subject of enormous scope that gets bigger all the time. To start our investigation of life, let's look at some properties that are shared by all living things.

The Properties of Life

How can you tell if something is alive?

Our definition of biology as the scientific study of life raises the obvious question: What is life? Or, to put it another way, what distinguishes living things from nonliving things? The phenomenon of **life** seems to defy a simple, one-sentence definition. Yet even a small child knows that a dog or a bug or a plant is alive, while a rock is not. We recognize life mainly by what living things do.

Figure 1.1 highlights seven of the properties and processes associated with life: (a) *Order*. All living things exhibit complex but ordered organization, as seen in the structure of a pinecone. (b) *Regulation*. The environment outside an organism may change drastically, but the organism can adjust its internal environment, keeping it within appropriate limits. When it senses its body temperature dropping, a lizard can bask on a rock to absorb heat. (c) *Growth and development*. Information carried by DNA controls the pattern of growth and development in all organisms, including the ostrich. (d) *Energy processing*. Organisms take in energy and use it to perform all of life's activities; they emit energy as heat. A puffin obtains energy by eating fish and then uses this energy to power swimming and other work. (e) *Response to the environment*. All organisms respond to environmental stimuli. A carnivorous Venus flytrap closes its leaves rapidly in response to the environmental stimulus of an insect touching the plant's sensory hairs. (f) *Reproduction*. Organisms reproduce their own kind. Thus, hippos reproduce only hippos—never snakes or puffins. (g) *Evolution*. Reproduction underlies the capacity of populations to change (evolve) over time. For example, the katydid has evolved in a way that provides camouflage in its environment. Evolutionary change is a central, unifying phenomenon of all life.

Life at Its Many Levels

One of the aspects of biology that makes it so interesting is the incredible range that the subject covers. To illustrate this point, Figure 1.2 takes you on a tour that spans the full scope of life. The top of the figure shows the global scale of the entire **biosphere**, which consists of all the environments on Earth that support life—including soil; oceans, lakes, and other bodies of water; and the lower atmosphere. At the other extreme of biological size and complexity are microscopic molecules such as DNA, the chemical responsible for inheritance. Going from bottom to top in the figure, you can see that it takes many molecules to build a cell, many cells to make a tissue, multiple tissues to make an organ, and so on. At each new level, novel properties emerge from the specific arrangement and interactions of the parts in an increasingly sophisticated system. Such properties are called emergent properties because they emerge as complexity increases. For example, life emerges at the level of the cell; a test tube full of molecules is not alive. The familiar saying that "the whole is greater than the sum of its parts" captures this idea.

From the interactions within the biosphere to the molecular machinery within cells, biologists are investigating life at its many levels. In the next section, we'll take a closer look at two biological levels near opposite ends of the size scale: ecosystems and cells. ✔

▼ Figure 1.1 **Some properties of life.**

(a) Order

(b) Regulation

(c) Growth and development

(d) Energy processing

1 Biosphere
Earth's biosphere includes all life and all the places where life exists.

2 Ecosystems
An ecosystem consists of all living organisms in a particular area and all the nonliving components of the environment with which life interacts, such as soil, water, and light.

3 Communities
All organisms in the tide pool (iguanas, crabs, seaweed, bacteria, and others) are collectively called a community.

4 Populations
Within communities are various populations, groups of interacting individuals of one species, such as a group of iguanas.

5 Organisms
An organism is an individual living thing, like this iguana.

6 Organ Systems and Organs
An organism's body consists of several organ systems, each of which contains two or more organs. For example, the iguana's circulatory system includes its heart and blood vessels.

10 Molecules and Atoms
Finally, we reach molecules, the chemical level in the hierarchy. Molecules are clusters of even smaller chemical units called atoms. Each cell consists of an enormous number of chemicals that function together to give the cell the properties we recognize as life. DNA, the molecule of inheritance and the substance of genes, is shown here as a computer graphic. Each sphere in the DNA model represents a single atom.

9 Organelles
Organelles are functional components of cells, such as the nucleus that houses the DNA.

7 Tissues
Each organ is made up of several different tissues, such as the heart muscle tissue shown here. A tissue consists of a group of similar cells performing a specific function.

8 Cells
The cell is the smallest unit that can display all the characteristics of life.

← Nucleus

← Atom

(e) Response to the environment

(f) Reproduction

(g) Evolution

Ecosystems

Life does not exist in a vacuum. Each organism interacts continuously with its environment, which includes other organisms as well as physical (nonliving) factors. Together, all the living organisms in a specific area, along with all the nonliving factors with which they interact, form an **ecosystem**. The roots of a tree, for example, absorb water and minerals from the soil. Leaves take in carbon dioxide gas from the air. Chlorophyll, the green pigment of the leaves, absorbs sunlight, which drives the plant's production of sugar from carbon dioxide and water. The tree releases oxygen to the air, and its roots help form soil by breaking up rocks. Both organism and environment are affected by the interactions between them. The tree also interacts with other living things, including microscopic organisms in the soil that are associated with the plant's roots and animals that eat its leaves and fruit.

The dynamics of any ecosystem depend on two main processes (**Figure 1.3**). The first major process is the recycling of chemical nutrients (represented by the light blue circle in the figure). For example, minerals that plants absorb from the soil can eventually be recycled to the soil by microorganisms that decompose leaf litter and other organic refuse. Within most ecosystems, there are three modes of nutrition: Producers are photosynthetic organisms, such as plants; consumers are the organisms, such as animals, that feed on plants, either directly (by eating plants) or indirectly (by eating animals that eat plants); decomposers, such as fungi and many bacteria, break down waste products and the remains of deceased organisms, changing complex dead material into simple nutrients that are recycled. The action of decomposers ensures that nutrients are recycled within an ecosystem.

How is an ecosystem like a recycling plant?

The second major process in an ecosystem is the flow of energy. Unlike chemical nutrients, energy doesn't get recycled. In fact, an ecosystem gains and loses energy constantly. Most ecosystems are solar powered (represented by the yellow, wavy arrow in the figure). The energy that enters an ecosystem as sunlight is captured by producers when plants and other photosynthesizers absorb the sun's energy and convert it to the chemical energy of sugars and other complex molecules (orange arrow). Chemical energy is then passed through a series of consumers and, eventually, decomposers, powering each organism in turn. In the process of these energy conversions between and within organisms, some energy is converted to heat, which is then lost from the system (red arrow). Thus, energy flows through an ecosystem, entering as light and exiting as heat.

The biosphere is enriched by a great variety of ecosystems. Examples include a tropical rain forest in South America, the deserts of the southwestern United States, the Great Barrier Reef off the eastern coast of Australia, and even a small pond that may exist on your campus or in your city. Even a woodland patch in New York's Central Park qualifies as an ecosystem, although it is small and artificial and may be overrun by human visitors. The fact is, humans are organisms that now have some presence, often disruptive, in all ecosystems throughout the biosphere. And the collective clout of 7 billion people and their machines affects the entire biosphere. For example, our fuel burning and forest chopping are changing the atmosphere and the planet's climate in ways that we do not yet fully understand, though we already know that our actions jeopardize the diversity of life on Earth. ☑

☑ CHECKPOINT

Within an ecosystem, _____ are recycled, whereas _____ flows through.

Answer: nutrients; energy

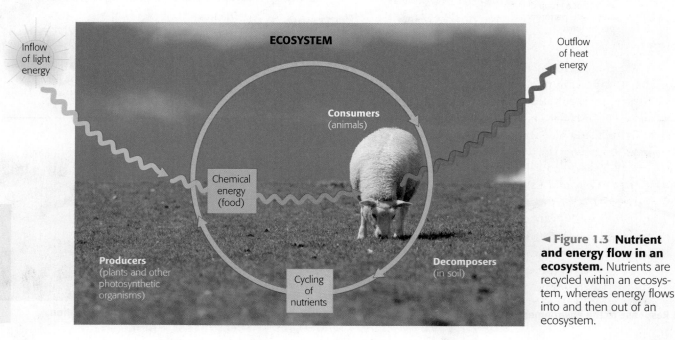

Inflow of light energy

ECOSYSTEM

Outflow of heat energy

Consumers (animals)

Chemical energy (food)

Producers (plants and other photosynthetic organisms)

Decomposers (in soil)

Cycling of nutrients

◄ **Figure 1.3 Nutrient and energy flow in an ecosystem.** Nutrients are recycled within an ecosystem, whereas energy flows into and then out of an ecosystem.

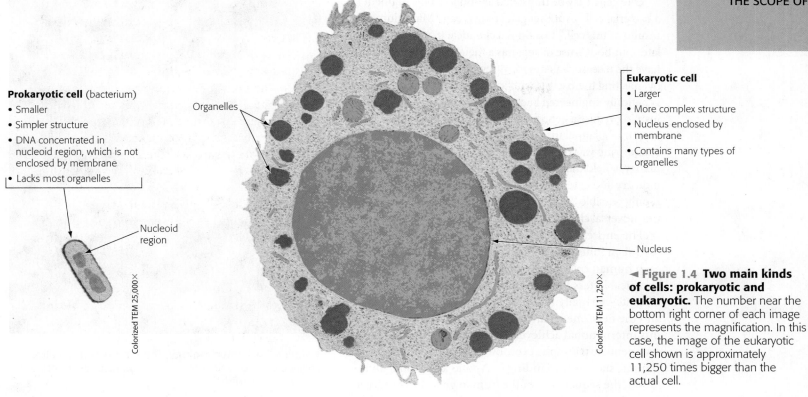

Prokaryotic cell (bacterium)
- Smaller
- Simpler structure
- DNA concentrated in nucleoid region, which is not enclosed by membrane
- Lacks most organelles

Organelles

Nucleoid region

Eukaryotic cell
- Larger
- More complex structure
- Nucleus enclosed by membrane
- Contains many types of organelles

Nucleus

Colorized TEM 25,000×

Colorized TEM 11,250×

◄ **Figure 1.4 Two main kinds of cells: prokaryotic and eukaryotic.** The number near the bottom right corner of each image represents the magnification. In this case, the image of the eukaryotic cell shown is approximately 11,250 times bigger than the actual cell.

Cells and Their DNA

Let's downsize now from ecosystems to cells. The cell has a special place in the hierarchy of biological organization: It is the level at which the properties of life emerge—the lowest level of structure that can perform all activities required for life.

All organisms are composed of cells. They occur singly as a great variety of unicellular (single-celled) organisms, such as amoebas and bacteria. Cells are also the subunits that make up multicellular organisms, such as humans and trees. In all cases, the cell is life's basic unit of structure and function. The ability of cells to divide to form new cells is the basis for all reproduction and for the growth and repair of multicellular organisms.

All cells share many characteristics. For example, every cell is enclosed by a membrane that regulates the passage of materials between the cell and its surroundings. And every cell uses DNA as its genetic information. But we can distinguish two basic types of cells: prokaryotic and eukaryotic **(Figure 1.4)**. The **prokaryotic cell** is much simpler and usually much smaller than the eukaryotic cell. The cells of bacteria are prokaryotic. Most other forms of life, including plants and animals, are composed of eukaryotic cells. In contrast to prokaryotic cells, a **eukaryotic cell** is subdivided by internal membranes into different functional compartments called organelles. For example, the nucleus houses DNA, the inherited material that directs the cell's activities. Prokaryotic cells also have DNA, but it is not packaged within a nucleus.

All cells use DNA as the chemical material of **genes**, the units of inheritance that transmit information from parent to offspring. Of course, bacteria and humans inherit different genes, but that information is encoded in a chemical language common to all organisms. In fact, the language of life has an alphabet of just four letters. The chemical names of DNA's four molecular building blocks are abbreviated as A, G, C, and T **(Figure 1.5)**.

An average-sized gene may be hundreds or thousands of chemical "letters" long. A gene's meaning to a cell is encoded in its specific sequence of these letters, just as the message of a sentence is encoded in its arrangement of letters selected from the 26 letters of the English alphabet.

► **Figure 1.5 The language of DNA.** Every molecule of DNA is constructed from four kinds of chemical building blocks that are chained together, shown here as simple shapes and letters.

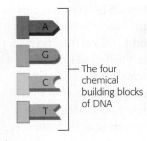

A

G

C

T

The four chemical building blocks of DNA

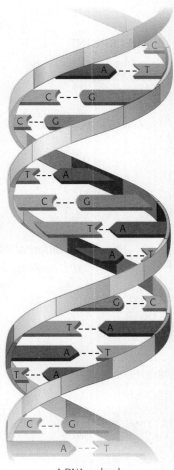

A DNA molecule

7

One gene may be translated as "Build a blue pigment in a bacterial cell." Another gene may mean "Make human insulin in this cell." Insulin is a chemical that helps regulate your body's use of sugar as a fuel. Some people who have the disease diabetes must regulate their sugar levels by injecting themselves with insulin, which is produced by genetically engineered bacteria. These bacteria can make insulin because a gene for human insulin production has been transplanted into their DNA. This example of genetic engineering was one of the earliest successes of biotechnology, a field that has transformed the pharmaceutical industry and extended millions of lives (Figure 1.6). And it is only possible because biological information is written in the universal chemical language of DNA.

The entire "book" of genetic instructions that an organism inherits is called its genome. The nucleus of each human cell packs a genome that is about 3 billion chemical letters long. In recent years, scientists have tabulated virtually the entire sequence of these letters, and the news media and world leaders have acclaimed this international achievement as one of the greatest scientific triumphs ever. But unlike past cultural zeniths, such as the landing of Apollo astronauts on the moon, the sequencing of the human genome is more a commencement than a climax. As the quest continues, biologists will learn the functions of thousands of genes and how their activities are coordinated in the development and functioning of an organism. Additionally, the genomes of other organisms (such as *E. coli* bacteria, dogs, and monkeys) have been sequenced, allowing scientists to compare the genomes of different species. The emerging field of genomics—a branch of biology that studies whole genomes—is a striking example of human curiosity about life at its many levels. ☑

▲ Figure 1.6 **Biotechnology.** These mice were genetically engineered to contain a gene for a glowing protein extracted from a jelly (jellyfish).

species range from 10 million to over 100 million. Whatever the actual number, the enormous diversity of life presents organizational challenges to biologists who study it.

Grouping Species: The Basic Concept

Biological diversity can be something to relish and preserve, but it can also be a bit overwhelming.

▼ Figure 1.7 **A small sample of biological diversity.** A fish called a yellow-ribbon sweetlip swims around a coral reef in Indonesia.

☑ CHECKPOINT

Name the two major kinds of cells. Which kind is your body made up of?

Answer: prokaryotic and eukaryotic; eukaryotic

Life in Its Diverse Forms

Diversity is a hallmark of life. The fish shown in **Figure 1.7** is just one of about 1.8 million species that biologists have identified and named (the scientific name for this fish is *Plectorhinchus polytaenia*). The diversity of known life includes at least 290,000 plants, 52,000 vertebrates (animals with backbones), and 1 million insects (more than half of all known forms of life). Biologists add thousands of newly identified species to the list each year. Estimates of the total number of

How many different species are there on Earth?

People have a tendency to group diverse items according to similarities. We may speak of "squirrels" and "butterflies," even though we recognize that each group actually includes many different species. We may even sort groups into broader categories, such as rodents (which include squirrels) and insects (which include butterflies). Taxonomy, the branch of biology that names and classifies species, is the arrangement of species into a hierarchy of broader and broader groups. Here we consider only the broadest units of classification.

The Three Domains of Life

On the broadest level, biologists divide the diversity of life into three domains: Bacteria, Archaea, and Eukarya (Figure 1.8). The first two domains, Bacteria and Archaea, identify two very different groups of organisms that have prokaryotic cells. All the eukaryotes (organisms with eukaryotic cells) are grouped into the domain Eukarya, which includes three kingdoms—Plantae, Fungi, and Animalia. Most members of the three kingdoms are multicellular. The kingdoms are distinguished partly by how the organisms obtain food. Plants produce their own sugars and other foods by photosynthesis. Fungi are mostly decomposers, obtaining food by digesting dead organisms and organic wastes. Animals obtain food by ingesting (eating) and digesting other organisms. (This, of course, is the kingdom to which we belong.) Those eukaryotes that do not fit into any of the three kingdoms are referred to as the protists. Most protists are single-celled; they include microscopic protozoans, such as amoebas. But protists also include certain multicellular forms, such as seaweeds. Scientists are in the process of organizing protists into multiple kingdoms, although they do not yet agree on exactly how to do this.

Unity in the Diversity of Life

If life is so diverse, how can biology have any unifying themes? What, for instance, can a tree, a mushroom, and a human possibly have in common? As it turns out, a great deal! Underlying the diversity of life is a striking unity, especially at the lower levels of biological organization. One of biology's major goals is to explain how such diversity arises while also accounting for characteristics common to different species. We have already seen one example: the universal genetic language of DNA. That fundamental language connects all kingdoms of life, even uniting prokaryotes such as bacteria with eukaryotes such as humans. What can account for this combination of unity and diversity in life? The scientific explanation is the biological process called evolution, which is our next topic. ☑

▼ Figure 1.8 **The three domains of life.**

DOMAIN BACTERIA

Colorized TEM 10,000X

DOMAIN ARCHAEA

TEM 18,500X

DOMAIN EUKARYA

Kingdom Plantae

Kingdom Fungi

Kingdom Animalia

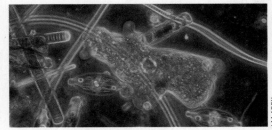
Protists (multiple kingdoms)
LM 150X

☑ CHECKPOINT

1. Name the three domains of life. To which do you belong?
2. Name three kingdoms found within the domain Eukarya. Name a fourth group within this domain.

Answers: **1.** *Bacteria, Archaea, Eukarya; Eukarya* **2.** *Plantae, Fungi, Animalia; the protists*

Evolution: Biology's Unifying Theme

The history of life, as documented by fossils and other evidence, is a saga of a constantly changing Earth billions of years old, inhabited by an evolving cast of living forms **(Figure 1.9)**. Life evolves. Just as you have a family history, each species is one twig of a branching tree of life extending back in time through ancestral species more and more remote. Species that are very similar, such as the brown bear and the polar bear, share a common ancestor that represents a relatively recent branch point on the tree of life **(Figure 1.10)**. But through an ancestor that lived much farther back in time, all bears are also related to squirrels, humans, and all other mammals. Hair and milk-producing mammary glands are two uniquely mammalian traits. Such similarities are what we would expect if all mammals descended from a common ancestor, a prototypical mammal. And mammals, reptiles, and all other vertebrates share a common ancestor even more ancient. Evidence of a still broader relationship can be found in similarities that are seen within all eukaryotic cells. Trace life back far enough, and there are only fossils of the primeval prokaryotes that inhabited Earth over 3 billion years ago. All of life is connected. And the basis for this kinship is evolution, the process that has transformed life on Earth from its earliest beginnings to the extensive diversity we see today. Evolution is the fundamental principle of life and the theme that unifies all of biology; it is the one idea that makes sense of everything we know about living organisms.

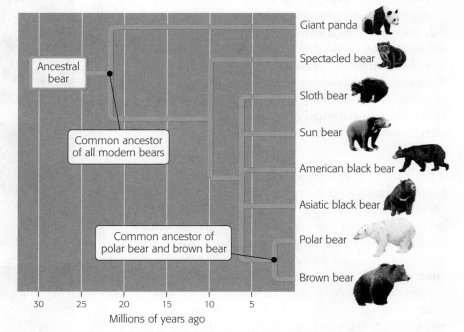

▲ **Figure 1.10 An evolutionary tree of bears.** This tree is a hypothesis (a tentative model) based on both the fossil record and a comparison of DNA sequences among modern bears.

Labels in figure: Giant panda, Spectacled bear, Sloth bear, Sun bear, American black bear, Asiatic black bear, Polar bear, Brown bear. Ancestral bear; Common ancestor of all modern bears; Common ancestor of polar bear and brown bear. Axis: 30, 25, 20, 15, 10, 5 — Millions of years ago

CHECKPOINT

☑ CHECKPOINT

What is the modern term for what Darwin called "descent with modification"?

Answer: evolution

▼ **Figure 1.9 Digging into the past.** A paleontologist excavates mammoth bones from a site in South Dakota.

The Darwinian View of Life

The evolutionary view of life came into focus in 1859 when English naturalist Charles Darwin published one of the most important and influential books ever written: *On the Origin of Species by Means of Natural Selection.* His book developed two main points. First, Darwin presented a large amount of evidence in support of the evolutionary view that species living today descended from a succession of ancestral species. Darwin called this process "descent with modification." It is an insightful phrase, as it captures the duality of life's unity (descent) and diversity (modification). In the Darwinian view, for example, the diversity of bears is based on different modifications of a common ancestor from which all bears descended. As the second main point in *The Origin of Species*, Darwin proposed a mechanism for descent with modification. He called this process natural selection. ☑

Natural Selection

Charles Darwin gathered important evidence for his theories during an around-the-world voyage. He was particularly struck by the diversity of animals on the Galápagos Islands, off the coast of Ecuador (**Figure 1.11**). Darwin regarded adaptation to the environment and the origin of new species as closely related processes. If some geographic barrier—an ocean separating islands, for instance—isolated two populations of a single species from each other, the populations could diverge more and more in appearance as each adapted to local environmental conditions. Over many generations, the two populations could become dissimilar enough to be designated separate species. The labeled branch point near the lower right of Figure 1.10 represents the point in time when two populations of one bear species began to diverge from each other, adapting to different climates and resulting in the evolution of the brown bear and the polar bear as two distinct species. Darwin realized that explaining such adaptation was the key to understanding descent with modification, or evolution. This focus on adaptation helped Darwin envision his concept of natural selection as the mechanism of evolution.

Darwin's Inescapable Conclusion

Darwin synthesized the theory of natural selection from two observations that by themselves were neither profound nor original. Others had the pieces of the puzzle, but Darwin saw how they fit together. Let's look at his logic:

Observation 1: **Overproduction and competition.** Any population can produce far more offspring than the environment can possibly support with available resources such as food and shelter. This overproduction leads to competition among the individuals of a population for these limited resources.

Observation 2: **Individual variation.** Individuals in a population of any species vary in many inherited traits. No two individuals in a population are exactly alike. You know that no two humans are exactly alike; careful observers find this kind of variation in populations of all species.

Conclusion: **Unequal reproductive success.** In the struggle for existence, those individuals with heritable traits best suited to the local environment are more likely to have the greatest reproductive success: They will survive and leave the greatest number of surviving, fertile offspring. Therefore, the very traits that enhance survival and reproductive success will be disproportionately represented in the next generation.

► **Figure 1.11 Charles Darwin (1809–1882), *The Origin of Species*, and blue-footed boobies on the Galápagos Islands.**

ON
THE ORIGIN OF SPECIES
BY MEANS OF NATURAL SELECTION,
ON THE
PRESERVATION OF FAVOURED RACES IN THE STRUGGLE
FOR LIFE.

By CHARLES DARWIN, M.A.,

LONDON:
JOHN MURRAY, ALBEMARLE STREET.
1859.

It is this unequal reproductive success that Darwin called **natural selection** because the environment "selects" only certain heritable traits from those already existing. And the product of natural selection is adaptation, the accumulation of favorable variations in a population over time. Returning to the example of bear evolution in Figure 1.10, one familiar adaptation is fur color. Polar bears and brown (grizzly) bears, as closely related as they are, each display an evolutionary adaptation (white and brown fur, respectively) that resulted from natural selection operating in their respective environments. Presumably, natural selection tended to favor the fur color that provided each bear lineage with the best camouflage in its home territory.

As the process leading to adaptation, natural selection is the mechanism of evolution. **Figure 1.12** presents a hypothetical example of a beetle population that colonizes a location where the soil has been blackened by a recent brush fire. Notice that natural selection works on preexisting variation (in shell color, in this case), enhancing the reproductive success of individuals with beneficial traits.

Observing Artificial Selection

Darwin found convincing evidence for the power of unequal reproduction in examples of artificial selection, the purposeful breeding of domesticated plants and animals by humans. People have been modifying other species for millennia by selecting breeding stock with certain traits. The plants we grow for food bear little resemblance to their wild ancestors; this is because we have customized crop plants through many generations of artificial selection by selecting different parts of the plant to accentuate as food. All the vegetables shown in **Figure 1.13a** (and more) have a common ancestor in one species of wild mustard (shown in the center of the figure). The power of selective breeding is especially apparent in our pets, which have been bred for looks and to be useful. For example, people in different cultures have customized hundreds of dog breeds as different as basset hounds and Saint Bernards, all descended from wolves **(Figure 1.13b)**. The tremendous variety of modern dogs reflects thousands of years of artificial selection. Darwin could see that in artificial selection, people take the place of the environment in screening the heritable traits of populations.

Why is there such a wide variety of dog breeds?

Observing Natural Selection

If artificial selection could achieve so much change so rapidly, Darwin reasoned, then natural selection should be capable of considerable adaptation of species over hundreds or thousands of generations. We now recognize many examples of natural selection in action. A classic example involves the finches (a kind of bird) of the Galápagos Islands. Over a span of two decades,

▼ **Figure 1.12 Natural selection.**

Population with varied inherited traits. Initially, the population varies extensively in the coloration of individual beetles, from very light gray to a dark charcoal color.

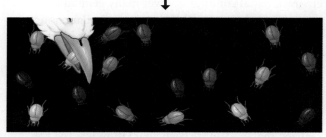

Elimination of individuals with certain traits. For hungry birds that prey on the beetles, it is easiest to spot the beetles that are lightest in color.

Reproduction of survivors. The selective predation favors survival and reproductive success of the darker beetles. Thus, genes for dark color are passed along to the next generation in greater frequency than genes for light color.

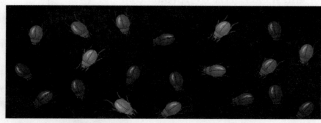

Increasing frequency of traits that enhance survival and reproductive success. Generation after generation, the beetle population adapts to its environment through natural selection.

researchers measured changes in beak size in a population of a species of ground finch that eats mostly small seeds. In dry years, when all seeds are in short supply, the birds must eat more large seeds. Birds with larger, stronger beaks have a feeding advantage and greater

▼ Figure 1.13 **Examples of artificial selection.**

(a) Vegetables descended from wild mustard

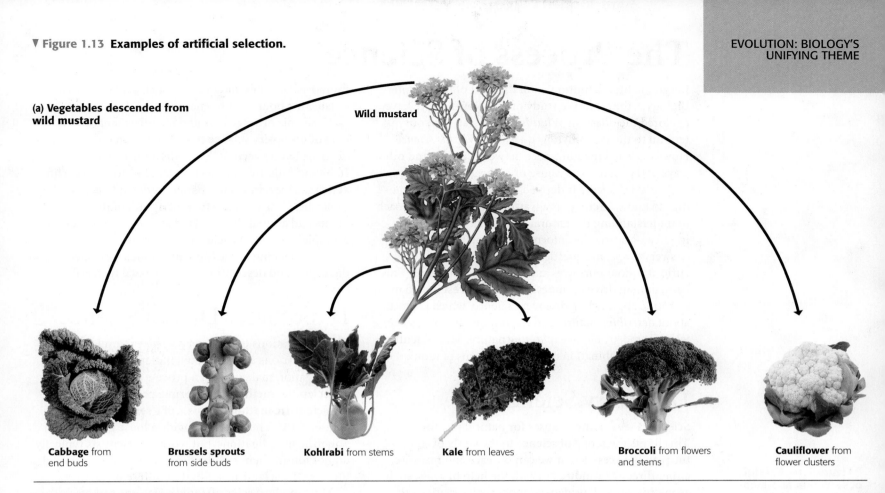

Wild mustard

Cabbage from end buds

Brussels sprouts from side buds

Kohlrabi from stems

Kale from leaves

Broccoli from flowers and stems

Cauliflower from flower clusters

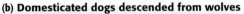

(b) Domesticated dogs descended from wolves

Gray wolves

Domesticated dogs

reproductive success, and the average beak depth for the population increases. During wet years, smaller beaks are more efficient for eating the abundant small seeds, and the average beak depth decreases. Such changes are measurable evidence of natural selection in action. At the end of this chapter, you'll read about another example: how the evolution of antibiotic resistance among bacteria is changing the way doctors prescribe drugs.

Darwin's publication of *The Origin of Species* fueled an explosion in biological research and knowledge that continues today. Over the past century and a half, a tremendous amount of evidence has accumulated in support of Darwin's theory of evolution by natural selection, making it one of biology's best-demonstrated, most comprehensive, and longest-lasting theories. At the end of every chapter of *Essential Biology*, we will highlight connections to evolution—the unifying theme of biology. ☑

☑ **CHECKPOINT**

What mechanism did Darwin propose for evolution? What three-word phrase summarizes this mechanism?

Answer: natural selection; unequal reproductive success

The Process of Science

Recall the first definition from the start of this chapter: Biology is the scientific study of life. Now that we have explored the question *What is life?* we can turn our attention to the next obvious question: *What is science?* How do we tell the difference between science and other ways of trying to make sense of nature?

The word *science* is derived from a Latin verb meaning "to know." **Science** is a way of knowing, an approach to understanding the natural world that is based on inquiry—a search for information, explanations, and answers to specific questions. It developed from our curiosity about ourselves and the world around us. This basic human drive to understand is manifest in two main scientific approaches: discovery science, which is mostly about *describing* nature, and hypothesis-driven science, which is mostly about *explaining* nature. Most scientists practice a combination of these two forms of inquiry.

Discovery Science

Scientists seek natural causes for natural phenomena. This limits the scope of science to the study of structures and processes that we can observe and measure, either directly or indirectly with the help of tools, such as microscopes. This dependence on observations that other people can confirm demystifies nature and distinguishes science from belief in the supernatural. Science can neither prove nor disprove that angels, ghosts, deities, or spirits, whether benevolent or evil, cause storms, rainbows, illnesses, or cures, for such explanations are outside the bounds of science.

Verifiable observations and measurements are the data of **discovery science (Figure 1.14)**. In our quest to describe nature accurately, we discover its structure. In biology, discovery science enables us to describe life at its many levels, from ecosystems down to cells and molecules. Darwin's careful description of the diverse plants and animals he collected in South America is an example of discovery science. A more recent example is the sequencing of the human genome, a detailed dissection and description of our genetic material.

Hypothesis-Driven Science

The observations of discovery science stimulate us to ask questions and seek explanations. Ideally, such investigation makes use of a process of inquiry called the scientific method. As a formal process of inquiry, the **scientific method** consists of a series of steps **(Figure 1.15)**. These steps provide a loose guideline for scientific investigations, but working scientists typically do not follow them rigidly; different scientists proceed through the scientific method in different ways.

Most modern scientific investigations can be described as **hypothesis-driven science**. A **hypothesis** is a tentative answer to a question—an explanation on trial. Although we don't think of it in those terms, we all use hypotheses in solving everyday problems. Let's

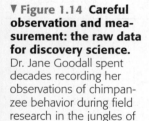

▼ Figure 1.14 **Careful observation and measurement: the raw data for discovery science.** Dr. Jane Goodall spent decades recording her observations of chimpanzee behavior during field research in the jungles of Tanzania.

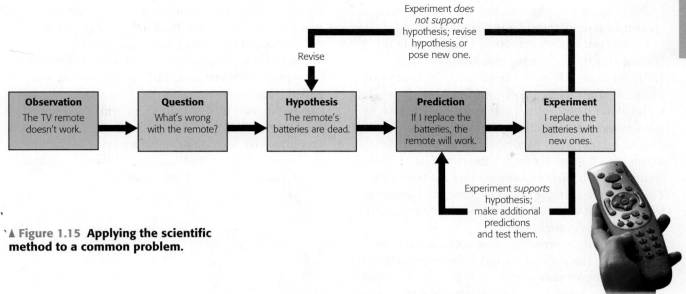

▲ Figure 1.15 Applying the scientific method to a common problem.

say, for example, that your TV remote fails to turn on your TV. That's an observation. The question is obvious: Why doesn't the remote work? An observation may give rise to many hypotheses, but we need to focus on one to begin an investigation. In this case, a reasonable hypothesis based on past experience is that the batteries in the remote are dead.

Once a hypothesis is formed, an investigator can use logic to test it. In the process of science, this logic usually takes the form of predictions about what experimental results or observations we should expect if a particular hypothesis (premise) is correct. We then test the hypothesis by performing an experiment to see whether or not the results are as predicted. This logical testing takes the form of "If . . . then" logic:

Observation: The TV remote doesn't work.

Question: What's wrong with the remote?

Hypothesis: The remote's batteries are dead.

Prediction: If I replace the batteries, then the remote will work.

Experiment: I replace the batteries with new ones.

Predicted result: The remote should work.

Let's say the remote still doesn't work. We can test an alternative hypothesis. Perhaps, for example, the TV is unplugged. We could also blame the dead remote on supernatural spirits, but that hypothesis is untestable and therefore outside the realm of science. ✓

☑ CHECKPOINT

If you spend a summer observing the squirrels on your campus and collecting data on their dietary habits, what kind of science are you performing? If you come up with a tentative explanation for their dietary behavior and then test your idea, what kind of science are you performing?

Answer: discovery science; hypothesis-driven science

Biology in Our Everyday Lives THE PROCESS OF SCIENCE

Are Trans Fats Bad for You?

One way to better understand the process of science is to examine a case study, an in-depth examination of an actual investigation. This particular case study is about the effects of one kind of dietary fat. Later chapters will include other case studies in the process of science, illustrating how discovery and hypothesis-driven science have been used in experiments both modern and classic. To

emphasize how the scientific method has been employed in each case, the key steps will be highlighted in blue text.

Dietary fat, a major component of the food we eat, comes in several different forms. Trans fats are a non-natural form of fat produced through a manufacturing process called hydrogenation (as in partially hydrogenated vegetable oil, which is often used in fried foods). Because trans fats add texture, increases shelf life, and is inexpensive to prepare, it was added to foods (such as margarine and shortening) in increasing amounts throughout the 1900s.

Fat was one dietary component examined in the Nurses' Health Study, a landmark study of over 120,000 female U.S. nurses begun in 1976. Every two years, the study participants completed questionnaires about their health status and dietary habits. In 1994, researchers examining the trove of collected data discovered that study participants who ate high levels of trans fats had nearly double the risk of heart disease compared with participants who ate little trans fats. This is a good example of discovery science: examination of a set of data gathered without a preconceived notion of what it might reveal.

While the data were suggestive, some researchers remained skeptical about the link between trans fats and health. In a hypothesis-driven study published in 2004, a research team started with the **observation** that human body fat (adipose tissue) retains traces of consumed dietary fats. This observation raised a **question**: Would the adipose tissue of heart attack patients be measurably different from the adipose tissue of a similar group of healthy patients? The researchers' **hypothesis** was that it would be, leading to the **prediction** that the body fat of healthy patients would contain less trans fats than the body fat of heart attack victims.

The researchers then set up an **experiment** to determine the amounts of different kinds of fat in the adipose tissue of 79 patients who had experienced a heart attack. These amounts were compared with data for 167 patients who had not experienced a heart attack but were similar to the first group in most other respects. Since trans fats are not produced by the body, the researchers assumed that any trans fats found in the adipose tissue had been consumed in the diet. Their **results** showed significantly

higher levels of trans fats in the bodies of the heart attack patients than in the healthier group **(Figure 1.16)**. Although other risk factors are also involved, these results added to the growing body of evidence that trans fats are unhealthy and should be avoided. Indeed, such evidence has led several countries (such as Australia and Denmark), some states (such as California), and some cities (such as New York City) to ban trans fats altogether. Trans fats have been eliminated from many foods, but you would do well to read nutrition labels and avoid trans fats as much as possible in your own diet.

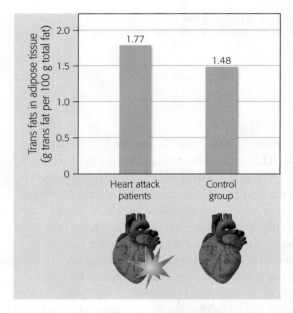

▲ **Figure 1.16 Levels of trans fats.** Results of an experiment that measured the levels of trans fats in the adipose tissue of 79 patients who had experienced a heart attack and 167 patients who had not (control group).

The trans fats study described in the Process of Science section is an example of a **controlled experiment**. An experiment of this type is designed to compare an experimental group (the patients who had a heart attack, in this case) with a control group (patients who did not have a heart attack). Ideally, the control group and the experimental group differ only in one factor the experiment is designed to test—in our example, the occurrence of a heart attack. Other factors—such as age, weight, and sex of the patients—were matched between the two sets of patients. Thus, the control group canceled out the effects of all variables other than the one being tested. The use of a controlled experiment enabled researchers to draw conclusions about the effect of just one variable—trans fats—on heart attack risk. ☑

Theories in Science

Many people associate facts with science, but accumulating facts is not the primary goal of science. A telephone book is an impressive catalog of factual information, but it has little to do with science. It is true that facts, in the form of verifiable observations and repeatable experimental results, are the prerequisites of science. What really advances science, however, are new theories that tie together a number of observations that previously seemed unrelated. The cornerstones of science are the explanations that apply to the greatest variety of phenomena. People like Newton, Darwin, and Einstein stand out in the history of science not because they discovered a great many facts, but because their theories had such broad explanatory power.

What is a scientific theory, and how is it different from a hypothesis? A scientific **theory** is much broader in scope than a hypothesis. This is a hypothesis: "White fur is an evolutionary adaptation that helps polar bears survive in an Arctic habitat." But this is a theory: "Adaptations to the local environment evolve by natural selection."

Because theories are so comprehensive, they only become widely accepted in science if they are supported by an accumulation of extensive and varied evidence. The use of the term *theory* in science for a comprehensive explanation supported by abundant evidence contrasts with our everyday usage, which equates theories more with speculations or hypotheses. Natural selection qualifies as a scientific theory because of its broad application and because it has been validated by a huge number of observations and experiments.

Scientific theories are not the only way of knowing nature, of course. A comparative religion course would be a good place to learn about the diverse legends that tell of a supernatural creation of Earth and its life. Science and religion are two very different ways of trying to make sense of nature. Art is still another way. A broad education should include exposure to all these different ways of viewing the world. Each of us synthesizes our worldview by integrating our life experiences and multidisciplinary education. As a science textbook and part of that broad education, *Essential Biology* showcases life in the scientific context of evolution, the one theme that continues to hold all of biology together, no matter how big and complex the subject becomes. ☑

The Culture of Science

It is not unusual for several scientists to ask the same questions. Such overlap contributes to the progressive and self-correcting qualities of science. Scientists build on what has been learned from earlier research, and they pay close attention to contemporary scientists working on the same problem. Scientists share information through publications, seminars, meetings, websites, blogs, and personal communication.

Both cooperation and competition characterize the scientific culture (**Figure 1.17**). Scientists working in the same research field subject one another's work to careful scrutiny. It is common for scientists to check the conclusions of others by attempting to repeat experiments. This obsession with evidence and confirmation helps characterize the scientific style of inquiry. Scientists are generally skeptics.

We have seen that science has two key features that distinguish it from other styles of inquiry: (1) a dependence on observations and measurements that others can verify and (2) the requirement that ideas

▲ Figure 1.17 **Science as a social process.** New England College neurobiologist Jim Newcomb (right) mentors a student in the methods of marine biology.

(hypotheses) are testable by experiments that others can repeat.

Science, Technology, and Society

Science and technology are interdependent. New technologies, such as more powerful microscopes and computers, advance science. And scientific discoveries can lead to new technologies. In most cases, technology applies scientific discoveries to the development of new goods and services. For example, about 60 years ago, two scientists, James Watson and Francis Crick, discovered the structure of DNA through the process of science. Their discovery eventually led to a variety of DNA technologies, including genetic engineering (see Figure 1.6) and the use of DNA profiling for investigating crimes (**Figure 1.18**). Perhaps Watson and Crick envisioned that their discovery would someday inform new technologies, but they could not have predicted exactly what the applications would be.

► Figure 1.18 **DNA technology and the law.** In 2007, DNA evidence helped to exonerate Jerry Miller of rape and kidnapping, crimes for which he spent 25 years wrongly imprisoned.

☑ **CHECKPOINT**

How does modern genetic engineering reflect a common ancestry for all life on Earth?

Answer: Genetic engineering is possible because all life uses chemically identical DNA, a result of our evolution from a common ancestor.

Technology has improved our standard of living in many ways, but it is a double-edged sword. Technology that keeps people healthier has enabled the population to grow more than tenfold in the past three centuries and to more than double to 7 billion in just the past 40 years. The environmental consequences are sometimes devastating. Acid rain, deforestation, global climate change, nuclear accidents, toxic wastes, and extinction of species are just a few of the repercussions of more and more people wielding more and more technology. Science can help us identify such problems and provide insight about what course of action may prevent further damage. But solutions to these problems depend upon politics, economics, culture, and the values of societies. Now that science and technology have become such powerful aspects of our culture, each of us has the responsibility to develop a reasonable amount of scientific literacy. The crucial relationship between science, technology, and society is a central theme of this book. ☑

Biology in Our Everyday Lives EVOLUTION CONNECTION

Evolution in Our Everyday Lives

To emphasize evolution as the core theme of biology, we end each chapter of *Essential Biology* with an Evolution Connection section. Evolution teaches us that the environment is a powerful selective force for traits that best adapt populations to their environments. But how does this affect your life? Our world is rich with examples of natural selection in action. One example that may directly affect you is the development of resistance to antibiotics in disease-causing bacteria.

Antibiotics are drugs that help cure certain infections by impairing the bacteria that cause them. Antibiotics have saved millions of human lives, but there's a dark side to their widespread use: It has driven the evolution of antibiotic-resistant populations of the very bacteria the drugs are meant to kill.

When an antibiotic is taken by a patient, it will usually kill most, but not all, of the infecting bacteria. The few bacteria among the varying members of a population that can survive the drug will have a survival advantage. In some cases, the mechanism of resistance in the bacteria is an ability to destroy the antibiotic—or even use the drug as food! Even though the drug kills most of the bacteria, those few bacteria that are resistant may soon multiply and become the norm in the population rather than the exception.

The evolution of antibiotic-resistant bacteria is a huge problem in public health. For example, methicillin-resistant *Staphlococcus aureus*, or MRSA, is a strain of a relatively common bacterium that has evolved resistance to several of the most potent antibiotics used to treat bacterial infections. Although most commonly spread in hospitals, MRSA is becoming an increasing problem among college athletes because of its potential to spread via skin-to-skin contact in locker rooms and during contact sports **(Figure 1.19)**.

The problem of antibiotic-resistant bacteria is influencing the way many physicians prescribe antibiotics. Doctors who understand that the abuse of these drugs is speeding the evolution of resistant bacteria are less likely to prescribe antibiotics needlessly—for instance, for a patient complaining of a common cold or flu, diseases caused by viruses (not bacteria), against which antibacterial drugs are powerless. Additionally, many farmers are reducing the use of antibiotics in animal feed, and many consumers are choosing to buy meats from animals raised without antibiotics. Some health professionals wonder if the increased use of antibacterial soaps contributes to the problem.

It is important to note that adaptation of bacteria to an environment containing an antibiotic does not mean that the drug *created* the antibiotic resistance trait. Instead, the environment screened the variations that already existed among individuals of a population and favored the individuals best suited to the present conditions. Throughout *Essential Biology*, you will learn more about how natural selection works and see other examples of how natural selection affects your life.

▲ **Figure 1.19 Natural selection in action.** Strains of the common bacterium *Staphylococcus aureus* (inset) that have evolved resistance to multiple antibiotics pose a significant health threat, particularly to hospitalized patients and college athletes.

Chapter Review

SUMMARY OF KEY CONCEPTS

 Go to **www.masteringbiology.com** for homework assignments, practice quizzes, Pearson eText, and more.

The Scope of Life

Biology is the scientific study of life. The study of biology encompasses a wide scale of size and a huge variety of life, both past and present.

The Properties of Life

All life displays a common set of characteristics:

Order

Regulation

Growth and development

Energy processing

Response to the environment

Reproduction

Evolution

Life at Its Many Levels

Within ecosystems, nutrients are recycled, but energy flows through. Cells are either prokaryotic (simple, small, and lacking membrane-enclosed organelles, such as the nucleus) or eukaryotic (more complex, larger, and containing a nucleus and other membrane-enclosed organelles). Both types of cells contain genes, the molecular units of inheritance.

Life in Its Diverse Forms

Biologists organize living organisms into three domains. The domain Eukarya is further divided into three kingdoms (distinguished partly by their means of obtaining food) and one catch-all group:

Life			
Prokaryotes		**Eukaryotes**	
		Plantae Fungi Animalia	Protists (all other eukaryotes)
		Three kingdoms	
Domain Bacteria	**Domain Archaea**	**Domain Eukarya**	

Evolution: Biology's Unifying Theme

The Darwinian View of Life

Charles Darwin established the ideas of evolution ("descent with modification") via natural selection (unequal reproductive success) in his 1859 publication *The Origin of Species*.

Natural Selection

Darwin formulated the theory of natural selection through a logical inference: Natural selection leads to adaptations to the environment, which—when passed from generation to generation—is the mechanism of evolution.

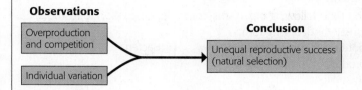

Observations

Overproduction and competition

Individual variation

Conclusion

Unequal reproductive success (natural selection)

The Process of Science

Discovery Science

Describing the natural world with verifiable data is the hallmark of discovery science.

Hypothesis-Driven Science

A scientist formulates a hypothesis (tentative explanation) to explain observations of the natural world. The hypothesis may then be tested via the steps of the scientific method:

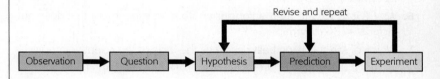

Revise and repeat

Observation → Question → Hypothesis → Prediction → Experiment

Theories in Science

A theory is a broad and comprehensive statement about the world that is supported by the accumulation of a great deal of verifiable evidence.

The Culture of Science

Scientists build on each other's work by always remaining skeptical and by seeking reproducible evidence to confirm ideas.

Science, Technology, and Society

Scientific advances promote new technologies, which in turn enable further scientific advances and useful applications to our lives.

SELF-QUIZ

1. Which of the following is *not* a characteristic of all living organisms?
   a. capable of self-reproduction
   b. composed of multiple cells
   c. complex yet organized
   d. energy utilization

2. Place the following levels of biological organization in order from smallest to largest: atom, biosphere, cell, ecosystem, molecule, organ, organism, population, tissue. Which is the smallest level capable of demonstrating all of the characteristics of life?

3. Plants use the process of photosynthesis to convert the energy in sunlight to chemical energy in the form of sugar. While doing so, they consume carbon dioxide and water and release oxygen. Explain how this process functions in both the cycling of chemical nutrients and the flow of energy through an ecosystem.

4. For each of the following organisms, match its description to its most likely domain and/or kingdom:

   a. A foot-tall organism capable of producing its own food from sunlight

   b. A microscopic, simple, nucleus-free organism found living in a riverbed

   c. An inch-tall organism growing on the forest floor that consumes material from dead leaves

   d. A thimble-sized organism that feeds on algae growing in a pond

   1. Bacteria

   2. Eukarya/Animalia

   3. Eukarya/Fungi

   4. Eukarya/Plantae

5. How does natural selection cause a population to become adapted to its environment over time?

6. Why is it difficult to draw a conclusion from an experiment that does not include a control group?

7. Which of the following best describes the logic of the scientific method?

   a. If I generate a testable hypothesis, tests and observations will support it.

   b. If my prediction is correct, it will lead to a testable hypothesis.

   c. If my observations are accurate, they will support my hypothesis.

   d. If my hypothesis is correct, I can expect certain test results.

8. Which of the following statements best distinguishes hypotheses from theories in science?

   a. Theories are hypotheses that have been proved.

   b. Hypotheses are tentative guesses; theories are correct answers to questions about nature.

   c. Hypotheses usually are narrow in scope; theories have broad explanatory power.

   d. Hypotheses and theories mean essentially the same thing in science.

9. _____ is the core idea that unifies all areas of biology.

10. Match each of the following terms to the phrase that best describes it.

   a. Natural selection

   b. Evolution

   c. Hypothesis

   d. Biosphere

   1. A testable idea

   2. Descent with modification

   3. Unequal reproductive success

   4. All life-supporting environments on Earth

Answers to these questions can be found in Appendix: Self-Quiz Answers.

THE PROCESS OF SCIENCE

11. The graph below shows the results of an experiment in which mice learned to run through a maze.

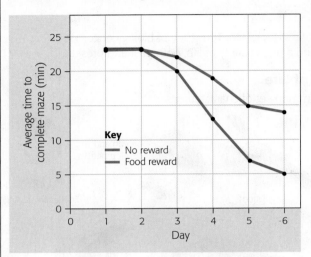

   a. State a hypothesis and prediction that you think this experiment may have been designed to test.

   b. Which was the control group and which the experimental group? Why was a control group needed?

   c. List some variables that must have been controlled so as not to affect the results.

   d. Do the data support the hypothesis you chose? Explain.

12. The fruits of wild species of tomato are tiny compared with the giant beefsteak tomatoes available today. This difference in fruit size is almost entirely due to the larger number of cells in the domesticated fruits. Plant biologists have recently discovered genes that are responsible for controlling cell division in tomatoes. Why would such a discovery be important to producers of other kinds of fruits and vegetables? To the study of human development and disease? To our basic understanding of biology?

BIOLOGY AND SOCIETY

13. The news media and popular magazines frequently report stories that are connected to biology. In the next 24 hours, record all such stories you hear or read about from three different sources and briefly describe the biological connections you perceive in each story.

14. If you pay attention, you will find yourself conducting many hypothesis-driven experiments each day. Over the next day, try to think of a good example where you performed a simple experiment to test a hypothesis about some observation. Write the experience out as a story, and then rewrite it using the steps of the scientific method (observation, question, hypothesis, prediction, and so on).

Unit 1
Cells

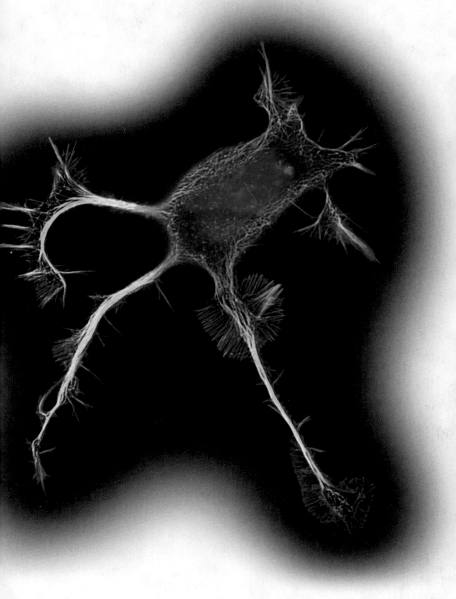

Chapter 2: **Essential Chemistry for Biology**

Chapter Thread: **Life's Dependence on Water**

Chapter 3: **The Molecules of Life**

Chapter Thread: **Lactose Intolerance**

Chapter 4: **A Tour of the Cell**

Chapter Thread: **Antibiotic-Resistant Bacteria**

Chapter 5: **The Working Cell**

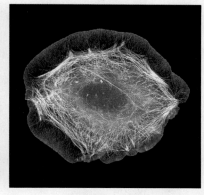

Chapter Thread: **Nanotechnology**

Chapter 6: **Cellular Respiration: Obtaining Energy from Food**

Chapter Thread: **Aerobic versus Anaerobic Lifestyles**

Chapter 7: **Photosynthesis: Using Light to Make Food**

Chapter Thread: **Green Energy**

2 Essential Chemistry for Biology

Human dependence on water.
All life, and the health of human civilization, depends on the availability of water.

Life's Dependence on Water BIOLOGY AND SOCIETY

More Precious than Gold

Drought is one of the most devasting natural disasters. A drought is a sustained period of abnormally dry weather that lasts long enough to change the environment. The effects of drought can include severe crop damage, shortages of drinking water, dust storms, famine, habitat loss, and mass migration. Even a mild drought can produce disruptions; most of us have experienced government-mandated water-saving measures, such as prohibitions on watering lawns and washing cars. In some areas, particularly in the southwestern United States, such water conservation measures have been in place for years.

Throughout human history, droughts have helped wipe out societies and even whole civilizations. A study of growth rings from a 1,100-year-old tree in Mexico suggests that a 25-year-long drought may have hastened the demise of the Mayan civilization. In the 1930s, a seven-year-long drought across the American prairie produced the Dust Bowl, resulting in millions of acres of lost farmland and a large westward migration of displaced people. More recently, a drought that lasted from 1987 to 1989 is considered the costliest natural disaster in our country's history, with agricultural losses totaling $39 billion. Certain parts of Africa, although historically lush, have experienced severe drought in the 21st century. The country of Sudan, for example, has suffered widespread famine, contributing to the ongoing social and political unrest in its drought-plagued Darfur region. As recently as 2009, a drought in the American Southwest (which hit California and Texas the hardest) caused more than $5 billion in agricultural losses. In the future, as global climate change accelerates, our most precious resource may be neither gold nor oil but fresh water.

Why are droughts so catastrophic? The reason is simple: Life cannot exist without water. Living organisms use water as the medium for the chemical reactions necessary to sustain life. Many questions about life are actually questions about chemicals and their interactions, making knowledge of chemistry essential to understanding biology. In this chapter, you will learn some essential chemistry that you can apply throughout your study of life. In the last section, we'll return to the crucial role that water plays in sustaining life on Earth.

Some Basic Chemistry

Why would a biology textbook include a chapter on chemistry? Well, take any biological system apart, and you eventually end up at the chemical level. In fact, you could think of your body as one big container of watery chemicals undergoing a continuous series of chemical reactions. Beginning at this basic biological level, let's explore the chemistry of life.

Matter: Elements and Compounds

All organisms and everything around them are made of matter, the physical "stuff" of the universe. Defined more formally, **matter** is anything that occupies space and has mass. Matter is found on Earth in three physical states: solid, liquid, and gas.

All matter is composed of chemical elements. An **element** is a substance that cannot be broken down into other substances by chemical reactions. There are 92 naturally occurring elements; examples are carbon, oxygen, and gold. Each element has a symbol derived from its English, Latin, or German name. For instance, the symbol for gold, Au, is from the Latin word *aurum*. All the elements—the 92 that occur naturally and several dozen that are human-made—are listed in the periodic table of the elements, a familiar fixture in any chemistry or biology lab (**Figure 2.1**; see Appendix: Periodic Table of Elements for a full version).

Of the 92 naturally occurring elements, 25 are essential to people (other organisms need fewer; plants, for example, typically need 17). Four of these elements—oxygen (O), carbon (C), hydrogen (H), and

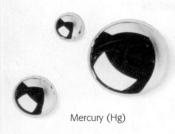

Mercury (Hg)

Copper (Cu)

Lead (Pb)

► **Figure 2.1 Abbreviated periodic table of the elements.** In the full periodic table (see Appendix: Periodic Table of Elements), each entry contains the element symbol in the center, with the atomic number above and the mass number below (both of these numbers are discussed on the facing page). The element highlighted here is carbon (C).

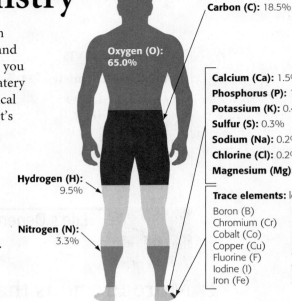

▲ **Figure 2.2 Chemical composition of the human body by weight.** Notice that just 4 elements make up 96% of your weight.

nitrogen (N)—make up about 96% of the weight of most cells (**Figure 2.2**). Much of the remaining 4% is accounted for by 7 elements, most of which are probably familiar to you, such as calcium (Ca) and phosphorus (P). Calcium, important for building strong bones and teeth, is found abundantly in milk and dairy products as well as sardines and green, leafy vegetables (kale and broccoli, for example). Phosphorus, a component of DNA, can be obtained by eating eggs, beans, and nuts.

Less than 0.01% of your weight is made up of 14 trace elements. **Trace elements** are required in only very small amounts, but you cannot live without them. The average person, for example, needs only a tiny speck of iodine each day. Iodine is an essential ingredient of a hormone produced by the thyroid gland, located in the neck. An iodine deficiency causes the thyroid gland to enlarge, a condition called goiter. Therefore, consuming foods that are naturally rich in iodine—such as kelp, green vegetables, and dairy products—prevents goiter. The addition of iodine to table salt ("iodized salt") has nearly eliminated goiter in industrialized nations, but many thousands of people in developing countries are still affected (**Figure 2.3**). Another trace element is fluorine, which (in the form of fluoride) is added to dental products and drinking water and helps maintain healthy bones and teeth. Many prepared foods are fortified with trace mineral elements. Look at the side of a cereal box and you'll probably see iron listed; you can actually see the iron youself if you crush the cereal and stir a magnet through it.

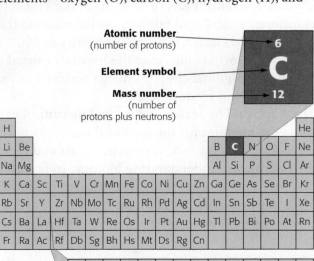

Elements can combine to form **compounds**, substances that contain two or more elements in a fixed ratio. In everyday life, compounds are much more common than pure elements. Familiar examples include table salt and water. Table salt is sodium chloride, NaCl, consisting of equal parts of the elements sodium (Na) and chlorine (Cl). A molecule of water, H_2O, has two atoms of hydrogen and one atom of oxygen. Most of the compounds in living organisms contain several different elements. DNA, for example, contains carbon, nitrogen, oxygen, hydrogen, and phosphorus. ☑

Atoms

Each element consists of one kind of atom, which is different from the atoms of other elements. An **atom**, named from a Greek word meaning "indivisible," is the smallest unit of matter that still retains the properties of an element. In other words, the smallest amount of the element carbon is one carbon atom. Just how small is this "piece" of carbon? It would take about a million carbon atoms to stretch across the period at the end of this sentence.

The Structure of Atoms

Atoms are composed of subatomic particles, of which the three most important are protons, electrons, and neutrons. A **proton** is a subatomic particle with a single unit of positive electrical charge (+). An **electron** is a subatomic particle with a single negative charge (−). A **neutron** is electrically neutral (has no charge).

Figure 2.4 shows two simplified models of an atom of the element helium (He), the "lighter-than-air" gas used in party balloons. Each atom of helium has 2 neutrons (○) and 2 protons (⊕) tightly packed into the **nucleus**, the atom's central core. Two electrons (⊖) move around the nucleus in a spherical cloud at nearly the speed of light. The electron cloud is much bigger than the nucleus.

▼ **Figure 2.4 Two simplified models of a helium atom.**

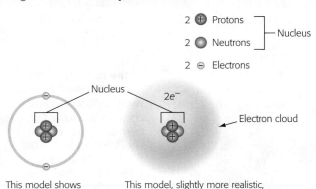

2 ⊕ Protons
2 ○ Neutrons — Nucleus
2 ⊖ Electrons

Nucleus

$2e^-$

Electron cloud

This model shows the subatomic particles in an atom of helium.

This model, slightly more realistic, shows the electrons as a spherical cloud of negative charge surrounding the nucleus.

▼ **Figure 2.3 The relationship between diet and goiter.**

Goiter, an enlargement of the thyroid gland, shown here in a Malaysian woman, can occur when a person's diet does not include enough iodine, a trace element.

Eating iodine-rich foods can prevent goiter.

In fact, if the atom were the size of a baseball stadium, the nucleus would be the size of a pea on the pitcher's mound and the electrons would be two gnats buzzing around the bleachers. The attraction between the negatively charged electrons and the positively charged protons keeps the electrons near the nucleus. When an atom has an equal number of protons and electrons (as helium does), its net electrical charge is zero and so the atom is neutral.

If an atom were the size of a baseball field, how big would its nucleus be?

Elements differ in the number of subatomic particles in their atoms. The number of protons in an atom, called the **atomic number**, determines which element it is. For example, helium always has 2 protons and thus an atomic number of 2. **Mass** is a measure of the amount of material in an object. A proton and a neutron have nearly identical mass. An electron has so little mass—only about 1/2,000 the mass of a proton—that it is usually approximated as zero. Therefore, an atom's **mass number** is just the sum of the number of protons and neutrons in its nucleus. For helium, the mass number is 4 (2 protons + 2 neutrons). Both the atomic number and the mass number can be read from the periodic table (see Figure 2.1 and Appendix: Periodic Table of Elements).

Isotopes

Some elements can exist in different forms called isotopes. The different **isotopes** of an element have the same numbers of protons and electrons but different numbers of neutrons; in other words, isotopes are forms of an element that differ in mass. For example, the

☑ **CHECKPOINT**

1. How many of the 92 naturally occurring elements are used in your body? Which four are the most abundant in living cells?
2. Which of the following are compounds: water (H_2O), oxygen gas (O_2), methane (CH_4)? Explain your choices.

Answers: 1. 25; oxygen, carbon, hydrogen, and nitrogen 2. H_2O and CH_4 are compounds, but O_2 is not because a compound must contain at least two different elements.

numbers of subatomic particles in three isotopes of carbon are shown in **Table 2.1**. Carbon-12 (named for its mass number), with 6 neutrons and 6 protons, makes up about 99% of all naturally occurring carbon. Most of the other 1% is carbon-13, with 7 neutrons and 6 protons. A third isotope, carbon-14, with 8 neutrons and 6 protons, occurs in minute quantities. Notice that all three isotopes have 6 protons—otherwise, they would not be carbon. Both carbon-12 and carbon-13 are stable isotopes, meaning that their nuclei remain intact more or less forever. The isotope carbon-14, on the other hand, is unstable, or radioactive. A **radioactive isotope** is one in which the nucleus decays spontaneously, giving off particles and energy.

Radioactive isotopes have many uses in biological research and medicine. Cells use radioactive isotopes the same way they use nonradioactive isotopes of the same element. Once the cell takes up a radioactive isotope, the location and concentration of the isotope can be detected because of the radiation it emits. This makes radioactive isotopes useful as tracers— biological spies, in effect—for monitoring the fate of atoms in living organisms. For example, a medical diagnostic tool called a PET scan works by detecting small amounts of radioactive materials introduced into the body **(Figure 2.5)**.

Although radioactive isotopes can be useful, radiation from decaying isotopes can damage cellular molecules and thus can pose serious health risks. In 1986, the explosion of a nuclear reactor at Chernobyl, Ukraine, released large amounts of radioactive isotopes, killing 30 people within a few weeks and exposing thousands to an increased risk of cancer. Likewise, scientists will carefully monitor the long-term health consequences of the 2011 post-tsunami Fukushima nuclear disaster in Japan.

Natural sources of radiation can also pose a threat. Radon, a radioactive gas, may cause lung cancer. Radon can contaminate buildings in regions where underlying rocks naturally contain the radioactive element uranium. Homeowners can buy a radon detector or hire a company to test their

Why is it a good idea to test your house for radon?

home to ensure that radon levels are safe. Such radon testing is now a standard step in most home purchases.

Electron Arrangement and the Chemical Properties of Atoms

Of the three subatomic particles we've discussed— protons, neutrons, and electrons—only electrons are directly involved in the chemical activity of an atom. Electrons vary in the amount of energy they possess. The farther an electron is from the nucleus, the greater its energy. Electrons do not move around an atom at just any energy level, but only at specific levels called electron shells. Depending on the number of electrons, an atom may have one, two, or more electron shells, with electrons in the outermost shell having the highest energy. Each shell can accommodate up to a specific number of electrons. The innermost shell is full with 2 electrons, while the second and third shells can each hold up to 8 electrons.

The number of electrons in the outermost shell determines the chemical properties of an atom. Atoms whose outer shells are not full tend to interact with other atoms— that is, to participate in chemical reactions. **Figure 2.6** shows the electron shells of four biologically important elements. Because the outer shells of all four atoms are not filled, these atoms react readily with other atoms. The hydrogen atom is highly reactive because it has only 1 electron in its single electron shell, which can accommodate 2 electrons. Atoms of carbon, nitrogen, and oxygen are also highly reactive because their outer shells, which can hold 8 electrons, are not filled. In contrast, the helium atom in Figure 2.4 has a single, first-level shell that is full with 2 electrons. As a result, helium is chemically unreactive. ☑

Table 2.1	Isotopes of Carbon		
	Carbon-12	**Carbon-13**	**Carbon-14**
Protons	6 ⎤ mass �—number	6 ⎤ mass —number	6 ⎤ mass —number
Neutrons	6 ⎦ 12	7 ⎦ 13	8 ⎦ 14
Electrons	6	6	6

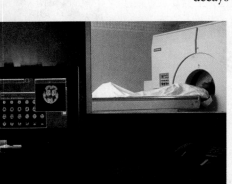

▲ **Figure 2.5 A PET scan.** This monitor shows the images produced by a PET scanner. PET scans can diagnose heart disorders and some cancers.

☑ **CHECKPOINT**

1. By definition all atoms of carbon have exactly 6 _____, but the number of _____ varies from one isotope to another.
2. As two atoms approach each other, which subatomic particles are the first to come into contact?

Answers: 1. protons; neutrons 2. the electrons of the outermost shells

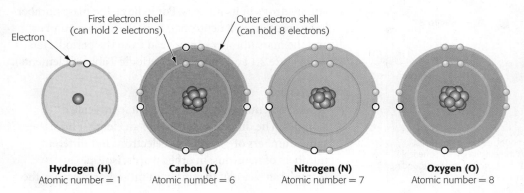

First electron shell (can hold 2 electrons)
Outer electron shell (can hold 8 electrons)
Electron

Hydrogen (H) Atomic number = 1

Carbon (C) Atomic number = 6

Nitrogen (N) Atomic number = 7

Oxygen (O) Atomic number = 8

◄ **Figure 2.6 Atoms of the four elements most abundant in living matter.** All four atoms are chemically reactive because their outermost electron shells are not filled. The small empty circles (o) in these diagrams represent unfilled "spaces" in the outer electron shells.

Chemical Bonding and Molecules

Chemical reactions enable atoms to give up or acquire electrons, thereby completing their outer electron shells. Atoms do this by either transferring or sharing their outermost electrons. These interactions usually result in atoms staying close together, held by attractions called **chemical bonds**. In this section, we will discuss three types of chemical bonds: ionic, covalent, and hydrogen bonds.

Ionic Bonds

Table salt is an example of how the transfer of electrons can bond atoms together. The two ingredients of table salt are the elements sodium (Na) and chlorine (Cl). When a chlorine atom strips an electron from a sodium atom, the electron transfer results in both atoms having full outer shells of electrons **(Figure 2.7)**. Before the electron transfer, each of these atoms is electrically neutral. Because electrons are negatively charged, the electron transfer moves one unit of negative charge from sodium to chlorine. Both atoms are now **ions**, atoms or molecules that are electrically charged as a result of gaining or losing electrons. The loss of an electron gives the sodium ion a charge of $+1$, while chlorine's gain of an electron gives it a charge of -1. The sodium ion (Na^+) and chloride ion (Cl^-) are held together by an **ionic bond**, the attraction between oppositely charged ions. Compounds, such as table salt, that are held together by ionic bonds are called ionic compounds. (Note that negatively charged ions often have names ending in "-ide," like "chloride" or "fluoride.") ☑

Covalent Bonds

In contrast to the complete *transfer* of electrons in ionic bonds, a **covalent bond** forms when two atoms *share* one or more pairs of outer-shell electrons. Covalent bonds are the strongest of the various bonds discussed here; they are the ones that hold atoms together in a **molecule**. For example, a covalent bond connects each hydrogen atom to the carbon atom in the molecule CH_4, a molecule called methane (the main component of natural gas). In **Figure 2.8**, you can see that each of the four hydrogen atoms in a molecule of

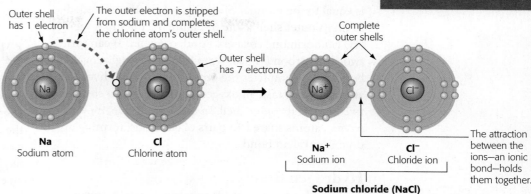

▼ **Figure 2.7 Electron transfer and ionic bonding.** When a sodium atom and a chlorine atom meet, the electron transfer between the two atoms results in two ions with opposite charges.

Outer shell has 1 electron

The outer electron is stripped from sodium and completes the chlorine atom's outer shell.

Outer shell has 7 electrons

Complete outer shells

Na
Sodium atom

Cl
Chlorine atom

Na⁺
Sodium ion

Cl⁻
Chloride ion

The attraction between the ions—an ionic bond—holds them together.

Sodium chloride (NaCl)

☑ CHECKPOINT

When a lithium ion (Li^+) joins a bromide ion (Br^-) to form lithium bromide, the resulting bond is a(n) _____ bond.

Answer: ionic

Name (molecular formula)	Electron configuration Shows how each atom completes its outer shell by sharing electrons	Structural formula Represents each covalent bond (a pair of shared electrons) with a line	Space-filling model Shows the shape of a molecule by symbolizing atoms with color-coded balls	Ball-and-stick model Represents atoms with "balls" and bonds with "sticks"
Hydrogen gas (H_2)	(H) (H)	H—H **Single bond** (a pair of shared electrons)		
Oxygen gas (O_2)	(O) (O)	O═O **Double bond** (two pairs of shared electrons)		
Methane (CH_4)	(H)(H)(C)(H)(H)	H—C—H with H above and below 		

◄ **Figure 2.8 Alternative ways to represent molecules.** A molecular formula, such as CH_4 or H_2O, tells you the number of each kind of atom in a molecule but not how they are attached together. This figure shows four common ways of representing the arrangement of atoms in molecules.

methane shares one pair of electrons with the single carbon atom.

The number of covalent bonds an atom can form is equal to the number of additional electrons needed to fill its outer shell. Note in Figure 2.8 that hydrogen (H) can form one covalent bond, oxygen (O) can form two, and carbon (C) can form four. The single covalent bond in H_2 completes the outer shells of both hydrogen atoms. In contrast, an oxygen atom needs two electrons to complete its outer shell. In an O_2 molecule, the two oxygen atoms share two pairs of electrons, forming a double covalent bond.

Hydrogen Bonds

A molecule of water (H_2O) consists of two hydrogen atoms joined to one oxygen atom by single covalent bonds (the "sticks" represent bonds between the atoms, which are shown as "balls"):

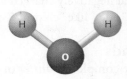

However, the electrons are not shared equally between the oxygen and hydrogen atoms. The two yellow arrows shown here indicate the stronger pull on the shared electrons that oxygen has compared with its hydrogen partners:

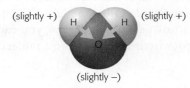

(slightly +)   (slightly +)

(slightly −)

The unequal sharing of negatively charged electrons, combined with its V shape, makes a water molecule polar. A **polar molecule** is one with an uneven distribution of charge. In the case of water, the oxygen end of the molecule has a slight negative charge, while the region around the two hydrogen atoms is slightly positive.

The polarity of water results in weak electrical attractions between neighboring water molecules. Because opposite charges attract, water molecules tend to orient such that a hydrogen atom from one water molecule is near the oxygen atom of an adjacent water

molecule. These weak attractions are called **hydrogen bonds (Figure 2.9)**. As you will see later in this chapter, the ability of water to form hydrogen bonds has many crucial implications for life on Earth.

Chemical Reactions

The chemistry of life is dynamic. Your cells are constantly rearranging molecules by breaking existing chemical bonds and forming new ones. Such changes in the chemical composition of matter are called **chemical reactions**. A simple example is the reaction between oxygen gas and hydrogen gas that forms water (this is an explosive reaction, which, fortunately, does not occur in your cells):

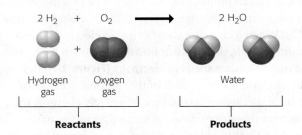

$2 H_2$ + O_2 → $2 H_2O$

Hydrogen gas   Oxygen gas   Water

Reactants   **Products**

Let's translate the chemical shorthand: Two molecules of hydrogen gas ($2 H_2$) react with one molecule of oxygen gas (O_2) to form two molecules of water ($2 H_2O$). The arrow indicates the conversion of the starting materials, the **reactants** ($2 H_2$ and O_2), to the **products** ($2 H_2O$).

Notice that the same numbers of hydrogen and oxygen atoms are present in reactants and products, although they are grouped differently. Chemical reactions cannot create or destroy matter, but only rearrange it.

These rearrangements usually involve the breaking of chemical bonds in reactants and the forming of new bonds in products.

The water molecules we have built here are a good conclusion to this section on basic chemistry. Water is a substance so important in biology that we'll take a closer look at its life-supporting properties in the next section. ✔

Hydrogen bond

(−)

(+)

H
O H

(+) (−)

(−)

(+)

Slightly positive charge

Slightly negative charge

(+) (−)

◀ **Figure 2.9 Hydrogen bonding in water.** The charged regions of the polar water molecules are attracted to oppositely charged areas of neighboring molecules. Each molecule can hydrogen-bond to a maximum of four partners.

☑ CHECKPOINT

Predict the formula for the compound that results when a molecule of sulfur trioxide (SO_3) combines with a molecule of water to produce a single molecule of product. (*Hint*: In chemical reactions, no atoms are gained or lost.)

Answer: H_2SO_4 (sulfuric acid), a component of acid rain.

Water and Life

Life on Earth began in water and evolved there for 3 billion years before spreading onto land. Modern life, even land-dwelling life, is still tied to water. You've had personal experience with this dependence on water every time you seek liquids to quench your thirst. Inside your body, your cells are surrounded by a fluid that's composed mostly of water, and your cells themselves range from 70% to 95% in water content.

The abundance of water is a major reason that Earth is habitable. Water is so common that it is easy to overlook the fact that it is an exceptional substance with many extraordinary properties **(Figure 2.10)**. We can trace water's unique life-supporting properties to the structure and interactions of its molecules.

Water's Life-Supporting Properties

The polarity of water molecules and the hydrogen bonding that results (see Figure 2.9) explain most of water's life-supporting properties. We'll explore four of those properties here: the cohesive nature of water, the ability of water to moderate temperature, the biological significance of ice floating, and the versatility of water as a solvent.

The Cohesion of Water

Water molecules stick together as a result of hydrogen bonding. Hydrogen bonds between molecules of liquid water last for only a few trillionths of a second, yet at any instant, many molecules are hydrogen-bonded to others. This tendency of molecules of the same kind to stick together, called **cohesion**, is much stronger for water than for most other liquids. The cohesion of water is important in the living world. Trees, for example, depend on cohesion to help transport water from their roots to their leaves **(Figure 2.11)**.

Related to cohesion is surface tension, a measure of how difficult it is to stretch or break the surface of a liquid. Hydrogen bonds give water unusually high surface tension, making it behave as though it were coated with an invisible film **(Figure 2.12)**. Other liquids have much weaker surface tension.

▲ **Figure 2.10 A watery world.** You can see each of the three physical states of water in this photograph: liquid water (which covers three-quarters of Earth's surface), ice, and water vapor (as fog and clouds).

Evaporation from the leaves

Flow of water

▲ **Figure 2.11 Cohesion and water transport in plants.** The evaporation of water from leaves pulls water upward from the roots through microscopic tubes in the trunk of the tree. Because of cohesion, the pulling force is relayed through the tubes all the way down to the roots. As a result, water rises against the force of gravity.

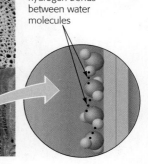

Microscopic water-conducting tubes

Cohesion due to hydrogen bonds between water molecules

Colorized SEM 150x

▼ **Figure 2.12 A raft spider walking on water.** The cumulative strength of hydrogen bonds between water molecules allows this spider to walk on pond water without breaking the surface.

How Water Moderates Temperature

If you've ever burned your finger on a metal pot while waiting for the water in it to boil, you know that water heats up much more slowly than metal. In fact, because of hydrogen bonding, water has a stronger resistance to temperature change than most other substances.

Temperature and heat are related but different. A swimmer crossing San Francisco Bay has a higher temperature than the water, but the bay contains far more heat because of its immense volume. **Heat** is the amount of energy associated with the movement of the atoms and molecules in a body of matter. **Temperature** measures the intensity of heat—that is, the average speed of molecules rather than the total amount of heat energy in a body of matter.

Why do days that are hot and humid feel so uncomfortable?

When water is heated, the heat energy first disrupts hydrogen bonds and then makes water molecules jostle around faster. The temperature of the water doesn't go up until the water molecules start to speed up. Because heat is first used to break hydrogen bonds rather than raise the temperature, water absorbs and stores a large amount of heat while warming up only a few degrees. Conversely, when water cools, hydrogen bonds form, a process that releases heat. Thus, water can release a relatively large amount of heat to the surroundings while the water temperature drops only slightly.

Earth's giant water supply—the oceans, seas, lakes, and rivers—enables temperatures to stay within limits that permit life by storing a huge amount of heat from the sun during warm periods and giving off heat to warm the air during cold conditions. That's why coastal areas generally have milder climates than inland regions. Water's resistance to temperature change also stabilizes ocean temperatures, creating a favorable environment for marine life.

Another way that water moderates temperature is by **evaporative cooling**. When a substance evaporates (changes physical state from a liquid to a gas), the surface of the liquid remaining behind cools down. This occurs because the molecules with the greatest energy (the "hottest" ones) tend to vaporize first. It's as if the five fastest runners on your track team quit school, lowering the average speed of the remaining team. Evaporative cooling helps prevent some land-dwelling creatures from overheating; it's why sweating helps you dissipate excess body heat **(Figure 2.13)**. And the old expression "It's not the heat, it's the humidity" has its basis in the difficulty of sweating water into air that is already saturated with water vapor.

The Biological Significance of Ice Floating

When most liquids get cold, their molecules move closer together. If the temperature is cold enough, the liquid freezes and becomes a solid. Water, however, behaves differently. When water molecules get cold enough, they move apart, with each molecule staying at "arm's length" from its neighbors, forming ice. A chunk of ice therefore has fewer molecules than an equal volume of liquid water; it floats because it is less dense than liquid water. Like water's other life-supporting properties, floating ice is a consequence of hydrogen bonding. In contrast to the short-lived and constantly-changing hydrogen bonds in liquid water, those in solid ice last longer, with each molecule bonded to four neighbors. As a result, ice is a spacious crystal **(Figure 2.14)**.

▲ **Figure 2.13 Sweating as a mechanism of evaporative cooling.**

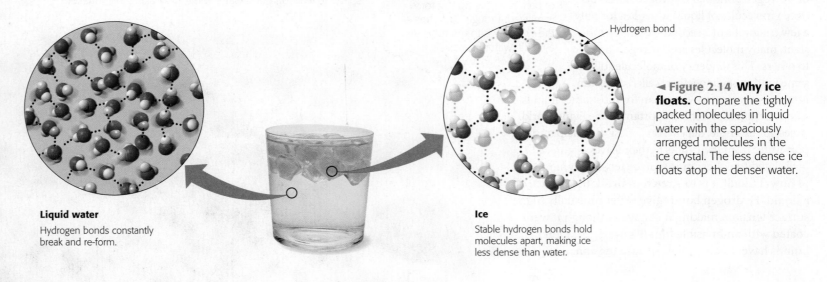

Liquid water
Hydrogen bonds constantly break and re-form.

Hydrogen bond

Ice
Stable hydrogen bonds hold molecules apart, making ice less dense than water.

◀ **Figure 2.14 Why ice floats.** Compare the tightly packed molecules in liquid water with the spaciously arranged molecules in the ice crystal. The less dense ice floats atop the denser water.

How does the ability of ice to float help support life on Earth? Imagine what would happen if ice was denser than water. If this were true, ice would sink during winter. All ponds, lakes, and even the oceans would eventually freeze solid. During summer, only the upper few inches of the oceans would thaw. Instead, when a deep body of water cools, the floating ice forms an insulating "blanket" over the liquid water, allowing life to persist under the frozen surface.

Water as the Solvent of Life

If you've ever enjoyed a glass of sweetened ice tea or added salt to soup, you know that you can dissolve sugar or salt in water. This results in a mixture known as a **solution**, a liquid consisting of a homogeneous mixture of two or more substances. The dissolving agent is called the **solvent**, and any substance that is dissolved is called a **solute**. When water is the solvent, the resulting solution is called an **aqueous solution**. The fluids of organisms are aqueous solutions. For example, blood, plant sap, and the fluid in and around cells are all aqueous solutions.

Water can dissolve an enormous variety of solutes necessary for life, providing a medium for chemical reactions. For example, water can dissolve salt ions, as shown in **Figure 2.15**. Each ion becomes surrounded by oppositely charged regions of water molecules. Solutes that are polar molecules, such as sugars, dissolve by orienting locally charged regions of their molecules toward water molecules in a similar way.

We have discussed four special properties of water. Next, we'll consider one way that water's unique structure can reveal important clues about the human brain. ☑

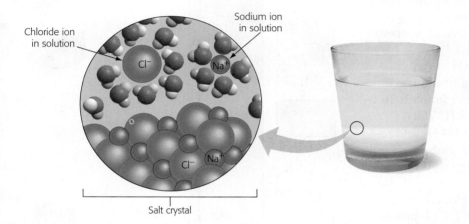

Chloride ion in solution
Sodium ion in solution
Cl⁻   Na⁺
Cl⁻   Na⁺
Salt crystal

◄ **Figure 2.15 A crystal of table salt (NaCl) dissolving in water.** As a result of electrical charge attractions, H_2O molecules surround the sodium and chloride ions, dissolving the crystal in the process.

 Life's Dependence on Water THE PROCESS OF SCIENCE

Can Exercise Boost Your Brain Power?

Biologists use a number of imaging techniques to reveal the body's inner structure. One such technique, magnetic resonance imaging (MRI), depends on the behavior of the hydrogen atoms in water molecules. MRI first aligns the hydrogen nuclei with powerful magnets, then knocks the nuclei out of alignment with a brief pulse of radio waves. In response, the hydrogen atoms give out faint radio signals of their own, which are picked up by the MRI scanner and translated by computer into an image. Since water is a major component of all of our soft tissues, MRI allows doctors to see regions of the body that are invisible to X-rays.

MRI has been particularly useful in studying the brain. One recent study began with the **observation** that the human brain shrinks as we age: About 20% of our brain matter is lost between ages 30 and 90, and the shrinkage is most prominent in brain areas responsible for memory and learning. Because exercise had been previously associated with improved memory, researchers from the University of Illinois asked the **question**, Can aerobic exercise slow or even reverse brain loss? Their **hypothesis** was that MRI scans would reveal differences between the brains of people who regularly exercised and those who did not. They made the **prediction** that the brains of active people would shrink less than the brains of less active people.

In their **experiment**, 29 research participants in their 60s and 70s participated for six months in an exercise program of three 1-hour aerobic training sessions per week. A control group of 29 participants (matched for age) engaged in a

program of nonaerobic whole-body stretching lasting the same duration. At the start and end of the program, MRI was used to scan the brains of all participants. The **results** of the experiment showed significant increases in brain volume in the aerobic group but not in the non-aerobic controls **(Figure 2.16)**. The researchers concluded that there may be a link between cardiovascular fitness and the retention of memory in aging adults. In other words, regular aerobic exercise may benefit both your body and your mind.

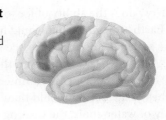

► Figure 2.16 **The effect of aerobic exercise on brain size.** The highlighted portion corresponds to regions of the brain that grew in aerobic exercise participants but not in a control group of non-aerobic exercisers.

Acids, Bases, and pH

In aqueous solutions, most of the water molecules are intact. However, some of the water molecules actually break apart into hydrogen ions (H^+) and hydroxide ions (OH^-). A balance of these two highly reactive ions is critical for the proper functioning of chemical processes within organisms.

A chemical compound that releases H^+ to a solution is called an **acid**. One example of a strong acid is hydrochloric acid (HCl), the acid in your stomach. In solution, HCl breaks apart into the ions H^+ and Cl^-. A **base** (or alkali) is a compound that accepts H^+ and removes them from solution. Some bases, such as sodium hydroxide (NaOH), do this by releasing OH^-, which combines with H^+ to form H_2O.

To describe the acidity of a solution, chemists use the **pH scale**, a measure of the hydrogen ion (H^+) concentration in a solution. The scale ranges from 0 (most acidic) to 14 (most basic). Each pH unit represents a tenfold change in the concentration of H^+ **(Figure 2.17)**. For example, lemon juice at pH 2 has 100 times more H^+ than an equal amount of tomato juice at pH 4. Aqueous solutions that are neither acidic nor basic (such as pure water) are said to be neutral; they have a pH of 7. They do contain some H^+ and OH^-, but the concentrations of the two ions are equal. The pH of the solution inside most living cells is close to 7.

Did you drink an acid today?

Even a slight change in pH can be harmful to an organism because the molecules in cells are extremely sensitive to H^+ and OH^- concentrations. Biological fluids contain **buffers**, substances that minimize changes in pH by accepting H^+ when that ion is in excess and donating H^+ when it is depleted. This buffering process, however, is not

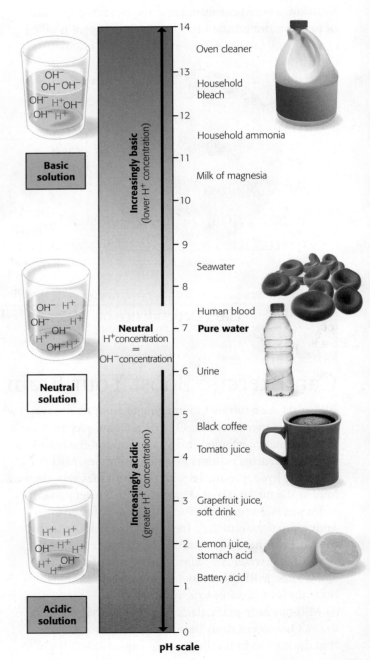

► Figure 2.17 **The pH scale.** A solution having a pH of 7 is neutral, meaning that its H^+ and OH^- concentrations are equal. The lower the pH below 7, the more acidic the solution, or the greater its excess of H^+ compared with OH^-. The higher the pH above 7, the more basic the solution, or the greater the deficiency of H^+ relative to OH^-.

Basic solution

OH^-
$OH^- OH^-$
$OH^- H^+ OH^-$
$OH^- H^+$

Neutral solution

$OH^- H^+$
$OH^- H^+$
$H^+ OH^-$
$OH^- H^+$

Acidic solution

$H^+ H^+$
$OH^- H^+ H^+$
$H^+ OH^-$
H^+

Increasingly basic (lower H^+ concentration)

Neutral
H^+ concentration = OH^- concentration

Increasingly acidic (greater H^+ concentration)

pH scale

14 — Oven cleaner
13 — Household bleach
12 — Household ammonia
11 — Milk of magnesia
10
9 — Seawater
8 — Human blood
7 — **Pure water**
6 — Urine
5 — Black coffee
4 — Tomato juice
3 — Grapefruit juice, soft drink
2 — Lemon juice, stomach acid
1 — Battery acid
0

foolproof, and changes in environmental pH can profoundly affect ecosystems. For example, much of the human-made CO_2 released into the atmosphere is absorbed by the oceans. When it combines with seawater, a chemical reaction produces an acid. The resulting ocean acidification can greatly change marine environments. This principle was illustrated by a 2008 study of the Mediterranean Sea near Naples, Italy. There, undersea volcanoes release high levels of CO_2 (**Figure 2.18**). Researchers found that the resulting acidification caused coral reef collapse and widespread death of marine organisms. This natural system suggests that high levels of dissolved human-made CO_2 could cause similar ecological disaster.

The effects of ocean acidification are daunting reminders that the chemistry of life is linked to the chemistry of the environment. It reminds us, too, that chemistry happens on a global scale, since industrial processes in one region of the world often cause acid precipitation to fall in another part of the world. ☑

◄ **Figure 2.18 The release of volcanic CO_2, causing undersea bubbling off the coast of Italy.**

☑ **CHECKPOINT**

Compared with a solution of pH 8, the same volume of a solution at pH 5 has _____ times more hydrogen ions (H^+). This second solution is considered a(n)_____.

Answer: 1,000; acid

Life's Dependence on Water   EVOLUTION CONNECTION

The Search for Extraterrestrial Life

Throughout this chapter, we have highlighted the importance of water to living systems. In fact, water is the substance that makes life as we know it possible.

One of the great questions facing humankind is: Has life evolved elsewhere in the universe? If it has, and if this life is at all similar to ours, then it, too, would depend on water. This explains why the search for water on other planets is such a priority for the U.S. space program.

Researchers at the National Aeronautics and Space Administration (NASA) have found evidence that water was once abundant on Mars. (Although Mars has clearly visible polar ice caps, no liquid water is known to flow there at present.) In January 2004, NASA landed two golf-cart-sized rovers on Mars. These robotic geologists determined the composition of rocks and sent back images of rock formations. One of the rovers detected a mineral that is formed only in the presence of water. Furthermore, pictures revealed physical evidence of the effects of liquid water flowing over the Martian surface in the past.

Images taken by NASA's *Mars Global Surveyor* spacecraft indicate that not only did the red planet have a water-filled ancient past, but liquid water may have flowed recently on its surface. In 2008, an analysis of Martian soil by the *Phoenix Mars Lander* (**Figure 2.19**) provided evidence that components of the soil had at one time been dissolved in water. As this chapter has shown, where there is water, there may indeed be life. The evidence for water on Mars raises the tantalizing possibility that microbial life may exist below the Martian surface.

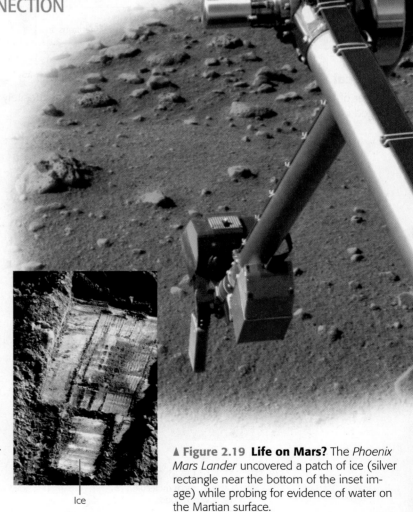

Ice

▲ **Figure 2.19 Life on Mars?** The *Phoenix Mars Lander* uncovered a patch of ice (silver rectangle near the bottom of the inset image) while probing for evidence of water on the Martian surface.

Chapter Review

SUMMARY OF KEY CONCEPTS

 Go to **www.masteringbiology.com** for homework assignments, practice quizzes, Pearson eText, and more.

Some Basic Chemistry

Matter: Elements and Compounds

Matter consists of elements and compounds, which are combinations of two or more elements. Of the 25 elements essential for life, oxygen, carbon, hydrogen, and nitrogen are the most abundant in living matter.

Atoms

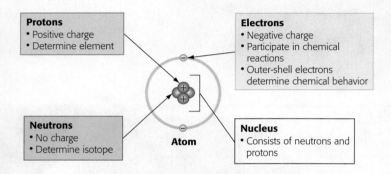

Protons
• Positive charge
• Determine element

Electrons
• Negative charge
• Participate in chemical reactions
• Outer-shell electrons determine chemical behavior

Neutrons
• No charge
• Determine isotope

Atom

Nucleus
• Consists of neutrons and protons

Chemical Bonding and Molecules

Transfer of one or more electrons produces attractions between oppositely charged ions:

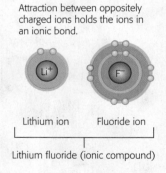

Attraction between oppositely charged ions holds the ions in an ionic bond.

Lithium ion   Fluoride ion

Lithium fluoride (ionic compound)

A molecule consists of two or more atoms connected by covalent bonds, which are formed by electron sharing:

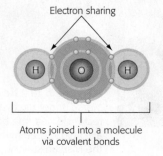

Electron sharing

Atoms joined into a molecule via covalent bonds

Water is a polar molecule; the slightly positively charged H atoms in one water molecule may be attracted to the partial negative charge of O atoms in neighboring water molecules, forming weak but important hydrogen bonds:

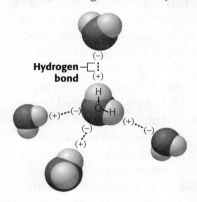

Hydrogen bond

Chemical Reactions

By breaking bonds in reactants and forming new bonds in products, chemical reactions rearrange matter.

Water and Life

Water's Life-Supporting Properties

The ability of leaves to pull water up microscopic tubes within trunks and stems is an example of how water's cohesion supports life. Water moderates temperature by absorbing heat in warm environments and releasing heat in cold environments. Evaporative cooling also helps stabilize the temperatures of oceans and organisms. Ice floats because it is less dense than liquid water, preventing the oceans from freezing solid. Blood and other biological fluids are aqueous solutions with a diversity of solutes dissolved in water, a versatile solvent.

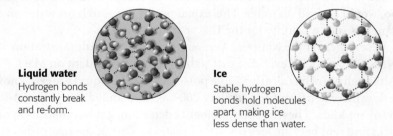

Liquid water
Hydrogen bonds constantly break and re-form.

Ice
Stable hydrogen bonds hold molecules apart, making ice less dense than water.

Acids, Bases, and pH

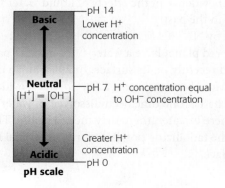

Basic — pH 14 Lower H^+ concentration

Neutral $[H^+] = [OH^-]$ — pH 7 H^+ concentration equal to OH^- concentration

Greater H^+ concentration

Acidic — pH 0

pH scale

SELF-QUIZ

1. An atom can be changed into an ion by adding or removing _____. An atom can be changed into a different isotope by adding or removing _____. But if you change the number of _____, the atom becomes a different element.

2. A nitrogen atom has 7 protons, and the most common isotope of nitrogen has 7 neutrons. A radioactive isotope of nitrogen has 9 neutrons. What are the atomic numbers and mass numbers of the stable and radioactive forms of nitrogen?

3. Why are radioactive isotopes useful as tracers in research on the chemistry of life?

4. A sulfur atom has 6 electrons in its third (outermost) shell, which can hold 8 electrons. As a result, it forms _____ covalent bonds with other atoms. (Provide a number.)

5. What is chemically nonsensical about this structure?

   H—C≡C—H

6. Why is it unlikely that two neighboring water molecules would be arranged like this?

7. Which of the following is not a chemical reaction?
   a. Sugar ($C_6H_{12}O_6$) and oxygen gas (O_2) combine to form carbon dioxide (CO_2) and water (H_2O).
   b. Sodium metal and chlorine gas unite to form sodium chloride.
   c. Hydrogen gas combines with oxygen gas to form water.
   d. Ice melts to form liquid water.

8. Some people in your study group say they don't understand what a polar molecule is. You explain that a polar molecule
   a. is slightly negative at one end and slightly positive at the other end.
   b. has an extra electron, giving it a positive charge.
   c. has an extra electron, giving it a negative charge.
   d. has covalent bonds.

9. Explain how the unique properties of water result from the fact that water is a polar molecule.

10. A can of cola consists mostly of sugar dissolved in water, with some carbon dioxide gas that makes it fizzy and makes the pH less than 7. Describe the cola using the following terms: solute, solvent, acidic, aqueous solution.

Answers to these questions can be found in Appendix: Self-Quiz Answers.

THE PROCESS OF SCIENCE

11. Animals obtain energy through a series of chemical reactions in which sugar ($C_6H_{12}O_6$) and oxygen gas (O_2) are reactants. This process produces water (H_2O) and carbon dioxide (CO_2) as waste products. How might you use a radioactive isotope to find out whether the oxygen in CO_2 comes from sugar or from oxygen gas?

12. The following diagram shows the arrangement of electrons around the nucleus of a fluorine atom (left) and a potassium atom (right). Predict what would happen if a fluorine atom and a potassium atom came into contact. What kind of bond do you think they would form?

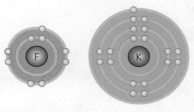

Fluorine atom   Potassium atom

BIOLOGY AND SOCIETY

13. Critically evaluate this statement: "It's paranoid and ignorant to worry about industry or agriculture contaminating the environment with chemical wastes; this stuff is just made of the same atoms that were already present in our environment."

14. A major source of the CO_2 that causes ocean acidification is emissions from coal-burning power plants. One way to reduce these emissions is to use nuclear power to produce electricity. The proponents of nuclear power contend that it is the only way that the United States can increase its energy production while reducing air pollution, because nuclear power plants emit little or no acid-precipitation-causing pollutants. What are some of the benefits of nuclear power? What are the possible costs and dangers? Do you think we ought to increase our use of nuclear power to generate electricity? Why or why not? If a new power plant were to be built near your home, would you prefer it to be a coal-burning plant or a nuclear plant? Why?

3 The Molecules of Life

Cheesy pizza.
Lactose digestion results from interactions between several classes of the body's molecules.

Lactose Intolerance BIOLOGY AND SOCIETY

Got Lactose?

You've probably seen ads meant to convince you that a milk mustache represents good health. Indeed, milk is a very healthy food because it's rich in protein, minerals, and vitamins. But for the majority of adults in the world, a glass of milk or a serving of milk-containing foods (such as cheesy pizza or ice cream) can cause bloating, gas, and other discomforts. These are symptoms of lactose intolerance, the inability to digest lactose, the main sugar found in milk.

For people with lactose intolerance, the problem starts when lactose enters the small intestine. To absorb this sugar, digestive cells there must produce a molecule called lactase. Lactase is an enzyme, a protein that helps drive chemical reactions—in this case, the breakdown of lactose into smaller sugars. People with lactose intolerance produce insufficient amounts or a defective version of the enzyme. Lactose that is not broken down in the small intestine passes into the large intestine, where bacteria feed on it and belch out gaseous by-products, producing uncomfortable symptoms. Sufficient lactase can thus mean the difference between delight and discomfort when someone feasts on an ice cream sundae.

What options are there for people with lactose intolerance? There is no treatment for the underlying cause: the decreased production of lactase. But symptoms can be controlled through diet. The first option is avoiding lactose-containing foods. Many substitutes are available, such as milk made from soy or from milk that has been pretreated with lactase. If you are lactose intolerant and pizza is your staple food, lactose-free cheese (made from soy) can be bought at most supermarkets, or you can make your own mozarella from lactose-free milk. Also, lactase in pill form can be taken along with food to ease digestion by artificially providing the enzyme that the body naturally lacks.

Lactose intolerance illustrates one way the interplay of biological molecules can affect your health. Such molecular interactions, repeated in countless variations, drive all biological processes. In this chapter, we'll explore the structure and function of large molecules that are essential to life. We'll start with an overview of carbon and then examine four classes of molecules: carbohydrates, lipids, proteins, and nucleic acids. Along the way, we'll look at where these molecules occur in your diet and the important roles they play in your body.

Organic Compounds

A cell is mostly water, but the rest of it consists mainly of carbon-based molecules. Carbon is unparalleled in its ability to form the skeletons of large, complex, diverse molecules that are necessary for life's functions. The study of carbon-based molecules, which are called **organic compounds**, lies at the heart of any study of life.

Could a cow someday fuel your car?

Carbon Chemistry

Why are carbon atoms so versatile as molecular ingredients? Recall that an atom's bonding ability is related to the number of electrons it must share to complete its outer shell. A carbon atom has 4 electrons in an outer shell that holds 8. Carbon completes its outer shell by sharing electrons with other atoms in four covalent bonds that can branch off in four directions. Because carbon can use one or more of its bonds to attach to other carbon atoms, it is possible to construct an endless diversity of carbon skeletons varying in size and branching pattern (**Figure 3.1**). Thus, molecules with multiple carbon "intersections" can form very elaborate shapes. The carbon atoms of organic compounds can also use one or more of their bonds to partner with other elements, most commonly hydrogen, oxygen, and nitrogen.

In terms of chemical composition, the simplest organic compounds are **hydrocarbons**, which contain only carbon and hydrogen atoms. And the simplest hydrocarbon is methane: CH_4, a single carbon atom bonded to four hydrogen atoms (**Figure 3.2**). Methane is one of the most abundant hydrocarbons in natural gas and is also produced by prokaryotes that live in swamps and in the digestive tracts of grazing animals, such as cows. Larger hydrocarbons (such as octane, with eight carbons) are the main molecules in the gasoline we burn in cars and other machines (**Figure 3.3**). Hydrocarbons are also important fuels in your body; the energy-rich parts of fat molecules have a hydrocarbon structure.

As you will see in subsequent chapters, a recurring theme in biology is the importance of the shape of molecules. Many vital processes within living organisms rely on the ability of molecules to recognize one another based on their shape.

The unique properties of an organic compound depend not only on its carbon skeleton but also on the atoms attached to the skeleton. In an organic compound, the groups of atoms directly involved in chemical

▼ Figure 3.2 **Methane, the simplest hydrocarbon.**

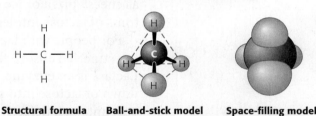

Structural formula   **Ball-and-stick model**   **Space-filling model**

▼ Figure 3.1 **Variations in carbon skeletons.** All of these examples are hydrocarbons, organic compounds consisting only of carbon and hydrogen. Notice that each carbon atom forms four bonds and each hydrogen atom forms one bond. Remember that one line represents a single bond (sharing of one pair of electrons) and two lines represent a double bond (sharing of two pairs of electrons).

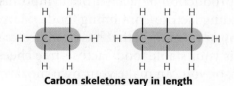

Carbon skeletons vary in length

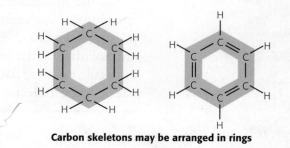

Carbon skeletons may have double bonds, which can vary in location

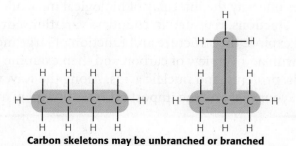

Carbon skeletons may be unbranched or branched

Carbon skeletons may be arranged in rings

▼ Figure 3.3 Hydrocarbons as fuel. Energy-rich hydrocarbons in gasoline provide fuel for machines, and energy-rich hydrocarbons in fats provide fuel for cells.

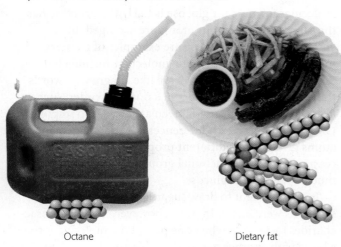

Octane   Dietary fat

reactions are called **functional groups**. Each functional group plays a particular role during chemical reactions. Two examples of functional groups are the hydroxyl group (—OH) and the carboxyl group (—COOH). Many biological molecules have two or more functional groups. Keeping in mind this basic scheme—carbon skeletons with functional groups—we are now ready to see how our cells make large molecules out of smaller ones.

Giant Molecules from Smaller Building Blocks

On a molecular scale, the members of three categories of large biological molecules—carbohydrates (such as those found in starchy foods like French fries and bagels), proteins (such as enzymes and the components of your hair), and nucleic acids (such as DNA)—are gigantic; in fact, biologists call them **macromolecules** (*macro* means "big"). Despite the size of macromolecules, their structures can be easily understood because they are **polymers**, large molecules made by stringing together many smaller molecules called **monomers**. A polymer is like a pearl necklace made by joining together many pearl monomers.

Cells link monomers together to form polymers through a **dehydration** reaction, a chemical reaction that removes a molecule of water (**Figure 3.4a**). For each monomer added to a chain, a water molecule (H_2O) is formed by the release of two hydrogen atoms and one oxygen atom. This same dehydration reaction occurs regardless of the specific monomers and the type of polymer the cell is producing.

Organisms not only make macromolecules but also break them down. For example, many molecules in your food are macromolecules. You must digest these giant molecules to make their monomers available to your cells, which can then rebuild the monomers into the macromolecules that make up your body. Converting macromolecules is like taking apart a car (food) made of Legos and then using the Legos (monomers) to assemble a new car (macromolecule) of your own design. The breakdown of polymers occurs by a process called **hydrolysis** (**Figure 3.4b**). Hydrolysis means to break (*lyse*) with water (*hydro*). Cells break bonds between monomers by adding water to them, a process that is essentially the reverse of a dehydration reaction. You've already heard of one example of a hydrolysis reaction: the breakdown of lactose into its monomers by the enzyme lactase. ☑

☑ CHECKPOINT

1. Chemical reactions that build _____ from _____ are called _____ reactions. _____ reverses these reactions.
2. When two molecules of glucose ($C_6H_{12}O_6$) are joined together, what are the formulas of the two products? (*Hint*: No atoms are gained or lost.)

Answers: **1.** polymers; monomers; dehydration; Hydrolysis **2.** $C_6H_{12}O_6 + C_6H_{12}O_6 \rightarrow C_{12}H_{22}O_{11} + H_2O$

▼ Figure 3.4 Synthesis and digestion of polymers. For simplicity, the only atoms shown in these diagrams are hydrogens and hydroxyl groups (—OH) in strategic locations.

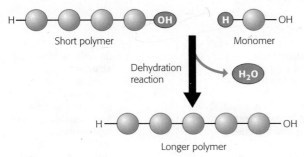

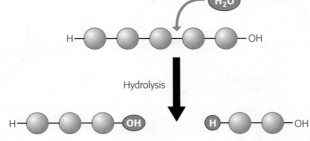

(a) Building a polymer chain. A polymer grows in length when an incoming monomer and the monomer at the end of the polymer each contribute atoms to form a water molecule. The monomers replace the lost covalent bonds with a bond to each other.

(b) Breaking a polymer chain. Hydrolysis reverses the process by adding a water molecule, which breaks the bond between two monomers, creating 2 smaller molecules from one bigger one.

Large Biological Molecules

The remainder of the chapter will introduce you to the four categories of large biological molecules: carbohydrates, lipids, proteins, and nucleic acids. For each category, we'll explore the structure and function of these large molecules by first learning about the smaller molecules used to build them.

Carbohydrates

Carbohydrates, commonly known as "carbs," are a class of molecules that includes sugars and polymers of sugars. Some examples are the small sugar molecules dissolved in energy drinks and the long starch molecules in spaghetti and bread. In animals, carbohydrates are a primary source of dietary energy and raw material for manufacturing other kinds of organic compounds; in plants, they serve as a building material for much of the plant body.

Monosaccharides

Simple sugars, or **monosaccharides** (from the Greek *mono*, single, and *sacchar*, sugar), are the monomers of carbohydrates; they cannot be broken down into smaller sugars. Common examples are glucose, found in sports drinks, and fructose, found in fruit. Both of these simple sugars are also in honey **(Figure 3.5)**. The

molecular formula for glucose is $C_6H_{12}O_6$. Fructose has the same formula, but its atoms are arranged differently. Glucose and fructose are examples of **isomers**, molecules that have the same molecular formula but different structures. Isomers are like anagrams—words that contain the same letters in a different order, such as *heart* and *earth*. Because molecular shape is so important, seemingly minor differences in the arrangement of atoms give isomers different properties. In this case, the rearrangement of functional groups makes fructose taste much sweeter than glucose.

It is convenient to draw sugars as if their carbon skeletons were linear. In water, however, many monosaccharides form rings when one part of the molecule forms a bond with another part of the molecule **(Figure 3.6)**. You'll notice this ring shape in the structure of many carbohydrates in this chapter.

Monosaccharides, particularly glucose, are the main fuel molecules for cellular work. Like an automobile engine consuming gasoline, your cells break down glucose molecules and extract their stored energy, giving off carbon dioxide as "exhaust." The rapid conversion of glucose to cellular energy is why an aqueous solution of glucose (often called dextrose) is given as an IV to sick or injured patients; the glucose provides an immediate energy source to tissues in need of repair. ✔

► **Figure 3.5**
Monosaccharides (simple sugars). These molecules have the two trademarks of sugars: several hydroxyl groups (—OH) and a carbonyl group (C=O). Glucose and fructose, which make honey sweet, are isomers.

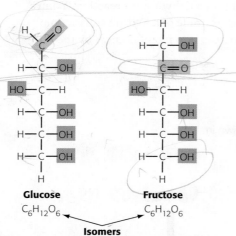
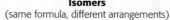

Glucose
$C_6H_{12}O_6$

Fructose
$C_6H_{12}O_6$

Isomers
(same formula, different arrangements)

▼ **Figure 3.6** **The ring structure of glucose.**

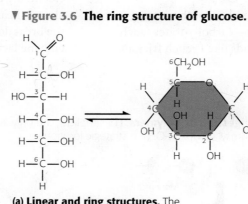

(a) Linear and ring structures. The carbon atoms are numbered so you can relate the linear and ring versions of the molecule. As the double arrows indicate, ring formation is a reversible process, but at any instant in an aqueous solution, most glucose molecules are rings.

(b) Abbreviated ring structure. In this book, we'll use this abbreviated ring symbol for glucose. Each unmarked corner represents a carbon and its attached atoms.

Disaccharides

A **disaccharide**, or double sugar, is constructed from two monosaccharides by a dehydration reaction. In the Biology and Society section, you learned about the disaccharide lactose, sometimes called "milk sugar." Lactose is made from the monosaccharides glucose and galactose (**Figure 3.7**). Another common disaccharide is maltose, naturally found in germinating seeds. It is used in making beer, malt whiskey and liquor, malted milk shakes, and malted milk ball candy. A molecule of maltose consists of two glucose monomers joined together.

The most common disaccharide is sucrose (table sugar), which consists of a glucose monomer linked to a fructose monomer. Sucrose is the main carbohydrate in plant sap, and it nourishes all the parts of the plant. Sugar manufacturers extract sucrose from the stems of sugarcane or the roots of sugar beets. However, sucrose is rarely used as a sweetener in processed foods in the United States. Much more common is high-fructose corn syrup, made through a commercial process that converts natural glucose in corn syrup to the much sweeter fructose. If you read the label on a soft drink can or bottle, you're likely to find that high-fructose corn syrup is one of the first ingredients listed (**Figure 3.8**).

The United States is one of the world's leading markets for sweeteners, and the average American consumes about 45 kilograms (kg)—a whopping 100 pounds—per year, mainly in the form of sucrose and high-fructose corn syrup. This national "sweet tooth" persists in spite of our growing awareness about how sugar can negatively affect our health. Sugar is a major cause of tooth decay. Moreover, high sugar consumption tends to replace eating more varied and nutritious foods. The description of sugars as "empty calories" is accurate in the sense that most sweeteners contain only negligible amounts of nutrients other than carbohydrates. For good health, we also require proteins, fats, vitamins, and minerals. And we need to include substantial amounts of complex carbohydrates—that is, polysaccharides—in our diet. Let's examine these macromolecules next.

Chances are you ate beets today—but in what?

▼ **Figure 3.7 Disaccharide (double sugar) formation.** To form a disaccharide, two simple sugars are joined by a dehydration reaction, in this case forming a bond between monomers of glucose and galactose to make the double sugar lactose.

Glucose   Galactose

OH H O

H₂O

Lactose

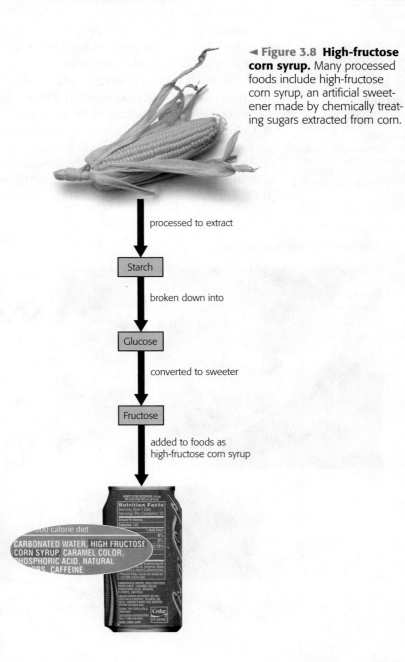

◄ **Figure 3.8 High-fructose corn syrup.** Many processed foods include high-fructose corn syrup, an artificial sweetener made by chemically treating sugars extracted from corn.

processed to extract

Starch

broken down into

Glucose

converted to sweeter

Fructose

added to foods as high-fructose corn syrup

CARBONATED WATER, HIGH FRUCTOSE CORN SYRUP, CARAMEL COLOR, PHOSPHORIC ACID, NATURAL FLAVORS, CAFFEINE

Polysaccharides

Complex carbohydrates, or **polysaccharides**, are long chains of sugars—polymers of monosaccharides. One familiar example is starch, a storage polysaccharide found in plants. **Starch** consists of long strings of glucose monomers (**Figure 3.9a**). Plant cells store starch, providing a sugar stockpile that can be broken down when needed. Potatoes and grains, such as wheat, corn, and rice, are the major sources of starch in our diet. Animals can digest starch because their digestive systems break the bonds between glucose monomers through hydrolysis reactions.

Animals store excess sugar in the form of a polysaccharide called **glycogen**. Like starch, glycogen is a polymer of glucose monomers, but glycogen is more extensively branched (**Figure 3.9b**). Most of your glycogen is stored in liver and muscle cells, which break down the glycogen to release glucose when you need energy. This is why some athletes "carbo load," consuming large amounts of starchy foods the night before an athletic event. The starch is converted to glycogen, which is then available for rapid use during physical activity the next day.

Cellulose, the most abundant organic compound on Earth, forms cable-like fibrils in the tough walls that enclose plant cells and is a major component of wood and other structural components of plants (**Figure 3.9c**). We take advantage of that structural strength when we use lumber as a building material. Cellulose is also a polymer of glucose, but its glucose monomers are linked together in a unique way. Unlike the glucose linkages in starch and glycogen, those in cellulose cannot be broken by animals. The cellulose in plant foods, which passes unchanged through our digestive tract, is commonly known as dietary fiber (your grandma might call it "roughage"). Because it remains undigested, fiber does not serve as a nutrient, but it does help keep your digestive system healthy. Among other benefits, the passage of cellulose stimulates cells lining the digestive tract to secrete mucus, which allows food to pass smoothly. Most Americans do not get the recommended levels of fiber in their diet. Foods rich in fiber include fruits and vegetables, whole grains, bran, and beans. Grazing animals and wood-eating insects such as termites are able to derive nutrition from cellulose because microorganisms inhabiting their digestive tracts break it down.

Monosaccharides (such as glucose or fructose) and disaccharides (such as sucrose or lactose) dissolve readily in water, forming sugary solutions. In contrast, cellulose does not dissolve in water, but water can adhere to its surface, which is why a fluffy bath towel (high in cellulose) is so water absorbent. Thus, almost all carbohydrates are **hydrophilic** ("water-loving") molecules. As you'll see next, not all biological molecules share this property. ☑

▼ **Figure 3.9 Polysaccharides.**

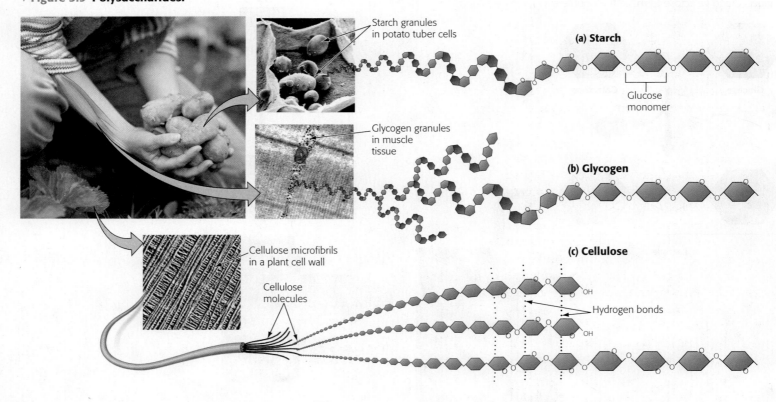

Starch granules in potato tuber cells

(a) Starch

Glucose monomer

Glycogen granules in muscle tissue

(b) Glycogen

Cellulose microfibrils in a plant cell wall

Cellulose molecules

(c) Cellulose

Hydrogen bonds

Lipids

In contrast to most biological molecules, **lipids** are **hydrophobic** ("water-fearing"); they do not mix with water. You've probably seen this chemical behavior when you combine oil and vinegar: The oil, which is a type of lipid, separates from the vinegar, which is mostly water (**Figure 3.10**). If you shake vigorously, you can force a temporary mixture long enough to douse your salad, but what remains in the bottle will quickly separate.

Unlike carbohydrates, proteins, and nucleic acids, lipids are neither macromolecules nor polymers. In fact, lipids are a diverse group of molecules made from different "building blocks." In this section, we'll look at two types of lipids: fats and steroids.

Fats

A typical **fat** consists of a glycerol molecule joined with three fatty acid molecules via dehydration reactions (**Figure 3.11**). The resulting fat is called a **triglyceride**, a term you may see on food labels or in the results of a blood test. The major portion of a fatty acid is a long hydrocarbon that stores a lot of energy, like the hydrocarbons of gasoline. In fact, a pound of fat packs more than twice as much energy as a pound of carbohydrate. The downside to this energy efficiency is that it is very difficult for a person trying to lose weight to "burn off" excess fat. It is important to understand that a reasonable amount of body fat is both normal and healthy as a fuel reserve. We stock these long-term food stores in specialized reservoirs called adipose cells, which swell and shrink when we deposit and withdraw fat from them. This adipose tissue, or "body fat," not only stores energy but also cushions vital organs and insulates us, helping maintain a warm body temperature even when the outside air is cold.

Notice in Figure 3.11b that the bottom fatty acid bends where there is a double bond in the carbon skeleton. That fatty acid is said to be **unsaturated** because it has fewer than the maximum number of hydrogens at the double bond. The other two fatty acids in the fat molecule lack double bonds in their hydrocarbon portions. Those fatty acids are **saturated**, meaning that they contain the maximum number of hydrogen atoms, giving them a straight shape. A saturated fat is one with all three of its fatty acid tails saturated. If one or more of the fatty acids is unsaturated, then it's an unsaturated fat, like the one in Figure 3.11b. A polyunsaturated fat has several double bonds within its fatty acids.

◄ **Figure 3.10 The separation of hydrophobic (oil) and hydrophilic (vinegar) components in salad dressing.**

Oil (hydrophobic)

Vinegar (hydrophilic)

Why is it so hard to lose body fat?

▼ **Figure 3.11 The synthesis and structure of a triglyceride molecule.**

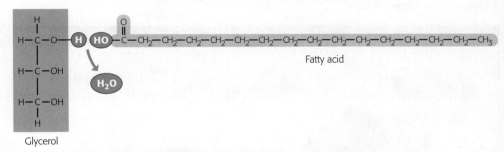

Glycerol

Fatty acid

(a) A dehydration reaction linking a fatty acid to glycerol

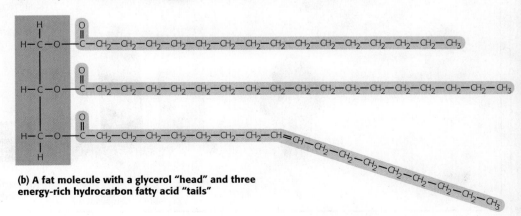

(b) A fat molecule with a glycerol "head" and three energy-rich hydrocarbon fatty acid "tails"

43

Most animal fats, such as lard and butter, have a relatively high proportion of saturated fatty acids. The linear shape of saturated fatty acids allows these molecules to stack easily (like bricks in a wall), so saturated fats tend to be solid at room temperature **(Figure 3.12)**. Diets rich in saturated fats may contribute to cardiovascular disease by promoting **atherosclerosis**. In this condition, lipid-containing deposits called plaque build up along the inside walls of blood vessels, reducing blood flow and increasing risk of heart attacks and strokes.

Plant and fish fats are relatively high in unsaturated fatty acids. The bent shape of unsaturated fatty acids makes them less likely to form solids (imagine trying to build a wall using irregularly bent bricks!), so most unsaturated fats are liquid at room temperature. Foods that are primarily unsaturated include vegetable oils (such as corn and canola oil) and fish oils (such as cod liver oil).

Although plant oils tend to be low in saturated fat, tropical plant fats are an exception. Cocoa butter, a main ingredient in chocolate, contains a mix of saturated and unsaturated fat. This gives chocolate a melting point near body temperature. Thus, chocolate stays solid at room temperature but melts in the mouth. This pleasing "mouth feel" is one of the reasons chocolate is so appealing.

Sometimes a food manufacturer wants to use a vegetable oil but needs the food product to be solid, as with margarine or peanut butter. To achieve this, the manufacturer can convert unsaturated fats to saturated fats by adding hydrogen, a process called **hydrogenation**. Unfortunately, hydrogenation also creates **trans fats**, a type of unsaturated fat that is particularly bad for your health. Since 2006, the U.S. Food and Drug Administration (FDA) has required trans fats to be listed on nutrition labels. But even if a label on a hydrogenated product says 0 grams (g) of trans fats per serving, the product might still have up to 0.5 g per serving. Any product with partially hydrogenated vegetable oil contains trans fats. (See the Process of Science section in Chapter 1—"Are Trans Fats Bad for You?"—for an investigation of the health effects of trans fats.) Due to the increased awareness of their unhealthy nature, trans fats are becoming less common as food manufacturers substitute other forms of fat.

Although saturated and trans fats should generally be avoided, it is not true that *all* fats are unhealthy. In fact, some fats perform important functions within the body and are beneficial and even essential to a healthy diet. For example, fats containing omega-3 fatty acids have been shown to reduce the risk of heart disease and relieve the symptoms of arthritis and inflammatory bowel disease. Some sources of these beneficial fats are nuts and oily fish such as salmon. ✓

Why does chocolate melt in your mouth but not in the package?

☑ **CHECKPOINT**

What are "unsaturated fats"? What kinds of unsaturated fat are particularly unhealthy? What kind of unsaturated fats are most healthful?

Answer: *fats with less than the maximum number of hydrogens because of double bonds between some carbons; trans fats; fats built from omega-3 fatty acids*

▼ **Figure 3.12 Types of fats.**

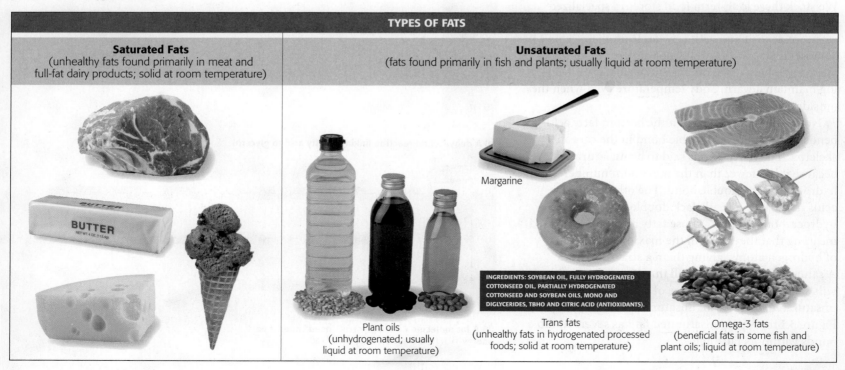

TYPES OF FATS

Saturated Fats
(unhealthy fats found primarily in meat and full-fat dairy products; solid at room temperature)

Unsaturated Fats
(fats found primarily in fish and plants; usually liquid at room temperature)

BUTTER

Margarine

INGREDIENTS: SOYBEAN OIL, FULLY HYDROGENATED COTTONSEED OIL, PARTIALLY HYDROGENATED COTTONSEED AND SOYBEAN OILS, MONO AND DIGLYCERIDES, TBHO AND CITRIC ACID (ANTIOXIDANTS).

Plant oils
(unhydrogenated; usually liquid at room temperature)

Trans fats
(unhealthy fats in hydrogenated processed foods; solid at room temperature)

Omega-3 fats
(beneficial fats in some fish and plant oils; liquid at room temperature)

Steroids

Although they are also hydrophobic, **steroids** are very different from fats in structure and function. All steroids have a carbon skeleton with four fused rings. Different steroids vary in the functional groups attached to this set of rings, and these chemical variations affect their function. One common steroid is cholesterol, which has a bad reputation because of its association with cardiovascular disease. However, cholesterol is an essential molecule in your body. It is a key component of the membranes that surround your cells. It is also the "base steroid" from which your body produces other steroids, such as the sex hormones estrogen and testosterone **(Figure 3.13)**.

The controversial drugs called anabolic steroids are synthetic variants of testosterone. In human males, testosterone causes buildup of muscle and bone mass during puberty and maintains masculine traits throughout life. Because anabolic steroids resemble testosterone, they mimic some of its effects. Anabolic steroids are prescribed to treat diseases that cause muscle wasting, such as cancer and AIDS. On the flip side, athletes can abuse anabolic steroids to build up their muscles quickly.

In recent years, the discovery that some athletes were using a performance-enhancing anabolic steroid called THG rocked the sports world. THG is a chemically modified ("designer") steroid intended to avoid detection by drug tests (hence its nickname, "the clear"). New tests revealed widespread use of THG and other steroids among athletes in many sports **(Figure 3.14)** and raised questions about the validity of home run records and other athletic accomplishments.

Using anabolic steroids is indeed a fast way to increase body size beyond what hard work alone can produce. But at what cost? Steroid abuse can cause violent mood swings ("roid rage"), depression, liver damage, high cholesterol, shrunken testicles, reduced sex drive, and infertility. These last symptoms occur because artificial anabolic steroids often cause the body to reduce its output of natural sex hormones. Most athletic organizations ban the use of anabolic steroids because of their many potential health hazards coupled with the unfairness of an artificial advantage. ☑

▼ **Figure 3.13 Examples of steroids.** The molecular structures of the steroids shown here are abbreviated by omitting all the atoms that make up the rings. The subtle difference between testosterone and estrogen influences the development of the anatomical and physiological differences between male and female mammals, including lions and humans.

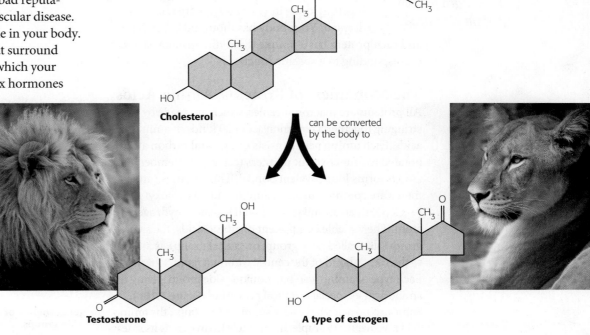

can be converted by the body to

Testosterone

A type of estrogen

▼ **Figure 3.14 Steroids and the modern athlete.** Baseball player Jose Canseco (left), an admitted user of performance-enhancing steroids, testifies before Congress during an inquiry into the abuse of drugs by professional athletes. After admitting that she had taken performance-enhancing drugs, track-and-field star Marion Jones (right) was stripped of her five Olympic medals. Note the similarity in chemical structure of testosterone (shown above) and THG (shown here).

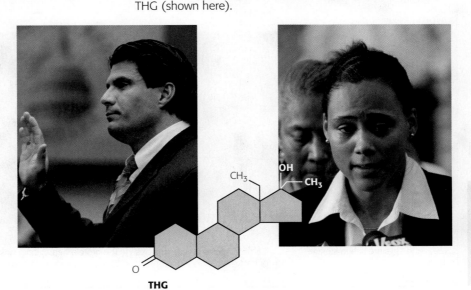

THG

☑ CHECKPOINT

What steroid acts as the molecular building block of the human steroid hormones?

Answer: cholesterol

Proteins

A **protein** is a polymer of amino acid monomers. Proteins are the most elaborate and diverse of life's molecules. Proteins account for more than 50% of the dry weight of most cells, and they are instrumental in almost everything cells do **(Figure 3.15)**. Chances are, if something is getting done in your body, there is a protein doing it. Your body has thousands of proteins, and each protein has a unique three-dimensional shape corresponding to a specific function.

How much protein is on your head?

The Monomers of Proteins: Amino Acids

All proteins are macromolecules, which are made by stringing together a common set of 20 kinds of amino acids. Each **amino acid** consists of a central carbon atom bonded to four covalent partners (carbon, remember, always forms four covalent bonds). Three of those attachments are common to all 20 amino acids: a carboxyl group (—COOH), an amino group (—NH$_2$), and a hydrogen atom. The variable component of amino acids, the side group (also called an R group, or radical group), is attached to the fourth bond of the central carbon **(Figure 3.16a)**. Each type of amino acid has a unique side group, giving that amino acid its special chemical properties **(Figure 3.16b)**. Some amino acids have very simple side groups; the amino acid glycine, for example, has a single hydrogen as its side group. Other amino acids have more complex side groups, some with branches or rings within them.

▼ **Figure 3.16 Amino acids.** The 20 amino acids vary only in their side groups, which give these monomers their unique properties.

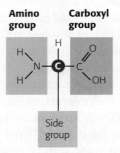

(a) The general structure of an amino acid.

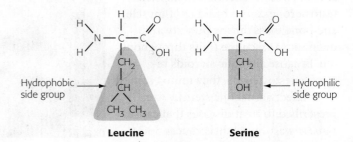

Leucine   **Serine**

(b) Examples of amino acids with hydrophobic and hydrophilic side groups. The side group of the amino acid leucine is pure hydrocarbon. That region of leucine is hydrophobic because hydrocarbons don't mix with water. In contrast, the side group of the amino acid serine has a hydroxyl group (—OH), which is hydrophilic.

▼ **Figure 3.15 Some types of proteins.**

MAJOR TYPES OF PROTEINS				
Structural Proteins (provide support)	**Storage Proteins** (provide amino acids for growth)	**Contractile Proteins** (help movement)	**Transport Proteins** (help transport substances)	**Enzymes** (help chemical reactions)
Structural proteins give hair and horns their toughness.	Seeds and eggs are rich in storage proteins.	Contractile proteins enable muscles to contract.	The protein hemoglobin within red blood cells transports oxygen.	Some cleaning products use enzymes to help break down molecules.

Proteins as Polymers

Cells link amino acid monomers together by—can you guess?—dehydration reactions. The bond between adjacent amino acids is called a **peptide bond** (Figure 3.17). The resulting long chain of amino acids is called a **polypeptide**. A protein is a polymer consisting of one or more polypeptides.

Your body has tens of thousands of different kinds of proteins. How is it possible to make such a huge variety of proteins from just 20 kinds of amino acids? The answer is arrangement. You know that you can make many different English words by varying the sequence of just 26 letters. Though the protein alphabet is slightly smaller (just 20 "letters"), the "words" are much longer, with a typical polypeptide being at least hundreds of amino acids in length. Just as each word is constructed from a unique succession of letters, each protein has a unique linear sequence of amino acids. This specific amino acid sequence—the "spelling" of a polypeptide— is called the protein's **primary structure** (Figure 3.18).

Changing a single letter can drastically affect the meaning of a word—"tasty" versus "nasty," for instance. Similarly, even a slight change in primary structure can affect a protein's ability to function. For example, the substitution of one amino acid for another at a particular position in hemoglobin, the blood protein that carries oxygen, causes sickle-cell disease, an inherited blood disorder (Figure 3.19). ✓

▼ **Figure 3.18 The primary structure (amino acid sequence) of a protein.** This chain, drawn in serpentine fashion so that it fits on the page, shows the primary structure of a protein called lysozyme. The names of the amino acids are given as their three-letter abbreviations.

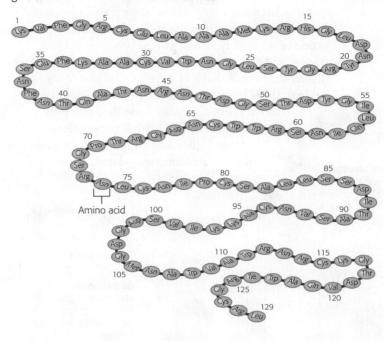

▼ **Figure 3.17 Joining amino acids.** A dehydration reaction links adjacent amino acids by a peptide bond.

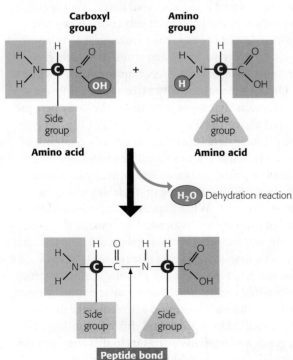

▼ **Figure 3.19 A single amino acid substitution in a protein causes sickle-cell disease.**

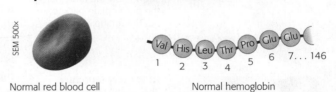

Normal red blood cell   Normal hemoglobin

(a) Normal hemoglobin. Red blood cells of humans are normally disk-shaped. Each cell contains millions of molecules of the protein hemoglobin, which transports oxygen from the lungs to other organs of the body. Next to the micrograph, you can see the first 7 of the 146 amino acids in a polypeptide chain of hemoglobin.

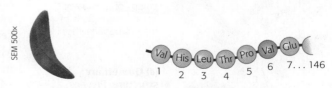

Sickled red blood cell   Sickle-cell hemoglobin

(b) Sickle-cell hemoglobin. A slight change in the primary structure of hemoglobin causes sickle-cell disease. The inherited substitution of one amino acid—valine in place of the amino acid glutamic acid—occurs at the 6th position of the polymer. Such abnormal hemoglobin molecules tend to crystallize, deforming some of the cells into a sickle shape. Someone with the disease suffers from dangerous episodes when the angular cells clog tiny blood vessels, impeding blood flow.

✓ CHECKPOINT

What are the monomers of all proteins?

Answer: amino acids

47

Protein Shape

At this point, you might be thinking that a polypeptide chain is the same thing as a protein, but that's not quite true. The distinction between the two is like the relationship between a long strand of yarn and a sweater that you could knit from the yarn. A functional protein is one or more polypeptide chains precisely twisted, folded, and coiled into a molecule of unique shape. If we dissect the overall shape of a protein, we can recognize at least three levels of structure: primary, secondary, and tertiary. Proteins with more than one polypeptide chain have a fourth level: quaternary structure. **Figure 3.20** shows how the levels of protein structure are related.

▼ Figure 3.20 The four levels of protein structure.

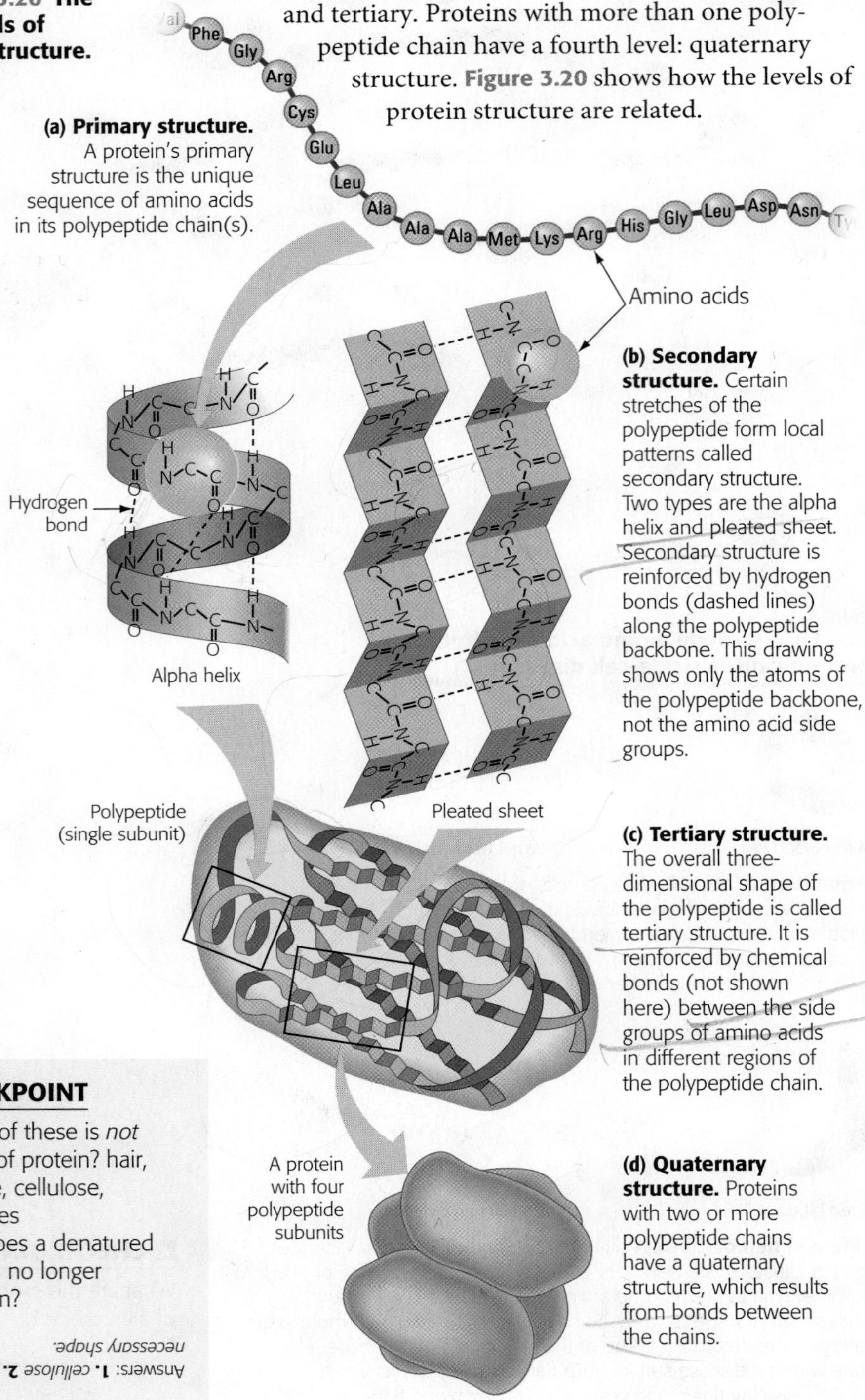

(a) Primary structure. A protein's primary structure is the unique sequence of amino acids in its polypeptide chain(s).

Amino acids

(b) Secondary structure. Certain stretches of the polypeptide form local patterns called secondary structure. Two types are the alpha helix and pleated sheet. Secondary structure is reinforced by hydrogen bonds (dashed lines) along the polypeptide backbone. This drawing shows only the atoms of the polypeptide backbone, not the amino acid side groups.

Hydrogen bond

Alpha helix

Pleated sheet

Polypeptide (single subunit)

(c) Tertiary structure. The overall three-dimensional shape of the polypeptide is called tertiary structure. It is reinforced by chemical bonds (not shown here) between the side groups of amino acids in different regions of the polypeptide chain.

A protein with four polypeptide subunits

(d) Quaternary structure. Proteins with two or more polypeptide chains have a quaternary structure, which results from bonds between the chains.

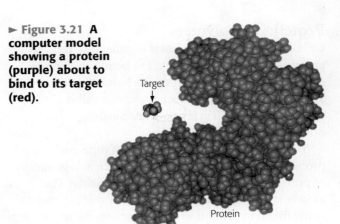

► Figure 3.21 A computer model showing a protein (purple) about to bind to its target (red).

Target

Protein

When a cell makes a polypeptide, the chain usually folds spontaneously to form the functional shape for that protein. It is a protein's three-dimensional shape that enables the molecule to carry out its specific function in a cell. In almost every case, a protein's function depends on its ability to recognize and bind to some other molecule. For example, the specific shape of lactase enables it to recognize and attach to lactose, its molecular target. With proteins, *function follows form*— that is, what a protein does is a consequence of its shape (Figure 3.21).

What Determines Protein Shape?

A protein's shape is sensitive to the surrounding environment. An unfavorable change in temperature, pH, or some other quality of the environment can cause a protein to unravel and lose its normal shape. This is called **denaturation** of the protein. If you cook an egg, the transformation of the egg white from clear to opaque is caused by proteins in the egg white denaturing. As the proteins fall apart, they separate and form a white solid. One of the reasons why extremely high fevers are so dangerous is that some proteins in the body become denatured above 104°F.

The primary structure of a protein—its sequence of amino acids—causes it to fold into its functional shape. Each kind of protein has a unique primary structure and therefore a unique shape that enables it to do a certain job in a cell. What happens if it folds incorrectly? Misfolded proteins are associated with many diseases, including some severe nervous system disorders, such as Alzheimer's disease, mad cow disease, and Parkinson's disease. But what determines a protein's primary structure? As noted earlier, a protein consists of one or more polypeptide chains. The amino acid sequence of each chain is specified by a gene. And this relationship between genes and proteins brings us to this chapter's last category of large biological molecules: nucleic acids. ☑

Nucleic Acids

Nucleic acids are macromolecules that store information and provide the instructions for building proteins. The name *nucleic* comes from the fact that DNA is found in the nuclei of eukaryotic cells. There are actually two types of nucleic acids: **DNA** (which stands for d̲e̲o̲xyribo̲n̲ucleic a̲cid) and **RNA** (for r̲ibo̲n̲ucleic a̲cid). The genetic material that humans and other organisms inherit from their parents consists of giant molecules of DNA. The DNA resides in the cell as one or more very long fibers called chromosomes. A **gene** is a specific stretch of DNA that programs the amino acid sequence of a polypeptide. Those programmed instructions, however, are written in a kind of chemical code that must be translated from "nucleic acid language" to "protein language" **(Figure 3.22)**. A cell's RNA molecules help make this translation (see Chapter 10).

Nucleic acids are polymers made from monomers called **nucleotides (Figure 3.23)**. Each nucleotide contains three parts. At the center of each nucleotide is a five-carbon sugar (blue in the figure), deoxyribose in DNA and ribose in RNA. Attached to the sugar is a negatively charged phosphate group (yellow) containing a phosphorus atom bonded to oxygen atoms (PO_4^-). Also attached to the sugar is a nitrogen-containing base (green) made of one or two rings. The sugar and phosphate are the same in all nucleotides; only the base varies. Each DNA nucleotide has one of four possible nitrogenous bases: adenine (abbreviated A), guanine (G), cytosine (C), or thymine (T) **(Figure 3.24)**. Thus, all genetic information is written in a four-letter alphabet.

▼ **Figure 3.23 A DNA nucleotide.** A DNA nucleotide monomer consists of three parts: a sugar (deoxyribose), a phosphate, and a nitrogenous (nitrogen-containing) base.

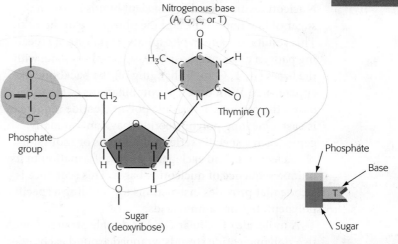

(a) Atomic structure

(b) Symbol used in this book

▼ **Figure 3.24 The nitrogenous bases of DNA.** Notice that adenine and guanine have double-ring structures. Thymine and cytosine have single-ring structures.

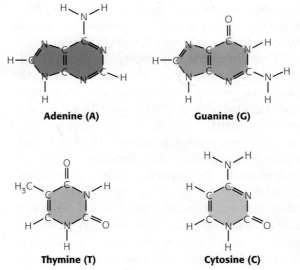

Adenine (A)   **Guanine (G)**

Thymine (T)   **Cytosine (C)**

▼ **Figure 3.22 Building a protein.** Within the cell, a gene (a segment of DNA) provides the directions to build a molecule of RNA, which can then be translated into a protein.

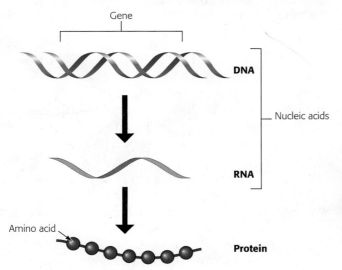

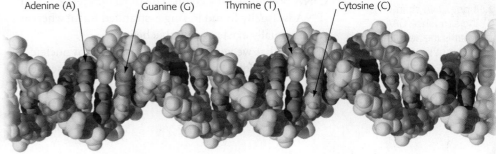

Space-filling model of DNA (showing the four bases in four different colors)

Dehydration reactions link nucleotide monomers into long chains called polynucleotides. In the case of DNA, these are called DNA strands (**Figure 3.25a**). Nucleotides are joined by covalent bonds between the sugar of one nucleotide and the phosphate of the next. This results in a **sugar-phosphate backbone**, a repeating pattern of sugar-phosphate-sugar-phosphate, with the bases (A, T, C, or G) hanging off the backbone like appendages. With different combinations of the four bases, the number of possible polynucleotide sequences is vast. One long polynucleotide may contain many genes, each a specific series of hundreds or thousands of nucleotides. And each gene stores information in its unique sequence of nucleotide bases. This sequence is a code that provides instructions for building a specific polypeptide from amino acids.

A molecule of cellular DNA is double-stranded, with two polynucleotide strands wrapped around each other to form a **double helix** (**Figure 3.25b**). In the central core of the helix, the bases along one DNA strand hydrogen-bond to bases along the other strand. The bonds are individually weak—they are hydrogen bonds, like those between water molecules—but collectively they zip the two strands together into a very stable double helix. Because of the way the functional groups hang off the bases, the base pairing in a DNA double helix is specific: The base A can pair only with T, and G can pair only with C. Thus, if you know the sequence of bases along one DNA strand, you also know the sequence along the complementary strand in the double helix. This unique base pairing is the basis of DNA's ability to act as the molecule of inheritance (as discussed in Chapter 10).

There are many similarities between DNA and RNA. Both are polymers of nucleotides, for example, and both are made of nucleotides consisting of a sugar, a phosphate, and a base. But there are three important differences. A first difference: as its name *ribonucleic acid* denotes, its sugar is ribose rather than deoxyribose. A second difference between RNA and DNA is that instead of the base thymine, RNA has a similar but distinct base called uracil (U) (**Figure 3.26**). Except for the presence of ribose and uracil, an RNA polynucleotide chain is identical to a DNA polynucleotide chain. The third difference is that RNA is usually found in single-stranded form, whereas DNA usually exists as a double helix.

Now that we've examined the structure of nucleic acids, we'll look at how a change in nucleotide sequence can affect protein production. ☑

☑ CHECKPOINT

1. DNA contains _____ polynucleotide strands, each composed of _____ kinds of nucleotides (Provide two numbers.).
2. If one DNA strand has the sequence GAATGC, what is the sequence of the other strand?

Answers: 1. two; four 2. CTTACG

▼ **Figure 3.25 The structure of DNA.** The base pairing in a DNA molecule is specific: A always pairs with T; G always pairs with C.

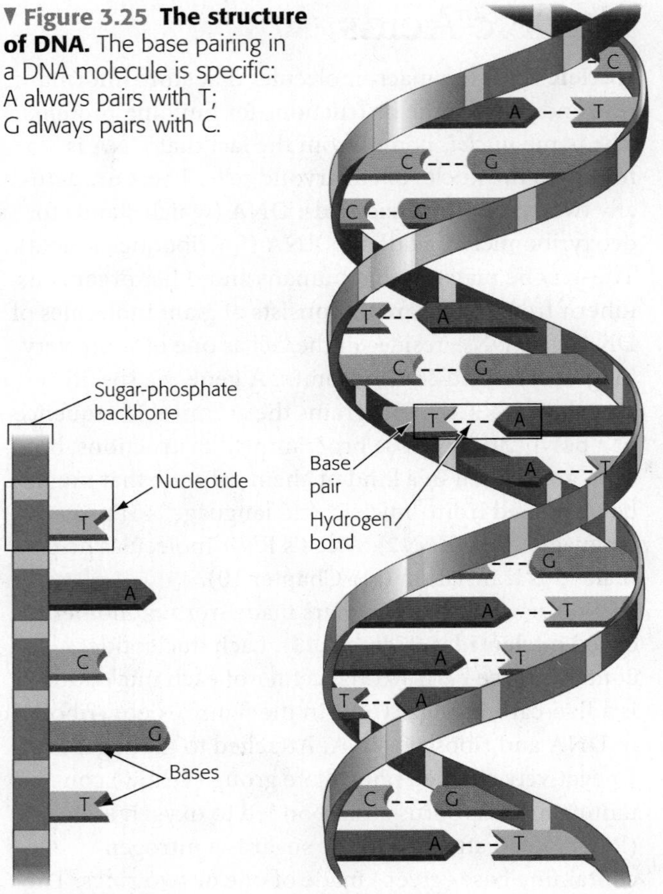

Sugar-phosphate backbone

Nucleotide

Bases

Base pair

Hydrogen bond

(a) DNA strand
(polynucleotide)

(b) Double helix
(two polynucleotide strands)

▼ **Figure 3.26 An RNA nucleotide.** Notice that this RNA nucleotide differs from the DNA nucleotide in Figure 3.23 in two ways: The RNA sugar is ribose rather than deoxyribose; and the base is uracil (U) instead of thymine (T). The other three kinds of RNA nucleotides have the bases A, C, and G, as in DNA.

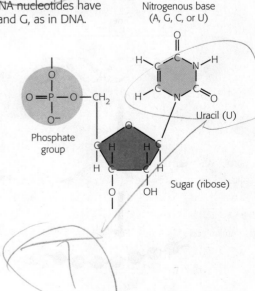

Nitrogenous base (A, G, C, or U)

Uracil (U)

Phosphate group

Sugar (ribose)

Does Lactose Intolerance Have a Genetic Basis?

The enzyme lactase, like all proteins, is encoded by a DNA gene. A reasonable hypothesis is that lactose-intolerant people have a defect in their lactase gene. However, this hypothesis is not supported by **observation**. Even though lactose intolerance runs in families, most lactose-intolerant people have a normal version of the lactase gene. This raises the **question**: What is the genetic basis for lactose intolerance?

In 2002, a group of Finnish and American scientists proposed the **hypothesis** that lactose intolerance can be correlated with a single nucleotide at a particular site within one chromosome. Based on their observations, they made the **prediction** that this site would be near, though not within, the lactase gene. In their **experiment**, they examined the genes of 196 lactose-intolerant people from nine Finnish families. Their **results** showed a 100% corre-lation between lactose intolerance and a nucleotide at a site

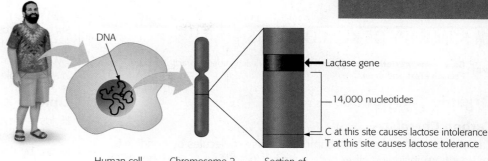

approximately 14,000 nucleotides away from the lactase gene—a relatively short distance in terms of the whole chromosome **(Figure 3.27)**. Other experiments showed that depending on the nucleotide sequence within this region of the DNA molecule, the action of the lactase gene is ramped up or down (in a way that likely involves producing a regulatory protein that interacts with the nucleotides near the lactase gene). This study shows how a small change in a DNA nucleotide sequence can have a major effect on the production of a protein and the well-being of an organism.

◄ **Figure 3.27 A genetic cause of lactose intoler-ance.** A 2002 study showed a correlation between lactose intolerance and a nucleotide at a specific location on one chromosome.

The Evolution of Lactose Intolerance in Humans

As you'll recall from the Biology and Society section, most of the world's population are lactose intolerant as adults and thus do not easily digest the milk sugar lactose. In fact, lactose intolerance is found in 80% of African Americans and Native Americans and 90% of Asian Americans but only in about 10% of Americans of northern European descent. And as discussed in the Process of Science section, lactose intolerance appears to have a genetic basis.

From an evolutionary perspective, it is reasonable to infer that lactose intolerance is rare among northern Europeans because the ability to tolerate lactose offered a survival advantage to their ancestors. In northern Europe's relatively cold climate, only one crop harvest a year is possi-ble. Therefore, animals were a main source of food for early humans in that region. Cattle were first domesticated in northern Europe about 9,000 years ago **(Figure 3.28)**. With milk and other dairy products at hand year-round, natural selection would have favored anyone with a mutation that

kept the lactase gene switched on. In other cultures where dairy products were not a staple in the diet, natural selection would not favor such a mutation.

Researchers wondered whether the genetic basis for lactose tolerance in northern Europeans might be present in other cultures that kept dairy herds. To find out, a 2006 study compared the genetic makeup and lactose tolerance of 43 ethnic groups in East Africa. The researchers identified three other genetic changes that keep the lactase gene permanently active. These mutations appear to have occurred beginning around 7,000 years ago, about the time that archaeological evidence shows domestication of cattle in these African regions.

Genetic changes that confer a selective advantage, such as surviving cold winters or withstanding drought by drinking milk, spread rapidly in these early peoples. Evolutionary and cultural history is thus recorded in the genes of such individuals' descendants and in their continuing ability to digest milk.

▲ **Figure 3.28 A prehistoric cave painting in Lascaux, France, of wild cattle.** This species, known as aurochs, became the first domesticated cattle in Europe. Aurochs migrated from Asia about 250,000 years ago but became extinct in 1627.

Chapter Review

SUMMARY OF KEY CONCEPTS

Go to **www.masteringbiology.com** for homework assignments, practice quizzes, Pearson eText, and more.

Organic Compounds

Carbon Chemistry

Carbon atoms can form large, complex, diverse molecules by bonding to four partners, including other carbon atoms. In addition to variations in the size and shape of carbon skeletons, organic compounds vary in the presence and locations of different functional groups.

Giant Molecules from Smaller Building Blocks

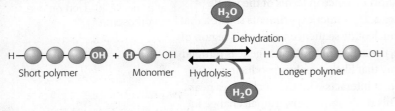

Large Biological Molecules

Large biological molecules	Functions	Components	Examples
Carbohydrates	Dietary energy; storage; plant structure	Monosaccharide	Monosaccharides: glucose, fructose; Disaccharides: lactose, sucrose; Polysaccharides: starch, cellulose
Lipids	Long-term energy storage (fats); hormones (steroids)	Components of a triglyceride	Fats (triglycerides); steroids (testosterone, estrogen)
Proteins	Enzymes, structure, storage, contraction, transport, etc.	Amino acid	Lactase (an enzyme); hemoglobin (a transport protein)
Nucleic acids	Information storage	Nucleotide	DNA, RNA

Carbohydrates

Simple sugars (monosaccharides) provide cells with energy and carbon skeletons for use in building other organic compounds. Double sugars (disaccharides), such as sucrose, consist of two monosaccharides joined by a dehydration reaction. Polysaccharides are long polymers of sugar monomers. Starch in plants and glycogen in animals are storage polysaccharides. The cellulose of plant cell walls is an example of a structural polysaccharide.

Lipids

Lipids are hydrophobic. Fats are the major form of long-term energy storage in animals. A molecule of fat, or triglyceride, consists of three fatty acids joined by a dehydration reaction to a glycerol. Most animal fats are saturated, meaning that their fatty acids have the maximum number of hydrogens. Plant oils contain mostly unsaturated fats, having fewer hydrogens in the fatty acids because of double bonding in the carbon skeletons. Steroids, including cholesterol and the sex hormones, are also lipids.

Proteins

There are 20 types of amino acids, the monomers of proteins. They are linked by dehydration reactions to form polymers called polypeptides. A protein consists of one or more polypeptides folded into a specific three-dimensional shape. Contributing to this shape are four levels of structure:

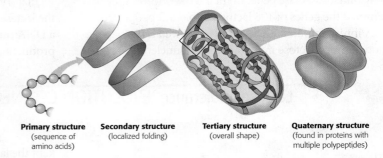

| Primary structure (sequence of amino acids) | Secondary structure (localized folding) | Tertiary structure (overall shape) | Quaternary structure (found in proteins with multiple polypeptides) |

Shape is sensitive to environment, and if a protein loses its shape because of an unfavorable environment, its function may also be lost.

Nucleic Acids

Nucleic acids include RNA and DNA. DNA takes the form of a double helix, two DNA strands (polymers of nucleotides) held together by hydrogen bonds between nucleotide components called bases. There are four kinds of DNA bases: adenine (A), guanine (G), thymine (T), and cytosine (C). A always pairs with T, and G always pairs with C. These base-pairing rules enable DNA to act as the molecule of inheritance. RNA has U (uracil) instead of T.

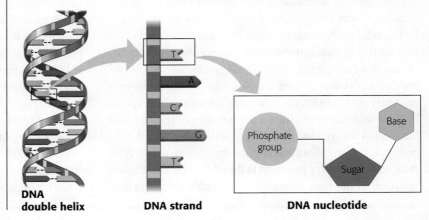

DNA double helix   **DNA strand**   **DNA nucleotide**

SELF-QUIZ

1. Draw the chemical structure of C_2H_4. (*Hint*: Each carbon has four bonds; each hydrogen has one.)

2. Monomers are joined together to form larger polymers through _____ reactions. This reaction releases a molecule of _____. Polymers are broken down into the monomers that make them up through the chemical reaction called _____.

3. Which of the following terms includes all the others in the list?
   a. polysaccharide
   b. carbohydrate
   c. monosaccharide
   d. disaccharide

4. One molecule of dietary fat is made by joining three molecules of _____ to one molecule of _____.

5. Which of the following statements about saturated fats is true?
   a. Saturated fats contain one or more double bonds along the hydrocarbon tails.
   b. Saturated fats contain the maximum number of hydrogens along the hydrocarbon tails.
   c. Saturated fats make up the majority of most plant oils.
   d. Saturated fats are typically healthier for you than unsaturated fats.

6. Humans and other animals cannot digest wood because they
   a. cannot digest any carbohydrates.
   b. cannot chew it fine enough.
   c. lack the enzyme needed to break down cellulose.
   d. get no nutrients from it.

7. Changing one amino acid within a protein could change what about a protein?
   a. the primary structure
   b. the overall shape of the protein
   c. the function of the protein
   d. all of the above

8. Most proteins can easily dissolve in water. Knowing that, where within the overall three-dimensional shape of a protein would you most likely find hydrophobic amino acids?

9. A shortage of phosphorus in the soil would make it especially difficult for a plant to manufacture
   a. DNA.
   b. proteins.
   c. cellulose.
   d. fatty acids.

10. A glucose molecule is to _____ as a nucleotide is to a _____.

11. Name three similarities between DNA and RNA. Name three differences.

12. What is the structure of a gene? What is the function of a gene?

Answers to these questions can be found in Appendix: Self-Quiz Answers.

THE PROCESS OF SCIENCE

13. A food manufacturer is advertising a new cake mix as fat-free. Scientists at the FDA are testing the product to see if it truly lacks fat. Hydrolysis of the cake mix yields glucose, fructose, glycerol, a number of amino acids, and several kinds of molecules with long hydrocarbon chains. Further analysis shows that most of the hydrocarbon chains have a carboxyl group at one end. What would you tell the food manufacturer if you were a spokesperson for the FDA?

14. Imagine that you have produced several versions of lactase, each of which differs from normal lactase by a single amino acid. Describe a test that could indirectly determine which of the versions significantly alters the three-dimensional shape of the protein.

BIOLOGY AND SOCIETY

15. Some amateur and professional athletes take anabolic steroids to help them build strength ("bulk up"). The health risks of this practice are extensively documented. Apart from these health issues, what is your opinion about the ethics of athletes using chemicals to enhance performance? Is this a form of cheating, or is it just part of the preparation required to stay competitive in a sport where anabolic steroids are commonly used? Defend your opinion.

16. Heart disease is the leading cause of death among people in the United States and other industrialized nations. Fast food is a major source of unhealthy fats that contribute significantly to heart disease. Imagine you're a juror sitting on a trial where a fast-food manufacturer is being sued for producing a harmful product. To what extent do you think manufacturers of unhealthy foods should be held responsible for the health consequences of their products? As a jury member, how would you vote?

17. Each year, industrial chemists develop and test thousands of new organic compounds for use as insecticides, fungicides, and weed killers. In what ways are these chemicals useful and important to us? In what ways can they be harmful? Is your general opinion of such chemicals positive or negative? What influences have shaped your feelings about these chemicals?

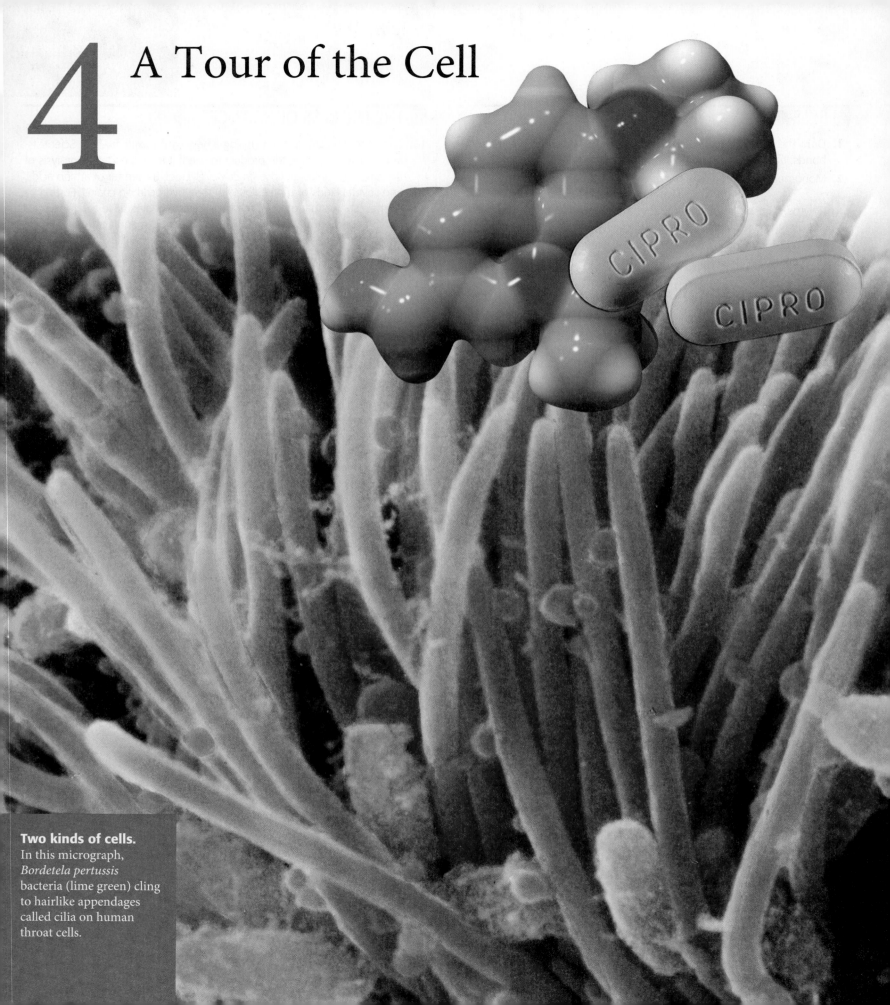

4 A Tour of the Cell

Two kinds of cells. In this micrograph, *Bordetela pertussis* bacteria (lime green) cling to hairlike appendages called cilia on human throat cells.

Antibiotic-Resistant Bacteria BIOLOGY AND SOCIETY

Antibiotics: Drugs that Target Bacterial Cells

Antibiotics—drugs that disable or kill infectious bacteria—are a marvel of modern medicine. Most antibiotics are naturally occurring chemicals derived from microorganisms. After the isolation of penicillin from mold in 1928, a revolution in human health rapidly followed. Fatality rates of many diseases (such as bacterial pneumonia and surgical infections) fell drastically, saving millions of lives. In fact, the improvement to human health was so fast and so profound that some doctors predicted the end of infectious diseases altogether. Alas, this did not come to pass, for reasons discussed at the end of the chapter.

The goal of antibiotic treatment is to harm invading bacteria while doing no damage to the human host. But how does an antibiotic zero in on its target among trillions of human cells? Most antibiotics achieve such precision by binding to structures found only in bacterial cells. For example, erythromycin and streptomycin bind to the bacterial ribosome, a vital cellular structure responsible for the production of proteins. The ribosomes of people are different enough from those of bacteria that the antibiotics bind only to bacterial ribosomes, leaving human ribosomes unaffected. Ciprofloxacin, the antibiotic of choice against anthrax-causing bacteria, targets an enzyme that bacteria need to maintain their chromosome structure. Your cells can survive just fine without this enzyme because human chromosomes have a sufficiently different makeup. Penicillin, ampicillin, and bacitracin disrupt the synthesis of cell walls, a structural feature found in most bacteria that is absent from the cells of humans and other animals.

The effect of antibiotics underscores the main point of this chapter: To understand how life works—whether in bacteria or in your own body—you first need to learn about cells. Cells are the smallest entities that can display all the characteristics of life. Many living organisms are single-celled; more complex organisms are multicelled. In this chapter, we'll explore the structure and function of cells. Along the way, we'll consider how antibiotics target specific cell structures of infectious bacteria.

The Microscopic World of Cells

Each cell in the human body is a miniature marvel of great complexity. If the space shuttle was reduced to microscopic size, its complexity would pale next to a living cell.

Organisms are either single-celled, such as most prokaryotes and protists, or multicelled, such as plants, animals, and most fungi. Your own body is a cooperative society of trillions of cells of many specialized types. Three examples are the muscle cells that keep your heart beating, the nerve cells that control your muscles, and the red blood cells that carry oxygen throughout your body. Everything you do—every action and every thought—reflects processes that occur at the cellular level. For exploring this world of cells, our main tools are microscopes.

What's the smallest object that can be seen in a microscope?

Microscopes as Windows on the World of Cells

Our understanding of nature often goes hand in hand with the invention and refinement of instruments that extend the human senses. For example, before microscopes were first used in the 1600s, no one knew that living organisms were composed of cells.

The type of microscope used by Renaissance scientists is the same kind of microscope found today in most biology classrooms: a **light microscope (LM)**. Visible light is projected through the specimen, such as a single-celled protist (**Figure 4.1**). Glass lenses enlarge the image and project it into a human eye or a camera.

Two important factors in microscopy are magnification and resolving power. **Magnification** is an increase in the object's image size compared with its actual size. The clarity of that magnified image depends on **resolving power**, the ability of an optical instrument to show two objects as separate. For example, what appears to the unaided eye as one star may be resolved as twin stars with a telescope. Each optical instrument—be it an eye, a telescope, or a microscope—has a limit to its resolving power. The normal human eye can resolve points as close together as 0.1 millimeter (mm), about the size of a very fine grain of sand. For light microscopes, the resolving power is about 0.2 micrometer (μm), the size of a small bacterial cell. This limits light microscopes to about 1,000× magnification. With greater magnification, an LM image becomes blurry.

Cells were first described in 1665 by the British scientist Robert Hooke, who used a microscope to examine a thin slice of oak tree bark. For the next two centuries, scientists found cells in every organism examined with a microscope. By the mid-1800s, this accumulation of evidence led to the **cell theory**, which states that all living things are composed of cells and that all cells come from other cells.

Our scientific knowledge of cell structure took a giant leap forward as biologists began using electron microscopes in the 1950s. Instead of using light, an

▼ **Figure 4.1 The protist *Paramecium* viewed with three different types of microscopes.** Photographs taken with microscopes are called micrographs. Throughout this textbook, micrographs will have size notations along the side. For example, "LM 1,000×" indicates that the micrograph was taken with a light microscope and the objects are magnified to 1,000 times their original size.

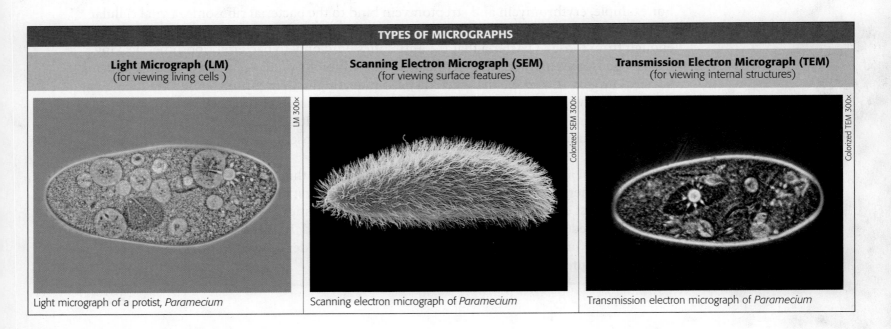

TYPES OF MICROGRAPHS

Light Micrograph (LM) (for viewing living cells)	**Scanning Electron Micrograph (SEM)** (for viewing surface features)	**Transmission Electron Micrograph (TEM)** (for viewing internal structures)

LM 300×

Colonized SEM 300×

Colonized TEM 300×

Light micrograph of a protist, *Paramecium*

Scanning electron micrograph of *Paramecium*

Transmission electron micrograph of *Paramecium*

electron microscope (EM) uses a beam of electrons to resolve objects. This gives electron microscopes 100-fold better resolution than light microscopes. **Figures 4.1b** and **4.1c** show images made with two kinds of electron microscopes: a **scanning electron microscope (SEM)**—used to study the detailed architecture of the cell surface—and a **transmission electron microscope (TEM)**—to study the internal structure of a cell.

The most powerful modern electron microscopes can distinguish objects as small as 0.2 nanometer (nm) **(Figure 4.2)**, which is about a million times smaller than the period at the end of this sentence. The highest-power electron micrographs you will see in this book have magnifications of about 100,000×. Such power can reveal many details within a cell **(Figure 4.3)**. However, preparing a specimen for an electron microscope usually requires killing and preserving the cell with a chemical fixative before it can be examined. Thus, the light microscope is still very useful as a window on living cells. ☑

▼ **Figure 4.2 An electron microscope.** An electron micrograph is formed by a beam of electrons that is generated at the top of the microscope's column and travels through the specimen being observed.

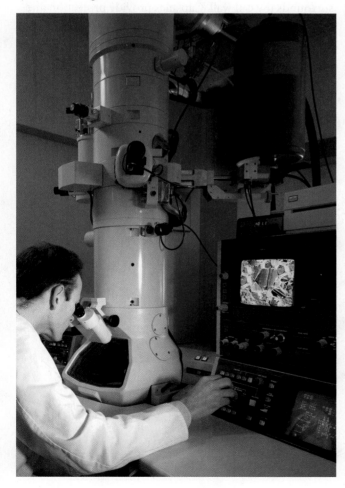

▼ **Figure 4.3 The size range of cells.** Starting at the top of this scale with 10 m (10 meters) and going down, each measurement along the left side marks a tenfold decrease in size.

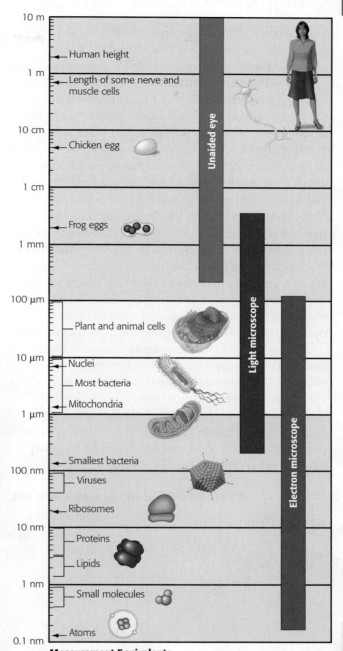

Measurement Equivalents

1 meter (m) = 100 cm = 1,000 mm = about 39.4 inches

1 centimeter (cm) = 10^{-2} ($\frac{1}{100}$) m = about 0.4 inch

1 millimeter (mm) = 10^{-3} ($\frac{1}{1,000}$) m = $\frac{1}{10}$ cm

1 micrometer (μm) = 10^{-6} m = 10^{-3} mm

1 nanometer (nm) = 10^{-9} m = 10^{-3} μm

☑ **CHECKPOINT**

Identify which type of microscope you would use to study (a) the internal structure of a dead human liver cell; (b) the finest details of surface texture of a human hair; and (c) the changes in shape of a living human white blood cell.

Answers: (a) transmission electron microscope; (b) scanning electron microscope; (c) light microscope

The Two Major Categories of Cells

The countless cells that exist on Earth fall into two basic categories: prokaryotic cells and eukaryotic cells.

What do you have in common with a mushroom?

Prokaryotic cells are found in organisms of the domains Bacteria and Archaea, known as prokaryotes (see Figures 1.4 and 1.8). Organisms of the domain Eukarya—protists, plants, fungi, and animals—are composed of **eukaryotic cells** and are called eukaryotes.

All cells have several features in common. They are all bounded by a barrier called a **plasma membrane**, which regulates the traffic of molecules between the cell and its surroundings. Inside all cells is a thick, jellylike fluid called the **cytosol**, in which cellular components are suspended. All cells have one or more **chromosomes** carrying genes made of DNA. And all cells have **ribosomes** that build proteins according to instructions from the genes. As mentioned in the Biology and Society section, some antibiotics—such as streptomycin—target prokaryotic ribosomes, crippling protein synthesis in the bacterial invaders but not in the eukaryotic host (that is, you).

Although they have many similarities, prokaryotic and eukaryotic cells differ in several important ways. Fossil evidence shows that prokaryotes were the first life on Earth, appearing more than 3.5 billion years ago. In contrast, the first eukaryotes did not appear until around 2.1 billion years ago. Prokaryotic cells are usually much smaller—about one-tenth the length of a typical eukaryotic cell—and are simpler in structure.

The most significant structural difference is that only eukaryotic cells have **organelles** ("little organs"), membrane-enclosed structures that perform specific functions. The most important organelle is the **nucleus**, which houses most of a eukaryotic cell's DNA and is surrounded by a double membrane. A prokaryotic cell lacks a nucleus; its DNA is coiled into a "nucleus-like" region called the **nucleoid**, which is not partitioned from the rest of the cell by membranes.

Consider this analogy: A eukaryotic cell is like an office that is separated into cubicles. Within each cubicle, a specific function is performed, thus dividing the labor among many internal compartments. The cubicle boundaries within eukaryotic cells are made from membranes that help maintain a unique chemical environment inside each cubicle. In contrast, the interior of a prokaryotic cell is like an open warehouse. The spaces for specific tasks are distinct but not separated by barriers.

Figure 4.4 depicts an idealized prokaryotic cell. Surrounding the plasma membrane of most prokaryotic cells is a rigid cell wall, which protects the cell and helps maintain its shape. Recall from the Biology and Society section that bacterial cell walls are the targets of some antibiotics. In some prokaryotes, a sticky outer coat called a capsule surrounds the cell wall. Capsules provide protection and help prokaryotes stick to surfaces. Capsules enable some infectious bacteria to evade engulfment by your immune system cells. Some prokaryotes have short projections called pili, which can also attach to surfaces. Many prokaryotic cells have flagella, long projections that propel them through their liquid environment. ✔

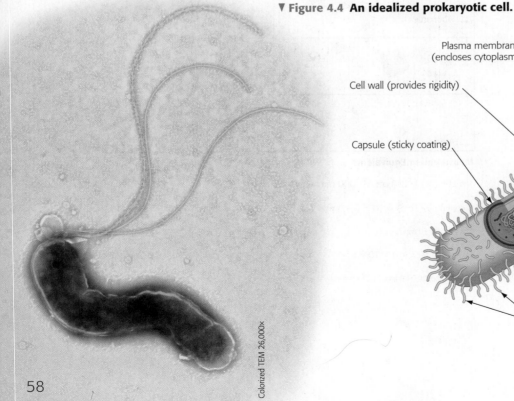

Colorized TEM 26,000x

▼ **Figure 4.4 An idealized prokaryotic cell.**

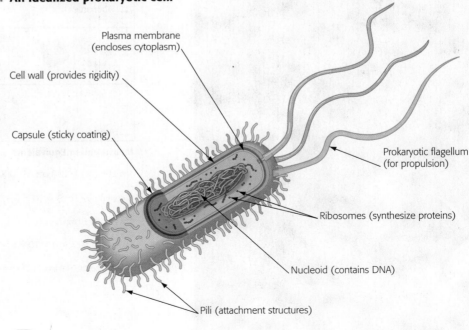

Plasma membrane (encloses cytoplasm)

Cell wall (provides rigidity)

Capsule (sticky coating)

Prokaryotic flagellum (for propulsion)

Ribosomes (synthesize proteins)

Nucleoid (contains DNA)

Pili (attachment structures)

An Overview of Eukaryotic Cells

All eukaryotic cells—whether from animals, plants, protists, or fungi—are fundamentally similar to one another and quite different from prokaryotic cells. **Figure 4.5** provides an overview of an idealized animal cell and plant cell. To keep from getting lost on our tour of the cell, we'll use miniature versions of these diagrams as road maps, highlighting the structure we're discussing. Notice that the structures are color-coded; we'll use this color scheme throughout *Essential Biology*.

The entire region of the cell between the nucleus and plasma membrane is called the **cytoplasm**. (This term is also used to refer to the interior of a prokaryotic cell.) The cytoplasm of a eukaryotic cell consists of various organelles suspended in the liquid cytosol. As you can see in Figure 4.5, most organelles are found in both animal and plant cells. But you'll notice some important differences—for example, only plant cells have chloroplasts (where photosynthesis occurs) and only animal cells have lysosomes (bubbles of digestive enzymes surrounded by membranes). In the rest of this section, we'll take a closer look at the architecture of eukaryotic cells, beginning with the plasma membrane. ☑

▼ **Figure 4.5 A view of an idealized animal cell and plant cell.** For now, the labels on the drawings are just words, but these organelles will come to life as we take a closer look at how each part of the cell functions.

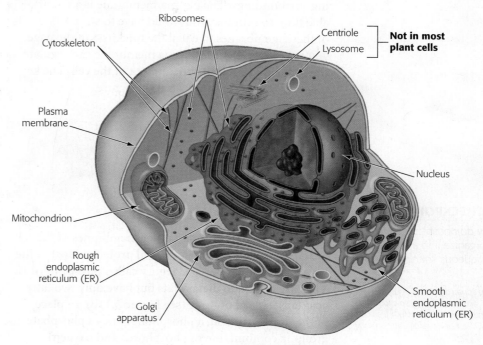

Ribosomes
Cytoskeleton
Centriole — Not in most plant cells
Lysosome
Plasma membrane
Nucleus
Mitochondrion
Rough endoplasmic reticulum (ER)
Golgi apparatus
Smooth endoplasmic reticulum (ER)

Idealized animal cell

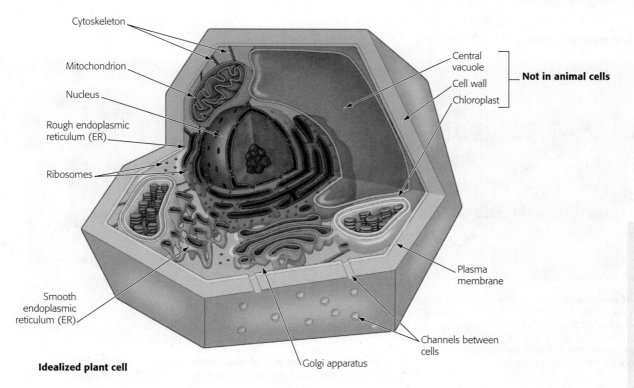

Cytoskeleton
Mitochondrion
Nucleus
Rough endoplasmic reticulum (ER)
Ribosomes
Central vacuole
Cell wall — Not in animal cells
Chloroplast
Plasma membrane
Smooth endoplasmic reticulum (ER)
Channels between cells
Golgi apparatus

Idealized plant cell

☑ CHECKPOINT

1. Name three structures in plant cells that animal cells lack.
2. Name two structures that may be found in animal cells but not in plant cells.

Answers: 1. chloroplasts, a central vacuole, and a cell wall 2. centrioles and lysosomes

Membrane Structure

Before we enter the cell to explore the organelles, let's make a quick stop at the surface of this microscopic world. The plasma membrane is the edge of life, the boundary that separates the living cell from its nonliving surroundings. The plasma membrane is a remarkable film, so thin that you would have to stack 8,000 of these membranes to equal the thickness of the page you're reading. Yet the plasma membrane can regulate the traffic of chemicals into and out of the cell. The key to how a membrane works is its structure.

The Plasma Membrane: A Fluid Mosaic of Lipids and Proteins

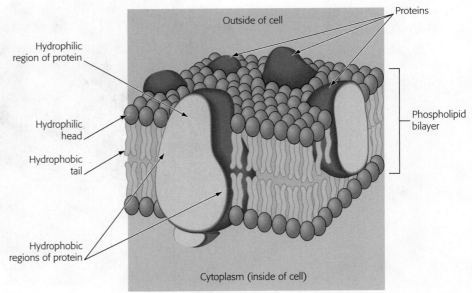

The plasma membrane and other membranes of the cell are composed mostly of lipids and proteins. Most of the lipids belong to a special category called **phospholipids**. They are related to dietary fats but have only two fatty acid tails instead of three (see Figure 3.11b). In place of the third fatty acid, a phospholipid has a phosphate group (a combination of phosphorus and oxygen).

The phosphate group is electrically charged, making it hydrophilic ("water-loving"). But the two fatty acid tails are hydrophobic ("water-fearing"). Thus, phospholipids have a chemical ambivalence in their interactions with water. The phosphate group head mixes with water, while the fatty acid tails avoid it. This makes phospholipids good membrane material. By forming a two-layered membrane, or **phospholipid bilayer**, the hydrophobic fatty acid tails of the molecules stay in the membrane interior away from water, while the hydrophilic phospholipid heads remain surrounded by water on the inside or outside of the cell **(Figure 4.6a)**. Embedded in the phospholipid bilayer of most membranes are proteins that help regulate traffic across the membrane and perform other functions **(Figure 4.6b)**. (You'll learn more about membrane proteins in Chapter 5.)

Membranes are not static sheets of molecules locked rigidly in place. The phospholipids and most of the proteins are free to drift about in the plane of the membrane. Thus, a membrane is a **fluid mosaic**—fluid because the molecules can move freely past one another and a mosaic because of the diversity of proteins that float like icebergs in the phospholipid sea. In the Process of Science section, we'll see how some bacteria can cause illness by piercing the plasma membrane. ☑

▼ **Figure 4.6 The plasma membrane structure.**

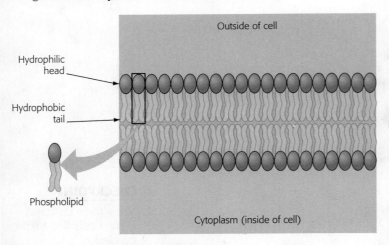

(a) Phospholipid bilayer of membrane. At the interface between two aqueous compartments, phospholipids arrange themselves into a bilayer. The symbol for a phospholipid that we'll use in this book looks like a lollipop with two wavy sticks. The "head" is the end with the phosphate group, and the two "tails" are hydrocarbons. The bilayer arrangement keeps the heads exposed to water while keeping the tails in the oily interior of the membrane.

(b) Fluid mosaic model of membrane. Membrane proteins, like the phospholipids, have both hydrophilic and hydrophobic regions.

What Makes a Superbug?

Some bacteria cause disease by rupturing the plasma membrane of human immune cells. One example is a common bacteria called *Staphylococcus aureus*. These bacteria, commonly found on the skin, are usually harmless but may multiply and spread, causing a "staph infection." Staph infections typically occur in hospitals and can cause serious, even life-threatening conditions, such as pneumonia or necrotizing fasciitis ("flesh-eating disease").

Most staph infections can be treated by antibiotics, including one called methicillin. But particularly dangerous strains of *S. aureus*—known as MRSA (for methicillin-resistant *S. aureus* or multi-drug-resistant SA)—are unaffected by these antibiotics. Recently, MRSA infections have become more common and have even turned up in nonhospital settings, such as gyms and schools. In 2007, scientists from the National Institutes of Health (NIH) studied one deadly MRSA strain. They began with the **observation** that other bacteria use a protein called PSM to disable human immune cells by forming holes that rip apart the plasma membrane. This led them to **question** whether PSM plays a role in MRSA infection **(Figure 4.7)**. Their **hypothesis** was that MRSA bacteria lacking the ability to produce PSM would be less deadly than normal MRSA strains.

In their **experiment**, they infected seven mice with a normal MRSA strain and eight mice with an MRSA strain genetically engineered to not produce PSM. The **results** over the next three days were striking: All seven mice infected with the normal MRSA strain died, while five of the eight mice infected with the strain that did not produce PSM survived. Under the electron microscope, immune cells from all of the dead mice showed holes within the plasma membrane. The researchers concluded that normal MRSA strains use the membrane-destroying PSM protein, but other

factors must come into play (possibly including other membrane-destroying proteins) because three mice died even in the absence of PSM. Active study of MRSA bacteria and how they interact with human cellular structures continues today.

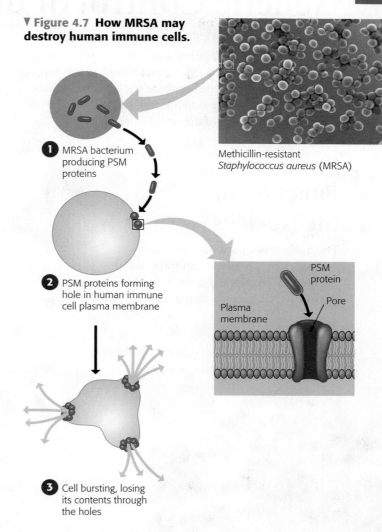

▼ **Figure 4.7 How MRSA may destroy human immune cells.**

Colonized SEM 1,300x

Methicillin-resistant *Staphylococcus aureus* (MRSA)

① MRSA bacterium producing PSM proteins

② PSM proteins forming hole in human immune cell plasma membrane

③ Cell bursting, losing its contents through the holes

PSM protein

Pore

Plasma membrane

Cell Surfaces

Surrounding their plasma membranes, plant cells have a cell wall made from cellulose fibers embedded in other molecules (see Figure 3.9c). The walls protect the cells, maintain cell shape, and keep cells from absorbing so much water that they burst. Plant cells are connected via channels that pass through the cell walls, joining the cytoplasm of each cell to that of its neighbors. These

channels allow water and other small molecules to move between cells, integrating the activities of a tissue.

Although animal cells lack a cell wall, most of them secrete a sticky coat called the **extracellular matrix**. This layer holds cells together in tissues, and it can also have protective and supportive functions. In addition, the surfaces of most animal cells contain **cell junctions**, structures that connect cells together into tissues, allowing them to function in a coordinated way. ☑

☑ **CHECKPOINT**

What polysaccharide is the primary component of plant cell walls?

Answer: cellulose

The Nucleus and Ribosomes: Genetic Control of the Cell

If we think of the cell as a factory, then the nucleus is its executive boardroom. The top managers are the genes, the inherited DNA molecules that direct almost all the business of the cell. Each gene is a stretch of DNA that stores the information necessary to produce a particular protein. Proteins then do most of the actual work of the cell.

Structure and Function of the Nucleus

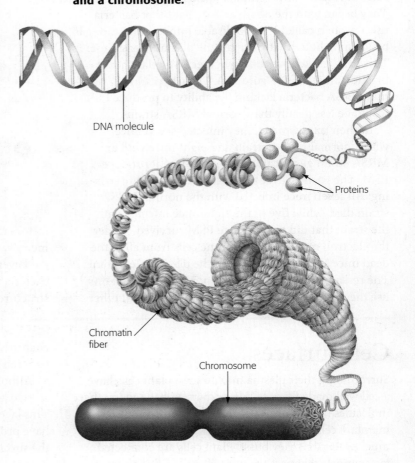

The nucleus is separated from the cytoplasm by a double membrane called the **nuclear envelope (Figure 4.8)**. Each membrane of the nuclear envelope is similar in structure to the plasma membrane. Pores in the envelope allow certain materials to pass between the nucleus and the cytoplasm. Within the nucleus, long DNA molecules and associated proteins form fibers called **chromatin**. Each long chromatin fiber constitutes one chromosome **(Figure 4.9)**. The number of chromosomes in a cell depends on the species; for example, each human body cell has 46 chromosomes, whereas rice cells have 24 and dog cells have 78 (see Figure 8.2 for more examples). The **nucleolus** (shown in Figure 4.8), a prominent structure within the nucleus, is the site where the components of ribosomes are made. We'll examine ribosomes next. ☑

☑ CHECKPOINT

What is the relationship between chromosomes and chromatin?

Answer: Chromosomes are made of chromatin, which is a combination of DNA and proteins.

▼ Figure 4.8 **The nucleus.**

Ribosomes | Chromatin fiber | Nuclear envelope | Nucleolus | Nuclear pore

TEM 7,000×

Surface of nuclear envelope

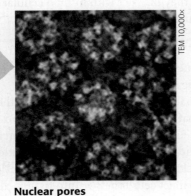

TEM 10,000×

Nuclear pores

▼ Figure 4.9 **The relationship between DNA, chromatin, and a chromosome.**

DNA molecule

Proteins

Chromatin fiber

Chromosome

Ribosomes

The small blue dots in the cells in Figure 4.5 and outside the nucleus in Figure 4.8 represent the ribosomes. As you'll see in the next section, ribosomes are responsible for protein synthesis (Figure 4.10). In eukaryotic cells, the components of ribosomes are made in the nucleus, then transported through the pores of the nucleus into the cytoplasm. It is in the cytoplasm that the ribosomes begin their work. Some are suspended in the cytosol, making proteins that remain within the fluid of the cell (Figure 4.11). Other ribosomes are attached to the outside of the nucleus or an organelle called the endoplasmic reticulum, making proteins that are incorporated into membranes or secreted by the cell. Free and bound ribosomes are structurally identical, and ribosomes can swing their locations, moving between the endoplasmic reticulum and the cytosol.

▼ **Figure 4.10** **A computer model of a ribosome synthesizing a protein.**

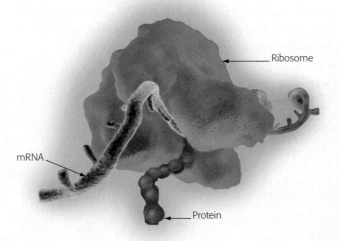
Ribosome
mRNA
Protein

▼ **Figure 4.11** **The locations of ribosomes.**

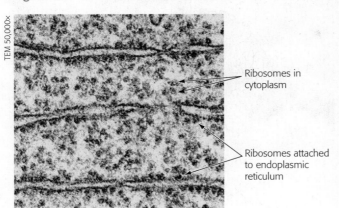
TEM 50,000×
Ribosomes in cytoplasm
Ribosomes attached to endoplasmic reticulum

How DNA Directs Protein Production

How do the DNA "executives" in the nucleus direct the "workers" in the cytoplasm? **Figure 4.12** shows the sequence of events during protein production in a eukaryotic cell (with the DNA and other structures being shown disproportionately large in relation to the nucleus). **1** DNA programs protein production in the cytoplasm by transferring its coded information to a molecule called messenger RNA (mRNA). Like a middle manager, the mRNA molecule then carries the order to "build this type of protein" from the nucleus to the cytoplasm. **2** The mRNA exits through pores in the nuclear envelope and travels to the cytoplasm, where it then binds to ribosomes. **3** The ribosome moves along the mRNA, translating the genetic message into a protein with a specific amino acid sequence. (You'll learn how the message is translated in Chapter 10.) ☑

▼ **Figure 4.12** **DNA → RNA → Protein.** Inherited genes in the nucleus control protein production and hence the activities of the cell.

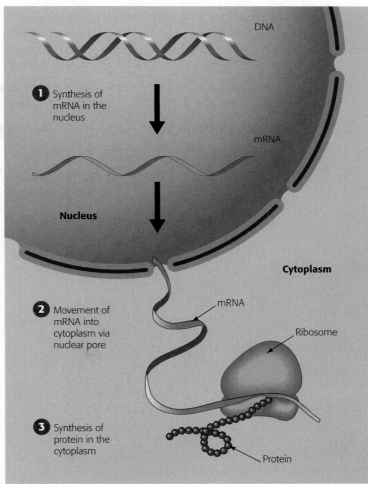
DNA
mRNA
1 Synthesis of mRNA in the nucleus
Nucleus
Cytoplasm
2 Movement of mRNA into cytoplasm via nuclear pore
mRNA
Ribosome
3 Synthesis of protein in the cytoplasm
Protein

☑ **CHECKPOINT**

1. What is the function of ribosomes?
2. What is the role of mRNA in making a protein?

Answers: 1. protein synthesis 2. A molecule of mRNA carries the genetic message from a gene (DNA) to ribosomes that translate it into protein.

The Endomembrane System: Manufacturing and Distributing Cellular Products

The cytoplasm of a eukaryotic cell is partitioned by organelle membranes (see Figure 4.5). Some of the organelles are connected to each other, either directly by their membranes or by transfer of membrane segments between them. Together, these organelles form the **endomembrane system**. This system includes the nuclear envelope, the endoplasmic reticulum, the Golgi apparatus, lysosomes, and vacuoles.

The Endoplasmic Reticulum

The **endoplasmic reticulum (ER)** is one of the main manufacturing facilities within a cell. It produces an enormous variety of molecules. Connected to the nuclear envelope, the ER forms an extensive labyrinth of tubes and sacs running throughout the cytoplasm **(Figure 4.13)**. A membrane separates the internal ER compartment from the cytosol. There are two components that make up the ER: rough ER and smooth ER. These two types of ER are physically connected but differ in structure and function.

Rough ER

The "rough" in **rough ER** refers to ribosomes that stud the outside of its membrane. One of the functions of rough ER is to make more membrane. Phospholipids made by enzymes of the rough ER are inserted into the ER membrane. In this way, the ER membrane grows, and portions of it are transferred to other parts of the cell. The ribosomes attached to the rough ER produce proteins that will be inserted into the growing ER membrane, transported to other organelles, and eventually exported. Cells that secrete a lot of protein—such as the cells of your salivary glands, which secrete enzymes into your mouth—are especially rich in rough ER. Some products manufactured by rough ER are dispatched to other locations in the cell by means of **transport vesicles**, sacs made of membrane that bud off from the rough ER **(Figure 4.14)**.

▼ **Figure 4.13 The endoplasmic reticulum (ER).** In this drawing (top) and micrograph (bottom), the flattened sacs of rough ER and the tubes of smooth ER are connected. Notice that the ER is also connected to the nuclear envelope.

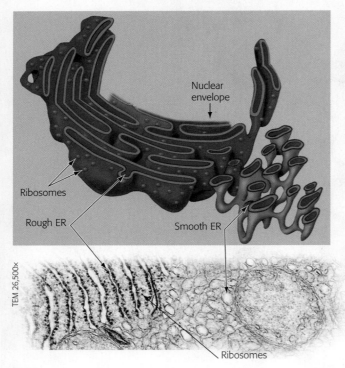

Nuclear envelope

Ribosomes

Rough ER

Smooth ER

TEM 26,500x

Ribosomes

▼ **Figure 4.14 How rough ER manufactures and packages secretory proteins.**

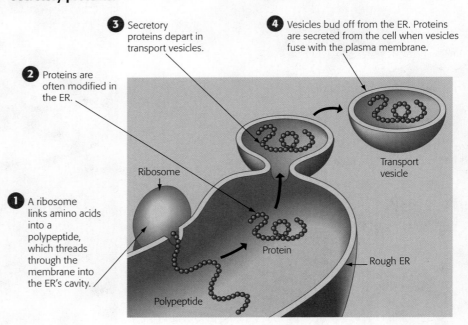

3 Secretory proteins depart in transport vesicles.

4 Vesicles bud off from the ER. Proteins are secreted from the cell when vesicles fuse with the plasma membrane.

2 Proteins are often modified in the ER.

1 A ribosome links amino acids into a polypeptide, which threads through the membrane into the ER's cavity.

Ribosome

Protein

Transport vesicle

Rough ER

Polypeptide

Smooth ER

The "smooth" in **smooth ER** refers to the fact that this organelle lacks the ribosomes that populate the surface of rough ER (see Figure 4.13). A diversity of enzymes built into the smooth ER membrane enables this organelle to perform many functions. One is the synthesis of lipids, including steroids (see Figure 3.13). For example, the cells in ovaries or testes that produce the steroid sex hormones are enriched with smooth ER. In liver cells, enzymes of the smooth ER detoxify circulating sedatives such as barbiturates, stimulants such as amphetamines, and some antibiotics (which is why they don't persist in the bloodstream after combating an infection). As liver cells are exposed to a drug, the amounts of smooth ER and its detoxifying enzymes increase. This can strengthen the body's tolerance of the drug, meaning that higher doses will be required in the future to achieve the desired effect. The growth of smooth ER in response to one drug can also increase tolerance of other drugs. Barbiturate use, such as frequently taking sleeping pills, may make certain antibiotics less effective by accelerating their breakdown in the liver. Furthermore, increased tolerance of drugs is one of the hallmarks of addiction—a potentially serious consequence of the continued use of certain drugs.

How does the liver detoxify drugs from the blood?

The Golgi Apparatus

Working in close partnership with the ER, the **Golgi apparatus**, an organelle named for its discoverer (Italian scientist Camillo Golgi), receives, refines, stores, and distributes chemical products of the cell **(Figure 4.15)**. Products made in the ER reach the Golgi apparatus in transport vesicles. The Golgi apparatus consists of a stack of membrane plates. **1** One side of a Golgi stack serves as a receiving dock for vesicles from the ER. **2** Proteins within a vesicle are usually modified by enzymes during their transit from the receiving to the shipping side of the Golgi apparatus. For example, molecular identification tags, such as phosphate groups, may be added that serve to mark and sort protein molecules into different batches for different destinations. **3** The shipping side of a Golgi stack is a depot from which finished products can be carried in transport vesicles to other organelles or to the plasma membrane. Vesicles that bind with the plasma membrane transfer proteins to it or secrete finished products to the outside of the cell. ☑

☑ CHECKPOINT

1. What makes rough ER rough?
2. What is the relationship between the Golgi apparatus and the ER in a protein-secreting cell?

Answers: 1. ribosomes attached to the membrane 2. The Golgi apparatus receives proteins from the ER via vesicles, processes the proteins, and then dispatches them in vesicles.

▼ **Figure 4.15 The Golgi apparatus.** This component of the endomembrane system consists of flattened sacs arranged something like a stack of pancakes. The number of stacks in a cell (from a few to hundreds) correlates with how active the cell is in secreting proteins.

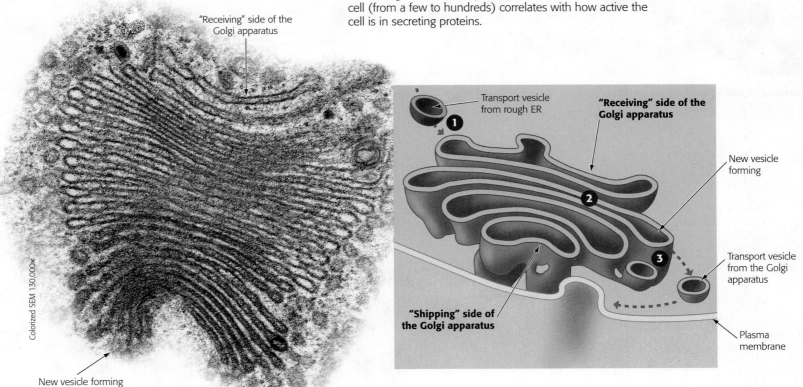

"Receiving" side of the Golgi apparatus

Colorized SEM 130,000×

New vesicle forming

Transport vesicle from rough ER

"Receiving" side of the Golgi apparatus

New vesicle forming

"Shipping" side of the Golgi apparatus

Transport vesicle from the Golgi apparatus

Plasma membrane

Lysosomes

A **lysosome** is a membrane-enclosed sac of digestive enzymes found in animal cells. Lysosomes are absent from most plant cells. Lysosomes develop from vesicles that bud off from the Golgi apparatus. Enzymes within a lysosome can break down large molecules such as proteins, polysaccharides, fats, and nucleic acids. The lysosome provides a compartment where the cell can digest these molecules safely, without unleashing these digestive enzymes on the cell itself.

Lysosomes have several types of digestive functions. Many cells engulf nutrients into tiny cytoplasmic sacs called food vacuoles. Lysosomes fuse with the food vacuoles, exposing the food to enzymes that digest it (**Figure 4.16a**). Small molecules that result from this digestion, such as amino acids, leave the lysosome and nourish the cell. Lysosomes also help destroy harmful bacteria. For example, our white blood cells ingest bacteria into vacuoles, and lysosomal enzymes that are emptied into these vacuoles rupture the bacterial cell walls. In addition, lysosomes break down the large molecules of damaged organelles. Without harming the cell, a lysosome can engulf and digest parts of another organelle, essentially recycling it by making its molecules available for the construction of new organelles (**Figure 4.16b**). Lysosomes also have sculpting functions in embryonic development. In an early human embryo, lysosomes release enzymes that digest webbing between fingers of the developing hand.

The importance of lysosomes to cell function and human health is made strikingly clear by hereditary disorders called lysosomal storage diseases. A person with such a disease is missing one or more of the digestive enzymes normally found within lysosomes. The abnormal lysosomes become engorged with indigestible substances, and this eventually interferes with other cellular functions. Most of these diseases are fatal in early childhood. In Tay-Sachs disease, lysosomes lack a lipid-digesting enzyme. As a result, nerve cells die as they accumulate excess lipids, ravaging the nervous system. Fortunately, storage diseases are rare. ☑

☑ CHECKPOINT

How can defective lysosomes result in excess accumulation of a particular chemical compound in a cell?

Answer: If the lysosomes lack an enzyme needed to break down the compound, the cell will accumulate an excess of that compound.

▼ **Figure 4.16 Two functions of lysosomes.**

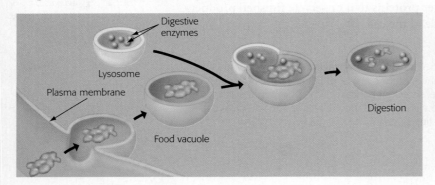

Digestive enzymes

Lysosome

Plasma membrane

Food vacuole

Digestion

(a) A lysosome digesting food

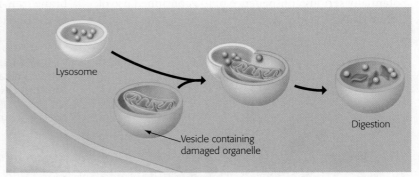

Lysosome

Vesicle containing damaged organelle

Digestion

(b) A lysosome breaking down the molecules of damaged organelles

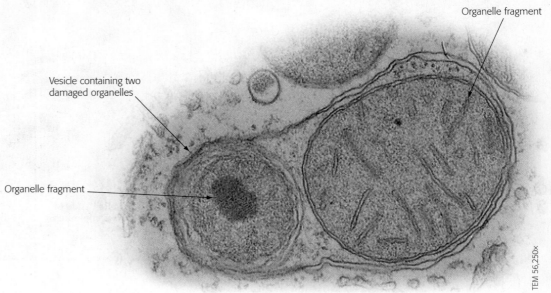

Organelle fragment

Vesicle containing two damaged organelles

Organelle fragment

TEM 56,250x

Vacuoles

Vacuoles are large sacs of membrane that bud from the ER, Golgi apparatus, or plasma membrane. Vacuoles have a variety of functions. For example, Figure 4.16a shows a food vacuole budding from the plasma membrane. Certain freshwater protists have contractile vacuoles that pump out excess water that flows into the cell from the outside environment **(Figure 4.17a)**.

Another type of vacuole is a **central vacuole**, which can account for more than half the volume of a mature plant cell **(Figure 4.17b)**. The central vacuole of a plant cell is a versatile compartment. It stores organic nutrients, such as proteins stockpiled in the vacuoles of seed cells. It also contributes to plant growth by absorbing water and causing cells to expand. In the cells of flower petals, central vacuoles may contain pigments that attract pollinating insects. Central vacuoles may also contain poisons that protect against plant-eating animals.

Figure 4.18 will help you review how organelles of the endomembrane system are related. Note that a product made in one part of the endomembrane system may exit the cell or become part of another organelle without crossing a membrane. Also note that membrane made by the ER can become part of the plasma membrane through the fusion of a transport vesicle. In this way, even the plasma membrane is related to the endomembrane system. ☑

☑ **CHECKPOINT**

Place the following cellular structures in the order they would be used in the production and secretion of a protein: Golgi apparatus, nucleus, plasma membrane, ribosome, transport vesicle.

Answer: nucleus, ribosome, transport vesicle, Golgi apparatus, plasma membrane

▼ **Figure 4.17 Two types of vacuoles.**

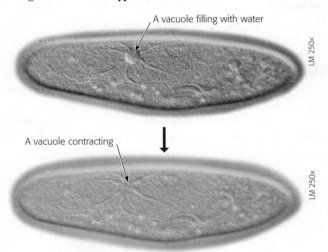

A vacuole filling with water

LM 250x

A vacuole contracting

LM 250x

(a) Contractile vacuole in *Paramecium*. A contractile vacuole fills with water and then contracts to pump the water out of the cell.

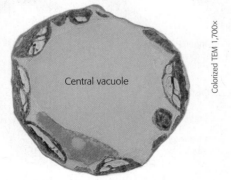

Central vacuole

Colorized TEM 1,700x

(b) Central vacuole in a plant cell. The central vacuole (colorized blue in this micrograph) is often the largest organelle in a mature plant cell.

▼ **Figure 4.18 Review of the endomembrane system.** The dashed arrows show some of the pathways of cell product distribution and membrane migration via transport vesicles.

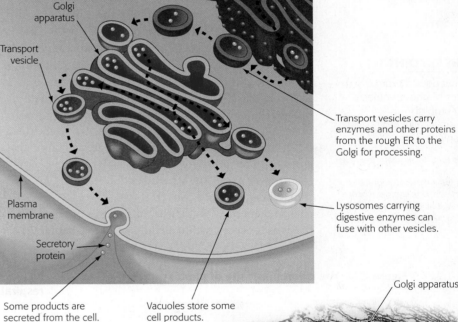

Rough ER

Golgi apparatus

Transport vesicle

Plasma membrane

Secretory protein

Transport vesicles carry enzymes and other proteins from the rough ER to the Golgi for processing.

Lysosomes carrying digestive enzymes can fuse with other vesicles.

Some products are secreted from the cell.

Vacuoles store some cell products.

Golgi apparatus

New vesicle forming

Transport vesicle from the Golgi apparatus

Plasma membrane

TEM 31,000x

67

Chloroplasts and Mitochondria: Energy Conversion

A cell requires a continuous energy supply to perform the work of life. Two organelles act as cellular power stations: chloroplasts and mitochondria.

Chloroplasts

Most of the living world runs on the energy provided by photosynthesis, the conversion of light energy from the sun to the chemical energy of sugar and other organic molecules. **Chloroplasts**, which are unique to the photosynthetic cells of plants and algae, are the organelles that perform photosynthesis.

A chloroplast is partitioned into three major compartments by internal membranes **(Figure 4.19)**. One compartment is the space between the two membranes that surround the chloroplast. The **stroma**, a thick fluid within the chloroplast, is the second compartment. Suspended in that fluid, the interior of a network of membrane-enclosed disks and tubes forms the third compartment. Notice in Figure 4.19 that the disks occur in interconnected stacks called **grana** (singular, *granum*). The grana are a chloroplast's solar power packs, the structures that trap light energy and convert it to chemical energy. (You'll learn the details of photosynthesis as it occurs within a chloroplast in Chapter 7.)

Which organelles have their own genes?

☑ CHECKPOINT

1. What does the process of photosynthesis accomplish?
2. What is cellular respiration?

Answers: **1.** *the conversion of light energy to chemical energy stored in food molecules* **2.** *a process that converts the chemical energy of sugars and other food molecules to chemical energy in the form of ATP*

Mitochondria

Mitochondria (singular, *mitochondrion*) are the organelles of cellular respiration in nearly all cells, harvesting energy from sugars and other food molecules and using it to produce another form of chemical energy called ATP (which stands for adenosine triphosphate). Cells use molecules of ATP as the direct energy source for most of their work. In contrast to chloroplasts, mitochondria are found in almost all eukaryotic cells, including those of plants and those in your body.

An envelope of two membranes encloses the mitochondrion, which contains a thick fluid called the **matrix (Figure 4.20)**. The inner membrane of the envelope has numerous infoldings called **cristae**. Many of the enzymes and other molecules that function in cellular respiration are embedded in the inner membrane. By increasing the surface area of this membrane, the cristae maximize ATP output. (You'll learn more about how mitochondria convert food energy to ATP energy in Chapter 6.)

Besides their ability to provide cellular energy, mitochondria and chloroplasts share another feature: They contain their own DNA that encodes some of their own proteins. This DNA is evidence that mitochondria and chloroplasts evolved from free-living prokaryotes in the distant past (see Chapter 15 for a discussion of this hypothesis). ☑

▼ **Figure 4.19** **The chloroplast: site of photosynthesis.**

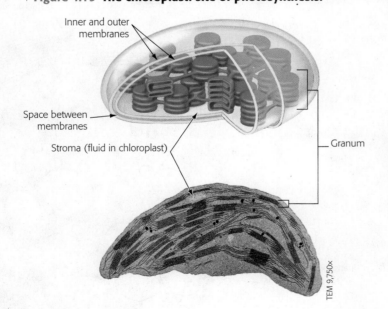

Inner and outer membranes
Space between membranes
Stroma (fluid in chloroplast)
Granum
TEM 9,750x

▼ **Figure 4.20** **The mitochondrion: site of cellular respiration.**

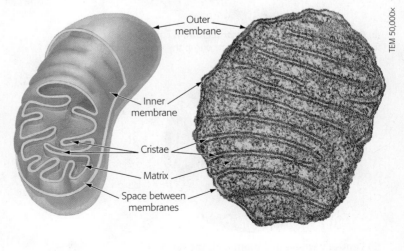

Outer membrane
Inner membrane
Cristae
Matrix
Space between membranes
TEM 50,000x

The Cytoskeleton: Cell Shape and Movement

If someone asked you to describe a house, you would most likely mention the various rooms and their locations. You probably would not think to mention the foundation and beams that support the house. Yet these structures perform an extremely important function. Similarly, cells have an infrastructure called the **cytoskeleton**, a network of fibers extending throughout the cytoplasm. The cytoskeleton serves as both skeleton and "muscles" for the cell, functioning in support and movement.

Maintaining Cell Shape

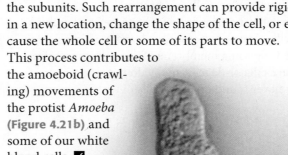

One function of the cytoskeleton is to give mechanical support to the cell and maintain its shape. This is especially important for animal cells, which lack rigid cell walls. The cytoskeleton contains several types of fibers made from different types of protein. One important type of fiber is the **microtubule (Figure 4.21a)**. Microtubules are straight, hollow tubes composed of proteins. The other kinds of cytoskeletal fibers, called intermediate filaments and microfilaments, are thinner and solid.

Just as the bony skeleton of your body helps fix the positions of your organs, the cytoskeleton provides anchorage and reinforcement for many organelles in a cell. For instance, the nucleus is often held in place by a cytoskeletal cage of filaments. Other organelles move along tracks made from microtubules. For example, a lysosome might reach a food vacuole by taking many small "baby steps" along a microtubule track. Microtubules also guide the movement of chromosomes when cells divide.

A cell's cytoskeleton is dynamic: It can quickly dismantle in one part of the cell by removing protein subunits and re-form in a new location by reattaching the subunits. Such rearrangement can provide rigidity in a new location, change the shape of the cell, or even cause the whole cell or some of its parts to move. This process contributes to the amoeboid (crawling) movements of the protist *Amoeba* **(Figure 4.21b)** and some of our white blood cells. ☑

▼ Figure 4.21 **The cytoskeleton.**

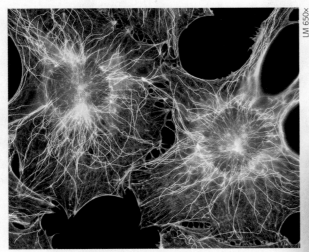

LM 650x

(a) Microtubules in the cytoskeleton. In this micrograph of animal cells, the cytoskeleton microtubules are labeled with a fluorescent yellow dye.

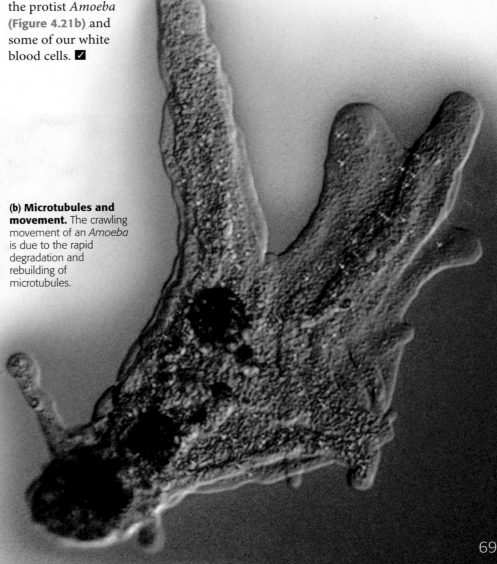

(b) Microtubules and movement. The crawling movement of an *Amoeba* is due to the rapid degradation and rebuilding of microtubules.

LM 220x

Cilia and Flagella

In some eukaryotic cells, microtubules are arranged into structures called flagella and cilia. Cilia and flagella are motile appendages—extensions from a cell that aid in movement. Eukaryotic **flagella** (singular, *flagellum*) propel cells through their undulating, whiplike motion. They often occur singly, such as in the sperm cells of humans and other animals (**Figure 4.22a**), but may also appear in groups on the outer surface of protists. **Cilia** (singular, *cilium*) are generally shorter and more numerous than flagella and promote movement by a coordinated back-and-forth motion, like the rhythmic oars of a crew team. Both cilia and flagella propel various protists through water (**Figure 4.22b**). Though different in length, number per cell, and beating pattern, cilia and flagella have the same basic architecture, with a core of microtubules wrapped in an extension of the plasma membrane. Although some animal cells have cilia or flagella, many do not, and they are almost never found on plant cells.

Some cilia extend from nonmoving cells that are part of a tissue layer. There, they move fluid over the tissue's surface. For example, cilia lining your windpipe clean your respiratory system by sweeping mucus with trapped debris out of your lungs (**Figure 4.22c**). Tobacco smoke can inhibit or destroy these cilia, interfering with the normal cleansing mechanisms and allowing more toxin-laden smoke particles to reach the lungs. Frequent coughing—common in heavy smokers—then becomes the body's attempt to cleanse the respiratory system.

Because human sperm rely on flagella for movement, it's easy to understand why problems with flagella can lead to male infertility. Interestingly, some men with a type of hereditary sterility also suffer from respiratory problems. The explanation lies in the similarities between flagella (found in sperm) and cilia (found lining the respiratory tract). Because of a defect in the structure of their flagella and cilia, their sperm cannot swim normally within the female reproductive tract to fertilize an egg (causing sterility) and their cilia do not sweep mucus out of their lungs (causing recurrent respiratory infections). ☑

How can defective flagella lead to male sterility?

☑ CHECKPOINT

Compare and contrast cilia and flagella.

Answer: Cilia and flagella have the same basic structure and help move cells or move fluid over cells. Cilia are short and numerous and move back and forth. Flagella are longer, often occurring singly, and they undulate.

▼ **Figure 4.22 Examples of flagella and cilia.**

(a) Flagellum of a human sperm cell. A eukaryotic flagellum undulates in a snakelike motion, driving a cell such as this sperm cell through its fluid environment.

Colorized SEM 5000×

(b) Cilia on a protist. Cilia are shorter and more numerous than flagella and move with a back-and-forth motion. As shown here, a dense nap of beating cilia covers *Paramecium*, a freshwater protist that can dart rapidly through its watery home.

Colorized SEM 500×

(c) Cilia lining the respiratory tract. The cilia lining your respiratory tract sweep mucus with trapped debris out of your lungs. This helps keep your airway clear and prevents infections.

Colorized SEM 3,000×

The Evolution of Antibiotic Resistance

As you read in the Biology and Society section, many antibiotics disrupt the cellular structures of invading microorganisms. This defensive mechanism is quite effective. In fact, when first introduced in the 1940s, penicillin appeared to be such a "wonder drug" that some doctors predicted the end of infections in people (Figure 4.23).

Why hasn't that optimistic prediction come true? The answer is both simple and profound: The rosy outlook does not take into account the force of evolution. Within a population of bacteria, random genetic changes result in slightly different proteins being produced in different bacteria. Some bacteria may produce a protein that reduces the effectiveness of an antibiotic. For example, a random change in a nucleotide sequence might lead to the production of an enzyme that deactivates or breaks down penicillin.

When an environment changes, natural selection favors individuals with beneficial genetic changes. In this case, the introduction of an antibiotic creates a pressure that favors resistant bacteria. Those individuals will survive and multiply, producing more of the same type of bacteria. Over time, drug-resistant bacteria, such as the MRSA strain discussed in the Process of Science section, become more common.

In what ways do we contribute to the problem of antibiotic resistance? Livestock producers add antibiotics to animal feed to promote growth and prevent illness. These practices may favor bacteria that resist standard antibiotics. Some doctors overprescribe antibiotics—for example, to patients with viral infections, which do not respond to such treatment. And some patients misuse prescribed antibiotics by prematurely stopping their medication. This misuse allows mutant bacteria that may be killed more slowly by the drug to survive and multiply.

The evolution of antibiotic-resistant bacteria is a serious public health concern. Nearly 100,000 people die each year in the United States from infections they contract in the hospital, often from antibiotic-resistant bacteria. Penicillin, effective against many bacterial infections in the 1940s, is virtually useless today in its original form. New drugs are developed but also continue to be rendered ineffective as resistant bacteria evolve. The medical community is engaged in an arms race against the powerful force of bacterial evolution. As of now, the ultimate victor remains to be determined.

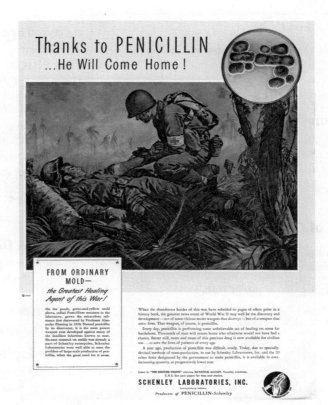

◄ Figure 4.23 **The changing role of antibiotics.** These two posters illustrate how the early promise of antibiotics (depicted in a poster from 1944) has given way to caution about their overuse (depicted in a poster from 2008).

Chapter Review

SUMMARY OF KEY CONCEPTS

The Microscopic World of Cells

Microscopes as Windows on the World of Cells

Using early microscopes, biologists discovered that all organisms are made of cells. Resolving power limits the useful magnification of microscopes. A light microscope (LM) has useful magnifications up to about 1,000×. Electron microscopes, both scanning (SEM) and transmission (TEM), are much more powerful.

The Two Major Categories of Cells

CATEGORIES OF CELLS	
Prokaryotic Cells	**Eukaryotic Cells**
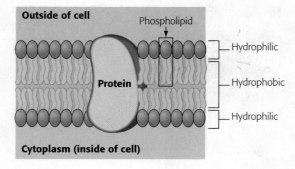	
• Smaller • Simpler • Most do not have organelles • Found in bacteria and archaea	• Larger • More complex • Have organelles • Found in protists, plants, fungi, animals

An Overview of Eukaryotic Cells

Many cellular functions are partitioned by membranes in the complex organization of eukaryotic cells. The largest organelle is usually the nucleus. Other organelles are located in the cytoplasm, the region between the nucleus and the plasma membrane.

Membrane Structure

The Plasma Membrane: A Fluid Mosaic of Lipids and Proteins

Outside of cell

Phospholipid

Hydrophilic

Protein

Hydrophobic

Hydrophilic

Cytoplasm (inside of cell)

Cell Surfaces

Most cells secrete an extracellular coat that helps protect and support the cell. The walls that encase plant cells support plants against the pull of gravity and also prevent cells from absorbing too much water. Animal cells are coated by a sticky extracellular matrix.

The Nucleus and Ribosomes: Genetic Control of the Cell

Structure and Function of the Nucleus

An envelope consisting of two membranes encloses the nucleus. Within the nucleus, DNA and proteins make up chromatin fibers; each very long fiber is a single chromosome. The nucleus also contains the nucleolus, which produces components of ribosomes.

Ribosomes

Ribosomes produce proteins in the cytoplasm.

How DNA Directs Protein Production

Genetic messages are transmitted to the ribosomes via messenger RNA (mRNA), which travels from the nucleus to the cytoplasm.

The Endomembrane System: Manufacturing and Distributing Cellular Products

The Endoplasmic Reticulum

The ER consists of membrane-enclosed tubes and sacs within the cytoplasm. Rough ER, named because of the ribosomes attached to its surface, makes membrane and secretory proteins. The functions of smooth ER include lipid synthesis and detoxification.

The Golgi Apparatus

The Golgi apparatus refines certain ER products and packages them in transport vesicles targeted for other organelles or export from the cell.

Lysosomes

Lysosomes, sacs containing digestive enzymes, aid digestion and recycling within the cell.

Vacuoles

Vacuoles include the contractile vacuoles that expel water from certain freshwater protists and the large, multifunctional central vacuoles of plant cells.

Chloroplasts and Mitochondria: Energy Conversion

Chloroplasts and Mitochondria

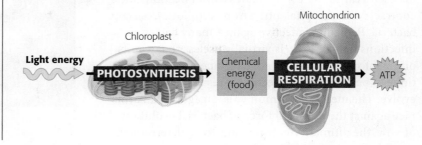

The Cytoskeleton: Cell Shape and Movement

Maintaining Cell Shape

Straight, hollow microtubules are an important component of the cytoskeleton, an organelle that gives support to, and maintains the shape of, cells.

Cilia and Flagella

Cilia and eukaryotic flagella are motile appendages made primarily of microtubules. Cilia are short and numerous and move the cell via coordinated beating. Flagella are long, often occur singly, and propel a cell through whiplike movements.

SELF-QUIZ

1. If you wanted to film the movement of chromosomes during cell division, the best choice for a microscope would be a
   a. light microscope, because of its magnifying power.
   b. transmission electron microscope, because of its resolving power.
   c. scanning electron microscope, because the chromosomes are on the cell surface.
   d. light microscope, because the specimen must be kept alive.

2. Using a light microscope to examine a thin section of a large spherical cell, you find that the cell is 0.3 mm in diameter. The nucleus is about one-fourth as wide. What would be the diameter of the nucleus in micrometers? (*Hint*: See Figure 4.3.)

3. You look into a light microscope and view an unknown cell. What might you see that would tell you whether the cell is prokaryotic or eukaryotic?
   a. a rigid cell wall
   b. a nucleus
   c. a plasma membrane
   d. ribosomes

4. Explain how each word in the term *fluid mosaic* describes the structure of a membrane.

5. Identify which of the following structures includes all the others in the list: rough ER, smooth ER, endomembrane system, the Golgi apparatus.

6. The ER has two distinct regions that differ in structure and function. Lipids are synthesized within the _____, and proteins are synthesized within the _____.

7. A type of cell called a lymphocyte makes proteins that are exported from the cell. You can track the path of these proteins within the cell from production through export by labeling them with radioactive isotopes. Identify which of the following structures would be radioactively labeled in your experiment, listing them in the order in which they would be labeled: chloroplasts, Golgi apparatus, plasma membrane, smooth ER, rough ER, nucleus, mitochondria.

8. Name two similarities in the structure or function of chloroplasts and mitochondria. Name two differences.

9. Match the following organelles with their functions:
   a. ribosomes   1. movement
   b. microtubules   2. photosynthesis
   c. mitochondria   3. protein synthesis
   d. chloroplasts   4. digestion
   e. lysosomes   5. cellular respiration

10. DNA controls the cell by transmitting genetic messages that result in protein production. Place the following organelles in the order that represents the flow of genetic information from the DNA through the cell: nuclear pores, ribosomes, nucleus, rough ER, Golgi apparatus.

11. Compare and contrast cilia and flagella.

Answers to these questions can be found in Appendix: Self-Quiz Answers.

THE PROCESS OF SCIENCE

12. The cells of plant seeds store oils in the form of droplets enclosed by membranes. Unlike the membranes you learned about in this chapter, the oil droplet membrane consists of a single layer of phospholipids rather than a bilayer. Draw a model for a membrane around an oil droplet. Explain why this arrangement is more stable than a bilayer.

13. Imagine that you are a pediatrician and one of your patients is a newborn who may have a lysosomal storage disease. You remove some cells from the patient and examine them under the microscope. What would you expect to see? Design a series of tests that could reveal whether the patient is indeed suffering from a lysosomal storage disease.

BIOLOGY AND SOCIETY

14. Doctors at a university medical center removed John Moore's spleen, which is a standard treatment for his type of leukemia. The disease did not recur. Researchers kept the spleen cells alive in a nutrient medium. They found that some cells produced a blood protein that showed promise as a treatment for cancer and AIDS. The researchers patented the cells. Moore sued, claiming a share in profits from any products derived from his cells. The U.S. Supreme Court ruled against Moore, stating that his lawsuit "threatens to destroy the economic incentive to conduct important medical research." Moore argued that the ruling left patients "vulnerable to exploitation at the hands of the state." Do you think Moore was treated fairly? What else would you like to know about this case that might help you decide?

5 The Working Cell

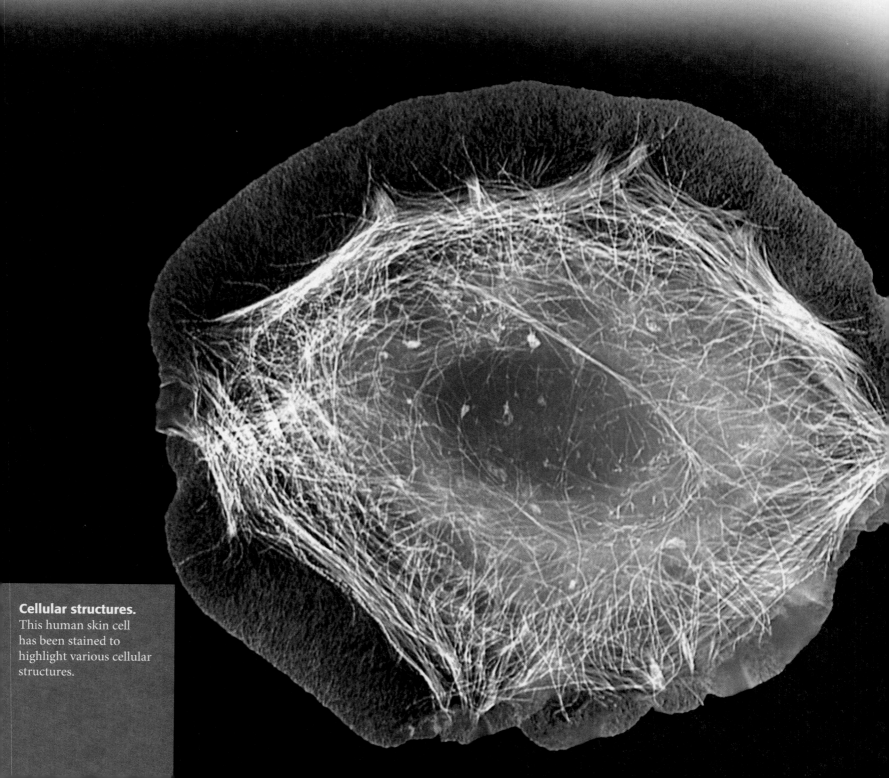

Cellular structures.
This human skin cell has been stained to highlight various cellular structures.

Nanotechnology BIOLOGY AND SOCIETY

Harnessing Cellular Structures

One of the most fascinating applications of modern science is nanotechnology, the manipulation of materials at the molecular scale. When designing devices of such small size, researchers often turn to living cells for inspiration. After all, you can think of a cell as a machine that continuously and efficiently performs a variety of functions, such as movement, energy processing, and production of various products. Let's consider one example of cell-based nanotechnology and see how it relates to three of the main concerns for working cells: energy, enzymes, and the plasma membrane.

Researchers at Cornell University are attempting to harvest the energy-producing capability of human sperm cells. Like other cells, a sperm cell generates energy by breaking down sugars and other molecules that pass through its plasma membrane. Enzymes within the cell carry out a process called glycolysis. During glycolysis, the energy released from the breakdown of glucose is used to produce molecules of ATP. Within a living sperm, the ATP produced during glycolysis and other processes provides the energy that propels the sperm through the female reproductive tract. In an attempt to harness this energy-producing system, the Cornell researchers attached three glycolysis enzymes to a computer chip. The enzymes continued to function in this artificial system, producing energy from sugar. The hope is that a larger set of enzymes can eventually be used to power microscopic robots. Perhaps such nanorobots could use glucose from the bloodstream to power the delivery of drugs to body tissues. This example is just one of many new technologies that may be built some day, inspired by the cells found in all living organisms.

This example of cell-based nanotechnology highlights the three main topics of this chapter. We'll explore how a cell uses energy, enzymes, and the plasma membrane to carry out the work of controlling its internal chemical environment. Along the way, we'll look at some other technologies that mimic the natural activities of living cells.

Some Basic Energy Concepts

Energy makes the world go round—both the larger world outside and the cellular world. But what exactly is energy? Our first step in understanding the working cell is to learn a few basic concepts about energy.

Conservation of Energy

Energy is defined as the capacity to cause change. Some forms of energy are used to perform work, such as moving an object against an opposing force—for example, gravity. In other words, energy is the ability to rearrange a collection of matter.

For example, imagine a diver climbing to the top of a platform and diving off **(Figure 5.1)**. To get to the top of the platform, the diver must perform work to overcome the opposing force of gravity. Specifically, chemical energy from food is converted to **kinetic energy**, the energy of motion. In this case, the kinetic energy takes the form of muscle movement.

What happens to the kinetic energy when the diver reaches the top of the platform? Has it disappeared?

The answer is no. You may be familiar with the principle of conservation of matter, which states that matter cannot be created or destroyed but can only be converted from one form to another. A similar principle, known as **conservation of energy**, states that it is not possible to destroy or create energy. Like matter, energy can only be converted from one form to another. A power plant, for example, does not make energy; it merely converts it from one form (such as energy stored in coal) to a more convenient form (such as electricity). That's what happens in the diver's climb up the steps. The kinetic energy of muscle movement is now stored in a form called potential energy. **Potential energy** is energy that an object has because of its location or structure, such as the energy contained by water behind a dam or by a compressed spring. In our example, the diver at the top of the platform has potential energy because of his elevated location. The act of diving off the platform into the water converts the potential energy back to kinetic energy. Life depends on countless similar conversions of energy from one form to another. ☑

☑ **CHECKPOINT**

How can an object at rest have energy?

Answer: It can have potential energy because of its location or structure.

▶ **Figure 5.1 Energy conversions during a dive.**

On the platform, the diver has more potential energy.

Climbing the steps converts kinetic energy of muscle movement to potential energy.

Diving converts potential energy to kinetic energy.

In the water, the diver has less potential energy.

Entropy

If energy cannot be destroyed, where has it gone when the diver hits the water? It has been converted to **heat**, a type of kinetic energy contained in the random motion of atoms and molecules. The friction between the body and its surroundings generated heat in the air and then in the water.

All energy conversions generate some heat. Although heat production does not destroy energy, it does make it less useful. Heat, of all energy forms, is the most difficult to "tame"—the most difficult to harness for useful work. Heat is energy in its most chaotic form, the energy of aimless molecular movement.

Entropy is a measure of the amount of disorder, or randomness, in a system. Every time energy is converted from one form to another, entropy increases. The energy conversions during the climb up the ladder and the dive from the platform increased entropy as the diver emitted heat to the surroundings. To climb up the steps again for another dive, the diver must use additional stored food energy. This conversion will also create heat and therefore increase entropy. ☑

Chemical Energy

How can molecules derived from the food we eat provide energy for our working cells? The molecules of food, gasoline, and other fuels have a special form of potential energy called **chemical energy**, which arises from the arrangement of atoms and can be released by a chemical reaction. Carbohydrates, fats, and gasoline have structures that make them especially rich in chemical energy.

Living cells and automobile engines use the same basic process to make the chemical energy stored in their fuels available for work **(Figure 5.2)**. In both cases, this process breaks organic fuel into smaller waste molecules that have much less chemical energy than the fuel molecules did, thereby releasing energy that can be used to perform work.

For example, the engine of an automobile mixes oxygen with gasoline in an explosive chemical reaction that breaks down the fuel molecules and pushes the pistons that eventually move the wheels. The waste products emitted from the car's exhaust pipe are mostly carbon dioxide and water. Only about 25% of the energy that an automobile engine extracts from its fuel is converted to

What do your cells have in common with a car's engine?

☑ CHECKPOINT

Which form of energy is most randomized and difficult to put to work?

Answer: heat

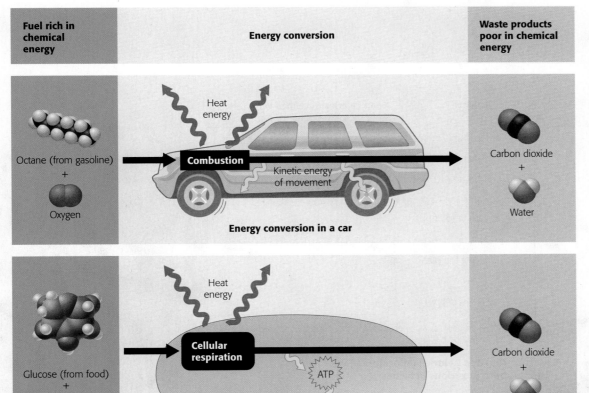

Fuel rich in chemical energy	Energy conversion	Waste products poor in chemical energy

Octane (from gasoline) + Oxygen — **Combustion** — Heat energy / Kinetic energy of movement → Carbon dioxide + Water

Energy conversion in a car

Glucose (from food) + Oxygen — **Cellular respiration** — Heat energy / ATP / Energy for cellular work → Carbon dioxide + Water

Energy conversion in a cell

◄ **Figure 5.2 Energy conversions in a car and a cell.** In both a car and a cell, the chemical energy of organic fuel molecules is harvested using oxygen. This chemical breakdown releases energy stored in the fuel molecules and produces carbon dioxide and water. The released energy can be used to perform work.

the kinetic energy of the car's movement. Most of the rest is converted to heat—so much that the engine would melt if the car's radiator and fan did not disperse excess heat into the atmosphere.

Cells also use oxygen in reactions that release energy from fuel molecules. As in a car engine, the "exhaust" is mostly carbon dioxide and water. The combustion of fuel in cells is called cellular respiration, which is a more gradual and efficient "burning" of fuel compared with the explosive combustion in an automobile engine. Cellular respiration is the energy-releasing chemical breakdown of fuel molecules and the storage of that energy in a form the cell can use to perform work. (We will discuss the details of cellular respiration in the next chapter.) You convert about 34% of your food energy to useful work, such as movement of your muscles. About 66% of the energy released by the breakdown of fuel molecules generates body heat. Humans and many other animals can use this heat to keep the body at an almost constant temperature (37°C, or 98.6°F, in the case of humans), even when the surrounding air is much colder. The liberation of heat energy also explains why you feel hot after exercise. Sweating and other cooling mechanisms enable your body to lose the excess heat, much as a car's radiator keeps the engine from overheating.

Why do dieters often feel cold?

☑ CHECKPOINT

According to Figure 5.3, how long would you have to ride your bicycle to burn off the energy in three slices of pepperoni pizza?

*Answer: a little over 1 hour
(1 slice = 181 Calories, so
3 slices = 543 Calories; 1 hour
of cycling consumes 490 Calories)*

Food Calories

Read any packaged food label and you'll find the number of calories in each serving of that food. Calories are units of energy. A **calorie** (cal) is the amount of energy that can raise the temperature of 1 gram (g) of water by 1°C. You could actually measure the caloric content of a peanut by burning it under a container of water to convert all of the stored chemical energy to heat and then measuring the temperature increase of the water.

Calories are tiny units of energy, so using them to describe the fuel content of foods is not practical. Instead, it's conventional to use kilocalories (kcal), units of 1,000 calories. In fact, the Calories (capital C) on a food package are actually kilocalories. For example, one peanut has about 5 kcal. That's a lot of energy, enough to increase the temperature of 1 kg (a little more than a quart) of water by 5°C. And just a handful of peanuts contains enough Calories, if converted to heat, to boil 1 kg of water. In living organisms, of course, food isn't used to boil water but instead to fuel the activities of life. **Figure 5.3** shows the number of Calories in several foods and how many Calories are burned off by some typical activities. ☑

▼ **Figure 5.3 Some caloric accounting.**

Food	Food Calories
Cheeseburger	295
Spaghetti with sauce (1 cup)	241
Baked potato (plain, with skin)	220
Fried chicken (drumstick)	193
Bean burrito	189
Pizza with pepperoni (1 slice)	181
Peanuts (1 ounce)	166
Apple	81
Garden salad (2 cups)	56
Popcorn (plain, 1 cup)	31
Broccoli (1 cup)	25

(a) Food Calories (kilocalories) in various foods

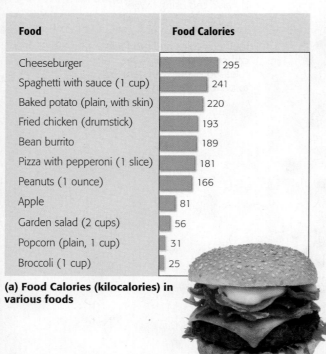

Activity	Food Calories consumed per hour by a 150-pound person*
Running (7 min/mi)	979
Dancing (fast)	510
Bicycling (10 mph)	490
Swimming (2 mph)	408
Walking (3 mph)	245
Dancing (slow)	204
Playing the piano	73
Driving a car	61
Sitting (writing)	28

*Not including energy necessary for basic functions, such as breathing and heartbeat

(b) Food Calories (kilocalories) we burn in various activities

ATP and Cellular Work

The carbohydrates, fats, and other fuel molecules we obtain from food do not drive work in our cells directly. Instead, the chemical energy released by the breakdown of organic molecules during cellular respiration is used to generate molecules of ATP. These molecules of ATP then power cellular work. ATP acts like an energy shuttle, storing energy obtained from food and then releasing it as needed at a later time.

The Structure of ATP

The abbreviation ATP stands for <u>a</u>denosine <u>t</u>riphosphate. **ATP** consists of an organic molecule called adenosine plus a tail of three phosphate groups (ⓟ) **(Figure 5.4)**. The triphosphate tail is the "business" end of ATP, the part that provides energy for cellular work. Each phosphate group is negatively charged. Negative charges repel each other. The crowding of negative charges in the triphosphate tail contributes to the potential energy of ATP. It's analogous to storing energy by compressing a spring; if you release the spring, it will relax, and you can use that springiness to do some useful work. For ATP power, it is release of the phosphate at the tip of the triphosphate tail that makes energy available to working cells. What remains is **ADP**, adenosine diphosphate (two phosphate groups instead of three, shown on the right side of Figure 5.4).

Phosphate Transfer

When ATP drives work in cells, phosphate groups don't just fly off into space. ATP energizes other molecules in cells by transferring phosphate groups to those molecules. This transfer of phosphate groups helps cells perform three main kinds of work: mechanical work, transport work, and chemical work.

Imagine a bicyclist pedaling up a hill. In the muscle cells of the rider's legs, ATP transfers phosphate groups to motor proteins. The proteins then change shape, causing the muscle cells to contract and perform mechanical work **(Figure 5.5a)**. ATP also enables the transport of ions and other dissolved substances across the membranes of the rider's nerve cells **(Figure 5.5b)**, helping them send signals to his legs. And ATP drives the chemical work of making some of a cell's large molecules **(Figure 5.5c)**. Notice again in Figure 5.5 that all these types of work occur when target molecules accept a phosphate group from ATP.

▼ **Figure 5.4 ATP power.** Each ⓟ in the triphosphate tail of ATP represents a phosphate group, a phosphorus atom bonded to oxygen atoms. The transfer of a phosphate from the triphosphate tail to other molecules provides energy for cellular work.

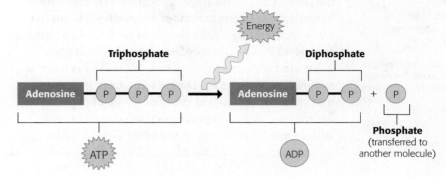

▼ **Figure 5.5 How ATP drives cellular work.** Each type of work shown here is powered when an enzyme transfers phosphate from ATP to a recipient molecule.

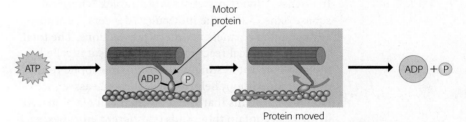

(a) Motor protein performing mechanical work (moving a muscle fiber)

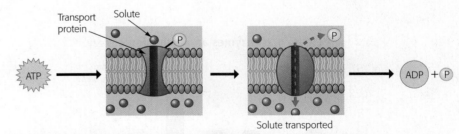

(b) Transport protein performing transport work (importing a solute)

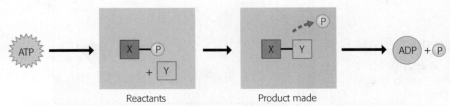

(c) Chemical reactants performing chemical work (promoting a chemical reaction)

The ATP Cycle

Your cells spend ATP continuously. Fortunately, it is a renewable resource. ATP can be restored by adding a phosphate group back to ADP. That takes energy, like recompressing a spring. And that's where food enters the story. The chemical energy that cellular respiration harvests from sugars and other organic fuels is put to work regenerating a cell's supply of ATP. Cellular work spends ATP, which is recycled when ADP and phosphate are combined using energy released by cellular respiration (**Figure 5.6**). Thus, energy from processes that yield energy, such as the breakdown of organic fuels, is transferred to processes that consume energy, such as muscle contraction and other cellular work.

▼ **Figure 5.6 The ATP cycle.**

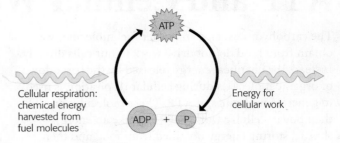

The third phosphate group acts as an energy shuttle within the ATP cycle. The ATP cycle can run at an astonishing pace: up to 10 million ATPs are consumed and recycled each second in a working muscle cell. ☑

Enzymes

As you've seen, a living organism contains a vast collection of chemicals, with countless chemical reactions constantly changing the organism's molecular makeup. In a sense, a living organism is a complex "chemical square dance," with the molecular "dancers" continually changing partners via chemical reactions. The total of all the chemical reactions in an organism is called **metabolism**. Interestingly, almost no metabolic reactions occur without help. Most require the assistance of **enzymes**, proteins that speed up chemical reactions. All living cells contain thousands of different enzymes, each promoting a different chemical reaction.

Activation Energy

For a chemical reaction to begin, chemical bonds in the reactant molecules must be broken. (The first step in swapping partners during a square dance is to let go of your current partner's hand.) This process requires that the molecules absorb energy from their surroundings. This energy is called **activation energy** because it activates the reactants and triggers the chemical reaction.

Enzymes enable metabolism to occur by reducing the amount of activation energy required to break the bonds of reactant molecules. If you think of the activation energy as a barrier to a chemical reaction, an enzyme's function is to lower that barrier (**Figure 5.7**). It does so by binding to reactant molecules and putting them under physical or chemical stress, making it easier to break their bonds and start a reaction. ☑

▼ **Figure 5.7 Enzymes and activation energy.**

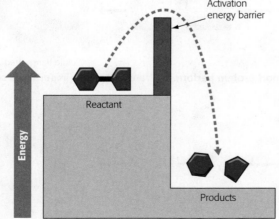

(a) Without enzyme. A reactant molecule must overcome the activation energy barrier before a chemical reaction can break the molecule into products.

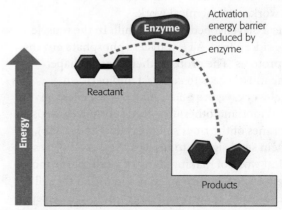

(b) With enzyme. An enzyme speeds the chemical reaction by lowering the activation energy barrier.

Can Enzymes Be Engineered?

Like all other proteins, enzymes are encoded by genes. **Observations** of genetic sequences suggest that many of our genes were formed through a type of molecular evolution: One ancestral gene duplicated, and the two copies diverged over time via random genetic changes, eventually becoming distinct genes for enzymes with different functions.

The natural evolution of enzymes raises a **question**: Can laboratory methods mimic this process through artificial selection? A group of researchers at two California biotechnology companies formed the **hypothesis** that an artificial process could be used to modify the gene that codes for the enzyme lactase (which breaks down the sugar lactose) into a new gene coding for a new enzyme with a new function. Their **experiment** used a procedure called directed evolution. In this process, many copies of the gene for the starting lactase enzyme were mutated at random (**Figure 5.8**). The researchers tested the enzymes resulting from these mutated genes to determine which enzymes best displayed a new activity (in this case, breaking down a different sugar). The genes for the enzymes that did show the new activity were then subjected to several more rounds of duplication, mutation, and screening.

After seven rounds, the **results** were clear: Directed evolution had produced a new enzyme with a novel function. Researchers have used similar methods to produce many artificial enzymes with desired properties. Directed evolution is another example of how scientists can mimic the natural processes of cells for useful purposes. Biomedical engineers may someday embed these artificial enzymes in nanotechnology devices with specific functions.

▼ **Figure 5.8 Directed evolution of an enzyme.** During seven rounds of directed evolution, the lactase enzyme gradually gained a new function.

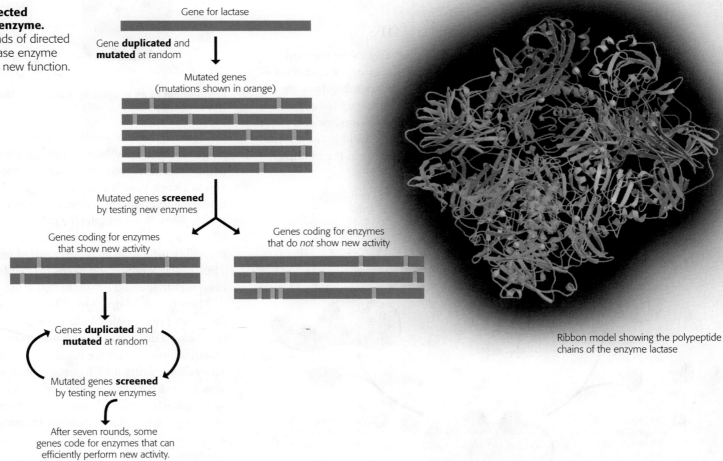

Gene for lactase

Gene **duplicated** and **mutated** at random

Mutated genes (mutations shown in orange)

Mutated genes **screened** by testing new enzymes

Genes coding for enzymes that show new activity

Genes coding for enzymes that do *not* show new activity

Genes **duplicated** and **mutated** at random

Mutated genes **screened** by testing new enzymes

After seven rounds, some genes code for enzymes that can efficiently perform new activity.

Ribbon model showing the polypeptide chains of the enzyme lactase

Induced Fit

An enzyme is very selective in the reaction it catalyzes. This selectivity is based on the enzyme's ability to recognize a certain reactant molecule, which is called the enzyme's **substrate**. And the ability of the enzyme to recognize and bind to its specific substrate depends on the enzyme's shape. A region of the enzyme called the **active site** has a shape and chemistry that fits the substrate molecule. When a substrate slips into this docking station, the active site changes shape slightly to embrace the substrate and catalyze the reaction. This interaction is called **induced fit** because the entry of the substrate induces the enzyme to change shape slightly, making the fit between substrate and active site snugger. Think of a handshake: As your hand makes contact with another hand, it changes shape slightly to make a better fit.

How is your hand like an enzyme?

After the products are released from the active site, the enzyme can accept another molecule of its substrate. In fact, the ability to function repeatedly is a key characteristic of enzymes. **Figure 5.9** follows the action of the enzyme sucrase, which hydrolyzes the disaccharide sucrose (the substrate). Like sucrase, many enzymes are named for their substrates, but with an -*ase* ending.

Enzyme Inhibitors

Certain molecules can inhibit a metabolic reaction by binding to an enzyme and disrupting its function **(Figure 5.10)**. Some of these **enzyme inhibitors** are actually substrate imposters that plug up the active site. (You can't shake a person's hand if someone else puts a banana in it first!) Other inhibitors bind to the enzyme at a site remote from the active site, but the binding

☑ CHECKPOINT

1. How does an enzyme recognize its substrate?
2. Name two ways that a molecule may inhibit an enzyme.

Answers: 1. The substrate and the enzyme's active site are complementary in shape and chemistry. 2. An inhibitor may bind to an enzyme in its active site, or it may bind in an alternate site that affects the active site.

▼ **Figure 5.9 How an enzyme works.** Our example is the enzyme sucrase, named for its substrate, sucrose.

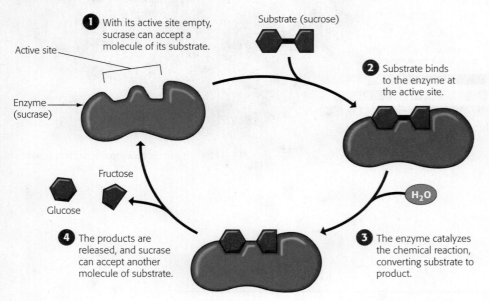

❶ With its active site empty, sucrase can accept a molecule of its substrate.

Active site

Enzyme (sucrase)

Substrate (sucrose)

❷ Substrate binds to the enzyme at the active site.

H_2O

Fructose

Glucose

❹ The products are released, and sucrase can accept another molecule of substrate.

❸ The enzyme catalyzes the chemical reaction, converting substrate to product.

▼ **Figure 5.10 Enzyme inhibitors.**

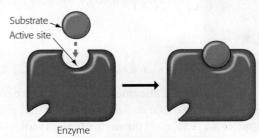

Substrate
Active site

Enzyme

(a) Enzyme and substrate binding normally

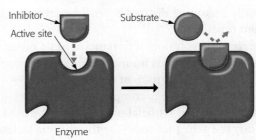

Inhibitor
Active site

Substrate

Enzyme

(b) Enzyme inhibition by a substrate imposter

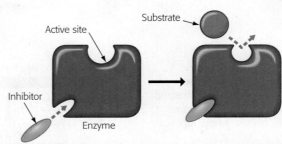

Substrate
Active site

Inhibitor

Enzyme

(c) Inhibition of an enzyme by a molecule that causes the active site to change shape

changes the enzyme's shape so that the active site no longer accepts the substrate. (Imagine trying to shake hands when someone else is tickling your ribs, causing you to clench your hand.) In some cases, the binding is reversible, enabling certain inhibitors to regulate metabolism. For example, if a cell is producing more of a certain product than it needs, that product may reversibly inhibit an enzyme required for its production. This feedback regulation keeps the cell from wasting resources that could be put to better use.

Many beneficial drugs work by inhibiting enzymes. Penicillin, for example, blocks the active site of an enzyme that bacteria use in making cell walls (see Chapter 4). Ibuprofen inhibits an enzyme involved in sending pain signals. Many cancer drugs inhibit enzymes that promote cell division. Many toxins and poisons are irreversible inhibitors. Nerve gases (a form of chemical warfare) bind to the active site of an enzyme vital to transmitting nerve impulses. The inhibition of this enzyme leads to rapid paralysis of vital functions and death. Many pesticides are toxic to insects because they irreversibly inhibit this same enzyme. ☑

Membrane Function

So far, we have discussed how cells control the flow of energy and how enzymes affect the pace of chemical reactions. In addition to these vital processes, cells must also regulate the flow of materials to and from the environment. In Chapter 4, you learned that the plasma membrane consists of a double layer of fat (a phospholipid bilayer) with embedded proteins (see Figure 4.6). **Figure 5.11** describes the major functions of these membrane proteins.

Transport proteins are membrane proteins that help move substances across a cell membrane. In this section, you'll learn about the most important mechanisms of transport across membranes.

Passive Transport: Diffusion across Membranes

Molecules are restless. They constantly vibrate and wander randomly. One result of this motion is **diffusion**, the movement of molecules spreading out evenly into the available space. Each molecule moves randomly, but the overall diffusion of a population of molecules is usually directional, from a region where the molecules are more concentrated to where they are less concentrated. For example, imagine many molecules of perfume inside a bottle. If you remove the bottle top, every molecule of perfume

▼ **Figure 5.11 Primary functions of membrane proteins.** In this diagram of two adjacent membranes, all six types of membrane proteins are shown for convenience. An actual cell may have just a few of these types of proteins.

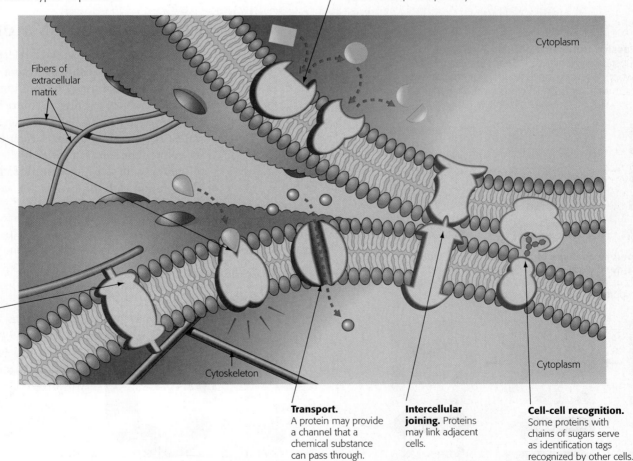

Enzymatic activity. This protein and the one next to it are enzymes, having an active site that fits a substrate. Enzymes may form an assembly line that carries out steps of a pathway.

Cytoplasm

Fibers of extracellular matrix

Cell signaling. A binding site fits the shape of a chemical messenger. The messenger may cause a change in the protein that relays the message to the inside of the cell.

Attachment to the cytoskeleton and extracellular matrix. Such proteins help maintain cell shape and coordinate changes.

Cytoskeleton

Cytoplasm

Transport. A protein may provide a channel that a chemical substance can pass through.

Intercellular joining. Proteins may link adjacent cells.

Cell-cell recognition. Some proteins with chains of sugars serve as identification tags recognized by other cells.

will move randomly about, but the overall movement will be out of the bottle. You could, with great effort, return the perfume to its bottle, but the molecules would never do that spontaneously.

For an example closer to a living cell, imagine a membrane separating pure water from a dye solution (**Figure 5.12**). Assume that this membrane has tiny holes that allow dye molecules to pass. Although each dye molecule moves randomly, there will be a net migration across the membrane to the side that began as pure water. Movement of the dye will continue until both solutions have equal concentrations. After that, there will be a dynamic equilibrium: Molecules will still be moving, but as many dye molecules move in one direction as in the other.

Diffusion across a membrane is an example of **passive transport**—passive because the cell does not expend any energy for it to happen. However, the cell membrane is selectively permeable, meaning that only certain substances are allowed to pass. For example, small molecules such as oxygen (O_2) generally pass through more readily than larger molecules such as amino acids. But

How does oxygen get from the air into your blood?

the membrane is relatively impermeable to even some very small substances, such as most ions, which are too hydrophilic to pass through the phospholipid bilayer. In passive transport, a substance diffuses down its **concentration gradient**, from where the substance is more concentrated to where it is less concentrated. In our lungs, for example, passive transport is the sole means by which O_2 enters the blood and CO_2 passes out of it.

Substances that do not cross membranes spontaneously—or do cross, but slowly—can be transported via proteins that act as corridors for specific molecules (see Figure 5.11). This assisted transport is called **facilitated diffusion**. For example, water molecules can move through the plasma membrane of some cells via transport proteins—each of which can allow the entry of 3 billion water molecules per second! Other specific transport proteins move glucose across cell membranes 50,000 times faster than diffusion. Even at this rate, facilitated diffusion is a type of passive transport because it does not require the cell to expend energy. As in all passive transport, the driving force is the concentration gradient. ✓

☑ **CHECKPOINT**

Why is facilitated diffusion a form of passive transport?

Answer: It uses proteins to transport materials down a concentration gradient without expending energy.

Osmosis and Water Balance

The diffusion of water across a selectively permeable membrane is called **osmosis** (**Figure 5.13**). Imagine a membrane separating two solutions with different concentrations of a solute. A **solute** is a substance that is dissolved in a liquid solvent, such as the salt in salt water. The membrane allows water to pass but not the solute. The solution with a higher concentration of solute is said to be **hypertonic** to the other solution. The solution with the lower solute concentration is said

▼ **Figure 5.12 Passive transport: diffusion across a membrane.** A substance will diffuse from where it is more concentrated to where it is less concentrated. Put another way, a substance tends to diffuse down its concentration gradient.

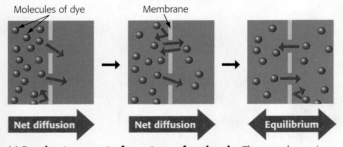

Molecules of dye   Membrane

Net diffusion   Net diffusion   Equilibrium

(a) Passive transport of one type of molecule. The membrane is permeable to these dye molecules, which diffuse down the concentration gradient. At equilibrium, the molecules are still restless, but the rate of transport is equal in both directions.

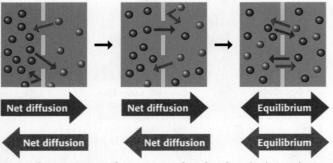

Net diffusion   Net diffusion   Equilibrium

Net diffusion   Net diffusion   Equilibrium

(b) Passive transport of two types of molecules. If solutions have two or more solutes, each will diffuse down its own concentration gradient.

▼ **Figure 5.13 Osmosis.** A membrane separates two solutions with different sugar concentrations. Water molecules can pass through the membrane, but sugar molecules cannot.

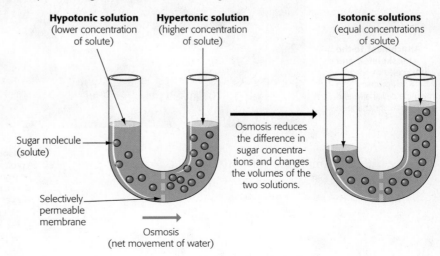

Hypotonic solution (lower concentration of solute)

Hypertonic solution (higher concentration of solute)

Isotonic solutions (equal concentrations of solute)

Sugar molecule (solute)

Osmosis reduces the difference in sugar concentrations and changes the volumes of the two solutions.

Selectively permeable membrane

Osmosis (net movement of water)

to be **hypotonic** to the other. Note that the hypotonic solution, by having the lower solute concentration, has the higher water concentration (less solute = more water). Therefore, water will diffuse across the membrane along its concentration gradient from an area of higher water concentration (hypotonic solution) to one of lower water concentration (hypertonic solution). This reduces the difference in solute concentrations and changes the volumes of the two solutions.

People can take advantage of osmosis to preserve foods. Salt is often applied to meats to cure them; the salt causes water to move out of the food toward the region of greater solute (salt) concentration. Food can also be preserved in honey because a high sugar concentration draws water out of food.

When the solute concentrations are the same on both sides of a membrane, water molecules will move at the same rate in both directions, so there will be no net change in solute concentration. Solutions of equal solute concentration are said to be **isotonic**. For example, many marine animals, such as sea stars and crabs, are isotonic to seawater, so they neither gain nor lose water. You may have seen this term on bottles of contact lens saline solution, which is formulated to have the same solute concentration as the fluid at the surface of the human eye, reducing irritation.

Water Balance in Animal Cells

The survival of a cell depends on its ability to balance water uptake and loss. When an animal cell, such as a red blood cell, is immersed in an isotonic solution, the cell's volume remains constant because the cell gains water at the same rate that it loses water (**Figure 5.14a**, top). But what happens if an animal cell is in contact with a hypotonic solution, which has a lower solute concentration than the cell? Due to osmosis, the cell would gain water, swell, and possibly burst (lyse) like an overfilled water balloon (**Figure 5.14b**, top). A hypertonic environment is also harsh on an animal cell; the cell shrivels from water loss (**Figure 5.14c**, top).

For an animal to survive a hypotonic or hypertonic environment, the animal must have a way to balance the uptake and loss of water. The control of water balance is called **osmoregulation**. For example, a freshwater fish has kidneys and gills that work constantly to prevent an excessive buildup of water in the body. Humans can suffer consequences of osmoregulation failure. Dehydration (consumption of too little water) can cause fatigue and even death. Drinking too much water—called hyponatremia or "water intoxication"—can also cause death by overdiluting necessary ions.

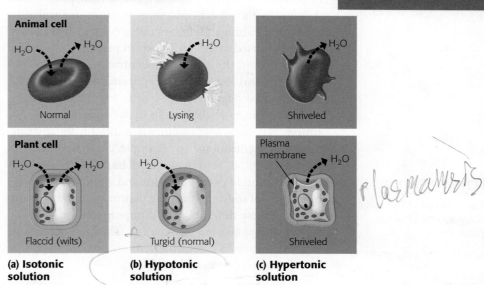

▼ Figure 5.14 **The behavior of animal and plant cells in different osmotic environments.**

Animal cell

Normal — Lysing — Shriveled

Plant cell

Plasma membrane

Flaccid (wilts) — Turgid (normal) — Shriveled

(a) Isotonic solution — **(b) Hypotonic solution** — **(c) Hypertonic solution**

Water Balance in Plant Cells

Problems of water balance are somewhat different for plant cells because of their rigid cell walls. A plant cell immersed in an isotonic solution is flaccid (floppy), and the plant wilts (Figure 5.14a, bottom). In contrast, a plant cell is turgid (very firm) and healthiest in a hypotonic environment, with a net inflow of water (Figure 5.14b, bottom). Although the elastic cell wall expands a bit, the back pressure it exerts prevents the cell from taking in too much water and bursting. Turgor is necessary for plants to retain their upright posture and the extended state of their leaves (Figure 5.15). However, in a hypertonic environment, a plant cell is no better off than an animal cell. As a plant cell loses water, it shrivels, and its plasma membrane pulls away from the cell wall (Figure 5.14c, bottom). This process, called plasmolysis, usually kills the cell. ✔

▼ Figure 5.15 **Plant turgor.** Watering a wilted plant will make it regain its turgor.

✔ CHECKPOINT

1. An animal cell shrivels when it is _____ compared with its environment.
2. The cells of a wilted plant are _____ compared with their environment.

Answers: 1. hypertonic 2. isotonic

Active Transport: The Pumping of Molecules across Membranes

In contrast to passive transport, **active transport** requires that a cell expend energy to move molecules across a membrane. Cellular energy (usually provided by ATP) is used to drive a transport protein that pumps a solute *against* the solute's concentration gradient— that is, in the direction that is opposite the way it would naturally flow (Figure 5.16).

Active transport allows cells to maintain internal concentrations of small solutes that differ from environmental concentrations. For example, compared with its surroundings, an animal nerve cell has a much higher concentration of potassium ions and a much lower concentration of sodium ions. The plasma membrane helps maintain these differences by pumping sodium out of the cell and potassium into the cell. This particular case of active transport (called the sodium-potassium pump) is vital to the nervous system. ☑

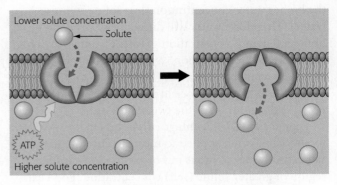

▲ **Figure 5.16 Active transport.** Transport proteins are specific in their recognition of atoms or molecules. This transport protein (purple) has a binding site that accepts only a certain solute. Using energy from ATP, the protein pumps the solute against its concentration gradient.

Exocytosis and Endocytosis: Traffic of Large Molecules

So far, we've focused on how water and small solutes enter and leave cells by moving through the plasma membrane. The story is different for large molecules such as proteins, which are much too big to fit through the membrane. Their traffic into and out of the cell depends on the ability of the cell to package large molecules inside sacs called vesicles. You have already seen an example of this: During protein production by the cell, secretory proteins exit the cell from transport vesicles that fuse with the plasma membrane, spilling the contents outside the cell (see Figures 4.14 and 4.18). That process is called **exocytosis** (Figure 5.17). When you cry, for

How are tears spilled?

example, cells in your tear glands use exocytosis to export the salty tears.

In **endocytosis**, a cell takes material in via vesicles that bud inward (Figure 5.18). For example, in a process called **phagocytosis** ("cellular eating"), a cell engulfs a particle and packages it within a food vacuole. Other times, a cell "gulps" droplets of fluid into vesicles. Endocytosis can also be triggered by the binding of certain external molecules to specific receptor proteins built into the plasma membrane. This binding causes the local region of the membrane to form a vesicle that transports the specific substance into the cell. In human liver cells, this process is used to take up cholesterol particles from the blood.

▼ **Figure 5.17 Exocytosis.**

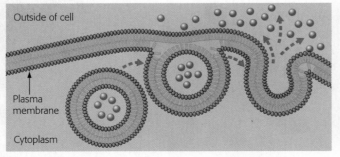

▼ **Figure 5.18 Endocytosis.**

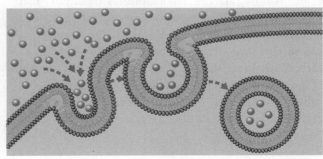

The Role of Membranes in Cell Signaling

In addition to transport, the plasma membrane and its embedded proteins play key roles in conveying signals from the external environment into the cell and also between cells. Communication begins when a receptor protein in the plasma membrane receives a stimulus, such as a hormone. This stimulus triggers a chain reaction in one or more molecules that function in transduction (passing the signal along). The proteins and other molecules of this **signal transduction pathway** relay the signal and convert it to chemical forms that can function within the cell. This signal may lead to various responses.

Figure 5.19 shows an example of cell signaling: signal reception, transduction, and response. When a person gets "psyched up" for an athletic contest, certain cells in the adrenal glands secrete a hormone called epinephrine (also called adrenaline) into the bloodstream. When that hormone reaches muscle cells, it is recognized by receptor proteins in the plasma membrane. This recognition triggers responses (such as the breakdown of glycogen into glucose) in the muscle cells without the hormone even entering. This chain of events is part of the "fight-or-flight" response that enables you to attack or run when in danger—or keep alert during an intense competition. ☑

▼ Figure 5.19 **An example of cell signaling.**

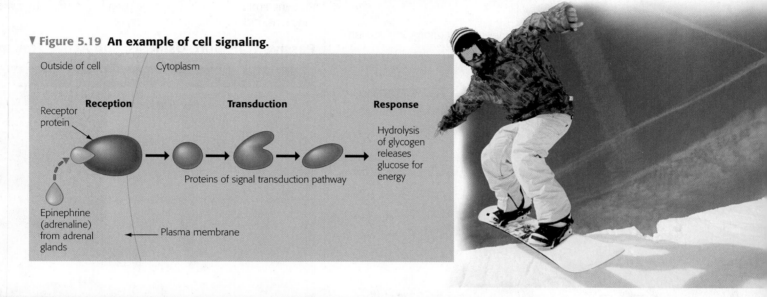

Nanotechnology EVOLUTION CONNECTION

The Origin of Membranes

Because all cells have a plasma membrane, it is logical to infer that membranes first formed early in the evolution of life on Earth. Phospholipids, their key ingredients, were probably among the first organic compounds that formed from chemical reactions on the early Earth. Once formed, they could self-assemble into simple membranes. When a mixture of phospholipids and water is shaken, for example, the phospholipids organize into bilayers, forming water-filled bubbles of membrane **(Figure 5.20)**. This assembly requires neither genes nor other information beyond the properties of the phospholipids themselves.

The tendency of lipids in water to spontaneously form membranes has led biomedical engineers to produce artificial vesicles called liposomes that can encase particular chemicals. In the future, these liposomes may deliver medications to specific sites within the body. Thus, membranes—like the other cellular components discussed in the Biology and Society and the Process of Science sections—have inspired novel nanotechnologies.

▼ Figure 5.20 **The spontaneous formation of membranes: a key step in the origin of life.**

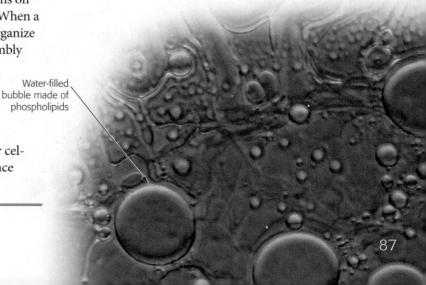

Water-filled bubble made of phospholipids

Chapter Review

SUMMARY OF KEY CONCEPTS

Some Basic Energy Concepts

Conservation of Energy

Machines and organisms can transform kinetic energy (energy of motion) to potential energy (stored energy) and vice versa. In all such energy transformations, total energy is conserved. Energy cannot be created or destroyed.

Entropy

Entropy is a measure of disorder, or randomness. Every energy conversion releases some randomized energy in the form of heat.

Chemical Energy

Molecules store varying amounts of potential energy in the arrangement of their atoms. Organic compounds are relatively rich in such chemical energy.

Food Calories

Food Calories, actually kilocalories, are units used to measure the amount of energy in our foods and the amount of energy we expend in various activities.

ATP and Cellular Work

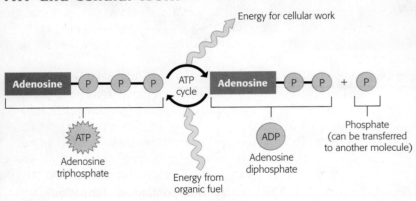

Enzymes

Activation Energy

Enzymes are biological catalysts that speed up metabolic reactions by lowering the activation energy required to break the bonds of reactant molecules.

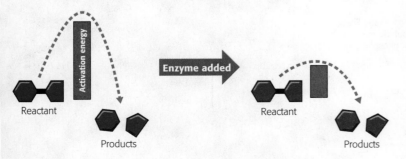

Induced Fit

The entry of a substrate into the active site of an enzyme causes the enzyme to change shape slightly, allowing for a better fit and thereby promoting the interaction of enzyme with substrate.

Enzyme Inhibitors

Enzyme inhibitors are molecules that can disrupt metabolic reactions by binding to enzymes, either at the active site or elsewhere.

Membrane Function

Proteins embedded in the plasma membrane perform a wide variety of functions, including regulating transport.

Passive Transport, Osmosis, and Active Transport

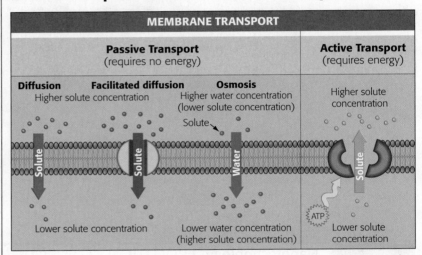

Most animal cells require an isotonic environment. Plant cells need a hypotonic environment, which keeps walled cells turgid. Osmoregulation is the control of water balance within a cell or organism.

Exocytosis and Endocytosis: Traffic of Large Molecules

Exocytosis is the secretion of large molecules within vesicles. Endocytosis is the import of large substances via vesicles into the cell.

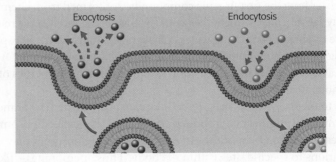

The Role of Membranes in Cell Signaling

Receptors on the cell surface trigger signal transduction pathways that control processes within the cell.

SELF-QUIZ

1. Describe the energy transformations that occur when you climb to the top of a stairway.

2. _____ is the capacity to perform work, while _____ is a measure of randomness.

3. The label on a candy bar says that it contains 150 Calories. If you could convert all of that energy to heat, you could raise the temperature of how much water by 15°C?

4. Why does removing a phosphate group from the triphosphate tail in a molecule of ATP release energy?

5. Your digestive system uses a variety of enzymes to break down large food molecules into smaller ones that your cells can assimilate. A generic name for a digestive enzyme is hydrolase. What is the chemical basis for that name? (*Hint*: Review Figure 3.4.)

6. Explain how an inhibitor can disrupt an enzyme's action without binding to the active site.

7. If someone at the other end of a restaurant smokes a cigarette, you may breathe in some smoke. The movement of smoke is similar to what type of transport?
   a. osmosis
   b. diffusion
   c. facilitated diffusion
   d. active transport

8. The total solute concentration in a red blood cell is about 2%. Sucrose cannot pass through a red blood cell's plasma membrane, but water and urea can. Osmosis will cause such a cell to shrink the most when the cell is immersed in which of the following?
   a. a hypertonic sucrose solution
   b. a hypotonic sucrose solution
   c. a hypertonic urea solution
   d. a hypotonic urea solution

9. Explain why it is not enough just to say that a solution is hypertonic.

10. What is the primary difference between passive and active transport in terms of concentration gradients?

11. Which of these types of cellular transport require(s) energy?
    a. facilitated diffusion
    b. active transport
    c. osmosis
    d. a and b

12. A _____ is a process that links the reception of a cell signal to a response within the cell.

Answers to these questions can be found in Appendix: Self-Quiz Answers.

THE PROCESS OF SCIENCE

13. HIV, the virus that causes AIDS, depends on an enzyme called reverse transcriptase in order to multiply. Reverse transcriptase reads a molecule of RNA and creates a molecule of DNA from it. A molecule of AZT, the first drug approved to treat AIDS, has a shape very similar to (but a bit different than) that of the DNA base thymine. Propose a model for how AZT inhibits HIV.

14. Gaining and losing weight are matters of caloric accounting: Calories in the food you eat minus Calories that you spend in activity. One pound of human body fat contains approximately 3,500 Calories. Using Figure 5.3, compare ways you could burn off those Calories. How far would you have to run, swim, or walk to burn the equivalent of 1 pound of fat, and how long would it take? Which method of burning Calories appeals the most to you? The least? How much of each food would you have to consume in order to gain a single pound? How does one pound's worth of food compare with one pound's worth of exercise? Does it seem like an even trade-off?

BIOLOGY AND SOCIETY

15. Obesity is a serious health problem for many Americans. Several popular diet plans advocate low-carbohydrate diets. Most low-carb dieters compensate by eating more protein and fat. What are the advantages and disadvantages of such a diet? Should the government regulate the claims of diet books? How should the claims be tested? Should diet proponents be required to obtain and publish data before making claims?

16. Lead acts as an enzyme inhibitor, and it can interfere with the development of the nervous system. One manufacturer of lead-acid batteries instituted a "fetal protection policy" that banned female employees of childbearing age from working in areas where they might be exposed to high levels of lead. These women were transferred to lower-paying jobs in lower-risk areas. Some employees challenged the policy in court, claiming that it deprived women of job opportunities available to men. The U.S. Supreme Court ruled the policy illegal. But many people are uncomfortable about the "right" to work in an unsafe environment. What rights and responsibilities of employers, employees, and government agencies are in conflict? What criteria should be used to decide who can work in a particular environment?

6 Cellular Respiration: Obtaining Energy from Food

Muscles in action. Sprinters, like all athletes, depend on cellular respiration to power their muscles.

Aerobic versus Anaerobic Lifestyles BIOLOGY AND SOCIETY

Marathoners versus Sprinters

Track-and-field athletes usually have a favorite event in which they excel. Some runners specialize in sprints of 100 or 200 meters. Others excel at longer races of 1,500, 5,000, or even 10,000 m. It is unusual to find a runner who competes equally well in both 100-m and 10,000-m races; most runners are more comfortable running races of particular lengths.

It turns out that there is a biological basis for such preferences. The muscles that move our legs contain two main types of muscle fibers: slow-twitch and fast-twitch. Slow-twitch muscle fibers can contract many times over a longer period but don't generate a lot of quick power for the body. They perform better in endurance exercises requiring slow, steady muscle activity, such as marathons. Fast-twitch muscle fibers can contract more quickly and powerfully than slow-twitch fibers but also fatigue much more quickly. They function best in short bursts of intense activity, such as sprints.

All human muscles contain both slow-twitch and fast-twitch fibers, but the percentage of each fiber type in a particular muscle varies from person to person. For example, the thigh muscles of most marathon runners contain more slow-twitch fibers, whereas sprinters have more fast-twitch fibers. These differences, which are genetically determined, undoubtedly help account for varying athletic capabilities. Thus, to a certain degree, champion marathoners and sprinters are born, not trained!

What makes these two types of muscle fibers perform differently? An important part of the answer is that they use different processes for making ATP, the molecule that supplies the energy for muscle contraction. While the cells in both types of muscle fiber break down glucose and use that chemical energy to produce ATP, slow-twitch fibers do it aerobically (using oxygen, O_2), while fast-twitch fibers can work anaerobically (without oxygen).

The series of chemical reactions that provides energy to muscles is also used by other cells. In fact, all your body cells need a continuous supply of energy for you to walk, talk, think—in short, to stay alive. In this chapter, you'll learn how cells harvest food energy and put it to work.

Energy Flow and Chemical Cycling in the Biosphere

Plants convert the energy of sunlight to the chemical energy of sugars and other organic molecules. This is accomplished via photosynthesis. **Photosynthesis** uses light energy from the sun to power a chemical process that builds organic molecules (as we'll discuss in Chapter 7).

Humans and other animals depend on this conversion for our food and more. You're probably wearing clothing made of a product of photosynthesis—cotton. Most of our homes are framed with lumber, which is wood produced by photosynthetic trees. Even textbooks are printed on a material (paper) that can be traced to photosynthesis in plants. But from an animal's point of view, photosynthesis is primarily about providing food.

Producers and Consumers

Plants and other **autotrophs** ("self-feeders") are organisms that make all their own organic matter—including carbohydrates, lipids, proteins, and nucleic acids—from nutrients that are entirely inorganic: carbon dioxide from the air and water and minerals from the soil. In other words, plants make their own food; they don't need to eat to gain energy to power their cellular processes. In contrast, humans and other animals are **heterotrophs** ("other-feeders"), organisms that cannot make organic molecules from inorganic ones. Therefore, we must eat organic material to get our nutrients and provide energy for life's processes.

Most ecosystems depend entirely on photosynthesis for food. For this reason, biologists refer to plants and other autotrophs as **producers**. Heterotrophs, in contrast, are **consumers**, because they obtain their food by eating plants or by eating animals that have eaten plants (Figure 6.1). We animals and other heterotrophs depend on autotrophs for organic fuel and for the raw organic materials we need to build our cells and tissues. ☑

Chemical Cycling between Photosynthesis and Cellular Respiration

The chemical ingredients for photosynthesis are carbon dioxide (CO_2), a gas that passes from the air into a plant via tiny pores, and water (H_2O), which is absorbed from the soil by the plant's roots (Figure 6.2). Inside leaf cells, tiny structures called chloroplasts use light energy to rearrange the atoms of these ingredients to produce sugars—most importantly glucose ($C_6H_{12}O_6$)—and

▼ Figure 6.1 **Producer and consumer.** A thrush (consumer) eats a fruit produced by a photosynthetic plant (producer).

other organic molecules. A by-product of photosynthesis is oxygen gas (O_2).

Both animals and plants use the organic products of photosynthesis as sources of energy. A chemical process called cellular respiration harvests energy that is stored in sugars and other organic molecules. Cellular respiration uses O_2 to help convert the energy stored in the chemical bonds of organic fuels to another source of chemical energy called ATP. Cells expend ATP for almost all their work. In both plants and animals, the production of ATP during cellular respiration occurs mainly in the organelles called mitochondria (see Figure 4.20).

Notice in Figure 6.2 that the waste products of cellular respiration are CO_2 and H_2O—the very same ingredients used

for photosynthesis. Plants store chemical energy via photosynthesis and then harvest this energy via cellular respiration. (Note that plants perform *both* photosynthesis to produce fuel molecules *and* cellular respiration to burn them, while animals perform *only* cellular respiration.) Plants usually make more organic molecules than they need for fuel. This photosynthetic surplus provides material for the plant to grow or can be stored, as starch in potatoes, for example. People have always taken advantage of plants' photosynthetic abilities by eating them. More recently, engineers have managed to tap into this energy reserve to produce liquid biofuels, primarily ethanol. Analyze nearly any food chain, and you can trace the energy and raw materials for growth back to solar-powered photosynthesis. ☑

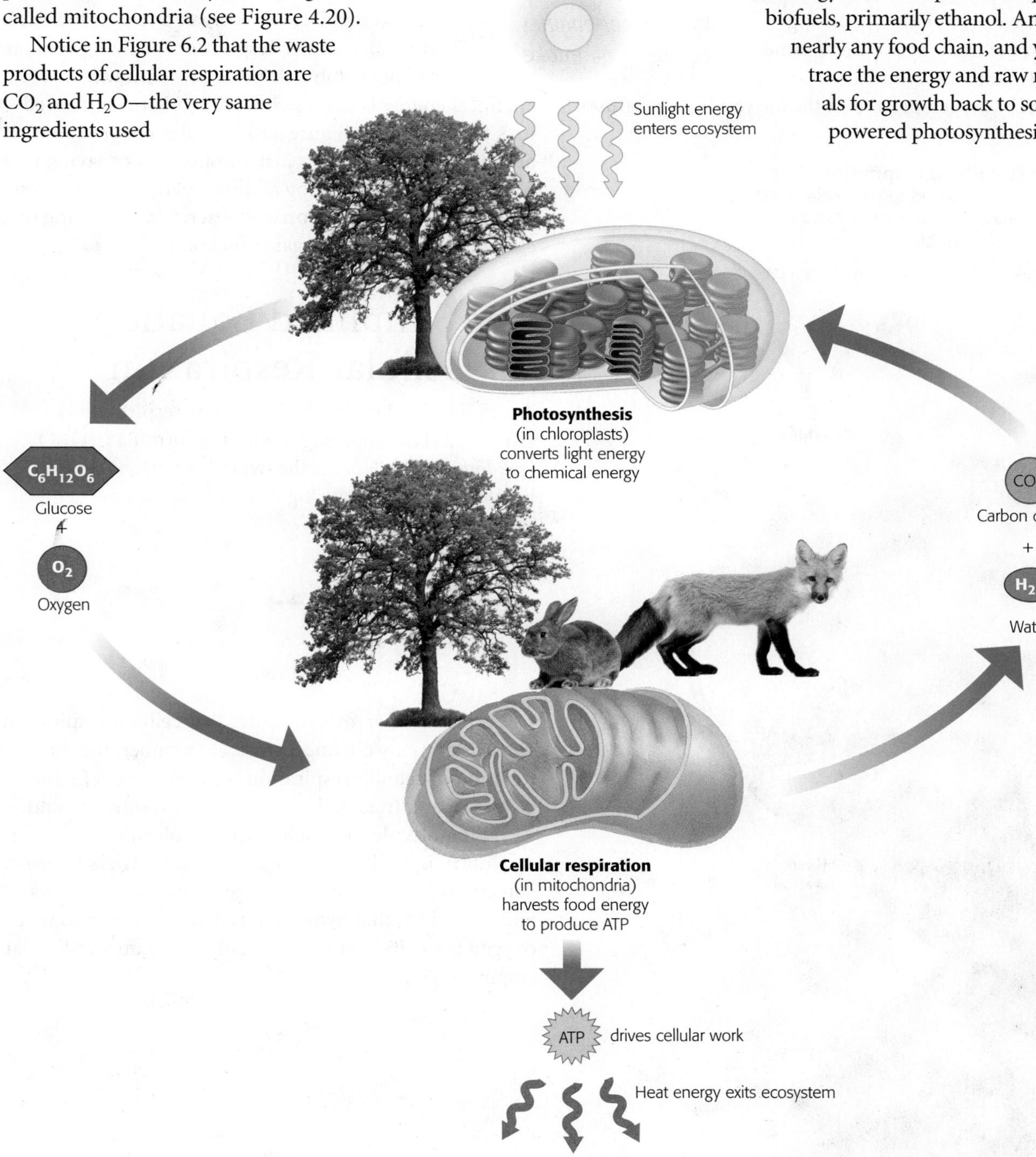

Sunlight energy enters ecosystem

Photosynthesis
(in chloroplasts) converts light energy to chemical energy

$C_6H_{12}O_6$
Glucose

O_2
Oxygen

CO_2
Carbon dioxide

+

H_2O
Water

Cellular respiration
(in mitochondria) harvests food energy to produce ATP

ATP drives cellular work

Heat energy exits ecosystem

◄ **Figure 6.2 Energy flow and chemical cycling in ecosystems.** Energy flows through an ecosystem, entering as sunlight and exiting as heat. In contrast, chemical elements are recycled within an ecosystem.

☑ **CHECKPOINT**

What is misleading about the following statement? "Plants have chloroplasts that perform photosynthesis, whereas animals have mitochondria that perform cellular respiration."

Answer: It implies that cellular respiration does not also occur in plants. It does.

Cellular Respiration:
Aerobic Harvest of Food Energy

We sometimes use the word *respiration* to mean breathing. While respiration on the organismal level should not be confused with cellular respiration, the two processes are closely related **(Figure 6.3)**. Cellular respiration requires a cell to exchange two gases with its surroundings. The cell takes in oxygen in the form of the gas O_2. It gets rid of waste in the form of the gas carbon dioxide, or CO_2. Breathing results in the exchange of these same gases between your blood and the outside air. Oxygen present in the air you inhale diffuses across the lining of your lungs and into your bloodstream. And the CO_2 in your bloodstream diffuses into your lungs and exits when you exhale. Every molecule of CO_2 that you exhale was originally formed in one of the mitochondria of your body's cells.

Why do car engines require an air intake?

Internal combustion engines, like the ones found in cars, use O_2 (via the air intakes) to break down gasoline. A cell also requires O_2 to break down its fuel (see Figure 5.2). Cellular respiration—a living version of internal combustion—is the main way that chemical energy is harvested from food and converted to ATP energy (see Figure 5.6). Cellular respiration is an **aerobic** process, which is just another way of saying that it requires oxygen. Putting all this together, we can now define **cellular respiration** as the aerobic harvesting of chemical energy from organic fuel molecules. ☑

▼ **Figure 6.3 How breathing is related to cellular respiration.**
When you inhale, you breathe in O_2. The O_2 is delivered to your cells, where it is used in cellular respiration. Carbon dioxide, a waste product of cellular respiration, diffuses from your cells to your blood and travels to your lungs, where it is exhaled.

Breathing

Lungs

O_2

CO_2

Muscle cells

Cellular respiration

The Simplified Equation for Cellular Respiration

A common fuel molecule for cellular respiration is glucose, a six-carbon sugar with the formula $C_6H_{12}O_6$ (see Figure 3.6). Here is the overall equation for what happens to glucose during cellular respiration:

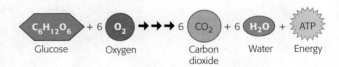

$$C_6H_{12}O_6 + 6\ O_2 \rightarrow \rightarrow \rightarrow 6\ CO_2 + 6\ H_2O + ATP$$

Glucose · Oxygen · Carbon dioxide · Water · Energy

The series of arrows indicates that cellular respiration consists of many chemical steps. Remember, the main function of cellular respiration is to generate ATP for cellular work. In fact, the process can produce around 32 ATP molecules for each glucose molecule consumed.

Notice that cellular respiration also transfers hydrogen atoms from glucose to oxygen, forming water. As you'll see next, that hydrogen transfer is the key to why oxygen is so vital to the harvest of energy during cellular respiration.

The Role of Oxygen in Cellular Respiration

In tracking the transfer of hydrogen from sugar to oxygen, we are also following the transfer of electrons. The atoms of sugar and other molecules are bonded together by shared electrons (see Figure 2.8). During cellular respiration, hydrogen and its bonding electrons change partners from sugar to oxygen, forming water as a product.

Redox Reactions

Chemical reactions that transfer electrons from one substance to another substance are called oxidation-reduction reactions, or **redox reactions** for short. The loss of electrons during a redox reaction is called **oxidation**. Glucose is oxidized during cellular respiration, losing electrons to oxygen. The acceptance of electrons during a redox reaction is called **reduction**. (Note that *adding* electrons is called *reduction*; negatively charged electrons added to an atom *reduce* the amount of positive charge of that atom.) Oxygen is reduced during cellular respiration, accepting electrons (and hydrogen) lost from glucose:

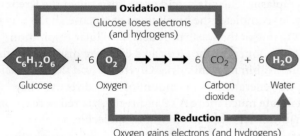

Oxidation
Glucose loses electrons (and hydrogens)

$C_6H_{12}O_6$ + 6 O_2 → → 6 CO_2 + 6 H_2O

Glucose   Oxygen   Carbon dioxide   Water

Reduction
Oxygen gains electrons (and hydrogens)

Water isn't the only thing produced when hydrogen and its bonding electrons change partners from glucose to oxygen; energy is released, too.

Why does electron transfer to oxygen release energy? In redox reactions, oxygen is an "electron grabber." An oxygen atom attracts electrons more strongly than almost any other type of atom. When electrons move (along with hydrogen) from glucose to oxygen, it is as though they are falling. They are not really falling in the sense of an apple dropping from a tree. However, in both cases, potential energy is unlocked. Instead of gravity, it is the attraction of electrons to oxygen that causes the "fall" and energy release during cellular respiration.

Figure 6.4 shows a simple example of a redox reaction: the reaction between hydrogen gas (H_2) and

oxygen gas (O_2), producing water (H_2O). The reaction releases a large amount of energy as the electrons of the hydrogen "fall" into their new bonds with oxygen. This reaction is actually quite explosive, and it would be difficult for a cell to capture such a burst of energy and put it to useful work. As you'll see shortly, cellular respiration is a more controlled "fall" of electrons—more like a stepwise cascade of electrons down an energy staircase. Instead of liberating food energy in a burst, cellular respiration unlocks chemical energy in smaller amounts that cells can put to productive use. ☑

NADH and Electron Transport Chains

Let's take a closer look at the path that electrons take on their way from glucose to oxygen (**Figure 6.5**). The first stop is a positively charged electron acceptor called NAD^+ (<u>n</u>icotinamide <u>a</u>denine <u>d</u>inucleotide) that cells make from niacin, a B vitamin. The transfer of electrons from organic fuel (food) to NAD^+ reduces it to **NADH** (the H represents the transfer of hydrogen along with the electrons). In our staircase analogy, the electrons have now taken one baby step down in their trip from glucose to oxygen. The rest of the staircase consists of an **electron transport chain**.

▼ Figure 6.5 The role of oxygen in harvesting food energy. In cellular respiration, electrons e^- "fall" in small steps from food to oxygen, producing water. NADH transfers electrons from food to an electron transport chain. The attraction of oxygen to electrons "pulls" the electrons down the chain.

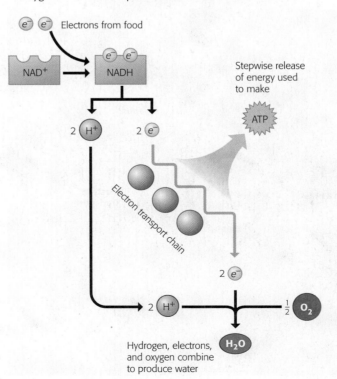

e^- e^- Electrons from food

NAD^+ → NADH e^- e^-

Stepwise release of energy used to make ATP

Electron transport chain

2 H^+ 2 e^-

2 e^-

2 H^+ $\frac{1}{2}$ O_2

H_2O

Hydrogen, electrons, and oxygen combine to produce water

▼ Figure 6.4 A simple redox reaction. An all-at-once redox reaction, such as the reaction of hydrogen and oxygen to form water, releases a burst of energy.

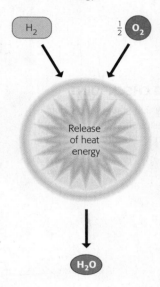

H_2 $\frac{1}{2}$ O_2

Release of heat energy

H_2O

☑ CHECKPOINT

During a redox reaction, the addition of electrons is called _____, while the removal of electrons is called _____.

Answer: reduction; oxidation

Each link in an electron transport chain is actually a molecule, usually a protein. In a series of redox reactions, each member of the chain first accepts and then donates electrons. With each transfer, the electrons give up a small amount of energy that can then be used indirectly to generate ATP. The first molecule of the chain accepts electrons from NADH. Thus, NADH carries electrons from glucose and other fuel molecules and deposits them at the top of an electron transport chain. The electrons cascade down the chain, from molecule to molecule, like an electron bucket brigade. The molecule at the bottom of the chain finally "drops" the electrons to oxygen. At the same time, oxygen picks up hydrogen, forming water.

The overall effect of all this transfer of electrons during cellular respiration is a "downward" trip for electrons from glucose to NADH to an electron transport chain to oxygen. During the stepwise release of chemical energy during electron transport, our cells make most of their ATP. It is actually oxygen, the "electron grabber," that makes it all possible. By pulling electrons down the

Why do animals drown so quickly?

transport chain from fuel molecules, oxygen functions somewhat like gravity pulling objects downhill. This is how the oxygen we breathe functions in our cells and why we cannot survive more than a few minutes without it. Viewed this way, drowning is deadly because it deprives cells of the final "electron grabbers" (oxygen) needed to drive cellular respiration.

An Overview of Cellular Respiration

Cellular respiration is an example of a metabolic pathway. That means that it is not a single chemical reaction, but a series of reactions. A specific enzyme catalyzes each reaction in a metabolic pathway. More than two dozen reactions are involved in cellular respiration. We can group them into three main metabolic stages: glycolysis, the citric acid cycle, and electron transport.

Figure 6.6 is a map that will help you follow the three stages of respiration and see where each stage occurs in your cells. During **glycolysis**, a molecule of glucose is split into two molecules of a compound called pyruvic acid. The enzymes for glycolysis are located in the cytoplasm. The **citric acid cycle** (also called the Krebs cycle) completes the breakdown of glucose all the way to CO_2, one of the waste products of cellular respiration. The enzymes for the citric acid cycle are dissolved in the fluid within mitochondria. Glycolysis and the citric acid cycle generate a small amount of ATP directly. They generate much more ATP indirectly, via redox reactions that transfer electrons from fuel molecules to NAD^+, forming NADH. The third stage of cellular respiration is **electron transport**. Electrons captured from food by the NADH formed in the first two stages "fall" down electron transport chains to oxygen. The proteins and other molecules that make up electron transport chains are embedded within the inner membrane of the mitochondria. Electron transport from NADH to oxygen releases the energy your cells use to make most of their ATP. ☑

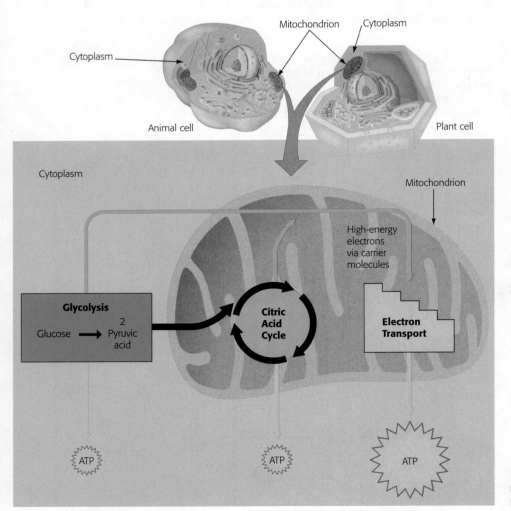

Cytoplasm

Mitochondrion   Cytoplasm

Cytoplasm

Animal cell   Plant cell

Cytoplasm   Mitochondrion

High-energy electrons via carrier molecules

Glycolysis

Glucose → 2 Pyruvic acid

Citric Acid Cycle

Electron Transport

ATP   ATP   ATP

◀ **Figure 6.6 A road map for cellular respiration.**

The Three Stages of Cellular Respiration

Now that you have a big-picture view of cellular respiration, let's examine the process in more detail. A small version of Figure 6.6 will help you keep the overall process of cellular respiration in plain view as we take a closer look at its three stages.

Stage 1: Glycolysis

The word *glycolysis* means "splitting of sugar." That is exactly what happens **(Figure 6.7)**. ❶ During glycolysis, a six-carbon glucose molecule is broken in half, forming two three-carbon molecules. Notice in Figure 6.7 that the initial split requires an energy investment of two ATP molecules per glucose. ❷ The three-carbon molecules then donate high-energy electrons to NAD$^+$, the electron carrier, forming NADH. ❸ In addition to NADH, glycolysis also makes four ATP molecules directly when

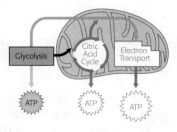

enzymes transfer phosphate groups from fuel molecules to ADP **(Figure 6.8)**. Glycolysis thus produces a net of two molecules of ATP per molecule of glucose. (This fact will become important during our discussion of fermentation.) What remains of the fractured glucose at the end of glycolysis are two molecules of pyruvic acid. The pyruvic acid still holds most of the energy of glucose, and that energy is harvested in the second stage of cellular respiration, the citric acid cycle.

▼ **Figure 6.8 ATP synthesis by direct phosphate transfer.** Glycolysis generates ATP when enzymes transfer phosphate groups directly from fuel molecules to ADP.

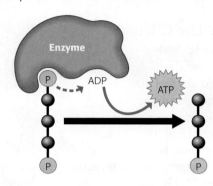

▼ **Figure 6.7 Glycolysis.** In glycolysis, a team of enzymes splits glucose, eventually forming two molecules of pyruvic acid. After investing 2 ATP at the start, glycolysis generates 4 ATP directly. More energy will be harvested later from high-energy electrons used to form NADH and from the 2 molecules of pyruvic acid.

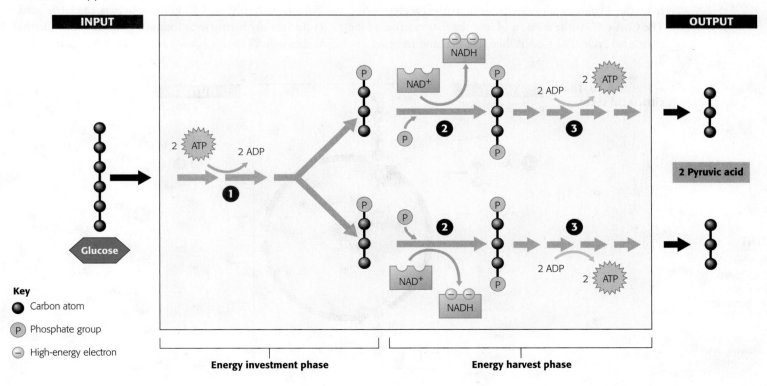

Key
- ● Carbon atom
- Ⓟ Phosphate group
- ⊖ High-energy electron

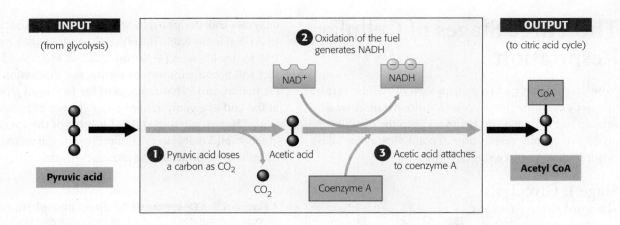

► **Figure 6.9 The link between glycolysis and the citric acid cycle: the conversion of pyruvic acid to acetyl CoA.** Remember that one molecule of glucose is split into two molecules of pyruvic acid. Therefore, the process shown here occurs twice.

Stage 2: The Citric Acid Cycle

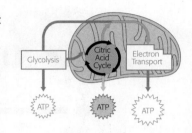

The two molecules of pyruvic acid, the fuel that remains after glycolysis, are not quite ready for the citric acid cycle. The pyruvic acid must be "groomed"—converted to a form the citric acid cycle can use **(Figure 6.9)**. **1** First, each pyruvic acid loses a carbon as CO_2. This is the first of this waste product we've seen so far in the breakdown of glucose. The remaining fuel molecules, each with only two carbons left, are called acetic acid (the acid that's in vinegar). **2** Oxidation of the fuel generates NADH. **3** Finally, each acetic acid is attached to a molecule called coenzyme A (CoA), an enzyme derived from the B vitamin pantothenic acid, to form acetyl CoA. The CoA escorts the acetic acid into the first reaction of the citric acid cycle. The CoA is then stripped and recycled.

The citric acid cycle finishes extracting the energy of sugar by dismantling the acetic acid molecules all the way down to CO_2 **(Figure 6.10)**. **1** Acetic acid joins a four-carbon acceptor molecule to form a six-carbon product called citric acid (for which the cycle is named). For every acetic acid molecule that enters the cycle as fuel, **2** two CO_2 molecules eventually exit as a waste product. Along the way, the citric acid cycle harvests energy from the fuel. **3** Some of the energy is used to produce ATP directly. However, the cycle captures much more energy in the form of **4** NADH and **5** a second, closely related electron carrier, $FADH_2$. **6** All the carbon atoms that entered the cycle as fuel are accounted for as CO_2 exhaust, and the four-carbon acceptor molecule is recycled. We have tracked only one acetic acid molecule through the citric acid cycle here. But since glycolysis splits glucose in two, the citric acid cycle actually turns twice for each glucose molecule that fuels a cell. ☑

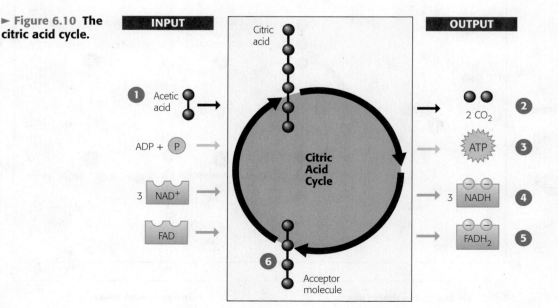

► **Figure 6.10 The citric acid cycle.**

Stage 3: Electron Transport

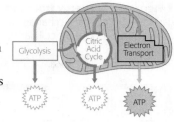

The molecules of electron transport chains are built into the inner membranes of mitochondria (see Figure 4.20). Because these membranes are highly folded, their large surface area can accommodate thousands of copies of the electron transport chain. Each chain functions as a chemical machine that uses the energy released by the "fall" of electrons to pump hydrogen ions (H^+) across the inner mitochondrial membrane. This pumping causes ions to become more concentrated on one side of the membrane than on the other. Such a difference in concentration stores potential energy.

The energy stored by electron transport behaves something like the water behind a dam. There is a tendency for hydrogen ions to gush back to where they are less concentrated, just as there is a tendency for water to flow downhill. The inner membrane temporarily "dams" hydrogen ions.

The energy of dammed water can be harnessed to perform work. Gates in a dam allow the water to rush downhill, turning giant turbines, and this work can be used to generate electricity. Your mitochondria have structures that act like turbines. Each of these miniature machines, called an **ATP synthase**, is constructed from protein built into the inner mitochondrial membrane, adjacent to the proteins of the electron transport chains. **Figure 6.11** shows a simplified view of how the energy previously stored in NADH and $FADH_2$ can now be used to generate ATP. ❶ NADH and ❷ $FADH_2$ transfer electrons to an electron transport chain. ❸ The electron transport chain uses this energy supply to pump H^+ across the inner mitochondrial membrane. ❹ Oxygen pulls electrons down the transport chain. ❺ The H^+ concentrated on one side of the membrane rushes back "downhill" through an ATP synthase. This action spins a component of the ATP synthase, just as water turns the turbines in a dam. ❻ The rotation activates parts of the synthase molecule that attach phosphate groups to ADP molecules to generate ATP.

The poison cyanide produces its deadly effect by binding to one of the protein complexes in the electron transport chain (marked by ☠ in Figure 6.11). When bound there, cyanide blocks the passage of electrons to oxygen. This blockage is like clogging a dam. As a result, no H^+ gradient is generated, and no ATP is made. Cells stop working, and the organism dies. Cyanide was the lethal agent in an infamous case of product tampering: the Tylenol murders of 1982. Seven people in the Chicago area died after ingesting Tylenol capsules that had been laced with cyanide. The perpetrator of that crime was never caught. ☑

How does cyanide kill?

☑ CHECKPOINT

What is the potential energy source that drives ATP production by ATP synthase?

Answer: a concentration gradient of H^+ across the inner membrane of a mitochondrion

▼ Figure 6.11 **How electron transport drives ATP synthase machines.**

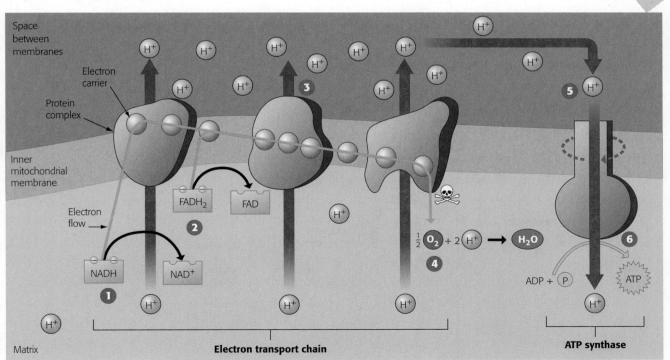

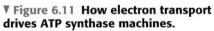

99

The Results of Cellular Respiration

Taking cellular respiration apart to see how all the molecular nuts and bolts of its metabolic machinery work, it's easy to lose sight of its overall function: to generate about 32 molecules of ATP per molecule of glucose (the actual number can vary by a few). **Figure 6.12** will help you add up the ATP molecules. Glycolysis and the citric acid cycle each contribute 2 ATP by directly making it. All of the rest of the ATP molecules are produced by the ATP synthase machines, powered by the "fall" of electrons from food to oxygen. The electrons are carried from the organic fuel to electron transport chains by NADH and $FADH_2$. Each electron pair "dropped" down a transport chain from NADH or $FADH_2$ can power the synthesis of a few ATP. To summarize, energy flows from glucose to carrier molecules and ultimately to ATP.

We have seen that glucose can provide the energy to make the ATP our cells use for all their work. The importance of glucose is underscored by the severity of diseases in which glucose balance is disturbed. Diabetes, which affects over 20 million Americans, is caused by an inability to properly regulate glucose levels in the blood due to problems with the hormone insulin. If left untreated, a glucose imbalance can lead to a variety of problems, including cardiovascular disease, coma, and even death.

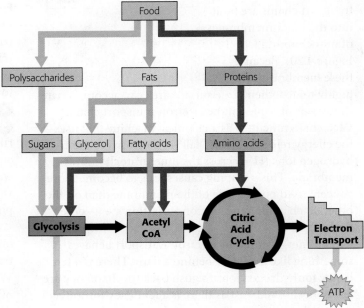

▼ **Figure 6.13 Energy from food.** The monomers from carbohydrates (polysaccharides and sugars), fats, and proteins can all serve as fuel for cellular respiration.

But even though we have concentrated on glucose as the fuel that is broken down during cellular respiration, respiration is a versatile metabolic furnace that can "burn" many other kinds of food molecules. **Figure 6.13** diagrams some metabolic routes for the use of carbohydrates, fats, and proteins as fuel for cellular respiration. ☑

▼ **Figure 6.12 A summary of ATP yield during cellular respiration.**

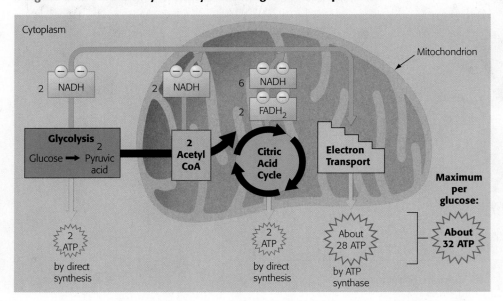

☑ **CHECKPOINT**

Which stage of cellular respiration produces the majority of ATP?

Answer: *electron transport*

Fermentation: Anaerobic Harvest of Food Energy

Although you must breathe to stay alive, some of your cells can work for short periods without oxygen. This **anaerobic** ("without oxygen") harvest of food energy is called **fermentation**.

Fermentation in Human Muscle Cells

As your muscles work, they require a constant supply of ATP, which is generated by cellular respiration. As long as your blood provides your muscle cells with enough O_2 to keep electrons "falling" down transport chains in mitochondria, your muscles will work aerobically. But under strenuous conditions, your muscles can spend ATP faster than your bloodstream can deliver O_2; when this happens, your muscle cells begin to work anaerobically. To stay within the aerobic zone, some athletes seek an unfair advantage by blood doping: artificially expanding their capacity to deliver O_2 to muscles by, for example, injecting excess red blood cells previously harvested from themselves or a donor.

After functioning anaerobically for about 15 seconds, muscle cells will begin to generate ATP by the process of fermentation. Fermentation relies on glycolysis, the first stage of cellular respiration. Glycolysis does not require

How does blood doping increase an athlete's aerobic capacity?

O_2 but does produce 2 ATP molecules for each glucose molecule broken down to pyruvic acid. That isn't very efficient compared with the 32 or so ATP molecules each glucose generates during cellular respiration, but it can energize muscles for a short burst. However, your cells will have to consume more glucose fuel per second, since so much less ATP per glucose molecule is generated under anaerobic conditions.

To harvest food energy during glycolysis, NAD^+ must be present as an electron acceptor (see Figure 6.7). This is no problem under aerobic conditions, because the cell regenerates NAD^+ when NADH drops its electron cargo down electron transport chains to O_2 (see Figure 6.5). However, this recycling of NAD^+ cannot occur under anaerobic conditions because there is no O_2 to accept the electrons. Instead, NADH disposes of electrons by adding them to the pyruvic acid produced by glycolysis **(Figure 6.14)**. This restores NAD^+ and keeps glycolysis working.

The addition of electrons to pyruvic acid produces a waste product called lactic acid. The lactic acid by-product is eventually transported to the liver, where liver cells convert it back to pyruvic acid. Exercise physiologists (biologists who study the effects of exercise on the body) have long speculated about the role that lactic acid plays in muscle fatigue, as you'll see next. ✔

✔ CHECKPOINT

How many molecules of ATP can be produced from one molecule of glucose during fermentation?

Answer: 2

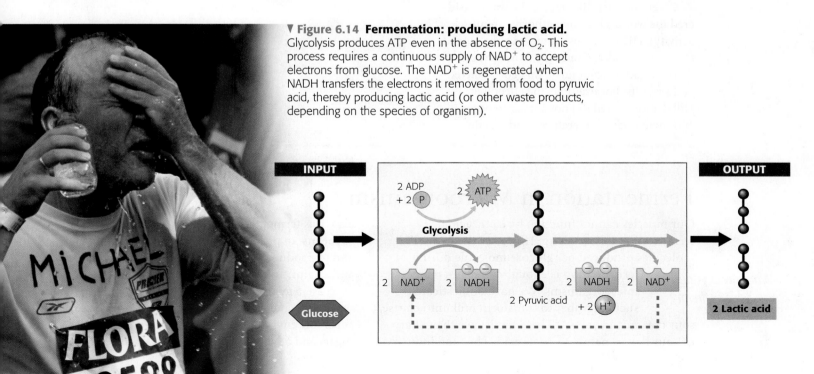

▼ Figure 6.14 **Fermentation: producing lactic acid.** Glycolysis produces ATP even in the absence of O_2. This process requires a continuous supply of NAD^+ to accept electrons from glucose. The NAD^+ is regenerated when NADH transfers the electrons it removed from food to pyruvic acid, thereby producing lactic acid (or other waste products, depending on the species of organism).

INPUT

2 ADP + 2 P   2 ATP

Glycolysis

2 NAD$^+$ 2 NADH   2 NADH   2 NAD$^+$

2 Pyruvic acid   + 2 H$^+$

Glucose

OUTPUT

2 Lactic acid

What Causes Muscle Burn?

You may have heard that the burn you feel after hard exercise ("Feel the burn! It's a *good* burn!") is due to the buildup of lactic acid in your muscles. This idea originated with the work of a British biologist named A.V. Hill. Considered one of the founders of the field of exercise physiology, Hill won a 1922 Nobel Prize for his investigations of muscle contraction.

In 1929, Hill performed a classic experiment that began with the **observation** that muscles produce lactic acid under anaerobic conditions. Hill asked the **question**, Does the buildup of lactic acid cause muscle fatigue? To find out, Hill developed a technique for electrically stimulating dissected frog muscles in a laboratory solution. He formed the **hypothesis** that a buildup of lactic acid would cause muscle activity to stop.

Hill's **experiment** tested frog muscles under two different sets of conditions (**Figure 6.15**). First, he showed that muscle performance declined when lactic acid could not diffuse away from the muscle tissue. Next, he showed that when lactic acid was allowed to diffuse away, performance improved significantly. These **results** led Hill to the conclusion that "lactic acid accumulation is the primary cause of failure" in muscle tissue.

Given his scientific stature (he was considered the world's leading authority on muscle activity), Hill's conclusion went unchallenged for many decades. Gradually, however, evidence began to accumulate that contradicted Hill's results. For example, the effect that Hill demonstrated did not appear to occur at human body temperature. And certain individuals who are unable to accumulate lactic acid have muscles that fatigue *more* rapidly, which is the opposite of what you would expect. Recent experiments have directly refuted Hill's conclusions. Today, the role of lactic acid in muscle fatigue remains a hotly debated topic.

The changing view of lactic acid's role in muscle fatigue illustrates an important point about the process of science: It is dynamic and subject to constant adjustment as new evidence is uncovered. This would not have surprised Hill, who himself wrote that the "built-in obsolescence" of scientific hypotheses is a necessary feature for the advancement of science.

▼ Figure 6.15 **A. V. Hill's 1929 apparatus for measuring muscle fatigue.**

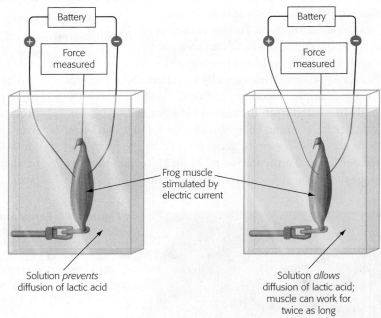

Frog muscle stimulated by electric current

Solution *prevents* diffusion of lactic acid

Solution *allows* diffusion of lactic acid; muscle can work for twice as long

Fermentation in Microorganisms

What gives yogurt its sour flavor?

Our muscles cannot function by lactic acid fermentation for very long. However, the two ATP molecules produced per glucose molecule during fermentation is enough to sustain many microorganisms. We have domesticated such microbes to transform milk into cheese, sour cream, and yogurt. These foods owe their sharp or sour flavor mainly to lactic acid. The food industry also uses fermentation to produce soy sauce from soybeans, to pickle cucumbers, olives, and cabbage, and to produce meat products like sausage, pepperoni, and salami.

Yeast, a microscopic fungus, is capable of both cellular respiration and fermentation. If you keep yeast cells in an anaerobic environment, they are forced to ferment sugars and other foods to stay alive. When yeast ferment,

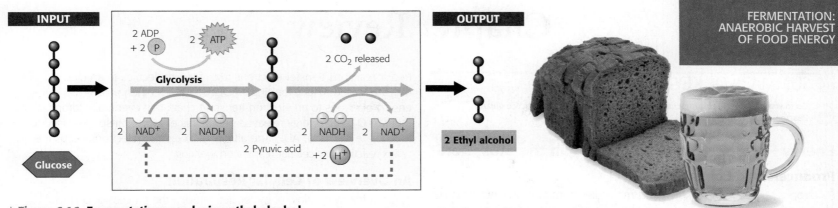

INPUT

2 ADP + 2 P → 2 ATP

Glycolysis

2 NAD⁺ 2 NADH

2 CO_2 released

2 NADH 2 NAD⁺

$Glucose$

2 Pyruvic acid +2 H⁺

OUTPUT

2 Ethyl alcohol

▲ Figure 6.16 **Fermentation: producing ethyl alcohol.**

they produce ethyl alcohol as a waste product instead of lactic acid **(Figure 6.16)**. This alcoholic fermentation also releases CO_2. For thousands of years, people have put yeast to work producing alcoholic beverages such as beer and wine. And as every baker knows, the CO_2 bubbles from fermenting yeast also cause bread dough to rise. (The alcohol produced in fermenting bread is burned off during baking.) ☑

Aerobic versus Anaerobic Lifestyles EVOLUTION CONNECTION

Life before and after Oxygen

In the Biology and Society and Process of Science sections, we have seen that living cells can generate ATP either aerobically (with oxygen via cellular respiration) or anaerobically (without oxygen via fermentation). Both of these processes start with glycolysis, the splitting of glucose to form pyruvic acid. Glycolysis is thus the universal energy-harvesting process of life.

The role of glycolysis in both respiration and fermentation has an evolutionary basis. Ancient prokaryotes probably used glycolysis to make ATP long before oxygen was present in Earth's atmosphere. The oldest known fossils of bacteria date back more than 3.5 billion years, but significant levels of O_2 did not accumulate in the atmosphere until about 2.7 billion years ago **(Figure 6.17)**. For almost a billion years, prokaryotes must have generated ATP exclusively from glycolysis.

The fact that glycolysis occurs in almost all organisms suggests that it evolved very early in ancestors common to all the domains of life. The location of glycolysis within the cell also implies great antiquity; the pathway does not require any of the membrane-enclosed organelles of the eukaryotic cell, which evolved more than a billion years after the prokaryotic cell. Glycolysis is a metabolic heirloom from early cells that continues to function in fermentation and as the first stage in the breakdown of organic molecules by cellular respiration.

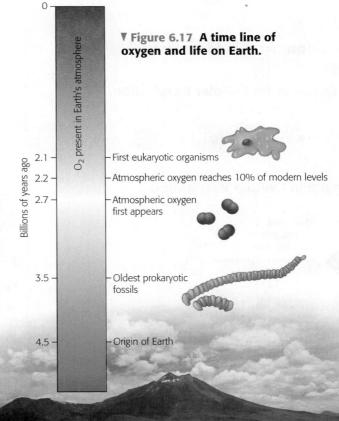

▼ Figure 6.17 **A time line of oxygen and life on Earth.**

O_2 present in Earth's atmosphere

Billions of years ago

0

2.1 — First eukaryotic organisms

2.2 — Atmospheric oxygen reaches 10% of modern levels

2.7 — Atmospheric oxygen first appears

3.5 — Oldest prokaryotic fossils

4.5 — Origin of Earth

Chapter Review

SUMMARY OF KEY CONCEPTS

(MB) Go to **www.masteringbiology.com** for homework assignments, practice quizzes, Pearson eText, and more.

Energy Flow and Chemical Cycling in the Biosphere

Producers and Consumers

Autotrophs (producers) make organic molecules from inorganic nutrients via photosynthesis. Heterotrophs (consumers) must consume organic material and obtain energy via cellular respiration.

Chemical Cycling between Photosynthesis and Cellular Respiration

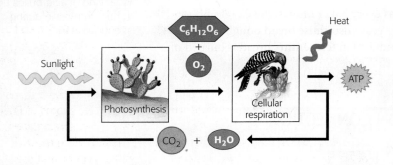

Cellular Respiration: Aerobic Harvest of Food Energy

The Simplified Equation for Cellular Respiration

The Role of Oxygen in Cellular Respiration

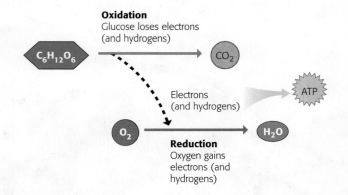

Redox reactions transfer electrons from food molecules to an electron acceptor called NAD^+, forming NADH. The NADH then passes the high-energy electrons to an electron transport chain that eventually "drops" them to O_2. The energy released during this electron transport is used to regenerate ATP from ADP. The affinity of oxygen for electrons keeps the redox reactions of cellular respiration working.

An Overview of Cellular Respiration

You can follow the flow of molecules through the process of cellular respiration in the following diagram:

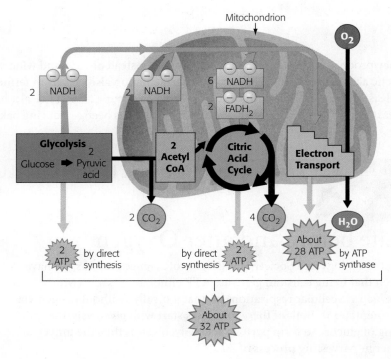

The electron transport chains pump H^+ across the inner mitochondrial membrane as electrons flow stepwise from NADH to O_2. Backflow of H^+ across the membrane powers the ATP synthases, which attach phosphate to ADP to make ATP.

Fermentation: Anaerobic Harvest of Food Energy

Fermentation in Human Muscle Cells

When muscle cells consume ATP faster than O_2 can be supplied for cellular respiration, they regenerate ATP by fermentation. The waste product under these anaerobic conditions is lactic acid. The ATP yield per glucose is much lower during fermentation (2 ATP) than during cellular respiration (about 32 ATP).

Fermentation in Microorganisms

Yeast and some other organisms can survive with or without O_2. Wastes from fermentation can be ethyl alcohol, lactic acid, or other compounds, depending on the species.

SELF-QUIZ

1. Which of the following statements is a correct distinction between autotrophs and heterotrophs?
   a. Only heterotrophs require chemical compounds from the environment.
   b. Cellular respiration is unique to heterotrophs.
   c. Only heterotrophs have mitochondria.
   d. Only autotrophs can live on nutrients that are entirely inorganic.

2. Why are plants called producers? Why are animals called consumers?

3. How is your breathing related to your cellular respiration?

4. Of the three stages of cellular respiration, which produces the most ATP molecules per glucose?

5. In glycolysis, _____ is oxidized and _____ is reduced.

6. The final electron acceptor of electron transport chains in mitochondria is _____.

7. The poison cyanide acts by blocking a key step in the electron transport chain. Knowing this, explain why cyanide kills so quickly.

8. Cells can harvest the most chemical energy from which of the following?
   a. an NADH molecule
   b. a glucose molecule
   c. six CO_2 molecules
   d. two pyruvic acid molecules

9. _____ is a metabolic pathway common to both fermentation and cellular respiration.

10. Sports physiologists at an Olympic training center want to monitor athletes to determine at what point their muscles are functioning anaerobically. They can do this by checking for a buildup of
    a. ADP.
    b. lactic acid.
    c. carbon dioxide.
    d. oxygen.

11. A glucose-fed yeast cell is moved from an aerobic environment to an anaerobic one. For the cell to continue to generate ATP at the same rate, approximately how much glucose must it consume in the anaerobic environment compared with the aerobic environment?

Answers to these questions can be found in Appendix: Self-Quiz Answers.

THE PROCESS OF SCIENCE

12. Your body makes NAD^+ from two B vitamins, niacin and riboflavin. You need only tiny amounts of these vitamins. The U.S. Food and Drug Administration's recommended dietary allowances are 20 mg daily for niacin and 1.7 mg daily for riboflavin. These amounts are thousands of times less than the amount of glucose your body needs each day to fuel its energy requirements. How many NAD^+ molecules are needed for the breakdown of each glucose molecule? Why do you think your daily requirement for these substances is so small?

BIOLOGY AND SOCIETY

13. Nearly all human societies use fermentation to produce alcoholic drinks such as beer and wine. The technology dates back to the earliest civilizations. Suggest a hypothesis for how people first discovered fermentation. In preindustrial cultures, why do you think wine was a more practical beverage than the grape juice from which it was made?

14. The consumption of alcohol by a pregnant woman can cause a series of birth defects called fetal alcohol syndrome (FAS). Symptoms of FAS include head and facial irregularities, heart defects, mental retardation, and behavioral problems. The U.S. Surgeon General's Office recommends that pregnant women abstain from drinking alcohol, and the government has mandated that a warning label be placed on liquor bottles. Imagine you are a server in a restaurant. An obviously pregnant woman orders a strawberry daiquiri. How would you respond? Is it the woman's right to make those decisions about her unborn child's health? Do you bear any responsibility in the matter? Is a restaurant responsible for monitoring the dietary habits of its customers?

7 Photosynthesis: Using Light to Make Food

Grown for Biofuel

Capturing solar energy. Sunlight drives the process of photosynthesis, which plants use to produce sugars. We can then convert these sugars to other substances, such as ethanol, that can power our vehicles.

Green Energy BIOLOGY AND SOCIETY

Biofuels

What's old is sometimes new again. Throughout our early history, people relied on plants as our primary source of energy, burning wood to produce heat and light. Then, as societies became industrialized, wood was largely displaced as an energy source by fossil fuels such as coal, gas, and oil. But now, as fossil fuel supplies dwindle and concerns are raised about global climate change, spiking oil prices, and the need for a domestic energy source, scientists are researching better ways to harness energy from biomass (living material). Some researchers focus on burning plant matter directly (for example, wood pellet boilers), while others focus on using plant material to produce biofuels that can be burned.

There are several types of biofuels. Bioethanol is a type of alcohol (the same type found in alcoholic drinks) that is made from wheat, corn, sugar beets, sugarcane, and other food crops. Starch made naturally by plants is converted to glucose and then fermented to ethanol by microorganisms (such as single-celled algae). Bioethanol can be used directly as a fuel source in specially designed vehicles, but it is more commonly used as a gasoline additive that can increase fuel efficiency while decreasing vehicle emissions. You may have noticed a sticker on the gas pump that declares the percentage of ethanol in the gas you are pumping; most cars today run on a blend of 85% gasoline and 15% ethanol. Many car manufacturers are producing flexible-fuel vehicles that can run on any combination of gasoline and bioethanol.

Cellulosic ethanol is a form of bioethanol made through the same fermentation process as bioethanol, but its primary ingredient is cellulose from nonedible plant material such as wood or grass. Biodiesel, the most common biofuel in Europe, is made from plant oils such as re-cycled frying oil. Like bioethanol, it can be used on its own or as an additive to standard diesel.

Whatever its form, when we derive energy from biomass or biofuels, we are actually tapping into the energy of the sun, which drives the process of photosynthesis in plants. Biofuels are just one way that people take advantage of plants' ability to capture solar energy. The topic of this chapter is photosynthesis, the process whereby plants use light to make sugars from carbon dioxide—sugars that are food for the plant and the starting point for most of our own food. First, we'll examine some basic concepts of photosynthesis; then we'll look at the specific mechanisms involved.

The Basics of Photosynthesis

Photosynthesis is a process whereby plants, algae (which are protists), and certain bacteria transform light energy into chemical energy, using carbon dioxide and water as starting materials. The chemical energy produced via photosynthesis is stored in the bonds of sugar molecules. Organisms that generate their own organic matter from inorganic ingredients are called autotrophs (see Chapter 6). Plants and other organisms that do this by photosynthesis—photosynthetic autotrophs—are the producers for most ecosystems **(Figure 7.1)**. This section presents an overview of photosynthesis, focusing on plants. Later, we'll take a closer look at some details of this process.

Chloroplasts: Sites of Photosynthesis

You have already learned that photosynthesis in plants and algae occurs within light-absorbing organelles called **chloroplasts** (see Chapter 4). All green parts of a plant have chloroplasts and can carry out photosynthesis. In most plants, however, the leaves have the most chloroplasts (about 500,000 per square millimeter of leaf surface) and are therefore the major locations of photosynthesis. Their green color is from **chlorophyll**, a light-absorbing molecule (a pigment) in the chloroplasts that plays a central role in converting solar energy to chemical energy.

Chloroplasts are concentrated in the interior cells of leaves **(Figure 7.2)**, with a typical cell containing 30–40 chloroplasts. Carbon dioxide (CO_2) enters a leaf, and oxygen (O_2) exits, by way of tiny pores called **stomata** (singular, *stoma*, meaning "mouth"). In addition to carbon dioxide, photosynthesis requires water, which is absorbed by the plant's roots and transported to the leaves, where veins carry it to the photosynthetic cells.

Membranes within the chloroplast form the framework where many of the reactions of photosynthesis occur. Like a mitochondrion, a chloroplast has a double-membrane envelope. The chloroplast's inner membrane encloses a compartment filled with **stroma**, a thick fluid. Suspended in the stroma are interconnected membranous sacs called **thylakoids**. The thylakoids are concentrated in stacks called **grana** (singular, *granum*). The chlorophyll molecules that capture light energy are built into the thylakoid membranes. The structure of a chloroplast—with its stacks of disks—aids its function by providing a large surface area for the reactions of photosynthesis. ✔

▼ Figure 7.1 **A diversity of photosynthetic autotrophs.**

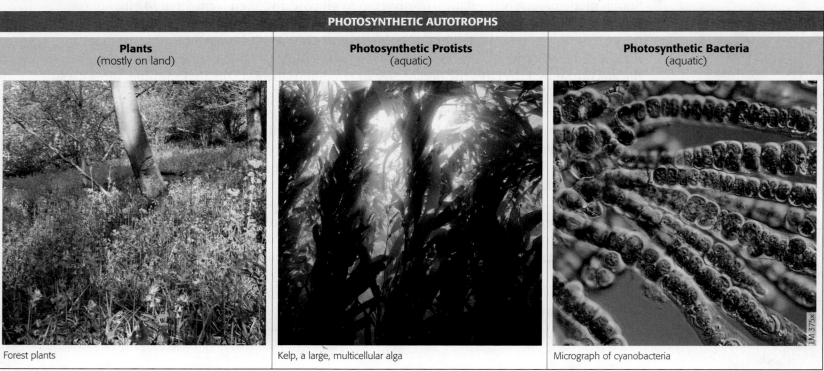

PHOTOSYNTHETIC AUTOTROPHS

Plants (mostly on land)	**Photosynthetic Protists** (aquatic)	**Photosynthetic Bacteria** (aquatic)
Forest plants	Kelp, a large, multicellular alga	Micrograph of cyanobacteria

LM 375×

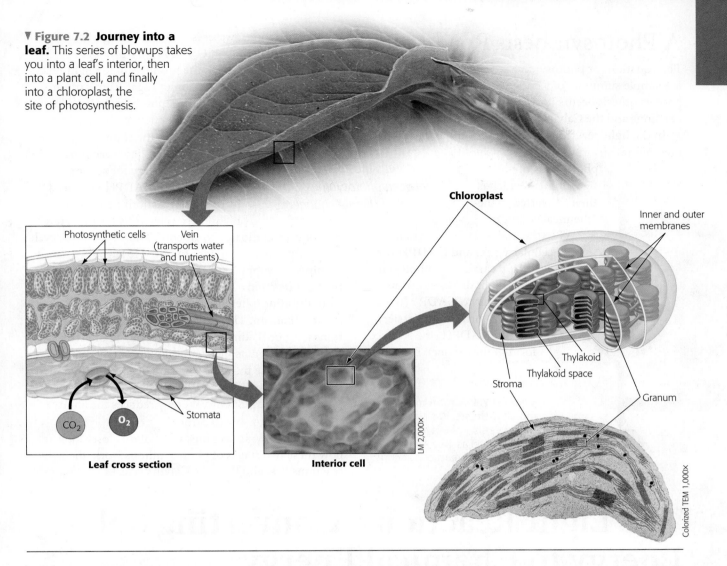

▼ Figure 7.2 **Journey into a leaf.** This series of blowups takes you into a leaf's interior, then into a plant cell, and finally into a chloroplast, the site of photosynthesis.

Chloroplast

Inner and outer membranes

Thylakoid

Thylakoid space

Stroma

Granum

Colorized TEM 1,000×

Photosynthetic cells

Vein (transports water and nutrients)

Stomata

CO_2 O_2

Leaf cross section

Interior cell

LM 2,000×

The Simplified Equation for Photosynthesis

The following chemical equation, simplified to highlight the relationship between photosynthesis and cellular respiration, provides a summary of the reactants and products of photosynthesis:

Light energy

$6 CO_2$ + $6 H_2O$ →→→ $C_6H_{12}O_6$ + $6 O_2$

Carbon dioxide   Water   **Photosynthesis**   Glucose   Oxygen gas

Notice that the reactants of photosynthesis—carbon dioxide (CO_2) and water (H_2O)—are the same as the waste products of cellular respiration (see Figure 6.2). Also notice that photosynthesis produces what respiration uses—glucose ($C_6H_{12}O_6$) and oxygen (O_2). In other words, photosynthesis recycles the "exhaust" of cellular respiration and rearranges its atoms to produce food and oxygen. Photosynthesis is a chemical transformation that requires a lot of energy, and sunlight absorbed by chlorophyll provides that energy.

You learned in Chapter 6 that cellular respiration is a process of electron transfer. A "fall" of electrons from food molecules to oxygen to form water releases the energy that mitochondria can use to make ATP (see Figure 6.5). The opposite occurs in photosynthesis: Electrons are boosted "uphill" and added to carbon dioxide to produce sugar. Hydrogen is moved along with the electrons being transferred from water to carbon dioxide. This transfer of hydrogen requires the chloroplast to split water molecules into hydrogen and oxygen. The hydrogen is transferred along with electrons to carbon dioxide to form sugar. The oxygen escapes through stomata in leaves into the atmosphere as O_2, a waste product of photosynthesis. ✓

In what sense do photosynthesis and cellular respiration form a complementary cycle?

✓ **CHECKPOINT**

What molecules are the inputs of photosynthesis? What molecules are the outputs?

Answer: CO_2 and H_2O; glucose and O_2

109

A Photosynthesis Road Map

The equation for photosynthesis on the previous page is a simple summary of a complex process. Actually, photosynthesis occurs in two multistep stages: the light reactions and the Calvin cycle (Figure 7.3).

In the **light reactions**, chlorophyll in the thylakoid membranes absorbs solar energy (the "photo" part of photosynthesis), which is then converted to the chemical energy of ATP (the molecule that drives most cellular work) and **NADPH** (an electron carrier). In photosynthesis, light drives electrons from water to NADP⁺ (the oxidized form of the carrier) to form NADPH (the reduced form of the carrier). During the light reactions, water is split, providing a source of electrons and giving off O_2 gas as a by-product.

The **Calvin cycle** uses the products of the light reactions to power the production of sugar from carbon dioxide (the "synthesis" part of photosynthesis). The enzymes that drive the Calvin cycle are dissolved in the stroma, the thick fluid within the chloroplast. ATP generated by the light reactions provides the energy for sugar synthesis. And the NADPH produced by the light reactions provides the high-energy electrons for the reduction of carbon dioxide to glucose. Thus, the Calvin cycle indirectly depends on light to produce sugar because it requires the supply of ATP and NADPH produced by the light reactions. The initial incorporation of carbon from the atmosphere into organic compounds is called **carbon fixation**. This process has important implications for global climate, since the removal of carbon from the air and its incorporation into plant material can help reduce the concentration of carbon dioxide in the atmosphere. Deforestation, which removes a lot of photosynthetic plant life, thereby reduces the ability of the biosphere to absorb carbon.

In the following sections, we'll take a closer look at how these two stages of photosynthesis work: the light reactions first and then the Calvin cycle. ☑

What's the connection between photosynthesis and global climate change?

◄ **Figure 7.3 A road map for photosynthesis.** We'll use a smaller version of this road map for orientation as we take a closer look at the light reactions and the Calvin cycle.

The Light Reactions: Converting Solar Energy to Chemical Energy

Chloroplasts are chemical factories powered by the sun. Let's look at how they convert sunlight to chemical energy.

The Nature of Sunlight

Sunlight is a type of energy called radiation or electromagnetic energy. Electromagnetic energy travels through space as rhythmic waves, like the ripples made by a pebble dropped into a pond. The distance between the crests of two adjacent waves is called a **wavelength**. The full range of radiation, from the very short wavelengths of gamma rays to the very long wavelengths of radio signals, is called the **electromagnetic spectrum (Figure 7.4)**.

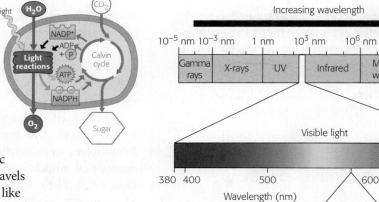

▲ **Figure 7.4 The electromagnetic spectrum.** The middle of the figure expands the thin slice of the spectrum that is visible to us as different colors of light, from about 380 nanometers (nm) to about 750 nm in wavelength. The bottom of the figure shows electromagnetic waves of one particular wavelength of visible light.

☑ **CHECKPOINT**

Name the two stages of photosynthesis in their proper order.

Answer: light reactions, Calvin cycle

Visible light is the fraction of the spectrum that our eyes see as different colors.

When sunlight shines on a pigmented material, certain wavelengths (colors) of the visible light are absorbed and disappear from the light that is reflected by the material. For example, we see a pair of jeans as blue because pigments in the fabric absorb the other colors, leaving only light in the blue part of the spectrum to be reflected from the fabric to our eyes.

The selective absorption of light by leaves explains why they appear green to us; light of that color is poorly absorbed by chloroplasts and is thus reflected or transmitted toward the observer (Figure 7.5). Since energy cannot be destroyed, the absorbed energy must be converted to other forms. Chloroplasts contain pigments that drive the conversion of some of the solar energy they absorb to chemical energy.

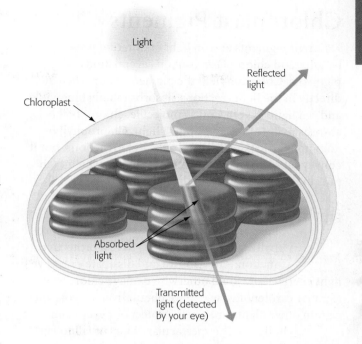

▶ **Figure 7.5 Why are leaves green?** Chlorophyll and other pigments in chloroplasts reflect or transmit green light while absorbing other colors.

Green Energy THE PROCESS OF SCIENCE

What Colors of Light Drive Photosynthesis?

In 1883, German biologist Theodor Engelmann made the **observation** that certain bacteria living in water tend to cluster in areas with higher oxygen concentrations. He already knew that light passed through a prism would separate into the different wavelengths (colors). Engelmann soon began to **question** whether he could use this information to determine which wavelengths of light work best for photosynthesis.

Engelmann's **hypothesis** was that oxygen-seeking bacteria would congregate near regions of algae performing the most photosynthesis (and hence producing the most oxygen). Engelmann began his **experiment** by laying a string of freshwater algal cells within a drop of water on a microscope slide. He then added oxygen-sensitive bacteria to the drop. Next, using a prism, he created a spectrum of light and shined it on the slide. His **results**, summarized in **Figure 7.6**, showed that most bacteria congregated around algae exposed to red-orange and blue-violet light, with very few bacteria moving to the area of green light. Other experiments have since verified that chloroplasts absorb light mainly in the blue-violet and red-orange part of the spectrum and that those wavelengths of light are the ones mainly responsible for photosynthesis.

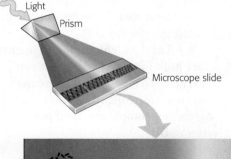

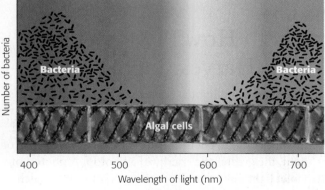

▲ **Figure 7.6 Investigating how light wavelength affects photosynthesis.** When algal cells are suspended in water on a microscope slide, oxygen-seeking bacteria migrate toward algae exposed to certain colors of light. These results suggest that blue-violet and orange-red wavelengths best drive photosynthesis, while green wavelengths do so only a little bit.

Chloroplast Pigments

Different pigments absorb light of different wavelengths, and chloroplasts contain several kinds of pigments. **Chlorophyll *a***, the pigment that participates directly in the light reactions, absorbs mainly blue-violet and red light. A very similar molecule, chlorophyll *b*, absorbs mainly blue and orange light. Chlorophyll *b* does not participate directly in the light reactions, but it conveys absorbed energy to chlorophyll *a*, which then puts the energy to work in the light reactions.

Chloroplasts also contain a family of yellow-orange pigments called carotenoids, which absorb mainly blue-green light. Some pass energy to chlorophyll *a*. Other carotenoids have a protective function: They absorb and dissipate excessive light energy that would otherwise damage chlorophyll. (Similar carotenoids, which we obtain from carrots and certain other plants, may help protect our eyes from bright light.) The spectacular colors of fall foliage in some parts of the world are due partly to the yellow-orange light reflected from carotenoids **(Figure 7.7)**. The falling autumn temperatures cause a decrease in the levels of chlorophyll, allowing the colors of the longer-lasting carotenoids to be seen in all their fall glory.

Why do some leaves turn color in the fall?

All of these chloroplast pigments are built into the thylakoid membranes (see Figure 7.2). There the pigments are organized into light-harvesting complexes called photosystems. ☑

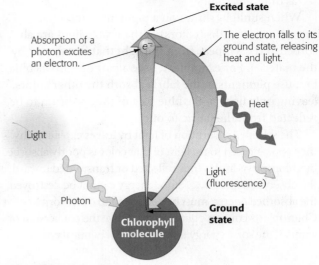

▼ Figure 7.8 Excited electrons in pigments.

Excited state

Absorption of a photon excites an electron.

The electron falls to its ground state, releasing heat and light.

Heat

Light

Light (fluorescence)

Photon

Chlorophyll molecule

Ground state

(a) Absorption of a photon

(b) Fluorescence of a glow stick. Breaking a vial within a glow stick starts a chemical reaction that excites electrons within a fluorescent dye. As the electrons fall from their excited state to the ground state, the excess energy is emitted as light.

▲ Figure 7.7 Photosynthetic pigments. Falling autumn temperatures cause a decrease in the levels of green chlorophyll within the leaves of leaf-bearing trees. This decrease allows the colors of the carotenoids to be seen.

How Photosystems Harvest Light Energy

Thinking about light as waves explains most of light's properties. However, light also behaves as discrete packets of energy called photons. A **photon** is a fixed quantity of light energy. The shorter the wavelength of light, the greater the energy of a photon. A photon of violet light, for example, packs nearly twice as much energy as a photon of red light.

When a pigment molecule absorbs a photon, one of the pigment's electrons gains energy. This electron is now said to be "excited"; that is, the electron has been raised from its starting state (called the ground state) to an excited state. The excited state is highly unstable, so an excited electron usually loses its excess energy and falls back to its ground state almost immediately **(Figure 7.8a)**. Most pigments merely release heat energy as their light-excited electrons fall back to their ground state. (That's why a surface with a lot of pigment, such as a black driveway, gets so hot on a sunny day.) But some pigments emit light as well as heat after absorbing photons. The fluorescent light emitted by a glow stick is caused by a chemical reaction that excites electrons of a fluorescent dye **(Figure 7.8b)**. The excited electrons quickly fall back down to their ground state, releasing energy in the form of fluorescent light.

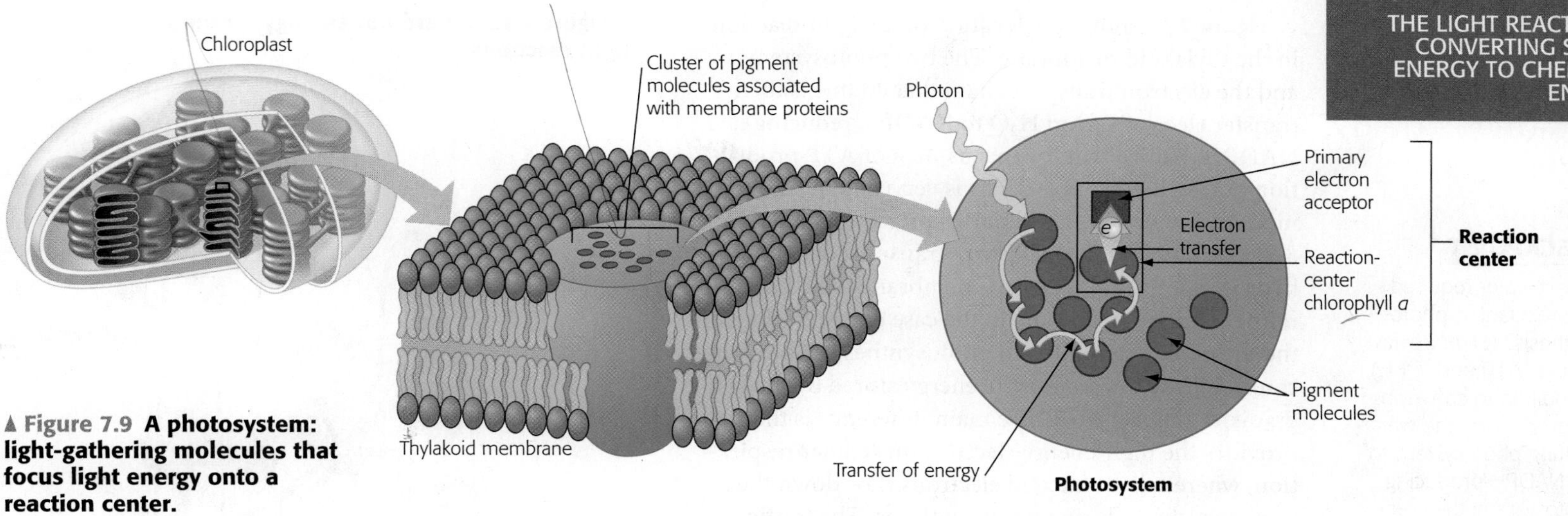

▲ **Figure 7.9 A photosystem: light-gathering molecules that focus light energy onto a reaction center.**

In the thylakoid membrane, chlorophyll molecules are organized with other molecules into photosystems. Each **photosystem** has a cluster of a few hundred pigment molecules, including chlorophylls *a* and *b* and some carotenoids **(Figure 7.9)**. This cluster of pigment molecules functions as a light-gathering antenna. When a photon strikes one of the pigment molecules, the energy jumps from molecule to molecule until it arrives at the **reaction center** of the photosystem. The reaction center consists of chlorophyll *a* molecules that sit next to another molecule called a **primary electron acceptor**. This primary electron acceptor traps the light-excited electron (e^-) from the chlorophyll *a* in the reaction center. Another team of molecules built into the thylakoid membrane then uses that trapped energy to make ATP and NADPH. ☑

☑ CHECKPOINT

What is the role of a reaction center during photosynthesis?

Answer: A reaction center transfers a light-excited photon from pigment molecules to molecules that can use this trapped energy to drive chemical reactions.

How the Light Reactions Generate ATP and NADPH

Two types of photosystems cooperate in the light reactions **(Figure 7.10)**. ❶ Photons excite electrons in the chlorophyll of the water-splitting photosystem. These photons are then trapped by the primary electron acceptor. The water-splitting photosystem replaces its light-excited electrons by extracting electrons from water. This is the step that releases O_2 during photosynthesis. ❷ Energized electrons from the water-splitting photosystem pass down an electron transport chain to the NADPH-producing photosystem. The chloroplast uses the energy released by this electron "fall" to make ATP. ❸ The NADPH-producing photosystem transfers its light-excited electrons to $NADP^+$, reducing it to NADPH.

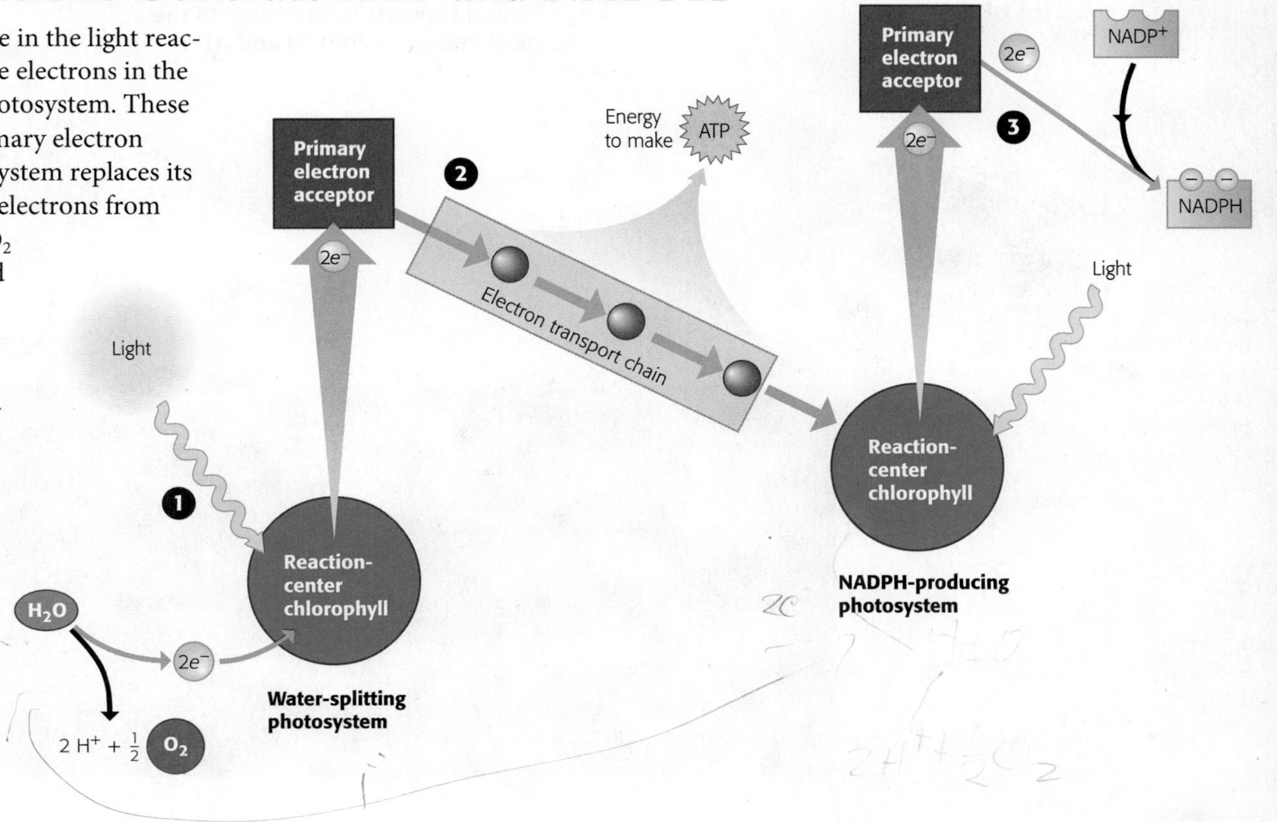

► **Figure 7.10 The light reactions of photosynthesis.** The orange arrows trace a light-driven flow of electrons from H_2O to NADPH. These electrons also produce ATP.

Figure 7.11 shows the location of the light reactions in the thylakoid membrane. The two photosystems and the electron transport chain that connects them transfer electrons from H_2O to $NADP^+$, reducing it to NADPH. Notice that the mechanism of ATP production during the light reactions is very similar to the mechanism we saw in cellular respiration (see Figure 6.11). In both cases, an electron transport chain pumps hydrogen ions (H^+) across a membrane—the inner mitochondrial membrane in the case of respiration and the thylakoid membrane in photosynthesis. And in both cases, ATP synthases use the energy stored by the H^+ gradient to make ATP. The main difference is that food provides the high-energy electrons in cellular respiration, whereas light-excited electrons flow down the transport chain during photosynthesis. The traffic of electrons shown in Figures 7.10 and 7.11 is analogous to the cartoon in **Figure 7.12**.

We have seen how the light reactions absorb solar energy and convert it to the chemical energy of ATP and NADPH. Notice again, however, that the light reactions did not produce any sugar. That's the job of the Calvin cycle, as we'll see next. ☑

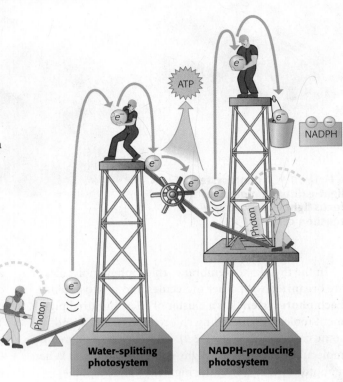

▼ **Figure 7.12 A hard-hat analogy for the light reactions.**

Water-splitting photosystem

NADPH-producing photosystem

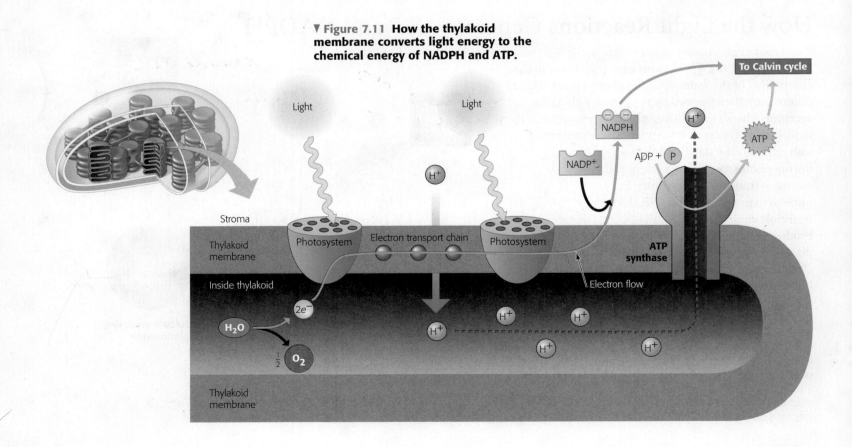

▼ **Figure 7.11 How the thylakoid membrane converts light energy to the chemical energy of NADPH and ATP.**

The Calvin Cycle: Making Sugar from Carbon Dioxide

The Calvin cycle functions like a sugar factory within a chloroplast. It is called a cycle because, like the citric acid cycle in cellular respiration, the starting material is regenerated. And with each turn of the cycle, there are chemical inputs and outputs. The inputs are CO_2 from the air as well as ATP and NADPH produced by the light reactions. Using carbon from CO_2, energy from ATP, and high-energy electrons from NADPH, the Calvin cycle constructs an energy-rich sugar molecule called glyceraldehyde 3-phosphate (G3P). The plant cell can then use G3P as the raw material to make the glucose and other organic compounds (such as cellulose and starch) that it needs. **Figure 7.13** presents the basics of the Calvin cycle, emphasizing inputs and outputs. Each ● symbol represents a carbon atom, and each (P) symbol represents a phosphate group. ☑

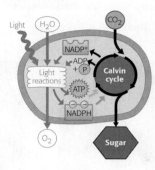

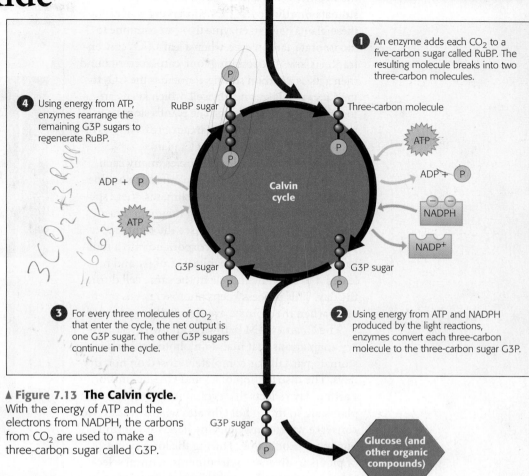

1 An enzyme adds each CO_2 to a five-carbon sugar called RuBP. The resulting molecule breaks into two three-carbon molecules.

4 Using energy from ATP, enzymes rearrange the remaining G3P sugars to regenerate RuBP.

3 For every three molecules of CO_2 that enter the cycle, the net output is one G3P sugar. The other G3P sugars continue in the cycle.

2 Using energy from ATP and NADPH produced by the light reactions, enzymes convert each three-carbon molecule to the three-carbon sugar G3P.

▲ **Figure 7.13 The Calvin cycle.** With the energy of ATP and the electrons from NADPH, the carbons from CO_2 are used to make a three-carbon sugar called G3P.

Green Energy EVOLUTION CONNECTION

Solar-Driven Evolution

Throughout this chapter, you've studied how plants convert solar energy to chemical energy via photosynthesis. Such "green energy" transformations are vital to our welfare and all of Earth's ecosystems.

You probably know that sunlight strikes Earth differently in different geographic regions. Because natural selection promotes the evolution of adaptations that best suit a local environment, it's not surprising that different modes of photosynthesis have evolved in different climates.

So far, we've focused on plants that use CO_2 directly from the air to drive the Calvin cycle. Such plants are called **C_3 plants** because the first organic compound produced in the Calvin cycle is a three-carbon

molecule (see Figure 7.13). C_3 plants are widely distributed and include such common crops as soybeans, oats, wheat, and rice. One problem that farmers face in growing C_3 plants, however, is that plants close their stomata on hot, dry days, helping to prevent dehydration. This adaptation reduces water loss but also prevents CO_2 from entering the leaves. As a result, CO_2 levels get very low in the leaves, and sugar production ceases. Thus, when the weather turns hot, the productivity of C_3 crops is significantly reduced because of their need to save water.

In hot, dry climates, alternative modes of incorporating carbon from CO_2 have evolved in some plants, allowing them to save water without shutting down photosynthesis. These species are categorized as either C_4 plants or CAM plants.

☑ CHECKPOINT

What is the function of NADPH in the Calvin cycle?

Answer: It provides the high-energy electrons that are added to CO_2 to form G3P (a sugar).

C_4 **plants** are so named because they incorporate carbon from CO_2 into a four-carbon compound before proceeding to the Calvin cycle (**Figure 7.14**, left side). When the weather is hot and dry, a C_4 plant keeps its stomata mostly closed, thus conserving water. But these plants have an enzyme that can continue to incorporate carbon even when a leaf's CO_2 concentration is low. The resulting four-carbon compound then acts as a carbon shuttle; it donates the CO_2 to the Calvin cycle in a nearby cell, which keeps on making sugars even though the plant's stomata are mostly closed. Corn and sugarcane are examples of some agriculturally important C_4 plants.

CAM plants include pineapples, many cacti, and succulent (water-storing) plants such as aloe and jade. Adapted to very dry climates, these species conserve water by opening their stomata and admitting CO_2 only at night (see the right side of Figure 7.14). The CO_2 is incorporated into a four-carbon compound that banks it at night and releases it to the Calvin cycle in the same cell during the day. This process keeps photosynthesis operating when the stomata are closed during the day.

The C_4 and CAM pathways are two evolutionary adaptations that maintain photosynthesis with stomata partially or completely closed on hot, dry days. The distribution of C_4 and CAM plants on Earth today reflects this evolutionary history; such plants are found in hot climates where the need to conserve water outweighs the need for continuous sugar production. During the long evolution of plants in diverse environments, natural selection has refined photosynthetic adaptations that enable these plants to continue producing food even in the arid conditions of their local environments. The cultivation of such plants where they thrive is yet another example of this chapter's theme: the ways that humans benefit from the "green energy" process of photosynthesis.

▼ **Figure 7.14** C_4 **and CAM photosynthesis.** The C_4 and CAM pathways are two evolutionary adaptations that maintain photosynthesis with stomata partially or completely closed on hot, dry days.

ALTERNATIVE PHOTOSYNTHETIC PATHWAYS

C_4 Pathway (example: sugarcane)

CAM Pathway (example: pineapple)

Carbon incorporation and the Calvin cycle occur in different types of cells.

Carbon incorporation and the Calvin cycle occur in the same cells at different times.

Chapter Review

SUMMARY OF KEY CONCEPTS

 Go to **www.masteringbiology.com** for homework assignments, practice quizzes, Pearson eText, and more.

The Basics of Photosynthesis

Photosynthesis is a process whereby light energy is transformed into chemical energy, which is stored as bonds in sugars made from carbon dioxide and water.

Chloroplasts: Sites of Photosynthesis

Chloroplasts contain a thick fluid called stroma surrounding a network of membranes called thylakoids.

The Simplified Equation for Photosynthesis

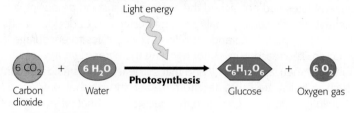

A Photosynthesis Road Map

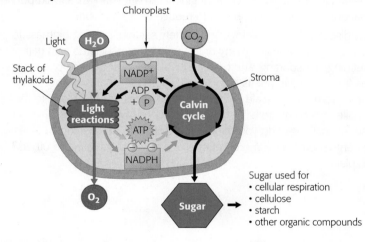

The Light Reactions: Converting Solar Energy to Chemical Energy

The Nature of Sunlight

Visible light is part of the spectrum of electromagnetic energy. It travels through space as waves. Different wavelengths of light appear as different colors; shorter wavelengths carry more energy.

Chloroplast Pigments

Pigment molecules absorb light energy of certain wavelengths and reflect other wavelengths. We see the reflected wavelengths as the color of the pigment. Several chloroplast pigments absorb light of various wavelengths and convey it to other pigments, but it is the green pigment chlorophyll *a* that participates directly in the light reactions.

How Photosystems Harvest Light Energy; How the Light Reactions Generate ATP and NADPH

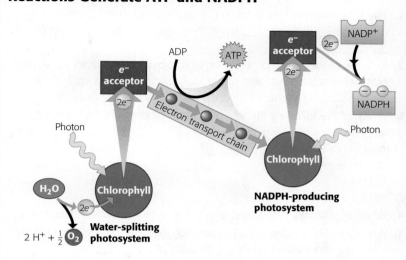

The Calvin Cycle: Making Sugar from Carbon Dioxide

Within the stroma (fluid) of the chloroplast, carbon dioxide from the air and ATP and NADPH produced during the light reactions are used to produce G3P, an energy-rich sugar molecule that can be used to make glucose and other organic molecules.

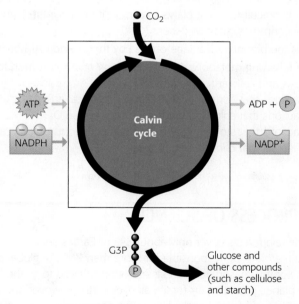

Evolution Connection: Solar-Driven Evolution

The photosynthetic adaptations of C_4 and CAM plants enable sugar production to continue even when stomata are closed, thereby reducing water loss in arid environments.

SELF-QUIZ

1. The light reactions take place in the structures of the chloroplast called the _____, while the Calvin cycle takes place in the _____.

2. In terms of the spatial organization of photosynthesis within the chloroplast, what is the advantage of the light reactions producing NADPH and ATP on the stroma side of the thylakoid membrane?

3. Which of the following are inputs to photosynthesis? Which are outputs?
   a. CO_2
   b. O_2
   c. sugar
   d. H_2O
   e. light

4. What color of light is the least effective in driving photosynthesis? Why?

5. When light strikes chlorophyll molecules, they lose electrons, which are ultimately replaced by splitting molecules of _____.

6. Which of the following are produced by reactions that take place in the thylakoids and are consumed by reactions in the stroma?
   a. CO_2 and H_2O
   b. $NADP^+$ and ADP
   c. ATP and NADPH
   d. glucose and O_2

7. The reactions of the Calvin cycle are not directly dependent on light, and yet they usually do not occur at night. Why?

8. Why is it difficult for most plants to carry out photosynthesis in very hot, dry environments, such as deserts?

9. What is the primary advantage offered by the C_4 and CAM pathways?

10. Of the following metabolic processes, which one is common to photosynthesis and cellular respiration?
    a. reactions that convert light energy to chemical energy
    b. reactions that split H_2O molecules and release O_2
    c. reactions that store energy by pumping H^+ across membranes
    d. reactions that convert CO_2 to sugar

Answers to these questions can be found in Appendix: Self-Quiz Answers.

THE PROCESS OF SCIENCE

11. Tropical rain forests cover only about 3% of Earth's surface, but they are estimated to be responsible for more than 20% of global photosynthesis. For this reason, rain forests are often referred to as the "lungs" of the planet, providing O_2 for life all over Earth. However, most experts believe that rain forests make little or no net contribution to global O_2 production. From your knowledge of photosynthesis and cellular respiration, can you explain why they might think this? (*Hint*: What happens to the energy stored as sugars in the body of a plant when that plant dies or parts of it are eaten by animals?)

12. Suppose you wanted to discover whether the oxygen atoms in the glucose produced by photosynthesis come from H_2O or CO_2. Explain how you could use a radioactive isotope to find out.

BIOLOGY AND SOCIETY

13. There is strong evidence that Earth is getting warmer because of an intensified greenhouse effect resulting from increased CO_2 emissions from industry, vehicles, and the burning of forests. Global climate change could influence agriculture, melt polar ice, and flood coastal regions. In response to these threats, 178 countries have accepted the Kyoto agreement, which calls for mandatory reductions of greenhouse gas emissions in 30 industrialized nations by 2012. As of late 2011, the United States had not signed the agreement, instead proposing a more modest set of voluntary goals allowing businesses to decide whether they wish to participate and providing tax incentives to encourage them to do so. The reasons given for rejecting the agreement are that it might hurt the American economy and that some less industrialized countries (such as India) are exempted from it, even though they produce a lot of pollution. Do you agree with this decision? In what ways might efforts to reduce greenhouse gases hurt the economy? How can those costs be weighed against the costs of global climate change? Should poorer nations carry an equal burden to reduce their emissions?

14. As discussed in the Biology and Society section, burning biomass to produce electricity avoids many of the problems associated with gathering, refining, transporting, and burning fossil fuels. Yet the use of biomass as fuel is not without its own set of problems. What challenges might arise from a large-scale conversion to biomass energy? How do these challenges compare with those encountered with fossil fuels? Which set of challenges do you think is more likely to be overcome? Does one energy source have more benefits and fewer costs than the others? Explain.

Unit 2
Genetics

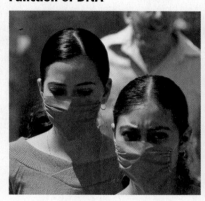

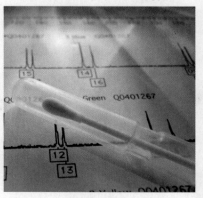

8 Cellular Reproduction: Cells from Cells

The Komodo dragon. The Komodo is the world's largest lizard and is found in the wild only on three islands in Indonesia. Komodo dragons can reproduce using two different types of cell division.

Life with and without Sex BIOLOGY AND SOCIETY

Virgin Birth of a Dragon

In 2002, zookeepers at the Chester Zoo in England were startled to discover that Flora, a female Komodo dragon (*Varanus komodoensis*), had laid a clutch of 25 eggs. It wasn't surprising that a captive Komodo dragon would breed. In fact, Flora was at the zoo for that very reason: She was one of two female Komodo dragons taking part in a captive breeding program intended to help repopulate the species.

What made Flora's clutch of eggs so remarkable is that she had not yet been in the company of any male, let alone mated with one. As far as anyone knew at that time, Komodo dragons, like the vast majority of animal species, create offspring through sexual reproduction involving the union of a male's sperm and a female's egg. But despite Flora's virginity, eight of her eggs developed normally and hatched into live, healthy Komodo dragons.

DNA analysis confirmed that Flora's offspring derived their genes solely from her. Her young must have been created by parthenogenesis, the production of offspring by a female without involvement of a male. Parthenogenesis is one form of asexual reproduction, the creation of a new generation without participation of sperm and egg. Although parthenogenesis is known to occur in some animals, it is rare among vertebrates (animals with backbones) and was never before seen in Komodo dragons. Soon, zoologists identified a second European Komodo who had borne young by parthenogenesis. This same Komodo dragon later bore additional offspring via sexual reproduction. Apparently, this species has evolved the potential to produce young through both asexual and sexual reproduction.

The ability of organisms to procreate is the one characteristic that best distinguishes living things from nonliving matter. The same cellular process—cell division—is at the heart of both asexual and sexual reproduction. The perpetuation of life depends on the production of new cells. Lizards born of parthenogenesis are the result of repeated cell divisions, as are eggs and sperm themselves. In this chapter, we'll look at how individual cells are copied and then see how cell reproduction underlies the process of sexual reproduction. During our discussion, we'll consider examples of asexual and sexual reproduction among both plants and animals.

What Cell Reproduction Accomplishes

When you hear the word *reproduction*, you probably think of the birth of new organisms. But reproduction actually occurs much more often at the cellular level. Consider the skin on your arm. Skin cells are constantly reproducing themselves and moving outward toward the surface, replacing dead cells that have rubbed off. This renewal of your skin goes on throughout your life. And when your skin is injured, additional cell reproduction helps heal the wound.

How does a new sea star grow from a lost arm?

When a cell undergoes reproduction, or **cell division**, the two "daughter" cells that result are genetically identical to each other and to the original "parent" cell. (Biologists traditionally use the word *daughter* in this context; it does not imply gender.) Before the parent cell splits into two, it duplicates its **chromosomes**, the structures that contain most of the cell's DNA. Then, during the division process, one set of chromosomes is distributed to each daughter cell. Each daughter cell receives identical sets of chromosomes from the lone, original parent cell.

As summarized in **Figure 8.1**, cell division plays several important roles in the lives of organisms. For example, within your body, millions of cells must divide every second to replace damaged or lost cells. Another function of cell division is growth. All of the trillions of cells in your body are the result of repeated cell divisions that began in your mother's body with a single fertilized egg cell.

Another vital function of cell division is reproduction. Many single-celled organisms, such as amoebas, reproduce by dividing in half, and the offspring are genetic replicas of the parent. Because it does not involve fertilization of an egg by a sperm, this type of reproduction is called **asexual reproduction**. Offspring produced by asexual reproduction inherit all of their chromosomes from a single parent.

Many multicellular organisms can reproduce asexually as well. For example, some sea star species have the ability to grow new individuals from fragmented pieces. And if you've ever grown a houseplant from a clipping, you've observed asexual reproduction in plants. In asexual reproduction, there is one simple principle of inheritance: The lone parent and each of its offspring have identical genes. The type of cell division responsible for asexual reproduction and for the growth and maintenance of multicellular organisms is called mitosis.

Sexual reproduction is different; it requires fertilization of an egg by a sperm. The production of **gametes**—egg and sperm—involves a special type of cell division called meiosis, which occurs only in reproductive organs (such as testes and ovaries in humans). As we'll discuss later, a gamete has only half as many chromosomes as the parent cell that gave rise to it.

In summary, two kinds of cell division are involved in the lives of sexually reproducing organisms: meiosis for reproduction and mitosis for growth and maintenance. The remainder of the chapter is divided into two main sections, one devoted to each type of cell division. ☑

☑ CHECKPOINT

Ordinary cell division produces two daughter cells that are genetically identical. Name three functions of this type of cell division.

Answer: cell replacement, growth of an organism, asexual reproduction of an organism

► **Figure 8.1 Three functions of cell division.**

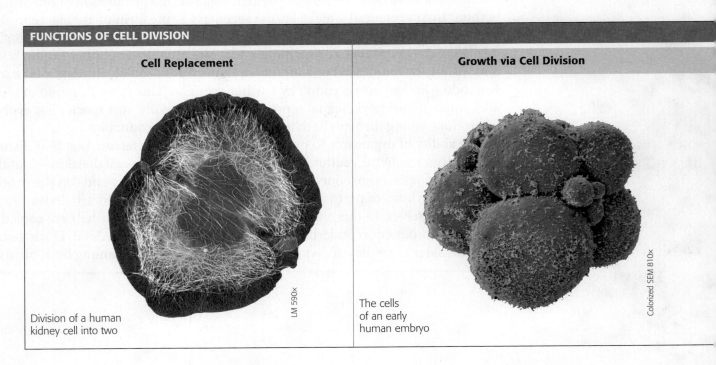

FUNCTIONS OF CELL DIVISION

Cell Replacement	Growth via Cell Division
Division of a human kidney cell into two	The cells of an early human embryo

LM 590x

Colorized SEM 810x

The Cell Cycle and Mitosis

Almost all of the genes of a eukaryotic cell—around 21,000 in humans—are located on chromosomes in the cell nucleus. (The main exceptions are genes on small DNA molecules found in mitochondria and chloroplasts.) Because chromosomes are the lead players in cell division, let's focus on them before turning our attention to the cell as a whole.

Eukaryotic Chromosomes

Each eukaryotic chromosome contains one very long DNA molecule, typically bearing thousands of genes. The number of chromosomes in a eukaryotic cell depends on the species (Figure 8.2). Chromosomes are made up of a material called **chromatin**, fibers composed of roughly equal amounts of DNA and protein molecules. The protein molecules help organize the chromatin and help control the activity of its genes.

Most of the time, the chromosomes exist as thin fibers that are much longer than the nucleus they are stored in. In fact, if stretched out, the DNA in just one of your cells would be taller than you! As a cell prepares to divide, its chromatin

▶ **Figure 8.2 The number of chromosomes in the cells of selected mammals.** Notice that humans have 46 chromosomes and that the number of chromosomes does not correspond to the size or complexity of an organism.

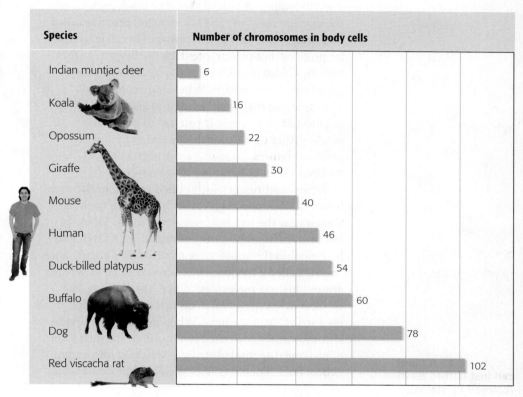

Species	Number of chromosomes in body cells
Indian muntjac deer	6
Koala	16
Opossum	22
Giraffe	30
Mouse	40
Human	46
Duck-billed platypus	54
Buffalo	60
Dog	78
Red viscacha rat	102

Asexual Reproduction

LM 250x

Reproduction of an amoeba

Fragmentation and regeneration of a sea star. The sea star on the right lost and replaced an arm. The severed arm grew into the new sea star on the left.

Reproduction of an African violet from a clipping (large leaf)

123

fibers coil up, forming compact chromosomes that can be viewed under a light microscope **(Figure 8.3)**. When a cell is not dividing, the chromosomes are too thin to be seen with a light micrograph.

How can yards' worth of DNA fit inside a microscopic nucleus?

Such long molecules of DNA can fit into the tiny nucleus because within each chromosome the DNA is packed into an elaborate, multilevel system of coiling and folding. A crucial aspect of DNA packing is the association of the DNA with small proteins called **histones**, found only in eukaryotes. (Bacteria have similar proteins, but prokaryotes lack the degree of DNA packing found in eukaryotes.) Why is it necessary for a cell's chromosomes to be compacted in this way? Imagine that your belongings are spread out around your room. If you had to move, you would gather up all your things and put them in small containers. Similarly, a cell must compact its DNA before it can move it to a new cell.

Figure 8.4 presents a simplified model for the main levels of DNA packing. At the first level of packing, shown near the top, histones attach to the DNA. In electron micrographs, the combination of DNA and histones has the appearance of beads on a string. Each "bead," called a **nucleosome**, consists of DNA wound around histone molecules. When not dividing, the DNA of active genes takes on this lightly packed, "beads on a string" arrangement. When preparing to divide, chromosomes condense even more. At the next level of packing, the beaded string is wrapped into a tight helical fiber. Then this fiber coils further into a thick

supercoil. Looping and folding can compact the DNA even more still, as you can see in the chromosome at the bottom of the figure. Viewed as a whole, Figure 8.4 gives a sense of how successive levels of coiling and folding enable a huge amount of DNA to fit into a cell's tiny nucleus.

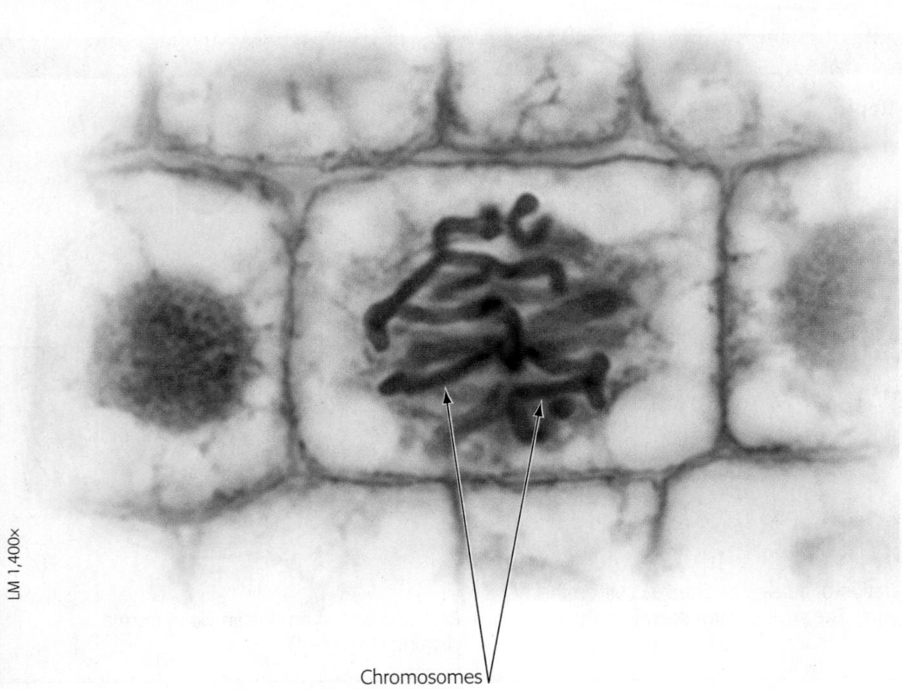

▼ **Figure 8.4** **DNA packing in a eukaryotic chromosome.** Successive levels of coiling of DNA and associated proteins ultimately results in highly compacted chromosomes.

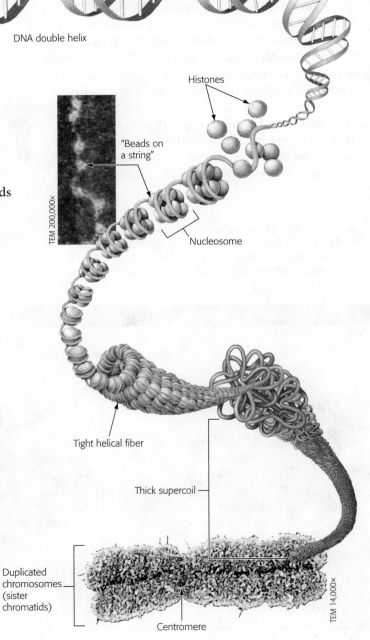

DNA double helix

Histones

"Beads on a string"

TEM 200,000×

Nucleosome

Tight helical fiber

Thick supercoil

Duplicated chromosomes (sister chromatids)

Centromere

TEM 14,000×

▼ **Figure 8.3** **A plant cell just before division (colored by stains).**

LM 1,400×

Chromosomes

Before a cell begins the division process, it duplicates all of its chromosomes. The DNA molecule of each chromosome is copied through the process of DNA replication (see Chapter 10), and new protein molecules attach as needed. The result is that—at this point—each chromosome consists of two copies called **sister chromatids**, which contain identical genes. At the bottom of Figure 8.4, you can see an electron micrograph of a human chromosome that has duplicated. The fuzzy appearance comes from the intricate twists and folds of the chromatin fibers. The two sister chromatids are joined together tightly at a narrow "waist" called the **centromere**.

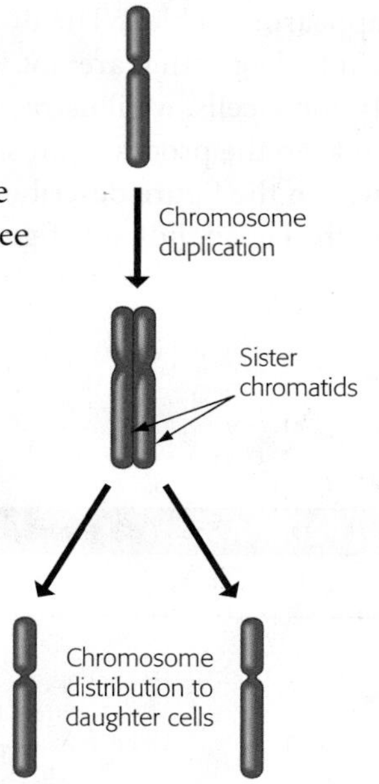

When the cell divides, the sister chromatids of a duplicated chromosome separate from each other **(Figure 8.5)**. Once separated from its sister, each chromatid is considered a full-fledged chromosome, and it is identical to the original chromosome. One of the new chromosomes goes to one daughter cell, and the other goes to the other daughter cell. In this way, each daughter cell receives a complete and identical set of chromosomes. A dividing human skin cell, for example, has 46 duplicated chromosomes, and each of the two daughter cells that result from it has 46 single chromosomes.

The Cell Cycle

The rate at which a cell divides depends on its role within the organism's body. Some cells divide once a day, others less often, and highly specialized cells, such as mature muscle cells, do not divide at all.

The ordered sequence of events that extends from the time a cell is first formed from a dividing parent cell until its own division into two cells is called the **cell cycle**. As **Figure 8.6** shows, most of the cell cycle is spent in **interphase**. Interphase is a time when a cell performs its normal functions within the organism. For example, a cell in your stomach lining might make and release enzyme molecules that aid in digestion. During interphase, a cell roughly doubles everything in its cytoplasm. It

▲ **Figure 8.5 Duplication and distribution of a single chromosome.** During cell reproduction, the cell duplicates each chromosome and distributes the two copies to the daughter cells.

increases its supply of proteins, increases the number of many of its organelles (such as mitochondria and ribosomes), and grows in size. Typically, interphase lasts for at least 90% of the cell cycle.

From the standpoint of cell reproduction, the most important event of interphase is chromosome duplication, when the DNA in the nucleus is precisely doubled. The period when this occurs is called the S phase (for DNA *synthesis*). The interphase periods before and after the S phase are called the G_1 and G_2 phases, respectively (G stands for *gap*). During G_2, each chromosome in the cell consists of two identical sister chromatids, and the cell during this period is preparing to divide.

The part of the cell cycle when the cell is actually dividing is called the **mitotic (M) phase**. It includes two overlapping stages, mitosis and cytokinesis. In **mitosis**, the nucleus and its contents, most importantly the duplicated chromosomes, divide and are evenly distributed, forming two daughter nuclei. During **cytokinesis**, the cytoplasm is divided in two. The combination of mitosis and cytokinesis produces two genetically identical daughter cells, each with a single nucleus, the surrounding cytoplasm with organelles, and a plasma membrane. ☑

☑ CHECKPOINT

1. A duplicated chromosome consists of two sister _____ joined together at the _____.

2. What are the two broadest divisions of the cell cycle? What two processes are involved in the actual duplication of the cell?

*Answers: **1.** chromatids; centromere **2.** interphase and the mitotic phase; mitosis and cytokinesis*

▼ **Figure 8.6 The eukaryotic cell cycle.** The cell cycle extends from the "birth" of a cell (just after the dark blue arrow at the bottom of the cycle), resulting from cell reproduction, to the time the cell itself divides in two. (During interphase, the chromosomes are diffuse masses of thin fibers; they do not actually appear in the rodlike form you see here.)

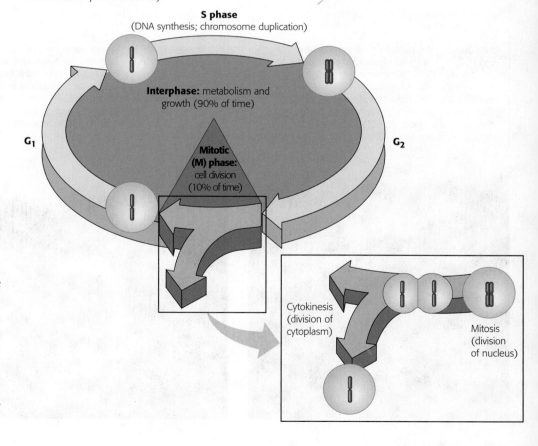

S phase
(DNA synthesis; chromosome duplication)

Interphase: metabolism and growth (90% of time)

G_1

G_2

Mitotic (M) phase: cell division (10% of time)

Cytokinesis (division of cytoplasm)

Mitosis (division of nucleus)

125

Mitosis and Cytokinesis

Figure 8.7 illustrates the cell cycle for an animal cell using drawings, descriptions, and photos. The micrographs running along the bottom row of the page show dividing cells from a salamander, with chromosomes appearing in blue. The drawings in the top row include details that are not visible in the micrographs. In these cells, we illustrate just four chromosomes to keep the process a bit simpler to follow. The text within the figure describes the events occurring at each stage. Study this figure carefully (it has a lot of

▼ **Figure 8.7 Cell reproduction: A dance of the chromosomes.** After the chromatin doubles during interphase, the elaborately choreographed stages of mitosis—prophase, metaphase, anaphase, and telophase—distribute the duplicate sets of chromosomes to two separate nuclei. Cytokinesis then divides the cytoplasm, yielding two genetically identical daughter cells.

INTERPHASE	PROPHASE

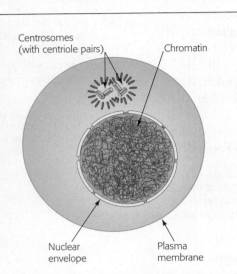

Centrosomes (with centriole pairs)

Chromatin

Nuclear envelope

Plasma membrane

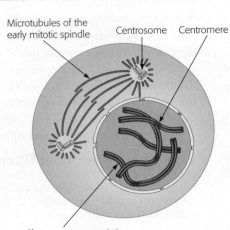

Microtubules of the early mitotic spindle

Centrosome   Centromere

Chromosome, consisting of two sister chromatids

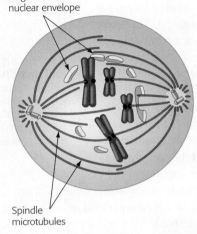

Fragments of nuclear envelope

Spindle microtubules

Interphase is the period of cell growth when the cell makes new molecules and organelles. At the point shown here, late interphase (G_2), the cytoplasm contains two centrosomes. Within the nucleus, the chromosomes are duplicated, but they cannot be distinguished individually because they are still in the form of loosely packed chromatin fibers.

During prophase, changes occur in both nucleus and cytoplasm. In the nucleus, the chromatin fibers coil, so that the chromosomes become thick enough to be seen individually with a light microscope. Each chromosome exists as two identical sister chromatids joined together at the narrow "waist" of the centromere. In the cytoplasm, the mitotic spindle

begins to form as microtubules grow out from the centrosomes, which are moving away from each other. Late in prophase, the nuclear envelope breaks into pieces. The spindle microtubules attach to the centromeres of the chromosomes and move the chromosomes toward the center of the cell.

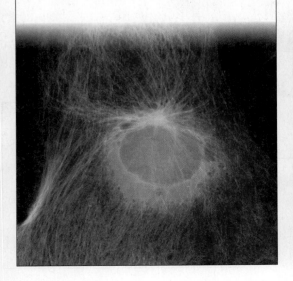

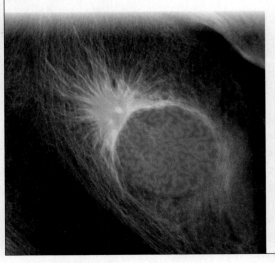

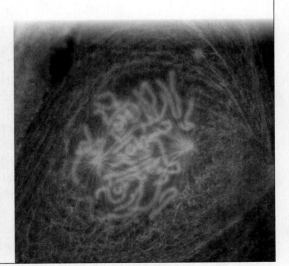

information and it's important!) and notice the striking changes in the nucleus and other cellular structures.

Biologists distinguish four main stages of mitosis: **prophase**, **metaphase**, **anaphase**, and **telophase**. The chromosomes are the stars of the mitotic drama, and their movements depend on the **mitotic spindle**, a football-shaped structure of microtubules (green in the micrographs) that guides the separation of the two sets of daughter chromosomes. The spindle microtubules grow from structures within the cytoplasm called **centrosomes**.

METAPHASE	ANAPHASE	TELOPHASE AND CYTOKINESIS

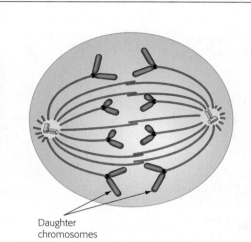

Spindle

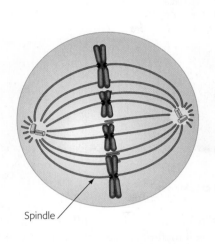

The mitotic spindle is now fully formed. The centromeres of all the chromosomes line up between the two poles of the spindle. For each chromosome, the microtubules of the mitotic spindle attached to the two sister chromatids pull toward opposite poles. This tug of war keeps the chromosomes in the middle of the cell.

Daughter chromosomes

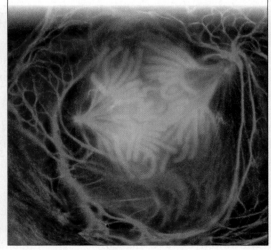

Anaphase begins suddenly when the sister chromatids of each chromosome separate. Each is now considered a full-fledged (daughter) chromosome. The chromosomes move toward opposite poles of the cell as the spindle microtubules shorten. Simultaneously, the microtubules not attached to chromosomes lengthen, pushing the poles farther apart and elongating the cell.

Nuclear envelope forming   Cleavage furrow

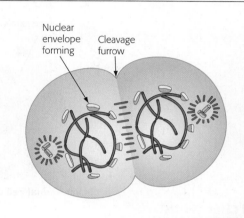

Telophase begins when the two groups of chromosomes have reached opposite ends of the cell. Telophase is the reverse of prophase: Nuclear envelopes form, the chromosomes uncoil, and the spindle disappears. Mitosis, the division of one nucleus into two genetically identical daughter nuclei, is now finished. Cytokinesis, the division of the cytoplasm, usually occurs with telophase. In animals, a cleavage furrow pinches the cell in two, producing two daughter cells.

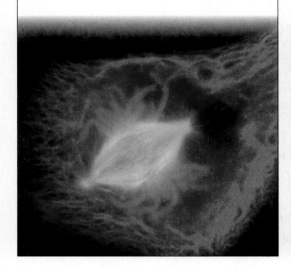

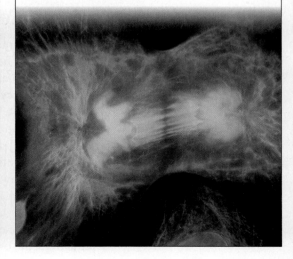

▼ **Figure 8.8** **Cytokinesis in animal and plant cells.**

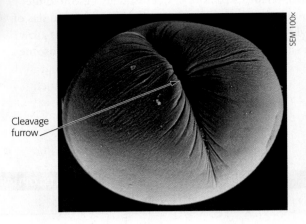

Cleavage
furrow

SEM 100x

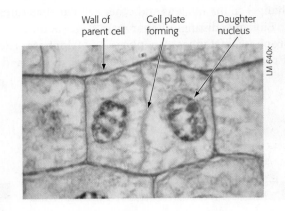

Wall of
parent cell

Cell plate
forming

Daughter
nucleus

LM 640x

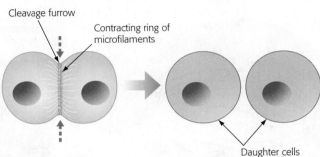

Cleavage furrow

Contracting ring of
microfilaments

Daughter cells

(a) Animal cell cytokinesis

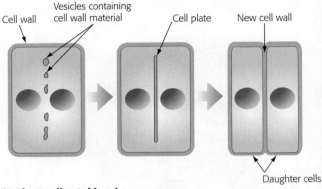

Cell wall

Vesicles containing
cell wall material

Cell plate

New cell wall

Daughter cells

(b) Plant cell cytokinesis

✓ CHECKPOINT

An organism called a
plasmodial slime mold is
one huge cytoplasmic mass
with many nuclei. Explain
how a variation in the cell
cycle could cause this
"monster cell" to arise.

*Answer: Mitosis occurs repeatedly
without cytokinesis*

Cytokinesis, the division of the cytoplasm into two cells, usually begins during telophase, overlapping the end of mitosis. In animal cells, the cytokinesis process is known as cleavage. The first sign of cleavage is the appearance of a **cleavage furrow**, an indentation at the equator of the cell. A ring of microfilaments in the cytoplasm just under the plasma membrane contracts, like the pulling of a drawstring on a hooded sweatshirt, deepening the furrow and pinching the parent cell in two **(Figure 8.8a)**.

Cytokinesis in a plant cell occurs differently. Vesicles containing cell wall material collect at the middle of the cell. The vesicles fuse, forming a membranous disk called the **cell plate**. The cell plate grows outward, accumulating more cell wall material as more vesicles join it. Eventually, the membrane of the cell plate fuses with the plasma membrane, and the cell plate's contents join the parental cell wall. The result is two daughter cells **(Figure 8.8b)**. ✓

Cancer Cells: Growing Out of Control

For a plant or animal to grow and maintain its tissues normally, it must be able to control the timing of cell division. The sequential events of the cell cycle are directed by a **cell cycle control system** that consists of specialized proteins within the cell. These proteins integrate information from the environment and from other body cells and send "stop" and "go-ahead" signals at certain key points during the cell cycle using signal transduction pathways (see Figure 5.19). For example, the cell cycle normally halts within the G_1 phase of interphase unless the cell receives a go-ahead signal via certain cell cycle control proteins. If that signal never arrives, the cell will switch into a permanently nondivididng state. Some of your nerve and muscle cells, for example, are arrested this way. If the go-ahead signal is received and the G_1 checkpoint is passed, the cell will usually complete the rest of the cycle.

What Is Cancer?

Cancer, which currently claims the lives of one out of every five people in the United States and other industrialized nations, is a disease of the cell cycle. Cancer cells do not respond normally to the cell cycle control system; they divide excessively and may invade other tissues of the body. If unchecked, cancer cells may continue to divide until they kill the host.

The abnormal behavior of cancer cells begins when a single cell undergoes transformation, a process that converts a normal cell to a cancer cell. Transformation occurs after a genetic change (mutation) in one or more genes that encode for proteins in the cell cycle control system. Because a transformed cell grows abnormally, the immune system generally recognizes and destroys it. However, if the cell evades destruction, it may proliferate to form a **tumor**, an abnormally growing mass of body cells. If the abnormal cells remain at the original site, the lump is called a **benign tumor**. Benign tumors can cause problems if they grow large and disrupt certain organs, such as the brain, but often they can be completely removed by surgery.

Why are some tumors worse than others?

In contrast, a **malignant tumor** is one that has begun to spread into neighboring tissues and other parts of the body **(Figure 8.9)**, displacing normal tissue and interrupting organ function. An individual with a malignant tumor is said to have **cancer**. Cancer cells may separate from the original tumor or secrete signal molecules that cause blood vessels to grow toward the tumor. A few tumor cells may then enter the blood or lymph vessels and move to other parts of the body, where they may proliferate and form new tumors. The spread of cancer cells beyond their original site is called **metastasis**. Cancers are named according to where they originate. Liver cancer, for example, always begins in liver tissue and may spread from there.

Cancer Treatment

Once a tumor starts growing in the body, how can it be treated? The three main types of cancer treatment are sometimes referred to as "slash, burn, and poison." Surgery to remove a tumor ("slash") is usually the first step. "Burn" and "poison" refer to treatments that attempt to stop cancer cells from dividing. In **radiation therapy** ("burn"), parts of the body that have cancerous tumors are exposed to concentrated beams of high-energy radiation, which can often harm cancer cells more than the normal cells of the body. However, there is sometimes enough damage to normal body cells to produce side effects, such as nausea and hair loss.

Chemotherapy ("poison"), the use of drugs to disrupt cell division, is used to treat widespread or metastatic tumors. Chemotherapy drugs work in a variety of ways. Some prevent cell division by interfering with the mitotic spindle. For example, paclitaxel (trade name Taxol) freezes the spindle after it forms, keeping it from functioning. Paclitaxel is made from a chemical discovered in the bark of the Pacific yew, a tree found mainly in the northwestern United States. It has fewer side effects than many other anticancer drugs and seems to be effective against some hard-to-treat cancers of the ovary and breast. Another drug, vinblastine, prevents the mitotic spindle from forming in the first place. Vinblastine was first obtained from the periwinkle plant, which is native to the tropical rain forests of Madagascar.

Cancer Prevention and Survival

Although cancer can strike anyone, there are certain lifestyle changes you can make to reduce your chances of developing cancer or increase your chances of surviving it. Not smoking, exercising adequately, avoiding overexposure to the sun, and eating a high-fiber, low-fat diet can all help reduce the likelihood of getting cancer. Seven types of cancer can be easily detected: skin and oral (via physical exam), breast (via self-exams or mammograms for higher-risk women), prostate (via rectal exam), cervical (via Pap smear), testicular (via self-exam), and colon (via colonoscopy). Regular visits to the doctor can help identify tumors early, which is the best way to increase the chance of successful treatment. ☑

▼ Figure 8.9 **Growth and metastasis of a malignant tumor of the breast.**

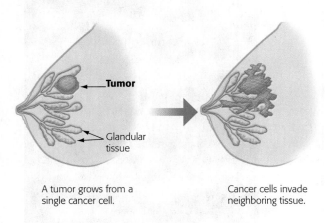

A tumor grows from a single cancer cell.

Cancer cells invade neighboring tissue.

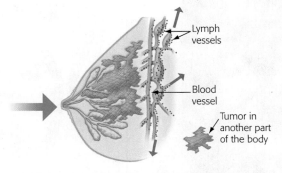

Lymph vessels

Blood vessel

Tumor in another part of the body

Metastasis: Cancer cells spread through lymph and blood vessels to other parts of the body.

Meiosis, the Basis of Sexual Reproduction

Only maple trees produce more maple trees, only goldfish make more goldfish, and only people make more people. These simple facts of life have been recognized for thousands of years and are reflected in the age-old saying, "Like begets like." But in a strict sense, "Like begets like" applies only to asexual reproduction, such as the cutting of the African violet in Figure 8.1. Because the offspring of asexual reproduction inherit all their DNA from a single parent, they are exact genetic replicas of that one parent and of each other, and their appearances are very similar.

How do your chromosomes compare with those of the president?

The family photo in **Figure 8.10** makes the point that in a sexually reproducing species, like does not exactly beget like. You probably resemble your parents more closely than you resemble strangers, but—unless you are an identical twin—you do not look exactly like your parents or your siblings. Each offspring of sexual reproduction inherits a unique combination of genes from its two parents, and this combined set of genes programs a unique combination of traits. As a result, sexual reproduction can produce tremendous variety among offspring.

Sexual reproduction depends on the cellular processes of meiosis and fertilization. But before discussing these processes, we need to return to chromosomes and the role they play in the life cycle of sexually reproducing organisms.

▼ **Figure 8.10 The varied products of sexual reproduction.** Every child inherits a unique combination of genes from his or her parents and displays a unique combination of traits.

Homologous Chromosomes

If we examine cells from different individuals of a single species—sticking to one gender, for now—we find that they have the same number and types of chromosomes. Viewed with a microscope, your chromosomes would look just like those of Angelina Jolie (if you're a woman) or Brad Pitt (if you're a man).

In humans, a typical body cell, called a **somatic cell**, has 46 chromosomes. If you break open a human cell in metaphase of mitosis, stain the chromosomes with dyes, take a picture with the aid of a microscope, and arrange the chromosomes in matching pairs, you produce a display called a **karyotype (Figure 8.11)**. Notice in the figure that each chromosome is duplicated, with two sister chromatids joined at the centromere. Notice also that almost every chromosome has a twin that resembles it in length and centromere position. The two chromosomes of such a matching pair, called **homologous chromosomes**, carry genes controlling the same inherited characteristics. For example, if a gene influencing freckles is located at a particular place on one chromosome—within the yellow band in the drawing in Figure 8.11, for instance—then the homologous chromosome has that same gene in the same location. However, the two homologous chromosomes may have different versions of the same gene. Let's restate this concept: A pair of homologous chromosomes has two nearly identical

▼ **Figure 8.11 Pairs of homologous chromosomes in a male karyotype.** This karyotype shows 22 completely homologous pairs (autosomes) and a 23rd pair that consists of an X chromosome and a Y chromosome (sex chromosomes). With the exception of X and Y, the homologous chromosomes of each pair match in size, centromere position, and staining pattern.

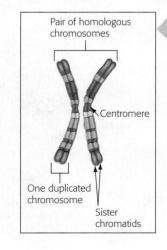

Pair of homologous chromosomes

Centromere

One duplicated chromosome

Sister chromatids

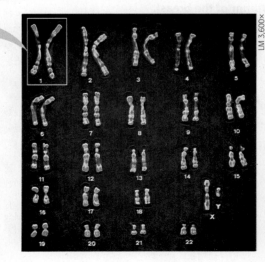

LM 3,600×

chromosomes, each of which consists of two identical sister chromatids after chromosome duplication (see the drawing in Figure 8.11). Altogether, each human has 23 pairs of homologous chromosomes. Other species have different numbers of chromosomes (see Figure 8.2), but those, too, usually match in pairs.

In human females, the 46 chromosomes fall neatly into 23 homologous pairs, with the members of each pair essentially identical in appearance. For a male, however, the chromosomes in one pair do not look alike. This nonmatching pair, only partly homologous, is the male's sex chromosomes. **Sex chromosomes** determine a person's sex (male versus female). In mammals, males have one X chromosome and one Y chromosome. Females have two X chromosomes. (Other organisms have different systems; in this chapter, we focus on humans.) The remaining chromosomes, found in both males and females, are called **autosomes**. For both autosomes and sex chromosomes, we inherit one chromosome of each pair from our mother and the other from our father.

Gametes and the Life Cycle of a Sexual Organism

The **life cycle** of a multicellular organism is the sequence of stages leading from the adults of one generation to the adults of the next. Having two sets of chromosomes, one inherited from each parent, is a key factor in the life cycle of humans and all other species that reproduce sexually. **Figure 8.12** shows the human life cycle, emphasizing the number of chromosomes.

Humans (as well as most other animals and many plants) are said to be **diploid** organisms because all body cells contain pairs of homologous chromosomes. The total number of chromosomes, 46 in humans, is the diploid number (abbreviated $2n$). The exceptions are the gametes, egg and sperm cells. Made by meiosis in an ovary or testis, each gamete has a single set of chromosomes: 22 autosomes plus a sex chromosome, either X or Y. A cell with a single chromosome set is called a **haploid** cell; it has only one member of each pair of homologous chromosomes. For humans, the haploid number, n, is 23.

In the human life cycle, a haploid sperm cell from the father fuses with a haploid egg cell from the mother in a process called **fertilization**. The resulting fertilized egg, called a **zygote**, is diploid. It has two sets of chromosomes, one set from each parent. The life cycle is completed as a sexually mature adult develops from the zygote. Mitotic cell division ensures that all somatic cells of the human body

receive a copy of all of the zygote's 46 chromosomes. Thus, every one of the trillions of cells in your body can trace its ancestry back through mitotic divisions to the single zygote produced when your father's sperm and your mother's egg fused about nine months before you were born.

All sexual life cycles involve an alternation of diploid and haploid stages. Producing haploid gametes by meiosis keeps the chromosome number from doubling in every generation. To illustrate, **Figure 8.13** tracks one pair of homologous chromosomes.

❶ Each of the chromosomes is duplicated during interphase (before mitosis).

❷ The first division, meiosis I, segregates the two chromosomes of the homologous pair, packaging them in separate (haploid) daughter cells. But each chromosome is still doubled. ❸ Meiosis II separates the sister chromatids. Each of the four daughter cells is haploid and contains only a single chromosome from the pair of homologous chromosomes.

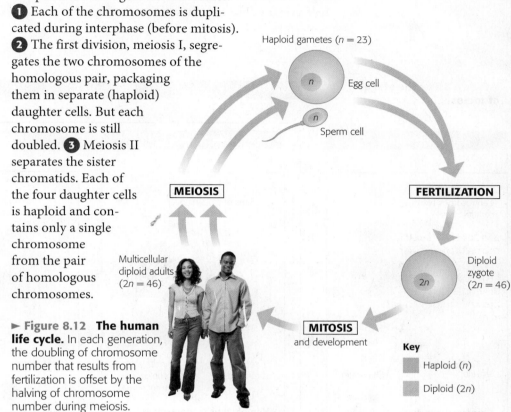

▶ Figure 8.12 **The human life cycle.** In each generation, the doubling of chromosome number that results from fertilization is offset by the halving of chromosome number during meiosis.

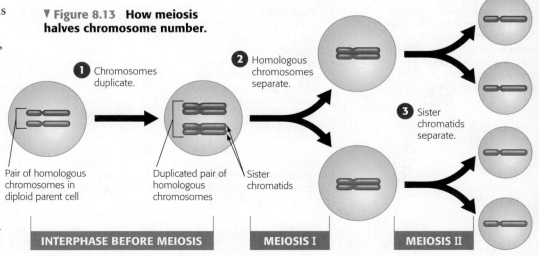

▼ Figure 8.13 **How meiosis halves chromosome number.**

❶ Chromosomes duplicate.

❷ Homologous chromosomes separate.

❸ Sister chromatids separate.

Pair of homologous chromosomes in diploid parent cell

Duplicated pair of homologous chromosomes

Sister chromatids

INTERPHASE BEFORE MEIOSIS

MEIOSIS I

MEIOSIS II

The Process of Meiosis

Meiosis, the process of cell division that produces haploid gametes in diploid organisms, resembles mitosis, but with two special features. The first is that the number of chromosomes is reduced to half. In meiosis, a cell that has duplicated its chromosomes undergoes two consecutive divisions, called meiosis I and meiosis II. Because one duplication of the chromosomes is followed by two divisions, each of the four daughter cells resulting from meiosis has a haploid set of chromosomes—half as many chromosomes as the starting cell.

The second special feature of meiosis is an exchange of genetic material—pieces of chromosomes—between homologous chromosomes. This exchange, called crossing over, occurs during the first prophase of meiosis. We'll look more closely at crossing over later. For now, study **Figure 8.14**, including the text below it, which describes the stages of meiosis in detail for a hypothetical animal cell containing four chromosomes.

As you go through Figure 8.14, keep in mind the difference between homologous chromosomes and sister chromatids: The two chromosomes of a homologous pair are individual chromosomes that were inherited

▼ **Figure 8.14** **The stages of meiosis.**

MEIOSIS I: HOMOLOGOUS CHROMOSOMES SEPARATE

INTERPHASE	PROPHASE I	METAPHASE I	ANAPHASE I

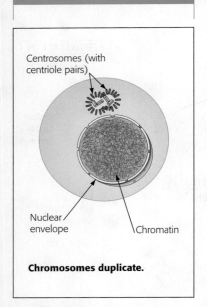

Centrosomes (with centriole pairs)

Nuclear envelope

Chromatin

Chromosomes duplicate.

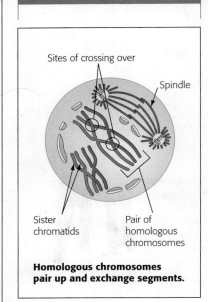

Sites of crossing over

Spindle

Sister chromatids

Pair of homologous chromosomes

Homologous chromosomes pair up and exchange segments.

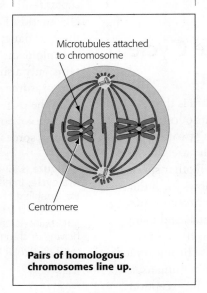

Microtubules attached to chromosome

Centromere

Pairs of homologous chromosomes line up.

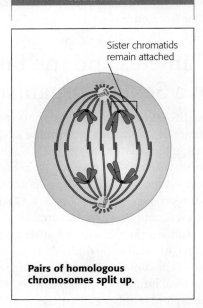

Sister chromatids remain attached

Pairs of homologous chromosomes split up.

Like mitosis, meiosis is preceded by an interphase during which the chromosomes duplicate. Each chromosome then consists of two identical sister chromatids. The chromosomes consist of uncondensed chromatin fibers.

Prophase I As the chromosomes coil up, special proteins cause the homologous chromosomes to stick together in pairs. The resulting structure has four chromatids. Within each set, chromatids of the homologous chromosomes exchange corresponding segments—they "cross over." Crossing over rearranges genetic information.

As prophase I continues, the chromosomes coil up further, a spindle forms, and the homologous pairs are moved toward the center of the cell.

Metaphase I At metaphase I, the homologous pairs are aligned in the middle of the cell. The sister chromatids of each chromosome are still attached at their centromeres, where they are anchored to spindle microtubules. Notice that for each chromosome pair, the spindle microtubules attached to one homologous chromosome come from one pole of the cell, and the microtubules attached to the other chromosome come from the opposite pole. With this arrangement, the homologous chromosomes are poised to move toward opposite poles of the cell.

Anaphase I The attachment between the homologous chromosomes of each pair breaks, and the chromosomes now migrate toward the poles of the cell. *In contrast to mitosis, the sister chromatids migrate as a pair instead of splitting up.* They are separated not from each other but from their homologous partners.

from different parents, one from the mother and one from the father. The members of a pair of homologous chromosomes in Figure 8.14 (and later figures) are identical in size and shape but colored differently (red versus blue) to remind you that they differ in this way. In the interphase just before meiosis, each chromosome duplicates to form sister chromatids that remain together until anaphase of meiosis II. Before crossing over occurs, sister chromatids are identical and carry the same versions of all their genes. ☑

LM 900x

Meiosis II in a lily cell

☑ CHECKPOINT

If a single diploid somatic cell with 18 chromosomes undergoes meiosis and produces sperm, the result will be _____ sperm, each with _____ chromosomes. (Provide two numbers.)

Answer: four, nine

MEIOSIS II: SISTER CHROMATIDS SEPARATE

| TELOPHASE I AND CYTOKINESIS | PROPHASE II | METAPHASE II | ANAPHASE II | TELOPHASE II AND CYTOKINESIS |

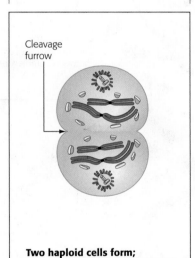

Cleavage furrow

Two haploid cells form; chromosomes are still doubled.

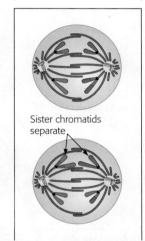

Sister chromatids separate

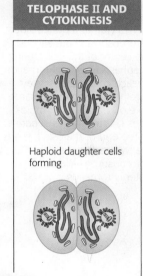

Haploid daughter cells forming

During another round of cell division, the sister chromatids finally separate; four haploid daughter cells result, containing single chromosomes.

Telophase I and Cytokinesis In telophase I, the chromosomes arrive at the poles of the cell. When they finish their journey, each pole has a haploid chromosome set, although each chromosome is still in duplicate form. Usually, cytokinesis occurs along with telophase I, and two haploid daughter cells are formed.

The Process of Meiosis II Meiosis II is essentially the same as mitosis. The important difference is that meiosis II starts with a haploid cell that has *not* undergone chromosome duplication during the preceding interphase.

During prophase II, a spindle forms and moves the chromosomes toward the middle of the cell. During metaphase II, the chromosomes are aligned as they are in mitosis, with the microtubules attached to the sister chromatids of each chromosome coming from opposite poles. In anaphase II, the centromeres of sister chromatids separate, and the sister chromatids of each pair move toward opposite poles of the cell. In telophase II, nuclei form at the cell poles, and cytokinesis occurs at the same time. There are now four haploid daughter cells, each with single chromosomes.

Review: Comparing Mitosis and Meiosis

You have now learned the two ways that cells of eukaryotic organisms divide. Mitosis, which provides for growth, tissue repair, and asexual reproduction, produces daughter cells that are genetically identical to the parent cell. Meiosis, needed for sexual reproduction, yields genetically unique haploid daughter cells—cells with only one member of each homologous chromosome pair.

For both mitosis and meiosis, the chromosomes duplicate only once, in the preceding interphase. Mitosis involves one division of the nucleus and cytoplasm, producing two diploid cells. Meiosis entails two nuclear and cytoplasmic divisions, yielding four haploid cells.

Figure 8.15 compares mitosis and meiosis, tracing these two processes for a diploid parent cell with four

▶ **Figure 8.15 Comparing mitosis and meiosis.** The events unique to meiosis occur during meiosis I: In prophase I, duplicated homologous chromosomes pair along their lengths, and crossing over occurs between homologous (nonsister) chromatids. In metaphase I, pairs of homologous chromosomes (rather than individual chromosomes) are aligned at the center of the cell. During anaphase I, sister chromatids of each chromosome stay together and go to the same pole of the cell as homologous chromosomes separate. At the end of meiosis I, there are two haploid cells, but each chromosome still has two sister chromatids.

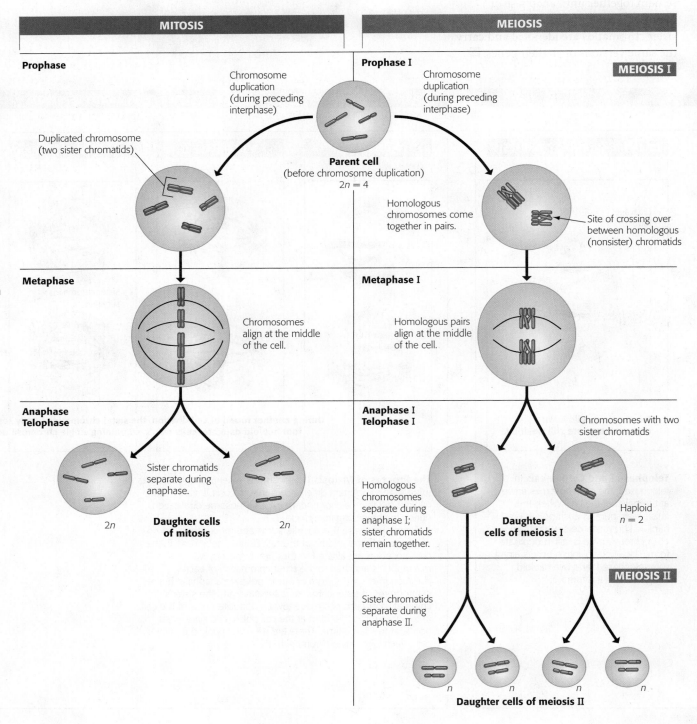

chromosomes. As before, homologous chromosomes are those matching in size. (Imagine that the red chromosomes were inherited from the mother and the blue chromosomes from the father.) Notice that all the events unique to meiosis occur during meiosis I. Meiosis II is virtually identical to mitosis in that it separates sister chromatids. But unlike mitosis, meiosis II yields daughter cells with a haploid set of chromosomes. ☑

The Origins of Genetic Variation

As we discussed earlier, offspring that result from sexual reproduction are genetically different from their parents and from one another. How does meiosis produce such genetic variation?

Independent Assortment of Chromosomes

Figure 8.16 illustrates one way in which meiosis contributes to genetic variety. The figure shows how the arrangement of homologous chromosomes at metaphase of meiosis I affects the resulting gametes. Once again, our example is from a diploid organism with four chromosomes (two pairs of homologous chromosomes), with colors used to differentiate homologous chromosomes (red for chromosomes inherited from the mother and blue for chromosomes from the father).

When aligned during metaphase I, the side-by-side orientation of each homologous pair of chromosomes (consisting of two sister chromatids) is a matter of chance—either the red or blue chromosome may be on the left or right. Thus, in this example, there are two possible ways that the chromosome pairs can align during metaphase I. In possibility 1, the chromosome pairs are oriented with both red chromosomes on the same side (blue/red and blue/red). In this case, each of the gametes produced at the end of meiosis II has only red or only blue chromosomes (combinations a and b). In possibility 2, the chromosome pairs are oriented differently (blue/red and red/blue). This arrangement produces gametes with one red and one blue chromosome (combinations c and d). Thus, with the two possible arrangements shown in this example, the organism will produce gametes with four different combinations of chromosomes. For a species with more than two pairs of chromosomes, such as humans, every chromosome pair orients independently of all the others at metaphase I. (Chromosomes X and Y behave as a homologous pair in meiosis.)

For any species, the total number of chromosome combinations that can appear in gametes is 2^n, where n is the haploid number. For the hypothetical organism in

☑ **CHECKPOINT**

True or false: Both mitosis and meiosis are preceded by chromosome duplication.

Answer: *true*

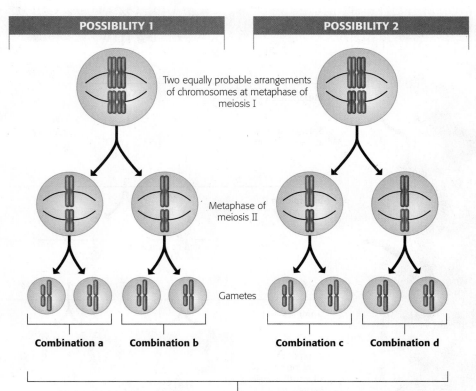

| POSSIBILITY 1 | POSSIBILITY 2 |

Two equally probable arrangements of chromosomes at metaphase of meiosis I

Metaphase of meiosis II

Gametes

Combination a **Combination b** **Combination c** **Combination d**

Because possibilities 1 and 2 are equally likely, the four possible types of gametes will be made in approximately equal numbers.

◄ **Figure 8.16 Results of alternative arrangements of chromosomes at metaphase of meiosis I.** The arrangement of chromosomes at metaphase I determines which chromosomes will be packaged together in the haploid gametes.

Figure 8.16, $n = 2$, so the number of chromosome combinations is 2^2, or 4. For a human ($n = 23$), there are 2^{23}, or about 8 million, possible chromosome combinations! This means that every gamete a person produces contains one of about 8 million possible combinations of maternal and paternal chromosomes.

Random Fertilization

How many possibilities are there when a gamete from one individual unites with a gamete from another individual during fertilization **(Figure 8.17)**? A human egg cell, representing one of about 8 million possibilities, is fertilized at random by one sperm cell, representing one of about 8 million other possibilities. By multiplying 8 million by 8 million, we find that a man and a woman can produce a diploid zygote with any of 64 trillion combinations of chromosomes! So we see that the random nature of fertilization adds a huge amount of potential variability to the offspring of sexual reproduction.

*In what sense are you
1 in 64,000,000,000,000?*

Crossing Over

So far, we have focused on genetic variety in gametes and zygotes at the whole-chromosome level. We'll now take a closer look at **crossing over**, the exchange of corresponding segments between nonsister chromatids of homologous chromosomes, which occurs during prophase I of meiosis. **Figure 8.18** shows crossing over between two homologous chromosomes and the resulting gametes. At the time that crossing over begins, homologous chromosomes are closely paired all along their lengths, with a precise gene-by-gene alignment. The sites of crossing over appear as X-shaped regions; each is called a **chiasma** (plural, *chiasmata*). The homologous chromatids remain attached to each other at chiasmata until anaphase I.

▼ **Figure 8.17 The process of fertilization: a close-up view.** Here you see many human sperm contacting an egg. Only one sperm can add its chromosomes to produce a zygote.

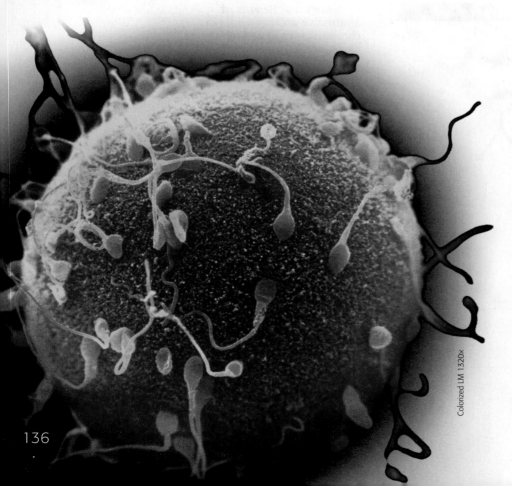

Colorized LM 1320x

▼ **Figure 8.18 The results of crossing over during meiosis for a single pair of homologous chromosomes.** A real cell has multiple pairs of homologous chromosomes that produce a huge variety of recombinant chromosomes in the gametes.

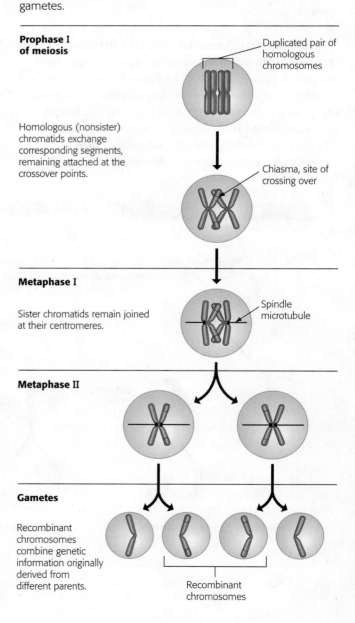

Prophase I of meiosis

Duplicated pair of homologous chromosomes

Homologous (nonsister) chromatids exchange corresponding segments, remaining attached at the crossover points.

Chiasma, site of crossing over

Metaphase I

Sister chromatids remain joined at their centromeres.

Spindle microtubule

Metaphase II

Gametes

Recombinant chromosomes combine genetic information originally derived from different parents.

Recombinant chromosomes

The exchange of segments between nonsister chromatids—one maternal chromatid and one paternal chromatid of a homologous pair—adds to the genetic variety resulting from sexual reproduction. In Figure 8.18, if there were no crossing over, meiosis could produce only two types of gametes. These would be the ones ending up with the "parental" types of chromosomes, either all blue or all red (as in Figure 8.16). With crossing over, gametes arise that have chromosomes that are part red and part blue. These chromosomes are called "recombinant" because they result from **genetic recombination**, the production of gene combinations different from those carried by the parental chromosomes.

Because most chromosomes contain thousands of genes, a single crossover event can affect many genes. When we also consider that multiple crossovers can occur in each pair of homologous chromosomes, it's not surprising that gametes and the offspring that result from them can be so varied. ☑

☑ **CHECKPOINT**

Name two events during meiosis that contribute to genetic variety among gametes. During what stages of meiosis does each occur?

Answer: crossing over between homologous chromosomes during prophase 1 and independent orientation/assortment of the pairs of homologous chromosomes at metaphase 1

Life with and without Sex THE PROCESS OF SCIENCE

Do All Animals Have Sex?

As discussed in the Biology and Society section, some species can reproduce via both sexual and asexual routes. But although some animal species can *also* reproduce asexually, very few animals reproduce *only* asexually. In fact, evolutionary biologists have traditionally considered asexual reproduction an evolutionary dead end (for reasons we'll discuss in the Evolution Connection section at the end of the chapter).

To investigate a case where asexual reproduction seemed to be the norm, researchers from Harvard University studied a group of animals called bdelloid rotifers (**Figure 8.19**). This class of nearly microscopic freshwater invertebrates includes more than 300 known species. Despite hundreds of years of **observations**, no one had ever found bdelloid rotifer males or evidence of sexual reproduction. But the possibility remained that bdelloids had sex very infrequently or that the males were impossible to recognize by appearance. Thus, the Harvard research team posed the **question**, Does this entire class of animals reproduce solely by asexual means?

The researchers formed the **hypothesis** that bdelloid rotifers have indeed thrived for millions of years despite a lack of sexual reproduction. But how to test it? In most species, the two versions of a gene in a pair of homologous chromosomes are very similar due to the constant trading of genes during sexual reproduction. If a species has survived without sex for millions of years, the researchers reasoned, then changes in the DNA sequences of homologous genes should accumulate independently, and the two versions of the genes should have significantly diverged from each other over time. This led to the **prediction** that bdelloid rotifers would display much more variation in their pairs of homologous genes than most organisms.

In a simple but elegant **experiment**, the researchers compared the sequences of a particular gene in bdelloid and non-bdelloid rotifers. Their **results** were striking. Among non-bdelloid rotifers that reproduce sexually, the two homologous versions of the gene were nearly identical, differing by only 0.5% on average. In contrast, the two versions of the same gene in bdelloid rotifers differed by 3.5–54%. These data provided strong evidence that bdelloid rotifers have evolved for millions of years without any sexual reproduction.

▶ **Figure 8.19**
A bdelloid rotifer.

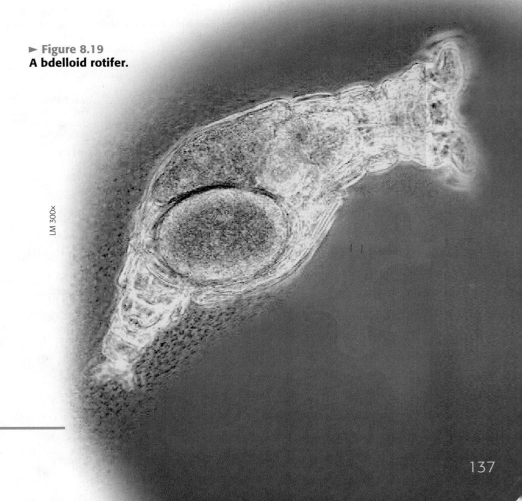

LM 500×

When Meiosis Goes Awry

So far, our discussion of meiosis has focused on the process as it normally and correctly occurs. But what happens when there is an error in the process? Such a mistake can result in genetic abnormalities that range from mild to severe to fatal.

How Accidents during Meiosis Can Alter Chromosome Number

Within the human body, meiosis occurs repeatedly as the testes or ovaries produce gametes. Almost always, the meiotic spindle distributes chromosomes to daughter cells without error. But occasionally there is a mishap, called a **nondisjunction**, in which the members of a chromosome pair fail to separate at anaphase. Nondisjunction can occur during meiosis I or II **(Figure 8.20)**. In either case, gametes with abnormal numbers of chromosomes are the result.

Figure 8.21 shows what can happen when an abnormal gamete produced by nondisjunction unites with a normal gamete during fertilization. When a normal sperm fertilizes an egg cell with an extra chromosome,

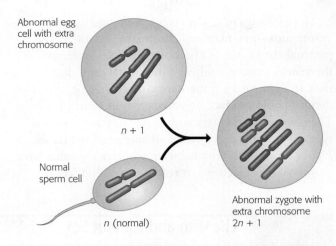

▲ **Figure 8.21   Fertilization after nondisjunction in the mother.**

the result is a zygote with a total of $2n + 1$ chromosomes. Mitosis then transmits the abnormality to all embryonic cells. If the organism survives, it will have an abnormal karyotype and probably a syndrome of disorders caused by the abnormal number of genes. ✓

▼ **Figure 8.20   Two types of nondisjunction.** In both examples in the figure, the cell at the top is diploid (2n), with two pairs of homologous chromosomes.

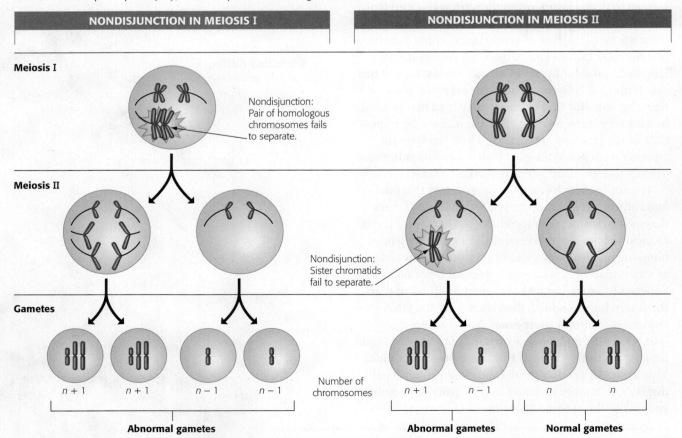

☑ CHECKPOINT

Explain how nondisjunction in meiosis could result in a diploid gamete.

Answer: A diploid gamete would result if there were nondisjunction of all the chromosomes during meiosis I or II.

Down Syndrome: An Extra Chromosome 21

Figure 8.11 showed a normal human complement of 23 pairs of chromosomes. Compare it with the karyotype in **Figure 8.22**; besides having two X chromosomes (because it's from a female), the karyotype in Figure 8.22 has three number 21 chromosomes, making 47 chromosomes in total. This condition is called **trisomy 21**.

In most cases, a human embryo with an atypical number of chromosomes is spontaneously aborted

▼ **Figure 8.22 Trisomy 21 and Down syndrome.** This child displays the characteristic facial features of Down syndrome. The karyotype (bottom) shows trisomy 21; notice the three copies of chromosome 21.

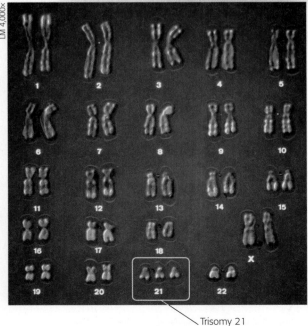

LM 4,000×

Trisomy 21

(miscarried) long before birth. However, some aberrations in chromosome number seem to upset the genetic balance less drastically, and individuals with such abnormalities can survive. These people usually have a characteristic set of symptoms, called a syndrome. A person with trisomy 21 has a condition called **Down syndrome** (named after John Langdon Down, who described it in 1866).

Affecting about 1 out of every 700 children, trisomy 21 is the most common chromosome number abnormality and the most common serious birth defect in the United States. Down syndrome includes characteristic facial features—frequently a fold of skin at the inner corner of the eye, a round face, and a flattened nose—as well as short stature, heart defects, and susceptibility to leukemia and Alzheimer's disease. People with Down syndrome usually have a life span shorter than normal. They also exhibit varying degrees of mental retardation. However, some individuals with the syndrome may live to middle age or beyond, and many are socially adept and can function well within society.

As indicated in **Figure 8.23**, the incidence of Down syndrome in the offspring of normal parents increases markedly with the age of the mother. Down syndrome affects less than 0.05% of children (fewer than 1 in 2,000) born to women under age 30. The risk climbs to 1% (10 in 1,000) for mothers at age 40 and is even higher (80 per 1,000) for women at age 50. Because of this relatively high risk, the fetuses of pregnant women age 35 and older are candidates for testing for trisomy 21 and other chromosomal abnormalities (see Chapter 9). ☑

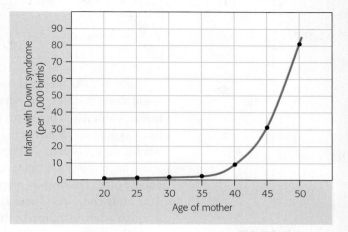

▲ **Figure 8.23 Maternal age and Down syndrome.** The chance of having a baby with Down syndrome rises with the age of the mother.

Abnormal Numbers of Sex Chromosomes

Nondisjunction in meiosis can lead to abnormal numbers of sex chromosomes, X and Y. Unusual numbers of sex chromosomes seem to upset the genetic balance less than unusual numbers of autosomes. This may be because the Y chromosome is very small and carries relatively few genes. Furthermore, mammalian cells normally operate with only one functioning X chromosome because other copies of the chromosome become inactivated in each cell (see Chapter 11).

☑ **CHECKPOINT**

According to Figure 8.23, how much more likely is a 45-year-old woman to have a child with Down syndrome than a 40-year-old woman?

Answer: three times (30 per 1,000 versus 10 per 1,000)

Table 8.1	Abnormalities of Sex Chromosome Number in Humans		
Sex Chromosomes	**Syndrome**	**Origins of Nondisjunction**	**Frequency in Population**
XXY	Klinefelter syndrome (male)	Meiosis in egg or sperm formation	$\frac{1}{2,000}$
XYY	None (normal male)	Meiosis in sperm formation	$\frac{1}{2,000}$
XXX	None (normal female)	Meiosis in egg or sperm formation	$\frac{1}{1,000}$
XO	Turner syndrome (female)	Meiosis in egg or sperm formation	$\frac{1}{5,000}$

Table 8.1 lists the most common human sex chromosome abnormalities. An extra X chromosome in a male, making him XXY, produces a condition called Klinefelter syndrome. If untreated, men with this disorder have male sex organs and normal intelligence, but the testes are abnormally small, the individual is sterile, and he often has breast enlargement and other feminine body contours. These symptoms can be reduced through administration of the sex hormone testosterone. Klinefelter syndrome is also found in individuals with more than three sex chromosomes, such as XXYY, XXXY, or XXXXY. These abnormal numbers of sex chromosomes result from multiple nondisjunctions.

Human males with a single extra Y chromosome (XYY) do not have any well-defined syndrome, although they tend to be taller than average. Females with an extra X chromosome (XXX) cannot be distinguished from XX females except by karyotype.

Females who are lacking an X chromosome are designated XO; the O indicates the absence of a second sex chromosome. These women have Turner syndrome. They have a characteristic appearance, including short stature and often a web of skin extending between the neck and shoulders. Women with Turner syndrome are of normal intelligence, but are sterile. If left untreated, they have poor development of breasts and other secondary sex characteristics. Administration of estrogen can alleviate those symptoms. The XO condition is the sole known case where having only 45 chromosomes is not fatal in humans.

Notice the crucial role of the Y chromosome in determining a person's sex. In general, a single Y chromosome is enough to produce "maleness," regardless of the number of X chromosomes. The absence of a Y chromosome results in "femaleness." ☑

☑ **CHECKPOINT**

Why is an individual more likely to survive with an abnormal number of sex chromosomes than an abnormal number of autosomes?

Answer: because the Y chromosome is very small and extra X chromosomes are inactivated

Life with and without Sex EVOLUTION CONNECTION

▼ **Figure 8.24 Sexual and asexual reproduction.** Many plants, such as this strawberry, have the ability to reproduce both sexually (via flowers that produce fruit) and asexually (via runners).

Runner ⟶

The Advantages of Sex

Throughout this chapter, we've examined cell division within the context of reproduction. Like the Komodo dragon discussed in the Biology and Society section, many species (especially among the plant kingdom) can reproduce both sexually and asexually **(Figure 8.24)**. An important advantage of asexual reproduction is that there is no need for a partner. Asexual reproduction may thus confer an evolutionary advantage when organisms are sparsely distributed (on an isolated island, for example) and unlikely to be able to meet a mate. Furthermore, if an organism is superbly suited to a stable environment, asexual reproduction has the advantage of passing on its entire genetic legacy intact. Asexual reproduction also eliminates the need to expend energy forming gametes and copulating with a partner.

In contrast to plants, the vast majority of animals reproduce by sexual means. There are exceptions, such as the few species that can reproduce via parthenogenesis and the bdelloid rotifers discussed in the Process of Science section. But most animals reproduce only through sex. Therefore, sex must enhance evolutionary fitness. But how? The answer remains elusive. Most hypotheses focus on the unique combinations of genes formed during meiosis and fertilization. By producing offspring of varied genetic makeup, sexual reproduction may enhance survival by speeding adaptation to a changing environment. Another idea is that shuffling genes during sexual reproduction might allow a population to rid itself of harmful genes more rapidly. But for now, one of biology's most basic questions—Why have sex?—remains a hotly debated topic that is the focus of much ongoing research and discussion.

Chapter Review

SUMMARY OF KEY CONCEPTS

 Go to **www.masteringbiology.com** for homework assignments, practice quizzes, Pearson eText, and more.

What Cell Reproduction Accomplishes

Cell reproduction, also called cell division, produces genetically identical daughter cells:

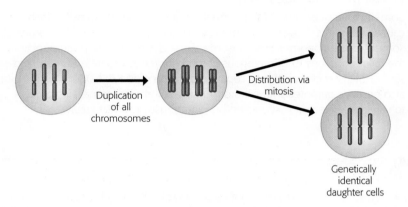

Duplication of all chromosomes

Distribution via mitosis

Genetically identical daughter cells

Some organisms use mitosis (ordinary cell division) to reproduce. This is called asexual reproduction, and it results in offspring that are genetically identical to the lone parent and to each other. Mitosis also enables multicellular organisms to grow and develop and to replace damaged or lost cells. Organisms that reproduce sexually, by the union of a sperm with an egg cell, carry out meiosis, a type of cell division that yields gametes with only half as many chromosomes as body (somatic) cells.

The Cell Cycle and Mitosis

Eukaryotic Chromosomes

The genes of a eukaryotic genome are grouped into multiple chromosomes in the nucleus. Each chromosome contains one very long DNA molecule, with many genes, that is wrapped around histone proteins. Individual chromosomes are coiled up and therefore visible with a light microscope only when the cell is in the process of dividing; otherwise, they are in the form of thin, loosely packed chromatin fibers. Before a cell starts dividing, the chromosomes duplicate, producing sister chromatids (containing identical DNA) joined together at the centromere.

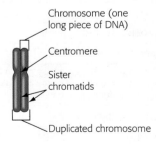

Chromosome (one long piece of DNA)

Centromere

Sister chromatids

Duplicated chromosome

The Cell Cycle

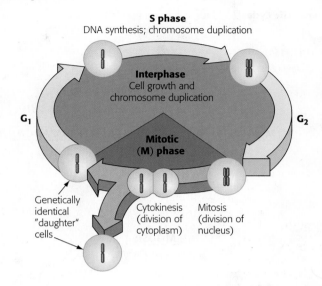

S phase
DNA synthesis; chromosome duplication

Interphase
Cell growth and chromosome duplication

G₁

G₂

Mitotic (M) phase

Genetically identical "daughter" cells

Cytokinesis (division of cytoplasm)

Mitosis (division of nucleus)

Mitosis and Cytokinesis

Mitosis is divided into four phases: prophase, metaphase, anaphase, and telophase. At the start of mitosis, the chromosomes coil up and the nuclear envelope breaks down (prophase). Next, a mitotic spindle made of microtubules moves the chromosomes to the middle of the cell (metaphase). The sister chromatids then separate and are moved to opposite poles of the cell (anaphase), where two new nuclei form (telophase). Cytokinesis overlaps the end of mitosis. In animals, cytokinesis occurs by cleavage, which pinches the cell in two. In plants, a membranous cell plate divides the cell in two. Mitosis and cytokinesis produce genetically identical cells.

Cancer Cells: Growing Out of Control

When the cell cycle control system malfunctions, a cell may divide excessively and form a tumor. Cancer cells may grow to form malignant tumors, invade other tissues (metastasize), and even kill the host. Surgery can remove tumors, and radiation and chemotherapy are effective as treatments because they interfere with cell division. You can increase the likelihood of surviving some forms of cancer through lifestyle changes and regular screenings.

Meiosis, the Basis of Sexual Reproduction

Homologous Chromosomes

The somatic cells (body cells) of each species contain a specific number of chromosomes; human cells have 46, made up of 23 pairs of homologous chromosomes. The chromosomes of a homologous pair carry genes for the same characteristics at the same places. Mammalian males have X and Y sex chromosomes (only partly homologous), while females have two X chromosomes.

Gametes and the Life Cycle of a Sexual Organism

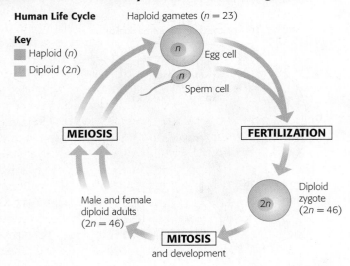

Human Life Cycle

Key
- Haploid (n)
- Diploid ($2n$)

Haploid gametes ($n = 23$)

n Egg cell

n Sperm cell

MEIOSIS

FERTILIZATION

Diploid zygote ($2n = 46$)

Male and female diploid adults ($2n = 46$)

MITOSIS
and development

The Process of Meiosis

Meiosis, like mitosis, is preceded by chromosome duplication. But in meiosis, the cell divides twice to form four daughter cells. The first division, meiosis I, starts with the pairing of homologous chromosomes. In crossing over, homologous chromosomes exchange corresponding segments. Meiosis I separates the members of the homologous pairs and produces two daughter cells, each with one set of (duplicated) chromosomes. Meiosis II is essentially the same as mitosis; in each of the cells, the sister chromatids of each chromosome separate.

Review: Comparing Mitosis and Meiosis

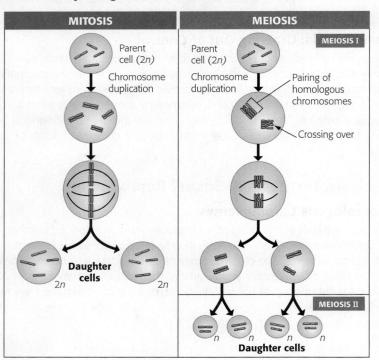

MITOSIS

MEIOSIS

MEIOSIS I

Parent cell ($2n$)

Chromosome duplication

Daughter cells $2n$ $2n$

Parent cell ($2n$)

Chromosome duplication

Pairing of homologous chromosomes

Crossing over

MEIOSIS II

n n n n

Daughter cells

The Origins of Genetic Variation

Because the chromosomes of a homologous pair come from different parents, they carry different versions of many of their genes. The large number of possible arrangements of chromosome pairs at metaphase of meiosis I leads to many different combinations of chromosomes in eggs and sperm. Random fertilization of eggs by sperm greatly increases the variation. Crossing over during prophase of meiosis I increases variation still further.

When Meiosis Goes Awry

Sometimes a person has an abnormal number of chromosomes, which causes problems. Down syndrome is caused by an extra copy of chromosome 21. The abnormal chromosome count is a product of nondisjunction, the failure of a pair of homologous chromosomes to separate during meiosis I or of sister chromatids to separate during meiosis II. Nondisjunction can also produce gametes with extra or missing sex chromosomes, which lead to varying degrees of malfunction but do not usually affect survival.

SELF-QUIZ

1. Which of the following is not a function of mitosis in humans?
   a. repair of wounds
   b. growth
   c. production of gametes from diploid cells
   d. replacement of lost or damaged cells

2. In what sense are the two daughter cells produced by mitosis identical?

3. Why is it difficult to observe individual chromosomes during interphase?

4. A biochemist measures the amount of DNA in cells growing in the laboratory. The quantity of DNA in a cell would be found to double
   a. between prophase and anaphase of mitosis.
   b. between the G_1 and G_2 phases of the cell cycle.
   c. during the M phase of the cell cycle.
   d. between prophase I and prophase II of meiosis.

5. Which two phases of mitosis are essentially opposites in terms of changes in the nucleus?

6. Complete the following table to compare mitosis and meiosis:

	Mitosis	Meiosis
a. Number of chromosomal duplications		
b. Number of cell divisions		
c. Number of daughter cells produced		
d. Number of chromosomes in daughter cells		
e. How chromosomes line up during metaphase		
f. Genetic relationship of daughter cells to parent cells		
g. Functions performed in the human body		

7. A chemical that disrupts microfilament formation would interfere with
   a. DNA replication.
   b. formation of the mitotic spindle.
   c. cleavage.
   d. crossing over.

8. If an intestinal cell in a dog contains 78 chromosomes, a dog sperm cell would contain _____ chromosomes.

9. A micrograph of a dividing cell from a mouse shows 19 chromosomes, each consisting of two sister chromatids. During which stage of meiosis could this picture have been taken? (Explain your answer.)

10. Tumors that remain at their site of origin are called _____, while tumors from which cells migrate to other body tissues are called _____.

11. A diploid body (somatic) cell from a fruit fly contains eight chromosomes. This means that _____ different combinations of chromosomes are possible in its gametes.

12. Although nondisjunction is a random event, there are many more individuals with an extra chromosome 21, which causes Down syndrome, than individuals with an extra chromosome 3 or chromosome 16. Propose an explanation for this.

Answers to these questions can be found in Appendix: Self-Quiz Answers.

THE PROCESS OF SCIENCE

13. A mule is the offspring of a horse and a donkey. A donkey sperm contains 31 chromosomes and a horse egg 32 chromosomes, so the zygote contains a total of 63 chromosomes. The zygote develops normally. The combined set of chromosomes is not a problem in mitosis, and the mule combines some of the best characteristics of horses and donkeys. However, a mule is sterile; meiosis cannot occur normally in its testes or ovaries. Explain why mitosis is normal in cells containing both horse and donkey chromosomes but the mixed set of chromosomes interferes with meiosis.

14. You prepare a slide with a thin slice of an onion root tip. You see the following view in a light microscope. Identify the stage of mitosis for each of the outlined cells, a–d.

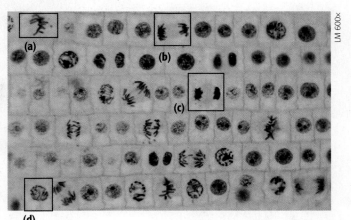

BIOLOGY AND SOCIETY

15. Every year, about a million Americans are diagnosed with cancer. This means that about 75 million Americans now living will eventually have cancer, and one in five will die of the disease. There are many kinds of cancers and many causes of the disease. For example, smoking causes most lung cancers. Overexposure to ultraviolet rays in sunlight causes most skin cancers. There is evidence that a high-fat, low-fiber diet is a factor in breast, colon, and prostate cancers. And agents in the workplace, such as asbestos and vinyl chloride, are also implicated as causes of cancer. Hundreds of millions of dollars are spent each year in the search for effective treatments for cancer, yet far less money is spent on preventing cancer. Why might this be true? What kinds of lifestyle changes can you make to help reduce your risk of cancer? What kinds of prevention programs could be initiated or strengthened to encourage these changes? What factors might impede such changes and programs? Should we devote more of our resources to treating cancer or to preventing it? Defend your position.

16. The practice of buying and selling gametes, particularly eggs from fertile women, is becoming increasingly common in the United States and some other industrialized countries. Do you have any objections to this type of transaction? Would you be willing to sell your gametes? At any price? Whether you are willing to do so or not, do you think that other people should be restricted from doing so?

9 Patterns of Inheritance

Canine genetics.
Dogs, such as these
Labrador retrievers, are
one of humankind's
longest running genetic
experiments.

Dog Breeding BIOLOGY AND SOCIETY

Our Longest-Running Genetic Experiment: Dogs

All of the cute canines shown in the photo on the left are purebred Labrador retrievers. If you were to mate two purebred Labs, you'd expect offspring that look much like these, displaying the traits that distinguish this breed—like a short, water-resistant coat and gentle eyes. This is a reasonable expectation because each purebred dog has a well-documented pedigree that includes several generations of ancestors with similar genetic makeup and appearance. But similarities among purebred Labs extend beyond mere appearance; Labradors are generally sweet tempered, playful, intelligent, and docile—traits that make these dogs the most popular breed in the U.S. and Canada. Such behavioral similarities suggest that dog breeders can select for personality as well as physical traits.

Purebred pooches are living proof that dogs are more than man's best friend: They are also one of our longest-running genetic experiments. Evidence (which we'll explore at the end of this chapter) suggests that people have selected and mated dogs with preferred traits for more than 15,000 years. Nearly every modern Lab, for example, can trace its ancestry back to a single breeding pair—named Avon and Ned—that were raised by the Duke of Buccleuch in England in the 1880s. These original dogs were chosen for their superb ability to retrieve objects from the water, a trait that is very useful to hunters of waterfowl. Similar choices were made for every modern dog breed. Over thousands of years, such genetic tinkering has led to the incredible variety of body types and behaviors we have today, from huge, docile Great Danes to tiny, spunky Chihuahuas.

Although people have been applying genetics for thousands of years—by breeding food crops (such as wheat, rice, and corn) as well as domesticated animals (such as cows, sheep, and goats)—the biological principles underlying genetics have only recently been understood. In this chapter, you will learn the basic rules of how genetic traits are passed from generation to generation and how the behavior of chromosomes (the topic of Chapter 8) accounts for these rules. In the process, you will learn how to predict the ratios of offspring with particular traits. At several points in the chapter, we'll return to the subject of dog breeding to help illustrate genetic principles.

Heritable Variation and Patterns of Inheritance

Heredity is the transmission of traits from one generation to the next. **Genetics**, the scientific study of heredity, began in the 1860s, when an Augustinian monk named Gregor Mendel **(Figure 9.1)** deduced its fundamental principles by breeding garden peas. Mendel lived and worked in an abbey in Brunn, Austria (now Brno, in the Czech Republic). Strongly influenced by his study of physics, mathematics, and chemistry at the University of Vienna, his research was both experimentally and mathematically rigorous, and these qualities were largely responsible for his success.

In a paper published in 1866, Mendel correctly argued that parents pass on to their offspring discrete "heritable factors" that are responsible for inherited traits, such as purple flowers or round seeds in pea plants. (It is interesting to note that Mendel's publication came just seven years after Darwin's 1859 publication of *On the Origin of Species*, making the 1860s a banner decade in the development of modern biology.) In his paper, Mendel stressed that the heritable factors (today called genes) retain their individual identities generation after generation, no matter how they are mixed up or temporarily masked.

▲ **Figure 9.1**
Gregor Mendel.

In an Abbey Garden

Mendel probably chose to study garden peas because they were easy to grow and they came in many readily distinguishable varieties. For example, one variety has purple flowers and another variety has white flowers. A heritable feature that varies among individuals, such as flower color, is called a **character**. Each variant of a character, such as purple or white flowers, is called a **trait**.

Perhaps the most important advantage of pea plants as an experimental model was that Mendel could strictly control their reproduction. The petals of a pea flower **(Figure 9.2)** almost completely enclose the egg-producing part (the carpel) and the sperm-producing parts (the stamens). Consequently, in nature, pea plants usually self-fertilize because sperm-carrying pollen grains released from the stamens land on the tip of the egg-containing carpel of the same flower. Mendel could ensure self-fertilization by covering a flower with a small bag so that no pollen from another plant could

reach the carpel. When he wanted cross-fertilization (fertilization of one plant by pollen from a different plant), he pollinated the plants by hand, as shown in **Figure 9.3**. Thus, whether Mendel let a pea plant self-fertilize or cross-fertilized it with a known source of pollen, he could always be sure of the parentage of his new plants.

Each of the characters Mendel chose to study, such as flower color, occurred in two distinct traits. Mendel worked with his plants until he was sure he had purebred varieties—that is, varieties for which self-fertilization produced offspring all identical to the parent. For instance, he identified a purple-flowered

▼ **Figure 9.2 The structure of a pea flower.** To reveal the reproductive organs—the stamens and carpel—one of the petals has been removed in this drawing.

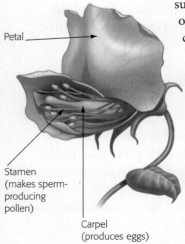

Petal

Stamen (makes sperm-producing pollen)

Carpel (produces eggs)

▼ **Figure 9.3 Mendel's technique for cross-fertilizing pea plants.**

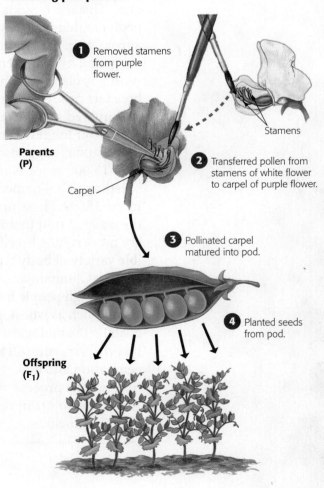

1 Removed stamens from purple flower.

Stamens

Parents (P)

Carpel

2 Transferred pollen from stamens of white flower to carpel of purple flower.

3 Pollinated carpel matured into pod.

4 Planted seeds from pod.

Offspring (F₁)

variety that, when self-fertilized, always produced off-spring plants that had all purple flowers.

Next Mendel was ready to ask what would happen when he crossed different purebred varieties with each other. For example, what offspring would result if plants with purple flowers and plants with white flowers were cross-fertilized as shown in Figure 9.3? The offspring of two different purebred varieties are called **hybrids**, and the cross-fertilization itself is referred to as a genetic **cross**. The parental plants are called the **P generation**, and their hybrid offspring are the **F₁ generation** (F for *filial*, from the Latin for "son" or "daughter"). When F₁ plants self-fertilize or fertilize each other, their offspring are the **F₂ generation**. ☑

Mendel's Law of Segregation

Mendel performed many experiments in which he tracked the inheritance of characters, such as flower color, that occur as two alternative traits **(Figure 9.4)**. The results led him to formulate several hypotheses about inheritance. Let's look at some of his experiments and follow the reasoning that led to his hypotheses.

▼ **Figure 9.4 The seven characters of pea plants studied by Mendel.** Each character comes in the two alternative traits shown here.

	Dominant	Recessive
Flower color	Purple	White
Flower position	Axial	Terminal
Seed color	Yellow	Green
Seed shape	Round	Wrinkled
Pod shape	Inflated	Constricted
Pod color	Green	Yellow
Stem length	Tall	Dwarf

☑ **CHECKPOINT**

Why was the development of purebred pea plant variet-ies critical to Mendel's work?

Answer: *Purebred varieties allowed Mendel to predict the outcome of specific crosses and therefore to run controlled experiments.*

Monohybrid Crosses

Figure 9.5 shows a cross between a purebred pea plant with purple flowers and a purebred pea plant with white flowers. This is called a **monohybrid cross** because the parent plants differ in only one character—flower color. Mendel saw that the F_1 plants all had purple flowers. Was the heritable factor for white flowers now lost as a result of the cross? By mating the F_1 plants with each other, Mendel found the answer to be no. Of the 929 F_2 plants, about three-fourths (705) had purple flowers and one-fourth (224) had white flowers; that is, there were about three purple F_2 plants for every white plant, or a 3:1 ratio of purple to white. Mendel figured out that the heritable factor for white flowers did not disappear in the F_1 plants, but was somehow hidden or masked when the purple-flower factor was present. He also deduced that the F_1 plants must have carried two factors for the flower-color character, one for purple and one for white. From these results and others, Mendel developed four hypotheses, listed here using modern terminology (including "gene" instead of "heritable factor"):

1. *There are alternative versions of genes that account for variations in inherited characters.* For example, the gene for flower color in pea plants exists in one form for purple and another for white. The alternative versions of a gene are called **alleles**.

2. *For each inherited character, an organism inherits two alleles, one from each parent.* These alleles may be the same or different. An organism that has two identical alleles for a gene is said to be **homozygous** for that gene (and is called a homozygote). An organism that has two different alleles for a gene is said to be **heterozygous** for that gene (and is called a heterozygote).

3. *If the two alleles of an inherited pair differ, then one determines the organism's appearance and is called the* **dominant allele**; *the other has no noticeable effect on the organism's appearance and is called the* **recessive allele**. Geneticists use uppercase italic letters to represent dominant alleles and lowercase italic letters to represent recessive alleles.

4. *A sperm or egg carries only one allele for each inherited character because the two alleles for a character segregate (separate) from each other during the production of gametes.* This statement is called the **law of segregation**. When sperm and egg unite at fertilization, each contributes its alleles, restoring the paired condition in the offspring.

Do Mendel's hypotheses account for the 3:1 ratio he observed in the F_2 generation? **Figure 9.6** illustrates Mendel's law of segregation, which explains the inheritance pattern shown in Figure 9.5. His hypotheses predict that when alleles segregate during gamete formation in the F_1 plants, half the gametes will receive a purple-flower allele (P) and the other half a white-flower allele (p). During pollination among the F_1 plants, the gametes unite randomly. An egg with a purple-flower allele has an equal chance of being fertilized by a sperm with a purple-flower allele or one with a white-flower allele (that is, a P egg may fuse with a P sperm or a p sperm). Because the same is true for an egg with a white-flower allele (a p egg with a P sperm or p sperm), there are a total of four equally likely combinations of sperm and egg.

The diagram at the bottom of Figure 9.6, called a **Punnett square**, repeats the cross shown in Figure 9.5 in a way that highlights the four possible combinations of gametes and the resulting four possible offspring in the F_2 generation. Each square represents an equally probable product of fertilization. For example, the box in the upper right corner of the Punnett square shows the genetic combination resulting from a p sperm fertilizing a P egg.

According to the Punnett square, what will be the physical appearance of these F_2 offspring? One-fourth of the plants have two alleles specifying purple flowers (PP); clearly, these plants will have purple flowers. One-half (two-fourths) of the F_2 offspring have

▼ **Figure 9.5 Mendel's cross tracking one character (flower color).** Note the 3:1 ratio of purple flowers to white flowers in the F_2 generation.

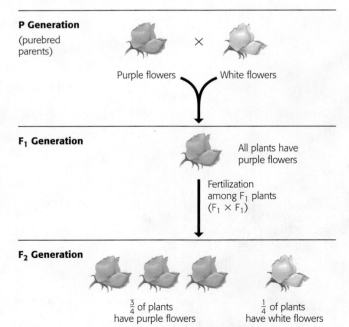

P Generation
(purebred parents)

Purple flowers × White flowers

F_1 Generation

All plants have purple flowers

Fertilization among F_1 plants ($F_1 \times F_1$)

F_2 Generation

$\frac{3}{4}$ of plants have purple flowers

$\frac{1}{4}$ of plants have white flowers

Figure 9.6 The law of segregation.

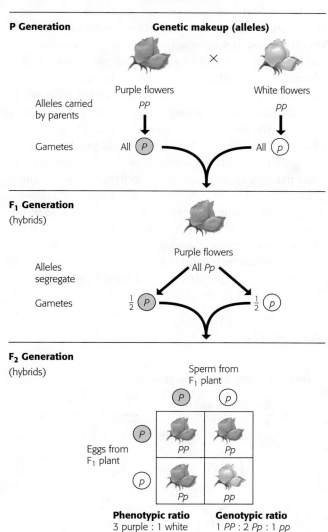

P Generation

Genetic makeup (alleles)

Purple flowers
PP

White flowers
pp

Alleles carried by parents

Gametes   All (P)   All (p)

F₁ Generation
(hybrids)

Purple flowers
All *Pp*

Alleles segregate

Gametes   ½ (P)   ½ (p)

F₂ Generation
(hybrids)

Sperm from F₁ plant
(P)   (p)

Eggs from F₁ plant
(P)
PP   *Pp*
(p)
Pp   *pp*

Phenotypic ratio   **Genotypic ratio**
3 purple : 1 white   1 *PP* : 2 *Pp* : 1 *pp*

Mendel found that each of the seven characters he studied had the same inheritance pattern: A parental trait disappeared in the F₁ generation, only to reappear in one-fourth of the F₂ offspring. The underlying mechanism is stated by Mendel's law of segregation: Pairs of alleles segregate (separate) during gamete formation; the fusion of gametes at fertilization creates allele pairs again. Research since Mendel's day has established that the law of segregation applies to all sexually reproducing organisms, including dogs and people.

Genetic Alleles and Homologous Chromosomes

Before continuing with Mendel's experiments, let's see how some of the concepts we discussed earlier (in Chapter 8) fit with what we've said about genetics so far. The diagram in **Figure 9.7** shows a pair of homologous chromosomes—chromosomes that carry alleles of the same genes. Recall that every diploid cell, whether from a pea plant or a person, has pairs of homologous chromosomes. One member of each pair comes from the organism's female parent and the other member of each pair comes from the male parent. Each labeled band on the chromosomes in the figure represents a gene **locus** (plural, *loci*), a specific location of a gene along the chromosome. You can see the connection between Mendel's law of segregation and homologous chromosomes: Alleles (alternative versions) of a gene reside at the same locus on homologous chromosomes. However, the two chromosomes may bear either identical alleles or different ones at any one locus. In other words, the organisms may be homozygous or heterozygous for the gene at that locus. We will return to the chromosomal basis of Mendel's law later in the chapter. ✓

✓ **CHECKPOINT**

1. Genes come in different versions called _____. What term describes the condition where the two copies are identical? What term describes the condition where the two copies are different?
2. If two plants have the same genotype, must they have the same phenotype? If two plants have the same phenotype, must they have the same genotype?
3. You carry two alleles for every trait. Where did these alleles come from?

Answers: 1. alleles; homozygous; heterozygous 2. Yes. No, one could be homozygous for the dominant allele, while the other is heterozygous. 3. One is from your father via his sperm and one is from your mother via her egg.

inherited one allele for purple flowers and one allele for white flowers (*Pp*); like the F₁ plants, these plants will also have purple flowers, the dominant trait. (Note that *Pp* and *pP* are equivalent and usually written as *Pp*.) Finally, one-fourth of the F₂ plants have inherited two alleles specifying white flowers (*pp*) and will express this recessive trait. Thus, Mendel's model accounts for the 3:1 ratio that he observed in the F₂ generation.

Geneticists distinguish between an organism's physical appearance, called its **phenotype** (such as purple or white flowers), and its genetic makeup, called its **genotype** (in our example, *PP*, *Pp*, or *pp*). Now we can see that Figure 9.5 shows only the phenotypes and Figure 9.6 both the genotypes and phenotypes in our sample cross. For the F₂ plants, the ratio of plants with purple flowers to those with white flowers (3:1) is called the phenotypic ratio. The genotypic ratio is 1(*PP*):2(*Pp*):1(*pp*).

Figure 9.7 The relationship between alleles and homologous chromosomes.
The matching colors of corresponding loci highlight the fact that homologous chromosomes carry alleles for the same genes at the same positions along their lengths.

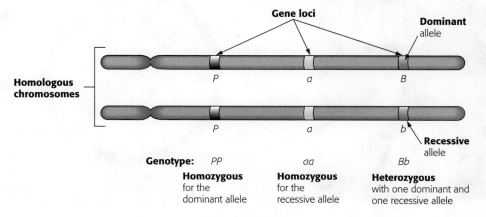

Gene loci

Dominant allele

Homologous chromosomes

P   *a*   *B*

P   *a*   *b*

Recessive allele

Genotype: *PP*   *aa*   *Bb*

Homozygous for the dominant allele

Homozygous for the recessive allele

Heterozygous with one dominant and one recessive allele

Mendel's Law of Independent Assortment

Two other pea plant characters Mendel studied were seed shape and seed color. Mendel's seeds were either round or wrinkled in shape and either yellow or green in color. From tracking these characters one at a time in monohybrid crosses, Mendel knew that the allele for round shape (designated R) was dominant to the allele for wrinkled shape (r) and that the allele for yellow seed color (Y) was dominant to the allele for green seed color (y). What would result from a **dihybrid cross**, the mating of parental varieties differing in two characters? Mendel crossed homozygous plants having round-yellow seeds (genotype $RRYY$) with plants having wrinkled-green seeds ($rryy$). As shown in **Figure 9.8**, the union of RY and ry gametes from the P generation yielded

hybrids heterozygous for both characters ($RrYy$)—that is, dihybrids. As we would expect, all of these offspring, the F_1 generation, had round-yellow seeds (the two dominant traits). But were the two characters transmitted from parents to offspring as a package, or was each character inherited independently of the other?

The question was answered when Mendel allowed fertilization to occur among the F_1 plants. If the genes for the two characters were inherited together (Figure 9.8a), then the F_1 hybrids would produce only the same two kinds of gametes that they received from their parents. In that case, the F_2 generation would show a 3:1 phenotypic ratio (three plants with round-yellow seeds for every one with wrinkled-green seeds), as in the Punnett square in Figure 9.8a. If, however, the two seed characters sorted independently, then the F_1 generation would produce four gamete genotypes—RY, rY, Ry, and ry—in equal quantities. The Punnett square in

▼ **Figure 9.8 Testing alternative hypotheses for gene assortment in a dihybrid cross.**

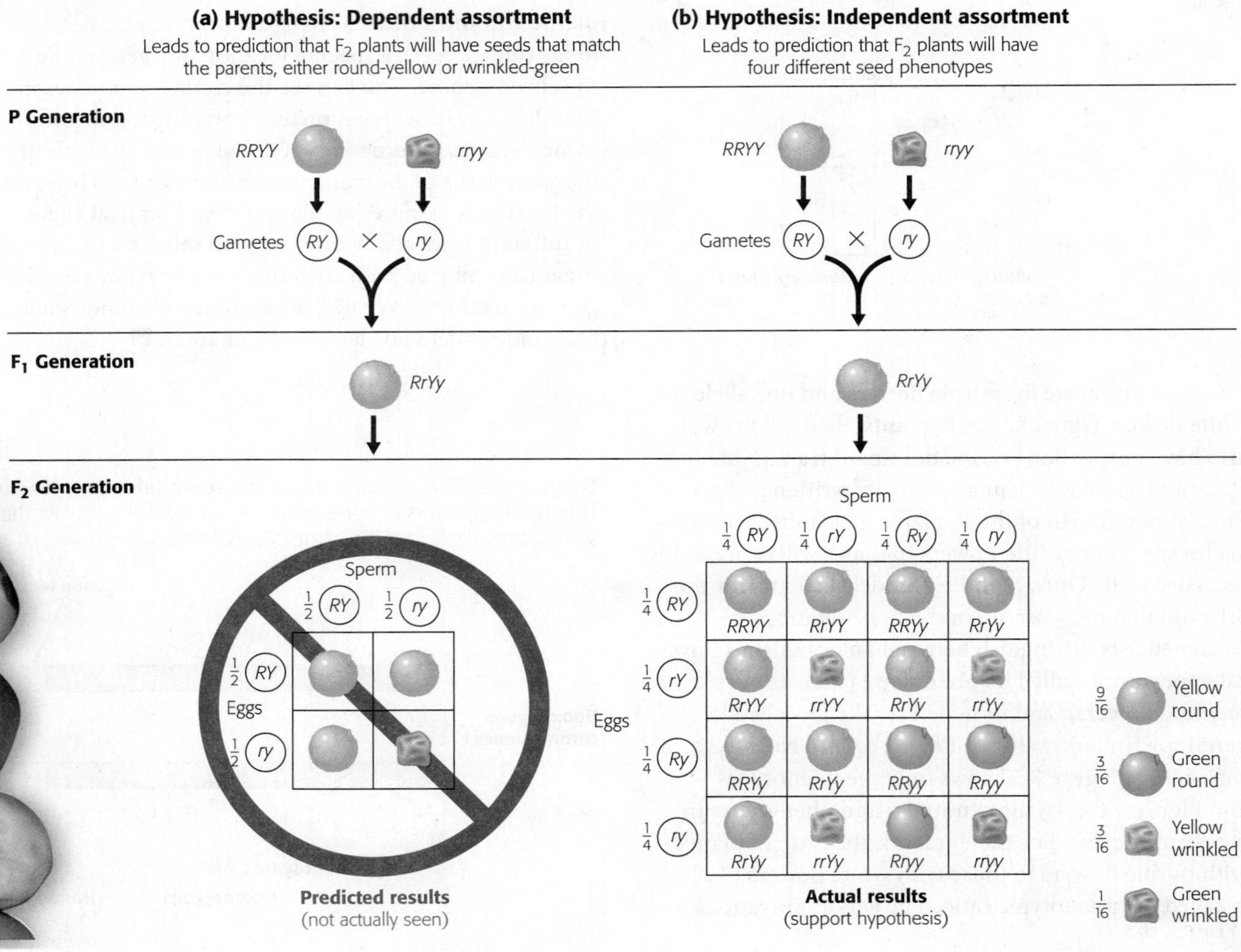

(a) Hypothesis: Dependent assortment
Leads to prediction that F_2 plants will have seeds that match the parents, either round-yellow or wrinkled-green

(b) Hypothesis: Independent assortment
Leads to prediction that F_2 plants will have four different seed phenotypes

P Generation

F₁ Generation

F₂ Generation

Predicted results
(not actually seen)

Actual results
(support hypothesis)

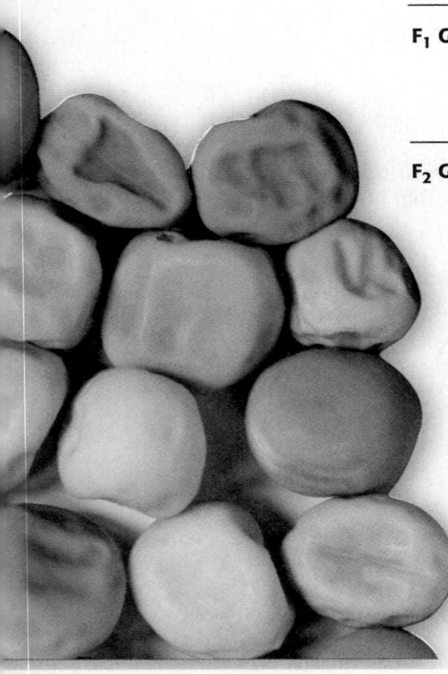

$\frac{9}{16}$ Yellow round

$\frac{3}{16}$ Green round

$\frac{3}{16}$ Yellow wrinkled

$\frac{1}{16}$ Green wrinkled

Figure 9.8b shows all possible combinations of alleles that can result in the F₂ generation from the union of four kinds of sperm with four kinds of eggs. If you study the Punnett square, you'll see that it predicts nine different genotypes in the F₂ generation. These nine genotypes will produce four different phenotypes in a ratio of 9:3:3:1.

The Punnett square in Figure 9.8b also reveals that a dihybrid cross is equivalent to two monohybrid crosses occurring simultaneously. From the 9:3:3:1 ratio, we can see that there are 12 plants with round seeds compared to 4 with wrinkled seeds, and 12 yellow-seeded plants compared to four green-seeded ones. These 12:4 ratios each reduce to 3:1, which is the F₂ ratio for a monohybrid cross. Mendel tried his seven pea characters in various dihybrid combinations and always observed a 9:3:3:1 ratio (or two simultaneous 3:1 ratios) of phenotypes in the F₂ generation. These results supported the hypothesis that *each pair of alleles segregates independently of the other pairs of alleles during gamete formation.* In other words, the inheritance of one character has no effect on the inheritance of another. This is called Mendel's **law of independent assortment**.

For another application of the law of independent assortment, examine **Figure 9.9**. The inheritance of two hereditary characters in Labrador retrievers is controlled by separate genes: black versus chocolate coat color, and normal vision versus the eye disorder progressive retinal atrophy (PRA). Black Labs have at least one copy of an allele called *B*, which gives their hairs densely packed granules of a dark pigment. The *B* allele is dominant to *b*, which leads to a less tightly packed distribution of pigment granules. As a result, the coats of dogs with genotype *bb* are chocolate in color. The allele that causes PRA, called *n*, is recessive to allele *N*, which is necessary for normal vision. Thus, only dogs of genotype *nn* become blind from PRA. If you mate two doubly heterozygous (*BbNn*) Labs (bottom of Figure 9.9), the phenotypic ratio of the offspring (F₂) is 9:3:3:1. These results resemble the F₂ results in Figure 9.8, demonstrating that the coat color and PRA genes are inherited independently. ☑

Why are there fewer chocolate Labs than black Labs?

▼ **Figure 9.9 Independent assortment of genes in Labrador retrievers.**
Blanks in the genotypes indicate alleles that can be either dominant or recessive.

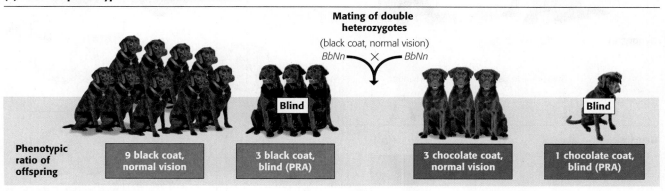

Phenotypes	Black coat, normal vision	Black coat, blind (PRA)	Chocolate coat, normal vision	Chocolate coat, blind (PRA)
Genotypes	*B_N_*	*B_nn*	*bbN_*	*bbnn*

(a) Possible phenotypes of Labrador retrievers

Mating of double heterozygotes
(black coat, normal vision)
BbNn — ✕ — *BbNn*

Phenotypic ratio of offspring	9 black coat, normal vision	3 black coat, blind (PRA)	3 chocolate coat, normal vision	1 chocolate coat, blind (PRA)

(b) A Labrador dihybrid cross

151

Using a Testcross to Determine an Unknown Genotype

Suppose you have a Labrador retriever with a chocolate coat. Consulting Figure 9.9, you can tell that its genotype must be *bb*, the only combination of alleles that produces the chocolate-coat phenotype. But what if you have a black Lab? It could have one of two possible genotypes—*BB* or *Bb*—and there is no way to tell which genotype is the correct one by looking at the dog. To determine your dog's genotype, you could perform a **testcross**, a mating between an individual of dominant phenotype but unknown genotype (your black Lab) and a homozygous recessive individual—in this case, a *bb* chocolate Lab.

Figure 9.10 shows the offspring that could result from such a mating. If, as shown on the left, the black Lab parent's genotype is *BB*, we would expect all the offspring to be black, because a cross between genotypes *BB* and *bb* can produce only *Bb* offspring. On the other hand, if the black Lab parent is *Bb*, we would expect both black (*Bb*) and chocolate (*bb*) offspring. Thus, the appearance of the offspring may reveal the original black dog's genotype. ☑

The Rules of Probability

Mendel's strong background in mathematics served him well in his studies of inheritance. For instance, he understood that genetic crosses obey the rules of probability—the same rules that apply to the tossing of coins, the rolling of dice, and the drawing of cards. An important lesson we can learn from coin tossing is that for each and every toss of the coin, the probability of heads is $\frac{1}{2}$. Even if heads has landed five times in a row, the probability of the next toss coming up heads is still $\frac{1}{2}$. In other words, the outcome of any particular toss is unaffected by what has happened on previous attempts. Each toss is an independent event.

If two coins are tossed simultaneously, the outcome for each coin is an independent event, unaffected by the other coin. What is the chance that both coins will land heads-up? The probability of such a dual event is the product of the separate probabilities of the independent events—for the coins, $\frac{1}{2} \times \frac{1}{2} = \frac{1}{4}$. This is called the **rule of multiplication**, and it holds true for independent events that occur in genetics as well as coin tosses, as shown in **Figure 9.11**. In our dihybrid cross of Labradors (see

▼ **Figure 9.11 Segregation of alleles and fertilization as chance events.** When heterozygotes (*Bb*) form gametes, segregation of alleles during sperm and egg formation is like two separately tossed coins (that is, two independent events).

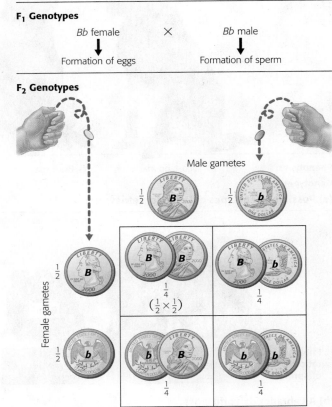

F₁ Genotypes

Bb female   ×   *Bb* male

Formation of eggs   Formation of sperm

F₂ Genotypes

Male gametes

Female gametes

▼ **Figure 9.10 A Labrador retriever testcross.** To determine the genotype of a black Lab, it can be crossed with a chocolate Lab (homozygous recessive, *bb*). If all the offspring are black, the black parent most likely had genotype *BB*. If half the offspring are chocolate, the black parent must be heterozygous (*Bb*).

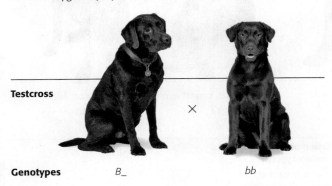

Testcross

Genotypes   *B_*   ×   *bb*

Two possible genotypes for the black dog:

BB   or   *Bb*

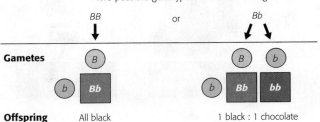

Gametes

Offspring   All black   1 black : 1 chocolate

☑ **CHECKPOINT**

If you mate a chocolate Lab with a black Lab of unknown genotype and you end up with a litter of three black puppies, do you know for certain the genotype of the black parent?

Answer: No. It could be BB and would always produce black puppies or Bb and just happened to have three black puppies in a row. Producing more puppies would increase confidence in the result.

Figure 9.9), the genotype of the F$_1$ dogs for coat color was *Bb*. What is the probability that a particular F$_2$ dog will have the *bb* genotype? To produce a *bb* offspring, both egg and sperm must carry the *b* allele. The probability that an egg from a *Bb* dog will have the *b* allele is $\frac{1}{2}$, and the probability that a sperm will have the *b* allele is also $\frac{1}{2}$. By the rule of multiplication, the probability that two *b* alleles will come together at fertilization is $\frac{1}{2} \times \frac{1}{2} = \frac{1}{4}$. This is exactly the answer given by the Punnett square in Figure 9.11. If we know the genotypes of the parents, we can predict the probability for any genotype among the offspring. By applying the rules of probability to segregation and independent assortment, we can solve some rather complex genetics problems. ☑

Family Pedigrees

Mendel's laws apply to the inheritance of many human traits. **Figure 9.12** illustrates alternative forms of three human characters that are each thought to be determined by simple dominant-recessive inheritance of one gene. (The genetic basis of many other human characters—such as eye and hair color—are much more complex and poorly understood.) If we call the dominant allele of any such gene *A*, the dominant phenotype results from either the homozygous genotype *AA* or the heterozygous genotype *Aa*. Recessive phenotypes result only from the homozygous genotype *aa*. In genetics, the word *dominant* does not imply that a phenotype is either normal or more common than a recessive phenotype; **wild-type traits** (those seen most often in nature) are not necessarily specified by dominant alleles. In genetics, dominance means that a heterozygote (*Aa*), carrying only a single copy of a dominant allele, displays the dominant phenotype. By contrast, the phenotype of the corresponding recessive allele is seen only in a homozygote (*aa*). Recessive traits may in fact be more common in the population than dominant ones. For example, the absence of freckles is more common than their presence.

How can human genetics be studied? Researchers working with pea plants or Labrador retrievers can perform test-crosses. But geneticists who study people obviously cannot control the mating of their research participants. Instead, they must analyze the results of matings that have already occurred. First, the geneticist collects as much information as possible about a family's history for a trait. Then the researcher assembles this information into a family tree, called a **pedigree**. (You may associate pedigrees with purebred animals such as racehorses and champion dogs, but they

Is your earlobe trait dominant or recessive?

☑ CHECKPOINT

Using a standard 52-card deck, what is the probability of being dealt an ace? What about being dealt an ace or a king? What about being dealt an ace and then another ace?

Answer: $\frac{1}{13}$ (4 aces / 52 cards); $\frac{2}{13}$ $(\frac{4}{52} + \frac{4}{52})$; $\frac{4}{52} \times \frac{3}{51}$ (since there are 3 aces left in a deck with 51 cards remaining) $= 0.0045$, or $\frac{1}{221}$

◄ **Figure 9.12 Examples of inherited human traits thought to be controlled by a single gene.**

DOMINANT TRAITS

Freckles

Widow's peak

Free earlobe

RECESSIVE TRAITS

No freckles

Straight hairline

Attached earlobe

can represent human matings just as well.) To analyze a pedigree, the geneticist applies logic and Mendel's laws.

Let's apply this approach to the example in **Figure 9.13**, a pedigree tracing the incidence of free versus attached earlobes. The letter *F* stands for the dominant allele for free earlobes, and *f* symbolizes the recessive allele for attached earlobes. In the pedigree, □ represents a male, ○ represents a female, colored symbols (■ and ●) indicate that the person has the trait being investigated (in this case, attached earlobes), and an unshaded symbol represents a person who does not have the trait (that person has free earlobes). The earliest (oldest) generation is at the top of the pedigree, and the most recent generation is at the bottom.

By applying Mendel's laws, we can deduce that the attached allele is recessive because that is the only way that Kevin can have attached earlobes when neither of his parents (Hal and Ina) do. We can therefore label all the individuals with attached earlobes in the pedigree (that is, all those with colored circles or squares) as homozygous recessive (*ff*).

Mendel's laws enable us to deduce the genotypes for most of the people in the pedigree. For example, Hal and Ina must have carried the *f* allele (which they passed on to Kevin) along with the *F* allele that gave them free earlobes. The same must be true of Aaron and Betty because they both have free earlobes but Fred and Gabe have attached earlobes. For each of these cases, Mendel's laws and simple logic allow us to definitively assign a genotype.

Notice that we cannot deduce the genotype of every member of the pedigree. For example, Lisa must have at least one *F* allele, but she could be *FF* or *Ff*. We cannot distinguish between these two possibilities using the available data. Perhaps future generations will provide the data that solves this mystery. ☑

Human Disorders Controlled by a Single Gene

The human genetic disorders listed in **Table 9.1** are known to be inherited as dominant or recessive traits controlled by a single gene. These disorders therefore show simple inheritance patterns like the ones Mendel studied in pea plants. The genes involved are all located on autosomes, chromosomes other than the sex chromosomes X and Y.

Recessive Disorders

Most human genetic disorders are recessive. They range in severity from harmless to life-threatening. Most people who have recessive disorders are born to normal parents who are both heterozygotes—that is, parents who are **carriers** of the recessive allele for the disorder but appear normal themselves.

Using Mendel's laws, we can predict the fraction of affected offspring that is likely to result from a marriage between two carriers. Consider a form of inherited deafness caused by a recessive allele. Suppose two heterozygous carriers (*Dd*) have a child. What is the probability that the child will be deaf? As the Punnett square in

▼ **Figure 9.13 A family pedigree showing inheritance of free versus attached earlobes.**

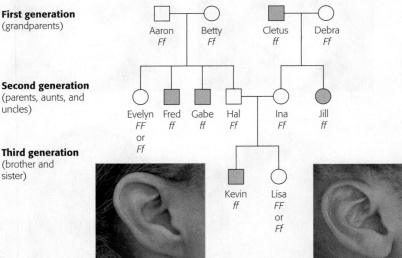

First generation (grandparents)

Aaron *Ff* — Betty *Ff*   Cletus *ff* — Debra *Ff*

Second generation (parents, aunts, and uncles)

Evelyn *FF* or *Ff*   Fred *ff*   Gabe *ff*   Hal *Ff*   Ina *Ff*   Jill *ff*

Third generation (brother and sister)

Kevin *ff*   Lisa *FF* or *Ff*

Female   Male

● ○   ■ □ Attached

○   □ Free

Table 9.1 Some Autosomal Disorders in People

Disorder	Major Symptoms	Incidence
Recessive Disorders		
Albinism	Lack of pigment in skin, hair, and eyes	$\frac{1}{22,000}$
Cystic fibrosis	Excess mucus in lungs, digestive tract, liver; increased susceptibility to infections; death in early childhood unless treated	$\frac{1}{1,800}$ European Americans
Phenylketonuria (PKU)	Accumulation of phenylalanine in blood; lack of normal skin pigment; mental retardation unless treated	$\frac{1}{100,000}$ in U.S. and Europe
Sickle-cell disease	Sickled red blood cells; damage to many tissues	$\frac{1}{500}$ African Americans
Tay Sachs disease	Lipid accumulation in brain cells; mental deficiency; blindness; death in childhood	$\frac{1}{3,500}$ European Jews
Dominant Disorders		
Achondroplasia	Dwarfism	$\frac{1}{25,000}$
Alzheimer's disease (one type)	Mental deterioration; usually strikes late in life	Not known
Huntington's disease	Mental deterioration and uncontrollable movements; strikes in middle age	$\frac{1}{25,000}$
Hypercholesterolemia	Excess cholesterol in blood; heart disease	$\frac{1}{500}$

Figure 9.14 shows, each child of two carriers has a $\frac{1}{4}$ chance of inheriting two recessive alleles. Thus, we can say that about one-fourth of the children of this couple are likely to be deaf. We can also say that a hearing child from such a family has a $\frac{2}{3}$ chance of being a carrier (that is, on average, two out of three of the offspring with the hearing phenotype will be *Dd*). We can apply this same method of pedigree analysis and prediction to any genetic trait controlled by a single gene.

The most common lethal genetic disease in the United States is **cystic fibrosis (CF)**. Affecting about 30,000 Americans and about 70,000 people worldwide, the recessive CF allele is carried by about 1 in 31

▼ **Figure 9.14 Predicted offspring when both parents are carriers for a recessive disorder.**

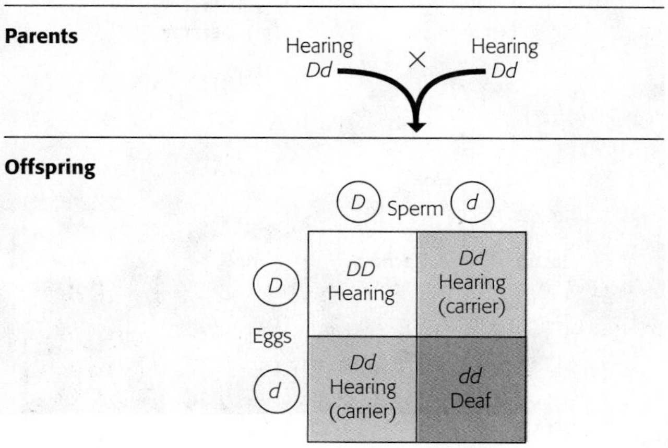

Americans. A person with two copies of this allele has cystic fibrosis, which is characterized by an excessive secretion of very thick mucus from the lungs, pancreas, and other organs. This mucus can interfere with breathing, digestion, and liver function and makes the person vulnerable to recurrent bacterial infections. Although there is no cure for this fatal disease, a special diet, antibiotics to prevent infection, frequent pounding of the chest and back to clear the lungs, and other treatments can greatly extend life. Once invariably fatal in childhood, advances in CF treatment have raised the median survival age of Americans with CF to 37.

Like cystic fibrosis, most genetic disorders are not evenly distributed across all ethnic groups. Such uneven distribution is the result of prolonged geographic isolation of certain populations. For example, the isolated lives of the early inhabitants of Martha's Vineyard (an island off the coast of Massachusetts) led to frequent marriages between blood relatives. Consequently, the frequency of an allele that caused deafness was high, and the deafness allele was rarely transmitted to outsiders.

With the increased mobility in most societies today, it is relatively unlikely that two carriers of a rare, harmful allele will meet and mate. However, the probability increases greatly if close blood relatives marry and have children. People with recent common ancestors are more likely to carry the same recessive alleles than are unrelated people. Therefore, a mating between close blood relatives, called **inbreeding**, is more likely to produce offspring homozygous for a harmful recessive trait.

Genetically speaking, why is it a bad idea to marry your first cousin?

Geticists have observed an increased incidence of harmful recessive traits among many types of inbred animals. Most lines of purebred dogs have known genetic defects. The Labrador retrievers discussed in the Biology and Society section, for example, are susceptible to hip dysplasia as well as blindness. The detrimental effects of inbreeding are also seen in some endangered species, such as cheetahs (see Chapter 13).

Dominant Disorders

A number of human disorders are caused by dominant alleles. Some are harmless, such as extra fingers and toes or digits that are webbed. A serious but nonlethal disorder caused by a dominant allele is **achondroplasia**, a form of dwarfism in which the head and torso develop normally but the arms and legs are short **(Figure 9.15)**. The homozygous dominant genotype (*AA*) causes death of the embryo, and therefore only heterozygotes (*Aa*), individuals with a single copy of the defective allele, have this disorder. This also means that a person with achondroplasia has a 50% chance of passing the condition on to any children **(Figure 9.16)**. Therefore, all those who do not have achondroplasia, more than 99.99% of the population, are homozygous for the recessive allele (*aa*). This example makes it clear that a dominant allele is not necessarily more common in a population than the corresponding recessive allele.

Dominant alleles that cause lethal disorders are much less common than lethal recessive alleles. One example is the allele that causes **Huntington's disease**, a degeneration of the nervous system that usually does not begin until middle age. Once the deterioration of the nervous system begins, it is irreversible and inevitably fatal. Because the allele for Huntington's disease is dominant, any child born to a parent with the allele has a 50% chance of inheriting the allele and the disorder. This example makes it clear that a dominant allele is not necessarily "better" than the corresponding recessive allele.

One way that geneticists study human traits is to find similar genes in animals, which can then be studied in greater detail through controlled matings and other experiments. Let's return to the chapter thread—dog breeding—to investigate the furry coats of man's best friend.

▼ **Figure 9.15**
Achondroplasia, a dominant trait.
Dr. Michael C. Ain, a pediatric orthopedic surgeon at the Johns Hopkins Children's Center, specializes in the repair of bone defects caused by achondroplasia and related disorders.

▼ **Figure 9.16 A family with and without achondroplasia.**
Amy Roloff (who has achondroplasia) and her husband Matt (who has an unrelated form of dwarfism) have four children. Zachary received Amy's achondroplasia allele while twin brother Jeremy, sister Molly Jo, and brother Jacob did not. The hypothetical Punnett square shows the offspring expected from a mating of a wild-type male with a dwarf female.

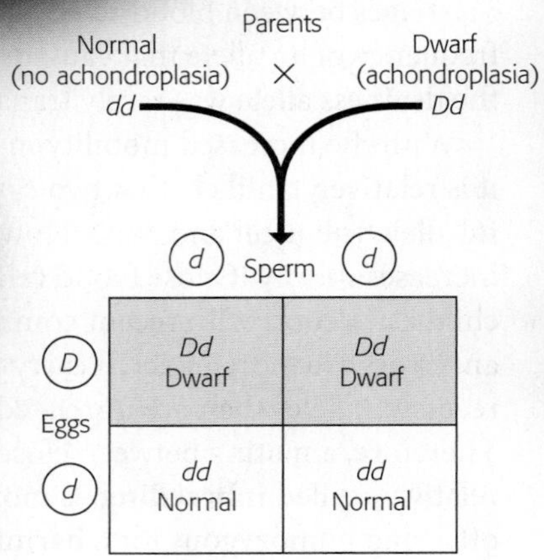

Dog Breeding THE PROCESS OF SCIENCE

What Is the Genetic Basis of Coat Variation in Dogs?

You've probably made the **observation** that compared with most mammals, dogs come in a wide variety of physical types. For instance, dog coats can be short or long, straight or curly or wire-haired (having a "moustache" and "eyebrows"). Sometimes a single breed, such as the fox terrier, may display two or more of these variations (**Figure 9.17**).

In 2005, the complete genome of a dog—the sequence of all the DNA of a female boxer named Tasha—was published. Since that time, canine geneticists have added a wealth of data from other breeds. In 2009, an international group of researchers set out to investigate the **question** of the genetic basis for canine coats. They proposed the **hypothesis** that a comparison of genes from a wide variety of dogs with different coats would identify the genes responsible. They made the **prediction** that mutations in just a few genes could account for the coat appearance. Their **experiment** compared DNA sequences in 622 dogs from dozens of breeds. Their **results** identified three genes that in different combinations produced seven different coat appearances, from

◄ **Figure 9.17 Smooth versus wired fox terrier.** The fox terrier, like several other breeds, comes in smooth (left) and wired (right) coats.

very short hair to full, thick, wired hair. The difference between the two dogs in the photo, for example, is due to a change in a single gene that regulates keratin, a protein that is one of the primary structural components of hair.

This experiment shows how the extreme range of phenotypes in dogs combined with the availability of genome sequences can be used to provide insight into interesting genetic questions. Indeed, similar research has uncovered the genetic basis of other dog traits, such as body size, hairlessness, and coat color.

Genetic Testing

Until relatively recently, the onset of symptoms was the only way to know if a person had inherited an allele that might lead to disease. Today, there are many tests that can detect the presence of disease-causing alleles in an individual's genome.

Most genetic tests are performed during pregnancy if the prospective parents are aware that they have an increased risk of having a baby with a genetic disease. Genetic testing before birth usually requires the collection of fetal cells. In amniocentesis, a physician uses a needle to extract about 2 teaspoonfuls of the fluid that bathes the developing fetus. In chorionic villus sampling, a physician inserts a narrow, flexible tube through the mother's vagina and into her uterus, removing some placental tissue. Once cells are obtained, they can be screened for genetic diseases.

Because amniocentesis and chorionic villus sampling have risks of complications, these techniques are usually reserved for situations in which the possibility of a genetic disease is significantly higher than average.

Newer genetic screening procedures involve isolating tiny amounts of fetal cells or DNA released into the mother's bloodstream. Although few reliable tests are yet available using this method, this promising and complication-free technology may soon replace more invasive procedures.

As genetic testing becomes more routine, geneticists are working to make sure that the tests do not cause more problems than they solve. Geneticists stress that patients seeking genetic testing should receive counseling both before and after to explain the test and to help them cope with the results. If fetal tests reveal a serious disorder, the parents must choose between terminating the pregnancy and preparing themselves for a baby with severe problems. Identifying a genetic disease early can give families time to prepare—emotionally, medically, and financially. Advances in biotechnology offer possibilities for reducing human suffering, but not before key ethical issues are resolved. The dilemmas posed by human genetics reinforce one of this book's themes: the immense social implications of biology. ☑

☑ CHECKPOINT

1. A man and a woman who are both carriers of cystic fibrosis have had three children without cystic fibrosis. If the couple has a fourth child, what is the probability that the child will have the disorder?
2. Peter is a 28-year-old man whose father died of Huntington's disease. Peter's mother shows no signs of the disease. What is the probability that Peter has inherited Huntington's disease?

Answers: 1. ¼ (The genotypes and phenotypes of their other children are irrelevant.) 2. ½

Variations on Mendel's Laws

Mendel's two laws explain inheritance in terms of discrete factors—genes—that are passed along from generation to generation according to simple rules of probability. These laws are valid for all sexually reproducing organisms, including garden peas, Labrador retrievers, and people. But just as the basic rules of musical harmony cannot account for all the rich sounds of a symphony, Mendel's laws stop short of explaining some patterns of genetic inheritance. In fact, for most sexually reproducing organisms, cases where Mendel's rules can strictly account for the patterns of inheritance are relatively rare. More often, the observed inheritance patterns are more complex. We will now add several extensions to Mendel's laws that help account for this complexity.

Incomplete Dominance in Plants and People

The F_1 offspring of Mendel's pea crosses always looked like one of the two parent plants. In such situations, the dominant allele has the same effect on the phenotype whether present in one or two copies. But for some characters, the appearance of F_1 hybrids falls between the phenotypes of the two parents, an effect called **incomplete dominance**. For instance, when red snapdragons are crossed with white snapdragons, all the F_1 hybrids have pink flowers **(Figure 9.18)**. And in the F_2 generation, the genotypic ratio and the phenotypic ratio are the same: 1:2:1.

We also see examples of incomplete dominance in people. One case involves a recessive allele (h) that causes **hypercholesterolemia**, dangerously high levels of cholesterol in the blood. Normal individuals are homozygous dominant, HH. Heterozygotes (Hh) have blood cholesterol levels about twice what is normal. They are very prone to cholesterol buildup in artery walls and may have heart attacks from blocked heart arteries by their mid-30s. Hypercholesterolemia is even more serious in homozygous individuals (hh). Homozygotes have about five times the normal amount of blood cholesterol and may have heart attacks as early as age 2. If we look at the molecular basis for hypercholesterolemia, we can understand the intermediate phenotype of heterozygotes **(Figure 9.19)**. The H allele specifies a cell-surface receptor protein that liver cells use to mop up excess low-density lipoprotein (LDL, or "bad cholesterol") from the blood. With only half as many receptors as HH individuals, heterozygotes can remove much less excess cholesterol.

▼ **Figure 9.18 Incomplete dominance in snapdragons.** Compare this diagram with Figure 9.6, where one of the alleles displays complete dominance.

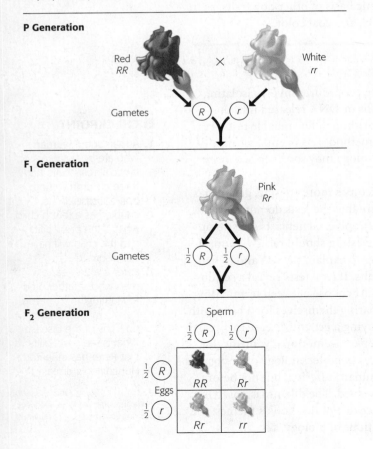

▼ **Figure 9.19 Incomplete dominance in human hypercholesterolemia.** LDL receptors on liver cells promote the breakdown of cholesterol carried in the bloodstream by LDL (low-density lipoproteins). This process helps prevent the accumulation of cholesterol in the arteries. Having too few receptors allows dangerous levels of LDL to build up in the blood.

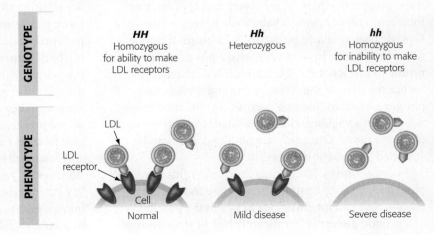

ABO Blood Groups: An Example of Multiple Alleles and Codominance

So far, we have discussed inheritance patterns involving only two alleles per gene (*H* versus *h*, for example). But most genes can be found in populations in more than two forms, known as multiple alleles. Although each individual carries, at most, two different alleles for a particular gene, in cases of multiple alleles, more than two possible alleles exist in the population.

The **ABO blood groups** in humans involve three alleles of a single gene. Various combinations of these three alleles produce four phenotypes: A person's blood type may be A, B, AB, or O. These letters refer to two carbohydrates, designated A and B, that may be found on the surface of red blood cells **(Figure 9.20)**. A person's red blood cells may be coated with carbohydrate A (giving them type A blood), carbohydrate B (type B), both (type AB), or neither (type O). (In case you are wondering, the "positive" and "negative" notations associated with blood types—referred to as the Rh blood group system—are due to inheritance of a separate, unrelated gene.)

Matching compatible blood groups is critical for safe blood transfusions. If a donor's blood cells have a carbohydrate (A or B) that is foreign to the recipient, then the recipient's immune system produces blood proteins called antibodies that bind to the foreign carbohydrates and cause the donor blood cells to clump together, potentially killing the recipient. The clumping reaction is also the basis of a blood-typing lab test.

The four blood groups result from various combinations of the three different alleles: I^A (for the ability to make substance A), I^B (for B), and *i* (for neither A nor B). Each person inherits one of these alleles from each parent. Because there are three alleles, there are six possible genotypes, as listed in Figure 9.20. Both the I^A and I^B alleles are dominant to the *i* allele. Thus, I^AI^A and I^Ai people have type A blood, and I^BI^B and I^Bi people have type B. Recessive homozygotes (*ii*) have type O blood with neither carbohydrate. Finally, people of genotype I^AI^B make *both* carbohydrates. In other words, the I^A and I^B alleles are **codominant**, meaning that both alleles are expressed in heterozygous individuals (I^AI^B) who have type AB blood. Be careful to distinguish codominance (the expression of both alleles) from incomplete dominance (the expression of one intermediate trait). ☑

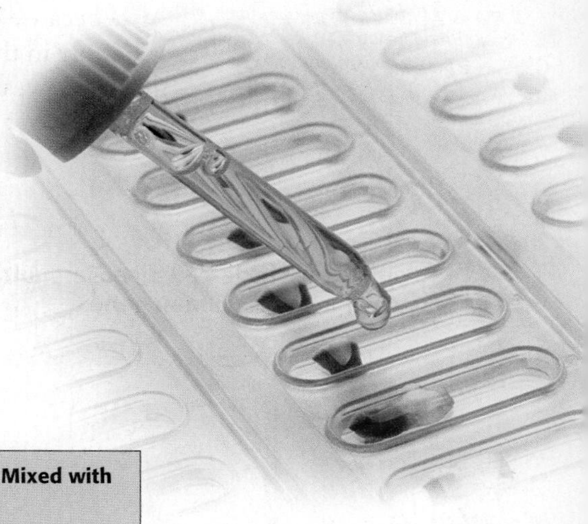

Why must a blood donor be carefully matched to a recipient?

▼ **Figure 9.20 Multiple alleles for the ABO blood groups.** The three versions of the gene responsible for blood type may produce carbohydrate A (allele I^A), carbohydrate B (allele I^B), or neither carbohydrate (allele *i*). Because each person carries two alleles, six genotypes are possible that result in four different phenotypes. The clumping reaction that occurs between antibodies and foreign blood cells is the basis of blood-typing (shown in the photograph at right) and of the adverse reaction that occurs when someone receives a transfusion of incompatible blood.

Blood Group (Phenotype)	Genotypes	Red Blood Cells	Antibodies Present in Blood	Reactions When Blood from Groups Below Is Mixed with Antibodies from Groups at Left			
				O	A	B	AB
A	I^AI^A or I^Ai	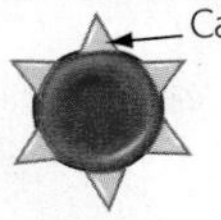 Carbohydrate A	Anti-B	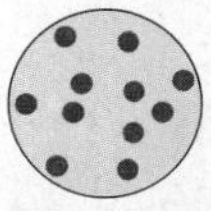	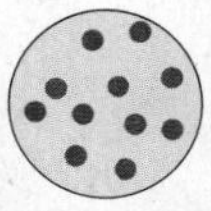	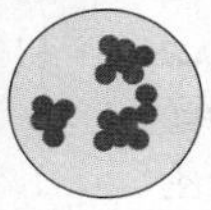	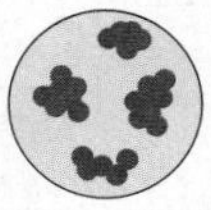
B	I^BI^B or I^Bi	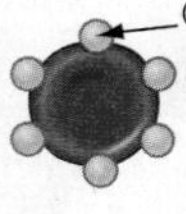 Carbohydrate B	Anti-A	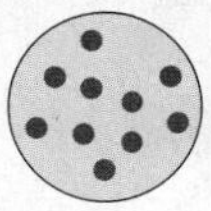	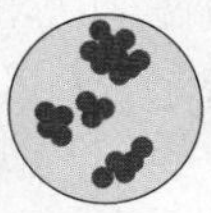	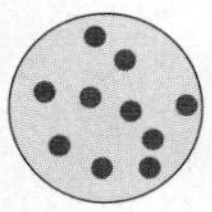	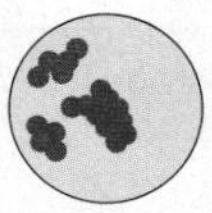
AB	I^AI^B	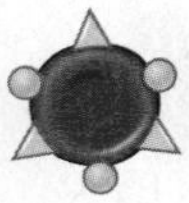	—	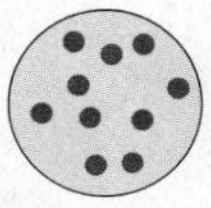	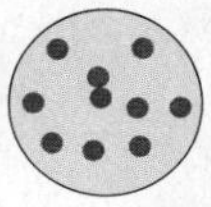	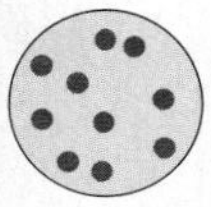	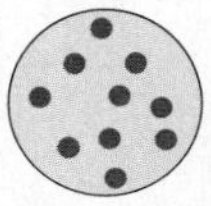
O	*ii*		Anti-A Anti-B	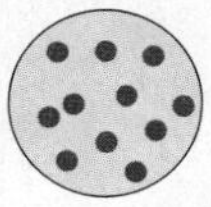	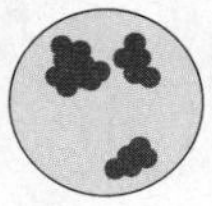	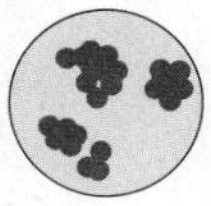	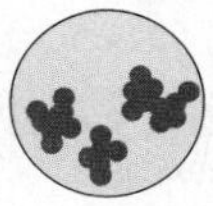

☑ **CHECKPOINT**

1. Why is a testcross unnecessary to determine whether a snapdragon with red flowers is homozygous or heterozygous?
2. Maria has type O blood and her sister has type AB blood. What are the genotypes of the girls' parents?

Answers: 1. Only plants homozygous for the dominant allele have red flowers; heterozygotes have pink flowers. 2. One parent is I^Ai, and the other parent is I^Bi.

Pleiotropy and Sickle-Cell Disease

Our genetic examples to this point have been cases in which each gene specifies only one hereditary character. But in many cases, one gene influences several characters, a property called **pleiotropy**.

An example of pleiotropy in humans that may be familiar to you is **sickle-cell disease** (sometimes called sickle-cell anemia), a disorder characterized by a diverse set of symptoms. The direct effect of the sickle-cell allele is to make red blood cells produce abnormal hemoglobin proteins (see Figure 3.19). These abnormal molecules tend to link together and crystallize, especially when the oxygen content of the blood is lower than usual because of high altitude, overexertion, or respiratory ailments. As the hemoglobin crystallizes, the normally disk-shaped red blood cells deform to a sickle shape with jagged edges **(Figure 9.21)**. Sickled cells are destroyed rapidly by the body, and their destruction may cause anemia and general weakening of the body. Also, because of their shape, sickled cells do not flow smoothly in the blood and tend to accumulate and clog tiny blood vessels. Blood flow to body parts is reduced, resulting in periodic fever, severe pain, and damage to the heart, brain, and kidneys. Blood transfusions and drugs may relieve some of the symptoms, but there is no cure, and sickle-cell disease kills about 100,000 people in the world annually.

In most cases, only people who are homozygous for the sickle-cell allele have sickle-cell disease. Heterozygotes, who have one sickle-cell allele and one normal allele, are usually healthy; hence, the disease is considered recessive. However, at the molecular level, the two alleles are actually codominant: Both alleles are expressed in heterozygous individuals, and their red blood cells contain both normal and abnormal hemoglobin. A simple blood test can distinguish homozygotes from heterozygotes. ☑

Polygenic Inheritance

Mendel studied genetic characters that could be classified on an either–or basis, such as purple or white flower color. However, many characters, such as human skin color and height, vary along a continuum in a population. Many such features result from **polygenic inheritance**, the additive effects of two or more genes on a single phenotypic character. (This is the logical opposite of pleiotropy, in which one gene affects several characters.)

There is evidence that height in people is controlled by several genes that are inherited separately. In actuality, human height is probably affected by a great number of genes, but we will simplify here. Let's consider three genes, with a tall allele for each (*A*, *B*, and *C*) contributing one "unit" of tallness to the phenotype and being incompletely dominant to the other alleles (*a*, *b*, and *c*). A person who is *AABBCC* would be very tall, while an *aabbcc* individual would be very short. An

☑ CHECKPOINT

How does sickle-cell disease exemplify the concept of pleiotropy?

Answer: Homozygotes for the sickle-cell allele have abnormal hemoglobin, and its effect on the shape of red blood cells leads to a cascade of traits affecting many organs of the body.

▼ Figure 9.21 **Sickle-cell disease: multiple effects of a single human gene.**

Individual homozygous for sickle-cell allele

Sickle-cell (abnormal) hemoglobin

Abnormal hemoglobin crystallizes into long flexible chains, causing red blood cells to become sickle-shaped.

Colorized SEM 4,000×

Sickled cells can lead to a cascade of symptoms, such as weakness, pain, organ damage, and paralysis.

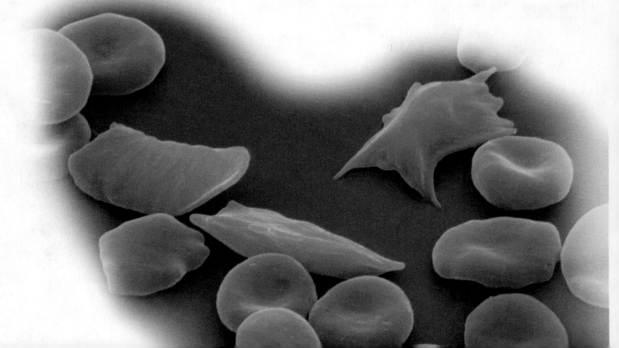

AaBbCc person would be of intermediate height. Because the alleles have an additive effect, the genotype *AaBbCc* would produce the same height as any other genotype with just three tallness alleles, such as *AABbcc*. The Punnett square in **Figure 9.22** shows all possible

▼ **Figure 9.22 A model for polygenic inheritance of height.** The seven bars in the graph at the bottom of the figure depict the relative numbers of each of the phenotypes in the F₂ generation. The bell-shaped curve indicates the distribution of an even greater variety of height phenotypes in the population that might result from the combination of heredity and environmental effects, such as diet and exercise.

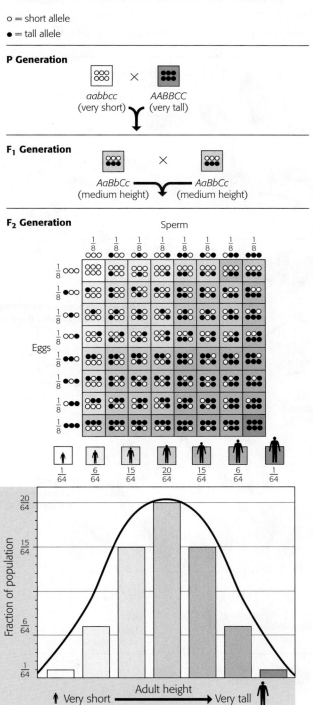

genotypes from a mating of two triple heterozygotes (*AaBbCd*). The row of figures below the Punnett square shows the seven height phenotypes that would theoretically result. This hypothetical example shows how inheritance of three genes could lead to seven different versions of a trait at the frequencies indicated by the bars in the graph. ☑

The Role of Environment

If we examine a real human population for height, we would see more height phenotypes than just seven. The true range might be similar to the entire distribution of height under the bell-shaped curve in Figure 9.22. In fact, no matter how carefully we characterize the genes for height, a purely genetic description will always be incomplete. This is because height is also influenced by environmental factors, such as nutrition and exercise.

Many phenotypic characters result from a combination of heredity and environment. For example, the leaves of a tree all have the same genotype, but they vary in size, shape, and color, depending on exposure to wind and sun and the tree's nutritional state. For people, exercise alters build; experience improves performance on intelligence tests; and social and cultural factors can greatly affect appearance. As geneticists learn more and more about our genes, it's becoming clear that many human characters—such as risk of heart disease, cancer, alcoholism, and schizophrenia—are influenced by both genes *and* environment.

Whether human characters are more influenced by genes or by the environment—nature or nurture—is a very old and hotly contested issue. For some characters, such as the ABO blood group, a given genotype mandates an exact phenotype, and the environment plays no role whatsoever. In contrast, the number of blood cells in a drop of your blood varies quite a bit, depending on such factors as the altitude, your physical activity, and whether or not you have a cold.

Simply spending time with identical twins will convince anyone that environment, and not just genes, affects a person's traits **(Figure 9.23)**. However, there is an important difference between these two sources of variation: Only genetic influences are inherited. Any effects of the environment are not passed to the next generation.

☑ **CHECKPOINT**
Based on the height model in Figure 9.22, put the following individuals in order by height, from shortest to tallest: *AAbbCC, aaBBcc, AabBCc, Aabbcc, AABBCC.*

Answer: *Aabbcc, aaBBcc, AabBCc, AAbbCC, AABBCC.*

▼ Figure 9.23 **As a result of environmental influences, even identical twins can look different.**

The Chromosomal Basis of Inheritance

It was not until many years after Mendel's death that biologists understood the significance of his work. Cell biologists worked out the processes of mitosis and meiosis in the late 1800s (see Chapter 8). Then, around 1900, researchers began to notice parallels between the behavior of chromosomes and the behavior of Mendel's "heritable factors" (what we now call genes). One of biology's most important concepts began to emerge.

The **chromosome theory of inheritance** states that genes are located at specific positions (loci) on chromosomes and that the behavior of chromosomes during meiosis and fertilization accounts for inheritance patterns. Indeed, it is chromosomes that undergo segregation and independent assortment during meiosis and thus account for Mendel's laws. **Figure 9.24** correlates the results of the dihybrid cross in Figure 9.8b with the movement of chromosomes through meiosis. Starting with two purebred parental plants, the diagram follows two genes on different chromosomes—one for seed shape (alleles *R* and *r*) and one for seed color (alleles *Y* and *y*)—through the F_1 and F_2 generations. ☑

► **Figure 9.24 The chromosomal basis of Mendel's laws.**

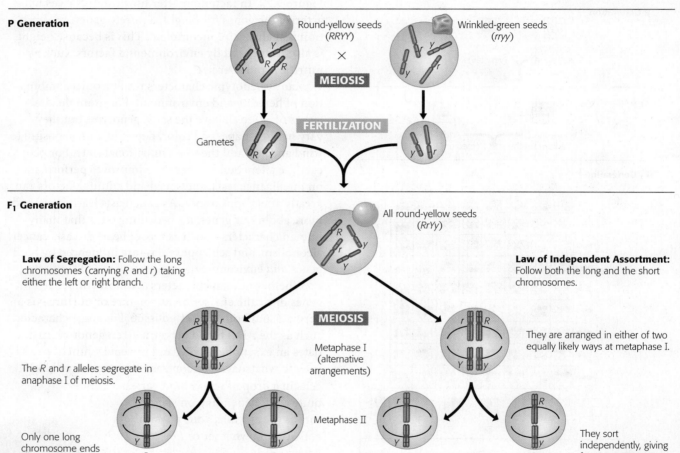

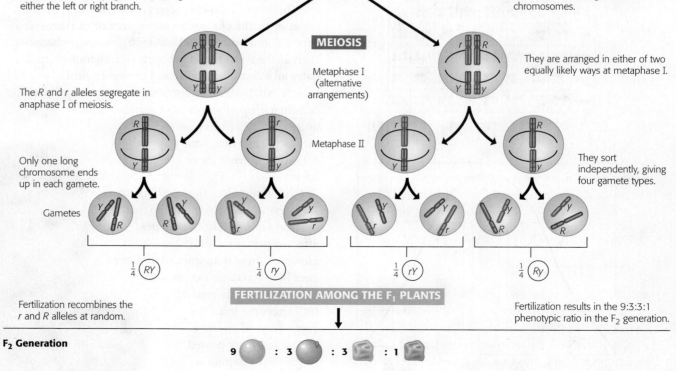

P Generation

Round-yellow seeds (*RRYY*) × Wrinkled-green seeds (*rryy*)

MEIOSIS

FERTILIZATION

Gametes

F₁ Generation

All round-yellow seeds (*RrYy*)

Law of Segregation: Follow the long chromosomes (carrying *R* and *r*) taking either the left or right branch.

Law of Independent Assortment: Follow both the long and the short chromosomes.

The *R* and *r* alleles segregate in anaphase I of meiosis.

MEIOSIS

Metaphase I (alternative arrangements)

They are arranged in either of two equally likely ways at metaphase I.

Metaphase II

Only one long chromosome ends up in each gamete.

They sort independently, giving four gamete types.

Gametes

$\frac{1}{4}$ *RY* $\frac{1}{4}$ *ry* $\frac{1}{4}$ *rY* $\frac{1}{4}$ *Ry*

FERTILIZATION AMONG THE F₁ PLANTS

Fertilization recombines the *r* and *R* alleles at random.

Fertilization results in the 9:3:3:1 phenotypic ratio in the F_2 generation.

F₂ Generation

9 : 3 : 3 : 1

Linked Genes

Realizing that genes are on chromosomes when they segregate enables us to extend Mendel's work in several important ways. For example, alleles that start out together on the same chromosome would be expected to travel together during meiosis and fertilization. In general, genes that are located close together on a chromosome, called **linked genes**, tend to be inherited as a set and therefore do not follow Mendel's law of independent assortment.

The most important early studies into linked genes took place in the New York City laboratory of American biologist Thomas Hunt Morgan. In the early 1900s, Morgan and his colleagues studied the fruit fly *Drosophila melanogaster* (**Figure 9.25**). Often seen flying around overripe fruit, *Drosophila* is a good research animal for studies of inheritance because it is easily and inexpensively grown and can produce several generations in a matter of months.

Wild-type *Drosophila* flies have gray bodies (genotype *GG*) and long wings (*LL*). Morgan cultivated purebred mutant (non–wild-type) fruit flies that had black bodies (*gg*) and short, underdeveloped wings (*ll*). He then performed a dihybrid testcross, crossing doubly heterozygous flies (*GgLl*) with double mutants (*ggll*). Morgan expected that the offspring would show equal numbers of all four possible phenotypes (¼ gray-long, ¼ gray-short, ¼ black-long, ¼ black-short).

In fact, Morgan's testcross produced equal numbers of two of the four expected phenotypes but far smaller numbers of the other two phenotypes. He found that 83% of the flies displayed the phenotypes of the parents (gray-long and black-short), while only 17% showed nonparental phenotypes (gray-short and black-long). Morgan reasoned that the genes for body color and wing shape were linked—in this case, *G* with *L* and *g* with *l*—causing them to be inherited together. Such linkage would mean that meiosis in the heterozygous fruit flies would yield gametes with only two genotypes (*GL* and *gl* but not *Gl* or *gL*). The large numbers of flies with gray-long and black-short traits in the experiment resulted from fertilization among the *GL* and *gl* gametes. ☑

Genetic Recombination: Crossing Over

But what of the smaller numbers of Morgan's gray-short and black-long flies? How could they be produced if the two genes involved are linked? We saw in Chapter 8 that during meiosis, crossing over between homologous chromosomes results in shuffled chromosome segments

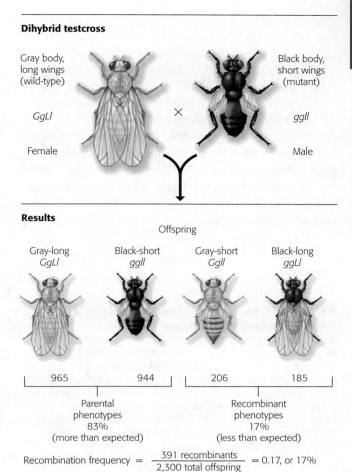

Dihybrid testcross

Gray body, long wings (wild-type) — *GgLl* — Female

×

Black body, short wings (mutant) — *ggll* — Male

Results

Offspring

Gray-long *GgLl*	Black-short *ggll*	Gray-short *Ggll*	Black-long *ggLl*
965	944	206	185

Parental phenotypes 83% (more than expected)

Recombinant phenotypes 17% (less than expected)

$$\text{Recombination frequency} = \frac{391 \text{ recombinants}}{2,300 \text{ total offspring}} = 0.17, \text{ or } 17\%$$

◄ **Figure 9.25 Thomas Morgan's experiment and results.** Among the 2,300 offspring of this dihybrid testcross, Morgan observed more than the expected parental phenotypes (gray-long and black-short) and fewer than expected nonparental phenotypes (gray-short and black-long).

in the haploid daughter cells (see Figure 8.18), thereby producing new combinations of alleles. **Figure 9.26** reviews crossing over, showing how two linked genes can give rise to four different gamete genotypes. Two of the gamete genotypes reflect the presence of parental-type chromosomes, which have not been altered by crossing

▼ **Figure 9.26 Review: Crossing over can produce recombinant gametes.**

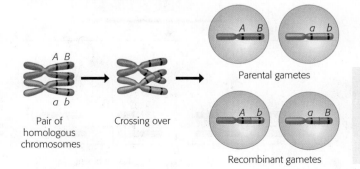

Pair of homologous chromosomes — *A B* / *a b*

Crossing over

Parental gametes — *A B* / *a b*

Recombinant gametes — *A b* / *a B*

☑ **CHECKPOINT**

What are linked genes?

Answer: genes located near each other on the same chromosome that tend to be inherited together

over. In contrast, the other two gamete genotypes are recombinant (nonparental). The chromosomes of these gametes carry new combinations of alleles that result from the exchange of chromosome segments during crossing over.

Morgan hypothesized that crossing over accounted for the observed nonparental offspring, those with the recombinant phenotypes (gray-short and black-long). Furthermore, the 17% of offspring with recombinant phenotypes must have resulted from fertilization involving recombinant gametes **(Figure 9.27)**. The percentage of recombinant offspring among the total is called the **recombination frequency** (see bottom of Figure 9.25).

Linkage Maps

While working with *Drosophila*, Alfred H. Sturtevant, one of Morgan's students, developed a way to use crossover data to map gene loci. This technique is based on the assumption that the chance of crossing over is approximately equal at all points along a chromosome. Sturtevant hypothesized that the farther apart two genes are on a chromosome, the higher the probability that a crossover will occur between them. His reasoning was elegantly simple: The greater the distance between two genes, the more points there are between them where crossing over can occur. (This assumption is not entirely accurate, but it is good enough to provide useful data.)

By applying Sturtevant's reasoning, geneticists can use recombination data to assign genes to relative positions on chromosomes—that is, to map genes. **Figure 9.28** shows some of the data used to map three linked genes (*g*, *c*, and *l*) that reside on one of the *Drosophila* chromosomes. Under the chromosome are the actual recombination frequencies (crossover frequencies) between these genes, taken two at a time: 17% between *g* and *l*, 9% between *g* and *c*, and 9.5% between *l* and *c*. Geneticists reasoned that these values represent the relative distances between the genes. Because the recombination frequencies between *g* and *c* and between *l* and *c* are approximately half the frequency between *g* and *l*, gene *c* must lie roughly midway between *g* and *l*. Thus, the sequence of these genes on their chromosome must be *g-c-l* (or the equivalent *l-c-g*). Such a diagram of relative gene locations is called a **linkage map**.

The linkage-mapping method has proved extremely valuable in establishing the relative positions of many genes in many organisms. The real beauty of the technique is that a wealth of information about genes can be learned simply by breeding and observing the organisms; no fancy equipment is required. ☑

▼ **Figure 9.27 Explaining the unexpected results from the dihybrid testcross in Figure 9.25.** The disproportionately large numbers of the parental phenotypes among the offspring is explained by gene linkage, the fact that the gene loci for the two characters are located nearby on the same chromosome and tend to remain together during meiosis and fertilization (*G* with *L* and *g* with *l*). As a result of crossing over, some of the gametes end up with recombinant chromosomes, carrying new combinations of alleles, either *Gl* or *gL*. When the recombinant gametes participate in fertilization, recombinant offspring can result.

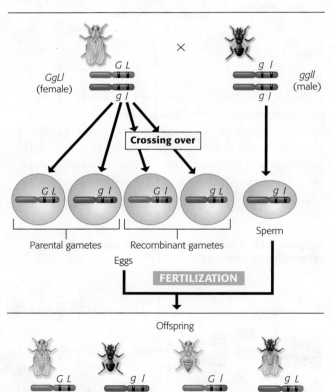

▼ **Figure 9.28 Using crossover data to map genes.** The three recessive alleles specify black body (*g*), cinnabar eyes (*c*), and short wings (*l*). The corresponding dominant alleles specify the wild-type traits of gray body, red eyes, and long wings.

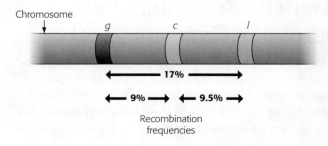

Sex Chromosomes and Sex-Linked Genes

The patterns of genetic inheritance we've discussed so far have always involved genes located on autosomes, not on the sex chromosomes. We're now ready to look at the role of sex chromosomes and the inheritance patterns exhibited by the characters they control. As you'll see, genes located on sex chromosomes produce some unusual patterns of inheritance.

Sex Determination in Humans

Many animals, including all mammals, have a pair of sex chromosomes—designated X and Y—that determine an individual's sex (Figure 9.29). Individuals with one X chromosome and one Y chromosome are males; XX individuals are females. Human males and females both have 44 autosomes (chromosomes other than sex chromosomes). As a result of chromosome segregation during meiosis, each gamete contains one sex chromosome and a haploid set of autosomes (22 in humans). All eggs contain a single X chromosome. Of the sperm cells, half contain an X chromosome and half contain a Y chromosome. An offspring's sex depends on whether the sperm cell that fertilizes the egg bears an X or a Y. ☑

Why was Henry VIII wrong to blame his wives for always producing daughters?

Sex-Linked Genes

Besides bearing genes that determine sex, the sex chromosomes also contain genes for characters unrelated to maleness or femaleness. A gene located on a sex chromosome is called a **sex-linked gene**. The human X chromosome contains more than a thousand genes, whereas the Y chromosome contains only about a dozen (and none of them are vital); therefore, most sex-linked genes are found on the X chromosome.

A number of human conditions, including red-green colorblindness, hemophilia, and a type of muscular dystrophy, result from sex-linked recessive alleles. **Red-green colorblindness** is a common sex-linked disorder that is caused by a malfunction of light-sensitive cells in the eyes. (Colorblindness is actually a large class of disorders involving several sex-linked genes, but we will focus on just one specific type of colorblindness here.) A person with normal color vision can see more than 150 colors. In contrast, someone with red-green colorblindness can see fewer than 25. Figure 9.30 shows a simple test for red-green colorblindness. Mostly males are affected, but heterozygous females have some defects.

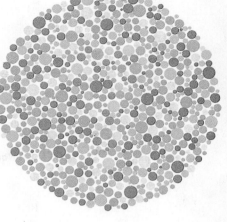

▲ Figure 9.30 **A test for red-green colorblindness.** Can you see a green numeral 7 against the reddish background? If not, you probably have some form of red-green colorblindness, a sex-linked trait.

▼ Figure 9.29 **The chromosomal basis of sex determination in humans.**
The micrograph at right shows human X and Y chromosomes in a duplicated state.

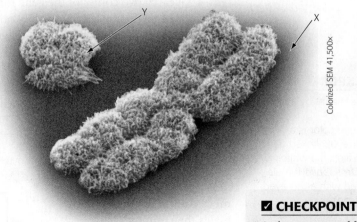

Colorized SEM 41,500×

▼ **Figure 9.31** **Inheritance of colorblindness, a sex-linked recessive trait.** We use an uppercase *N* for the dominant, normal color-vision allele and *n* for the recessive, colorblind allele. To indicate that these alleles are on the X chromosome, we show them as superscripts to the letter X. The Y chromosome does not have a gene locus for vision; therefore, the male's phenotype results entirely from the sex-linked gene on his single X chromosome.

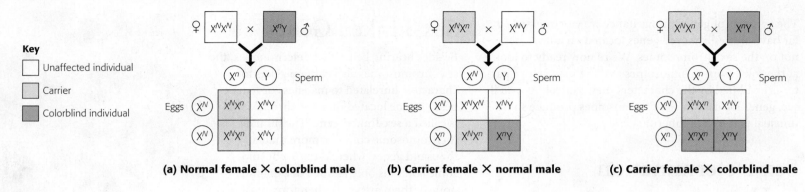

Key
- Unaffected individual
- Carrier
- Colorblind individual

(a) **Normal female × colorblind male**

(b) **Carrier female × normal male**

(c) **Carrier female × colorblind male**

Because they are located on the sex chromosomes, sex-linked genes exhibit unusual inheritance patterns. **Figure 9.31a** illustrates what happens when a colorblind male has offspring with a homozygous female with normal color vision. All the children have normal color vision, suggesting that the allele for wild-type (normal) color vision is dominant. If a female carrier mates with a male who has normal color vision, the classic 3:1 phenotypic ratio of normal color vision to colorblindness appears among the children (**Figure 9.31b**). However, there is a surprising twist: The colorblind trait shows up only in males. All the females have normal vision, while half the males are colorblind and half are normal. This is because the gene involved in this inheritance pattern is located exclusively on the X chromosome; there is no corresponding locus on the Y. Thus, females (XX) carry two copies of the gene for this character, while males (XY) carry only one. Because the colorblindness allele is recessive, a female will be colorblind only if she receives that allele on both X chromosomes (**Figure 9.31c**). For a male, however, a single copy of the recessive allele confers colorblindness. For this reason, recessive sex-linked traits are expressed much more frequently in men than in women. For example, colorblindness is about 20-fold more common among males than among females. This inheritance pattern is why people often say that certain genes "skip a generation"—because they are passed from a male to a female carrier (who does not express it) back to a male.

Hemophilia is a sex-linked recessive trait with a long, well-documented history. Hemophiliacs bleed excessively when injured because they have inherited an abnormal allele for a factor involved in blood clotting. The most seriously affected individuals may bleed to death after relatively minor bruises or cuts. A high incidence of hemophilia plagued the royal families of Europe. Queen Victoria (1819–1901) of England was a carrier of the hemophilia allele. She passed it on to one of her sons and two of her daughters. Through marriage, her daughters then introduced the disease into the royal families of Prussia, Russia, and Spain. In this way, the age-old practice of strengthening international alliances by marriage effectively spread hemophilia through the royal families of several nations (**Figure 9.32**). ☑

Why are there so few colorblind women?

CHECKPOINT

1. What is meant by a sex-linked gene?
2. White eye color is a recessive sex-linked trait in fruit flies. If a white-eyed *Drosophila* female is mated with a red-eyed (wild-type) male, what do you predict for the numerous offspring?

Answers: 1. a gene that is located on a sex chromosome, usually the X chromosome 2. All female offspring will be heterozygous ($X^R X^r$), with red eyes; all male offspring will be white-eyed ($X^r Y$).

▼ **Figure 9.32** **Hemophilia in the royal family of Russia.** The photograph shows Queen Victoria's granddaughter Alexandra, her husband Nicholas, who was the last czar of Russia, their son Alexis, and their daughters. In the pedigree, half-colored symbols represent heterozygous carriers of the hemophilia allele and fully colored symbols represent a person with hemophilia.

Barking Up the Evolutionary Tree

As we've seen throughout this chapter, dogs are more than man's best friend: They are also one of our longest-running genetic experiments. About 15,000 years ago, in East Asia, people began to cohabit with ancestral canines that were predecessors of both modern wolves and dogs. As people moved into permanent, geographically isolated settlements, populations of canines were separated from one another and eventually became inbred.

Different groups of people chose dogs with different traits, depending on their needs. Herders selected dogs that were good at controlling flocks. Hunters chose dogs that were good at retrieving prey. A 2010 study indicated that small dogs were first bred within early agricultural settlements of the Middle East around 12,000 years ago. Continued over millennia, such genetic tinkering has resulted in a diverse array of dog body types and behaviors. In each breed, a distinct genetic makeup results in a distinct set of physical and behavioral traits.

As discussed in the Process of Science section, our understanding of canine evolution took a big leap forward when researchers sequenced the complete genome of a dog. Using the genome sequence and a wealth of other data, canine geneticists produced an evolutionary tree based on a genetic analysis of 85 breeds (Figure 9.33). The analysis shows that the canine family tree includes a series of well-defined branch points. Each fork represents a purposeful selection by people that produced a genetically distinct subpopulation with specific desired traits.

The genetic tree shows that the most ancient breeds, those most closely related to the wolf, are Asian species such as the shar-pei and Akita. Subsequent genetic splits created distinct breeds in Africa (basenji), the Arctic (Alaskan malamute and Siberian husky), and the Middle East (Afghan hound and saluki). The remaining breeds, primarily of European ancestry, were developed most recently and can be grouped by genetic makeup into those bred for guarding (for example, the rottweiler), herding (such as sheepdogs), and hunting (including the Labrador retriever and beagle). The formulation of an evolutionary tree for the domestic dog shows that new technologies can provide important insights into genetic and evolutionary questions about life on Earth.

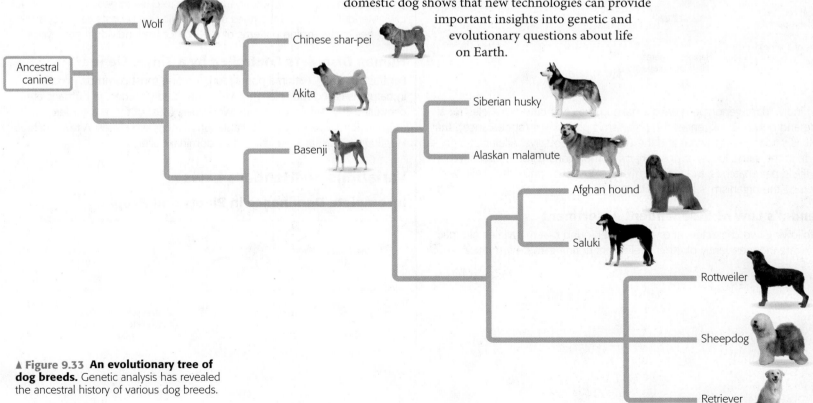

▲ **Figure 9.33 An evolutionary tree of dog breeds.** Genetic analysis has revealed the ancestral history of various dog breeds.

Chapter Review

SUMMARY OF KEY CONCEPTS

 Go to **www.masteringbiology.com** for homework assignments, practice quizzes, Pearson eText, and more.

Heritable Variation and Patterns of Inheritance

Gregor Mendel was the first to study genetics, the science of heredity, by analyzing patterns of inheritance. He emphasized that heritable factors (genes) retain permanent identities.

In an Abbey Garden

Mendel started with purebred varieties of pea plants representing two alternative variants of a hereditary character, such as flower color. He then crossed the different varieties and traced the inheritance of traits from generation to generation.

Mendel's Law of Segregation

Pairs of alleles separate during gamete formation; fertilization restores the pairs.

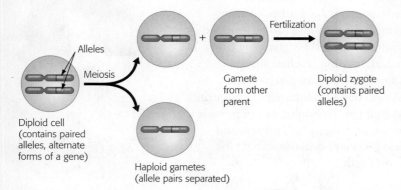

If an individual's genotype (genetic makeup) has two different alleles for a gene and only one influences the organism's phenotype (appearance), that allele is said to be dominant and the other allele recessive. Alleles of a gene reside at the same locus, or position, on homologous chromosomes. When the allele pair matches, the organism is homozygous; when the alleles are different, the organism is heterozygous.

Mendel's Law of Independent Assortment

By following two characters at once, Mendel found that the alleles of a pair segregate independently of other allele pairs during gamete formation.

Using a Testcross to Determine an Unknown Genotype

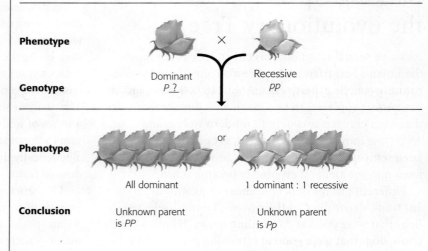

The Rules of Probability

Inheritance follows the rules of probability. The chance of inheriting a recessive allele from a heterozygous parent is $\frac{1}{2}$. The chance of inheriting it from both of two heterozygous parents is $\frac{1}{2} \times \frac{1}{2} = \frac{1}{4}$, illustrating the rule of multiplication for calculating the probability of two independent events.

Family Pedigrees

The inheritance of many human traits, from freckles to genetic diseases, follows Mendel's laws and the rules of probability. Geneticists can use family pedigrees to determine patterns of inheritance and individual genotypes.

Human Disorders Controlled by a Single Gene

For traits that vary within a population, the one most commonly found in nature is called the wild type. Many inherited disorders in humans are controlled by a single gene with two alleles. Most of these disorders, such as cystic fibrosis, are caused by autosomal recessive alleles. A few, such as Huntington's disease, are caused by dominant alleles.

Variations on Mendel's Laws

Incomplete Dominance in Plants and People

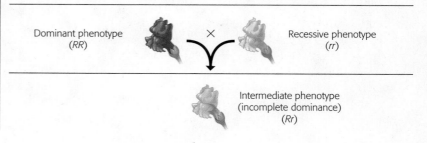

ABO Blood Groups: An Example of Multiple Alleles and Codominance

Within a population, there are often multiple kinds of alleles for a character, such as the three alleles for the ABO blood groups. The alleles determining the A and B blood factors are codominant; that is, both are expressed in a heterozygote.

Pleiotropy and Sickle-Cell Disease

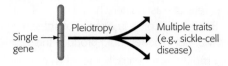

The presence of two copies of the sickle-cell allele at a single gene locus brings about the many symptoms of sickle-cell disease.

Polygenic Inheritance

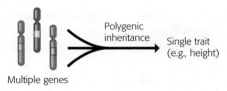

The Role of Environment

Many phenotypic characters result from a combination of genetic and environmental effects, but only genetic influences are biologically heritable.

The Chromosomal Basis of Inheritance

Genes are located on chromosomes. The behavior of chromosomes during meiosis and fertilization accounts for inheritance patterns.

Linked Genes

Certain genes are linked: They tend to be inherited as a set because they lie close together on the same chromosome.

Genetic Recombination: Crossing Over

Crossing over can separate linked genes producing gametes with recombinant chromosomes and offspring with recombinant phenotypes.

Linkage Maps

The fact that crossing over between linked genes is more likely to occur between genes that are farther apart enables geneticists to map the relative positions of genes on chromosomes.

Sex Chromosomes and Sex-Linked Genes
Sex Determination in Humans

In humans, sex is determined by whether a Y chromosome is present. A person who inherits two X chromosomes develops as a female. A person who inherits one X and one Y chromosome develops as a male.

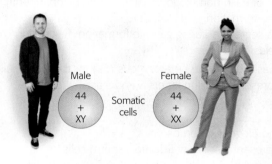

Sex-Linked Genes

Genes on the sex chromosomes (most often the X) are said to be sex-linked. Their inheritance pattern reflects the fact that females have two homologous X chromosomes, but males have only one X chromosome. Most sex-linked human disorders, such as red-green colorblindness and hemophilia, are due to recessive alleles and are seen mostly in males. A male receiving a single sex-linked recessive allele from his mother will have the disorder; a female has to receive the allele from both parents to be affected.

Sex-Linked Traits				
Female: Two alleles	Genotype	$X^N X^N$	$X^N X^n$	$X^n X^n$
	Phenotype	Normal female	Carrier female	Affected female (rare)
Male: One allele	Genotype	$X^N Y$		$X^n Y$
	Phenotype	Normal male		Affected male

SELF-QUIZ

1. The genetic makeup of an organism is called its _____, and the physical traits of an organism are called its _____.

2. Which of Mendel's laws is represented by each statement?
   a. Alleles of each homologous pair separate independently during gamete formation.
   b. Alleles segregate during gamete formation; fertilization creates pairs of alleles once again.

3. Edward was found to be heterozygous (*Ss*) for the sickle-cell trait. The alleles represented by the letters *S* and *s* are
   a. on the X and Y chromosomes.
   b. linked.
   c. on homologous chromosomes.
   d. both present in each of Edward's sperm cells.

4. Whether an allele is dominant or recessive depends on
   a. how common the allele is, relative to other alleles.
   b. whether it is inherited from the mother or the father.
   c. whether it or another allele determines the phenotype when both are present.
   d. whether or not it is linked to other genes.

5. Two fruit flies with eyes of the usual red color are crossed, and their offspring are as follows: 77 red-eyed males, 71 ruby-eyed males, 152 red-eyed females. The gene that controls whether eyes are red or ruby is _____, and the allele for ruby eyes is _____.
   a. autosomal (carried on an autosome); dominant
   b. autosomal; recessive
   c. sex-linked; dominant
   d. sex-linked; recessive

6. All the offspring of a white hen and a black rooster are gray. The simplest explanation for this pattern of inheritance is
   a. pleiotropy.
   b. sex linkage.
   c. codominance.
   d. incomplete dominance.

7. A man who has type B blood and a woman who has type A blood could have children of which of the following phenotypes? (*Hint*: Review Figure 9.20.)
   a. A, B, or O
   b. AB only
   c. AB or O
   d. A, B, AB, or O

8. Duchenne muscular dystrophy is a sex-linked recessive disorder characterized by a progressive loss of muscle tissue. Neither Rudy nor Carla has Duchenne muscular dystrophy, but their first son does have it. If the couple has a second child, what is the probability that he or she will also have the disease?

9. In fruit flies, the genes for wing shape and body stripes are linked. In a fly whose genotype is *WwSs*, *W* is linked to *S*, and *w* is linked to *s*. But this fly produces gametes with four different combinations of gametes. What process is responsible for this? Of the four types of gametes, which are parental-type gametes? Which are recombinant gametes?

10. Adult height in people is at least partially hereditary; tall parents tend to have tall children. But people come in a range of sizes, not just tall or short. What extension of Mendel's model could produce this variation in height?

11. A purebred brown mouse is repeatedly mated with a purebred white mouse, and all their offspring are brown. If two of these brown offspring are mated, what fraction of the F$_2$ mice will be brown?

12. How could you determine the genotype of one of the brown F$_2$ mice in problem 11? How would you know whether a brown mouse is homozygous? Heterozygous?

13. Tim and Jan both have freckles (a dominant trait), but their son Michael does not. Show with a Punnett square how this is possible. If Tim and Jan have two more children, what is the probability that *both* of them will have freckles?

14. Incomplete dominance is seen in the inheritance of hypercholesterolemia. Mack and Toni are both heterozygous for this character, and both have elevated levels of cholesterol. Their daughter Katerina has a cholesterol level six times normal; she is apparently homozygous, *hh*. What fraction of Mack and Toni's children are likely to have elevated but not extreme levels of cholesterol, like their parents? If Mack and Toni have one more child, what is the probability that the child will suffer from the more serious form of hypercholesterolemia seen in Katerina?

15. A female fruit fly with forked bristles on her body is mated with a male fly with normal bristles. Their offspring are 121 females with normal bristles and 138 males with forked bristles. Explain the inheritance pattern for this trait.

16. Both parents of a boy are phenotypically normal, but their son suffers from hemophilia, a sex-linked recessive disorder. Draw a pedigree that shows the genotypes of the three individuals. What fraction of the couple's children are likely to suffer from hemophilia? What fraction are likely to be carriers?

17. Heather was surprised to discover that she suffered from red-green colorblindness. She told her biology professor, who said, "Your father is colorblind too, right?" How did her professor know this? Why did her professor not say the same thing to the colorblind males in the class?

Answers to these questions can be found in Appendix: Self-Quiz Answers.

THE PROCESS OF SCIENCE

18. In 1981, a stray cat with unusual curled-back ears was adopted by a family in Lakewood, California. Hundreds of descendants of this cat have since been born, and cat fanciers hope to develop the "curl" cat into a show breed. The curl allele is apparently dominant and carried on an autosome. Suppose you owned the first curl cat and wanted to develop a purebred variety. Describe tests that would determine whether the curl gene is dominant or recessive and whether it is autosomal or sex-linked.

19. Imagine that you have a large collection of fruit flies divided into ten different strains. Each strain is purebred (homozygous) and differs from wild-type flies in just one character. The only special equipment available is a magnifying glass that lets you determine the sex and readily observable traits of a fly, a large number of bottles to perform controlled matings, and an anesthetic liquid that enables you to examine and sort live flies. Using only this equipment, how much could you learn about the genetic makeup of the flies? Describe a series of experiments that would give you knowledge about fruit fly genetics.

BIOLOGY AND SOCIETY

20. Gregor Mendel never saw a gene, yet he concluded that "heritable factors" were responsible for the patterns of inheritance he observed in peas. Similarly, maps of *Drosophila* chromosomes (and the very idea that genes are carried on chromosomes) were conceived by observing the patterns of inheritance of linked genes, not by observing the genes directly. Is it legitimate for biologists to claim the existence of objects and processes they cannot actually see? How do scientists know whether an explanation is correct?

21. Many infertile couples turn to in vitro fertilization to try to have a baby. In this technique, sperm and ova are collected and used to create eight-cell embryos for implantation into a woman's uterus. At the eight-cell stage, one of the fetal cells can be removed without causing harm to the developing fetus. Once removed, the cell can be genetically tested. Some couples may know that a particular genetic disease runs in their family. They might wish to avoid implanting any embryos with the disease-causing genes. Do you think this is an acceptable use of genetic testing? What if a couple wanted to use genetic testing to select embryos for traits unrelated to disease, such as freckles? Do you think that couples undergoing in vitro fertilization should be allowed to perform whatever genetic tests they wish? Or do you think that there should be limits on what tests can be performed? How do you draw the line between genetic tests that are acceptable and those that are not?

10 The Structure and Function of DNA

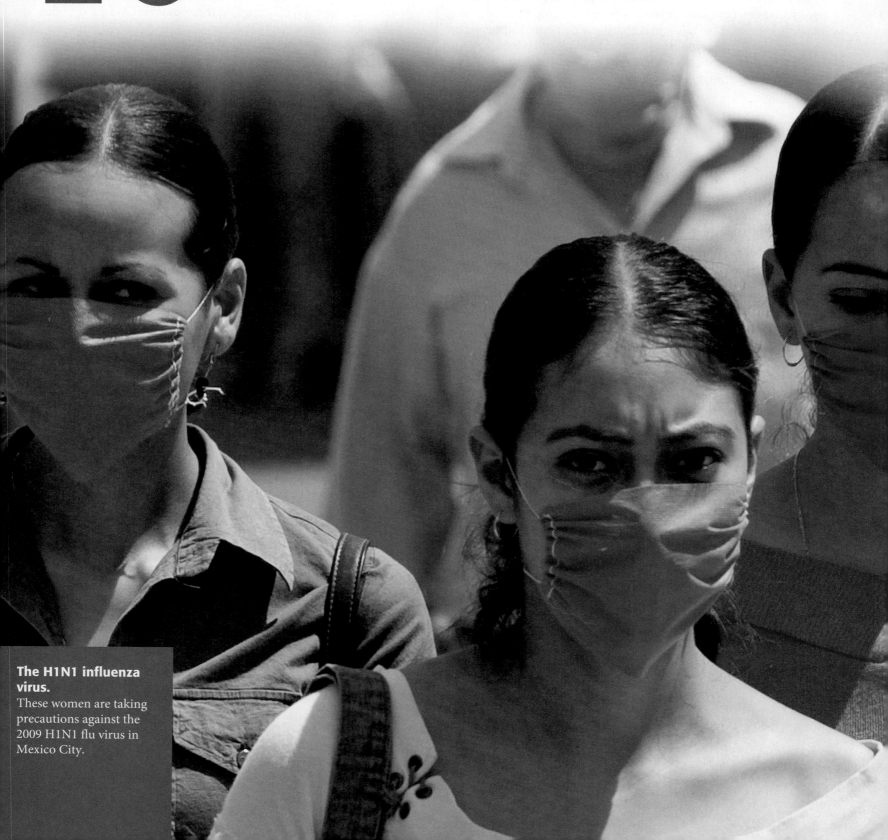

The H1N1 influenza virus.
These women are taking precautions against the 2009 H1N1 flu virus in Mexico City.

 The Deadliest Virus BIOLOGY AND SOCIETY

Mix-and-Match Viruses

In 2009, a cluster of unusual flu cases broke out around Mexico City. Despite a near total shutdown of the city, the new viral strain, called 2009 H1N1, quickly spread to California and Texas. This strain was originally misnamed the "swine flu"; in fact, pigs had little impact on the spread of this virus, which, like most flu viruses, is passed from person to person through respiratory fluids. Nonetheless, the new strain received nearly constant media attention and caused considerable worry among the general public. In June 2009, the World Health Organization (WHO) declared H1N1 a pandemic (global epidemic) and unveiled a massive effort to contain it.

Scientists soon determined that H1N1 was a hybrid flu strain, made when a previously known flu virus (which itself originated through a combination of viruses from birds, swine, and people) mixed with an Asian swine flu virus. This novel combination of genes produced some unusual features in the H1N1 strain. Most significantly, it infected young, healthy people, whereas the flu usually affects the elderly or people who are already sick. Many countries participated in coordinated response, including widespread distribution of a new vaccine. As a result, the virus was contained, and WHO declared the pandemic over in August 2010. Although exact numbers are difficult to produce, WHO estimates that this virus killed about 18,000 people.

You may wonder, What's the big deal about the flu? Don't we all get the flu from time to time? While you may think of the flu as merely a seasonal inconvenience, the influenza virus may be the deadliest pathogen known to science. Each year in the United States, over 20,000 people die from influenza infection. And that is in a good year. Once every few decades, a new strain explodes on the scene, causing pandemics and widespread death. H1N1 pales in comparison to the deadliest outbreak: the pandemic of 1918–1919, which in just 18 months killed about 40 million people worldwide—that's more people than have died of AIDS since it was discovered over 30 years ago.

The flu virus, like all viruses, consists of a relatively simple structure of nucleic acid (RNA in this case) and protein. Therefore, combating any virus requires a detailed understanding of life at the molecular level. In this chapter, we will explore the structure of DNA, how it replicates and mutates, and how it controls the cell by directing the synthesis of RNA and protein.

DNA: Structure and Replication

DNA was known to be a chemical in cells by the late 1800s, but Mendel and other early geneticists did all their work without any knowledge of DNA's role in heredity. By the late 1930s, experimental studies had convinced most biologists that one specific kind of molecule, rather than a complex chemical mixture, is the basis of inheritance. Attention focused on chromosomes, which were already known to carry genes. By the 1940s, scientists knew that chromosomes consist of two types of chemicals: DNA and protein. And by the early 1950s, a series of discoveries had convinced the scientific world that DNA was the molecule that acts as the hereditary material. This breakthrough ushered in the field of **molecular biology**, the study of heredity at the molecular level.

What came next was one of the most celebrated quests in the history of science: the effort to figure out the structure of DNA. A good deal was already known about DNA. Scientists had identified all its atoms and knew how they were bonded to one another. What was not understood was the specific three-dimensional arrangement of atoms that gives DNA its unique properties—the capacity to store genetic information, copy it, and pass it

from generation to generation. A race was on to discover how the structure of this molecule could account for its role in heredity. We will describe that momentous discovery shortly. First, let's review the underlying chemical structure of DNA and its chemical cousin RNA.

DNA and RNA Structure

Both DNA and RNA are nucleic acids, which consist of long chains (polymers) of chemical units (monomers) called **nucleotides**. (For an in-depth refresher, see the information on nucleic acids in Chapter 3, particularly Figures 3.22–3.26.) A diagram of a nucleotide polymer, or **polynucleotide**, is shown in **Figure 10.1**. This sample polynucleotide chain shows only one of many possible arrangements of the four different types of nucleotides (abbreviated A, C, T, and G) that make up DNA. Polynucleotides can be very long and may have any sequence of nucleotides, so a large number of polynucleotide chains are possible.

Nucleotides are joined together by covalent bonds between the sugar of one nucleotide and the phosphate of the next. This results in a **sugar-phosphate backbone**, a repeating pattern of sugar-phosphate-sugar-phosphate.

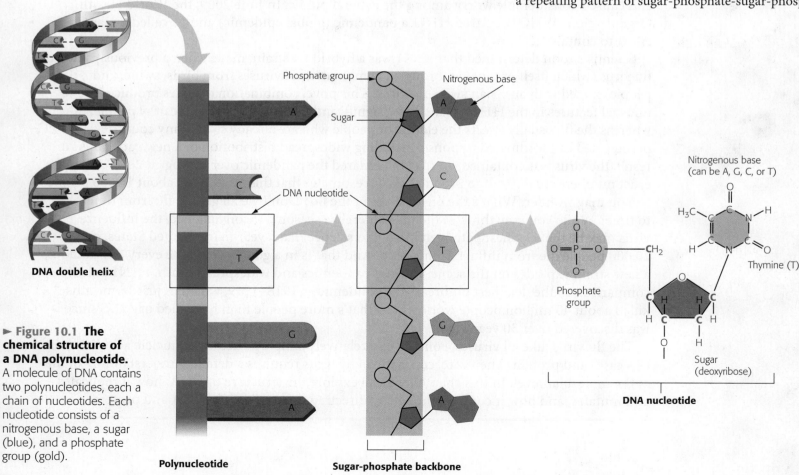

► **Figure 10.1 The chemical structure of a DNA polynucleotide.** A molecule of DNA contains two polynucleotides, each a chain of nucleotides. Each nucleotide consists of a nitrogenous base, a sugar (blue), and a phosphate group (gold).

DNA double helix

Phosphate group

Nitrogenous base

Sugar

DNA nucleotide

A

C

T

G

A

Polynucleotide

Sugar-phosphate backbone

Nitrogenous base (can be A, G, C, or T)

H_3C

Thymine (T)

Phosphate group

Sugar (deoxyribose)

DNA nucleotide

The nitrogenous bases are arranged like ribs that project from this backbone. Moving from left to right across Figure 10.1, we can zoom in to see that each nucleotide consists of three components: a nitrogenous base, a sugar (blue), and a phosphate group (gold). Examining a single nucleotide even more closely, we see the chemical structure of its three components. The phosphate group, with a phosphorus atom (P) at its center, is the source of the *acid* in nucleic acid. The phosphate has given up a hydrogen ion, H^+, leaving a negative charge on one of its oxygen atoms. The sugar has five carbon atoms (shown in red): four in its ring and one extending above the ring. The ring also includes an oxygen atom. The sugar is called *deoxyribose* because, compared with the sugar ribose, it is missing an oxygen atom. The full name for **DNA** is *deoxyribonucleic acid*, with *nucleic* referring to DNA's location in the nuclei of eukaryotic cells. The nitrogenous base (thymine, in our example) has a ring of nitrogen and carbon atoms with various chemical groups attached. In contrast to the acidic phosphate group, nitrogenous bases are basic; hence their name.

The four nucleotides found in DNA differ only in their nitrogenous bases (see Figure 3.24 for a review). The bases can be divided into two types. **Thymine (T)** and **cytosine (C)** are single-ring structures. **Adenine (A)** and **guanine (G)** are larger, double-ring structures. Instead of thymine, RNA has a similar base called **uracil (U)**. And RNA contains a slightly different sugar than DNA (ribose instead of deoxyribose). Other than that, RNA and DNA polynucleotides have the same chemical structure. **Figure 10.2** is a computer graphic of a piece of RNA polynucleotide about 20 nucleotides long. ✔

Cytosine
Uracil
Adenine
Guanine
Phosphate
Sugar (ribose)

► **Figure 10.2 An RNA polynucleotide.**
The yellow used for the phosphorus atoms and the blue of the sugar atoms make it easy to spot the sugar-phosphate backbone.

✔ CHECKPOINT
Compare and contrast the chemical components of DNA and RNA.

Answer: Both are polymers of nucleotides (a sugar + a nitrogenous base + a phosphate group). In RNA, the sugar is ribose; in DNA, it is deoxyribose. Both RNA and DNA have the bases A, G, and C, but DNA has T and RNA has U.

Watson and Crick's Discovery of the Double Helix

The celebrated partnership that solved the puzzle of DNA structure began soon after a 23-year-old newly minted American Ph.D. named James D. Watson journeyed to Cambridge University in England. There, a more senior scientist named Francis Crick was studying protein structure with a technique called X-ray crystallography. While visiting the laboratory of Maurice Wilkins at King's College in London, Watson saw an X-ray image of DNA produced by Wilkins's colleague Rosalind Franklin. A careful study of the image enabled Watson to figure out that the basic shape of DNA is a helix (spiral) with a uniform diameter. The thickness of the helix suggested that it was made up of two polynucleotide strands—in other words, a **double helix**. But how were the nucleotides arranged in the double helix?

Using wire models, Watson and Crick began trying to construct a double helix that would conform both to Franklin's data and to what was then known about the chemistry of DNA **(Figure 10.3)**. Watson placed the backbones on the outside of the model, forcing the nitrogenous bases to swivel to the interior of the molecule. It then occurred to him that the four kinds of bases might pair in a specific way. This idea of *specific base pairing* was a flash of inspiration that enabled Watson and Crick to solve the DNA puzzle.

▼ **Figure 10.3 Discoverers of the double helix.**

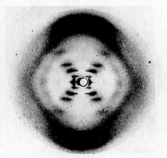

James Watson (left) and **Francis Crick.** The discoverers of the structure of DNA are shown in 1953 with their model of the double helix.

Rosalind Franklin (top). By generating X-ray images of DNA (bottom), Franklin provided Watson and Crick with some key data about the structure of DNA.

At first, Watson imagined that the bases paired like with like—for example, A with A, C with C. But that kind of pairing did not fit with the fact that the DNA molecule has a uniform diameter. An AA pair (made of two double-ringed bases) would be almost twice as wide as a CC pair (made of two single-ringed bases), resulting in an uneven molecule. It soon became apparent that a double-ringed base on one strand must always be paired with a single-ringed base on the opposite strand.

Moreover, Watson and Crick realized that the chemical structure of each kind of base dictated the pairings even more specifically. Each base has chemical groups that can best form hydrogen bonds with just one appropriate partner. Adenine can best form hydrogen bonds with thymine, and guanine with cytosine. In the biologist's shorthand: A pairs with T, and G pairs with C. A is also said to be "complementary" to T, and G to C.

You can picture the model of the DNA double helix proposed by Watson and Crick as a rope ladder having rigid, wooden rungs, with the ladder twisted into a spiral (**Figure 10.4**). Figure 10.5 shows three more detailed representations of the double helix. The ribbonlike diagram in **Figure 10.5a** symbolizes the bases with shapes that emphasize their complementarity. **Figure 10.5b** is a more chemically precise version showing only four base pairs, with the helix untwisted and the individual hydrogen bonds specified by dashed lines. **Figure 10.5c** is a computer model showing part of a double helix in atomic detail.

Although the base-pairing rules dictate the side-by-side combinations of nitrogenous bases that form the rungs of the double helix, they place no restrictions on the sequence of nucleotides along the length of a DNA strand. In fact, the sequence of bases can vary in countless ways.

► **Figure 10.4 A rope-ladder model of a double helix.** The ropes at the sides represent the sugar-phosphate backbones. Each wooden rung stands for a pair of bases connected by hydrogen bonds.

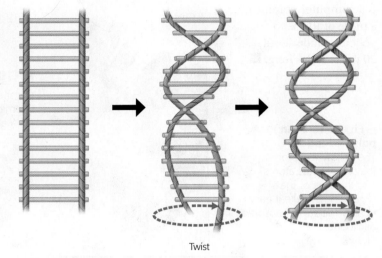

Twist

▼ Figure 10.5 **Three representations of DNA.**

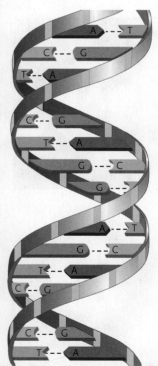

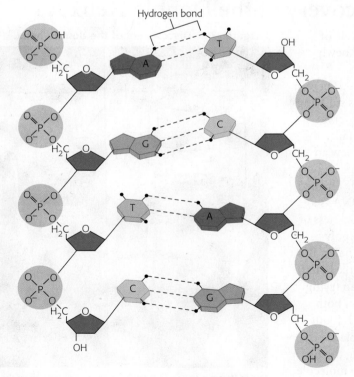

Hydrogen bond

(a) Ribbon model. The sugar-phosphate backbones are blue ribbons, and the bases are complementary shapes in shades of green and orange.

(b) Atomic model. In this more chemically detailed structure, you can see the individual hydrogen bonds (dashed lines). You can also see that the strands run in opposite directions: Notice that the sugars on the two strands are upside down with respect to each other.

(c) Computer model. Each atom is shown as a sphere, creating a space-filling model.

In April 1953, Watson and Crick rocked the scientific world with a succinct paper proposing their molecular model for DNA in the British scientific journal *Nature*. Few milestones in the history of biology have had as broad an impact as their double helix, with its AT and CG base pairing. In 1962, Watson, Crick, and Wilkins received the Nobel Prize for their work. (Franklin deserved the prize as well, but she had died from cancer in 1958; Nobel prizes are never awarded posthumously.)

In their 1953 paper, Watson and Crick wrote that the structure they proposed "immediately suggests a possible copying mechanism for the genetic material." In other words, the structure of DNA also points toward a molecular explanation for life's unique properties of reproduction and inheritance, as we see next.

DNA Replication

When a cell or a whole organism reproduces, a complete set of genetic instructions must pass from one generation to the next. For this to occur, there must be a means of copying the instructions. Watson and Crick's model for DNA structure immediately suggested to them that each DNA strand serves as a mold, or template, to guide reproduction of the other strand. The logic behind the Watson-Crick proposal for how DNA is copied is quite simple. If you know the sequence of bases in one strand of the double helix, you can very easily determine the sequence of bases in the other strand by applying the base-pairing rules: A pairs with T (and T with A), and G pairs with C (and C with G). For example, if one polynucleotide has the sequence AGTC, then the complementary polynucleotide in that DNA molecule must have the sequence TCAG.

Figure 10.6 shows how this model can account for the direct copying of a piece of DNA. The two strands of parental DNA separate, and each becomes a template for the assembly of a complementary strand from a supply of free nucleotides. The nucleotides are lined up one at a time along the template strand in accordance with the base-pairing rules. Enzymes link the nucleotides to form the new DNA strands. The completed new molecules, identical to the parental molecule, are known as daughter DNA molecules (no gender should be inferred from this name).

Although the general mechanism of DNA replication is conceptually simple, the actual process is complex and requires the cooperation of more than a dozen enzymes and other proteins. The enzymes that make the covalent bonds between the nucleotides of a new DNA strand are called **DNA polymerases**. As an incoming nucleotide base-pairs with its complement on the template strand, a DNA polymerase adds it to the end of the growing daughter strand (polymer). The process is both fast and

amazingly accurate; typically, DNA replication proceeds at a rate of 50 nucleotides per second, with fewer than one in a billion incorrectly paired. In addition to their roles in DNA replication, DNA polymerases and some of the associated proteins are also involved in repairing damaged DNA. DNA can be harmed by toxic chemicals in the environment or by high-energy radiation, such as X-rays and ultraviolet light.

DNA replication begins at specific sites on a double helix, called origins of replication. It then proceeds in both directions, creating what are called replication "bubbles" **(Figure 10.7)**. The parental DNA strands open up as daughter strands elongate on both sides of each bubble. The DNA molecule of a typical eukaryotic chromosome has many origins where replication can start simultaneously, shortening the total time needed for the process. Eventually, all the bubbles merge, yielding two completed double-stranded daughter DNA molecules.

DNA replication ensures that all the body cells in a multicellular organism carry the same genetic information. It is also the means by which genetic information is passed along to offspring. ☑

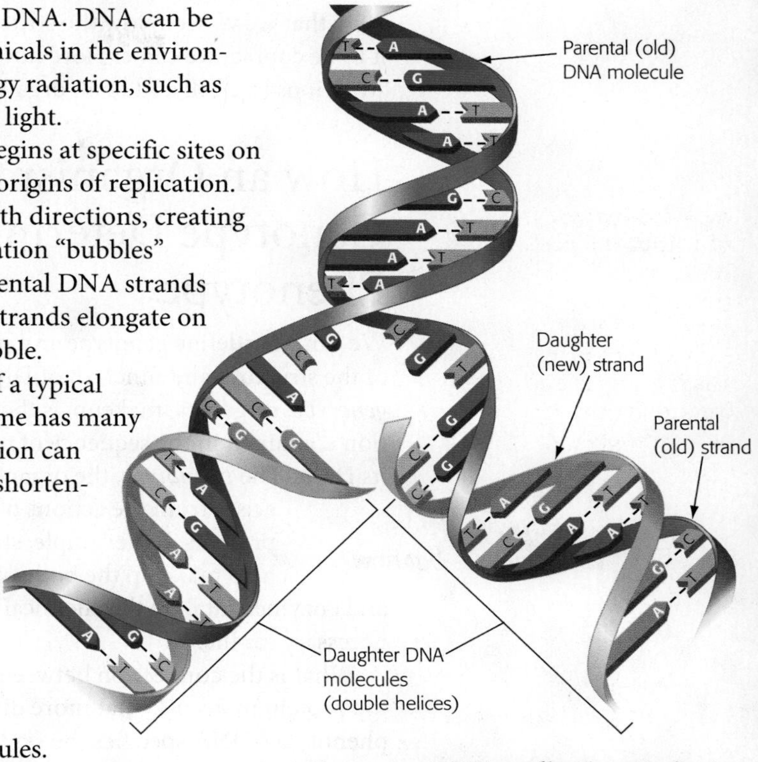

Parental (old) DNA molecule

Daughter (new) strand

Parental (old) strand

Daughter DNA molecules (double helices)

▲ **Figure 10.6 DNA replication.** Replication results in two daughter DNA molecules, each consisting of one old strand and one new strand. The parental DNA untwists as its strands separate, and the daughter DNA rewinds as it forms.

▼ Figure 10.7 **Multiple "bubbles" in replicating DNA.**

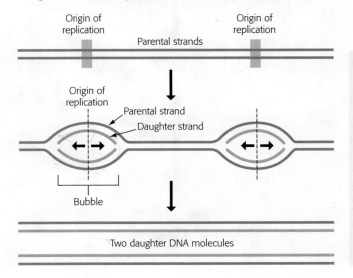

Origin of replication

Origin of replication

Parental strands

Origin of replication

Parental strand

Daughter strand

Bubble

Two daughter DNA molecules

☑ CHECKPOINT

1. How does complementary base pairing make DNA replication possible?
2. What enzymes connect nucleotides together during DNA replication?

Answers: 1. When the two strands of the double helix separate, each serves as a template on which nucleotides can be arranged by specific base pairing into new complementary strands. 2. DNA polymerases

The Flow of Genetic Information from DNA to RNA to Protein

Now that we've seen how the structure of DNA allows it to be copied, we can explore how DNA provides instructions to a cell and to an organism as a whole.

How an Organism's Genotype Determines Its Phenotype

We can now define genotype and phenotype in terms of the structure and function of DNA. An organism's *genotype*, its genetic makeup, is the heritable information contained in the sequence of nucleotide bases in its DNA. The *phenotype*, the organism's physical traits,

Your genes determine who you are—but how?

arises from the actions of a wide variety of proteins. For example, structural proteins help make up the body of an organism, and enzymes catalyze the chemical reactions that are necessary for life.

What is the connection between the genotype and the protein molecules that more directly determine the phenotype? DNA specifies the synthesis of proteins. However, a gene does not build a protein directly, but rather dispatches instructions in the form of RNA, which in turn programs protein synthesis. This fundamental concept in biology (termed the "central dogma" by Francis Crick) is summarized in **Figure 10.8**. The

molecular "chain of command" is from DNA in the nucleus (purple area in the figure) to RNA to protein synthesis in the cytoplasm (blue-green). The two main stages are **transcription**, the transfer of genetic information from DNA into an RNA molecule, and **translation**, the transfer of the information from RNA into a protein.

The relationship between genes and proteins was first proposed in 1909, when English physician Archibald Garrod suggested that genes dictate phenotypes through enzymes, the proteins that speed chemical reactions. Garrod hypothesized that inherited diseases reflect a person's inability to make a particular enzyme. He gave as one example the hereditary condition called alkaptonuria, in which the urine appears dark red because it contains a chemical called alkapton. Garrod reasoned that normal individuals have an enzyme that breaks down alkapton, whereas alkaptonuric individuals lack the enzyme. Research conducted decades later proved him right.

The major breakthrough in demonstrating the relationship between genes and enzymes came in the 1940s from the work of American geneticists George Beadle and Edward Tatum with the bread mold *Neurospora crassa* (**Figure 10.9**). Beadle and Tatum studied strains of the mold that were unable to grow on the usual growth medium. Each of these strains turned out to lack an enzyme in a metabolic pathway that synthesized an amino acid called arginine. Beadle and Tatum also showed that each mutant was defective in a single gene. Accordingly, they hypothesized that the function of an individual

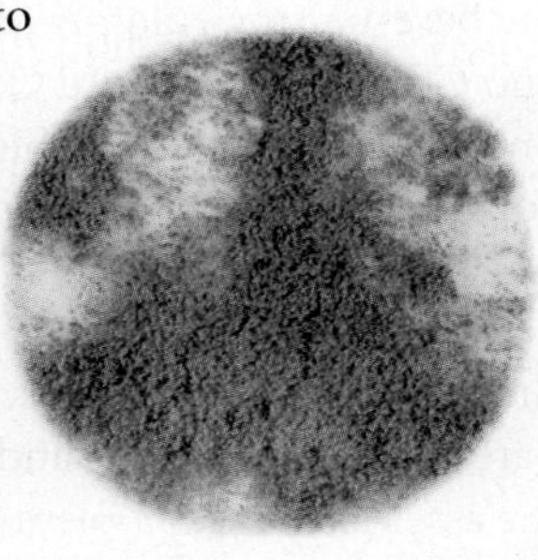

▲ **Figure 10.9** **The bread mold *Neurospora crassa* has a fuzzy appearance.**

gene is to dictate the production of a specific enzyme.

The "one gene–one enzyme" hypothesis has since been modified. First it was extended beyond enzymes to include all types of proteins. For example, keratin (the structural protein of your hair) is the product of a gene. Then it was discovered that many proteins have two or more different polypeptide chains (see Figure 3.20d); in such cases, each polypeptide is specified by its own gene. Thus, Beadle and Tatum's hypothesis is now stated as follows: the function of a gene is to dictate the production of a polypeptide. ☑

► **Figure 10.8** **The flow of genetic information in a eukaryotic cell.** A sequence of nucleotides in the DNA is transcribed into a molecule of RNA in the cell's nucleus. The RNA travels to the cytoplasm, where it is translated into the specific amino acid sequence of a protein.

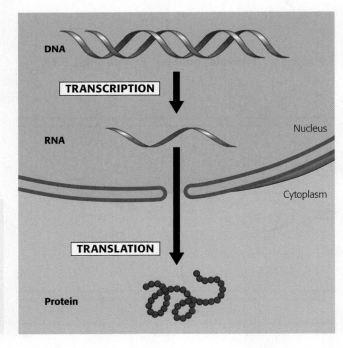

DNA

TRANSCRIPTION

RNA

Nucleus

Cytoplasm

TRANSLATION

Protein

☑ **CHECKPOINT**

What are transcription and translation?

Answer: Transcription is the transfer of genetic information from DNA to RNA. Translation is the use of the information in an RNA molecule for the synthesis of a polypeptide.

From Nucleotides to Amino Acids: An Overview

Genetic information in DNA is transcribed into RNA and then translated into polypeptides, which then fold into proteins. But how do these processes occur? Transcription and translation are linguistic terms, and it is useful to think of nucleic acids and proteins as having languages. To understand how genetic information passes from genotype to phenotype, we need to see how the chemical language of DNA is translated into the different chemical language of proteins.

What exactly is the language of nucleic acids? Both DNA and RNA are polymers made of nucleotide monomers strung together in specific sequences that convey information, much as specific sequences of letters convey information in English. In DNA, the monomers are the four types of nucleotides, which differ in their nitrogenous bases (A, T, C, and G). The same is true for RNA, although it has the base U instead of T.

The language of DNA is written as a linear sequence of nucleotide bases, a sequence such as the blue sequence you see on the enlarged DNA strand in **Figure 10.10**. Specific sequences of bases, each with a beginning and an end, make up the genes on a DNA strand. A typical gene consists of thousands of nucleotides in a specific sequence.

When a segment of DNA is transcribed, the result is an RNA molecule. The process is called transcription because the nucleic acid language of DNA has simply been rewritten (transcribed) as a sequence of bases of RNA; the language is still that of nucleic acids. The nucleotide bases of the RNA molecule are complementary to those on the DNA strand. As you will soon see, this is because the RNA was synthesized using the DNA as a template.

Translation is the conversion of the nucleic acid language to the polypeptide language. Like nucleic acids, polypeptides are polymers, but the monomers that make them up—the letters of the polypeptide alphabet—are the 20 amino acids common to all organisms (represented as purple shapes in Figure 10.10). Again, the language is written in a linear sequence. In this case, the sequence of nucleotides of the RNA molecule dictates the sequence of amino acids of the polypeptide. But remember, RNA is only a messenger; the genetic information that dictates the amino acid sequence originates in DNA.

What are the rules for translating the RNA message into a polypeptide? In other words, what is the correspondence between the nucleotides of an RNA molecule and the amino acids of a polypeptide? Keep in mind that there are only four different kinds of nucleotides in DNA (A, G, C, T) and RNA (A, G, C, U). In translation, these four must somehow specify 20 amino acids. If each nucleotide base coded for one amino acid, only 4 of the 20 amino acids could be accounted for. In fact, triplets of bases are the smallest "words" of uniform length that can specify all the amino acids. There can be 64 (that is, 4^3) possible code words of this type—more than enough to specify the 20 amino acids. Indeed, there are enough triplets to allow more than one coding for each amino acid. For example, the base triplets AAA and AAG both code for the same amino acid.

Experiments have verified that the flow of information from gene to protein is based on a triplet code. The genetic instructions for the amino acid sequence of a polypeptide chain are written in DNA and RNA as a series of three-base words called **codons**. Three-base codons in the DNA are transcribed into complementary three-base codons in the RNA, and then the RNA codons are translated into amino acids that form a polypeptide. As summarized in Figure 10.10, one DNA codon (three nucleotides) → one RNA codon (three nucleotides) → one amino acid. Next we turn to the codons themselves. ☑

▼ **Figure 10.10 Transcription of DNA and translation of codons.** This figure focuses on a small region of one of the genes carried by a DNA molecule. The enlarged segment from one strand of gene 3 shows its specific sequence of bases. The red strand and purple chain represent the results of transcription and translation, respectively.

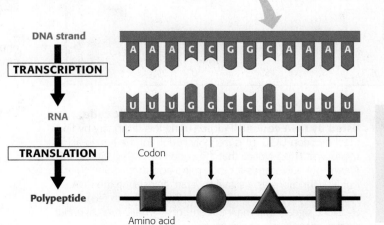

☑ CHECKPOINT

How many nucleotides are necessary to code for a polypeptide that is 100 amino acids long?

Answer: 300

The Genetic Code

During the 1960s, scientists cracked the **genetic code**, the set of rules that convert a nucleotide sequence in RNA to an amino acid sequence. As **Figure 10.11** shows, 61 of the 64 triplets code for amino acids. The triplet AUG has a dual function: It codes for the amino acid methionine (Met) and can also provide a signal for the start of a polypeptide chain. Three codons (UAA, UGA, and UAG) do not designate amino acids. They are the stop codons that instruct the ribosomes to end the polypeptide.

Notice in Figure 10.11 that a given RNA triplet always specifies a given amino acid. For example, although codons UUU and UUC both specify phenylalanine, neither of them ever represents any other amino acid. The codons in the figure are the triplets found in RNA. They have a straightforward, complementary relationship to the codons in DNA.

How is it that genetic engineers can mix and match DNA from different species?

The nucleotides making up the codons occur in a linear order along the DNA and RNA, with no gaps separating the codons.

The genetic code is nearly universal, shared by organisms from the simplest bacteria to the most complex plants and animals. The universality of the genetic vocabulary suggests that it arose very early in evolution and was passed on over the eons to all the organisms living on Earth today. In fact, such universality is the key to modern DNA technologies. Because diverse organisms share a common genetic code, it is possible to program one species to produce a protein from another species by transplanting DNA (**Figure 10.12**). This allows scientists to mix and match genes from various species—a procedure with many useful applications. Besides having practical purposes, a shared genetic vocabulary also reminds us of the evolutionary kinship that connects all life on Earth. ✔

✔ CHECKPOINT

An RNA molecule contains the nucleotide sequence CCAUUUACG. Using Figure 10.11, translate this sequence into the corresponding amino acid sequence.

Answer: Pro-Phe-Thr

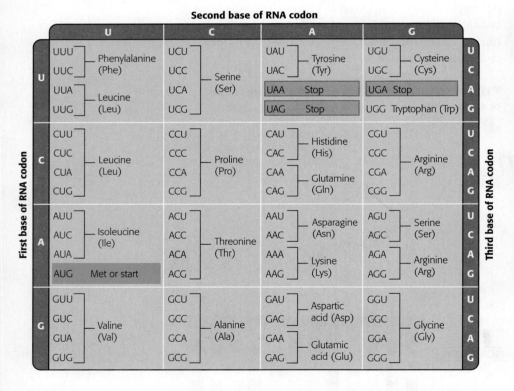

Second base of RNA codon

	U	C	A	G	
U	UUU ⎤ Phenylalanine (Phe) UUC ⎦ UUA ⎤ Leucine (Leu) UUG ⎦	UCU ⎤ UCC UCA Serine (Ser) UCG ⎦	UAU ⎤ Tyrosine (Tyr) UAC ⎦ UAA Stop UAG Stop	UGU ⎤ Cysteine (Cys) UGC ⎦ UGA Stop UGG Tryptophan (Trp)	U C A G
C	CUU ⎤ CUC CUA Leucine (Leu) CUG ⎦	CCU ⎤ CCC CCA Proline (Pro) CCG ⎦	CAU ⎤ Histidine (His) CAC ⎦ CAA ⎤ Glutamine (Gln) CAG ⎦	CGU ⎤ CGC CGA Arginine (Arg) CGG ⎦	U C A G
A	AUU ⎤ AUC Isoleucine (Ile) AUA ⎦ AUG Met or start	ACU ⎤ ACC ACA Threonine (Thr) ACG ⎦	AAU ⎤ Asparagine (Asn) AAC ⎦ AAA ⎤ Lysine (Lys) AAG ⎦	AGU ⎤ Serine (Ser) AGC ⎦ AGA ⎤ Arginine (Arg) AGG ⎦	U C A G
G	GUU ⎤ GUC GUA Valine (Val) GUG ⎦	GCU ⎤ GCC GCA Alanine (Ala) GCG ⎦	GAU ⎤ Aspartic acid (Asp) GAC ⎦ GAA ⎤ Glutamic acid (Glu) GAG ⎦	GGU ⎤ GGC GGA Glycine (Gly) GGG ⎦	U C A G

First base of RNA codon (left axis) — *Third base of RNA codon* (right axis)

▲ Figure 10.11 **The dictionary of the genetic code, listed by RNA codons.** Practice using this dictionary by finding the codon UGG. (It is the only codon for the amino acid tryptophan, Trp.) Notice that the codon AUG (highlighted in green) not only stands for the amino acid methionine (Met), but also functions as a signal to "start" translating the RNA at that place. Three of the 64 codons (highlighted in red) function as "stop" signals that mark the end of a genetic message, but do not encode any amino acids.

▲ Figure 10.12 **Mice expressing a foreign gene.** This photo shows the results of an experiment in which researchers incorporated a jelly (jellyfish) gene for a protein called green fluorescent protein (GFP) into the DNA of mice. The mouse in the middle lacks the gene for GFP; the other mice have it.

Transcription: From DNA to RNA

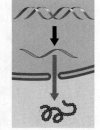

Let's look more closely at transcription, the transfer of genetic information from DNA to RNA. An RNA molecule is transcribed from a DNA template by a process that resembles the synthesis of a DNA strand during DNA replication. **Figure 10.13a** is a close-up view of this process. As with replication, the two DNA strands must first separate at the place where the process will start. In transcription, however, only one of the DNA strands serves as a template for the newly forming RNA molecule; the other strand is unused. The nucleotides that make up the new RNA molecule take their place one at a time along the DNA template strand by forming hydrogen bonds with the nucleotide bases there. Notice that the RNA nucleotides follow the usual base-pairing rules, except that U, rather than T, pairs with A. The RNA nucleotides are linked by the transcription enzyme **RNA polymerase**.

Figure 10.13b is an overview of the transcription of an entire gene. Special sequences of DNA nucleotides tell the RNA polymerase where to start and where to stop the transcribing process.

❶ Initiation of Transcription

The "start transcribing" signal is a nucleotide sequence called a **promoter**, which is located in the DNA at the beginning of the gene. A promoter is a specific place where RNA polymerase attaches. The first phase of transcription, called initiation, is the attachment of RNA polymerase to the promoter and the start of RNA

synthesis. For any gene, the promoter dictates which of the two DNA strands is to be transcribed (the particular strand varies from gene to gene).

❷ RNA Elongation

During the second phase of transcription, elongation, the RNA grows longer. As RNA synthesis continues, the RNA strand peels away from its DNA template, allowing the two separated DNA strands to come back together in the region already transcribed.

❸ Termination of Transcription

In the third phase, termination, the RNA polymerase reaches a special sequence of bases in the DNA template called a **terminator**. This sequence signals the end of the gene. At this point, the polymerase molecule detaches from the RNA molecule and the gene, and the DNA strands rejoin.

In addition to producing RNA that encodes amino acid sequences, transcription makes two other kinds of RNA that are involved in building polypeptides. We discuss these kinds of RNA a little later. ☑

☑ CHECKPOINT

How does RNA polymerase "know" where to start transcribing a gene?

Answer: It recognizes the gene's promoter, a specific nucleotide sequence.

▼ **Figure 10.13 Transcription.**

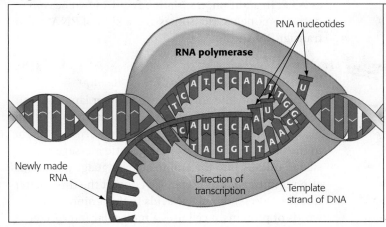

(a) **A close-up view of transcription.** As RNA nucleotides base-pair one by one with DNA bases on one DNA strand (called the template strand), the enzyme RNA polymerase (orange) links the RNA nucleotides into an RNA chain.

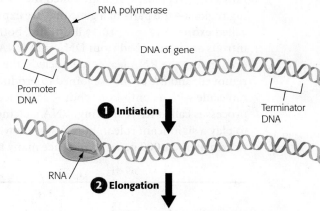
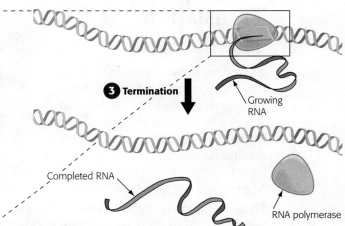

(b) **Transcription of a gene.** The transcription of an entire gene occurs in three phases: initiation, elongation, and termination of the RNA. The section of DNA where the RNA polymerase starts is called the promoter; the place where it stops is called the terminator.

The Processing of Eukaryotic RNA

In the cells of prokaryotes, which lack nuclei, the RNA transcribed from a gene immediately functions as **messenger RNA (mRNA)**, the molecule that is translated into protein. But this is not the case in eukaryotic cells. The eukaryotic cell not only localizes transcription in the nucleus but also modifies, or processes, the RNA transcripts there before they move to the cytoplasm for translation by the ribosomes.

One kind of RNA processing is the addition of extra nucleotides to the ends of the RNA transcript. These additions, called the **cap** and **tail**, protect the RNA from attack by cellular enzymes and help ribosomes recognize the RNA as mRNA.

Another type of RNA processing is made necessary in eukaryotes by noncoding stretches of nucleotides that interrupt the nucleotides that actually code for amino acids. It is as if nonsense words were randomly interspersed in a story. Most genes of plants and animals, it turns out, include such internal noncoding regions, which are called **introns**. The coding regions—the parts of a gene that are expressed—are called **exons**. As **Figure 10.14** illustrates, both exons and introns are transcribed from DNA into RNA. However, before the RNA leaves the nucleus, the introns are removed, and the exons are joined to produce an mRNA molecule with a continuous coding sequence. This process is called **RNA splicing**. RNA splicing is believed to play a significant role in humans in allowing our approximately 21,000 genes to produce many thousands

Do your genes contain gobbledygook?

☑ CHECKPOINT

Why is a final mRNA often shorter than the DNA gene that coded for it?

Answer: because introns are removed from the RNA

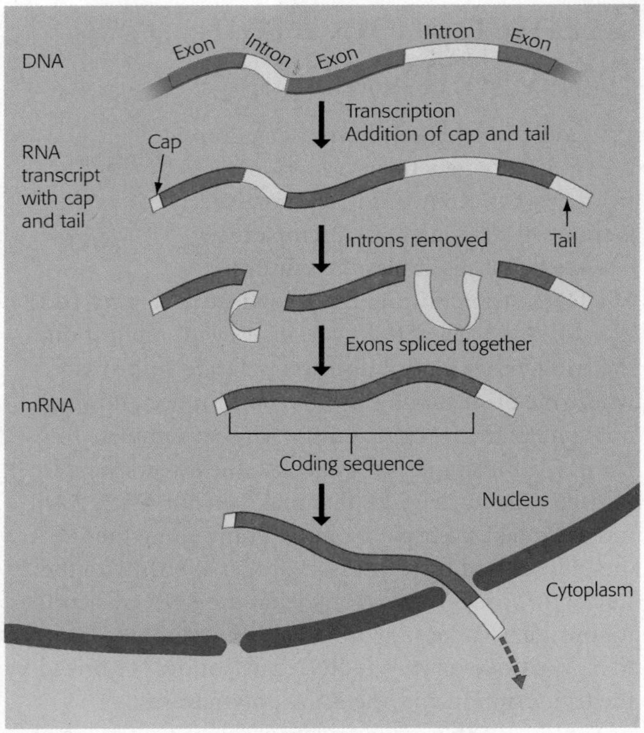

▲ **Figure 10.14 The production of messenger RNA (mRNA) in a eukaryotic cell.** Note that the molecule of mRNA that leaves the nucleus is substantially different from the molecule of RNA that was first transcribed from the gene. In the cytoplasm, the coding sequence of the final mRNA will be translated.

DNA

Transcription
Addition of cap and tail

RNA transcript with cap and tail

Cap

Introns removed   Tail

Exons spliced together

mRNA

Coding sequence

Nucleus

Cytoplasm

more polypeptides. This is accomplished by varying the exons that are included in the final mRNA.

With capping, tailing, and splicing completed, the "final draft" of eukaryotic mRNA is ready for translation. ☑

Translation: The Players

As we have already discussed, translation is a conversion between different languages—from the nucleic acid language to the protein language—and it involves more elaborate machinery than transcription.

Messenger RNA (mRNA)

The first important ingredient required for translation is the mRNA produced by transcription. Once it is present, the machinery used to translate mRNA requires enzymes and sources of chemical energy, such

as ATP. In addition, translation requires two heavy-duty components: ribosomes and a kind of RNA called transfer RNA.

Transfer RNA (tRNA)

Translation of any language into another language requires an interpreter, someone or something that can recognize the words of one language and convert them to the other. Translation of the genetic message carried in mRNA into the amino acid language of proteins also requires an interpreter. To convert the three-letter words (codons) of nucleic acids to the amino acid words of proteins, a cell uses a molecular interpreter, a type of RNA called **transfer RNA (tRNA)**, depicted in **Figure 10.15**.

▼ Figure 10.15 The structure of tRNA. At one end of the tRNA is the site where an amino acid will attach (purple), and at the other end is the three-nucleotide anticodon where the mRNA will attach (light green).

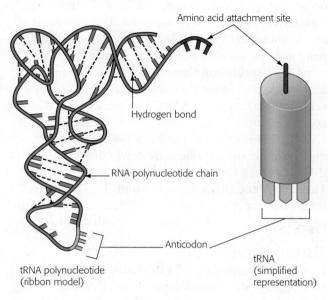

Amino acid attachment site

Hydrogen bond

RNA polynucleotide chain

Anticodon

tRNA polynucleotide (ribbon model)

tRNA (simplified representation)

A cell that is producing proteins has in its cytoplasm a supply of amino acids. But amino acids themselves cannot recognize the codons arranged in sequence along messenger RNA. It is up to the cell's molecular interpreters, tRNA molecules, to match amino acids to the appropriate codons to form the new polypeptide. To perform this task, tRNA molecules must carry out two distinct functions: (1) pick up the appropriate amino acids and (2) recognize the appropriate codons in the mRNA. The unique structure of tRNA molecules enables them to perform both tasks.

As shown on the left in Figure 10.15, a tRNA molecule is made of a single strand of RNA—one polynucleotide chain—consisting of about 80 nucleotides. The chain twists and folds upon itself, forming several double-stranded regions in which short stretches of RNA base-pair with other stretches. At one end of the folded molecule is a special triplet of bases called an **anticodon**. The anticodon triplet is complementary to a codon triplet on mRNA. During translation, the anticodon on the tRNA recognizes a particular codon on the mRNA by using base-pairing rules. At the other end of the tRNA molecule is a site where one specific kind of amino acid attaches. Although all tRNA molecules are similar, there are slightly different versions of tRNA for each amino acid.

Ribosomes

Ribosomes are the organelles that coordinate the functioning of the mRNA and tRNA and actually make polypeptides. As you can see in **Figure 10.16a**, a ribosome consists of two subunits. Each subunit is made up of proteins and a considerable amount of yet another kind of RNA, **ribosomal RNA (rRNA)**. A fully assembled ribosome has a binding site for mRNA on its small subunit and binding sites for tRNA on its large subunit. **Figure 10.16b** shows how two tRNA molecules get together with an mRNA molecule on a ribosome. One of the tRNA binding sites, the P site, holds the tRNA carrying the growing polypeptide chain, while another, the A site, holds a tRNA carrying the next amino acid to be added to the chain. The anticodon on each tRNA base-pairs with a codon on the mRNA. The subunits of the ribosome act like a vise, holding the tRNA and mRNA molecules close together. The ribosome can then connect the amino acid from the tRNA in the A site to the growing polypeptide. ☑

▼ Figure 10.16 The ribosome.

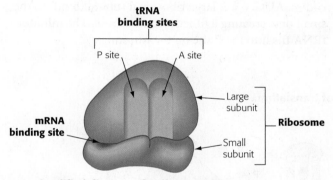

tRNA binding sites

P site   A site

mRNA binding site

Large subunit

Ribosome

Small subunit

(a) A simplified diagram of a ribosome. Notice the two subunits and sites where mRNA and tRNA molecules bind.

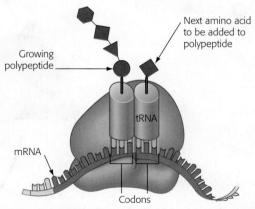

Growing polypeptide

Next amino acid to be added to polypeptide

tRNA

mRNA

Codons

(b) The "players" of translation. When functioning in polypeptide synthesis, a ribosome holds one molecule of mRNA and two molecules of tRNA. The growing polypeptide is attached to one of the tRNAs.

☑ CHECKPOINT

What is an anticodon?

Answer: An anticodon is the base triplet of a tRNA molecule that couples the tRNA to a complementary codon in the mRNA. The base pairing of anticodon to codon is a key step in translating mRNA to a polypeptide.

Translation: The Process

Translation is divided into the same three phases as transcription: initiation, elongation, and termination.

Initiation

This first phase brings together the mRNA, the first amino acid with its attached tRNA, and the two subunits of a ribosome. An mRNA molecule, even after splicing, is longer than the genetic message it carries (**Figure 10.17**). Nucleotide sequences at either end of the molecule (pink) are not part of the message, but along with the cap and tail in eukaryotes, they help the mRNA bind to the ribosome. The initiation process determines exactly where translation will begin so that the mRNA codons will be translated into the correct sequence of amino acids. Initiation occurs in two steps, as shown in **Figure 10.18**. ❶ An mRNA molecule binds to a small ribosomal subunit. A special initiator tRNA then binds to the **start codon**, where translation is to begin on the mRNA. The initiator tRNA carries the amino acid methionine (Met); its anticodon, UAC, binds to the start codon, AUG. ❷ A large ribosomal subunit binds to the small one, creating a functional ribosome. The initiator tRNA fits into the P site on the ribosome.

Elongation

Once initiation is complete, amino acids are added one by one to the first amino acid. Each addition occurs in the three-step elongation process shown in **Figure 10.19**. ❶ **Codon recognition**. The anticodon of an incoming tRNA molecule, carrying its amino acid, pairs with the mRNA codon in the A site of the ribosome. ❷ **Peptide bond formation**. The polypeptide leaves the tRNA in the P site and attaches to the amino acid on the tRNA in the A site. The ribosome catalyzes bond formation. Now the chain has one more amino acid. ❸ **Translocation**. The P site tRNA now leaves the ribosome, and the ribosome moves the remaining tRNA, carrying the growing polypeptide, to the P site. The mRNA and tRNA move as a unit. This movement brings into the A site the next mRNA codon to be translated, and the process can start again with step 1.

Termination

Elongation continues until a **stop codon** reaches the ribosome's A site. Stop codons—UAA, UAG, and UGA—do not code for amino acids but instead tell translation to stop. The completed polypeptide, typically several hundred amino acids long, is freed, and the ribosome splits back into its subunits. ☑

▼ **Figure 10.17 A molecule of mRNA.**

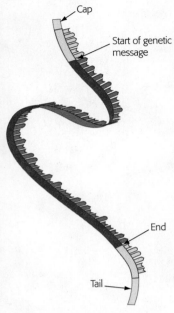

Cap

Start of genetic message

End

Tail

☑ CHECKPOINT

Which of the following does not participate directly in translation: ribosomes, transfer RNA, messenger RNA, DNA?

Answer: DNA

▼ **Figure 10.18 The initiation of translation.**

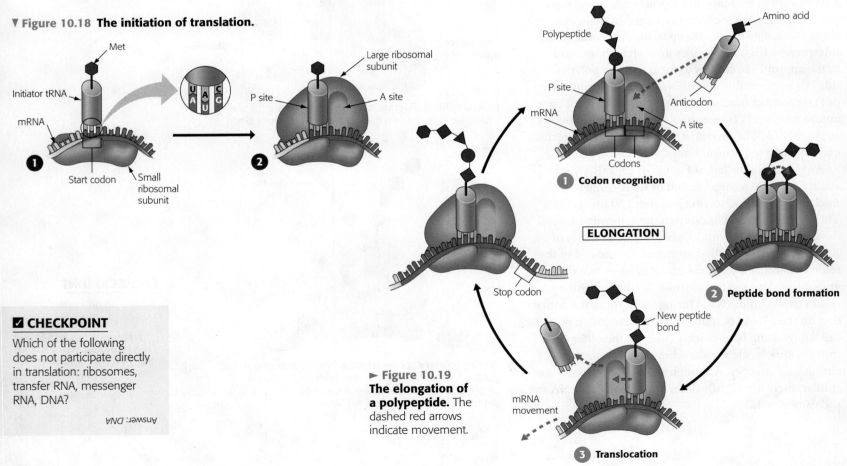

Met

Initiator tRNA

mRNA

Start codon

Small ribosomal subunit

P site

A site

Large ribosomal subunit

Polypeptide

P site

mRNA

Codons

❶ **Codon recognition**

Amino acid

Anticodon

A site

ELONGATION

❷ **Peptide bond formation**

New peptide bond

Stop codon

mRNA movement

❸ **Translocation**

► **Figure 10.19 The elongation of a polypeptide.** The dashed red arrows indicate movement.

Review:
DNA → RNA → Protein

Figure 10.20 reviews the flow of genetic information in the cell, from DNA to RNA to protein. In eukaryotic cells, transcription (DNA → RNA) occurs in the nucleus, and the RNA is processed before it enters the cytoplasm. Translation (RNA → protein) is rapid; a single ribosome can make an average-sized polypeptide in less than a minute. As it is made, a polypeptide coils and folds, assuming a three-dimensional shape, its tertiary structure.

What is the overall significance of transcription and translation? These are the processes whereby genes control the structures and activities of cells—or, more broadly, the way the genotype produces the phenotype. The chain of command originates with the information in a gene, a specific sequence of nucleotides in DNA. The gene dictates the transcription of a complementary sequence of nucleotides in mRNA. In turn, mRNA specifies the sequence of amino acids in a polypeptide. Finally, the proteins that form from the polypeptides determine the appearance and capabilities of the cell and organism.

For decades, the DNA → RNA → protein pathway was believed to be the sole means by which genetic information controls traits. In recent years, however, this notion has been challenged by discoveries that point to more complex roles for RNA. We will explore some of these special properties of RNA in Chapter 11. ✓

☑ **CHECKPOINT**

1. Transcription is the synthesis of _____, using _____ as a template.
2. Translation is the synthesis of _____, with one _____ determining each amino acid in the sequence.
3. Which organelle coordinates translation?

Answers: 1. mRNA; DNA 2. protein (polypeptides); codon 3. ribosomes

▼ **Figure 10.20 A summary of transcription and translation.** This figure summarizes the main stages in the flow of genetic information from DNA to protein in a eukaryotic cell.

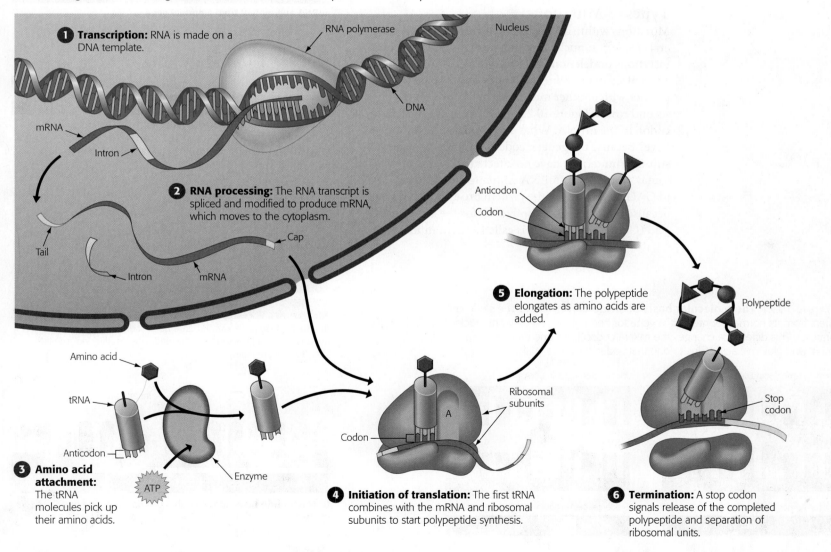

1 Transcription: RNA is made on a DNA template.

RNA polymerase

Nucleus

DNA

mRNA

Intron

Tail

Intron

mRNA

Cap

2 RNA processing: The RNA transcript is spliced and modified to produce mRNA, which moves to the cytoplasm.

Anticodon

Codon

Polypeptide

5 Elongation: The polypeptide elongates as amino acids are added.

Amino acid

tRNA

Anticodon

ATP

Enzyme

3 Amino acid attachment: The tRNA molecules pick up their amino acids.

Codon

A

Ribosomal subunits

4 Initiation of translation: The first tRNA combines with the mRNA and ribosomal subunits to start polypeptide synthesis.

Stop codon

6 Termination: A stop codon signals release of the completed polypeptide and separation of ribosomal units.

Mutations

Since discovering how genes are translated into proteins, scientists have been able to describe many heritable differences in molecular terms. For instance, sickle-cell disease can be traced to a change in a single amino acid in one of the polypeptides in the hemoglobin protein (see Figure 3.19). This difference is caused by a single nucleotide difference in the DNA coding for that polypeptide **(Figure 10.21)**.

How can a molecular "typo" make you sick?

Any change in the nucleotide sequence of DNA is called a **mutation**. Mutations can involve large regions of a chromosome or just a single nucleotide pair, as in sickle-cell disease. Occasionally, a base substitution leads to an improved protein or one with new capabilities that enhance the success of the mutant organism and its descendants. Much more often, though, mutations are harmful. Let's consider how mutations involving only one or a few nucleotide pairs can affect gene translation.

Types of Mutations

Mutations within a gene can be divided into two general categories: nucleotide substitutions and nucleotide insertions or deletions **(Figure 10.22)**. A substitution is the replacement of one nucleotide and its base-pairing partner with another nucleotide pair. For example, in the second row in Figure 10.22, A replaces G in the fourth codon of the mRNA. What effect can a substitution have? Because the genetic code is redundant, some substitution mutations have no effect at all. For example, if a mutation causes an mRNA codon to change from GAA to GAG, no change in the protein product would result because GAA and GAG both code for the same amino acid (Glu). Such a change is called a silent mutation.

Other substitutions involving a single nucleotide do change the amino acid coding. Such mutations are called missense mutations. For example, if a mutation causes an mRNA codon to change from GGC to AGC, the resulting protein will have a serine (Ser) instead of a glycine (Gly) at this position. Some missense mutations have little or no effect on the shape or function of the resulting protein, but others, as we saw in the sickle-cell case, cause changes in the protein that prevent it from performing normally.

▼ **Figure 10.22 Three types of mutations and their effects.** Mutations are changes in DNA, but they are shown here in mRNA and the polypeptide product.

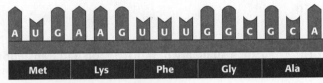

mRNA and protein from a normal gene

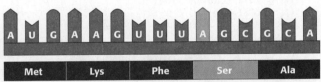

(a) Base substitution. Here, an A replaces a G in the fourth codon of the mRNA. The result in the polypeptide is a serine (Ser) instead of a glycine (Gly). This amino acid substitution may or may not affect the protein's function.

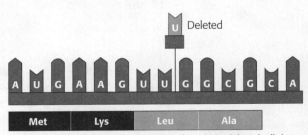

(b) Nucleotide deletion. When a nucleotide is deleted, all the codons from that point on are misread. The resulting polypeptide is likely to be completely nonfunctional.

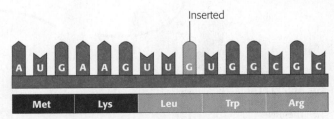

(c) Nucleotide insertion. As with a deletion, inserting one nucleotide disrupts all codons that follow, most likely producing a nonfunctional polypeptide.

▼ **Figure 10.21 The molecular basis of sickle-cell disease.** The sickle-cell allele differs from its normal counterpart, a gene for hemoglobin, by only one nucleotide (orange). This difference changes the mRNA codon from one that codes for the amino acid glutamic acid (Glu) to one that codes for valine (Val).

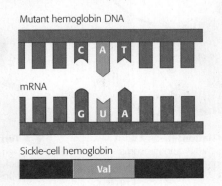

Some substitutions, called nonsense mutations, change an amino acid codon into a stop codon. For example, if an AGA (Arg) codon is mutated to a UGA (stop) codon, the result will be a prematurely terminated protein, which probably will not function properly.

Mutations involving the deletion or insertion of one or more nucleotides in a gene often have disastrous effects (see Figure 10.22b and c). Because mRNA is read as a series of nucleotide triplets during translation, adding or subtracting nucleotides may alter the triplet grouping of the genetic message. All the nucleotides that are "downstream" of the insertion or deletion will be regrouped into different codons. For example, consider an mRNA molecule containing the sequence AAG-UUU-GGC-GCA; this codes for Lys-Phe-Gly-Ala. If a U is missing in the second codon (as a result of a deletion in the DNA), the resulting sequence will be AAG-UUG-GCG-CA, which codes for Lys-Leu-Ala (see Figure 10.22b). The altered polypeptide is likely to be nonfunctional. Inserting one or two nucleotides would have a similarly profound effect.

Mutagens

What causes mutations? Mutagenesis, the creation of mutations, can occur in a number of ways. Spontaneous mutations result from errors during DNA replication or recombination. Other sources of mutation are physical and chemical agents called **mutagens**. The most common physical mutagen is high-energy radiation, such as X-rays and ultraviolet (UV) light. Chemical mutagens are of various types. One type, for example, consists of chemicals that are similar to normal DNA bases but that base-pair incorrectly when incorporated into DNA. For example, the anti-AIDS drug AZT works because its structure is similar enough to thymine that viral polymerases incorporate it into newly synthesized DNA, but different enough that the drug blocks further replication.

Many mutagens can act as carcinogens, agents that cause cancer. What can you do to avoid exposure to mutagens? Several lifestyle practices can help, including not smoking and wearing protective clothing and sunscreen to minimize direct exposure to the sun's UV rays. But such precautions are not foolproof, and it is not possible to avoid mutagens (such as UV radiation and secondhand smoke) entirely.

Although mutations are often harmful, they can also be extremely useful, both in nature and in the laboratory. Mutations are one source of the rich diversity of genes in the living world, a diversity that makes evolution by natural selection possible **(Figure 10.23)**. Mutations are also essential tools for geneticists. Whether naturally occurring or created in the laboratory, mutations are responsible for the different alleles needed for genetic research. ☑

▼ **Figure 10.23 Mutations and diversity.** Mutations are one source of the diversity of life visible in this scene from the big island of Hawaii.

☑ **CHECKPOINT**

1. What would happen if a mutation changed a start codon to some other codon?
2. What happens when one nucleotide is lost from the middle of a gene?

Answers: 1. mRNA transcribed from the mutated gene would be nonfunctional because ribosomes would not initiate translation. 2. In the mRNA, the reading of the triplets downstream from the deletion is shifted, leading to a long string of incorrect amino acids in the polypeptide.

Viruses and Other Noncellular Infectious Agents

Viruses share some of the characteristics of living organisms, such as having genetic material in the form of nucleic acid packaged within a highly organized structure. A virus is generally not considered alive, however, because it is not cellular and cannot reproduce on its own. In a sense, a **virus** is nothing more than "genes in a box": a bit of nucleic acid wrapped in a protein coat **(Figure 10.24)**. A virus can

Is a virus a living creature?

survive only by infecting a living cell and directing the cell's molecular machinery to make more viruses. In this section, we'll look at viruses that infect different types of host organisms, starting with bacteria.

Bacteriophages

Viruses that attack bacteria are called **bacteriophages** ("bacteria-eaters"), or **phages** for short. **Figure 10.25** shows a micrograph of a bacteriophage called T4 infecting an *E. coli* bacterium. The phage consists of a molecule of DNA enclosed within an elaborate structure made of proteins. The "legs" of the phage (called tail fibers) bend when they touch the cell surface. The tail is a hollow rod enclosed in a springlike sheath. As the legs bend, the spring compresses, the bottom of the rod punctures the cell membrane, and the viral DNA passes from inside the head of the virus into the cell.

Once they infect a bacterium, most phages enter a reproductive cycle called the **lytic cycle**. The lytic cycle gets its name from the fact that after many copies of the phage are produced within the bacterial cell, the bacterium lyses (breaks open). Some viruses can also reproduce by an alternative route—the **lysogenic cycle**.

▼ **Figure 10.24 Adenovirus.** A virus that infects the human respiratory system, an adenovirus consists of DNA enclosed in a protein coat shaped like a 20-sided polyhedron, shown here in a computer-generated model that is magnified approximately 500,000 times the actual size. At each corner of the polyhedron is a protein spike, which helps the virus attach to a susceptible cell.

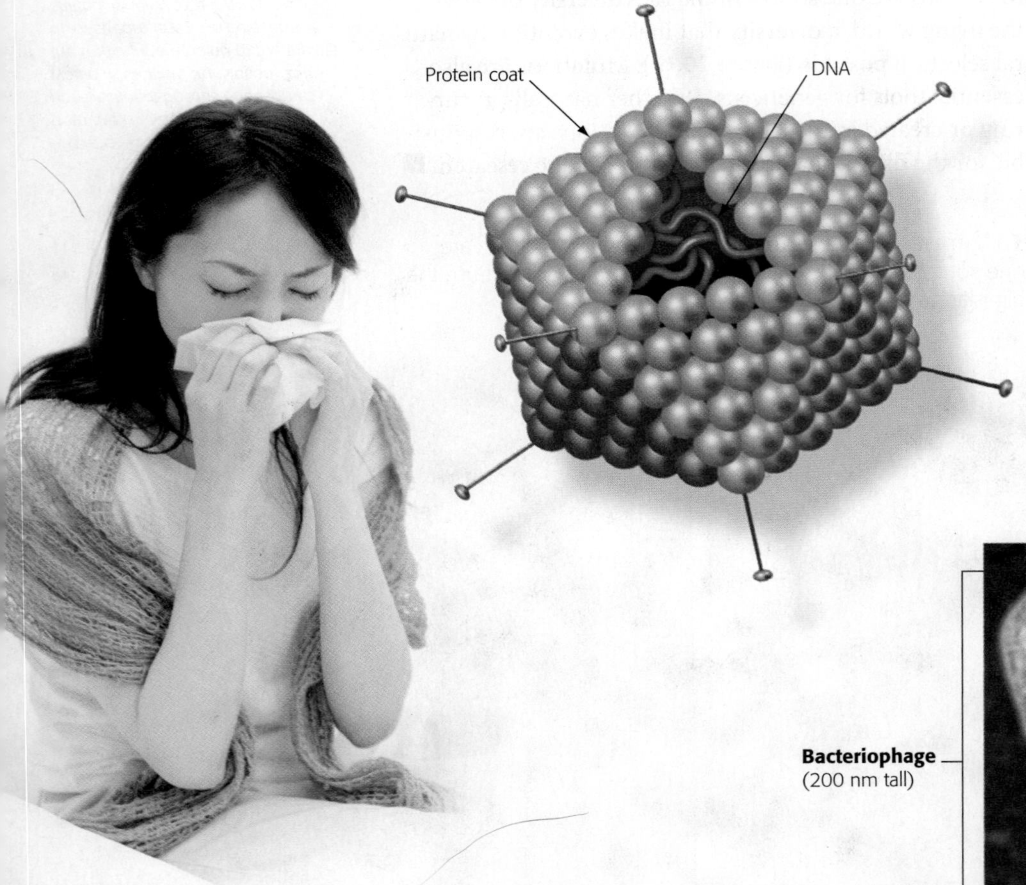

Protein coat

DNA

▼ **Figure 10.25 Bacteriophages (viruses) infecting a bacterial cell.**

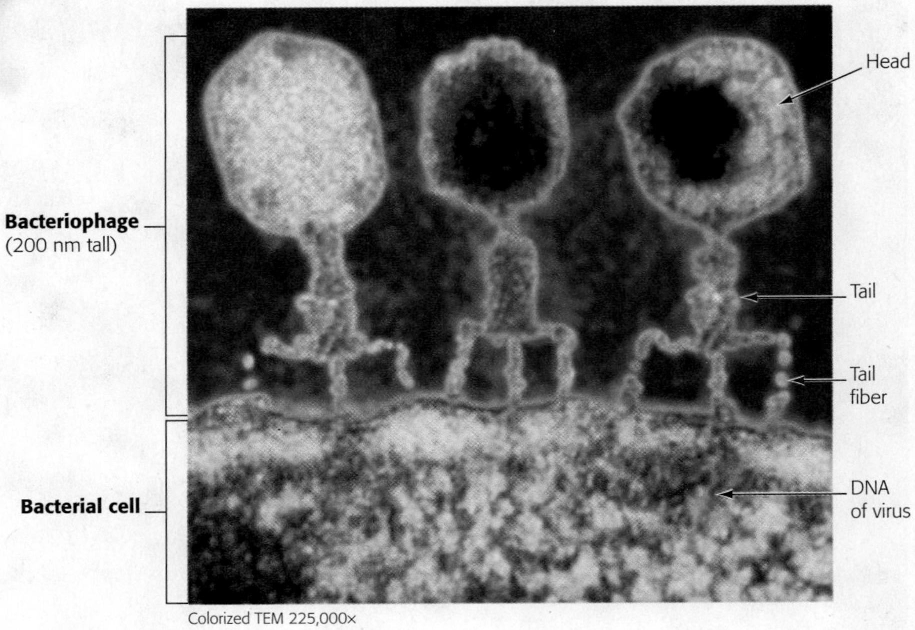

Bacteriophage
(200 nm tall)

Bacterial cell

Head

Tail

Tail fiber

DNA of virus

Colorized TEM 225,000×

During a lysogenic cycle, viral DNA replication occurs without phage production or the death of the cell.

Figure 10.26 illustrates the two kinds of cycles for a phage named lambda that can infect *E. coli* bacteria. Lambda has a head (containing DNA) and a tail. At the start of infection, **①** lambda binds to the outside of a bacterium and injects its DNA inside. **②** The injected lambda DNA forms a circle. In the lytic cycle, this DNA immediately turns the cell into a virus-producing factory. **③** The cell's own machinery for DNA replication, transcription, and translation is hijacked by the virus and used to produce copies of the virus. **④** The cell lyses, releasing the new phages.

In the lysogenic cycle, **⑤** the viral DNA is inserted into the bacterial chromosome. Once there, the phage DNA is referred to as a **prophage**, and most of its genes are inactive. Survival of the prophage depends on the reproduction of the cell where it resides. **⑥** The host cell replicates the prophage DNA along with its cellular DNA and then, upon dividing, passes on both the prophage and the cellular DNA to its two daughter cells. A single infected bacterium can quickly give rise to a large population of bacteria that all carry prophages. The prophages may remain in the bacterial cells indefinitely. **⑦** Occasionally, however, a prophage leaves its chromosome; this event may be triggered by environmental conditions such as exposure to a mutagen. Once separate, the lambda DNA usually switches to the lytic cycle, which results in the production of many copies of the virus and lysing of the host cell.

Sometimes the few prophage genes active in a lysogenic bacterial cell can cause medical problems. For example, the bacteria that cause diphtheria, botulism, and scarlet fever would be harmless to people if it were not for the prophage genes they carry. Certain of these genes direct the bacteria to produce toxins that make people ill. ☑

▼ **Figure 10.26 Alternative phage reproductive cycles.** Certain phages can undergo alternative reproductive cycles. After entering the bacterial cell, the phage DNA can either integrate into the bacterial chromosome (lysogenic cycle) or immediately start the production of progeny phages (lytic cycle), destroying the cell. Once it enters a lysogenic cycle, the phage's DNA may be carried in the host cell's chromosome for many generations.

☑ **CHECKPOINT**

Describe one way some viruses can perpetuate their genes without destroying the cells they infect.

Answer: Some viruses can insert their DNA into the DNA of the cell they infect. The viral DNA is replicated along with the cell's DNA every time the cell divides.

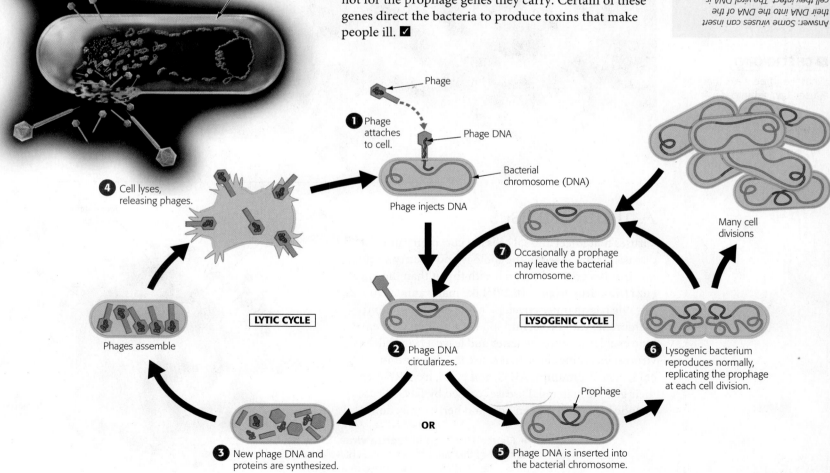

Phage lambda

E. coli

① Phage attaches to cell.

Phage

Phage DNA

Bacterial chromosome (DNA)

Phage injects DNA

④ Cell lyses, releasing phages.

LYTIC CYCLE

Phages assemble

③ New phage DNA and proteins are synthesized.

OR

② Phage DNA circularizes.

⑦ Occasionally a prophage may leave the bacterial chromosome.

LYSOGENIC CYCLE

Prophage

⑤ Phage DNA is inserted into the bacterial chromosome.

⑥ Lysogenic bacterium reproduces normally, replicating the prophage at each cell division.

Many cell divisions

189

Plant Viruses

Viruses that infect plant cells can stunt plant growth and diminish crop yields. Most known plant viruses have RNA rather than DNA as their genetic material. Many of them, like the tobacco mosaic virus shown in **Figure 10.27**, are rod-shaped with a spiral arrangement of proteins surrounding the nucleic acid.

▼ **Figure 10.27 Tobacco mosaic virus.** The photo shows the mottling of leaves in tobacco mosaic disease. The rod-shaped virus causing the disease has RNA as its genetic material.

To infect a plant, a virus must first get past the plant's outer protective layer of cells (the epidermis). For this reason, a plant damaged by wind, chilling, injury, or insects is more susceptible to infection than a healthy plant. Some insects carry and transmit plant viruses, and farmers and gardeners may spread plant viruses through the use of pruning shears and other tools. Also, infected plants may pass viruses to their offspring.

There is no cure for most viral plant diseases, and agricultural scientists focus on preventing infection and on breeding or genetically engineering varieties of crop plants that resist viral infection. In Hawaii, for example, the spread of papaya ringspot potyvirus (PRSV) by aphids wiped out the papaya (Hawaii's second largest crop) in certain island regions. But since 1998, farmers have been able to plant a genetically engineered PRSV-resistant strain of papaya, and papayas have been reintroduced into their old habitats. ☑

Tobacco mosaic virus

RNA
Protein

☑ **CHECKPOINT**

What are three ways that viruses can get into a plant?

Answer: through lesions caused by injuries, transfer by insects that feed on the plant, and contaminated farming or gardening tools

Animal Viruses

Viruses that infect animal cells are common causes of disease. As discussed in the Biology and Society section, no virus is a greater human health threat than the influenza (flu) virus **(Figure 10.28)**. Like many animal viruses, this one has an outer envelope made of phospholipid membrane, with projecting spikes of protein. The envelope enables the virus to enter and leave a host cell. Many viruses, including those that cause the flu, common cold, measles, mumps, AIDS, and polio, have RNA as their genetic material. Diseases caused by DNA viruses include hepatitis, chicken pox, and herpes infections.

► **Figure 10.28 An influenza virus.** The genetic material of this virus consists of eight separate molecules of RNA, each wrapped in a protein coat.

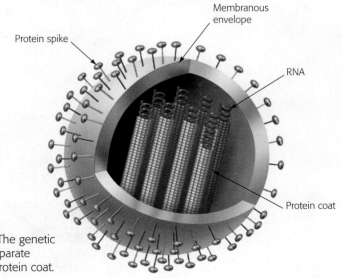

Protein spike

Membranous envelope

RNA

Protein coat

Figure 10.29 shows the reproductive cycle of a typical enveloped RNA virus: the mumps virus. Once a common childhood disease characterized by fever and swelling of the salivary glands, mumps has become quite rare in industrialized nations due to widespread vaccination. When the virus contacts a susceptible cell, protein spikes on its outer surface attach to receptor proteins on the cell's plasma membrane. **1** The viral envelope fuses with the cell's membrane, allowing the protein-coated RNA to enter the cytoplasm. **2** Enzymes then remove the protein coat. **3** An enzyme that entered the cell as part of the virus uses the virus's RNA genome as a template for making complementary strands of RNA. The new strands have two functions: **4** They serve as

mRNA for the synthesis of new viral proteins, and **5** they serve as templates for synthesizing new viral genome RNA. **6** The new coat proteins assemble around the new viral RNA. **7** Finally, the viruses leave the cell by cloaking themselves in plasma membrane. In other words, the virus obtains its envelope from the cell, leaving the cell without necessarily lysing it.

Not all animal viruses reproduce in the cytoplasm. For example, herpesviruses—which cause chicken pox, shingles, cold sores, and genital herpes—are enveloped DNA viruses that reproduce in a host cell's nucleus, and they get their envelopes from the cell's nuclear membrane. Copies of the herpesvirus DNA usually remain behind in the nuclei of certain nerve cells. There they remain dormant until some sort of stress, such as a cold, sunburn, or emotional stress, triggers virus production, resulting in unpleasant symptoms. Once acquired, herpes infections may flare up repeatedly throughout a person's life. Over 75% of American adults are thought to carry herpes simplex 1 (which causes cold sores), and over 20% carry herpes simplex 2 (which causes genital herpes).

The amount of damage a virus causes the body depends partly on how quickly the immune system responds to fight the infection and partly on the ability of the infected tissue to repair itself. We usually recover completely from colds because our respiratory tract tissue can efficiently replace damaged cells by mitosis. In contrast, the poliovirus attacks nerve cells, which are not usually replaceable. The damage to such cells by polio is permanent. In such cases, the only medical option is to prevent the disease with vaccines.

How effective are vaccines? We'll examine this question next using the example of the flu vaccine. ☑

Why does a herpes infection last forever?

☑ **CHECKPOINT**

Why is infection by herpesvirus permanent?

Answer: because herpesvirus leaves viral DNA in the nuclei of nerve cells

▼ **Figure 10.29 The reproductive cycle of an enveloped virus.** This virus is the one that causes mumps. Like the flu virus, it has a membranous envelope with protein spikes, but its genome is a single molecule of RNA.

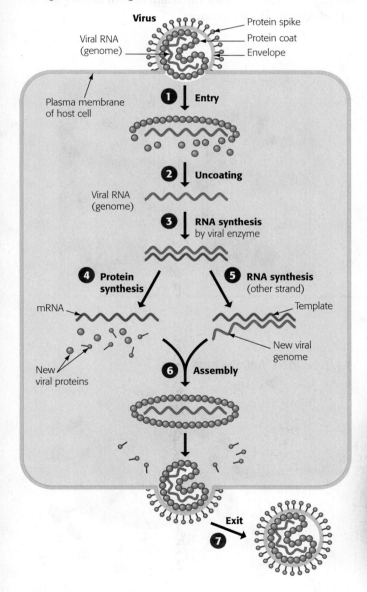

Virus
Protein spike
Protein coat
Envelope
Viral RNA (genome)
Plasma membrane of host cell

1 Entry

2 Uncoating

Viral RNA (genome)

3 RNA synthesis by viral enzyme

4 Protein synthesis

5 RNA synthesis (other strand)

mRNA
Template
New viral proteins
New viral genome

6 Assembly

Exit

7

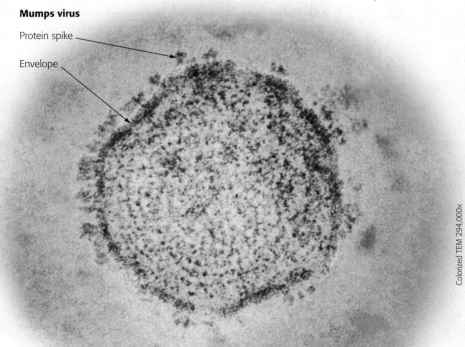

Mumps virus

Protein spike
Envelope

Colorized TEM 294,000x

Do Flu Vaccines Protect the Elderly?

Yearly flu vaccinations are recommended for nearly all people over the age of six months. But how can we be sure they are effective? Epidemiologists (who study the distribution, causes, and control of diseases in populations) have made the **observation** that vaccination rates among the elderly rose from 15% in 1980 to 65% in 1996. This observation has led them to ask the **question:** Do flu vaccines decrease the mortality rate among those elderly people who receive them? To find out, researchers investigated data from the general population. Their main **hypothesis** was that elderly people who were immunized would have fewer hospital stays and deaths during the winter after vaccination. Their **experiment** followed tens of thousands of people over the age of 65 during the ten flu seasons of the 1990s. The **results** are summarized in **Figure 10.30**. People who were vaccinated had a 27% less chance of being hospitalized during the next flu season and a 48% less chance of dying. But could some factor other than flu shots be at play? For example, maybe people who choose to be vaccinated are healthier for other reasons. As a control, the researchers examined health data for the summer (when flu is not a factor). During these months, there was no difference in the hospitalization rates and only 16% fewer deaths for the immunized, suggesting that flu vaccines provide a significant health benefit among the elderly during the flu season.

► **Figure 10.30 The effect of flu vaccines on the elderly.** Receiving a flu vaccine greatly reduced the risk of hospitalization and death in the flu season following the shot. The reduction was much smaller or nonexistent in later summer months.

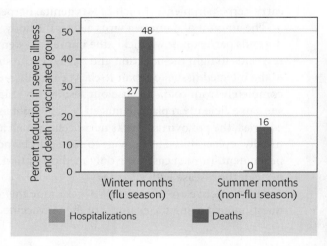

HIV, the AIDS Virus

The devastating disease **AIDS** (acquired immunodeficiency syndrome) is caused by **HIV** (human immunodeficiency virus), an RNA virus with some special twists. In outward appearance, HIV **(Figure 10.31)** resembles the flu or mumps virus. Its envelope enables HIV to enter and leave a cell much the way the mumps virus does. But HIV has a different mode of reproduction. It is a **retrovirus**, an RNA virus that reproduces by means of a DNA molecule. Retroviruses are so named because they reverse the usual DNA → RNA flow of genetic information. These viruses carry molecules of an enzyme called **reverse transcriptase**, which catalyzes reverse transcription: the synthesis of DNA on an RNA template.

▼ **Figure 10.31 HIV, the AIDS virus.**

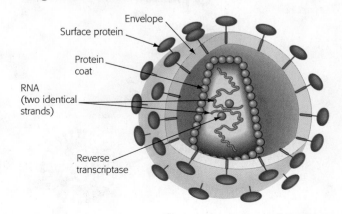

Figure 10.32 illustrates what happens after HIV RNA is uncoated in the cytoplasm of a cell. The reverse transcriptase (green) ❶ uses the RNA as a template to make a DNA strand and then ❷ adds a second, complementary DNA strand. ❸ The resulting double-stranded viral DNA then enters the cell nucleus and inserts itself into the chromosomal DNA, becoming a **provirus**. Occasionally, the provirus is ❹ transcribed into RNA and ❺ translated into viral proteins. ❻ New viruses assembled from these components eventually leave the cell and can then infect other cells. This is the standard reproductive cycle for retroviruses.

HIV infects and eventually kills several kinds of white blood cells that are important in the body's immune system. The loss of such cells causes the body to become susceptible to other infections that it would normally be able to fight off. Such secondary infections cause the syndrome (a collection of symptoms) that eventually kills AIDS patients. Since it was first recognized in 1981, HIV has infected tens of millions of people worldwide, resulting in millions of deaths.

| *Why is HIV so deadly?* |

While there is no cure for AIDS, its progression can be slowed by two categories of anti-HIV drugs. Both types of medicine interfere with the reproduction of the virus. The first type inhibits the action of enzymes called proteases, which help produce the final versions of HIV proteins. The second type, which includes the drug AZT, inhibits the action of the HIV enzyme reverse transcriptase. The key to AZT's effectiveness is its shape. The shape of a molecule of AZT is very similar to the shape of part of the T (thymine) nucleotide **(Figure 10.33)**. In fact, AZT's shape is so similar to the T nucleotide that AZT can bind to reverse transcriptase, essentially taking the place of T. But unlike thymine, AZT cannot be incorporated into a growing DNA chain. Thus, AZT "gums up the works," interfering with the synthesis of HIV DNA. Because this synthesis is an essential step in the reproductive cycle of HIV, AZT may block the spread of the virus within the body.

Many HIV-infected people in the United States and other industrialized countries take a "drug cocktail" that contains both reverse transcriptase inhibitors and protease inhibitors, and the combination seems to be much more effective than the individual drugs in keeping the virus at bay and extending patients' lives. However, even in combination, the drugs do not completely rid the body of the virus. Typically, HIV reproduction and the symptoms of AIDS return if a patient discontinues the medications. Because AIDS has no cure yet, prevention (namely, the avoidance of unprotected sex and needle sharing) is the only healthy option. ☑

▼ **Figure 10.32 The behavior of HIV nucleic acid in an infected cell.**

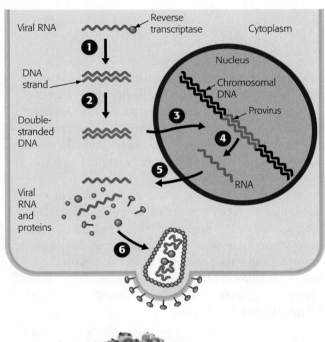

Viral RNA
Reverse transcriptase
Cytoplasm
❶
DNA strand
❷
Double-stranded DNA
Nucleus
Chromosomal DNA
❸
Provirus
❹
❺
RNA
Viral RNA and proteins
❻

HIV (red dots) infecting a white blood cell

SEM 5,500×

☑ CHECKPOINT

Why is HIV called a retrovirus?

Answer: Because it synthesizes DNA from its RNA genome. This is the reverse ("retro") of the usual DNA → RNA information flow.

▼ **Figure 10.33 AZT and the T nucleotide.** The anti-HIV drug AZT (right) has a chemical shape very similar to part of the T (thymine) nucleotide of DNA.

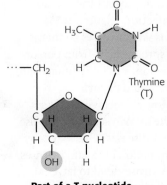

Thymine (T)

Part of a T nucleotide

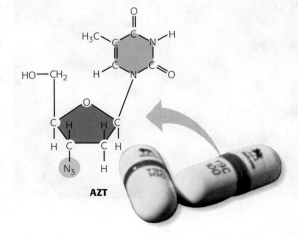

AZT

Viroids and Prions

Viruses may be small and simple, but they dwarf two other classes of pathogens: viroids and prions. Viroids are small circular RNA molecules that infect plants. Viroids do not encode proteins but can nonetheless replicate in host plant cells, apparently using cellular enzymes. These small RNA molecules seem to cause disease by interfering with the regulatory systems that control plant growth.

Even stranger are infectious proteins called **prions**. Prions cause a number of brain diseases in various animal species, including scrapie in sheep and goats, chronic wasting disease in deer and elk, and mad cow disease (formally called bovine spongiform encephalopathy or BSE), which infected over 2 million cattle in the United Kingdom in the 1980s **(Figure 10.34)**. In humans, prions cause an extremely rare disease called Creutzfeldt-Jakob disease. A prion is thought to be a misfolded form of a protein normally present in brain cells. When the prion enters a cell containing the normal form of protein, the prion somehow converts the normal protein molecules to the misfolded prion version. To date, there is no known cure for prion diseases, so the only hope for avoiding future illnesses lies in understanding and preventing the process of infection. ☑

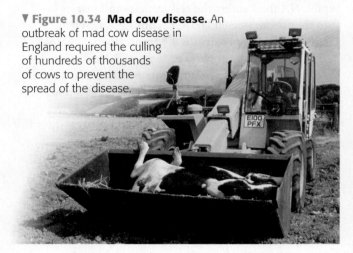

▼ Figure 10.34 **Mad cow disease.** An outbreak of mad cow disease in England required the culling of hundreds of thousands of cows to prevent the spread of the disease.

☑ CHECKPOINT

What makes prions so unusual as pathogens?

Answer: Prions, unlike any other infectious agent, have no nucleic acid (DNA or RNA).

The Deadliest Virus EVOLUTION CONNECTION

Emerging Viruses

Viruses that suddenly come to the attention of medical scientists are called **emerging viruses**. H1N1 (discussed in the Biology and Society section) is one example; another is avian flu. In 1997, at least 18 people in Hong Kong were infected with a strain of flu virus previously seen only in birds. A mass culling of all of Hong Kong's 1.5 million domestic birds appeared to stop that outbreak. Beginning in 2002, however, new cases of human infection by this bird strain spread to Europe and Africa, infecting over 400 people and killing over 250 of them. Over 100 million birds have either died from the disease or been killed to prevent the spread of infection **(Figure 10.35)**. If this virus evolves so that it can spread easily from person to person, a major human outbreak could occur.

How do such viruses burst on the human scene, giving rise to new diseases? One way is by the mutation of existing viruses. RNA viruses tend to have unusually high rates of mutation because errors in replicating their RNA genomes are not subject to proofreading mechanisms that help reduce errors during DNA replication. Some mutations enable existing viruses to evolve into new strains that can cause disease in individuals who have developed resistance to the ancestral virus. This is why we need yearly flu vaccines: Mutations create new influenza virus strains to which people have no immunity.

New viral diseases also arise from the spread of existing viruses from one host species to another. Scientists estimate that about three-quarters of new human diseases have originated in other animals. The avian flu is a prime example. The spread of a viral disease from a small, isolated population can also lead to widespread epidemics. For instance, AIDS went unnamed and virtually unnoticed for decades before it began to spread around the world. In this case, technological and social factors, including affordable international travel, blood transfusions, sexual promiscuity, and the abuse of intravenous drugs, allowed a previously rare human disease to become a global scourge.

Acknowledging the persistent threat that viruses pose to human health, geneticist and Nobel Prize winner Joshua Lederberg once warned: "We live in evolutionary competition with microbes. There is no guarantee that we will be the survivors." If we ever do manage to control HIV, influenza, and other emerging viruses, this success will likely arise from our understanding of molecular biology.

▼ Figure 10.35 **Rounding up ducks in India to help prevent the spread of the Avian flu virus.**

Chapter Review

SUMMARY OF KEY CONCEPTS

 Go to **www.masteringbiology.com** for homework assignments, practice quizzes, Pearson eText, and more.

DNA: Structure and Replication

DNA and RNA Structure

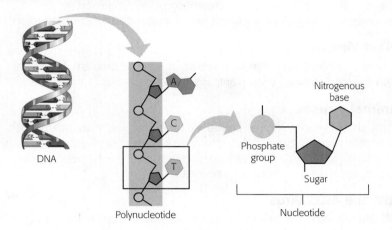

DNA

Polynucleotide

Nucleotide

Nitrogenous base

Phosphate group

Sugar

	DNA	RNA
Nitrogenous base	C G A T	C G A U
Sugar	Deoxy-ribose	Ribose
Number of strands	2	1

Watson and Crick's Discovery of the Double Helix

Watson and Crick worked out the three-dimensional structure of DNA: two polynucleotide strands wrapped around each other in a double helix. Hydrogen bonds between bases hold the strands together. Each base pairs with a complementary partner: A with T, and G with C.

DNA Replication

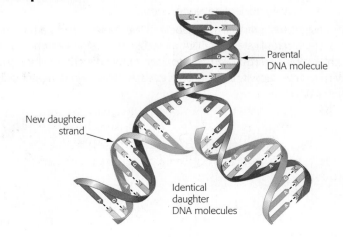

Parental DNA molecule

New daughter strand

Identical daughter DNA molecules

The Flow of Genetic Information from DNA to RNA to Protein

How an Organism's Genotype Determines Its Phenotype

The information constituting an organism's genotype is carried in the sequence of its DNA bases. Studies of inherited metabolic defects first suggested that phenotype is expressed through proteins.

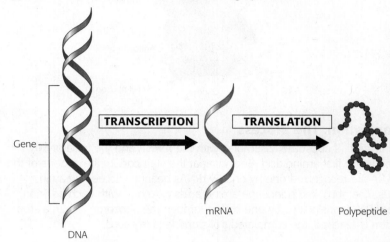

Gene

TRANSCRIPTION

TRANSLATION

DNA

mRNA

Polypeptide

From Nucleotides to Amino Acids: An Overview

The DNA of a gene is transcribed into RNA using the usual base-pairing rules, except that an A in DNA pairs with U in RNA. In the translation of a genetic message, each triplet of nucleotide bases in the RNA, called a codon, specifies one amino acid in the polypeptide.

The Genetic Code

In addition to codons that specify amino acids, the genetic code has one codon that is a start signal and three that are stop signals for translation. The genetic code is redundant: There is more than one codon for most amino acids.

Transcription: From DNA to RNA

In transcription, RNA polymerase binds to the promoter of a gene, opens the DNA double helix there, and catalyzes the synthesis of an RNA molecule using one DNA strand as a template. As the single-stranded RNA transcript peels away from the gene, the DNA strands rejoin.

The Processing of Eukaryotic RNA

The RNA transcribed from a eukaryotic gene is processed before leaving the nucleus to serve as messenger RNA (mRNA). Introns are spliced out, and a cap and tail are added.

Translation: The Players

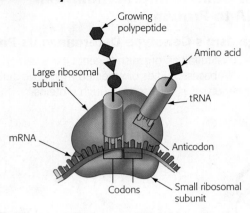

Translation: The Process

In initiation, a ribosome assembles with the mRNA and the initiator tRNA bearing the first amino acid. Beginning at the start codon, the codons of the mRNA are recognized one by one by tRNAs bearing succeeding amino acids. The ribosome bonds the amino acids together. With each addition, the mRNA translocates by one codon through the ribosome. When a stop codon is reached, the completed polypeptide is released.

Review: DNA → RNA → Protein

Figure 10.20 summarizes transcription, RNA processing, and translation. The sequence of codons in DNA, via the sequence of codons in mRNA, spells out the primary structure of a polypeptide.

Mutations

Mutations are changes in the DNA base sequence, caused by errors in DNA replication or recombination or by mutagens. Substituting, deleting, or inserting nucleotides in a gene has varying effects on the polypeptide and organism.

Type of Mutation	Effect
Substitution of one DNA base for another	**Silent** mutations result in no change to amino acids.
	Missense mutations swap one amino acid for another.
	Nonsense mutations change an amino acid codon to a stop codon.
Insertions or **deletions** of DNA nucleotides	These mutations can alter the triplet grouping of codons and greatly change the amino acid sequence.

Viruses and Other Noncellular Infectious Agents

Viruses can be regarded as genes packaged in protein.

Bacteriophages

When phage DNA enters a lytic cycle inside a bacterium, it is replicated, transcribed, and translated. The new viral DNA and protein molecules then assemble into new phages, which burst from the cell. In the lysogenic cycle, phage DNA inserts into the cell's chromosome and is passed on to generations of daughter cells. Much later, it may initiate phage production.

Plant Viruses

Viruses that infect plants can be a serious agricultural problem. Most have RNA genomes. Viruses enter plants via breaks in the plant's outer layers.

Animal Viruses

Many animal viruses, such as flu viruses, have RNA genomes; others, such as hepatitis viruses, have DNA. Some animal viruses "steal" a bit of cell membrane as a protective envelope. Some, such as the herpesvirus, can remain latent inside cells for long periods.

HIV, the AIDS Virus

HIV is a retrovirus. Inside a cell it uses its RNA as a template for making DNA, which is then inserted into a chromosome.

Viroids and Prions

Even smaller than viruses, viroids are small molecules of RNA that can infect plants. Prions are infectious proteins that cause a number of degenerative brain diseases in humans and other animals.

SELF-QUIZ

1. A molecule of DNA contains two polymer strands called _____, made by bonding together many monomers called _____. Each monomer contains three parts: a _____, a _____, and a _____.

2. Which of the following correctly ranks nucleic acid structures in order of size, from largest to smallest?
   a. gene, chromosome, nucleotide, codon
   b. chromosome, gene, codon, nucleotide
   c. nucleotide, chromosome, gene, codon
   d. chromosome, nucleotide, gene, codon

3. A scientist inserts a radioactively labeled DNA molecule into a bacterium. The bacterium replicates this DNA molecule and distributes one daughter molecule (double helix) to each of two daughter cells. How much radioactivity will the DNA in each of the two daughter cells contain? Why?

4. The nucleotide sequence of a DNA codon is GTA. In an mRNA molecule transcribed from this DNA, the codon has the sequence _____. In the process of protein synthesis, a tRNA pairs with the mRNA codon. The nucleotide sequence of the tRNA anticodon is _____. The amino acid attached to the tRNA is _____. (See Figure 10.11.)

5. Describe the process by which the information in a gene is transcribed and translated into a protein. Correctly use these terms in your description: tRNA, amino acid, start codon, transcription, mRNA, gene, codon, RNA polymerase, ribosome, translation, anticodon, peptide bond, stop codon.

6. Match the following molecules with the cellular process or processes in which they are primarily involved.

   a. ribosomes   **1.** DNA replication
   b. tRNA   **2.** transcription
   c. DNA polymerases   **3.** translation
   d. RNA polymerase
   e. mRNA

7. A geneticist finds that a particular mutation has no effect on the polypeptide encoded by the gene. This mutation probably involves
   a. deletion of one nucleotide.
   b. alteration of the start codon.
   c. insertion of one nucleotide.
   d. substitution of one nucleotide.

8. Scientists have discovered how to put together a bacteriophage with the protein coat of phage A and the DNA of phage B. If this composite phage were allowed to infect a bacterium, the phages produced in the cell would have
   a. the protein of A and the DNA of B.
   b. the protein of B and the DNA of A.
   c. the protein and DNA of A.
   d. the protein and DNA of B.

9. How do some viruses reproduce without ever having DNA?

10. HIV requires an enzyme called _____ to convert its RNA genome to a DNA version.

11. Why is reverse transcriptase a particularly good target for anti-AIDS drugs? (*Hint*: Would you expect such a drug to harm the human host?)

Answers to these questions can be found in Appendix: Self-Quiz Answers.

THE PROCESS OF SCIENCE

12. A cell containing a single chromosome is placed in a medium containing radioactive phosphate, making any new DNA strands formed by DNA replication radioactive. The cell replicates its DNA and divides. Then the daughter cells (still in the radioactive medium) replicate their DNA and divide, resulting in a total of four cells. Sketch the DNA molecules in all four cells, showing a normal (nonradioactive) DNA strand as a solid line and a radioactive DNA strand as a dashed line.

13. In a classic 1952 experiment, biologists Alfred Hershey and Martha Chase labeled two batches of bacteriophages, one with radioactive sulfur (which only tags protein) and the other with radioactive phosphorus (which only tags DNA). In separate test tubes, they allowed each batch of phages to bind to nonradioactive bacteria and inject its DNA. After a few minutes, they separated the bacterial cells from the viral parts that remained outside the bacterial cells and measured the radioactivity of both portions. What results do you think they obtained? How would these results help them to determine which viral component—DNA or protein—was the infectious portion?

BIOLOGY AND SOCIETY

14. Scientists at the National Institutes of Health (NIH) have worked out thousands of sequences of genes and the proteins they encode, and similar analysis is being carried out at universities and private companies. Knowledge of the nucleotide sequences of genes might be used to treat genetic defects or produce lifesaving medicines. NIH and some U.S. biotechnology companies have applied for patents on their discoveries. In Britain, the courts have ruled that a naturally occurring gene cannot be patented. Do you think individuals and companies should be able to patent genes and gene products? Before answering, consider the following: What are the purposes of a patent? How might the discoverer of a gene benefit from a patent? How might the public benefit? What negative effects might result from patenting genes?

15. Your college roommate seeks to improve her appearance by visiting a tanning salon. How would you explain the dangers of this to her?

11 How Genes Are Controlled

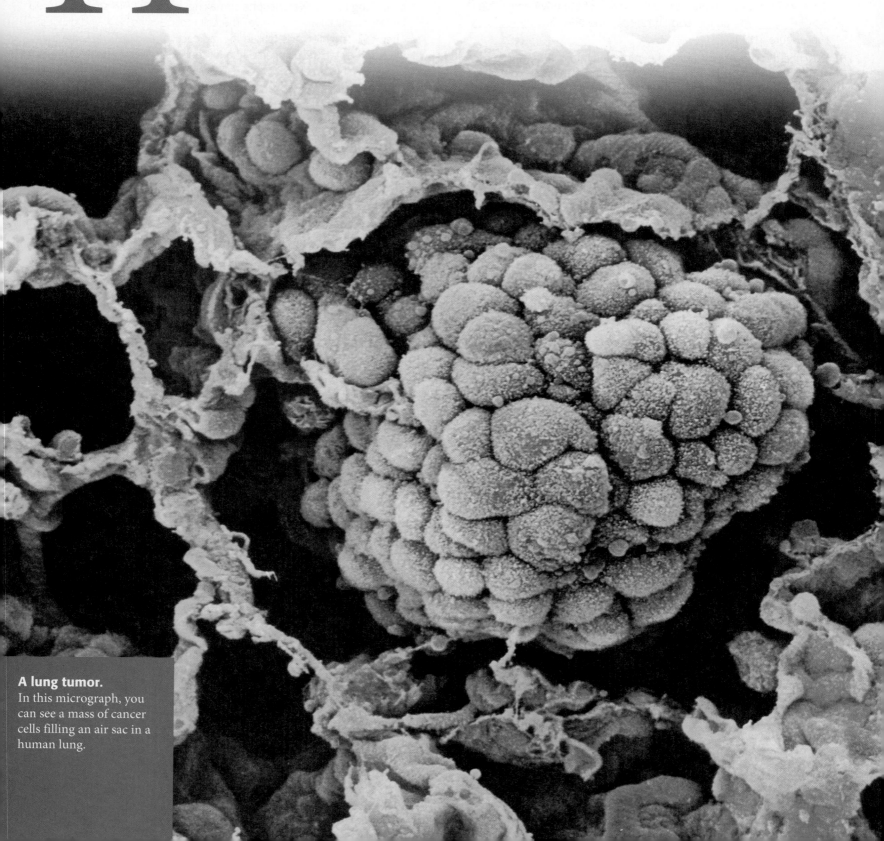

A lung tumor.
In this micrograph, you can see a mass of cancer cells filling an air sac in a human lung.

Cancer BIOLOGY AND SOCIETY

Tobacco's Smoking Gun

When European explorers returned from their first voyages to the Americas, they brought back tobacco, a common trade item among Native Americans. The novelty of smoking quickly spread through Europe, and the southern United States soon became a major tobacco producer. By the 1950s, about half of all Americans smoked over a pack of cigarettes each day. Little credence was paid to health risks; in fact, cigarette advertising often touted the "health benefits" of tobacco. Smoking was pervasive in American society.

But doctors began to notice a disturbing trend: As tobacco use increased, so did the rate of lung cancer. This disease was rare in 1930, but by 1955 it had become the deadliest form of cancer among American men. In fact, by 1990, lung cancer was killing more than twice as many men each year as any other type of cancer. But a few vocal skeptics, mostly supported by the tobacco industry, doubted the link between smoking and cancer. They pointed out that the evidence was purely statistical or based on animal studies; no direct proof had been found that tobacco smoke causes cancer in humans.

The "smoking gun" of proof was found in 1996 when researchers added one component of tobacco smoke, called BPDE, to human lung cells growing in the lab. In these cells, the researchers showed, BPDE binds to DNA within a gene called *p53*, which codes for a protein that normally helps suppress the formation of tumors. The researchers proved that BPDE causes mutations in the *p53* gene that deactivate the protein and lead to tumors. This work directly linked a chemical in tobacco smoke to the formation of human lung tumors. This evidence linking cigarettes to cancer was impossible to ignore.

How can a mutation in a gene lead to cancer? It turns out that many cancer-associated genes encode proteins that turn other genes on or off. When these proteins malfunction, the cell may become cancerous. In fact, the ability to properly control which genes are active at any given time is crucial to normal cell function. How genes are controlled and how the regulation of genes affects cells and organisms are the subjects of this chapter. You'll soon find out that these topics deeply affect your life.

How and Why Genes Are Regulated

In a multicellular organism, every somatic (body) cell is produced by repeated rounds of mitosis, starting from a zygote, the original cell that formed after fusion of sperm and egg. Since a cell's genes are duplicated with each round of the cell cycle, every body cell has the same DNA as the zygote. To put it simply: Every somatic cell contains every gene.

If every cell contains identical genetic instructions, how do cells become different from one another? Cells with the same genetic information can develop into cells with different structures and functions only if gene activity is regulated. Control mechanisms must turn *on* certain genes while other genes remain turned *off* in a particular cell. In other words, individual cells must undergo **cellular differentiation**—that is, they must become specialized in structure and function. It is **gene regulation**, the turning on and off of genes, that leads to this specialization.

Patterns of Gene Expression in Differentiated Cells

What does it mean to say that genes are active or inactive, turned on or off? Genes determine the nucleotide sequence of specific mRNA molecules, and mRNA in turn determines the sequence of amino acids in proteins (DNA→RNA→protein; see Chapter 10). A gene that is turned on is being transcribed into mRNA, and that message is being translated into specific proteins. The overall process by which genetic information flows from genes to proteins—that is, from genotype to phenotype—is called **gene expression**.

Because all the differentiated cells in an individual organism contain the same genes, the differences among the cells must result from the selective expression of genes—that is, from the pattern of genes turned on in a given cell at a given time. Such regulation of gene expression plays a central role in the development of a unicellular zygote into a multicellular organism. During embryonic growth, groups of cells follow diverging pathways, and each group becomes a particular kind of tissue. In the mature organism, each cell type—nerve or pancreas, for instance—has a different pattern of turned-on genes. This is like a company-wide book of procedures; every worker has the complete manual, but each worker reads only those few sections that are relevant to his or her job.

Figure 11.1 shows the patterns of gene expression for four genes in three different specialized cells of an adult human. Note that the genes for "housekeeping" enzymes, such as those that provide energy via glycolysis, are "on" in all the cells. In contrast, the genes for some proteins, such as insulin and hemoglobin, are expressed only by particular kinds of cells. One protein, hemoglobin, is not expressed in any of the cell types shown in the figure. ☑

Gene Regulation in Bacteria

To understand how a cell can regulate gene expression, consider the relatively simple case of bacteria. In the course of their lives, bacteria must regulate their genes in response to environmental changes. For example,

☑ CHECKPOINT

If your nerve cells and skin cells have the same genes, how can they be so different?

Answer: Each cell type expresses different genes than the other cell type.

► **Figure 11.1 Patterns of gene expression in three types of human cells.** Different types of cells express different combinations of genes. The specialized proteins whose genes are represented here are an enzyme involved in glucose digestion; an antibody, which aids in fighting infection; insulin, a hormone made in the pancreas; and the oxygen transport protein hemoglobin, which is expressed only in red blood cells.

Key

✓ Active gene

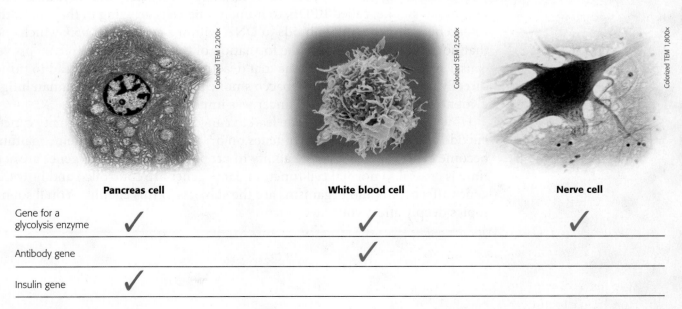

	Pancreas cell	White blood cell	Nerve cell
Gene for a glycolysis enzyme	✓	✓	✓
Antibody gene		✓	
Insulin gene	✓		
Hemoglobin gene			

when a nutrient is plentiful, bacteria do not squander valuable resources to make it from scratch. Bacterial cells that can conserve resources and energy have a survival advantage over cells that are unable to do so. Thus, natural selection has favored bacteria that express only the genes whose products are needed by the cell.

Imagine an *Escherichia coli* bacterium living in your intestines. It will be bathed in various nutrients, depending on what you eat. If you drink a milk shake, for example, there will be a sudden rush of the sugar lactose. In response, *E. coli* will express three genes for enzymes that enable the bacterium to absorb and digest this sugar. After the lactose is gone, *E. coli* turns the genes off; it does not waste its energy continuing to produce these enzymes when they are not needed. Thus, a bacterium can adjust its gene expression to changes in the environment.

How does the presence or absence of lactose influence the activity of the genes that code for the lactose enzymes? The key is the way the three genes are organized: They are adjacent in the DNA and turned on and off as a single unit. This regulation is achieved through short stretches of DNA that help turn all three genes on and off at once, coordinating their expression. Such a cluster of genes with related functions, along with the DNA control sequences, is called an **operon** (**Figure 11.2**). The operon considered here, the *lac* (short for lactose) operon, was first described in the 1960s by French biologists François Jacob and Jacques Monod. The *lac* operon illustrates principles of gene regulation that apply to a wide variety of prokaryotic genes.

How do DNA control sequences turn genes on or off? One control sequence, called a **promoter** (green in the figure), is the site where the enzyme RNA polymerase attaches and initiates transcription—in our example, transcription of the genes for lactose enzymes. Between the promoter and the enzyme genes, a DNA segment called an **operator** (yellow) acts as a switch that is turned on or off, depending on whether a specific protein is bound there. The operator and protein together determine whether RNA polymerase can attach to the promoter and start transcribing the genes (light blue). In the *lac* operon, when the operator switch is turned on, all the enzymes needed to metabolize lactose are made at once.

The top half of Figure 11.2 shows the *lac* operon in "off" mode, its status when there is no lactose around. Transcription is turned off because ❶ a protein called a **repressor** (🦀) binds to the operator (〰) and ❷ physically blocks the attachment of RNA polymerase (🕹) to the promoter (▭).

The bottom half of Figure 11.2 shows the operon in "on" mode, when lactose is present. The lactose (⬤)

interferes with attachment of the *lac* repressor to the operator by ❶ binding to the repressor and ❷ changing the repressor's shape. In its new shape (🦀), the repressor cannot bind to the operator, and the operator switch remains on. ❸ RNA polymerase is no longer blocked, so it can now bind to the promoter and from there ❹ transcribe the genes for the lactose enzymes into mRNA. ❺ Translation produces all three lactose enzymes (purple).

Many operons have been identified in bacteria. Some are quite similar to the *lac* operon, while others have somewhat different mechanisms of control. For example, operons that control amino acid synthesis cause bacteria to stop making these molecules when they are already present in the environment, saving materials and energy for the cells. In these cases, the amino acid *activates* the repressor. Armed with a variety of operons, *E. coli* and other prokaryotes can thrive in frequently changing environments. ✔

✔ CHECKPOINT

A mutation in *E. coli* makes the *lac* operator unable to bind the active repressor. How would this mutation affect the cell? Why would this effect be a disadvantage?

Answer: The cell would wastefully produce the enzymes for lactose metabolism continuously, even in the absence of lactose.

▼ **Figure 11.2 The *lac* operon of *E. coli.***

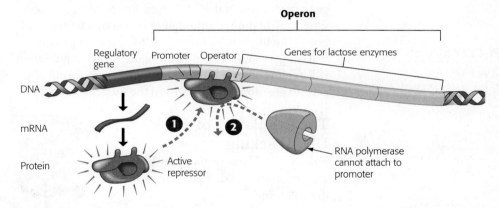

Operon turned off (lactose absent)

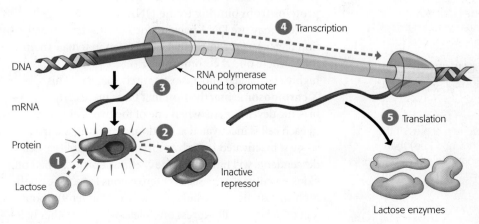

Operon turned on (lactose inactivates repressor)

Gene Regulation in Eukaryotic Cells

Eukaryotes, especially multicellular ones, have more so-phisticated mechanisms than bacteria for regulating the expression of their genes. This is not surprising because a prokaryote, being a single cell, does not require the elaborate regulation of gene expression that leads to cell specialization in multicellular eukaryotic organisms. A bacterium does not have blood cells that need to be different from muscle cells, for example.

The pathway from gene to protein in eukaryotic cells is a long one, providing a number of points where the process can be turned on or off, speeded up or slowed down. Picture the series of pipes that carry water from your local reservoir to a faucet in your home. At various

How is gene expression like plumbing?

points, valves control the flow of water. We use this analogy in **Figure 11.3** to illustrate the flow of genetic information from a eukaryotic chromosome—a reservoir of genetic information—to an active protein that has been made in the cell's cytoplasm. The multiple mechanisms that control gene expression are analogous to the control valves in your water pipes. In the figure, each control knob indicates a gene expression "valve." All these knobs represent possible control points, although only one or a few control points are likely to be important for a typical protein.

Using a reduced version of Figure 11.3 as a guide, we will explore several ways that eukaryotes can control gene expression, starting within the nucleus.

The Regulation of DNA Packing

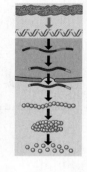

Eukaryotic chromosomes may be in a more or less condensed state, with the DNA and accompanying proteins more or less tightly wrapped together (see Chapter 8). DNA packing tends to prevent gene expression by preventing RNA polymerase and other transcription proteins from binding to the DNA.

Cells may use DNA packing for the long-term inactivation of genes. One intriguing case is seen in female mammals, where one X chromosome in each somatic cell is highly compacted and almost entirely inactive. This **X chromosome inactivation** first takes place early in embryonic development, when one of the two X chromosomes in each cell is inactivated at random. After one X chromosome is inactivated in each embryonic cell, all of that cell's descendants will have the same X chromosome turned off. Consequently, if a female is heterozygous for a gene on the X chromosome (a sex-linked gene; see Chapter 9), about half of her cells will express one allele, while the other half will express the alternate allele (**Figure 11.4**). ☑

▼ **Figure 11.3 The gene expression "pipeline" in a eukaryotic cell.** Each valve in the pipeline represents a stage at which the pathway from chromosome to functioning protein can be regulated.

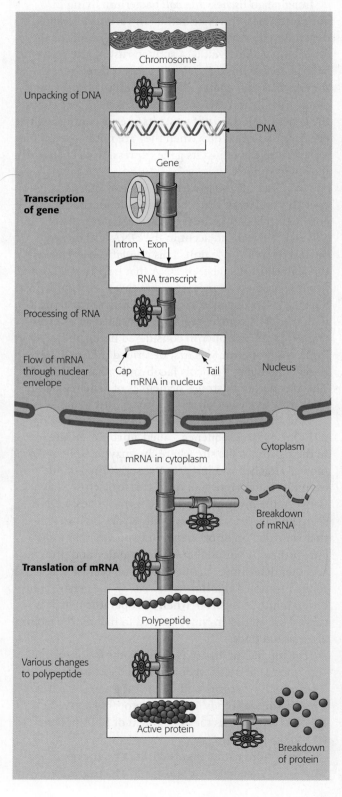

Chromosome

Unpacking of DNA

DNA

Gene

Transcription of gene

Intron Exon

RNA transcript

Processing of RNA

Flow of mRNA through nuclear envelope

Cap   Tail
mRNA in nucleus

Nucleus

Cytoplasm

mRNA in cytoplasm

Breakdown of mRNA

Translation of mRNA

Polypeptide

Various changes to polypeptide

Active protein

Breakdown of protein

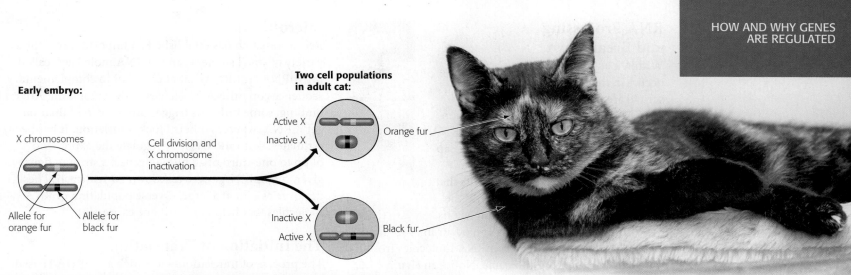

Early embryo:

X chromosomes

Allele for orange fur

Allele for black fur

Cell division and X chromosome inactivation

Two cell populations in adult cat:

Active X
Inactive X
Orange fur

Inactive X
Active X
Black fur

▲ **Figure 11.4 X chromosome inactivation: the tortoiseshell pattern on a cat.** The tortoiseshell gene is on the X chromosome, and the tortoiseshell phenotype requires the presence of two different alleles, one for orange fur and one for non-orange (black) fur. If a female is heterozygous for the tortoiseshell gene, orange patches are formed by populations of cells in which the X chromosome with the orange allele is active; black patches have cells in which the X chromosome with the non-orange allele is active.

The Initiation of Transcription

The initiation of transcription (whether transcription starts or not) is the most important stage for regulating gene expression. In both prokaryotes and eukaryotes, regulatory proteins bind to DNA and turn the transcription of genes on and off. Unlike prokaryotic genes, however, most eukaryotic genes have individual promoters and other control sequences. That is, eukaryotic genes are generally not organized into groups as operons.

As seen in **Figure 11.5**, transcriptional regulation in eukaryotes is complex, typically involving many proteins (collectively called **transcription factors**, purple in the figure) acting in concert to bind to DNA sequences called **enhancers** (yellow) and to the promoter (green). The DNA-protein assembly promotes the binding of RNA polymerase (orange) to the promoter. Genes coding for related enzymes, such as those in a metabolic pathway, may share a specific kind of enhancer (or collection of enhancers), allowing these genes to be activated at the same time. Not shown in the figure are repressor proteins, which may bind to DNA sequences called **silencers**, inhibiting the start of transcription.

In fact, repressor proteins that turn genes off are less common in eukaryotes than **activators**, proteins that turn genes on by binding to DNA. Activators act by

making it easier for RNA polymerase to bind to the promoter. The use of activators is efficient because a typical animal or plant cell needs to turn on (transcribe) only a small percentage of its genes, those required for the cell's specialized structure and function. The "default" state for most genes in multicellular eukaryotes seems to be off, with the exception of "housekeeping" genes for routine activities such as glucose metabolism. ☑

☑ **CHECKPOINT**

Of all the control points of DNA expression shown in Figure 11.3, which is under the tightest regulation?

Answer: the initiation of transcription

▼ **Figure 11.5 A model for turning on a eukaryotic gene.** A large assembly of proteins and several control sequences in the DNA are involved in initiating the transcription of a eukaryotic gene.

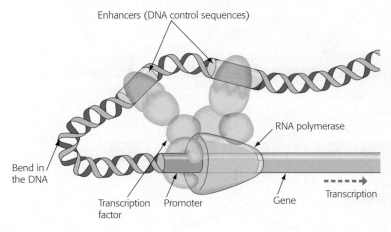

Enhancers (DNA control sequences)

RNA polymerase

Bend in the DNA

Transcription factor

Promoter

Gene

Transcription

RNA Processing and Breakdown

Within a eukaryotic cell, transcription occurs in the nucleus, where RNA transcripts are processed into mRNA before moving to the cytoplasm for translation by the ribosomes (see Figure 10.20). RNA processing includes the addition of a cap and a tail, as well as the removal of any introns—noncoding DNA segments that interrupt the genetic message—and the splicing together of the remaining exons.

Within a cell, exon splicing can occur in more than one way, generating different mRNA molecules from the same starting RNA molecule. Notice in **Figure 11.6**, for example, that one mRNA ends up with the green exon and the other with the brown exon. With this sort of **alternative RNA splicing**, an organism can produce more than one type of polypeptide from a single gene. A typical human gene contains about ten exons; nearly all genes are spliced in at least two different ways, and some are spliced hundreds of different ways.

After an mRNA is produced in its final form, its "lifetime" can be highly variable, from hours to weeks to months. Controlling the timing of mRNA breakdown provides another opportunity for regulation. But all mRNAs are eventually broken down and their parts recycled.

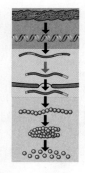

How can your 20,000 genes produce more than 100,000 kinds of protein?

☑ CHECKPOINT

After a gene is transcribed in the nucleus, how is the transcript converted to mRNA? After the mRNA reaches the cytoplasm, what are four control mechanisms that can regulate the amount of active protein in the cell?

Answer: by RNA processing, including the addition of cap and tail and RNA splicing; control by microRNAs, initiation of translation, activation of the protein, and breakdown of the protein

microRNAs

Recent research has established an important role for a variety of small single-stranded RNA molecules, called microRNAs (miRNAs), that can bind to complementary sequences on mRNA molecules in the cytoplasm. After binding, some miRNAs trigger breakdown of their target mRNA, whereas others block translation. It has been estimated that miRNAs may regulate the expression of up to one-third of all human genes, a striking figure given that miRNAs were unknown 20 years ago. These discoveries hint at a large, diverse population of RNA molecules that help regulate gene expression.

The Initiation of Translation

The process of translation—in which an mRNA is used to make a protein—offers additional opportunities for control by regulatory molecules. Red blood cells, for instance, have a protein that prevents the translation of hemoglobin mRNA unless the cell has a supply of heme, an iron-containing chemical group essential for hemoglobin function.

Protein Activation and Breakdown

The final opportunities for regulating gene expression occur after translation. Post-translational control mechanisms in eukaryotes often involve cutting polypeptides into smaller, active final products. The hormone insulin, for example, is synthesized as one long, inactive polypeptide **(Figure 11.7)**. After translation, an enzyme removes an interior section, leaving two shorter chains that make up the active insulin molecule.

Another control mechanism operating after translation is the selective breakdown of proteins. Some proteins that trigger metabolic changes in cells are broken down within a few minutes or hours. This regulation allows a cell to adjust the kinds and amounts of its proteins in response to changes in its environment. ☑

▼ **Figure 11.6 Alternative RNA splicing: producing multiple mRNAs from the same gene.** Two different cells can use the same DNA gene to synthesize different mRNAs and proteins. The cells might be from different tissues or the same type of cell at different times in the organism's life. In this example, one mRNA has ended up with exon 3 (brown) and the other with exon 4 (green). These mRNAs, which are just two of many possible outcomes, can then be translated into different proteins.

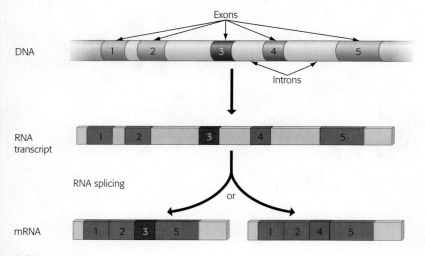

▼ **Figure 11.7 The formation of an active insulin molecule.** Only in its final form does insulin act as a hormone.

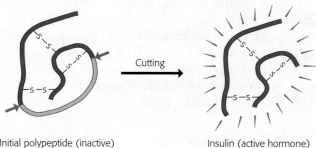

Initial polypeptide (inactive)　　Insulin (active hormone)

Cell Signaling

So far, we have considered gene regulation only within a single cell. In a multicellular organism, the process can cross cell boundaries. A cell can produce and secrete chemicals, such as hormones, that affect gene regulation in another cell.

A signal molecule can act by binding to a receptor protein and initiating a **signal transduction pathway**, a series of molecular changes that converts a signal received outside a cell to a specific response inside the target cell (as you saw in Figure 5.19). **Figure 11.8** shows an example of cell-to-cell signaling in which the target cell's response is the transcription (turning on) of a gene. ❶ First, the signaling cell secretes the signal molecule (◖). ❷ This molecule binds to a specific receptor protein (◖) embedded in the target cell's plasma membrane. ❸ The binding activates a signal transduction pathway consisting of a series of relay proteins (green) within the target cell. Each relay molecule activates the next. ❹ The last relay molecule in the series activates a transcription factor (◖) that ❺ triggers the transcription of a specific gene. ❻ Translation of the mRNA produces a protein that can then perform the function originally called for by the signal. ✔

✔ **CHECKPOINT**

How can a signal molecule from one cell alter gene expression in a target cell without entering the target cell?

Answer: by binding to a receptor protein in the membrane of the target cell and triggering a signal transduction pathway that activates transcription factors

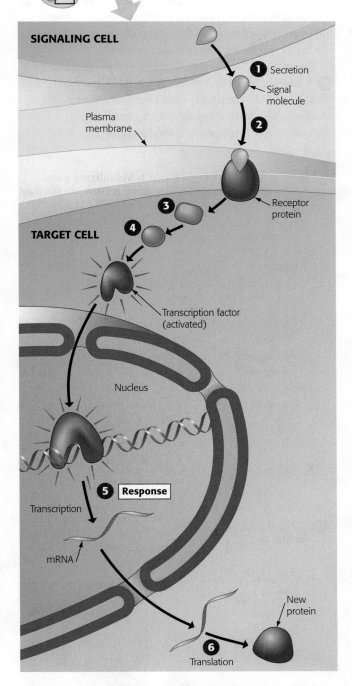

▲ Figure 11.8 **A cell-signaling pathway that turns on a gene.** The coordination of cellular activities in a multicellular organism depends on cell-to-cell signaling that helps regulate genes.

Labels in figure: SIGNALING CELL; Secretion; Signal molecule; Plasma membrane; Receptor protein; TARGET CELL; Transcription factor (activated); Nucleus; Response; Transcription; mRNA; New protein; Translation

Homeotic Genes

Cell-to-cell signaling and the control of gene expression are most important during early embryonic development, when a single-celled zygote develops into a multicellular organism. Master control genes called **homeotic genes** regulate groups of other genes that determine what body parts will develop in which locations. For example, one set of homeotic genes in fruit flies instructs cells in the midbody to form legs. Elsewhere, these homeotic genes remain turned off, while others are turned on. Mutations in homeotic genes can produce bizarre effects. For example, fruit flies with mutations in homeotic genes may have extra sets of legs growing from their head (**Figure 11.9**).

▶ Figure 11.9 **The effect of homeotic genes.** The strange mutant fruit fly shown at the bottom results from a mutation in a homeotic (master control) gene.

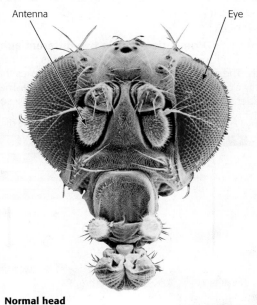

Labels: Antenna; Eye; **Normal head**; Extra pair of legs; **Mutant fly with extra legs growing from head**

One of the most significant biological discoveries in recent years is that similar homeotic genes help direct embryonic development in nearly every eukaryotic organism examined so far, including yeasts, plants, earthworms, frogs, chickens, mice, and humans. **Figure 11.10** highlights some striking similarities in the chromosomal locations and developmental roles of homeotic genes in two quite different animals: a fruit fly and a mouse. The colored segments represent homeotic genes that are very similar in both animals. Notice that the fruit fly and mouse chromosomes have the same order of homeotic genes, corresponding to analogous body regions in both animals. These similarities suggest that these homeotic genes arose very early in the history of life and that the genes have remained remarkably unchanged over eons of animal evolution. The evolution and role of homeotic genes is a very active and exciting area of research. ☑

DNA Microarrays: Visualizing Gene Expression

Scientists who study gene regulation often want to determine which genes are on or off in a particular cell. A **DNA microarray** is a glass slide with thousands of different kinds of single-stranded DNA fragments attached to wells in a tightly spaced array (grid). Each DNA fragment is obtained from a particular gene; a single microarray thus carries DNA from thousands of genes, perhaps even all the genes of an organism.

Figure 11.11 outlines how microarrays are used.

❶ A researcher collects all of the mRNA transcribed from genes in a particular type of cell at a given moment. This collection of mRNA is mixed with reverse transcriptase, a viral enzyme that

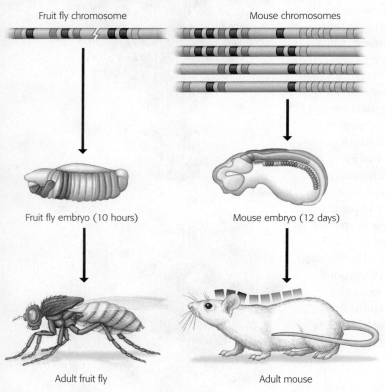

▼ **Figure 11.10 Homeotic genes in two different animals.** At the top of the figure are portions of chromosomes that carry homeotic genes. The colored boxes represent homeotic genes that have especially close DNA sequences in fruit flies and mice. The same color coding identifies the parts of the animals affected by these genes.

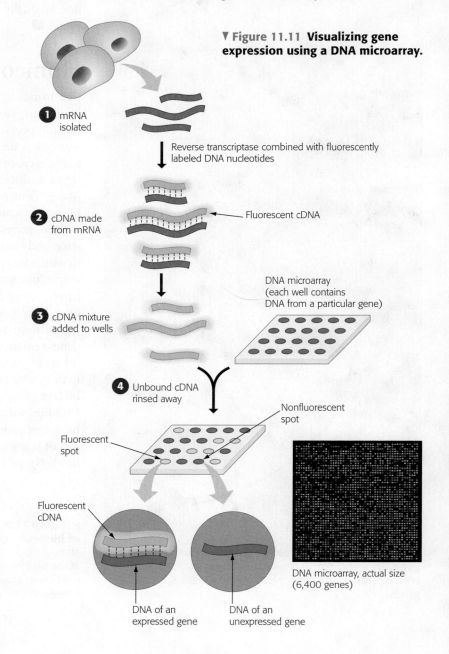

▼ **Figure 11.11 Visualizing gene expression using a DNA microarray.**

② produces DNA that is complementary to each mRNA sequence. This **complementary DNA (cDNA)** is synthesized using nucleotides that have been modified to fluoresce (glow). The fluorescent cDNA collection thus represents all of the genes being actively transcribed in the cell. ③ A small amount of the fluorescently labeled cDNA mixture is added to the DNA fragment in each well of the microarray. If a molecule in the cDNA mixture is complementary to a DNA fragment at a particular location on the grid, the cDNA molecule binds to it, becoming fixed there. ④ After unbound cDNA is rinsed away, the remaining cDNA glows in the microarray. The pattern of glowing spots enables the researcher to determine which genes were being transcribed in the starting cells. Researchers can thus learn which genes are active in different tissues, at different times, or in tissues from individuals in different states of health. ☑

☑ **CHECKPOINT**

What is cDNA? Do you have any in your cells?

Answer: cDNA is DNA synthesized from mRNA. cDNA is artificially produced and does not exist naturally in your cells.

Cloning Plants and Animals

Now that we have examined how gene expression is regulated, we will devote the rest of this chapter to how gene regulation affects two important processes: cloning and cancer.

The Genetic Potential of Cells

One of the most important take-home lessons from this chapter is that most cells express only a small percentage of their genes. So how do we know that all the genes are still present? And if all the genes are still there, do differentiated cells retain the potential to express them?

One way to approach these questions is to see if a differentiated cell can be stimulated to generate a whole new organism. In plants, this ability is common. For example, if you have ever grown a plant from a small cutting, you've seen evidence that a differentiated plant cell can undergo cell division and give rise to all the tissues of an adult plant. On a larger scale, the technique described in **Figure 11.12** can be used to produce hundreds or thousands of genetically identical organisms—clones—from the cells of a single plant.

Plant cloning is now used extensively in agriculture. For some plants, such as orchids, cloning is the only commercially practical means of reproducing plants. In other cases, cloning has been used to reproduce a plant with specific desirable traits, such as high fruit yield or resistance to disease. Seedless plants (such as seedless grapes) cannot reproduce sexually, leaving cloning as the sole means of mass-producing these common foods.

A similar, naturally occurring process in animals is **regeneration**, the regrowth of lost body parts. When a salamander loses a leg, for example, certain cells in the leg stump reverse their differentiated state, divide, and then differentiate again to give rise to a new leg. Many other animals, especially among the invertebrates, can regenerate lost parts, and isolated pieces of a few relatively simple animals can dedifferentiate and then develop into an entirely new organism (see Figure 8.1).

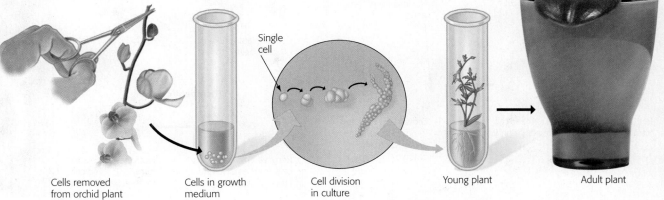

► **Figure 11.12 Test-tube cloning of an orchid.** Tissue removed from the stem of an orchid plant and placed in growth medium may begin dividing and eventually grow into an adult plant. The new plant is a genetic duplicate of the parent plant. This process proves that mature plant cells can reverse their differentiation and develop into all the specialized cells of an adult plant.

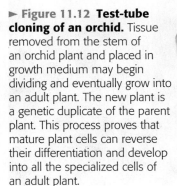

Cells removed from orchid plant

Cells in growth medium

Single cell

Cell division in culture

Young plant

Adult plant

Reproductive Cloning of Animals

Animal cloning is achieved through a procedure called **nuclear transplantation (Figure 11.13)**. First performed in the 1950s on frog embryos, nuclear transplantation involves replacing the nucleus of an egg cell or a zygote with a nucleus removed from an adult body cell. The recipient cell may then begin to divide. Repeated cell divisions form a blastocyst, a hollow ball of about 100 cells that is an early stage in normal animal development. At this point, the blastocyst may be used for different purposes, as indicated by the two branches in Figure 11.13.

If the animal to be cloned is a mammal, further development requires implanting the blastocyst into the uterus of a surrogate mother (Figure 11.13, upper branch). The resulting animal will be a "clone" (genetic copy) of the donor. This type of cloning is called **reproductive cloning** because it results in the birth of a new animal.

In 1996, Scottish researcher Ian Wilmut and his colleagues used reproductive cloning to produce the first mammal cloned from an adult cell, a sheep named Dolly. The researchers used an electric shock to fuse specially treated adult sheep udder cells with 277 eggs from which they had removed the nuclei. After several days of growth, 29 of the resulting embryos were implanted in the uteruses of surrogate mothers. One of the embryos developed into Dolly. As expected, Dolly resembled her genetic parent, the nucleus donor, not the egg donor or the surrogate mother.

Practical Applications of Reproductive Cloning

In the years since Dolly's landmark birth, researchers have cloned many species of mammals, including mice, horses, dogs, mules, cows, pigs, rabbits, ferrets, and cats **(Figure 11.14a)**. Why would anyone want to do this? In agriculture, farm animals with specific sets of desirable traits might be cloned to produce herds with these traits. In research, genetically identical animals can provide perfect "control animals" for experiments. The pharmaceutical industry is experimenting with cloning animals for potential medical use. For example, the pigs in **Figure 11.14b** are clones that lack a gene for a protein that can cause immune system rejection in humans. Organs from such pigs may one day be used in human patients who need transplants.

Perhaps the most intriguing use of reproductive cloning is to restock populations of endangered animals. Among the rare animals that have been cloned are a wild mouflon (a small European sheep), a banteng (a Javanese cow), a gaur (an Asian ox), and gray wolves **(Figure 11.14c)**. The 2003 cloning of a banteng, whose numbers have dwindled to just a few in the wild, is a remarkable case. Using frozen cells from a zoo-raised banteng that had died 23 years prior, scientists transplanted nuclei from the frozen cells

▼ **Figure 11.13 Cloning by nuclear transplantation.** In nuclear transplantation, a nucleus from an adult body cell is injected into a nucleus-free egg cell. The resulting embryo may then be used to produce a new organism (reproductive cloning, shown in the upper branch) or to provide stem cells (therapeutic cloning, lower branch). The lamb in the photograph is the famous Dolly, shown with her surrogate mother.

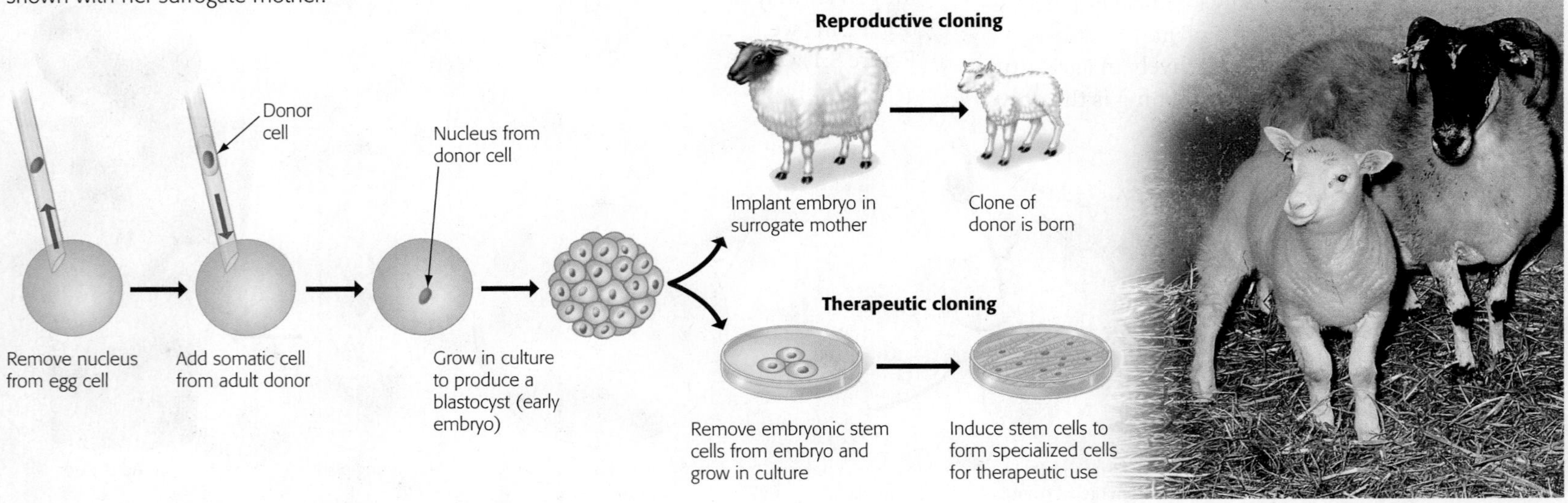

into nucleus-free eggs from dairy cows. The resulting embryos were implanted into surrogate cows, leading to

Can cloning reverse extinction?

the birth of a healthy baby banteng. This success shows that it is possible to produce a baby even when a female of the donor species is unavailable. Scientists may someday be able to use similar cross-species methods to clone an animal from a recently extinct species.

The use of cloning to repopulate endangered species holds tremendous promise. However, cloning may also create new problems. Conservationists object that cloning may detract from efforts to preserve natural habitats. They correctly point out that cloning does not increase genetic diversity and is therefore not as beneficial to endangered species as natural reproduction. Cloned animals may be less healthy than those arising from a fertilized egg. In 2003, Dolly was euthanized after suffering complications from a lung disease that is normally seen only in much older sheep, although no one is sure whether her illness was related to her unusual birth. Other cloned animals have exhibited defects such as susceptibility to obesity, pneumonia, liver failure, and premature death.

Human Cloning

The cloning of various mammals has heightened speculation that humans could be cloned. Critics point out the many practical and ethical objections to human cloning. Practically, cloning of mammals is extremely difficult and inefficient. Only a small percentage of cloned embryos develop normally, and they appear less healthy than naturally born kin. Ethically, the discussion about whether or not people should be cloned—and if so, under what circumstances—is far from settled. Consensus on this topic is unlikely anytime soon. Meanwhile, the research and the debate continue. ✓

☑ CHECKPOINT

Suppose a nucleus from an adult body cell of a black mouse is injected into an egg removed from a white mouse, and then the embryo is implanted into a brown mouse. What would be the color of the resulting cloned mice?

Answer: black, the color of the nucleus donor

▼ **Figure 11.14 Reproductive cloning of mammals.**

(a) The first cloned cat. CC ("Copy Cat") and her lone parent (left).

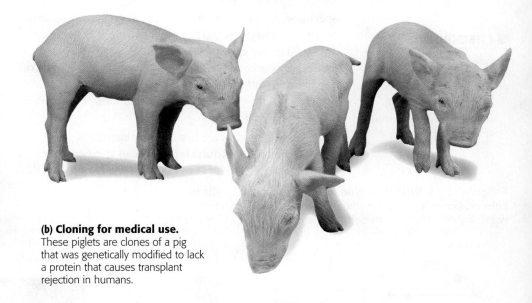

(b) Cloning for medical use. These piglets are clones of a pig that was genetically modified to lack a protein that causes transplant rejection in humans.

(c) Clones of endangered animals

Mouflon lamb with mother   Banteng   Gaur   Gray wolf

Therapeutic Cloning and Stem Cells

The lower branch of Figure 11.13 shows the process of **therapeutic cloning**. The purpose of this procedure is not to produce a living organism but rather to produce embryonic stem cells.

Embryonic Stem Cells

In mammals, **embryonic stem cells (ES cells)** are derived from blastocysts. During development in the uterus, embryonic stem cells differentiate, giving rise to all the specialized cells in the body. When removed from an early embryo and grown in laboratory culture, embryonic stem cells can divide indefinitely. The right conditions—such as the presence of certain growth-stimulating proteins—can (hypothetically) induce changes in gene expression that cause the cells to develop into a particular cell type **(Figure 11.15)**. If scientists can discover the right conditions, they may be able to grow cells for the repair of injured or diseased organs. Some people speculate, for example, that ES cells may one day be used to replace cells damaged by spinal cord injuries or heart attacks. The use of embryonic stem cells in therapeutic cloning is controversial, however, because the removal of ES cells destroys the embryo.

Adult Stem Cells

Embryonic stem cells are not the only stem cells available to researchers. **Adult stem cells** can also generate replacements for some of the body's cells. Unlike ES cells, adult stem cells are partway along the road to differentiation. In the body, adult stem cells usually give rise to only a few related types of specialized cells. For example, stem cells in bone marrow generate different kinds of blood cells. Because no embryonic tissue is involved in their harvest, adult stem cells may provide an ethically less problematic therapy than ES cells. However, some researchers think that only the more versatile ES cells are likely to lead to groundbreaking advances in human health.

Umbilical Cord Blood Banking

Another source of stem cells is blood collected from the umbilical cord and placenta at birth. Such stem cells appear to be partially differentiated, less so than adult stem cells, more so than embryonic stem cells. To obtain these cells, a physician inserts a needle into the umbilical cord and extracts 1/4 to 1/2 cup of blood **(Figure 11.16)**. The cells are then frozen and kept in a blood bank, where they are available if needed for medical treatment. In 2005, doctors reported that an infusion of umbilical cord blood stem cells from a compatible (but unrelated) donor appeared to cure some babies of Krabbe's disease, a usually fatal inherited disorder of the nervous system. Other people have received cord blood as a treatment for leukemia. To date, however, most attempts at umbilical cord blood therapy have not been successful. At present, the American Academy of Pediatrics recommends cord blood banking only for babies born into families with a known genetic risk. So far, the promise of cord blood banking vastly exceeds the accomplishments. ✔

Why do some parents save their baby's umbilical cord blood?

▼ **Figure 11.15 Differentiation of embryonic stem cells in culture.** Scientists hope to someday discover growth conditions that will stimulate cultured stem cells to differentiate into specialized cells.

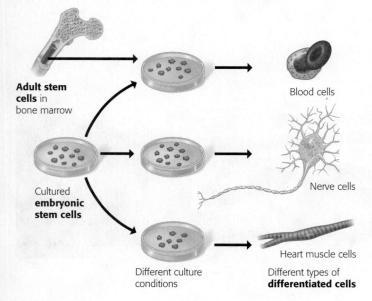

Adult stem cells in bone marrow

Cultured embryonic stem cells

Different culture conditions

Blood cells

Nerve cells

Heart muscle cells

Different types of **differentiated cells**

▼ **Figure 11.16 Umbilical cord blood banking.** Just after birth, a doctor may collect blood from a newborn's umbilical cord. The umbilical cord blood (inset), rich in stem cells, is stored for possible future use.

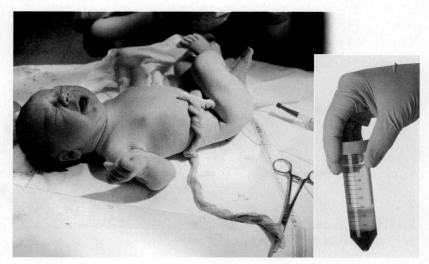

The Genetic Basis of Cancer

Cancer is a variety of diseases in which cells escape from the control mechanisms that normally limit their growth and division (as introduced in Chapter 8). This escape involves changes in gene expression.

Genes That Cause Cancer

One of the earliest clues to the role of genes in cancer was the discovery in 1911 of a virus that causes cancer in chickens. Recall that viruses are simply "genes in a box," molecules of DNA or RNA surrounded by protein. Viruses that cause cancer can become permanent residents in host cells by inserting their nucleic acid into the DNA of host chromosomes. Researchers have identified a number of viruses that harbor genes that if inserted into a host cell can make the cell cancerous. A gene that causes cancer is called an **oncogene** ("tumor gene").

Oncogenes and Tumor-Suppressor Genes

In 1976, American molecular biologists J. Michael Bishop, Harold Varmus, and their colleagues made a startling discovery. They found that a cancer-causing chicken virus contains an oncogene that is an altered version of a normal chicken gene. Subsequent research has shown that the chromosomes of many animals, including humans, contain genes that can be converted to oncogenes. A normal gene with the potential to become an oncogene is called a **proto-oncogene**. (These terms can be confusing, so let's repeat them: A *proto-oncogene* is a normal, healthy gene that, if changed, can become a cancer-causing *oncogene*.) A cell can acquire an oncogene from a virus or from the mutation of one of its own proto-oncogenes.

How can a change in a gene cause cancer? Searching for the normal roles of proto-oncogenes in the cell, researchers found that many of these genes code for **growth factors**—proteins that stimulate cell division—or for other proteins that affect the cell cycle. When all these proteins are functioning normally, in the right amounts at the right times, they help keep the rate of cell division at an appropriate level. When they malfunction—if a growth factor becomes hyperactive, for example—cancer (uncontrolled cell growth) may result.

For a proto-oncogene to become an oncogene, a mutation must occur in the cell's DNA. **Figure 11.17** illustrates three kinds of changes in DNA that can produce active oncogenes. In all three cases, abnormal gene expression stimulates the cell to divide excessively.

Changes in genes whose products inhibit cell division are also involved in cancer. These genes are called **tumor-suppressor genes** because the proteins they encode normally help prevent uncontrolled cell growth **(Figure 11.18)**. Any mutation that keeps a growth-inhibiting protein from being made or from functioning may contribute to the development of cancer. Researchers have identified many mutations in both tumor-suppressor and growth factor genes that are associated with cancer, as we'll discuss next.

▼ **Figure 11.17 How a proto-oncogene can become an oncogene.**

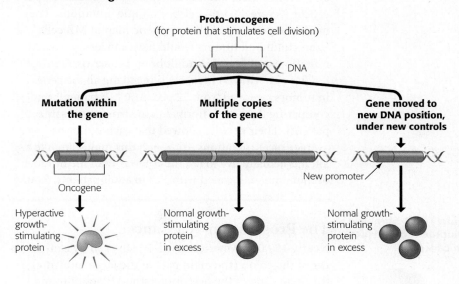

▼ **Figure 11.18 Tumor-suppressor genes.**

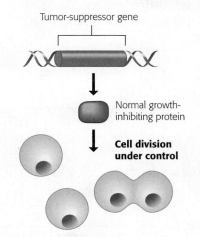

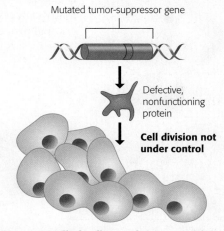

(a) Normal cell growth. A tumor-suppressor gene normally codes for a protein that inhibits cell growth and division. In this way, the gene helps prevent cancerous tumors from arising.

(b) Uncontrolled cell growth (cancer). When a mutation in a tumor-suppressor gene makes its protein defective, cells that are usually under the control of the normal protein may divide excessively, forming a tumor.

Cancer THE PROCESS OF SCIENCE

Are Childhood Tumors Special?

Medical researchers have made many **observations** of specific mutations that can lead to cancer. They therefore **question** whether different kinds of cancers are associated with specific mutations. A large research team led by the Johns Hopkins Kimmel Cancer Center in Baltimore formed the **hypothesis** that young patients with medulloblastoma (MB)—the most common pediatric brain cancer and the deadliest form of childhood cancer (**Figure 11.19**)—harbor unique mutations. They made the **prediction** that a genetic map of MB cells from childhood tumors would have cancer-associated mutations not found in adult brain cancer tissue.

The **experiment** involved sequencing all the genes in tumors removed from 22 pediatric MB patients and comparing them with normal tissue from these same patients. Their **results** showed that each tumor had an average of 11 mutations. Although this may seem like a lot, it is actually five to ten times fewer than the number of mutations associated with MB in adult patients. Young

MB patients therefore seem to have fewer, but deadlier, mutations. When they investigated the role that the mutated genes play, the research team found that some help control DNA packing, whereas others play a role in the development of organs. The researchers hope that this new knowledge about the genetic basis of MB may be used to develop new therapies for this often fatal disease.

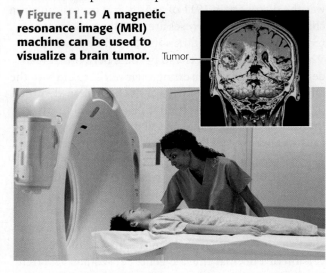

▼ **Figure 11.19** **A magnetic resonance image (MRI) machine can be used to visualize a brain tumor.** Tumor

▼ **Figure 11.20** **Stepwise development of a typical colon cancer.**

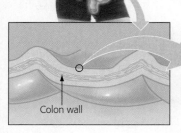

The Progression of a Cancer

Nearly 150,000 Americans will be stricken by cancer of the colon (the main part of the large intestine) this year. One of the best-understood types of human cancer, colon cancer illustrates an important principle about how cancer develops: More than one mutation is needed to produce a full-fledged cancer cell. As in many cancers, the development of colon cancer is a gradual process.

As shown in **Figure 11.20**, ❶ colon cancer begins when an oncogene arises through mutation, causing unusually frequent division of normal-looking cells in the colon lining. ❷ Later, additional DNA mutations (such as the inactivation of a tumor-suppressor gene) cause the growth of a small benign tumor (called a polyp) in the colon wall. ❸ Further mutations eventually lead to formation of a malignant tumor—a tumor that has the potential to metastasize (spread).

Colon wall

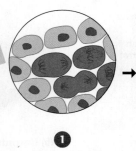

Colon wall

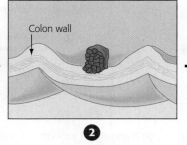

❶ ❷ ❸

Cellular changes:	Increased cell division	Growth of benign tumor	Growth of malignant tumor
DNA changes:	Oncogene activated	Tumor-suppressor gene inactivated	Second tumor-suppressor gene inactivated

The development of a malignant tumor is accompanied by a gradual accumulation of mutations that convert proto-oncogenes to oncogenes and knock out tumor-suppressor genes (Figure 11.21). The requirement for several DNA mutations—usually four or more—explains why cancers can take a long time to develop. This requirement may also help explain why the incidence of cancer increases with age; the longer we live, the more likely we are to accumulate mutations that cause cancer.

"Inherited" Cancer

Most mutations that lead to cancer arise in the organ where the cancer starts—the colon, for example. Because these mutations do not affect the cells that give rise to eggs or sperm, they are not passed from parent to child. Sometimes, however, a cancer-causing mutation occurs in a cell that gives rise to gametes and is therefore passed on from generation to generation. Such mutations predispose the people who inherit them to developing cancer. Such cancer is said to be familial or inherited. But even familial cancers don't appear unless the person acquires additional mutations in the susceptible tissue.

One well-studied inherited cancer gene is *BRCA1* (pronounced "braca-1"), the normal allele of which encodes a tumor-suppressor protein. Certain alleles of *BRCA1* are associated with breast cancer, a disease that strikes one out of every ten American women (Figure 11.22). Some *BRCA1* mutations give a woman an 80% risk of developing breast or ovarian cancer during

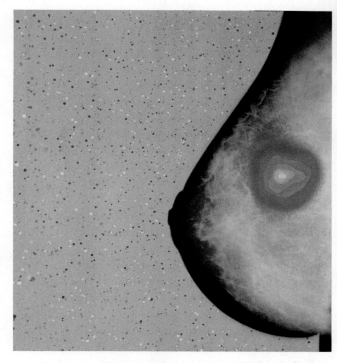

▲ **Figure 11.22 Breast cancer.** In this mammogram, normal breast tissue appears as greenish-blue, while the tumor is highlighted in yellow and red.

her lifetime. In recent years, tests for *BRCA1* mutations have become available. Unfortunately, these tests are of limited use because surgical removal of the breasts and/or ovaries is the only preventive option currently available to women who carry the mutant genes. ☑

▼ **Figure 11.21 Accumulation of mutations in the development of a cancer cell.**
Mutations leading to cancer accumulate in a lineage of cells. In this figure, colors distinguish the normal cells from cells with one or more mutations, leading to increased cell division and cancer. Once a cancer-promoting mutation occurs (orange band on chromosome), it is passed to all the descendants of the cell carrying it.

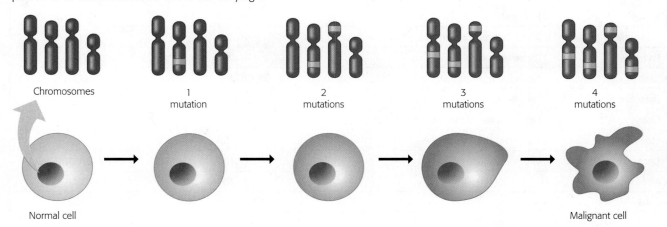

Chromosomes   1 mutation   2 mutations   3 mutations   4 mutations

Normal cell   Malignant cell

☑ CHECKPOINT

How can a mutation in a tumor-suppressor gene contribute to the development of cancer?

Answer: A mutated tumor-suppressor gene may produce a defective protein unable to function in a pathway that normally inhibits cell division and therefore normally suppresses tumors.

Cancer Risk and Prevention

Cancer is the second-leading cause of death (after heart disease) in most industrialized countries. Death rates due to certain forms of cancer have decreased in recent years, but the overall cancer death rate is still on the rise, currently increasing at about 1% per decade.

Most cancers arise from mutations that are caused by **carcinogens**, cancer-causing agents found in the environment. Mutations often result from decades of exposure to carcinogens. One of the most potent carcinogens is ultraviolet (UV) radiation. Excessive exposure to UV radiation from the sun can cause skin cancer, including a deadly type called melanoma.

What can you do to lower your risk of cancer?

The one substance known to cause more cases and types of cancer than any other is tobacco. By a wide margin, more people die from lung cancer (nearly 160,000 Americans in 2011) than from any other form of cancer. Most tobacco-related cancers are due to smoking, but inhaling secondhand smoke also poses a risk. As **Table 11.1** indicates, tobacco use, sometimes in combination with alcohol consumption, causes several types of cancer. In nearly all cases, cigarettes are the main culprit, but smokeless tobacco products (chewing tobacco, or "dip") are linked to cancer of the mouth and throat. Exposure to some of the most lethal carcinogens is often a matter of individual choice: Tobacco use, the consumption of alcohol, and excessive time spent in the sun are all avoidable behaviors that affect cancer risk.

Some food choices significantly reduce a person's cancer risk. For instance, eating 20–30 g of plant fiber daily (about the amount found in 7 apples, which is twice the amount the average American consumes) while eating less animal fat may help prevent colon cancer. There is also evidence that certain substances in fruits and vegetables, including vitamins C and E and certain compounds related to vitamin A, may help protect against a variety of cancers. Cabbage and its relatives, such as broccoli and cauliflower, are thought to be especially rich in substances that help prevent cancer, although some of the specific substances have not yet been identified. Determining how diet influences cancer has become an important focus of nutrition research.

The battle against cancer is being waged on many fronts, and there is reason for optimism in the progress being made. It is especially encouraging that we can help reduce our risk of acquiring some of the most common forms of cancer by the choices we make in our daily lives. ☑

Table 11.1	Cancer in the United States (Ranked by Number of Cases)		
Cancer	**Known or Likely Carcinogens or Factors**	**Estimated Cases (2011)**	**Estimated Deaths (2011)**
Prostate	Testosterone; possibly dietary fat	241,000	33,700
Breast	Estrogen; possibly dietary fat	233,000	40,000
Lung	Cigarette smoke	221,000	157,000
Colon and rectum	High dietary fat; low dietary fiber	141,000	49,400
Skin	Ultraviolet light	76,300	12,000
Lymphomas	Viruses (for some types)	75,200	20,600
Bladder	Cigarette smoke	69,300	15,000
Kidney	Cigarette smoke	60,900	13,100
Uterus	Estrogen	46,500	8,100
Leukemias	X-rays; benzene; viruses (for some types)	44,600	21,800
Pancreas	Cigarette smoke	44,000	37,700
Liver	Alcohol; hepatitis viruses	26,200	19,600
Brain and nerve	Trauma; X-rays	22,300	13,100
Ovary	Large number of ovulation cycles	22,000	15,500
Stomach	Table salt; cigarette smoke	21,500	10,300
Cervix	Viruses; cigarette smoke	12,700	4,300
All other types		239,200	100,800
Total		1,596,700	572,000

Source: *Cancer Facts and Figures 2011* (American Cancer Society Inc.).

☑ **CHECKPOINT**

Of all known behavioral factors, which one causes the most cancer cases and deaths?

Answer: *tobacco use*

Cancer EVOLUTION CONNECTION

The Evolution of Cancer in the Body

The theory of evolution describes natural selection acting on populations of organisms. Recently, medical researchers have been using an evolutionary perspective to gain insight into the development of tumors, such as the bone tumor shown in **Figure 11.23**. Evolution drives the growth of a tumor—which can be thought of as a population of cancer cells—and also affects how those cells respond to cancer treatments.

Recall that there are several assumptions behind Darwin's theory of natural selection (see Chapter 1). Let's consider how each one can be applied to cancer. First, all evolving populations have the potential to produce more offspring than can be supported by the environment. Cancer cells, with their uncontrolled growth, clearly demonstrate such overproduction. Second, there must be variation among individuals of the population. Studies of tumor cell DNA, like the one described in the Process of Science section, show genetic variability within tumors. Finally, variations in the population must affect survival and reproductive success. Indeed, the accumulation of mutations in cancer cells renders them less susceptible to normal mechanisms of reproductive control. Mutations that enhance survival of malignant cancer cells are passed on to that cell's descendants. In short, a tumor evolves.

Viewing the progression of cancer through the lens of evolution helps explain why there is no easy "cure" for cancer but may also pave the way for novel therapies. For example, some researchers are attempting to "prime" tumors for treatment by increasing the reproductive success of only those cells that will be susceptible to a chemotherapy drug. Our understanding of cancer, like all other aspects of biology, benefits from an evolutionary perspective.

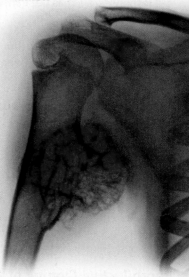

▼ **Figure 11.23** **X-ray of shoulder and upper arm, revealing a large bone tumor.**

Chapter Review

SUMMARY OF KEY CONCEPTS

 Go to **www.masteringbiology.com** for homework assignments, practice quizzes, Pearson eText, and more.

How and Why Genes Are Regulated

Patterns of Gene Expression in Differentiated Cells

The various types of cells in a multicellular organism arise due to different combinations of genes being turned on and off via gene regulation in each cell type.

Gene Regulation in Bacteria

An operon is a cluster of genes with related functions together with their promoter and other DNA sequences that control their transcription. The *lac* operon allows *E. coli* to produce enzymes for lactose use only when the sugar is present.

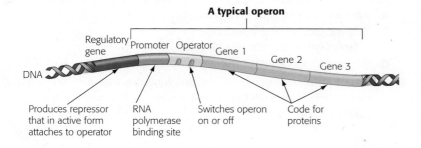

A typical operon

Regulatory gene / Promoter / Operator / Gene 1 / Gene 2 / Gene 3

DNA

Produces repressor that in active form attaches to operator

RNA polymerase binding site

Switches operon on or off

Code for proteins

Gene Regulation in Eukaryotic Cells

In the nucleus of eukaryotic cells, there are several possible control points in the pathway of gene expression.

- DNA packing tends to block gene expression, presumably by preventing access of transcription proteins to the DNA. An extreme example is X chromosome inactivation in the cells of female mammals.

- The most important control point in both eukaryotes and prokaryotes is at gene transcription. Various regulatory proteins interact with DNA and with each other to turn the transcription of eukaryotic genes on or off.

- There are also opportunities for the control of eukaryotic gene expression after transcription, when introns are cut out of the RNA and a cap and tail are added to process RNA transcripts into mRNA.

- In the cytoplasm, presence of microRNAs may block the translation of an mRNA, and various proteins may regulate the start of translation.

- Finally, the cell may activate the finished protein in various ways (for instance, by cutting out portions). Eventually, the protein may be selectively broken down.

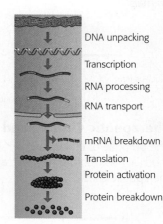

DNA unpacking

Transcription

RNA processing

RNA transport

mRNA breakdown

Translation

Protein activation

Protein breakdown

Cell Signaling

Cell-to-cell signaling is key to the development and functioning of multicellular organisms. Signal transduction pathways convert molecular messages to cell responses, such as the transcription of particular genes.

Homeotic Genes

Evidence for the evolutionary importance of gene regulation is apparent in homeotic genes, master genes that regulate other genes that in turn control embryonic development.

DNA Microarrays: Visualizing Gene Expression

DNA microarrays can be used to determine which genes are turned on in a particular cell type.

Cloning Plants and Animals

The Genetic Potential of Cells

Most differentiated cells retain a complete set of genes, so an orchid plant, for example, can be made to grow from a single orchid cell. Under special conditions, animals can also be cloned.

Reproductive Cloning of Animals

Nuclear transplantation is a procedure whereby a donor cell nucleus is inserted into a nucleus-free egg. First demonstrated in frogs in the 1950s, reproductive cloning was used in 1996 to clone a sheep from an adult mammary cell and has since been used to create many other cloned animals.

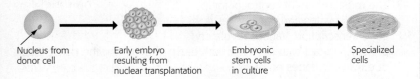

Nucleus from donor cell — Early embryo resulting from nuclear transplantation — Embryo implanted in surrogate mother — Clone of nucleus donor

Therapeutic Cloning and Stem Cells

The purpose of therapeutic cloning is to produce embryonic stem cells for medical uses. Both embryonic and adult stem cells show promise for future therapeutic uses.

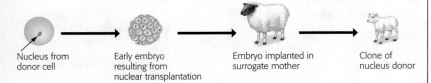

Nucleus from donor cell — Early embryo resulting from nuclear transplantation — Embryonic stem cells in culture — Specialized cells

The Genetic Basis of Cancer

Genes That Cause Cancer

Cancer cells, which divide uncontrollably, can result from mutations in genes whose protein products regulate the cell cycle.

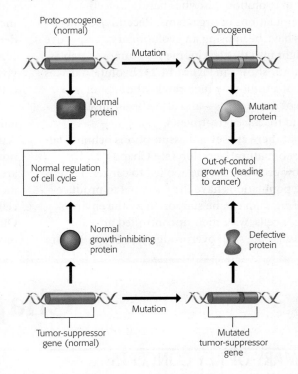

Many proto-oncogenes and tumor-suppressor genes code for proteins active in signal transduction pathways regulating cell division. Mutations of these genes cause malfunction of the pathways. Cancers result from a series of genetic changes in a cell lineage. Researchers have gained insight into the genetic basis of breast cancer by studying families in which a disease-predisposing mutation is inherited.

Cancer Risk and Prevention

Reducing exposure to carcinogens (which induce cancer-causing mutations) and making other healthful lifestyle choices can help reduce cancer risk.

SELF-QUIZ

1. Your bone cells, muscle cells, and skin cells look different because
   a. different kinds of genes are present in each kind of cell.
   b. they are present in different organs.
   c. different genes are active in each kind of cell.
   d. different mutations have occurred in each kind of cell.

2. A group of prokaryotic genes with related functions that are regulated as a single unit, along with the control sequences that perform this regulation, is called a(n) _____.

3. The regulation of gene expression must be more complex in multicellular eukaryotes than in prokaryotes because
   a. eukaryotic cells are much larger.
   b. in a multicellular eukaryote, different cells are specialized for different functions.
   c. prokaryotes are restricted to stable environments.
   d. eukaryotes have fewer genes, so each gene must do several jobs.

4. A eukaryotic gene was inserted into the DNA of a bacterium. The bacterium then transcribed this gene into mRNA and translated the mRNA into protein. The protein produced was useless and contained many more amino acids than the protein made by the eukaryotic cell. Why?
   a. The mRNA was not spliced as it is in eukaryotes.
   b. Eukaryotes and prokaryotes use different genetic codes.
   c. Repressor proteins interfered with transcription and translation.
   d. Ribosomes were not able to bind to tRNA.

5. How does dense packing of DNA in chromosomes prevent gene expression?

6. What evidence demonstrates that differentiated cells in a plant or animal retain their full genetic potential?

7. The most common procedure for cloning an animal is _____.

8. What is learned from a DNA microarray?

9. Which of the following is a valid difference between embryonic stem cells and the stem cells found in adult tissues?
   a. In laboratory culture, only adult stem cells are immortal.
   b. In nature, only embryonic stem cells give rise to all the different types of cells in the organism.
   c. Only adult stem cells can be made to differentiate in the laboratory.
   d. Only embryonic stem cells are in every tissue of the adult body.

10. Name three potential sources of stem cells.

11. What is the difference between oncogenes and proto-oncogenes? How can one turn into the other? What function do proto-oncogenes serve?

12. A mutation in a single gene may cause a major change in the body of a fruit fly, such as an extra pair of legs or wings. Yet it takes many genes to produce a wing or leg. How can a change in just one gene cause such a big change in the body? What are such genes called?

Answers to these questions can be found in Appendix: Self-Quiz Answers.

THE PROCESS OF SCIENCE

13. Study the depiction of the *lac* operon in Figure 11.2. Normally, the genes are turned off when lactose is not present. Lactose activates the genes, which code for enzymes that enable the cell to use lactose. Mutations can alter the function of this operon; in fact, the effects of various mutations enabled Jacob and Monod to figure out how the operon works. Predict how the following mutations would affect the function of the operon in the presence and absence of lactose:
   a. mutation of regulatory gene; repressor will not bind to lactose
   b. mutation of operator; repressor will not bind to operator
   c. mutation of regulatory gene; repressor will not bind to operator
   d. mutation of promoter; RNA polymerase will not attach to promoter

14. The human body has a far greater variety of proteins than genes, a fact that seems to highlight the importance of alternative RNA splicing, which allows several different mRNAs to be made from a single gene. Suppose you have samples of two types of adult cells from one person. Design an experiment using microarrays to determine whether or not the different gene expression is due to alternative RNA splicing.

15. Because a cat must have both orange and non-orange alleles to be tortoiseshell (see Figure 11.4), we would expect only female cats, which have two X chromosomes, to be tortoiseshell. Normal male cats (XY) can carry only one of the two alleles. Male tortoiseshell cats are rare and usually sterile. What might you guess their genotype to be?

16. Design a DNA microarray experiment that measures the difference in gene expression between normal colon cells and cells from a colon tumor.

BIOLOGY AND SOCIETY

17. A chemical called dioxin is produced as a by-product of certain chemical manufacturing processes. Trace amounts of this substance were present in Agent Orange, a defoliant sprayed on vegetation during the Vietnam War. There has been a continuing controversy over its effects on soldiers exposed to Agent Orange during the war. Animal tests have suggested that dioxin can cause cancer, liver and thymus damage, immune system suppression, and birth defects; at high dosage it can be lethal. But such animal tests are inconclusive; a hamster is not affected by a dose that can kill a much larger guinea pig, for example. Researchers have discovered that dioxin enters a cell and binds to a protein that in turn attaches to the cell's DNA. How might this mechanism help explain the variety of dioxin's effects on different body systems and in different animals? How might you determine whether a particular individual became ill as a result of exposure to dioxin? Do you think this information is relevant in the lawsuits of soldiers suing over exposure to Agent Orange? Why or why not?

18. There are genetic tests available for several types of "inherited cancer." The results from these tests cannot usually predict that someone will get cancer within a particular amount of time. Rather, they indicate only that a person has an increased risk of developing cancer. For many of these cancers, lifestyle changes cannot decrease a person's risk. Therefore, some people consider the tests useless. If your close family had a history of cancer and a test were available, would you want to get screened? Why or why not? What would you do with this information? If a sibling decided to get screened, explain whether you would want to know the results.

12 DNA Technology

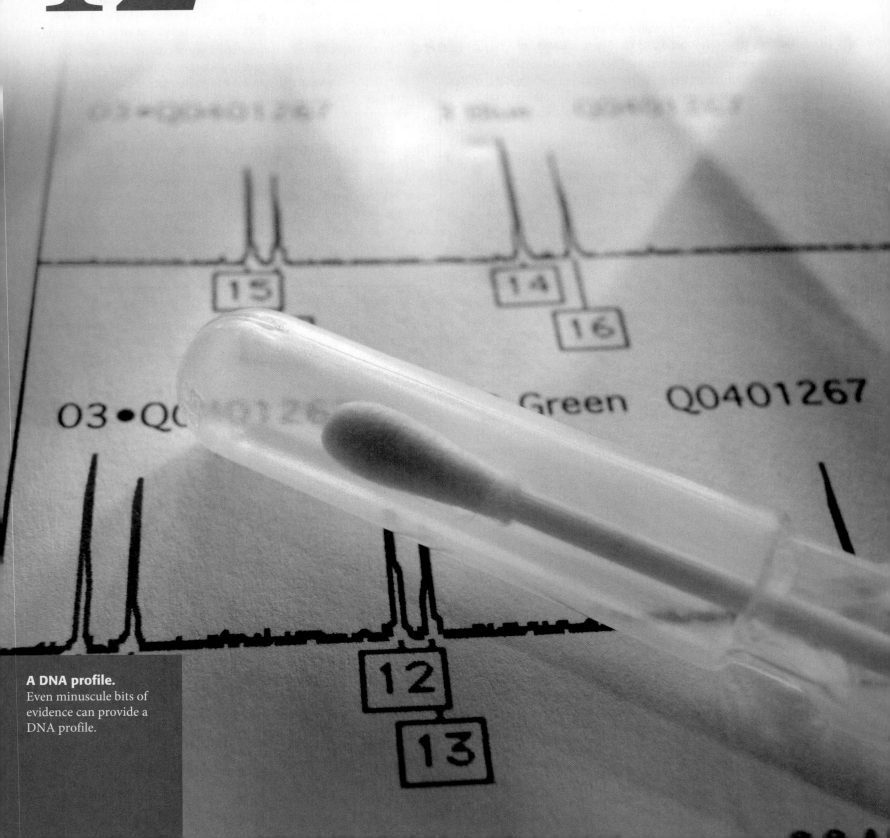

A DNA profile.
Even minuscule bits of
evidence can provide a
DNA profile.

DNA Profiling BIOLOGY AND SOCIETY

DNA, Guilt, and Innocence

It was a horrific crime: Early in the morning of May 3, 1992, a 3-year-old girl sleeping in her Mississippi home was abducted, raped, murdered, and thrown into a creek. A tiny semen sample was recovered at the crime scene. Police arrested the mother's boyfriend, who had been babysitting the girl that night. Although police could not conclusively match the crime scene sample to the suspect, the jury found the circumstantial evidence compelling. He was convicted of the crime and sentenced to death.

How can a biological sample be used to provide evidence of guilt? Modern forensic investigations hinge on a simple fact: The cells of every person (except identical twins) contain unique DNA. DNA profiling is the analysis of DNA samples to determine whether they come from the same individual. Although the semen sample from the 1992 crime scene was insufficient for DNA profiling at the time, new methods allowed a DNA profile to be determined in 2001. The results this time were conclusive: The semen at the crime scene did *not* match the man originally convicted of the crime.

Several years later, the DNA profile obtained from the crime scene was matched to a different man. The second man soon confessed to the crime and to the nearly identical 1990 murder of another 3-year-old girl, for which a third man was serving jail time. After years of legal maneuvering, the two wrongly convicted men were freed in 2008, exonerated based on the DNA evidence.

A steady stream of stories such as the one told here demonstrates the relevance of DNA technology to forensic science. Even beyond the courtroom, DNA technology has led to some of the most remarkable scientific advances in recent years: Corn and other crops, such as soybeans and tomatoes, have been genetically modified to produce their own insecticides; human genes are being compared with those of other animals to help shed light on what makes us distinctly human; and significant advances have been made toward detecting and curing fatal genetic diseases. This chapter will describe these and other uses of DNA technology and explain how various DNA techniques are performed. Along the way, we'll also examine some of the social, legal, and ethical issues that lie at the intersection of biology and society.

Recombinant DNA Technology

You may think of **biotechnology**, the manipulation of organisms or their components to make useful products, as a modern phenomenon, but it actually dates back to the dawn of civilization. Consider such ancient practices as using yeast to make bread and the selective breeding of livestock. But when people use the term *biotechnology* today, they are usually referring to **DNA technology**, modern laboratory techniques for studying and manipulating genetic material. Using these methods, scientists can modify specific genes and move them between organisms as different as bacteria, plants, and animals.

Are there any products of biotechnology in your lunch?

In the 1970s, the field of biotechnology exploded with the invention of methods for making recombinant DNA in the laboratory. **Recombinant DNA** is constructed when scientists combine pieces of DNA from two different sources—often from different species—to form a single DNA molecule. Recombinant DNA technology is widely used in **genetic engineering**, the direct manipulation of genes for practical purposes. Scientists have genetically engineered bacteria to mass-produce a variety of useful chemicals, from cancer drugs to pesticides. Scientists have also transferred genes from bacteria to plants and from one animal species to another **(Figure 12.1)**. Such engineering can serve a variety of purposes, from basic research (What does this gene do?) to medical applications (Can we create animal models for this human disease?). ✓

☑ CHECKPOINT

What is biotechnology? What is recombinant DNA?

Answer: the manipulation of organisms or their parts to produce a useful product; a molecule containing DNA from two different sources, often different species

▼ **Figure 12.1 Glowing fish.** Genetic engineers produced glowing fish by transferring a gene for a fluorescent protein originally obtained from jellies ("jellyfish").

Applications: From Humulin to Foods to "Pharm" Animals

By transferring the gene for a desired protein into a bacterium, yeast, or other kind of cell that is easy to grow in culture, scientists can produce large quantities of useful proteins that are present naturally only in small amounts. In this section, you'll learn about some applications of recombinant DNA technology.

Making Humulin

Humulin is human insulin produced by genetically modified bacteria **(Figure 12.2)**. In humans, insulin is a protein normally made by the pancreas. Insulin functions as a hormone and helps regulate the level of glucose in the blood. If the body fails to produce enough insulin, the result is type 1 diabetes. There is no cure, so people with this disease must inject themselves daily with doses of insulin for the rest of their lives.

Because human insulin is not readily available, diabetes was historically treated using insulin from cows and pigs. This treatment was problematic, however. Pig and cow insulins can cause allergic reactions in people because their chemical structures differ slightly from that of human insulin. In addition, by the 1970s, the supply of beef and pork pancreas available for insulin extraction could not keep up with the demand.

In 1978, scientists working at the biotechnology company Genentech chemically synthesized two genes, one for each of the polypeptides of the active form of human insulin (see Figure 11.7). Because the amino acid sequences of the two insulin polypeptides were already known, it was easy to use the genetic code (see Figure 10.11) to determine nucleotide sequences that would encode for them. Researchers synthesized DNA fragments and linked them

▶ **Figure 12.2
Humulin, human insulin produced by genetically modified bacteria.**

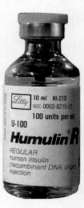

to form the insulin genes. In 1979, they succeeded in inserting these artificial genes into *Escherichia coli* host cells. Under proper growing conditions, these bacteria cranked out large quantities of the human protein.

In 1982, Humulin hit the market as the world's first genetically engineered pharmaceutical product. Today, it is produced around the clock in gigantic fermentation vats filled with a liquid culture of bacteria. Each day, more than 4 million people with diabetes use the insulin collected, purified, and packaged at such facilities **(Figure 12.3)**.

Insulin is just one of many human proteins produced by genetically modified bacteria. Another example is human growth hormone (HGH). Abnormally low levels of this hormone during childhood and adolescence can cause dwarfism. Because growth hormones from other animals are not effective in people, HGH was an early target of genetic engineers. Before genetically engineered HGH became available in 1985, children with an HGH deficiency could only be treated with scarce and expensive supplies of HGH obtained from human cadavers.

Besides bacteria, yeast and mammalian cells can also be used to produce medically valuable human proteins. For example, genetically modified mammalian cells growing in laboratory cultures are currently used to produce a hormone called erythropoietin (EPO) that stimulates production of red blood cells. EPO is used to treat anemia; unfortunately, some athletes abuse the drug to seek the advantage of artificially high levels of oxygen-carrying red blood cells (a practice called "blood doping").

DNA technology is also helping medical researchers develop vaccines. A **vaccine** is a harmless variant or derivative of a disease-causing microbe—such as a bacterium or virus—that is used to prevent an infectious disease. When a person is inoculated, the vaccine stimulates the immune system to develop lasting defenses against the microbe. For many viral diseases, the only

way to prevent serious harm from the illness is to use vaccination to prevent the illness in the first place. One approach to vaccine production is to use genetically engineered yeast cells to make large amounts of a protein found on the microbe's outer surface. The vaccine against hepatitis B, a disabling and sometimes fatal liver disease, is made in this way.

Genetically Modified (GM) Foods

Since ancient times, people have selectively bred agricultural crops to make them more useful (see Figure 1.13a). Today, DNA technology is quickly replacing traditional breeding programs as scientists work to improve the productivity of agriculturally important plants and animals. Scientists have produced many varieties of **genetically modified (GM) organisms**, organisms that have acquired one or more genes by artificial means. If the newly acquired gene is from another organism, typically of another species, the recombinant organism is called a **transgenic organism**.

In the United States today, roughly half the corn crop and more than three-quarters of the soybean and cotton crops are genetically modified. **Figure 12.4** shows corn that has been genetically engineered to resist attack by an insect called the European corn borer (shown in the inset). Growing insect-resistant plants reduces the need for chemical insecticides. In another example, modified strawberry plants produce bacterial proteins that act as a natural antifreeze, protecting the plants from cold weather, which can harm the delicate crop. Potatoes and rice have been experimentally modified to produce harmless proteins derived from the cholera bacterium; researchers hope that these modified foods will one day serve as an edible vaccine against cholera, a disease that kills thousands of children in developing nations every year. In India, the insertion of a natural but rare saltwater-resistance gene has enabled new varieties of rice to thrive in water three times as salty as seawater, allowing food to be grown in drought-stricken or flooded regions.

▼ Figure 12.3 **A factory that produces genetically engineered insulin.**

▼ Figure 12.4 **Genetically modified corn.** The corn plants in this field carry a bacterial gene that helps prevent infestation by the European corn borer (inset).

▲ **Figure 12.5 Genetically modified rice.** "Golden rice 2," the yellow grains shown here alongside ordinary rice, has been genetically modified to produce high levels of beta-carotene, a molecule that the body converts to vitamin A.

Scientists are also using genetic engineering to improve the nutritional value of crop plants. One example is "golden rice 2," a transgenic variety of rice that carries genes from daffodils and corn (**Figure 12.5**). This rice could help prevent vitamin A deficiency and resulting blindness, especially in developing nations that depend on rice as a staple crop. However, controversy surrounds the use of GM foods, as we'll discuss at the end of the chapter. ☑

"Pharm" Animals

Figure 12.6 shows a transgenic pig that carries a gene for human hemoglobin. The pig-produced hemoglobin can be isolated and used in human blood transfusions. Because transgenic animals are difficult to produce, researchers may create a single transgenic animal and then breed or clone it. The resulting herd of transgenic animals could then serve as a grazing pharmaceutical factory—"pharm" animals.

DNA technology may eventually replace traditional animal breeding. Scientists might, for example, identify a gene that causes the development of larger muscles (which make up most of the meat we eat) in one variety of cattle and transfer it to other cattle or even to chickens. In 2006, University of Pittsburgh researchers genetically modified pigs to carry a roundworm gene whose protein converts less healthy fatty acids to omega-3 fatty acids. Meat from the modified pigs contains four to five times as much healthy omega-3 fat as regular pork. Unlike transgenic plants, however, transgenic animals are currently used only to produce potentially useful proteins; as of 2011, no transgenic animals are sold as food, although the Food and Drug Administration has issued regulatory guidelines for their eventual introduction.

Recombinant DNA technology serves many roles today and will certainly play an even larger part in our future. In the next section, you'll learn how scientists create and manipulate recombinant DNA.

Recombinant DNA Techniques

Although recombinant DNA techniques can be performed using many types of cells, bacteria are the workhorses of modern biotechnology. To manipulate genes in the laboratory, biologists often use bacterial **plasmids**, which are small, circular DNA molecules that replicate (duplicate) separately from the larger bacterial chromosome (**Figure 12.7**). Because plasmids can carry virtually any gene and are passed from one generation of bacteria to the next, they are key tools for **gene cloning**, the production of multiple identical copies of a gene-carrying piece of DNA. Gene-cloning methods are central to the production of useful products from genetically engineered organisms.

Consider a typical genetic engineering challenge: A molecular biologist at a pharmaceutical company identifies a gene of interest that codes for a valuable protein, such as a potential new drug. The biologist wants to manufacture the protein on a large scale. **Figure 12.8** illustrates a way to accomplish this by using recombinant DNA techniques.

To start, the biologist isolates two kinds of DNA: ❶ bacterial plasmids that will serve as **vectors** (gene carriers) and ❷ DNA from another organism that includes the gene of interest (along with other unwanted genes). This other DNA may be from any type of organism, even a human. ❸ The researcher uses an enzyme to cut the two kinds of DNA. Each plasmid is cut in only one place; the other DNA is cut into many fragments, one of which carries the gene of interest. The figure shows the processing of just three of these DNA fragments and three plasmids, but actually millions of

▼ **Figure 12.7 Bacterial plasmids.** The micrograph shows a bacterial cell that has been ruptured, revealing one long chromosome and several smaller plasmids. The inset is an enlarged view of a single plasmid.

◄ **Figure 12.6 A genetically modified swine.**

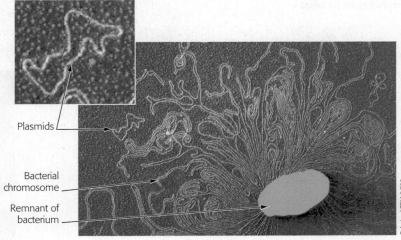

Plasmids

Bacterial chromosome

Remnant of bacterium

Colorized TEM 2,700x

▼ **Figure 12.8 Using recombinant DNA technology to produce useful products.**

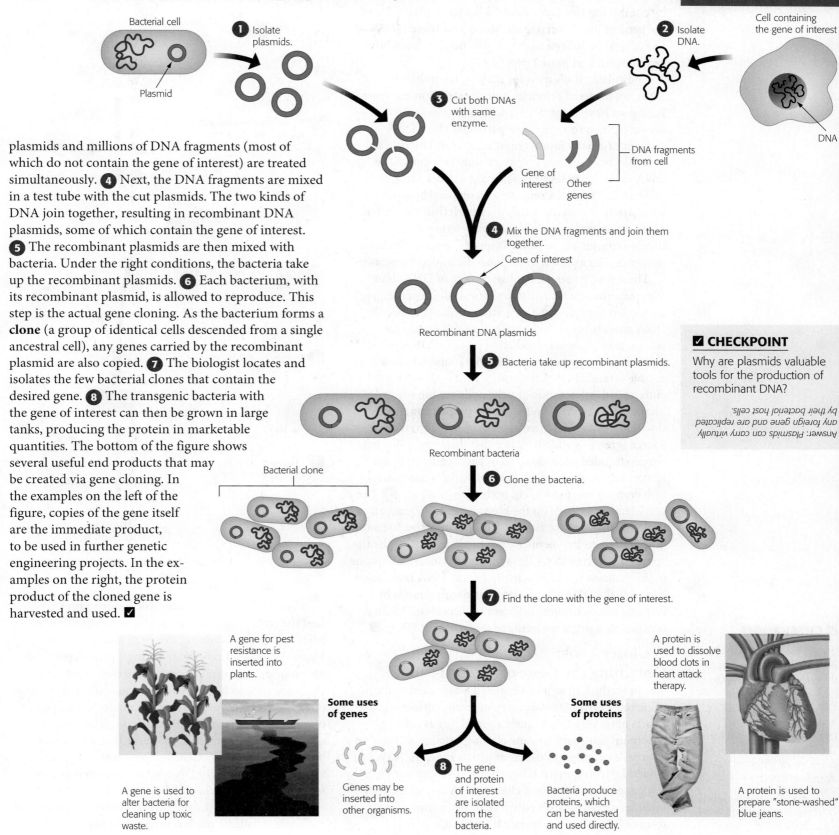

plasmids and millions of DNA fragments (most of which do not contain the gene of interest) are treated simultaneously. ❹ Next, the DNA fragments are mixed in a test tube with the cut plasmids. The two kinds of DNA join together, resulting in recombinant DNA plasmids, some of which contain the gene of interest. ❺ The recombinant plasmids are then mixed with bacteria. Under the right conditions, the bacteria take up the recombinant plasmids. ❻ Each bacterium, with its recombinant plasmid, is allowed to reproduce. This step is the actual gene cloning. As the bacterium forms a **clone** (a group of identical cells descended from a single ancestral cell), any genes carried by the recombinant plasmid are also copied. ❼ The biologist locates and isolates the few bacterial clones that contain the desired gene. ❽ The transgenic bacteria with the gene of interest can then be grown in large tanks, producing the protein in marketable quantities. The bottom of the figure shows several useful end products that may be created via gene cloning. In the examples on the left of the figure, copies of the gene itself are the immediate product, to be used in further genetic engineering projects. In the examples on the right, the protein product of the cloned gene is harvested and used. ☑

Bacterial cell

❶ Isolate plasmids.

Plasmid

❷ Isolate DNA.

Cell containing the gene of interest

DNA

❸ Cut both DNAs with same enzyme.

DNA fragments from cell

Gene of interest

Other genes

❹ Mix the DNA fragments and join them together.

Gene of interest

Recombinant DNA plasmids

❺ Bacteria take up recombinant plasmids.

Recombinant bacteria

Bacterial clone

❻ Clone the bacteria.

❼ Find the clone with the gene of interest.

A gene for pest resistance is inserted into plants.

A protein is used to dissolve blood clots in heart attack therapy.

Some uses of genes

Some uses of proteins

A gene is used to alter bacteria for cleaning up toxic waste.

Genes may be inserted into other organisms.

❽ The gene and protein of interest are isolated from the bacteria.

Bacteria produce proteins, which can be harvested and used directly.

A protein is used to prepare "stone-washed" blue jeans.

☑ **CHECKPOINT**

Why are plasmids valuable tools for the production of recombinant DNA?

Answer: Plasmids can carry virtually any foreign gene and are replicated by their bacterial host cells.

A Closer Look: Cutting and Pasting DNA with Restriction Enzymes

As you saw in Figure 12.8, recombinant DNA is created by combining two ingredients: a bacterial plasmid and the gene of interest. To understand how these DNA molecules are spliced together, you need to learn how enzymes cut and paste DNA.

The cutting tools used for making recombinant DNA are bacterial enzymes called **restriction enzymes**. Biologists have identified hundreds of restriction enzymes, each recognizing a particular short DNA sequence (usually four to eight nucleotides long). For example, one restriction enzyme only recognizes the DNA sequence GAATTC, whereas another recognizes GGATCC. The DNA sequence recognized by a particular restriction enzyme is called a **restriction site**. After a restriction enzyme binds to its restriction site, it cuts the two strands of the DNA at specific points within the sequence, like a pair of highly specific molecular scissors.

The top of **Figure 12.9** shows a piece of DNA (blue) that contains one recognition sequence for a particular restriction enzyme. ❶ The restriction enzyme cuts the DNA strands between the bases A and G within the recognition sequence, producing pieces of DNA called **restriction fragments**. The staggered cuts yield two double-stranded DNA fragments with single-stranded ends, called "sticky ends." Sticky ends are the key to joining DNA restriction fragments originating from different sources. ❷ Next, a piece of DNA from another source (green) is added. Notice that the green DNA has single-stranded ends identical in base sequence to the sticky ends on the blue DNA because the same restriction enzyme was used to cut both types of DNA. ❸ The complementary ends on the blue and green fragments stick together by base pairing. ❹ The union between the blue and green fragments is then made permanent by the "pasting" enzyme **DNA ligase**. This enzyme, which is one of the proteins the cell normally uses in DNA replication, connects the DNA pieces into continuous strands by forming bonds between adjacent nucleotides. The final outcome is a single molecule of recombinant DNA. ☑

A Closer Look: Obtaining the Gene of Interest

The procedure shown in Figure 12.8 can yield millions of recombinant plasmids carrying many different segments of foreign DNA. Such a procedure is called a "shotgun" approach to gene cloning because it "hits" an enormous number of different pieces of DNA. A typical cloned DNA fragment is big enough to carry one or a few genes. A collection of cloned DNA fragments that includes an organism's entire genome (a complete set of its genes) is called a **genomic library**.

☑ CHECKPOINT

If you mix a restriction enzyme that cuts within the sequence AATC with DNA of the sequence CGAATCTAGCAATCGCGA, how many restriction fragments will result? (For simplicity, the sequence of only one of the two DNA strands is listed.)

Answer: Cuts at two restriction sites will yield three restriction fragments.

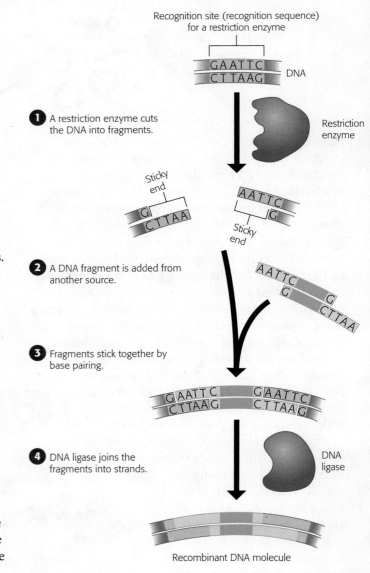

▼ Figure 12.9 **Cutting and pasting DNA.** The production of recombinant DNA requires two enzymes: a restriction enzyme, which cuts the original DNA molecules into pieces, and DNA ligase, which pastes the pieces together.

Recognition site (recognition sequence) for a restriction enzyme

GAATTC
CTTAAG DNA

❶ A restriction enzyme cuts the DNA into fragments.

Restriction enzyme

Sticky end

G   AATTC
CTTAA   G

Sticky end

❷ A DNA fragment is added from another source.

AATTC   G
G   CTTAA

❸ Fragments stick together by base pairing.

GAATTC   GAATTC
CTTAAG   CTTAAG

❹ DNA ligase joins the fragments into strands.

DNA ligase

Recombinant DNA molecule

After you've created a genomic library, you have to find the right "book"—that is, you must identify the bacterial clone containing a desired gene (step 7 in Figure 12.8). Methods for detecting a gene depend on base pairing between the gene and a complementary sequence on another nucleic acid molecule, either DNA or RNA. When at least part of the nucleotide sequence of a gene is known, this information can be used to advantage. For example, if we know that a gene contains the sequence TAGGCT, a biologist can synthesize a short single strand of DNA with a complementary sequence (ATCCGA) and label it with a radioactive isotope or fluorescent dye. This labeled complementary molecule is called a **nucleic acid probe** because it is used to find a specific gene or other nucleotide sequence within a mass of DNA. (In actual practice, probe molecules are considerably longer than six nucleotides.) When a radioactive DNA probe is added to the DNA of various clones, it tags the correct molecule—finds the right book in the library—by base-pairing to the complementary sequence in the gene of interest (**Figure 12.10**). After a probe detects the desired clone within a library, more of the tagged cells can be grown, resulting in the production of large quantities of the gene of interest.

Another approach to obtaining a gene of interest is to synthesize it. One method uses reverse transcriptase, a viral enzyme that can synthesize DNA by using an mRNA template (see Chapter 10). **Figure 12.11** shows the steps involved. A eukaryotic cell ❶ transcribes the gene of interest and ❷ processes the transcript, removing introns and splicing exons together to produce mRNA. A researcher then ❸ isolates the mRNA in a test tube and ❹ makes single-stranded DNA from it using reverse transcriptase. ❺ DNA polymerase is then used to synthesize a second DNA strand.

When the researcher starts with an mRNA mixture from a particular cell type, the DNA that results from this procedure, called complementary DNA (cDNA), represents only those genes that were actually transcribed in the starting cells. Because cDNA molecules lack introns, they are shorter than the full version of the genes and therefore easier to work with.

A final approach is to synthesize a gene of interest from scratch. Automated DNA-synthesizing machines can accurately and rapidly produce customized DNA molecules of any sequence up to lengths of a few hundred nucleotides (**Figure 12.12**). ☑

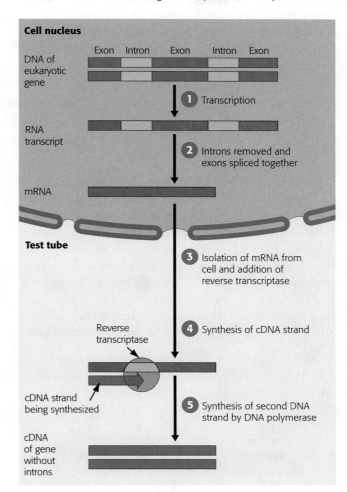

▼ **Figure 12.11 Making a gene from eukaryotic mRNA.** Using the enzyme reverse transcriptase (shown in green), a researcher can produce an artificial DNA gene (cDNA, in blue) from a molecule of messenger RNA (mRNA, in red).

Cell nucleus

DNA of eukaryotic gene — Exon Intron Exon Intron Exon

❶ Transcription

RNA transcript

❷ Introns removed and exons spliced together

mRNA

Test tube

❸ Isolation of mRNA from cell and addition of reverse transcriptase

Reverse transcriptase

❹ Synthesis of cDNA strand

cDNA strand being synthesized

❺ Synthesis of second DNA strand by DNA polymerase

cDNA of gene without introns

☑ **CHECKPOINT**

Name three ways a gene of interest can be obtained.

Answer: The gene can be isolated from a genomic library, produced from mRNA using reverse transcriptase, or synthesized from scratch.

▼ **Figure 12.10 How a DNA probe tags a gene.** The probe is a short, radioactive, single-stranded molecule of DNA or RNA. When it is mixed with single-stranded DNA from a gene with a complementary sequence, it attaches by hydrogen bonds (shown by the small red dots), "labeling" the gene.

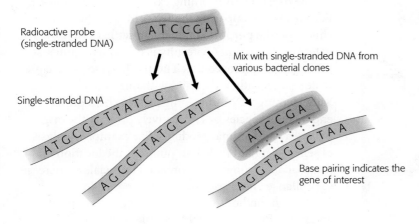

Radioactive probe (single-stranded DNA) — A T C C G A

Mix with single-stranded DNA from various bacterial clones

Single-stranded DNA

ATGCGCTTATCG
AGCCTTATGCAT

ATCCGA
AGGTAGGCTAA

Base pairing indicates the gene of interest

▶ **Figure 12.12 A DNA synthesizer.** This synthesizer constructs molecules of DNA from a programmed sequence, using solutions of the four DNA nucleotides (stored in the bottles beneath the machine).

DNA Profiling and Forensic Science

As discussed in the Biology and Society section, the analysis of DNA samples to determine whether they come from the same individual, known as **DNA profiling**, can help in criminal investigations. Indeed, DNA profiling has rapidly transformed the field of **forensics**, the scientific analysis of evidence for crime scene investigations and other legal proceedings. To produce a DNA profile, scientists compare sequences in the genome that vary from person to person. Like a gene, a noncoding genetic sequence is more likely to be a match between relatives than between unrelated individuals.

How have the techniques of DNA technology revolutionized forensics?

Figure 12.13 presents an overview of a typical investigation using DNA profiling. ❶ First, DNA samples are isolated from the crime scene, suspects, victims, or other evidence. ❷ Next, selected sequences from each DNA sample are amplified (copied many times) to produce a large sample of DNA fragments. ❸ Finally, the amplified DNA regions are compared using a gel (a method we'll discuss later). All together, these steps provide data about which samples are from the same individual and which samples are unique. ✔

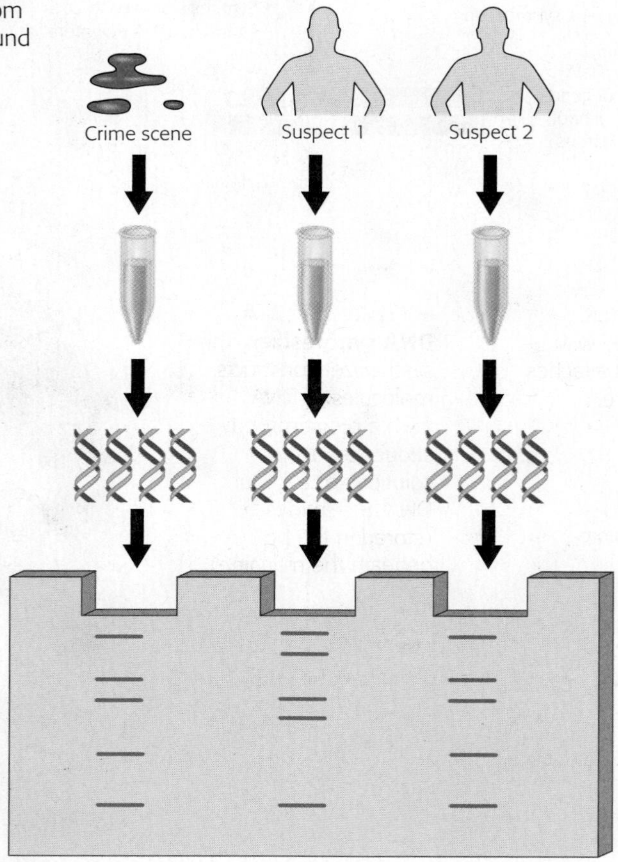

Investigating Murder, Paternity, and Ancient DNA

Since its introduction in 1986, DNA profiling has become a standard tool of forensics and has provided crucial evidence in many famous cases. DNA profiling first came to widespread attention during the O. J. Simpson murder trial. In this case, DNA analysis proved that blood in Simpson's car belonged to the victims and that blood at the crime scene belonged to Simpson. (The jury did not find the DNA evidence alone to be sufficient to convict the suspect, and Simpson was found not guilty.) And during the investigation that led up to his impeachment, President Bill Clinton repeatedly denied that he had sexual relations with Monica Lewinsky—until DNA profiling proved that his semen was on her dress. Of course, DNA evidence can prove innocence as well as guilt. As of 2011, lawyers at the Innocence Project, a nonprofit legal organization located in New York City, have helped to exonerate more than 270 convicted criminals in 34 states, including 17 who were on death row. In more than a third of these cases, DNA profiling has also identified the true perpetrators.

DNA profiling can also be used to identify murder victims. The largest such effort in history took place after the World Trade Center attack on September 11, 2001. Forensic scientists in New York City worked for years to identify more than 20,000 samples of victims' remains. DNA profiles of tissue samples from the disaster site were matched to DNA profiles from tissue known to be from the victims. If no sample of a victim's DNA was available, blood samples from close relatives were used to confirm identity through near matches. More than half of the victims identified at the World Trade Center site were recognized solely by DNA evidence, providing closure to many grieving families.

The use of DNA profiling extends beyond crimes. For instance, comparing the DNA of a mother, her child, and the purported father can settle a question of paternity. Sometimes paternity is of historical interest: DNA profiling proved that Thomas Jefferson or a close male relative fathered a child with one of his slaves, Sally Hemings. DNA profiling can also help protect endangered species by conclusively proving the origin of contraband animal products. For example, analysis of seized elephant tusks can pinpoint the location of the poaching, allowing enforcement officials to increase surveillance and prosecute those responsible.

Modern methods of DNA profiling are so specific and powerful that the DNA samples can be in a partially

☑ CHECKPOINT

DNA profiling depends on analyzing genetic markers. What is a genetic marker?

Answer: A genetic marker is any sequence in the genome that varies from person to person.

▶ **Figure 12.13 Overview of DNA profiling.** In this example, DNA from suspect 1 does not match DNA found at the crime scene, but DNA from suspect 2 does match.

Crime scene   Suspect 1   Suspect 2

❶ DNA isolated

❷ DNA amplified

❸ DNA compared

degraded state. This allows DNA analysis to be applied in a great number of ways. In evolution research, the technique has been used to study DNA recovered from an ancient mummified human and from a 30-million-year-old plant fossil. A 2005 study determined that DNA extracted from a 27,000-year-old Siberian mammoth was 98.6% identical to DNA from modern African elephants. One of the strangest cases of DNA profiling is that of Cheddar Man, a 9,000-year-old skeleton found in a cave near Cheddar, England **(Figure 12.14)**. DNA was extracted from his tooth and used to construct a DNA profile. The results suggested that Cheddar Man was a direct ancestor (through approximately 300 generations) of a present-day schoolteacher who lived only half a mile from the cave!

▶ **Figure 12.14 Cheddar Man.**
Analysis of DNA extracted from "Cheddar Man"—a 9,000-year-old skeleton found in an English cave—suggested that he was a direct ancestor of a local schoolteacher (shown in the inset).

DNA Profiling Techniques

In this section, you'll learn about techniques for making a DNA profile (steps 2 and 3 in Figure 12.13).

The Polymerase Chain Reaction (PCR)

The **polymerase chain reaction (PCR)** is a technique by which a specific segment of DNA can be targeted and copied quickly and precisely. Through PCR, a scientist can obtain enough DNA from even minute amounts of blood or other tissue to allow a DNA profile to be constructed.

In principle, PCR is simple. A DNA sample is mixed with nucleotides, the DNA replication enzyme DNA polymerase, and a few other ingredients. The solution is then exposed to cycles of heating (to separate the DNA strands) and cooling (to allow double-stranded DNA to re-form). During these cycles, specific regions of each molecule of DNA are replicated, doubling the amount of that DNA **(Figure 12.15)**. The key to automated PCR is an unusually heat-stable DNA polymerase, first isolated from prokaryotes living in hot springs. Unlike most proteins, this enzyme can withstand the heat at the start of each cycle. Beginning with a single DNA molecule, automated PCR can generate hundreds of billions of copies in a few hours. ☑

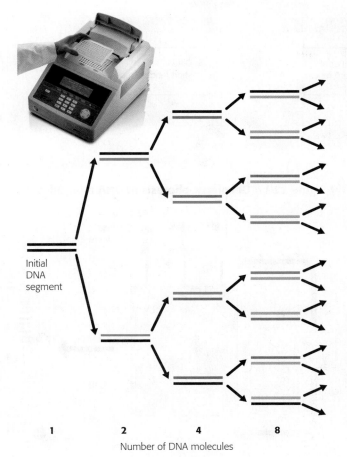

1 2 4 8
Number of DNA molecules

◀ **Figure 12.15 DNA amplification by PCR.** The polymerase chain reaction (PCR) is a method for making many copies of a specific segment of DNA. Each round of PCR, performed on a table-top thermal cycler (shown at top), doubles the total quantity of DNA.

☑ **CHECKPOINT**
Why is only the slightest trace of DNA at a crime scene often sufficient for forensic analysis?

Answer: because PCR can be used to produce enough molecules for analysis

Short Tandem Repeat (STR) Analysis

How do you prove that two samples of DNA come from the same person? You could compare the entire genomes found in the two samples. But such an approach would be extremely impractical, requiring a lot of time and money. Instead, forensic scientists typically compare about a dozen short segments of noncoding repetitive DNA. **Repetitive DNA**, which makes up much of the DNA that lies between genes in humans, consists of nucleotide sequences that are present in multiple copies in the genome. Some of this DNA consists of short sequences repeated many times tandemly (one after another); such a series of repeats is called a **short tandem repeat (STR)**. For example, one person might have the sequence AGAT repeated 12 times in a row at one place in the genome, the sequence GATA repeated 35 times at a second place, and so on; another person is likely to have the same sequences at the same places but with a different number of repeats. These stretches of repetitive DNA are more likely to be an exact match between relatives than between unrelated individuals.

STR analysis is a method of DNA profiling that compares the lengths of STR sequences at specific sites in the genome. Most commonly, STR analysis compares the number of repeats of specific four-nucleotide DNA sequences at 13 sites scattered throughout the genome. Each repeat site, which typically contains from 3 to 50 four-nucleotide repeats in a row, varies widely from person to person. In fact, some STRs used in the standard procedure have up to 80 variations in the number of repeats. In the United States, the number of repeats at each site is entered into a database called CODIS (Combined DNA Index System) administered by the Federal Bureau of Investigation. Law enforcement agencies around the world can access CODIS to search for matches to DNA samples they have obtained from crime scenes or suspects.

Consider the two samples of DNA shown in **Figure 12.16**. Imagine that the top DNA segment was obtained at a crime scene and the bottom from a suspect's blood. The two segments have the same number of repeats at the first site: 7 repeats of the four-nucleotide DNA sequence AGAT (in orange). Notice, however, that they differ in the number of repeats at the second site: 8 repeats of GATA (in purple) in the crime scene DNA, compared with 13 repeats in the suspect's DNA. To create a DNA profile, a scientist uses PCR to specifically amplify the regions of DNA that include these STR sites. The resulting fragments are then compared. Next we'll look at how this comparison is made. ☑

Gel Electrophoresis

The lengths of DNA fragments can be compared using **gel electrophoresis**, a method for sorting macromolecules—usually proteins or nucleic acids—primarily by their electrical charge and size. **Figure 12.17** shows how gel electrophoresis separates DNA fragments obtained from

▼ **Figure 12.16 Short tandem repeat (STR) sites.** Scattered throughout the genome, STR sites contain tandem repeats of four-nucleotide sequences. The number of repetitions at each site can vary from individual to individual. In this figure, both DNA samples have the same number of repeats (7) at the first STR site, but different numbers (8 versus 13) at the second.

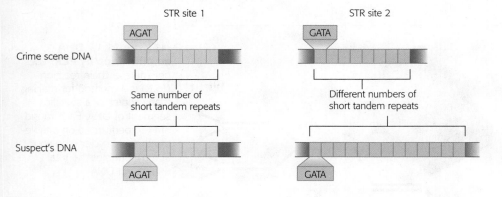

▼ **Figure 12.17 Gel electrophoresis of DNA molecules.**

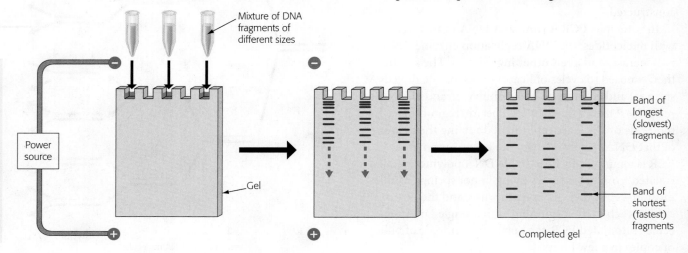

☑ **CHECKPOINT**

What are STRs, and why are they useful for DNA profiling?

Answer: STRs (short tandem repeats) are nucleotide sequences repeated many times in a row within the human genome. STRs are valuable for DNA profiling because different people have different numbers of repeats at the various STR sites.

different sources. A DNA sample from each source is placed in a separate well (hole) at one end of a flat, rectangular gel, a thin slab of jellylike material that acts as a molecular sieve. A negatively charged electrode is then attached to the DNA-containing end of the gel and a positive electrode to the other end. Because the phosphate (PO_4^-) groups of nucleotides give DNA fragments a negative charge, the fragments move through the gel toward the positive pole. However, longer DNA fragments move more slowly through the thicket of polymer fibers in the gel than do shorter DNA fragments. Over time, shorter molecules move farther through the gel than longer molecules. Gel electrophoresis thus separates DNA fragments by length. When the current is turned off, a series of bands is left in each "lane" of the gel. Each band is a collection of DNA fragments of the same length. The bands can be made visible by staining, by exposure onto photographic film (if the DNA is radioactively labeled), or by measuring fluorescence (if the DNA is labeled with a fluorescent dye).

Figure 12.18 shows the gel that would result from using gel electrophoresis to separate the DNA fragments from the example in Figure 12.16. The differences in the locations of the bands reflect the different lengths of the DNA fragments. This gel would provide evidence that the crime scene DNA did not come from the suspect. Because gel electrophoresis reveals similarities and differences between DNA samples, DNA profiling can provide evidence of either guilt or innocence. ☑

RFLP Analysis

Gel electrophoresis has many uses besides STR analysis. One application is RFLP analysis. RFLP (pronounced "rif-lip") stands for restriction fragment length polymorphism. In this method, the DNA molecules to be compared are exposed to a restriction enzyme **(Figure 12.19)**. The resulting restriction fragments are separated and made visible on a gel. In this case, both the number and location of bands indicate whether the original DNA samples had identical nucleotide sequences at the sites shown.

☑ **CHECKPOINT**

You use a restriction enzyme to cut a DNA molecule that has three copies of the enzyme's recognition sequence clustered near one end. When you separate the restriction fragments by gel electrophoresis, how do you expect the bands to appear?

Answer: three bands near the positive pole at the bottom of the gel (small fragments) and one band near the negative pole at the top of the gel (large fragment)

▼ **Figure 12.19 RFLP analysis.** The DNA segments shown have nucleotide sequences that differ at one base pair (orange boxes). A particular restriction enzyme may therefore cut the segments at different places. In this case, the difference in DNA sequence results in three restriction fragments from the first DNA sample and two from the second. This difference, revealed by gel electrophoresis, indicates that the two DNA samples come from different individuals.

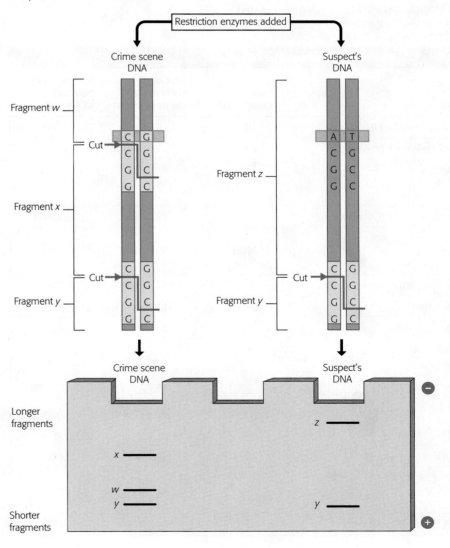

▼ **Figure 12.18 Visualizing STR fragment patterns.** This figure shows the bands that would result from gel electrophoresis of the STR sites illustrated in Figure 12.16. Notice that one of the bands from the crime scene DNA does not match one of the bands from the suspect's DNA. (A gel from an actual DNA profile would typically contain more than just two bands in each lane.)

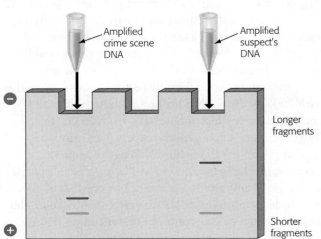

Genomics and Proteomics

In 1995, a team of scientists announced that it had determined the nucleotide sequence of the entire genome of *Haemophilus influenzae*, a bacterium that can cause several human diseases, including pneumonia and meningitis. **Genomics**, the study of complete sets of genes (genomes), was born.

The first targets of genomics research were bacteria, which have relatively little DNA. The *H. influenzae* genome, for example, contains 1.8 million nucleotides and 1,709 genes. But soon the attention of genomics researchers turned toward more complex organisms with much larger genomes **(Table 12.1)**. As of 2011, the genomes of more than 1,700 species have been published, and more than 8,000 are in progress. The majority of organisms sequenced to date are prokaryotes, including *E. coli* and more than 1,000 other bacteria (some of medical importance) and more than 100 archaea. Over 100 eukaryotic genomes have also been completed.

Baker's yeast (*Saccharomyces cerevisiae*) was the first eukaryote to have its full sequence determined, and the roundworm *Caenorhabditis elegans* was the first multicellular organism. Other sequenced animals include the fruit fly (*Drosophila melanogaster*) and lab rat (*Ratus norvegicus*), both model organisms for genetics research. Among the sequenced plants are *Arabidopsis thaliana*, a type of mustard plant used as a model organism, and rice (*Oryza sativa*) and potato (*Solanum tuberosum*), two of the world's most economically important crops. Next we'll discuss a particularly notable example of a sequenced animal genome—our own.

The Human Genome Project

The **Human Genome Project** was a massive scientific endeavor to determine the nucleotide sequence of all the DNA in the human genome and to identify the location and sequence of every gene. The project began in 1990 as an effort by government-funded researchers from six countries. Several years into the project, private companies, chiefly Celera Genomics, joined the effort. At the completion of the project, more than 99% of the genome had been determined to 99.999% accuracy. (There remain a few hundred gaps of unknown sequence that will require special methods to figure out.) This ambitious project has provided a wealth of data that may illuminate the genetic basis of what it means to be human.

The chromosomes in the human genome (22 autosomes plus the X and Y sex chromosomes) contain approximately 3 billion nucleotide pairs of DNA. To try to get a sense of this quantity of DNA, imagine that its nucleotide sequence is printed in letters (A, T, C, and G) in books the size of this textbook. The sequence would fill a stack of books 18 stories high! However, the biggest surprise from the Human Genome Project is the relatively small number of human genes—currently estimated to be about 21,000—very close to the number found in a roundworm! This number of genes is well below estimates made before the results of the project were known. In fact, a friendly betting pool set up in the year 2000 by the world's leading genome researchers included a wide range of guesses—from 26,000 to 150,000. Every single genome expert overestimated!

Our genome was a major challenge to sequence because, like the genomes of most complex eukaryotes, only a small amount of our total DNA consists of genes that code for proteins, tRNAs, or rRNAs. Most complex eukaryotes have a huge amount of noncoding DNA—about 98% of human DNA is of this type. Some of this

Table 12.1	Some Important Sequenced Genomes		
Organism	**Year Completed**	**Size of Genome (in base pairs)**	**Approximate Number of Genes**
Haemophilus influenzae (bacterium)	1995	1.8 million	1,700
Saccharomyces cerevisiae (yeast)	1996	12 million	5,800
Escherichia coli (bacterium)	1997	4.6 million	4,400
Caenorhabditis elegans (roundworm)	1998	97 million	19,100
Drosophila melanogaster (fruit fly)	2000	180 million	13,700
Arabidopsis thaliana (mustard plant)	2000	120 million	25,500
Oryza sativa (rice)	2002	430 million	40,000
Homo sapiens (human)	2003	3.0 billion	21,000
Rattus norvegicus (lab rat)	2004	2.8 billion	20,000
Pan troglodytes (chimpanzee)	2005	3.1 billion	20,000
Macaca mulatta (macaque)	2007	2.9 billion	22,000
Ornithorhynchus anatinus (duck-billed platypus)	2008	1.8 billion	18,500
Solanum tuberosum (potato)	2011	844 million	39,000

noncoding DNA is made up of gene control sequences such as promoters, enhancers, and microRNAs (see Chapter 11). Other noncoding regions include introns and repetitive DNA (some of which is used in DNA profiling). Some noncoding DNA is important to our health, with certain regions known to carry disease-causing mutations. But the function (if there is any) of most noncoding DNA remains unknown. Biologists used to refer to noncoding DNA as "junk DNA," but it is now generally accepted that much of this DNA plays some (still mysterious) role.

The potential benefits of having a complete map of the human genome are enormous. Already, hundreds of disease-associated genes have been identified. One example is the gene that is mutated in an inherited type of Parkinson's disease, a debilitating brain disorder that causes tremors of increasing severity (Figure 12.20). Data from the Human Genome Project mapped some cases of Parkinson's disease to a specific gene. Interestingly, an altered version of the protein encoded by this gene has also been tied to Alzheimer's disease, suggesting a link between these two brain disorders. Moreover, the same gene is also found in rats, where it plays a role in the sense of smell, and in zebra finches, where it is thought to be involved in song learning. Cross-species comparisons such as these may uncover clues about the role played by the normal version of the protein in the human brain. And such knowledge could eventually lead to treatment for Parkinson's disease. ☑

Tracking the Anthrax Killer

In October 2001, a 63-year-old Florida man died from inhalation anthrax, a disease caused by breathing spores of the bacterium *Bacillus anthracis*. As the first victim of this disease in the United States since 1976 (and coming so soon after the 9/11 terrorist attacks the month before), his death was immediately suspicious. By the end of the year, four more people had died from anthrax. Law enforcement officials realized that someone was sending anthrax spores through the mail (Figure 12.21). The United States was facing an unprecedented bioterrorist attack.

In the investigation that followed, one of the most helpful clues turned out to be the anthrax spores themselves. Investigators compared the genomes of the mailed anthrax spores with several laboratory strains. They quickly established that all of the mailed spores were genetically identical, suggesting that a single perpetrator was behind all the attacks. Furthermore, they were able to match the deadly spores with a laboratory subtype isolated at the U.S. Army Medical Research Institute of Infectious Diseases in Fort Detrick, Maryland. A second, more comprehensive analysis of the spores used in the attack was completed in 2008. This analysis found four unique mutations in the mailed anthrax and traced the mutations to a single flask at the army facility. Based in part on this evidence, the FBI named an army research scientist as a suspect in the case. Although never charged, that suspect committed suicide in 2008; the case remains officially unsolved.

How did the FBI track down the anthrax killer?

☑ CHECKPOINT

1. Approximately how many nucleotides and genes are contained in the human genome?
2. Name three types of DNA that do not code for another molecule.

Answers: 1. about 3 billion nucleotides and 21,000 genes 2. introns, repetitive DNA, and gene control sequences

▼ Figure 12.20 **The fight against Parkinson's disease.** Boxer Muhammad Ali and actor Michael J. Fox—both of whom have Parkinson's disease—testify before the Senate on the status of federal funding for Parkinson's research.

▼ Figure 12.21 **The 2001 anthrax attacks.** In 2001, envelopes containing anthrax spores caused five deaths.

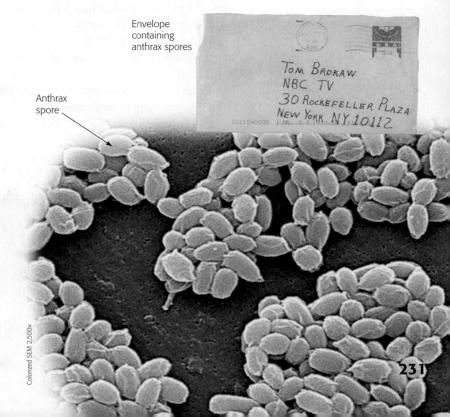

Envelope containing anthrax spores

Anthrax spore

Tom Brokaw
NBC TV
30 Rockefeller Plaza
New York, NY 10112

Colorized SEM 2,500x

The anthrax investigation is just one example of the new field of bioinformatics, the application of computational tools to molecular biology. In 1991, sequence data provided strong evidence that a Florida dentist transmitted HIV to several patients. In 1993, after a cult released anthrax spores in downtown Tokyo, genomic analysis showed why their attack didn't kill anyone: They had used a harmless veterinary vaccine strain. And investigation of the West Nile virus outbreak in 1999 proved that a single natural strain of virus was infecting both birds and people. Bioinformatics has even allowed geneticists to produce a family tree of dog breeds (see the Evolution Connection section in Chapter 9).

Bioinformatics can also reveal similarities and differences in organisms more closely related to humans. In 2005, researchers completed the genome sequence for our closest living relative on the evolutionary tree of life, the chimpanzee (*Pan troglodytes*). Comparisons with human DNA revealed that we share 96% of our genome with our closest animal relative. Genomic scientists are currently finding and studying the important differences, shedding scientific light on the age-old question of what makes us human.

How similar is your DNA to the DNA of a chimp?

Genome-Mapping Techniques

Today, entire genomes are most often sequenced using the **whole-genome shotgun method**. The first step in this method is to chop the entire genome into fragments using restriction enzymes. Next, all the fragments are cloned and sequenced. Finally, computers running specialized mapping software reassemble the millions of overlapping short sequences into a single continuous sequence for every chromosome—an entire genome **(Figure 12.22)**.

The DNA sequences determined by the Human Genome Project have been deposited in a database that is available on the World Wide Web. (You can browse it yourself at the website for the National Center for Biotechnology Information.) Scientists use software to scan and analyze the sequences for genes, control elements, and other features. The result is a genetic map containing all the genes and their locations on chromosomes. Next comes the most exciting challenge: figuring out the functions of the genes and other sequences and how they work together to direct the structure and function of a living organism. This challenge and the applications of the new knowledge should keep scientists busy well into the twenty-first century.

The human genome sequenced by government-funded scientists was actually a reference genome compiled from a group of individuals. The genome sequenced by Celera consisted primarily of DNA from scientist

▼ **Figure 12.22 Genome sequencing.** In the photo at the bottom, a technician performs a step in the whole-genome shotgun method (depicted in the diagram).

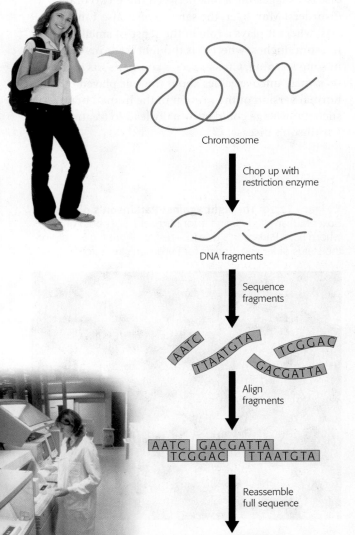

Chromosome

Chop up with restriction enzyme

DNA fragments

Sequence fragments

AATC
TTAATGTA
TCGGAC
GACGATTA

Align fragments

AATC GACGATTA
TCGGAC TTAATGTA

Reassemble full sequence

AATCGGACGATTAATGTA

Craig Venter, the company's president. As of 2011, the complete genomes of a handful of other individuals—including James Watson, codiscoverer of the structure of DNA—have also been sequenced. Scientists have even begun to gather sequence data from our extinct relatives, such as a nearly complete genome, published in 2010, from a Neanderthal. The more human genomes we have, the more insight we can gain into what makes each person unique. We may soon enter an age of "personal genomics," where individual genetic differences among people will be put to routine medical use. Some of these seemingly minuscule differences can actually be a matter of life and death, as we'll see next.

DNA Profiling THE PROCESS OF SCIENCE

Can Genomics Cure Cancer?

Lung cancer, which kills more Americans every year than any other type of cancer, has long been the target of searches for effective chemotherapy drugs. One drug used to treat lung cancer, called gefitinib, targets the protein encoded by the *EGFR* gene. This protein is found on the surface of cells that line the lungs and is also found in lung cancer tumors.

Unfortunately, treatment with gefitinib is ineffective for many patients. While studying the effectiveness of gefitinib, researchers at the Dana-Farber Cancer Institute in Boston made the **observation** that a few patients actually responded quite positively to the drug. This posed a **question:** Are genetic differences among lung cancer patients responsible for the differences in gefitinib's effectiveness? The researchers' **hypothesis** was that mutations in the *EGFR* gene were causing the different responses to gefitinib. The team made the **prediction** that DNA profiles focusing on the *EGFR* gene would reveal different DNA sequences in the tumors of responsive patients compared with the tumors of unresponsive patients. The researchers' **experiment** involved sequencing the *EGFR* gene in cells extracted from the tumors of five patients who responded to the drug and four who did not.

The **results** were quite striking: All five tumors from gefitinib-responsive patients had mutations in *EGFR*, whereas none of the other four tumors did (**Figure 12.23**). These results suggest that doctors can use DNA profiling techniques to screen lung cancer patients for those who are most likely to benefit from treatment with this drug. In broader terms, this work suggests that genomics may bring about a revolution in the treatment of disease by allowing therapies to be custom-tailored to the genetic makeup of each patient.

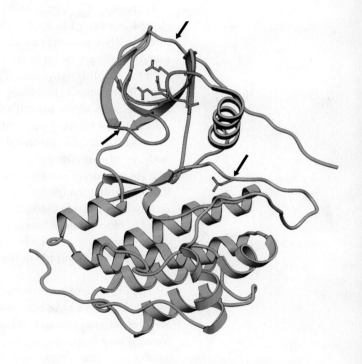

▲ Figure 12.23 **The *EGFR* protein: Fighting cancer with genomics.** Mutations (located at sites indicated by black arrows) in the *EGFR* protein can affect the ability of a cancer-fighting drug to destroy lung tumors. Here, the amino acid backbone of the protein is shown in green, with some important regions highlighted in orange, blue, and red.

Proteomics

The successes in the field of genomics have encouraged scientists to begin similar systematic studies of the full protein sets (proteomes) that genomes encode, an approach called **proteomics**. The number of different proteins in humans far exceeds the number of different genes (about 100,000 proteins versus about 21,000 genes). And since proteins, not genes, actually carry out the activities of the cell, scientists must study when and where proteins are produced and how they interact to understand the functioning of cells and organisms.

Genomics and proteomics are enabling biologists to approach the study of life from an increasingly holistic (whole-system) perspective. Biologists are now compiling catalogs of genes and proteins—that is, listings of all the "parts" that contribute to the operation of cells, tissues, and organisms. As such catalogs become complete, researchers are shifting their attention from the individual parts to how these parts function as a whole in biological systems. Such analyses may have many practical applications. For example, proteins associated with specific diseases may be used to aid diagnosis (by developing tests that search for a particular combination of proteins) and treatment (by designing drugs that interact with the proteins involved). ☑

☑ CHECKPOINT

What is the difference between genomics and proteomics?

Answer: Genomics concerns the complete set of an organism's genes, whereas proteomics concerns the complete set of an organism's proteins.

233

Human Gene Therapy

Human gene therapy is a recombinant DNA procedure intended to treat disease by altering an afflicted person's genes. In some cases, a mutant version of a gene may be replaced or supplemented with the normal allele. This could potentially correct a genetic disorder, perhaps permanently. In other cases, genes are inserted and expressed only long enough to treat a medical problem.

Figure 12.24 summarizes one approach to human gene therapy. ❶ A gene from a normal individual is cloned, converted to an RNA version, and then inserted into the RNA genome of a harmless virus. ❷ Bone marrow cells are taken from the patient and infected with the recombinant virus. ❸ The virus inserts a DNA copy of its genome, including the normal human gene, into the DNA of the patient's cells. ❹ The engineered cells are then injected back into the patient. The normal gene is transcribed and translated within the patient's body, producing the desired protein. Ideally, the non-mutant version of the gene would be inserted into cells that multiply throughout a person's life. Bone marrow cells, which include the stem cells that give rise to all the types of blood cells, are prime candidates. If the procedure succeeds, the cells will multiply permanently and produce a steady supply of the missing protein, curing the patient.

The promise of gene therapy thus far exceeds actual results, but there have been some successes. In 2009, an international research team conducted a trial that focused on a form of progressive blindness linked to a defect in a gene responsible for producing light-detecting pigments in the eye. The researchers found that a single injection of a virus carrying the normal gene into one eye of affected children improved vision in that eye, sometimes enough to allow normal functioning. The other eye was left untreated as a control.

From 2000 to 2011, gene therapy also cured 22 children with severe combined immunodeficiency (SCID), a fatal inherited disease caused by a defective gene that prevents development of the immune system, requiring patients to remain isolated within protective "bubbles." Unless treated with a bone marrow transplant, which is effective only 60% of the time, SCID patients quickly die from infections by microbes that most of us easily fend off. In these cases, researchers periodically removed immune system cells from the patients' blood, infected them with a virus engineered to carry the normal allele of the defective gene, then reinjected the blood into the patient. The treatment cured the patients of SCID, but there have been some serious side effects: Four of the treated patients developed leukemia, and one died after the inserted gene activated an oncogene (see Chapter 11), creating cancerous blood cells. Gene therapy remains promising, but there is very little evidence to date of safe and effective application. Active research continues, with new, tougher safety guidelines in place that are meant to prevent the problems of the past. ☑

▼ Figure 12.24 **One approach to human gene therapy.**

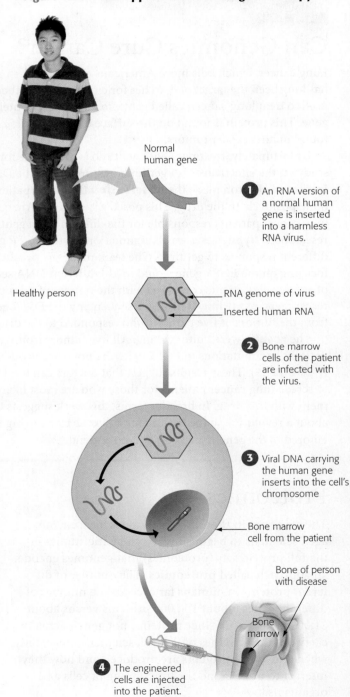

Normal human gene

Healthy person

❶ An RNA version of a normal human gene is inserted into a harmless RNA virus.

RNA genome of virus

Inserted human RNA

❷ Bone marrow cells of the patient are infected with the virus.

❸ Viral DNA carrying the human gene inserts into the cell's chromosome

Bone marrow cell from the patient

Bone of person with disease

Bone marrow

❹ The engineered cells are injected into the patient.

☑ CHECKPOINT

Why are bone marrow stem cells ideally suited as targets for gene therapy?

Answer: because bone marrow stem cells multiply throughout a person's life

Safety and Ethical Issues

As soon as scientists realized the power of DNA technology, they began to worry about potential dangers. Early concerns focused on the possibility of creating hazardous new disease-causing organisms. What might happen, for instance, if cancer-causing genes were transferred into infectious bacteria or viruses? To address such concerns, scientists developed a set of guidelines that have become formal government regulations in the United States and some other countries.

One safety measure is a set of strict laboratory procedures to protect researchers from infection by engineered microbes and to prevent microbes from accidentally leaving the laboratory (Figure 12.25). In addition, strains of microbes to be used in recombinant DNA experiments are genetically crippled to ensure that they cannot survive outside the laboratory. Finally, certain obviously dangerous experiments have been banned. Today, most public concern about possible hazards centers not on recombinant microbes but on genetically modified (GM) foods.

What steps are being taken by scientists to prevent the release of a "super germ"?

The Controversy over Genetically Modified Foods

GM strains account for a significant percentage of several staple crops. Controversy about the safety of these foods is an important political issue (Figure 12.26). For example, the European Union has suspended the introduction of new GM crops and considered banning the import of all GM foodstuffs. In the United States and other countries where the GM revolution has proceeded more quietly than in Europe, the labeling of GM foods is now being debated but has not yet become law.

Advocates of a cautious approach fear that crops carrying genes from other species might harm the environment or be hazardous to human health (by, for example, introducing new allergens, molecules that can cause allergic reactions, into foods). A major concern is that transgenic plants might pass their new genes to close relatives in nearby wild areas. We know that lawn and

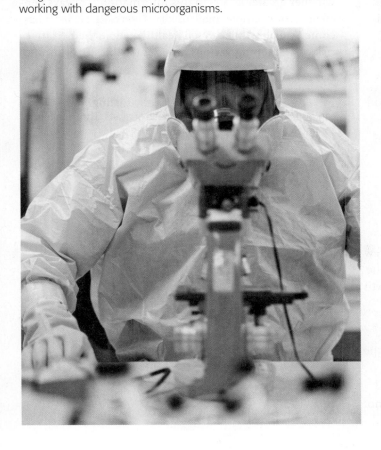

▼ **Figure 12.25 Maximum-security laboratory.** A scientist in a high-containment laboratory wears a biohazard suit, used for working with dangerous microorganisms.

▶ **Figure 12.26 Opposition to genetically modified organisms (GMOs).** This photo shows tractors destroying a Belgian field of genetically modified crop. The Belgian Minister for Consumer Protection ordered the destruction as part of a widespread opposition to GM crops. The sign translates to "GMO, no thanks! Yes to biodiversity."

crop grasses, for example, commonly exchange genes with wild relatives via pollen transfer. If domestic plants carrying genes for resistance to herbicides, diseases, or insect pests pollinated wild plants, the offspring might become "superweeds" that would be very difficult to control. However, researchers may be able to prevent the escape of such plant genes in various ways—for example, by engineering plants so that they cannot breed. Concern has also been raised that the widespread use of GM seeds may reduce natural genetic diversity, leaving crops susceptible to catastrophic die-offs in the event of a sudden change to the environment or introduction of a new pest.

The U.S. National Academy of Sciences released a study finding no scientific evidence that transgenic crops pose any special health or environmental risks. But the authors of the study also recommended more stringent long-term monitoring to watch for unanticipated environmental impacts.

Should widespread DNA profiling be used to try to end violent crime?

Negotiators from 130 countries (including the United States) agreed on a Biosafety Protocol that requires exporters to identify GM organisms present in bulk food shipments and allows importing countries to decide whether the shipments pose environmental or health risks. This agreement has been hailed as a breakthrough by environmentalists.

Today, governments and regulatory agencies throughout the world are grappling with how to facilitate the use of biotechnology in agriculture, industry, and medicine while ensuring that new products and procedures are safe. In the United States, all genetic engineering projects are evaluated for potential risks by a number of regulatory agencies, including the Food and Drug Administration, the Environmental Protection Agency, the National Institutes of Health, and the Department of Agriculture. ☑

✓ CHECKPOINT

What is the main concern about adding genes for herbicide resistance to crop plants?

Answer: the possibility that the genes could escape, via cross-pollination, to wild plants that are closely related to the crop species

Ethical Questions Raised by DNA Technology

DNA technology raises legal and ethical questions—few of which have clear answers. Consider, for example, the treatment of dwarfism with injections of human growth hormone (HGH) produced by genetically engineered cells. Should parents of short but hormonally normal children be able to seek HGH treatment to make their kids taller? If not, who decides which children are "tall enough" to be excluded from treatment?

Genetic engineering of gametes (sperm or ova) and zygotes has been accomplished in lab animals. It has not been attempted in humans because such a procedure

would raise very difficult ethical questions. Should we try to eliminate genetic defects in our children and their descendants? Should we interfere with evolution in this way? From a long-term perspective, the elimination of unwanted versions of genes from the gene pool could backfire. Genetic variety is a necessary ingredient for the adaptation of a species as environmental conditions change with time. Genes that are damaging under some conditions may be advantageous under others (one example is the sickle-cell allele—see the Evolution Connection section at the end of Chapter 13). Are we willing to risk making genetic changes that could be detrimental to our species in the future? We may have to face such questions soon.

Similarly, advances in genetic profiling raise privacy issues. If we were to create a DNA profile of every person at birth, then theoretically we could match nearly every violent crime to a perpetrator because it is virtually impossible for someone to commit a violent crime without leaving behind DNA evidence. Furthermore, having a complete profile database could help with the identification of crime victims or remains. But are we, as a society, prepared to sacrifice our genetic privacy, even for such worthwhile goals?

As more information becomes available about our personal genetic makeup, many people question whether greater access to this information is always beneficial. For example, mail-in kits **(Figure 12.27)** have become available that can tell healthy people their relative risk of developing various diseases (such as Parkinson's

▼ **Figure 12.27 Personalized genetic testing.** This kit can be used to send saliva for genetic analysis. The results can indicate a person's risk of developing certain diseases.

and Crohn's) later in life. Some argue that such information helps families to prepare. Others say that the tests prey on our fears without offering any real benefit because certain diseases, such as Parkinson's, are not currently preventable or treatable. Other tests, however, such as for breast cancer risk, may help a person make changes that can prevent disease. How can we identify truly useful tests?

There is also a danger that information about disease-associated genes could be abused. One issue is the possibility of discrimination and stigmatization. In response, Congress passed the Genetic Information Nondiscrimination Act of 2008. Title I of the act prohibits insurance companies from requesting or requiring genetic information during an application for health insurance. Title II provides similar protections in employment. But even with such safeguards in place,

can we fully prevent genetic information from being used in a discriminatory manner?

A much broader ethical question is how do we really feel about wielding one of nature's powers—the evolution of new organisms? Some might ask if we have any right to alter an organism's genes—or to create new organisms.

The benefits to people and the environment must also be considered. For example, bacteria are being engineered to clean up mining wastes and other pollutants that threaten the soil, water, and air. Since these organisms may be the only feasible solutions to some of our most pressing environmental problems, many people think this type of genetic engineering should be encouraged.

DNA technologies raise many complex issues that have no easy answers. It is up to you, as a "citizen scientist," to make informed choices. ✓

☑ **CHECKPOINT**

Why does genetically modifying a human gamete raise different ethical questions than genetically modifying a human somatic (body) cell?

Answer: A genetically modified somatic cell will affect only the patient. Modifying a gamete will affect an unborn individual as well as all of his or her descendants.

DNA Profiling EVOLUTION CONNECTION

The Y Chromosome as a Window on History

Barring mutations, the human Y chromosome passes essentially intact from father to son. By comparing Y DNA, researchers can learn about the ancestry of human males. DNA profiling can thus provide data about recent human evolution.

In 2003, geneticists discovered that about 8% of males currently living in central Asia have Y chromosomes of striking genetic similarity. Further analysis traced their common genetic heritage to a single man living about 1,000 years ago. In combination with historical records, the data led to the speculation that the Mongolian ruler Genghis Khan **(Figure 12.28)** may have been responsible for the spread of the chromosome to nearly 16 million men living today. A similar study of Irish men in 2006 suggested that nearly 10% of them were descendants of Niall of the Nine Hostages, a warlord who lived during the 1400s. Another study of Y DNA seemed to confirm the claim by the Lemba people of southern Africa that they are descended from ancient Jews. Sequences of Y DNA distinctive of the Jewish priestly caste called Kohanim are found at high frequencies among the Lemba.

Comparison of Y chromosome DNA profiles is part of a larger effort to learn more about the human genome. Other research efforts are extending genomic studies to many more species. These studies will advance our understanding of all aspects of biology, including health and ecology, as well as evolution. In fact, comparisons of the completed genome sequences of bacteria, archaea, and eukaryotes first supported the theory that these are the three fundamental domains of life—a topic we discuss further in the next unit, "Evolution and Diversity."

▲ **Figure 12.28** **Genghis Khan.**

Chapter Review

SUMMARY OF KEY CONCEPTS

 Go to **www.masteringbiology.com** for homework assignments, practice quizzes, Pearson eText, and more.

Recombinant DNA Technology

DNA technology, the manipulation of genetic material, is a relatively new branch of biotechnology, the use of organisms to make helpful products. DNA technology often involves the use of recombinant DNA, the combination of nucleotide sequences from two different sources.

Applications: From Humulin to Foods to "Pharm" Animals

Recombinant DNA techniques have been used to create genetically modified organisms, organisms that carry artificially introduced genes. Nonhuman cells have been engineered to produce human proteins, genetically modified food crops, and transgenic farm animals. A transgenic organism is one that carries artificially introduced genes, typically from a different species.

Recombinant DNA Techniques

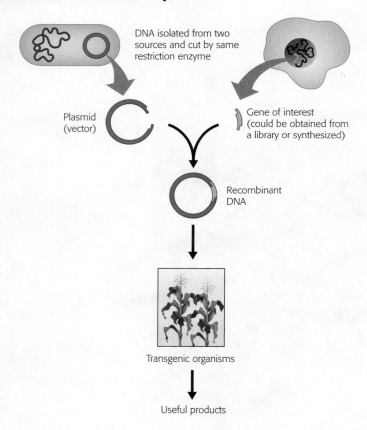

DNA isolated from two sources and cut by same restriction enzyme

Plasmid (vector)

Gene of interest (could be obtained from a library or synthesized)

Recombinant DNA

Transgenic organisms

Useful products

DNA Profiling and Forensic Science

Forensics, the scientific analysis of legal evidence, has been revolutionized by DNA technology. DNA profiling is used to determine whether two DNA samples come from the same individual.

Investigating Murder, Paternity, and Ancient DNA

DNA profiling can be used to establish innocence or guilt of a criminal suspect, identify victims, determine paternity, and contribute to basic research.

DNA Profiling Techniques

Short tandem repeat (STR) analysis compares DNA fragments using the polymerase chain reaction (PCR) and gel electrophoresis.

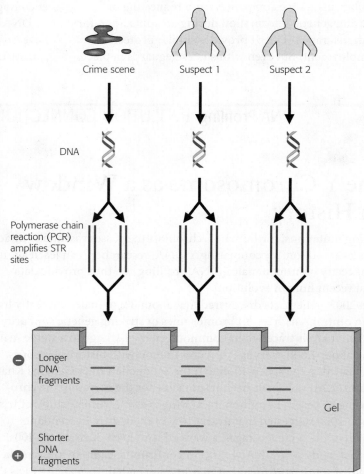

Crime scene   Suspect 1   Suspect 2

DNA

Polymerase chain reaction (PCR) amplifies STR sites

Longer DNA fragments

Shorter DNA fragments

Gel

DNA fragments compared by gel electrophoresis
(Bands of shorter fragments move faster toward the positive pole.)

Genomics and Proteomics

The Human Genome Project

The nucleotide sequence of the human genome is providing a wealth of useful data. The 24 different chromosomes of the human genome contain about 3 billion nucleotide pairs and 21,000 genes. The majority of the genome consists of noncoding DNA.

Tracking the Anthrax Killer

Comparing genomes can aid criminal investigations and basic research.

Genome-Mapping Techniques

The whole-genome shotgun method involves sequencing DNA fragments from an entire genome and then assembling the sequences.

Proteomics

Success in genomics has given rise to proteomics, the systematic study of the full set of proteins found in organisms.

Human Gene Therapy

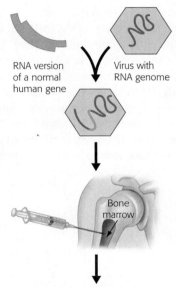

RNA version of a normal human gene

Virus with RNA genome

Bone marrow

A normal human gene is transcribed and translated in a patient, potentially curing the genetic disease permanently

Gene therapy trials have focused on a number of inherited diseases, with both success and failures achieved to date.

Safety and Ethical Issues

The Controversy over Genetically Modified Foods

The debate about genetically modified crops centers on whether they might harm humans or damage the environment by transferring genes through cross-pollination with other species.

Ethical Questions Raised by DNA Technology

We as a society and as individuals must become educated about DNA technologies to address the ethical questions raised by their use.

SELF-QUIZ

1. Suppose you wish to create a large batch of the protein lactase using recombinant DNA. Place the following steps in the order you would have to perform them.
   a. Find the clone with the gene for lactase.
   b. Insert the plasmids into bacteria and grow the bacteria into clones.
   c. Isolate the gene for lactase.
   d. Create recombinant plasmids, including one that carries the gene for lactase.

2. Why is an artificial gene that is made using reverse transcriptase often shorter than the natural form of the gene?

3. A carrier that moves DNA from one cell to another, such as a plasmid, is called a _____.

4. In making recombinant DNA, what is the benefit of using a restriction enzyme that cuts DNA in a staggered fashion?

5. A paleontologist has recovered a bit of organic material from the 400-year-old preserved skin of an extinct dodo. She would like to compare DNA from the sample with DNA from living birds. The most useful method for initially increasing the amount of dodo DNA available for testing is _____.

6. Why do DNA fragments containing STR sites from different people tend to migrate to different locations during gel electrophoresis?

7. What feature of a DNA fragment causes it to move through a gel during electrophoresis?
   a. the electrical charges of its phosphate groups
   b. its nucleotide sequence
   c. the hydrogen bonds between its base pairs
   d. its double helix shape

8. After a gel electrophoresis procedure is run, the pattern of bars in the gel shows
   a. the order of bases in a particular gene.
   b. the presence of various-sized fragments of DNA.
   c. the order of genes along particular chromosomes.
   d. the exact location of a specific gene in a genomic library.

9. Name the steps of the whole-genome shotgun method.

10. Put the following steps of human gene therapy in the correct order.
    a. Virus is injected into patient.
    b. Human gene is inserted into a virus.
    c. Normal human gene is isolated and cloned.
    d. Normal human gene is transcribed and translated in the patient.

Answers to these questions can be found in Appendix: Self-Quiz Answers.

THE PROCESS OF SCIENCE

11. A biochemist hopes to find a gene in human liver cells that codes for a blood-clotting protein. The nucleotide sequence of a small part of the gene is CTGGACTGACA. Briefly explain how to obtain the desired gene.

12. Some scientists once joked that when the DNA sequence of the human genome was complete, "we can all go home" because there would be nothing left for genetic researchers to discover. Why haven't they all "gone home"?

BIOLOGY AND SOCIETY

13. In the not-too-distant future, gene therapy may be used to treat many inherited disorders. What do you think are the most serious ethical issues to face before human gene therapy is used on a large scale? Explain.

14. Today, it is fairly easy to make transgenic plants and animals. What are some safety and ethical issues raised by this use of recombinant DNA technology? What are some dangers of introducing genetically engineered organisms into the environment? What are some reasons for and against leaving such decisions to scientists? Who should make these decisions?

15. In October 2002, the government of the African nation of Zambia announced that it was refusing to distribute 15,000 tons of corn donated by the United States, enough corn to feed 2.5 million Zambians for three weeks. The government rejected the corn because it was likely to contain genetically modified kernels. The government made the decision after its scientific advisers concluded that the studies of the health risks posed by GM crops "are inconclusive." Do you agree with this assessment? Do you think that it is a good justification for refusing the donated corn? At the time of the government's decision, Zambia was facing food shortages, and 35,000 Zambians were expected to die from starvation over the next six months. In light of this, do you think it was morally acceptable for the government to refuse the food? How do the relative risks posed by GM crops compare with the relative risks posed by starvation?

16. In 1983, a 10-year-old girl was kidnapped from her home, raped, and murdered. A jury convicted a local teenager of the crimes and sentenced him to death for the brutal killing. In 1995, DNA analysis proved that semen found near the scene could not have come from the man accused. After 12 years on death row, he was exonerated and released from prison. His case, which took place in Illinois, was far from unique. From 1977 to 2000, 12 convicts were executed and 13 exonerated. In 2000, the governor of Illinois declared a moratorium on all executions in his state because the death penalty system was "fraught with errors." Do you support the Illinois governor's decision? What rights should death penalty inmates have with regard to DNA testing of old evidence? Who should pay for this additional testing?

Unit 3
Evolution and Diversity

Chapter 13: **How Populations Evolve**

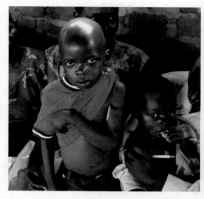

Chapter Thread: **Evolution in Action**

Chapter 14: **How Biological Diversity Evolves**

Chapter Thread: **Mass Extinctions**

Chapter 15: **The Evolution of Microbial Life**

Chapter Thread: **How Life Began**

Chapter 16: **Plants, Fungi, and the Move onto Land**

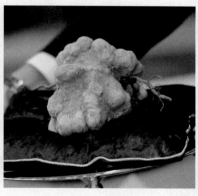

Chapter Thread: **Plant-Fungus Symbiosis**

Chapter 17: **The Evolution of Animals**

Chapter Thread: **Human Evolution**

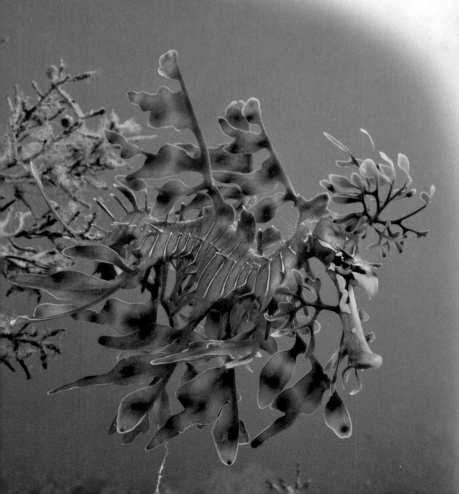

13 How Populations Evolve

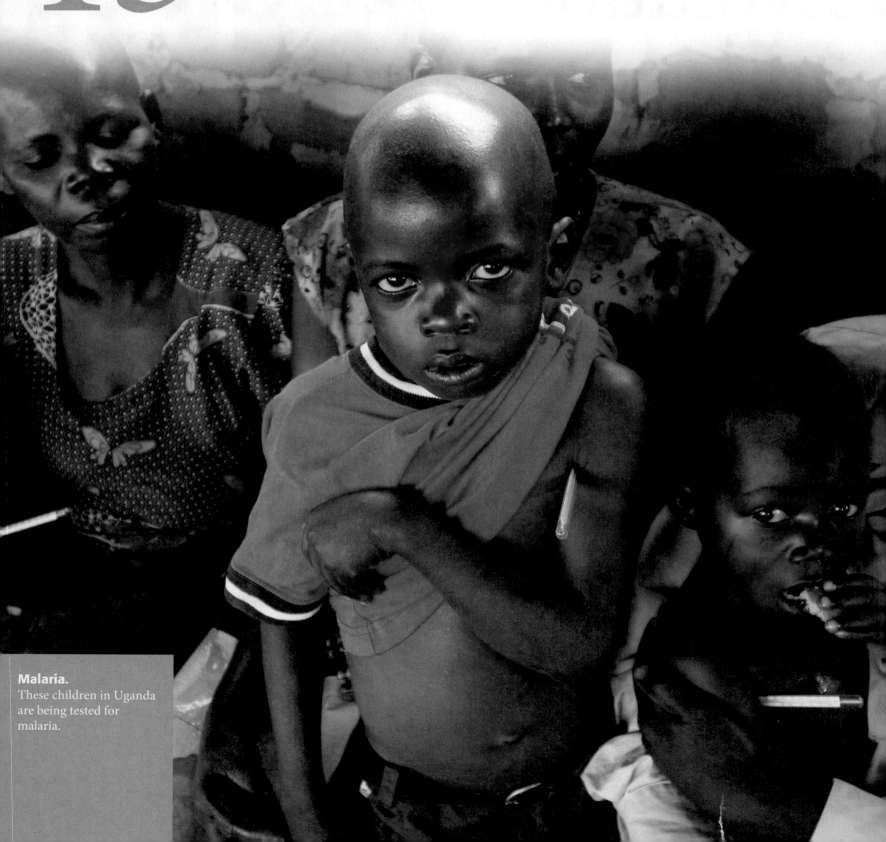

Malaria.
These children in Uganda are being tested for malaria.

Evolution in Action BIOLOGY AND SOCIETY

Mosquitoes, Microbes, and Malaria

What does actor George Clooney have in common with George Washington, Ernest Hemingway, Christopher Columbus, and Mother Teresa? They all survived bouts with malaria, a disease caused by a protozoan parasite that is one of the worst killers in human history. In the 1960s, the World Health Organization (WHO) launched a campaign to eradicate malaria. It was defeated by the microbe's secret weapon: evolution. Today, malaria causes more than a million deaths and 250 million cases of miserable illness each year.

The campaign against malaria focused on killing the mosquitoes that carry the protozoan from person to person. DDT, a widely used pesticide, was deployed in massive spraying operations. But in one location after another, early success was followed by rebounding mosquito populations. Although the lethal chemical killed most of the mosquitoes immediately, survivors gave rise to new populations. Many of the survivors, it turned out, carried an allele (alternate form of a gene) that coded for an enzyme that destroys DDT. The enzyme gave those mosquitoes a huge advantage wherever DDT was applied, and they passed the allele on to their offspring. In each generation, the proportion of DDT-resistant insects in the population increased, making subsequent sprayings less effective. This is an example of evolution in action, a change in allele frequency in response to environmental changes.

Evolution has also hindered our efforts to alleviate the suffering of malaria victims. At the same time that DDT was being celebrated as a miracle pesticide, a drug called chloroquine was hailed as the miracle cure for malaria. Through a similar process of adaptation to environmental change—in this case, the chloroquine encountered in the human body—the malaria parasite evolved resistance to the drug. At present, the most effective drug is artemisinin, a compound extracted from a plant used in traditional Chinese medicine. As you might expect, though, artemisinin-resistant malaria has already been detected.

An understanding of evolution informs all of biology, from exploring life's molecules to analyzing ecosystems. And applications of evolutionary biology are transforming medicine, agriculture, biotechnology, and conservation biology. In this chapter, you'll read about evolution in action: verifiable, measurable examples of evolution that affect our world.

Charles Darwin and *The Origin of Species*

Biology came of age on November 24, 1859, the day Charles Darwin published *On the Origin of Species by Means of Natural Selection*. In one respect, Darwin's book was similar to volumes written by other naturalists—an assemblage of facts about the natural world, including the characteristics, habitats, behaviors, and geographic distributions of diverse species of plants and animals. Three broad observations emerged from these facts (**Figure 13.1**):

- the rich diversity of life
- the similarities that allow the classification of organisms into groups nested within broader groups
- the striking ways in which organisms are suited to their environments

Unlike other authors, Darwin proposed a hypothesis, a scientific explanation for his observations. Among the hundreds of pages devoted to the evidence supporting his hypothesis, Darwin also made testable predictions and reported the results of numerous experiments he had performed. Darwin hypothesized that present-day species are the descendants of ancient ancestors that they still resemble in some ways. Over time, differences accumulated by a process that Darwin called "descent with modification," his phrase for evolution (**Figure 13.2**). He also proposed a mechanism for how life evolves: natural selection.

Natural selection is a process in which organisms with certain inherited traits are more likely to survive and reproduce than are individuals with other traits (see Figure 1.12). As a result of natural selection, a **population**—a group of individuals of the same species living in the same place at the same time—can change over generations. Natural selection leads to **evolutionary adaptation**, a population's increase in the frequency of traits suited to the environment. (The term *adaptation* can also refer to the trait itself; for example, the flower mantid's camouflage is an adaptation that helps it ambush prey.) In modern terms, we would

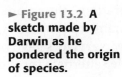
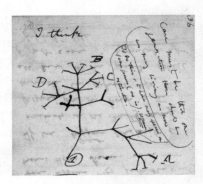

► **Figure 13.2 A sketch made by Darwin as he pondered the origin of species.**

▼ **Figure 13.1 Key observations about life.**

(a) The diversity of life. The 70 square miles of this rain forest in Madagascar is home to 77 species of birds, 25 species of mammals, nearly 100 species of reptiles and amphibians, more than a thousand species of plants, and countless species of insects, fungi, and microbes.

(b) Patterns of similarities. All species of flowers have the same basic parts, but the shapes and numbers of the parts differ and can be used to classify flowers into narrower groups.

(c) An insect suited to its environment. Camouflage helps this Malaysian flower mantid ambush prey.

say that the genetic composition of the population has changed over time, and that is one way of defining **evolution**. But we can also use the term *evolution* on a much grander scale to mean all of biological history, from the earliest microbes to the enormous diversity of organisms that live on the Earth today. ☑

Darwin's Cultural and Scientific Context

The view of life developed by Darwin in *The Origin of Species* was fundamentally different from the prevailing scientific and cultural views of his time. To help you appreciate the radical nature of Darwin's ideas, let's place them in their historical context.

The Idea of Fixed Species

The Greek philosopher Aristotle, whose ideas had an enormous impact on Western culture, generally held the view that species are fixed, permanent forms that do not evolve. Judeo-Christian culture fortified this idea with a literal interpretation of the biblical book of Genesis, which tells the story of each form of life being individually created in its present-day form. In the 1600s, religious scholars used biblical accounts to estimate the age of Earth at 6,000 years. Thus, the idea that all living species came into being relatively recently and are unchanging in form dominated the intellectual climate of the Western world for centuries.

At the same time, however, naturalists were also grappling with the interpretation of **fossils**—imprints or remains of organisms that lived in the past. Although fossils were thought to be the remains of living creatures, many were puzzling. For example, if "snake-stones" **(Figure 13.3a)** were the coiled bodies of snakes, then why were none ever found with an intact head? Could some fossils represent species that had become extinct? Stunning discoveries in the early 1800s, including fossilized skeletons of a gigantic sea creature dubbed an ichthyosaur, or fish-lizard **(Figure 13.3b)**, convinced many naturalists that extinctions had indeed occurred.

Lamarck and Evolutionary Adaptations

Fossils told of other changes in the history of life, too. Naturalists compared fossil forms with living species and noted patterns of similarities and differences. In the early 1800s, French naturalist Jean-Baptiste de Lamarck suggested that the best explanation for these observations is that life evolves. Lamarck explained evolution as the refinement of traits that equip organisms to perform successfully in their environments. He proposed that by using or not using its body parts, an individual may develop certain traits that it passes on to its offspring. For example, some birds have powerful beaks that enable them to crack tough seeds. Lamarck suggested that these strong beaks are the cumulative result of ancestors exercising their beaks during feeding and passing that acquired beak power on to offspring. However, simple observations provide evidence against the inheritance of acquired traits: A carpenter who builds up strength and stamina through a lifetime of pounding nails with a heavy hammer will not pass enhanced biceps on to children. Although Lamarck's idea of *how* species evolve was mistaken, his proposal that species evolve as a result of interactions between organisms and their environments helped set the stage for Darwin.

☑ **CHECKPOINT**

How did Darwin's *The Origin of Species* differ from other books that described the natural world?

Answer: *Darwin proposed a scientific explanation for his observations.*

▼ **Figure 13.3 Perplexing fossils.**

(a) "Snakestone." This fossil is actually a mollusc called an ammonite, an extinct relative of the present-day nautilus (see Figure 17.13). Ammonites of this type ranged in size from about several inches to more than 7 feet in diameter.

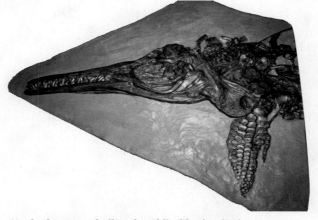

(b) Ichythyosaur skull and paddle-like forelimb. These marine reptiles—some more than 50 feet long—ruled the oceans for 155 million years before becoming extinct about 90 million years ago. The enormous eye is thought to be an adaptation to the dim light of the deep sea.

The Voyage of the *Beagle*

Charles Darwin was born in 1809, on the same day as Abraham Lincoln. Even as a boy, Darwin's consuming interest in nature was evident. When he was not reading nature books, he was in the fields and forests fishing, hunting, and collecting insects. His father, an eminent physician, could see no future for a naturalist and sent Charles to the University of Edinburgh to study medicine. But Charles, who was only 16 years old at the time, found medical school boring and distasteful. He left Edinburgh without a degree and then enrolled at Christ College at Cambridge University, intending to become a minister. Darwin received his B.A. degree—which included courses in biology—in 1831. Soon after, his botany professor recommended him to Captain Robert FitzRoy, who was preparing the survey ship HMS *Beagle* for a voyage around the world. It was a tour that would have a profound effect on Darwin's thinking and eventually on the thinking of the entire world.

How did Charles Darwin go from being an average student to being the most famous person in the history of biology?

Darwin was 22 years old when he sailed from Great Britain on the *Beagle* in December 1831 **(Figure 13.4)**. The main mission of the voyage was to chart poorly known stretches of the South American coastline. Darwin spent most of his time on shore collecting thousands of specimens of fossils and living plants and animals. He noted the unique adaptations of organisms that inhabited such diverse environments as the Brazilian jungles, the grasslands of the Argentine pampas, and the desolate and frigid lands at the southern tip of South America.

In spite of their unique adaptations, the plants and animals throughout the continent all had a definite South American stamp, very distinct from the life-forms of Europe. That in itself may not have surprised Darwin. But the plants and animals living in temperate regions of South America seemed more closely related to species living in tropical regions of that continent than to species living in temperate regions of Europe. And the South American fossils Darwin found, though clearly different species from living ones, were distinctly South American in their resemblance to the living plants and animals of that continent. These observations led Darwin to wonder if contemporary South American species owed their features to descent from ancestral species on that continent.

Darwin was particularly intrigued by the geographic distribution of organisms on the Galápagos Islands. The Galápagos are relatively young volcanic islands about 900 km (540 miles) off the Pacific coast of South America. Most of the animals that inhabit these remote

▼ **Figure 13.4 The voyage of the *Beagle*.**

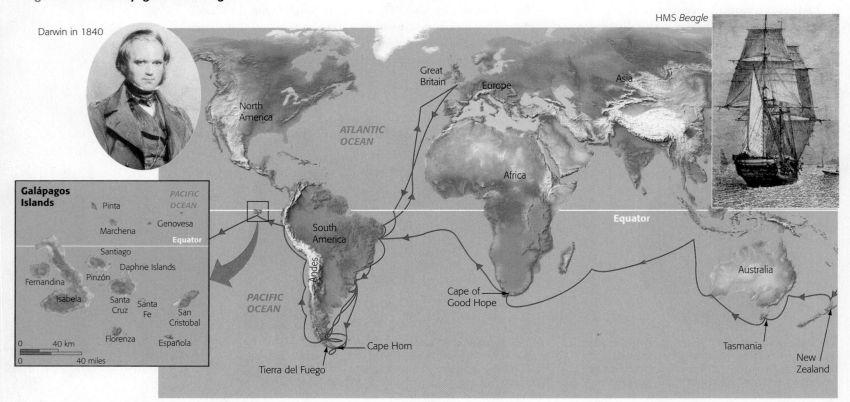

islands are found nowhere else in the world, but they resemble species living on the South American mainland (Figure 13.5).

While on his voyage, Darwin was strongly influenced by the newly published *Principles of Geology*, by Scottish geologist Charles Lyell. The book presented the case for an ancient Earth sculpted by gradual geologic processes that continue today. Having witnessed an earthquake that raised part of the coastline of Chile almost a meter, Darwin realized that natural forces gradually changed Earth's surface and that these forces still operate. Thus, the growth of mountains as a result of earthquakes could account for the presence of marine snail fossils he collected on mountaintops in the Andes.

By the time Darwin returned to Great Britain five years after the *Beagle* set sail, his experiences and reading had led him to seriously doubt that Earth and all its living organisms had been specially created only a few thousand years earlier. The evidence assembled by Lyell and other geologists implied that Earth must be very old—on the order of millions, rather than thousands, of years old—and constantly changing. (Modern scientists have determined that Earth is roughly 4.6 *billion* years old.) The extended time scale, Darwin reasoned, would allow for gradual changes to occur in species as well as in geologic features. Darwin began to analyze his collections and to discuss them with colleagues. He continued to read, correspond with other scientists, and maintain extensive journals of his observations, studies, and thoughts.

Descent with Modification

By the early 1840s, Darwin had composed a long essay describing the major features of his theory of evolution. He realized that his ideas would cause a social furor, however, and therefore delayed publishing his essay. Then, in the mid-1850s, Alfred Wallace, a British naturalist doing fieldwork in Indonesia, developed ideas almost identical to Darwin's. When Wallace sent Darwin a manuscript describing his own concept of natural selection, Darwin wrote, "All my originality . . . will be smashed." To resolve Darwin's dilemma, two of his colleagues presented Wallace's paper and excerpts from Darwin's earlier essay together to the scientific community. With the publication in 1859 of *The Origin of Species*, Darwin presented the world with an avalanche of evidence and a strong, logical argument for evolution.

As noted earlier, Darwin made two main points in *The Origin of Species*. First, he presented evidence that each living species descended from a succession of ancestral species. In the first edition of his book, he did not use the word *evolution*, referring instead to "descent with modification." Darwin hypothesized that as the descendants of the earliest organisms spread into various habitats over millions of years, they were modified (changed) by accumulating adaptations to diverse ways of life. Darwin's second main point was that natural selection is the mechanism for descent with modification. Before we look more closely at Darwin's theory of natural selection, let's examine the evidence for evolution. ✔

▼ **Figure 13.5** **A marine iguana (right), an example of the unique species inhabiting the Galápagos.** Darwin noticed that Galápagos marine iguanas—with a flattened tail that aids in swimming—are similar to, but distinct from, land-dwelling iguanas on the islands and on the South American mainland (left).

Evidence of Evolution

Evolution leaves observable signs. Such clues to the past are essential to any historical science. Historians of human civilization can study written records from earlier times. But they can also piece together the evolution of societies by recognizing vestiges of the past in modern cultures. Even if we did not know from written documents that Spaniards colonized the Americas, we would deduce this from the Hispanic stamp on Latin American culture. Similarly, biological evolution has left evidence in today's organisms, as well as in fossils.

In this section, we will examine five of the many lines of evidence in support of evolution. One of them—fossils—is a historical record. The other four—biogeography, comparative anatomy, comparative embryology, and molecular biology—encompass historical vestiges of evolution evident in modern life.

✔ CHECKPOINT

Why are older fossils generally in deeper rock layers than younger fossils?

Answer: *Sedimentation places younger rock layers on top of older ones.*

The Fossil Record

Over millions of years, sand and silt that eroded from the land were carried by rivers and deposited in the oceans, piling up and compressing older deposits below into rock. Some dead organisms that settled along with the sediments left imprints in the rocks. Thus, each rock layer, or stratum (plural, *strata*), bears a unique set of fossils representing a local sampling of the organisms that lived and died when that sediment was deposited. Younger strata are on top of older ones, so the positions of fossils in the strata reveal their relative age. (The ages of fossils can be confirmed using radiometric dating—see Figure 14.15.) The **fossil record** is this ordered sequence of fossils as they appear in the rock layers, marking the passage of geologic time **(Figure 13.6)**.

The fossil record reveals the appearance of organisms in a historical sequence. The oldest known fossils, dating from about 3.5 billion years ago, are prokaryotes. This fossil evidence fits with the molecular and cellular evidence that prokaryotes are the ancestors of all life. Fossils in younger layers of rock reveal the evolution of various groups of eukaryotic organisms.

In *The Origin of Species*, Darwin predicted that the fossil record would include transitional forms that link past and present. Paleontologists (scientists who study fossils) have indeed discovered many such fossils. For example, a series of transitional fossils provides evidence that birds descended from one branch of dinosaurs. Another example is a series of transitional whale fossils connecting these aquatic mammals to four-legged land mammals. Whales living today have forelegs in the form of flippers but lack hind legs. The hypothesis that whales evolved from terrestrial (land-dwelling) ancestors predicts a four-limbed beginning for whales. Paleontologists digging in Egypt, Pakistan, and North America have uncovered a series of remarkable fossils of extinct mammals that document the transition from life on land to life in the sea **(Figure 13.7)**. Some whale ancestors had a type of anklebone that is otherwise unique to the group of land mammals that includes pigs, hippos, cows, camels, and deer. The anklebone similarity strongly suggests that whales (as well as dolphins and porpoises) are most closely related to this group of land mammals. ✔

▼ **Figure 13.6 Strata of sedimentary rock at the Grand Canyon.** The Colorado River has cut through more than a mile of rock, exposing sedimentary strata that are like huge pages from the book of life. Each stratum entombs fossils that represent some of the organisms from that period of Earth's history.

▼ **Figure 13.7 A transitional fossil linking past and present.** Shown here are fossilized leg bones of *Basilosaurus*, an ancient whale. Like other extinct whales, *Basilosaurus* was already aquatic and no longer used its legs to support its weight.

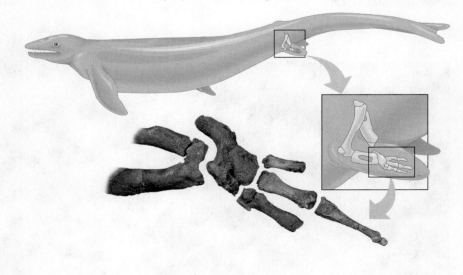

Biogeography

It was **biogeography**, the geographic distribution of species, that first suggested to Darwin that today's organisms evolved from ancestral forms. Consider, for example, Darwin's visit to the Galápagos Islands. Darwin noted that the Galápagos animals resembled species of the South American mainland more than they resembled animals on similar but distant islands. He hypothesized that the Galápagos species evolved from animals that migrated from South America. These immigrants eventually gave rise to new species as they became adapted to their new environment.

Many other examples from biogeography seem baffling without an evolutionary perspective. Consider the diversity of marsupials in Australia (**Figure 13.8**). Australia is home to many kinds of marsupials (mammals that complete embryonic development outside the uterus, typically in a mother's pouch) but relatively few placental mammals (mammals that complete embryonic development in the uterus). This is not because Australia is inhospitable to placental mammals. Humans have introduced rabbits, foxes, and many other placental mammals to Australia, and these introduced species have thrived to the point of becoming ecological and economic nuisances. The prevailing hypothesis is that the unique Australian wildlife evolved on that island continent in isolation from regions where early placental mammals diversified.

The geographic distribution of species makes little sense if we imagine that species were individually placed in suitable environments. In the Darwinian view, we find species where they are because they evolved from ancestors that inhabited those regions.

Why are marsupial mammals so common in Australia and so uncommon everywhere else?

▼ Figure 13.8 **Biogeography.** The continent of Australia is home to many unique plants and animals, such as these marsupials, mammals that evolved in relative isolation from other continents where placental mammals diversified.

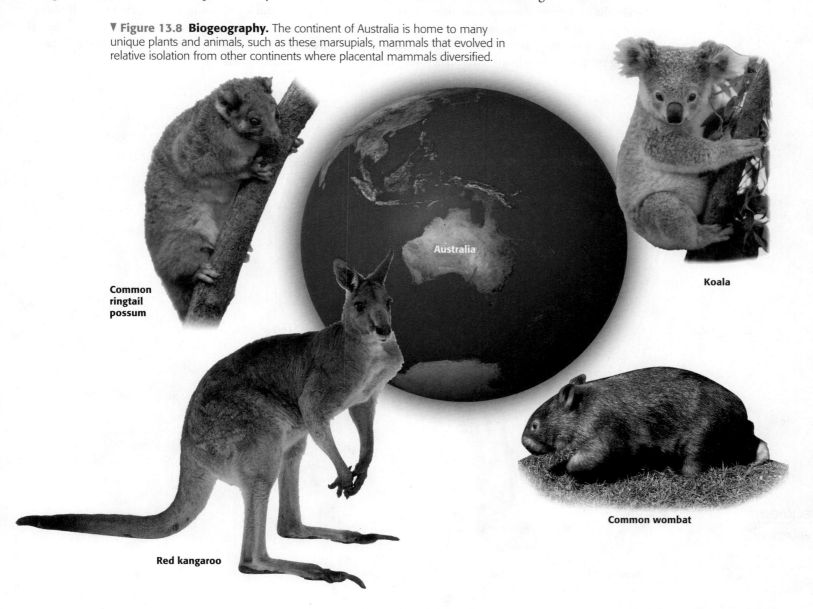

Common ringtail possum

Australia

Koala

Red kangaroo

Common wombat

Comparative Anatomy

The comparison of body structures in different species is called **comparative anatomy**. Biologists have observed many anatomical similarities among species. For example, the same skeletal elements make up the forelimbs of humans, cats, whales, and bats, even though the functions of these forelimbs differ greatly; clearly, a whale's flipper does not do the same job as a bat's wing. Scientists interpret these similarities as an indication of common ancestry. The arms, forelegs, flippers, and wings of these different mammals are variations on anatomical structures of an ancestral organism, structures that over millions of years have become adapted to different functions. These adaptations account for the observed similarities in structures despite different uses. Such similarity in structure due to common ancestry is called **homology**. The forelimbs of diverse mammals are therefore known as homologous structures **(Figure 13.9)**.

How is your arm similar to a whale's flipper?

Comparative anatomy attests that evolution is a remodeling process in which ancestral structures become modified as they take on new functions—the kind of process that Darwin referred to as descent with modification. The historical constraints of this modification are evident in anatomical imperfections. For example, the human spine and knee joint were derived from ancestral structures that supported four-legged mammals. Consequently, almost none of us will reach old age without experiencing knee or back problems. If these structures had first taken form specifically to support our bipedal posture, we would expect them to be less subject to sprains, spasms, and other common injuries.

Some of the most interesting homologous structures are "leftover" structures of marginal, if any, importance to the organism. These **vestigial structures** are remnants of features that served important functions in the organism's ancestors, such as the rear leg bones evident in ancient whale fossils (see Figure 13.7). In another example, the skeletons of some snakes retain vestiges of the pelvis and leg bones of walking ancestors. If limbs were a hindrance to ancient snakes' way of life, natural selection would favor snake descendants with successively smaller limbs. ☑

▼ **Figure 13.9 Homologous structures: anatomical signs of descent with modification.** The forelimbs of all mammals are constructed from the same skeletal elements. (Homologous bones in each of these four mammals are colored the same.) The hypothesis that all mammals descended from a common ancestor predicts that their forelimbs, though diversely adapted, would be variations on a common anatomical theme.

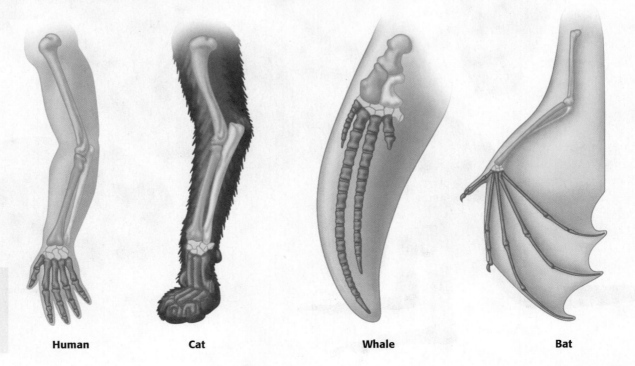

Human **Cat** **Whale** **Bat**

☑ **CHECKPOINT**

What is homology?

Answer: similarity between species that is due to shared ancestry

Comparative Embryology

Comparing early stages of development in different animal species reveals additional homologies not visible in adult organisms. For example, all vertebrate embryos have a developmental stage in which structures called pharyngeal pouches appear on the sides of the throat. At this stage, the embryos of fishes, frogs, snakes, birds, and apes—indeed, all vertebrates—look more alike than different (Figure 13.10). The different classes of vertebrates take on more distinctive features as development progresses. For example, pharyngeal pouches develop into gills in fishes but into parts of the ear and throat in humans.

Molecular Biology

The hereditary background of an organism is documented in its DNA and in the proteins encoded by the DNA (see Chapter 10). If two species have genes with nucleotide sequences that match closely, biologists conclude that these sequences are homologous and must have been inherited from a relatively recent common ancestor (Figure 13.11). In contrast, the greater the number of sequence differences between species, the less likely they share a close common ancestor. Molecular comparisons between diverse organisms have allowed biologists to develop hypotheses about the evolutionary divergence of branches on the tree of life. For example, genetic analyses first suggested that the domain Archaea is more closely related to the eukaryotes than it is to the domain Bacteria.

Darwin's boldest hypothesis was that *all* forms of life are related to some extent through branching evolution from the earliest organisms. About 100 years after Darwin made his claim, molecular biology began providing strong evidence for evolution: All forms of life use the same genetic language of DNA and RNA, and the genetic code (how RNA triplets are translated into amino acids) is nearly universal. This genetic language has been passed along through all the branches of evolution since its beginnings in an early form of life. ☑

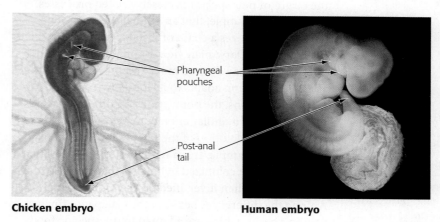

▼ Figure 13.10 **Evolutionary signs from comparative embryology.** At the early stage of development shown here, the kinship of vertebrates is unmistakable. Notice, for example, the pharyngeal pouches and tails in both the chicken embryo and the human embryo.

Pharyngeal pouches

Post-anal tail

Chicken embryo　　　　**Human embryo**

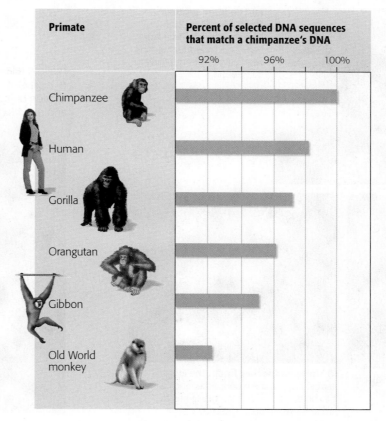

▼ Figure 13.11 **Genetic relationships among some primates.** The bars in this diagram show the percent of selected DNA sequences that match between a chimpanzee and other primates, the animal group that includes monkeys, apes, and humans. For example, note that the selected DNA sequences of chimps and humans are better than a 98% match. In contrast, the DNA sequences of chimps and Old World monkeys (such as macaques, mandrills, baboons, and rhesus monkeys) have less than a 93% match.

Primate	Percent of selected DNA sequences that match a chimpanzee's DNA
	92%　　96%　　100%
Chimpanzee	
Human	
Gorilla	
Orangutan	
Gibbon	
Old World monkey	

☑ CHECKPOINT

Name the five lines of evidence for evolution presented in this section.

Answer: the fossil record, biogeography, comparative anatomy, comparative embryology, molecular biology

Natural Selection

Darwin perceived adaptation to the environment and the origin of new species as closely related processes. Imagine, for example, that an animal species from a mainland colonizes a chain of distant, relatively isolated islands. In the Darwinian view, populations on the different islands may diverge more and more in appearance as each population adapts to its local environment. Over many generations, the populations on different islands could become dissimilar enough to be designated as separate species. Evolution of the finches on the Galápagos Islands is an example. It is a reasonable hypothesis that the islands were colonized by finches that strayed from elsewhere and then diversified on the different islands. Among the differences between the Galápagos finches are their beaks, which are adapted to the specific foods available on each species' home island **(Figure 13.12)**. Darwin anticipated that explaining how such adaptations arise is the key to understanding evolution. And his theory of natural selection remains our best explanation for the formation of new adaptations. ☑

☑ CHECKPOINT

How did Darwin hypothesize that adaptation is related to the origin of new species?

Answer: Populations in different environments adapt to local conditions. Over time, the populations might become dissimilar enough to be designated as separate species.

Darwin's Theory of Natural Selection

Darwin based his theory of natural selection on two key observations, both of which had already been noted by scientists. First, he recognized that all species tend to produce excessive numbers of offspring **(Figure 13.13)**. Darwin deduced that because natural resources are limited, the production of more individuals than the environment can support leads to a "struggle for existence" (competition) among the individuals of a population. In most cases, only a small percentage of offspring will survive in each generation. Many eggs are laid, young born, and seeds spread, but only a tiny fraction complete their development and leave offspring of their own. The rest are starved, eaten, frozen, diseased, unmated, or unable to reproduce for other reasons.

The second key observation that led Darwin to natural selection was his awareness of variation among individuals of a population. Just as no two people in a human population are alike, individual variation abounds in all species **(Figure 13.14)**. Much of this variation is heritable. Siblings share more traits with

▼ **Figure 13.12 Galápagos finches with beaks adapted for specific diets.**

(a) The large ground finch. This species of Galápagos finch has a large beak specialized for cracking seeds that fall from plants to the ground.

▼ **Figure 13.13 Overproduction of offspring.** This sea slug, a mollusc related to snails (see Figure 17.13), is laying thousands of eggs embedded in the pink ribbon around its body. Only a tiny fraction of the eggs will actually give rise to offspring that survive and reproduce.

(b) The warbler finch. The smaller beak of the warbler finch is used to grasp insects.

(c) The woodpecker finch. The long, narrow beak of the woodpecker finch allows it to hold tools such as cactus spines to probe for wood-boring insects.

▲ **Figure 13.14 Color variation within a population of Asian lady beetles.**

each other and with their parents than they do with less closely related members of the population.

From these two observations, Darwin arrived at the conclusion that defines natural selection: Individuals whose inherited traits are better suited to the local environment are more likely than other individuals to survive and reproduce. In other words, the individuals that function best should leave the most surviving offspring. Darwin's genius was in connecting two observations that anyone could make and drawing a conclusion that could explain how adaptations evolve.

Does evolution produce perfect organisms?

Observation 1: Overproduction and competition. Populations of all species have the potential to produce many more offspring than the environment can possibly support with food, space, and other resources. This overproduction makes competition among individuals inevitable.

Observation 2: Individual variation. Individuals in a population vary in many heritable traits.

Conclusion: Unequal reproductive success. Those individuals with heritable traits best suited to the local environment generally leave a larger share of surviving, fertile offspring.

Darwin's insight was both simple and profound. The environment screens a population's inherent variability. Unequal success in reproduction (natural selection) leads to an accumulation of the favored traits in the population over generations (evolution). In other words, natural selection promotes evolutionary adaptations.

It is important to emphasize three key but subtle points about evolution by natural selection. The first point is that individuals do not evolve, even though natural selection occurs through interactions between individual organisms and their environment. Evolution refers to generation-to-generation changes in populations (as you'll see in the next section).

The second key point is that natural selection can amplify or diminish only traits that are heritable. An organism may become modified through interactions with the environment during its lifetime, and those acquired traits may help it survive. But unless these traits are coded for in the genes of the organism's gametes (sperm or egg), they cannot be passed on to offspring and therefore will not affect the reproductive success of the next generation.

The third key point is that evolution is not goal directed; it does not lead to perfectly adapted organisms. Natural selection is the result of environmental factors that vary from place to place and from time to time. A trait that is favorable in one situation may be useless—or even detrimental—in different circumstances. For example, some genetic mutations that happen to endow mosquitoes with resistance to the pesticide DDT also reduce a mosquito's growth rate. Before DDT was introduced, the resistance allele was a handicap. But after DDT became part of the environment, the mutant alleles were advantageous, and natural selection increased their frequency in mosquito populations. This example also shows that significant evolutionary change can occur in a short time—something we'll stress again in the next section. ✓

Natural Selection in Action

Natural selection and evolution are observable. You learned about one unsettling example in the Biology and Society section: the evolution of pesticide resistance within insect species. Pesticides control insects and prevent them from eating crops, transmitting diseases such as malaria, or just annoying us. But widespread use has led to the evolution of pesticide-resistant insect populations **(Figure 13.15)**. The evolution of antibiotic-resistant bacteria is another example of natural selection in action (see Chapter 1). More recently, doctors have documented an increase in drug-resistant strains of HIV, the virus that causes AIDS. The unifying thread woven throughout this chapter is that evolution and natural selection did not operate only in the distant past, but are observable today. Let's look at another example of evolution in action.

☑ CHECKPOINT
Explain why the following statement is incorrect: "Pesticides cause pesticide resistance in insects."

Answer: An environmental factor does not create new traits such as pesticide resistance, but favors traits that are already represented in the population.

▼ **Figure 13.15 Evolution of pesticide resistance in insect populations.** By spraying crops with poisons to kill insect pests, people have unwittingly favored the reproductive success of insects with inherent resistance to the poisons.

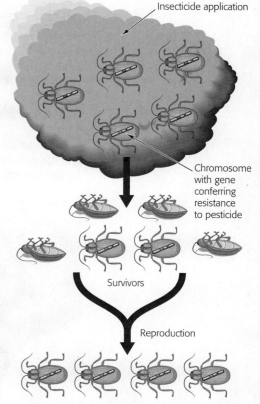

Insecticide application

Chromosome with gene conferring resistance to pesticide

Survivors

Reproduction

Additional applications of the same pesticide will be less effective, and the frequency of resistant insects in the population will grow.

Evolution in Action THE PROCESS OF SCIENCE

Does Predation Drive the Evolution of Lizard Horn Length?

One recent and particularly elegant demonstration of evolution in action involved the flat-tailed horned lizard *Phrynosoma mcalli*, a desert inhabitant of the American Southwest. The lizard's main predator, a bird called the shrike, attacks by biting a lizard's neck just behind the skull, severing the spine. The shrike then carries the dead prey to a convenient place, such as a fence or branch, impales it, and eats it **(Figure 13.16)**.

Evolutionary biologists at Utah State University and Indiana University made the **observation** that the flat-tailed horned lizard defends against attack by thrusting its head backward, stabbing the shrike with the spiked horns that protrude from the rear and sides of the skull. This led the researchers to **question** whether longer horn length and spread represented a survival advantage. Their **hypothesis** was that it did, so they formed the **prediction** that live horned lizards would have longer and more widely spread horns than killed ones.

The **experiment** to test this hypothesis was simple: The researchers measured the length of rear horns and the tip-to-tip spread distance of side horns from the skulls of 29 killed lizards (found where they had been impaled) and 155 live lizards. Their **results**, shown in the graph in Figure 13.15, indicate that the average horn length and spread of live lizards is about 10% greater than that of killed lizards (note that each blue bar is about 10% taller than the corresponding orange bar). The researchers concluded that defensive behavior against predators is one factor driving natural selection of horn length among this lizard species. Thus, evolution—in this case of the length of lizard horns—is observable and measurable in the world around us today.

◄ **Figure 13.16 The effect of predation on the evolution of lizard horn length.** Researchers measured the horns of lizards killed by birds and compared them with the horns of live lizards. The fact that the length of the rear horns and the spread of the side horns are both significantly greater in live lizards than in killed lizards suggests that horn length is an adaptation that is evolving in response to predation by birds.

(a) A flat-tailed horned lizard. The lizards use the spiky horns that protrude from the back and sides of the skull to ward off attacks.

(b) The remains of a lizard impaled by a shrike. After killing a lizard, the bird often impales the lizard on a fence or branch.

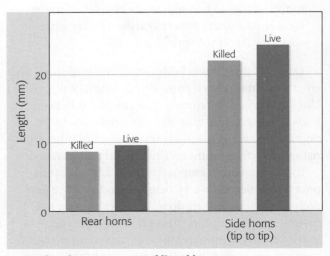

(c) Results of measurement of lizard horns.

Evolutionary Trees

In Darwin's view, the history of life is analogous to a tree. Patterns of descent branch off from a common trunk, the first organism, to the tips of millions of twigs representing the species living today. At each fork of the evolutionary tree is an ancestor common to all evolutionary branches extending from that fork. Closely related species share many traits because their lineage of common descent traces to a recent fork of the tree of life. Biologists represent these patterns of descent with an **evolutionary tree**, although today they usually turn the trees sideways as in **Figure 13.17**.

Homologous structures, both anatomical and molecular, can be used to determine the branching sequence of an evolutionary tree. Some homologous structures, such as the genetic code, are shared by all species because they date to the deep ancestral past. In contrast, traits that evolved more recently are shared by smaller groups of organisms. For example, all tetrapods (from the Greek *tetra*, four, and *pod*, foot) have the same basic limb bone structure illustrated in Figure 13.9, but their ancestors do not.

Figure 13.17 is an evolutionary tree of tetrapods (amphibians, mammals, and reptiles, including birds) and their closest living relatives, the lungfishes. In this diagram, each branch point represents the common ancestor of all species that descended from it. For example, lungfishes and tetrapods descended from ancestor **1**. Three homologies are shown by the blue dots on the tree—tetrapod limbs, the amnion (a protective embryonic membrane), and feathers. Tetrapod limbs were present in common ancestor **2** and hence are found in its descendants (the tetrapods). The amnion was present in ancestor **3** and thus is shared only by mammals and reptiles, which are known as amniotes. Feathers were present only in ancestor **6** and hence are found only in birds.

Evolutionary trees are hypotheses reflecting our current understanding of patterns of evolutionary descent. Some trees are more speculative because sufficient data are not yet available. Other trees are based on a convincing combination of fossil, anatomical, and DNA data. ✔

▼ **Figure 13.17 An evolutionary tree of tetrapods (four-limbed animals).**

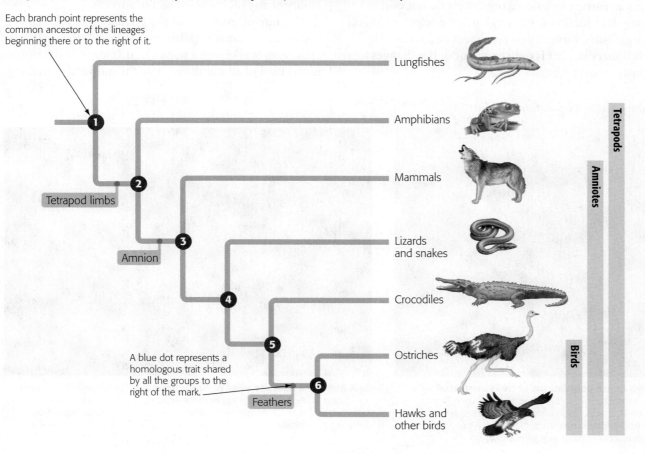

Each branch point represents the common ancestor of the lineages beginning there or to the right of it.

Tetrapod limbs

Amnion

A blue dot represents a homologous trait shared by all the groups to the right of the mark.

Feathers

Lungfishes

Amphibians

Mammals

Lizards and snakes

Crocodiles

Ostriches

Hawks and other birds

Tetrapods

Amniotes

Birds

The Modern Synthesis: Darwinism Meets Genetics

Natural selection requires hereditary processes that Darwin could not explain. How do the variations that are the raw material for natural selection arise in a population? And how are these variations passed along from parents to offspring? Darwin and Gregor Mendel lived and worked around the same time. In fact, by breeding peas in his abbey garden, Mendel illuminated the very hereditary processes required for natural selection to work. However, Mendel's discoveries went unappreciated by the scientific community during his lifetime. Mendelism and Darwinism finally came together in the mid-1900s, decades after both scientists had died. This fusion of genetics with evolutionary biology came to be known as the **modern synthesis** (here, the term *synthesis* means "combination"). One of its key elements is an emphasis on the biology of populations.

Populations as the Units of Evolution

As noted earlier, individual organisms do not evolve during their lifetimes. Although natural selection affects an organism's survival and reproductive success, the evolutionary impact is only apparent in the changes in a population over time.

One population may be isolated from other populations of the same species, with little interbreeding and thus little exchange of alleles between them. Such isolation is common for populations in geographically separated areas—for example, widely separated islands, unconnected lakes, or mountain ranges separated by lowlands. However, populations are not usually so isolated, and they rarely have sharp boundaries **(Figure 13.18a)**. One population center may blur into another in a region of overlap, where members of both populations are present but less numerous. Nevertheless, individuals are more concentrated in the population centers and are more likely to breed with other locals **(Figure 13.18b)**. Therefore, organisms of a population are generally more closely related to one another than to members of other populations.

A population is the smallest biological unit that can evolve. In the Biology and Society section and Figure 13.15, you saw that natural selection can affect pesticide resistance in populations of insects. That impact is measured by the change in the relative numbers of resistant insects over a span of generations, not by the ability of any individual insect to survive.

In studying evolution at the population level, biologists focus on what is called the **gene pool**, the total collection of alleles in a population at any one time (that is, the total of all the alleles in all the individuals making

▼ Figure 13.18 **Populations.**

(a) Two dense populations of trees separated by a lake. Interbreeding occurs when wind blows pollen between the populations. Nevertheless, trees are more likely to breed with members of the same population than with trees on the other side of the lake.

(b) A nighttime satellite view of North America. Notice the lights of human population centers, or cities. People move around, of course, and there are suburban and rural communities between cities, but people are more likely to choose mates locally.

up the population). For many genes, there are two or more alleles (versions of the gene) in the gene pool. For example, in an insect population, there may be one allele that codes for an enzyme that breaks down a certain pesticide and one for a version of the enzyme that does not. In fields sprayed with pesticide, the first allele will increase in frequency and the other allele will decrease in frequency. When the relative frequencies of alleles in a population change like this over a number of generations, evolution is occurring on its smallest scale. Later we'll look at the causes of evolution within a population. But first let's explore the sources of genetic variation. ☑

Genetic Variation in Populations

You have no trouble recognizing your friends in a crowd. People vary in appearance, reflecting the individual differences in their genomes. Individual variation abounds in all species **(Figure 13.19)**. In addition to visible differences, most populations vary greatly at the molecular level. For example, you cannot tell someone's blood group (A, B, AB, or O) just by looking at that person, but biochemical analyses can reveal such variations.

Not all variation in a population is heritable. Phenotype—the expressed traits of an organism—results from a combination of the genotype, which is inherited, and many environmental influences. For instance, a strength-training program can build up your muscle mass beyond what would naturally occur from your genetic makeup. However, you would not pass this environmentally induced physique on to your offspring. Only the genetic component of variation is relevant to natural selection.

If your parents spend a lot of money on orthodontia for you, will your children inherit nice, straight teeth?

Many of the variable traits in a population result from the combined effect of several genes. This polygenic ("many genes") inheritance produces traits that vary more or less continuously—in human height, for instance, from very short individuals to very tall ones. By contrast, other features, such as human blood group, are determined by a single gene locus, with different alleles producing one of only a few distinct phenotypes; there are no in-between types. Next, we'll focus on the sources of different alleles.

Sources of Genetic Variation

Mutations and sexual reproduction, both involving random processes, produce genetic variation. Let's examine each of these processes in detail.

Mutations, random changes in the nucleotide sequence of DNA (see Figure 10.22), can result in new alleles. For example, a mutation in a gene may substitute one nucleotide for another. If such a change affects the protein's function, the mutation will probably be harmful. A random mutation is like a shot in the dark; it is not likely to improve a genome any more than shooting a bullet through the hood of a car is likely to improve engine performance.

☑ **CHECKPOINT**

What is the smallest biological unit that can evolve?

Answer: a population

► **Figure 13.19 Variation in a garter snake population.** These four garter snakes, which belong to the same species, were all captured in one Oregon field. The behavior of each physical type is correlated with its coloration. When approached, spotted snakes, which blend in with their background, generally freeze. In contrast, snakes with stripes, which make it difficult to judge the speed of motion, usually flee rapidly when approached.

On rare occasions, however, a mutant allele may actually enhance reproductive success. This kind of effect is more likely when the environment is changing in such a way that alleles that were once disadvantageous are favorable under the new conditions. We already considered one example, the changing fortune of the DDT resistance allele in insect populations.

A new mutation that is transmitted in gametes can immediately change the gene pool of a population by replacing one allele with another. For any given gene locus, mutation alone has little effect on a large population in a single generation. This is because a mutation at any given gene locus is a very rare event. However, the cumulative impact of mutations across the genome can be significant because an individual has thousands of genes, and many populations have thousands or millions of individuals.

Organisms with very short generation spans, such as bacteria, can evolve rapidly with mutation as the only source of genetic variation. Bacteria multiply so quickly that natural selection can increase a population's frequency of a beneficial mutation in just hours or days. For most animals and plants, however, their long generation times prevent new mutations from significantly affecting overall genetic variation in the short term. Consequently, in sexually reproducing organisms, most of the genetic variation in a population results from the unique combination of alleles that each individual inherits. (Of course, the origin of the variation in those alleles is past mutation.)

Fresh assortments of existing alleles arise every generation from three random components of sexual reproduction: independent orientation of homologous chromosomes at metaphase I of meiosis (see Figure 8.16), random fertilization, and crossing over (see Figure 8.18).

Do mutations occur in response to a changing environment?

☑ CHECKPOINT

Which process, mutation or sexual reproduction, results in most of the generation-to-generation variability in human populations? Why?

Answer: sexual reproduction, because humans have a relatively long generation span and mutations have relatively little effect in a single generation

During prophase I of meiosis, pairs of homologous chromosomes, one set inherited from each parent, trade some of their genes by crossing over, and then each pair separates into gametes independently of other chromosome pairs. Gametes from one individual vary extensively in their genetic makeup, and each zygote made by a mating pair has a unique assortment of alleles resulting from the random union of sperm and egg.

While the processes that generate genetic variation—mutation and events during sexual reproduction—are random, natural selection (and hence evolution) is not. The environment selectively promotes the propagation of those genetic combinations that enhance survival and reproductive success. ☑

Analyzing Gene Pools

As described earlier, a gene pool consists of all the alleles in a population at any one time. The gene pool is the reservoir from which the next generation of organisms draws its alleles.

Imagine a wildflower population with two varieties that are different colors (**Figure 13.20**). An allele for red flowers, which we will symbolize by R, is dominant to an allele for white flowers, symbolized by r. These are the only two alleles for flower color in the gene pool of this hypothetical plant population. Now, let's say that 80%, or 0.8, of all flower-color loci in the gene pool have the R allele. We'll use the letter p to represent the relative frequency of the R allele in the population. Thus, $p = 0.8$. Because there are only two alleles in this example, the r allele must be present at the other 20% (0.2) of the gene pool's flower-color loci. Let's use the letter q for the frequency of the r allele in the population. For the wildflower population, $q = 0.2$. And since there are only two alleles for flower color, we can express their frequencies as follows:

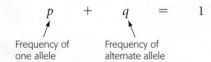

$$p \quad + \quad q \quad = \quad 1$$

Frequency of one allele | Frequency of alternate allele

Notice that if we know the frequency of either allele in the gene pool, we can subtract it from 1 to calculate the frequency of the other allele.

From the frequencies of alleles, we can also calculate the frequencies of different genotypes in the population if the gene pool is completely stable (not evolving). In the wildflower population, what is the probability of producing an RR individual by "drawing" two R alleles from the pool of gametes? Here we apply the rule of multiplication that you learned in Chapter 9 (review Figure 9.11). The probability of drawing an R sperm

▼ Figure 13.20 **A population of wildflowers with two varieties of color.**

multiplied by the probability of drawing an R egg is $p \times p = p^2$, or $0.8 \times 0.8 = 0.64$. In other words, 64% of the plants in the population will have the RR genotype. Applying the same math, we also know the frequency of rr individuals in the population: $q^2 = 0.2 \times 0.2 = 0.04$. Thus, 4% of the plants are rr, giving them white flowers. Calculating the frequency of heterozygous individuals, Rr, is trickier. That's because the heterozygous genotype can form in two ways, depending on whether the sperm or egg supplies the dominant allele. So the frequency of the Rr genotype is $2pq$, which is $2 \times 0.8 \times 0.2 = 0.32$. In our imaginary wildflower population, 32% of the plants are Rr, with red flowers. **Figure 13.21** reviews these calculations graphically.

Now we can write a general formula for calculating the frequencies of genotypes in a gene pool from the frequencies of alleles, and vice versa:

$$p^2 + 2pq + q^2 = 1$$

p^2: Frequency of homozygotes for one allele
$2pq$: Frequency of heterozygotes
q^2: Frequency of homozygotes for alternate allele

Notice that the frequencies of all genotypes in the gene pool must add up to 1. This formula is called the Hardy-Weinberg formula, named for the two scientists who derived it in 1908.

▼ **Figure 13.21 A mathematical swim in the gene pool.** Each of the four boxes in the Punnett square corresponds to a probable "draw" of alleles from the gene pool.

Allele frequencies
p = 0.8 (R)
q = 0.2 (r)
Eggs
R
p = 0.8
r
q = 0.2
Sperm
R
p = 0.8
r
q = 0.2
RR
p² = 0.64
Rr
pq = 0.16
Rr
pq = 0.16
rr
q² = 0.04
Genotype frequencies
p² = 0.64 (RR)
2pq = 0.32 (Rr)
q² = 0.04 (rr)

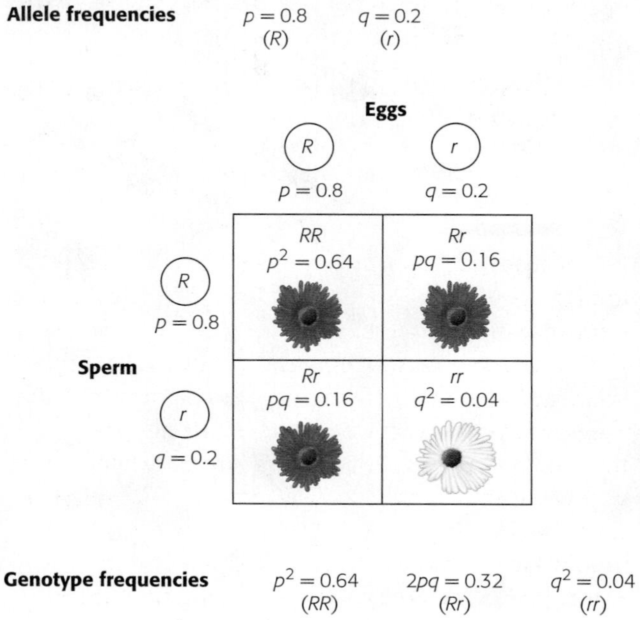

Population Genetics and Health Science

Public health scientists use the Hardy-Weinberg formula to calculate the percentage of a human population that carries the allele for certain inherited diseases. Consider phenylketonuria (PKU), which is an inherited inability to break down the amino acid phenylalanine. If untreated, the disorder causes severe mental retardation. PKU occurs in about 1 out of 10,000 babies born in the United States. Newborn babies are now routinely tested for PKU, and symptoms can be prevented if individuals living with the disease follow a strict diet (**Figure 13.22**).

PKU is caused by a recessive allele (that is, one that must be present in two copies to produce the phenotype). Thus, we can represent the frequency of individuals in the U.S. population born with PKU with the q^2 term in the Hardy-Weinberg formula. For one PKU occurrence per 10,000 births, $q^2 = 0.0001$. Therefore, q, the frequency of the recessive allele in the population, equals the square root of 0.0001, or 0.01. And p, the frequency of the dominant allele, equals $1 - q$, or 0.99.

Now let's calculate the frequency of carriers, who are heterozygous individuals who carry the PKU allele in a single copy and may pass it on to offspring. Carriers are represented in the formula by $2pq$: $2 \times 0.99 \times 0.01$, or 0.0198. Thus, the Hardy-Weinberg formula tells us that about 2% of the U.S. population are carriers for the PKU allele. Estimating the frequency of a harmful allele is essential for any public health program dealing with genetic diseases.

Diet
INGREDIENTS: SORBITOL, MAGNESIUM STEARATE, ARTIFICIAL FLAVOR,
ASPARTAME† (SWEETENER),
ARTIFICIAL COLOR (YELLOW 5 LAKE, BLUE 1 LAKE), ZINC GLUCONATE.
†PHENYLKETONURICS: CONTAINS PHENYLALANINE

▲ **Figure 13.22 A warning to individuals with PKU.** People with PKU (phenylketonuria) must strictly regulate their dietary intake of the amino acid phenylalanine. In addition to natural sources, phenylalanine is found in aspartame, a common artificial sweetener. The frequency of the PKU allele is high enough to warrant warnings on foods that contain phenylalanine.

Microevolution as Change in a Gene Pool

As stated earlier, evolution can be measured as changes in the genetic composition of a population over time. It helps, as a basis of comparison, to know what to expect if a population is *not* evolving. A nonevolving population is in genetic equilibrium, which is also known as **Hardy-Weinberg equilibrium**. The population's gene pool remains constant. From generation to generation, the frequencies of alleles (p and q) and genotypes (p^2, $2pq$, and q^2) are unchanged. Sexual shuffling of genes cannot by itself change a large gene pool.

One of the products of the modern synthesis was a definition of evolution that is based on the genetics of populations: Evolution is a generation-to-generation change in a population's frequencies of alleles. Because this is evolution viewed on the smallest scale, it is sometimes referred to as **microevolution**. ☑

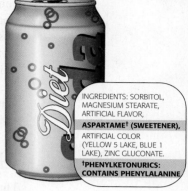

☑ CHECKPOINT

1. Which term in the Hardy-Weinberg formula ($p^2 + 2pq + q^2 = 1$) corresponds to the frequency of individuals with *no* alleles for the recessive disease PKU?
2. Define microevolution.

Answers: **1.** p^2 **2.** *Microevolution is a change in a population's frequencies of alleles.*

Mechanisms of Evolution

Now that we understand that evolution can be evident in changes in a population's genetic makeup from generation to generation (microevolution), we come to an obvious question: What mechanisms can change a gene pool? Natural selection is the most important, because it is the only process that promotes adaptation. But we'll also look at two other mechanisms of evolutionary change: genetic drift, which is due to chance, and gene flow, the exchange of alleles between neighboring populations.

Genetic Drift

Flip a coin 1,000 times, and a result of 700 heads and 300 tails would make you very suspicious about that coin. But flip a coin 10 times, and an outcome of 7 heads and 3 tails would seem within reason. With a smaller sample, there is a greater chance of deviation from an idealized result—in this case, an equal number of heads and tails.

Let's apply coin toss logic to a population's gene pool. If a new generation draws its alleles at random from the previous generation, then the larger the population (the sample size), the better the new generation will represent the gene pool of the previous generation. Thus,

one requirement for a gene pool to maintain the status quo is a large population size. The gene pool of a small population may not be accurately represented in the next generation because of sampling error. The changed gene pool is analogous to the erratic outcome from a small sample of coin tosses.

Figure 13.23 applies this concept of sampling error to a small population of wildflowers. Chance causes the frequencies of the alleles for red (*R*) and white (*r*) flowers to change over the generations. And that fits our definition of microevolution. This evolutionary mechanism, a change in the gene pool of a population due to chance, is called **genetic drift**. But what would cause a population to shrink down to a size where there is genetic drift? Two ways this can occur are the bottleneck effect and the founder effect.

The Bottleneck Effect

Disasters such as earthquakes, floods, and fires may kill large numbers of individuals, producing a small surviving population that is unlikely to have the same genetic makeup as the original population. By chance, certain alleles may be overrepresented among the survivors. Other

▼ **Figure 13.23 Genetic drift.** This hypothetical wildflower population consists of only ten plants. Due to random change over the generations, genetic drift can eliminate some alleles, as is the case for the *r* allele in generation 3 of this imaginary population.

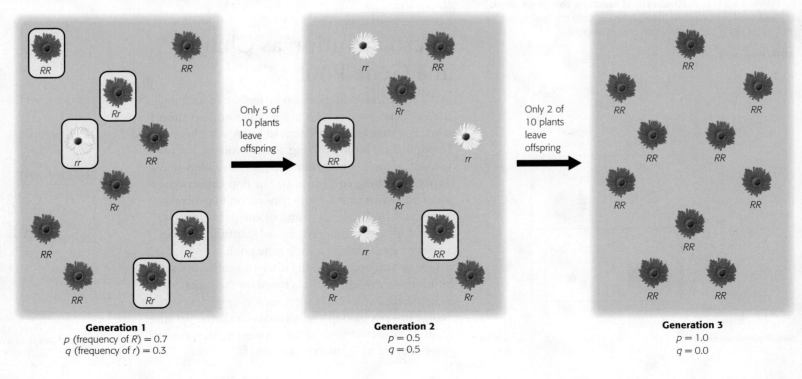

Generation 1
p (frequency of *R*) = 0.7
q (frequency of *r*) = 0.3

Only 5 of 10 plants leave offspring

Generation 2
p = 0.5
q = 0.5

Only 2 of 10 plants leave offspring

Generation 3
p = 1.0
q = 0.0

alleles may be underrepresented. And some alleles may be eliminated. Chance may continue to change the gene pool for many generations until the population is again large enough for sampling errors to be insignificant.

The analogy in **Figure 13.24** illustrates why genetic drift due to a drastic reduction in population size is called the **bottleneck effect**.

▼ **Figure 13.24 The bottleneck effect.** The colored marbles in this analogy represent three alleles in an imaginary population. Shaking just a few of the marbles through the bottleneck is like an environmental disaster that drastically reduces the size of a population. Compared with the predisaster population, purple marbles are overrepresented in the new population, green marbles are underrepresented, and orange marbles are absent—all by chance. Similarly, a population that passes through a "bottleneck" event emerges with reduced variability.

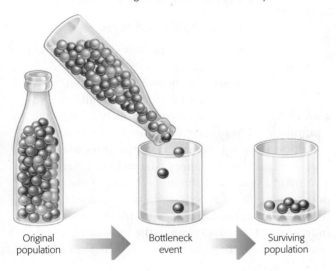

| Original population | Bottleneck event | Surviving population |

Passing through a "bottleneck"—a severe reduction in population size—decreases the overall genetic variability in a population because at least some alleles are likely to be lost from the gene pool. An important application of this concept is the potential loss of individual variation, and hence adaptability, in drastically reduced populations of endangered species, such as the cheetah **(Figure 13.25)**. The fastest of all running animals, cheetahs are magnificent cats that were once widespread in Africa and Asia. Like many African mammals, the number of cheetahs fell dramatically during the last ice age (around 10,000 years ago). At that time, the species suffered a severe bottleneck, possibly as a result of disease, human hunting, and periodic droughts. Evidence suggests that the South African cheetah population suffered a second bottleneck during the 1800s, when farmers hunted the animals to near extinction. Today, only a few small populations of cheetahs exist in the wild. Genetic variability in these populations is very low compared with populations of other mammals. This lack of variability, coupled with an increasing loss of habitat, makes the cheetah's future precarious. The cheetahs remaining in Africa are being crowded into nature preserves and parks as human demands on the land increase. Along with crowding comes an increased potential for the spread of disease. With so little variability, the cheetah has a reduced capacity to adapt to such environmental challenges. Captive breeding programs are already under way and may be required for the cheetah's long-term survival. However, the species' pre-bottleneck genetic diversity can never be restored. ☑

☑ **CHECKPOINT**

Would you expect modern cheetahs to have more genetic variation or less genetic variation than cheetahs did 1,000 years ago?

Answer: less, because the bottleneck effect reduces genetic variability

▼ **Figure 13.25 Implications of the bottleneck effect in conservation biology.** Some endangered species, such as the cheetah, have low genetic variability. As a result, they are less adaptable to environmental changes, such as new diseases, than are species with a greater resource of genetic variation.

The Founder Effect

Genetic drift is also likely when a few individuals colonize an isolated island, lake, or other new habitat. The smaller the colony, the less its genetic makeup will match the gene pool of the larger population from which the colonists emigrated. If the colony succeeds, random drift will continue to affect the frequency of alleles until the population is large enough for genetic drift to be minimal.

The type of genetic drift resulting from the establishment of a small, new population whose gene pool differs from that of the parent population is called the **founder effect**. The founder effect undoubtedly contributed to the evolutionary divergence of the finches and other organisms that arrived as strays on the remote Galápagos Islands that Darwin visited.

The founder effect also explains the relatively high frequency of certain inherited disorders in some small human populations. For example, in 1814, a group of 15 people founded a British colony on Tristan da Cunha, a cluster of small islands in the middle of the Atlantic Ocean **(Figure 13.26)**. Apparently, one of the colonists carried a recessive allele for retinitis pigmentosa, a progressive form of blindness. Of the 240 descendants who still lived on the islands in the 1960s, 4 had retinitis pigmentosa, and 9 others were heterozygous carriers with one copy of the recessive allele. The frequency of the retinitis pigmentosa allele was ten times higher on Tristan da Cunha than in the British population from which the founders came.

▼ **Figure 13.26 Residents of Tristan da Cunha in the early 1900s.** The island of Tristan da Cunha, located in the middle of the Atlantic Ocean, is listed in *Guinness World Records* as the world's most remote inhabited island. The genetic isolation of the island's residents resulted in a disproportionately high rate of hereditary blindness.

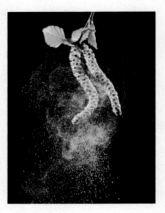

▲ **Figure 13.27 Gene flow.** The pollen of some plants can be carried by the wind for hundreds of miles, allowing gene flow to occur between distant populations.

Gene Flow

Another source of evolutionary change, separate from genetic drift, is **gene flow**, where a population may gain or lose alleles when fertile individuals move into or out of the population or when gametes (such as plant pollen) are transferred between populations **(Figure 13.27)**. Gene flow tends to reduce differences between populations. For example, because people today move more freely about the world than in the past, gene flow has become an important agent of evolutionary change in previously isolated human populations. ☑

Natural Selection: A Closer Look

Genetic drift, gene flow, and even mutation can cause evolution, but they do not necessarily lead to adaptation. In fact, random drift, migrant alleles, and shot-in-the-dark mutations are unlikely to improve a population's fit to its environment. Of all causes of evolution, only natural selection promotes adaptation. And such evolutionary adaptation, remember, is a blend of chance and sorting—chance in the random generation of genetic variability, and sorting in the unequal reproductive success among the varying individuals. Darwin explained the basics of natural selection. But it took the modern synthesis to fill in the details.

Hardy-Weinberg equilibrium, which defines a nonevolving population, demands that all individuals in a population be equal in their ability to survive and reproduce. This condition is probably never actually met. On average, individuals that function best in the environment leave the most offspring and therefore have a disproportionate impact on the gene pool. When farmers began spraying their fields with pesticides, resistant pests started outreproducing other members of the insect populations. The spraying increased the frequency of alleles for pesticide resistance in the insect gene pools. As a result, evolution by natural selection occurred.

Evolutionary Fitness

The phrases "struggle for existence" and "survival of the fittest" are misleading if we take them to mean direct competitive contests between individuals. There *are* animal species in which individuals lock horns or otherwise

▲ **Figure 13.28 Relative fitness of some flowering plants depends in part on competition in attracting pollinators.**

fight one another to determine mating privilege. But the causes of reproductive success are generally more subtle. Plants in a wildflower population, for example, may differ in reproductive success because some attract more pollinators—perhaps the result of slight differences in flower color, shape, or fragrance (**Figure 13.28**). A frog may produce more eggs than her neighbors because she is better at catching insects for food. These examples point to an evolutionary definition of **relative fitness**: the contribution an individual makes to the gene pool of the next generation *relative to* the contributions of other individuals. Thus, the fittest individuals in the context of evolution are those that produce the largest numbers of viable, fertile offspring and thus pass on the most alleles to the next generation. ✔

Three General Outcomes of Natural Selection

Imagine a population of mice with individuals ranging in fur color from very light to very dark gray. If we graph the number of mice in each color category, we get a bell-shaped curve like the one shown at the top of **Figure 13.29**. If natural selection favors certain fur-color phenotypes over others, the population of mice will change over the generations. Three general outcomes are possible, depending on which phenotypes are favored. These three modes of natural selection are called directional selection, disruptive selection, and stabilizing selection.

Directional selection shifts the overall makeup of a population by selecting in favor of one extreme phenotype—the darkest mice, for example (**Figure 13.29a**). Directional selection is most common when the local environment changes or when organisms migrate to a new

environment. An actual example is the shift of insect populations toward a greater frequency of pesticide-resistant individuals.

Disruptive selection can lead to a balance between two or more contrasting phenotypes in a population (**Figure 13.29b**). A patchy environment, which favors different phenotypes in different patches, is one situation associated with disruptive selection. The variations seen in the snake population in Figure 13.19 result from disruptive selection.

Stabilizing selection favors intermediate phenotypes (**Figure 13.29c**). It typically occurs in relatively stable environments, where conditions tend to reduce physical variation. This evolutionary conservatism works by selecting against the more extreme phenotypes. For example, stabilizing selection keeps the majority of human birth weights between 3 and 4 kg (approximately 6.5 to 9 pounds). For babies much lighter or heavier than this, infant mortality is greater.

☑ CHECKPOINT

What is the best measure of relative fitness?

Answer: the number of fertile offspring an individual leaves

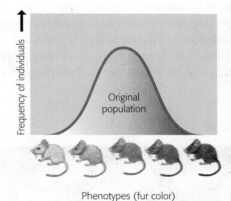

◄ **Figure 13.29 Three possible outcomes for selection working on fur color in imaginary populations of mice.** The large downward arrows symbolize the pressure of natural selection working against certain phenotypes.

Frequency of individuals

Original population

Phenotypes (fur color)

Original population   Evolved population

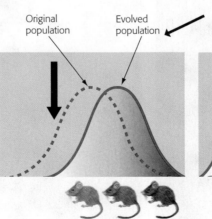

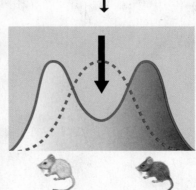

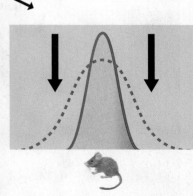

(a) Directional selection shifts the overall makeup of the population by favoring variants at one extreme. In this case, the trend is toward darker color, perhaps because the landscape has been shaded by the growth of trees, making darker mice less noticeable to predators.

(b) Disruptive selection favors variants at opposite extremes over intermediate individuals. Here, the relative frequencies of very light and very dark mice have increased. Perhaps the mice have colonized a patchy habitat where a background of light soil is studded with dark rocks.

(c) Stabilizing selection culls extreme variants from the population, in this case eliminating individuals that are unusually light or dark. The trend is toward reduced phenotypic variation and increased frequency of an intermediate phenotype.

Of the three selection modes, stabilizing selection prevails most of the time, resisting change in well-adapted populations. Evolutionary spurts occur when a population is stressed by a change in the environment or by migration to a new place. When challenged with a new set of environmental problems, a population either adapts through natural selection or dies off in that locale. The fossil record tells us that the population's extinction is the most common result. Those populations that do survive crises may change enough to be designated new species. (You'll learn more about this in Chapter 14.) ☑

Sexual Selection

Darwin was the first to explore the implications of **sexual selection**, a form of natural selection in which individuals with certain traits are more likely than other individuals to obtain mates. The males and females of an animal species obviously have different reproductive organs. But they may also have secondary sexual traits, noticeable differences not directly associated with reproduction or survival. This distinction in appearance, called **sexual dimorphism**, is often manifested in a size difference. Among male vertebrates, sexual dimorphism may also be evident in adornment, such as manes on lions, antlers on deer, or colorful plumage on peacocks and other birds (**Figure 13.30a**).

In some species, secondary sex structures may be used to compete with members of the same sex (usually males) for mates. Contests may involve physical combat, but are more often ritualized displays (**Figure 13.30b**). Such selection is common in species where the winner acquires a harem of mates—an obvious boost to that male's evolutionary fitness.

In a more common type of sexual selection, individuals of one sex (usually females) are choosy in selecting their mates. Males with the largest or most colorful adornments are often the most attractive to females. The extraordinary feathers of a peacock's tail are an example of this sort of "choose me!" statement. Every time a female chooses a mate based on a certain appearance or behavior, she perpetuates the alleles that caused her to make that choice and allows a male with that particular phenotype to perpetuate his alleles.

What is the advantage to females of being choosy? One hypothesis is that females prefer male traits that are correlated with "good" alleles. In several bird species, research has shown that traits preferred by females, such as bright beaks or long tails, are related to overall male health. This link—between alleles and health—brings us to this chapter's final example of evolution in action.

☑ CHECKPOINT

The thickness of fur in a bear population increases over several generations as the climate in the region becomes colder. This is an example of which type of selection: directional, disruptive, or stabilizing?

Answer: directional

▼ **Figure 13.30 Sexual dimorphism.**

(a) Sexual dimorphism in a finch species. Among vertebrates, including this pair of green-winged Pytilia (native to Africa), males (right) are usually the showier sex.

(b) Competing for mates. Male Spanish ibex engage in nonlethal combat for the right to mate with females.

An Evolutionary Response to Malaria

Like all organisms, our own species has been shaped by natural selection. We can't observe human evolutionary change over a short time span, however. While organisms such as mosquitoes produce new generations of offspring in a matter of weeks, our generation span is measured in decades. Nevertheless, we can see the results of past natural selection in present-day humans.

Malaria, the devastating disease you learned about in the Biology and Society section of this chapter, must have had a powerful selective effect on human populations. The disease first emerged as a serious threat to people in Africa just 10,000 years ago, long after humans had established populations around the globe. Consequently, we expect to see an evolutionary response in populations from malarial regions, but not elsewhere.

What kind of adaptation could protect people against malaria? After the protozoan invades the human body, it enters red blood cells, using the hemoglobin (a protein that transports oxygen) within to fuel its own reproduction. Thus, a mutation that denies the parasite this critical resource would be beneficial. One such mutation results in an abnormal form of hemoglobin, called sickle hemoglobin, which distorts the shape of red blood cells (Figure 13.31). An individual who has one copy of this allele (a heterozygote) is relatively resistant to malaria. It is not an ideal solution—possessing two sickle-cell alleles is usually fatal, and even heterozygotes may have health problems under certain circumstances. But then, adaptations are often compromises.

On the map in Figure 13.31, the dotted areas indicate locations with a high incidence of malaria—environments where the sickle-cell allele should be favored. As you can see, the highest allele frequencies are indeed found in those regions. People whose ancestors came from malarial regions are also more likely to carry the sickle-cell allele. For example, about one in ten black Americans has a single copy of the allele, a vestige of west African roots. Other malarial regions also have a high frequency of the sickle-cell allele. And sickle hemoglobin is not the only evolutionary response to malaria. Several other mutations are thought to protect against the disease as well. One example is a group of inherited blood disorders called thalassemias, which are common in people from malarial regions of Africa, Asia, and the Mediterranean.

This example of the intersection of evolutionary biology and health science is a reminder that biology is the foundation of all medicine. And evolution is the foundation of all biology.

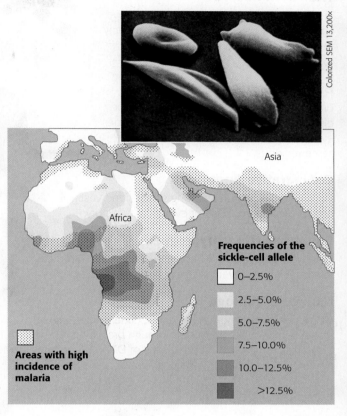

▼ Figure 13.31 **Mapping malaria and the sickle-cell allele.** The inset shows sickled red blood cells.

Colorized SEM 13,200x

Asia

Africa

Frequencies of the sickle-cell allele

- 0–2.5%
- 2.5–5.0%
- 5.0–7.5%
- 7.5–10.0%
- 10.0–12.5%
- >12.5%

Areas with high incidence of malaria

Chapter Review

SUMMARY OF KEY CONCEPTS

(MB) Go to **www.masteringbiology.com** for homework assignments, practice quizzes, Pearson eText, and more.

Charles Darwin and *The Origin of Species*

Charles Darwin established the ideas of evolution and natural selection in his 1859 publication *On the Origin of Species by Means of Natural Selection*.

Darwin's Cultural and Scientific Context

During his around-the-world voyage on the *Beagle*, Darwin observed adaptations of organisms that inhabited diverse environments. In particular,

Darwin was struck by the geographic distribution of organisms on the Galápagos Islands, off the South American coast. When Darwin considered his observations in light of new evidence for a very old Earth that changed slowly, he arrived at ideas that were at odds with the long-held notion of a young Earth populated by unchanging species.

Descent with Modification

Darwin made two proposals in *The Origin of Species*: (1) Existing species descended from ancestral species, and (2) natural selection is the mechanism of evolution.

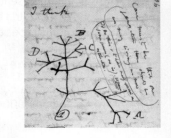

Evidence of Evolution

The Fossil Record

The fossil record shows that organisms have appeared in a historical sequence, and many fossils link ancestral species with those living today.

Biogeography

Biogeography, the study of the geographic distribution of species, suggests that species evolved from ancestors that inhabited the same region.

Comparative Anatomy

Homologous structures among species and vestigial organs provide evidence of evolutionary history.

Comparative Embryology

Closely related species often have similar stages in their embryonic development.

Molecular Biology

All species share a common genetic code, suggesting that all forms of life are related through branching evolution from the earliest organisms. Comparisons of DNA and proteins provide evidence of evolutionary relationships.

Natural Selection

Darwin's Theory of Natural Selection

Individuals best suited for a particular environment are more likely to survive and reproduce than less fit individuals.

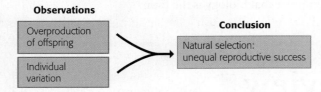

Observations

Overproduction of offspring

Individual variation

Conclusion

Natural selection: unequal reproductive success

Natural Selection in Action

Natural selection can be observed in the evolution of pesticide-resistant insects, drug-resistant microbes, and horned lizards, among many other organisms.

Evolutionary Trees

An evolutionary tree represents a succession of related species, with the most recent at the tips of the branches. Each branch point represents a common ancestor of all species that radiate from it.

The Modern Synthesis: Darwinism Meets Genetics

The modern synthesis fused genetics (Mendelism) and evolutionary biology (Darwinism) in the mid-1900s.

Populations as the Units of Evolution

A population, members of the same species living in the same time and place, is the smallest biological unit that can evolve. Population genetics emphasizes the extensive genetic variation within populations and tracks the genetic makeup of populations over time.

Genetic Variation in Populations

Polygenic ("many genes") inheritance produces traits that vary continuously, whereas traits determined by one genetic locus may be present in two or more distinct forms. Mutation and sexual reproduction produce genetic variation. Individual mutations have little short-term effect on a large gene pool, but in the long term, mutation is the source of genetic variation.

Analyzing Gene Pools

A gene pool consists of all the alleles in all the individuals making up a population. The Hardy-Weinberg formula can be used to calculate the frequencies of genotypes in a gene pool from the frequencies of alleles, and vice versa:

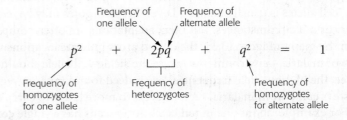

Frequency of one allele   Frequency of alternate allele

$$p^2 + 2pq + q^2 = 1$$

Frequency of homozygotes for one allele   Frequency of heterozygotes   Frequency of homozygotes for alternate allele

Population Genetics and Health Science

The Hardy-Weinberg formula can be used to estimate the frequency of a harmful allele, which is useful information for public health programs dealing with genetic diseases.

Microevolution as Change in a Gene Pool

Microevolution is generation-to-generation change in allele frequencies in a population.

Mechanisms of Evolution

Genetic Drift

Genetic drift is a change in the gene pool of a small population due to chance. A bottleneck event (a drastic reduction in population size) and the founder effect (occurring in a new population started by a few individuals) are two situations leading to genetic drift.

Gene Flow

A population may gain or lose alleles by gene flow, which is genetic exchange with another population.

Natural Selection: A Closer Look

Of all causes of evolution, only natural selection promotes evolutionary adaptations. Relative fitness is the contribution an individual makes to the gene pool of the next generation relative to the contributions of other individuals. The outcome of natural selection may be directional, disruptive, or stabilizing.

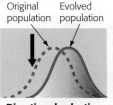 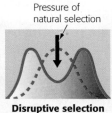 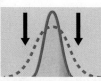

Original population   Evolved population   Pressure of natural selection

Directional selection   **Disruptive selection**   **Stabilizing selection**

Sexual Selection

Secondary sexual traits (such as sex-specific plumage or behaviors) can promote sexual selection, a type of natural selection in which mating preferences are determined by inherited traits.

SELF-QUIZ

1. Which of the following is a true statement about Charles Darwin?
   a. He was the first to discover that living things can change, or evolve.
   b. He based his theory on the inheritance of acquired traits.
   c. He proposed natural selection as the mechanism of evolution.
   d. He was the first to realize that Earth is more than 6,000 years old.

2. How did the insights of Lyell and other geologists influence Darwin's thinking about evolution?

3. In a population with two alleles for a particular genetic locus, B and b, the allele frequency of B is 0.7. If this population is in Hardy-Weinberg equilibrium, the frequency of heterozygotes is _____, the frequency of homozygous dominants is _____, and the frequency of homozygous recessives is _____.

4. Define fitness from an evolutionary perspective.

5. The processes of _____ and _____ generate variation, and _____ produces adaptation to the environment.
   a. sexual reproduction . . . natural selection . . . mutation
   b. mutation . . . sexual reproduction . . . genetic drift
   c. genetic drift . . . mutation . . . sexual reproduction
   d. mutation . . . natural selection . . . sexual reproduction
   e. mutation . . . sexual reproduction . . . natural selection

6. As a mechanism of evolution, natural selection can be most closely equated with
   a. random mating.
   b. genetic drift.
   c. unequal reproductive success.
   d. gene flow.

7. Compare and contrast how the bottleneck effect and the founder effect can lead to genetic drift.

8. In a particular bird species, individuals with average-sized wings survive severe storms more successfully than other birds in the same population with longer or shorter wings. Of the three general outcomes of natural selection (directional, disruptive, or stabilizing), this example illustrates _____.

9. Which of the following statements is (are) true about a population in Hardy-Weinberg equilibrium? (More than one may be true.)
   a. The population is quite small.
   b. The population is not evolving.
   c. Gene flow between the population and surrounding populations does not occur.
   d. Natural selection is not occurring.

10. What environmental factor accounts for the relatively high frequency of the sickle-cell allele in tropical Africa?

Answers to these questions can be found in Appendix: Self-Quiz Answers.

THE PROCESS OF SCIENCE

11. A population of snails has recently become established in a new region. The snails are preyed on by birds that break the snails open on rocks, eat the soft bodies, and leave the shells. The snails occur in both striped and unstriped forms. In one area, researchers counted both live snails and broken shells. Their data are summarized here:

	Striped Shells	Unstriped Shells
Number of live snails	264	296
Number of broken snail shells	486	377
Total	750	673

Based on these data, which snail form is more subject to predation by birds? Predict how the frequencies of striped and unstriped individuals might change over the generations.

12. Imagine that the presence or absence of stripes on the snails from the previous question is determined by a single gene locus, with the dominant allele (S) producing striped snails and the recessive allele (s) producing unstriped snails. Combining the data from both the living snails and broken shells, calculate the following: the frequency of the dominant allele, the frequency of the recessive allele, and the number of heterozygotes in the observed groups.

BIOLOGY AND SOCIETY

13. To what extent are people in a technological society exempt from natural selection? Explain your answer.

14 How Biological Diversity Evolves

A critically endangered species. Hunting and habitat loss have brought this black and white ruffed lemur, found only in the rain forests of eastern Madagascar, to the edge of extinction.

Mass Extinctions BIOLOGY AND SOCIETY

The Sixth Mass Extinction

The fossil record reveals that the evolutionary history of life on Earth has been episodic, with long, relatively stable periods punctuated by brief, cataclysmic ones. During these upheavals, new species formed and others died out in great numbers.

Extinctions are inevitable in a changing world, but the fossil record reveals a few instances of great change, times when the majority of life on Earth—between 50% and 90% of living species—suddenly died out, vanishing forever. Scientists have documented five such mass extinctions during the last 540 million years. Today, human activities are modifying the global environment to such an extent that many species are disappearing at an alarming rate. In the past 400 years—a very short time on a geologic scale—more than 1,000 species are known to have become extinct. Scientists estimate that this is 100 to 1,000 times the extinction rate seen in most of the fossil record.

Are we witnessing a sixth mass extinction? In an extensive analysis published in *Nature* in 2011, researchers compared data from the fossil record of the "big five" mass extinctions with data from the modern era. The good news is that the current loss of biodiversity does not yet qualify as a mass extinction. The bad news is that we're teetering on the brink. The loss of species that are now at critical risk of extinction—like the black-and-white ruffed lemur pictured on the facing page—would push our planet into a period of mass extinction. When the researchers include species that are endangered or threatened (lower categories of risk) in their calculations, the picture becomes very grim indeed. In contrast to the ancient mass extinctions, which unfolded over hundreds of thousands of years, a human-driven sixth mass extinction could be completed in just a few centuries. And, as with prior mass extinctions, life on Earth may take millions of years to recover.

The fossil record also shows a creative side to the destruction. Mass extinctions can pave the way for the evolution of many diverse species from a common ancestor. Accordingly, we'll begin this chapter by discussing the birth of new species and then examine how biologists trace the evolution of biological diversity and classify living organisms.

The Origin of Species

Natural selection, a microevolutionary mechanism, explains the striking ways in which organisms are suited to their environment. But what accounts for the tremendous diversity of life, the millions of species that have existed during Earth's history? This question intrigued Darwin, who referred to it in his diary as "that mystery of mysteries—the first appearance of new beings on this Earth."

When, as a young man, Darwin visited the Galápagos Islands (see Figure 13.4), he realized that he was visiting a place of origins. Though the volcanic islands were geologically young, they were already home to many plants and animals known nowhere else in the world. Among these unique inhabitants were giant tortoises **(Figure 14.1)**, for which the Galápagos are named (*galápago* means "tortoise" in Spanish), marine iguanas (see Figure 13.5), and numerous species of small birds called finches (see Figure 13.12). Surely, Darwin thought, not all of these species could have been among the original colonists. Some of them must have evolved later on, the myriad descendants of the original colonists, modified by natural selection from those original ancestors.

In the century and a half since the publication of Darwin's *On the Origin of Species by Means of Natural Selection*, new discoveries and technological advances—especially in molecular biology—have given scientists a wealth of new information about the evolution of life on Earth. For example, researchers have explained the

What would Darwin learn from modern evolutionary biology?

genetic patterns underlying the homology of vertebrate limbs and the varied beak shapes of Galápagos finches. Tens of thousands more fossil discoveries have been cataloged, including many of the transitional (intermediate) forms predicted by Darwin. In a fascinating convergence of old and new techniques, researchers have even been able to investigate the genetic material of certain fossils, including our ancient relatives, the Neanderthals (see Figure 17.42). New dating methods have confirmed that Earth is billions of years old, much older than even the most radical geologists of Darwin's time proposed. As you'll learn in this chapter, these dating methods have also enabled researchers to determine the ages of fossils and rocks, providing valuable insight into evolutionary relationships between groups of organisms. In addition, our enhanced understanding of geologic processes, such as the changing positions of continents, explains some of the geographic distributions of organisms and fossils that puzzled Darwin and his contemporaries.

In this chapter, you'll learn how evolution has woven the rich tapestry of life, beginning with **speciation**, the process in which one species splits into two or more species. Other topics include the origin of evolutionary novelty, such as the wings and feathers of birds and the large brains of humans, and the impact of mass extinctions, which clear the way for new adaptive explosions, such as the diversification of mammals following the disappearance of most of the dinosaurs.

▼ **Figure 14.1 Galápagos tortoises.** The size and shape of the shell vary between populations found on different islands.

What Is a Species?

Species is a Latin word meaning "kind" or "appearance." Indeed, we learn to distinguish between the kinds of plants and animals—between dogs and cats, for example, or between roses and dandelions—from differences in their appearance. Although the basic idea of species as distinct life-forms seems intuitive, devising a more formal definition is not so easy.

One way of defining a species (and the main definition used in this book) is the **biological species concept (Figure 14.2)**. It defines a **species** as a group of populations whose members have the potential to interbreed with one another in nature to produce fertile offspring (offspring that can reproduce). Geography and culture may conspire to keep a Manhattan businesswoman and a Mongolian dairyman apart. But if the two did meet and mate, they could have viable babies that develop into fertile adults because all humans belong to the same species. In contrast, humans and chimpanzees, despite having a shared evolutionary history, are distinct species because they do not interbreed.

We cannot apply the biological species concept to all situations. For example, basing the definition of species on reproductive compatibility excludes organisms that only reproduce asexually (producing offspring from a single parent). Fossils aren't doing any sexual reproduction either, so they cannot be evaluated by the biological species concept.

In response to such challenges, biologists have developed several other ways to define species. For example, most of the 1.8 million species named to date have been classified based on measurable physical traits. Another approach identifies species in terms of the ecological resources they use, focusing on unique adaptations to particular roles in a biological community. Yet another classification scheme defines a species as the smallest group of individuals sharing a common ancestor and forming one branch on the tree of life.

Each species concept is useful, depending on the situation and the questions being asked. The biological species concept, however, is particularly useful when focusing on how discrete groups of organisms may arise and be maintained by reproductive isolation. Next, we'll look at reproductive isolation more closely because it is such an essential factor in the evolution of so many species. ☑

☑ CHECKPOINT

According to the biological species concept, what defines a species?

Answer: the ability of its members to interbreed with one another and produce fertile offspring in a natural setting

▼ **Figure 14.2** **The biological species concept is based on reproductive compatibility rather than physical similarity.**

Similarity between different species. The eastern meadowlark (left) and the western meadowlark (right) are very similar in appearance, but they are separate species and do not interbreed.

Diversity within one species. Humans, as diverse in appearance as we are, belong to a single species (*Homo sapiens*) and can interbreed.

Reproductive Barriers between Species

Clearly, a fly will not mate with a frog or a fern. But what prevents closely related species from interbreeding? What, for example, maintains the species boundary between the eastern meadowlark and the western meadowlark (shown in Figure 14.2)? Their geographic ranges overlap in the Great Plains region, and they are so similar that only expert birders can tell them apart. And yet, these two bird species do not interbreed.

A **reproductive barrier** is anything that prevents individuals of closely related species from interbreeding. Let's examine the different kinds of reproductive barriers that isolate the gene pools of species **(Figure 14.3)**. We can classify reproductive barriers as either prezygotic or post-zygotic, depending on whether they block interbreeding before or after the formation of zygotes (fertilized eggs).

Prezygotic barriers prevent mating or fertilization between species **(Figure 14.4)**. The barrier may be time based (temporal isolation). For example, western spotted skunks breed in the fall, but the eastern species breeds in late winter. Temporal isolation keeps the species from mating even where they coexist on the Great Plains. In other cases, species live in the same region but not in the same habitats (habitat isolation). For example, one species of North American garter snake lives mainly in water, while a closely related species lives on land. Traits that enable individuals to recognize potential mates, such as a particular odor, coloration, or courtship ritual, can also function as reproductive barriers (behavioral isolation). In many bird species, for example, courtship behavior is so elaborate that individuals

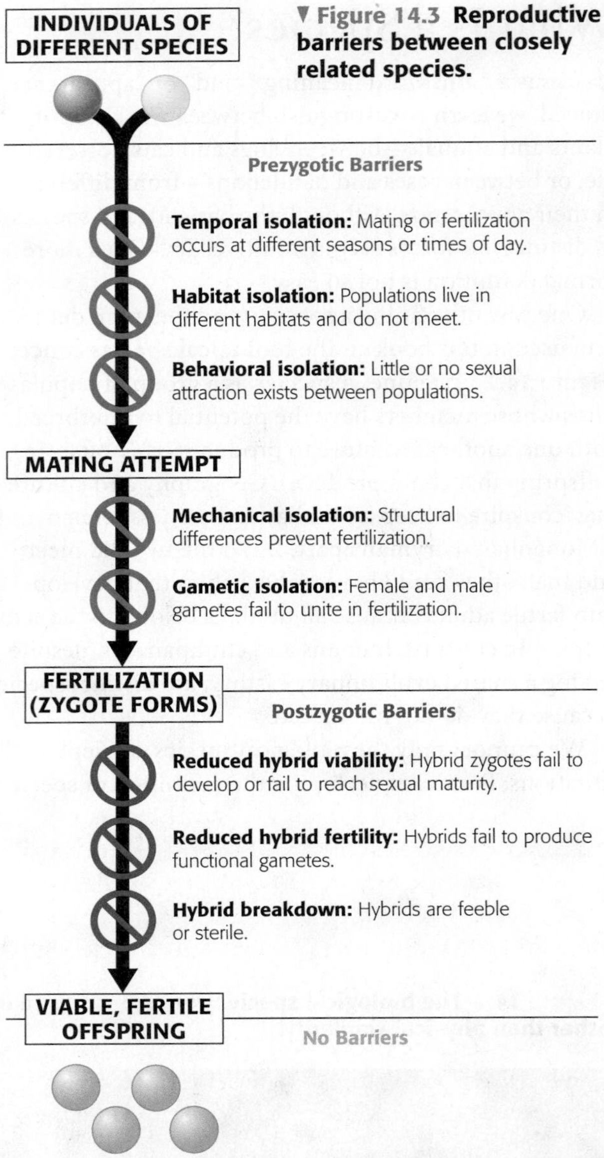

▼ Figure 14.3 Reproductive barriers between closely related species.

INDIVIDUALS OF DIFFERENT SPECIES

Prezygotic Barriers

Temporal isolation: Mating or fertilization occurs at different seasons or times of day.

Habitat isolation: Populations live in different habitats and do not meet.

Behavioral isolation: Little or no sexual attraction exists between populations.

MATING ATTEMPT

Mechanical isolation: Structural differences prevent fertilization.

Gametic isolation: Female and male gametes fail to unite in fertilization.

FERTILIZATION (ZYGOTE FORMS)

Postzygotic Barriers

Reduced hybrid viability: Hybrid zygotes fail to develop or fail to reach sexual maturity.

Reduced hybrid fertility: Hybrids fail to produce functional gametes.

Hybrid breakdown: Hybrids are feeble or sterile.

VIABLE, FERTILE OFFSPRING

No Barriers

► Figure 14.4 Prezygotic barriers. Prezygotic barriers prevent mating or fertilization.

PREZYGOTIC BARRIERS

Temporal Isolation

These two closely related species of skunks mate at different times of the year.

Habitat Isolation

These two closely related species of garter snakes do not mate because one lives in the water while the other lives on land.

are unlikely to mistake a bird of a different species as one of their kind. In still other cases, the egg-producing and sperm-producing structures of different species are anatomically incompatible (mechanical isolation). For example, the two closely related species of snails in Figure 14.4 cannot join their male and female sex organs because their shells spiral in opposite directions. In still other cases, gametes (eggs and sperm) of different species are incompatible, preventing fertilization (gametic isolation). Gametic isolation is very important when fertilization is external. Male and female sea urchins of many species release eggs and sperm into the sea, but fertilization occurs only if species-specific molecules on the surface of egg and sperm attach to each other.

Postzygotic barriers operate if interspecies mating actually occurs and results in hybrid zygotes **(Figure 14.5)**. (In this context, "hybrid" means that the egg comes from one species and the sperm from another species.) In some cases, hybrid offspring die before reaching reproductive maturity (reduced hybrid viability). For example, although certain closely related salamander species will hybridize, the offspring fail to develop normally because of genetic incompatibilities between the two species. In other cases of hybridization, offspring may become vigorous adults, but are infertile (reduced hybrid fertility). A mule, for example, is the hybrid offspring of a female horse and a male donkey. Mules are sterile—they cannot successfully breed with each other. Thus, horses and donkeys remain distinct species. In other cases, the first-generation hybrids are viable and fertile, but when these hybrids mate with one another or with either parent species, the offspring are feeble or sterile (hybrid breakdown). For example, different species of cotton

plants can produce fertile hybrids, but the offspring of the hybrids do not survive.

In summary, reproductive barriers form the boundaries around closely related species. In most cases, it is not a single reproductive barrier but some combination of two or more that keeps species isolated. Next, we examine situations that make reproductive isolation and speciation possible. ✔

▼ **Figure 14.5 Postzygotic barriers.** Postzygotic barriers prevent development of fertile adults.

POSTZYGOTIC BARRIERS

Reduced Hybrid Viability	Reduced Hybrid Fertility	Hybrid Breakdown

Some species of salamander can hybridize, but their offspring do not develop fully or, like this one, are frail and will not survive long enough to reproduce.

Horse

Donkey

Mule

The hybrid offspring of a horse and a donkey is a mule, which is sterile.

The rice hybrids at the left and right are fertile, but plants of the next generation (middle) are small and sterile.

Behavioral Isolation	Mechanical Isolation	Gametic Isolation

Galápagos blue-footed boobies mate only after a specific ritual of high stepping that advertises a mate's bright blue feet.

Because these snails' shells spiral in opposite directions, their genital openings (indicated by arrows) cannot be aligned and mating cannot occur.

Gametes of these red and purple urchins are unable to fuse because proteins on the surface of the eggs and sperm cannot bind to one another.

Mechanisms of Speciation

A key event in the origin of many species occurs when a population is somehow cut off from other populations of the parent species. With its gene pool isolated, the splinter population can follow its own evolutionary course. Changes in its allele frequencies caused by genetic drift and natural selection will not be diluted by alleles entering from other populations (gene flow). Such reproductive isolation can result from two general scenarios: allopatric ("different country") speciation and sympatric ("same country") speciation **(Figure 14.6)**. In **allopatric speciation**, the initial block to gene flow is a geographic barrier that physically isolates the splinter population. In contrast, **sympatric speciation** is the origin of a new species without geographic isolation. The splinter population becomes reproductively isolated even though it is right in the midst of the parent population.

How does a new species get started?

Allopatric Speciation

Several geologic processes can fragment a population into two or more isolated populations. A mountain range may emerge and gradually split a population of organisms that can inhabit only lowlands. A land bridge, such as the Isthmus of Panama, may form and separate the marine life on either side. A large lake may subside and form several smaller lakes, with their populations now isolated. Allopatric speciation can also occur if individuals colonize a new, geographically remote area and become isolated from the parent population. An example is the speciation that occurred on the Galápagos Islands following initial colonization by immigrant organisms after volcanoes built the islands.

How formidable must a geographic barrier be to keep allopatric populations apart? The answer depends partly on the ability of the organisms to move about. Birds, mountain lions, and coyotes can cross mountain ranges, rivers, and canyons. Nor do such barriers hinder the windblown pollen of pine trees or the spread of seeds carried by animals capable of crossing the barrier. In contrast, small rodents may find a deep canyon or a wide river an impassable barrier **(Figure 14.7)**.

Allopatric speciation is more common for a small, isolated population because it is more likely than a large population to have its gene pool changed substantially by both genetic drift and natural selection. For example, in less than 2 million years, the few foreign animals and plants that first colonized the Galápagos Islands gave rise to all the species now found there. But for each

▼ Figure 14.6 **Two modes of speciation.**

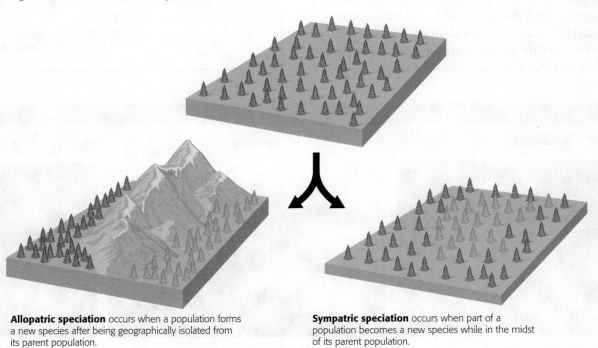

Allopatric speciation occurs when a population forms a new species after being geographically isolated from its parent population.

Sympatric speciation occurs when part of a population becomes a new species while in the midst of its parent population.

Ammospermophilus harrisii

Ammospermophilus leucurus

▲ **Figure 14.7 Allopatric speciation of antelope squirrels on opposite rims of the Grand Canyon.** Harris's antelope squirrel (*Ammospermophilus harrisii*) is found on the south rim of the Grand Canyon. Just a few miles away on the north rim is the closely related white-tailed antelope squirrel (*Ammospermophilus leucurus*). Birds and other organisms that can disperse easily across the canyon have not diverged into different species on opposite rims.

small, isolated population that becomes a new species, many more simply perish in their new environment. Life on the frontier is harsh, and most pioneer populations become extinct.

Even if a small, isolated population survives, it does not necessarily evolve into a new species. The population may adapt to its local environment and begin to look very different from the ancestral population, but

that doesn't necessarily make it a new species. Speciation occurs with the evolution of reproductive barriers between the isolated population and its parent population. In other words, if speciation occurs during geographic separation, the new species cannot breed with its ancestral population, even if the two populations should come back into contact at some later time **(Figure 14.8).** ☑

▶ **Figure 14.8 Has speciation occurred during geographic isolation?** In this diagram, the arrows track populations over time. The mountain symbolizes a period of geographic isolation. The two parts of the figure show the two possibilities when populations come back together after a long period of separation.

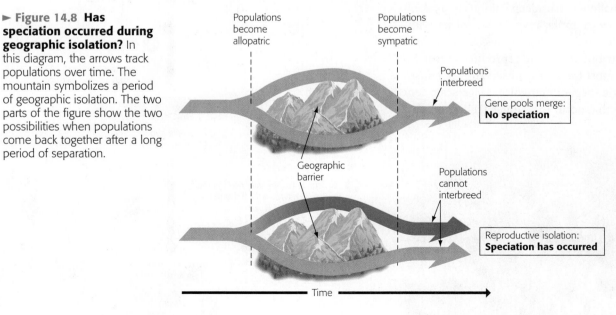

Populations become allopatric

Populations become sympatric

Populations interbreed

Gene pools merge:
No speciation

Geographic barrier

Populations cannot interbreed

Reproductive isolation:
Speciation has occurred

Time

Sympatric Speciation

Sympatric speciation occurs in populations that live in the same geographic area. How can a subpopulation become reproductively isolated while in the midst of its parent population?

An accident during cell division that results in an extra set of chromosomes is a common route to sympatric speciation in plants. A new species that evolves this way has polyploid cells, meaning that each cell has more than two sets of chromosomes. The new species cannot produce fertile hybrids with its parent species. This is a good example of sympatric speciation because reproductive isolation has occurred in a single generation, without geographic isolation.

Polyploids do not always come from a single parent species. In fact, most polyploid species arise from the hybridization of two parent species. This mechanism of sympatric speciation accounts for many of the plant species we grow for food, including oats, potatoes, bananas, peanuts, barley, plums, apples, sugarcane, coffee, and wheat. Wheat makes a good case study. The most widely cultivated plant in the world, what we call wheat is actually represented by 20 species. People began domesticating wheat from wild grasses at least 11,000 years ago in the Middle East. **Figure 14.9** traces the evolutionary path from that first cultivated wheat species to bread wheat, the most important wheat species today.

Biologists have also identified cases in which subpopulations appear to be in the process of sympatric speciation. In some cases, subgroups of a population evolve adaptations for exploiting food sources in different habitats, such as the shallow versus deep habitats of a lake. In another example, a type of sexual selection in which females choose mates based on color has contributed to rapid reproductive isolation. But the most frequently observed mechanism of sympatric speciation involves large-scale genetic changes that occur in a single generation. ☑

☑ CHECKPOINT

What mechanism accounts for most observed instances of sympatric speciation? Why might this be the case?

Answer: Accidents of cell division that result in polyploidy produces "instant" reproductive isolation.

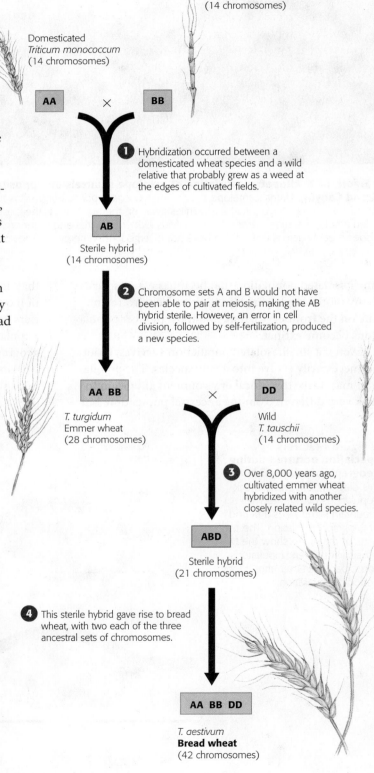

▼ **Figure 14.9 The evolution of wheat.** The uppercase letters in this diagram represent not alleles but sets of chromosomes that can be traced in the evolution of wheat, or *Triticum*. Interestingly, the AABB hybrid, emmer wheat (*Triticum turgidum*), is still grown widely in Eurasia and western North America and is used mainly for making pasta.

Wild *Triticum*
(14 chromosomes)

Domesticated
Triticum monococcum
(14 chromosomes)

AA × **BB**

1 Hybridization occurred between a domesticated wheat species and a wild relative that probably grew as a weed at the edges of cultivated fields.

AB

Sterile hybrid
(14 chromosomes)

2 Chromosome sets A and B would not have been able to pair at meiosis, making the AB hybrid sterile. However, an error in cell division, followed by self-fertilization, produced a new species.

AA BB × **DD**

T. turgidum
Emmer wheat
(28 chromosomes)

Wild
T. tauschii
(14 chromosomes)

3 Over 8,000 years ago, cultivated emmer wheat hybridized with another closely related wild species.

ABD

Sterile hybrid
(21 chromosomes)

4 This sterile hybrid gave rise to bread wheat, with two each of the three ancestral sets of chromosomes.

AA BB DD

T. aestivum
Bread wheat
(42 chromosomes)

What Is the Pace of Speciation?

Biologists continue to make field observations and devise experiments to study evolution in progress. However, much of the evidence of evolution comes from the fossil record, the chronicle of extinct organisms engraved in layers of rock over millions of years of geologic time. What does this record say about the process of speciation?

Many fossil species appear suddenly in a layer of rock, persist essentially unchanged through several layers (strata), and then disappear as abruptly as they appeared. The term **punctuated equilibria** describes these long periods of little apparent change (equilibria) interrupted (punctuated) by relatively brief periods of rapid change.

Figure 14.10 shows two patterns for the pace of speciation that scientists have observed in the fossil record: the punctuated pattern and the gradual pattern. In a punctuated pattern of speciation, there are no transitional stages in the lineages. The new species change little, if at all, once they appear. In the gradual pattern of speciation, differences evolve little by little in populations as the species become adapted to their local environments, and new species (represented by the two butterflies at the far right) evolve slowly from the ancestral population. That is, big changes (speciations) occur by the steady accumulation of many small changes.

What do punctuated and gradual patterns tell us about how long it takes new species to form? Suppose that a species survived for 5 million years, but most of the changes in its body features occurred during the first 50,000 years of its existence, just 1% of its overall history. Time periods this short often cannot be distinguished in fossil strata. Thus, based on its fossils, the species would seem to have appeared suddenly and continued with little change before becoming extinct. Although such a species may have originated more slowly than its fossils suggest, a punctuated pattern indicates that speciation occurred relatively rapidly. For species whose fossils show much more gradual change, we cannot tell exactly when a new biological species formed. It is likely that speciation in such groups occurred relatively slowly, perhaps taking millions of years.

How often do species evolve abruptly and then remain essentially unchanged for most of their existence? Rapid speciation is certainly known to occur. As we saw earlier, sudden speciation can occur by polyploidy in plants and even occasionally in a few animals. And genetic drift and natural selection can significantly alter the gene pool of a small, isolated population in just a few hundred generations.

Regardless of the pace of speciation, as species diverge, differences accumulate and become more pronounced, eventually leading to the formation of new groups of organisms that differ greatly from their ancestors. Furthermore, as one group produces many new species, another group may lose species to extinction. The cumulative effects of multiple speciation and extinction events have helped to shape the dramatic changes documented in the fossil record. This type of evolution is the subject of the next section. ☑

How long does it take for a new species to evolve?

▼ **Figure 14.10 Two patterns for the pace of speciation.**

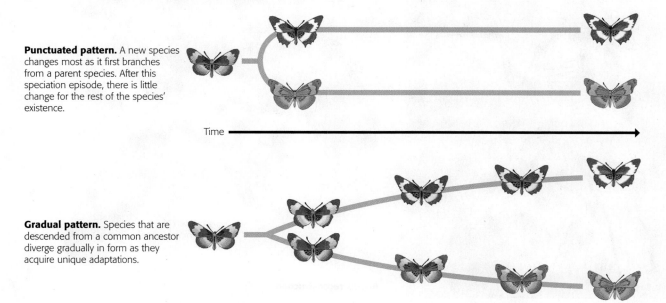

Punctuated pattern. A new species changes most as it first branches from a parent species. After this speciation episode, there is little change for the rest of the species' existence.

Time →

Gradual pattern. Species that are descended from a common ancestor diverge gradually in form as they acquire unique adaptations.

☑ CHECKPOINT

How does the punctuated pattern account for the relative rarity of transitional fossils linking newer species to older ones?

Answer: In the punctuated pattern, the time required for speciation in most cases is relatively short compared with the overall duration of the species' existence. Thus, on the vast geologic time scale of the fossil record, the transition of one species to another seems abrupt.

The Evolution of Biological Novelty

The two squirrels in Figure 14.7 are different species, but they are very similar animals that live very much the same way. How do we account for the dramatic differences between dissimilar groups—squirrels and elephants, for example? How do we explain such evolutionary products as flight in birds and braininess in humans? In the rest of this chapter, you'll learn about **macroevolution**, evolutionary change above the species level, including the origin of evolutionary novelty and new groups of species, and the impact of mass extinctions on the diversity of life and its subsequent recovery.

Adaptation of Old Structures for New Functions

Birds are derived from a lineage of earthbound reptiles (Figure 14.11). How could flying animals evolve from flightless ancestors? More generally, how do major novelties—new biological structures and functions—evolve? One way evolutionary novelty arises is when structures that originally played one role gradually acquire a different role. Structures that evolve in one context but become adapted for another function are called exaptations. This term suggests that a structure can become adapted to alternative functions; it does not mean that a structure somehow evolves in anticipation of future use. New features can arise gradually via intermediate stages, each functioning in the organism's current context.

Exaptation can account for the evolution of novel structures. Consider the evolution of birds from a dinosaur ancestor. Birds have lightweight skeletons with honeycombed bones, a feature found in their dinosaur ancestors. Since the fossil record clearly indicates that light bones predated flight, they must have had some function on the ground. The ancestors of birds were small, agile, bipedal dinosaurs that would have benefited from a light frame. Moreover, a winglike form with feathers would have increased the surface area of the forelimbs. These enlarged forelimbs were adapted for flight after functioning in some other capacity, such as thermal regulation, courtship displays, or camouflage (roles that wings still play today). The first flights may have been only glides or extended hops as the animal pursued prey or fled from a predator. As flight evolved, animals with better-adapted feathers and wings would have had a selective advantage.

According to Harvard zoologist Karel Liem, "Evolution is like modifying a machine while it's running." The concept that biological novelties can evolve by the remodeling of old structures is in the Darwinian tradition of large changes being an accumulation of many small changes that result from natural selection. ☑

▶ **Figure 14.11 An extinct bird.** Called *Archaeopteryx* ("ancient wing"), this animal lived near tropical lagoons in central Europe about 150 million years ago. Like birds today, it had flight feathers, but otherwise it was more like some small bipedal (two-legged) dinosaurs of its era. *Archaeopteryx* probably relied mainly on gliding from trees. Despite its feathers, *Archaeopteryx* is not considered an ancestor of today's birds. Instead, it probably represents an extinct side branch of the bird lineage.

Fossil

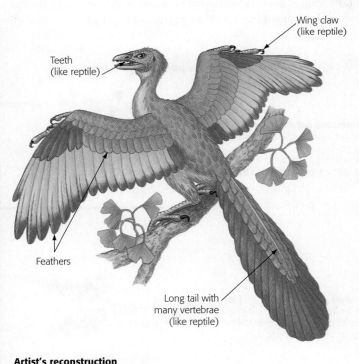

Teeth
(like reptile)

Wing claw
(like reptile)

Feathers

Long tail with
many vertebrae
(like reptile)

Artist's reconstruction

Evo-Devo: Development and Evolutionary Novelty

Gradual evolutionary remodeling, such as the accumulation of flight adaptations in birds, probably involves a large number of genetic changes in populations. In other cases of macroevolution, just a few genetic changes can become magnified into major structural differences between organisms. Such cases are of particular interest to scientists working in the field of **evo-devo**, or evolutionary developmental biology, which studies the evolution of developmental processes in multicellular organisms.

Homeotic genes, the master control genes, program development by controlling the rate, timing, and spatial pattern of changes in an organism's form as it develops from a zygote into an adult. These genes determine such basic developmental events as where a pair of wings or legs will appear on a fruit fly (see Figure 11.9). A subtle change in the developmental program can have profound effects. Accordingly, changes in the number, nucleotide sequence, and regulation of homeotic genes have led to the huge diversity in body forms. Many striking evolutionary transformations are the result of a change in the rate or timing of developmental events. Consider, for example, the evolution of tetrapods (animals with backbones and four limbs) from fishes. The location within a developing limb where certain homeotic genes are expressed is initially the same in both fishes and tetrapods. A second region of expression in the developing tetrapod limb, however, produces the extra skeletal elements that develop into foot bones. Thus, changes in the expression of these genes appear to have led to the evolution of walking legs from the paired fins of fishes.

How could feet evolve from fins?

Duplications of homeotic genes probably facilitated the origin of new body shapes in animals, including the evolution of vertebrates (animals with backbones) from invertebrates (animals without backbones). For example, consider the homeotic genes of a fruit fly (an invertebrate) and a mouse (a vertebrate). A fruit fly has a single cluster of homeotic genes that direct the development of major body parts, whereas a mouse has four clusters of these genes (see Figure 11.10). Two duplications of these gene clusters appear to have occurred in the evolution of vertebrates from invertebrates. Mutations in these duplicated genes may then have led to the origin of novel vertebrate characteristics. For instance, some genes may have taken on new roles, such as directing the development of a backbone, jaws, and limbs.

The animal in **Figure 14.12**, a salamander called an axolotl, illustrates a developmental phenomenon called **paedomorphosis**, which is the retention into adulthood of features that were solely juvenile in ancestral species. The axolotl grows to full size and reproduces without losing its external gills, a juvenile feature in most species of salamanders.

Paedomorphosis has also been important in human evolution. Humans and chimpanzees are even more alike in body form as fetuses than they are as adults. In the fetuses of both species, the skulls are rounded and the jaws are small, making the face rather flat (**Figure 14.13**). As development proceeds, uneven bone growth makes the chimpanzee skull sharply angular, with heavy browridges and massive jaws. The adult chimpanzee has much greater jaw strength than we have, and its teeth are proportionately larger. In contrast, the adult human has a skull with decidedly rounded, more fetus-like contours. Put another way, our skull is paedomorphic; it retains fetal features even after we are mature. Our large skull is one of our most distinctive features. Our large, complex brain, which fills that bulbous skull, is another. The human brain is proportionately larger than the chimpanzee brain because growth of the organ is switched off much later in human development. Compared with the brain of a chimpanzee, our brain continues to grow for several more years, which can be interpreted as the prolonging of a juvenile process.

Gills

▲ **Figure 14.12 Paedomorphosis.** The axolotl, a salamander, becomes an adult (shown here) and reproduces while retaining certain tadpole characteristics, including gills.

▼ **Figure 14.13 Comparison of human and chimpanzee skull development.** Starting with fetal skulls that are very similar (left), the differential growth rates of the bones making up the skulls produce adult heads with very different proportions. The grid lines will help you relate the fetal skulls to the adult skulls.

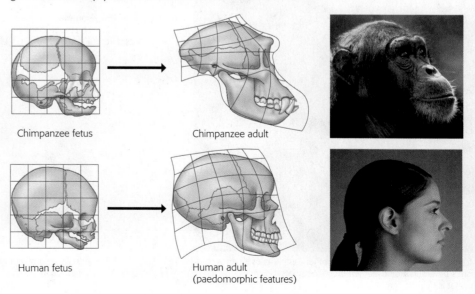

Chimpanzee fetus

Chimpanzee adult

Human fetus

Human adult (paedomorphic features)

Earth History and Macroevolution

Having examined how new species and evolutionary adaptations arise, we are ready to turn our attention to the history of biological diversity. Macroevolution is closely tied to the history of Earth.

Geologic Time and the Fossil Record

The fossil record, the sequence in which fossils appear in rock strata, is an archive of macroevolution. **Figure 14.14** surveys some of the diverse ways that organisms can fossilize. Sedimentary rocks are the richest sources of fossils and provide a record of life on Earth in their strata (see Figure 13.6). The fossils in each stratum of sedimentary rock are a local sample of the organisms that existed at the time the sediment was deposited.

By studying many sites over the past two centuries, geologists have established a **geologic time scale** that divides Earth's history into a sequence of geologic periods. The time line presented in **Table 14.1** is separated into four broad divisions: the Precambrian (a general term for the time before about 540 million years ago), followed by the Paleozoic, Mesozoic, and Cenozoic eras. Each of these divisions represents a distinct age in the history of Earth and its life.

▼ Figure 14.14 **A gallery of fossils.**

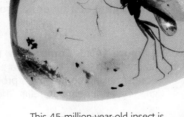

Sedimentary fossils are formed when minerals seep into and replace organic matter. This petrified (stone) tree in Arizona's Petrified Forest National Park is about 190 million years old.

Sedimentary rocks are the richest hunting grounds for paleontologists, scientists who study fossils. This researcher is excavating a fossilized dinosaur skeleton from sandstone in Dinosaur National Monument, located in Utah and Colorado.

This 45-million-year-old insect is embedded in amber (hardened resin from a tree).

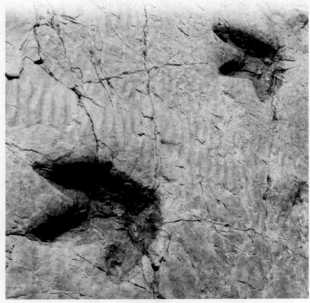

Trace fossils are footprints, burrows, and other remnants of an ancient organism's behavior. A dinosaur left these footprints 120 million years ago in what is now northern Spain.

These tusks belong to a whole 23,000-year-old mammoth, which scientists discovered in Siberian ice in 1999.

Table 14.1   **The Geologic Time Scale**

Geologic Time	Period	Epoch	Age (millions of years ago)	Some Important Events in the History of Life
Cenozoic era	Quaternary	Recent 	0.01	Historical time
		Pleistocene	1.8	Ice ages; humans appear 
	Tertiary	Pliocene	5	Origin of genus *Homo* 
		Miocene	23	Continued speciation of mammals and angiosperms 
		Oligocene	34	Origins of many primate groups, including apes 
		Eocene	56	Angiosperm dominance increases; origins of most living mammalian orders 
		Paleocene	65	Major speciation of mammals, birds, and pollinating insects 
Mesozoic era	Cretaceous		145	Flowering plants (angiosperms) appear; many groups of organisms, including most dinosaur lineages, become extinct at end of period (Cretaceous extinctions) 
	Jurassic		200	Gymnosperms continue as dominant plants; dinosaurs become dominant 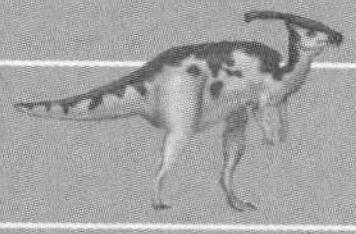
	Triassic		251	Cone-bearing plants (gymnosperms) dominate landscape; speciation of dinosaurs, early mammals, and birds 
Paleozoic era	Permian		299	Extinction of many marine and terrestrial organisms (Permian extinctions); speciation of reptiles; origins of mammal-like reptiles and most living orders of insects 
	Carboniferous		359	Extensive forests of vascular plants; first seed plants; origin of reptiles; amphibians become dominant 
	Devonian		416	Diversification of bony fishes; first amphibians and insects 
	Silurian		444	Early vascular plants dominate land 
	Ordovician		488	Marine algae are abundant; colonization of land by diverse fungi, plants, and animals 
	Cambrian		542	Origin of most living animal phyla (Cambrian explosion) 
Precambrian			600	Diverse algae and soft-bodied invertebrate animals appear 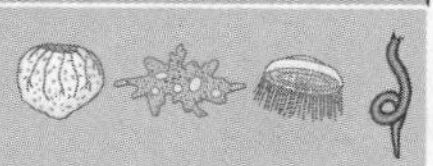
			635	Oldest animal fossils
			2,100	Oldest eukaryotic fossils
			2,700	Oxygen begins accumulating in atmosphere
			3,500	Oldest fossils known (prokaryotes)
			4,600	Approximate time of origin of Earth

Relative Time Span

Cenozoic

Mesozoic

Paleozoic

Pre-cambrian

The boundaries between eras are marked by mass extinctions, when many forms of life disappeared from the fossil record and were replaced by species that diversified from the survivors. For example, most of the animals that lived during the late Precambrian became extinct at the end of that era. The following period, the Cambrian, is characterized by a great diversity of fossilized animals that are absent in rocks of the late Precambrian.

Fossils are reliable chronological records only if we can determine their ages. The record of the rocks reveals only the *relative* ages of fossils and therefore the order in which groups of species evolved. However, the series of sedimentary layers alone does not tell us the

How do scientists know how old fossils are?

absolute ages of the embedded fossils. The rock strata are analogous to the layers of wallpaper you might peel from the walls of a very old house. You could determine the sequence in which the wallpapers had been applied, but not the year that each layer was added. Geologists use a variety of methods to determine the ages of rocks and the fossils they contain. The most common method is **radiometric dating (Figure 14.15)**, which is based on the decay of radioactive isotopes, including isotopes of carbon, potassium, and uranium. (Recall that isotopes are alternative forms of elements; see Table 2.1.) The dates in the geologic time scale in Table 14.1 were established by radiometric dating. ☑

☑ CHECKPOINT

Use Table 14.1 to estimate how long prokaryotes inhabited Earth before eukaryotes evolved.

Answer: about 1,800 million years, or 1.8 billion years

▼ **Figure 14.15 Radiometric dating.** Amounts of radioactive isotopes can be measured by the radiation they emit as they decompose to more stable atoms. Paleontologists use this clocklike decay to date fossils.

Radioactive decay of carbon-14.
Carbon-14 is a radioactive isotope with a half-life of 5,600 years. From the time an organism dies, it takes 5,600 years for half of the radioactive carbon-14 to decay; half of the remainder is present after another 5,600 years; and so on.

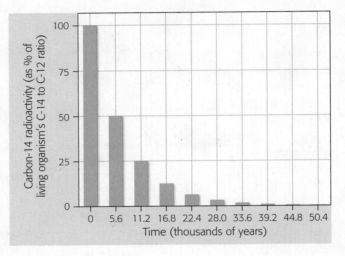

How carbon-14 dating is used to determine the vintage of a fossilized clam shell.

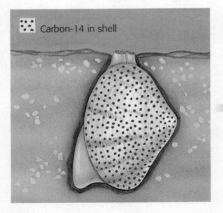

❶ A living organism, in this case a clam, assimilates the different isotopes of each element in proportions determined by their relative abundances in the environment. Carbon-14 is taken up in trace quantities, along with much larger quantities of the more common carbon-12.

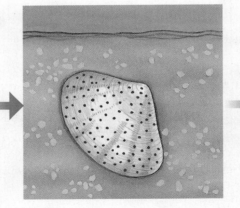

❷ After the clam dies, it is covered with sediment, and its shell eventually becomes consolidated into a layer of rock as the sediment is compressed. From the time the clam dies and ceases to assimilate carbon, the amount of carbon-14 relative to carbon-12 in the fossil declines due to radioactive decay.

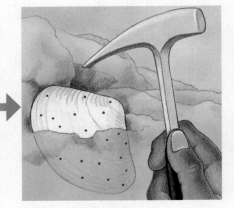

❸ After the clam fossil is found, its age can be determined by measuring the ratio of the two isotopes to learn how many half-life reductions have occurred since it died. For example, if the ratio of carbon-14 to carbon-12 in this fossil clam was found to be 25% of that of a living organism, this fossil would be about 11,200 years old (see graph above).

Plate Tectonics and Macroevolution

The continents are not locked in place. They drift about Earth's surface like passengers on huge, irregularly shaped plates of crust floating on a flexible layer of hot, underlying material called the mantle. When two landmasses are embedded in different plates, their positions relative to each other change. For example, North America and Europe are presently drifting apart at a rate of about 2 cm (about 0.75 inch) per year. Violent geologic activities such as earthquakes, volcanic eruptions, and massive upheavals that build mountains are common in regions where plates collide or scrape past each other (Figure 14.16).

Plate movements rearrange geography constantly, but two chapters in the continuing saga of continental drift had an especially strong influence on life. About 250 million years ago, near the end of the Paleozoic era, plate movements brought all the previously separated landmasses together into a supercontinent called Pangaea, which means "all land" (Figure 14.17). Imagine some of the possible effects on life. Species that had been evolving in isolation came together and competed. As the landmasses joined over millions of years, the total amount of shoreline was reduced. There is also evidence that the ocean basins increased in depth, lowering sea level and draining the shallow coastal seas. Then, as now, most marine species inhabited shallow waters, and the formation of Pangaea destroyed a considerable amount of that habitat. It was probably a long, traumatic period for terrestrial life as well. The continental interior, which was drier and had a more erratic climate than the coastal regions, increased in area substantially when the land came together. Changing ocean currents also undoubtedly affected land life as well as sea life. Thus, the formation of Pangaea had a tremendous environmental impact that reshaped biological diversity by causing extinctions and providing new opportunities for diversification of the survivors.

The second dramatic chapter in the history of continental drift began during the mid-Mesozoic era. Pangaea started to break up, causing geographic isolation of colossal proportions. As the continents drifted apart, each became a separate evolutionary arena as climates changed and the organisms of the different biogeographic realms diverged.

The pattern of continental separations is the solution to many puzzles of biogeography. For example, paleontologists have discovered matching fossils of Mesozoic reptiles in Ghana (West Africa) and Brazil. These two parts of the world, now separated by 3,000 km (1,864 miles) of ocean, were contiguous during the early Mesozoic era. Plate tectonics also explains much about the current distribution of organisms. For example, the mammals of Australia contrast so sharply with those of the rest of the world because the plate on which Australia rests drifted away from other plates early in the evolutionary history of mammals, leaving marsupials free to evolve in isolation on that con- (see Figure 13.8). ✓

✓ **CHECKPOINT**

How many continents did Earth have at the time of Pangaea?

Answer: one

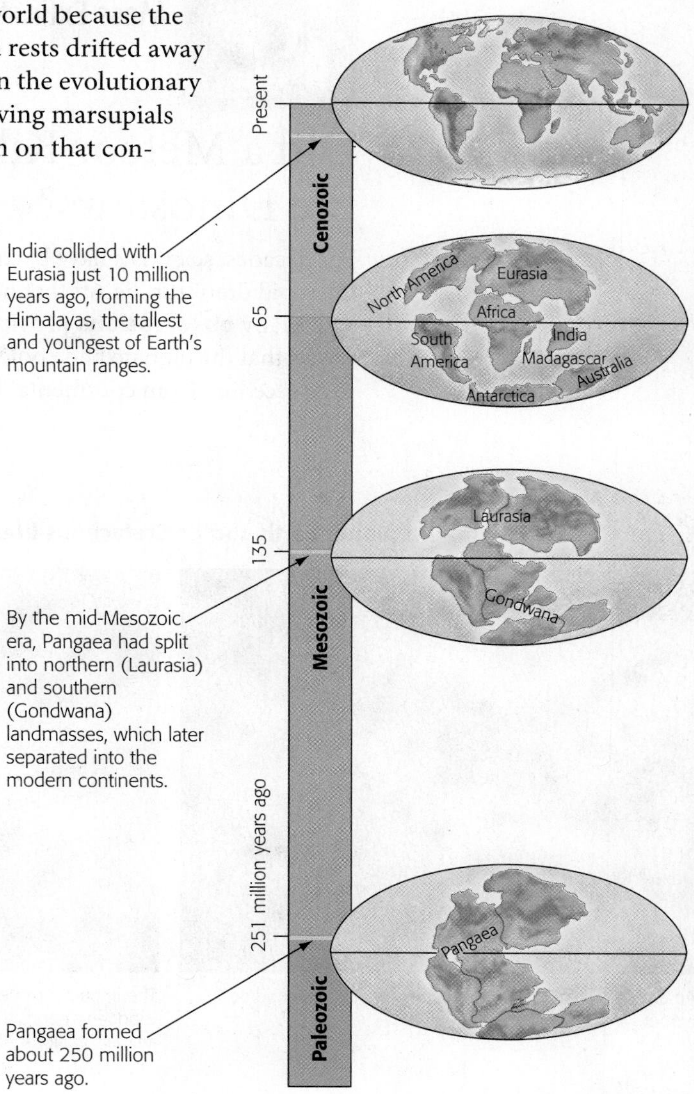

◀ **Figure 14.16 A tsunami caused by an earthquake off the coast of Japan in March 2011.** Japan sits atop four different plates. Frequent earthquakes occur as the plates move and bump against each other.

▶ **Figure 14.17 The history of plate tectonics.** The continents continue to drift, though not at a rate that's likely to cause any motion sickness for their passengers.

India collided with Eurasia just 10 million years ago, forming the Himalayas, the tallest and youngest of Earth's mountain ranges.

By the mid-Mesozoic era, Pangaea had split into northern (Laurasia) and southern (Gondwana) landmasses, which later separated into the modern continents.

Pangaea formed about 250 million years ago.

Present

65

135

251 million years ago

Cenozoic

Mesozoic

Paleozoic

North America · Eurasia · Africa · South America · India · Madagascar · Antarctica · Australia

Laurasia · Gondwana

Pangaea

283

Mass Extinctions and Explosive Diversifications of Life

As discussed in the Biology and Society section, the fossil record reveals that five mass extinctions have occurred over the last 540 million years. In each of these events, 50% or more of Earth's species died out. Of all the mass extinctions, those marking the ends of the Permian and Cretaceous periods have been the most intensively studied.

The Permian mass extinction, at about the time the merging continents formed Pangaea, claimed about 96% of marine species and took a tremendous toll on terrestrial life as well. Equally notable is the mass extinction at the end of the Cretaceous period. For 150 million years prior, dinosaurs dominated Earth's land and air, whereas mammals were few and small, resembling today's rodents. Then, about 65 million years ago, most of the dinosaurs became extinct, leaving behind only the descendants of one lineage, the birds. Remarkably, the massive die-off (which also included half of all other species) occurred in less than 10 million years—a brief period in geologic time.

But there is a flip side to the destruction. Each massive dip in species diversity has been followed by explosive diversification of certain survivors. Extinctions seem to have provided the surviving organisms with new environmental opportunities. For example, mammals existed for at least 75 million years before undergoing an explosive increase in diversity just after the Cretaceous period. Their rise to prominence was undoubtedly associated with the void left by the extinction of the dinosaurs. The world would be a very different place today if many dinosaur lineages had escaped the Cretaceous extinctions or if none of the mammals had survived.

 Mass Extinctions THE PROCESS OF SCIENCE

Did a Meteor Kill the Dinosaurs?

For decades, scientists have been debating the cause of the rapid dinosaur die-off that occurred 65 million years ago. Many **observations** provide clues. The fossil record shows that the climate had cooled and that shallow seas were receding from continental lowlands. It also shows that many plant species died out. Perhaps the most telling evidence was discovered by physicist Luis Alvarez and his geologist son Walter Alvarez, both of the University of California, Berkeley. In 1980, they found that rock deposited around 65 million years ago contains a thin layer of clay rich in iridium, an element very rare on Earth but common in meteors and other extraterrestrial material that occasionally falls to Earth. This discovery led the Alvarez team to ask the following **question**: Is

▼ **Figure 14.18 Trauma for planet Earth and its Cretaceous life.**

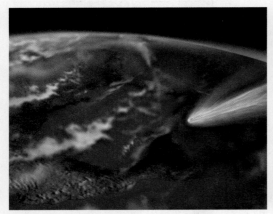

An artist's representation of the impact of an asteroid or comet.

The impact's immediate effect was most likely a cloud of hot vapor and debris that could have killed many of the plants and animals in North America within hours.

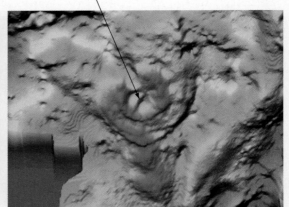

Chicxulub crater

The 65-million-year-old Chicxulub impact crater is located in the Caribbean Sea near the Yucatán Peninsula of Mexico. The horseshoe shape of the crater and the pattern of debris in sedimentary rocks indicate that an asteroid or comet struck at a low angle from the southeast.

the iridium layer the result of fallout from a huge cloud of dust that billowed into the atmosphere when a large meteor or asteroid hit Earth?

The father and son formed the **hypothesis** that the mass extinction 65 million years ago was caused by the impact of an extraterrestrial object. This hypothesis makes a clear **prediction**: A huge impact crater of the right age should be found somewhere on Earth's surface. (This is a good example of using verifiable observations rather than a direct **experiment** to test a hypothesis; see Chapter 1.) In 1981, two petroleum geologists found the **results** predicted by the Alvarezes' hypothesis: the Chicxulub crater, located near Mexico's Yucatán Peninsula in the Caribbean Sea **(Figure 14.18)**. This impact site, about 180 km wide (about 112 miles) and dating from the predicted time, was created when a meteor or asteroid about 10 km in diameter (about 6 miles) slammed into Earth, releasing thousands of times more energy than is stored in the world's combined stockpile of nuclear weapons. Such a cloud could have blocked sunlight and disturbed climate severely for months, perhaps killing off many plant species and, later, the animals that depended on those plants for food.

Debate continues about whether this impact alone caused the dinosaurs to die out or whether other factors—such as continental movements or volcanic activity—also contributed. Most scientists agree, however, that the collision that created the Chicxulub crater could indeed have been a major factor in global climatic change and mass extinctions.

Classifying the Diversity of Life

Systematics is a discipline of biology that focuses on classifying organisms and determining their evolutionary relationships. Systematics includes **taxonomy**, which is the identification, naming, and classification of species.

Some Basics of Taxonomy

Assigning scientific names to species is an essential part of systematics. Common names such as monkey, fly, and pea may work well in everyday communication, but they can be ambiguous because there are many species of each of these organisms. And some common names are misleading. For example, consider the following so-called "fishes": jellyfish (a cnidarian), crayfish (a crustacean), and silverfish (an insect).

Using an agreed-upon formal naming system eases communication among scientists, allows researchers to unambiguously identify an organism, and makes it easier to recognize when a new species is discovered. The formal taxonomic system used by biologists today dates back to Carolus Linnaeus (1707–1778), a Swedish physician and botanist (plant specialist). Linnaeus's system has two main characteristics: a two-part name for each species and a hierarchical classification of species into broader groups of organisms.

Naming Species

Linnaeus's system assigns to each species a two-part Latinized name, or **binomial**. The first part of a binomial is the **genus** (plural, *genera*) to which the species belongs. The second part of a binomial is unique for each species within the genus. The two parts must be used together to name a species. For example, the scientific name for the leopard is *Panthera pardus*. Notice that the first letter of the genus is capitalized and that the whole binomial is italicized and given a Latin ending. For example, a newly discovered spider in the genus *Aptostichus* was named *Aptostichus stephencolberti*, after the television personality. The scientific name of our own species, *Homo sapiens*, which Linnaeus assigned in a show of optimism, means "wise man."

Hierarchical Classification

In addition to naming species, a major objective of systematics is to group species into an ordered hierarchy of categories. The first step of such a hierarchical classification is built into the binomial. We group species that are closely related into the same genus. For example, the leopard (*Panthera pardus*) belongs to a genus that also contains three other cats: the lion (*Panthera leo*), the tiger (*Panthera tigris*), and the jaguar (*Panthera onca*) **(Figure 14.19)**. Grouping species is natural for us, at least in concept. We might lump together several trees we recognize as oaks and distinguish them from several other species of trees we call maples. Indeed, oaks and maples belong to separate genera. Biology's taxonomic scheme formalizes our tendency to group related objects as a way of structuring our view of the world.

▼ Figure 14.19 **The four species within the genus *Panthera*.**

Leopard (*Panthera pardus*)

Tiger (*Panthera tigris*)

Lion (*Panthera leo*)

Jaguar (*Panthera onca*)

► **Figure 14.20 Hierarchical classification.** Taxonomy classifies species—the least inclusive groups—into increasingly broad categories. *Panthera pardus* is one of four species (yellow boxes) in the genus *Panthera*; *Panthera* is one of 18 genera (orange boxes) in the family Felidae, and so on.

Leopard (*Panthera pardus*)

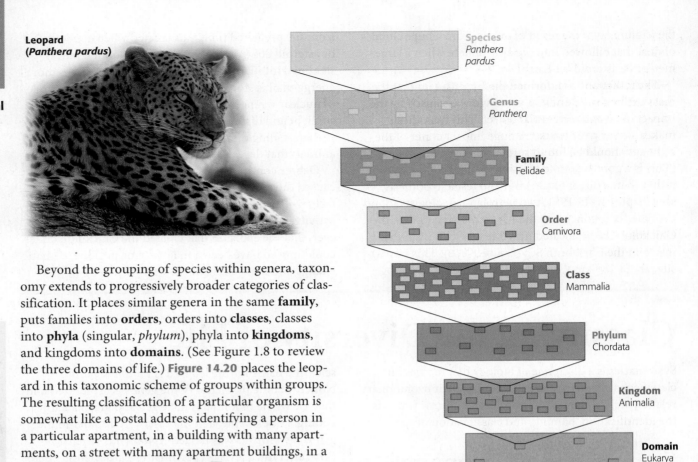

Species
Panthera pardus

Genus
Panthera

Family
Felidae

Order
Carnivora

Class
Mammalia

Phylum
Chordata

Kingdom
Animalia

Domain
Eukarya

Beyond the grouping of species within genera, taxonomy extends to progressively broader categories of classification. It places similar genera in the same **family**, puts families into **orders**, orders into **classes**, classes into **phyla** (singular, *phylum*), phyla into **kingdoms**, and kingdoms into **domains**. (See Figure 1.8 to review the three domains of life.) **Figure 14.20** places the leopard in this taxonomic scheme of groups within groups. The resulting classification of a particular organism is somewhat like a postal address identifying a person in a particular apartment, in a building with many apartments, on a street with many apartment buildings, in a city with many streets, and so on. ☑

Classification and Phylogeny

Ever since Darwin, systematics has had a goal beyond simple organization: to have classification reflect evolutionary relationships. In other words, how an organism is named and classified should reflect its place within the evolutionary tree of life. Biologists use **phylogenetic trees** to depict hypotheses about the evolutionary history of species. These branching diagrams reflect the hierarchical classification of groups nested within more inclusive groups. The tree in **Figure 14.21** shows the classification of some carnivores and their probable evolutionary relationships. Note that each branch point represents the divergence of two lineages from a common ancestor.

Sorting Homology from Analogy
Homologous structures in different species may vary in form and function but exhibit fundamental similarities because they evolved from the same structure in a common ancestor. Among the vertebrates, for instance, the whale forelimb is adapted for steering in

▼ **Figure 14.21 The relationship of classification and phylogeny for some members of the order Carnivora.** The hierarchical classification is reflected in the finer and finer branching of the phylogenetic tree. Each branch point in the tree represents an ancestor common to species to the right of that branch point.

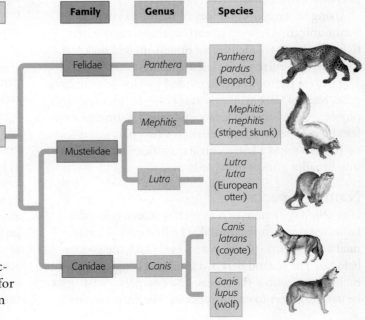

Order	Family	Genus	Species
Carnivora	Felidae	*Panthera*	*Panthera pardus* (leopard)
	Mustelidae	*Mephitis*	*Mephitis mephitis* (striped skunk)
		Lutra	*Lutra lutra* (European otter)
	Canidae	*Canis*	*Canis latrans* (coyote)
			Canis lupus (wolf)

the water, whereas the bat wing is adapted for flight. Nonetheless, there are many basic similarities in the bones supporting these two structures (see Figure 13.9). Thus, homologous structures are one of the best sources of information for phylogenetic relationships. The greater the number of homologous structures between two species, the more closely the species are related.

There are pitfalls in the search for homology: Not all likeness is inherited from a common ancestor. Species from different evolutionary branches may have certain structures that are superficially similar if natural selection has shaped analogous adaptations. This is called **convergent evolution**. Similarity due to convergence is called **analogy**, not homology. For example, the wings of insects and those of birds are analogous flight equipment: They evolved independently and are built from entirely different structures.

To develop phylogenetic trees and classify organisms according to evolutionary history, we must use only homologous similarities. This guideline is generally straightforward, but there can be complications. Adaptation can obscure homologies, and convergence can create misleading similarities. Comparing the embryonic development of two species can often reveal homology that is not apparent in the mature structures (for example, see Figure 13.10).

There is another clue to distinguishing homology from analogy: The more complex two similar structures are, the less likely it is they evolved independently. For example, compare the skulls of a human and a chimpanzee (see Figure 14.13). Although each is a fusion of many bones, they match almost perfectly, bone for bone. It is highly improbable that such complex structures matching in so many details could have separate origins. Most likely, the genes required to build these skulls were inherited from a common ancestor. ☑

How can we tell whether similar structures evolved independently or from a common ancestor?

Molecular Biology as a Tool in Systematics

If homology reflects common ancestry, then comparing the genes and gene products (proteins) of organisms gets right to the heart of their evolutionary relationships. Sequences of nucleotides in DNA are inherited, and they program corresponding sequences of amino acids in proteins. At the molecular level, the evolutionary divergence of species parallels the accumulation of differences in their genomes. The more recently two species have branched from a common ancestor, the more similar their DNA and amino acid sequences should be.

Today, the amino acid sequences for many proteins and the nucleotide sequences for a rapidly increasing number of genomes are in databases that are available on the Internet (see Table 12.1). These databases have

fostered a boom in systematics as researchers use them to compare the hereditary information of different species in search of homology at its most basic level.

Molecular systematics provides a new way to test hypotheses about the phylogeny of species. The strongest support for any such hypothesis is agreement between molecular data and other means of tracing phylogeny, such as evaluating anatomical homology and analyzing the fossil record. And some fossils are preserved in such a way that DNA fragments can be extracted for comparison with living organisms (Figure 14.22).

The Cladistic Revolution

Systematics entered a vigorous new era in the 1960s. Just as molecular methods became readily available for comparing species, computer technology that could crunch a wealth of data helped usher in a new approach to systematics called cladistics.

In cladistics, organisms are grouped by common ancestry. A **clade** (from the Greek word for "branch") consists of an ancestral species and all its evolutionary descendants—a distinct branch in the tree of life. Thus, identifying clades makes it possible to construct classification schemes that reflect the branching pattern of evolution.

Cladistics is based on the Darwinian concept of "descent with modification from a common ancestor"—species have some characteristics in common with their ancestors, but they also differ from them. To identify clades, scientists compare an ingroup with an outgroup (Figure 14.23). The ingroup (for example, the three mammals in Figure 14.23) is the group of species that is actually being analyzed. The outgroup (in Figure 14.23, the iguana, representing reptiles) is a species or group of species known to have diverged before the

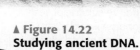

▲ **Figure 14.22**
Studying ancient DNA. Some sedimentary fossils, such as this 40-million-year-old leaf, retain DNA and other organic material that scientists can analyze.

☑ CHECKPOINT

Our forearms and a bat's wings are derived from the same ancestral prototype; thus, they are _____. In contrast, the wings of a bat and the wings of a bee are derived from totally unrelated structures; thus, they are _____.

Answer: homologous; analogous

► **Figure 14.23**
A simplified example of cladistics.

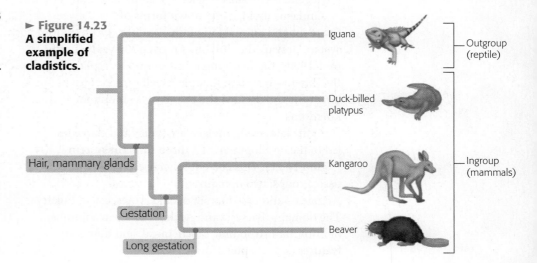

Iguana — Outgroup (reptile)

Duck-billed platypus

Kangaroo — Ingroup (mammals)

Beaver

Hair, mammary glands

Gestation

Long gestation

lineage that contains the groups being studied. By comparing members of the ingroup with each other and with the outgroup, we can determine what characteristics distinguish the ingroup from the outgroup. All the mammals in the ingroup have hair and mammary glands. These were present in the ancestral mammal, but not in the outgroup. But gestation, the carrying of offspring in the uterus within the female parent, is absent from the duck-billed platypus (which lays eggs with a shell). From this absence we might infer that the duck-billed platypus represents an early branch point in the mammalian clade. Proceeding in this manner, we can construct a phylogenetic tree. Each branch represents the divergence of two groups from a common ancestor, with the emergence of a lineage possessing one or more new features. The sequence of branching represents the order in which they evolved and when groups last shared a common ancestor. In other words, cladistics focuses on the changes that define the branch points in evolution.

Cladistics has become the most widely used method in systematics. This approach clarifies evolutionary relationships that were not always apparent in other taxonomic classifications. For instance, biologists traditionally placed birds and reptiles in separate classes of vertebrates (class Aves and class Reptilia, respectively). This classification, however, is inconsistent with

cladistics. An inventory of homologies indicates that birds and crocodiles make up one clade, and lizards and snakes form another. If we go back as far as the ancestor that crocodiles share with lizards and snakes to make up a clade, then the class Reptilia must also include birds. The tree in **Figure 14.24** is thus more consistent with cladistics than with traditional classifications. ☑

▼ **Figure 14.24 How cladistics is shaking phylogenetic trees.** Strict application of cladistics sometimes produces phylogenetic trees that conflict with classical taxonomy.

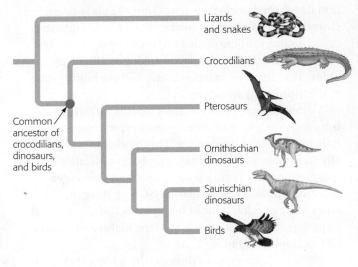

Classification: A Work in Progress

Phylogenetic trees are hypotheses about evolutionary history. Like all hypotheses, they are revised (or in some cases rejected) based on new evidence. Molecular systematics and cladistics are combining to remodel phylogenetic trees and challenge traditional classifications.

Linnaeus divided all known forms of life between the plant and animal kingdoms, and the two-kingdom system prevailed in biology for over 200 years. In the mid-1900s, the two-kingdom system was replaced by a five-kingdom system that placed all prokaryotes in one kingdom and divided the eukaryotes among four other kingdoms.

In the late 1900s, molecular studies and cladistics led to the development of a **three-domain system** (**Figure 14.25**). This current scheme recognizes three basic groups: two domains of prokaryotes—Bacteria and Archaea—and one domain of eukaryotes, called Eukarya. The domains Bacteria and Archaea differ in a number of important structural, biochemical, and functional features (see Chapter 15).

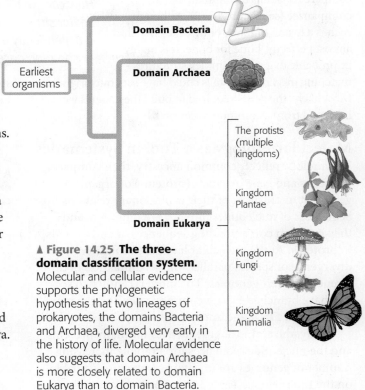

▲ **Figure 14.25 The three-domain classification system.** Molecular and cellular evidence supports the phylogenetic hypothesis that two lineages of prokaryotes, the domains Bacteria and Archaea, diverged very early in the history of life. Molecular evidence also suggests that domain Archaea is more closely related to domain Eukarya than to domain Bacteria.

The domain Eukarya is currently divided into kingdoms, but the exact number of kingdoms is still under debate. Biologists generally agree on the kingdoms Plantae, Fungi, and Animalia. These kingdoms consist of multicellular eukaryotes that differ in structure, development, and modes of nutrition. Plants make their own food by photosynthesis. Fungi live by decomposing the remains of other organisms and absorbing small organic molecules. Most animals live by ingesting food and digesting it within their bodies.

The remaining eukaryotes, the protists, include all those that do not fit the definition of plant, fungus, or animal—effectively, a taxonomic grab bag. Most protists are unicellular (amoebas, for example). But the protists also include certain large, multicellular organisms that are believed to be direct descendants of unicellular protists. For example, many biologists classify the seaweeds as protists because they are more closely related to some single-celled algae than they are to true plants.

It is important to understand that classifying Earth's diverse species is a work in progress as we learn more about organisms and their evolution. Charles Darwin envisioned the goals of modern systematics when he wrote in *The Origin of Species*, "Our classifications will come to be, as far as they can be so made, genealogies." ☑

☑ **CHECKPOINT**
What lines of evidence caused biologists to develop the three-domain system of classification?

Answer: molecular studies and cladistics

Mass Extinctions EVOLUTION CONNECTION

Rise of the Mammals

In this chapter, you've read about mass extinctions and their effects on the evolution of life on Earth. In the fossil record, each mass extinction was followed by a period of evolutionary change. Many new species arose as survivors became adapted to occupy new habitats or fill community roles vacated by extinctions.

For example, fossil evidence indicates that the number of mammal species increased dramatically after the extinction of most of the dinosaurs around 65 million years ago **(Figure 14.26)**. Although mammals originated 180 million years ago, fossils older than 65 million years indicate that they were mostly small and not very diverse. Early mammals may have been eaten or outcompeted by the larger and more diverse dinosaurs. With the disappearance of most of the dinosaurs, mammals expanded greatly in both diversity and size, filling the ecological roles once occupied by dinosaurs. Had it not been for the dinosaur extinction, mammals may never have expanded their territories and become the predominant land animals. Therefore, we humans may owe our existence to the demise of older species. Through the process of evolution by natural selection, this pattern of death and renewal is repeated throughout the history of life on Earth.

▼ Figure 14.26 **The increase in mammalian species after the extinction of dinosaurs.** Although mammals originated nearly 150 million years ago, they did not begin to widely diverge until after the demise of the dinosaurs.

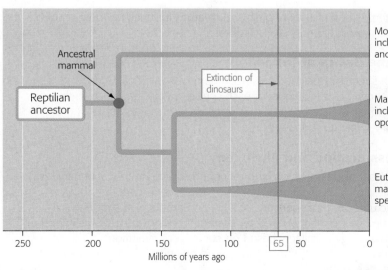
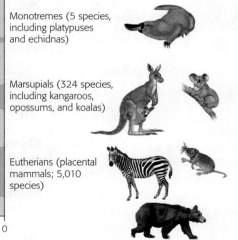

Ancestral mammal
Extinction of dinosaurs
Reptilian ancestor
Monotremes (5 species, including platypuses and echidnas)
Marsupials (324 species, including kangaroos, opossums, and koalas)
Eutherians (placental mammals; 5,010 species)

250   200   150   100   65   50   0
Millions of years ago

American black bear

Chapter Review

SUMMARY OF KEY CONCEPTS

 Go to **www.masteringbiology.com** for homework assignments, practice quizzes, Pearson eText, and more.

The Origin of Species

What Is a Species?

The diversity of life evolved through speciation, the process in which one species splits into two or more species. According to the biological species concept, a species is a group of populations whose members have the potential to interbreed in nature to produce fertile offspring. The biological species concept is just one of several possible ways to define species.

Reproductive Barriers between Species

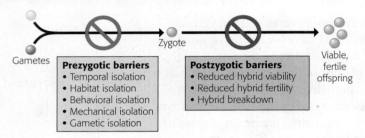

Gametes
Zygote
Viable, fertile offspring

Prezygotic barriers
• Temporal isolation
• Habitat isolation
• Behavioral isolation
• Mechanical isolation
• Gametic isolation

Postzygotic barriers
• Reduced hybrid viability
• Reduced hybrid fertility
• Hybrid breakdown

Mechanisms of Speciation

When the gene pool of a population is severed from other gene pools of the parent species, the splinter population can follow its own evolutionary course.

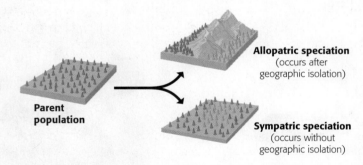

Parent population

Allopatric speciation
(occurs after geographic isolation)

Sympatric speciation
(occurs without geographic isolation)

Hybridization leading to polyploids is a common mechanism of sympatric speciation in plants.

What Is the Pace of Speciation?

In the punctuated equilibria pattern, the time required for speciation is relatively short compared with the overall duration of the species' existence. This pattern accounts for the relative rarity of transitional fossils linking newer species to older ones.

The Evolution of Biological Novelty

Macroevolution refers to evolutionary change above the species level, including the origin of evolutionary novelty and new groups of species and the impact of mass extinctions on the diversity of life and its subsequent recovery.

Adaptation of Old Structures for New Functions

An exaptation is a structure that evolves in one context and gradually becomes adapted for other functions.

Evo-Devo: Development and Evolutionary Novelty

A subtle change in the genes that control a species' development can have profound effects. In paedomorphosis, for example, the adult retains body features that were strictly juvenile in ancestral species.

Earth History and Macroevolution

Geologic Time and the Fossil Record

Geologists have established a geologic time scale with four broad divisions: Precambrian, Paleozoic, Mesozoic, and Cenozoic. The most common method for determining the ages of fossils is radiometric dating.

Plate Tectonics and Macroevolution

About 250 million years ago, plate movements brought all the landmasses together into the supercontinent Pangaea, causing extinctions and providing new opportunities for the survivors to diversify. About 180 million years ago, Pangaea began to break up, causing geographic isolation.

Mass Extinctions and Explosive Diversifications of Life

The fossil record reveals long, relatively stable periods punctuated by mass extinctions followed by explosive diversification of certain survivors. For example, during the Cretaceous extinctions, about 65 million years ago, the world lost an enormous number of species, including most of the dinosaurs. Mammals greatly increased in diversity after the Cretaceous period.

Classifying the Diversity of Life

Systematics, the study of biological diversity, includes taxonomy, which is the identification, naming, and classification of species.

Some Basics of Taxonomy

Each species is assigned a two-part name. The first part is the genus, and the second part is unique for each species within the genus. In the taxonomic hierarchy, domain > kingdom > phylum > class > order > family > genus > species.

Classification and Phylogeny

The goal of classification is to reflect phylogeny, the evolutionary history of species. Classification is based on the fossil record, homologous structures, and comparisons of DNA and amino acid sequences. Homology (similarity based on shared ancestry) must be distinguished from analogy (similarity based on convergent evolution). Cladistics uses shared characteristics to group related organisms into clades—distinctive branches in the tree of life.

Classification: A Work in Progress

Biologists currently classify life into a three-domain system:

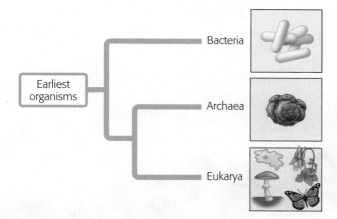

SELF-QUIZ

1. Distinguish between microevolution, speciation, and macroevolution.

2. Bird guides once listed the myrtle warbler and Audubon's warbler as distinct species that lived side by side in parts of their ranges. However, recent books describe them as the eastern and western forms of a single species, the yellow-rumped warbler. Apparently, the two kinds of warblers
   a. live in the same areas.
   b. successfully interbreed.
   c. are almost identical in appearance.
   d. are merging to form a single species.

3. Identify each of the following reproductive barriers as prezygotic or postzygotic.
   a. One lilac species lives on acidic soil, another on basic soil.
   b. Mallard and pintail ducks mate at different times of year.
   c. Two species of leopard frogs have different mating calls.
   d. Hybrid offspring of two species of jimsonweed always die before reproducing.
   e. Pollen of one kind of pine tree cannot fertilize another kind.

4. Why is a small, isolated population more likely to undergo speciation than a large one?

5. Many species of plants and animals adapted to desert conditions probably did not arise there. Their success in living in deserts could be due to _____, structures that originally had one use but became adapted for different functions.

6. Mass extinctions
   a. cut the number of species to the few survivors left today.
   b. resulted mainly from the separation of the continents.
   c. occurred regularly, about every million years.
   d. were followed by diversification of the survivors.

7. The animals and plants of India are almost completely different from the species in nearby Southeast Asia. Why might this be true?
   a. They have become separated by convergent evolution.
   b. The climates of the two regions are completely different.
   c. India is in the process of separating from the rest of Asia.
   d. India was a separate continent until relatively recently.

8. Place these levels of classification in order from least inclusive to most inclusive: class, domain, family, genus, kingdom, order, phylum, species.

9. A paleontologist estimates that when a particular rock formed, it contained 12 mg of the radioactive isotope potassium-40. The rock now contains 3 mg of potassium-40. The half-life of potassium-40 is 1.3 billion years. From this information, you can conclude that the rock is approximately _____ billion years old.

10. In the three-domain system, which two domains contain prokaryotic organisms?

Answers to these questions can be found in Appendix: Self-Quiz Answers.

THE PROCESS OF SCIENCE

11. Imagine you are conducting fieldwork and discover two groups of mice living on opposite sides of a river. Assuming that you will not disturb the mice, design a study to determine whether these two groups belong to the same species. If you could capture some of the mice and bring them to the lab, how might that affect your experimental design?

BIOLOGY AND SOCIETY

12. Experts estimate that human activities cause the extinction of hundreds or thousands of species every year. The natural rate of extinction is thought to be a few species per year. As we continue to alter the global environment, the resulting extinction will probably rival that at the end of the Cretaceous period. Most biologists are alarmed at this prospect. What are some reasons for their concern? Considering that life has endured numerous mass extinctions and has always bounced back, how is the present mass extinction different? What might be some consequences for the surviving species?

15 The Evolution of Microbial Life

Signs of life.
These present-day rocky outcrops closely resemble fossils of prokaryotes at the dawn of life.

How Life Began BIOLOGY AND SOCIETY

Has Life Been Created in the Lab?

In *The Origin of Species*, Charles Darwin described the emergence of new species as a consequence of natural selection acting on existing species. But if you take his argument back to its logical start, you arrive at the ultimate mystery: How did life first arise on Earth?

Some biologists seek insight into this question through experiments on artificial systems. In 2010, a team led by Craig Venter (known for his role in sequencing the human genome— see Chapter 12) achieved a milestone in the burgeoning new field of synthetic biology. The researchers synthesized from scratch the entire genome of a small bacterium known as *Mycoplasma mycoides* and then transplanted the artificial genome into the cells of a closely related species called *Mycoplasma capricolum*. The newly installed genome took over the recipient cells and began cranking out *M. mycoides* proteins and reproducing to make more cells containing the synthetic *M. mycoides* genome. To verify that the synthetic genome was indeed in charge of the new cells, the researchers inserted several "watermarks" in its DNA, strings of bases encrypting messages that translate into English rather than amino acids. One of the watermarks, a quotation from physicist Richard Feynman, expresses one reason for pursuing this line of research: "What I cannot build, I cannot understand." Artificial life-forms may help answer fundamental questions about the origins of life in nature. Venter and others in the field also have more pragmatic—and potentially lucrative—goals. They hope to engineer artificial organisms that can be safely manipulated—a bacterial strain, for example, that might clean up toxic wastes or generate biofuels but be unable to survive outside specific conditions (so that it wouldn't spread out of control).

The Venter team's success at rebooting cells with a synthetic genome was a technical tour de force rather than an act of creation: The genome they built was plagiarized from existing life and transplanted to an off-the-shelf cell. Thus, the question, How did life begin? has yet to be answered. Although it may never be answered with certainty, the question continues to fascinate scientists. Accordingly, this chapter starts with a discussion of some of the key events in the history of life on Earth. We'll then discuss the origins, structures, and diversity of microbes (a term generally used to describe microscopic organisms), starting with the prokaryotes and then moving on to the protists.

Major Episodes in the History of Life

This chapter is the first of three that survey Earth's life-forms and their evolution. This section helps to set the stage by giving a brief overview of the major events in the history of life on Earth.

Life began when Earth was young. The planet formed about 4.6 billion years ago, and its crust began to solidify about 4 billion years ago. A few hundred million years later, by 3.5 billion years ago, Earth was already inhabited by a diversity of organisms **(Figure 15.1)**. Those earliest organisms were all **prokaryotes**, their cells lacking true nuclei. Within the next billion years, two distinct groups of prokaryotes—bacteria and archaea—diverged.

An oxygen revolution began about 2.7 billion years ago. Photosynthetic prokaryotes that split water molecules released oxygen gas, profoundly changing Earth's atmosphere (see the Evolution Connection section at the end of Chapter 6). The accumulation of O_2 in the atmosphere doomed many prokaryotic groups. Among the survivors, a diversity of metabolic modes evolved, including cellular respiration, which uses O_2 in extracting energy from food (see Chapter 6). All of this metabolic evolution occurred during the almost 2 billion years that prokaryotes had Earth to themselves.

The oldest eukaryotic fossils are about 2.1 billion years old. **Eukaryotes** are composed of one or more cells that contain nuclei and many other organelles absent in prokaryotic cells. The eukaryotic cell evolved from a prokaryotic community, a host cell containing even smaller prokaryotes. The mitochondria of our cells and those of every other eukaryote are descendants of those smaller prokaryotes, as are the chloroplasts of plants and algae.

The evolution of more complex cells launched a period of tremendous diversification of eukaryotic forms. These new organisms were the protists. Represented today by a great diversity of species, protists are mostly microscopic and unicellular. Examples you may recognize include algae, amoebas, and *Paramecium*.

The next great event in the evolution of life was multicellularity. As discussed in this chapter's Evolution Connection section, the first multicellular eukaryotes evolved at least 1.2 billion years ago as colonies of single-celled organisms. Their modern descendants

▼ **Figure 15.1 Some major episodes in the history of life.** The timing of events shown on this phylogenetic tree is based on fossil evidence and molecular analysis. (Review Figure 14.23 for a reminder of how to read and interpret phylogenetic trees.)

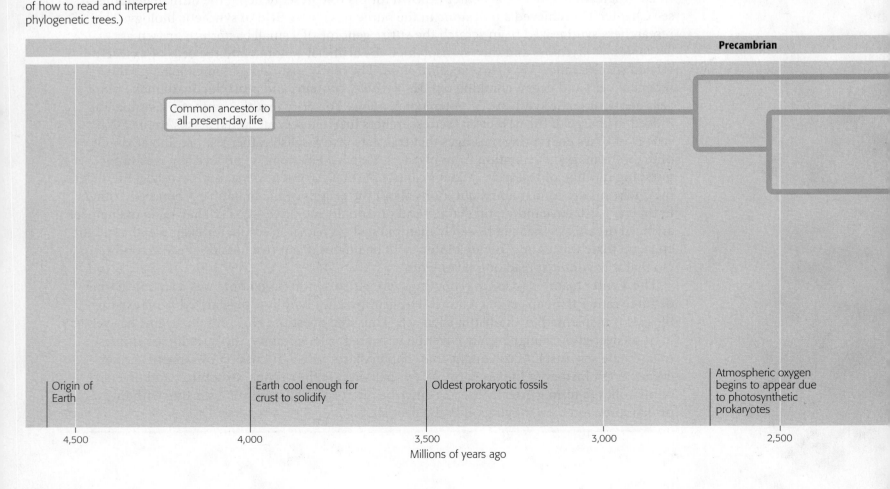

include multicellular protists, such as seaweeds. Other evolutionary branches stemming from the ancient protists gave rise to animals, fungi, and plants.

The greatest diversification of animals was the so-called Cambrian explosion. The Cambrian was the first period of the Paleozoic era, which began about 540 million years ago (see Table 14.1). The earliest animals lived in late-Precambrian seas, but they diversified extensively over a span of just 10 million years during the early Cambrian. In fact, all the major animal body plans—as well as all the major groups—had evolved by the end of that evolutionary eruption.

For over 85% of biological history—life's first 3 billion years—life was confined mostly to aquatic habitats. The colonization of land was a major milestone in the history of life. Plants and fungi together led the way about 500 million years ago. Plants transformed the landscape, creating new opportunities for all life-forms, especially herbivorous (plant-eating) animals and their predators.

The evolutionary venture onto land included vertebrate animals in the form of the first amphibians. These prototypes of today's frogs and salamanders descended from air-breathing fish with fleshy fins that could support the animal's weight on land. Further evolution by natural selection led to the appearance of reptiles and

mammals. Among the mammals are the primates, the animal group that includes humans and their closest relatives, apes and monkeys.

Figure 15.2 uses the analogy of a clock ticking down from the origin of Earth 4.6 billion years ago to the present to summarize the major events in the history of life. As the figure makes clear, to trace the history of life on Earth, we must go back to the origin and diversification of microbes, starting with the prokaryotes (yellow band).

▶ Figure 15.2 **A clock analogy for the major events in the history of life on Earth.**

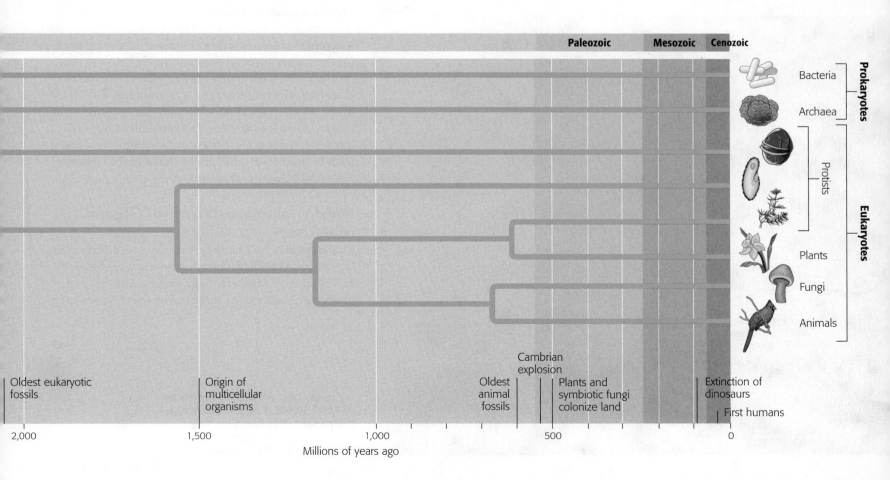

The Origin of Life

Although we'll never know for sure how life on Earth began, in this section we'll discuss hypotheses for the formation of the first life. Then we'll talk about its subsequent early evolution.

Resolving the Biogenesis Paradox

From the time of the ancient Greeks until well into the 1800s, it was commonly believed that life could regularly arise from nonliving matter, an idea called **spontaneous generation**. Many people believed, for instance, that flies arose from rotting meat and fish from ocean mud. Then, in 1862, experiments by Louis Pasteur confirmed what many others had suspected: All life today, including microbes, arises only by the reproduction of preexisting life. This "life-from-life" principle is called **biogenesis**.

But wait! If life always arises from previous life, then how could the first organisms arise? Although there is no evidence that spontaneous generation occurs today,

it could have early in Earth's history, when conditions were very different. For instance, the O_2 in today's atmosphere is a corrosive agent that tends to disrupt chemical bonds, thereby preventing the formation of complex molecules—but O_2 wasn't present in the ancient atmosphere. And such energy sources as lightning, volcanic activity, and ultraviolet sunlight were all more intense on the early Earth than they are today. So life did not begin on a planet anything like the modern Earth, but on a young Earth that was a very different world (**Figure 15.3**). Most biologists now think that chemical and physical processes in Earth's primordial environment could have led to very simple cells through a sequence of stages. Debate abounds about the nature of those stages. ☑

A Four-Stage Hypothesis for the Origin of Life

According to one hypothesis for the origin of life, the first organisms were products of chemical evolution in four stages: (1) the abiotic (nonliving) synthesis of small organic molecules, such as amino acid and nucleotide monomers; (2) the joining of these small molecules into macromolecules, including proteins and nucleic acids; (3) the packaging of all these molecules into pre-cells, droplets with membranes that maintained an internal chemistry different from the surroundings; and (4) the origin of self-replicating molecules that eventually made inheritance possible. This is all speculative, of course, but what makes it a valid scientific hypothesis is that it leads to predictions that can be tested in the laboratory. Let's take a closer look at each of these four stages.

Stage 1: Abiotic Synthesis of Organic Monomers

This stage was the first to be extensively studied in the laboratory. We'll begin our investigation of chemical evolution with a breakthrough experiment that first brought this idea to the forefront of scientific thinking.

◄ **Figure 15.3 An artist's rendition of Earth about 3 billion years ago.** The pad-like objects in the scene represent colonies of prokaryotes known from the fossil record.

Can Biological Monomers Form Spontaneously?

In 1953, University of Chicago scientist Harold Urey and his 23-year-old graduate student Stanley Miller conducted what is now considered a classic experiment. They began with the **observation** that modern biological macromolecules (DNA, protein, carbohydrates, and so on) are all composed of elements (primarily oxygen, hydrogen, carbon, and nitrogen) that were present in abundance on early Earth. This led to the **question**, Could biological molecules arise spontaneously under conditions like those on the early Earth? Miller and Urey began with the **hypothesis** that a closed system designed to simulate such conditions in the laboratory could produce biologically important organic molecules from inorganic ingredients.

Figure 15.4 shows the apparatus they created to test their hypothesis. A flask of warmed water simulated the primordial sea. An "atmosphere"—in the form of gases added to a reaction chamber—contained hydrogen gas (H_2), methane (CH_4), ammonia (NH_3), and water vapor (H_2O). To mimic the prevalent lightning of the early Earth, sparks were discharged into the chamber. A condenser cooled the atmosphere, causing water and any dissolved compounds to "rain" into the miniature "sea." Miller and Urey's **prediction** was that organic molecules would form and accumulate during this **experiment**.

Miller and Urey's **results** made front-page news. After the apparatus had run for a week, an abundance of organic molecules essential for life, including amino acids, the monomers of proteins, had collected in the "sea." These laboratory experiments, which have been repeated and extended by other scientists, support the idea that organic molecules could have arisen abiotically on the early Earth.

Researchers are also exploring other hypotheses about the origin of organic molecules. One hypothesis is based on observations of submerged volcanoes and deep-sea hydrothermal vents—gaps in Earth's crust where hot water and minerals gush into the deep oceans (see Figure 15.6). These undersea environments, rather than the atmosphere, may have provided the chemical resources for life's beginning. Another hypothesis for the origin of life omits the abiotic synthesis of organic monomers, proposing instead that meteorites provided a "starter set" of organic molecules. This hypothesis is based on observations of 4.5-billion-year-old meteorite fragments, which were found to contain a variety of organic molecules, including amino acids, sugars, and uracil (one of the building blocks of RNA).

▼ Figure 15.4 **The abiotic production of organic molecules: a laboratory simulation of early-Earth chemistry.**

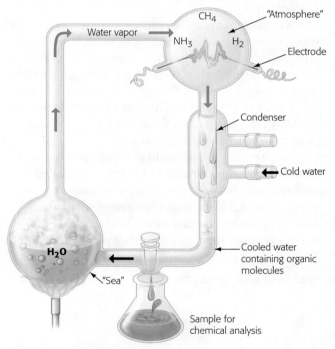

Miller and Urey's experiment

Stage 2: Abiotic Synthesis of Polymers

Once small organic molecules were present, how were they linked together to form polymers such as proteins and nucleic acids without the help of enzymes and other cellular equipment? Researchers have brought about such polymerization by dripping solutions of organic monomers onto hot sand, clay, or rock. The heat vaporizes the water in the solutions and concentrates the monomers on the underlying material. Some of the monomers then spontaneously bond together to form polymers. On the early Earth, raindrops or waves may have splashed dilute solutions of organic monomers onto fresh lava or other hot rocks and then washed polypeptides and other polymers back into the sea. There they could accumulate in great quantities (since no life existed to consume them). ✔

✔ CHECKPOINT

What is the name of the chemical reaction whereby monomers are linked together into polymers? (*Hint*: Review Figure 3.4.)

Answer: *dehydration reaction*

Stage 3: Formation of Pre-Cells

According to the four-stage hypothesis, a key step in the origin of life was the isolation of a collection of abiotically created molecules within a membrane. We'll call these molecular aggregates pre-cells—not really cells, but molecular packages with some of the properties of life. Within a confined space, certain combinations of molecules could be concentrated and interact more efficiently. Furthermore, the internal environment of a pre-cell could differ from its surroundings.

Laboratory experiments demonstrate that pre-cells could have formed spontaneously from abiotically produced organic compounds (see Figure 5.20). Such pre-cells produced in the laboratory display some lifelike properties: They have a selectively permeable surface, can grow by absorbing molecules from their surroundings, and swell or shrink when placed in solutions of different salt concentrations.

Stage 4: Origin of Self-Replicating Molecules

Life is defined partly by the process of inheritance, which is based on self-replicating molecules. Today's cells store their genetic information as DNA. They transcribe the information into RNA and then translate RNA messages into specific enzymes and other proteins (see Figure 10.10). This mechanism of information flow probably emerged gradually through a series of small changes to much simpler processes.

What were the first genes like? One hypothesis is that they were short strands of RNA that replicated without the assistance of proteins. In laboratory experiments, short RNA molecules can assemble spontaneously from nucleotide monomers in the absence of enzymes **(Figure 15.5)**. The result is a population of RNA

molecules, each with a random sequence of monomers. Some of the molecules self-replicate, but their success at this reproduction varies. What happens can be described as molecular evolution: The RNA varieties that replicate fastest increase their frequency in the population.

In addition to the experimental evidence, there is another reason the idea of RNA genes in the primordial world is plausible. Cells actually have RNAs that can act as enzymes; they are called ribozymes. Perhaps early ribozymes catalyzed their own replication. That would help with the "chicken and egg" paradox of which came first, enzymes or genes. Maybe the "chicken and egg" came together in the same RNA molecules. The molecular biology of today may have been preceded by an ancient "RNA world." ☑

Was there life before DNA?

From Chemical Evolution to Darwinian Evolution

If pre-cells with self-replicating RNA (and later DNA) did form on a young Earth, they would be refined by natural selection. Mutations, errors in the copying of the "genes," would result in variation among the pre-cells. And the most successful of these pre-cells would grow, divide (reproduce), and continue to evolve. Of course, the gap between such pre-cells and even the simplest of modern cells is enormous. But with millions of years of incremental changes through natural selection, these molecular cooperatives could have become more and more cell-like. The point at which we stop calling them pre-cells and start calling them living cells is as fuzzy as our understanding of how life originated. But we do know that prokaryotes were already flourishing at least 3.5 billion years ago and that all branches of life arose from those ancient prokaryotes.

☑ **CHECKPOINT**

What are ribozymes? Why are they a logical step in the formation of life?

Answer: A ribozyme is an RNA molecule that functions as an enzyme. Ribozymes can perform some of the functions of both DNA and protein.

▼ Figure 15.5 **Self-replication of RNA "genes."**

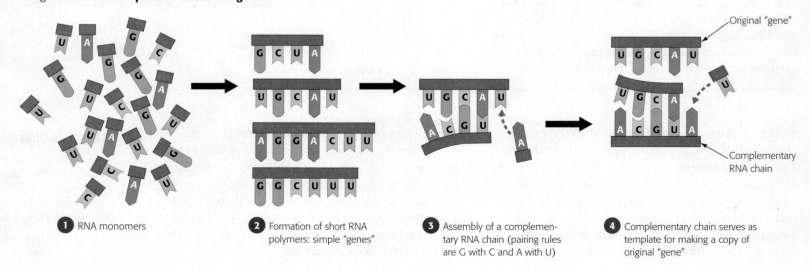

1 RNA monomers

2 Formation of short RNA polymers: simple "genes"

3 Assembly of a complementary RNA chain (pairing rules are G with C and A with U)

4 Complementary chain serves as template for making a copy of original "gene"

Prokaryotes

The history of prokaryotic life is a success story spanning billions of years. Prokaryotes lived and evolved all alone on Earth for about 2 billion years. They have continued to adapt and flourish on an evolving Earth and in turn have helped to change the planet. In this section, you will study prokaryotic structure and function, diversity, effects on people, and ecological significance.

They're Everywhere!

Today, prokaryotes are found wherever there is life, including in and on the bodies of multicellular organisms. The collective biological mass (biomass) of prokaryotes is at least ten times that of all eukaryotes. Prokaryotes also thrive in habitats too cold, too hot, too salty, too acidic, or too alkaline for any eukaryote (Figure 15.6). Scientists are just beginning to investigate the extensive prokaryotic diversity in the oceans. Biologists have even discovered prokaryotes living on the walls of a gold mine 3.3 km (2 miles) below Earth's surface.

Though individual prokaryotes are small organisms (Figure 15.7), they are giants in their collective impact on Earth and its life. We hear most about the relatively few species that cause illness. Bacterial infections are responsible for about half of all human diseases, including tuberculosis, cholera, many sexually transmitted infections, and certain types of food poisoning. However, prokaryotic life is much more than just a rogues' gallery. Benign or beneficial prokaryotes are far more common than harmful ones. For example, people have long used bacteria to produce various types of food, converting milk to cheese, yogurt, and sour cream. In addition, each of us harbors several hundred species of prokaryotes in and on our bodies. Many of the bacteria that live on our skin perform helpful housekeeping functions, such as decomposing dead skin cells. Some of our intestinal residents supply essential vitamins and enable us to obtain nutrition from food molecules that we couldn't otherwise digest. Bacteria also guard the body against microbial intruders.

It would be hard to overstate the importance of prokaryotes to the health of the environment. Prokaryotes living in the soil and at the bottom of lakes, rivers, and oceans help to decompose dead organisms and other organic waste material, returning vital chemical elements to the environment. If prokaryotes were to disappear, the chemical cycles that sustain life would come to a halt, and all forms of eukaryotic life would also be doomed. In contrast, prokaryotic life would undoubtedly persist in the absence of eukaryotes, as it once did for 2 billion years.

Prokaryotes cause disease, so wouldn't we be better off without them?

◄ **Figure 15.6 A window to early life?** An instrument on the research submarine *Alvin* samples the water around a hydrothermal vent more than 1.5 km (about a mile) below the ocean's surface. Prokaryotes that live near the vent use the emitted gases as an energy source. This environment, which is very dark, hot, and under high pressure, is among the most extreme in which life exists today.

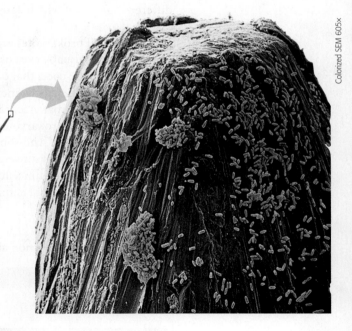

► **Figure 15.7 Bacteria on the point of a pin.** The orange rods are individual bacteria, each about 5 µm long, on the point of a pin. Besides highlighting their tiny size, this micrograph will help you understand why a pin prick can cause infection.

Colorized SEM 605x

299

The Structure and Function of Prokaryotes

Prokaryotes have a cellular organization fundamentally different from that of eukaryotes. Whereas eukaryotic cells have a membrane-enclosed nucleus and numerous other membrane-enclosed organelles, prokaryotic cells lack these structural features (see Figures 4.4 and 4.5). And nearly all species of prokaryotes have cell walls exterior to their plasma membranes. Despite the simplicity of the cell structures, though, prokaryotes display an enormous range of diversity. In this section, you'll learn about aspects of their form, reproduction, and nutrition that help these organisms survive in their environments.

Prokaryotic Forms

Determining cell shape by microscopic examination is an important step in identifying a prokaryote. The micrographs in **Figure 15.8** show the three most common shapes. Spherical prokaryotic cells are called **cocci** (singular, *coccus*). Rod-shaped prokaryotes are called **bacilli** (singular, *bacillus*). A third prokaryotic cell shape is spiral or curved. These include spirochetes, different species of which cause syphilis and Lyme disease.

Although all prokaryotes are unicellular, the cells of some species usually exist as groups of two or more cells. For example, cocci that occur in clusters are called staphylococci. Other cocci, including the bacterium that causes strep throat, occur in chains; they are called streptococci. Some prokaryotes grow branching chains of cells (**Figure 15.9a**). And some species even exhibit a simple division of labor among specialized types of cells (**Figure 15.9b**). Among unicellular species, moreover, there are some giants that actually dwarf most eukaryotic cells (**Figure 15.9c**).

▼ Figure 15.9 **A diversity of prokaryotic shapes and sizes.**

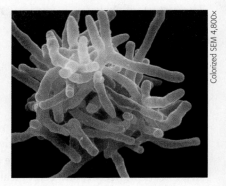

(a) Actinomycete. An actinomycete is a mass of branching chains of rod-shaped cells. These bacteria are common in soil, where they secrete antibiotics that inhibit the growth of other bacteria. Various antibiotic drugs, such as streptomycin, are obtained from actinomycetes.

Colorized SEM 4,800×

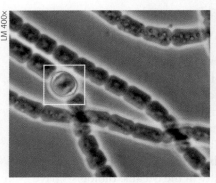

(b) Cyanobacteria. These photosynthetic cyanobacteria exhibit division of labor. The box highlights a cell that converts atmospheric nitrogen to ammonia, which can then be incorporated into amino acids and other organic compounds.

LM 400×

(c) Giant bacterium. The larger white blob in this photo is the marine bacterium *Thiomargarita namibiensis*. This prokaryotic cell is over 0.5 mm in diameter, about the size of the fruit fly's head below it.

LM 18×

▼ Figure 15.8 **Three common shapes of prokaryotic cells.**

SHAPES OF PROKARYOTIC CELLS		
Spherical (cocci)	**Rod-shaped (bacilli)**	**Spiral**
Colorized SEM 10,000×	Colorized SEM 10,000×	Colorized TEM 30,000×

About half of all prokaryotic species are mobile. Many of those that travel have one or more flagella that propel the cells away from unfavorable places or toward more favorable places, such as nutrient-rich locales.

In many natural environments, prokaryotes attach to surfaces in a highly organized colony called a **biofilm**. A biofilm may consist of one or several species of prokaryotes, and it may include protists and fungi as well. As a biofilm becomes larger and more complex, it develops into a "city" of microbes. Communicating by chemical signals, members of the community engage in division of labor, including defense against invaders, among other activities.

Biofilms can form on almost any type of surface, such as rocks, organic material (including living tissue), metal, and plastic. A biofilm known as dental plaque (Figure 15.10) can cause tooth decay. Biofilms are common among bacteria that cause disease in humans. For instance, ear infections and and urinary tract infections are often the result of biofilm-forming bacteria. Biofilms of harmful bacteria can also form on implanted medical devices such as catheters, replacement joints, or pacemakers. The structure of biofilms makes these infections especially difficult to defeat. Antibiotics may not be able to penetrate beyond the outer layer of cells, leaving much of the community intact.

Prokaryotic Reproduction

Many prokaryotes can reproduce at a phenomenal rate if conditions are favorable. The cells copy their DNA almost continuously and divide again and again by the process of **binary fission**. Dividing by binary fission, a single cell becomes 2 cells, which then become 4, 8, 16, and so on. Some species can produce a new generation in only 20 minutes under optimal conditions. If reproduction continued unchecked at this rate, a single prokaryote could give rise to a colony outweighing Earth in only three days! Also, each time DNA is replicated prior to binary fission, spontaneous mutations occur. As a result, rapid reproduction generates a great deal of genetic variation in a prokaryotic population. If the environment changes, an individual that possesses a beneficial gene can quickly take advantage of the new conditions. For example, exposure to antibiotics may select for antibiotic resistance in a bacterial population (see the Evolution Connection at the end of Chapter 4).

Fortunately, few prokaryotic populations can sustain exponential growth for long. Environments are usually limiting in resources such as food and space. Prokaryotes also produce metabolic waste products that may eventually pollute the colony's environment. Still, you can understand why certain bacteria can make you sick so soon after infection or why food can spoil so rapidly.

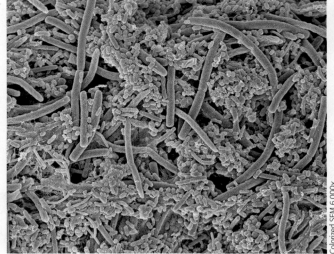

◄ Figure 15.10 **Dental plaque, a biofilm that forms on teeth.**

Colorized SEM 6,000×

Refrigeration retards food spoilage not because the cold kills bacteria, but because most microorganisms reproduce very slowly at such low temperatures.

Some prokaryotes can survive during very harsh conditions by forming specialized cells called endospores. An **endospore** is a thick-coated, protective cell produced within the prokaryotic cell when the prokaryote is exposed to unfavorable conditions (Figure 15.11). The endospore can survive all sorts of trauma and extreme heat or cold. Not even boiling water kills most of these resistant cells. And when the environment becomes more hospitable, the endospore can absorb water and resume growth. To ensure that all cells, including endospores, are killed when laboratory equipment is sterilized, microbiologists use an appliance called an autoclave, a pressure cooker that uses high-pressure steam at a temperature of 121°C (250°F). The food-canning industry employs similar methods to kill endospores of dangerous soil bacteria such as *Clostridium botulinum*, the cause of the potentially fatal disease botulism. ✔

► Figure 15.11 **An endospore in an anthrax bacterium.** This prokaryote is *Bacillus anthracis*, the notorious bacterium that produces the disease called anthrax in cattle, sheep, and people. There are actually two cells here, one inside the other. The outer cell produced the specialized dormant inner cell, the endospore.

Endospore

Colorized TEM 35,000×

Prokaryotic Nutrition

When classifying diverse organisms, biologists often use the phrase "mode of nutrition" to describe how an organism obtains energy and carbon, the two main resources needed for synthesizing organic compounds. Species that obtain energy from light are called photo-trophs, while species that obtain energy from environmental chemicals are called chemotrophs. Species that obtain carbon from the inorganic compound carbon dioxide (CO_2) are called autotrophs, while species that obtain carbon from at least one organic nutrient—the sugar glucose, for instance—are called heterotrophs. We can combine energy source (phototroph versus chemotroph) and carbon source (autotroph versus heterotroph) to group all organisms according to the four major modes of nutrition shown in **Figure 15.12**. Two of these modes—photoautotrophs (such as most plants), and chemoheterotrophs (such as most animals)—are dominant among multicellular organisms. The other two modes are used only by certain prokaryotes. ☑

◀ **Figure 15.12**
Modes of nutrition.

MODES OF NUTRITION

	Energy source	
	Light	**Chemical**

Carbon source

CO_2

Photoautotrophs
These organisms are photosynthesizers that use light to drive the synthesis of organic compounds from CO_2. Photoautotrophs include plants and algae.

Elodea, an aquatic plant

Chemoautotrophs
These organisms extract energy from inorganic substances such as ammonia, NH_3. All chemoautotrophs are prokaryotes.

Colorized TEM 8,750×

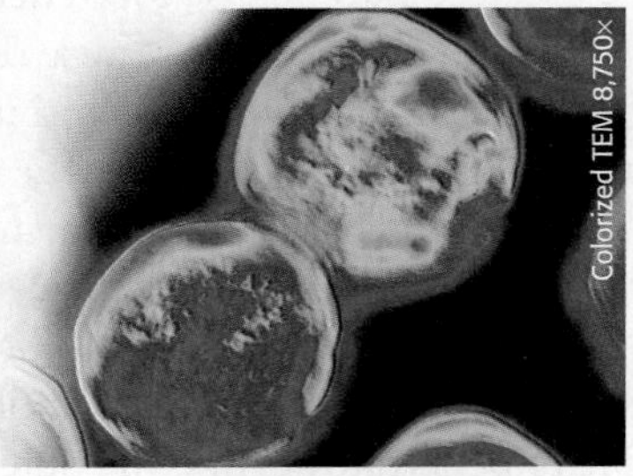

Bacteria from a hot spring

Organic compounds

Photoheterotrophs
These organisms harness energy from light but must obtain carbon in organic form. All photoheterotrophs are prokaryotes.

Colorized TEM 6,000×

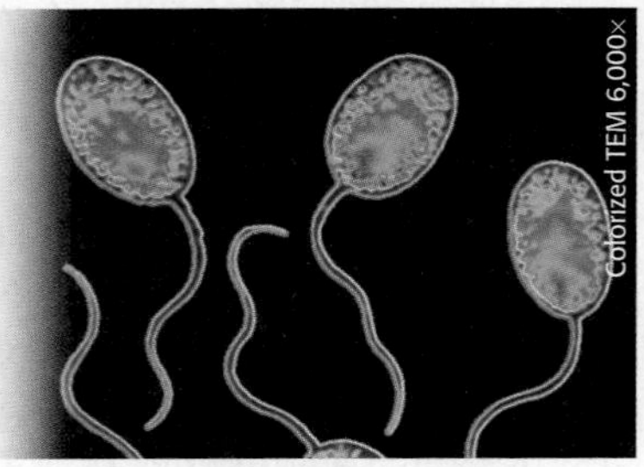

Rhodopseudomonas

Chemoheterotrophs
These organisms consume organic molecules for both energy and carbon. Chemoheterotrophs include some prokaryotes and protists and all fungi and animals.

Kingfisher with prey

☑ CHECKPOINT

A bacterium requires only water and the amino acid methionine to grow and lives in very deep caves where no light penetrates. Based on its mode of nutrition, this species would be classified as a
_____.

Answer: chemoheterotroph

The Two Main Branches of Prokaryotic Evolution: Bacteria and Archaea

By comparing diverse prokaryotes at the molecular level, biologists have identified two major branches of prokaryotic evolution: **bacteria** and **archaea**. Thus, life is organized into three domains—**Bacteria**, **Archaea**, and **Eukarya** (review Figure 14.25). Although bacteria and archaea have prokaryotic cell organization in common, they differ in many structural and physiological characteristics. Some of these differences suggest that archaea are more closely related to eukaryotes than they are to bacteria. In this section, we'll focus on the special characteristics of archaea before turning our attention to bacteria.

The term *archaea* ("ancient") refers to the antiquity of this group's origin from the earliest cells. Even today, many species of archaea inhabit extreme environments, such as hot springs and salt ponds. Few other modern organisms (if any) can survive in some of these environments, which may resemble habitats on the early Earth.

Biologists refer to some archaea as "extremophiles," meaning "lovers of the extreme." There are extreme halophiles ("salt lovers"), archaea that thrive in such environments as Utah's Great Salt Lake, the Dead Sea, and seawater-evaporating ponds used to produce salt

(Figure 15.13a). There are also extreme thermophiles ("heat lovers") that live in very hot water (Figure 15.13b); some archaea even populate the deep-ocean vents that gush water hotter than 100°C (212°F), such as the one shown in Figure 15.6. Also among the archaea are the methanogens, which live in anaerobic (oxygen-free) environments and give off methane as a waste product. They are abundant in the mud at the bottom of lakes and swamps. You may have seen methane, also called marsh gas, bubbling up from a swamp. Great numbers of methanogens also inhabit the digestive tracts of animals. In humans, intestinal gas is largely the result of their metabolism. More importantly, methanogens aid digestion in cattle, deer, and other animals that depend heavily on cellulose for their nutrition. Normally, bloating does not occur in these animals because they regularly expel large volumes of gas produced by the methanogens. (And that may be more than you wanted to know about these gas-producing microbes!)

▼ Figure 15.13 **Archaeal "extremophiles."**

(a) Salt-loving archaea. This is an aerial photo of commercial salt-producing ponds at the edge of San Francisco Bay. The colors of the ponds result from dense growth of the harmless prokaryotes that thrive when the salinity of the water reaches five to eight times that of seawater.

(b) Heat-loving archaea. In this photo, you can see orange colonies of heat-loving prokaryotes growing near Grand Prismatic Spring in Yellowstone National Park, Wyoming.

Bacteria and Disease

In this section, we'll consider some aspects of disease-causing bacteria. Keep in mind, though, that only a minority of prokaryotes are harmful—many more are beneficial.

Bacteria That Cause Disease

We are constantly exposed to bacteria, some of which are potentially harmful (Figure 15.14). Bacteria and other organisms that cause disease are called **pathogens**. We're healthy most of the time because our body's defenses check the growth of pathogen populations. Occasionally, the balance shifts in favor of a pathogen, and we become ill. Even some of the bacteria that are normal residents of the human body can make us sick when our defenses have been weakened by poor nutrition or a viral infection.

Most pathogenic bacteria cause disease by producing a poison—either an exotoxin or an endotoxin. **Exotoxins** are proteins that bacterial cells secrete into their environment. For example, *Staphylococcus aureus* (abbreviated *S. aureus*) produces several exotoxins. Although *S. aureus* is commonly found on the skin and in the nasal passages, if it enters the body through a wound, it can cause serious disease. One of its exotoxins causes layers of skin to slough off ("flesh-eating disease"); another can produce a potentially deadly disease called toxic shock syndrome. Food may also be contaminated with *S. aureus* exotoxins, which are so potent that a millionth of a gram causes vomiting and diarrhea.

Endotoxins are chemical components of the outer membrane of certain bacteria. All endotoxins induce the same general symptoms: fever, aches, and sometimes a dangerous drop in blood pressure (septic shock). Septic shock triggered by an endotoxin of the pathogen that causes bacterial meningitis can kill a healthy person in a matter of days, or even hours. Because the bacteria are easily transmitted among people living in close contact, many colleges require students to be vaccinated against this disease. Other examples of endotoxin-producing bacteria include the species of *Salmonella* that cause food poisoning and typhoid fever.

How do bacteria make us sick?

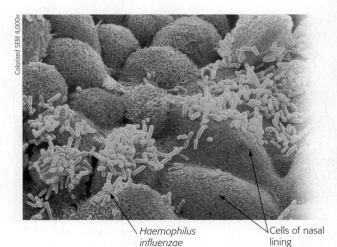

Colorized SEM 4,000×

Haemophilus influenzae

Cells of nasal lining

◄ Figure 15.14 **Bacteria that cause pneumonia.** *Haemophilus influenzae*, shown here on cells lining the interior of a human nose, causes pneumonia and other lung infections, which kill about 4 million people worldwide per year. Most victims are children in less industrialized countries, where malnutrition lowers resistance to all pathogens.

During the last century, following the discovery that "germs" cause disease, the incidence of bacterial infections declined, particularly in more industrialized nations. Sanitation is generally the most effective way to prevent bacterial disease. The installation of water treatment and sewage systems continues to be a public health priority throughout the world. Antibiotics have been discovered that can cure most bacterial diseases. However, resistance to widely used antibiotics has evolved in many of these pathogens. (For example, Figure 4.7 explains antibiotic-resistant *S. aureus*.)

In addition to sanitation and antibiotics, a third defense against bacterial disease is education. A case in point is Lyme disease, which is caused by a spirochete bacterium carried by ticks (**Figure 15.15**). Disease-carrying ticks live on deer and field mice but also bite humans. Lyme disease usually starts as a red rash shaped like a bull's-eye around a tick bite. Antibiotics can cure the disease if administered within a month of exposure. If untreated, Lyme disease can cause debilitating arthritis, heart disease, and nervous system disorders. So far, the best defense is public education about avoiding tick bites and the importance of seeking treatment if a rash develops. The Centers for Disease Control and Prevention recommends that you avoid vegetation in tick-infested areas, wear light-colored clothing when walking through brush so that you can easily see any ticks, and use an appropriate insect repellent. ☑

☑ CHECKPOINT

How can an exotoxin be harmful even after bacteria are killed?

Answer: Exotoxins are secreted poisons that can remain harmful even when the bacteria that secrete them are gone.

▼ **Figure 15.15 Lyme disease, a bacterial disease transmitted by ticks.** The bacterium that causes Lyme disease (shown in micrograph at right) is carried from deer to humans by ticks.

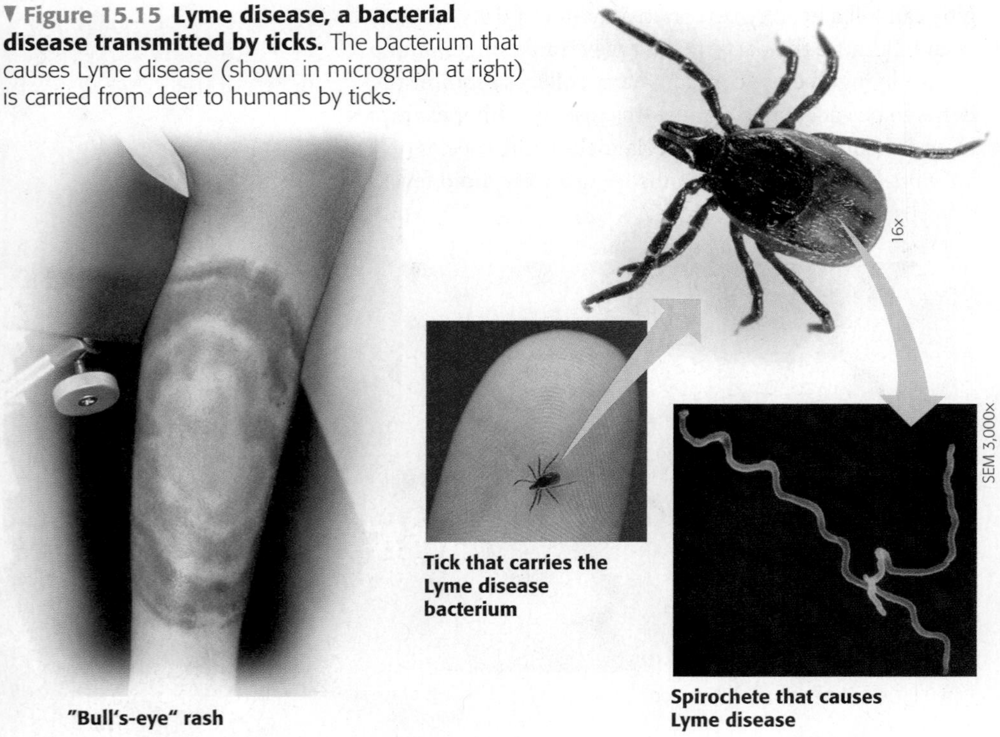

"Bull's-eye" rash

Tick that carries the Lyme disease bacterium

16×

Spirochete that causes Lyme disease

SEM 3,000×

Biological Weapons

In October 2001, endospores of the bacterium that causes anthrax (see Figure 15.11) were mailed to members of the news media and the U.S. Senate. When anthrax endospores enter the lungs, they germinate, and the bacteria multiply, producing an exotoxin that eventually accumulates to lethal levels in the blood. Although the bacteria can be killed by certain antibiotics, the antibiotics don't eliminate the toxin already in the body. As a result, inhalation anthrax has a very high death rate. The attacks in 2001, which resulted in five deaths, raised public awareness of the potential for biological agents such as viruses and bacteria to be used as weapons.

The bacterium that causes plague is also among the biological agents that are considered the highest-priority threats. Plague bacteria are carried by rodents in many parts of the world and are transmitted by fleas. People contract the disease when they are bitten by infected fleas. When diagnosed in time, plague can be treated by antibiotics. In the untreated bubonic form of plague, egg-size swellings called buboes grow in the armpits, groin, and neck, and black blotches appear where the bacteria proliferate in clots under the skin (**Figure 15.16**). If bacteria spill into the bloodstream, death from the bacterial toxins is certain. In the pneumonic form of plague, the bacteria infect cells in the lungs, becoming airborne as the disintegrating lung tissue is coughed out in droplets. As a result, pneumonic plague is easily transmitted from person to person and can become epidemic, the worst scenario for an attack by biological weapons.

Another bacterium considered to have dangerous potential as a weapon is *Clostridrium botulinum*. Unlike other biological agents, the weapon form of *C. botulinum* is the exotoxin it produces, botulinum, rather than the living microbes. Botulinum, which blocks transmission of the nerve signals that cause muscle contraction, is the deadliest poison on earth. Thirty grams of pure toxin, a bit more than an ounce, could kill every person in the United States.

▼ **Figure 15.16 Swellings characteristic of bubonic plague.**

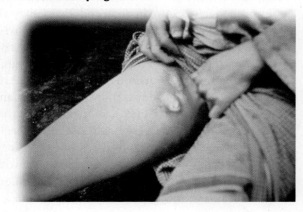

The Ecological Impact of Prokaryotes

Pathogenic bacteria are in the minority among prokaryotes. Far more common are species that are essential to our well-being, either directly or indirectly. Let's turn our attention now to the vital role that prokaryotes play in sustaining the biosphere.

Prokaryotes and Chemical Recycling

Not too long ago, the atoms making up the organic molecules in your body were part of inorganic compounds found in soil, air, and water, as they will be again. Life depends on the recycling of chemical elements between the biological and physical components of ecosystems. Prokaryotes play essential roles in these chemical cycles. For example, nearly all the nitrogen that plants use to make proteins and nucleic acids comes from prokaryotic metabolism in the soil. In turn, animals get their nitrogen compounds from plants.

Another vital function of prokaryotes, mentioned earlier in the chapter, is the breakdown of organic wastes and dead organisms. Prokaryotes decompose organic matter and, in the process, return elements to the environment in inorganic forms that can be used by other organisms. If it were not for such decomposers, carbon, nitrogen, and other elements essential to life would become locked in the organic molecules of corpses and waste products. (You'll learn more about the role that prokaryotes play in chemical cycling in Chapter 20.)

Prokaryotes and Bioremediation

People have put the metabolically diverse prokaryotes to work in cleaning up the environment. **Bioremediation** is the use of organisms to remove pollutants from water, air, or soil. One example of bioremediation is the use of prokaryotic decomposers to treat our sewage. Raw sewage is first passed through a series of screens and shredders, and solid matter settles out from the liquid waste. This solid matter, called sludge, is then gradually added to a culture of anaerobic prokaryotes, including both bacteria and archaea. The microbes decompose the organic matter in the sludge, converting it to material that can be used as landfill or fertilizer. The liquid wastes may then be passed through a trickling filter system consisting of a long horizontal bar that slowly rotates, spraying liquid wastes onto a bed of rocks **(Figure 15.17)**. Aerobic prokaryotes and fungi growing on the rocks remove much of the organic matter from the liquid. The outflow from the rock bed is then sterilized and released back into the environment.

Bioremediation has also become an important tool for cleaning up toxic chemicals released into the soil and water by industrial processes. Naturally occurring prokaryotes capable of degrading pollutants such as oil, solvents, and pesticides are often present in contaminated soil, but their activity is limited by environmental factors such as nutrient availability. In **Figure 15.18**, workers are spraying an oil-polluted beach in Alaska with fertilizers to stimulate soil bacteria to speed up the breakdown of oil. Chemical dispersants were used in the massive Gulf of Mexico oil spill in 2010. Like detergents that help clean greasy dishes, these chemicals break oil into smaller droplets that offer more surface area for microbial attack. Prokaryotes are also helping to decontaminate old mining sites where the soil and water are laced with heavy metals and other poisons. We are just beginning to explore the great potential that prokaryotes offer for bioremediation. In the future, genetically engineered microbes may be put to work cleaning up the wide variety of toxic waste products that continue to accumulate in our landscapes and landfills.

The various modes of nutrition and metabolic pathways we find in organisms living today are all variations on themes that evolved in prokaryotes during their long reign as Earth's exclusive inhabitants. The subsequent breakthroughs in evolution were mostly structural, including the origin of the eukaryotic cell and the diversification of the protists. ✔

> *Can prokaryotes clean up our environmental messes?*

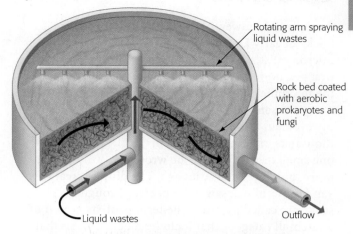

▲ **Figure 15.17 Putting microbes to work in sewage treatment facilities.** This is a trickling filter system, which uses bacteria, archaea, and fungi to treat liquid wastes after sludge is removed.

Labels: Rotating arm spraying liquid wastes; Rock bed coated with aerobic prokaryotes and fungi; Liquid wastes; Outflow

☑ CHECKPOINT

How do bacteria help restore the atmospheric CO_2 required by plants for photosynthesis?

Answer: By decomposing the organic molecules of dead organisms and organic refuse such as leaf litter, bacteria release carbon from the organic matter in the form of CO_2

▼ **Figure 15.18 Treatment of an oil spill in Alaska.** A worker is spraying fertilizers onto an oil-soaked beach. The fertilizers stimulate growth of naturally occurring bacteria that initiate the breakdown of the oil.

Protists

Anton van Leeuwen-hoek, an early Dutch microscopist, was the first person to describe the microbial world: "No more pleasant sight has met my eye than this of so many thousands of living creatures in one small drop of water," he wrote more than three centuries ago. The diverse creatures van Leeuwenhoek saw as he peered through his microscope are called protists. The term **protists** is a bit of a catch-all category that includes all eukaryotes that are not fungi, animals, or plants. Most, but not all, are unicellular. Because their cells are eukaryotic, even the simplest protists are much more complex than any prokaryote.

The fossil record indicates that the first eukaryotes evolved from prokaryotes around 2 billion years ago. These primal eukaryotes were not only the predecessors of the great variety of modern protists; they were also ancestral to all other eukaryotes—plants, fungi, and animals. So before we sample the wide diversity of present-day protists, let's look at how it all began.

The Origin of Eukaryotic Cells

Membrane-enclosed organelles are a distinguishing feature of eukaryotic cells. How did these complex cells arise from prokaryotic ancestors? A widely accepted theory is that eukaryotic cells evolved through a combination of two processes. In one process, the eukaryotic cell's endomembrane system—all of the membrane-enclosed organelles except mitochondria and chloroplasts (review Figure 4.18)—evolved from inward folds of the plasma membrane of a prokaryotic cell **(Figure 15.19a)**.

A second process, called endosymbiosis, generated mitochondria and chloroplasts. **Symbiosis** ("living together") is a close association between organisms of two or more species, and **endosymbiosis** refers to one species living inside another host species. Chloroplasts and mitochondria seem to have evolved from small symbiotic prokaryotes (symbionts) that established residence within other, larger host prokaryotes **(Figure 15.19b)**. These small prokaryotes may have gained entrance to the larger cell as undigested prey or as internal parasites. In a world that was becoming increasingly aerobic, a cell that was itself an anaerobe would have benefited from aerobic endosymbionts that turned the oxygen to advantage. And a heterotrophic host could derive nourishment from photosynthetic endosymbionts. As the host and endosymbionts became increasingly interdependent, they would have become single organisms with inseparable parts.

Extensive evidence supports the endosymbiosis model. Present-day mitochondria and chloroplasts are similar to prokaryotic cells in a number of ways. For example, both types of organelles contain small amounts of DNA, RNA, and ribosomes that resemble prokaryotic versions more than eukaryotic ones. They also replicate their own DNA and reproduce within the cell by a process resembling the binary fission of prokaryotes. ☑

☑ **CHECKPOINT**

Which organelles of eukaryotic cells probably descended from endosymbiotic bacteria?

Answer: *mitochondria and chloroplasts*

▼ **Figure 15.19** **A two-stage hypothesis for the evolution of eukaryotes through endosymbiosis.**

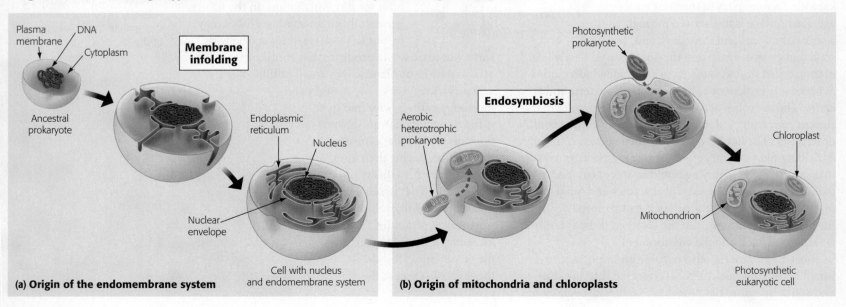

(a) Origin of the endomembrane system

(b) Origin of mitochondria and chloroplasts

The Diversity of Protists

The origin of the eukaryotic cell made more complex organisms possible, and a vast variety of protists evolved. Given that the term *protist* is a catch-all category, it shouldn't be surprising that the protists are a mixed bag of organisms. They are all eukaryotes, but they are so diverse that it is hard to name any other general characteristics about them. Biologists used to classify all protists in a kingdom called Protista, but recent molecular and cellular studies have shaken the foundations of protist taxonomy. It is now clear that there are multiple clades of protists, with some lineages more closely related to plants, fungi, or animals than they are to other protists. While our knowledge of the evolutionary relationships among these diverse groups remains incomplete, *protists* is still a convenient term to refer to eukaryotes that are not plants, animals, or fungi.

One mark of protist diversity is the variety of ways they obtain their nutrition. Some protists are autotrophs, producing their food by photosynthesis. Photosynthetic protists belong to an informal category called **algae** (singular, *alga*). Algae may be unicellular, colonial, or multicellular, such as the one shown in **Figure 15.20a**. Other protists are heterotrophs, acquiring their food from other organisms. Some heterotrophic protists eat bacteria or other protists; some are fungus-like and obtain organic molecules by absorption. Still others are parasitic. A **parasite** derives its nutrition from a living host, which is harmed by the interaction. For example, the parasitic trypanosomes shown among human red blood cells in **Figure 15.20b** cause sleeping sickness, a debilitating

What do all protists have in common?

disease common in parts of Africa. Yet other protists are mixotrophs, capable of both photosynthesis and heterotrophy. *Euglena* **(Figure 15.20c)**, a common inhabitant of pond water, can change its mode of nutrition, depending on availability of light and nutrients.

Protist habitats are also diverse. Most protists are aquatic, living in oceans, lakes, and ponds **(Figure 15.21)**. They are found almost anywhere there is moisture, including terrestrial habitats such as damp soil and leaf litter. Others reside in the bodies of various host organisms in mutually beneficial relationships. For example, coral reefs are made possible by the unicellular algae that inhabit the bodies of reef-building coral animals.

▼ **Figure 15.21 A diversity of protists in a drop of pond water.**

LM 240×

▼ **Figure 15.20 Protist modes of nutrition.**

(a) An autotroph: *Caulerpa,* a multicellular alga

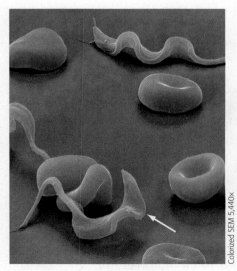

Colorized SEM 5,440×

(b) A heterotroph: parasitic trypanosome

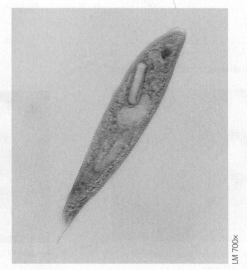

LM 700×

(c) A mixotroph: *Euglena*

And without the protists that inhabit their intestinal tract, termites would not be able to damage houses: Termite endosymbionts digest the tough cellulose in the wood.

Because the classification of protists remains a work in progress, our brief survey of protists is not organized to correspond with any hypothesis about phylogeny. Instead, we'll look at four major categories of protists, grouped by lifestyle: protozoans, slime molds, unicellular and colonial algae, and seaweeds.

Protozoans

Protists that live primarily by ingesting food are called **protozoans (Figure 15.22)**. Protozoans thrive in all types of aquatic environments. Most species eat bacteria or other protozoans, but some can absorb nutrients dissolved in the water. Protozoans that live as parasites in animals, though in the minority, cause some of the world's most harmful diseases.

Flagellates are protozoans that move by means of one or more flagella. Most species are free-living (nonparasitic). However, this group also includes some nasty parasites that make people sick. An example is *Giardia*, a common waterborne parasite that causes severe diarrhea. People most often pick up *Giardia* by drinking water contaminated with feces containing the parasite. For example, a swimmer in a lake or river might accidentally ingest water, or a hiker might drink contaminated water from a seemingly pristine stream. (Boiling the water first will kill *Giardia*.) Another flagellate is *Trichomonas*, a common sexually transmitted parasite. The parasite travels through the reproductive tract by moving its flagella and undulating part of its membrane. In women, these protozoans feed on white blood cells and bacteria living on the cells lining the vagina. *Trichomonas* also infects the cells lining the male reproductive tract, but limited availability of food results in very small population sizes. Consequently, males typically have no symptoms of infection.

Amoebas are characterized by great flexibility in their body shape and the absence of permanent organelles for locomotion. Most species move and feed by means of **pseudopodia** (singular, *pseudopodium*), temporary extensions of the cell. Amoebas can assume virtually any shape as they creep over rocks, sticks, or mud at the bottom of a pond or ocean. One species of parasitic amoeba causes amoebic dysentery, a disease that is responsible for an estimated 100,000 deaths worldwide every year. Other protozoans with pseudopodia include the **forams**, which have shells. The pseudopodia extend through small pores in the shell. Although they are single-celled, the largest forams grow to a diameter of several centimeters. Ninety percent of forams that have been identified are fossils.

Apicomplexans are all parasitic, and some cause serious human diseases. They are named for a structure at their apex (tip) that is specialized for penetrating host cells and tissues. This group of protozoans includes *Plasmodium*, the parasite that causes malaria (see the Biology and Society essay in Chapter 13). Another apicomplexan is *Toxoplasma*. Millions of people in the United States carry *Toxoplasma* in their intestinal tracts but don't become sick because the immune system keeps the parasite in check. However, a woman who is newly infected with *Toxoplasma* during pregnancy can pass the parasite to her unborn child, who may suffer damage to the nervous system as a result. *Toxoplasma* can also cause serious disease in individuals whose immune systems are impaired, such as AIDS patients.

Ciliates are protozoans named for their hair-like structures called cilia, which provide movement for the protist and sweep food into its mouth. Nearly all ciliates are free-living (nonparasitic) and include both heterotrophs and mixotrophs. If you have had the opportunity to explore protist diversity in a droplet of pond water, you may have seen the common freshwater ciliate *Paramecium*. ✔

☑ CHECKPOINT

What three modes of locomotion occur among protozoans?

Answer: movement using flagella, cilia, and pseudopodia

▼ Figure 15.22 **A diversity of protozoans.**

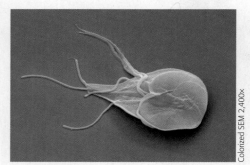

A flagellate: *Giardia*. This flagellated protozoan parasite can colonize and reproduce within the human intestine, causing disease.

Colorized SEM 2,400×

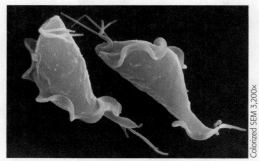

Another flagellate: *Trichomonas*. This common sexually transmitted parasite causes an estimated 5 million new infections each year.

Colorized SEM 3,200×

An amoeba. This amoeba is beginning to wrap pseudopodia around an algal cell in preparation for engulfing it.

Colorized TEM 2,300×

Slime Molds

These protists are more attractive than their name implies. Slime molds resemble fungi in appearance and lifestyle, but the similarities are due to convergent evolution; slime molds are more closely related to amoebas than to fungi. The weblike body of a slime mold, like that of a fungus, is an adaptation that increases exposure to the environment. This suits the role of these organisms as decomposers. The two main groups of these protists are plasmodial slime molds and cellular slime molds.

Plasmodial slime molds are named for the feeding stage in their life cycle, an amoeboid mass called a plasmodium (**Figure 15.23**)—not to be confused with *Plasmodium*, the apicomplexan parasite that causes malaria. You can find plasmodial slime molds among the leaf litter and other decaying material on a forest floor, and you won't need a microscope to see them. A plasmodium can measure several centimeters across,

with its network of fine filaments taking in bacteria and bits of dead organic matter amoeboid style. Large as it is, the plasmodium is actually a single cell with many nuclei.

The study of **cellular slime molds** raises a question about what it means to be an individual organism, given the different forms they can take during their successive life stages (**Figure 15.24**). The feeding stage of a cellular slime mold consists of ❶ solitary amoeboid cells. They function individually, using their pseudopodia to creep through organic matter and engulf bacteria. But when food is in short supply, the amoeboid cells swarm together to form ❷ a slug-like colony that moves and functions as a single unit. After a brief period of mobility, the colony ❸ extends a stalk and develops into a multicellular reproductive structure. ☑

☑ **CHECKPOINT**

Which protozoans are most similar in their movement to the unicellular stage of slime molds?

Answer: amoebas

▼ **Figure 15.23 A plasmodial slime mold.** The weblike form of the slime mold's feeding stage is an adaptation that enlarges the organism's surface area, increasing its contact with food, water, and oxygen.

▼ **Figure 15.24 Life stages of a cellular slime mold.**

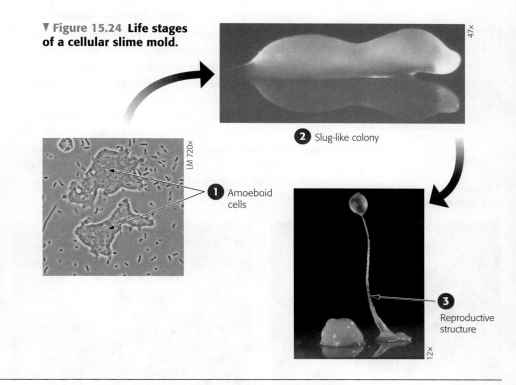

❷ Slug-like colony

❶ Amoeboid cells

❸ Reproductive structure

A foram. A foram cell secretes a shell made of organic material hardened with calcium carbonate. The shells of fossilized forams are a major component of limestone.

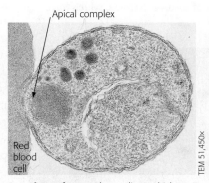

Apical complex

Red blood cell

An apicomplexan. *Plasmodium*, which causes malaria, enters red blood cells of its human host. The parasite feeds on the host cell from within, eventually destroying it.

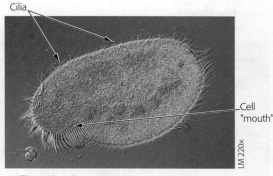

Cilia

Cell "mouth"

A ciliate. The ciliate *Paramecium* uses its cilia to move through pond water. Cilia lining the oral groove keep a current of water containing food moving toward the cell "mouth."

309

Unicellular and Colonial Algae

Algae are photosynthetic protists whose chloroplasts support food chains in freshwater and marine ecosystems. Researchers are currently trying to harness their ability to convert light energy to chemical energy for another purpose—to produce biofuels. We'll look at three groups of unicellular algae—dinoflagellates, diatoms, and green algae—and one type of colonial algae.

Many unicellular algae are components of **plankton**, the communities of organisms, mostly microscopic, that drift or swim weakly near the surfaces of ponds, lakes, and oceans. Dinoflagellates are abundant in the vast aquatic pastures of plankton. Each **dinoflagellate** species has a characteristic shape reinforced by external plates made of cellulose (**Figure 15.25a**). The beating of two flagella in perpendicular grooves produces a spinning movement. Dinoflagellate blooms—population explosions—sometimes cause warm coastal waters to turn pinkish orange, a phenomenon known as a red tide. Toxins produced by some red-tide dinoflagellates have caused massive fish kills, especially in the tropics, and are poisonous to humans as well.

Diatoms have glassy cell walls containing silica, the mineral used to make glass (**Figure 15.25b**). The cell wall consists of two halves that fit together like the bottom and lid of a shoe box. Diatoms store their food reserves in the form of an oil that provides buoyancy, keeping diatoms floating as plankton near the sunlit surface. Massive accumulations of fossilized diatoms make up thick sediments known as diatomaceous earth, which is mined for its use as a filtering material, an abrasive, and a natural insecticide.

Green algae are named for their grass-green chloroplasts. Unicellular green algae flourish in most freshwater lakes and ponds, as well as many home pools and aquariums. Some species are flagellated, such as *Chlamydomonas* (**Figure 15.25c**). The green algal group also includes colonial forms, such as *Volvox*, shown in **Figure 15.25d**. Each *Volvox* colony is a hollow ball of flagellated cells (the small green dots in the photo) that are very similar to certain unicellular green algae. The balls within the balls in Figure 15.25d are daughter colonies that will be released when the parent colonies rupture. Of all photosynthetic protists, green algae are the most closely related to plants. (We'll examine the evidence of this evolutionary relationship in the next chapter.)

Seaweeds

Defined as large, multicellular marine algae, **seaweeds** grow on rocky shores and just offshore beyond the zone of the pounding surf. Their cell walls have slimy and rubbery substances that cushion their bodies against the agitation of the waves. Some seaweeds are as large and complex as many plants. And though the word *seaweed* implies a plantlike appearance, the similarities between these algae and plants are a consequence of convergent evolution. In fact, the closest relatives of seaweeds are certain unicellular algae, which is why many biologists include seaweeds with the protists. Seaweeds are classified into three different groups (**Figure 15.26**), based partly on the types of pigments present in their chloroplasts: green algae, red algae, and brown algae (some of which are known as kelp).

Many coastal people, particularly in Asia, harvest seaweeds for food. For example, in Japan and Korea, some seaweed species, including brown algae called kombu, are ingredients in soups. Other seaweeds, such as red algae called nori, are used to wrap sushi. Marine algae are rich in iodine and other essential minerals. However, much of their organic material consists of unusual polysaccharides that humans cannot digest, which prevents seaweeds from becoming staple foods. They are eaten mostly for their rich tastes and unusual textures. The gel-forming substances in the cell walls of seaweeds are widely used as thickeners for such processed foods as puddings, ice cream, and salad dressing. The seaweed extract called agar provides the gel-forming base for the media microbiologists use to culture bacteria in petri dishes and for a type of gel commonly used to perform gel electrophoresis (as shown in Figure 12.17). ☑

☑ CHECKPOINT

1. What metabolic process mainly distinguishes algae from protozoans?
2. Are seaweeds plants?

Answers: 1. photosynthesis 2. No, they are large, multicellular marine algae.

▼ **Figure 15.25 Unicellular and colonial algae.**

(a) A dinoflagellate, with its wall of protective plates

SEM 1,065×

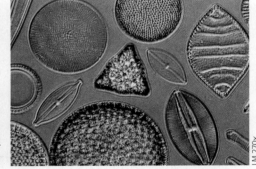

(b) A sample of diverse diatoms, which have glassy walls

LM 270×

(c) *Chlamydomonas*, a unicellular green alga with a pair of flagella

Colorized SEM 1,750×

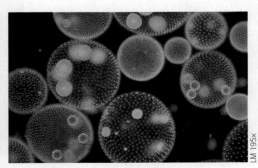

(d) *Volvox*, a colonial green alga

LM 195×

▼ **Figure 15.26 The three major groups of seaweeds.**

Green algae. This sea lettuce is an edible species that inhabits the intertidal zone, where the land meets the ocean. In addition to seaweeds, green algae include unicellular and colonial species.

Red algae. These seaweeds are most abundant in the warm coastal waters of the tropics. Because their chloroplasts have special pigments that absorb the blue and green light that penetrates best through water, red algae can generally live in the deepest water.

Brown algae. This group includes the largest seaweeds, known as kelp, which grow as marine "forests" in relatively deep water beyond the intertidal zone.

How Life Began EVOLUTION CONNECTION

The Origin of Multicellular Life

An orchestra can play a greater variety of musical compositions than a violin soloist can. Put simply, increased complexity makes more variations possible. Thus, the origin of the eukaryotic cell led to an evolutionary radiation of new forms of life. Unicellular protists, which are organized on the complex eukaryotic plan, are much more diverse in form than the simpler prokaryotes. The evolution of multicellular bodies crossed another threshold in structural organization.

Multicellular organisms are fundamentally different from unicellular ones. In a unicellular organism, all of life's activities are carried out by a single cell. In contrast, a multicellular organism has various specialized cells that perform different functions—such as feeding, waste disposal, gas exchange, and protection—and are dependent on each other.

The evolutionary links between unicellular and multicellular life were probably colonial forms, in which unicellular protists stuck together as loose federations of independent cells **(Figure 15.27)**. The gradual transition from colonies to true multicellular organisms involved the cells becoming increasingly interdependent

as a division of labor evolved. We can see one level of specialization and cooperation in the colonial green alga *Volvox* (see Figure 15.25d). *Volvox* produces gametes (sperm and ova), which depend on nonreproductive (somatic) cells while developing. Cells in truly multicellular organisms are specialized for many more nonreproductive functions.

Multicellularity evolved many times among the ancestral stock of protists, leading to new waves of biological diversification. The diverse seaweeds are examples of their descendants, and so are plants, fungi, and animals. In the next chapter, we'll trace the long evolutionary movement of plants and fungi onto land.

▼ **Figure 15.27 A model for the evolution of multicellular organisms from unicellular protists.**

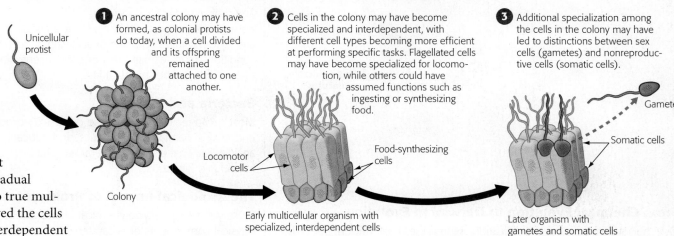

Unicellular protist

1 An ancestral colony may have formed, as colonial protists do today, when a cell divided and its offspring remained attached to one another.

Colony

2 Cells in the colony may have become specialized and interdependent, with different cell types becoming more efficient at performing specific tasks. Flagellated cells may have become specialized for locomotion, while others could have assumed functions such as ingesting or synthesizing food.

Locomotor cells

Food-synthesizing cells

Early multicellular organism with specialized, interdependent cells

3 Additional specialization among the cells in the colony may have led to distinctions between sex cells (gametes) and nonreproductive cells (somatic cells).

Gamete

Somatic cells

Later organism with gametes and somatic cells

Chapter Review

SUMMARY OF KEY CONCEPTS

 Go to **www.masteringbiology.com** for homework assignments, practice quizzes, Pearson eText, and more.

Major Episodes in the History of Life

Major episode	Millions of years ago
Plants and fungi colonize land	500
All major animal phyla established	530
First multicellular organisms	1,200
Oldest eukaryotic fossils	1,800
Accumulation of O₂ in atmosphere	2,400
Oldest prokaryotic fossils	3,500
Origin of Earth	4,600

The Origin of Life

Resolving the Biogenesis Paradox

All life today arises only by the reproduction of preexisting life. However, most biologists think it is possible that chemical and physical processes in Earth's primordial environment produced the first cells through a series of stages.

A Four-Stage Hypothesis for the Origin of Life

One scenario suggests that the first organisms were products of chemical evolution in four stages:

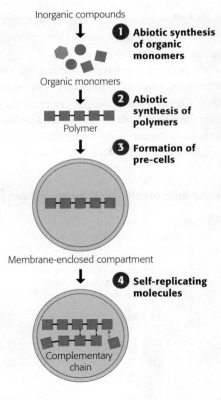

Inorganic compounds

① **Abiotic synthesis of organic monomers**

Organic monomers

② **Abiotic synthesis of polymers**

Polymer

③ **Formation of pre-cells**

Membrane-enclosed compartment

④ **Self-replicating molecules**

Complementary chain

From Chemical Evolution to Darwinian Evolution

Over millions of years, natural selection favored the most efficient pre-cells, which evolved into the first prokaryotic cells.

Prokaryotes

They're Everywhere!

Prokaryotes are found wherever there is life and greatly outnumber eukaryotes. Prokaryotes thrive in habitats where eukaryotes cannot live. A few prokaryotic species cause serious disease, but most are either benign or beneficial to other forms of life.

The Structure and Function of Prokaryotes

Prokaryotic cells lack nuclei and other membrane-enclosed organelles. Most have cell walls. Prokaryotes exhibit three common shapes.

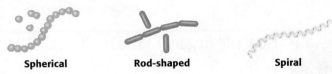

Spherical   **Rod-shaped**   **Spiral**

About half of all prokaryotic species are mobile, most of these using flagella to move. Some prokaryotes can survive extended periods of harsh conditions by forming endospores. Many prokaryotes can reproduce by binary fission at high rates if conditions are favorable, but growth is usually restricted by limited resources.

Prokaryotes exhibit all four major modes of nutrition.

Nutritional Mode	Energy Source	Carbon Source
Photoautotroph	Sunlight	CO₂
Chemoautotroph	Inorganic chemicals	CO₂
Photoheterotroph	Sunlight	Organic compounds
Chemoheterotroph	Organic compounds	Organic compounds

The Two Main Branches of Prokaryotic Evolution: Bacteria and Archaea

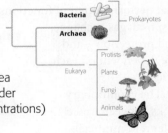

The prokaryotic lineage includes domains Bacteria and Archaea. Many archaea are "extremophiles" capable of surviving under conditions (such as high heat or salt concentrations) that would kill other forms of life.

Bacteria and Disease

Most pathogenic bacteria cause disease by producing exotoxins or endotoxins. Sanitation, antibiotics, and education are the best defenses against bacterial disease. Several bacteria have the potential to be formidable weapons.

The Ecological Impact of Prokaryotes

Prokaryotes help recycle chemical elements between the biological and physical components of ecosystems. People use prokaryotes to remove pollutants from water, air, and soil in the process called bioremediation.

Protists

The Origin of Eukaryotic Cells

The nucleus and endomembrane system of eukaryotes probably evolved from infoldings of the plasma membrane of ancestral prokaryotes. Mitochondria and chloroplasts probably evolved from symbiotic prokaryotes that took up residence inside larger cells, a process called endosymbiosis.

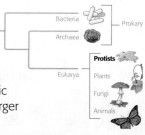

The Diversity of Protists

Protists are unicellular eukaryotes and their closest multicellular relatives.

- Protozoans (including flagellates, amoebas, apicomplexans, and ciliates) primarily live in aquatic environments and ingest their food.
- Slime molds (including plasmodial slime molds and cellular slime molds) resemble fungi in appearance and lifestyle as decomposers, but are not at all closely related.
- Unicellular algae (including dinoflagellates, diatoms, and unicellular green algae) are photosynthetic protists that support food chains in freshwater and marine ecosystems.
- Seaweeds—which include green, red, and brown algae—are large, multicellular marine algae that grow on and near rocky shores.

SELF-QUIZ

1. Place these events in the history of life on Earth in the order that they occurred.
   a. colonization of land by animals
   b. colonization of land by plants and fungi
   c. diversification of animals (Cambrian explosion)
   d. origin of eukaryotes
   e. origin of humans
   f. origin of multicellular organisms
   g. origin of prokaryotes

2. Place the following steps in the origin of life in the order that they are hypothesized to have occurred.
   a. integration of abiotically produced molecules into membrane-enclosed pre-cells
   b. origin of the first molecules capable of self-replication
   c. abiotic joining of organic monomers into polymers
   d. abiotic synthesis of organic monomers
   e. natural selection among pre-cells

3. DNA replication relies on the enzyme DNA polymerase. Why does this suggest that the earliest genes were made from RNA?

4. Contrast exotoxins with endotoxins.

5. What is the difference between autotrophs and heterotrophs in terms of the source of their organic compounds?

6. The bacteria that cause tetanus can be killed only by prolonged heating at temperatures considerably above boiling. What does this suggest about tetanus bacteria?

7. To what nutritional classification do you belong? To what nutritional classification does a mushroom belong? (*Hint:* Review Figure 15.12.)

8. Why are protists especially important to biologists investigating the evolution of eukaryotic life?

9. Of the following, which describes protists most inclusively?
   a. multicellular eukaryotes
   b. protozoans
   c. eukaryotes that are not plants, fungi, or animals
   d. single-celled organisms closely related to bacteria

10. Which algal group is most closely related to plants?
    a. diatoms
    b. green algae
    c. dinoflagellates
    d. seaweeds

Answers to these questions can be found in Appendix: Self-Quiz Answers.

THE PROCESS OF SCIENCE

11. Imagine you are on a team designing a moon base that will be self-contained and self-sustaining. Once supplied with building materials, equipment, and organisms from Earth, the base will be expected to function indefinitely. One of the members of your team has suggested that everything sent to the base be chemically treated or irradiated so that no bacteria of any kind are present. Do you think this is a good idea? Predict some of the consequences of eliminating all bacteria from an environment.

12. Your classmate says that organisms that require oxygen existed before photosynthetic organisms. Do you support this idea? Explain why or why not.

BIOLOGY AND SOCIETY

13. Many local newspapers publish a weekly list of restaurants that have been cited by inspectors for poor sanitation. Locate such a report and highlight the cases that are probably associated with food contamination by pathogenic prokaryotes.

14. What do you think should be done to prevent attacks by terrorists using biological weapons?

16 Plants, Fungi, and the Move onto Land

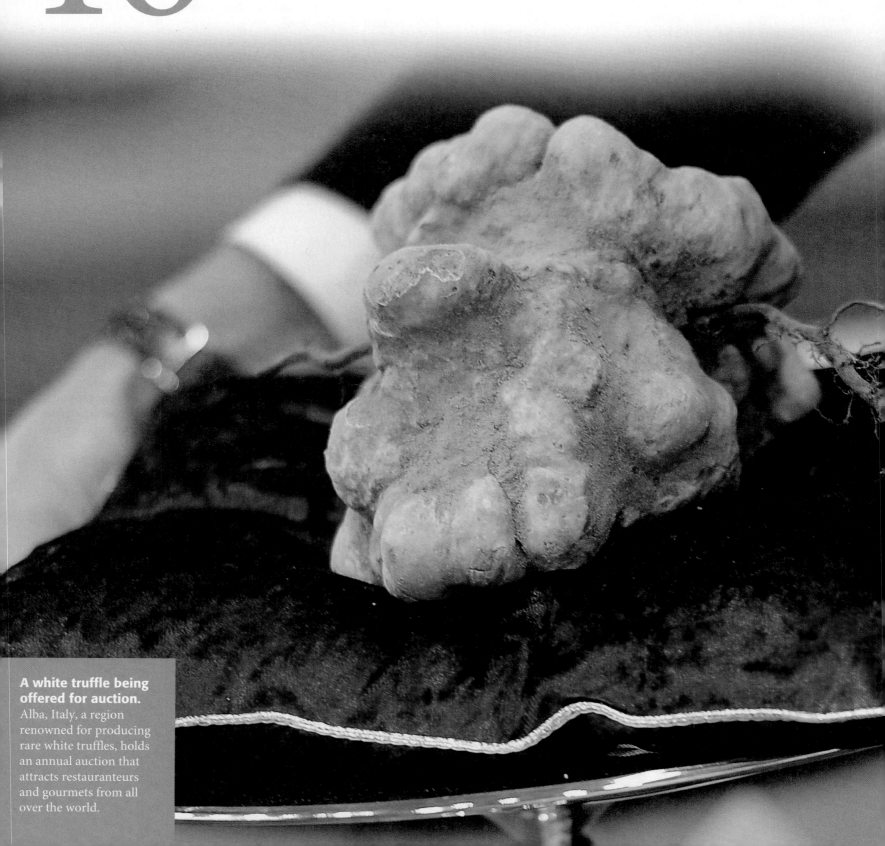

A white truffle being offered for auction. Alba, Italy, a region renowned for producing rare white truffles, holds an annual auction that attracts restauranteurs and gourmets from all over the world.

Plant-Fungus Symbiosis BIOLOGY AND SOCIETY

The Diamond of the Kitchen

To the untrained eye, a truffle (the fungus, not the chocolate) is an unappealing lump that you probably wouldn't eat on a dare. But despite their unappetizing appearance, truffles are treasured by gourmets as "diamonds of the kitchen." They command prices up to hundreds of dollars per ounce for the best specimens. A 3.3-pound white truffle—an unusually large individual of the rarest variety—brought a record $330,000 at auction. What's the attraction? Rather than their taste, truffles are prized for their powerful scent, which has been described as earthy or moldy. A little truffle goes a long way. Chefs only need to add a few shavings from a truffle to infuse a dish with its delectable essence.

Truffles are the subterranean reproductive bodies of certain fungi. Their job is to produce spores, single cells that are capable of growing into a new fungus, just as a seed can grow into a new plant. It is generally advantageous for seeds or spores to start their lives in a new place, away from the ground inhabited by their parents. And that's where the potent truffle smell comes in. Attracted by the heady aroma, animals excavate and eat the fungi and later deposit the hardy spores in their feces. Human noses are not sensitive enough to locate the buried treasures, so truffle hunters use pigs or trained dogs to sniff out their quarry.

Besides being culinary gems, truffles represent the essential role of fungi as the hidden power behind the throne of the plant kingdom. The roots of most plants are surrounded—in some cases even permeated—by a finely woven web of fungal filaments. Truffles, for example, have such a relationship with certain species of trees. This association is an example of **symbiosis**, an interaction in which one species lives in or on another species. The ultrathin filaments reach into pockets between the soil grains that are too small for roots to enter, absorbing water and inorganic nutrients and passing them to the plant. The plant returns the favor by supplying the fungus with sugars and other organic molecules. This relationship between fungus and root is evident on some of the oldest plant fossils, suggesting that the mutually beneficial symbiosis was crucial to the colonization of land.

Colonizing Land

Plants are terrestrial (land-dwelling) organisms. It is true that some, such as water lilies, have returned to the water, but they evolved from terrestrial ancestors (just as several species of aquatic mammals, such as whales, evolved from terrestrial mammals). In this section, we'll discuss some of the adaptations that allowed plants to move onto land.

Terrestrial Adaptations of Plants

Why aren't seaweeds considered plants?

What exactly is a plant? A **plant** is a multicellular eukaryote that makes organic molecules by photosynthesis; that is, they are photoautotrophs (see Figure 15.12). Photosynthesis distinguishes plants from the animal and fungal kingdoms. But what about large algae, including seaweeds, which

we classified as protists in the preceding chapter? They, too, are multicellular, eukaryotic, and photosynthetic. What distinguishes plants from algae is a set of structural and reproductive terrestrial adaptations.

Structural Adaptations

Living on land poses different problems than living in water (**Figure 16.1**). In terrestrial habitats, the resources that a photosynthetic organism needs are found in two very different places. Light and carbon dioxide are mainly available in the air, while water and mineral nutrients are found mainly in the soil. Thus, the complex bodies of plants are specialized to take advantage of these two environments by having both aerial leaf-bearing organs called **shoots** and subterranean organs called **roots**.

As you learned in the Biology and Society section, most plants have symbiotic fungi associated with their roots. These root-fungus combinations are called **mycorrhizae** ("fungus roots") (**Figure 16.2**). For their part, the fungi absorb water and essential minerals from the soil and provide these materials to the plant. The sugars produced by the plant nourish the fungi. Mycorrhizae are key adaptations that made it possible for plants to live on land.

Shoots also show structural adaptations to the terrestrial environment. Leaves are the main photosynthetic organs of most plants. Exchange of carbon dioxide (CO_2) and oxygen (O_2) between the atmosphere and the

▼ Figure 16.1 **Structural adaptations of algae and plants.**

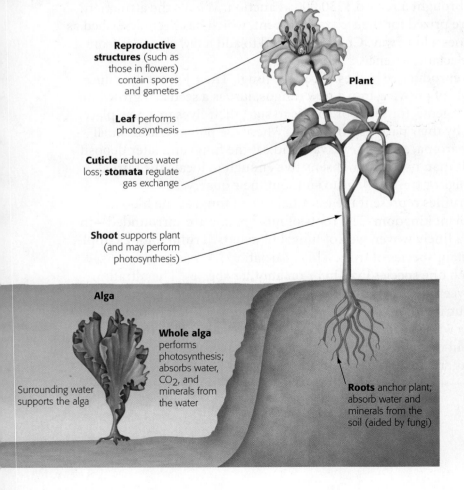

Reproductive structures (such as those in flowers) contain spores and gametes

Plant

Leaf performs photosynthesis

Cuticle reduces water loss; **stomata** regulate gas exchange

Shoot supports plant (and may perform photosynthesis)

Alga

Whole alga performs photosynthesis; absorbs water, CO_2, and minerals from the water

Surrounding water supports the alga

Roots anchor plant; absorb water and minerals from the soil (aided by fungi)

▼ Figure 16.2 **Mycorrhizae: symbiotic associations of fungi and roots.** The finely branched filaments of the fungus (white in the photo) provide an extensive surface area for absorption of water and minerals from the soil.

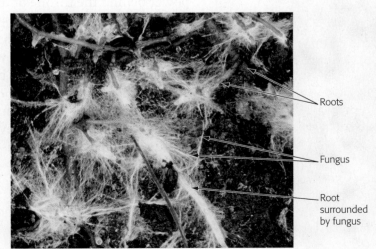

Roots

Fungus

Root surrounded by fungus

photosynthetic interior of a leaf occurs via **stomata** (singular, *stoma*), the microscopic pores found on a leaf's surface (see Figure 7.2). A waxy layer called the **cuticle** coats the leaves and other aerial parts of most plants, helping the plant body retain water (see Figure 18.8b).

Differentiation of the plant body into shoot and root systems solved one problem but created new ones. For the shoot system to stand up straight in the air, it must have support. This is not a major problem in the water: Huge seaweeds do not need skeletons because the surrounding water buoys them. An important terrestrial adaptation of plants is **lignin**, a chemical that hardens cell walls. Imagine what would happen to you if your skeleton were to suddenly turn mushy. A tree would also collapse if it were not for its "skeleton," its framework of lignin-rich cell walls.

Specialization of the plant body into shoots and roots also introduced the problem of transporting vital materials between the distant organs. The terrestrial equipment of most plants includes **vascular tissue**, a system of tube-shaped cells that branch throughout the plant **(Figure 16.3)**. The vascular tissue actually has two types of tissues specialized for transport: **xylem**, consisting of dead cells with tubular cavities for transporting water and minerals from roots to leaves; and **phloem**, consisting of living cells that distribute sugars from the leaves to the roots and other nonphotosynthetic parts of the plant.

Reproductive Adaptations

Adapting to land also required a new mode of reproduction. For algae, the surrounding water ensures that gametes (sperm and eggs) and developing offspring stay moist. The aquatic environment also provides a means of dispersing the gametes and offspring. Plants, however, must keep their gametes and developing offspring from drying out in the air. Plants (and some algae) produce their gametes in protective structures that are called **gametangia** (singular, *gametangium*). A gametangium has a jacket of protective cells surrounding a moist chamber where gametes can develop without dehydrating.

For most plants, sperm reach the eggs by traveling inside pollen grains, which are carried by wind or animals. The egg remains within tissues of the mother plant and is fertilized there. In plants, but not algae, the zygote (fertilized egg) develops into an embryo while still contained within the female parent, which protects the embryo and keeps it from dehydrating **(Figure 16.4)**. Most plants rely on wind or animals, such as fruit-eating birds or mammals, to disperse their offspring, which are in the form of embryos contained in seeds. ✓

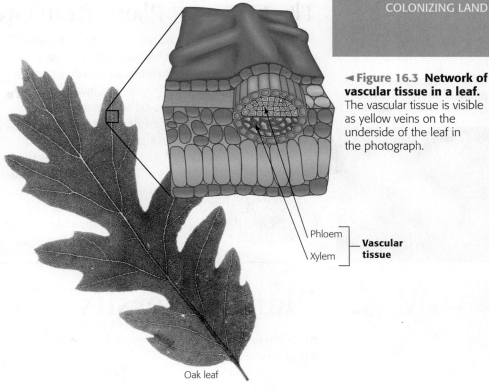

◄ **Figure 16.3 Network of vascular tissue in a leaf.** The vascular tissue is visible as yellow veins on the underside of the leaf in the photograph.

Phloem

Xylem

Vascular tissue

Oak leaf

▼ **Figure 16.4 The protected embryo of a plant.** Internal fertilization, with sperm and egg combining within a moist chamber on the mother plant, is an adaptation for living on land. The female parent continues to nurture and protect the plant embryo, which develops from the zygote.

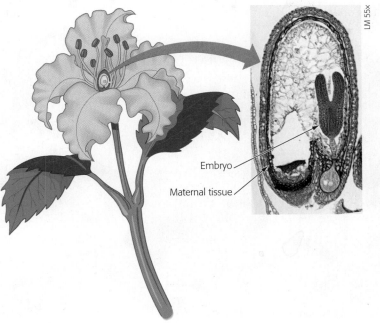

LM 55x

Embryo

Maternal tissue

✓ CHECKPOINT

Name some adaptations of plants for living on land.

Answer: any of the following: cuticle; stomata; vascular tissue; lignin-hardened cell walls; gametangia, which protect gametes; protected embryos; and differentiation of the body into aerial shoots and subterranean roots

317

The Origin of Plants from Green Algae

The algal ancestors of plants carpeted moist fringes of lakes or coastal salt marshes over 500 million years ago. These shallow-water habitats were subject to occasional drying, and natural selection would have favored algae that could survive periodic droughts. Some species accumulated adaptations that enabled them to live permanently above the water line. A modern-day lineage of green algae, the **charophytes (Figure 16.5)**, may resemble

▼ **Figure 16.5 Two species of charophytes, the closest algal relatives of plants.**

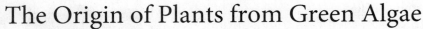

LM 265x

one of these early plant ancestors. Plants and present-day charophytes probably evolved from a common ancestor.

Adaptations making life on dry land possible had accumulated by about 475 million years ago, the age of the oldest known plant fossils. The evolutionary novelties of these first land plants opened the new frontier of a terrestrial habitat. Early plant life would have thrived in the new environment. Bright sunlight was abundant on land, the atmosphere had a wealth of carbon dioxide, and at first there were relatively few pathogens and plant-eating animals. The stage was set for an explosive diversification of plant life.

Plant Diversity

As we survey the diversity of modern plants, remember that the past is the key to the present. The history of the plant kingdom is a story of adaptation to diverse terrestrial habitats.

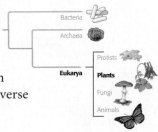

▼ **Figure 16.6 Highlights of plant evolution.** This phylogenetic tree highlights the evolution of structures that allowed plants to move onto land; these structures still exist in modern plants. As we survey the diversity of plants, miniature versions of this tree will help you place each plant group in its evolutionary context.

Highlights of Plant Evolution

The fossil record chronicles four major periods of plant evolution, which are also evident in the diversity of modern plants **(Figure 16.6)**. Each stage is marked by the evolution of structures that opened new opportunities on land.

1 After plants originated from an algal ancestor approximately 475 million years ago, early diversification gave rise to nonvascular plants, including mosses, liverworts, and hornworts. These plants, called **bryophytes**, lack true roots and leaves. Bryophytes also lack lignin, the wall-hardening material that enables other plants to stand tall. Without lignified cell walls, bryophytes have weak upright support. The most familiar bryophytes are **mosses**. A mat of moss actually consists of many plants growing in a tight pack, holding one another up. Gametangia, which protect the gametes and embryos, are a terrestrial adaptation that originated in bryophytes.

2 The second period of plant evolution, begun about 425 million years ago, was the diversification of

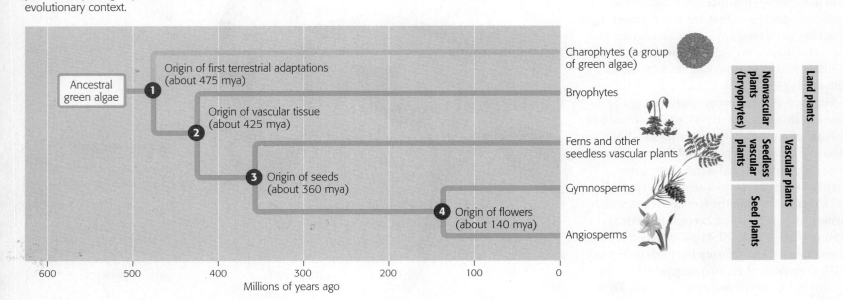

plants with vascular tissue. The presence of conducting tissues hardened with lignin allowed vascular plants to grow much taller, rising above the ground to achieve significant height. The earliest vascular plants lacked seeds. Today, this seedless condition is retained by **ferns** and a few other groups of vascular plants.

❸ The third major period of plant evolution began with the origin of the seed about 360 million years ago. Seeds advanced the colonization of land by further protecting plant embryos from drying and other hazards. A **seed** consists of an embryo packaged along with a store of food within a protective covering. The seeds of early seed plants were not enclosed in any specialized chambers. These plants gave rise to the **gymnosperms** ("naked seeds"). Today, the most widespread and diverse

gymnosperms are the **conifers**, consisting mainly of cone-bearing trees, such as pines.

❹ The fourth major episode in the evolutionary history of plants was the emergence of flowering plants, or **angiosperms** ("contained seeds"), at least 140 million years ago. The **flower** is a complex reproductive structure that bears seeds within protective chambers called ovaries. This contrasts with the naked seeds of gymnosperms. The great majority of living plants—some 250,000 species—are angiosperms, including all our fruit and vegetable crops, grains and other grasses, and most trees.

With these highlights as our framework, we are now ready to survey the four major groups of modern plants: bryophytes, ferns, gymnosperms, and angiosperms **(Figure 16.7).** ☑

▼ Figure 16.7 **The major groups of plants.**

PLANT DIVERSITY			
Bryophytes (nonvascular plants)	**Ferns** (seedless vascular plants)	**Gymnosperms** (naked-seed plants)	**Angiosperms** (flowering plants)

Bryophytes

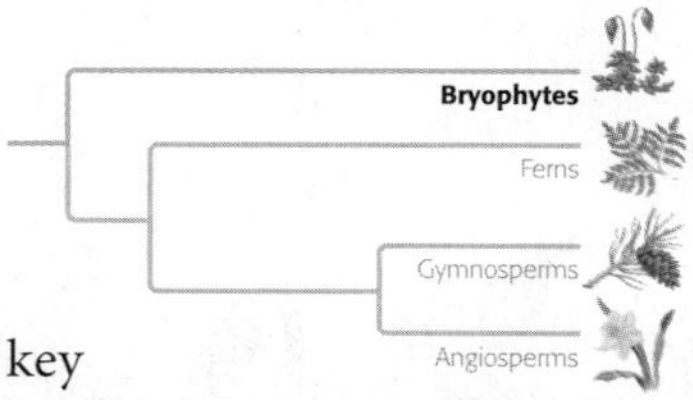

Mosses, which are bryophytes, may sprawl as low mats over acres of land **(Figure 16.8).** Mosses display two of the key terrestrial adaptations that made the move onto land possible: (1) a waxy cuticle that helps prevent dehydration and (2) the retention of developing embryos within the mother plant's gametangium. However, mosses are not totally liberated from their ancestral aquatic habitat. Mosses need water to reproduce because their sperm need to swim to reach eggs within the female gametangium. (A film of rainwater or dew is enough moisture for the sperm to travel.) In addition,

Bryophytes
Ferns
Gymnosperms
Angiosperms

▼ Figure 16.8 **A peat moss bog in Scotland.** Mosses are bryophytes, which are nonvascular plants. Sphagnum mosses, collectively called peat moss, carpet at least 3% of Earth's land surface. They are most commonly found in high northern latitudes. The ability of peat moss to absorb and retain water makes it an excellent addition to garden soil.

because most mosses have no vascular tissue to carry water from soil to aerial parts of the plant, they need to live in damp, shady places.

If you examine a mat of moss closely, you can see two distinct forms of the plant. The green, sponge-like plant that is the more obvious is called the **gametophyte**. Careful examination will reveal the other form of the moss, called a **sporophyte**, growing out of a gametophyte as a stalk with a capsule at its tip (**Figure 16.9**). The cells of the gametophyte are haploid—they have one set of chromosomes (see Figure 8.12). In contrast, the sporophyte is made up of diploid cells (with two chromosome sets). These two different stages of the plant life cycle are named for the types of reproductive cells they produce. Gametophytes produce gametes (sperm and eggs), while sporophytes produce spores. A **spore** is a haploid cell that can develop into a new individual without fusing with another cell (two gametes must fuse to form a zygote). Spores usually have tough coats that enable them to survive in harsh environments. Seedless plants, including mosses and ferns, disperse their offspring as spores rather than as multicellular seeds.

The gametophyte and sporophyte are alternating generations that take turns producing each other. Gametophytes produce gametes that unite to form zygotes, which develop into new sporophytes. And sporophytes produce spores that give rise to new gametophytes. This type of life cycle, called **alternation of generations**, occurs only in plants and multicellular green algae (**Figure 16.10**). Among plants, mosses and other bryophytes are unique in having the gametophyte as the larger, more obvious plant. As we continue our survey of plants, we'll see an increasing dominance of the sporophyte as the more highly developed generation. ☑

▼ Figure 16.9 The two forms of a moss. The feathery plant we generally know as a moss is the gametophyte. The stalk with the capsule at its tip is the sporophyte.

Spore capsule

Sporophytes

Gametophytes

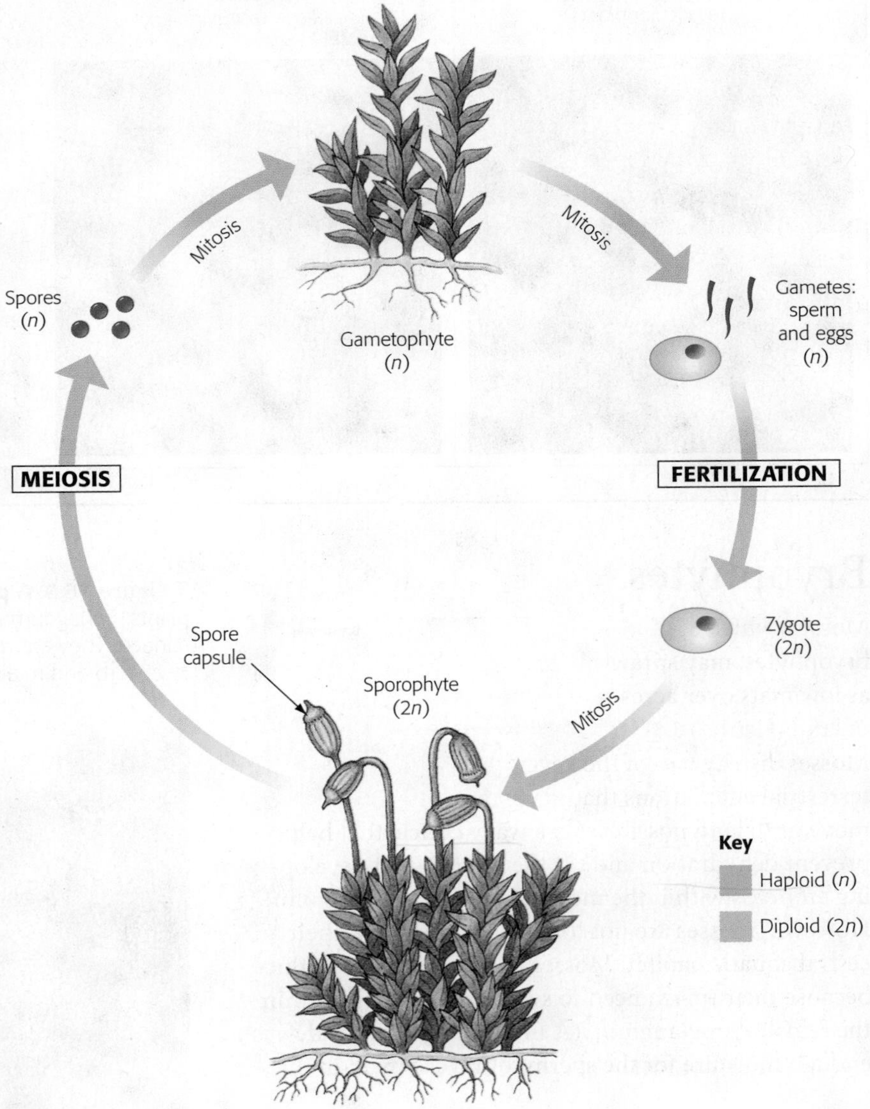

► Figure 16.10 Alternation of generations. Plants have life cycles very different from ours. Each of us is a diploid individual; the only haploid stages in the human life cycle, as for nearly all animals, are sperm and eggs. By contrast, plants have alternating generations: Diploid (2*n*) individuals (sporophytes) and haploid (*n*) individuals (gametophytes) generate each other in the life cycle.

Mitosis

Mitosis

Spores (*n*)

Gametophyte (*n*)

Gametes: sperm and eggs (*n*)

MEIOSIS

FERTILIZATION

Spore capsule

Sporophyte (2*n*)

Zygote (2*n*)

Mitosis

Key

Haploid (*n*)

Diploid (2*n*)

Ferns

Ferns took terrestrial adaptation to the next level with the evolution of vascular tissue. Ferns are by far the most diverse seedless vascular plants, with more than 12,000 known species. However, the sperm of ferns, like those of mosses, have flagella and must swim through a film of water to fertilize eggs. Most ferns inhabit the tropics, although many species are found in temperate forests, such as many woodlands in the United States (Figure 16.11).

During the Carboniferous period, from about 360 to 300 million years ago, ancient ferns were part of a much greater diversity of seedless plants that formed vast, swampy tropical forests over much of what is now Eurasia and North America (Figure 16.12). As the plants died, they fell into stagnant wetlands and did not decay completely. Their remains formed thick organic deposits. Later, seawater flooded the swamps, marine sediments covered the organic deposits, and pressure and heat gradually converted them to coal. Coal is black sedimentary rock made up of fossilized plant material. Like coal, oil and natural gas also formed from the remains of long-dead organisms; thus, all three are known as **fossil fuels**. Since the Industrial Revolution, coal has been a crucial source of energy for people. However, burning these fossil fuels releases CO_2 and other greenhouse gases into the atmosphere, contributing to global climate change. ☑

▼ **Figure 16.11 Ferns (seedless vascular plants).** The ferns in the foreground are growing on the forest floor in Redwood National Park, California. The fern generation familiar to us is the sporophyte generation. You would have to crawl on the forest floor and explore with careful hands and sharp eyes to find fern gametophytes (upper right), tiny plants growing on or just below the soil surface.

New sporophyte

Gametophyte

Spore capsule

"Fiddlehead" (young leaf ready to unfurl)

◄ **Figure 16.12 A "coal forest" of the Carboniferous period.** This painting, based on fossil evidence, reconstructs one of the great seedless forests. Most of the large trees belong to ancient groups of seedless vascular plants that are represented by just a few present-day species. The plants near the base of the trees are ferns.

☑ CHECKPOINT

Why are ferns able to grow taller than mosses?

Answer: Vascular tissue hardened with lignin allows ferns to stand taller and transport nutrients farther.

Gymnosperms

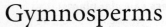

"Coal forests" dominated
the North American and
Eurasian landscapes until
near the end of the
Carboniferous period. At that
time, the global climate turned drier
and colder, and the vast swamps began to disappear.
This climatic change provided an opportunity for seed
plants, which can complete their life cycles on dry land
and withstand long, harsh winters. Of the earliest seed
plants, the most successful were the gymnosperms, and several kinds grew along
with the seedless plants in the Carboniferous swamps. Their descendants include the conifers,
or cone-bearing plants. Let's take a closer look at the
conifers before discussing the adaptations that allowed
seed plants to dominate the land.

*What is the oldest tree
in the United States?*

Conifers

Perhaps you have had the fun of hiking or skiing
through a forest of conifers, the most common gymnosperms. Pines, firs, spruces, junipers, cedars,
and redwoods are all conifers. A broad band of
coniferous forests covers much of northern Eurasia and North America and extends southward in mountainous regions (Figure 16.13).
Today, about 190 million acres of coniferous
forests in the United States, mostly in the
western states and Alaska, are designated
national forests.

Conifers are among the tallest, largest,
and oldest organisms on Earth. Coastal
redwoods, native to the northern California
coast, are the world's tallest trees—up to 110 m, the
height of a 33-story building. Giant sequoias, relatives
of redwoods that grow in the Sierra Nevada mountains
of California, are massive. One, known as the General
Sherman tree, is about 84 m (275 feet) high and outweighs the combined weight of a dozen space shuttles.
Bristlecone pines, another species of California conifer,
are among the oldest organisms alive. One bristlecone
pine is more than 4,600 years old; it was a young tree
when people invented writing.

Nearly all conifers are evergreens, meaning they retain leaves throughout the year. Even during winter, they
perform a limited amount of photosynthe-
sis on sunny days. And when spring comes,
conifers already have fully developed leaves
that can take advantage of the sunnier days. The needle-
shaped leaves of pines and firs are also adapted to survive
dry seasons. A thick cuticle covers the leaf, and the stomata are located in pits, further reducing water loss.

Coniferous forests are highly productive; you probably use products harvested from them every day. For
example, conifers provide much of our lumber for
building and wood pulp for paper production. What we
call wood is actually an accumulation of vascular tissue
with lignin, which gives the tree structural support.

Terrestrial Adaptations of Seed Plants

Compared with ferns, most gymnosperms have three
additional adaptations that make survival in diverse
terrestrial habitats possible: (1) further reduction of the
gametophyte, (2) pollen, and (3) seeds.

The first adaptation is an even greater development
of the diploid sporophyte compared with the haploid
gametophyte generation (Figure 16.14). A pine tree
or other conifer is actually a sporophyte with tiny

▼ **Figure 16.13 A
coniferous forest in Tetlin
National Wildlife Refuge,
Alaska.** Coniferous forests
are widespread in northern
North America and Eurasia;
conifers also grow in the
Southern Hemisphere, though
they are less numerous there.

► **Figure 16.14
Three variations
on alternation
of generations
in plants.**

Key

Haploid (*n*)

Diploid (2*n*)

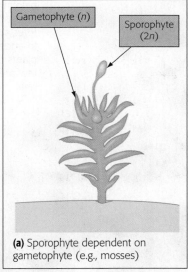

(a) Sporophyte dependent on
gametophyte (e.g., mosses)

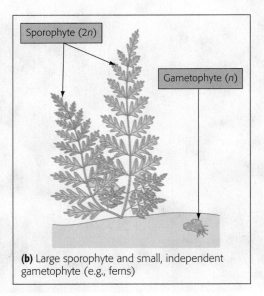

(b) Large sporophyte and small, independent
gametophyte (e.g., ferns)

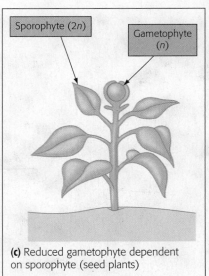

(c) Reduced gametophyte dependent
on sporophyte (seed plants)

gametophytes living in its cones (**Figure 16.15**). In contrast to what is seen in bryophytes and ferns, gymnosperm gametophytes are totally dependent on and protected by the tissues of the parent sporophyte.

A second adaptation of seed plants to dry land came with the evolution of pollen. A **pollen grain** is actually the much-reduced male gametophyte; it houses cells that will develop into sperm. In the case of conifers, wind carries the pollen from male to female cones, where eggs develop within female gametophytes. This mechanism for sperm transfer contrasts with the swimming sperm of mosses and ferns. In seed plants, this use of tough, airborne pollen that carries sperm to egg is a terrestrial adaptation that led to even greater success and diversity of plants on land.

The third important terrestrial adaptation of seed plants is the seed itself. A seed consists of a plant embryo packaged along with a food supply within a protective coat. Seeds develop from structures called **ovules** (**Figure 16.16**). In conifers, the ovules are located on the scales of female cones. Conifers and other gymnosperms, lacking ovaries, bear their seeds "naked" on the cone scales (though the seeds do have protective coats). Once released from the parent plant, the seed can remain dormant for days, months, or even years. Under favorable conditions, the seed can then **germinate**, or sprout: Its embryo emerges through the seed coat as a seedling. Some seeds drop close to their parents, while others are carried far by the wind or animals. ☑

▼ **Figure 16.15 A pine tree, the sporophyte, bearing two types of cones containing gametophytes.** Each scale of the female cone is actually a modified leaf that bears a structure called an ovule containing a female gametophyte. Male cones release clouds of millions of pollen grains, the male gametophytes. Some of these pollen grains land on female cones on trees of the same species. The sperm can fertilize eggs in the ovules of the female cones. The ovules eventually develop into seeds.

Scale

Ovule-producing cones; the scales contain female gametophytes

Pollen-producing cones; they produce male gametophytes

Ponderosa pine

▼ **Figure 16.16 From ovule to seed.**

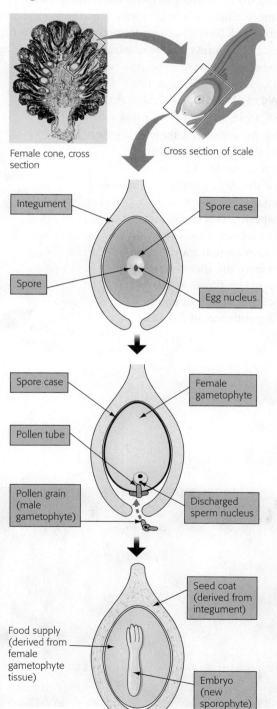

Female cone, cross section

Cross section of scale

Key
Haploid (*n*)
Diploid (2*n*)

Integument

Spore case

Spore

Egg nucleus

(a) Ovule. The sporophyte produces spores within a tissue surrounded by a productive integument, which may be multilayered.

Spore case

Female gametophyte

Pollen tube

Pollen grain (male gametophyte)

Discharged sperm nucleus

(b) Fertilized ovule. The spore develops into a female gametophyte, which produces one or more eggs. When a pollen grain enters the ovule through a special pore in the integument, it discharges sperm cells that fertilize eggs.

Seed coat (derived from integument)

Food supply (derived from female gametophyte tissue)

Embryo (new sporophyte)

(c) Seed. Fertilization initiates the transformation of ovule to seed. The fertilized egg (zygote) develops into an embryo; the rest of the gametophyte forms a tissue that stockpiles food; and the integument of the ovule hardens to become the seed coat.

Angiosperms

Angiosperms dominate
the modern landscape.
There are about 250,000
angiosperm species versus
about 700 species of gym-
nosperms. Several unique adaptations
account for the success of angiosperms. For example,
refinements in vascular tissue make water transport
even more efficient in angiosperms than in gymnosperms. Of all terrestrial adaptations, however, it is the
flower that accounts for the unparalleled success of the
angiosperms.

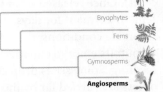

Flowers, Fruits, and the Angiosperm Life Cycle

No organism makes a showier display of its
sex life than the angiosperm.
From roses to dandelions,
flowers display a plant's
sex organs. For many
angiosperms, this showiness
helps to attract insects and
other animals that transfer
pollen from the sperm-bearing
organs of one flower to the
egg-bearing organs of another.
This dependence on animals
for pollen transfer targets the pollen to other plants of
the same species, rather than relying on uncertain winds
to blow the pollen around.

A flower is a short stem bearing modified leaves
that are attached in concentric circles at its base
(**Figure 16.17**). The outer layer consists of the **sepals**,
which are usually green. They enclose the flower before
it opens (think of the green "wrapping" on a rosebud).
When the sepals are peeled away, the next layer is the
petals, which are often colorful and help to attract
insects and other pollinators. Plucking off the petals
reveals the **stamens**, the male reproductive structures. Pollen grains develop in the **anther**, a sac at the
top of each stamen. At the center of the flower is the
carpel, the female reproductive structure. It includes
the **ovary**, a protective chamber
containing one or more ovules,
in which eggs develop. The
sticky tip of the carpel,
called the **stigma**, traps
pollen. As you can see in
Figure 16.18, the basic
structure of a flower can
exist in many beautiful
variations.

Stamen
Anther
Filament

Petal
Stigma
Style
Ovary
Carpel

Ovule
Sepal

◀ **Figure 16.17 Structure
of a flower.**

▼ **Figure 16.18 A diversity of flowers.**

Pansy

Bleeding heart

California poppy

Water lily

▼ **Figure 16.19** **The angiosperm life cycle.**

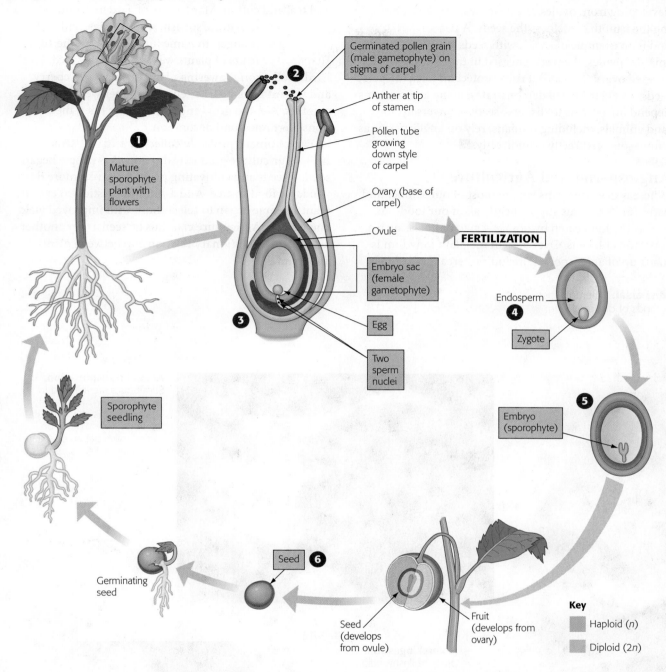

Germinated pollen grain (male gametophyte) on stigma of carpel

Anther at tip of stamen

Pollen tube growing down style of carpel

Ovary (base of carpel)

Ovule

FERTILIZATION

Embryo sac (female gametophyte)

Egg

Two sperm nuclei

Endosperm

Zygote

Embryo (sporophyte)

Mature sporophyte plant with flowers

Sporophyte seedling

Germinating seed

Seed

Seed (develops from ovule)

Fruit (develops from ovary)

Key

Haploid (*n*)

Diploid (2*n*)

Figure 16.19 highlights key stages in the angiosperm life cycle. **1** The flower is part of the sporophyte plant. As in gymnosperms, the pollen grain is the male gametophyte of angiosperms. The female gametophyte—the embryo sac—is located within an ovule, which in turn resides within a chamber of the ovary. **2** A pollen grain that lands on the sticky stigma of a carpel extends a tube down to the ovule and **3** deposits two sperm nuclei within the embryo sac. This **double fertilization** is an angiosperm characteristic. One sperm cell fertilizes an egg in the embryo sac. **4** This produces a zygote, which **5** develops into an embryo. The second sperm cell "fertilizes" another female gametophyte cell, which then develops into a nutrient-storing tissue called **endosperm**, which nourishes the embryo. Double fertilization therefore synchronizes the development of the embryo and food reserves within an ovule. **6** The whole ovule develops into a seed. The seed's enclosure within an ovary is what distinguishes angiosperms from gymnosperms, which have a naked seed.

Why does it take two sperm to fertilize a flower?

325

A **fruit** is the ripened ovary of a flower. As seeds are developing from ovules, the ovary wall thickens, forming the fruit that encloses the seeds. A pea pod is an example of a fruit with seeds (mature ovules, the peas) encased in the ripened ovary (the pod). Fruits protect and help disperse seeds. As **Figure 16.20** demonstrates, many angiosperms depend on animals to disperse seeds. Conversely, most land animals, including humans, rely on angiosperms as a food source, directly or indirectly. ☑

When is a vegetable also a fruit?

Angiosperms and Agriculture

Whereas gymnosperms supply most of our lumber and paper, angiosperms supply nearly all of our food—as well as the food eaten by domesticated animals, such as cows and chickens. Over 90% of the plant kingdom is made up of angiosperms, including cereal grains such as wheat and corn, citrus and other fruit trees, coffee and tea, and cotton. Many types of garden produce—tomatoes, squash, strawberries, and oranges, to name just a few—are the edible fruits of plants we have domesticated. Fine hardwoods from flowering plants such as oak, cherry, and walnut trees supplement the lumber we get from conifers. We also grow angiosperms for fiber, medications, perfumes, and decoration.

Early humans probably collected wild seeds and fruits. Agriculture gradually developed as people began sowing seeds and cultivating plants to have a more dependable food source. And as they domesticated certain plants, people began to select those with improved yield and quality. Agriculture can thus be seen as yet another facet of the evolutionary relationship between plants and animals.

☑ CHECKPOINT

What are the four main parts of a flower? Where do pollen grains develop? Where do eggs develop?

Answer: sepals, petals, stamens, carpels; in the anther within the stamen; in the ovary within the carpel

▼ **Figure 16.20 Fruits and seed dispersal.** Different types of fruits are adapted for different methods of dispersal.

Wind dispersal. Some angiosperms depend on wind for seed dispersal. Here, milkweed pods open to release masses of seeds (brown) carried by silken parachutes (part of the seed coat).

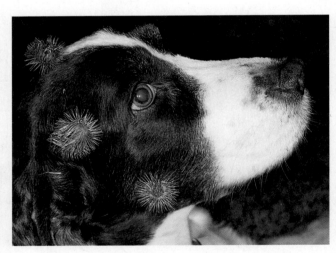

Animal transportation. Some fruits are adapted to hitch free rides on animals. The cockleburs attached to the fur of this dog may be carried miles before opening and releasing seeds.

Animal ingestion. Many angiosperms produce fleshy, edible fruits that are attractive to animals as food. When a weasel eats a berry, it digests the fleshy part of the fruit, but most of the tough seeds pass unharmed through the animal's digestive tract. The weasel later deposits the seeds, along with a fertilizer supply, some distance from where it ate the fruit.

Plant Diversity as a Nonrenewable Resource

The exploding human population, with its demand for space and natural resources, is extinguishing plant species at an unprecedented rate. The problem is especially critical in the tropics, where more than half the human population live and population growth is fastest. Tropical rain forests are being destroyed at a frightening pace. The most common cause of this destruction is large-scale slash-and-burn clearing of forest for agricultural use (Figure 16.21). Fifty million acres, an area about the size of the state of Washington, are cleared each year, a rate that could completely eliminate Earth's tropical forests within 25 years. As the forest disappears, so do species of plants that are found nowhere else. Insects and other rain forest animals that depend on these plants are also vanishing. The toll is greatest in the tropics because that is where most species live; but environmental assault seems to be a general human tendency. Europeans eliminated most of their forests centuries ago, and habitat destruction is now endangering many species in North America. What is lost is irreplaceable—entire ecosystems that provide medicinal plants, food, timber, and clean water and air.

Many people have ethical concerns about contributing to the extinction of living forms. But there are also practical reasons to be concerned about the loss of plant diversity. As already mentioned, we depend on plants for thousands of products, including food, building materials, and medicines (Table 16.1). More than 120 prescription drugs are extracted from plants. However, researchers have investigated only a fraction of the 300,000 known plant species as potential sources of medicine. Pharmaceutical companies were led to most of these species by local peoples who use the plants in preparing their traditional medicines.

Scientists are now rallying to slow the loss of plant diversity, in part by offering less destructive ways for people to benefit from forests. The goal of such efforts is to encourage management practices that use forests as resources without damaging them. The solutions we propose must be economically realistic; people who live where there are tropical rain forests must be able to make a living. But if the only goal is profit for the short term, then we will continue to slash and burn until the forests are gone. We need to appreciate the rain forests and other ecosystems as living treasures that can regenerate only slowly. Only then will we learn to work with them in ways that preserve their biological diversity for the future.

Throughout our survey of plants in this chapter, we have seen how entangled the botanical world is with other terrestrial life. We switch our attention now to that other group of organisms that moved onto land with plants: the kingdom Fungi. ☑

☑ CHECKPOINT

In what way are forests renewable resources? In what way are they not?

Answer: Forests are renewable in the sense that new trees can grow where old growth has been removed by logging. Habitats that are permanently destroyed cannot be replaced, however, so forests must be harvested in a sustainable manner.

▼ Figure 16.21 **Slash-and-burn clearing of a tropical forest in Brazil.**

Table 16.1	A Sampling of Medicines Derived from Plants		
Compound	**Source**		**Example of Use**
Atropine	Belladonna plant		Pupil dilator in eye exams
Digitalin	Foxglove		Heart medication
Menthol	Eucalyptus tree		Ingredient in cough medicines
Morphine	Opium poppy		Pain reliever
Quinine	Quinine tree		Malaria preventive
Paclitaxel (Taxol)	Pacific yew		Ovarian cancer drug
Tubocurarine	Curare tree		Muscle relaxant during surgery
Vinblastine	Periwinkle		Leukemia drug

Source: Adapted from Randy Moore et al., Botany, 2nd ed. Dubuque, IA: Brown, 1998, Table 2.2, p. 37.

Fungi

The word *fungus* often evokes unpleasant images. Fungi rot timbers, spoil food, and afflict people with athlete's foot and worse. However, ecosystems would collapse without fungi to decompose dead organisms, fallen leaves, feces, and other organic materials. Fungi recycle vital chemical elements back to the environment in forms that other organisms can assimilate. And you have already learned that nearly all plants have mycorrhizae, fungus-root associations that help plants absorb minerals and water from the soil. In addition to these ecological roles, fungi have been used by people in various ways for centuries. We eat fungi (mushrooms and truffles, for instance), culture fungi to produce antibiotics and other drugs, add them to dough to make bread rise, culture them in milk to produce a variety of cheeses, and use them to ferment beer and wine.

Fungi are eukaryotes, and most are multicellular, but many have body structures and modes of reproduction unlike those of any other organism **(Figure 16.22)**. Molecular studies indicate that fungi and animals arose from a common ancestor around 1.5 billion years ago. The oldest undisputed fossils of fungi, however, are only about 460 million years old, perhaps because the ancestors of terrestrial fungi were microscopic and fossilized poorly. Despite appearances, a mushroom is more closely related to you than it is to any plant!

Biologists who study fungi have described over 100,000 species, and there may be as many as 1.5 million. Classifying fungi is an ongoing area of research. (One widely accepted phylogenetic tree divides the kingdom Fungi into five groups.) You are probably familiar with several kinds of fungi, including mushrooms, mold, and yeast. In this section, we'll discuss the characteristics common to all fungi and then survey their wide-ranging ecological impact. ✔

☑ CHECKPOINT

Name three ways that we benefit from fungi in our environment.

Answer: Fungi help recycle nutrients by decomposing dead organisms; mycorrhizae help plants absorb water and nutrients; some fungi serve us as food.

▼ **Figure 16.22 A gallery of diverse fungi.**

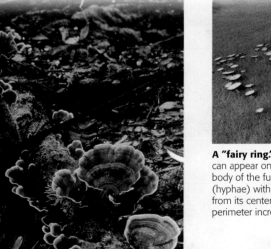

Orange fungi. These are the reproductive structures of a fungus that absorbs nutrients as it decomposes a fallen tree on a forest floor.

A "fairy ring." Some mushroom-producing fungi poke up "fairy rings," which can appear on a lawn overnight. A ring develops at the edge of the main body of the fungus, which consists of an underground mass of tiny filaments (hyphae) within the ring. As the underground fungal mass grows outward from its center, the diameter of the fairy ring produced at its expanding perimeter increases annually.

Colorized SEM 2,800x

Mold. Molds grow rapidly on their food sources, which are often our food sources as well. The mold on this orange reproduces asexually by producing chains of microscopic spores (inset) that are dispersed via air currents.

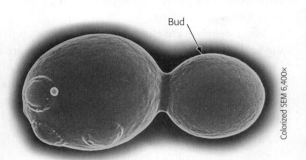

Bud

Colorized SEM 6,400x

Budding yeast. Yeasts are unicellular fungi. This yeast cell is reproducing asexually by a process called budding.

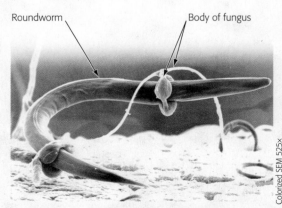

Roundworm   Body of fungus

Colorized SEM 525x

Predatory fungus. This predatory fungus traps and feeds on tiny roundworms in the soil. The fungus is equipped with hoops that can constrict around a worm in less than a second.

Characteristics of Fungi

We'll begin our look at the structure and function of fungi with an overview of how fungi obtain nutrients.

Fungal Nutrition

Fungi are chemoheterotrophs (see Figure 15.12) that acquire their nutrients by **absorption**. In this mode of nutrition, small organic molecules are absorbed from the surrounding medium. A fungus digests food outside its body by secreting powerful digestive enzymes into the food. The enzymes decompose complex molecules to simpler compounds that the fungus can absorb. Fungi absorb nutrients from such nonliving organic material as fallen logs, animal corpses, and the wastes of live organisms.

Fungal Structure

The bodies of most fungi are constructed of thread-like filaments called **hyphae** (singular, *hypha*). Fungal hyphae are minute threads of cytoplasm surrounded by a plasma membrane and cell wall. The cell walls of fungi differ from the cellulose walls of plants. Fungal cell walls are usually built mainly of chitin, a strong but flexible polysaccharide that is also found in the external skeletons of insects. Most fungi have multicellular hyphae, which consist of chains of cells separated by cross-walls with pores. In many fungi, cell-to-cell channels allow ribosomes, mitochondria, and even nuclei to flow between cells.

Fungal hyphae branch repeatedly, forming an interwoven network called a **mycelium** (plural, *mycelia*), the feeding structure of the fungus **(Figure 16.23)**. Fungal mycelia usually escape our notice because they are often subterranean, but they can be huge. In fact, scientists have discovered that the mycelium of one humongous fungus in Oregon is 5.5 km—that's 3.4 miles!—in diameter and spreads through 2,200 acres of forest. This fungus is at least 2,600 years old and weighs hundreds of tons, qualifying it as one of Earth's oldest and largest organisms.

A mycelium maximizes contact with its food source by mingling with the organic matter it is decomposing and absorbing. A bucketful of rich organic soil may contain as much as a kilometer of hyphae. A fungal mycelium grows rapidly, adding hyphae as it branches within its food. The great majority of fungi are nonmotile; they cannot run, swim, or fly in search of food. But the mycelium makes up for the lack of mobility by swiftly extending the tips of its hyphae into new territory. ☑

Fungal Reproduction

The mushroom in Figure 16.23 is actually made up of tightly packed hyphae. Mushrooms arise from an underground mycelium. While the mycelium obtains food from organic material via absorption, the function of the mushroom is reproduction. Unlike a truffle, which employs animals to disperse its spores, a mushroom pops up above ground to disperse its spores on air currents.

Fungi typically reproduce by releasing haploid spores that are produced either sexually or asexually. The output of spores is mind-boggling. For example, puffballs, which are the reproductive structures of certain fungi, can spew clouds containing trillions of spores. Easily carried by wind or water, spores germinate to produce mycelia if they land in a moist place where there is food. Spores thus function in dispersal and account for the wide geographic distribution of many species of fungi. The airborne spores of fungi have been found more than 160 km (100 miles) above Earth. Closer to home, try leaving a slice of bread out for a week and you will observe the furry mycelia that grow from the invisible spores raining down from the surrounding air.

How does bread get moldy?

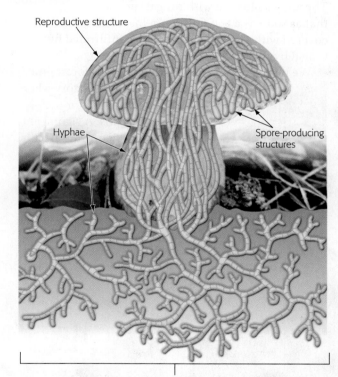
Reproductive structure

Hyphae

Spore-producing structures

Mycelium

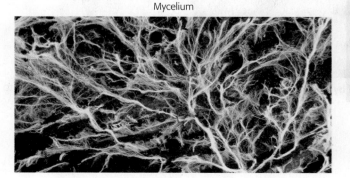

◄ **Figure 16.23 The fungal mycelium.** A mushroom consists of tightly packed hyphae that extend upward from a much more massive mycelium of hyphae growing underground. The photo shows a mycelium made up of the cottony threads that decompose organic litter.

☑ **CHECKPOINT**

Describe how the structure of a fungal mycelium reflects its function.

Answer: The extensive network of hyphae puts a large surface area in contact with the food source.

329

The Ecological Impact of Fungi

Fungi have been major players in terrestrial communities ever since plants and fungi together moved onto land. Let's examine a few examples of how fungi continue to have an enormous ecological impact, including numerous interactions with people.

Fungi as Decomposers

Fungi and bacteria are the principal decomposers that keep ecosystems stocked with the inorganic nutrients essential for plant growth. Without decomposers, carbon, nitrogen, and other elements would accumulate in nonliving organic matter. Plants and the animals they feed would starve because elements taken from the soil would not be returned.

Fungi are well adapted as decomposers of organic refuse. Their invasive hyphae enter the tissues and cells of dead organisms and digest polymers, including the cellulose of plant cell walls. A succession of fungi, in concert with bacteria and, in some environments, invertebrate animals, is responsible for the complete breakdown of organic litter. The air is so loaded with fungal spores that as soon as a leaf falls or an insect dies, it is covered with spores and soon after infiltrated by fungal hyphae.

What kind of "worm" is actually a fungus?

We may applaud fungi that decompose forest litter or dung, but it's a different story when molds attack our fruit or our shower curtains. A significant amount of the world's fruit harvest is lost each year to fungal attack. And a wood-digesting fungus does not distinguish between a fallen oak limb and the oak planks of a boat. During the Revolutionary War, the British lost more ships to fungal rot than to enemy attack. What's more, soldiers stationed in the tropics during World War II watched as their tents, clothing, boots, and binoculars were destroyed by molds.

Parasitic Fungi

Parasitism is a relationship in which two species live in contact and one organism benefits while the other is harmed. Parasitic fungi absorb nutrients from the cells or body fluids of living hosts. Of the 100,000 known species of fungi, about 30% make their living as parasites.

About 50 species of fungi are known to be parasitic in humans and other animals. Among the diseases that fungi cause in people are yeast infections of the lungs, some of which can be fatal, and vaginal yeast infections. Other fungal parasites produce a skin disease called ringworm, so named because it appears as circular red areas on the skin. Most commonly, ringworm fungus attacks the feet and causes intense itching and sometimes blisters. This condition, known as athlete's foot, is highly contagious but can be treated with fungicidal lotions and powders.

The great majority of fungal parasites infect plants. In some cases, fungi that infect plants have literally changed the landscape. For example, American chestnut and American elm trees, once common in forests, fields, and city streets, were devastated by fungal epidemics (**Figure 16.24a**). Fungi are also serious agricultural pests, and some of the fungi that attack food crops are toxic to humans. The seed heads of many kinds of grain and grasses, including rye, wheat, and oats, are sometimes infected with fungal growths called ergots (**Figure 16.24b**). Consumption of flour made from ergot-infested grain can cause hallucinations, temporary insanity, and death. In fact, lysergic acid, the raw material from which the hallucinogenic drug LSD is made, has been isolated from ergots. This fact may help explain a centuries-old mystery, as we'll see next.

(a) An American elm tree killed by Dutch elm disease fungus

(b) Ergots

◄ **Figure 16.24 Parasitic fungi that cause plant disease.** (a) The parasitic fungus that causes Dutch elm disease evolved with European species of elm trees, and it is relatively harmless to them. But it has been deadly to American elms since it was accidentally introduced after World War I. (b) Ergots, parasitic fungi, are the dark structures on these rye seed heads.

Did a Fungus Lead to the Salem Witch Hunt?

In January 1692, eight young girls in the town of Salem, Massachusetts, began to act bizarrely. The girls suffered from incomprehensible speech, odd skin sensations, convulsions, and hallucinations. The worried community blamed the girls' symptoms on witchcraft and began to accuse one another. By the time the hysteria ended that autumn, more than 150 villagers had been accused of witchcraft, and 20 of them had been hanged. Finding the cause behind the "Salem witch hunt" has long intrigued historians.

In 1976, a University of California psychology graduate student offered a new explanation. She began with the **observation** that the symptoms reported by the girls were consistent with ergot poisoning **(Figure 16.25)**. This led her to **question** whether an ergot outbreak could have been behind the witch hunt. The researcher tested her **hypothesis** by examining the historical records, making the **prediction** that facts consistent with ergot poisoning would be uncovered.

Her **results** were suggestive, though not conclusive. Agricultural records confirm that rye—the principal host for ergot—grew abundantly around Salem at that time and that the growing season of 1691 had been particularly warm and wet, conditions under which ergot thrives. This suggests that the rye crop consumed during the winter of 1691–1692 could easily have been contaminated. The summer of 1692, when the accusations began to die down, was dry, consistent with an ergot die-off. Most importantly, the reported symptoms appear consistent with those of ergot poisoning. These clues suggest (but do not prove) that the girls, and perhaps others in Salem, were in the grips of ergot-induced illness. Some historians dispute this idea, and other hypotheses have been proposed. Conclusive evidence may never be found, but this story reinforces the unifying thread of this chapter—the importance of the interaction of plants and fungi—and illustrates how the scientific method can be applied in a wide variety of academic disciplines.

▼ **Figure 16.25 Ergot and the Salem witch hunt.** Ergot poisoning may have been the catalyst for the Salem witch hunt of 1692.

Commercial Uses of Fungi

It would not be fair to fungi to end our discussion with an account of diseases. In addition to their positive global impact as decomposers, fungi also have a number of practical uses for people.

Most of us have eaten mushrooms, although we may not have realized that we were ingesting the reproductive extensions of subterranean fungi. Your grocery store probably stocks Portobello, shiitake, and oyster mushrooms along with common button mushrooms. If you like to cook with mushrooms, you can buy a mushroom "garden"— mycelium embedded in a rich food source—that makes it easy to grow your own. Some enthusiasts gather edible fungi from fields and forests **(Figure 16.26)**, but only experts should dare to eat wild fungi. Some poisonous species resemble edible ones, and there are no simple rules to help the novice distinguish one from the other.

Other fungi are used in food production. The distinctive flavors of certain kinds of cheeses, including Roquefort and blue cheese, come from the fungi used to ripen them. And people have used yeasts (unicellular fungi) for thousands of years to produce alcoholic beverages and cause bread to rise (see Figure 6.16).

▼ **Figure 16.26 Fungi eaten by people.**

Chicken of the woods. This fleshy shelf fungus is said to taste like chicken.

Chanterelle mushrooms. Gourmet mushrooms are highly prized by chefs for their earthy flavors and interesting textures.

Giant puffball. These humongous fungi can grow to more than 2 feet in diameter. They are only edible when immature, before the spores form. Beware: Deadly fungi often resemble small puffballs.

☑ **CHECKPOINT**

1. What is athlete's foot?
2. What do you think is the natural function of the antibiotics that fungi produce in their native environments?

Answers: 1. Athlete's foot is infection of the foot's skin with ringworm fungus. 2. The antibiotics block the growth of microorganisms, especially bacteria, that compete with the fungi for nutrients and other resources.

Fungi are medically valuable as well. Some fungi produce antibiotics that are used to treat bacterial diseases. In fact, the first antibiotic discovered was penicillin, made by the common mold *Penicillium* **(Figure 16.27)**. And in 2007, researchers discovered that several varieties of fungi that attack hazelnut trees produce a powerful anticancer drug.

As sources of medicines and food, as decomposers, and as partners with plants in mycorrhizae, fungi play vital roles in life on Earth. ☑

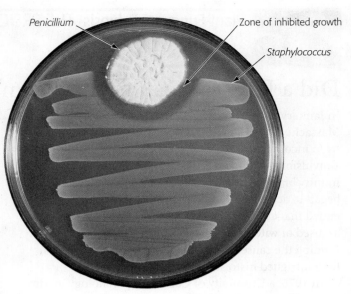

► **Figure 16.27 Fungal production of an antibiotic.** Penicillin is made by the common mold *Penicillium*. In this petri dish, the clear area between the mold and the growing *Staphylococcus* bacteria is where the antibiotic produced by the *Penicillium* inhibits the growth of the bacteria.

Plant-Fungus Symbiosis EVOLUTION CONNECTION

Mutually Beneficial Symbiosis

▼ **Figure 16.28 Lichens: symbiotic associations of fungi and algae.** Lichens generally grow very slowly, sometimes less than a millimeter per year. Some lichens are thousands of years old, rivaling the oldest plants as Earth's elders. The close relationship between the fungal and algal partners is evident in the microscopic blowup of a lichen.

Discussing fungi in the same chapter as plants may seem to indicate that these two kingdoms are close relatives. Actually, as we've discussed, fungi are more closely related to animals than to plants. But the success of plants on land and the great diversity of fungi are interconnected; neither could have populated the land without the other.

Evolution is not just about the origin and adaptation of individual species. Relationships between species are also an evolutionary product. For example, prokaryotes partner with a variety of organisms in mutually beneficial symbioses. Eukaryotic cells evolved from symbiosis among prokaryotes (see Figure 15.19). Bacteria living in the roots of certain plants provide nitrogen compounds to their host and receive food in exchange. We even have our own symbiotic bacteria that help keep our skin healthy and produce certain vitamins in our intestines. Particularly relevant to this chapter is the symbiotic association of fungi and plant roots—mycorrhizae—that made life's move onto land possible.

Lichens, symbiotic associations of unicelleular algae or photosynthetic bacteria held in a mass of fungal hyphae, are striking examples of how intimate these relationships can be. At a distance, it is easy to mistake lichens for mosses or other simple plants growing on rocks, rotting logs, or trees **(Figure 16.28)**. The partners are so closely entwined that they appear to be a single organism. The fungus receives food from its photosynthetic partner. The fungal mycelium, in turn, provides a suitable habitat for the algae, helping the algae absorb and retain water and minerals. The merger is so complete that lichens are actually named as species, as though they were individual organisms.

After protists and plants, fungi is the third group of eukaryotes that we have surveyed so far. Strong evidence suggests that they evolved from protist ancestors that also gave rise to the fourth and most diverse group of eukaryotes: the animals, the topic of the next chapter.

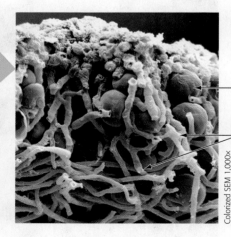

Algal cell

Fungal hyphae

Colorized SEM 1,000x

Chapter Review

SUMMARY OF KEY CONCEPTS

 Go to **www.masteringbiology.com** for homework assignments, practice quizzes, Pearson eText, and more.

Colonizing Land

Terrestrial Adaptations of Plants

Plants are multicellular photosynthetic eukaryotes with adaptations for living on land.

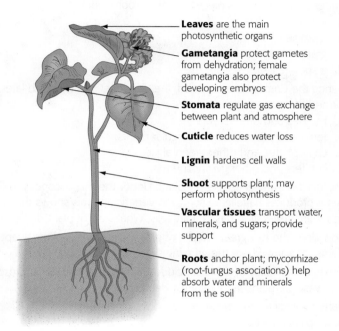

Leaves are the main photosynthetic organs

Gametangia protect gametes from dehydration; female gametangia also protect developing embryos

Stomata regulate gas exchange between plant and atmosphere

Cuticle reduces water loss

Lignin hardens cell walls

Shoot supports plant; may perform photosynthesis

Vascular tissues transport water, minerals, and sugars; provide support

Roots anchor plant; mycorrhizae (root-fungus associations) help absorb water and minerals from the soil

The Origin of Plants from Green Algae

Plants evolved from a group of multicellular green algae called charophytes.

Plant Diversity

Highlights of Plant Evolution

Four major periods of plant evolution are marked by terrestrial adaptations.

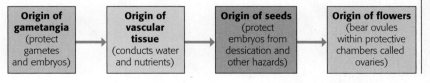

Origin of gametangia (protect gametes and embryos) → **Origin of vascular tissue** (conducts water and nutrients) → **Origin of seeds** (protect embryos from dessication and other hazards) → **Origin of flowers** (bear ovules within protective chambers called ovaries)

Bryophytes

 The most familiar bryophytes are mosses. Mosses display two key terrestrial adaptations: a waxy cuticle that prevents dehydration and the retention of developing embryos within the mother plant's gametangia. Mosses are most common in moist environments because their sperm must swim to the eggs and because they lack lignin in their cell walls and thus cannot stand tall. Bryophytes are unique among plants in having the gametophyte as the dominant generation in the life cycle.

Ferns

 Ferns are seedless plants that have vascular tissues but still use flagellated sperm to fertilize eggs. During the Carboniferous period, giant ferns were among the plants that decayed to thick deposits of organic matter, which were gradually converted to coal.

Gymnosperms

 A drier and colder global climate near the end of the Carboniferous period favored the evolution of the first seed plants. The most successful were the gymnosperms, represented by conifers. Needle-shaped leaves with thick cuticles and sunken stomata are adaptations to dry conditions. Conifers and most other gymnosperms have three additional terrestrial adaptations: (1) further reduction of the haploid gametophyte and greater development of the diploid sporophyte, (2) sperm-bearing pollen, which doesn't require water for transport, and (3) seeds, which consist of a plant embryo packaged along with a food supply inside a protective coat.

Angiosperms

Angiosperms supply nearly all our food and much of our fiber for textiles. The evolution of the flower and more efficient water transport help account for the success of the angiosperms. The dominant stage is a sporophyte with gametophytes in its flowers. The female gametophyte is located within an ovule, which in turn resides within a chamber of the ovary. Fertilization of an egg in the female gametophyte produces a zygote, which develops into an embryo. The whole ovule develops into a seed. The seed's enclosure within an ovary is what distinguishes angiosperms from gymnosperms, which have naked seeds. A fruit is the ripened ovary of a flower. Fruits protect and help disperse seeds. Angiosperms are a major food source for animals, while animals aid plants in pollination and seed dispersal. Agriculture constitutes a unique kind of evolutionary relationship among plants, people, and other animals.

Plant Diversity as a Nonrenewable Resource

The exploding human population, with its demand for space and natural resources, is causing the extinction of plant species at an unprecedented rate. Scientists are researching how to slow this loss and help us learn to work with forests in ways that preserve their biological diversity.

Fungi

Characteristics of Fungi

Fungi are unicellular or multicellular eukaryotes; they are chemoheterotrophs that digest their food externally and absorb the nutrients from the environment. They are more closely related to animals than to plants. A fungus usually consists of a mass of threadlike hyphae, forming a mycelium. The cell walls of fungi are mainly composed of chitin. Although most fungi are nonmotile, a mycelium can grow very quickly, extending the tips of its hyphae into new territory. Mushrooms are reproductive structures that extend from the underground mycelium. Fungi reproduce and disperse by releasing spores that are produced either sexually or asexually.

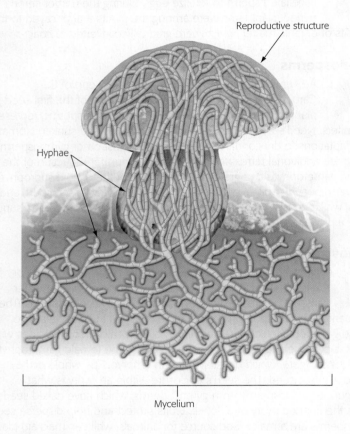

Reproductive structure

Hyphae

Mycelium

The Ecological Impact of Fungi

Fungi and bacteria are the principal decomposers of ecosystems. Many molds destroy fruit, wood, and human-made materials. About 50 species of fungi are known to be parasites of people and other animals. Fungi are also commercially important as food and in baking, beer and wine production, and the manufacture of antibiotics.

Evolution Connection: Mutually Beneficial Symbiosis

Lichens, in which algae are surrounded by fungal hyphae, are an example of a mutually beneficial symbiotic relationship.

SELF-QUIZ

1. Which of the following structures is common to all four major plant groups: vascular tissue, flowers, seeds, cuticle, pollen?

2. Angiosperms are distinguished from all other plants because only angiosperms have reproductive structures called _____.

3. Complete the following analogies:
   a. Gametophyte is to haploid as _____ is to diploid.
   b. _____ are to conifers as flowers are to _____.
   c. Ovule is to seed as ovary is to _____.

4. Under a microscope, a piece of a mushroom would look most like
   a. jelly.
   b. a tangle of string.
   c. grains of sand.
   d. a sponge.

5. During the Carboniferous period, the dominant plants, which later formed the great coal beds, were mainly
   a. mosses and other bryophytes.
   b. ferns and other seedless vascular plants.
   c. charophytes and other green algae.
   d. conifers and other gymnosperms.

6. You discover a new species of plant. Under the microscope, you find that it produces flagellated sperm. A genetic analysis shows that its dominant generation has diploid cells. What kind of plant do you have?

7. How does the evergreen nature of pines and other conifers adapt the plants for living where the growing season is very short?

8. Which of the following terms includes all others in the list? angiosperm, fern, vascular plant, gymnosperm, seed plant

9. Plant diversity is greatest in
   a. tropical forests.
   b. the temperate forests of Europe.
   c. deserts.
   d. the oceans.

10. What is a fruit?

11. Lichens are symbionts of photosynthetic _____ with _____.

12. Contrast the heterotrophic nutrition of a fungus with your own heterotrophic nutrition.

Answers to these questions can be found in Appendix: Self-Quiz Answers.

THE PROCESS OF SCIENCE

13. In April 1986, an accident at a nuclear power plant in Chernobyl, Ukraine, scattered radioactive fallout for hundreds of miles. In assessing the biological effects of the radiation, researchers found mosses to be especially valuable as organisms for monitoring the damage. Radiation damages organisms by causing mutations. Explain why it is faster to observe the genetic effects of radiation on mosses than on other types of plants. Imagine that you are conducting tests shortly after a nuclear accident. Using potted moss plants as your experimental organisms, design an experiment to test the hypothesis that the frequency of mutations decreases with the organism's distance from the source of radiation.

14. You discover what you think may be one extremely large underground fungal mycelium living beneath your campus. How could you prove that it is, in fact, one individual organism spread across a very large area, as opposed to a group of separate organisms?

BIOLOGY AND SOCIETY

15. Why are tropical rain forests being destroyed at such an alarming rate? What kinds of social, technological, and economic factors are responsible? Most forests in more industrialized Northern Hemisphere countries have already been cut. Do the more industrialized nations have a right to pressure the less industrialized nations in the Southern Hemisphere to slow or stop the destruction of their forests? Defend your answer. What kinds of benefits, incentives, or programs might slow the assault on the rain forests?

16. Imagine you were charged with the task of managing a coniferous forest. How would you balance the need for productive use of the forest (to provide lumber, for example) with preservation of its diversity? What activities would you allow or prohibit in the forest (for example, snowmobiling, logging, hiking, mushroom harvesting, mining, camping, grazing, making campfires)? How would you defend your choices to the public?

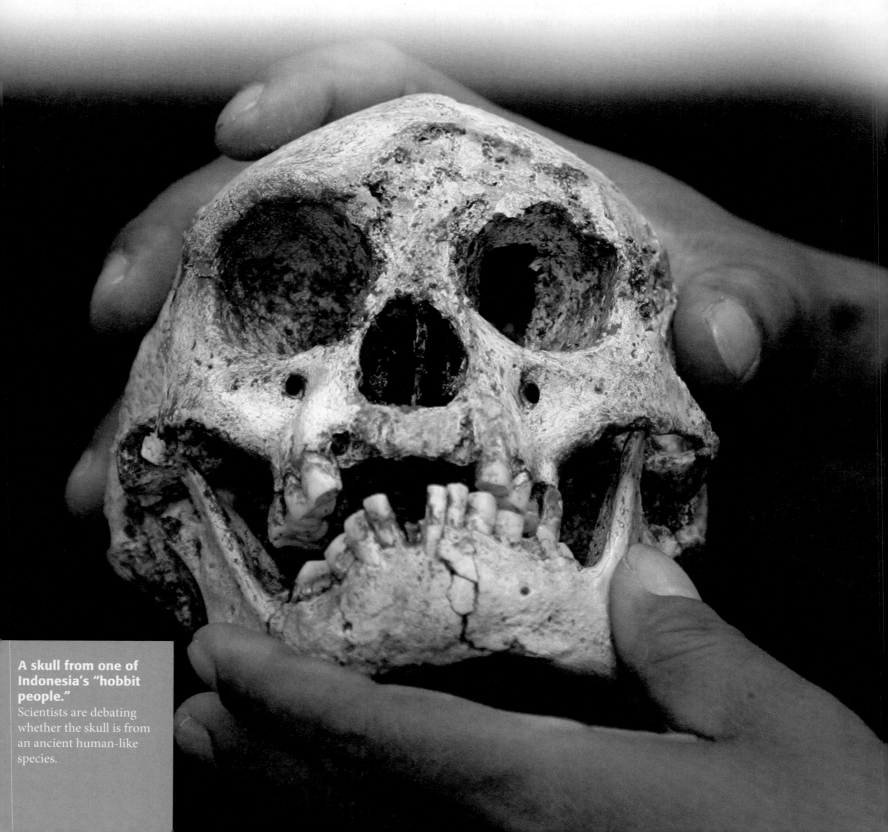

17 The Evolution of Animals

A skull from one of Indonesia's "hobbit people." Scientists are debating whether the skull is from an ancient human-like species.

Human Evolution BIOLOGY AND SOCIETY

The Discovery of the Hobbit People

In 2003, Australian anthropologists digging on the Indonesian island of Flores stumbled upon bones of some highly unusual people, including the nearly complete skeleton of an adult female. Next to a modern woman, this fully grown individual would stand about waist-high. Features of her skull, such as the shape and thickness of the bones, were human-like, but its size was proportional to her tiny body, and her brain was the size of a chimpanzee's. Surprisingly, the bones were accompanied by tools for hunting and butchering animals, along with evidence of cooking fires. Most astonishing of all, the remains dated to roughly 18,000 years ago, a time when scientists had thought that *Homo sapiens* was the only surviving human species. Since the initial discovery, researchers have unearthed the bones of a dozen or so more of these miniature humans.

The discoverers attributed their astonishing find to a previously unknown species, which they named *Homo floresiensis* and nicknamed "hobbits." They speculated that a band of ancestral humans arrived on Flores millions of years ago from Africa and, within the isolated environment of the island, evolved into the diminuitive *Homo floresiensis*. There is precedent for animal evolution of this type: Biologists have discovered island-bound dwarf populations of deer, elephants, and hippos. One hypothesis is that a lack of predators favors the evolution of smaller, more energy-efficient forms. Controversy erupted as soon as the team announced their findings. Skeptical scientists suggested that the bones were from *Homo sapiens* with diseases that cause skeletal malformations. As you'll find out in the Process of Science section, the more scientists learn about the "hobbit" people, the more puzzling their findings become.

Homo sapiens and *Homo floresiensis* are just two of the over 1 million species of animals that have been named and described by biologists. This amazing diversity arose through hundreds of millions of years of evolution as natural selection shaped animal adaptations to Earth's many environments. In this chapter, we'll look at the 9 most abundant and widespread of the roughly 35 phyla (major groups) in the kingdom Animalia. We'll give special attention to the major milestones in animal evolution and conclude by reconnecting with the fascinating subject of human evolution.

The Origins of Animal Diversity

Animal life began in Precambrian seas with the evolution of multicellular creatures that ate other organisms. We are among their descendants.

What Is an Animal?

Animals are eukaryotic, multicellular, heterotrophic organisms that obtain nutrients by eating. This mode of nutrition contrasts animals with plants and other organisms that construct organic molecules through photosynthesis. It also contrasts with fungi, which obtain nutrients by absorption after digesting the food outside their bodies (see Figure 16.23). Most animals digest their food within their bodies after ingesting other organisms, dead or alive, whole or by the piece **(Figure 17.1)**.

Animal cells lack the cell walls that provide strong support in the bodies of plants and fungi. And most animals have muscle cells for movement and nerve cells that control the muscles. The most complex animals can use their muscular and nervous systems for many functions other than eating. Some species even use massive networks of nerve cells called brains to think.

Most animals are diploid and reproduce sexually; eggs and sperm are the only haploid cells. The life cycle of a sea star **(Figure 17.2)** includes basic stages found in most animal life cycles. ❶ Male and female adult animals make haploid gametes by meiosis, and ❷ an egg and a sperm fuse, producing a zygote. ❸ The zygote divides by mitosis, forming ❹ an early embryonic stage

called a **blastula**, which is usually a hollow ball of cells. ❺ In most animals, one side of the blastula folds inward, forming a stage called a **gastrula**. ❻ The gastrula develops into a saclike embryo with a two-layered wall and an opening at one end. After the gastrula stage, many animals develop directly into adults. ❼ Others, such as the sea star, develop into a **larva**, an immature individual that looks different from the adult animal. (A tadpole, for another example, is a larval frog.) ❽ The larva undergoes a major change of body form, called **metamorphosis**, in becoming an adult capable of reproducing sexually. ☑

☑ CHECKPOINT

What mode of nutrition distinguishes animals from fungi, both of which are heterotrophs?

Answer: ingestion (eating)

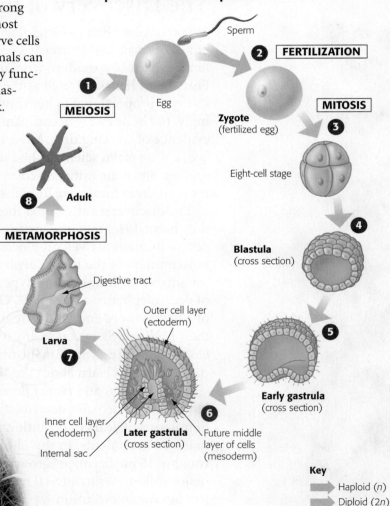

▼ Figure 17.2 **The life cycle of a sea star as an example of animal development.**

Sperm

MEIOSIS

Egg

❶

❷ **FERTILIZATION**

Zygote
(fertilized egg)

MITOSIS

❸

Eight-cell stage

❹

Blastula
(cross section)

❺

Early gastrula
(cross section)

❻

Future middle layer of cells (mesoderm)

Later gastrula
(cross section)

Inner cell layer (endoderm)

Internal sac

Outer cell layer (ectoderm)

❼ **Larva**

Digestive tract

METAMORPHOSIS

❽ **Adult**

Key

Haploid (*n*)

Diploid (2*n*)

▼ Figure 17.1 **Nutrition by ingestion, the animal way of life.** Few animals ingest a piece of food as large as the gazelle being eaten by this rock python. The snake will spend two weeks or more digesting its meal.

Early Animals and the Cambrian Explosion

Scientists hypothesize that animals evolved from a colonial, flagellated protist (**Figure 17.3**). Although molecular data point to a much earlier origin, the oldest animal fossils that have been found are 550–575 million years old. Animal evolution must have already been under way for some time prior to that—the fossils reveal a variety of shapes, and sizes range from 1 cm to 1 m in length (**Figure 17.4**).

Animal diversification appears to have accelerated rapidly from 535 to 525 million years ago, during the Cambrian period. Because so many animal body plans and new phyla appear in the fossils from such an evolutionarily short time span, biologists call this episode the Cambrian explosion. The most celebrated source of Cambrian fossils is located in British Columbia, Canada. The Burgess Shale, as it is known, provided a cornucopia of perfectly preserved animal fossils. In contrast to the Precambrian animals, many Cambrian animals had hard parts such as shells, and many are clearly related to existing animal groups. For example, scientists have classified more than a third of the species found in the Burgess Shale as arthropods, the group that includes present-day crabs, shrimps, and insects (**Figure 17.5**). Other fossils are more difficult to place. Some are downright weird, like the spiky creature near the center of the drawing, known as *Hallucigenia*, and *Opabinia*, the five-eyed predator grasping a worm with the long, flexible appendage that protrudes in front of its mouth.

What ignited the Cambrian explosion? Scientists have proposed several hypotheses, including increasingly complex predator-prey relationships and an increase in atmospheric oxygen. But whatever the cause of the rapid diversification, it is likely that the set of "master control" genes—the genetic framework for complex bodies—was already in place (see Figure 11.10). Much of the diversity in body form among the animal phyla is associated with variations in where and when these genes are expressed within developing embryos.

In the last half billion years, animal evolution has to a large degree merely generated variations of the animal forms that originated in the Cambrian seas. Continuing research will help test hypotheses about the Cambrian explosion. But even as the explosion becomes less mysterious, it will seem no less wondrous. ☑

◄ Figure 17.3 Hypothetical common ancestor of animals. As you'll learn shortly, the individual cells of this colonial flagellated protist resemble the feeding cells of sponges.

◄ Figure 17.4 Precambrian animals. All of the oldest animal fossils are impressions of soft-bodied animals. Most of them do not appear to be related to any living group of animals.

Dickinsonia costata (about 8 cm across)

Spriggina floundersi (about 3 cm long)

▼ Figure 17.5 A Cambrian seascape. This drawing is based on fossils from the Burgess Shale. The flat-bodied animals are ancient arthropods called trilobites. A photo of fossil trilobites is shown at the right.

☑ CHECKPOINT

Why is animal evolution during the early Cambrian referred to as an "explosion"?

Answer: because a great diversity of animals evolved in a relatively short time span

Animal Phylogeny

Historically, biologists have categorized animals by "body plan"—general features of body structure. Distinctions between body plans are used to help infer the evolutionary relationships between animal groups. More recently, a wealth of genetic data has allowed evolutionary biologists to modify and refine groups. **Figure 17.6** represents a set of hypotheses about the evolutionary relationships between nine major animal phyla based on structural and genetic similarities.

▶ **Figure 17.6 An overview of animal phylogeny.** Only 9 of the more than 30 animal phyla (the exact number is not agreed upon) are included in the tree and in the text. The branching takes into account the body plan of the organisms as well as genetic data.

▼ **Figure 17.7 Body symmetry.**

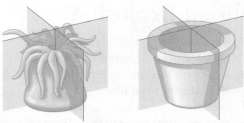

Radial symmetry. Parts radiate from the center, so any slice through the central axis divides into mirror images.

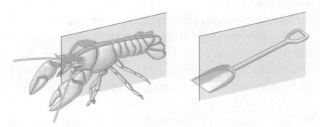

Bilateral symmetry. Only one slice can divide left and right sides into mirror-image halves.

A major branch point in animal evolution distinguishes sponges from all other animals based on structural complexity. Unlike more complex animals, sponges lack true tissues, groups of similar cells that perform a function (such as nervous tissue). A second major evolutionary split is based on body symmetry: radial versus bilateral **(Figure 17.7)**. To understand this difference, imagine a pail and shovel. The pail has **radial symmetry**, identical all around a central axis. The shovel has **bilateral symmetry**, which means there's only one way to split it into two equal halves—right down the midline. A bilateral animal has a definite "head end" that first encounters food, danger, and other stimuli when traveling. In most bilateral animals, a nerve center in the form of

a brain is at the head end, near a concentration of sense organs such as eyes. Thus, bilateral symmetry is an adaptation that aids movement, such as crawling, burrowing, or swimming. Indeed, many radial animals are stationary, whereas most bilateral animals are mobile.

The evolution of body cavities also helped lead to more complex animals. A **body cavity** is a fluid-filled space separating the digestive tract from the outer body wall. The cavity enables the internal organs to grow and move independently of the outer body wall, and the fluid cushions them from injury. In soft-bodied animals such as earthworms, the fluid is under pressure and functions as a hydrostatic skeleton. Of the phyla shown in Figure 17.6, only sponges, cnidarians, and flatworms lack a body cavity.

Among animals with a body cavity, there are differences in how the cavity develops **(Figure 17.8)**. In all cases, the cavity is at least partly lined by a middle layer of tissue, called mesoderm, which develops between the inner (endoderm) and outer (ectoderm) layers of the gastrula embryo. If the body cavity is not completely lined by tissue derived from mesoderm, it is called a **pseudocoelom**. Among the animal phyla discussed in this chapter, only the roundworms (nematodes) have a pseudocoelom. A true **coelom**, the type of body cavity humans and many other animals have, is completely lined by tissue derived from mesoderm. (Despite its name, a pseudocoelom functions just like a coelom.)

With the overview of animal evolution in Figure 17.6 as our guide, we're ready to take a closer look at the nine most numerous animal phyla. ✔

Tree labels (Figure 17.6):
- Ancestral protist
- No true tissues — Sponges
- Radial symmetry — Cnidarians
- Tissues
- Bilateral symmetry — Molluscs, Flatworms, Annelids, Roundworms, Arthropods, Echinoderms, Chordates

✔ CHECKPOINT

1. In terms of key body features, chordates are most like which other animal phylum?
2. A round pizza displays _____ symmetry, whereas a slice of pizza displays _____ symmetry.

Answers: 1. echinoderms 2. radial; bilateral

▼ **Figure 17.8 Body plans of bilateral animals.** The various organ systems of these animals develop from the three tissue layers that form in the embryo.

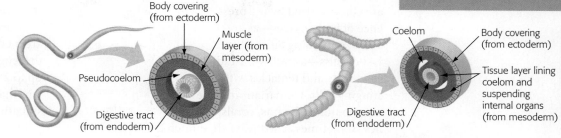

(a) No body cavity: for example, flatworm

(b) Pseudocoelom: a body cavity only partially lined by the mesoderm, the middle tissue layer; for example, roundworm

(c) True coelom: a fluid-filled body cavity completely lined by mesoderm; for example, annelid

Major Invertebrate Phyla

Living as we do on land, our sense of animal diversity is biased in favor of vertebrates, animals with a backbone, such as amphibians, reptiles, and mammals. However, vertebrates make up less than 5% of all animal species. If we were to sample the animals in an aquatic habitat, such as a pond, tide pool, or coral reef, or if we were to consider the millions of insects that share our terrestrial world, we would find ourselves in the realm of **invertebrates**, animals without backbones. We give special attention to the vertebrates simply because we humans are among the backboned ones. However, by exploring the other 95% of the animal kingdom—the invertebrates—we'll discover an astonishing diversity of beautiful creatures that too often escape our notice.

Sponges

Sponges were once grouped into the single phlyum Porifera. However, genetic evidence now suggests that there are multiple phyla. Sponges are stationary animals that appear so immobile that you might mistake them for plants. The simplest of all animals, sponges probably evolved very early from colonial protists. Sponges range in height from about 1 cm to 2 m. They have no nerves or muscles, but their individual cells can sense and react to changes in the environment. The cell layers of sponges are loose associations of relatively unspecialized cells that are not considered true tissues. Of the 9,000 or so species of sponges, only about 100 live in fresh water; the rest are marine.

The body of a sponge resembles a sac perforated with holes. Water is drawn through the pores into a central cavity and then flows out of the sponge through a larger opening **(Figure 17.9)**. Cells called choanocytes have flagella that sweep water through the sponge's porous body. Choanocytes trap bacteria and other food particles in mucus and then engulf the food by endocytosis (see Figure 5.18). Cells called amoebocytes pick up food from the choanocytes, digest it, and carry the nutrients to other cells. Amoebocytes also manufacture the fibers that make up a sponge's skeleton. In some sponges, these fibers are sharp and spur-like. Other sponges have softer, more flexible skeletons; these pliant, honeycombed skeletons are often used as natural sponges in the bath or to wash cars. ☑

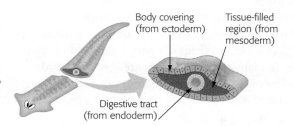

Sponges
Cnidarians
Molluscs
Flatworms
Annelids
Roundworms
Arthropods
Echinoderms
Chordates

▼ **Figure 17.9 Anatomy of a sponge.** To obtain enough food to grow by 3 ounces, a sponge must filter roughly 275 gallons of water through its body.

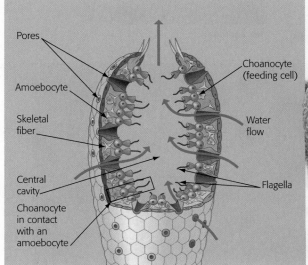

Pores

Amoebocyte

Skeletal fiber

Central cavity

Choanocyte in contact with an amoebocyte

Choanocyte (feeding cell)

Water flow

Flagella

Cnidarians

Cnidarians (phylum Cnidaria) are characterized by the presence of body tissues—as are all the remaining animals we will discuss—as well as by radial symmetry and tentacles with stinging cells. Cnidarians include sea anemones, hydras, corals, and jellies (sometimes called jellyfish, though they are not fish). Most of the 10,000 cnidarian species are marine.

The basic body plan of a cnidarian is a sac with a central digestive compartment, the **gastrovascular cavity**. A single opening to this cavity functions as both mouth and anus. This basic body plan has two variations: the stationary **polyp** and the floating **medusa (Figure 17.10)**. Polyps adhere to larger objects and extend their tentacles,

waiting for prey. Examples of the polyp body plan are hydras, sea anemones, and corals. A medusa (plural, *medusae*) is a flattened, mouth-down version of the polyp. It moves freely by a combination of passive drifting and contractions of its bell-shaped body. The largest jellies are medusae with tentacles 60–70 m long (more than half the length of a football field) dangling from an umbrella up to 2 m in diameter. There are some species of cnidarians that live only as polyps, others only as medusae, and still others that pass through both a medusa stage and a polyp stage in their life cycle.

Cnidarians are carnivores that use tentacles arranged in a ring around the mouth to capture prey and push the food into the gastrovascular cavity, where digestion begins. The undigested remains are eliminated through the mouth/anus. The tentacles are armed with batteries of cnidocytes ("stinging cells") that function in defense and in the capture of prey **(Figure 17.11)**. The phylum Cnidaria is named for these stinging cells. ☑

☑ **CHECKPOINT**

In what fundamental way does the body plan of a cnidarian differ from that of all other animals?

Answer: *The body of a cnidarian is radially symmetric.*

▼ **Figure 17.10 Polyp and medusa forms of cnidarians.** Note that cnidarians have two tissue layers, distinguished in the diagrams by blue and yellow. The gastrovascular cavity has only one opening, which functions as both mouth and anus.

Mouth/anus

Tentacle

Gastrovascular cavity

Polyp form

Coral

Sea anemone

Hydra

Gastrovascular cavity

Mouth/anus

Tentacle

Medusa form

Jelly

▼ **Figure 17.11 Cnidocyte action.** When a trigger on a tentacle is stimulated by touch, a fine thread shoots out from a capsule. Some cnidocyte threads entangle prey, while others puncture the prey and inject a poison.

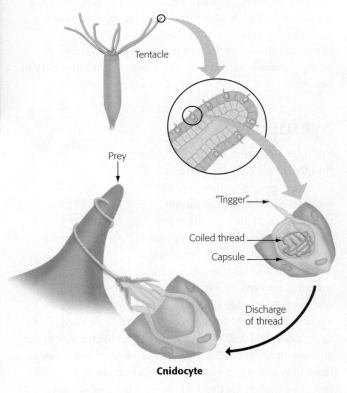

Tentacle

Prey

"Trigger"

Coiled thread

Capsule

Discharge of thread

Cnidocyte

Molluscs

Snails and slugs, oysters and clams, and octopuses and squids are all **molluscs** (phylum Mollusca). Molluscs are soft-bodied animals, but most are protected by a hard shell. Slugs, squids, and octopuses have reduced shells, most of which are internal, or they have lost their shells completely during their evolution. Many molluscs feed by using a file-like organ called a **radula** to scrape up food. Garden snails use their radulas like tiny saws to cut pieces out of leaves.

There are 93,000 known species of molluscs, with most being marine animals. All molluscs have a similar body plan **(Figure 17.12)**. The body has three main parts: a muscular foot, usually used for movement; a visceral mass containing most of the internal organs; and a fold of tissue called the mantle. The **mantle** drapes over the visceral mass and secretes the shell if one is present. The three major groups of molluscs are gastropods, bivalves, and cephalopods **(Figure 17.13)**.

Most **gastropods**, including snails, are protected by a single spiraled shell into which the animal can retreat when threatened. Slugs and sea slugs lack shells. Many gastropods have a distinct head with eyes at the tips of tentacles (think of a garden snail). Marine, freshwater, and terrestrial gastropods make up about three-quarters of the living mollusc species.

The **bivalves**, including clams, oysters, mussels, and scallops, have shells divided into two halves hinged together. None of the bivalves have a radula. There are both marine and freshwater species, with most being sedentary, using their muscular foot for digging and anchoring in sand or mud.

Cephalopods are all marine animals and generally differ from gastropods and sedentary bivalves in that their bodies are fast and agile. A few have large, heavy shells, but in most the shell is small and internal (as in squids) or missing (as in octopuses). Cephalopods have large brains and sophisticated sense organs, which contribute to their success as mobile predators. They use beak-like jaws and a radula to crush or rip prey apart. The mouth is at the base of the foot, which is drawn out into several long tentacles for catching and holding prey. The giant squid, which averages about 10 m in length, was thought to be the largest living invertebrate until an even larger species was discovered in the ocean depths near Antarctica. Scientists estimate that this massive cephalopod, dubbed the colossal squid, grows to an average length of 13 m—as long as a school bus. A specimen caught in 2007 weighed almost half a ton. ☑

What do you call a squid that's even larger than a giant squid?

◄ **Figure 17.12 The general body plan of a mollusc.** Note the body cavity (a true coelom, though a small one) and the complete digestive tract, with both mouth and anus.

Visceral mass — Coelom, Kidney, Heart, Reproductive organs, Digestive tract, Shell, Mantle, Mantle cavity, Anus, Gill, Radula, Mouth, Foot, Nerve cords

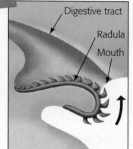

Digestive tract, Radula, Mouth

☑ CHECKPOINT

Classify these molluscs: A garden snail is an example of a _____; a clam is an example of a _____; a squid is an example of a _____.

Answer: gastropod; bivalve; cephalopod

▼ **Figure 17.13 Mollusc diversity.**

MAJOR GROUPS OF MOLLUSCS

Gastropods	Bivalves (hinged shell)	Cephalopods (large brain and tentacles)

Snail (spiraled shell)

Sea slug (no shell)

Scallop. This scallop has many eyes (small round structures) peering out between the two halves of the hinged shell.

Octopus. Octopuses live on the seafloor, where they search for crabs and other food. They have no shell. The brain of an octopus is larger and more complex, proportionate to body size, than that of any other invertebrate.

Nautilus. The shell of the nautilus is a coiled series of chambers. The animal inhabits only the outermost chamber; the others contain gas and fluid that enable the nautilus to regulate its buoyancy.

Sponges, Cnidarians, **Molluscs**, Flatworms, Annelids, Roundworms, Arthropods, Echinoderms, Chordates

Flatworms

Flatworms (phylum Platy-helminthes) are the simplest animals with bilateral symmetry. True to their name, these worms are ribbonlike and range from about 1 mm to about 20 m (about 65 feet) in length. Most flatworms have a gastrovascular cavity with a single opening. There are about 20,000 species of flatworms living in marine, freshwater, and damp terrestrial habitats **(Figure 17.14)**.

The gastrovascular cavity of free-living flatworms called planarians is highly branched, providing an extensive surface area for the absorption of nutrients. When the animal feeds, a muscular tube projects through the mouth and sucks food in. Planarians live on the under-surfaces of rocks in freshwater ponds and streams.

Parasitic flatworms include blood flukes called schistosomes, which are a major health problem in the tropics. These worms have suckers that attach to the inside of the blood vessels near the human host's intestines. Infection by these flatworms causes a long-lasting disease called schistosomiasis or blood fluke disease, with such symptoms as severe abdominal pain, anemia, and dysentery. Although schistosomes are not found in the United States, more than 200 million people around the world are infected by these parasites each year.

Tapeworms parasitize many vertebrates, including people. Most tapeworms have a very long, ribbonlike body with repeated parts. There is no mouth and no gastrovascular cavity. The head of a tapeworm is armed with suckers and hooks that lock the worm to the intestinal lining of the host. Bathed in partially digested food in the intestines of its host, the tapeworm simply absorbs nutrients across its body surface. Behind the head is a long ribbon of units that are little more than sacs of sex organs. At the back of the worm, mature units containing thousands of eggs break off and leave the host's body with the feces. People can become infected with tapeworms by eating undercooked beef, pork, or fish containing tapeworm larvae. The larvae are microscopic, but the adults can reach lengths of 2 m in the intestine. Such large tapeworms can cause intestinal blockage and rob enough nutrients from the host to cause nutritional deficiencies. Fortunately, an orally administered drug can kill the adult worms. ☑

A tapeworm doesn't have a mouth, so how does it eat?

Sponges
Cnidarians
Molluscs
Flatworms
Annelids
Roundworms
Arthropods
Echinoderms
Chordates

☑ CHECKPOINT

Flatworms are the simplest animals to display a body plan that is _____.

Answer: *bilaterally symmetric*

▼ **Figure 17.14 Flatworm diversity.**

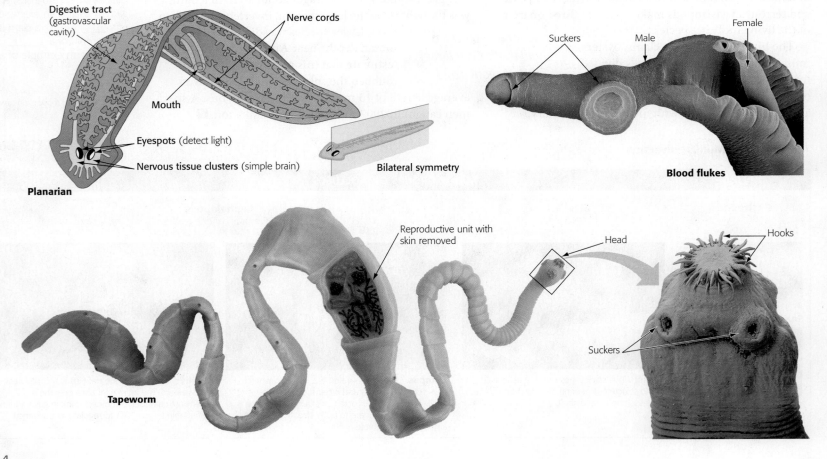

Digestive tract (gastrovascular cavity)

Nerve cords

Mouth

Eyespots (detect light)

Nervous tissue clusters (simple brain)

Bilateral symmetry

Planarian

Suckers

Male

Female

Blood flukes

Reproductive unit with skin removed

Head

Hooks

Suckers

Tapeworm

Annelids

Annelids (phylum Annelida) are worms that have **body segmentation**, which is the subdivision of the body along its length into a series of repeated parts called segments. In annelids, the segments look like a set of fused rings. There are about 16,000 annelid species, ranging in length from less than 1 mm to the 3-m giant Australian earthworm. Annelids live in damp soil, the sea, and most freshwater habitats. There are three main groups: earthworms, polychaetes, and leeches **(Figure 17.15)**.

Annelids exhibit two characteristics shared by all other bilateral animals except flatworms. One is a **complete digestive tract**, which is a digestive tube with two openings: a mouth and an anus. A complete digestive tract can process food and absorb nutrients as a meal moves in one direction from one specialized digestive organ to the next. In people, for example, the mouth, stomach, and intestines act as digestive organs. A second characteristic is a body cavity, which in this case is a coelom (a body cavity completely lined by mesoderm-derived tissue; see Figure 17.8c).

Earthworms, like all annelids, are segmented both externally and internally **(Figure 17.16)**. Many of the internal structures are repeated, segment by segment. The coelom (body cavity) is partitioned by walls (only two segment walls are fully shown here). The nervous system (yellow in the figure) and organs that dispose of fluid wastes (green) are repeated in each segment. The digestive tract, however, is not segmented; it passes through the segment

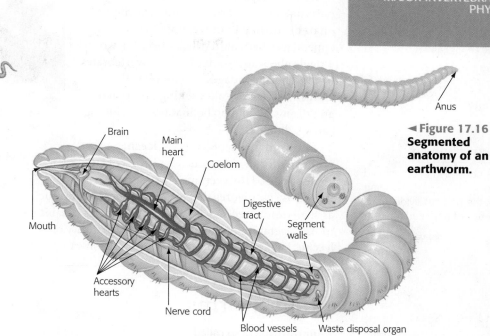

◄ **Figure 17.16**
Segmented anatomy of an earthworm.

walls from the mouth to the anus. Segmental blood vessels include one main heart and five pairs of accessory hearts.

Earthworms eat their way through the soil, extracting nutrients as the soil passes through the digestive tract. Undigested material, mixed with mucus secreted into the digestive tract, is eliminated as castings through the anus. Farmers and gardeners value earthworms because the animals aerate the soil, and the castings improve the texture of the soil. Charles Darwin estimated that each acre of British farmland contained about 50,000 earthworms that produced 18 tons of castings per year.

▼ **Figure 17.15 Annelid diversity.**

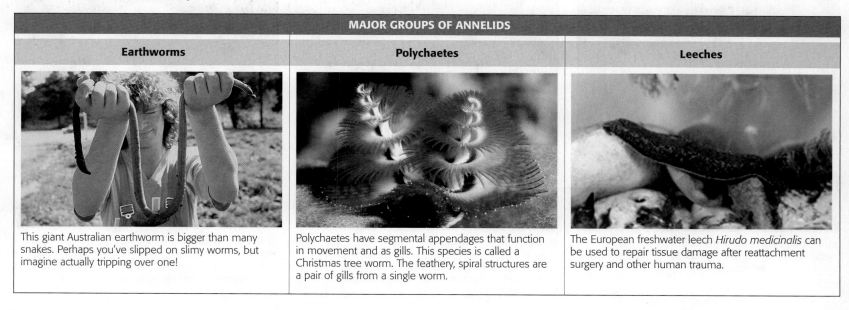

MAJOR GROUPS OF ANNELIDS

Earthworms	Polychaetes	Leeches
This giant Australian earthworm is bigger than many snakes. Perhaps you've slipped on slimy worms, but imagine actually tripping over one!	Polychaetes have segmental appendages that function in movement and as gills. This species is called a Christmas tree worm. The feathery, spiral structures are a pair of gills from a single worm.	The European freshwater leech *Hirudo medicinalis* can be used to repair tissue damage after reattachment surgery and other human trauma.

In contrast to earthworms, most **polychaetes** are marine, mainly crawling on or burrowing in the seafloor. Segmental appendages with hard bristles help the worm wriggle about in search of small invertebrates to eat. The appendages also increase the animal's surface area for taking up oxygen and disposing of metabolic wastes, including carbon dioxide.

The third group of annelids, **leeches**, are notorious for the bloodsucking habits of some species. However, most species are free-living carnivores that eat small invertebrates such as snails and insects. A few terrestrial species inhabit moist vegetation in the tropics, but the majority of leeches live in fresh water. A European freshwater

Medicinal leech

species called *Hirudo medicinalis* is used for the treatment of circulatory complications. Most commonly, leeches are applied after reconstructive microsurgery in which limbs or digits are reattached. Because arteries (which transport blood into a reattached area) are easier to reconnect than veins (which transport blood out), blood can pool in the reattached area and stagnate, starving the healing tissue of oxygen. Medicinal leeches have razor-like jaws with hundreds of tiny teeth that cut through the skin. They secrete saliva containing an anesthetic and an anticoagulant into the wound. The anesthetic makes the bite virtually painless, and the anticoagulant prevents clotting as the leech drains excess blood from the wound. ✔

✔ **CHECKPOINT**

The body plan of an annelid displays _____, meaning that the body is divided into a series of repeated regions.

Answer: segmentation

Roundworms

Roundworms (also called **nematodes**, members of the phylum Nematoda) get their common name from their cylindrical body, which is usually tapered at both ends **(Figure 17.17)**. Roundworms are among the most numerous and widespread of all animals. About 25,000 species of roundworms are known, and perhaps ten times that number actually exist. Roundworms range in length from about 1 mm to 1 m. They are found in

most aquatic habitats, in wet soil, and as parasites in the body fluids and tissues of plants and animals.

Free-living roundworms are important decomposers. They live virtually everywhere there is decaying organic matter, and their numbers are huge. Ninety thousand nematodes were found in a single rotting apple. In 2011, researchers even found nematodes living 2 miles underground, where they survive by grazing on microbes. Other species of nematodes thrive as parasites in plants and animals. Some are major agricultural pests that attack the roots of plants. At least 50 parasitic roundworm species infect people; they include pinworms, hookworms, and the parasite that causes trichinosis. ✔

Sponges
Cnidarians
Molluscs
Flatworms
Annelids
Roundworms
Arthropods
Echinoderms
Chordates

✔ **CHECKPOINT**

Which phylum is most closely related to the roundworms? (*Hint*: Refer to the phylogenetic tree.)

Answer: arthropods

▼ **Figure 17.17 Roundworm diversity.**

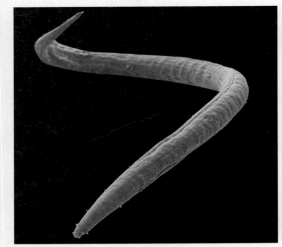

(a) A free-living roundworm. This species has the classic roundworm shape: cylindrical with tapered ends. The ridges indicate muscles that run the length of the body.

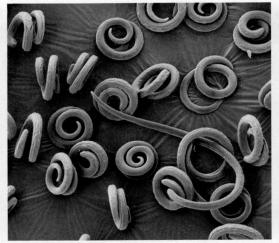

(b) Parasitic roundworms in pork. The potentially fatal disease trichinosis is caused by eating undercooked pork infected with *Trichinella* roundworms. The worms (shown here in pork tissue) burrow into a person's intestine and then invade muscle tissue.

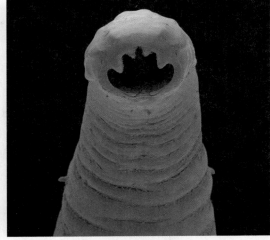

(c) Head of hookworm. Hookworms sink their hooks into the wall of the host's small intestine and feed on blood. Although the worms are small (less than 1 cm), a severe infestation can cause serious anemia.

Arthropods

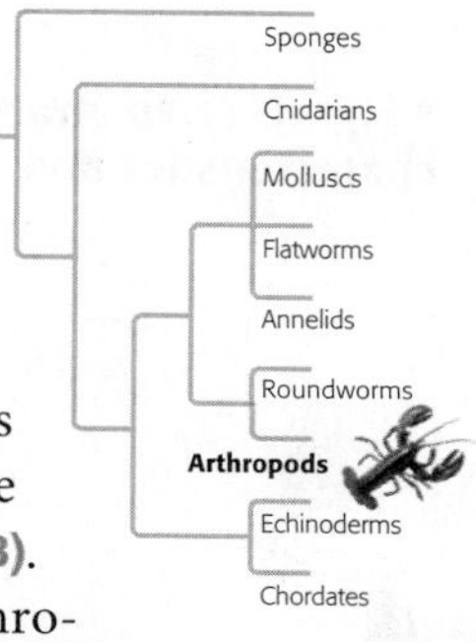

Arthropods (phylum Arthropoda) are named for their jointed appendages. Crustaceans (such as crabs and lobsters), arachnids (such as spiders and scorpions), and insects (such as grasshoppers and moths) are examples of arthropods **(Figure 17.18)**. Zoologists estimate that the total arthropod population numbers about a billion billion (10^{18}) individuals—that's about 150 million arthropods for each person! Researchers have identified over a million arthropod species, mostly insects. In fact, two out of every three species of life that have been scientifically described are arthropods. And arthropods are represented in nearly all habitats of the biosphere. In species diversity, distribution, and sheer numbers, arthropods must be regarded as the most successful animal phylum.

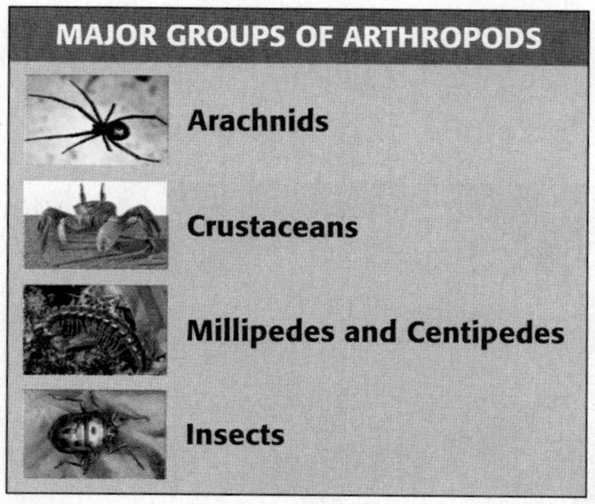

Sponges
Cnidarians
Molluscs
Flatworms
Annelids
Roundworms
Arthropods
Echinoderms
Chordates

◄ **Figure 17.18 Arthropod diversity.**

MAJOR GROUPS OF ARTHROPODS
Arachnids
Crustaceans
Millipedes and Centipedes
Insects

General Characteristics of Arthropods

Arthropods are segmented animals. In contrast with the repeating similar segments of annelids, however, arthropod segments and their appendages have become specialized for a great variety of functions. This evolutionary flexibility contributed to the great diversification of arthropods. Specialization of segments (or of fused groups of segments) provides for an efficient division of labor among body regions. For example, the appendages of different segments may be adapted for walking, feeding, sensory reception, swimming, or defense **(Figure 17.19)**.

The body of an arthropod is completely covered by an **exoskeleton**, an external skeleton. This coat is constructed from layers of protein and a polysaccharide called chitin. The exoskeleton can be a thick, hard armor over some parts of the body (such as the head), yet be paper-thin and flexible in other locations (such as the joints). The exoskeleton protects the animal and provides points of attachment for the muscles that move the appendages. There are, of course, advantages to wearing hard parts on the outside. Our own skeleton is interior to most of our soft tissues, an arrangement that doesn't provide much protection from injury. But our skeleton does offer the advantage of being able to grow along with the rest of our body. In contrast, a growing arthropod must occasionally shed its old exoskeleton and secrete a larger one. This process, called molting, leaves the animal temporarily vulnerable to predators and other dangers. The next five pages explore the major groups of arthropods. ☑

☑ CHECKPOINT

What is the primary difference between your skeleton and a crab's skeleton?

Answer: Your skeleton is interior, whereas a crab has an exterior skeleton (an exoskeleton).

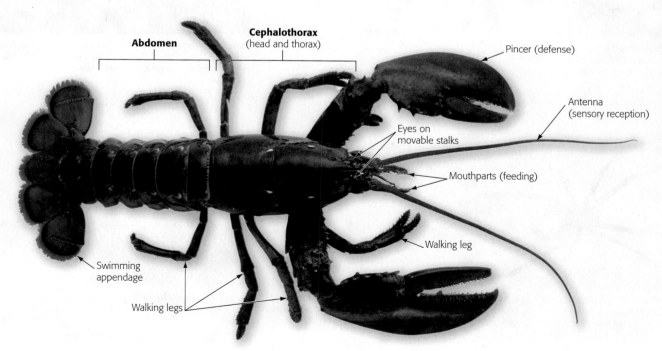

Abdomen

Cephalothorax (head and thorax)

Pincer (defense)

Antenna (sensory reception)

Eyes on movable stalks

Mouthparts (feeding)

Walking leg

Swimming appendage

Walking legs

◄ **Figure 17.19 Anatomy of a lobster, a crustacean.** The whole body, including the appendages, is covered by an exoskeleton. The body is segmented, but this characteristic is obvious only in the abdomen.

Arachnids

Most **arachnids** live on land. Scorpions, spiders, ticks, and mites are examples (Figure 17.20). Arachnids usually have four pairs of walking legs and a specialized pair of feeding appendages. In spiders, these feeding appendages are fang-like and equipped with poison glands. As a spider uses these appendages to immobilize and dismantle its prey, it spills digestive juices onto the torn tissues and sucks up its liquid meal.

▼ **Figure 17.20 Arachnid characteristics and diversity.**

Pair of feeding appendages

Leg (four pairs)

Pair of silk-spinning appendages

Scorpion. Scorpions have a pair of large pincers that function in defense and food capture. The tip of the tail bears a poisonous stinger. Scorpions sting people only when prodded or stepped on.

Dust mite. This microscopic house dust mite is a ubiquitous scavenger in our homes. Dust mites are harmless except to people who are allergic to the mites' feces.

Spider. Like most spiders, including the tarantula in the large photo, this black widow spins a web of liquid silk, which solidifies as it comes out of specialized glands. A black widow's venom can kill small prey but is rarely fatal to humans.

Wood tick. Wood ticks and other species carry bacteria that cause Rocky Mountain spotted fever. Lyme disease is carried by several different species of ticks.

Crustaceans

Crustaceans are nearly all aquatic, including delectable species of crabs, lobsters, crayfish, and shrimps (Figure 17.21). Barnacles, which anchor themselves to rocks, boat hulls, and even whales, are also crustaceans. One group of crustaceans, the isopods, is represented on land by pill bugs. All of these animals exhibit the arthropod characteristic of multiple pairs of specialized appendages.

▼ Figure 17.21 **Crustacean characteristics and diversity.**

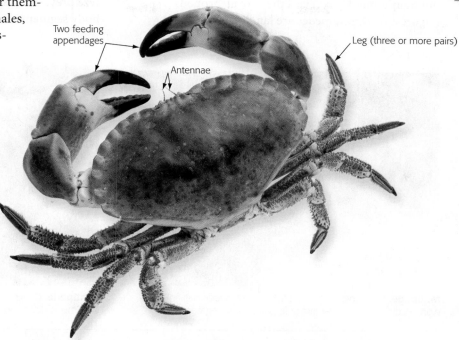

Two feeding appendages

Antennae

Leg (three or more pairs)

Crab. Ghost crabs are common along shorelines throughout the world. They scurry along the surf's edge and then quickly bury themselves in sand.

Shrimp. Naturally found in Pacific waters from Africa to Asia, giant prawns are widely cultivated as food.

Pill bug. Commonly found in moist locations with decaying leaves, such as under logs, pill bugs get their name from their tendency to roll up into a tight ball when they sense danger.

Crayfish. The red swamp crayfish, cultivated worldwide for food, becomes a pest when released outside of its native range in the southeastern United States.

Barnacles. Barnacles are stationary crustaceans with exoskeletons hardened into shells by calcium carbonate (lime). The jointed appendages projecting from the shell capture small plankton.

Millipedes and Centipedes

Millipedes and **centipedes** have similar segments over most of the body and superficially resemble annelids, but their jointed legs reveal they are arthropods (**Figure 17.22**). Millipedes are landlubbers that eat decaying plant matter. They have two pairs of short legs per body segment. Centipedes are terrestrial carnivores, with a pair of poison claws used in defense and to paralyze prey, such as cockroaches and flies. Each of their body segments bears a single pair of legs.

► **Figure 17.22 Millipedes and centipedes.**

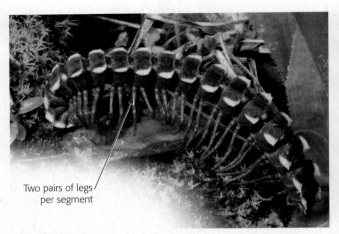

Two pairs of legs per segment

Millipede. Like most millipedes, this blue millipede has an elongated body with two pairs of legs per trunk segment.

One pair of legs per segment

Centipede. Centipedes can be found in dirt and leaf litter. Their venomous claws can harm cockroaches and spiders, but not people.

Insect Anatomy

Like the grasshopper in **Figure 17.23**, most **insects** have a three-part body: head, thorax, and abdomen. The head usually bears a pair of sensory antennae and a pair of eyes. The mouthparts of insects are adapted for particular kinds of eating—for example, for biting and chewing plant material in grasshoppers; for lapping up fluids in houseflies; and for piercing skin and sucking blood in mosquitoes. Most adult insects have three pairs of legs and one or two pairs of wings, all extending from the thorax.

Flight is obviously one key to the great success of insects. An animal that can fly can escape many predators, find food and mates, and disperse to new habitats much faster than an animal that must crawl on the ground. Because their wings are extensions of the exoskeleton and not true appendages, insects can fly without sacrificing legs. By contrast, the flying vertebrates—birds and bats—have one of their two pairs of legs modified for wings, which explains why these vertebrates are generally not very swift on the ground.

▼ **Figure 17.23 Anatomy of a grasshopper.**

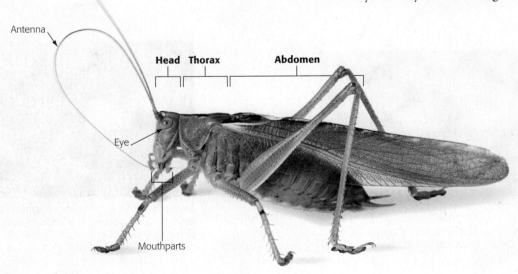

Antenna

Head Thorax Abdomen

Eye

Mouthparts

Insect Diversity

In species diversity, insects outnumber all other forms of life combined (Figure 17.24). They live in almost every terrestrial habitat and in fresh water, and flying insects fill the air. Insects are rare in the seas, where crustaceans are the dominant arthropods. The oldest insect fossils date back to about 400 million years ago. Later, the evolution of flight sparked an explosion in insect variety.

▼ Figure 17.24 **Insect diversity.**

Rhinoceros beetle. Only males have a "horn," which is used for fighting other males and for digging.

Red-and-black-striped stink bug. Members of this large insect family give off a foul-smelling liquid when disturbed.

Greater arid-land katydid. Often called the red-eyed devil, this scary-looking predator displays its wings and spiny legs when threatened.

Trilobite beetle. This beetle is found in the tropical rain forests of India and Southeast Asia.

Praying mantis. There are over 2,000 species of praying mantises throughout the world.

Jeweled beetle. Light reflected from varying thicknesses of chitin produces the brilliant colors of this beetle.

Buckeye butterfly. The eyespots on the wings of this butterfly may startle predators.

Rainbow bush locust. This colorful relative of grasshoppers is found in Madagascar.

Many insects undergo metamorphosis in their development. In the case of grasshoppers and some other insect groups, the young resemble adults but are smaller and have different body proportions. The animal goes through a series of molts, each time looking more like an adult, until it reaches full size. In other cases, insects have distinctive larval stages specialized for eating and growing that are known by such names as maggots (fly larvae), grubs (beetle larvae), or caterpillars (larvae of moths and butterflies). The larval stage looks entirely different from the adult stage, which is specialized for dispersal and reproduction. Metamorphosis from the larva to the adult occurs during a pupal stage **(Figure 17.25)**.

Forensic entomologists (forensic scientists who study insects) use their knowledge of insect life cycles to help solve criminal cases. For example, blowfly maggots feed on decaying flesh. Female blowflies, which can smell a dead body from up to a mile away, typically arrive and lay their eggs in a fresh corpse within

minutes. By knowing the length of each stage in the life cycle of a blowfly, an entomologist can determine how much time has passed since death occurred.

Animals so numerous, diverse, and widespread as insects are bound to affect the lives of all other terrestrial organisms, including people, in many ways. On the one hand, we depend on bees, flies, and other insects to pollinate our crops and orchards. On the other hand, insects are carriers of the microbes that cause many human diseases, such as malaria and West Nile disease. Insects also compete with people for food by eating our field crops. Trying to minimize their losses, farmers in the United States spend billions of dollars each year on pesticides, spraying crops with massive doses of insecticide poisons. But try as they might, not even humans have significantly challenged the preeminence of insects and their arthropod kin. As renowned entomologist Thomas Eisner put it: "Bugs are not going to inherit the Earth. They own it now. So we might as well make peace with the landlord." ☑

When a killer dumps a body outdoors, who (or what) is first to arrive on the scene?

☑ **CHECKPOINT**
Which major arthropod group is mainly aquatic? Which is the most numerous?

Answer: *crustaceans; insects*

▼ **Figure 17.25 Metamorphosis of a monarch butterfly.**

The **larva (caterpillar)** spends its time eating and growing, molting as it grows.

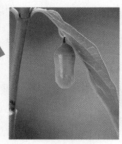

After several molts, the larva becomes a **pupa** encased in a cocoon.

Within the pupa, the larval organs break down and adult organs develop from cells that were dormant in the larva.

Finally, the **adult** emerges from the cocoon.

The butterfly flies off and reproduces, nourished mainly by calories stored when it was a caterpillar.

Echinoderms

The **echinoderms** (phylum Echinodermata) are named for their spiny surfaces (*echin* is Greek for "spiny"). Among the echinoderms are sea stars, sea urchins, sea cucumbers, and sand dollars **(Figure 17.26)**.

Echinoderms include about 7,000 species, all of them marine. Most move slowly, if at all. Echinoderms lack body segments, and most have radial symmetry as adults. Both the external and the internal parts of a sea star, for instance, radiate from the center like the spokes of a wheel. In contrast to the adult, the larval stage of echinoderms is bilaterally symmetric. This supports other evidence that echinoderms are not closely related to other radial animals, such as cnidarians, that never show bilateral symmetry. Most echinoderms have an **endoskeleton** (interior skeleton) constructed from hard plates just beneath the skin. Bumps and spines of this endoskeleton account for the animal's rough or prickly surface. Unique to echinoderms is the **water vascular system**, a network of water-filled canals that circulate water throughout the echinoderm's body, facilitating gas exchange (the entry of O_2 and the removal of CO_2) and waste disposal. The water vascular system also branches into extensions called tube feet. A sea star or sea urchin pulls itself slowly over the seafloor using its suction-cup-like tube feet. Sea stars also use their tube feet to grip prey during feeding.

Looking at sea stars and other adult echinoderms, you may think they have little in common with humans and other vertebrates. But as shown by the phylogenetic tree at the left, echinoderms share an evolutionary branch with chordates, the phylum that includes vertebrates. Analysis of embryonic development can differentiate the echinoderms and chordates from the evolutionary branch that includes molluscs, flatworms, annelids, roundworms, and arthropods. With this context in mind, we're now ready to make the transition from invertebrates to vertebrates. ☑

Sponges
Cnidarians
Molluscs
Flatworms
Annelids
Roundworms
Arthropods
Echinoderms
Chordates

☑ CHECKPOINT

Contrast the skeleton of an echinoderm with that of an arthropod.

Answer: An echinoderm has an endoskeleton; an arthropod has an exoskeleton.

▼ Figure 17.26 **Echinoderm diversity.**

Sea star. When a sea star encounters an oyster or clam, it grips the mollusc's shell with its tube feet (see inset) and positions its mouth next to the narrow opening between the two halves of the prey's shell. The sea star then pushes its stomach out through its mouth and the crack in the mollusc's shell.

Sea urchin. In contrast to sea stars, sea urchins are spherical and have no arms. If you look closely, you can see the long tube feet projecting among the spines. Unlike sea stars, which are mostly carnivorous, sea urchins mainly graze on seaweed and other algae.

Tube feet

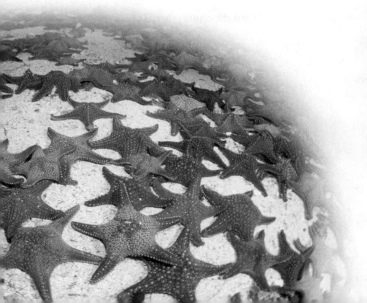

Sea cucumber. On casual inspection, this sea cucumber does not look much like other echinoderms. However, a closer look would reveal many echinoderm traits, including five rows of tube feet.

Sand dollar. Live sand dollars have a skin of movable spines covering a rigid skeleton. A set of five pores (arranged in a star pattern) allows seawater to be drawn into the sand dollar's body.

353

Vertebrate Evolution and Diversity

Most of us are curious about our family ancestry. Biologists are also interested in the larger question of tracing human ancestry within the animal kingdom. In this section, we trace the evolution of the vertebrates, the group that includes humans and their closest relatives. All vertebrates have endoskeletons, a characteristic shared with most echinoderms. However, vertebrate endoskeletons are unique in having a cranium (skull) and a backbone, a series of bones called vertebrae (singular, *vertebra*), for which the group is named **(Figure 17.27)**. Our first step in tracing the vertebrate lineage is to determine where vertebrates fit in the animal kingdom.

▼ **Figure 17.27 A vertebrate endoskeleton.** This snake skeleton, like those of all vertebrates, has a cranium (skull) and a backbone consisting of vertebrae.

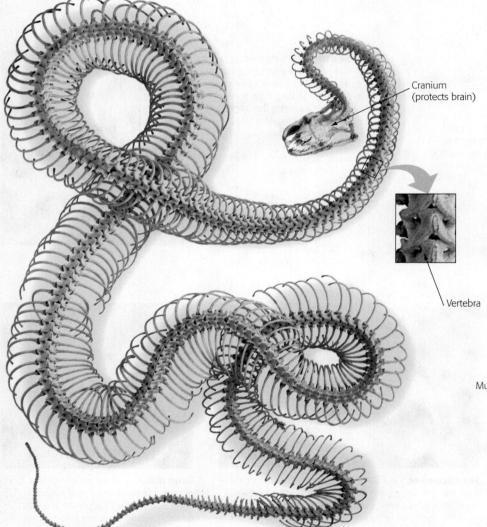

Cranium
(protects brain)

Vertebra

Characteristics of Chordates

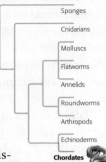

Sponges
Cnidarians
Molluscs
Flatworms
Annelids
Roundworms
Arthropods
Echinoderms
Chordates

The last phylum in our survey of the animal kingdom is the phylum Chordata. **Chordates** share four key features that appear in the embryo and sometimes in the adult **(Figure 17.28)**. These four chordate characteristics are (1) a **dorsal, hollow nerve cord**; (2) a **notochord**, which is a flexible, longitudinal rod located between the digestive tract and the nerve cord; (3) **pharyngeal slits**, which are grooves in the pharynx, the region of the digestive tube just behind the mouth; and (4) a **post-anal tail**, which is a tail to the rear of the anus. Though these chordate characteristics are often difficult to recognize in the adult animal, they are always present in chordate embryos. For example, the notochord, for which our phylum is named, persists in adult humans only in the form of the cartilage disks that function as cushions between the vertebrae. Back injuries described as "ruptured disks" or "slipped disks" refer to these notochord remnants.

Body segmentation is another chordate characteristic. Chordate segmentation is apparent in the backbone of vertebrates (see Figure 17.27) and is also evident in the segmental muscles of all chordates (see the chevron-shaped—>>>>>—muscles in the lancelet in Figure 17.29). Segmental musculature is not so obvious in adult humans unless one is motivated enough to sculpt those "washboard abs."

Three groups of chordates are invertebrates. Two of these groups, **tunicates** and **lancelets**, have no cranium **(Figure 17.29)**. The third group—hagfishes—have a cranium. (Hagfishes will be described shortly.) All other

▼ **Figure 17.28 Chordate characteristics.**

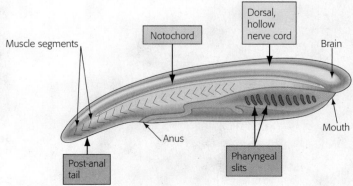

Muscle segments

Notochord

Dorsal,
hollow
nerve cord

Brain

Anus

Post-anal
tail

Pharyngeal
slits

Mouth

chordates are **vertebrates**, which retain the basic chordate characteristics but have additional features that are unique—including, of course, the backbone. **Figure 17.30** is an overview of chordate and vertebrate evolution that will provide a context for our survey. ☑

▼ **Figure 17.29 Chordates that have no cranium or vertebrae.**

Mouth

Tail

Lancelet. This marine invertebrate owes its name to its bladelike shape. Only a few centimeters long, lancelets wiggle backward into the gravel, leaving their mouth exposed, and filter tiny food particles from the seawater.

Tunicates. The tunicate, or sea squirt, is a stationary animal that filters food from the water. These pastel sea squirts get their nickname from their coloration and the fact that they can quickly expel water to startle intruders.

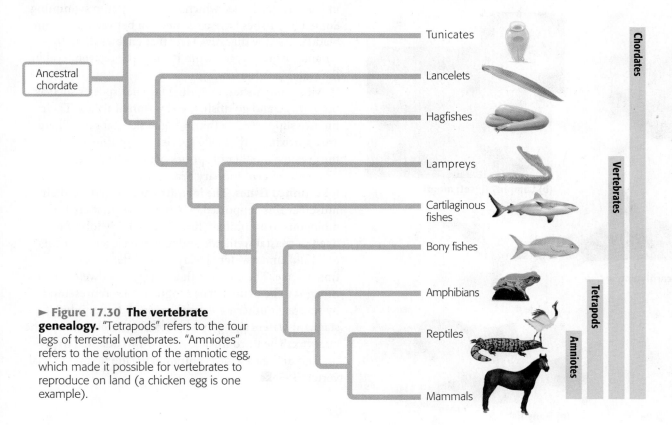

Tunicates

Ancestral chordate

Lancelets

Hagfishes

Lampreys

Cartilaginous fishes

Bony fishes

Amphibians

Reptiles

Mammals

Chordates

Vertebrates

Tetrapods

Amniotes

► **Figure 17.30 The vertebrate genealogy.** "Tetrapods" refers to the four legs of terrestrial vertebrates. "Amniotes" refers to the evolution of the amniotic egg, which made it possible for vertebrates to reproduce on land (a chicken egg is one example).

☑ **CHECKPOINT**

During our early embryonic development, what four features do we share with invertebrate chordates such as lancelets?

Answer: (1) dorsal, hollow nerve cord; (2) notochord; (3) pharyngeal slits; (4) post-anal tail

Fishes

The first vertebrates were aquatic and probably evolved during the early Cambrian period about 542 million years ago. In contrast with most other vertebrates, they lacked jaws, hinged bone structures that work the mouth.

Two types of jawless fishes survive today: hagfishes and lampreys. As noted earlier, hagfishes are invertebrates but have a cranium. Present-day hagfishes scavenge dead or dying animals on the cold, dark seafloor. When threatened, a hagfish exudes an enormous amount of slime from special glands on the sides of its body (Figure 17.31a). Recently, hagfishes have become endangered because their skin is used to make "eel-skin" belts, purses, and boots. Unlike hagfishes, lampreys are vertebrates. Some lampreys are parasites that use their jawless mouths as suckers to attach to the sides of large fish and draw blood (Figure 17.31b).

We know from the fossil record that the first jawed vertebrates were fishes that evolved about 470 million years ago. They had two pairs of fins, making them agile swimmers. Some early fishes were active predators up to 10 m in length that could chase prey and bite off chunks of flesh. Even today, most fishes are carnivores.

Cartilaginous fishes, such as sharks and rays, have a flexible skeleton made of cartilage (Figure 17.31c). Most sharks are adept predators because they are fast swimmers with streamlined bodies, acute senses, and powerful jaws. A shark does not have keen eyesight, but its sense of smell is very sharp. In addition, special electrosensors on the head can detect minute electrical fields produced by muscle contractions in nearby animals. Sharks also have a lateral line system, a row of sensory organs running along each side of the body. Sensitive to changes in water pressure, the lateral line system enables a shark to detect minor vibrations caused by animals swimming in its neighborhood. There are about 750 living species of cartilaginous fishes, nearly all of them marine.

The skeletons of bony fishes are reinforced by calcium (Figure 17.31d). Bony fishes have a lateral line system, a keen sense of smell, and excellent eyesight. On each side of the head, a protective flap called the operculum (plural, opercula) covers a chamber housing the gills, feathery external organs that extract oxygen from water. Movement of the operculum allows the fish to breathe without swimming. By contrast, sharks lack opercula and must swim to pass water over their gills. The need to move water over the gills is why a shark must keep moving to stay alive. Also unlike sharks, bony fishes have an organ that helps keep them buoyant—the swim bladder, a gas-filled sac. Thus, many bony fishes can conserve energy by remaining almost motionless, in contrast to sharks, which sink if they stop swimming. Some bony fishes have a connection between the swim bladder and the digestive tract that enables them to gulp air and extract oxygen from it when the oxygen level in the water gets too low.

Most bony fishes, including familiar species such as tuna, trout, and goldfish, are ray-finned fishes. Their fins are supported by thin, flexible skeletal rays. There are approximately 27,000 species of ray-finned fishes, the greatest number of species of any vertebrate group.

A second evolutionary branch includes the lobe-finned fishes. The lobe-fins are named for their muscular fins supported by stout bones that are homologous to amphibian limb bones. Early lobe-fins lived in coastal wetlands and may have used their fins to "walk" underwater. Today, three lineages of lobe-fins survive. The coelacanth is a deep-sea dweller once thought to be extinct. The lungfishes are represented by several Southern Hemisphere species that inhabit stagnant waters and gulp air into lungs connected to the pharynx. The third lineage of lobe-fins adapted to life on land and gave rise to amphibians, the first terrestrial vertebrates. ✓

Cladogram labels:
Tunicates
Lancelets
Hagfishes
Lampreys
Cartilaginous fishes
Bony fishes
Amphibians
Reptiles
Mammals

✓ CHECKPOINT

A shark has a _____ skeleton, whereas a tuna has a _____ skeleton.

Answer: cartilaginous; bony

▼ Figure 17.31 **Fish diversity.**

(a) Hagfish

(b) Lamprey (inset: mouth)

(c) Shark, a cartilaginous fish

Lateral line   Operculum

(d) Bony fish

Amphibians

In Greek, the word *amphibios* means "living a double life." Most **amphibians** exhibit a mixture of aquatic and terrestrial adaptations. Most species are tied to water because their eggs, lacking shells, dry out quickly in the air. A frog may spend much of its time on land, but it lays its eggs in water. An egg develops into a larva called a tadpole, a legless, aquatic algae-eater with gills, a lateral line system resembling that of fishes, and a long-finned tail. In changing into a frog, the tadpole undergoes a radical metamorphosis **(Figure 17.32a)**. When a young

Tunicates
Lancelets
Hagfishes
Lampreys
Cartilaginous fishes
Bony fishes
Amphibians
Reptiles
Mammals

frog crawls onto shore and begins life as a terrestrial insect-eater, it has four legs, air-breathing lungs instead of gills, external eardrums, and no lateral line system. But even as adults, amphibians are most abundant in damp habitats, such as swamps and rain forests. This is partly because amphibians depend on their moist skin to supplement lung function in exchanging gases with the environment. Thus, even those frogs that are adapted to relatively dry habitats spend much of their time in humid burrows or under piles of moist leaves. The amphibians of today, including frogs and salamanders, account for about 12% of all living vertebrates, or about 6,000 species **(Figure 17.32b)**.

Amphibians were the first vertebrates to colonize land. They descended from fishes that had lungs and fins with muscles and skeletal supports strong enough to enable some movement, however clumsy, on land **(Figure 17.33)**. The fossil record chronicles the evolution of four-limbed amphibians from fishlike ancestors. Terrestrial vertebrates—amphibians, reptiles, and mammals—are collectively called **tetrapods**, which means "four feet." ☑

▼ Figure 17.32 Amphibian diversity.

(a) Tadpole and adult gray tree frog

Malaysian horned frog

Texas barred tiger salamander
(b) Frogs and salamanders: the two major groups of amphibians

▼ Figure 17.33 The origin of tetrapods.

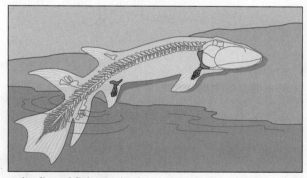

Lobe-finned fish. Fossils of some lobe-finned fishes have skeletal supports extending into their fins.

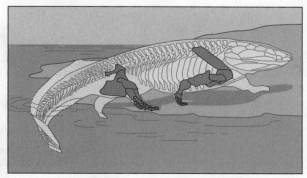

Early amphibian. Fossils of early amphibians have limb skeletons that probably functioned in helping them move on land.

357

Reptiles

Reptiles (including birds) and mammals are **amniotes**. The evolution of amniotes from an amphibian ancestor included many adaptations for living on land. The adaptation that gives the group its name is the **amniotic egg**, a fluid-filled egg with a waterproof shell that encloses the developing embryo. The amniotic egg functions as a self-contained "pond" that enables amniotes to complete their life cycle on land.

The **reptiles** include snakes, lizards, turtles, crocodiles, alligators, and birds, along with a number of extinct groups, including most of the dinosaurs **(Figure 17.34)**. The European grass snake in Figure 17.34 displays two reptilian adaptations to living on land: scaled waterproof skin, preventing dehydration in dry air, and amniotic eggs with shells, providing a watery, nutritious internal environment where the embryo can develop. These adaptations allowed reptiles to break their ancestral ties to aquatic habitats. Reptiles cannot breathe through their dry skin and so obtain most of their oxygen through their lungs.

Tunicates
Lancelets
Hagfishes
Lampreys
Cartilaginous fishes
Bony fishes
Amphibians
Reptiles
Mammals

Nonbird Reptiles

Nonbird reptiles are sometimes referred to as "cold-blooded" animals because they do not use their metabolism extensively to control body temperature. Reptiles do regulate body temperature, but largely through behavioral adaptations. For example, many lizards regulate their internal temperature by basking in the sun when the air is cool and seeking shade when the air is too warm. Because lizards and other nonbird reptiles absorb external heat rather than generating much of their own, they are said to be **ectotherms**, a term more accurate than "cold-blooded." By heating directly with solar energy rather than through the metabolic breakdown of food, a nonbird reptile can survive on less than 10% of the calories required by a mammal of equivalent size.

As successful as reptiles are today, they were far more widespread, numerous, and diverse during the Mesozoic era, which is sometimes known as the "age of reptiles." Reptiles diversified extensively during that era, producing a dynasty that lasted until about 65 million years ago. Dinosaurs, the most diverse reptile group, included the largest animals ever to inhabit land. Some were gentle giants that lumbered about while browsing vegetation. Others were voracious carnivores that chased their larger prey on two legs.

The age of reptiles began to fade about 70 million years ago. Around that time, the global climate became cooler and more variable. This was a period of mass extinctions that claimed all the dinosaurs by about 65 million years ago, except for one lineage (see Table 14.1). That lone surviving lineage is represented today by the reptilian group we know as birds. ☑

▼ **Figure 17.34 Reptile diversity.**

Snake. The shells of nonbird reptile eggs are leathery and flexible. This European grass snake is nonvenomous. When threatened, it may hiss and strike. If the bluff fails, it goes limp, pretending to be dead.

Turtle. The common box turtle, found throughout the eastern United States, can live for 100 years.

Lizard. The Gila monster, a desert-dweller of the Southwest, is the only venomous lizard native to the United States. Although large (up to 2 feet long), it moves too slowly to pose any danger to people.

Birds

Although **birds** were previously placed in their own class—class Aves—recent genetic and fossil evidence show that they are reptiles, having evolved from a lineage of small, two-legged dinosaurs called theropods. But today birds look quite different from reptiles because of their feathers and other distinctive flight equipment. Almost all of the 10,000 living bird species are airborne. The few flightless species, including the ostrich and the penguin, evolved from flying ancestors.

Where does the phrase "scarcer than hen's teeth" come from?

Appreciating the avian world is all about understanding flight. Almost every element of bird anatomy is modified in some way that enhances flight. The bones have a honeycombed structure that makes them strong but light. (The wings of airplanes have the same basic construction.) For example, a huge seagoing species called the frigate bird has a wingspan of more than 2 m (6.6 feet), but its whole skeleton weighs only about 113 g (a mere 4 ounces). Another adaptation that reduces the weight of birds is the absence of some internal organs found in other vertebrates. Female birds, for instance, have only one ovary instead of a pair. Also, today's birds are toothless, an adaptation that trims the weight of the head, preventing uncontrolled nosedives. Birds do not chew food in the mouth but grind it in the gizzard, a chamber of the digestive tract near the stomach.

Flying requires a great expenditure of energy and an active metabolism. Unlike other reptiles, birds are **endotherms**, meaning they use their own metabolic heat to maintain a warm, constant body temperature.

A bird's most obvious flight equipment is its wings. Bird wings are airfoils that illustrate the same principles of aerodynamics as the wings of an airplane **(Figure 17.35)**. A bird's flight motors are its powerful breast muscles, which are anchored to a keel-like breastbone. It is mainly these flight muscles that we call "white meat" on chicken and turkey breasts. Some birds, such as eagles and hawks, have wings adapted for soaring on air currents and flap their wings only occasionally. Other birds, including hummingbirds, excel at maneuvering but must flap continuously to stay aloft. Feathers are made of the same protein that forms the scales of reptiles. Feathers may have functioned first as insulation, helping birds retain body heat, only later being adapted as flight gear. ✔

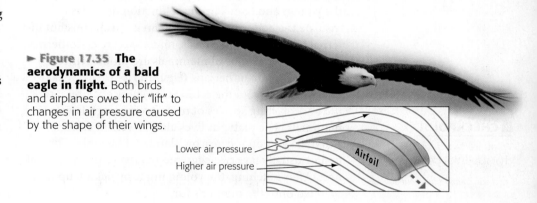

► **Figure 17.35 The aerodynamics of a bald eagle in flight.** Both birds and airplanes owe their "lift" to changes in air pressure caused by the shape of their wings.

Lower air pressure

Higher air pressure

Airfoil

Crocodile. Found throughout central and southern Africa, the Nile crocodile can grow up to 20 feet long and weigh nearly 2,000 pounds.

Birds. These red-crowned cranes, native to China, are performing an elaborate courtship dance.

Dinosaur. This *Herrarasaurus* skeleton is from a carnivorous biped discovered in Argentina.

Mammals

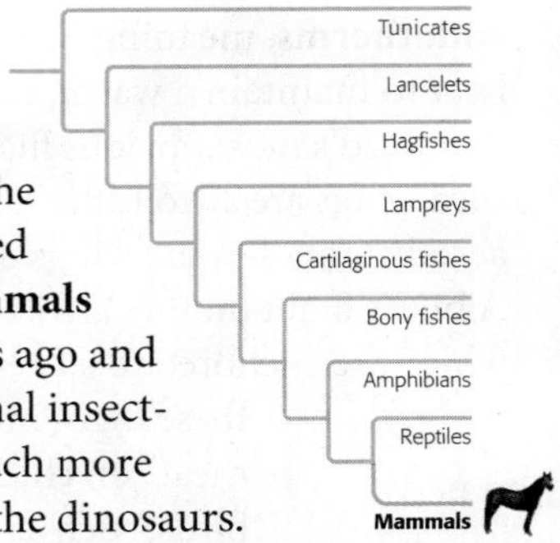

There are two major lineages of amniotes: one that led to the reptiles and one that produced the mammals. The first **mammals** arose about 200 million years ago and were probably small, nocturnal insect-eaters. Mammals became much more diverse after the downfall of the dinosaurs. Most mammals are terrestrial. These include nearly 1,000 species of winged mammals, the bats. And the roughly 80 species of dolphins, porpoises, and whales are totally aquatic. The blue whale—an endangered mammal that grows to lengths of nearly 30 m (about as long as a basketball court)—is the largest animal that has ever lived. Mammals have two unique characteristics: mammary glands (which produce milk that nourishes the young) and hair. The main function of hair is to insulate the body and help maintain a warm, constant internal temperature; like birds, mammals are endotherms.

The major groups of mammals are monotremes, marsupials, and eutherians **(Figure 17.36)**. The duck-billed platypus and the echidna, or spiny anteater, are the only existing species of **monotremes**, egg-laying mammals. The platypus lives along rivers in eastern Australia and on the nearby island of Tasmania. The female usually lays two eggs and incubates them in a leaf nest. After hatching, the young nurse by licking up milk secreted onto the mother's fur.

Most mammals are born rather than hatched. During pregnancy in marsupials and eutherians, the embryos are nurtured inside the mother by an organ called the **placenta**. Consisting of both embryonic and maternal tissues, the placenta joins the embryo to the mother within the uterus. The embryo receives oxygen and nutrients from maternal blood that flows close to the embryonic blood system in the placenta.

Marsupials, the so-called pouched mammals, include kangaroos, koalas, and opossums. These mammals have a brief pregnancy and give birth to tiny embryonic offspring that complete development while attached to the mother's nipples. The nursing young of most marsupials are housed in an external pouch on the mother's abdomen. Nearly all marsupials live in Australia, New Zealand, and North and South America. Australia has been a marsupial sanctuary for much of the past 60 million years. Australian marsupials have diversified extensively, filling terrestrial habitats that on the other continents are occupied by eutherian mammals.

Eutherians are also called **placental mammals** because their placentas provide a more intimate and longer-lasting association between the mother and her developing young than do marsupial placentas. Eutherians make up almost 95% of the 5,300 species of living mammals. Dogs, cats, cows, rodents, rabbits, bats, and whales are all examples of eutherian mammals. One of the eutherian groups is the primates, which include monkeys, apes, and humans. ☑

☑ **CHECKPOINT**

What are two defining characteristics of mammals?

Answer: mammary glands and hair

▼ **Figure 17.36 Mammalian diversity.**

MAJOR GROUPS OF MAMMALS		
Monotremes (hatched from eggs)	**Marsupials** (embryonic at birth)	**Eutherians** (fully developed at birth)
Monotremes, such as this duck-billed platypus, are the only mammals that lay eggs. Like other mammals, platypus mothers nourish their young with milk.	The young of marsupials are born very early in their development. The newborn kangaroo will finish its growth while nursing from a nipple in its mother's pouch.	In eutherians (placental mammals), young develop within the uterus of the mother. There they are nurtured by the flow of blood through the dense network of vessels in the placenta. This newborn foal is coated by remnants of the placenta.

The Human Ancestry

We have now traced animal phylogeny to the **primates**, the mammalian group that includes us—*Homo sapiens*—and our closest kin. To understand what that means, we must follow our ancestry back to the trees, where some of our most treasured traits originated.

The Evolution of Primates

Primate evolution provides a context for understanding human origins. The fossil record supports the hypothesis that primates evolved from insect-eating mammals during the late Cretaceous period, about 65 million years ago. Those early primates were small, arboreal (tree-dwelling) mammals. Thus, primates were first distinguished by characteristics that were shaped, through natural selection, by the demands of living in the trees. For example, primates have limber shoulder joints, which make it possible to swing from branch to branch. The agile hands of primates can hang on to branches and manipulate food. Nails have replaced claws in many primate species, and the fingertips are very sensitive. The eyes of primates are close together on the front of the face. The overlapping fields of vision of the two eyes enhance depth perception, an obvious advantage when swinging in trees. Excellent eye-hand coordination is also important for arboreal maneuvering. Parental care is essential for young animals in the trees. Mammals devote more energy to caring for their young than most other vertebrates, and primates are among the most attentive parents of all mammals. Most primates have single births and nurture their offspring for a long time. Although humans never lived in trees, we retain in modified form many traits that originated there.

Taxonomists divide the primates into three main groups **(Figure 17.37)**. The first includes lemurs, lorises, and pottos. These primates live in Madagascar, southern Asia, and Africa. Tarsiers, small nocturnal tree-dwellers found only in Southeast Asia, form the second group of primates. The third group of primates, **anthropoids**, includes monkeys and apes. All monkeys in the New World (the Americas) are arboreal and are distinguished by prehensile (grasping) tails that function as an extra appendage for swinging. If you see a monkey in a zoo swinging by its tail, you know it's from the New World. Although some Old World (African and Asian) monkeys are also arboreal, their tails are not prehensile. And many Old World monkeys, including baboons, macaques, and mandrills,

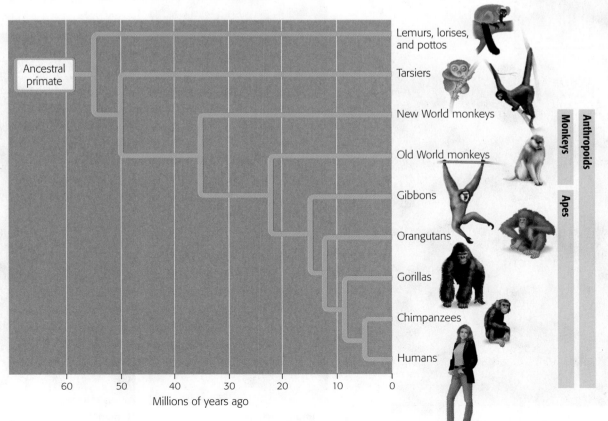

◄ **Figure 17.37 Primate phylogeny.**

Lemurs, lorises, and pottos

Tarsiers

New World monkeys

Old World monkeys

Gibbons

Orangutans

Gorillas

Chimpanzees

Humans

Ancestral primate

Millions of years ago

60   50   40   30   20   10   0

Monkeys

Apes

Anthropoids

are mainly ground-dwellers. Anthropoids also have a fully opposable thumb; that is, they can touch the tips of all four fingers with their thumb.

Our closest anthropoid relatives are the nonhuman apes: gibbons, orangutans, gorillas, and chimpanzees. They live only in tropical regions of the Old World. Except for some gibbons, apes are larger than monkeys, with relatively long arms,

What's the difference between apes and monkeys?

short legs, and no tail. Although all apes are capable of living in trees, only gibbons and orangutans are primarily arboreal. Gorillas and chimpanzees are highly social. Apes have larger brains proportionate to body size than monkeys, and their behavior is more adaptable. And, of course, the apes include humans. **Figure 17.38** shows examples of primates.

▼ **Figure 17.38 Primate diversity.**

Red ruffed lemur

Tarsier

Black spider monkey
(New World monkey)

Gibbon (ape)

Orangutan (ape)

Patas monkey (Old World monkey)

Gorilla (ape)

Chimpanzee (ape)

Human

The Emergence of Humankind

Humanity is one very young twig on the tree of life. In the continuum of life spanning 3.5 billion years, the fossil record and molecular systematics indicate that humans and chimpanzees have shared a common African ancestry for all but the last 5–7 million years (see Figure 17.37). Put another way, if we compressed the history of life to a year, the human branch has existed for only 18 hours.

Some Common Misconceptions

Certain misconceptions about human evolution persist in the minds of many, long after these myths have been debunked by the fossil evidence. Let's first dispose of the myth that our ancestors were chimpanzees or any other modern ape. Although 5–7 million years is a brief time span relative to the 3.5-billion-year history of life, it is ample time for speciation. Since diverging from a common, less specialized ancestor, chimpanzees and humans have evolved separately for hundreds of thousands of generations. Thus, chimps are not our parent species, but more like our phylogenetic cousins.

Another misconception envisions human evolution as a ladder with a series of steps leading directly from an ancestral anthropoid to *Homo sapiens*. This is often illustrated as a parade of fossil **hominins** (members of the human family) becoming progressively more modern as they march across the page. If human evolution is a parade, then it is a disorderly one, with many splinter groups having traveled down dead ends. At times in hominin history, several human species coexisted (**Figure 17.39**). Human phylogeny is more like a multibranched bush than a ladder, with our species being the tip of the only twig that still lives.

One more myth is that various human characteristics, such as upright posture and an enlarged brain, evolved in unison. A popular image is of early humans as half-stooped, half-witted cave-dwellers. In fact, the fossil record reveals that different human features evolved at different rates, with erect posture, or bipedalism, leading the way. Our pedigree includes ancestors who walked upright but had ape-sized brains.

Although we can dismiss these misconceptions about human evolution, many fascinating questions about our ancestry still remain. With each new hominin fossil, scientists get a little closer to solving the puzzle of how we became human. In the following pages, you'll learn about some of the important clues that have been discovered so far.

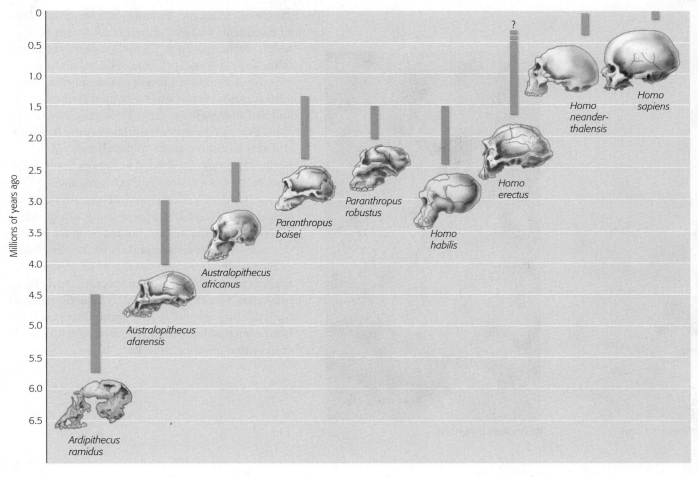

◄ **Figure 17.39 A time line of human evolution.** The orange bars indicate the time span during which each species lived. Notice that there have been times when two or more hominin species coexisted. The skulls are all drawn to the same scale so you can compare the sizes of craniums and hence brains.

Australopithecus and the Antiquity of Bipedalism

Present-day humans and chimpanzees clearly differ in two major physical features: Humans are bipedal (walk upright) and have much larger brains. When did these features emerge? In the early 1900s, scientists hypothesized that increased brain size was the initial change that separated hominins from other apes. That hypothesis was overturned when a team of researchers in Ethiopia unearthed a stunning 3.24-million-year-old female hominin that had a small brain and walked on two legs **(Figure 17.40a)**. Officially named *Australopithecus afarensis*, but nicknamed Lucy by her discoverers, the individual was only about 3 feet tall and with a head about the size of a softball. Corroborating evidence of early bipedalism was found soon after—the footprints of two upright-walking hominins preserved in a 3.6-million-year-old layer of volcanic ash **(Figure 17.40b)**. Lucy represents just one of several species of *Australopithecus* discovered to date. The first analysis of the most recent addition to the genus, *Australopithecus sediba*, was published in 2010.

Scientists are now certain that bipedalism is a very old trait. Another lineage known as "robust"

▼ **Figure 17.40 The antiquity of upright posture.**

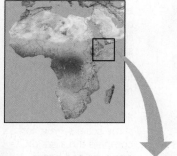

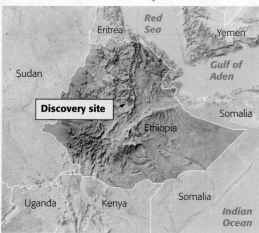

(a) Afar region of Ethiopia, where Lucy was discovered

(b) Ancient footprints

australopiths—including *Paranthropus boisei* and *Paranthropus robustus* in Figure 17.39—were also small-brained bipeds. So was *Ardipithecus ramidus*, the oldest hominin shown in Figure 17.39.

Homo habilis and the Evolution of Inventive Minds

Enlargement of the human brain is first evident in fossils from East Africa dating to about 2.4 million years ago. Thus, the fundamental human trait of an enlarged brain evolved a few million years after bipedalism. As evolutionary biologist Stephen Jay Gould put it, "Mankind stood up first and got smart later."

Anthropologists have found skulls with brain capacities intermediate in size between those of the latest *Australopithecus* species and those of *Homo sapiens*. Simple handmade stone tools are sometimes found with the larger-brained fossils, which have been dubbed *Homo habilis* ("handy man"). After walking upright for about 2 million years, humans were finally beginning to use their manual dexterity and big brains to invent tools that enhanced their hunting, gathering, and scavenging on the African savanna.

Homo erectus and the Global Dispersal of Humanity

The first species to extend humanity's range from Africa to other continents was *Homo erectus*. Skeletons of *Homo erectus* dating to 1.8 million years ago found in the former Soviet republic of Georgia represent the oldest known fossils of hominins outside Africa. *Homo erectus* was taller than *Homo habilis* and had a larger brain capacity. Intelligence enabled this species to continue succeeding in Africa and also to survive in the colder climates of the north. *Homo erectus* resided in huts or caves, built fires, made clothes from animal skins, and designed stone tools. In anatomical and physiological adaptations, *Homo erectus* was poorly equipped for life outside the tropics, but made up for the deficiencies with cleverness and social cooperation.

Eventually, *Homo erectus* migrated to populate many regions of Asia and Europe, moving as far as Indonesia. Could the "hobbits" (*Homo floresiensis*) from the Biology and Society section have evolved from a long-isolated group of *Homo erectus*? We'll explore that question next. ☑

Who Were the Hobbit People?

How do scientists test hypotheses about events that occurred in the distant past? One approach involves using fossils, the historical record of life on Earth. Researchers have discovered thousands of fossils from at least 20 species of extinct hominins. If you have watched TV shows like *Bones*, in which forensic scientists use skeletal remains to solve crimes, you know that even a small piece of a skeleton can provide a wealth of information to an expert. Researchers have applied this method of hypothesis testing to the scientific debate over the "hobbit" people.

The first **observations** made by the researchers who discovered hominin fossils on the island of Flores revealed that the new fossils did not belong to any known species. This led researchers to ask the **question**, "Where does this hominin fit in our evolutionary history?" The scientists formed the **hypothesis** that the hobbits evolved from an isolated population of *Homo erectus*, the ancient hominin whose far-flung migrations predated those of *Homo sapiens*. They made the **prediction** that key traits of the new species, such as its skull characteristics and body proportions, would resemble those of a miniature *Homo erectus* individual. Rather than a controlled **experiment**, the investigation consisted of making detailed measurements and other observations of the new fossils and comparing them with data from *Homo erectus* fossils. The initial **results** supported their hypothesis.

As you have learned, however, preliminary conclusions are often overturned by new evidence. In the past several years, further analyses have been carried out, and additional specimens have been examined. Many scientists now think that the evidence supports an alternative hypothesis:

Homo floresiensis is most closely related to *Homo habilis*, a smaller and more ancient species than *Homo erectus*. Other researchers continue to test the hypothesis that the hobbits are not a species at all, but a *Homo sapiens* population with a disorder that caused bone malformations.

How can scientists determine which hypothesis is correct? By accumulating further evidence. While some researchers continue to excavate the site where *Homo floresiensis* was discovered **(Figure 17.41)**, others are widening the search to additional locations. The most helpful information would come from finding a second skull or unearthing bones or teeth from which DNA could be extracted and analyzed. Meanwhile, the mystery of the hobbit people continues.

▼ **Figure 17.41 Searching for hobbits.** Researchers continue to excavate Liang Bua Cave, on the Indonesian island of Flores, where *Homo floresiensis* was discovered.

Homo neanderthalensis

Whether or not it was the immediate ancestor of *Homo floresiensis*, *Homo erectus* did give rise to regionally diverse descendants in Europe and Asia. Among these descendants was *Homo neanderthalensis*—commonly called Neanderthals. This species had a large brain and hunted big game with tools made from stone and wood. Neanderthals were living in Europe as far back as 350,000 years ago and later spread to the Near East; but by 28,000 years ago, the species was extinct.

Since the first discovery of fossilized remains in the Neander Valley in Germany 150 years ago, people have

Do you have a little Neanderthal in you?

wondered whether Neanderthals are related to us. Through DNA analysis, researchers have shown that the last common ancestor of humans and Neanderthals lived around 500,000 years ago. However the full Neanderthal genome sequence, completed in 2010, suggests that Neanderthals may have interbred with some populations of *Homo sapiens*. Scientists also learned that the individuals whose DNA was sequenced had pale skin and red hair **(Figure 17.42)**. Further analysis of Neanderthal DNA will undoubtedly reveal more details about the physical appearance and physiology of these intriguing hominins.

▲ **Figure 17.42 An artist's rendering of a Neanderthal.**

The Origin and Dispersal of *Homo sapiens*

The oldest known fossils of our own species, *Homo sapiens*, were discovered in Ethiopia and date from 160,000 to 195,000 years ago. These early humans lacked the heavy browridges of *Homo erectus* and *Homo neanderthalensis* and were more slender, suggesting that they belong to a distinct lineage. The Ethiopian fossils support molecular evidence about the origin of humans: DNA studies strongly suggest that all living humans can trace their ancestry back to a single African *Homo sapiens* lineage that began 160,000 to 200,000 years ago.

Fossil evidence suggests that our species emerged from Africa in one or more waves, spreading first into Asia and then to Europe and Australia (**Figure 17.43**). The oldest fossils of *Homo sapiens* outside Africa date back about 50,000 years. The date of the first arrival of humans in the New World is uncertain, although the generally accepted evidence suggests a minimum of 15,000 years ago.

Certain uniquely human traits have allowed for the development of human societies. The primate brain continues to grow after birth, and the period of growth is longer for a human than for any other primate. The extended period of human development also lengthens the time parents care for their offspring, which contributes to the child's ability to benefit from the experiences of earlier generations. This is the basis of **culture**—social transmission of accumulated knowledge, customs, beliefs, and art over generations (**Figure 17.44**). The major means of this transmission is language, spoken and written. Humans have evolved culturally as well as biologically.

Nothing has had a greater impact on life on Earth than *Homo sapiens*. The global consequences of human evolution have been enormous. Cultural evolution made modern *Homo sapiens* a new force in the history of life—a species that could defy its physical limitations. We do not have to wait to adapt to an environment through natural selection; we simply change the environment to meet our needs.

We are the most numerous and widespread of all large animals, and wherever we go, we bring environmental change faster than many species can adapt; the rate of extinctions during the 1900s was 50 times greater than the average for the past 100,000 years. In the next unit, on ecology, we'll examine the interactions of humans—as well as other species—with the environment. ☑

▼ **Figure 17.43 The spread of *Homo sapiens* (dates given as years before present, BP).**

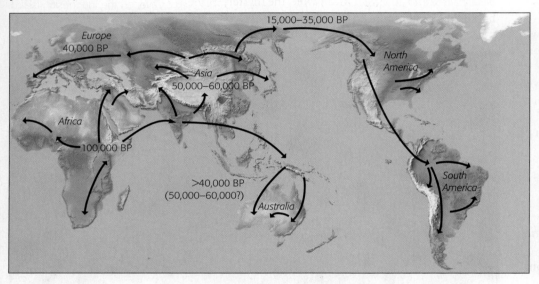

- Europe 40,000 BP
- 15,000–35,000 BP
- North America
- Asia 50,000–60,000 BP
- Africa
- 100,000 BP
- >40,000 BP (50,000–60,000?)
- Australia
- South America

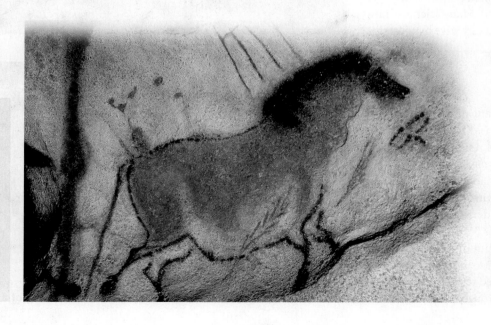

◄ **Figure 17.44 Art history goes back a long way.** Beautiful ancient art, such as this 30,000-year-old cave painting, is just one example of our cultural roots in early societies.

Human Evolution EVOLUTION CONNECTION

Are We Still Evolving?

Imagine that you could take a time machine 100,000 years into the past and bring back a *Homo sapiens* man. If you dressed him in jeans and a T-shirt and took him for a stroll around campus, chances are that no one would look twice. Did we stop evolving after becoming *Homo sapiens*? In some ways, yes. The human body has not changed much in the past 100,000 years. And by the time *Homo sapiens* began to travel out of Africa, all of the complex characteristics that define our humanity, including our big-brained intelligence and our capacity for language and symbolic thought, had already evolved.

But as humans wandered far from their site of origin and settled in diverse environments, populations encountered different selective forces. Some traits of people today reflect evolutionary responses of ancient ancestors to their environment, including disease, diet, and physical factors. For example, certain populations evolved sickle hemoglobin as an adaptation to the deadly disease malaria (see the Evolution Connection section of Chapter 13). Populations that kept dairy herds evolved the ability to digest lactose as adults (see the Evolution Connection section of Chapter 3). One of the most striking differences among people is skin color **(Figure 17.45)**. The loss of skin pigmentation in humans who migrated north from Africa is thought to be an adaptation to low levels of ultraviolet (UV) radiation in northern latitudes. Dark pigment blocks the UV radiation necessary for synthesizing vitamin D—essential for proper bone development—in the skin. Recent research has turned up numerous other examples of adaptations that enabled us to colonize Earth's varied environments. For instance, Tibetans live at altitudes up to 14,000 feet (2.6 miles), where the air has 40% less oxygen than at sea level. Researchers have identified genes that have undergone evolutionary changes in response to this challenging environment **(Figure 17.46)**. Despite evolutionary tweaks such as these, however, we remain a single species.

▼ **Figure 17.45 People with different adaptations to UV radiation.**

▼ **Figure 17.46 Tibetans, a population adapted to living at high altitude.**

Chapter Review

SUMMARY OF KEY CONCEPTS

 Go to **www.masteringbiology.com** for homework assignments, practice quizzes, Pearson eText, and more.

The Origins of Animal Diversity

What Is an Animal?

Animals are eukaryotic, multicellular, heterotrophic organisms that obtain nutrients by ingestion. Most animals reproduce sexually and develop from a zygote to a blastula and then to a gastrula. After the gastrula stage, some develop directly into adults, whereas others pass through a larval stage.

Early Animals and the Cambrian Explosion

Animals probably evolved from a colonial, flagellated protist. Precambrian animals were soft-bodied. Animals with hard parts appeared during the Cambrian period. Between 535 and 525 million years ago, animal diversity increased rapidly.

Animal Phylogeny

Major branches of animal evolution are defined by two key evolutionary differences: the presence or absence of tissues and radial versus bilateral body symmetry. A body cavity (coelom) at least partly lined by mesoderm evolved in a number of later branches.

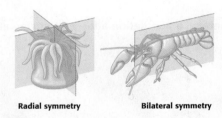

Radial symmetry   **Bilateral symmetry**

Major Invertebrate Phyla

This tree shows the eight major invertebrate phyla, as well as chordates, which include a few invertebrates.

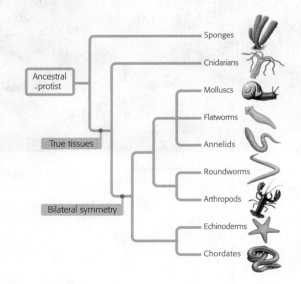

Sponges

Sponges (multiple phyla) are stationary animals with porous bodies but no true tissues. Specialized cells draw water through pores in the sides of the body and trap food particles.

Cnidarians

Cnidarians (phylum Cnidaria) have radial symmetry, a gastrovascular cavity with a single opening, and tentacles with stinging cnidocytes. The body is either a stationary polyp or a floating medusa.

Molluscs

Molluscs (phylum Mollusca) are soft-bodied animals often protected by a hard shell. The body has three main parts: a muscular foot, a visceral mass, and a fold of tissue called the mantle.

MOLLUSCS		
Gastropods	**Bivalves**	**Cephalopods**

Flatworms

Flatworms (phylum Platyhelminthes) are the simplest bilateral animals. They may be free-living (such as planarians) or parasitic (such as tapeworms).

Annelids

Annelids (phylum Annelida) are segmented worms with complete digestive tracts. They may be free-living or parasitic.

Roundworms

Roundworms, also called nematodes (phylum Nematoda), are unsegmented and cylindrical with tapered ends. They may be free-living or parasitic.

Arthropods

Arthropods (phylum Arthropoda) are segmented animals with an exoskeleton and specialized, jointed appendages.

ARTHROPODS			
Arachnids	**Crustaceans**	**Millipedes and Centipedes**	**Insects**

Echinoderms

Echinoderms (phylum Echinodermata) are stationary or slow-moving marine animals that lack body segments and possess a unique water vascular system. Bilaterally symmetric larvae usually change to radially symmetric adults. Echinoderms have a bumpy endoskeleton.

Vertebrate Evolution and Diversity

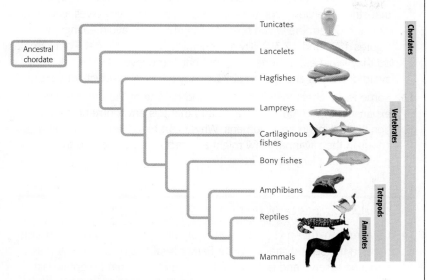

Characteristics of Chordates

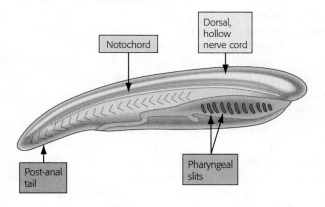

Tunicates and lancelets are invertebrate chordates. The vast majority of chordates are vertebrates, possessing a cranium and backbone.

Fishes

Hagfishes have skulls but lack vertebrae. Lampreys are jawless vertebrates. Cartilaginous fishes, such as sharks, are mostly predators with powerful jaws and a flexible skeleton made of cartilage. Bony fishes have a stiff skeleton reinforced by calcium. Bony fishes are further classified into ray-finned fishes and lobe-finned fishes (including lungfishes).

Amphibians

Amphibians are tetrapod vertebrates that usually deposit their eggs (lacking shells) in water. Aquatic larvae typically undergo a radical metamorphosis into the adult stage. Their moist skin requires that amphibians spend much of their adult life in humid environments.

Reptiles

Reptiles are amniotes, vertebrates that develop in a fluid-filled egg enclosed by a shell. Reptiles include terrestrial ectotherms with lungs and waterproof skin covered by scales. Scales and amniotic eggs enhanced reproduction on land. Birds are endothermic reptiles with wings, feathers, and other adaptations for flight.

Mammals

Mammals are endothermic vertebrates with mammary glands and hair. There are three major groups: Monotremes lay eggs; marsupials use a placenta but give birth to tiny embryonic offspring that usually complete development while attached to nipples inside the mother's pouch; and eutherians, or placental mammals, use their placenta in a longer-lasting association between the mother and her developing young.

MAMMALS		
Monotremes	**Marsupials**	**Eutherians**

The Human Ancestry

The Evolution of Primates

The first primates were small, arboreal mammals that evolved from insect-eating mammals about 65 million years ago. Anthropoids consist of New World monkeys (with prehensile tails), Old World monkeys (without prehensile tails), apes, and humans.

The Emergence of Humankind

Chimpanzees and humans evolved from a common ancestor about 5–7 million years ago. Species of the genus *Australopithecus*, which lived at least 4 million years ago, walked upright and had a small brain. Enlargement of the human brain in *Homo habilis* came later, about 2.4 million years ago. *Homo erectus* was the first species to extend humanity's range from its birthplace in Africa to other continents. *Homo erectus* gave rise to regionally diverse descendants, such as the Neanderthals (*Homo neanderthalensis*). Current data indicate a relatively recent dispersal of modern Africans that gave rise to today's human diversity.

SELF-QUIZ

1. Bilateral symmetry in the animal kingdom is best correlated with
   a. an ability to sense equally in all directions.
   b. the presence of a skeleton.
   c. motility and active predation and escape.
   d. development of a true coelom.

2. The cavity between your outer body wall and your digestive tract that is fully lined by mesoderm is an example of a true _____. Roundworms have a _____, a body cavity not completely lined by mesoderm.

CHAPTER 17

3. Identify which of the following categories includes all others in the list: arthropod, arachnid, insect, butterfly, crustacean, millipede.

4. The oldest group of tetrapods is the _____.

5. Reptiles are much more extensively adapted to life on land than amphibians because reptiles
  a. have a complete digestive tract.
  b. lay eggs that are enclosed in shells.
  c. are endothermic.
  d. go through a larval stage.

6. What is the name of the phylum to which humans belong? For what anatomical structure is the phylum named? Where in your body is a derivative of this anatomical structure found?

7. Fossils suggest that the first major trait distinguishing human primates from other primates was _____.

8. Which of the following types of animals is not included in the human ancestry? (*Hint*: See Figure 17.30.)
  a. a bird
  b. a bony fish
  c. an amphibian
  d. a primate

9. Put the following list of species in order, from the oldest to the most recent: *Homo erectus*, *Australopithecus* species, *Homo habilis*, *Homo sapiens*.

10. Match each of the following animals to its phylum:
  a. human   1. Echinodermata
  b. leech   2. Arthropoda
  c. sea star   3. Cnidaria
  d. lobster   4. Chordata
  e. sea anemone   5. Annelida

Answers to these questions can be found in Appendix: Self-Quiz Answers.

THE PROCESS OF SCIENCE

11. Imagine that you are a marine biologist. As part of your exploration, you dredge up an unknown animal from the seafloor. Describe some of the characteristics you should look at to determine the phylum to which the creature should be assigned.

12. Many people describe themselves as vegetarians. Strictly speaking, vegetarians eat only plant products. Most vegetarians are not, in fact, that strict. Interview acquaintances who describe themselves as vegetarians and determine which taxonomic groups they avoid eating (see Figures 17.6 and 17.30). Try to generalize about their diet. For example, do they avoid eating vertebrates but eat some invertebrates? Do they avoid only birds and mammals? Do they eat dairy products or eggs?

13. Some researchers think that drying and cooling of the climate caused expansion of the African savanna and that this environment favored upright walking in early humans. Why might bipedalism be advantageous in the savanna? How might an erect posture relate to the evolution of a larger brain?

BIOLOGY AND SOCIETY

14. Coral reefs harbor a greater diversity of animals than any other environment in the sea. Australia's Great Barrier Reef has been protected as a marine reserve and is a mecca for scientists and nature enthusiasts. Elsewhere, such as in Indonesia and the Philippines, coral reefs are in danger. Many reefs have been depleted of fish, and runoff from the shore has covered coral with sediment. Nearly all the changes in the reefs can be traced back to human activities. What kinds of activities do you think might be contributing to the decline of the reefs? What are some reasons to be concerned about this decline? Do you think the situation is likely to improve or worsen in the future? Why? What might the local people do to halt the decline? Should the more industrialized countries help? Why or why not?

15. The human body has not changed much in the last 100,000 years, but human culture has changed a great deal. As a result of our culture, we change the environment at a rate far greater than the rate at which many species, including our own, can evolve. What evidence of rapid environmental change do you see regularly? What aspects of human culture are responsible for these changes? Do you see any evidence of a decrease in the rate of human-caused environmental changes?

Unit 4
Ecology

18 An Introduction to Ecology and the Biosphere

A polar bear on Arctic ice.
Global climate change is shrinking the permanent sea ice that polar bears use as hunting platforms.

Global Climate Change BIOLOGY AND SOCIETY

Penguins and Polar Bears in Peril

The scientific debate is over. The great majority of scientists now agree that the global climate is changing. In the past few years, climate change has also become a hot topic for the general public. Articles and documentaries appear regularly, and it seems as if every magazine on the newsstand—including such unlikely publications as *Elle* and *Sports Illustrated*—has featured at least one cover story on climate change. What do we know about climate change now, and what can we expect for the future?

Average global temperatures have risen 0.8°C (about 1.4°F) over the past century, mostly over the last 30 years. The northernmost regions of the Northern Hemisphere and the Antarctic Peninsula have heated up the most. In parts of Alaska, for example, winter temperatures have risen by 5–6°F. The permanent Arctic sea ice is shrinking; each summer brings thinner ice and more open water. Polar bears, which stalk their prey on ice and need to store up body fat for the warmer months when there is no ice, are showing signs of starvation as their winter hunting grounds melt away. At the other end of the planet, diminishing sea ice near the Antarctic Peninsula limits the access of Adélie penguins to their food supply, and spring blizzards of unprecedented frequency and severity are taking a heavy toll on their eggs and chicks. But the warming trend isn't the whole story of climate change. Precipitation patterns have also changed, bringing longer and more intense drought to some regions. In other areas, a greater proportion of the total precipitation is falling in torrential downpours that cause flooding.

Any predictions that scientists make now about the future ecological impact of global climate change are based on incomplete information. Much remains to be discovered about species diversity and about the complex interactions of organisms (living things) with each other and with their environments. There is overwhelming evidence that human enterprises are responsible for the changes that are occurring. How we respond to this crisis will determine whether circumstances improve or worsen. And the process begins with understanding the basic concepts of ecology, which we start to explore in this chapter.

An Overview of Ecology

In your study of biology so far, you have learned about the diversity of life on Earth and about the molecular and cellular structures and processes that make life tick. **Ecology**, the scientific study of the interactions between organisms and their environments, offers a different perspective on life—biology from the skin out, so to speak.

Humans have always had an interest in other organisms and their environments. As hunters and gatherers, prehistoric people had to learn where and when game and edible plants could be found in greatest abundance. Naturalists, from Aristotle to Darwin and beyond, made the process of observing and describing organisms in their natural habitats an end in itself rather than simply a means of survival. We can still gain valuable insight from this discovery-based approach of watching nature and recording its structure and processes (Figure 18.1). As you might expect, field research, whether discovery-based natural history or hypothesis-driven science, is fundamental to ecology. But ecologists also test hypotheses using laboratory experiments, where conditions can be simplified and controlled. And some ecologists take a theoretical approach, devising mathematical and computer models, which enable them to simulate large-scale experiments that are impossible to conduct in the field.

Will ecologists solve our environmental problems?

▼ **Figure 18.1 Discovery science in a rain forest canopy.** A biologist collects insects in a rain forest on the eastern slope of the Andes mountain range in Argentina.

Ecology and Environmentalism

Technological innovations have enabled people to colonize just about every environment on Earth. Even so, our survival depends on Earth's resources, which have been profoundly altered by human activities (Figure 18.2). Global climate change is just one of the many environmental issues that have stirred public concern in recent decades. Some of our industrial and agricultural practices have contaminated the air, soil, and water. Our relentless quest for land and other resources has endangered a lengthy list of plant and animal species and has even driven some to extinction.

The science of ecology can provide the understanding needed to solve environmental problems. But these problems cannot be solved by ecologists alone, because they require making decisions based on values and ethics. On a personal level, each of us makes daily choices that affect our ecological impact. And legislators and corporations, motivated by environmentally aware voters and consumers, must address questions that have wider implications: How should land use be regulated? Should we try to save all species or just certain ones? What alternatives to environmentally destructive practices can be developed? How can we balance environmental impact with economic needs?

▼ **Figure 18.2 Human impact on the environment.** A man paddles a canoe through a trash-clogged waterway in Manila, capital of the Philippines.

A Hierarchy of Interactions

Many different factors can potentially affect an organism's interaction with its environment. **Biotic factors**—all of the organisms in the area—make up the living component of the environment. Other organisms may compete with an individual for food and other resources, prey upon it, or change its physical and chemical environment. **Abiotic factors** make up the environment's nonliving component and include chemical and physical factors, such as temperature, light, water, minerals, and air. An organism's **habitat**, the specific environment it lives in, includes the biotic and abiotic factors of its surroundings.

When we study the interactions between organisms and their environments, it is convenient to divide ecology into four increasingly comprehensive levels: organismal ecology, population ecology, community ecology, and ecosystem ecology.

An **organism** is an individual living thing. **Organismal ecology** is concerned with the evolutionary adaptations that enable organisms to meet the challenges posed by their abiotic environments. The distribution of organisms is limited by the abiotic conditions they can tolerate. For example, amphibians such as the salamander in **Figure 18.3a** are not found in cold climates because they gain most of their body warmth by absorbing heat from their surroundings. Temperature and precipitation shifts due to global climate change have already affected the distributions of some salamander species, and many more will feel the impact in the coming decades.

The next level of organization in ecology is the **population**, a group of individuals of the same species living in a particular geographic area. **Population ecology** concentrates mainly on factors that affect population density and growth **(Figure 18.3b)**. Biologists who study endangered species are especially interested in this level of ecology.

A **community** consists of all the organisms that inhabit a particular area; it is an assemblage of populations of different species. Questions in **community ecology** focus on how interactions between species, such as predation and competition, affect community structure and organization **(Figure 18.3c)**.

An **ecosystem** includes all the abiotic factors in addition to the community of species in a certain area. For example, a savanna ecosystem includes not only the organisms, such as diverse plants and animals, but also the soil, water sources, sunlight, and other abiotic factors of the environment. In **ecosystem ecology**, questions concern energy flow and the cycling of chemicals among the various biotic and abiotic factors **(Figure 18.3d)**.

▼ **Figure 18.3 Examples of questions at different levels of ecology.**

(a) Organismal ecology. What range of temperatures can a red salamander tolerate?

(b) Population ecology. What factors affect the survival of emperor penguin chicks?

(c) Community ecology. How do predators such as this beech marten affect the diversity of rodents in a community?

(d) Ecosystem ecology. What processes recycle vital chemical elements such as nitrogen within a savanna ecosystem in Africa?

The **biosphere** is the global ecosystem—the sum of all the planet's ecosystems, or all of life and where it lives. The most complex level in ecology, the biosphere includes the atmosphere to an altitude of several kilometers, the land down to water-bearing rocks about 1,500 m (almost a mile) deep, lakes and streams, caves, and the oceans to a depth of several kilometers. But despite its grand scale, organisms within the biosphere are linked; events in one part may have far-reaching effects. ✔

✔ CHECKPOINT

What does the ecosystem level of classification have in common with the community level of classification? What does the ecosystem level include that the community level does not?

Answer: all the biotic factors of the area; the abiotic factors of the area

Living in Earth's Diverse Environments

Whether you have seen the world by traveling or through television and movies, you have probably noticed that there are striking regional patterns in the distribution of life. For example, some terrestrial areas, such as the tropical forests of South America and Africa, are home to plentiful plant life, whereas other areas, such as deserts, are relatively barren. Coral reefs are alive with vibrantly colored organisms; other parts of the ocean appear empty by comparison.

The distribution of life varies on a local scale, too. In the aerial view of a New Zealand wilderness in **Figure 18.4**, we can see a mixture of forest, a large lake, a meandering river, and mountains. Within these different environments, variation occurs on an even smaller scale. For example, we would find that the lake has several different habitats, and each habitat has a characteristic community of organisms.

▼ **Figure 18.4 Local variation of the environment in a New Zealand wilderness.**

Abiotic Factors of the Biosphere

Patterns in the distribution of life mainly reflect differences in the abiotic factors of the environment. In this section, let's look at several major abiotic factors that influence where organisms live.

Energy Source

All organisms require a usable source of energy to live. Solar energy from sunlight, captured by chlorophyll during the process of photosynthesis, powers most ecosystems. In the image shown in **Figure 18.5**, colors are keyed to the relative abundance of chlorophyll. Green areas on land indicate high densities of plant life. Orange areas on land, including the Sahara region of Africa and much of the western United States, are much less productive. Green regions of the ocean contain an abundance of algae and photosynthetic bacteria compared to darker regions.

Lack of sunlight is seldom the most important factor limiting plant growth for terrestrial ecosystems, although shading by trees does create intense competition for light among plants growing on forest floors. In many aquatic environments, however, light cannot penetrate beyond certain depths. As a result, most photosynthesis in a body of water occurs near the surface.

Surprisingly, life also thrives in environments that are completely dark. A mile or more below the ocean's surface lies the unique world of hydrothermal vents, sites near the adjoining edges of giant plates of Earth's crust where molten rock and hot gases surge upward from Earth's interior. Towering chimneys, some as tall as a nine-story building, emit scalding water and hot gases **(Figure 18.6)**. These ecosystems are powered by chemoautotrophic bacteria (see Figure 15.12) that derive energy from the oxidation of inorganic chemicals such as hydrogen sulfide. Bacteria with similar metabolic talents support communities of cave-dwelling organisms.

If the sun stopped shining, would all life on Earth go extinct?

▼ **Figure 18.5
Distribution of life in the biosphere.** In this image of Earth, colors are keyed to the relative abundance of chlorophyll, which correlates with the regional densities of photosynthetic organisms.

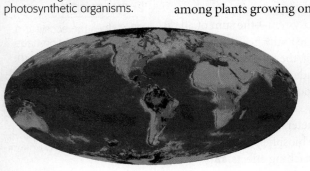

▼ **Figure 18.6 A deep-sea hydrothermal vent.** "Black smokers" west of Vancouver Island spew plumes of hot gases from Earth's interior. Giant tube worms (inset), annelids that may grow to 2 m long, are members of the vent community.

Temperature

Temperature is an important abiotic factor because of its effect on metabolism. Few organisms can maintain a sufficiently active metabolism at temperatures close to 0°C (32°F), and temperatures above 45°C (113°F) destroy the enzymes of most organisms. Most organisms function best within a specific range of environmental temperatures. For example, the American pika (Figure 18.7) has a high body temperature well suited to the chilly climate of its mountain habitat. On warm days, however, pikas must take refuge in crevices where pockets of cold air prevent fatal over-heating. In winter, pikas depend on a blanket of snow to insulate their shelters from the perilous cold.

▲ Figure 18.7 **An American pika.** This diminutive relative of rabbits lives at high elevations in the western United States and Canada.

Water

Water is essential to all life. For terrestrial organisms, the primary threat is drying out in the air. Many land animals have watertight coverings that reduce water loss, such as reptilian scales, and most plants have waxy coatings on their leaves and other aerial parts (Figure 18.8). Aquatic organisms are surrounded by water, but they face problems of water balance if their own solute concentration does not match that of their surroundings (see Figure 5.14).

Inorganic Nutrients

The distribution and abundance of photosynthetic organisms, including plants, algae, and photosynthetic bacteria, depend on the availability of inorganic nutrients such as compounds of nitrogen and phosphorus. Plants obtain these nutrients from the soil. Soil structure, pH, and nutrient content often play major roles in determining the distribution of plants. In many aquatic ecosystems, low levels of nitrogen and phosphorus limit the growth of algae and photosynthetic bacteria.

Other Aquatic Factors

Several abiotic factors are important in aquatic, but not terrestrial, ecosystems. While terrestrial organisms have a plentiful supply of oxygen from the air, aquatic organisms must depend on oxygen dissolved in water. This is a critical factor for many species of fish. Cold, fast-moving water has a higher oxygen content than warm or stagnant water. Salinity (saltiness), currents, and tides also play a role in many aquatic ecosystems.

Other Terrestrial Factors

Some abiotic factors affect terrestrial, but not aquatic, ecosystems. For example, wind is often an important abiotic factor on land. Wind increases an organism's rate of water loss by evaporation. The resulting increase in evaporative cooling can be advantageous on a hot summer day, but it can cause dangerous wind chill in the winter. In some ecosystems, frequent occurrences of natural disturbances such as storms or fire play a role in the distribution of organisms. ☑

☑ CHECKPOINT

Why is solar energy such an important factor for most ecosystems?

Answer: Solar energy captured by the process of photosynthesis provides most of the organic fuel and building material for the organisms in those ecosystems.

▼ Figure 18.8 **Watertight coverings.**

(a) Scales on a basilisk lizard.

(b) Beaded water droplets showing the water repellency of the leaf's waxy coating.

The Evolutionary Adaptations of Organisms

The ability of organisms to live in Earth's diverse environments demonstrates the close relationship between the fields of ecology and evolutionary biology. Charles Darwin was an ecologist, although he predated the word *ecology*. It was the geographic distribution of organisms and their exquisite adaptations to specific environments that provided Darwin with evidence for evolution. Evolutionary adaptation via natural selection results from the interactions of organisms with their environments, which brings us back to our definition of ecology. Thus, events that occur in the short term, during the course of an individual's lifetime, may translate into effects over the longer scale of evolutionary time. For example, because the availability of water affects a plant's growth and ultimately its reproductive success, precipitation has an impact on the gene pool of a plant population. After a period of lower-than-average rainfall, drought-resistant individuals may be more prevalent in a plant population. Organisms also evolve in response to biotic interactions, such as predation and competition. ☑

☑ CHECKPOINT

How are the fields of ecology and evolution linked?

Answer: *The process of evolutionary adaptation via natural selection results from the interactions of organisms with their environments (ecology).*

Adjusting to Environmental Variability

The abiotic factors in a habitat may vary from year to year, seasonally, or over the course of a day. An individual's abilities to adjust to environmental changes that occur during its lifetime are themselves adaptations refined by natural selection. For instance, if you see a bird on a cold day, it may look unusually fluffy **(Figure 18.9)**. Small muscles in the skin raise the bird's feathers, a physiological response that traps insulating pockets of air. Some species of birds adjust to seasonal cold by growing heavier feathers. And some bird species respond to the onset of cold weather by migrating to warmer regions—a behavioral response.

Note that these responses occur during the lifetime of an individual, so they are not examples of evolution, which is change in a population over time.

▼ Figure 18.9 **A gray-headed chickadee demonstrating its physiological response to cold weather.**

Physiological Responses

Like birds, mammals can adjust to a cold day by contracting skin muscles—in this case attached to hairs—to create a temporary layer of insulation. (Our own muscles do this, too, but we just get "goose bumps" instead of a furry insulation.) The blood vessels in the skin also constrict, which slows the loss of body heat. In both cases, the adjustment occurs in just seconds.

Why do we get goose bumps when we're cold?

A gradual, though still reversible, physiological adjustment that occurs in response to an environmental change is called **acclimation**. For example, suppose you moved from Boston, which is essentially at sea level, to the mile-high city of Denver, where there is less oxygen. One physiological response to your new environment would be a gradual increase in the number of your red blood cells, which transport O_2 from your lungs to other parts of your body. Acclimation can take days or weeks. This is why high-altitude climbers, such as those attempting to scale Mount Everest, need extended stays at a high-elevation base camp before proceeding to the summit.

The ability to acclimate is generally related to the range of environmental conditions a species naturally experiences. Species that live in very warm climates, for example, usually cannot acclimate to extreme cold. Among vertebrates, birds and mammals can generally tolerate the greatest temperature extremes because, as endotherms, they use their metabolism to regulate internal temperature. In contrast, ectothermic reptiles can only tolerate a more limited range of temperatures **(Figure 18.10)**.

▼ Figure 18.10 **The number of lizard species in different regions of the contiguous United States.** Notice that there are fewer and fewer lizard species in more northern regions. This reflects lizards' ectothermic physiology, which depends on environmental heat for keeping the body warm enough for the animal to be active.

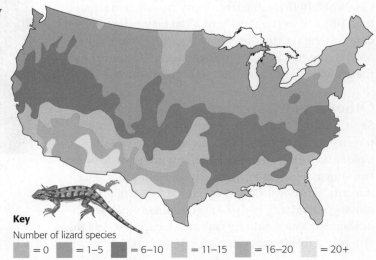

Key

Number of lizard species

■ = 0   ■ = 1–5   ■ = 6–10   ■ = 11–15   ■ = 16–20   ■ = 20+

Anatomical Responses

Many organisms respond to environmental challenge with some type of change in body shape or structure. When the change is reversible, the response is an example of acclimation. Many mammals, for example, grow a heavier coat of fur before the winter cold sets in and shed it when summer comes. In some animals, fur or feather color changes seasonally as well, camouflaging the animal against winter snow and summer vegetation (Figure 18.11).

Other anatomical changes are irreversible over the lifetime of an individual. Environmental variation can affect growth and development so much that there may be remarkable differences in body shape within a population. You can see an example in Figure 18.12, which shows the "flagging" that wind causes in certain trees. In general, plants are more anatomically changeable than animals. Rooted and unable to move to a better location, plants rely entirely on their anatomical and physiological responses to survive environmental fluctuations.

▲ Figure 18.11 **The arctic fox in winter and summer coats.**

▼ Figure 18.12 **Wind as an abiotic factor that shapes trees.** The mechanical disturbance of the prevailing wind hinders limb growth on the windward side of this fir tree near the timberline in the Rocky Mountains, while limbs on the other side grow normally. This anatomical response is an evolutionary adaptation that reduces the number of limbs that are broken during strong winds.

Behavioral Responses

In contrast to plants, most animals can respond to an unfavorable change in the environment by moving to a new location. Such movement may be fairly localized. For example, many desert ectotherms, including reptiles, maintain a reasonably constant body temperature by shuttling between sun and shade. Some animals are capable of migrating great distances in response to such environmental cues as the changing seasons. Many migratory birds overwinter in Central and South America, returning to northern latitudes to breed during summer. And we humans, with our large brains and available technology, have an especially rich range of behavioral responses available to us (Figure 18.13). ☑

☑ CHECKPOINT

What is acclimation?

Answer: a gradual, reversible change in anatomy or physiology in response to an environmental change

▼ Figure 18.13 **Behavioral responses have expanded the geographic range of humans.** Dressing for the weather is a thermoregulatory behavior unique to people.

Biomes

The abiotic factors you learned about in the previous section are largely responsible for the distribution of life on Earth. (You'll learn about the role of biotic factors in species distribution in Chapter 20.) Using various combinations of these factors, ecologists have categorized Earth's environments into biomes. A **biome** is a major terrestrial or aquatic life zone, characterized by vegetation type in terrestrial biomes and the physical environment in aquatic biomes. In this section, we'll briefly survey the aquatic biomes, followed by the terrestrial biomes.

Aquatic biomes, which occupy roughly 75% of Earth's surface, are determined by their salinity and other physical factors. Freshwater biomes (lakes, streams and rivers, and wetlands) typically have a salt concentration of less than 1%. The salt concentrations of marine biomes (oceans, intertidal zones, coral reefs, and estuaries) are generally around 3%.

Freshwater Biomes

Freshwater biomes cover less than 1% of Earth, and they contain a mere 0.01% of its water. But they harbor a disproportionate share of biodiversity—an estimated 6% of all described species. Moreover, we depend on freshwater biomes for drinking water, crop irrigation, sanitation, and industry.

Freshwater biomes fall into two broad groups: standing water, which includes lakes and ponds, and flowing water, such as rivers and streams. The difference in water movement results in profound differences in ecosystem structure.

Lakes and Ponds

Standing bodies of water range from small ponds only a few square meters in area to large lakes, such as North America's Great Lakes, that are thousands of square kilometers (Figure 18.14).

◄ **Figure 18.14 A satellite view of the Great Lakes.**

In lakes and large ponds, the communities of plants, algae, and animals are distributed according to the depth of the water and its distance from shore (Figure 18.15). Shallow water near shore and the upper layer of water away from shore make up the **photic zone**, so named because light is available for photosynthesis. Microscopic algae and cyanobacteria grow in the photic zone, joined by rooted plants and floating plants such as water lilies in the photic area near shore. If a lake or pond is deep enough or murky enough, it has an **aphotic zone**, where light levels are too low to support photosynthesis.

The **benthic realm** is at the bottom of all aquatic biomes. Made up of sand and organic and inorganic sediments, the benthic realm is occupied by communities of organisms that are collectively called benthos. (If you have ever waded barefoot into a pond or lake, you have felt the benthos squish between your toes.) Dead material that "rains" down from the productive surface waters of the photic zone is a major source of food for the benthos.

The mineral nutrients nitrogen and phosphorus typically regulate the growth of **phytoplankton**, the collective name for microscopic algae and cyanobacteria in aquatic biomes. Many lakes and ponds are affected by large inputs of nitrogen and phosphorus from sewage and runoff from fertilized lawns and farms. These nutrients often produce heavy growth of algae, which reduces light penetration. When the algae die and decompose, a pond or lake can suffer serious oxygen depletion, killing fish that are adapted to high-oxygen conditions. ☑

▼ **Figure 18.15 Zones in a lake.**

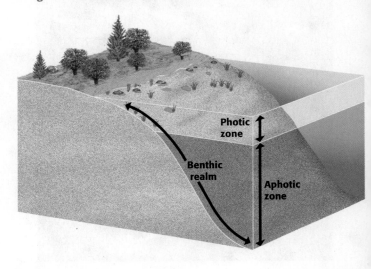

Photic zone

Benthic realm

Aphotic zone

▲ **Figure 18.16 A stream in the Appalachian Mountains.**

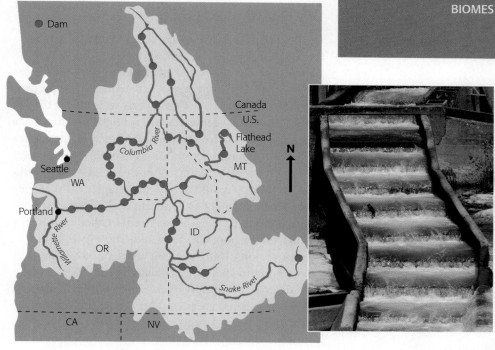

▲ **Figure 18.17 Damming the Columbia River basin.** This map shows only the largest of the 250 dams that have altered freshwater ecosystems throughout the Pacific Northwest. These great concrete obstacles make it difficult for salmon to swim upriver to their breeding streams, though many dams now have "fish ladders" that provide detours (inset).

Rivers and Streams

Rivers and streams, which are bodies of flowing water, generally support quite different communities of organisms than lakes and ponds (**Figure 18.16**). A river or stream changes greatly between its source (perhaps a spring or snowmelt in the mountains) and the point at which it empties into a lake or the ocean. Near a source, the water is usually cold, low in nutrients, and clear. The channel is often narrow, with a swift current that does not allow much silt to accumulate on the bottom. The current also inhibits the growth of phytoplankton; most of the organisms found here are supported by the photosynthesis of algae attached to rocks or by organic material (such as leaves) carried into the stream from the surrounding land. The most abundant benthic animals are usually insects that eat algae, leaves, or one another. Trout are often the predominant fishes, locating their food, including insects, mainly by sight in the clear water.

Downstream, a river or stream typically widens and slows. There the water is usually warmer and may be murkier because of sediments and phytoplankton suspended in it. Worms and insects that burrow into mud are often abundant, as are waterfowl, frogs, and catfish and other fishes that find food more by scent and taste than by sight.

People have altered rivers by constructing dams to control flooding, to provide reservoirs of drinking water, or to generate hydroelectric power. In many cases, dams have completely changed the downstream ecosystems, altering the rate and volume of water flow and affecting fish and invertebrate populations (**Figure 18.17**). Many streams and rivers have also been affected by pollution from human activities.

Wetlands

A **wetland** is a transitional biome between an aquatic ecosystem and a terrestrial one. Freshwater wetlands include swamps, bogs, and marshes (**Figure 18.18**). Covered with water either permanently or periodically, wetlands support the growth of aquatic plants and are rich in species diversity. Migrating waterfowl and many other birds depend on wetland "pit stops" for food and shelter during their journeys. In addition, wetlands provide water storage areas that reduce flooding and improve water quality by trapping pollutants such as metals and organic compounds in their sediments.

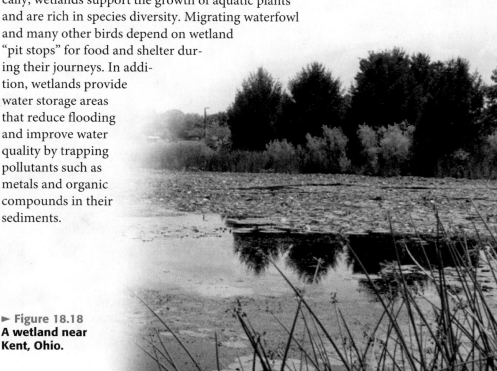

► **Figure 18.18 A wetland near Kent, Ohio.**

381

Marine Biomes

Gazing out over a vast ocean, you might think that it is the most uniform environment on Earth. But marine habitats can be as different as night and day. The deepest ocean, where hydrothermal vents are located, is perpetually dark. In contrast, the vivid coral reefs nearer the surface are utterly dependent on sunlight. Habitats near shore are different from those in mid-ocean, and the seafloor hosts different communities than the open waters.

As in freshwater biomes, the seafloor is known as the benthic realm **(Figure 18.19)**. The **pelagic realm** of the oceans includes all open water. In shallow areas, such as the submerged parts of continents, called continental shelves, the photic zone includes both pelagic and benthic regions. In these sunlit areas, photosynthesis by phytoplankton and multicellular algae provides energy for a diverse community of animals. Sponges, burrowing worms, clams, sea anemones, crabs, and echinoderms inhabit the benthos. **Zooplankton** (free-floating animals, including many microscopic ones), fishes, marine mammals, and many other types of animals are abundant in the pelagic photic zone.

The **coral reef** biome occurs in the photic zone of warm tropical waters in scattered locations around the globe **(Figure 18.20)**. A coral reef is built up slowly by successive generations of coral animals—a diverse group of cnidarians that secrete a hard external skeleton—and by multicellular algae encrusted with limestone. Unicellular algae live within the coral's cells, providing the coral with food. The physical structure and productivity of coral reefs support a huge variety of invertebrates and fishes.

The photic zone extends down a maximum of 200 m (about 656 feet) in the ocean. Although there is not enough light for photosynthesis between 200 and 1,000 m (down a little more than half a mile), some light does reach these depths of the aphotic zone. This dimly lit world, sometimes called the twilight zone, is dominated by a fascinating variety of small fishes and crustaceans. Food sinking from the photic zone provides some sustenance for these animals. In addition, many of them migrate to the surface at night to feed. Some fishes in the twilight zone have enlarged eyes, enabling them to see in the very dim light, and light-emitting organs that attract mates and prey.

Below 1,000 m, the ocean is completely and permanently dark. Adaptation to this environment has produced many bizarre-looking creatures. Most of the benthic organisms here are deposit feeders, animals that consume dead organic material on the seafloor. Crustaceans, polychaete worms, sea anemones, and echinoderms such as sea cucumbers, sea stars, and sea

▼ **Figure 18.19 Ocean life.** (Zone depths and organisms not drawn to scale.)

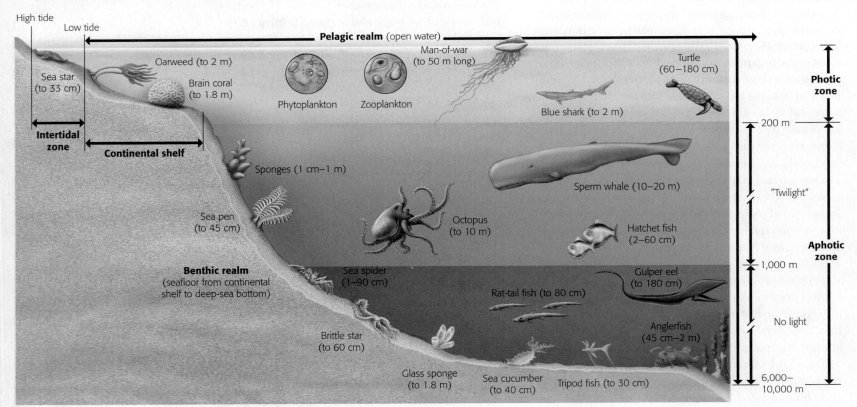

▲ Figure 18.20 **A coral reef in the Red Sea off the coast of Egypt.**

urchins are common. Food is scarce, however. The density of animals is low except at hydrothermal vents, the prokaryote-powered ecosystems mentioned earlier (see Figure 18.6).

The marine environment also includes distinctive biomes where the ocean interfaces with land or with fresh water. In the **intertidal zone**, where the ocean meets land, the shore is pounded by waves during high tide and exposed to the sun and drying winds during low tide **(Figure 18.21)**. The rocky inter-tidal zone is home to many sedentary organisms, such as algae, barnacles, and mussels, which attach to rocks and are thus prevented from being washed away. On sandy beaches, suspension-feeding worms, clams, and preda-tory crustaceans bury themselves in the ground.

Have you heard about the Great Pacific Garbage Patch?

Figure 18.22 shows an **estuary**, a transition area between a river and the ocean. The saltiness of estuar-ies ranges from nearly that of fresh water to that of the ocean. With their waters enriched by nutrients from the river, estuaries, like freshwater wetlands, are among the most productive areas on Earth. Oysters, crabs, and many fishes live in estuaries or reproduce in them. Estu-aries are also crucial nesting and feeding areas for water-fowl. Mudflats and salt marshes are extensive coastal wetlands that often border estuaries.

For centuries, people viewed the ocean as a limitless resource, harvesting its bounty with increasingly effective and indiscriminate technologies and using it as a dump-ing ground for wastes. The negative effects of these practices are now becoming clear. Populations of commercial fish species are declining. Plastic debris floats beneath the surface of vast swaths of the Pacific Ocean, concentrated by converging currents in a region dubbed the "Great Pacific Garbage Patch." Many marine habitats are polluted by nutrients or toxic chemicals; it will be

years before the full extent of damage from the massive Deepwater Horizon oil spill in the Gulf of Mexico in 2010 is known. Because of their proximity to land, estuaries are especially vulnerable. Many have been completely replaced by development on landfill; other threats include pollution and alteration of freshwater inflow. Coral reefs are imperiled by ocean acidification and rising sea surface temperatures due to global warming. Meanwhile, our knowledge of marine biomes is woefully incomplete. A massive international census of marine life, completed in 2010, announced the discovery of more than 6,000 new species. ☑

☑ CHECKPOINT

What are phytoplankton? Why are they essential to other oceanic life?

Answer: Phytoplankton are photosynthetic algae and bacteria. They are food for animals in the photic zone; those animals in turn may become food for animals in the aphotic zone.

▼ Figure 18.22 **Waterfowl in an estuary on the southeast coast of England.**

How Climate Affects Terrestrial Biome Distribution

Terrestrial biomes are determined primarily by climate, especially temperature and rainfall. Before we survey these biomes, let's look at the broad patterns of global climate that help explain their locations.

Earth's global climate patterns are largely the result of the input of radiant energy from the sun and the planet's movement in space. Because of its curvature, Earth receives an uneven distribution of solar energy (**Figure 18.23**). The equator receives the greatest intensity of solar radiation. As it is heated by the direct rays of the sun, air at the equator rises. It then cools, forms clouds, and drops rain (**Figure 18.24**). This largely explains why rain forests are concentrated in the **tropics**—the region from the Tropic of Cancer to the Tropic of Capricorn.

After losing moisture over equatorial zones, dry high-altitude air masses spread away from the equator until they cool and descend again at latitudes of about 30° north and south. Many of the world's great deserts— the Sahara in North Africa and the Arabian on the Arabian Peninsula, for example—are centered at these latitudes because of the dry air they receive.

Latitudes between the tropics and the Arctic Circle and the Antarctic Circle are called **temperate zones**. Generally, these regions have milder climates than the tropics or the polar regions. Notice in Figure 18.24 that some of the descending dry air heads into the latitudes above 30°. At first these air masses pick up moisture, but they tend to drop it as they cool at higher latitudes. This is why the north and south temperate zones tend to be relatively wet. Coniferous forests dominate the landscape at the wet but cool latitudes around 60° north.

Proximity to large bodies of water and the presence of landforms such as mountain ranges also affect climate. Oceans and large lakes moderate climate by absorbing heat when the air is warm and releasing heat to cold air. Mountains affect climate in two major ways. First, air temperature drops as elevation increases. As a result, driving up a tall mountain offers a quick tour of several biomes. **Figure 18.25** shows the scenery you might encounter on a journey from the scorching lowlands of the Sonoran Desert to a cool coniferous forest at an elevation of 11,000 feet above sea level.

▼ **Figure 18.23 Uneven heating of Earth.**

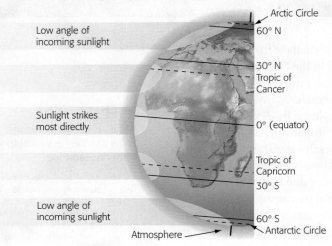

Low angle of incoming sunlight

Arctic Circle
60° N

30° N
Tropic of Cancer

Sunlight strikes most directly

0° (equator)

Tropic of Capricorn
30° S

Low angle of incoming sunlight

60° S
Antarctic Circle

Atmosphere

► **Figure 18.25 The effect of altitude on vegetation.** The zones shown are typical of the Sonoran Desert region in southwestern North America.

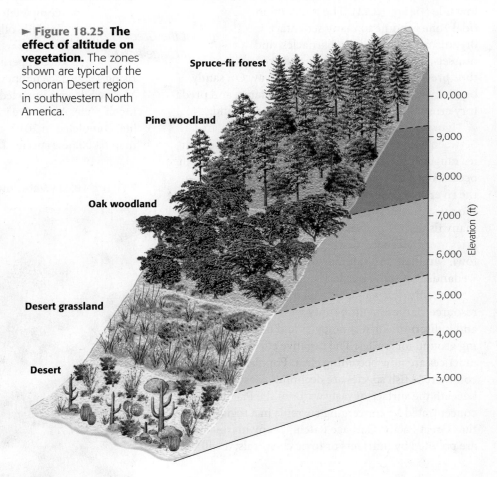

Spruce-fir forest

Pine woodland

Oak woodland

Desert grassland

Desert

10,000

9,000

8,000

7,000

6,000

5,000

4,000

3,000

Elevation (ft)

▼ **Figure 18.24 How uneven heating of Earth produces various climates.**

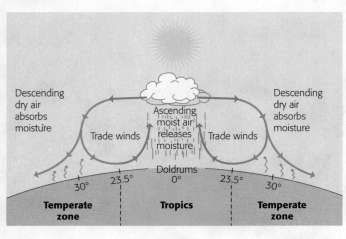

Descending dry air absorbs moisture

Ascending moist air releases moisture

Descending dry air absorbs moisture

Trade winds

Trade winds

Doldrums

30°   23.5°   0°   23.5°   30°

Temperate zone

Tropics

Temperate zone

Second, mountains can block the flow of cool, moist air from a coast, causing radically different climates on opposite sides of a mountain range. In the example shown in **Figure 18.26**, moist air moves in off the Pacific Ocean and encounters the Coast Range in California. Air flows upward, cools at higher altitudes, and drops a large amount of rainfall. The world's tallest trees, the coastal redwoods, thrive here. Precipitation increases again farther inland as the air moves up and over higher mountains (the Sierra Nevada). On the eastern side of the Sierra, there is little precipitation, and the dry descending air also absorbs moisture. This effect, called a rain shadow, is responsible for the desert that covers much of central Nevada. ☑

▼ **Figure 18.26 How mountains affect rainfall.**

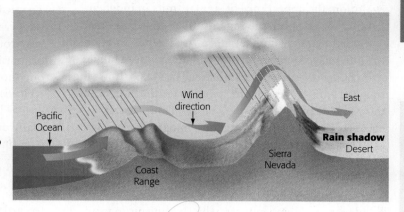

Terrestrial Biomes

Terrestrial ecosystems are grouped into biomes primarily on the basis of their vegetation type **(Figure 18.27)**. By providing food, shelter, and nesting sites for animals, as well as much of the organic material for the decomposers that recycle mineral nutrients, plants build the foundation for the communities of organisms typical of each biome. The geographic distribution of plants, and thus of biomes, largely depends on climate, with temperature and rainfall often the key factors determining the kind of biome that exists in a particular region. If the climate in two geographically separate areas is similar, the same type of biome may occur in both. Coniferous forests, for instance, extend in a broad band across North America, Europe, and Asia. There is local variation within each biome, giving the vegetation a patchy, rather than a uniform, appearance. For example, in northern coniferous forests, snowfall may break branches and small trees, causing openings where broadleaf trees such as aspen and birch can grow. Local storms and fires also create openings in many biomes.

Each biome is characterized by a type of biological community rather than an assemblage of particular species. For example, the groups of species living in the deserts of southwestern North America and in the Sahara Desert of Africa are different, but both groups are adapted to desert conditions. Organisms in widely

▶ **Figure 18.27 A map of the major terrestrial biomes.** Although this map has sharp boundaries, biomes actually grade into one another. We'll use smaller versions of this map, highlighted by color coding, during our closer look at the terrestrial biomes in the next several pages.

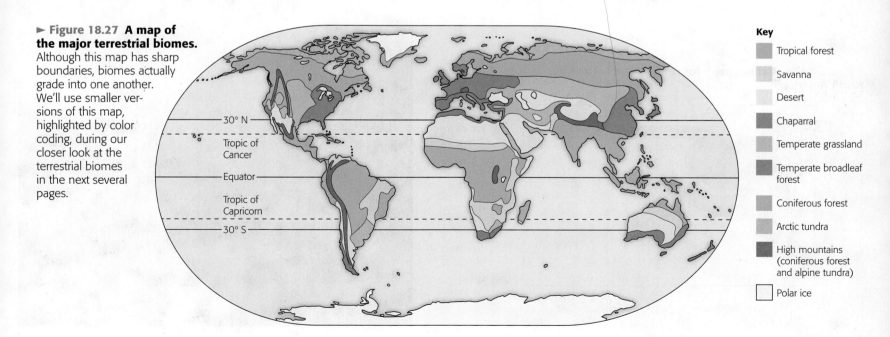

Key

- Tropical forest
- Savanna
- Desert
- Chaparral
- Temperate grassland
- Temperate broadleaf forest
- Coniferous forest
- Arctic tundra
- High mountains (coniferous forest and alpine tundra)
- Polar ice

separated biomes may look alike because of convergent evolution, the appearance of similar traits in independently evolved species living in similar environments.

Figure 18.28 is a climograph, a visual representation of the differences in precipitation and temperature ranges that characterize terrestrial biomes. The *x*-axis shows the range of annual average precipitation for the biome, and the *y*-axis displays the biome's range of annual average temperature. By studying the climograph plots, we can see how these abiotic factors compare in different biomes. For example, organisms that live in temperate broadleaf forests must have adaptations that allow them to cope with a wide range of temperatures, while organisms in tropical forests experience very little temperature variation. Although the range of precipitation in temperate broadleaf forests is similar to that of northern coniferous forests, the lower range of temperatures in northern coniferous forests reveals a significant difference in the abiotic environments of these two biomes.

Today, concern about global warming is generating intense interest in the effect of climate on vegetation patterns. Using powerful new tools such as satellite imagery, scientists are documenting shifts in latitude of biome borders, decreases in snow and ice coverage, and changes in the length of the growing season. At the same time, many natural biomes have been fragmented and altered by human activity. We'll discuss both of these issues after we survey the major terrestrial biomes, beginning near the equator and generally approaching the poles.

How much rain does it take to make a rain forest?

Tropical Forest

Tropical forests occur in equatorial areas where the temperature is warm and days are 11–12 hours long year-round. The type of vegetation is determined primarily by rainfall. Tropical rain forests, like the one shown in **Figure 18.29**, receive 200–400 cm (6.6 to 13 *feet*!) of rain per year.

The layered structure of tropical rain forests provides many different habitats. Treetops form a closed canopy over one or two layers of smaller trees and a shrub understory. Few plants grow in the deep shade of the forest floor. Many trees are covered by woody vines growing toward the light. Other plants, such as orchids, gain access to sunlight by growing on the branches or trunks of tall trees. Scattered trees reach full sunlight by towering above the canopy. Many of the animals also dwell in trees, where food is abundant. Monkeys, birds, insects, snakes, bats, and frogs find food and shelter many meters above the ground.

Rainfall is less plentiful in other tropical forests. Tropical dry forests predominate in lowland areas that have a prolonged dry season or scarce rainfall at any time. The plants found there are a mixture of thorny shrubs and trees and succulents. In regions with distinct wet and dry seasons, tropical deciduous trees are common. ☑

▼ **Figure 18.29 Tropical rain forest in Borneo.**

▼ **Figure 18.28 A climograph for some major biomes in North America.**

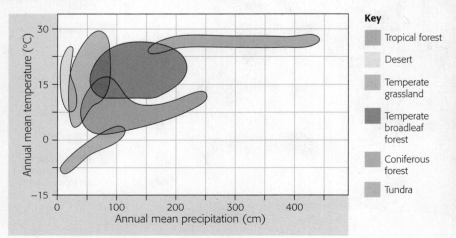

Key
- Tropical forest
- Desert
- Temperate grassland
- Temperate broadleaf forest
- Coniferous forest
- Tundra

Savanna

Savannas, such as the one shown in **Figure 18.30**, are dominated by grasses and scattered trees. The temperature is warm year-round. Rainfall averages 30–50 cm (roughly 12–20 inches) per year, with dramatic seasonal variation.

Fire, caused by lightning or human activity, is an important abiotic factor in the savanna. The grasses survive burning because the growing points of their shoots are below ground. Other plants have seeds that sprout rapidly after a fire. Poor soil and lack of moisture, along with fire and grazing animals, prevent the establishment of most trees. The luxuriant growth of grasses and small broadleaf plants during the rainy season provides a rich food source for plant-eating animals.

Many of the world's large grazing mammals and their predators inhabit savannas. African savannas are home to zebras and many species of antelope, as well as to lions and cheetahs. Several species of kangaroo are the dominant grazers of Australian savannas. Oddly, though, the large grazers are not the dominant plant-eaters in savannas. That distinction belongs to insects, especially ants and termites. Other animals include burrowers such as mice, moles, gophers, and ground squirrels.

Desert

Deserts are the driest of all biomes, characterized by low and unpredictable rainfall—less than 30 cm (about 12 inches) per year. Some deserts are very hot, with daytime soil surface temperatures above 60°C (140°F) and large daily temperature fluctuations. Other deserts, such as those west of the Rocky Mountains and the Gobi Desert, spanning northern China and southern Mongolia, are relatively cold. Air temperatures in cold deserts may fall below −30°C (−22°F).

Desert vegetation typically includes water-storing plants such as cacti and deeply rooted shrubs. Various snakes, lizards, and seed-eating rodents are common inhabitants. Arthropods such as scorpions and insects also thrive in the desert. Evolutionary adaptations of desert plants and animals include a remarkable array of mechanisms that conserve water. For example, the "pleated" stem of saguaro cacti **(Figure 18.31)** enables the plants to expand when they absorb water during wet periods. Some desert mice *never* drink, deriving all their water from the metabolic breakdown of the seeds they eat. Protective adaptations that deter feeding by mammals and insects, such as spines on cacti and poisons in the leaves of shrubs, are common in desert plants. ☑

☑ CHECKPOINT

1. How does the savanna climate vary seasonally?
2. What abiotic factor characterizes deserts?

Answers: 1. Temperature stays about the same year-round, but rainfall varies dramatically. 2. Rainfall is low and unpredictable.

▼ **Figure 18.30** **Savanna in the Serengeti Plain in Tanzania.**

Temperature range | Precipitation | Fire

▼ **Figure 18.31** **Sonoran Desert.**

Temperature range | Precipitation

Chaparral

The climate that supports **chaparral** vegetation results mainly from cool ocean currents circulating offshore, producing mild, rainy winters and hot, dry summers. As a result, this biome is limited to small coastal areas, some in California (**Figure 18.32**). The largest region of chaparral surrounds the Mediterranean Sea; in fact, Mediterranean is another name for this biome. Dense, spiny, evergreen shrubs dominate chaparral. Annual plants are also common during the wet winter and spring months. Animals characteristic of the chaparral are deer, fruit-eating birds, seed-eating rodents, and lizards and snakes.

Chaparral vegetation is adapted to periodic fires caused by lightning. Many plants contain flammable chemicals and burn fiercely, especially where dead brush has accumulated. After a fire, shrubs use food reserves stored in the surviving roots to support rapid shoot regeneration. Some chaparral plants produce seeds that will germinate only after a hot fire. The ashes of burned vegetation fertilize the soil with mineral nutrients, promoting regrowth of the plant community. Houses do not fare as well. The firestorms that race through the densely populated canyons of Southern California can be devastating to the human inhabitants.

Why don't grasslands have any trees?

Temperate Grassland

Temperate grasslands have some of the characteristics of tropical savannas, but they are mostly treeless, except along rivers or streams, and are found in regions of relatively cold winter temperatures. Rainfall, averaging between 25 and 75 cm per year (approximately 10–30 inches), with frequent severe droughts, is too low to support forest growth. Periodic fires and grazing by large mammals also prevent invasion by woody plants. These grazers include the bison and pronghorn in North America, the wild horses and sheep of the Asian steppes, and kangaroos in Australia. As in the savanna, however, the dominant plant-eaters are invertebrates, especially grasshoppers and soil-dwelling nematodes.

Without trees, many birds nest on the ground. Many small mammals, such as rabbits, voles, ground squirrels, prairie dogs, and pocket gophers, dig burrows to escape predators. Temperate grasslands like the one shown in **Figure 18.33** once covered much of central North America.

Because grassland soil is both deep and rich in nutrients, these habitats provide fertile land for agriculture. Most grassland in the United States has been converted to cropland or pasture, and very little natural prairie exists today. ✔

▼ **Figure 18.32 Chaparral in California.**

▼ **Figure 18.33 Temperate grassland in Saskatchewan, Canada.**

Temperate Broadleaf Forest

Temperate broadleaf forests occur throughout midlatitudes where there is sufficient moisture to support the growth of large trees. Annual precipitation is relatively high at 75–150 cm (30–60 inches) and typically distributed evenly around the year. Annual temperature varies over a wide range, with hot summers and cold winters. In the Northern Hemisphere, dense stands of deciduous trees are trademarks of temperate forests, such as the one pictured in **Figure 18.34**. Deciduous trees drop their leaves before winter, when temperatures are too low for effective photosynthesis and water lost by evaporation is not easily replaced from frozen soil.

Why do deciduous trees drop their leaves in the fall?

Numerous invertebrates live in the soil and the thick layer of leaf litter that accumulates on the forest floor. Some vertebrates, such as mice, shrews, and ground squirrels, burrow for shelter and food, while others, including many species of birds, live in the trees. Predators include bobcats, foxes, black bears, and mountain lions. Many mammals that inhabit these forests enter a dormant winter state called hibernation, and some bird species migrate to warmer climates.

Virtually all the original temperate broadleaf forests in North America were destroyed by logging or cleared for agriculture or development. These forests tend to recover after disturbance, however, and today we see deciduous trees growing in undeveloped areas over much of their former range.

Coniferous Forest

Cone-bearing evergreen trees such as pine, spruce, fir, and hemlock dominate **coniferous forests** in the Northern Hemisphere. (Other kinds of conifers grow in parts of South America, Africa, and Australia.) The northern coniferous forest, or **taiga (Figure 18.35)**, is the largest terrestrial biome on Earth, stretching in a broad band across North America and Asia south of the Arctic Circle. Taiga is also found at cool, high elevations in more temperate latitudes—for example, in much of the mountainous region of western North America. The taiga is characterized by long, snowy winters and short, wet summers that are sometimes warm. The slow decomposition of conifer needles in the thin, acidic soil makes few nutrients available for plant growth. The conical shape of many conifers prevents too much snow from accumulating on their branches and breaking them. Animals of the taiga include moose, elk, hares, bears, wolves, grouse, and migratory birds. The Asian taiga is home to the dwindling number of Siberian tigers that remain in the wild.

The **temperate rain forests** of coastal North America (from Alaska to Oregon) are also coniferous forests. Warm, moist air from the Pacific Ocean supports this unique biome, which, like most coniferous forests, is dominated by a few tree species, typically hemlock, Douglas fir, and redwood. These forests are heavily logged, and the old-growth stands of trees are rapidly disappearing. ☑

▼ **Figure 18.34**
Temperate broadleaf forest in Vermont in autumn.

▼ **Figure 18.35**
Northern coniferous forest in Finland, with the sky lit by the northern lights.

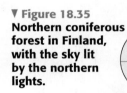

Tundra

Tundra covers expansive areas of the Arctic between the taiga and polar ice. **Permafrost** (permanently frozen subsoil), bitterly cold temperatures, and high winds are responsible for the absence of trees and other tall plants in the arctic tundra shown in **Figure 18.36**. The arctic tundra receives very little annual precipitation. However, water cannot penetrate the underlying permafrost, so melted snow and ice accumulate in pools on the shallow topsoil during the short summer.

Tundra vegetation includes small shrubs, grasses, mosses, and lichens. When summer arrives, annual plants grow quickly and flower in a rapid burst. Caribou, musk oxen, wolves, and small rodents called lemmings are among the mammals found in the arctic tundra. Many migratory animals use the tundra as a summer breeding ground. During the brief but productive warm season, the marshy ground supports the aquatic larvae of insects, providing food for migratory waterfowl, and clouds of mosquitoes often fill the tundra air.

High winds and cold temperatures create plant communities called alpine tundra on very high mountaintops at all latitudes, including the tropics. Although these communities are similar to arctic tundra, there is no permafrost beneath alpine tundra.

Polar Ice

Polar ice covers the land at high latitudes north of the arctic tundra in the Northern Hemisphere and in Antarctica in the Southern Hemisphere **(Figure 18.37)**. The temperature in these regions is extremely cold year-round, and precipitation is very low. Only a small portion of these landmasses is free of ice or snow, even during the summer. Nevertheless, small plants, such as mosses and lichens, eke out a living, and invertebrates such as nematodes, mites, and wingless insects called springtails inhabit the frigid soil. Nearby sea ice provides feeding platforms for large animals such as polar bears (in the Northern Hemisphere), penguins (in the Southern Hemisphere), and seals. Seals, penguins, and other marine birds visit the land to rest and breed. The polar marine biome provides the food that sustains these birds and mammals. In the Antarctic, penguins feed at sea, eating a variety of fish, squids, and small shrimplike crustaceans known as krill. Antarctic krill, an important food source for many species of fish, seals, squids, seabirds, and filter-feeding whales as well as penguins, depend on sea ice for breeding and as a refuge from predators. As the amount and duration of sea ice decline as a consequence of global climate change, krill habitat is shrinking. ☑

▼ Figure 18.36 **Arctic tundra in eastern Alaska.**

▼ Figure 18.37 **Polar ice in Antarctica.**

The Water Cycle

Biomes are not self-contained units. Rather, all parts of the biosphere are linked by the global water cycle, illustrated in **Figure 18.38**, and by nutrient cycles (see Chapter 20). Consequently, events in one biome may reverberate throughout the biosphere.

As you learned earlier in this chapter, water and air move in global patterns driven by solar energy. Precipitation and evaporation continuously move water between the land, oceans, and the atmosphere. Water also evaporates from plants, which pull it from the soil in a process called transpiration.

Over the oceans, evaporation exceeds precipitation. The result is a net movement of water vapor to clouds that are carried by winds from the oceans across the land. On land, precipitation exceeds evaporation and transpiration. The excess precipitation may stay on the surface, or it may trickle through the soil to become groundwater. Both surface water and groundwater eventually flow back to the sea, completing the water cycle.

Just as the water draining from your shower carries dead skin cells from your body along with the day's grime, the water washing over and through the ground carries traces of the land and its history. For example, water flowing from land to the sea carries with it silt (fine soil particles) and chemicals such as fertilizers and pesticides.

Erosion from coastal development has caused silt to muddy the waters of some coral reefs, dimming the light available to the photosynthetic algae that power the reef community. Chemicals in surface water may travel hundreds of miles by stream and river to the ocean, where currents then carry them even farther from their point of origin. For instance, traces of pesticides and chemicals from industrial wastes have been found in marine mammals in the Arctic and in deep-sea octopuses and squids. Airborne pollutants such as nitrogen oxides and sulfur oxides, which combine with water to form acid precipitation, are also distributed by the water cycle.

Human activity also affects the global water cycle itself in a number of important ways. One of the main sources of atmospheric water is transpiration from the dense vegetation making up tropical rain forests. The destruction of these forests changes the amount of water vapor in the air. Pumping large amounts of groundwater to the surface for irrigation increases the rate of evaporation over land and may deplete groundwater supplies. In addition, global warming affects the water cycle in complex ways that will have far-reaching effects on precipitation patterns. We'll consider some of these environmental impacts in the following sections. ☑

▼ Figure 18.38 **The global water cycle.**

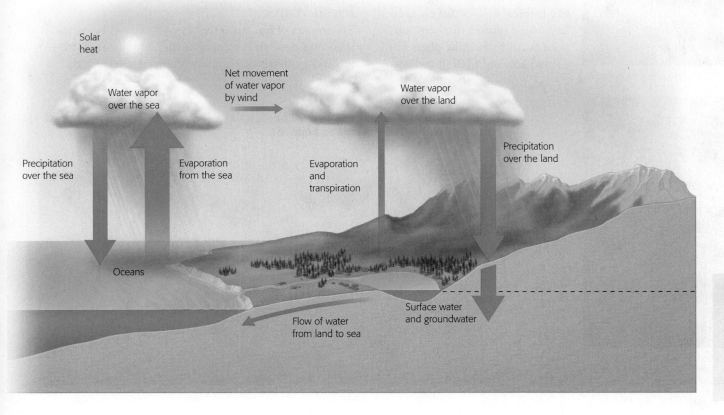

☑ CHECKPOINT

What is the main way that living organisms contribute to the water cycle?

Answer: Plants move water from the ground to the air via transpiration.

Human Impact on Biomes

For hundreds of years, people have been using increasingly effective technologies to capture or produce food, to extract resources from the environment, and to build cities. It is now clear that the environmental costs of these enterprises are staggering. In this section, you'll see some examples of how human activities are affecting forest and freshwater resources. Throughout the remainder of this unit, you'll learn about the role of ecological knowledge in achieving **sustainability**, the goal of developing, managing, and conserving Earth's resources in ways that meet the needs of people today without compromising the ability of future generations to meet their needs.

Forests

The map in Figure 18.27 shows the terrestrial biomes that would be expected to flourish under the prevailing climatic conditions. However, about three-quarters of Earth's land surface has been altered by thousands of years of human occupation. Most of the land that we've appropriated is used for agriculture; another hefty chunk is covered by the asphalt and concrete of development. Changes in vegetation are especially dramatic in regions like tropical forests that escaped large-scale human intervention until recently. Satellite photos of a small area in Brazil show how thoroughly a landscape can be altered in a short amount of time (**Figure 18.39**).

Every year, more and more forested land is cleared for agriculture. You might think that this land is needed to feed new mouths as the human population continues to grow, but that's not entirely the case. Unsustainable agricultural practices have degraded much of the world's cropland so severely that it is unusable. Researchers estimate that replacing worn-out farmland accounts for up to 80% of the deforestation occurring today. Tropical forests, such as the one in **Figure 18.40**, are also being cleared to grow palm oil for biofuel. Other forests are being lost to logging, mining, and air pollution, problems that are hitting coniferous forests especially hard. (As we mentioned in the previous section, most temperate broadleaf forests were replaced by human enterprises long ago.) Land that hasn't been directly converted to food production and living space also bears the imprint of our presence. Roads penetrate regions that are otherwise unaltered, bringing pollution to the wilderness, providing avenues for new diseases to emerge, and slicing vast tracts of biome into segments that are too small to support a full array of species.

Land uses that provide resources such as food, fuel, and shelter are clearly beneficial to us. But natural ecosystems also provide services that support the human population—purification of air and water, nutrient cycling, and recreation, to name just a few. (We'll return to the topic of ecosystem services in Chapter 20.)

Fresh Water

The impact of human activities on freshwater ecosystems may pose an even greater threat to life on Earth—including ourselves—than the damage to terrestrial

▼ **Figure 18.39 Satellite photos of the Rondonia area of the Brazilian rain forest.**

1975. In 1975, the forest in this remote region was virtually intact.

2001. Same area in 2001, after a paved highway through the region brought loggers and farmers. The "fishbone" pattern marks the new network of roads carved through the forest.

▼ **Figure 18.40 Clearcutting in the Chocó, a unique region of coastal rain forest that extends from Panama to Equador.**

ecosystems. Freshwater ecosystems are being polluted by large amounts of nitrogen and phosphorus compounds that run off from heavily fertilized farms or from livestock feedlots. A wide variety of other pollutants, such as industrial wastes, also contaminate freshwater habitats, drinking water, and groundwater. Some regions of the world face dire shortages of water as a result of the overuse of groundwater for irrigation, extended droughts (partially caused by global climate change), or poor water management practices.

Las Vegas, the population center of Clark County, Nevada, is one example of a city whose water resources are increasingly stressed by drought and overuse. Figure 18.41a is a satellite photo of Las Vegas in 1973, when the population of Clark County was 319,400. Figure 18.41b shows the same area less than 30 years later, when the population had swelled to 1,620,748. In contrast to the disappearance of greenery in the photos of Brazilian rain forest, the mark of human activities in Figure 18.41b is the notable expansion of greenery—the result of watering lawns and golf courses. Las Vegas is situated in a high valley in the Mojave Desert. Where does it get the water to turn barren desert into green fields?

Las Vegas taps underground aquifers for some water, but its main water supply is Lake Mead. Lake Mead is an enormous reservoir formed by the Hoover Dam on the Colorado River, which in turn receives almost all of its water from snowmelt in the Rocky Mountains. With decreased annual snowfall, attributable largely to global warming, the flow of the Colorado has greatly diminished. The water level in Lake Mead has dropped drastically (Figure 18.42), and parched cities and farms farther downstream are pleading for more water.

To ensure an adequate water supply for the future, Las Vegas must look elsewhere to satisfy its needs. Among other options, Las Vegas is eyeing the abundant supply of groundwater in the northern end of the valley where it lies. Although sparsely populated, that area is home to many ranchers whose livelihoods depend on the groundwater. It is also home to numerous endangered species. Not surprisingly, environmentalists and residents of the north valley are resisting efforts to pipe its groundwater to Las Vegas.

Nevada is just one of many places where the hard realities of climate change are beginning to affect daily life. Battles over water resources are shaping up throughout the arid West and Southwest of the United States, where changing precipitation patterns due to global warming are projected to continue the drought for many years to come. In other regions of the world, including China, India, and North Africa, the increasing demands of economic, agricultural, and population growth are straining water resources that are already scarce.

While policymakers are dealing with current crises and planning how to manage resources in the future, researchers are seeking methods of sustainable agriculture and water use. Basic ecological research is an essential component of ensuring that sufficient food and water will be available for people now—and for the generations to come. Next, we take a closer look at a major threat to sustainability: global climate change. ☑

▼ Figure 18.42 **Low water level in Lake Mead.** The white "bathtub ring" is caused by mineral deposits on rocks that were once submerged.

▼ Figure 18.41 **Satellite photos of Las Vegas, Nevada.**

(a) May 1973

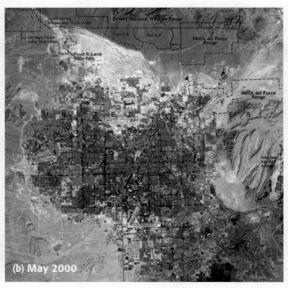

(b) May 2000

Global Climate Change

Rising concentrations of carbon dioxide (CO_2) and certain other gases in the atmosphere are changing global climate patterns. This was the overarching conclusion of the assessment report released by the Intergovernmental Panel on Climate Change (IPCC) in 2007. Thousands of scientists and policymakers from more than 100 countries participated in producing the report, which is based on data published in hundreds of scientific papers. Thus, there is no debate among scientists about whether climate change is occurring. In this section, you'll learn why it is occurring, how it is affecting the biosphere, and what you can do about it.

The Greenhouse Effect and Global Warming

Why is Earth's atmosphere becoming warmer? A useful analogy is a greenhouse, which is used to grow plants when the weather outside is too cold. Its transparent glass or plastic walls allow solar radiation to pass through, but some of the heat that accumulates inside the building is trapped by the glass. On a smaller scale, think how hot it gets in a closed car on a sunny day. Similarly, certain gases in Earth's atmosphere are transparent to solar radiation but absorb or reflect heat. Some of these so-called **greenhouse gases** are natural, including CO_2, water vapor, and methane. Others, such as chlorofluorocarbons (CFCs, found in some aerosol sprays and refrigerants), are synthetic. As **Figure 18.43** shows, greenhouse gases act as a blanket that traps heat in the atmosphere. For this reason, the increase in global temperatures is often called the **greenhouse effect**. This natural heating effect is highly beneficial. Without it, the average air temperature on Earth would be a frigid −18°C (−2.4°F), far too cold for most life as we know it. However, increasing the insulation that the blanket provides is making Earth overly warm.

The signature effect of rapidly increasing greenhouse gases is the steady increase in the average global temperature, which has risen 0.8°C (1.4°F) over the last 100 years, with 75% of that increase occurring over the last three decades. Further increases of 2–4.5°C are likely by the end of this century, according to the 2007 IPPC report. Ocean temperatures are also rising, in deeper layers as well as at the surface. But the temperature increases are not distributed evenly around the globe. The largest increases are in the northernmost regions of the Northern Hemisphere and parts of Antarctica (**Figure 18.44**). ☑

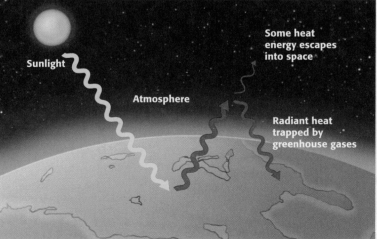

▼ **Figure 18.43 The greenhouse effect.** The atmosphere traps heat in the same way that glass keeps heat inside a greenhouse.

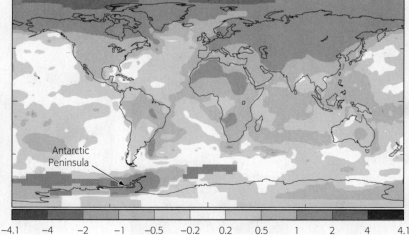

▼ **Figure 18.44 Differences in average temperatures during 2001–2010 compared with long-term averages during 1951–1981, in °C.** The largest temperature increases are shown in red. Gray indicates regions for which no data are available.

The Accumulation of Greenhouse Gases

After many years of data collection and debate, the vast majority of scientists are confident that human activities have caused the rising concentrations of greenhouse gases. Major sources of emissions include agriculture, landfills, and the burning of wood and fossil fuels (oil, coal, and natural gas).

Let's take a closer look at CO_2, the dominant greenhouse gas. For 650,000 years, the atmospheric concentration of CO_2 did not exceed 300 parts per million (ppm); the concentration before the Industrial Revolution was 280 ppm. Today, atmospheric CO_2 is nearly 390 ppm and still rising (Figure 18.45). The levels of other greenhouse gases have increased dramatically, too. As you saw in Figure 6.2, CO_2 is removed from the atmosphere by the process of photosynthesis and stored in organic molecules such as carbohydrates. These molecules are eventually broken down by cellular respiration, releasing CO_2. Overall, uptake of CO_2 by photosynthesis roughly equals the release of CO_2 by cellular respiration (Figure 18.46). However, extensive deforestation has significantly decreased the incorporation of CO_2 into organic material. At the same time, CO_2 is flooding into the atmosphere from the burning of fossil fuels and wood, a process that releases CO_2 from organic material much more rapidly than cellular respiration.

CO_2 is also exchanged between the atmosphere and the surface waters of the oceans. For decades, the oceans have acted as massive sponges, soaking up considerably more CO_2 than they have released. But now, the excess CO_2 has made the oceans more acidic, a change that could have a profound effect on marine communities. Many marine animals, including corals, many species of plankton, and many molluscs, will be unable to build their shells or exoskeletons as ocean acidification worsens. Their demise will remove critical links from marine food webs and ultimately damage marine ecosystems around the world. ☑

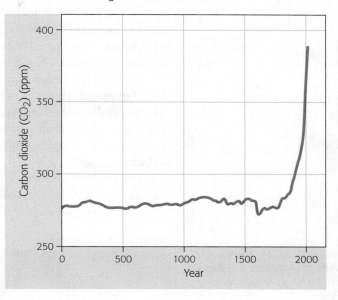

▼ Figure 18.45 **Atmospheric concentration of CO_2.** Notice that the concentration was relatively stable until the Industrial Revolution, which began in the late 1700s.

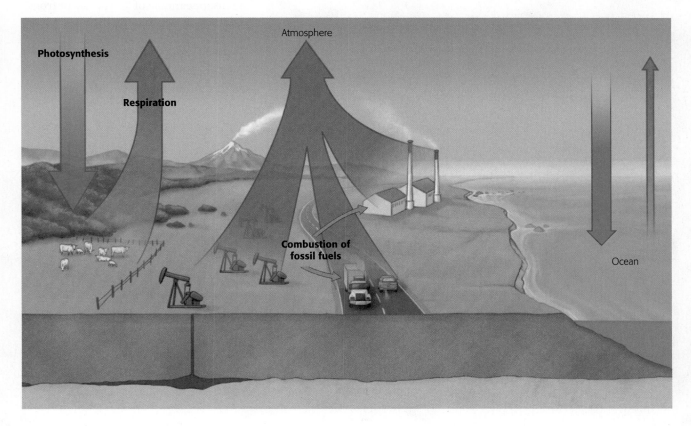

◄ Figure 18.46 **How CO_2 enters and leaves the atmosphere.**

Photosynthesis

Respiration

Atmosphere

Combustion of fossil fuels

Ocean

☑ CHECKPOINT

What is the major source of CO_2 released by human activities?

Answer: burning fossil fuels

How Does Climate Change Affect Species Distribution?

As you've learned in this chapter, abiotic factors of the environment are fundamental determinants of where organisms live. It stands to reason that changes in temperature and precipitation patterns will have a significant effect on the distribution of life. With rising temperatures, the ranges of many species have already shifted toward the poles or to higher elevations. For example, shifts in the ranges of many bird species have been reported; the Inuit peoples living north of the Arctic Circle have sighted robins in the region for the first time.

Let's examine how a team of ecologists investigated the impact of climate change on European butterflies. Using the **observation** that the average temperature in Europe has risen 0.8°C (about 1.4°F) and that butterflies are sensitive to temperature change, the researchers asked the **question**: Have the ranges of butterflies changed in response to the temperature changes? This question led to the **hypothesis** that butterfly range boundaries are shifting in line with the warming trend. The researchers **predicted** that butterfly species will be establishing new populations to the north of their former ranges, and populations at the southern edges of their ranges will become extinct. The **experiment** involved analyzing historical data on the ranges of 35 species of butterflies in Europe. The **results** showed that more than 60% of the species have pushed their northern range boundaries poleward over the last century, some by as much as 150 miles. The southern boundaries have simultaneously contracted for some species, but not for others. **Figure 18.47** shows the range shift for the species *Argynnis paphia*.

While some organisms have the dispersal ability and the room for northward population shifts, species that live on mountaintops or in polar regions have nowhere to go. For example, researchers in Costa Rica have reported the disappearance of 20 species of frogs and toads as warmer Pacific Ocean temperatures reduce the dry-season mists in their mountain habitats. And as we mentioned in the Biology and Society section, animals at both poles are also at risk.

▶ **Figure 18.47 Northward shift of *Argynnis paphia*.** On the map, orange represents the butterfly's range in 1970; its 1997 range is shown in light green.

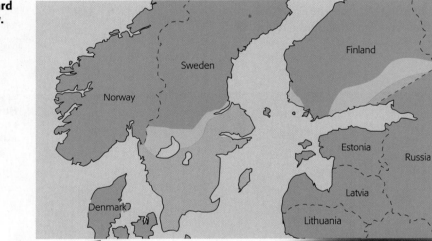

Argynnis paphia (silver-washed fritillary butterfly)

Effects of Climate Change on Ecosystems

The sentiment expressed by the poet John Donne that "no man is an island" is equally true for every other species in nature: Every species needs others to survive. Climate change is knocking some of these interactions out of sync. In many plants and animals, life cycle events are triggered by warming temperatures. Across the Northern Hemisphere, the warm temperatures of spring are arriving earlier. Satellite images show earlier greening of the landscape, and flowering occurs sooner. A variety of species, including birds and frogs, have begun their breeding seasons earlier. But for other species, the environmental cue that spring has arrived is day length, which is not affected by climate change. Consequently, the winter white fur of snowshoe hares may be conspicuous against a greening landscape, or plants may bloom before pollinators have emerged.

So what if global warming makes spring come early—isn't that a good thing?

The combined effects of climate change on forest ecosystems in western North America have spawned catastrophic wildfire seasons (**Figure 18.48**). In these regions, spring snowmelt in the mountains releases water into streams that sustain forest moisture levels over the summer dry season. With the earlier arrival of spring, snowmelt begins earlier and dwindles away before the dry season ends. As a result, the fire season is lasting longer. Meanwhile, bark beetles, which bore into conifers to lay their eggs, have benefited from global warming. Healthy trees can fight off the pests, but drought-stressed trees are too weak to resist (**Figure 18.49**). As a bonus for the beetles, the warmer weather allows them to reproduce twice a year rather than once. In turn, vast numbers of dead trees add fuel to a fire. Wildfires burn longer, and the number of acres burned has increased dramatically.

The map of terrestrial biomes (see Figure 18.27), which is primarily determined by temperature and rainfall, is also changing. Melting permafrost is shifting the boundary of the tundra northward as shrubs and conifers are able to stretch their ranges into the previously frozen ground. Prolonged droughts are extending the boundaries of deserts. Scientists also predict that great expanses of the Amazonian rain forest will gradually become savanna as increased temperatures dry out the soil.

Global climate change has significant consequences for people, too, as changing temperature and precipitation patterns affect food production, the availability of fresh water, and the structural integrity of buildings and roads. All projections point to an even greater impact in the future. Unlike other species, however, humans can take action to reduce greenhouse gas emissions and maybe even reverse the warming trend. ☑

▼ Figure 18.49 **Pines in Colorado infested by bark beetles.** Red or light-colored foliage indicates dead or dying trees. Green trees are still healthy.

▼ Figure 18.48 **A wildfire in northern Los Angeles County, July 2010.**

☑ **CHECKPOINT**

How have bark beetles benefited from global warming?

Answer: Drought-stressed trees are less resistant to the beetles; with a longer warm season, beetles can reproduce twice in a year rather than once.

397

Looking to Our Future

Emissions of greenhouse gases continue to rise. In the United States, for example, total emissions increased more than 13% from 1990 to 2008. At this rate, further climate change is inevitable. However, with effort, ingenuity, and international cooperation, we may be able to begin reducing emissions.

Given the vast scope and complexity of the problem, you might think that your own actions would have little impact on greenhouse gas emissions. But it was the collective activities of individuals that caused—and are still causing—emissions to rise. The amount of greenhouse gas emitted as a result of the actions of a single individual is that person's **carbon footprint** (from the fact that the most important greenhouse gas is CO_2). A carbon footprint can be estimated using a set of rough calculations; several different calculators are available online.

Home energy use is one major contributor to the carbon footprint. It's easy to reduce your energy consumption by turning off the lights, TV, and other electrical appliances when they aren't in use. Unplug "vampire" devices—electronics such as cell phone chargers, videogame consoles, and other computer, video, and audio equipment that draw electricity even when they aren't being used. You can also switch to energy-efficient lightbulbs.

Are vampire devices consuming electricity while you sleep?

Transportation is another significant part of the carbon footprint. If you have a car, keep it well maintained, consolidate trips, share rides with friends, and use alternative means of transportation whenever possible.

Manufactured goods are a third category in the carbon footprint. Every item you purchase generated its own carbon footprint in the process of going from raw materials to store shelves. You can reduce your carbon emissions by not buying unnecessary goods and by recycling—or better yet, reusing—items instead of putting them in the trash (**Figure 18.50**). Landfills are the largest human-related source of methane, a greenhouse gas more potent than CO_2. The methane is released by bacteria that decompose (break down) landfill waste.

Changes in your eating habits can also shrink your carbon footprint. Like landfills, the digestive system of cattle depends on methane-producing bacteria. The methane released by cattle and by the bacteria that decompose their manure accounts for about 20% of methane emissions in the United States. Thus, replacing beef and dairy products in your diet with fish, chicken, eggs, and vegetables reduces your carbon footprint. In addition, eating locally grown fresh foods may lower the greenhouse gas emissions that result from food processing and transportation (**Figure 18.51**). Many websites offer additional suggestions for reducing your carbon footprint. ☑

☑ CHECKPOINT

What is a personal carbon footprint?

Answer: the amount of greenhouse gas that a person is responsible for emitting

▼ Figure 18.50 **Turning trash into treasure.** If you have things that you no longer need, don't trash them when you move out of your dorm or apartment. Environmentally conscious students at the University of North Carolina collect and sell discarded items, donating the proceeds to charity.

▼ Figure 18.51 **Eating locally grown foods may reduce your carbon footprint—and they taste good, too!**

Climate Change as an Agent of Natural Selection

Environmental change has always been a part of life; in fact, it is a key ingredient of evolutionary change. Will evolutionary adaptation counteract the negative effects of climate change on organisms? Researchers have documented microevolutionary shifts in a few populations, including red squirrels, a few bird species, and a tiny mosquito **(Figure 18.52a)**. It appears that some populations, especially those with high genetic variability and short life spans, may avoid extinction by means of evolutionary adaptation. However, evolutionary adaptation is unlikely to save long-lived species such as polar bears and penguins that are experiencing rapid habitat loss **(Figure 18.52b)**. The rate of climate change is incredibly fast compared with major climate shifts in evolutionary history. If climate change continues on its present course, thousands of species—the IPCC estimates as much as 30% of all plants and animals—will face extinction by midcentury.

▼ Figure 18.52 **Which species will survive climate change?**

(a) Pitcher plant mosquito. The pitcher plant mosquito, pictured inside the carnivorous plant for which it is named, may be able to evolve quickly enough.

(b) Adélie penguin. Adélie penguins, which live on the rapidly warming Antarctic Peninsula, are not likely to make it.

Chapter Review

SUMMARY OF KEY CONCEPTS

(MB) Go to **www.masteringbiology.com** for homework assignments, practice quizzes, Pearson eText, and more.

An Overview of Ecology

Ecology is the scientific study of interactions between organisms and their environments. The environment includes abiotic (nonliving) and biotic (living) components. Ecologists use observation, experiments, and computer models to test hypothetical explanations of these interactions.

Ecology and Environmentalism

Human activities have had an impact on all parts of the biosphere. Ecology provides the basis for understanding and addressing these environmental problems.

A Hierarchy of Interactions

Ecologists study interactions at four increasingly complex levels.

Organismal ecology (individual) → Population ecology (group of individuals) → Community ecology (all organisms in a particular area) → Ecosystem ecology (all organisms and abiotic factors)

Living in Earth's Diverse Environments

The biosphere is an environmental patchwork in which abiotic factors affect the distribution and abundance of organisms.

Abiotic Factors of the Biosphere

These include the availability of sunlight, water, nutrients, and temperature. In aquatic habitats, dissolved oxygen, salinity, current, and tides are also important. Additional factors in terrestrial environments include wind and fire.

The Evolutionary Adaptations of Organisms

Adaptation via natural selection results from the interactions of organisms with their environments.

Adjusting to Environmental Variability

Organisms also have adaptations that enable them to cope with environmental variability, including physiological, behavioral, and anatomical responses to changing conditions.

Biomes

A biome is a major terrestrial or aquatic life zone.

Freshwater Biomes

Freshwater biomes include lakes, ponds, rivers, streams, and wetlands. Lakes vary, depending on depth, with regard to light penetration, temperature, nutrients, oxygen levels, and community structure. Rivers change greatly from their source to the point at which they empty into a lake or ocean.

Marine Biomes

Marine life is distributed into distinct realms (benthic and pelagic) and zones (photic, aphotic, and intertidal) according to the depth of the water, degree of light penetration, distance from shore, and open water versus deep-sea bottom. The coral reef biome, which occurs in warm tropical waters above the continental shelf, has an abundance of biological diversity. A biome found near hydrothermal vents in the deep ocean is powered by chemical energy from Earth's interior instead of sunlight. Estuaries, located where a freshwater river or stream merges with the ocean, are one of the most biologically productive environments on Earth.

How Climate Affects Terrestrial Biome Distribution

The geographic distribution of terrestrial biomes is based mainly on regional variations in climate. Climate is largely determined by the uneven distribution of solar energy on Earth. Proximity to large bodies of water and the presence of landforms such as mountains also affect climate.

Terrestrial Biomes

Most biomes are named for major physical or climatic features and for their predominant vegetation. The major terrestrial biomes include tropical forest, savanna, desert, chaparral, temperate grassland, temperate broadleaf forest, coniferous forest, tundra, and polar ice. If the climate in two geographically separate areas is similar, the same type of biome may occur in both.

The Water Cycle

The global water cycle links aquatic and terrestrial biomes. Human activities are disrupting the water cycle.

Human Impact on Biomes

Land use by humans has altered vast tracts of forest and degraded the services provided by natural ecosystems. Unsustainable agricultural practices have depleted cropland fertility. Human activities have polluted freshwater ecosystems, which are vital for life. Agriculture, population growth, drought, and declining snowfall are all factors in the rapid depletion of freshwater resources in some regions.

Global Climate Change

The Greenhouse Effect and Global Warming

So-called greenhouse gases, including CO_2 and methane, increase the amount of heat retained in Earth's atmosphere. The accumulation of these gases has caused increases in the average global temperature.

The Accumulation of Greenhouse Gases

Human activities, especially the burning of fossil fuels, are responsible for the rise in greenhouse gases over the past century. Release of CO_2 has exceeded the amount that can be absorbed by natural processes.

Effects of Climate Change on Ecosystems

Climate change is disrupting interactions between species. Devastating wildfires are among the effects of climate change in certain ecosystems. Climate change is also shifting biome boundaries.

Looking to Our Future

Each person has a carbon footprint—that person's responsibility for a portion of global greenhouse gas emissions. We can take action to reduce our carbon footprints.

SELF-QUIZ

1. Place these levels of ecological study in order, from the least to the most comprehensive: community ecology, ecosystem ecology, organismal ecology, population ecology.

2. Name several abiotic factors that might affect the community of organisms living inside a home fish tank.

3. The formation of goose bumps on your skin in cold weather is an example of a (an) _____ response, while seasonal migration is an example of a (an) _____ response.

4. Which of the following sea creatures might be described as a pelagic animal of the aphotic zone?
   - a. a coral reef fish
   - b. a giant clam near a deep-sea hydrothermal vent
   - c. an intertidal snail
   - d. a deep-sea squid
   - e. a species of phytoplankton

5. Identify the following biomes on the climograph below: tundra, coniferous forest, desert, grassland, temperate broadleaf forest, and tropical rain forest.

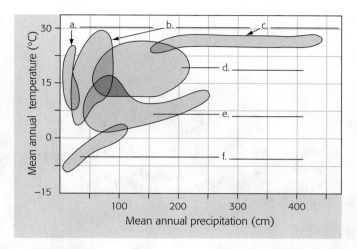

6. We are on a coastal hillside on a hot, dry summer day among evergreen shrubs that are adapted to fire. We are most likely standing in a _____ biome.

7. What three abiotic factors account for the rarity of trees in arctic tundra?

8. What human activity is responsible for the greatest amount of deforestation?

9. What is the greenhouse effect? How is the greenhouse effect related to global warming?

10. The recent increase in atmospheric CO_2 concentration is mainly a result of an increase in
   a. primary productivity.
   b. the absorption of heat radiating from Earth.
   c. the burning of fossil fuels and wood.
   d. cellular respiration by the increasing human population.

11. What populations of organisms are most likely to survive climate change via evolutionary adaptation?

Answers to these questions can be found in Appendix: Self-Quiz Answers.

THE PROCESS OF SCIENCE

12. Design a laboratory experiment to measure the effect of water temperature on the population growth of a certain phytoplankton species from a pond.

13. Some people are not convinced that human-induced global climate change is a real phenomenon. Using your knowledge of the scientific process (see Chapter 1) and the information from this chapter, develop arguments you could use to explain the scientific basis for saying that global climate change is truly occurring and that people are responsible for it.

BIOLOGY AND SOCIETY

14. Near Lawrence, Kansas, there was a rare patch of the original North American temperate grassland that had never been plowed. It was home to numerous native grasses, annual plants, and grassland animals. Among the species present were two endangered plants. Environmental activists thought the area should be set aside as a nature preserve, and they started to raise money to save the patch of land. In 1990, the owner of the land plowed it, stating that there are no federal laws protecting endangered plants on private grasslands and that he did not want to be told what he could do with his property. What issues and values are in conflict in this situation? How could this story have had a more satisfactory ending for all concerned? What would you have done if you were an environmental activist? If you were the farmer?

15. Land clearing for agricultural use is responsible for most of the deforestation that is currently taking place. Agriculture also pumps enormous amounts of groundwater for irrigation and pollutes surface waters with nitrogen via runoff. But agriculture also supplies the world's food. Are the environmental consequences of agriculture simply the price we must pay to eat? What are the long-term costs? Suggest some ways to alleviate the environmental impact of agriculture.

16. Research your country's per capita (per person) carbon emissions. Calculate your own carbon footprint and compare it with the average for your country. Make a list of actions you are willing to take to reduce your personal carbon footprint. What actions could you take to persuade others to reduce their carbon footprints?

17. In the summer of 2007, unprecedented drought conditions brought the city of Atlanta, Georgia, within weeks of running out of water. Most of Atlanta's water comes from Lake Lanier, a reservoir that the Army Corps of Engineers created by damming the Chattahoochee River. With Lake Lanier drying up from lack of rainfall, Georgia petitioned the Corps, which manages the dam, to reduce the amount of water released downstream. The Corps refused, citing its obligation under the Endangered Species Act to protect the habitats of a species of sturgeon (a fish) and two species of mussel (a mollusc). Objections were also raised by Alabama and Florida, where hundreds of towns, recreational facilities, and power plants depend on the water released downstream. Some people thought that Atlanta authorities had brought the water shortage on themselves by allowing developers to build without considering whether adequate water was available. Florida also argued that reduction of freshwater inflows would harm its oyster fisheries. How would you prioritize the competing claims on the water from Lake Lanier? Who should allocate scarce water resources? How can cities and states plan more wisely for future shortages?

19 Population Ecology

A red lionfish.
This beautiful but deadly invader is a threat to coral reef communities, such as this one in the Bahamas.

Biological Invasions BIOLOGY AND SOCIETY

Invasion of the Lionfish

Lionfish, with their graceful, flowing fins, bold stripes, and eye-catching array of spines, are striking members of tropical reef communities. They are also favorites of saltwater aquarium enthusiasts—especially the red lionfish, a native to the coral reefs of the South Pacific and Indian Oceans. There are a few drawbacks to owning a red lionfish, however. The spines are venomous and can inflict an intensely painful sting. Lionfish are merciless predators, so any tankmates must be chosen with care. And they are large. A 2-inch juvenile can rapidly become an 18-inch adult that requires, at minimum, a 120-gallon tank. Apparently, some aquarium owners who regretted their purchase released their lionfish into the wild.

Freed from the competitors and predators of their native reefs as well as their tanks, red lionfish have multiplied exponentially. Within a few years of the first sightings off the southeastern coast of Florida, lionfish populations had spread up the East Coast. They have since invaded islands and coastlines throughout the Atlantic and Caribbean regions and are now swarming into the Gulf of Mexico. The speed of the onslaught has stunned scientists, who are just beginning to document its devastating effects on native ecosystems. Lionfish consume prodigious numbers of fish, including species that are key to maintaining the legendary diversity of reef communities and juveniles of economically important fishes such as grouper and snapper. Some biologists think our best hope of stopping the lionfish invasion is for *us* to consume *them*. The National Oceanic and Atmospheric Administration (NOAA) has launched an "Eat Lionfish" campaign to encourage human predation on the tasty fish.

For as long as people have traveled the globe, they have carried—intentionally or accidentally—thousands of species to new habitats. Many of these non-native species have established populations that spread far and wide, leaving environmental havoc in their wake. We humans, too, have multiplied and spread far from our point of origin, and we have radically changed our environment. As you explore population ecology in this chapter, you'll also learn about trends in human population growth and other applications of this area of ecological research.

An Overview of Population Ecology

Ecologists usually define a **population** as a group of individuals of a single species that occupy the same general area. These individuals rely on the same resources, are influenced by the same environmental factors, and are likely to interact and breed with one another. For example, the lionfish that live in the vicinity of a specific reef are a population.

Population ecology is concerned with changes in population size and the factors that regulate populations over time. A population ecologist might describe a population in terms of its size (number of individuals), age structure (proportion of individuals of different ages), or density (number of individuals per unit area or volume) **(Figure 19.1)**. Population ecologists also study population dynamics, the interactions between biotic and abiotic factors that cause variation in population size. One important aspect of population dynamics—and a major topic for this chapter—is population growth.

Can population ecologists help solve real-world problems?

Population ecology also plays a key role in applied research. For example, it provides critical information for identifying and saving endangered species. Population ecology is being used to develop sustainable fisheries throughout the world and to manage wildlife populations. Studying the population ecology of pests and pathogens provides insight into controlling how they spread. Population ecologists also study human population growth, one of the most critical environmental issues of our time.

Let's consider what a snapshot of a population might look like. The first question is, Which individuals are included in this population? A population's geographic boundaries may be natural, as with lionfish inhabiting a particular coral reef. But ecologists often define a population's boundaries in more arbitrary ways that fit their research questions. For example, an ecologist studying the contribution of asexual reproduction to the population growth of sea anemones might define a population as all the anemones of one species in a particular tide pool. Another researcher studying the effects of hunting on deer might define a population as all the deer within a particular state. Yet another researcher, attempting to determine which segment of the human population will be most affected by the AIDS epidemic, might study the HIV infection rate of the human population in one nation or throughout the world.

▼ **Figure 19.1 Gentoo penguin (Pygoscelis papua) in the nest with an egg, New Island, Falkland Islands, east of the tip of South America.**

Population Density

Our snapshot of a population would include **population density**, the number of individuals of a species per unit area or volume of the habitat: the number of largemouth bass per cubic kilometer (km^3) of a lake, for example, or the number of oak trees per square kilometer (km^2) in a forest, or the number of nematodes per cubic meter (m^3) in the forest's soil. In rare cases, an ecologist can actually count all the individuals within the boundaries of the population. For example, we could count the total number of oak trees (say, 200) in a forest covering 50 km^2 (about 19 square miles). The population density would be the total number of trees divided by the area, or 4 trees per square kilometer (4/km^2).

In most cases, however, it is impractical or impossible to count all individuals in a population. Instead, ecologists use a variety of sampling techniques to estimate population density. For example, they might estimate the density of alligators in the Florida Everglades based on a count of individuals in a few sample plots of 1 km^2 each. Generally speaking, the larger the number and size of sample plots, the more accurate the estimates. Population densities may also be estimated by indicators such as number of bird nests or rodent burrows **(Figure 19.2)** rather than by actual counts of organisms.

Keep in mind that population density is not a constant number. It changes when individuals are born or die and when new individuals enter the population (immigration) or leave it (emigration).

Population Age Structure

The **age structure** of a population—the distribution of individuals in different age-groups—reveals information that is not apparent from population density. For instance, age structure can provide insight into the history of a population's survival or reproductive success and how it relates to environmental factors. **Figure 19.3** shows the age structure of males in a population of cactus finches on the Galápagos Islands in 1987. (See Figure 13.12 for other examples of Galápagos finches.) Four-year-old birds, born in 1983, made up almost half the population, while no 2- or 3-year-olds were present at all. Why was there such dramatic variation? For their food, cactus finches depend on vegetation, which in turn depends on rainfall. The 1983 baby boom resulted from unusually wet weather that produced abundant food. Severe droughts in 1984 and 1985 limited the food supply, preventing reproduction and causing many deaths. As we'll see later in this chapter, age structure is also a useful tool for predicting future changes in a population. ☑

☑ **CHECKPOINT**

What does an age structure show?

Answer: the distribution of individuals in different age-groups

▼ **Figure 19.2 An indirect census of a prairie dog population.** We could get a rough estimate of the number of prairie dogs in this colony in Saskatchewan, Canada, by counting the number of burrows constructed by the rodents and then multiplying by the number of animals using a typical burrow.

▼ **Figure 19.3 Age structure for the males in a population of large cactus finches (inset) on one of the Galápagos Islands in 1987.**

Life Tables and Survivorship Curves

Life tables track survivorship, the chance of an individual in a given population surviving to various ages. The life insurance industry uses life tables to predict how long, on average, a person of a given age will live. Starting with a population of 100,000 people, **Table 19.1** shows the number who are expected to be alive at the beginning of each age interval, based on death rates in 2006. For example, 93,750 out of 100,000 people are expected to live to age 50. The chance of them surviving to age 60, shown in the last column of the same row, is 0.939; about 94% of 50-year-olds will reach the age of 60. The chance of 80-year-olds surviving to age 90, however, is only 0.386. Population ecologists have adopted this technique and constructed life tables to help them understand the structure and dynamics of various plant and animal species. By identifying the most vulnerable stage of the life cycle, life table data may also help conservationists develop effective measures to protect species whose populations are declining.

Ecologists represent life table data graphically in a **survivorship curve**, a plot of the number of individuals still alive at each age in the maximum life span **(Figure 19.4)**. By using a percentage scale instead of actual ages on the *x*-axis, we can compare species with widely varying life spans on the same graph. The curve for the human population (red) shows that most people survive to the older age intervals. Ecologists refer to the shape of this curve as Type I survivorship. Species

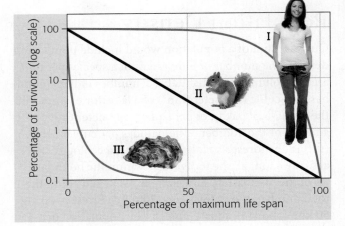

▲ Figure 19.4 **Three idealized types of survivorship curves.**

that exhibit a Type I curve—humans and many other large mammals—usually produce few offspring but give them good care, increasing the likelihood that they will survive to maturity.

In contrast, a Type III curve (blue) indicates low survivorship for the very young, followed by a period when survivorship is high for those few individuals who live to a certain age. Species with this type of survivorship curve usually produce very large numbers of offspring but provide little or no care for them. Some species of fish, for example, produce millions of eggs at a time, but most of these offspring die as larvae from predation or other causes. Many invertebrates, including oysters, also have Type III survivorship curves.

A Type II curve (black) is intermediate, with survivorship constant over the life span. That is, individuals are no more vulnerable at one stage of the life cycle than another. This type of survivorship has been observed in some invertebrates, lizards, and rodents. ☑

Life History Traits as Evolutionary Adaptations

A population's pattern of survivorship is a key feature of its **life history**, the set of traits that affect an organism's schedule of reproduction and survival. Let's take a closer look now at how natural selection affects the reproductive patterns that evolve in populations.

Key life history traits include the age at first reproduction, the frequency of reproduction, the number of offspring, and the amount of parental care given. For a given population in a particular environment, natural selection will favor the combination of life history traits that maximizes an individual's output of viable, fertile

☑ CHECKPOINT

Sea turtles lay their eggs in nests on sandy beaches. Although a single nest may contain as many as 200 eggs, only a small proportion of the hatchlings survive the journey from the beach to the open ocean. Once sea turtles have matured, however, the mortality rate is low. What type of survivorship do sea turtles exhibit?

Answer: Type III

Table 19.1	Life Table for the U.S. Population in 2006		
	Number Living at Start of Age Interval	Number Dying During Interval	Chance of Surviving Interval
Age Interval	(*N*)	(*D*)	$1-(D/N)$
0–10	100,000	853	0.991
10–20	99,147	400	0.996
20–30	98,747	988	0.990
30–40	97,759	1,264	0.987
40–50	96,495	2,745	0.972
50–60	93,750	5,693	0.939
60–70	88,057	11,396	0.871
70–80	76,661	22,460	0.707
80–90	54,201	33,303	0.386
90+	20,898	20,898	0.000

offspring. In other words, life history traits, like anatomical features, are shaped by evolutionary adaptation.

Natural selection cannot maximize all life history traits simultaneously because an organism has limited time, energy, and nutrients. For example, an organism that gives birth to a large number of offspring will not be able to provide a great deal of parental care. Consequently, the combination of life history traits represents trade-offs that balance the demands of reproduction and survival. Because selection pressures vary, life histories are very diverse. Nevertheless, ecologists have observed some patterns that are useful for understanding how natural selection influences life history characteristics.

Why do some animals produce hundreds of young, others only a few?

One life history pattern is typified by small-bodied, short-lived animals (for example, insects and small rodents) that develop and reach sexual maturity rapidly, have a large number of offspring, and offer little or no parental care. In plants, "parental care" is measured by the amount of nutritional material stocked in each seed. Many small, nonwoody plants (dandelions, for example) produce thousands of tiny seeds. Such organisms have an **opportunistic life history**, one that enables the plant or animal to take immediate advantage of favorable conditions. In general, populations with this life history pattern exhibit a Type III survivorship curve.

In contrast, some organisms have an **equilibrial life history**, a pattern of developing and reaching sexual maturity slowly and producing few, well-cared-for offspring. Organisms that have an equilibrial life history are typically larger-bodied, longer-lived species (for example, bears and elephants). Populations with this life history pattern exhibit a Type I survivorship curve. Plants with comparable life history traits include certain trees. For example, coconut palms produce relatively few seeds that are well stocked with nutrient-rich material. **Table 19.2** compares key traits of opportunistic and equilibrial life history patterns.

What accounts for the differences in life history patterns?

Some ecologists hypothesize that the potential survival rate of the offspring and the likelihood that the adult will live to reproduce again are the critical factors. In a harsh, unpredictable environment, where the adult may have just one good shot at reproduction, it may be an advantage to invest in quantity rather than quality. On the other hand, in an environment where favorable conditions are more dependable, an adult is more likely to survive to reproduce again. Seeds are more likely to fall on fertile ground, and newly emerged animals are more likely to survive to adulthood. In that case, it may be more advantageous for the adult to invest its energy in producing a few well-cared-for offspring at a time.

Of course, there is much more diversity in life history patterns than the two extremes described here. Nevertheless, the contrasting patterns are useful for understanding the interactions between life history traits and our next topic, population growth. ☑

☑ **CHECKPOINT**

How does the term *opportunistic* capture the key characteristics of that life history pattern?

Answer: An opportunistic life history is characterized by an ability to produce a large number of offspring very rapidly when the environment affords a temporary opportunity for a burst of reproduction.

Dandelions have an opportunistic life history.

Elephants have an equilibrial life history.

Table 19.2	Some Life History Characteristics of Opportunistic and Equilibrial Populations	
Characteristic	**Opportunistic Populations (such as many wildflowers)**	**Equilibrial Populations (such as many large mammals)**
Climate	Relatively unpredictable	Relatively predictable
Maturation time	Short	Long
Life span	Short	Long
Death rate	Often high	Usually low
Number of offspring per reproductive episode	Many	Few
Number of reproductions per lifetime	Usually one	Often several
Timing of first reproduction	Early in life	Later in life
Size of offspring or eggs	Small	Large
Parental care	Little or none	Often extensive

Population Growth Models

Population size fluctuates as new individuals are born or immigrate into an area and others die or emigrate out of an area. Some populations—for example, trees in a mature forest—are relatively constant over time. Other populations change rapidly, even explosively. Consider a single bacterium that divides every 20 minutes. There would be two bacteria after 20 minutes, four after 40 minutes, eight after 60 minutes, and so on. In just 12 hours, the population would approach 70 billion cells. If reproduction continued for a day and a half—a mere 36 hours—there would be enough bacteria to form a layer a foot deep over the entire Earth! Population ecologists use idealized models to investigate how the size of a particular population may change over time under different conditions. We'll describe two simple mathematical models that illustrate fundamental concepts of population growth.

The Exponential Population Growth Model: The Ideal of an Unlimited Environment

Exponential population growth describes the expansion of a population in an ideal, unlimited environment. In the exponential model, the population size of each new generation is calculated by multiplying the current population size by a constant factor that represents the number of births minus the number of deaths. Let's look at how such a population grows. In **Figure 19.5**, we begin with a population of 20 rabbits, indicated on the *y*-axis. Each month, there are more rabbit births than deaths; as a result, the population size increases each month.

Notice in Figure 19.5 that each increase is larger than the previous one—that is, the *rate* of population growth increases with population size. The increasing rate of population growth produces a J-shaped curve that is typical of exponential growth. The slope of the curve represents the growth rate of the population. At the outset, when the population is small, the curve is almost flat: Over the first 4 months, the population increases by a total of only 37 individuals, an average of 9.25 births per month. By the end of 7 months, the growth rate has increased to an average of 15 births per month. The largest growth is seen in the period from 10 to 12 months, when an average of 85 rabbits are born each month. Thus, exponential population growth is like compound interest on a savings account: The principal (population size) grows faster with each interest payment (the individuals added to the population).

Exponential population growth is common in certain situations. For example, a disturbance such as a fire, flood, hurricane, drought, or cold snap may suddenly reduce the size of a population. Organisms that have opportunistic life history patterns can rapidly take advantage of the lack of competition and quickly recolonize the habitat by exponential population growth. Human activity can also be a major cause of disturbance, and plants and animals with opportunistic life history traits commonly occupy road cuts, freshly cleared fields and woodlots, and poorly maintained lawns. However, no natural environment can sustain exponential growth indefinitely. ☑

▼ **Figure 19.5 Exponential growth of a rabbit population.**

☑ **CHECKPOINT**

Why does the exponential model of population growth produce a curve shaped like a J?

Answer: The rate of population growth increases as population size increases.

The Logistic Population Growth Model: The Reality of a Limited Environment

Most natural environments do not have an unlimited supply of the resources needed to sustain population growth. Environmental factors that restrict population growth are called **limiting factors**. Limiting factors ultimately control the number of individuals that can occupy a habitat. Ecologists define **carrying capacity** as the maximum population size that a particular environment can sustain. In **logistic population growth**, the growth rate decreases as the population size approaches carrying capacity. When the population is at carrying capacity, the growth rate is zero.

You can see the effect of limiting factors in the graph in **Figure 19.6**, which shows the growth of a population of fur seals on St. Paul Island, off the coast of Alaska. (For simplicity, only the mated bulls were counted. Each has a harem of females, as shown in the photograph.) Before 1925, the seal population on the island remained low—between 1,000 and 4,500 mated bulls—because of uncontrolled hunting. After hunting was controlled, the population increased rapidly until about 1935, when it began to level off and started fluctuating around a population size of about 10,000 bull seals—the carrying capacity for St. Paul Island. In this instance, the main limiting factor was the amount of space suitable for breeding territories.

The carrying capacity for a population varies, depending on the species and the resources available in the habitat. For example, carrying capacity might be considerably less than 10,000 for a fur seal population on a smaller island with fewer breeding sites. Even in one location, it is not a fixed number. Organisms interact with other organisms in their communities, including predators, pathogens, and food sources, and these interactions may affect carrying capacity. Changes in abiotic factors may also increase or decrease carrying capacity. In any case, the concept of carrying capacity expresses an essential fact of nature: Resources are finite.

Ecologists hypothesize that selection for organisms exhibiting equilibrial life history patterns occurs in environments where the population size is at or near carrying capacity. Because competition for resources is keen under these circumstances, organisms gain an advantage by allocating energy to their own survival and to the survival of their descendants.

Figure 19.7 compares logistic growth (blue) with exponential growth (red). As you can see, the logistic curve is J-shaped at first, but gradually levels off to resemble an S shape as carrying capacity is reached. Both the logistic model and the exponential model are theoretical ideals of population growth. No natural population fits either one perfectly. However, these models are useful starting points for studying population growth. Ecologists use them to predict how populations will grow in certain environments and as a basis for constructing more complex models. ☑

▼ Figure 19.6 **Logistic growth of a seal population.**

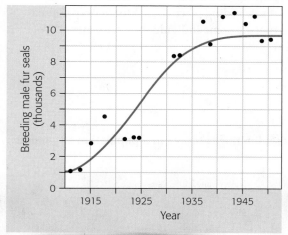

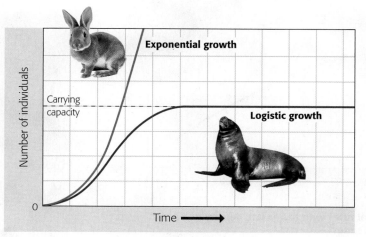

◄ Figure 19.7 **Comparison of exponential and logistic growth.**

409

Regulation of Population Growth

Now let's take a closer look at how population growth is regulated in nature. What stops a population from continuing to increase after reaching carrying capacity?

Density-Dependent Factors

Several **density-dependent factors**—limiting factors whose intensity is related to population density—

How do organisms "know" when the population has reached carrying capacity?

can limit growth in natural populations. The most obvious is **intraspecific competition**, the competition between individuals of the same species for the same limited resources.

As a limited food supply is divided among more and more individuals, birth rates may decline as individuals have less energy available for reproduction. In the study shown in **Figure 19.8a**, clutch size (the number of eggs a female bird lays at one time) declined as the population density, and therefore the number of competitors, increased.

Density-dependent factors often depress a population's growth by increasing the death rate. In a laboratory experiment with flour beetles, for example, survivorship declined with increasing population density (**Figure 19.8b**). In a natural setting, plants that are growing close together may experience increased mortality. And those that do survive will produce fewer flowers, fruits, and seeds than uncrowded individuals. In an animal population, the death rate may climb as a result of increased disease transmission under crowded conditions or the accumulation of toxic waste products. Predation may also be an important cause of density-dependent mortality. A predator may concentrate on and capture more of a particular kind of prey as that prey becomes abundant.

A limited resource may be something other than food or nutrients. In many vertebrates that defend a territory, the availability of space may limit reproduction. For instance, the number of nesting sites on rocky islands may limit the population size of oceanic birds such as gannets, which maintain breeding territories (**Figure 19.9**). Or, like a game of musical chairs, the number of safe hiding places may limit a prey population by exposing some individuals to a greater risk of predation.

▼ Figure 19.8 **Density-dependent regulation of population growth.**

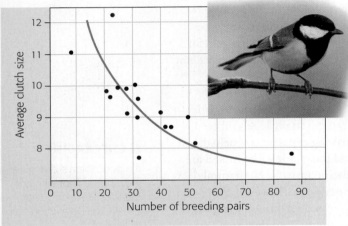

(a) **Decreasing birth rate with increasing density in a population of great tits**

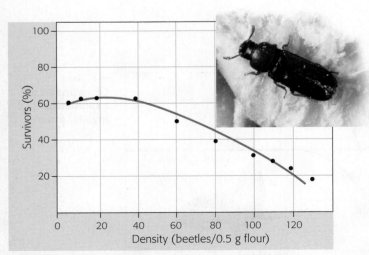

(b) **Decreasing survival rates with increasing density in a population of flour beetles**

▼ Figure 19.9 **Space as a limiting resource in a population of gannets.**

Density-Independent Factors

In many natural populations, abiotic factors such as weather may limit or reduce population size well before other limiting factors become important. A population-limiting factor whose intensity is unrelated to population density is called a **density-independent factor**. If we look at the growth curve of such a population, we see something like exponential growth followed by a rapid decline rather than a leveling off. **Figure 19.10** shows this effect for a population of aphids, insects that feed on the sugary sap of plants. These and many other insects undergo virtually exponential growth in the spring and then rapidly die off when the weather turns hot and dry in the summer. A few individuals may remain, allowing population growth to resume if favorable conditions return. In some populations of insects—many mosquitoes and grasshoppers, for instance—the adults die off entirely, leaving behind eggs that will initiate population growth the following year. In addition to seasonal changes in the weather, environmental disturbances, such as fire, floods, and storms, can affect a population's size regardless of its density.

Over the long term, most populations are probably regulated by a complex interaction of density-dependent and density-independent factors. Although some populations remain fairly stable in size and are presumably close to a carrying capacity that is determined by biotic factors such as competition or predation, most populations for which we have long-term data do fluctuate.

Population Cycles

Some populations of insects, birds, and mammals undergo dramatic fluctuations in density with remarkable regularity. "Booms" characterized by rapid exponential growth are followed by "busts," during which the population falls back to a minimal level. Lemmings, small rodents that live in the tundra, are a striking example. In lemming populations, boom-and-bust growth cycles occur every three to four years. Some researchers hypothesize that natural changes in the lemmings' food supply may be the underlying cause. Another hypothesis is that stress from crowding during the "boom" may cause the "bust" by reducing reproduction via physiological mechanisms.

Figure 19.11 illustrates another example—the cycles of the snowshoe hare and the lynx. The lynx is one of the main predators of the snowshoe hare in the far northern forests of Canada and Alaska. About every ten years, both hare and lynx populations show a rapid increase followed by a sharp decline. What causes these boom-and-bust cycles? Since ups and downs in the two populations seem to almost match each other on the graph, does this mean that changes in one directly affect the other? For the hare cycles, there are three main hypotheses. First, cycles may be caused by winter food shortages that result from overgrazing. Second, cycles may be due to predator-prey interactions. Many predators other than lynx, such as coyotes, foxes, and great-horned owls, eat hares, and together these predators might overexploit their prey. Third, cycles may be affected by a combination of food resource limitation and excessive predation. Recent field studies support the hypothesis that the ten-year cycles of the snowshoe hare are largely driven by excessive predation, but are also influenced by fluctuations in the hare's food supplies. Long-term studies are the key to unraveling the complex causes of such population cycles. ☑

> ### ☑ CHECKPOINT
> List some density-dependent factors that limit population growth.
>
> *Answer: food and nutrient limitations, insufficient space for territories or nests, increase in disease and predation, accumulation of toxins*

▼ Figure 19.10 **Weather change as a density-independent factor limiting growth of an aphid population.**

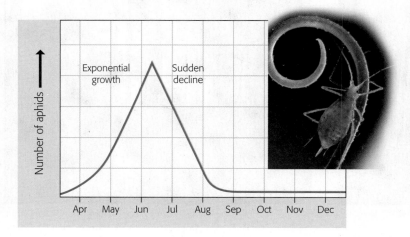

▼ Figure 19.11 **Population cycles of the snowshoe hare and the lynx.**

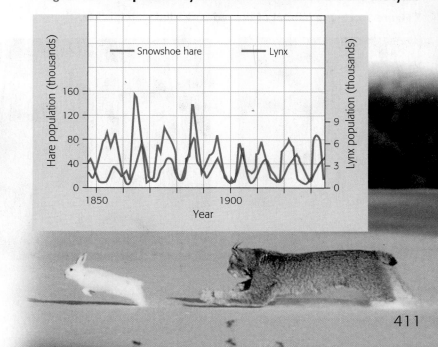

411

Applications of Population Ecology

To a great extent, we have converted Earth's natural ecosystems to ecosystems that produce goods and services for our own benefit. In some cases, we try to increase populations of organisms that we wish to harvest and decrease populations of organisms that we consider pests. Other efforts are aimed at saving populations that are perilously close to extinction. Principles of population ecology help guide us toward these various resource management goals.

Conservation of Endangered Species

The U.S. Endangered Species Act has defined an **endangered species** as one that is "in danger of extinction throughout all or a significant portion of its range." **Threatened species** are defined as those that are likely to become endangered in the foreseeable future. Endangered and threatened species are characterized by population sizes that are highly reduced or steadily declining. The challenge for conservationists is to determine the circumstances that threaten a species with extinction and try to remedy the situation.

The case of the endangered red-cockaded woodpecker is an example of how conservationists rescued a species on the brink of extinction by identifying and correcting the factors responsible for reducing its populations (**Figure 19.12**). The red-cockaded woodpecker requires longleaf pine forests, where it drills its nest holes in mature, living pine trees. Originally found throughout the southeastern United States, the numbers of red-cockaded woodpeckers declined as suitable habitats were lost to logging and agriculture. Moreover, we have altered the composition of many of the remaining forests by suppressing the fires that are a natural occurrence in these ecosystems. Research has revealed that breeding birds tend to abandon nests when vegetation among the pines is thick and higher than about 4.5 m (15 feet). Apparently, the birds require a clear flight path between their home trees and the neighboring feeding grounds.

The recent recovery of the red-cockaded woodpecker from near-extinction to sustainable populations is largely due to recognizing and manipulating the key factors that regulate the bird's population growth. For example, controlled fires that reduce forest undergrowth help maintain mature pine trees and thus woodpecker populations as well. ✓

Sustainable Resource Management

A goal of wildlife managers, fishery biologists, and foresters is to gather the maximum amount of crop while sustaining the productivity of the resource for future harvests. This means maintaining a high population growth rate to replenish the population. According to the logistic growth model, the fastest growth rate occurs when the

Once a species is "endangered," how can it be saved from extinction?

✓ CHECKPOINT

What was a key factor in the recovery of red-cockaded woodpecker populations?

Answer: removal of understory vegetation by controlled burns

▼ Figure 19.12 **The habitat of the red-cockaded woodpecker.**

A red-cockaded woodpecker perches at the entrance to its nest in a longleaf pine tree.

High, dense undergrowth impedes the woodpeckers' access to feeding grounds.

Low undergrowth offers birds a clear flight path between nest sites and feeding grounds.

population size is at roughly half the carrying capacity of the habitat. Theoretically, a resource manager should achieve the best results by harvesting the population down to this level. However, the logistic model assumes that growth rate and carrying capacity are stable over time. Calculations based on these assumptions, which are not realistic for some populations, may lead to unsustainably high harvest levels that ultimately deplete the resource. In addition, human economic and political pressures often outweigh ecological concerns, and scientific information is frequently insufficient.

Fish, the only wild animals still hunted on a large scale, are particularly vulnerable to overharvesting. For example, in the northern Atlantic cod fishery, estimates of cod stocks were too high, and the practice of discarding young cod (not of legal size) at sea caused a higher mortality rate than was predicted. The fishery collapsed in 1992 and has not recovered (**Figure 19.13**).

Until the 1970s, marine fisheries concentrated on species such as cod that inhabit the continental shelves (see Figure 18.19). As these resources dwindled, attention turned to deeper waters, most commonly the continental slopes below 600 m. In many of these new fisheries, however, catches are initially high but then quickly fall off as stocks are depleted. Deeper waters are colder, and food is relatively scarce. Fishes that are adapted to this environment, such as Chilean sea bass and orange roughy, typically grow more slowly, take longer to reach maturity, and have a lower reproductive rate than continental shelf species. Sustainable catch rates can't be estimated without knowing these essential life history traits for the target species. In addition, knowledge of population ecology alone is not sufficient; sustainable fisheries also require knowledge of community and ecosystem characteristics. ☑

☑ **CHECKPOINT**
Why do managers try to maintain populations of fish and game species at about half their carrying capacity?

Answer: to prevent overharvesting yet maintain lower population levels so that growth rate is high

▼ **Figure 19.13** **The collapse of the northern cod fishery off Newfoundland.** As of 2010, the fishery had not recovered.

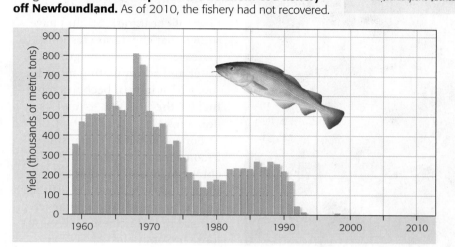

Invasive Species

Like the lionfish featured in the Biology and Society section, organisms that are introduced into non-native habitats can have a devastating effect on the ecosystem. An **invasive species** is a non-native species that has spread far beyond the original point of introduction and causes environmental or economic damage by colonizing and dominating suitable habitats. In the United States alone, there are hundreds of invasive species, including plants, mammals, birds, fishes, arthropods, and molluscs. Worldwide, there are thousands more. Regardless of where you live, an invasive plant or animal is probably living nearby. Invasive species are a leading cause of local extinctions. And the economic costs of invasive species are enormous—an estimated $137 billion a year in the United States.

Not every organism that is introduced to a new habitat is successful, and not every species that survives in its new habitat becomes invasive. There is no single explanation for why any non-native species turns into a damaging pest, but invasive species typically exhibit an opportunistic life history pattern. A female lionfish, for example, is sexually mature at a year old and can produce 2 million eggs per year.

The life history traits of cheatgrass (*Bromus tectorum*, **Figure 19.14**), an invasive plant of the arid western United States, have enabled its spectacular success as well. Its seeds were accidentally carried into the United States with grain from Asia and then spread by livestock. Currently, cheatgrass covers more than 60 million acres of rangeland that was formerly dominated by native grasses and sagebrush, and it claims an estimated 4,000 more acres every day. Cheatgrass seeds sprout during fall rains, and the roots continue to grow underground through the winter. Already established when the warm spring weather arrives, dense clumps of cheatgrass deprive native species or crops of soil moisture and mineral nutrients. It also produces seeds earlier and in greater abundance than its competitors. After

▼ **Figure 19.14** **Cheatgrass, an invasive plant.**

cheatgrass seeds mature in early summer, the plants become extremely dry and flammable, creating abundant fuel that is easily ignited by lightning or a stray spark. Cheatgrass fires are more intense and occur much more frequently than the fires that native plants have evolved to tolerate. After a few fire cycles, the native plants are gone, robbing more than 150 species of birds and mammals of the food and shelter they derive from sagebrush. Global climate change is also hastening the transition of rangeland into fields of cheatgrass. Studies have shown that cheatgrass responds to increased CO_2 levels by growing faster and accumulating more tissue, which in turn becomes more fuel for the fires that extend its domain.

▼ **Figure 19.15 A Burmese python.** This 9-foot-long snake was captured in Florida after devouring a pet cat.

How did Burmese pythons invade the Florida Everglades? Will they spread to the rest of the country?

For a non-native organism to become invasive, the biotic and abiotic factors of the new environment must be compatible with the organism's needs and tolerances. For example, Burmese pythons set loose in South Florida—either accidently released by damaging storms or deliberately freed by disenchanted pet owners—found a hot, humid climate similar to their native area. Prey such as birds, mammals, reptiles, and amphibians are readily available, especially in the Everglades. As a result, South Florida is now home to a burgeoning population of the giant reptiles **(Figure 19.15)**. Burmese pythons released in a less favorable environment might survive for a short time, but would not be able to establish a population. ☑

☑ **CHECKPOINT**

What distinguishes invasive species from organisms that are introduced to non-native habitats but do not become invasive?

Answer: Invasive species spread far from where they are introduced, and they cause environmental or economic damage.

Biological Control of Pests

The absence of biotic factors such as pathogens, predators, or herbivores that suppress population growth rate by increasing mortality may also contribute to the success of invasive species. Accordingly, efforts to eliminate or control these troublesome organisms often focus on **biological control**, the intentional release of a natural enemy to attack a pest population. Agricultural researchers have long been interested in identifying potential biological agents to control insects, weeds, and other organisms that reduce crop yield.

Biological control has been effective in numerous instances, especially with invasive insects and plants. In one classic success story, beetles were brought in to combat St. John's wort, a perennial (long-lived) European weed that invaded the western United States. By the 1940s, St. John's wort (also known as Klamath weed) had overgrown millions of acres of rangeland and pasture, leaving few edible plants for grazing livestock. Researchers imported leaf beetles from the plant's native region that feed exclusively on St. John's wort. The shiny, pea-sized insects reduced the weed to less than 5 percent of its former abundance, restoring the land's value to ranchers.

One potential pitfall of biological control is the danger that an imported control agent may be as invasive as its target. One cautionary tale comes from introducing the mongoose **(Figure 19.16)** to control rats. Rats that originated in India and northern Asia were accidentally transported around the world and became invasive in many places. For sugarcane growers, rat infestation meant massive crop damage. Cane planters imported the small Indian mongoose, a fierce little carnivore, to deal with the problem. In time, mongooses were introduced to dozens of natural habitats, including all of the largest Caribbean and Hawaiian islands—and became invasive themselves. Mongooses are not picky eaters, and they have voracious appetites. On island after island, populations of reptiles, amphibians, and ground-nesting birds have declined or vanished as mongoose populations have grown and spread. They also prey on domestic poultry and ruin crops, costing millions of dollars a year. Clearly, rigorous research is needed to assess the safety and efficacy of potential biological control agents.

◄ **Figure 19.16 A small Indian mongoose eating a nene (Hawaiian goose), Hawaii's endangered state bird.**

Can Biological Control Defeat Kudzu?

Let's take a brief look at the search for a biological agent to control kudzu, an invasive vine known as "the plant that ate the South" (Figure 19.17). In the 1930s, the U.S. Department of Agriculture distributed plantings of this Asian import to help control erosion along road cuts and irrigation canals. Today, kudzu covers an estimated 31,000 square kilometers (roughly the combined area of Maryland and Delaware). With its formidable growth rate of up to a foot per day, kudzu climbs over forest trees and blankets the ground in dense greenery. The shoots die back in winter but quickly regenerate from the roots in the spring. Cold winters have limited its acquisition of new territory—the roots don't survive being frozen. However, as global climate change brings warmer winters, kudzu is advancing farther north.

Unlike many invasive species, kudzu does have natural enemies in the United States, but it easily outgrows the damage they inflict. Researchers are investigating the possibility that one of these native pathogens or insects could be manipulated to provide effective control. Several possibilities have already been tested and discarded. For example, experiments showed that larvae of a species of moth have a prodigious appetite for kudzu. Further investigation, however, proved that the larvae actually preferred soybeans—an important crop species closely related to kudzu. At present, a fungal pathogen called *Myrothecium verrucaria* appears to be a promising candidate.

Researchers chose to test *M. verrucaria* because of **observations** that it causes severe disease in other weeds belonging to the same family as kudzu. Preliminary tests in a greenhouse, in controlled environment chambers, and in small outdoor plantings established that *M. verrucaria* kills kudzu when a high enough concentration of *M. verrucaria* spores is sprayed on the plants along with a "wetting agent" (a soap-like substance that reduces the surface tension of water). These findings led them to ask the **question**, Will *M. verrucaria* treatment work on an established stand of kudzu in a natural setting? Their **hypothesis** was that the *M. verrucaria* treatment that was most effective in the small outdoor plantings would also be most effective in a natural setting. Their **prediction** was that the greatest kudzu mortality would result from the treatment that sprayed the highest concentration of spores in combination with a wetting agent. The **results** of this field experiment, which are shown in **Figure 19.18**, support the hypothesis. However, these experiments are only the initial steps toward biological control of kudzu. A great deal of research is needed to ensure that the method is safe, effective, and practical.

▼ **Figure 19.17** **Kudzu (*Pueraria lobata*).** Unseen in this photo are the plants that have died for lack of sunlight beneath the large kudzu leaves.

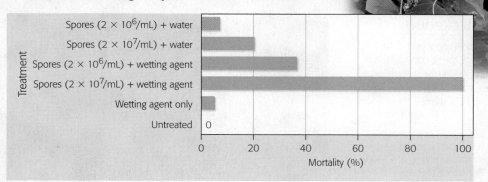

▼ **Figure 19.18** **Biological control of a natural infestation of kudzu with the fungus *Myrothecium verrucaria*.**

Treatment:
- Spores (2×10^6/mL) + water
- Spores (2×10^7/mL) + water
- Spores (2×10^6/mL) + wetting agent
- Spores (2×10^7/mL) + wetting agent
- Wetting agent only
- Untreated — 0

Mortality (%): 0, 20, 40, 60, 80, 100

Integrated Pest Management

In contrast to enterprises such as fisheries, which harvest resources from natural ecosystems, agricultural operations create their own highly managed ecosystems. A typical crop population consists of genetically similar individuals (a monoculture) planted in close proximity to each other—a banquet laid out for the many plant-eating animals and pathogenic bacteria, viruses, and fungi in the community. The tilled, fertile ground nurtures weeds as well as crops. Thus, farmers wage an eternal war against pests that compete with their crop for soil minerals, water, and light; that siphon nutrients from the growing plants; or that consume their leaves, roots, fruits, or seeds. At home, you may be engaged in combat against pests on a smaller scale as you attempt to eradicate the weeds, insects, fungi, and bacteria that attack your lawn and garden or the mosquitoes that make your summer evenings miserable.

Like invasive species, most crop pests have an opportunistic life history pattern that enables them to rapidly take advantage of a favorable habitat. The history of agriculture abounds with examples of devastating pest outbreaks. For example, the boll weevil (Figure 19.19) is an insect that feeds on cotton plants both as larvae and as adults. Its unstoppable spread across the southern United States in the early 1900s severely damaged local economies and had a lasting impact on the region. The folklore of the invasion includes the song "The Boll Weevil Blues," which has been recorded by many artists, including the White Stripes. Fungi (Figure 19.20), bacteria, nematodes, and other plant-eating insects can cause massive damage as well.

When synthetic herbicides and insecticides such as DDT were developed in the 1940s, they quickly became the method of choice in agriculture. However, chemical solutions to pest problems bring numerous problems of their own. These chemicals are pollutants that can be carried great distances by air or water currents. In addition, natural selection may result in populations that are not affected by a pesticide (see Figure 13.15). Furthermore, most insecticides kill both the pest and their natural predators. Because prey species often have a higher reproductive rate than predators, pest populations rapidly rebound before their predators can reproduce. There may be other unintended damage as well, such as killing pollinators that are essential for both agricultural and natural ecosystems.

Integrated pest management (IPM) uses a combination of biological, chemical, and cultural methods for sustainable control of agricultural pests. Researchers are also investigating IPM approaches to invasive species. IPM relies on knowledge of the population ecology of the pest and its associated predators and parasites, as well as plant growth dynamics. In contrast to traditional methods of pest control, IPM advocates tolerating a low level of pests rather than attempting total eradication. Thus, many pest control measures are aimed at lowering the habitat's carrying capacity for the pest population by using pest-resistant varieties and mixed-species plantings and rotating crops to deprive the pest of a dependable food source. Biological control is also used when possible. Pesticides are applied when necessary, but adherence to the principles of IPM prevents the overuse of chemicals. ☑

▼ Figure 19.20 **Tomatoes stricken by blight fungus.**

▼ Figure 19.19 **A boll weevil on a damaged boll (seed pod) of a cotton plant.**

☑ **CHECKPOINT**

Why is integrated pest management considered a more sustainable method of pest control than the use of chemicals alone?

Answer: Use of pesticides may result in resistant pest populations, which makes the pesticides less effective. Also, pesticide use is unsustainable in the long run because of problems with pollution.

Human Population Growth

The History of Human Population Growth

Now that we have examined the regulation of population growth in other organisms, what about our own species? Let's begin by looking at the history of the human population and then consider some current and future trends in population growth.

In the few seconds it takes you to read this sentence, approximately 19 babies will be born somewhere in the world and 8 people will die. An imbalance between births and deaths is the cause of population growth (or decline), and as the line graph in **Figure 19.21** shows, the human population is expected to continue increasing for at least the next several decades. The bar graph in Figure 19.21 tells a different part of the story. The number of people added to the population each year has been declining since the 1980s. How do we explain these patterns of human population growth?

Is human population growth speeding up or slowing down?

Let's begin with the rise in world population from approximately 480 million people in 1500 to the current population of more than 6.9 billion. In the exponential population growth model introduced earlier in this chapter, we assumed that the *rate* of population growth was constant—births and deaths were roughly equal. As a result, population growth depended only on the size of the existing population. Throughout most of human history, this assumption held true. Although parents had many children, mortality was also high. As a result, human population growth was initially very slow. (If we

extended the *x*-axis of Figure 19.21 back in time to year 1, when the population was roughly 300 million, the line would be almost flat for 1,500 years.) The 1 billion mark was not reached until the early 1800s. As economic development in Europe and the United States led to advances in nutrition and sanitation, and later, medical care, people took control of their population's growth rate. At first, the death rate decreased while the birth rate remained the same. The net rate of increase rose, and population growth began to pick up steam by the beginning of the 1900s. By midcentury, improvements in nutrition, sanitation, and health care had spread to the developing world, spurring growth at a breakneck pace as birth rates far outstripped death rates.

As the world population skyrocketed from 2 billion in 1927 to 3 billion just 33 years later, some scientists became alarmed. They feared that Earth's carrying capacity would be reached and that density-dependent factors would maintain that population size through human suffering and death. But the overall growth rate peaked in 1962. In the more developed nations, advanced medical care continued to improve survivorship, but effective contraceptives held down the birth rate. As a result, the overall growth rate of the world's population began a downward trend as the difference between birth rate and death rate decreased.

Because economic development has occurred at different times in different regions, worldwide population growth rates reflect a mosaic of the changes occurring in different countries. In the most developed nations, the overall growth rates are near zero **(Table 19.3)**. In the developing world, on the other hand, death rates have dropped, but high birth rates persist. As a result, these populations are growing rapidly. Of the more than 75 million people added to the world each year, over 72 million are in developing nations. ☑

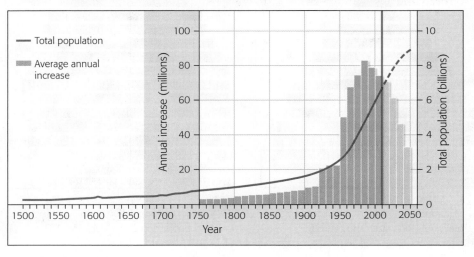

▼ **Figure 19.21** **Five centuries of human population growth, projected to 2050.**

Table 19.3	Population Trends in 2010		
Population	**Birth Rate per 1,000**	**Death Rate per 1,000**	**Growth Rate (%)**
World	19.3	8.2	1.1
More developed countries	11.0	10.3	0.3
Less developed countries	21.1	7.7	1.3

Age Structures

Age structures, which were introduced at the beginning of this chapter, are helpful for predicting a population's future growth. **Figure 19.22** shows the estimated and projected age structures of Mexico's population in 1985, 2010, and 2035. In these diagrams, the area to the left of each vertical line represents the number of males in each age-group; females are represented on the right side of the line. The three different colors represent the portion of the population in their prereproductive years (0–14), prime reproductive years (15–44), and postreproductive years (45 and older). Within each of these broader groups, each horizontal bar represents the population in a 5-year age-group.

In 1985, each age-group was larger than the one above it, indicating a high birth rate. The pyramidal shape of this age structure is typical of a population that is growing rapidly. In 2010, the population's growth rate was lower; notice that the youngest (bottommost) three age-groups are roughly the same size. However, the population continues to be affected by its earlier expansion. This situation, which results from the increased proportion of women of childbearing age in the population, is known as **population momentum**. Girls 0–14 years old in the 1985 age structure (outlined in pink) are in their reproductive prime in 2010, and girls who were 0–14 years old in 2010 (outlined in blue) will carry the legacy of rapid growth forward to 2035. Putting the brakes on a rapidly expanding population is like

stopping a freight train; the actual event takes place long after the decision to do it was made. Even when fertility is reduced to replacement rate (an average of two children per female), the total population size will continue to increase for several decades. Thus, the percentage of individuals under the age of 15 gives a rough idea of future growth. In the less developed countries, about 29% of the population is in this age-group. In contrast, roughly 16% of the population of more developed nations is under the age of 15. Population momentum also explains why the total population size in Figure 19.21 continues to increase even though fewer people are added to the population each year.

Age structure diagrams may also indicate social conditions. For instance, an expanding population has an increasing need for schools, employment, and infrastructure. A large elderly population requires that extensive resources be allotted to health care. Let's look at trends in the age structure of the United States from 1985 to 2035 **(Figure 19.23)**. The noticeable bulge in the 1985 population (yellow screen) corresponds to the "baby boom" that lasted for about two decades after World War II ended in 1945. The large number of children swelled school enrollments, prompting construction of new schools and creating a demand for teachers. On the other hand, graduates who were born near the end of the boom faced stiff competition for jobs. Because they make up such a large segment of the population, boomers have had an enormous influence on social, economic, and political trends. They also

▼ Figure 19.22 **Population momentum in Mexico.**

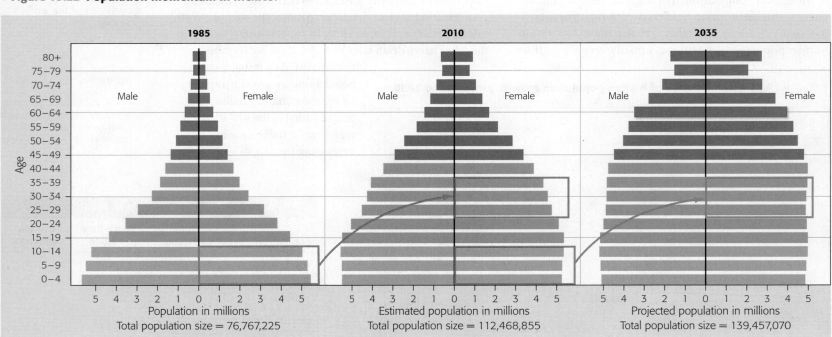

▼ **Figure 19.23** **Age structures for the United States in 1985, 2010 (estimated) and 2035 (projected).**

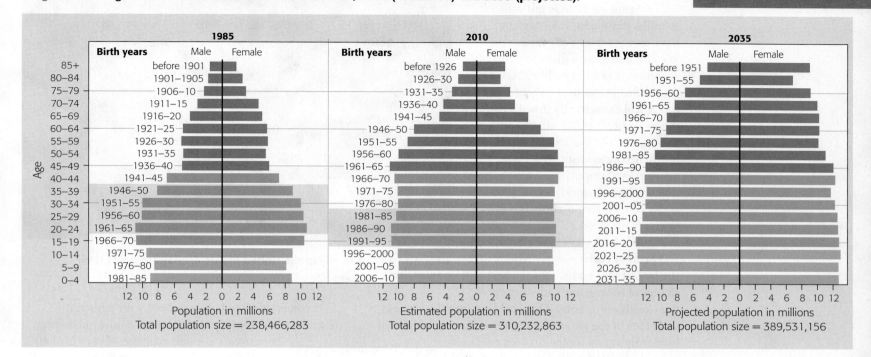

produced a boomlet of their own, seen in the 0–4 age-group in 1985 and the bump (pink screen) in the 2010 age structure.

Where are the baby boomers now? The leading edge has reached retirement age, which will place pressure on programs such as Medicare and Social Security. In 2010, 60% of the U.S. population was between 20 and 64, the ages most likely to be in the workforce, and 13% was over 65. In 2035, the percentages are projected to be 54 and 20, respectively. In part, the increase in the elderly population results from people living longer. The percentage of the population over 80, which was 2.5% in 1985, is projected to rise to nearly 6% in 2035 and 7.4%—more than 32 million people—in 2050. ☑

Our Ecological Footprint

Figure 19.21 shows that the world's population is growing exponentially, but at a slower rate than it did in the last century. The rate of increase, as well as population momentum, predicts that the populations of most developing nations will continue to increase for the foreseeable future. The U.S. Census Bureau projects a global population of 8 billion by 2025 and 9.5 billion by the middle of the century. But these numbers are only part of the story. Trillions of bacteria can live in a petri dish *if* they have sufficient resources. What is Earth's

carrying capacity for the human population? Are there sufficient resources to sustain 8 or 9 billion people?

To accommodate all the people expected to live on our planet in the coming decades and improve the diets of those who are currently malnourished or undernourished, world food production must increase dramatically. But agricultural lands are already under pressure. Overgrazing by the world's growing herds of livestock is turning vast areas of grassland into desert. Water use has risen sixfold over the past 70 years, causing rivers to run dry, water for irrigation to be depleted, and levels of groundwater to drop. Changes in precipitation patterns due to global warming are already causing food shortages in some regions of the world.

An **ecological footprint** is one approach to understanding resource availability and usage. The footprint is an estimate of the amount of land and water required to provide the raw materials an individual or a nation consumes, including food, fuel, fresh water, housing, and waste disposal. When the total area of ecologically productive land and water on Earth is divided by the global population, we each have a share of about 2.1 global hectares (1 ha = 2.47 acres; a global hectare is a hectare with world-average ability to produce resources and absorb wastes). In 2006, the average ecological footprint for the world's population was 2.6 gha. We have already overshot the planet's capacity to sustain us.

The ecological footprint of the United States (9 gha per person) is almost twice what its own land and resources can support (4.4 gha per person); in other words, it has an enormous ecological deficit. Looking at **Figure 19.24**, it is not difficult to understand why—Americans have an abundance of possessions. We also consume a disproportionate amount of food and fuel. Overall, the United States uses 23% of Earth's ecological capacity. By this measure, the ecological impact of affluent nations such as the United States is potentially as damaging as the unrestrained population growth in the developing world. So the problem is not just overpopulation, but also overconsumption.

Figure 19.25 shows the ecological footprint of each country. Notice that the largest footprints—the darkest shades of orange and red—belong to the wealthiest nations. The world's richest countries, with 15% of the global population, account for 36% of humanity's total footprint. Some researchers estimate that providing everyone with the same standard of living enjoyed in the United States would require the resources of three additional planet Earths.

▲ **Figure 19.24 A family in the United States displays some of their possessions.**

Are we living beyond our ecological means?

If you would like to learn about your personal resource consumption, a number of online quizzes can provide a rough estimate of your ecological footprint. Like carbon footprint calculators (described in Chapter 18), these tools are useful for learning how to reduce your environmental impact. ☑

▼ **Figure 19.25 A world map color-coded by ecological footprint.**

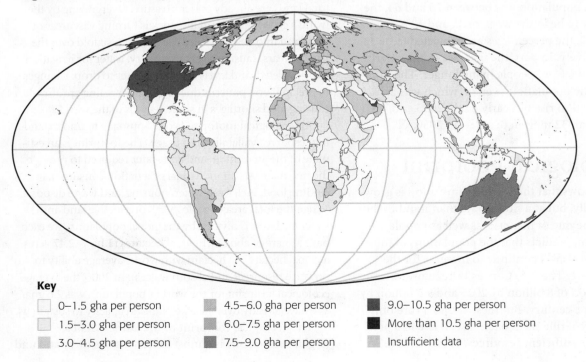

Key

☐ 0–1.5 gha per person	4.5–6.0 gha per person	9.0–10.5 gha per person
1.5–3.0 gha per person	6.0–7.5 gha per person	More than 10.5 gha per person
3.0–4.5 gha per person	7.5–9.0 gha per person	Insufficient data

Biological Invasions EVOLUTION CONNECTION

Humans as an Invasive Species

The magnificent pronghorn antelope (*Antilocapra americana*) is the descendant of ancestors that roamed the open plains and shrub deserts of North America millions of years ago (Figure 19.26). With strides that cover 6 m (20 feet) or more at its top speed of 97 km/h (60 mph), it is easily the fastest mammal on the continent. The pronghorn's speed is more than a match for its major predator, the wolf, which typically takes adults that have been weakened by age or illness. What selection pressure promoted such extravagant speed? Ecologists hypothesize that the pronghorn's ancestors were running from the now-extinct American cheetah, a fleet-footed predator that bore some similarities to the more familiar African cheetah.

Cheetahs were not the only danger in the pronghorn's environment. During the Pleistocene epoch, which lasted from 1.8 million to 10,000 years ago, North America was also home to an intimidating list of other predators: lions, jaguars, saber-toothed cats with canines up to 7 inches long, and towering short-faced bears, which stood 11 feet tall and weighed ¾ of a ton. There were plenty of potential prey for these fearsome predators, including massive ground sloths, bison with horns that spread 10 feet, elephant-like mammoths, a variety of horses and camels, and several species of pronghorns.

Of all these species of large mammals, only *Antilocapra americana* remained at the end of the Pleistocene. The others went extinct during a relatively brief period of time that coincided with the spread of humans throughout North America. Although the cause of the extinctions has been hotly disputed, many scientists think that the human invasion, combined with climate change at the end of the last ice age, was responsible. Taken together, changes in the biotic and abiotic environments happened too rapidly for an evolutionary response by these large mammals.

The role of humans in the Pleistocene extinctions was merely a preview of things to come. The human population continues to increase, colonizing almost every corner of the globe. Like other invasive species, we change the environment of the other organisms that share our habitats. As the scope and speed of human-induced environmental changes increase, extinctions are occurring at an accelerating pace. This rapid loss of biodiversity will be our unifying thread in the next chapter.

▼ Figure 19.26 **A pronghorn antelope racing across the North American plains.**

Chapter Review

Go to **www.masteringbiology.com** for homework assignments, practice quizzes, Pearson eText, and more.

SUMMARY OF KEY CONCEPTS

An Overview of Population Ecology

A population consists of members of a species living in the same place at the same time. Population ecology focuses on the factors that influence a population's size, growth rate, density, and structure.

Population Density

Population density, the number of individuals of a species per unit area or volume, can be estimated by a variety of sampling techniques.

Population Age Structure

A graph showing the distribution of individuals in different age-groups often provides useful information about the population.

Life Tables and Survivorship Curves

A population's pattern of mortality is a key feature of life history. A life table tracks survivorship and mortality in a population. Survivorship curves can be classified into three general types, depending on the rate of mortality over the entire life span.

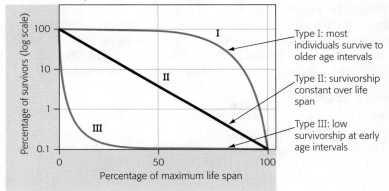

Type I: most individuals survive to older age intervals

Type II: survivorship constant over life span

Type III: low survivorship at early age intervals

Life History Traits as Evolutionary Adaptations

Life history traits are shaped by evolutionary adaptation; they may vary within a species and may change as the environmental context changes. Most populations probably fall between the extreme opportunistic life histories (reach sexual maturity rapidly; produce many offspring; little or no parental care) of many insects and the equilibrial life histories (develop slowly and produce few, well-cared-for offspring) of many larger-bodied species.

Population Growth Models

The Exponential Population Growth Model: The Ideal of an Unlimited Environment

Exponential population growth is the accelerating increase that occurs when growth is unlimited. The exponential model predicts that the larger a population becomes, the faster it grows. Exponential growth in nature is generally a short-lived consequence of organisms being introduced to a new or under-exploited environment.

The Logistic Population Growth Model: The Reality of a Limited Environment

Logistic population growth occurs when growth is slowed by limiting factors. The logistic model predicts that a population's growth rate will be small when the population size is either small or large, and highest when the population is at an intermediate level relative to the carrying capacity.

Regulation of Population Growth

Over the long term, most population growth is limited by a mixture of density-independent and density-dependent factors. Density-dependent factors intensify as a population increases in density, increasing the death rate, decreasing the birth rate, or both. Density-independent factors affect the same percentage of individuals regardless of population size. Some populations have regular boom-and-bust cycles.

Applications of Population Ecology

Conservation of Endangered Species

Endangered and threatened species are characterized by very small population sizes. One approach to conservation is identifying and attempting to supply the critical combination of habitat factors needed by the population.

Sustainable Resource Management

According to the logistic growth model, a population's highest growth rate occurs when the population size is half the carrying capacity. For some populations, harvesting at this level produces sustainable yields. However, some populations don't meet the assumptions of the logistic model. Thorough scientific knowledge is needed to estimate yields that are truly sustainable.

Invasive Species

Invasive species are non-native organisms that spread far beyond their original point of introduction and cause environmental and economic damage. Typically, invasive species have an opportunistic life history pattern, and many are superior to native species at obtaining resources.

Biological Control of Pests

Biological control, the intentional release of a natural enemy to attack a pest population, is sometimes effective against invasive species. However, prospective control agents can themselves become invasive. Researchers are currently investigating whether a fungal pathogen could be used to control kudzu, an invasive plant.

Integrated Pest Management

Crop scientists have developed integrated pest management (IPM) strategies, combinations of biological, chemical, and cultural methods to deal with agricultural pests. IPM may prove useful at combating invasive species, too.

Human Population Growth

The History of Human Population Growth

The human population grew rapidly during the 1900s and currently stands at more than 6.9 billion. A shift from high birth and death rates to low birth and death rates has lowered the rate of growth in more developed countries. In developing nations, death rates have dropped, but birth rates are still high.

Age Structures

The age structure of a population affects its future growth. The wide base of the age structure of Mexico in 1985—the 0–14 age-group—predicts continued population growth in the next generation. Population momentum is the continued growth that occurs (despite fertility having been reduced to replacement rate) as a result of girls in the 0–14 age-group of a previously expanding population reaching their childbearing years. Age structures may also indicate social and economic trends, as in the age structure on the right below.

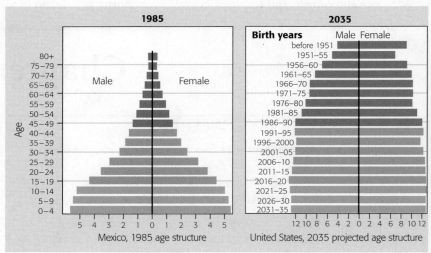

Our Ecological Footprint

The ecological footprint represents the amount of land needed to support an individual's or nation's resource needs. The carrying capacity of the world may already be smaller than the population's ecological footprint. There is a huge disparity between resource consumption in more developed and less developed nations.

SELF-QUIZ

1. What two values would you need to know to figure out the human population density of your community?

2. If members of a species produce a large number of offspring but provide minimal parental care, then a Type _____ survivorship curve is expected. In contrast, if members of a species produce few offspring and provide them with long-standing care, then a Type _____ survivorship curve is expected.

3. Label the following characteristics as typical of opportunistic (O) or equilibrial (E) life history patterns:
   _____ produce many offspring per reproductive episode
   _____ typical of habitats that have unpredictable climate or frequent disturbances
   _____ life span typically long
   _____ maturation time short
   _____ often provide extensive care to offspring

4. Use this graph of the idealized exponential and logistic growth curves to complete the following.

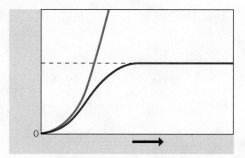

   a. Label the axes and curves on the graph.
   b. What does the dotted line represent?
   c. For each curve, indicate and explain where population growth is the most rapid.
   d. Which of these curves better represents global human population growth?

5. Which of the following describes the effects of a density-dependent limiting factor?
   a. A forest fire kills all the pine trees in a patch of forest.
   b. Early rainfall triggers the explosion of a locust population.
   c. Drought decimates a wheat crop.
   d. Rabbits multiply, and their food supply begins to dwindle.

6. Which life history pattern is typical of invasive species?

7. Skyrocketing growth of the human population since the beginning of the Industrial Revolution appears to be mainly a result of
   a. migration to thinly settled regions of the globe.
   b. better nutrition boosting the birth rate.
   c. a drop in the death rate due to better nutrition and health care.
   d. the concentration of humans in cities.

8. How does the age structure of the human population explain the current surplus in the Social Security fund?

9. According to the ecological footprint study produced in 2006,
   a. the carrying capacity of the world is 10 billion.
   b. the carrying capacity of the world would increase if all people ate more meat.
   c. the current demand on global resources by more developed countries is less than the resources available in those countries.
   d. the United States has a larger ecological footprint than its own resources can provide.
   e. nations with the largest ecological footprints have the fastest population growth rates.

Answers to these questions can be found in Appendix: Self-Quiz Answers.

THE PROCESS OF SCIENCE

10. If researchers establish that *Myrothecium verrucaria* is an effective biological control agent against kudzu, they must then demonstrate that the pathogen will not harm desirable species such as soybeans (a close relative of kudzu). Describe experiments that could fulfill this purpose.

11. Propose a hypothesis to explain why North American mammals such as cheetahs, short-faced bears, and ground sloths did not survive the changes in their environment through evolutionary adaptation.

BIOLOGY AND SOCIETY

12. The tiger, mountain gorilla, spotted owl, giant panda, snow leopard, and grizzly bear are all endangered by human encroachment on their environments. Another thing these animals have in common is that they all have equilibrial life history traits. Why might they be more easily endangered than animals with opportunistic life history traits? What general type of survivorship curve would you expect these species to exhibit? Explain your answer.

13. Many people regard the rapid population growth of less developed countries as our most serious environmental problem. Others think that resource consumption in more developed countries is actually a greater threat to the environment. What kinds of problems result from these two issues? Which do you think is the greater environmental threat?

20 Communities and Ecosystems

Coastal marsh.
Wetlands in the Atchafalaya National Wildlife Refuge in Louisiana provide valuable ecosystem services.

Biodiversity in Decline BIOLOGY AND SOCIETY

Why Biodiversity Matters

As the human population has expanded, hundreds of species have become extinct and thousands more are threatened with extinction. These changes represent a loss in biological diversity, or *biodiversity*. Biodiversity loss goes hand in hand with the disappearance of natural ecosystems. Only about a quarter of Earth's land surfaces remain untouched by human alterations. We see the evidence of our impact on natural ecosystems every day. We live and work in altered landscapes. And though we may be less aware of it, our impact on the oceans is also extensive.

What is the value of biodiversity? Most people appreciate the direct benefits provided by certain ecosystems. For example, you probably know that we use resources—such as water, wood, and fish—that come from natural or near-natural ecosystems. These resources have economic value, as the massive 2010 oil spill in the Gulf of Mexico dramatically demonstrated. Billions of dollars were lost by fishing, recreation, and other industries as a result of the disaster. But human well-being also depends on less obvious services that healthy ecosystems provide. The coastal wetlands affected by the Gulf oil spill normally act as a buffer against hurricanes, reduce the impact of flooding, and filter pollutants. The wetlands also furnish nesting sites for birds and marine turtles and breeding areas and nurseries for a wide variety of fish and shellfish. Natural ecosystems provide other services as well—such as recycling nutrients, preventing erosion and mudslides, controlling agricultural pests, and pollinating crops. Some scientists have attempted to assign an economic value to these benefits. They arrived at an average annual value of ecosystem services of $33 trillion, almost twice the global gross national product for the year they published their results. Although rough, these estimates make the important point that we cannot afford to take biodiversity for granted.

In this chapter, we'll examine the interactions among organisms and how those relationships determine the features of communities. On a larger scale, we'll explore the dynamics of ecosystems. Finally, we'll consider how scientists are working to save biodiversity. And throughout the chapter, you'll learn how an understanding of ecology can help us manage Earth's resources wisely.

The Loss of Biodiversity

As mentioned previously, **biodiversity** is short for biological diversity, the variety of living things that you learned about in Unit 3. It includes genetic diversity, species diversity, and ecosystem diversity. Thus, the loss of biodiversity encompasses more than just the fate of individual species.

Genetic Diversity

When species are lost, so are their unique genes. The genetic diversity within a population is the raw material that makes microevolution and adaptation to the environment possible. If local populations are lost, then the number of individuals in the species declines, and so do the genetic resources for that species. Severe reduction in genetic variation threatens the survival of a species. The enormous genetic diversity of all the organisms on Earth has great potential benefit for people, too. Many researchers and biotechnology leaders are enthusiastic about the potential that genetic "bioprospecting" holds for future development of new medicines, industrial chemicals, and other products. Bioprospecting may also hold the key to the world's food supply. For example, researchers are currently scrambling to stop the spread of a deadly new strain of wheat stem rust, a fungal pathogen that has devastated harvests in eastern Africa and central Asia. At least 75% of the wheat varieties planted worldwide are susceptible to this pathogen, but researchers hope to find a resistance gene in the wild relatives of wheat **(Figure 20.1)**. ☑

Species Diversity

In view of the damage we are doing to the biosphere, ecologists believe that we are pushing species toward extinction at an alarming rate. The present rate of species loss may be as much as 100 times higher than at any time in the past 100,000 years. Some researchers estimate that at the current rate of destruction, over half of all currently living plant and animal species will be gone by the end of this century. **Figure 20.2** shows two recent victims. Here are some examples of where things stand:

- Approximately 12% of the 10,027 known bird species and 21% of the 5,490 known mammalian species in the world are threatened with extinction.

- More than 20% of the known freshwater fishes in the world have either become extinct during human history or are seriously threatened.

- Roughly 30% of all known amphibian species are either near extinction or endangered.

- Of the approximately 20,000 known plant species in the United States, 200 species have become extinct since dependable records have been kept, and 790 species are endangered or threatened.

▼ Figure 20.1 **Einkorn wheat, one of the wild relatives of modern cultivated varieties.**

☑ **CHECKPOINT**

How does the loss of genetic diversity endanger a population?

Answer: A population with decreased genetic diversity has less ability to evolve in response to environmental change.

▼ Figure 20.2 **Recent additions to the list of human-caused extinctions.**

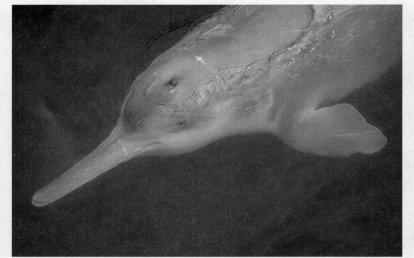

A Chinese river dolphin. Last sighted in 2002, this former resident of the Yangtze River is presumed extinct after a thorough 2006 search failed to find any.

Golden toads. These small frogs, unique to high-altitude Costa Rican cloud forests, have not been seen since 1989. The males shown here are gathered near a puddle to wait for mates.

Ecosystem Diversity

Ecosystem diversity is the third component of biological diversity. Recall that an ecosystem includes both the organisms and the abiotic factors in a particular area. Because of the network of interactions among populations of different species within an ecosystem, the loss of one species can have a negative effect on the entire ecosystem. The disappearance of natural ecosystems results in the loss of **ecosystem services**, functions performed by an ecosystem that directly or indirectly benefit people. These vital services include air and water purification, climate regulation, and erosion control. For example, forests absorb and store carbon from the atmosphere, a service that vanishes when forests are destroyed or degraded (see Figure 18.39). Coral reefs not only are rich in species diversity **(Figure 20.3)** but also provide a wealth of benefits to people, including food, storm protection, and recreation. An estimated 20% of the world's coral reefs have already been destroyed by human activities. A study published in 2011 found that 75% of the remaining reefs are threatened, a percentage expected to top 90% by 2030 if current abuses continue. ☑

▼ **Figure 20.3 A coral reef, a colorful display of biodiversity.**

Causes of Declining Biodiversity

Ecologists have identified four main factors responsible for the loss of biodiversity: habitat destruction and fragmentation, invasive species, overexploitation, and pollution. The ever-expanding size and dominance of the human population are at the root of all four factors. In addition, scientists expect global climate change to become a leading cause of extinctions in the near future (see Chapter 18).

Habitat Destruction

The massive destruction and fragmentation of habitats caused by agriculture, urban development, forestry, and mining pose the single greatest threat to biodiversity **(Figure 20.4)**. According to the International Union for the Conservation of Nature, which compiles information on the conservation status of species worldwide, habitat destruction affects more than 85% of all birds, mammals, and amphibians that are threatened with extinction. We'll take a closer look at the consequences of habitat fragmentation later in this chapter.

Invasive Species

Ranking second behind habitat loss as a cause of biodiversity loss is the introduction of invasive species. Uncontrolled population growth of human-introduced species to non-native habitats has caused havoc when the introduced species have competed with, preyed on, or parasitized native species (see Chapter 19). The lack of interactions with other species that could keep the newcomers in check is often a key factor in a non-native species becoming invasive.

☑ CHECKPOINT

When ecosystems are destroyed, the services they provide are lost. What are some examples of ecosystem services?

Answer: Possible answers are mentioned in the Biology and Society section as on this page. Services include air and water purification; climate regulation; erosion control; recreation; and resources used by people, such as wood, water, and food.

▼ **Figure 20.4 Habitat destruction.** In a controversial method known as mountaintop removal, mining companies blast the tops off of mountains and then scoop out coal. The earth removed from the mountain is dumped into a neighboring valley.

Overexploitation

Unsustainable marine fisheries (see Figure 19.13) demonstrate how people can overexploit wildlife by harvesting at rates that exceed the ability of populations to rebound. Among the many terrestrial species whose numbers have been drastically reduced by excessive commercial harvesting, poaching, or sport hunting are the American bison, Galápagos tortoises, and tigers. Overharvesting also threatens some plants, including rare trees such as mahogany and rosewood that produce valuable wood.

Pollution

Air and water pollution **(Figure 20.5)** is a contributing factor in declining populations of hundreds of species worldwide. The global water cycle can transport pollutants from terrestrial to aquatic ecosystems hundreds of miles away. Pollutants that are emitted into the atmosphere may be carried aloft for thousands of miles before falling to earth in the form of acid precipitation. ☑

☑ **CHECKPOINT**

What are the four main causes of declining biodiversity?

Answer: habitat destruction, invasive species, overexploitation, and pollution

▲ **Figure 20.5 A pelican stuck in oil from the 2010 Gulf of Mexico disaster.** Wildlife is often the most visible casualty of pollution, but the impact extends throughout the ecosystem.

Community Ecology

On your next walk through a field or woodland, or even across campus or your own backyard, observe the variety of species present. You may see birds in trees, butterflies on flowers, dandelions in the grass of a lawn, or lizards darting for cover as you approach. Each of these organisms interacts with other organisms as it goes about looking for food, nesting sites, living space, or shelter. An organism's biotic environment includes not just individuals from its own population, but also populations of other species living in the same area. Ecologists call such an assemblage of species living close enough together for potential interaction a **community**. In **Figure 20.6**, the lion, the zebra, the hyena, the vultures, the plants, and the unseen microbes are all members of an ecological community in Kenya.

Interspecific Interactions

Our study of communities begins with **interspecific interactions**—that is, interactions between species. Interspecific interactions can be classified according to the effect on the populations concerned, which may be helpful (**+**) or harmful (**−**). In some cases, two populations in a community vie for a resource such as food or space. The effect of this interaction is generally negative for both species (**−/−**)—neither species has access to the full range of resources offered by the habitat. On the other hand, some interspecific interactions benefit both parties (**+/+**). For example, the interactions between flowers and their pollinators are mutually beneficial. In a third type of interspecific interaction, one species exploits another species as a source of food. The effect of this interaction is clearly beneficial to one population and harmful to the other (**+/−**). In the next several pages, you will learn more about these interspecific interactions and how they affect communities. We will also look at some examples of interspecific interactions as powerful agents of natural selection.

▼ **Figure 20.6 Diverse species interacting in a Kenyan savanna community.**

Interspecific Competition (−/−)

In the logistic model of population growth (see Figure 19.6), increasing population density reduces the amount of resources available for each individual. This intraspecific (within-species) competition for limited resources ultimately limits population growth. In **interspecific competition** (between-species competition), the population growth of a species may be limited by the population densities of competing species as well as by the density of its own population.

What determines whether populations in a community compete with each other? Each species has an **ecological niche**, defined as its total use of the biotic and abiotic resources in its environment. For example, the ecological niche of a small bird called the Virginia's warbler **(Figure 20.7a)** includes its nest sites and nest-building materials, the insects it eats, and climatic conditions such as the amount of precipitation and the temperature and humidity that enable it to survive. In other words, the ecological niche encompasses everything the Virginia's warbler needs for its existence. The ecological niche of the orange-crowned warbler **(Figure 20.7b)** includes some of the same resources used by the Virginia's warbler. Consequently, when these two species inhabit the same area, they are competitors.

Ecologists investigated the effects of interspecific competition between populations of these two birds in a community in central Arizona. When they removed either Virginia's warblers or orange-crowned warblers from the study site, members of the remaining species were significantly more successful in raising their offspring. This study showed that interspecific competition can have a direct, negative effect on reproductive fitness.

If the ecological niches of two species are too similar, they cannot coexist in the same place. Ecologists call this the **competitive exclusion principle**, a concept introduced by Russian ecologist G. F. Gause, who demonstrated this effect with an elegant series of experiments. Gause used two closely related species of protists, *Paramecium caudatum* and *P. aurelia*. First, he established the carrying capacity for each species separately under the conditions used to culture (grow) them in the laboratory **(Figure 20.8**, top graph). Then he cultured the two species in the same habitat. Within two weeks, the *P. caudatum* population had crashed (bottom graph). Gause concluded that the requirements of these two species were so similar that the superior competitor—in this case, *P. aurelia*—deprived *P. caudatum* of essential resources. ☑

▼ **Figure 20.8 Competitive exclusion in laboratory populations of *Paramecium*.**

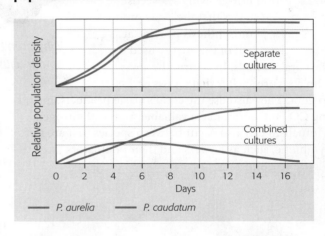

Paramecium aurelia

LM 200×

Paramecium caudatum

LM 200×

▼ **Figure 20.7 Species that use similar resources.**

(a) Virginia's warbler

(b) Orange-crowned warbler

☑ CHECKPOINT

In another experiment, Gause found that *Paramecium caudatum* and *P. bursaria* could coexist in the same habitat, but both populations were smaller than when each species occupied the habitat alone. How would you explain these results?

Answer: Competition between P. caudatum and P. bursaria reduces the resources available to each population—some aspects of their ecological niches are similar. However, neither species outcompetes the other for essential resources.

Mutualism (+/+)

In **mutualism**, both species benefit from an interaction. Some mutualisms occur between symbiotic species—those in which the organisms have a close physical association with each other. For example, in the symbiotic root-fungus associations known as mycorrhizae (see the Biology and Society essay in Chapter 16), the fungus delivers mineral nutrients to the plant and receives organic nutrients in return. Coral reef ecosystems depend on the mutualism between certain species of coral animals and millions of unicellular algae that live in the cells of each coral polyp **(Figure 20.9)**. Reefs are constructed by successive generations of colonial corals that secrete an external calcium carbonate skeleton. The formation of the skeleton must outpace erosion and competition for space from fast-growing seaweeds. The sugars that the algae produce by photosynthesis provide at least half of the energy used by the coral animals. In return, the algae gain a secure shelter that allows access to light. They also use the coral's waste products, including CO_2 and ammonia, a valuable source of nitrogen. Mutualism can also occur between species that are not symbiotic, such as flowers and their pollinators (see Figure 13.28).

▲ **Figure 20.9 Mutualism.** Coral polyps are inhabited by unicellular algae.

▼ **Figure 20.10 Cryptic coloration.** Camouflage conceals the pygmy seahorse from predators.

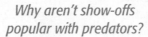

Why aren't show-offs popular with predators?

Predation (+/−)

Predation refers to an interaction in which one species (the predator) kills and eats another (the prey). Because predation has such a negative impact on the reproductive success of the prey, numerous adaptations for predator avoidance have evolved in prey populations through natural selection. For example, some prey species, like the pronghorn antelope, run fast enough to escape their predators (see the Evolution Connection section in Chapter 19). Others, like rabbits, flee into shelters. Still other prey species rely on mechanical defenses, such as the porcupine's sharp quills or the hard shells of clams and oysters.

Adaptive coloration is a type of defense that has evolved in many species of animals. Camouflage, called **cryptic coloration**, makes potential prey difficult to spot against its background **(Figure 20.10)**. **Warning coloration**, bright patterns of yellow, red, or orange in combination with black, often marks animals with effective chemical defenses. Predators learn to associate these color patterns with undesirable consequences, such as a noxious taste or painful sting, and avoid potential prey with similar markings. The vivid colors of the poison dart frog **(Figure 20.11)**, an inhabitant of Costa Rican rain forests, warn of noxious chemicals in the frog's skin.

A prey species may also gain significant protection through mimicry, a "copycat" adaptation in which one species looks like another. For example, the pattern of alternating red, yellow, and black rings of the harmless scarlet king snake resembles the bold color pattern of the venomous eastern coral snake **(Figure 20.12)**. Some insects have combined protective coloration with adaptations of body structures in elaborate disguises. For instance, there are insects that resemble twigs, leaves, and bird droppings. Some

▼ **Figure 20.11 Warning coloration of a poison dart frog.**

▲ **Figure 20.12 Mimicry in snakes.** The color pattern of the nonvenomous scarlet king snake (left) is similar to that of the venomous eastern coral snake (right).

even do a passable imitation of a vertebrate. For example, the colors on the dorsal side of certain caterpillars are an effective camouflage, but when disturbed, the caterpillar flips over to reveal the snakelike eyes of its ventral side **(Figure 20.13)**. Eyespots that resemble vertebrate eyes are common in several groups of moths and butterflies. A flash of these large "eyes" startles would-be predators. In other species, an eyespot may deflect a predator's attack away from vital body parts.

Herbivory (+/−)

Herbivory is the consumption of plant parts or algae by an animal. Although herbivory is not usually fatal to plants, a plant whose body parts have been partially eaten by an animal must expend energy to replace the loss. Consequently, numerous defenses against herbivores have evolved in plants. Spines and thorns are obvious anti-herbivore devices, as anyone who has plucked a rose from a thorny rosebush or brushed against a spiky cactus knows. Chemical toxins are also very common in plants. Like the chemical defenses of

animals, toxins in plants are distasteful, and herbivores learn to avoid them. Among such chemical weapons are the poison strychnine, produced by a tropical vine called *Strychnos toxifera*; morphine, from the opium poppy; nicotine, produced by the tobacco plant; mescaline, from peyote cactus; and tannins, from a variety of plant species. Other defensive compounds that are not toxic to humans but may be distasteful to herbivores are responsible for the familiar flavors of peppermint, cloves, and cinnamon **(Figure 20.14)**. Some plants even produce chemicals that cause abnormal development in insects that eat them. Chemical companies have taken advantage of the poisonous properties of certain plants to produce pesticides. For example, nicotine is used as an insecticide. ☑

▼ **Figure 20.14 Flavorful plants.**

Peppermint. Parts of the peppermint plant yield a pungent oil.

Cloves. The cloves used in cooking are the flower buds of this plant.

▼ **Figure 20.13 An insect mimicking a snake.** When disturbed, this sphinx moth larva flips over (left) and resembles a snake (right).

Cinnamon. Cinnamon comes from the inner bark of this tree.

431

Parasites and Pathogens (+/−)

Both plants and animals may be victimized by parasites or pathogens. These interactions are beneficial to one species (the parasite or pathogen) and harmful to the other, known as the host. A **parasite** lives on or in a **host** from which it obtains nourishment. Pathogens are disease-causing bacteria, viruses, fungi, or protists that can be thought of as microscopic parasites. Invertebrate parasites include flatworms, such as flukes and tapeworms, and a variety of roundworms, which live inside a host organism's body. External parasites, such as ticks, lice, mites, and mosquitoes, attach to their victims temporarily to feed on blood or other body fluids. Plants are also attacked by parasites, including roundworms and aphids, tiny insects that tap into the phloem to suck plant sap (see Figure 19.10). In any parasite population, reproductive success is greatest for individuals that are best at locating and feeding on their hosts. For example,

some aquatic leeches first locate a host by detecting movement in the water and then confirm its identity based on the host's body temperature and chemical cues on its skin.

Non-native pathogens, whose impact can be rapid and dramatic, have provided some opportunities to investigate the effects of pathogens on communities. In one example, ecologists studied the consequences of the epidemic of chestnut blight, a disease caused by a protist. The loss of chestnuts, massive canopy trees that once dominated many forest communities in North America, had a significant impact on community composition and structure. Trees such as oaks and hickories that had formerly competed with chestnuts became more numerous; overall, the diversity of tree species increased. Dead chestnut trees also furnished niches for other organisms, such as insects, cavity-nesting birds, and, eventually, decomposers. ☑

Trophic Structure

Now that we have looked at how populations in a community interact with one another, let's consider the community as a whole. The feeding relationships among the various species in a community are referred to as its **trophic structure**. A community's trophic structure determines the passage of energy and nutrients from plants and other photosynthetic organisms to herbivores and then to predators. The sequence of food transfer between trophic levels is called a **food chain**.

Figure 20.15 shows two food chains, one terrestrial and one aquatic. At the bottom of both chains is the trophic level that supports all others. This level consists of autotrophs, which ecologists call **producers**. Photosynthetic producers transform light energy to chemical energy stored in the bonds of organic compounds. Plants are the main producers on land. In water, the producers are mainly photosynthetic protists and cyanobacteria, collectively called phytoplankton. Multicellular algae and aquatic plants are also important producers in shallow waters. In a few communities, such as those surrounding hydrothermal vents, the producers are chemosynthetic prokaryotes.

All organisms in trophic levels above the producers are heterotrophs, or **consumers**, and all consumers depend directly or indirectly on the output of producers. **Herbivores**, which eat plants, algae, or phytoplankton, are the **primary consumers**. Primary consumers on land include grasshoppers and many other insects, snails, and certain vertebrates, such as grazing mammals and birds that eat seeds and fruits. In aquatic environments, primary consumers include a variety of

▼ **Figure 20.15 Examples of food chains.** The arrows trace the transfer of food from one trophic level to the next in terrestrial and aquatic communities.

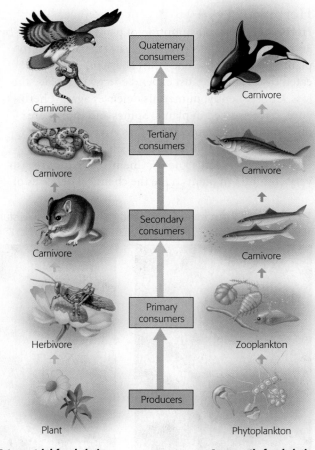

Quaternary consumers

Tertiary consumers

Secondary consumers

Primary consumers

Producers

Carnivore · Carnivore · Carnivore · Herbivore · Plant

Carnivore · Carnivore · Carnivore · Zooplankton · Phytoplankton

A terrestrial food chain   **An aquatic food chain**

zooplankton (mainly protists and microscopic animals such as small shrimps) that eat phytoplankton.

Above the primary consumers, the trophic levels are made up of **carnivores**, which eat the consumers from the level below. On land, **secondary consumers** include many small mammals, such as the mouse shown in Figure 20.15 eating an herbivorous insect, and a great variety of birds, frogs, and spiders, as well as lions and other large carnivores that eat grazers. In aquatic communities, secondary consumers are mainly small fishes that eat zooplankton. Higher trophic levels include **tertiary consumers** (third-level consumers), such as snakes that eat mice and other secondary consumers. Most communities have secondary and tertiary consumers. As the figure indicates, some also have a higher level—**quaternary consumers** (fourth-level consumers). These include hawks in terrestrial communities and killer whales in the marine environment. There are no fifth-level consumers—you'll find out why shortly.

Figure 20.15 shows only those consumers that eat living organisms. Some consumers derive their energy from **detritus**, the dead material left by all trophic levels, including animal wastes, plant litter, and dead bodies. Different organisms consume detritus in different stages of decay. **Scavengers**, which are large animals such as crows and vultures, feast on carcasses left behind by predators or speeding cars. The diet of **detritivores** is made up primarily of decaying organic material. Earthworms and millipedes are examples of detritivores. **Decomposers**, mainly prokaryotes and fungi, secrete enzymes that digest molecules in organic material and convert them to inorganic forms. Enormous numbers of microscopic decomposers in the soil and in the mud at the bottom of lakes and oceans break down organic materials to inorganic compounds—the raw materials used by plants and phytoplankton to make new organic materials that may eventually become food for consumers. Many gardeners keep a compost pile, using the services of detritivores and decomposers to break down organic material from kitchen scraps and yard trimmings (**Figure 20.16**).

▼ **Figure 20.16 Adding compost to a garden.** As it decays, the rich organic material of compost provides a slow-release source of inorganic nutrients for plants.

Biological Magnification

Organisms can't metabolize many of the toxins produced by industrial wastes or applied as pesticides; after consumption, the chemicals remain in the body. These toxins become concentrated as they pass through a food chain, a process called **biological magnification**. **Figure 20.17** shows the biological magnification of chemicals called PCBs (organic compounds used in electrical equipment until 1977) in a Great Lakes food chain. Zooplankton—represented by the base of the pyramid—feed on phytoplankton contaminated by PCBs in the water. Smelt (small fish) feed on contaminated zooplankton. Because each smelt consumes many zooplankton, the concentration of PCBs is higher in smelt than in zooplankton. For the same reason, the concentration of PCBs in trout is higher than in smelt. The top-level predators—herring gulls in this example—have the highest concentrations of PCBs in the food chain and are the organisms most severely affected by any toxic compounds in the environment. In this case, fewer of the contaminated eggs hatched, resulting in a decline in the reproductive success of herring gulls. Many other synthetic chemicals that cannot be degraded by microorganisms, including DDT and mercury, can also become concentrated through biological magnification. Since people are top-level predators, too, eating fish from contaminated waters can be dangerous.

◄ **Figure 20.17 Biological magnification of PCBs in a Great Lakes food chain in the early 1960s.**

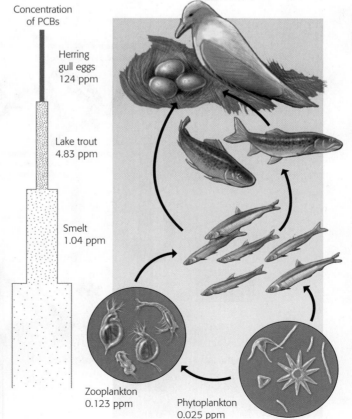

Concentration of PCBs

Herring gull eggs 124 ppm

Lake trout 4.83 ppm

Smelt 1.04 ppm

Zooplankton 0.123 ppm

Phytoplankton 0.025 ppm

Food Webs

Few, if any, communities are so simple that they are characterized by a single unbranched food chain. Several types of primary consumers usually feed on the same plant species, and one species of primary consumer may eat several different plants. Such branching of food chains occurs at the other trophic levels as well. Thus, the feeding relationships in a community are woven into elaborate **food webs**.

Consider the grasshopper mouse in **Figure 20.18**, the secondary consumer shown crunching on a grasshopper in Figure 20.15. Its diet also includes plants, making it a primary consumer, too. It is an **omnivore**, an animal that eats producers as well as consumers of different levels. The rattlesnake that eats the mouse also feeds on more than one trophic level. The blue arrow leading to the rattlesnake indicates that it eats primary consumers—it is a secondary consumer. The purple arrow shows that it eats secondary consumers, so it is also a tertiary consumer. Sound complicated? Actually, Figure 20.18 shows a simplified food web. An actual food web would involve many more organisms at each trophic level, and most of the animals would have a more diverse diet than shown in the figure. ☑

► **Figure 20.18 A simplified food web for a Sonoran desert community.** As in the food chains of Figure 20.15, the arrows in this web indicate "who eats whom," the direction of nutrient transfers. We also continue the color coding introduced in Figure 20.15 for the trophic levels and food transfers.

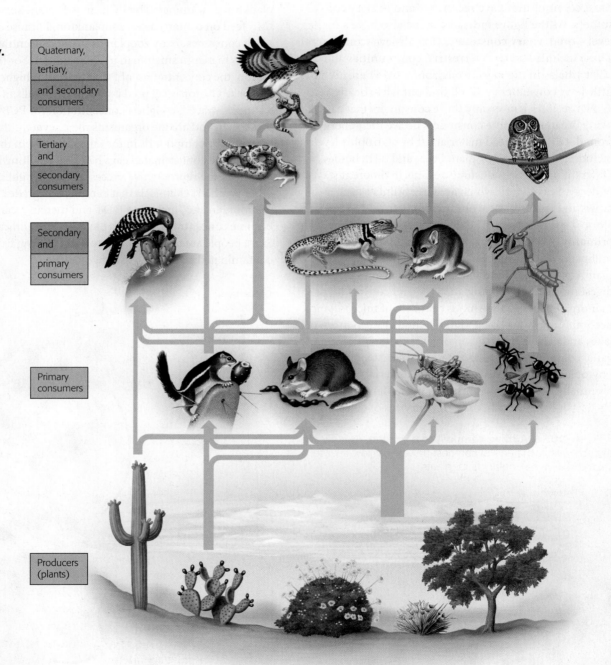

Quaternary, tertiary, and secondary consumers

Tertiary and secondary consumers

Secondary and primary consumers

Primary consumers

Producers (plants)

☑ CHECKPOINT

You're eating a pizza. At which trophic level(s) are you feeding?

Answer: You're a primary consumer when you eat flour (in the crust) and tomato sauce, and you're a secondary consumer when you eat cheese or meat on the pizza.

Species Diversity in Communities

The **species diversity** of a community—the variety of species that make up the community—has two components. The first component is **species richness**, or the number of different species in the community. The other component is the **relative abundance** of the different species, the proportional representation of each species in a community. To understand why both components are important for describing species diversity, imagine walking through the woodlands shown in **Figure 20.19**. On the path through woodland A, you would pass by four different species of trees, but most of the trees you encounter would be the same species. Now imagine walking on a path through woodland B. You would see the same four species of trees that you saw in woodland A—the species richness of the two woodlands is the same. However, woodland B might seem more diverse to you because no single species predominates. As **Figure 20.20** shows, the relative abundance of one species in woodland A is much higher than the relative abundances of the other three species. In woodland B, all four species are equally abundant. As a result, species diversity is greater in woodland B. Because plants provide food and shelter for many animals, a diverse plant community promotes animal diversity.

Although the abundance of a dominant species such as a forest tree can have an impact on the diversity of

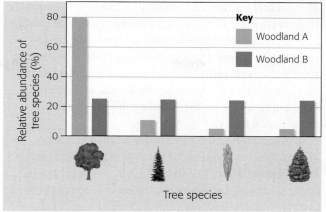

◄ **Figure 20.20 Relative abundance of tree species in woodlands A and B.**

▼ **Figure 20.19 Which woodland is more diverse?**

Woodland A

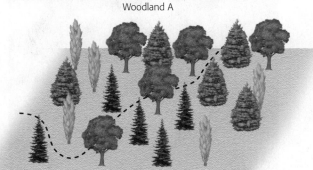

Woodland B

other species in the community, a nondominant species may also exert control over community composition. A **keystone species** is a species whose impact on its community is much larger than its total mass or abundance indicates. The term *keystone species* was derived from the wedge-shaped stone at the top of an arch that locks the other pieces in place. If the keystone is removed, the arch collapses. A keystone species occupies an ecological niche that holds the rest of its community in place.

To investigate the role of a potential keystone species in a community, ecologists compare diversity when the species is present or absent. Experiments by Robert Paine in the 1960s were among the first to provide evidence of the keystone species effect. Paine manually removed a predator, a sea star of the genus *Pisaster* (**Figure 20.21**), from experimental areas within the intertidal zone of the Washington coast. The result was that *Pisaster*'s main prey, a mussel, outcompeted many of the other shoreline organisms (algae, barnacles, and snails, for instance) for the important resource of space on the rocks. The number of different organisms present in experimental areas dropped from more than 15 species to fewer than 5 species.

Ecologists have identified other species that play a key role in ecosystem structure. For instance, the decline of sea otters off the western coast of Alaska allowed populations of sea urchins, their main prey, to increase. The abundance of urchins, which consume seaweeds such as kelp, has resulted in the loss of many of the kelp "forests" (see Figure 15.26) and the diversity of marine life that they support. In many ecosystems, however, ecologists are just beginning to understand the complex relationships among species; the value of an individual species may not be apparent until it is gone. ✓

▼ **Figure 20.21 A *Pisaster* sea star.**

✓ CHECKPOINT

How could a community appear to have relatively little diversity even though it is rich in species?

Answer: if one or a few of the diverse species accounted for almost all the organisms in the community, with the other species being rare

Disturbances in Communities

Most communities are constantly changing in response to disturbances. **Disturbances** are episodes that damage biological communities, at least temporarily, by destroying organisms and altering the availability of resources such as mineral nutrients and water. Examples of natural disturbances are storms, fire, floods, and droughts, but people are by far the most significant agents of disturbance today.

Understanding the effects of disturbance is especially important because of the potential impact on the human population. For instance, one consequence of human-caused disturbance is the emergence of previously unknown infectious diseases. Three-quarters of emerging diseases have jumped to humans from another vertebrate species. In many cases, people come into contact with the pathogens through activities such as clearing land for agriculture, road building, or hunting in previously isolated ecosystems. HIV, which may have been transmitted to people from the blood of primates butchered for food, is probably the best-known example. Others include potentially fatal hemorrhagic fevers, such as Ebola. Habitat destruction may also cause pathogen-carrying animals to venture closer to human dwellings in search of food.

Small-scale natural disturbances often have positive effects on a biological community. For example, when a large tree falls in a windstorm, it creates new habitats

Where do deadly new diseases like Ebola come from?

(Figure 20.22). More light may now reach the forest floor, giving small seedlings the opportunity to grow; or the depression left by the tree's roots may fill with water and be used as egg-laying sites by frogs, salamanders, and numerous insects. ☑

Ecological Succession

Communities change drastically following a severe disturbance that strips away vegetation and even soil. The disturbed area may be colonized by a variety of species, which are gradually replaced by a succession of other species, in a process called **ecological succession**.

When ecological succession begins in a virtually lifeless area with no soil, it is called **primary succession** (Figure 20.23). Examples of such areas are cooled lava flows on volcanic islands and the rubble left by a retreating glacier. Often the only life-forms initially present are autotrophic bacteria. Lichens and mosses, which grow from windblown spores, are commonly the first multicellular photosynthesizers to colonize the area. Soil develops gradually as rocks weather and organic matter accumulates from the decomposed remains of the early colonizers. Lichens and mosses are eventually overgrown by grasses and shrubs that sprout from seeds blown in from nearby areas or carried in by animals. Finally, the area is colonized by plants that become the community's prevalent form of vegetation. Primary succession can take hundreds or thousands of years.

▼ **Figure 20.22 A small-scale disturbance.** When this tree fell during a windstorm, its root system and the surrounding soil uplifted, resulting in a depression that filled with water. The dead tree, the root mound, and the water-filled depression are new habitats.

▼ **Figure 20.23 Primary succession under way on a lava flow in Volcanoes National Park, Hawaii.**

Secondary succession occurs where a disturbance has destroyed an existing community but left the soil intact. For example, secondary succession occurs as areas recover from floods or fires **(Figure 20.24)**. Disturbances that lead to secondary succession are also caused by human activities. Even before colonial times, people were clearing the temperate deciduous forests of eastern North America for agriculture and settlements. Some of this land was later abandoned as the soil was depleted of its chemical nutrients or the residents moved west to new territories. Whenever human intervention stops, secondary succession begins. ☑

▼ **Figure 20.24 Secondary succession after a fire.**

☑ **CHECKPOINT**

What is the main abiotic factor that distinguishes primary from secondary succession?

Answer: absence of soil (primary succession) versus presence of soil (secondary succession) at the onset of succession

Ecosystem Ecology

In addition to the community of species in a given area, an **ecosystem** includes all the abiotic factors, such as energy, soil characteristics, and water. Let's look at a small-scale ecosystem—a terrarium—to see how the community interacts with these abiotic factors **(Figure 20.25)**. A terrarium microcosm exhibits the two major processes that sustain all ecosystems: energy flow and chemical cycling. **Energy flow** is the passage of energy through the components of the ecosystem. **Chemical cycling** is the use and reuse of chemical elements such as carbon and nitrogen within the ecosystem.

Energy enters the terrarium in the form of sunlight (yellow arrows). Plants (producers) convert light energy to chemical energy through the process of photosynthesis. Animals (consumers) take in some of this chemical energy in the form of organic compounds when they eat the plants. Detritivores and decomposers in the soil obtain chemical energy when they feed on the dead remains of plants and animals. Every use of chemical energy by organisms involves a loss of some energy to the surroundings in the form of heat (red arrows). Because so much of the energy captured by photosynthesis is lost as heat, this ecosystem would run out of energy if it were not powered by a continuous inflow of energy from the sun.

In contrast to energy flow, chemical cycling (blue arrows in Figure 20.25) involves the transfer of materials within the ecosystem. While most ecosystems have a constant input of energy from sunlight or another source, the supply of the chemical elements used to construct molecules is limited. Chemical elements such as carbon and nitrogen are cycled between the abiotic components of the ecosystem, including air, water, and soil, and the biotic components of the ecosystem (the community). Plants acquire these elements in inorganic form from the air and soil and fix them into organic molecules. Animals, such as the snail in Figure 20.25, consume some of these organic molecules. When the plants and animals become detritus, decomposers return most of the elements to the soil and air in inorganic form. Some elements are also returned to the air and soil as the by-products of plant and animal metabolism.

In summary, both energy flow and chemical cycling involve the transfer of substances through the trophic levels of the ecosystem. However, energy flows through, and ultimately out of, ecosystems, whereas chemicals are recycled within and between ecosystems.

▼ **Figure 20.25 A terrarium ecosystem.** Though it is small and artificial, this sealed terrarium illustrates the two major ecosystem processes: energy flow and chemical cycling.

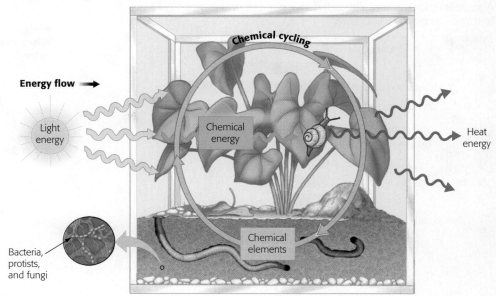

Energy Flow in Ecosystems

All organisms require energy for growth, maintenance, reproduction, and, in many species, locomotion. In this section, we take a closer look at energy flow through ecosystems. Along the way, we'll answer two key questions: What limits the length of food chains? and How do lessons about energy flow apply to people's use of resources?

Primary Production and the Energy Budgets of Ecosystems

Each day, Earth receives about 10^{19} kcal of solar energy, the energy equivalent of about 100 million atomic bombs. Most of this energy is absorbed, scattered, or reflected by the atmosphere or by Earth's surface. Of the visible light that reaches plants, algae, and cyanobacteria, only about 1% is converted to chemical energy by photosynthesis.

Ecologists call the amount, or mass, of living organic material in an ecosystem the **biomass**. The rate at which an ecosystem's producers convert solar energy to the chemical energy stored in biomass is called **primary production**. The primary production of the entire biosphere is roughly 165 billion tons of biomass per year.

Different ecosystems vary considerably in their primary production **(Figure 20.26)** as well as in their contribution to the total production of the biosphere. Tropical rain forests are among the most productive terrestrial ecosystems and contribute a large portion of the planet's overall production of biomass. Coral reefs

also have very high production, but their contribution to global production is small because they cover such a small area. Interestingly, even though the open ocean has very low production, it contributes the most to Earth's total net primary production because of its huge size—it covers 65% of Earth's surface area. Whatever the ecosystem, primary production sets the spending limit for the energy budget of the entire ecosystem because consumers must acquire their organic fuels from producers. Now let's see how this energy budget is divided among the different trophic levels in an ecosystem's food web. ☑

Ecological Pyramids

When energy flows as organic matter through the trophic levels of an ecosystem, much of it is lost at each link in the food chain. Consider the transfer of organic matter from plants (producers) to herbivores (primary consumers). In most ecosystems, herbivores manage to eat only a fraction of the plant material produced, and they can't digest all of what they do consume. For example, a caterpillar feeding on leaves passes about half the energy in the leaves as feces **(Figure 20.27)**. Another 35% of the energy is expended in cellular respiration. Only about 15% of the energy in the caterpillar's food is transformed into caterpillar biomass. Only this biomass (and the energy it contains) is available to the consumer that eats the caterpillar.

Figure 20.28, called a **pyramid of production**, illustrates the cumulative loss of energy with each transfer in a food chain. Each tier of the pyramid represents all of the organisms in one trophic level, and the width of each tier indicates how much of the chemical energy of the tier below is actually incorporated into the organic matter of that trophic level. Note that producers convert

☑ **CHECKPOINT**

Deserts and semidesert scrub cover about the same amount of surface area as tropical rain forests but contribute less than 1% of Earth's primary production, while rain forests contribute 22%. Explain this difference.

Answer: Primary production is measured in g/m²/yr. A square meter of tropical rain forest produces more than 20 times as much biomass as a square meter of desert and semidesert scrub.

▼ **Figure 20.26 Primary production of different ecosystems.** Primary production is the amount of biomass created by the producers of an ecosystem over a unit of time, in this case a year. Aquatic ecosystems are color-coded blue in these histograms; terrestrial ecosystems are green.

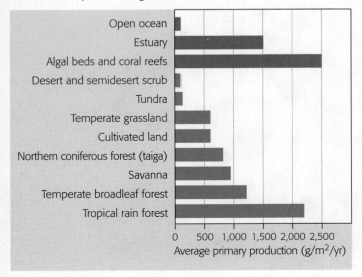

► **Figure 20.27 What becomes of a caterpillar's food?** Only about 15% of the calories of plant material this herbivore consumes will be stored as biomass available to the next link in the food chain.

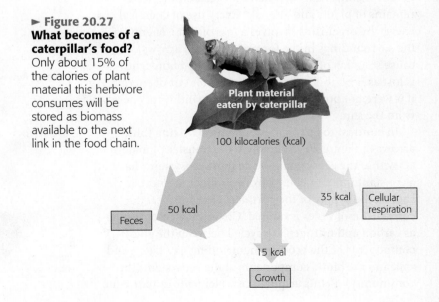

▼ Figure 20.28 **An idealized pyramid of production.**

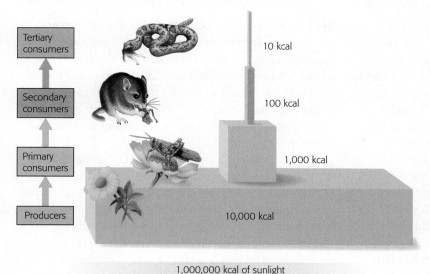

- Tertiary consumers — 10 kcal
- Secondary consumers — 100 kcal
- Primary consumers — 1,000 kcal
- Producers — 10,000 kcal

1,000,000 kcal of sunlight

only about 1% of the energy in the sunlight available to them to primary production. In this generalized pyramid, 10% of the energy available at each trophic level becomes incorporated into the next higher level. Actual efficiencies of energy transfer are usually in the range of 5–20%. In other words, 80–95% of the energy at one trophic level never reaches the next.

An important implication of this stepwise decline of energy in a trophic structure is that the amount of energy available to top-level consumers is small compared with that available to lower-level consumers. Only a tiny fraction of the energy stored by photosynthesis flows through a food chain to a tertiary consumer, such as a snake feeding on a mouse. This explains why top-level consumers such as lions and hawks require so much geographic territory: It takes a lot of vegetation to support trophic levels so many steps removed from photosynthetic production. You can also understand why most food chains are

limited to three to five levels; there is simply not enough energy at the very top of an ecological pyramid to support another trophic level. There are, for example, no nonhuman predators of lions, eagles, and killer whales; the biomass in populations of these top-level consumers is insufficient to supply yet another trophic level with a reliable source of nutrition.

Ecosystem Energetics and Human Resource Use

The dynamics of energy flow apply to the human population as much as to other organisms. The two production pyramids in **Figure 20.29** are based on the same generalized model used to construct Figure 20.28, with roughly 10% of the energy in each trophic level available for consumption by the next trophic level. The pyramid on the left shows energy flow from producers (represented by corn) to people as primary consumers—vegetarians. The pyramid on the right illustrates energy flow from the same corn crop, with people as secondary consumers, eating beef. Clearly, the human population has less energy available to it when people eat at higher trophic levels than as primary consumers.

Eating meat of any kind is both economically and environmentally expensive. Compared with growing plants for direct human consumption, producing meat usually requires that more land be cultivated, more water be used for irrigation, more fossil fuels be burned, and more chemical fertilizers and pesticides be applied to croplands used for growing grain. In many countries, people cannot afford to buy meat and are vegetarians by necessity. As countries become more affluent, the demand for meat increases—and so do the environmental costs of food production. ☑

Are vegetarians greener?

▼ Figure 20.29 **Food energy available to the human population at different trophic levels.**

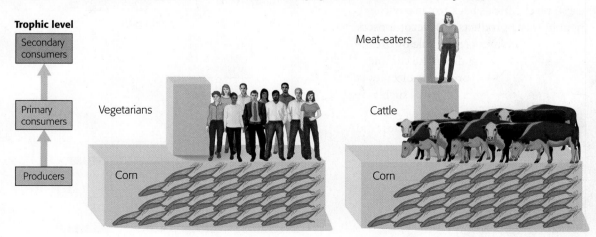

Trophic level

- Secondary consumers
- Primary consumers
- Producers

Vegetarians — Corn

Meat-eaters — Cattle — Corn

Chemical Cycling in Ecosystems

The sun (or in some cases Earth's interior) supplies ecosystems with a continual input of energy, but aside from an occasional meteorite, there are no extraterrestrial sources of chemical elements. Life, therefore, depends on the recycling of chemicals. While an organism is alive, much of its chemical stock changes continuously, as nutrients are acquired and waste products are released. Atoms present in the complex molecules of an organism at the time of its death are returned to the environment by the action of decomposers, replenishing the pool of inorganic nutrients that plants and other producers use to build new organic matter **(Figure 20.30)**. In a sense, each living thing only borrows an ecosystem's chemical elements, returning what is left in its body after it dies. Let's take a closer look at how chemicals cycle between organisms and the abiotic components of ecosystems.

☑ CHECKPOINT

What is the role of abiotic reservoirs in biogeochemical cycles? What are the three major abiotic reservoirs?

Answer: Abiotic reservoirs are sources of the nutrients used by producers for synthesizing organic molecules. The atmosphere, soil, and water are the three major abiotic reservoirs.

The General Scheme of Chemical Cycling

Because chemical cycles in an ecosystem involve both biotic components (organisms and nonliving organic material) and abiotic (geologic and atmospheric) components, they are called **biogeochemical cycles**. **Figure 20.31** is a general scheme for the cycling of a mineral nutrient within an ecosystem. Note that the cycle has an **abiotic reservoir** (white box) where a chemical accumulates or is stockpiled outside of living organisms. The atmosphere, for example, is an abiotic reservoir for carbon. Phosphorus, on the other hand, is available only from the soil. The water of aquatic ecosystems contains dissolved carbon, nitrogen, and phosphorus compounds.

Let's trace our way around our general biogeochemical cycle. ❶ Producers incorporate chemicals from the abiotic reservoir into organic compounds. ❷ Consumers feed on the producers, incorporating some of the chemicals into their own bodies. ❸ Both producers and consumers release some chemicals back to the environment in waste products. ❹ Decomposers play a central role by breaking down the complex organic molecules in detritus such as plant litter, animal wastes, and dead organisms. The products of this metabolism are inorganic molecules that replenish the abiotic reservoirs. Geologic processes such as erosion and the weathering of rock also contribute to the abiotic reservoirs. Producers use the inorganic molecules from abiotic reservoirs as raw materials for synthesizing new organic molecules (carbohydrates and proteins, for example), and the cycle continues.

▼ **Figure 20.30 Plant growth on fallen tree.** In the temperate rain forest of Olympic National Park, in Washington State, plants—including other trees—quickly take advantage of the mineral nutrients supplied by decomposing "nurse logs."

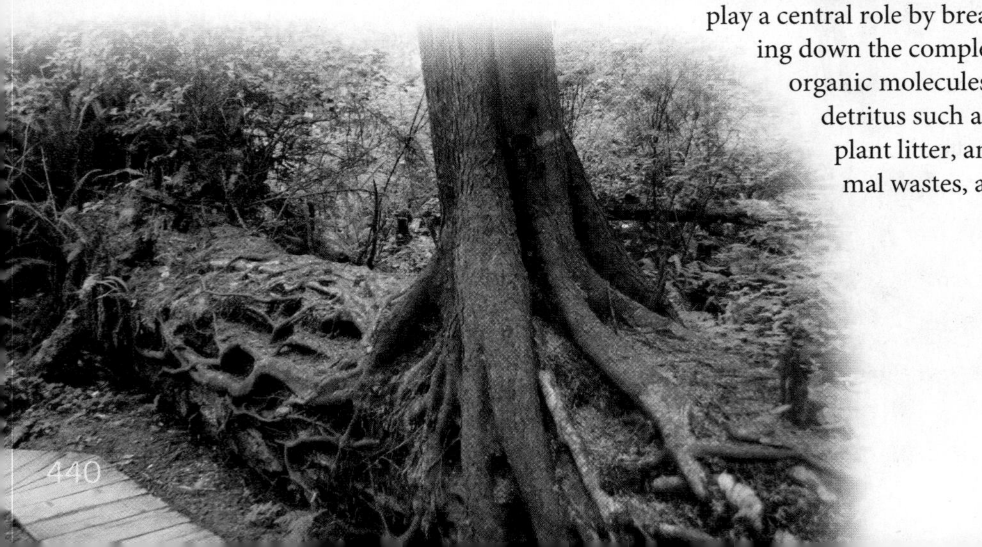

Biogeochemical cycles can be local or global. Soil is the main reservoir for nutrients in a local cycle, such as phosphorus. In contrast, for those chemicals that spend part of their time in gaseous form—carbon and nitrogen are examples—the cycling is essentially global. For instance, some of the carbon a plant acquires from the air may have been released into the atmosphere by the respiration of a plant or animal on another continent.

Now let's examine three important biogeochemical cycles more closely: the cycles for carbon, phosphorus, and nitrogen. As you study the cycles, look for the four basic steps we described, as well as the geologic processes that may move chemicals around and between ecosystems. In all the diagrams, the main abiotic reservoirs appear in white boxes. ☑

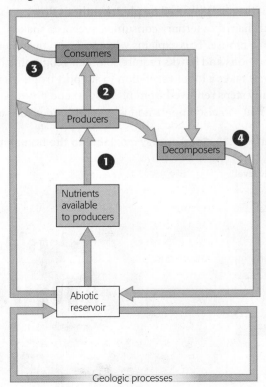

▼ **Figure 20.31 General scheme for biogeochemical cycles.**

The Carbon Cycle

Carbon, the major ingredient of all organic molecules, has an atmospheric reservoir and cycles globally. Other abiotic reservoirs of carbon include fossil fuels and dissolved carbon compounds in the oceans. The reciprocal metabolic processes of photosynthesis and cellular respiration, which you may recall from previous chapters, are mainly responsible for the cycling of carbon between the biotic and abiotic worlds (**Figure 20.32**). **1** Photosynthesis removes CO_2 from the atmosphere and incorporates it into organic molecules, which are **2** passed along the food chain by consumers. **3** Cellular respiration returns CO_2 to the atmosphere. **4** Decomposers break down the carbon compounds in detritus; that carbon, too, is eventually released as CO_2. On a global scale, the return of CO_2 to the atmosphere by respiration closely balances its removal by photosynthesis. However, increasing levels of CO_2 caused by **5** the burning of wood and fossil fuels (coal and petroleum) are contributing to global climate change (see Figure 18.46).

The Phosphorus Cycle

Organisms require phosphorus as an ingredient of nucleic acids, phospholipids, and ATP and (in vertebrates) as a mineral component of bones and teeth. In contrast to the carbon cycle and the other major biogeochemical cycles, the phosphorus cycle does not have an atmospheric component. Rocks are the only source of phosphorus for terrestrial ecosystems; in fact, rocks that have high phosphorus content are mined for fertilizer.

At the center of **Figure 20.33**, **1** the weathering (breakdown) of rock gradually adds inorganic phosphate (PO_4^{3-}) to the soil. **2** Plants absorb dissolved phosphate from the soil and assimilate it by building the phosphorus atoms into organic compounds. **3** Consumers obtain phosphorus in organic form by eating plants. **4** Phosphates are returned to the soil by the action of decomposers on animal waste and the remains of dead plants and animals. **5** Some of the phosphates drain from terrestrial ecosystems into the sea, where they may settle and eventually become part of new rocks. Phosphorus removed from the cycle in this way will not be available to living organisms until **6** geologic processes uplift the rocks and expose them to weathering.

Phosphates move from land to aquatic ecosystems much more rapidly than they are replaced, and soil characteristics may also decrease the amount of phosphate available to plants. As a result, phosphate is a limiting factor in many terrestrial ecosystems. Farmers and gardeners often use phosphate fertilizer, such as crushed phosphate rock or bone meal (finely ground bones from slaughtered livestock or fish), to boost plant growth.

▼ **Figure 20.32 The carbon cycle.**

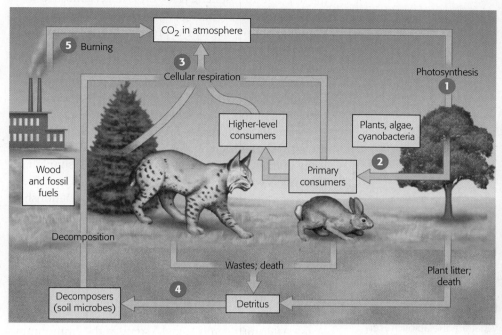

▼ **Figure 20.33 The phosphorus cycle.**

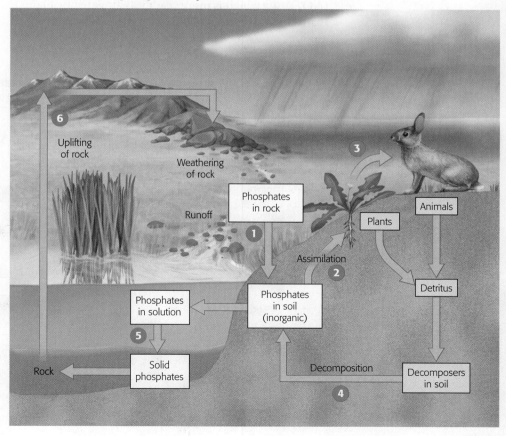

The Nitrogen Cycle

As an ingredient of proteins and nucleic acids, nitrogen is essential to the structure and functioning of all organisms. Nitrogen has two abiotic reservoirs, the atmosphere and the soil. The atmospheric reservoir is huge; almost 80% of the atmosphere is nitrogen gas (N_2). However, plants cannot use nitrogen gas. The process of **nitrogen fixation** converts gaseous N_2 to nitrogen compounds that plants can assimilate. Most of the nitrogen available in natural ecosystems comes from biological fixation performed by certain bacteria. Without these organisms, the reservoir of usable soil nitrogen would be extremely limited.

Figure 20.34 illustrates the actions of two types of nitrogen-fixing bacteria. **1** Some bacteria live symbiotically in the roots of certain species of plants, supplying their hosts with a direct source of usable nitrogen. The largest group of plants with this mutualistic relationship is the legumes, a family that includes peanuts and soybeans. Many farmers improve soil fertility by alternating crops of legumes, which add nitrogen to the soil, with plants such as corn that require nitrogen fertilizer. **2** Free-living nitrogen-fixing bacteria in soil or water convert N_2 to ammonia (NH_3), which then picks up another H^+ to become ammonium (NH_4^+).

3 After nitrogen is "fixed," some of the ammonium is taken up and used by plants. **4** Nitrifying bacteria in the soil also convert some of the ammonium to nitrate (NO_3^-), **5** which is more readily assimilated by plants. Plants use this nitrogen to make molecules such as amino acids, which are then incorporated into proteins.

6 When an herbivore (represented here by a rabbit) eats a plant, it digests the proteins into amino acids and then uses the amino acids to build the proteins it needs. Higher-order consumers get nitrogen from the organic molecules of their prey. Because animals form nitrogen-containing waste products during protein metabolism, consumers excrete some nitrogen into the soil or water. The urine that rabbits and other mammals excrete contains urea, a nitrogen compound that is widely used as fertilizer.

Organisms that are not consumed eventually die and become detritus, which is decomposed by bacteria and fungi. **7** Decomposition releases ammonium from organic compounds back into the soil, replenishing that abiotic reservoir. Under low-oxygen conditions, however, **8** soil bacteria known as denitrifying bacteria strip the oxygen atoms from nitrates, releasing N_2 back into the atmosphere and depleting the soil of usable nitrogen.

Human activities are disrupting the nitrogen cycle by adding more nitrogen to the biosphere each year than natural processes do. Combustion of fossil fuels and modern agricultural practices are two major sources of nitrogen. For example, many farmers use enormous amounts of synthetic nitrogen fertilizer to supplement natural nitrogen. However, less than half the fertilizer applied is actually used by the crop plants. Some nitrogen escapes to the atmosphere, where it forms nitrous oxide (N_2O), a gas that contributes to global warming. And as you'll learn next, nitrogen fertilizers also pollute aquatic systems. ☑

☑ CHECKPOINT

What are the abiotic reservoirs of nitrogen? In what form does nitrogen occur in each reservoir?

Answer: atmosphere: N_2; soil: NH_4^+ and NO_3^-

▼ Figure 20.34 **The nitrogen cycle.**

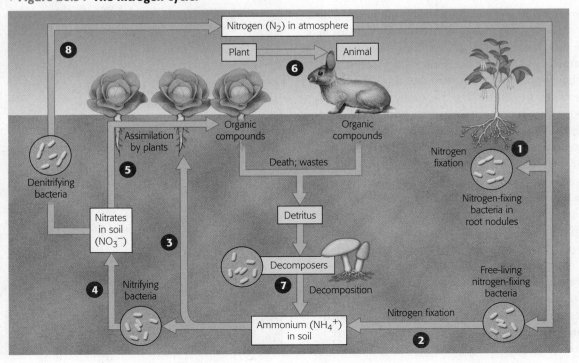

Nutrient Pollution

Low nutrient levels, especially of phosphorus and nitrogen, often limit the growth of algae and cyanobacteria in aquatic ecosystems. Nutrient pollution occurs when human activities add excess amounts of these chemicals to aquatic ecosystems.

In many areas, phosphate pollution comes from agricultural fertilizers and runoff of animal waste from livestock feedlots (where hundreds of animals are penned together). Phosphates are also a common ingredient in dishwasher detergents, making the outflow from sewage treatment facilities—which also contains phosphorus from human waste—a major source of phosphate pollution. Phosphate pollution of lakes and rivers results in heavy growth of algae and cyanobacteria **(Figure 20.35)**. Microbes consume a great deal of oxygen as they decompose the extra biomass, a process that depletes the water of oxygen. These changes lead to reduced diversity of aquatic species and a much less appealing body of water.

Why are high-phosphate dishwasher detergents banned in many states?

Agricultural sources of nitrogen include feedlots and the large amounts of inorganic nitrogen fertilizers that are routinely applied to crops. Lawns and golf courses also receive sizable applications of nitrogen fertilizers. Crop and lawn plants take up some of the nitrogen compounds, and denitrifiers convert some to atmospheric N_2, but nitrate is not bound tightly by soil particles and is easily washed out of the soil by rain or irrigation. As a result, chemical fertilizers often exceed the soil's natural recycling capacity. Nitrogen pollution may also come from sewage treatment facilities when extreme conditions (such as unusual storms) or malfunctioning equipment prevent them from meeting water quality standards.

In an example of how far-reaching this problem can be, nitrogen runoff from midwestern farm fields has been linked to an annual summer "dead zone" in the Gulf of Mexico **(Figure 20.36)**. Vast algal blooms extend outward from where the Mississippi River deposits its nutrient-laden waters. As the algae die, decomposition of the huge quantities of biomass diminishes the supply of dissolved oxygen over an area that ranges from 13,000 km² (roughly the area of Connecticut) to 22,000 km² (about the area of Michigan). Oxygen depletion disrupts benthic communities, displacing fish and invertebrates that can move and killing organisms that are attached to the substrate. More than 400 recurring and permanent coastal dead zones totaling approximately 245,000 km² have been documented worldwide. ☑

☑ CHECKPOINT

How does the excessive addition of mineral nutrients to a pond eventually result in the loss of most fish in the pond?

Answer: Overfertilization by nutrient pollution initially causes population explosions of algae and the organisms that feed on them. The respiration of so much life, especially of the microbes decomposing all the organic refuse, consumes most of the lake's oxygen, which the fish require.

▼ **Figure 20.35 Algal growth resulting from nutrient pollution.** The flat green area in this photo is not a lawn, but rather the surface of a polluted pond.

▼ **Figure 20.36 The Gulf of Mexico dead zone.**

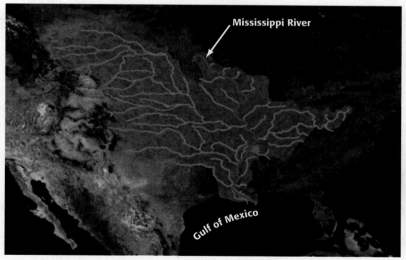

Mississippi River

Gulf of Mexico

Light blue lines represent rivers draining into the Mississippi River (shown in dark blue). Nitrogen runoff carried by these rivers ends up in the Gulf of Mexico. In the images below, red and orange indicate high concentrations of phytoplankton. Bacteria feeding on dead phytoplankton deplete the water of oxygen, creating a "dead zone."

Gulf of Mexico

Summer

Gulf of Mexico

Winter

Conservation and Restoration Biology

As we have seen in this unit, many of the environmental problems facing us today have been caused by human enterprises. But the science of ecology is not just useful for telling us how things have gone wrong. Ecological research is also the foundation for finding solutions to these problems and for reversing the negative consequences of ecosystem alteration. Thus, we end the ecology unit by highlighting these beneficial applications of ecological research.

Conservation biology is a goal-oriented science that seeks to understand and counter the loss of biodiversity. Conservation biologists recognize that biodiversity can be sustained only if the evolutionary mechanisms that have given rise to species and communities of organisms continue to operate. Thus, the goal is not simply to preserve individual species but to sustain ecosystems, where natural selection can continue to function, and to maintain the genetic variability on which natural selection acts. The expanding field of **restoration ecology** uses ecological principles to develop methods of returning degraded areas to their natural state.

Biodiversity "Hot Spots"

Conservation biologists are applying their understanding of population, community, and ecosystem dynamics in establishing parks, wilderness areas, and other legally protected nature reserves. Choosing locations for these protected zones often focuses on **biodiversity hot spots**. These relatively small areas have a large number of endangered and threatened species and an exceptional concentration of **endemic species**, species that are found nowhere else. Together, the "hottest" of Earth's biodiversity hot spots, shown in **Figure 20.37**, total less than 1.5% of Earth's land surface but are home to a third of all species of plants and vertebrates. For example, all lemurs are endemic to Madagascar, a large island off the eastern coast of Africa that is home to more than 50 species of lemurs. In fact, almost all of the mammals, reptiles, amphibians, and plants that inhabit Madagascar are endemic. There are also hot spots in aquatic ecosystems, such as certain river systems and coral reefs. Because biodiversity hot spots can also be hot spots of extinction, they rank high on the list of areas demanding strong global conservation efforts.

Concentrations of species provide an opportunity to protect many species in very limited areas. However, the "hot spot" designation tends to favor the most noticeable organisms, especially vertebrates and plants. Invertebrates and microorganisms are often overlooked. Furthermore, species endangerment is a global problem, and focusing on hot spots should not detract from efforts to conserve habitats and species diversity in other areas. Finally, even the protection of a nature reserve does not shield organisms from the effects of climate change or other threats, such as invasive species or infectious disease. The golden toad you saw in Figure 20.2 went extinct despite living in a protected reserve—a victim of changing weather patterns, airborne pollution, and disease. To stem the tide of biodiversity loss, we will have to address environmental problems globally as well as locally. ☑

▼ Figure 20.37 **Earth's terrestrial biodiversity hot spots (purple).**

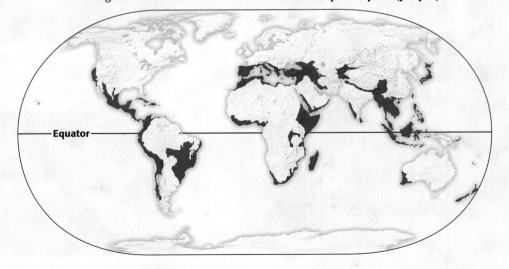

Equator

Conservation at the Ecosystem Level

Most conservation efforts in the past have focused on saving individual species, and this work continues. (You have already learned about one example, the red-cockaded woodpecker; see Figure 19.12.) More and more, however, conservation biology aims at sustaining the biodiversity of entire communities and ecosystems. On an even broader scale, conservation biology considers the biodiversity of whole landscapes. Ecologically, a **landscape** is a regional assemblage of interacting ecosystems, such as an area with forest, adjacent fields, wetlands, streams, and streamside habitats. **Landscape ecology** is the application of ecological principles to the study of land-use patterns. Its goal is to make ecosystem conservation a functional part of the planning for land use.

▼ **Figure 20.38 Edges between ecosystems within a landscape.**

Natural edges. Forests border grassland ecosystems in Lake Clark National Park, Alaska.

Edges created by human activity. Pronounced edges (roads) surround clear-cuts in this photograph of a heavily logged rain forest in Malaysia.

Edges between ecosystems are prominent features of landscapes, whether natural or altered by people **(Figure 20.38)**. Such edges have their own sets of physical conditions—such as soil type and surface features—that differ from the ecosystems on either side of them. Edges also may have their own type and amount of disturbance. For instance, the edge of a forest often has more blown-down trees than a forest interior because the edge is less protected from strong winds. Because of their specific physical features, edges also have their own communities of organisms. Some organisms thrive in edges because they require resources found only there. For instance, whitetail deer browse on woody shrubs found in edge areas between woods and fields, and their populations often expand when forests are logged or interrupted by development.

Edges can have both positive and negative effects on biodiversity. A recent study in a tropical rain forest in western Africa indicated that natural edge communities are important sites of speciation. On the other hand, landscapes where human activities have produced edges often have fewer species.

Another important landscape feature, especially where habitats have been severely fragmented, is the **movement corridor**, a narrow strip or series of small clumps of suitable habitat connecting otherwise isolated patches. In places where there is extremely heavy human impact, artificial corridors are sometime constructed **(Figure 20.39)**. Corridors can promote dispersal and help sustain populations, and they are especially important to species that migrate between different habitats seasonally. But a corridor can also be harmful—as, for example, in the spread of disease, especially among small subpopulations in closely situated habitat patches. ✔

Why do some animals prefer living on the edge?

✔ CHECKPOINT

How is a landscape different from an ecosystem?

Answer: A landscape is more inclusive in that it consists of several interacting ecosystems in the same region.

► **Figure 20.39 An artificial corridor.** This bridge over a road provides an artificial corridor for animals in Banff National Park, Canada.

How Does Tropical Forest Fragmentation Affect Biodiversity?

Long-term studies are essential for learning how we might best conserve biodiversity and other natural resources. One site for such studies is the Biological Dynamics of Forest Fragmentation Project (BDFFP), a 1,000-km^2 ecological "laboratory" located deep in the Amazonian forest of Brazil. When the project was begun in 1979, laws required landowners who cleared forest for ranching or other agricultural operations to leave scattered tracts of untouched forest. Biologists recruited some of these landowners to create reserves in isolated fragments of 1 ha (roughly 2.5 acres), 10 ha, and 100 ha. **Figure 20.40** shows some of these forest "islands." Before each area was isolated from the main forest, a small army of specialists inventoried the organisms present and measured the trees.

Hundreds of researchers have used the BDFFP sites to investigate the effects of forest fragmentation on all levels of ecological study. The initial **observations** for these investigations were gleaned from the results of other ecological studies—for example, the effects of fragmentation in temperate forests or differences in the biodiversity of small islands compared with mainland ecosystems. These observations led many researchers to ask the **question**, How does fragmentation of tropical forests affect species diversity within the fragments? Based on previous research on numerous species, a reasonable **hypothesis** might be: Species diversity declines as the size of the forest fragment decreases. An ecologist studying large predators such as jaguars and pumas, which require large hunting territories, might therefore make the **prediction** that predators will only be found in the largest areas. The BDFFP is unique because it allows researchers to test their predictions with new observations that compare species diversity in forest fragments with a comparable control: species diversity in the same area when it was intact. An undisturbed area of 25,400 acres is also available for comparison with fragmented areas. In addition, data can be collected over a period of years or even decades.

Since the BDFFP was established, scientists have studied many different groups of plants and animals. In general, the **results** have shown that fragmentation of forest into smaller pieces leads to a decline in species diversity. Species richness decreases as a result of local extinctions of many species of large mammals, insects, and insectivorous birds. The population density of remaining species often declines. Researchers also documented edge effects, such as those described in the previous section. Changes in abiotic factors along the fragment edges, including increased wind disturbance, higher temperature, and decreased soil moisture, played a role in community alterations. For example, ecologists found that tree mortality was higher than normal at fragment edges. They also observed changes in the composition of communities of invertebrates that inhabit the soil and leaf litter.

▼ **Figure 20.40 Fragments of forest in the Amazon that were created as part of the Biological Dynamics of Forest Fragmentation Project.** The patch of forest on the right is a 1-ha fragment.

Restoring Ecosystems

One of the major strategies in restoration ecology is **bioremediation**, the use of living organisms to detoxify polluted ecosystems. For example, bacteria have been used to clean up old mining sites and oil spills (see Figure 15.18). Researchers are also investigating the potential of using plants to remove toxic substances such as heavy metals and organic pollutants (for example, PCBs) from contaminated soil **(Figure 20.41)**.

Some restoration projects have the broader goal of returning ecosystems to their natural state, which may involve replanting vegetation, fencing out non-native animals, or removing dams that restrict water flow. Hundreds of restoration projects are currently under way in the United States. One of the most ambitious endeavors is the Kissimmee River Restoration Project in south-central Florida.

The Kissimmee River was once a meandering shallow river that wound its way from Lake Kissimmee southward into Lake Okeechobee. Periodic flooding of the river covered a wide floodplain during about half of the year, creating wetlands that provided habitat for large numbers of birds, fishes, and invertebrates. And as the floods deposited the river's load of nutrient-rich silt on the floodplain, they boosted soil fertility and maintained the water quality of the river.

Between 1962 and 1971, the U.S. Army Corps of Engineers converted the 166-km wandering river to a straight canal 9 m deep, 100 m wide, and 90 km long. This project, designed to allow development on the floodplain, drained approximately 31,000 acres of wetlands, with significant negative impacts on fish and wetland bird populations. Without the marshes to help filter and reduce agricultural runoff, the river transported phosphates and other excess nutrients from Lake Okeechobee to the Everglades ecosystem to the south.

The restoration project involves removing water control structures such as dams, reservoirs, and channel modifications and filling in about 35 km of the canal **(Figure 20.42)**. The first phase of the project was completed in 2004. The photo shows a section of the Kissimmee canal that has been plugged, diverting flow into the remnant river channels. Birds and other wildlife have returned in unexpected numbers to the 11,000 acres of wetlands that have been restored. The marshes are filled with native vegetation, and game fishes again swim in the river channels. ☑

▼ **Figure 20.41 Bioremediation using plants.** A researcher from the U.S. Department of Agriculture investigates the use of canola plants to reduce toxic levels of selenium in contaminated soil.

▼ **Figure 20.42 The Kissimmee River Restoration Project.**

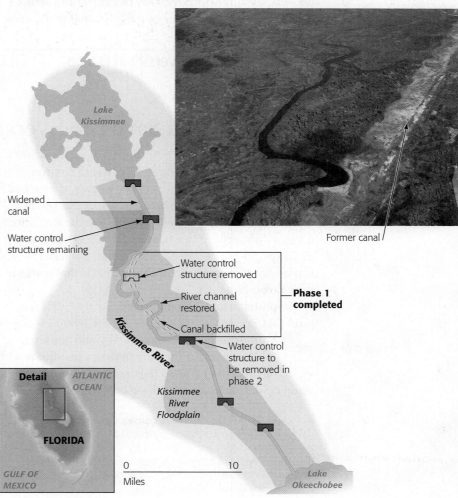

447

The Goal of Sustainable Development

The demand for the "provisioning" services of ecosystems, such as food, wood, and water, is increasing as the world population grows and becomes more affluent. Although these demands are currently being met, they are satisfied at the expense of other critical ecosystem services, such as climate regulation and protection against natural disasters. Clearly, we have set ourselves and the rest of the biosphere on a precarious path into the future. How can we best manage Earth's resources to ensure that all generations inherit an adequate supply of natural and economic resources and a relatively stable environment?

Many nations, scientific associations, corporations, and private foundations have embraced the concept of **sustainable development**. The Ecological Society of America, the world's largest organization of ecologists, endorses a research agenda called the Sustainable Biosphere Initiative. The goal of this initiative is to acquire the ecological information necessary for the responsible development, management, and conservation of Earth's resources. The research agenda includes the search for ways to sustain the productivity of natural and artificial ecosystems and studies of the relationship between biological diversity, global climate change, and ecological processes.

Sustainable development depends on more than continued research and application of ecological knowledge. It also requires that we connect the life sciences with the social sciences, economics, and humanities. Conservation of biodiversity is only one side of sustainable development; the other key factor is improving the human condition. Public education and the political commitment and cooperation of nations are essential to the success of this endeavor.

An awareness of our unique ability to alter the biosphere and jeopardize the existence of other species, as well as our own, may help us choose a path toward a sustainable future. The risk of a world without adequate natural resources for all its people is not a vision of the distant future. It is a prospect for your children's lifetime, or perhaps even your own. But although the current state of the biosphere is grim, the situation is far from hopeless. Now is the time to take action by aggressively pursuing greater knowledge about the diversity of life on our planet and by working toward long-term sustainability. ☑

☑ CHECKPOINT

What is meant by sustainable development?

Answer: development that ensures an adequate supply of natural and economic resources for future generations

Biodiversity in Decline   EVOLUTION CONNECTION

Can Biophilia Save Biodiversity?

For millions of years, the diversity of life has flourished via evolutionary adaptation in response to environmental change. For many species, however, the pace of evolution can't match the breakneck speed at which humans are changing the environment (see the Evolution Connection sections in Chapters 18 and 19). Perhaps those species are doomed to extinction. Or perhaps they can be saved by one human characteristic that works in their favor: biophilia.

Biophilia, which literally means "love of life," is a term that Edward O. Wilson, one of the world's foremost experts on biodiversity and conservation, uses for the human desire to affiliate with other life in its many forms **(Figure 20.43)**. People develop close relationships with pets, nurture houseplants,

Are you a biophiliac?

► Figure 20.43 **Doing what comes naturally.** Edward O. Wilson has helped teach scientists and the general public a greater respect for Earth's biodiversity. This photograph finds biophiliac Wilson in the woods near Massachusetts's Walden Pond, a landscape immortalized by another great naturalist and writer, Henry David Thoreau.

invite avian visitors with backyard feeders, and flock to zoos, gardens, and nature parks **(Figure 20.44)**. Our attraction to pristine landscapes with clean water and lush vegetation is also testimony to our biophilia. Wilson proposes that our biophilia is innate, an evolutionary product of natural selection acting on a brainy species whose survival depended on a close connection to the environment and a practical appreciation of plants and animals. We evolved in natural environments rich in biodiversity, and we still have an affinity for such settings. Our behavior reflects remnants of our ancestral attachment to nature and the diversity of life.

It will come as no surprise that many biologists have embraced the concept of biophilia. After all, these are people who have turned their passion for nature into careers. But biophilia strikes a chord with biologists for another reason. If biophilia is evolutionarily embedded in our genome, then there is hope that we can become better custodians of the biosphere. If we all pay more attention to our biophilia, a new environmental ethic could catch on among individuals and societies. And that ethic is a resolve never to knowingly allow a single species to become extinct as a result of our actions or any ecosystem to be destroyed as long as there are reasonable ways to prevent it. Yes, we should be motivated to preserve biodiversity because we depend on it for food, medicine, building materials, fertile soil, flood control, habitable climate, drinkable water, and breathable air. But maybe we can also work harder to prevent the extinction of other forms of life just because it is the ethical thing for us to do. Again, Wilson sounds the call: "Right now, we're pushing the species of the world through a bottleneck. We've got to make it a major moral principle to get as many of them through this as possible. It's the challenge now and for the rest of the century. And there's one good thing about our species: We like a challenge!"

Biophilia is a fitting capstone for this unit. Modern biology is the scientific extension of our human tendency to feel connected to and curious about all forms of life. We are most likely to save what we appreciate, and we are most likely to appreciate what we understand. We hope that our discussion of biodiversity has deepened your biophilia and broadened your education.

▼ **Figure 20.44 Biophilia.** Whether we seek other organisms in their own habitats or invite them into ours, we clearly find pleasure in the diversity of life.

Chapter Review

SUMMARY OF KEY CONCEPTS

 Go to **www.masteringbiology.com** for homework assignments, practice quizzes, Pearson eText, and more.

The Loss of Biodiversity

THE COMPONENTS OF BIODIVERSITY		
Genetic Diversity	**Species Diversity**	**Ecosystem Diversity**
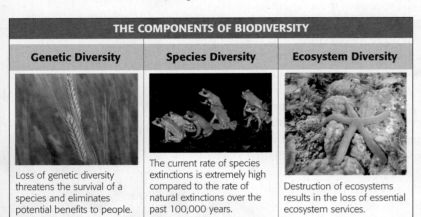		
Loss of genetic diversity threatens the survival of a species and eliminates potential benefits to people.	The current rate of species extinctions is extremely high compared to the rate of natural extinctions over the past 100,000 years.	Destruction of ecosystems results in the loss of essential ecosystem services.

Causes of Declining Biodiversity

Habitat destruction is the leading cause of extinctions. Invasive species, overexploitation, and pollution are also significant factors.

Community Ecology

Interspecific Interactions

Populations in a community interact in a variety of ways that can be generally categorized as being beneficial (**+**) or harmful (**−**) to the populations. Because **+/−** interactions (exploitation of one species by another species) may have such a negative impact on the individual that is harmed, defensive evolutionary adaptations are common.

Trophic Structure

The trophic structure of a community defines the feeding relationships among organisms. These relationships are sometimes organized into food chains or food webs. Toxins may accumulate by the process of biological magnification as they are passed up a food chain to the top predators.

Increasing PCB concentration

Species Diversity in Communities

Diversity within a community includes species richness and relative abundance of different species. A keystone species is a species that has a great impact on the composition of the community despite relatively low abundance or biomass.

Disturbances in Communities

Disturbances are episodes that damage communities, at least temporarily, by destroying organisms or altering the availability of resources such as mineral nutrients and water. People are the most significant cause of disturbances today.

Ecological Succession

The sequence of changes in a community after a disturbance is called ecological succession. Primary succession occurs where a community arises in a virtually lifeless area with no soil. Secondary succession occurs where a disturbance has destroyed an existing community but left the soil intact.

INTERACTIONS BETWEEN SPECIES IN A COMMUNITY					
Interspecific Interaction	**Effect on Species 1**	**Effect on Species 2**	**Interspecific Interaction**	**Effect on Species 1**	**Effect on Species 2**
Competition	−	−	Exploitation	**+**	**−**
			Predation	**+**	**−**
Mutualism	**+**	**+**	Herbivory	**+**	**−**
			Parasites and Pathogens		

Ecosystem Ecology

Energy Flow in Ecosystems

An ecosystem is a biological community and the abiotic factors with which the community interacts. Energy must flow continuously through an ecosystem, from producers to consumers and decomposers. Chemical elements can be recycled between an ecosystem's living community and the abiotic environment. Trophic relationships determine an ecosystem's routes of energy flow and chemical cycling.

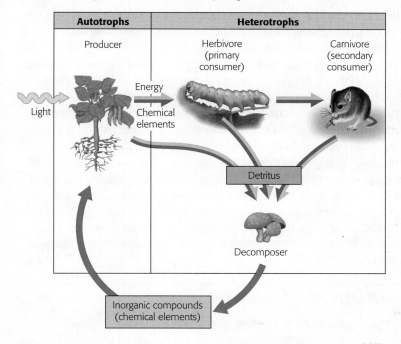

Primary production is the rate at which plants and other producers build biomass. Ecosystems vary considerably in their productivity. Primary production sets the spending limit for the energy budget of the entire ecosystem because consumers must acquire their organic fuels from producers. In a food chain, only about 10% of the biomass at one trophic level is available to the next, resulting in a pyramid of production.

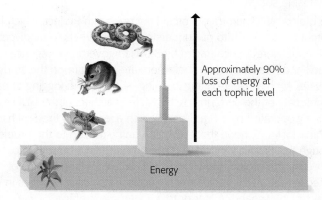

When people eat producers instead of consumers, less photosynthetic production is required, which reduces the impact on the environment.

Chemical Cycling in Ecosystems

Biogeochemical cycles involve biotic and abiotic components. Each circuit has an abiotic reservoir through which the chemical cycles. Some chemical elements require "processing" by certain microorganisms before they are available to plants as inorganic nutrients. A chemical's specific route through an ecosystem varies with the element and the trophic structure of the ecosystem. Phosphorus is not very mobile and is cycled locally. Carbon and nitrogen spend part of their time in gaseous form and are cycled globally. Runoff of nitrogen and phosphorus, especially from agricultural land, causes algal blooms in aquatic ecosystems, lowering water quality and sometimes depleting the water of oxygen.

Conservation and Restoration Biology

Biodiversity "Hot Spots"

Conservation biology is a goal-oriented science that seeks to counter the loss of biodiversity. The front lines for conservation biology are biodiversity "hot spots," relatively small geographic areas that are especially rich in endangered species.

Conservation at the Ecosystem Level

Increasingly, conservation biology aims at sustaining the biodiversity of entire communities, ecosystems, and landscapes. Edges between ecosystems are prominent features of landscapes, with positive and negative effects on biodiversity. Corridors can promote dispersal and help sustain populations.

Restoring Ecosystems

In some cases, toxic substances such as heavy metals can be removed from an ecosystem by microbes or plants. Ecologists are working to revitalize some ecosystems by planting native vegetation, removing barriers to wildlife, and other means. The Kissimmee River Restoration Project is an attempt to undo the ecological damage done when the river was engineered into straight channels.

The Goal of Sustainable Development

Balancing the needs of people with the health of the biosphere, sustainable development has the goal of long-term prosperity of human societies and the ecosystems that support them.

Evolution Connection:
Biophilia and an Environmental Ethic

Biophilia is a term used by biologist E. O. Wilson to describe the innate affinity people have for nature and for other organisms. Wilson—and many other biologists—hope that our biophilia will help us develop an environmental ethic of preserving biodiversity.

SELF-QUIZ

1. Currently, the number one cause of biodiversity loss is _____.

2. According to the concept of competitive exclusion,
   a. two species cannot coexist in the same habitat.
   b. extinction or emigration is the only possible result of competitive interactions.
   c. intraspecific competition results in the success of the best-adapted individuals.
   d. two species cannot share the same niche in a community.

3. The concept of trophic structure emphasizes the
   a. prevalent form of vegetation.
   b. keystone species concept.
   c. feeding relationships within a community.
   d. species richness of the community.

4. Match each organism with its trophic level (you may choose a level more than once).
   a. alga   1. decomposer
   b. grasshopper   2. producer
   c. zooplankton   3. tertiary consumer
   d. eagle   4. secondary consumer
   e. fungus   5. primary consumer

5. Why are the top predators in food chains most severely affected by pesticides such as DDT?

6. Over a period of many years, grass grows on a sand dune, then shrubs grow, and then eventually trees grow. This is an example of ecological _____.

7. According to the pyramid of production, why is eating grain-fed beef a relatively inefficient means of obtaining the energy trapped by photosynthesis?

8. Local conditions, such as heavy rainfall or the removal of plants, may limit the amount of nitrogen, phosphorus, or calcium available to a particular terrestrial ecosystem, but the amount of carbon available to the ecosystem is seldom a problem. Why?

9. A _____ is a local grouping of interacting ecosystems with several adjacent habitats.

10. Movement corridors are
    a. the routes taken by migratory animals.
    b. strips or clumps of habitat that connect isolated fragments.
    c. landscapes that include several different ecosystems.
    d. edges or boundaries between ecosystems.
    e. buffer zones that protect the long-term viability of protected areas.

Answers to these questions can be found in Appendix: Self-Quiz Answers.

THE PROCESS OF SCIENCE

11. An ecologist studying desert plants performed the following experiment. She staked out two identical plots that included a few sagebrush plants and numerous small annual wildflowers. She found the same five wildflower species in similar numbers in both plots. Then she enclosed one of the plots with a fence to keep out kangaroo rats, the most common herbivores in the area. After two years, four species of wildflowers were no longer present in the fenced plot, but one wildflower species had increased dramatically. The unfenced control plot had not changed significantly in species composition. Using the concepts discussed in the chapter, what do you think happened?

12. Imagine that you have been chosen as the biologist for the design team implementing a self-contained space station to be assembled in orbit. It will be stocked with the organisms you choose, creating an ecosystem that will support you and five other people for two years. Describe the main functions you expect the organisms to perform. List the types of organisms you would select, and explain why you chose them.

13. Biologists in the United States are concerned that populations of many migratory songbirds, such as warblers, are declining. Evidence suggests that some of these birds might be victims of pesticides. Most of the pesticides implicated in songbird mortality have not been used in the United States since the 1970s. Suggest a hypothesis to explain the current decline in songbird numbers. Design an experiment that could test your hypothesis.

BIOLOGY AND SOCIETY

14. Some organizations are starting to envision a sustainable society—one in which each generation inherits sufficient natural and economic resources and a relatively stable environment. The Worldwatch Institute, an environmental policy organization, estimates that we must reach sustainability by the year 2030 to avoid economic and environmental collapse. In what ways is our current system not sustainable? What might we do to work toward sustainability, and what are the major roadblocks to achieving it? How would your life be different in a sustainable society?

15. The Biological Dynamics of Forest Fragmentation Project, which has contributed so much to our understanding of threats to biodiversity, is itself endangered. Encouraged by Brazilian government agencies, urban sprawl and intensive forest settlement are closing in on the study site. Activities such as clear-cutting, burning, hunting, and logging threaten the integrity of the surrounding forest. Researchers at the BDFFP, which is jointly operated by a Brazilian research agency and the Smithsonian Tropical Institute, hope that they can bring attention to the problem through the Brazilian media and pressure the government into protecting the project. How would you argue the importance of protecting the BDFFP against ecologically destructive activities in a letter to a newspaper editor or to a government official?

Unit 5
Animal Structure and Function

Chapter 21: **Unifying Concepts of Animal Structure and Function**

Chapter Thread: **Controlling Body Temperature**

Chapter 22: **Nutrition and Digestion**

Chapter Thread: **Controlling Your Weight**

Chapter 23: **Circulation and Respiration**

Chapter Thread: **Athletic Endurance**

Chapter 24: **The Body's Defenses**

Chapter Thread: **HIV and AIDS**

Chapter 25: **Hormones**

Chapter Thread: **Steroid Abuse**

Chapter 26: **Reproduction and Development**

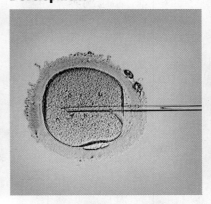

Chapter Thread: **High-Tech Babies**

Chapter 27: **Nervous, Sensory, and Locomotor Systems**

Chapter Thread: **Extrahuman Senses**

21 Unifying Concepts of Animal Structure and Function

Keeping cool.
Sweating and drinking water are two ways of cooling the human body.

Controlling Body Temperature BIOLOGY AND SOCIETY

An Avoidable Tragedy

August 20, 2008, started off as a normal day for the football team at Pleasure Ridge Park High School. True, the day was sweltering, with a heat index of 94, but such conditions are common during Kentucky summers. However, this day turned tragic when Max Gilpin, a healthy 15-year-old sophomore offensive lineman, began to have trouble breathing during the team's routine training and collapsed. By the time he reached the hospital, his body temperature was 107 degrees Fahrenheit. Max died three days later from heat stroke. As heartbreaking as it is, this case is hardly unique: Heat illness is a leading cause of death and injury among U.S. high school athletes, affecting nearly 10,000 each year.

When you play or work hard, your muscles produce a lot of heat. In response, a temperature control center in your brain initiates responses that help keep your internal temperature near its normal value (about 37°C, or 99°F). Sweating cools your skin by evaporation and blood vessels near the skin surface expand, allowing more heat to be released. But what if the heat worsens? Surface blood vessels widen to their maximum, and excessive sweating may cause dehydration. Both of these responses could lower blood pressure enough to cause you to faint. This set of symptoms, called heat exhaustion, represents the body's final attempt to cool itself. To avoid heat exhaustion, you should drink plenty of water and rest if you feel lightheaded or your skin flushes excessively.

Under extreme conditions, a severely elevated body temperature can disrupt the brain's control center. When the body loses its ability to self-regulate, sweating stops and the skin becomes hot and dry. The body's organs begin to fail as a result of the extreme heat, and brain damage and death can quickly follow unless the body is rapidly cooled and provided with fluids. This condition, called heat stroke, is caused by a total breakdown of the body's internal temperature control system.

In this unit, you will learn how your body works, including its self-regulating mechanisms. We'll concentrate on humans but offer comparisons to other animals to provide examples of different solutions to a common set of problems. How, for example, do creatures as diverse as hydras, halibut, and humans regulate body temperature or obtain food? By learning about various evolutionary adaptations common to animals, you will better understand your own body. To set the stage for the rest of the unit, this chapter begins with a description of basic animal structure, from cells to tissues to organs to organ systems. Next, these structural principles will be applied to two examples of how animals regulate their internal environment: the control of temperature and the control of water and solute movement.

The Structural Organization of Animals

Life is characterized by a hierarchy of organization. In animals, individual cells are grouped into tissues, which in turn are grouped into organs, which participate in organ systems, which together make up the entire organism (Figure 21.1). Parts of the body at each level of the hierarchy act together to perform the functions of life, such as regulating an animal's internal environment. For example, regulation of your body temperature requires the cooperation of several levels of body organization. The brain, an organ, sends signals via the nervous system that trigger specific changes in tissues (such as the narrowing or widening of capillaries near the skin) and individual cells (such as an increase or decrease in glucose metabolism). The result is a change within the whole body. ☑

Form Fits Function

Which is the better tool: a hammer or a screwdriver? The answer, of course, depends on what you're trying to do. Given a choice of tools, you would not use a hammer to loosen a screw or a screwdriver to pound a nail. How a device works is correlated with its structure: Form fits function. A chair, for example, must have a surface to sit on and a stable base to support that surface.

▼ Figure 21.1 **Structural hierarchy in a human.**

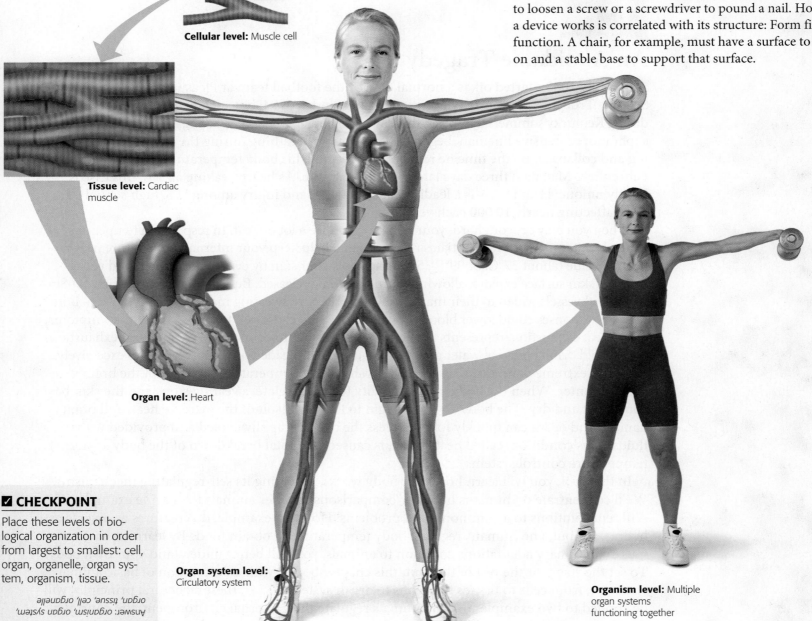

Cellular level: Muscle cell

Tissue level: Cardiac muscle

Organ level: Heart

Organ system level: Circulatory system

Organism level: Multiple organ systems functioning together

☑ CHECKPOINT

Place these levels of biological organization in order from largest to smallest: cell, organ, organelle, organ system, organism, tissue.

Answer: organism, organ system, organ, tissue, cell, organelle

These structural elements are dictated by the task that the chair must perform. The same principle applies to life at its many structural levels, from cells to organisms. Analyzing a biological structure gives us clues about what it does and how it works. Conversely, knowing the function of a structure provides insight about its construction. In exploring life at its many levels, we will discover functional elegance at every turn (Figure 21.2).

When discussing structure and function, biologists distinguish anatomy from physiology. **Anatomy** is the study of the structure of an organism's parts. **Physiology** is the study of the function of those parts. For example, an anatomist might study the arrangement of blood vessels near the surface of the skin, whereas a physiologist might study how those blood vessels widen in response to a sudden rise in temperature. Despite their different approaches, the two disciplines serve the same purpose: to better understand the connections between structure and function.

The correlation of form (structure) and function is a fundamental principle of biology that is evident at all levels of life's hierarchy; it is a principle that will guide us throughout our study of animals. But this rule of "design" does not mean that such biological tools as a bird's wings, a fish's gills, or a mammal's blood vessels are products of purposeful invention. Here the analogy to household tools such as hammers and screwdrivers fails because those tools were designed with specific goals. It is natural selection that refines biological equipment to the current environment. It does so by screening for the most effective variations among individuals of a population—those variations that are most advantageous in the local environment. Generations of selecting for what works best in a particular environment will fit form to function without any goal-oriented plan. Thus, the form–function principle is just another facet of biology's unifying theme: evolution. ☑

Tissues

The cell is the basic unit of all living organisms. In almost all animals, including humans, cells rarely act alone but instead are grouped into tissues. A **tissue** is an integrated group of similar cells that performs a specific function. The cells composing a tissue are specialized; they have an overall structure that enables them to perform a specific task.

Some tissues consist of living cells surrounded by a meshwork of nonliving fibers. The cells of other tissues are held together by a sticky substance that coats the cells or by special junctions that fuse the cells together. An animal has four main categories of tissue: epithelial tissue, connective tissue, muscle tissue, and nervous tissue. As you'll see, the structure of each type of tissue relates to its specific function.

▼ **Figure 21.2 Form fits function.**

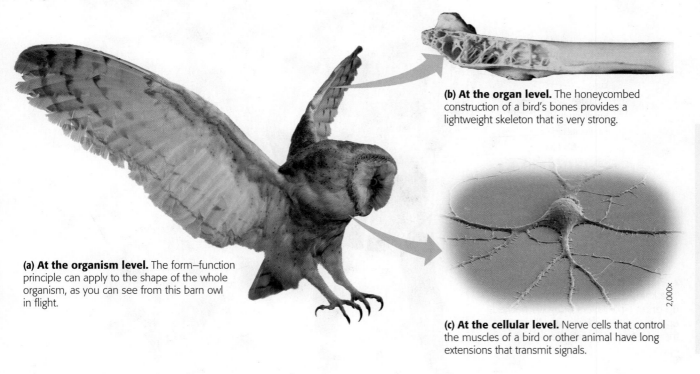

(a) At the organism level. The form–function principle can apply to the shape of the whole organism, as you can see from this barn owl in flight.

(b) At the organ level. The honeycombed construction of a bird's bones provides a lightweight skeleton that is very strong.

(c) At the cellular level. Nerve cells that control the muscles of a bird or other animal have long extensions that transmit signals.

2,000x

☑ **CHECKPOINT**

1. What is the difference between anatomy and physiology?
2. Explain how a tennis racket illustrates the "form fits function" principle.

Answers: 1. Anatomy is the study of structure, whereas physiology is the study of function. 2. To aid the function of hitting a ball, a tennis racket has a handle for gripping, a large head to strike the ball, and strings to provide bounce.

Epithelial Tissue

The tissue that covers the surface of the body and lines organs is called **epithelial tissue**, also known as **epithelium (Figure 21.3)**. The epidermis (outer layer of skin) and the linings of the heart, blood vessels, and digestive tract are examples. Epithelial tissue is made of sheets of tightly packed cells that are fused together. The architecture of an epithelium illustrates how structure fits function at the tissue level. For example, your epidermis contains dense layers of tightly bound epithelial cells, forming a protective barrier that surrounds your body and helps protect its internal environment from external threats.

The body continuously renews the cells of epithelial tissue, shedding old cells and growing new ones. For example, cells of the epidermis continuously fall off and are renewed about every two weeks. Such turnover requires rapid cell division, which increases the risk of an error in cell division that leads to cancer. And compared with other body tissues, epithelium that contacts the environment directly is exposed to much higher levels of carcinogens (smoke in the lungs and UV light on the skin, for example). Consequently, about 80% of all cancers (including skin, lung, and breast cancer) arise in epithelial tissue. Cancers of the epithelium are called carcinomas.

Connective Tissue

In contrast to epithelium, with its tightly packed cells, **connective tissue** has a sparse population of cells scattered throughout a jellylike material called the **extracellular matrix**. The matrix consists of a web of protein fibers embedded in a liquid (as in blood), jelly (as in fat tissue), or solid (as in bone).

The structure of connective tissue corresponds to its function: to bind and support other tissues. For example, the epithelial tissue of your skin (epidermis) lies on top of a layer of connective tissue called the dermis, which contains the blood vessels and extracellular fluids that nourish the epidermis.

Figure 21.4 illustrates six of the major types of connective tissue. The most widespread connective tissue in the body of vertebrates (animals with backbones, including humans) is **loose connective tissue (Figure 21.4a)**. It binds epithelia to underlying tissues and holds organs in place, similar to the way that packing peanuts can prevent shipped merchandise from sliding around. This connective tissue is held together by a mesh of protein fibers that provide great strength and elasticity. For example, if someone pinches your cheek, it is protein fibers that

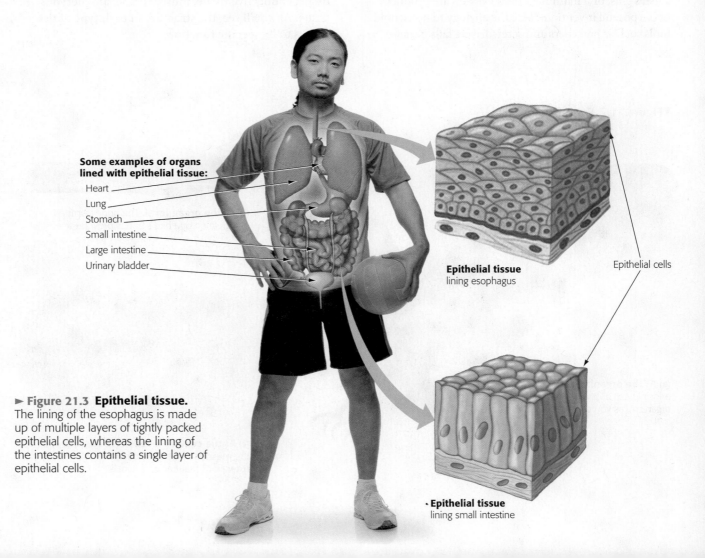

Some examples of organs
lined with epithelial tissue:

Heart
Lung
Stomach
Small intestine
Large intestine
Urinary bladder

Epithelial tissue
lining esophagus

Epithelial cells

Epithelial tissue
lining small intestine

► Figure 21.3 **Epithelial tissue.**
The lining of the esophagus is made up of multiple layers of tightly packed epithelial cells, whereas the lining of the intestines contains a single layer of epithelial cells.

keep your flesh in place and allow it to quickly snap back. A decrease in production of one of these proteins (collagen) as we age can result in skin wrinkles; some people inject collagen in an attempt to restore smooth skin.

Adipose tissue stores fat in closely packed cells **(Figure 21.4b)**. This tissue stockpiles energy while also padding and insulating the body. Each adipose cell contains a large globule of fat (mostly triglycerides—see Figure 3.11b); the cell swells when fat is stored and shrinks when fat is used for energy. Gaining body fat involves increasing the size of your fat cells, not creating new fat cells.

Blood is a connective tissue consisting of red and white blood cells suspended in a liquid called plasma **(Figure 21.4c)**. Blood functions mainly in transporting substances from one part of the body to another and also plays a major role in immunity.

The other three types of connective tissue have cells suspended in dense matrices. **Fibrous connective tissue** has a dense matrix of collagen. It forms tendons, which attach muscles to bones, and ligaments, which join bones together at joints **(Figure 21.4d)**. The matrix of **cartilage** is strong but flexible **(Figure 21.4e)**. Use your finger to flip your outer ear, and you'll get the idea of how cartilage functions as a flexible, boneless skeleton. The cartilaginous fishes—which include sharks and rays—have skeletons made entirely from cartilage. Cartilage is often found at the end of bones where it forms shock-absorbing pads. Cartilage has no blood vessels, so injuries to it (football knee injuries, for example) tend to heal very slowly, if at all. **Bone** is a rigid connective tissue with a matrix of collagen fibers hardened with deposits of calcium salts. This combination makes bone hard without being brittle **(Figure 21.4f)**.

Why are knee injuries often long-lasting?

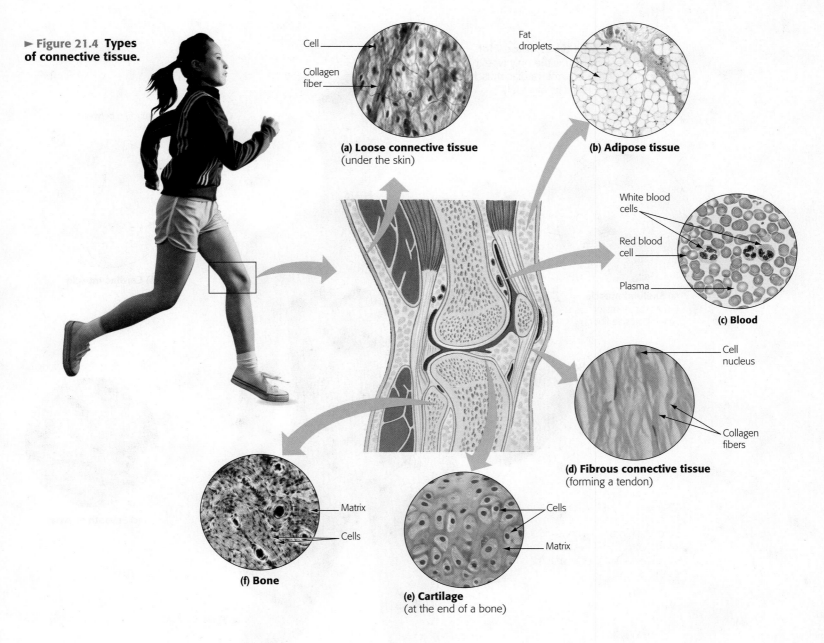

▶ **Figure 21.4 Types of connective tissue.**

Cell
Collagen fiber

(a) Loose connective tissue (under the skin)

Fat droplets

(b) Adipose tissue

White blood cells
Red blood cell
Plasma

(c) Blood

Cell nucleus
Collagen fibers

(d) Fibrous connective tissue (forming a tendon)

Matrix
Cells

(f) Bone

Cells
Matrix

(e) Cartilage (at the end of a bone)

Muscle Tissue

Muscle is the most abundant tissue in most animals. In fact, what we call "meat" on the menu is mostly animal muscle. **Muscle tissue** consists of bundles of long, thin, cylindrical cells called muscle fibers. Each cell has specialized proteins arranged into a structure that contracts (pulls in) when the cell is stimulated by a signal from a nerve. Humans and other vertebrates have three types of this contractile tissue, each with a slightly different structure: skeletal muscle, cardiac (heart) muscle, and smooth muscle.

Skeletal muscle is attached to your bones by tendons and is responsible for your voluntary movements, such as walking and talking (Figure 21.5a). This type of muscle is said to be striated (striped) because the contractile proteins form a banded pattern. Adults have a fixed number of these cells. Weight training does not increase the number of muscle cells but instead enlarges those already present.

What effect does working out have on your muscles?

Cardiac muscle is found only in heart tissue **(Figure 21.5b)**. The contraction of the cardiac muscle produces the heartbeat. Cardiac muscle cells are branched and joined to one another, appearing like one large interconnected mass of muscle. This structure allows the contraction signal to be propagated quickly to all muscle cells at once, producing a coordinated beat. Cardiac muscle is an involuntary muscle, meaning that your heart contracts without any conscious control on your part.

In contrast to skeletal muscle and cardiac muscle, **smooth muscle** is named for its lack of obvious stripes **(Figure 21.5c)**. Found in the walls of such organs as the intestines and blood vessels, smooth muscle is involuntary. For example, you have no control over the dilation of your blood vessels in response to heat, a response that causes you to flush. Smooth muscle contracts more slowly than skeletal muscle, but it can remain contracted for a longer time.

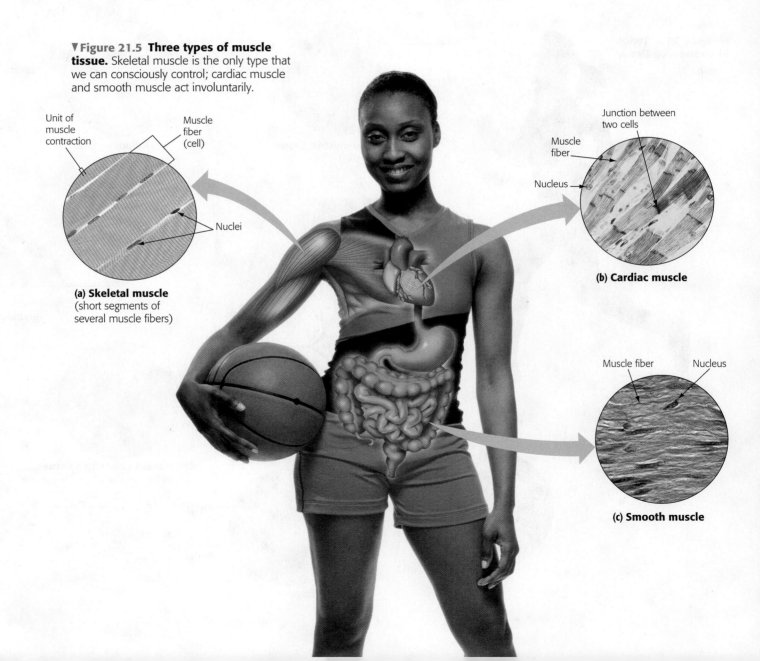

▼ **Figure 21.5 Three types of muscle tissue.** Skeletal muscle is the only type that we can consciously control; cardiac muscle and smooth muscle act involuntarily.

Unit of muscle contraction

Muscle fiber (cell)

Nuclei

(a) Skeletal muscle (short segments of several muscle fibers)

Junction between two cells

Muscle fiber

Nucleus

(b) Cardiac muscle

Muscle fiber

Nucleus

(c) Smooth muscle

Nervous Tissue

Most animals are active creatures that respond rapidly to stimuli from their environment. For example, if you touch a very hot object, your arm quickly jerks away. This response requires information to be relayed from one part of the body to another. It is **nervous tissue** that makes such communication possible. Nervous tissue is found in your brain and spinal cord, as well as in the nerves that connect them to all other parts of your body.

The basic unit of nervous tissue is the **neuron**, or nerve cell **(Figure 21.6)**. With their long extensions, neurons can transmit electrical signals very rapidly over long distances. For example, neurons in the sciatic nerve of your leg may be as long as 1 m (3.3 feet), running all the way from the base of your spinal cord to the tips of your toes. You are wired for action—and for thinking, since it is the network of neurons in your brain that functions as your mind. ☑

▼**Figure 21.6 Nervous tissue.** Here you see the body's network of nervous tissue, to the right, and its basic unit, the neuron, to the left. Each neuron has extensions that receive signals, a cell body, and an extension that transmits signals. These signals are transmitted throughout the brain, the spinal cord, and the network of nerves (cable-like bundles of neurons) that connect to all other parts of the body.

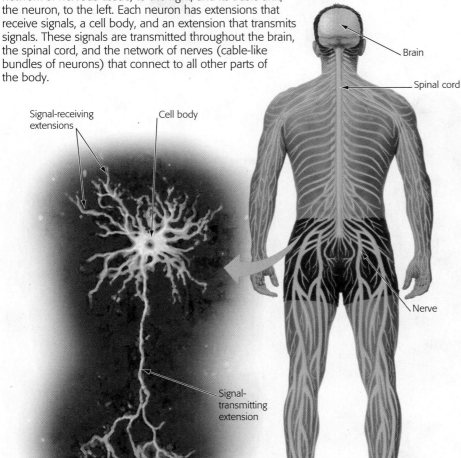

Signal-receiving extensions

Cell body

Brain

Spinal cord

Nerve

Signal-transmitting extension

LM 1,000×

Organs and Organ Systems

After tissues, the next level in the structural hierarchy is the organ. An **organ** consists of two or more tissues packaged into one working unit that performs a specific function. Your heart, brain, and small intestine are examples of organs. At each level of the hierarchy, functions emerge from the collective interaction of the structures at lower levels. An organ performs functions that none of its component tissues can carry out alone.

To see how multiple tissues coordinate a single organ, examine the layered arrangement of tissues in the wall of the small intestine in **Figure 21.7**. The inside wall is lined with epithelial tissue (top layer of cells in figure) that secretes mucus. Underneath this layer are two layers of connective tissue—one containing blood capillaries and lymph vessels—separated by two layers of smooth muscle. A final layer of epithelial tissue forms the outside surface. Neurons regulate the rhythmic contractions of the intestinal muscles, propelling food.

☑ **CHECKPOINT**

Name the four types of tissue found in most organs.

Answer: epithelial, connective, muscle, and nervous

► **Figure 21.7 Tissue layers of the small intestine, an organ.**

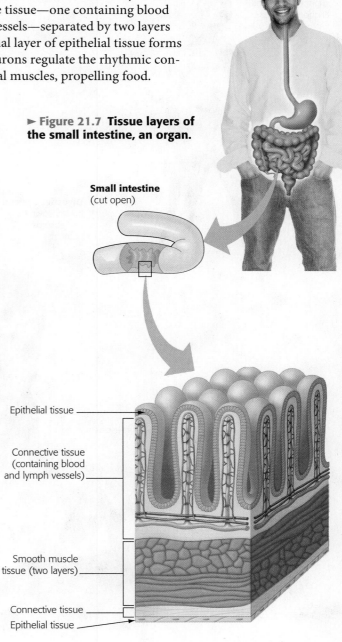

Small intestine (cut open)

Epithelial tissue

Connective tissue (containing blood and lymph vessels)

Smooth muscle tissue (two layers)

Connective tissue

Epithelial tissue

The organs of humans and most other animals are organized into **organ systems**, teams of organs that work together to perform vital body functions. The components of an organ system can be physically connected or they can be dispersed within the body. An example of an organ system is your circulatory system, which transports materials throughout your body. Its main organs are the heart and blood vessels (arteries, veins, and capillaries). **Figure 21.8** presents an overview of 11 major organ systems in vertebrates.

An organism depends on the coordination of all its organ systems for survival. For instance,

▼ **Figure 21.8 Organ systems of a vertebrate.**

Skeletal system:
supports body and anchors muscles

Bone

Cartilage

Circulatory system:
transports substances throughout body

Heart

Blood vessels

Respiratory system:
exchanges O_2 and CO_2 between blood and air

Nasal cavity

Pharynx

Larynx

Trachea

Bronchus

Lung

Digestive system:
breaks down food and absorbs nutrients

Mouth

Esophagus

Liver

Stomach

Large intestine

Small intestine

Anus

Urinary system:
rids body of certain wastes

Kidney

Ureter

Urinary bladder

Urethra

Muscular system:
moves the body

Skeletal muscles

the action of muscle cells can produce body heat, raising your internal temperature. Cells within your nervous system can sense the temperature change and send signals that cause blood vessels of your circulatory system to widen, releasing heat. The failure of any organ system will jeopardize the entire animal because organ systems are so interwoven and dependent on each other. Your body is a whole, living unit that is greater than the sum of its parts. In the next section, we'll look at how the body's organ systems interact with the external environment. ☑

☑ **CHECKPOINT**

Your stomach is a(n) _____ , whereas your digestive system is a(n) _____ .

Answer: organ; organ system

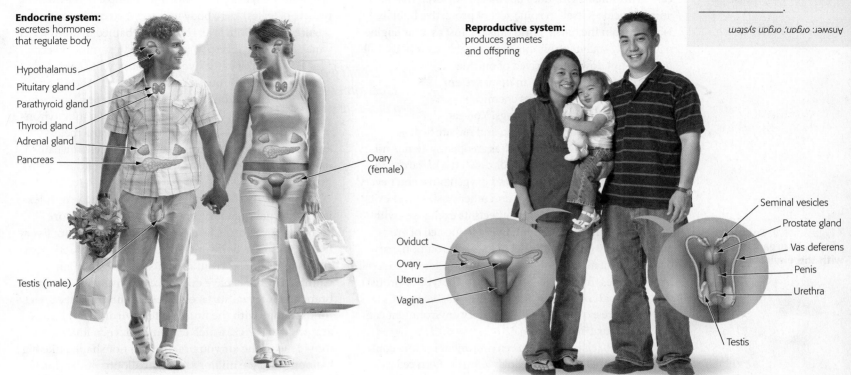

Endocrine system:
secretes hormones that regulate body

Hypothalamus
Pituitary gland
Parathyroid gland
Thyroid gland
Adrenal gland
Pancreas
Testis (male)

Ovary (female)

Reproductive system:
produces gametes and offspring

Oviduct
Ovary
Uterus
Vagina

Seminal vesicles
Prostate gland
Vas deferens
Penis
Urethra
Testis

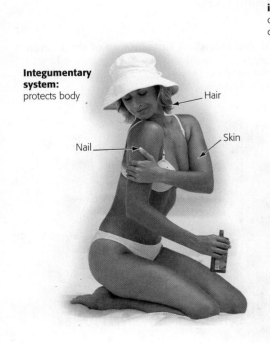

Integumentary system:
protects body

Hair
Nail
Skin

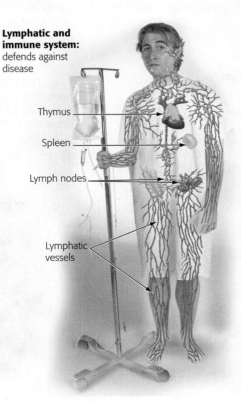

Lymphatic and immune system:
defends against disease

Thymus
Spleen
Lymph nodes
Lymphatic vessels

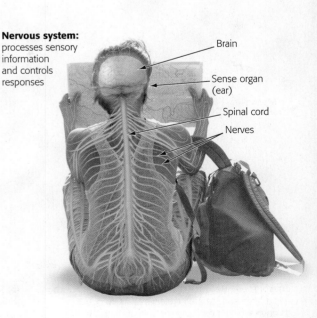

Nervous system:
processes sensory information and controls responses

Brain
Sense organ (ear)
Spinal cord
Nerves

463

Exchanges with the External Environment

Most animals are covered with a protective layer that separates the external world from the internal chemical environment. This does not mean, however, that an animal encloses itself in some sort of protective bubble, isolated from the harsh world outside. Just as a car engine will quickly stall if the air intake is clogged, your body will quickly shut down if deprived of outside oxygen. Every organism is an **open system** that continuously exchanges chemicals and energy with its surroundings. You eat, breathe, defecate, urinate, sweat, and radiate heat— all examples of how you operate as an open system. And the exchange of materials extends down the hierarchy to each individual cell: Nutrients and oxygen must enter every living cell, and carbon dioxide and other wastes must exit.

Why doesn't a parasitic tapeworm require a digestive system?

An animal's size and shape affects its exchanges with its surrounding environment. Every living cell of an animal's body must be bathed in a watery solution, partly because substances must be dissolved in water to cross cell membranes. In a single-celled amoeba (a type of protist), every part of its body borders the outside world, where exchange with the watery environment can occur (**Figure 21.9a**).

Exchange with the environment is more complicated for multicellular animals. Each cell in a multicellular organism has a plasma membrane where exchange of materials can occur. But this exchange only works if all the cells of the animal have access to a suitable watery environment. A hydra (a simple pond-dwelling relative of jellies) has a body wall only two cell layers thick (**Figure 21.9b**). Both layers of cells are bathed in pond water, which enters the digestive sac through the mouth. Every cell of the hydra can thus exchange materials through direct contact with the watery environment. A flat body shape is another way of maximizing exposure to the environment. For instance, a tapeworm may be several meters long, but because it is very thin, most of its cells are bathed in the body fluid of the worm's host, from which it obtains nutrients directly.

Simple body shapes do not allow for much complexity in internal organization. But animals with more complex body forms face the same basic problem: Every living cell in the body must be bathed in fluid and have access to resources from the outside environment. Complex animals have evolved extensively folded or branched internal surfaces that maximize surface area for exchange with the immediate environment. For example, your lungs, which exchange oxygen and carbon dioxide with the air you breathe, are not shaped like big balloons but like millions of tiny balloons at the tips of finely branched air tubes (**Figure 21.10**). The epithelium of the lungs has a very large total surface area—about the size of a tennis court.

▼ **Figure 21.9 Contact of simple organisms with the environment.**

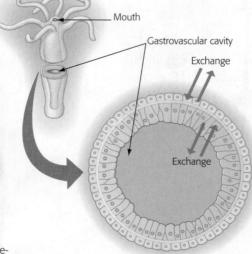

Mouth

Gastrovascular cavity

Exchange

Exchange

Exchange

(a) Single cell. The entire surface area of a single-celled organism, such as this amoeba, contacts the environment. Because of its small size, the organism has a large surface area (relative to its volume) through which it exchanges materials with the external world.

(b) Two cell layers. Although a hydra is multicellular, each one of its cells touches an aqueous environment. The body has only two cell layers, both exposed to water.

▼ **Figure 21.10 The branched surface area of the human lung.** This plastic model shows the tiny air tubes of the lungs (white) and the thin blood vessels (red) that transport gases between the heart and lungs.

Figure 21.11 shows a schematic model of an animal body, highlighting the three organ systems—digestive, respiratory, and urinary—that exchange materials with the external environment. Notice also the vital role of the circulatory system: It connects to nearly every organ system as it transports needed materials from the environment to the body's tissues and carries wastes away. Looking at the figure, you can see how nutrients that are absorbed from the digestive tract are distributed throughout the body by the circulatory system. The heart that pumps blood through the circulatory system requires nutrients absorbed from food by the digestive tract and also oxygen (O_2) obtained from the air by the respiratory system. And absorption of nutrients inevitably produces wastes that must be excreted by the urinary system. The circulatory system thereby provides an internal conduit that joins the systems that connect with the outside world. ☑

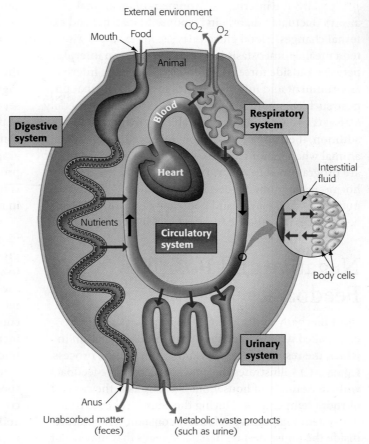

▶ **Figure 21.11 Exchange between the external environment and the internal environment of complex animals.** The blue arrows indicate the exchange of materials between the circulatory system and three other systems and between the circulatory system and body cells.

☑ **CHECKPOINT**

Is your body an open or closed system? Why?

Answer: Your body is an open system because the digestive, respiratory, and urinary systems are in direct contact with the external environment.

Regulating the Internal Environment

In this section, you'll learn how animals adjust to a changing environment. We'll look in particular at how they regulate temperature and control the movement of water and solutes.

Homeostasis

One of the body's most important functions is to stay relatively unchanged even when the world around it changes. The internal environment of vertebrates includes the **interstitial fluid** that fills the spaces between cells and exchanges nutrients and wastes with microscopic blood vessels (see Figure 21.11). It is important that the composition of the interstitial fluid remain relatively constant no matter what occurs in the outside world.

Homeostasis, which literally means "steady state," is the tendency to maintain relatively constant conditions in the internal environment even when the external environment changes. In the face of large external

changes, the mechanisms of homeostasis normally maintain internal conditions within a range that the animal's metabolism can tolerate **(Figure 21.12)**. For example, your internal body temperature normally fluctuates by less than a degree, whether you are making an angel in the cold winter snow or a cannonball into a pool in the hot summer sun. Losing the ability to maintain homeostasis can have significant health consequences. Diabetes, for example, is a loss of glucose homeostasis in the blood.

▼ **Figure 21.12 Homeostasis.**

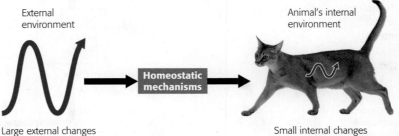

External environment

Large external changes

Homeostatic mechanisms

Animal's internal environment

Small internal changes

Actually, the internal environment of an animal always fluctuates slightly in response to internal and external changes. Blood glucose levels, for example, rise after a meal. Homeostasis is a dynamic state, an interplay between outside forces that tend to change the internal environment and internal control mechanisms that oppose such changes. Changes do occur, but they generally stay within a range that is tolerable for living cells. In addition, there are times during the development of an animal when major changes in the internal environment are programmed to occur. For example, the balance of hormones in human blood changes radically during puberty or pregnancy, and body temperature may rise a few degrees in response to a bacterial infection.

Negative and Positive Feedback

Most mechanisms of homeostasis depend on a principle called **negative feedback**, a form of regulation in which the results of a process inhibit that same process. **Figure 21.13** illustrates the concept of negative feedback with an example of household homeostasis, the control of room temperature. During the winter, a home heating system maintains a relatively constant temperature inside the house despite drastic changes that may occur outside. A key component of this system is a control center—a thermostat—that monitors temperature and switches the heater on and off. Whenever room temperature drops below the set point (the temperature at which the thermostat is set, 20°C in the figure), the thermostat switches the heater on (bottom pathway in Figure 21.13). When the temperature rises above the set point, the thermostat switches the heater off (top pathway). The basic principle of negative feedback is simple: The result (increased room temperature, for example) of a process (heating of the air) inhibits that very process (by switching the heater off). Negative feedback is the most common mechanism of homeostatic control in animals.

Less commonly, organisms use **positive feedback**, in which the results of a process intensify that same process. For example, during the labor that leads up to childbirth, chemical signals cause the muscles of the uterus to contract. This contraction stimulates the release of more such chemicals, which cause more contractions, and so on, in a positive-feedback loop of increasing intensity. The result is climactic muscle contractions that push the baby from the womb.

In the rest of this section, we'll examine several specific examples of homeostasis. We'll first discuss the control of temperature and the control of water gain and loss in a variety of animals. We'll then focus on the human urinary system—an organ system that performs several homeostatic roles. ☑

► Figure 21.13 **An example of negative feedback: control of room temperature.** This is an example of negative feedback because the result of the process (heat) shuts that process down.

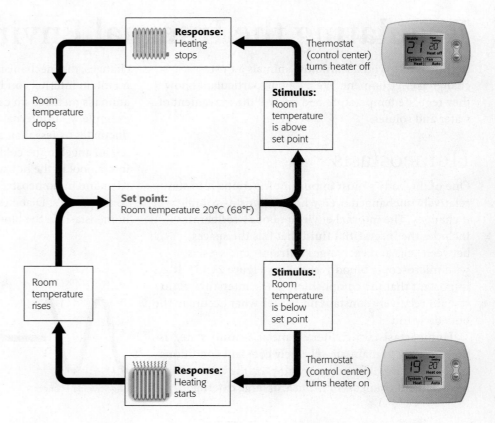

☑ CHECKPOINT

When you flush a toilet, water begins to refill the tank. The rising water level lifts a float. When the float reaches a certain height, it stops more water from entering the tank. This is an example of what kind of homeostatic control? Why?

Answer: This is an example of negative feedback because the result of a process (water filling the tank) inhibits that same process.

Thermoregulation

As you saw in the Biology and Society section, the maintenance of internal body temperature is important in animals. This homeostatic mechanism is called **thermoregulation**. As you walk from a warm building to the outside on a cold winter day, your body's temperature will barely fluctuate, despite the drastic change in temperature in the environment around you. The ability to maintain a body temperature substantially warmer than the surrounding environment is characteristic of **endotherms**, animals such as mammals and birds that derive most of their body heat from their own metabolism. In contrast, **ectotherms**, which include most invertebrates, fishes, amphibians, and nonbird reptiles, obtain their body heat primarily by absorbing it from their surroundings.

You have a number of structures and mechanisms that aid in thermoregulation. As shown in **Figure 21.14**, your brain has a control center that maintains your body temperature near 37°C (98.6°F). When your body temperature falls below normal, your brain's control center sends signals that trigger changes that will bring it back to normal: Blood vessels near your body's surface constrict (conserving heat) and muscles contract, causing you to shiver (producing heat). When body temperature gets too high, the control center sends signals to dilate the blood vessels near your skin and activate sweat glands, allowing excess heat to escape. Like a home controlled by a thermostat, the temperature of the body does not stay completely constant but fluctuates up and down within an acceptable range.

Why do you shiver when you are cold?

Fever, an abnormally high internal temperature, is a body-wide response that usually indicates an ongoing fight against infection. When your immune system cells encounter invading microbes, the cells release chemicals that travel through the bloodstream to your brain. These chemicals stimulate your brain's thermostatic control center to raise the body's internal temperature, producing a fever. Many people mistakenly believe that the invading microbes themselves cause a fever. In fact, the cause is usually the body's fight *against* the microbes. A fever of more than 40°C (104°F) may be life-threatening because a temperature that high can damage body proteins. A moderate fever of 38–39°C (100–102°F), however, discourages bacterial growth and speeds the body's internal defenses. A moderate fever thus helps protect the body's internal environment against potentially harmful invaders from the external environment.

We are endotherms and so can generate body heat to warm ourselves. Ectotherms generally cannot. But there are exceptions to this rule, as we'll see next in the Process of Science section. ☑

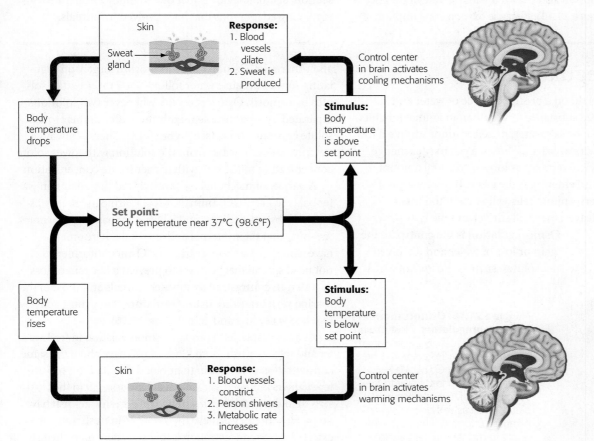

◄ **Figure 21.14**
Thermoregulation in the human body. By comparing this figure with Figure 21.13, you can see how similar negative-feedback controls moderate the temperatures of a room and your body. The control center for body temperature is located in the brain.

Skin
Sweat gland

Response:
1. Blood vessels dilate
2. Sweat is produced

Control center in brain activates cooling mechanisms

Stimulus: Body temperature is above set point

Body temperature drops

Set point: Body temperature near 37°C (98.6°F)

Body temperature rises

Stimulus: Body temperature is below set point

Control center in brain activates warming mechanisms

Skin

Response:
1. Blood vessels constrict
2. Person shivers
3. Metabolic rate increases

☑ **CHECKPOINT**

Name two features of the human body that help release heat and two features that help keep the body warm.

Answer: Examples include sweating and dilation of blood vessels to release heat; shivering and constriction of blood vessels to keep the body warm.

467

How Does a Python Warm Her Eggs?

As just described, ectotherms usually absorb heat from their surroundings. Under certain circumstances, however, some ectotherms can generate their own body heat. An example is the Burmese python (*Python molurus bivittatus*), a very large snake native to the rain forests of southeastern Asia. Like most snakes, it reproduces by laying eggs. Researchers at the Bronx Zoo, in New York City, made the **observation** that a female Burmese python incubating her eggs wraps her body around them, raises her body temperature, and frequently contracts the muscles in her coils. They formed the **hypothesis** that the muscle contractions elevate the snake's body temperature.

To test their hypothesis, they performed a simple **experiment**. They placed a python and her eggs in a chamber. As they varied the chamber's temperature, they monitored the python's muscle contractions and oxygen uptake, a measure of her rate of cellular respiration. Their **results** showed that the python's oxygen consumption increased when the temperature in the chamber decreased. Her oxygen consumption also changed with the rate of muscle contraction **(Figure 21.15)**. Because oxygen consumption

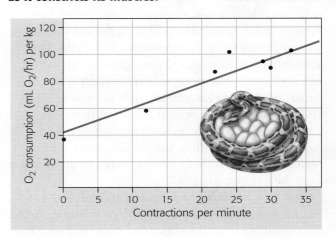

▼ **Figure 21.15 Oxygen consumed by a Burmese python as it constricts its muscles.**

generates heat through cellular respiration and increases with the rate of muscle contraction, the researchers concluded that the muscle contractions were the source of the Burmese python's elevated body temperature during egg incubation. As you'll see in the Evolution Connection section, such behavior is just one of many temperature-regulating adaptations that have evolved in animals.

Osmoregulation

Living cells depend on a precise balance of water and solutes (dissolved substances). Whether an animal inhabits land, fresh water, or salt water, its cells cannot survive if too much water enters or leaves. That is, a cell may exchange water with the environment as long as the total amount leaving and entering is the same. If too much water enters, animal cells will burst; if too much leaves, they will shrivel and die.

Osmoregulation is the control of the gain or loss of water and dissolved solutes, such as the ions of NaCl

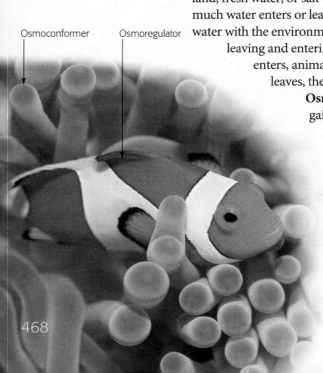

Osmoconformer   Osmoregulator

◄ **Figure 21.16 Osmoconformers and osmoregulators.** Most marine invertebrates (such as the sea anemone whose tentacles are visible here) are osmoconformers, which have water concentrations similar to their surroundings. Most marine vertebrates (such as this clown fish) are osmoregulators, which use mechanisms to maintain water balance.

and other salts. Osmoregulation is based largely on regulating solutes because water follows the movement of solutes by osmosis. Osmosis occurs whenever two solutions separated by a permeable membrane differ in their total solute concentrations (see Figure 5.13). There is always a net movement of water from the solution with lower solute concentration to the one with higher solute concentration.

A variety of mechanisms have evolved that maintain water balance in aquatic animals. Most marine invertebrates—such as lobsters, scallops, and jellies—are **osmoconformers**, meaning that their internal and external environments have similar solute concentrations. Osmoconformers do not need special mechanisms to prevent a net gain or loss of water. In contrast, all freshwater animals and most of the marine vertebrates are **osmoregulators**: They must actively regulate water loss and gain **(Figure 21.16)**.

As an example, let's compare osmoregulation in freshwater and saltwater fish. Both kinds of fish have about the same concentration of solutes in their blood despite their very different environments: Saltwater fish have less salt in their tissues than the water they swim in, while freshwater fish have more. How do they achieve this control? In fresh water, the external solute concentration is low, so water enters the fish by osmosis. To compensate, freshwater fish take up solutes via the digestive system and gills and produce large amounts of dilute urine. In contrast, osmoregulators that live in salt water lose water by osmosis. In response, saltwater fish take in water by drinking, pump out ions via the gills, and produce only small amounts of concentrated urine.

All land animals are osmoregulators. Most land animals gain water from eating and drinking and lose it through urinating, defecating, breathing, and perspiring. The primary challenge facing land-dwelling osmoregulators is to avoid becoming dehydrated. As we'll see in the next section, our kidneys play a major role in regulating water balance. ☑

Homeostasis in the Urinary System

The human urinary system plays a central role in forming and excreting waste-carrying urine while regulating the amount of water and solutes in body fluids. The main processing centers are the two kidneys. Each is a compact organ, a bit smaller than a fist, located on either side of the abdomen. The kidneys contain nearly 100 miles of thin tubes called **tubules** and an intricate network of capillaries (tiny blood vessels). Every day, all of your blood passes through the capillaries of your kidneys hundreds of times. As the blood circulates, a fraction of it is filtered, and the plasma (the liquid portion) enters the kidney tubules. Once there, the plasma is called **filtrate**. The filtrate contains valuable substances that need to be reclaimed (such as water and glucose) and other substances that need to be disposed of. Chief among the waste products to be excreted is

urea, a nitrogen-containing compound produced from the breakdown of proteins and nucleic acids. Humans must dispose of urea, but we cannot simply excrete all of the filtrate as urine; if we did, we would lose vital nutrients and dehydrate rapidly. Instead, our kidneys refine the filtrate, concentrating the wastes and returning most of the water and useful solutes to the blood.

The anatomy of the human urinary system is shown in Figure 21.17. Starting with the whole system in **Figure 21.17a**, blood to be filtered enters each kidney via a blood vessel called the renal artery. Filtered blood leaves the kidney in the renal vein. **Figure 21.17b** shows a cutaway view of a kidney. Within the kidney, the renal artery branches into millions of thin blood vessels. **Figure 21.17c** shows one branch of the renal artery supplying blood to a nephron via a network of capillaries. A **nephron** consists of a tubule and its associated blood vessels. Each kidney contains about a million nephrons.

The nephrons carry out the functions of the urinary system. Blood pressure forces water and solutes from the blood through a filter at the start of the nephron tubule, creating filtrate. As the filtrate then passes through the tubule, water and needed nutrients are reabsorbed into the bloodstream and wastes are secreted into the filtrate. The filtrate becomes more and more concentrated, resulting in a relatively small quantity of **urine**. At the end of the tubule, urine leaves the nephron via a collecting duct. Urine collects in the kidney and then leaves via the **ureter**. Urine is stored in the **urinary bladder** (visible in Figure 21.17a). Periodically, urine is expelled from the urinary bladder via the **urethra**, a tube that empties near the vagina in females and through the penis in males.

☑ **CHECKPOINT**

Name two ways that water enters your body and four ways that water leaves your body.

Answer: Water enters via eating and drinking and leaves via breathing, sweating, urinating, and defecating.

▼ **Figure 21.17 Anatomy of the human urinary system.**

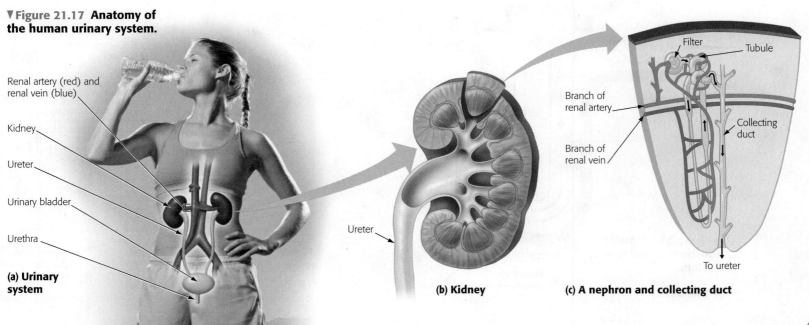

Renal artery (red) and renal vein (blue)

Kidney

Ureter

Urinary bladder

Urethra

(a) Urinary system

Ureter

(b) Kidney

Filter

Tubule

Branch of renal artery

Branch of renal vein

Collecting duct

To ureter

(c) A nephron and collecting duct

Figure 21.18 summarizes the functions performed by each nephron. First, during **filtration**, water and other small molecules are forced from the blood through a capillary wall into the beginning of a kidney tubule, forming filtrate. Next, in **reabsorption**, water and valuable solutes are reclaimed from the filtrate and returned to the blood. In **secretion**, certain substances, such as some ions and drugs, are transported into the filtrate. What remains after filtration, reabsorption, and secretion is the urine. Finally, in **excretion**, urine passes from the kidneys to the outside.

Why is kidney failure inevitably fatal if untreated?

The body controls its concentration of water and dissolved molecules through hormones that act on the kidney's nephrons. When the solute concentration of body fluids rises too high (indicating that not enough water is present), the brain increases levels of a hormone called ADH (antidiuretic hormone) in the blood. This hormone signals the nephrons to reabsorb more water from the filtrate, effectively increasing the body's water content. Conversely, when body fluids become too dilute, blood levels of ADH drop, the kidneys reabsorb less water, and the excreted urine becomes much more dilute. This is why your urine is very clear after you have been drinking a lot of water. Diuretics, such as alcohol, are substances that inhibit the release of ADH and therefore cause excessive urinary water loss. Drinking alcohol will make you urinate more frequently, and the resulting dehydration contributes to the symptoms of a hangover.

Kidney failure, the inability of the kidneys to filter blood, can be caused by injury, illness (such as high blood pressure or diabetes), or prolonged use of pain relievers (including over-the-counter medicines such as aspirin), alcohol, or other drugs. If the kidneys fail, the body is unable to rid itself of wastes. A person with one functioning kidney can lead a normal life, but if both kidneys fail, the buildup of toxic wastes will lead to certain and rapid death. One option is to place the person on **dialysis**, filtration of the blood by a machine that mimics the action of a nephron **(Figure 21.19)**. Blood from an artery enters a series of selectively permeable tubes. Urea and excess fluids pass from the blood into a dialyzing solution, while necessary salts and other substances transfer the opposite way. The machine discards the used dialyzing solution as wastes accumulate. Dialysis treatment is life sustaining for people with kidney failure, but it is costly, takes a lot of time (about 4–6 hours three times a week), and must be continued for life. Alternatively, a kidney from a living compatible donor (usually a relative) or a deceased organ donor can be transplanted into a person with kidney failure. Unfortunately, the number of people who need kidneys is much greater than the number of kidneys available, and the average wait for a kidney donation in the United States is three to five years.

Throughout our study of animal form and function in this unit, you will see many other examples of how mechanisms of homeostasis moderate changes in the internal environment despite larger fluctuations in the external environment. You will also see many other examples of what happens when homeostatic controls fail. ☑

☑ CHECKPOINT

Name the four processes that occur as kidney tubules process blood and create urine.

Answer: filtration, reabsorption, secretion, excretion

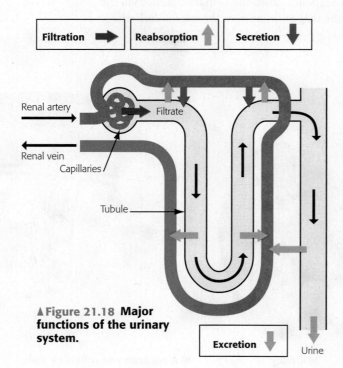

▲ Figure 21.18 Major functions of the urinary system.

Filtration ➡ | Reabsorption ⬆ | Secretion ⬇

Renal artery
Filtrate
Renal vein
Capillaries
Tubule
Excretion ⬇
Urine

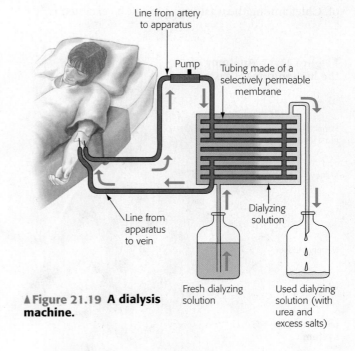

▲ Figure 21.19 A dialysis machine.

Line from artery to apparatus
Pump
Tubing made of a selectively permeable membrane
Line from apparatus to vein
Dialyzing solution
Fresh dialyzing solution
Used dialyzing solution (with urea and excess salts)

Adaptations for Thermoregulation

Natural selection has promoted a wide variety of adaptations—anatomical, physiological, and behavioral—that help animals cope with heat gained from or lost to the environment (Figure 21.20). A major anatomical adaptation in mammals and birds is insulation, consisting of hair (often called fur), feathers, or fat layers. A thin coat of fur in the summer often becomes a thick, insulating coat during the winter. Also, most land mammals and birds react to cold by raising their fur or feathers; this adaptation traps a thicker layer of air next to the warm skin, improving the insulation. In people, our muscles raise our hair in the cold, causing goose bumps, a vestige from our furry ancestors. Aquatic mammals (such as seals) and aquatic birds (such as penguins) have a thick insulating layer of fat called blubber.

Some adaptations are physiological. In cold weather, hormonal changes tend to boost the metabolic rate of birds and mammals, increasing their heat production. Simply moving around more or shivering also produces heat as a metabolic by-product of the contraction of skeletal muscles. Honeybees survive cold winters by clustering together and shivering in their hive. Their metabolic activity generates enough heat to keep the cluster alive. Panting and sweating are examples of physiological adaptations that greatly increase cooling.

A variety of behavioral responses can regulate body temperature. Some birds and butterflies migrate seasonally to more suitable climates. Other animals, such as desert lizards, bask in the sun when it is cold and find cool, damp areas or burrows when it is hot. Honeybees cool their hive during hot weather by transporting water into it and fanning with their wings. Many animals cool themselves by bathing, and a few even spread saliva on their bodies. Some mammals, such as ground squirrels and chipmunks, drastically reduce their body temperature and metabolic rate by hibernating in burrows during the winter, thereby conserving energy. All of these mechanisms—anatomical, physiological, and behavioral—demonstrate how a single selection pressure (the need to thermoregulate) can drive the evolution of a multitude of adaptations in a wide variety of environments.

▼ Figure 21.20 **Methods of thermoregulation in animals.**

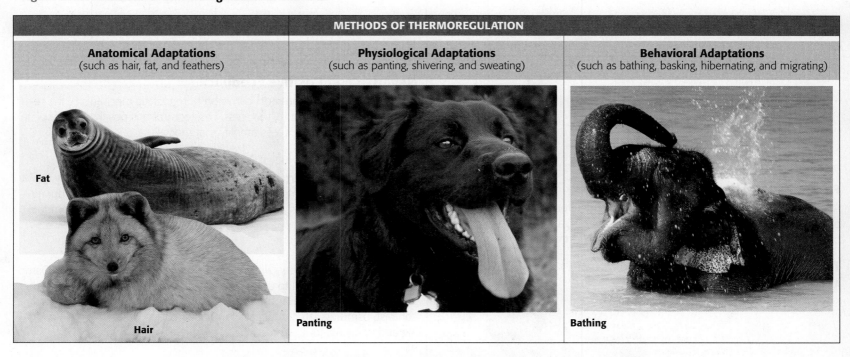

METHODS OF THERMOREGULATION		
Anatomical Adaptations (such as hair, fat, and feathers)	**Physiological Adaptations** (such as panting, shivering, and sweating)	**Behavioral Adaptations** (such as bathing, basking, hibernating, and migrating)
Fat / Hair	Panting	Bathing

471

Chapter Review

SUMMARY OF KEY CONCEPTS

The Structural Organization of Animals

HIERARCHICAL ORGANIZATION OF ANIMALS		
Level	**Description**	**Example**
Cell	The basic unit of all living organisms	Muscle cell
Tissue	A collection of similar cells performing a specific function	Cardiac muscle
Organ	Multiple tissues forming a structure that performs a specific function	Heart
Organ system	A team of organs that work together	Circulatory system
Organism	A living being, which depends on the coordination of all structural levels for homeostasis and survival	Person

Form Fits Function

At every level, the structure of a body part is correlated with the task it must perform. Anatomy is the study of the structure of organisms, whereas physiology is the study of the function of an organism's structures.

Tissues

Animals have four main kinds of tissue.

Muscle (contracts)

Connective (supports organs)

Epithelial (covers body surfaces and organs)

Nervous (relays and integrates information)

Organs and Organ Systems

An organ is a collection of tissues that together perform a specific function; an organ system is a group of organs that together provide a vital function for the organism. Figure 21.8 summarizes the 11 major human organ systems.

Exchanges with the External Environment

All animals are open systems, exchanging chemicals and energy with the environment. Every cell of a simple organism can exchange materials through direct contact with the environment. Large and complex body shapes require indirect exchange between extensively branched internal structures and the environment, usually via a circulatory system.

Regulating the Internal Environment

Homeostasis

Homeostasis is the body's tendency to maintain relatively constant internal conditions despite large fluctuations in the external environment.

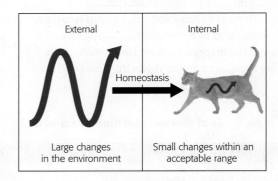

Negative and Positive Feedback

In negative feedback, the most common homeostatic mechanism, the results of a process inhibit that process. Less common is positive feedback, in which the results of a process amplify that process.

Thermoregulation

In thermoregulation, homeostatic mechanisms regulate internal body temperature. Endotherms are warmed primarily by heat generated during metabolism. Ectotherms are warmed primarily by heat absorbed from the environment.

Osmoregulation

All organisms balance the gain or loss of water and dissolved solutes. Osmoconformers do not tend to undergo a net gain or loss of water because their internal and external environments have similar solute concentrations. In contrast, osmoregulators must actively regulate their water balance—by drinking and urinating, for example.

Homeostasis in the Urinary System

The urinary system expels wastes and regulates solute and water balance. The following diagram summarizes the structure and function of the nephron, the functional unit of the kidney.

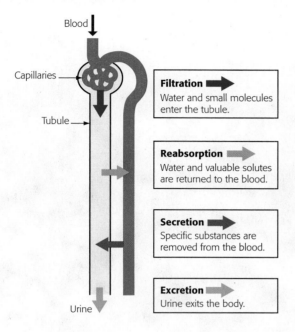

Blood

Capillaries

Tubule

Filtration ▶
Water and small molecules enter the tubule.

Reabsorption ▶
Water and valuable solutes are returned to the blood.

Secretion ▶
Specific substances are removed from the blood.

Excretion ▶
Urine exits the body.

Urine

SELF-QUIZ

1. List as many units of structural hierarchy in your body as you can, in order from smallest to largest.

2. How might body shape affect whether an animal requires a circulatory system?

3. Which of the following best illustrates homeostasis?
   a. Most adult human beings are between 5 and 6 feet tall.
   b. The lungs and intestines have large surface areas for exchange.
   c. When the concentration of water in the blood goes up, the kidneys expel more water.
   d. When oxygen in the blood decreases, you may feel light-headed.

4. Most human cells are surrounded by an aqueous solution called

   _____.

5. Stimulation of a nerve cell causes sodium ions to leak into the cell, and the sodium influx triggers the inward leaking of even more sodium. This is an example of _____ feedback. An increase in the concentration of glucose in the blood stimulates the pancreas to secrete insulin, a hormone that lowers blood glucose concentrations. This is an example of _____ feedback.

6. What is the main difference between endotherms and ectotherms?

7. Like most vertebrates, you are a(n) _____; your body must actively regulate the gain or loss of water. In contrast, a lobster is a(n) _____, living in an environment with a solute concentration similar to that of its body.

8. Which of the following is not one of the homeostatic functions of the kidney?
   a. reabsorption
   b. filtration
   c. excretion
   d. ingestion

9. Drinking alcohol makes you urinate more frequently because
   a. alcohol contains caffeine.
   b. alcohol inhibits the release of ADH, a hormone that increases water reabsorption in the kidneys.
   c. alcohol inhibits the release of ADH, a hormone that decreases water reabsorption in the kidneys.
   d. alcohol causes more water to filter from the blood into the kidneys.

10. What happens to most of the water that passes from the blood into the kidneys by filtration? What happens to the rest of it?

Answers to these questions can be found in Appendix: Self-Quiz Answers.

THE PROCESS OF SCIENCE

11. Eastern tent caterpillars (*Malacosoma americanum*) live in sizable groups in silk nests, or tents, typically in cherry and apple trees. They emerge early in the spring, when daily temperatures fluctuate from freezing to hot. Early in the morning, these black caterpillars rest in a tightly packed group on the east-facing surface of the tent. In midafternoon, the group is found on the tent undersurface, each caterpillar hanging from the tent by a few of its legs. Propose a hypothesis to explain this behavior. How could you test it?

BIOLOGY AND SOCIETY

12. The kidneys remove many drugs from the blood, and these substances show up in the urine. Some employers require a urine drug test at the time of hiring and/or at intervals during employment. Should an employee have the right to refuse a urine test? Should every job be subject to mandatory drug testing? If not, which jobs should be subject to testing? Would you take a drug test for a job? Why or why not?

13. Kidneys were the first organs to be successfully transplanted. A donor can live a normal life with a single kidney, making it possible for individuals to donate a kidney to an ailing relative or even an unrelated individual. Should a person be allowed to sell a kidney? Why or why not? What are some ethical issues raised by organ commerce?

22 Nutrition and Digestion

The key to maintaining a healthy weight. Eating a healthy diet and staying active are the only reliable ways to achieve and maintain a proper weight.

Controlling Your Weight BIOLOGY AND SOCIETY

The "Secret" to Shedding Pounds

Americans are obsessed with weight. About 50 million Americans (one in seven) go on a diet each year. Weight loss is a growth industry, with the leading weight loss programs boasting millions of members. Although Americans spend billions of dollars each year on diets and related products, only about 5% of dieters are able to reach their goal weight and maintain it for the long term.

For many of us, the obsession with weight loss is understandable. More than a third of American adults are obese (very overweight), and obesity is estimated to contribute to 300,000 deaths per year in the United States through increased incidence of heart disease, diabetes, cancer, and other health problems. Young adults are often particularly susceptible to sudden weight gain because the switch to independent living in college can lead to changes in diet and activity levels, often for the worse. And the problem is not limited to the United States: The United Nations World Health Organization recognizes obesity as a major global health problem. For most of us, therefore, it is healthy and proper to put effort into controlling our weight.

But with the wealth of fad diets with bogus claims, it can be difficult for you to know the best way to shed pounds. The good news is that there really is no trick to managing your weight: Add up the calories from the food you eat and then subtract the calories that your body burns. If you take in more by eating than you burn by activity, you will gain weight. If you burn more than you take in, you will lose weight. Weight control can be summed up in a five-word "secret": Eat less and exercise more! This is easier said than done, but the principle is sound and simple.

Caloric balance alone does not ensure good nutrition. Food must also provide the raw materials from which you build your body. You are what you eat: Your health and appearance depend on the quality of your diet and the proper functioning of your digestive system. This chapter focuses on essential concepts of digestion and nutrition, beginning with an overview of how animals process food. Next, we'll focus on the structure and function of the human digestive system. Along the way, we'll come back to the topic of weight loss as a reminder of the importance of this topic.

Overview of Animal Nutrition

Every mealtime reminds us that we must eat other organisms to acquire organic nutrients. Food provides the raw materials that animals, including people, need to build tissue and fuel cellular work. However, food primarily consists of large, complex molecules that are not in a form an animal's cells can use. Thus, the body must break down these nutrients—digest them—to make them useful.

Animal Diets

All animals eat other organisms, dead or alive, whole or by the piece. Beyond that generalization, however, animal diets vary extensively (Figure 22.1). **Herbivores**, such as cattle, gorillas, and sea urchins, feed mainly on plants or algae. **Carnivores**, such as lions, snakes, and spiders, mainly eat other animals. **Omnivores**, such as crows, cockroaches, and people, regularly eat animals as well as plants or algae. ☑

☑ CHECKPOINT

A chicken eats corn and bugs. That makes it a(n) ___________.

Answer: omnivore

The Four Stages of Food Processing

Think of the fate of one of your meals—such as a slice of pizza—and you'll start to get a sense of the four stages of food processing: ingestion, digestion, absorption, and elimination. **Ingestion** is just another word for eating. You ingest pizza when you bite off a piece. **Digestion** is the breakdown of food into molecules small enough for the body to absorb. The tomato sauce on a pizza, for example, is broken down to simple sugars and amino acids. **Absorption** is the uptake of the small nutrient molecules by cells. For instance, amino acids made available by the breakdown of the cheese protein in pizza are absorbed by cells lining the small intestine and transferred to the bloodstream, which distributes them throughout the body. **Elimination** is the disposal of undigested materials left over from food.

▼ **Figure 22.1 Animal diets.** Animals can be classified into three broad groups according to their diet.

ANIMAL DIETS		
Herbivore (mainly eats plants or algae)	**Carnivore** (mainly eats animals)	**Omnivore** (regularly eats animals as well as plants or algae)

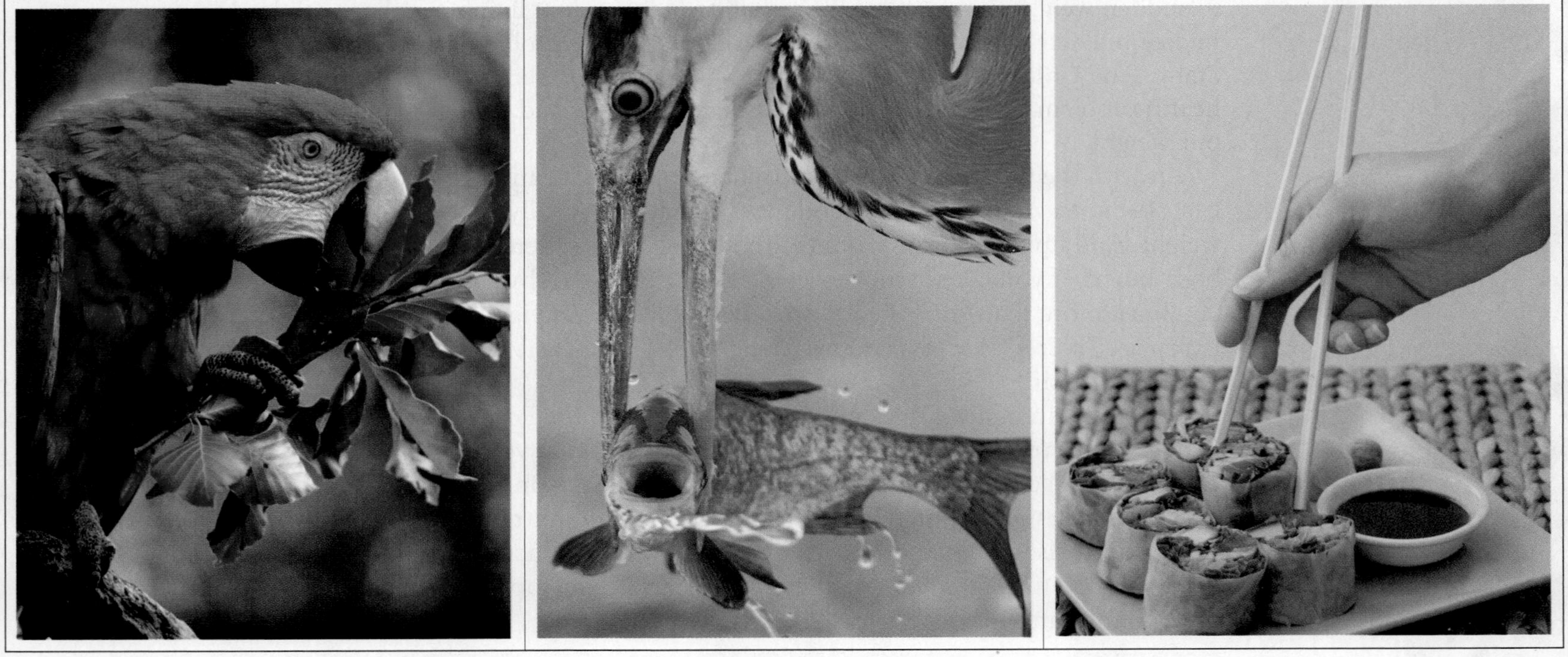

Digestion: A Closer Look

Digestion usually begins with physical processes such as chewing. Such mechanical digestion breaks chunks of food into small pieces, exposing them to chemical digestion, the breakdown of food by digestive enzymes. Food molecules that are polymers, such as carbohydrates and proteins, are broken down via chemical digestion into monomers (see Chapter 3). For instance, starch is digested to its component glucose monomers.

The dismantling of food molecules is necessary for two reasons. First, these molecules are too large to cross the membranes of animal cells; they must be broken down into molecules that are small enough for cells to absorb. Second, most food molecules—the proteins in cheese, for example—are different from the molecules that make up an animal's body. Your body does not directly use the protein that you eat but instead dismantles it and uses the pieces (amino acids) to build its own new proteins (Figure 22.2).

Chemical digestion happens via hydrolysis, chemical reactions that break down large biological molecules by the addition of water molecules (see Figure 3.4b). Like most of life's chemical reactions, digestion requires enzymes (Figure 22.3). For example, lipases are enzymes that digest fats, such as those found in pizza's cheese and meat. ☑

☑ **CHECKPOINT**

1. Place the four stages of food processing in their proper order: absorption, digestion, elimination, ingestion.
2. Food molecules are broken down into smaller molecules by enzymes that catalyze chemical reactions known as _____ reactions.

Answers: 1. *ingestion, digestion, absorption, elimination* 2. *hydrolysis*

▼ **Figure 22.2 From cheese protein to human protein.**

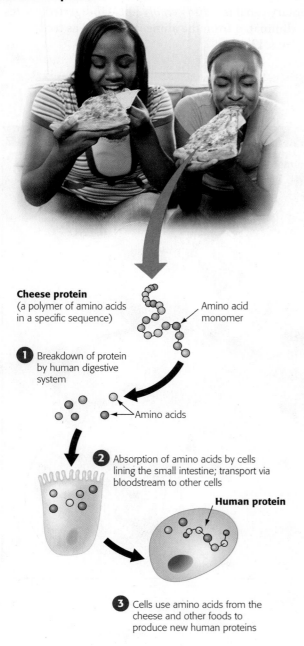

Cheese protein
(a polymer of amino acids in a specific sequence)

Amino acid monomer

❶ Breakdown of protein by human digestive system

Amino acids

❷ Absorption of amino acids by cells lining the small intestine; transport via bloodstream to other cells

Human protein

❸ Cells use amino acids from the cheese and other foods to produce new human proteins

▼ **Figure 22.3 Chemical digestion: hydrolysis of food molecules.**
Digestive enzymes catalyze the breakdown of various types of food molecules by the addition of water molecules.

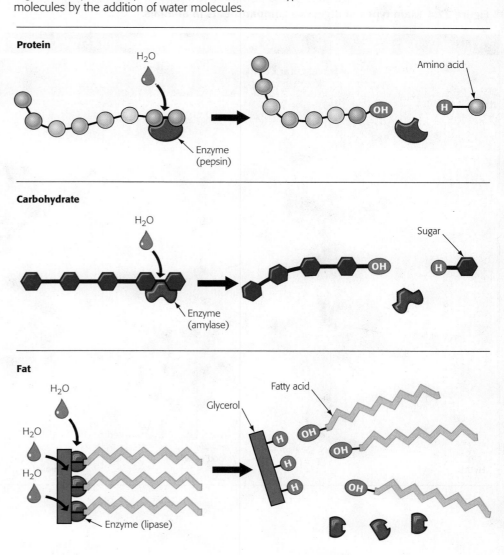

Protein

H_2O

Amino acid

OH

Enzyme (pepsin)

Carbohydrate

H_2O

Sugar

OH

Enzyme (amylase)

Fat

H_2O

Fatty acid

Glycerol

H_2O

H_2O

Enzyme (lipase)

Digestive Compartments

How do animals digest their food without digesting their own cells and tissues? After all, digestive enzymes break down the same kinds of biological molecules that make up the animal body, and it is obviously important to avoid digesting yourself! A common solution to this problem has evolved in animals: Chemical digestion proceeds safely within some kind of compartment.

Digestion within a cell is the simplest type. In this process, a cell engulfs food by phagocytosis, forming a vacuole. This food vacuole then fuses with a lysosome containing enzymes, forming a digestive compartment (see Figure 4.16a). As food is digested, small food molecules pass through the vacuole membrane into the cytoplasm and nourish the cell. This type of digestion is common in protists, but sponges are the only animals that digest food solely within their cells.

Most animals use a digestive compartment to process food (**Figure 22.4**). Such compartments allow animals to digest pieces of food that are much larger than a single cell. Simpler animals, including cnidarians (such as hydras and jellies) and flatworms, have a **gastrovascular cavity**, a digestive compartment with a single opening that functions as both the entrance for food and the exit for undigested wastes.

The vast majority of animals, including earthworms and humans, have a digestive tube with two separate openings, a mouth at one end and an anus at the other. Such a tube is called an **alimentary canal**, or **digestive tract**. Food moves through specialized regions that digest and absorb nutrients in a stepwise fashion. You know what an assembly line is; an alimentary canal is a *disassembly* line. Undigested wastes are eliminated from the alimentary canal as feces via the anus. ☑

☑ **CHECKPOINT**

What is the main difference between gastrovascular cavities and alimentary canals?

Answer: *Gastrovascular cavities have just one opening; alimentary canals have two (mouth and anus).*

▼ **Figure 22.4 Main types of digestive compartments in animals.**

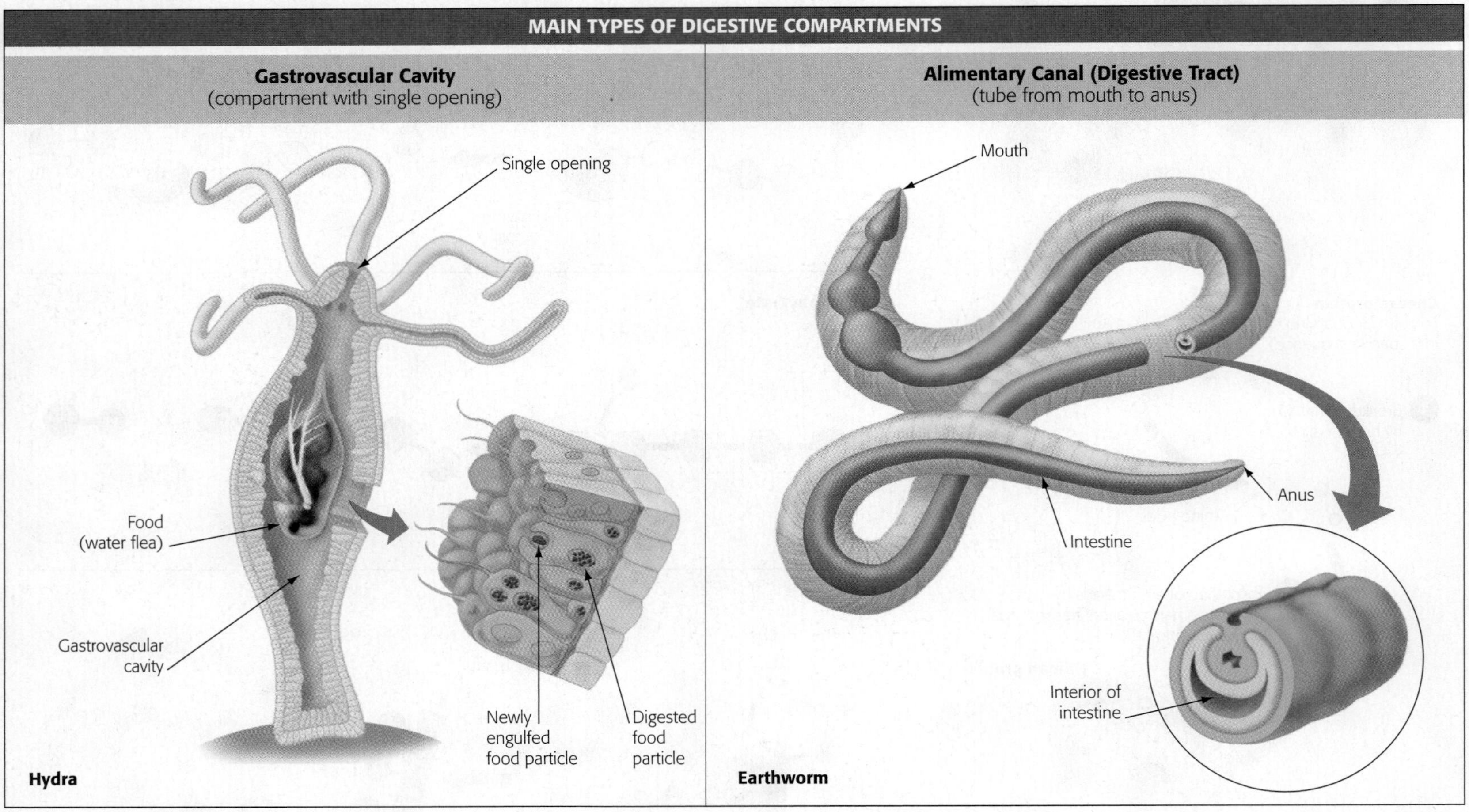

MAIN TYPES OF DIGESTIVE COMPARTMENTS

Gastrovascular Cavity
(compartment with single opening)

Single opening

Food
(water flea)

Gastrovascular
cavity

Newly engulfed food particle

Digested food particle

Hydra

Alimentary Canal (Digestive Tract)
(tube from mouth to anus)

Mouth

Anus

Intestine

Interior of intestine

Earthworm

A Tour of the Human Digestive System

We are now ready to follow our slice of pizza through the human alimentary canal, from mouth to anus. It's important to have a good map of the human digestive system so we don't get lost in there.

System Map

The human digestive system (Figure 22.5) consists of an alimentary canal (also called the gut) and several accessory organs (salivary glands, pancreas, liver, and gallbladder). The accessory organs secrete digestive chemicals into the alimentary canal via ducts (thin tubes). The human alimentary canal totals about 9 m (30 feet) in length. Such a long tube fits within a human body because it folds back and forth over itself with many switchbacks.

The alimentary canal is divided into specialized digestive organs along its length: mouth (oral cavity) → pharynx → esophagus → stomach → small intestine → large intestine (colon and rectum) → anus. You'll get a closer look at the structure and function of the digestive organs on our journey through the alimentary canal. As you reach each organ during our tour, look back at Figure 22.5 to find exactly where you are. First stop: the mouth.

The Mouth

The **mouth** (also known as the **oral cavity**) is where we ingest (take in) food and begin to digest it (Figure 22.6). Mechanical digestion begins here as our teeth cut, smash, and grind the food. Chewing makes food easier to swallow and exposes more surfaces of the food to digestive juices. Typically, an adult person has 32 teeth, which include bladelike incisors (that help bite off pieces of food), pointed canines (for ripping and tearing—think of the fangs of a dog or a wolf), and premolars and molars (for crushing and grinding). The last set of molars are called wisdom teeth; some people must have them removed if they push on other teeth. Chemical digestion also begins in the mouth with the secretion of saliva from **salivary glands**. Saliva contains the digestive enzyme salivary amylase. This enzyme breaks down starch, a major ingredient in pizza crust.

The muscular **tongue** is very busy during mealtime. Besides tasting the food, the tongue shapes it into a ball and pushes this food ball to the back of the mouth. Swallowing moves food into the pharynx. ☑

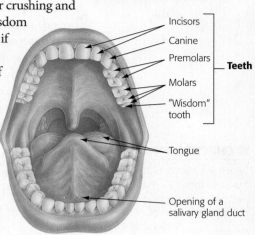

▼ Figure 22.6 **The human mouth and its teeth.**

- Incisors
- Canine
- Premolars — **Teeth**
- Molars
- "Wisdom" tooth
- Tongue
- Opening of a salivary gland duct

► Figure 22.5 **The human digestive system.** The human digestive system consists of the alimentary canal (black labels) and accessory organs (blue labels).

ACCESSORY ORGANS

Salivary glands

Liver
Gallbladder
Pancreas

ALIMENTARY CANAL

- Oral cavity (mouth)
- Tongue
- Pharynx
- Esophagus
- Stomach
- Small intestine
- Colon of large intestine
- Appendix
- Rectum
- Anus

☑ CHECKPOINT

In the oral cavity, chewing functions in _____ digestion, and salivary amylase initiates the chemical digestion of _____.

Answer: mechanical; starch (or polysaccharides)

The Pharynx

The chamber called the **pharynx**, located in your throat, is an intersection of the pathways for swallowing and breathing. The pharynx connects the mouth to the esophagus (part of the digestive system). But the pharynx also opens to the trachea, or windpipe, which leads to the lungs (part of the respiratory system). When you're not swallowing, the trachea entrance is open and you can breathe (**Figure 22.7**, left). Air enters the larynx (also called the voice box), flows past the vocal chords, through the trachea, and to your lungs. Men generally have larger larynxes and therefore more prominent Adam's apples (which are formed by cartilage on the outside of the larynx).

When you swallow, a reflex moves the opening of the trachea upward and tips a door-like flap called the epiglottis to close the trachea entrance (see Figure 22.7, right). Like a crossing guard at a dangerous intersection, the epiglottis directs the closing of the trachea, ensuring that the food will go down the esophagus. You can see this action in the bobbing of your Adam's apple every time you swallow. Occasionally, food begins to "go down the wrong pipe," which irritates the lining of the trachea and triggers a strong coughing reflex that helps keep your airway clear of food.

The Esophagus

The **esophagus** is a muscular tube that connects the pharynx to the stomach. Your esophagus moves food

▼ **Figure 22.7 The epiglottis controls whether the pharynx is open to the lungs (left) or the stomach (right).**

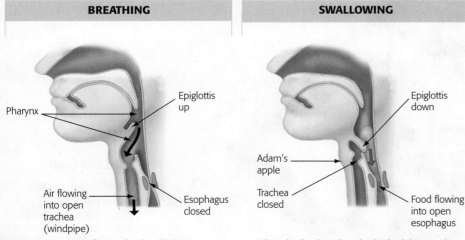

BREATHING	SWALLOWING

When you're not swallowing food or drink, air travels freely through the trachea (black arrows). The esophagus is closed.

When the food reaches the back of the mouth, a swallowing reflex is triggered. The top of the trachea rises against the epiglottis, closing the air passage, while the esophagus opens. Food travels down the esophagus (green arrow).

▼ **Figure 22.8 The esophagus and peristalsis.** Muscles of the esophageal wall contract just behind the food ball and relax just ahead of it.

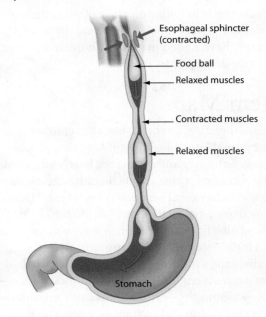

by **peristalsis**, alternating waves of muscular contraction and relaxation that squeeze the food ball along the esophagus (**Figure 22.8**). It is this action that allows a lapping animal to swallow even when its head is lower than its stomach (like a cat at a water dish or a giraffe at a watering hole). Peristalsis propels food throughout the length of the alimentary canal. ☑

The Stomach

We do not have to eat constantly because the human **stomach** is a large organ that can store enough food to sustain us for several hours (**Figure 22.9**). With its elastic wall and accordion-like folds, the stomach can stretch to hold about 2 liters (L)—more than half a gallon!—of food and drink.

The cells lining the stomach's interior secrete a digestive fluid called **gastric juice**. Gastric juice is made up of strong acid, digestive enzymes, and mucus. The acid in gastric juice is hydrochloric acid, and it is concentrated enough to dissolve iron nails. Gastric juice also contains **pepsin**, an enzyme that breaks proteins into smaller pieces.

When food passes from the esophagus into the stomach, the muscular stomach walls begin to churn, mixing the food and gastric juice into a thick soup called **chyme**. At the downstream end of the stomach, a sphincter (a ring of muscle) regulates the transfer of chyme from the stomach to the small intestine. With the chyme leaving the stomach only a squirt at a time, it takes about 2–6 hours for the stomach to empty after a meal, long enough for stomach acids and pepsin to begin digestion. (Continued contraction of stomach muscles after the stomach is empty causes the "stomach growling" that lets everyone know you are hungry.)

With all of that acid, what keeps the stomach from digesting itself? Mucus coating the stomach lining helps protect it from gastric juices and from abrasive materials in the food. Timing is also a factor: Nerve and hormone signals regulate secretion of gastric juice so that it is discharged only when food is in the stomach. Even with these safeguards, gastric juice can still erode the stomach lining, requiring the production of new cells by cell division. In fact, your stomach replaces its lining completely about once every three days.

Stomach Ailments

Gastric juice can be harmful. Occasional backflow of chyme causes pain in the esophagus, commonly but inaccurately called "heartburn" (it should really be called "esophageal burn"). Some people suffer this backflow frequently and severely enough to harm the lining of the esophagus, a condition known as acid reflux or GERD (gastroesophageal reflux disease).

If the stomach lining is eroded by gastric juice faster than it can regenerate, painful open sores called gastric ulcers can form in the stomach wall. The cause of most ulcers is not stress, as was once thought, but infection of the stomach lining by an acid-tolerant bacterium called *Helicobacter pylori*. The metabolism of these bacteria damages the coat of mucus, making the lining more accessible to gastric juice. In severe ulcers, the erosion can produce a hole in the stomach wall and cause

life-threatening internal bleeding and infection. (The cause of ulcers was established in 1984 when biologist Barry Marshall experimented on himself by drinking beef soup laced with *H. pylori* bacteria; although Marshall eventually won a 2005 Nobel Prize for his work, we do not recommend this kind of experimentation!) Most stomach ulcers are treated with antibiotics. Affected people can also get relief by taking medications that contain bismuth, which helps reduce ulcer symptoms and may kill some bacteria.

Weight Loss Surgeries

Some people who are severely obese can shed pounds by diet and exercise. But others who cannot are candidates for weight loss surgery. The most common weight loss surgery in the United States (with about 150,000 operations each year) is gastric bypass. Staples are used to reduce the stomach to about the size of a chicken egg, and the first 18 inches of the small intestine are bypassed by attaching the downstream intestine directly to the reduced stomach pouch **(Figure 22.10)**. As a result, patients quickly feel full, and the body's ability to absorb food is reduced. When accompanied by a healthy lifestyle, weight loss surgeries are successful in 90% of patients. However, all surgeries carry risks (there is about a 1% mortality rate), and patients must carefully monitor their diet to ensure proper nutrition. Weight loss surgeries can be effective, but many health professionals recommend them only as a last resort. ☑

☑ CHECKPOINT

Why are antibiotics an effective treatment for most gastric ulcers?

Answer: The antibiotics kill bacteria that damage the stomach lining.

▼Figure 22.9 **The human stomach.**

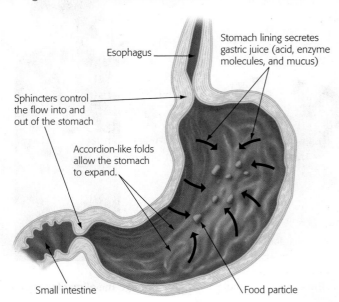

▼Figure 22.10 **Gastric bypass surgery.** An incision is made in the small intestine about 18 inches from where it joins the stomach. The free end of the intestine is then attached to the smaller stomach pouch, which now has a significantly reduced capacity to store food.

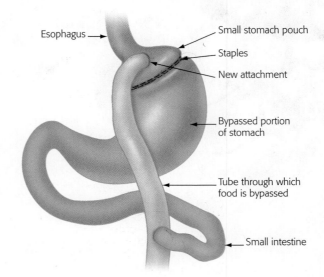

The Small Intestine

The **small intestine**, at a length of about 6 m (about 20 feet), is the longest part of the alimentary canal. Although this intestine isn't small in length, it is small in diameter—only 2.5 cm (about the width of a quarter) across, compared with the large intestine, which is 5 cm across. The small intestine is the major organ for chemical digestion and for absorption of nutrients into the bloodstream.

Chemical Digestion in the Small Intestine

What shape is our pizza in by the time it reaches the small intestine? At that point, mechanical digestion has turned the pizza into a thick, nutrient-rich soup. Chemical digestion by salivary amylase and gastric pepsin has initiated breakdown of the pizza's starch and proteins. Now the small intestine takes over with an arsenal of enzymes that dismantle the food molecules into smaller molecules. These enzymes are mixed with chyme in the first 25 cm or so (about a foot) of the small intestine, the region called the **duodenum**.

The duodenum receives digestive juices from the pancreas, liver, gallbladder, and the intestinal lining itself **(Figure 22.11)**. The **pancreas** is a large gland that secretes pancreatic juice into the duodenum via a duct. Pancreatic juice neutralizes the stomach acid that enters

What are gallstones and what causes them?

the duodenum, and it contains enzymes that aid in digestion. As peristalsis propels the mix along the small intestine, these enzymes contribute to the continuing breakdown of food molecules.

Bile is a juice produced by the **liver**, stored in the **gallbladder**, and secreted through a duct into the duodenum. Bile contains salts that break up fats into small droplets that are more susceptible to dismantling by digestive enzymes. Bile sometimes crystallizes to form gallstones, which can cause pain by obstructing the gallbladder or its ducts. Often the only cure is surgical removal of the gallbladder, which usually has no long-lasting effect on digestion because the liver still produces and secretes bile.

Absorption of Nutrients

In the small intestine, the broken-down food molecules are ready for absorption into the body. Wait a minute! Aren't these nutrients already in the body? Not really. The alimentary canal is a tube running through the body, and its cavity is continuous with the great outdoors. The doughnut analogy shown in **Figure 22.12** should convince you that this is so. Until nutrients actually cross the tissue lining the alimentary canal to enter the bloodstream, they are still *outside* the body. If it were not for nutrient absorption, we could eat and digest huge meals but still starve.

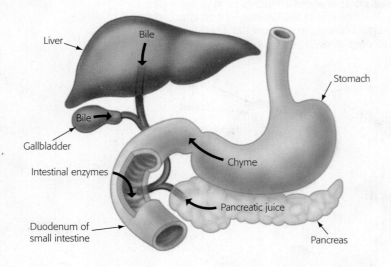

▼**Figure 22.11 The duodenum.** Chyme squirted from the stomach into the duodenum is mixed with digestive juices from the pancreas, liver, gallbladder, and the lining of the duodenum itself.

Liver
Bile
Gallbladder
Bile
Intestinal enzymes
Duodenum of small intestine
Chyme
Stomach
Pancreatic juice
Pancreas

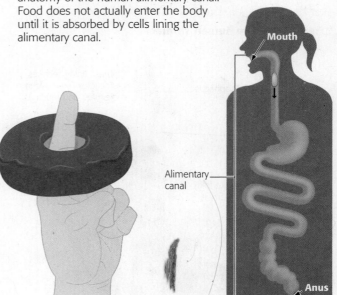

▼**Figure 22.12 Nutrients within the small intestine are not yet inside the body.** Imagine an elongated doughnut that's analogous to the "tube-within-a-tube" anatomy of the human alimentary canal. Food does not actually enter the body until it is absorbed by cells lining the alimentary canal.

Mouth
Alimentary canal
Anus

A finger through a hole   **Food through the alimentary canal**

Most digestion is complete by the time what's left of the pizza reaches the end of the duodenum. The next several meters of the small intestine are specialized for nutrient absorption. The structure of the intestinal lining, or epithelium, fits this function (Figure 22.13). The surface area of this epithelium is huge—roughly 300 m², the size of a tennis court. The intestinal lining not only has large folds, like the stomach, but also has finger-like outgrowths called villi (singular, *villus*), making the epithelium something like the absorptive surface of a fluffy bath towel. Each cell of the epithelium adds even more surface by having microscopic projections called microvilli. Across this expansive surface of intestinal epithelium, nutrients are transported into the network of small blood vessels and lymphatic vessels in the core of each villus.

Normally, the small intestine is free of microorganisms. But improper sanitation can lead to infection by various bacteria. The disease cholera, for example, is caused by ingestion of the bacterium *Vibrio cholera*. As it multiplies in the small intestine, this bacterium releases a toxin that leads to profuse watery vomiting and diarrhea, which in turn can lead to dehydration and eventually death. Cholera is primarily found in developing nations, where inadequate sanitation can lead to outbreaks. Cholera often appears after a natural disaster, when many people are displaced without proper sanitation. The 2010 earthquake in Haiti, for example, was followed by a cholera epidemic.

After nutrients have crossed the cell membranes of the microvilli, they are finally *inside* the body, where the bloodstream and lymph carry them away to distant cells. But our tour of the digestive system is not over yet, because we still have to visit the large intestine. ✓

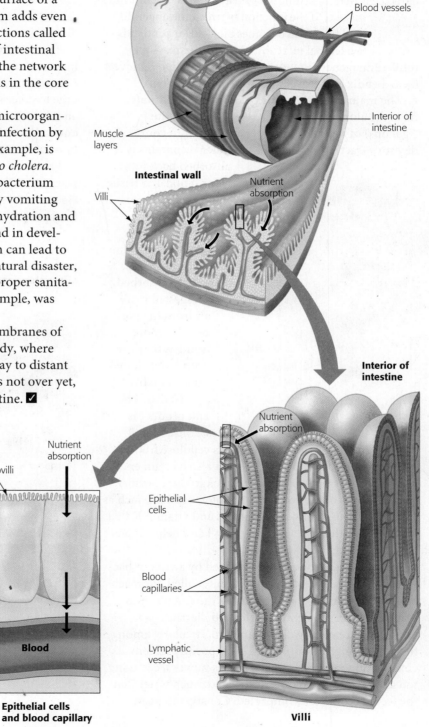

Blood vessels

Interior of
intestine

Muscle
layers

Intestinal wall

Villi

Nutrient
absorption

**Interior of
intestine**

Microvilli

Nutrient
absorption

Blood

**Epithelial cells
and blood capillary**

Nutrient
absorption

Epithelial
cells

Blood
capillaries

Lymphatic
vessel

Villi

► Figure 22.13 **The small intestine and nutrient absorption.** Folds with projections (villi) that have even smaller projections (microvilli) give the small intestine an enormous surface area for nutrient absorption (black arrows). Most nutrients are transported across the microvilli into blood capillaries.

The Large Intestine

At only 1.5 m (5 feet) in length, the **large intestine**, the main portion of which is called the **colon**, is shorter than the small intestine but is called "large" because it is almost twice as wide (about 5 cm). Where the two organs join, a sphincter controls the passage of what's left of a meal **(Figure 22.14)**. Nearby is a small finger-like extension called the **appendix**. The appendix contains white blood cells that make minor contributions to the immune system. If the junction between the appendix and the colon becomes blocked, appendicitis—a bacterial infection of the appendix—may result. Emergency surgery is usually required to remove the appendix and prevent the spread of infection.

Why is a burst appendix a medical emergency?

The main function of the colon is to absorb water from the alimentary canal. About 7 L (not quite 2 gallons) of digestive juice per day spill into your digestive tract. About 90% of the water it contains is absorbed back into your blood and tissue fluids, with the small intestine reclaiming much of the water and the colon finishing the job. As water is absorbed, undigested materials from the meal become more solid as they are conveyed along the colon by peristalsis. The end product is **feces**, consisting of undigested material (such as cellulose from peppers on a pizza). The feces also contain enormous numbers of intestinal prokaryotes, normal inhabitants of the colon. Some colon bacteria, such as *Escherichia coli*, produce B vitamins and vitamin K that are absorbed through your colon wall and help supplement your diet.

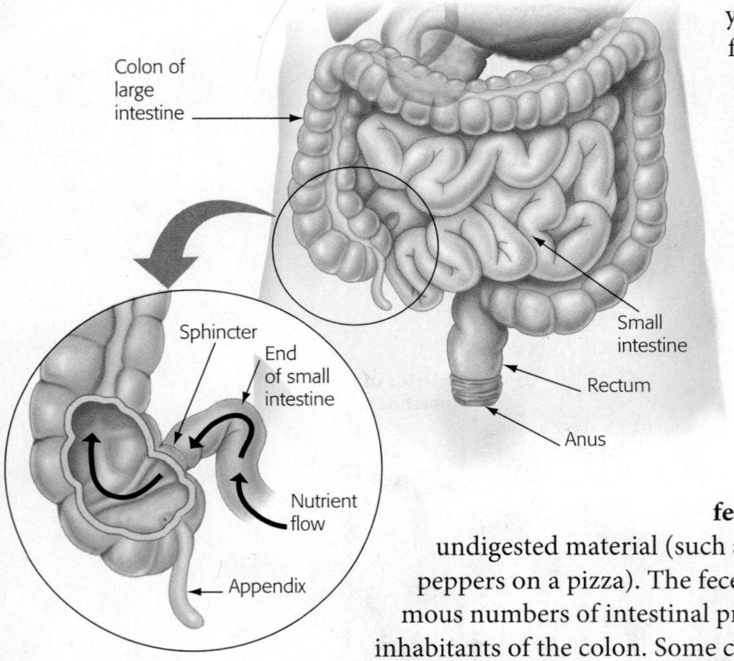

If the lining of the colon is irritated by a viral or bacterial infection (sometimes mistakenly called "stomach bugs"), diarrhea may result because the colon cannot reabsorb water efficiently. Prolonged diarrhea can cause life-threatening dehydration, particularly among the very young and very old. The opposite problem, constipation, occurs when peristalsis moves feces along too slowly and the colon reabsorbs so much water that the feces become too compacted. Constipation can result from lack of exercise or from a diet that does not include enough plant fiber.

Several intestinal disorders are characterized by inflammation (painful swelling) of the intestinal wall. Celiac disease results when gluten, a protein found in wheat, triggers an immune reaction that leads to swelling and a lack of nutrient absorption. The only treatment is a lifelong gluten-free diet. An inappropriate immune response also causes Crohn's disease, a chronic inflammation that can periodically flare up along any part of the alimentary canal. Investigating the cause and treatment of Crohn's disease is an active area of medical research.

The **rectum**, the last 15 cm (6 inches) of the large intestine, stores feces until they can be eliminated. Contractions of the colon and the rectum create the urge to defecate. Two rectal sphincters, one voluntary and the other involuntary, regulate the opening of the **anus**. When the voluntary sphincter is relaxed, contractions of the rectum expel feces.

From entrance to exit, we have now followed a pizza slice all the way through the alimentary canal. **Figure 22.15** stretches out the tube to help you review food processing along its length. ✔

▼ **Figure 22.14 The large intestine and its connection to the small intestine.**

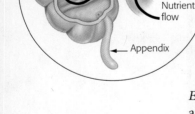

Colon of large intestine

Small intestine

Rectum

Anus

Sphincter

End of small intestine

Nutrient flow

Appendix

▼ **Figure 22.15 Review of food processing in the human alimentary canal.**

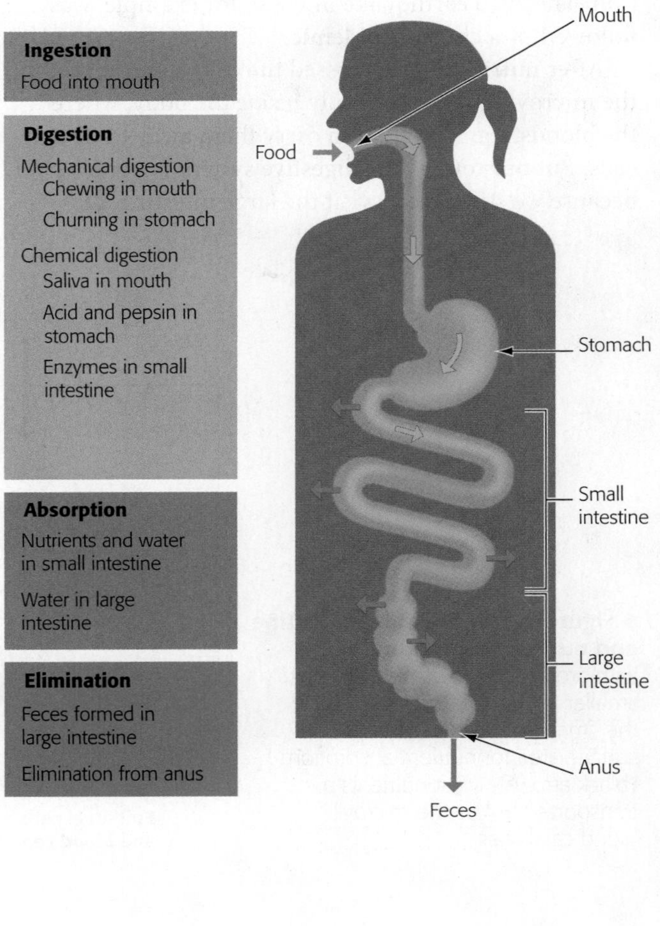

Ingestion
Food into mouth

Digestion
Mechanical digestion
  Chewing in mouth
  Churning in stomach
Chemical digestion
  Saliva in mouth
  Acid and pepsin in stomach
  Enzymes in small intestine

Absorption
Nutrients and water in small intestine
Water in large intestine

Elimination
Feces formed in large intestine
Elimination from anus

Mouth

Food

Stomach

Small intestine

Large intestine

Anus

Feces

✔ **CHECKPOINT**

What is the main function of the large intestine?

Answer: water reabsorption

Human Nutritional Requirements

For any animal, proper nutrition provides fuel for cellular work, materials for building molecules, and essential nutrients for health. A healthy human diet is rich in whole grains, vegetables, fruits, and calcium, along with moderate quantities of protein from lean meat, eggs, nuts, or beans. Nutritionists recommend limited consumption of fats and sugars (primarily to help maintain a healthy weight) as well as salt.

Food as Fuel

Cells can extract energy stored in the organic molecules of food through the process of cellular respiration (described in detail in Chapter 6) and expend that energy as cellular work. Using oxygen, cellular respiration breaks down sugar and other food molecules. This process generates many molecules of ATP for cells to use as a direct source of energy and releases carbon dioxide and water as waste "exhaust" **(Figure 22.16)**.

Calories

Calories are a measure of the energy stored in your food as well as the energy you expend during daily activities. One **calorie** is the amount of energy required to raise the temperature of a gram of water by 1°C. But such a tiny amount of energy is not very useful from a human perspective. We can scale up with the **kilocalorie** (1 **kcal** = 1,000 calories). Now, for a wrinkle in these definitions: The "Calories" (with an uppercase C) listed on food labels are actually kilocalories. So the 280 or so Calories in a slice of thick-crust pepperoni pizza are actually 280 kcal. That's a whole lot of fuel for making ATP. However, about 60% of our food energy is lost as heat that dissipates to the environment. You know this effect from being in a crowded room; each person produces as much heat as a 75-watt light bulb.

Metabolic Rate

How fast do we "burn" our food? The rate of energy consumption by the body is called **metabolic rate**. Your metabolic rate is equal to your **basal metabolic rate (BMR)**, the amount of energy it takes just to maintain your basic body functions, plus any additional energy consumption above that base rate. BMRs for people average about 1,300–1,500 kcal per day for adult females and 1,600–1,800 kcal per day for adult males. The more active you are, the greater your actual metabolic rate and the greater the number of calories your body uses per day. Metabolic rate also depends on other factors, such as body size, age, stress level, and heredity.

The examples in **Table 22.1** give you an idea of the amount of activity that it takes to use up the kilocalories in several common foods. As discussed in the Biology and Society section, balancing the calories you take in (via your diet) and the calories you expend (via exercise) can help you manage your weight. Caloric balance, however, does not ensure good nutrition, and food is our source of substance as well as our source of energy. ☑

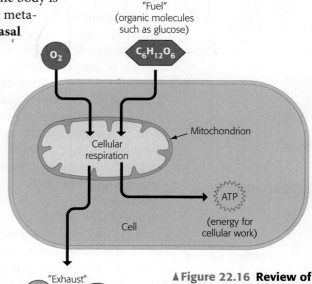

▲ **Figure 22.16** **Review of cellular respiration.** Within each mitochondrion, a series of chemical reactions extracts energy from fuel molecules and generates ATP, a chemical that provides energy for most cellular work.

Table 22.1	Exercise Required to Burn the Calories (kcal) in Common Foods		
	Jogging (9 min/mi)	Playing Soccer	Walking (2 min/mi)
kcal "burned" per hour*	775	477	245
Ice cream (1 cup, premium style), 500 kcal	39 min	1 hr, 3 min	2 hr, 2 min
Cheeseburger (quarter-pound), 417 kcal	32 min	52 min	1 hr, 42 min
Pepperoni pizza (1 large slice), 280 kcal	22 min	35 min	1 hr, 8 min
Soft drink (12 oz), 152 kcal	12 min	19 min	37 min
Apple (medium), 100 kcal	8 min	13 min	24 min
Whole wheat bread (1 slice), 65 kcal	5 min	8 min	16 min
*These data are estimated for a person weighing 68 kg (150 pounds).			

☑ CHECKPOINT

1. What cellular process ultimately uses the energy stored in food molecules?
2. If you eat 1,000 Calories in a day, would you be likely to gain weight?

Answers: 1. cellular respiration 2. No. Chances are your basal metabolic rate is higher than that, so you would lose a bit of weight.

Food as Building Material

Even if you have stopped growing, your health depends on the continuous repair and maintenance of your tissues. The building materials required for such work are provided by the small organic molecules (monomers) produced during the digestion of food. Your cells can reassemble those smaller molecules into various large biological molecules (polymers), such as your own unique proteins and DNA.

Within limits, your metabolism can change organic material from one form to another and compensate for nutrients that are lacking in your diet. For instance, if a cell has a shortage of a particular amino acid, it may be able to make that amino acid from an excess supply of another amino acid. However, certain substances—the **essential nutrients**—cannot be made from any other materials, so the body needs to receive them in preassembled form. A healthful diet must include adequate amounts of all of the essential nutrients: essential amino acids, vitamins, minerals, and essential fatty acids. ☑

What makes red beans and rice so healthy?

Essential Amino Acids

All proteins are built from 20 different kinds of amino acids (see Figure 3.16). Twelve of the 20 amino acids can be manufactured by the adult body from other compounds. The other eight are **essential amino acids**: They must be obtained from the diet because human cells cannot make them. (Infants also require a ninth, histidine.)

Different foods contain different proportions of amino acids. Animal proteins, such as those in meat, eggs, and milk, are said to be "complete" because they provide adequate amounts of all the essential amino acids. In contrast, most plant proteins are incomplete, meaning they are deficient in one or more of the essential amino acids. If you are a vegetarian (by choice or, as for much of the world's population, by economic necessity), the key to good nutrition is to eat a variety of plants that together provide all of the essential amino acids. The combination of a grain and a legume (such as beans, peanuts, or peas) often provides the right balance **(Figure 22.17)**. Most societies have a staple meal that includes such a combination.

▼ **Figure 22.17 Essential amino acids from a vegetarian diet.**

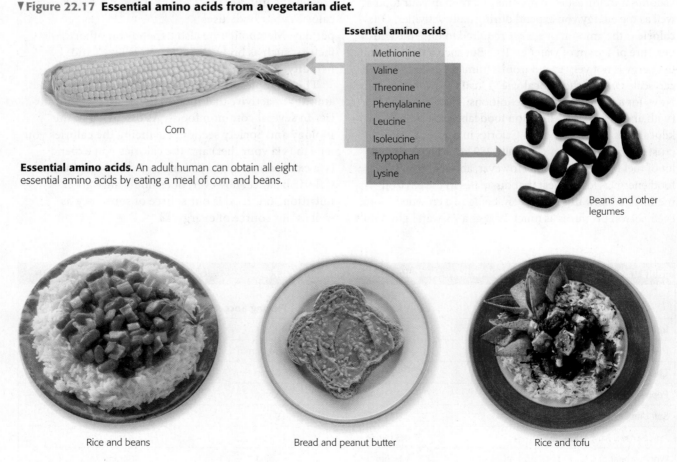

Essential amino acids

Corn

Methionine
Valine
Threonine
Phenylalanine
Leucine
Isoleucine
Tryptophan
Lysine

Beans and other legumes

Essential amino acids. An adult human can obtain all eight essential amino acids by eating a meal of corn and beans.

Rice and beans

Bread and peanut butter

Rice and tofu

Complete meals. Many societies have a staple meal that provides a complete set of essential amino acids by combining a grain with a legume.

Vitamins

Organic molecules that are required in the diet in very small amounts are called **vitamins**. For example, one tablespoon of vitamin B_{12} can provide the daily requirement of nearly a million people. There are 13 vitamins essential to human health **(Table 22.2)**. Most are needed because they assist enzymes.

Deficiencies in any essential vitamin can cause serious health problems.

People who eat a balanced diet should be able to obtain enough of all needed nutrients in their food. For others, vitamin supplements can fill in the gaps, but supplements should not be used indiscriminately because overdoses of some vitamins (such as A, D, and K) can be harmful. ☑

Table 22.2	Vitamins	
Vitamin	**Major Dietary Sources**	**Interesting Facts**
Water-Soluble Vitamins		
Vitamin B_1 (thiamine)	Pork, legumes, peanuts, whole grains	Too little thiamin leads to the disease beriberi; refined grains (like polished white rice) lack thiamin.
Vitamin B_2 (riboflavin)	Dairy products, organ meats, enriched grains, vegetables	Deficiency causes photophobia (aversion to light).
Niacin	Nuts, meats, fish, grains	High doses reduce cholesterol but can cause hot flashes. Too little leads to the disease pellagra, which can be deadly.
Vitamin B_6 (pyridoxine)	Common in most foods: meats, vegetables, whole grains, milk, legumes	Deficiency is rare.
Pantothenic acid	Most foods: meats, fish, dairy, whole grains	Deficiency is rare but can lead to fatigue.
Folic acid (folate)	Green leafy vegetables, oranges, nuts, legumes, whole grains, fortified foods	Recommended for women of childbearing age because it cuts in half the risk of some birth defects involving development of the spinal cord.
Vitamin B_{12}	Animal products: meats, eggs, dairy	It's hard for vegans to get enough B_{12} in their diet, and some intestinal disorders (such as Crohn's disease or celiac disease) may cause deficiencies.
Biotin	Legumes, most vegetables, meats, milk, liver, egg yolks	For most people, adequate levels are provided by intestinal bacteria.
Vitamin C (ascorbic acid)	Raw fruits and vegetables, especially citrus fruits, broccoli, cabbage, tomatoes, green peppers, strawberries	Many animals can produce their own vitamin C, but humans cannot. Deficiency causes the disease scurvy, which was a significant health problem during the era of lengthy sea voyages.
Fat-Soluble Vitamins		
Vitamin A	Dark green and orange vegetables and fruits, dairy products	Too little in the diet can lead to vision loss. Too much can cause yellow/orange skin.
Vitamin D	Fortified dairy products, egg yolk; also made in human skin in presence of sunlight	Aids calcium absorption. Too little causes rickets (bone deformities).
Vitamin E (tocopherol)	Green leafy vegetables, oils, nuts, seeds, wheat germ	Deficiency is rare.
Vitamin K	Green vegetables, vegetable oils	Needed for blood clotting. Produced by intestinal bacteria, so newborns and people taking long-term antibiotics may be deficient.

☑ **CHECKPOINT**

Why do vegetarians have to be particularly careful to get proper amounts of the essential amino acids?

Answer: because few plant products contain all of them

Minerals

The organic molecules in our diet, such as carbohydrates, fats, and proteins, provide the four chemical elements most abundant in our body: carbon, oxygen, hydrogen, and nitrogen. We also require smaller amounts of 21 other chemical elements (see Figure 2.2) that are acquired mainly in the form of inorganic nutrients called **minerals**. Like vitamin deficiencies, mineral deficiencies can cause health problems. For example, calcium is needed as a building material for your bones and teeth and for the proper functioning of nerves and muscles. It can be obtained from dairy products, legumes, and dark green vegetables such as spinach. Too little calcium can result in the degenerative bone disease osteoporosis.

Mineral excesses can also cause problems. For example, we require sodium for our nerves and muscles to function, but the average American consumes about 20 times the required amount of sodium, mainly in the form of salt (sodium chloride) added to processed foods. Excess sodium can contribute to high blood pressure.

Essential Fatty Acids

Which fats are good for you?

Our cells make fats and other lipids by combining fatty acids with other molecules, such as glycerol (see Figure 3.11). We can make most of the required fatty acids, in turn, from simpler molecules; those we cannot make, called **essential fatty acids**, we must obtain in our diet. One essential fatty acid, linoleic acid (one of the omega-6

family of fatty acids), is especially important because it is needed to make some of the phospholipids of cell membranes. Most diets furnish ample amounts of the essential fatty acids, so deficiencies are rare.

Decoding Food Labels

To help consumers assess the nutritional value of packaged foods, the U.S. Food and Drug Administration (FDA) requires two blocks of information on labels **(Figure 22.18)**. One lists the ingredients (by weight) from greatest amount to least. The other lists key nutrients, emphasizing the ones associated with disease and the ones associated with a healthy diet. You should note the serving size and adjust the rest of the nutritional information to reflect your actual serving. For example, if the serving size is 1 cup of cereal but you're eating 2 cups, double all of the other values. You'll see a wide variety of data—including Calories, fat, cholesterol, carbohydrates, fiber, protein, vitamins, and minerals—expressed as amounts per serving and as percentages of a daily value. (Daily values are based on a 2,000-Calorie-per-day diet; these values are therefore "one-size-fits-all" numbers that should be used only as rough guidelines.) If you pay attention, you'll find that serving sizes are often surprising; a single cookie or a snack-sized bag of chips may actually contain multiple servings and therefore many more calories than a quick glance would indicate. Reading food labels carefully can help you make informed choices about what you put into your body. ☑

▶ **Figure 22.18 FDA-required food labels.**

INGREDIENTS: Organic Whole Wheat Flour, Water, Organic Agave Syrup, Organic Cracked Wheat, Organic Vital Wheat Gluten, Organic High Oleic Sunflower Oil/Safflower Oil, Sea Salt, Organic Cultured Whole Spelt Flour, Organic Oat Flour, Organic Barley Malt, Yeast, Organic Soy Oil, Lactic Acid, Soy Lecithin, Ascorbic Acid, Natural Enzymes.

CONTAINS: WHEAT, SOY

Nutrition Facts

Serving Size 1 Slice (37g/1.3oz)
Servings Per Container 18

Amount Per Serving

Calories 100   Calories from Fat 10

	% Daily Value*
Total Fat 1g	1%
Saturated Fat 0g	0%
Trans Fat 0g	
Polyunsaturated Fat 0g	
Monounsaturated Fat 0g	
Cholesterol 0mg	0%
Sodium 150mg	6%
Total Carbohydrate 18g	6%
Dietary Fiber 3g	11%
Sugars 2g	
Protein 4g	

Vitamin A	0%	Vitamin C	0%
Calcium	0%	Iron	4%
Thiamine	6%	Riboflavin	2%
Niacin	6%	Folate	2%
Vitamin B₆	4%		

*Percent Daily Values are based on a 2,000 calorie diet. Your daily values may be higher or lower depending on your calorie needs.

☑ CHECKPOINT

1. What is the difference between vitamins and minerals?
2. How many slices of the bread in Figure 22.18 would an average person have to eat to obtain the daily value of fiber?

Answers: 1. Both are required in the diet for proper health, but vitamins are organic compounds, whereas minerals are elements. 2. nine slices

Nutritional Disorders

Considering the central role that nutrients play in a healthy body, it is not surprising that dietary problems can have severe health consequences. In this section, we examine some common nutritional disorders.

Malnutrition

Living in an industrialized country where food is plentiful and most people can afford a decent diet, we may find it hard to relate to starvation. But 800 million people around the world—nearly three times the population of the United States—must cope with hunger. As difficult as it is to imagine, 14,000 children under the age of 5 starve to death *each day*.

The main type of nutritional deficiency is **malnutrition**, health problems caused by an improper or insufficient diet. Malnutrition may be caused by inadequate intake or medical problems (such as metabolic or digestive abnormalities). On a global scale, protein deficiency—insufficient intake of one or more essential amino acids—causes the most suffering, mainly in less industrialized countries.

Protein deficiency is most common where there is a great gap between food supply and population size. The most reliable sources of essential amino acids are animal products, but these foods are expensive. People forced by economic necessity to get almost all their calories from a single plant staple, such as corn or potatoes, will suffer deficiencies of essential amino acids.

Most victims of protein deficiency are children, who are likely to develop poorly both physically and mentally—if they even survive infancy. The resulting syndrome is called kwashiorkor, from the Ghanaian word for "rejected one," a reference to the onset of the disease when a child is weaned from its mother's milk and placed on a starchy diet after a sibling is born **(Figure 22.19)**. The problem of protein deficiency in some less industrialized countries has been compounded by a trend away from breast-feeding altogether.

Eating Disorders

Millions of Americans, mostly female, are affected by malnutrition because of an eating disorder. **Anorexia nervosa** is characterized by self-starvation due to an intense fear of gaining weight, even when the person is underweight. **Bulimia** is a behavioral pattern of binge eating followed by purging through induced vomiting, abuse of laxatives, or excessive exercise. Both disorders are characterized by an obsession with body weight and shape and can result in serious health problems.

The causes of anorexia and bulimia are unknown, but certain people may be more prone to develop eating disorders than others because of differences in genetics, psychology, and brain chemistry. Culture also seems to be a factor: Anorexia and bulimia occur almost exclusively in affluent industrialized countries, where food is plentiful but thinness is idealized. Treatment options include counseling and antidepressant medications. Some people suffering from anorexia and bulimia eventually develop healthy eating habits without treatment. But for many, dysfunctional nutrition becomes a long-term problem that can impair health and even lead to death. ☑

☑ CHECKPOINT

What is the difference between anorexia and bulimia?

Answer: Anorexia is self-starvation; bulimia is a pattern of binge eating and purging.

▼ **Figure 22.19 Kwashiorkor in a Sudanese boy.**
Kwashiorkor, a form of malnutrition caused by inadequate protein in the diet, causes fluid to enter the abdominal cavity, producing swelling of the belly.

Obesity

In the United States and many other industrialized countries, overnourishment is the nutritional disorder of greatest concern. **Obesity** is defined as a too-high **body mass index (BMI)**, a ratio of weight to height. About one-third of all Americans are obese, and another one-third are overweight (a BMI that is between normal and obese). Obesity increases the risk of heart attack, diabetes, and several other diseases.

What does your BMI say about you?

It is important to realize that not being as slim or well toned as a magazine model does not mean that you are obese. Researchers continue to debate how heavy we can be before we are considered unhealthy. And keep in mind that BMI is only an approximation that does not, for example, take into account body mass from muscle versus body mass from fat. Reflecting this uncertainty, BMI charts show a range of acceptable values **(Figure 22.20)**. Further complicating matters, a tendency toward obesity is inherited to some extent, as we'll see next. ☑

☑ CHECKPOINT

What BMI category is a person who is 6 feet 4 inches tall and weighs 230 pounds?

Answer: overweight

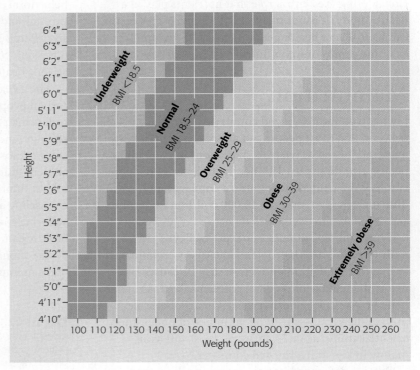

▼ **Figure 22.20 Body mass index (BMI): one measure of healthy weight.**

Controlling Your Weight THE PROCESS OF SCIENCE

Can a Gene Make You Fat?

Several decades ago, researchers made the **observation** that a mutation in a particular gene in mice leads to a significant increase in body fat **(Figure 22.21)**. An obvious **question** about this so-called *obese* gene is: How does a small change in DNA cause such a large change in the body? Researchers at Rockefeller University, in New York City, formed the **hypothesis** that the mutant mice become overweight because their defective *obese* gene fails to produce a protein called leptin, which helps control body weight. They made the **prediction** that injecting leptin into mutant mice would overcome the effects of the defective *obese* gene.

Their **experiment** is summarized in **Figure 22.22.** The researchers injected some mutant and normal mice with leptin and injected others with saline (as a control).

▼ **Figure 22.21 A ravenous rodent.** The obese mouse on the left has a defect in a gene that normally produces an appetite-regulating protein.

Their **results** were striking: Mutant mice that received leptin ended the study weighing about half as much as those that received saline (compare the top two bars in Figure 22.22). Normal mice receiving leptin lost weight compared with those receiving saline, but the difference was not as large (compare the bottom two bars). The researchers concluded that leptin helps regulate body weight in mice.

How do these results apply to people? Although leptin is present in human blood, the *obese* gene is only one of more than 100 genes that contribute to the complex weight maintenance system seen in humans. So far, this complexity has prevented formulation of effective drugs to treat obesity. More important, genetics only partially explains why certain people must fight hard to control their weight, whereas others can eat all they want without gaining a pound. Genetic defects can't produce obesity without a large intake of fattening foods. The best way to maintain a healthy weight is to eat a balanced diet and get plenty of exercise.

▼ **Figure 22.22 The effect of leptin on mice with the obese gene.** This graph shows the final average weight of normal and mutant mice after receiving injections of saline and leptin.

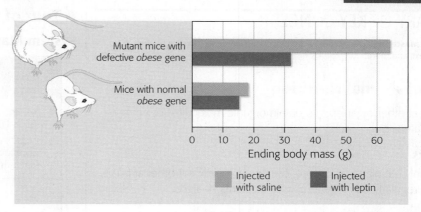

Mutant mice with defective *obese* gene

Mice with normal *obese* gene

Ending body mass (g)
0 10 20 30 40 50 60

Injected with saline   Injected with leptin

Controlling Your Weight EVOLUTION CONNECTION

Fat and Sugar Cravings

The majority of Americans consume too many of the high-calorie foods that contribute to obesity. Even though we all know that we need to limit the amount of fats and sugars in our diet, it sure is hard, isn't it? Most of us crave fatty or sweet foods: cheeseburgers, chips, fries, ice cream, candy. For many of us, such foods are satisfying in a way that other foods are not.

Why do we hunger for unhealthy foods? The seemingly un-helpful trait of craving fat and sugar makes more sense from an evolutionary standpoint. In the natural world, overnourishment is usually an advantage. It is only within the last 100 years that large numbers of people have had access to a reliable supply of food. For most of human history, our ancestors were continually in danger of starvation. On the African savanna, fatty or sweet foods were probably hard to find. In such a feast-or-famine existence, natural selection may have favored individuals who gorged themselves on the rare occasions when rich, fatty foods were available. With their ample reserves, they were more likely than thinner peers to survive the inevitable famines.

Perhaps our modern taste for fats and sugars reflects the advantage it conveyed in our evolutionary history. Of course, today most people typically hunt and gather in grocery stores, restaurants, and cafeterias **(Figure 22.23)**. Although we know it is unhealthful, many of us find it difficult to overcome the ancient survival behavior of stockpiling for the next famine.

▼ **Figure 22.23 Modern hunter-gatherers.**

491

Chapter Review

SUMMARY OF KEY CONCEPTS

MB Go to **www.masteringbiology.com** for homework assignments, practice quizzes, Pearson eText, and more.

Overview of Animal Nutrition

Animals must eat other organisms to obtain organic molecules for energy and building materials.

Animal Diets

Herbivores mainly eat plants and algae, carnivores mainly eat other animals, and omnivores regularly eat animals as well as plants or algae.

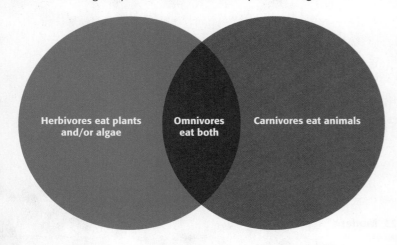

The Four Stages of Food Processing

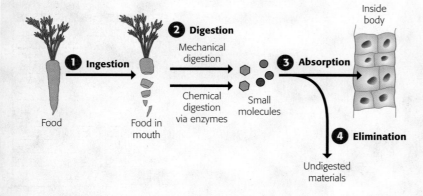

Digestive Compartments

In animals, the breakdown of food occurs within food vacuoles (membrane-enclosed compartments within cells), a gastrovascular cavity (a digestive compartment with a single opening), or an alimentary canal, also called a digestive tract (a tube with two separate openings: mouth and anus).

A Tour of the Human Digestive System

System Map

Alimentary canal	Accessory organs	Digestion		Absorption
		Mechanical	Chemical	
Mouth (oral cavity)	Salivary glands	Chewing	Salivary amylase	
Pharynx and esophagus				
Stomach		Churning	Acid and pepsin (in gastric juice)	
Small intestine	Liver, gallbladder, pancreas		Other enzymes	Nutrients and water
Large intestine				Water
Anus				

The Mouth, The Pharynx, The Esophagus

Within the mouth (oral cavity), teeth function in mechanical digestion, breaking food into smaller pieces. Salivary amylase, an enzyme in saliva, initiates chemical digestion by starting the breakdown of starch into sugars. The pharynx within the throat chamber leads to both the digestive and respiratory systems. When you swallow, the epiglottis closes the trachea and opens the esophagus. The esophagus connects the pharynx to the stomach and moves food along via rhythmic muscular contractions called peristalsis.

The Stomach

This elastic organ stores food, functions in mechanical digestion by churning, and uses gastric juice for chemical digestion. Mucus secreted by the cells of the stomach lining helps protect the stomach from self-digestion. Sphincters regulate the passage of food into and out of the stomach.

The Small Intestine

Small in diameter but very long, the small intestine is the main organ of chemical digestion and nutrient absorption. Most chemical digestion occurs in the duodenum, the first part of the small intestine, where chyme from the stomach mixes with pancreatic juice, bile, and a digestive juice secreted by the intestinal lining. These digestive juices include enzymes for dismantling large food molecules into small molecules. The rest of the small intestine is specialized for absorbing these small molecules. Across the large surface area of the intestinal lining, with its microvilli upon villi, intestinal cells transport nutrients into capillaries of the circulatory system.

The Large Intestine

The colon, wider and shorter than the small intestine, makes up most of the large intestine. The large intestine finishes reclaiming water that entered the alimentary canal with digestive juices. When undigested wastes reach the rectum, most water has been reabsorbed into the blood. Feces are stored in the rectum until eliminated via the anus.

Human Nutritional Requirements

Food as Fuel

Our metabolic rate depends on basal metabolic rate (energy expenditure at complete rest) plus energy burned by additional activity.

Food as Building Material

To repair and maintain tissues, we need building blocks from the breakdown of organic molecules. We also need four types of preassembled essential nutrients.

Essential Nutrients			
Essential Amino Acids	**Vitamins**	**Minerals**	**Essential Fatty Acids**
Required for protein production	Organic molecules required in very small amounts	Essential chemical elements from inorganic compounds	Required to make cell membranes

Decoding Food Labels

The U.S. Food and Drug Administration requires labels on packaged foods that list ingredients in descending order of abundance and provide information about Calories and specific nutrients.

Nutritional Disorders

Malnutrition

Malnutrition results from inadequate intake of one or more essential nutrients. Protein deficiency is the most common dietary deficiency in less industrialized countries. Malnutrition can be caused by anorexia nervosa (self-starvation) or bulimia (binge eating and purging).

Obesity

Defined as an inappropriately high ratio of weight to height, obesity is the most common nutritional disorder in most industrialized countries. About one-third of all Americans are obese, putting them at higher risk for heart disease and diabetes.

SELF-QUIZ

1. Imagine that a new species of large animal has just been discovered. Most animals have an alimentary canal, but this animal *appears* to rely entirely on food vacuoles. Why is this unlikely?

2. A friend says, "It's not eating that causes you to gain weight, it's absorption." Is that statement true?

3. _____ is the mechanical and chemical breakdown of food into small molecules, whereas _____ is the uptake of these small molecules by the body's cells.

4. Why don't astronauts in zero gravity have trouble swallowing?

5. Which class of large biological molecules is primarily broken down in the stomach? What enzyme is responsible?

6. What type of organism is responsible for most stomach ulcers? If the ulcers are detected early, how can they be treated?

7. Most chemical digestion occurs in the _____ as a result of the activity of enzymes made by the _____.
   a. stomach; oral cavity
   b. pancreas; stomach
   c. large intestine; small intestine
   d. small intestine; pancreas

8. Explain how treatment of a chronic infection with antibiotics for an extended period of time can cause a vitamin K deficiency.

9. If you maintain a normal activity level and consume the same number of calories needed for your basal metabolic rate, you will
   a. gain weight.
   b. lose weight.
   c. stay the same weight.
   d. lose weight but quickly regain it.

10. Why is the amount of oxygen you consume proportional to your metabolic rate?

11. Imagine that you and a friend both eat according to FDA nutritional guidelines, but you are a vegetarian and your friend is not. Why do you have to be more concerned about the nutritional content of your food than your friend does? What can you do to address this concern?

12. A friend takes megadoses of vitamin supplements. Which vitamin excess could pose the largest threat?
    a. A
    b. thiamin (B1)
    c. C
    d. folic acid

Answers to these questions can be found in Appendix: Self-Quiz Answers.

THE PROCESS OF SCIENCE

13. The FDA recommends that about 12% of our daily calories come from protein. How do we know if our diet is in accordance with those regulations? Nutritional labels typically tell how many Calories are from fat but don't specify how many Calories are from other nutrients. Proteins have approximately 4 Calories per gram. Read this cookie label and calculate the percentage of calories from protein.

Nutrition Facts	
Serving Size 1 Cookie (28 g /1 oz)	
Servings Per Container 8	
Amount Per Serving	
Calories 140 Calories from Fat 60	
	% Daily Value*
Total Fat 7g	**11%**
Saturated Fat 3g	**15%**
Trans Fat 0g	
Cholesterol 10mg	**3%**
Sodium 80mg	**3%**
Total Carbohydrate 18g	**6%**
Dietary Fiber 1g	**4%**
Sugars 10g	
Protein 2g	

14. Describe some nutritional and digestive problems a patient might face after gastric bypass surgery.

BIOLOGY AND SOCIETY

15. How could you test the claims of companies that sell weight loss supplements? Should these companies be accountable for false claims?

16. Should insurance companies pay for gastric bypass surgeries?

23 Circulation and Respiration

The demand for stamina.
Triathletes require world-class circulatory and respiratory systems to maintain their pace over extended periods.

Athletic Endurance BIOLOGY AND SOCIETY

Avoiding "The Wall"

What does it take to be an elite endurance athlete? To be sure, it takes guts, determination, and dedication. But is that all? From a biological standpoint, what it really takes to be an Iron Man is the ability to deliver a steady supply of oxygen to muscle cells over an extended period of time. So to be a marathoner or a long-distance swimmer, you must have world-class circulatory and respiratory systems.

To understand this claim, we need to understand what goes on within the body of an endurance athlete. To perform work over an extended period—over the course of a 26-mile run, for example—muscle cells require a steady supply of oxygen (O_2) and must be able to rid themselves of carbon dioxide (CO_2) waste. As long as there is enough O_2 reaching the muscle tissue and enough CO_2 being removed, well-trained athletes can perform at a steady pace for hours. What limits the speed and stamina of most endurance athletes is not the strength of their muscles but the ability of their heart and lungs to deliver oxygen at a steady rate. If the heart and lungs can't deliver enough oxygen, an athlete will hit "the wall" and be unable to continue.

It isn't surprising that endurance athletes put considerable effort into training their bodies to deliver more oxygen over longer periods of time. One way they do this is through endurance training. We all know that training for an athletic activity (say, jogging) allows us to perform the activity better and longer in the near future. Elite athletes who need a more intensive regimen often turn to high-altitude training. The lower atmospheric pressure at high altitude means that fewer molecules of O_2 are taken into the body with each breath. By training under these conditions, athletes hope that the body will adapt to need less O_2. If it does, these adaptations will make competing at normal altitude easier. Some athletes even train or sleep in low-oxygen chambers that simulate high altitudes. Still others turn to cheating by blood doping (injecting red blood cells to increase the number of them in circulation) or taking drugs that artificially increase the red blood cell count. Because red blood cells carry oxygen, having more of them aids endurance.

Properly functioning circulatory and respiratory systems are essential not just to athletes but to all of us. In fact, a failure of either system can result in rapid death. The two systems are such close partners that we will explore them in a single chapter. For each of the two systems, we'll start by considering general challenges and survey the variety of ways these are addressed. We'll then take a closer look at each system in humans. Throughout the discussion, we'll examine what may happen when these systems fail and consider medical options to maintain health.

Unifying Concepts of Animal Circulation

Every organism must exchange materials and energy with its environment. In simple animals, such as hydras and jellies, nearly all the cells are in direct contact with the outside world. Thus, every body cell can easily exchange materials with the environment by **diffusion**, the spontaneous movement of molecules from an area of higher concentration to an area of lower concentration (see Figure 5.12). However, most animals are too large or too complex for

exchange to take place by diffusion alone. In such animals, a **circulatory system** facilitates the exchange of materials, providing a rapid, long-distance internal transport system that brings resources close enough to cells for diffusion to occur. Once there, the resources that cells need, such as nutrients and O_2, enter the cytoplasm through the plasma membrane. And metabolic wastes, such as CO_2, diffuse from the cells to the circulatory system for disposal. ☑

Open and Closed Circulatory Systems

All but the simplest animals have a circulatory system with three main components: a central pump, a vascular system (a set of tubes), and a circulating fluid. Two main types of circulatory systems have evolved in animals. Many invertebrates, including most molluscs and all arthropods, have an **open circulatory system**. The system is called "open" because fluid is pumped through open-ended tubes and flows out among the cells **(Figure 23.1a)**.

Nearly all other animals have a **closed circulatory system** in which blood stays within a set of tubes and is distinct from the interstitial fluid, the fluid that fills the spaces around cells **(Figure 23.1b)**. One or more hearts

pump blood into large tubes that branch into smaller ones winding through the organs. Earthworms, octopuses, and vertebrates (including humans) are some examples of animals with a closed circulatory system.

The closed circulatory system of humans and other vertebrates, consisting of a heart and blood vessels, is called a **cardiovascular system** (from the Greek *kardia*, heart, and Latin *vas*, vessel). The fish in Figure 23.1b illustrates the main features of a cardiovascular system. The heart receives blood in a chamber called the **atrium** (plural, *atria*). A second chamber called the **ventricle** pumps blood away from the heart. Blood is confined in three

▼ Figure 23.1 **Open and closed circulatory systems.**

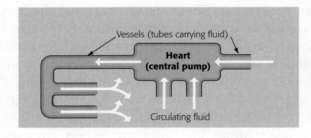

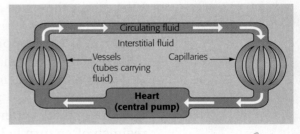

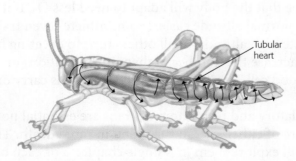

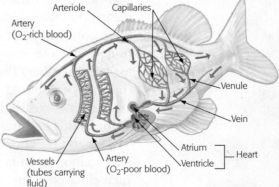

(a) Open circulatory system. In an open system, the heart pumps circulating fluid into body tissues, where nutrients diffuse directly into body cells. Contractions of body muscles move the fluid toward the tail.

(b) Closed circulatory system. In a closed system, blood is contained within vessels, separate from the interstitial fluid bathing the cells. In a fish, blood is pumped from the heart to the gills, then to capillaries in body tissues, and finally back to the heart.

main types of blood vessels: arteries, capillaries, and veins. **Arteries** carry blood away from the heart, branching into smaller **arterioles** as they approach the organs. The blood then flows from arterioles into networks of tiny vessels called **capillaries** that run through nearly every organ and tissue in the body. The thin walls of capillaries allow exchange between the blood and interstitial fluid. Capillaries are the functional center of the circulatory system: This is where materials are transferred to and from surrounding tissues. You can think of this as a kind of postal system: Many people and machines are involved in bringing your mail, but the actual transfer back and forth takes place at your mailbox. As blood flows out of the capillaries, it enters **venules**, which in turn converge into larger **veins** that return blood back to the heart, completing the circuit. ☑

☑ CHECKPOINT

Place the following in the order that describes how blood travels from the heart to cells throughout the body and back to the heart: capillaries, arteries, arterioles, venules, and veins.

Answer: Heart → arteries → arterioles → capillaries → venules → veins → heart

The Human Cardiovascular System

Recall that most animals have a circulatory system consisting of three main components: a pump, a vascular system, and a circulating fluid. In the human cardiovascular system, the central pump is the heart, the vascular system consists of the blood vessels, and the circulating fluid is the blood.

The Path of Blood

In humans and other terrestrial vertebrates, the cardiovascular system is organized into a **double circulation system**, with blood flowing in two loops, or circuits.

The **pulmonary circuit** carries blood between the heart and the lungs (**Figure 23.2a**). In the lungs, carbon dioxide diffuses from the blood into the lungs, while oxygen diffuses from the lungs into the blood. The pulmonary circuit then returns this oxygen-rich blood back to the heart. As shown in **Figure 23.2b**, the **systemic circuit** carries blood between the heart and the rest of the body. The blood supplies oxygen and nutrients to body tissues and organs and picks up carbon dioxide and other wastes from them. At the end of this circuit, the oxygen-poor blood returns to the heart via the systemic circuit.

▼ **Figure 23.2 Double circulation.** It is important to note that in the body, both of these circuits work simultaneously. The pulmonary circuit sends blood to the lungs at the same time the systemic circuit sends blood to the body.

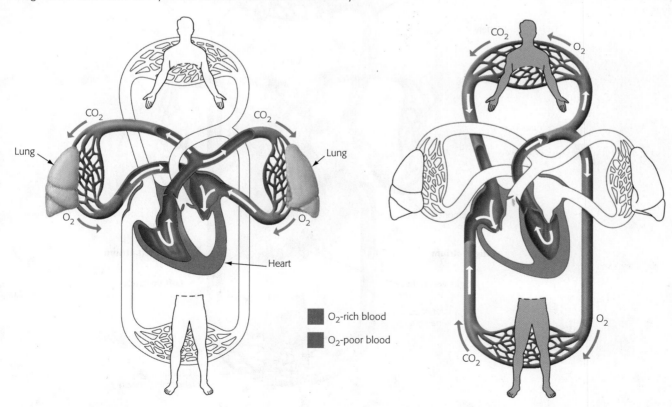

Lung

CO_2 CO_2

Lung

O_2 O_2

Heart

CO_2 O_2

O_2

CO_2

■ O_2-rich blood

■ O_2-poor blood

(a) Pulmonary circuit. In organisms with double circulation, the pulmonary circuit transports blood between the heart and lungs.

(b) Systemic circuit. The systemic circuit transports blood between the heart and the rest of the body.

How long does it take for blood to travel from your heart to your fingertips and back?

Figure 23.3 traces the path of blood in the human cardiovascular system as it makes one complete trip around the body. The pulmonary and systemic circuits operate simultaneously: The two ventricles pump almost in unison, sending some blood through the pulmonary circuit and the rest through the systemic circuit at the same time. It takes the blood in your body about 1 minute to travel through the circulatory system—less time than it will take you to read about it!

Let's start at ❶ the right atrium, where two large veins empty O_2-poor blood from the body into the heart. The blood is then pumped to ❷ the right ventricle, which pumps the O_2-poor blood to the lungs via ❸ two pulmonary arteries. ❹ As the blood flows through capillaries in the lungs, CO_2 diffuses out of the blood and O_2 diffuses into the blood. The newly O_2-rich blood then flows through ❺ the pulmonary veins to ❻ the left atrium of the heart, completing the pulmonary circuit.

Next, the blood is pumped a short distance from the left atrium to ❼ the left ventricle. Oxygen-rich blood leaves the left ventricle through ❽ the aorta, the largest blood vessel in the body, with a diameter about as big as a quarter. Branching from the aorta are the coronary arteries that supply the heart itself and several large arteries that lead to ❾ the head and arms and the abdominal region and legs. Within each organ, arteries lead to arterioles that branch into capillaries that penetrate the tissues. Diffusion of O_2 into the cells and CO_2 out of the cells takes place across the thin walls of the capillaries. Downstream, the capillaries join into venules, which convey the blood back into veins. Oxygen-poor blood from the upper body and head is channeled into ❿ a large vein called the superior vena cava (in this case, "superior" means "sitting above"), and oxygen-poor blood from the lower body flows into ⓫ the inferior ("below") vena cava. The superior vena cava and inferior vena cava complete the systemic circuit by returning blood to the heart.

In the next section, you'll learn about the structure and function of each of the components of the human cardiovascular system and how these components work together. You may find it useful to refer back to Figure 23.3 as you learn about the details of each component. ☑

► **Figure 23.3 A trip through the human cardiovascular system.**
Note that the left side of the heart is on the right side of the figure—and vice versa—because the body is viewed from the front.

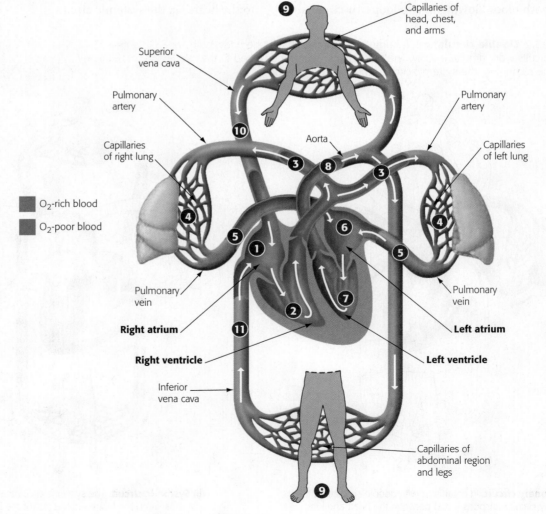

O₂-rich blood

O₂-poor blood

Capillaries of head, chest, and arms

Superior vena cava

Pulmonary artery

Aorta

Pulmonary artery

Capillaries of right lung

Capillaries of left lung

Pulmonary vein

Pulmonary vein

Right atrium

Left atrium

Right ventricle

Left ventricle

Inferior vena cava

Capillaries of abdominal region and legs

How the Heart Works

The hub of the human cardiovascular system is the **heart**, a muscular organ about the size of a fist located under the breastbone. Remember that humans have a double circulation system, with the pulmonary circuit pumping blood between the heart and lungs and the systemic circuit transporting blood between the heart and the rest of the body. This double circuit is supported by a four-chambered heart (**Figure 23.4**).

The atria collect blood returning to the heart and pump it a short distance into the ventricles. The ventricles then pump the blood out of the heart to the other body organs. The ventricles are much more powerful than the atria (which makes sense, given their harder task). Four valves in the heart prevent backflow and keep blood moving in the correct direction. The right atrium receives oxygen-poor blood from body tissues via two large veins, and the right ventricle pumps it to the lungs. The left atrium receives oxygen-rich blood from the lungs, and the left ventricle pumps it out to body organs via the arteries. Thus, the structure of a four-chambered heart prevents oxygen-rich and oxygen-poor blood from mixing. ☑

The Cardiac Cycle

The muscles of the heart relax and contract rhythmically in what is called the **cardiac cycle**. One heart beat makes up one complete circuit of the cardiac cycle. In a healthy adult at rest, the number of beats per minute, or **heart rate**, ranges between 70 and 80. Through superior conditioning, endurance athletes can achieve resting heart rates in the 50s or 60s.

The relaxation phase of the heart cycle is known as **diastole**; the contraction phase is called **systole**. **Figure 23.5** follows the heart through a cycle, which lasts only 0.8 second. ❶ During diastole, which lasts about 0.4 second, blood returning to the heart flows into all four chambers. ❷ During the first 0.1 second of systole, the atria contract, forcing all the blood into the ventricles. ❸ In the last 0.3 second of systole, the ventricles contract, pumping blood out of the heart and into the aorta and pulmonary arteries.

As it beats, the heart makes a distinctive "lubb-dupp, lubb-dupp" sound as the heart valves snap shut. You can hear this sound with a stethoscope or by pressing your ear against a friend's chest. A trained ear can also detect the sound of a **heart murmur**, which may indicate a defect in one or more of the valves. A serious murmur sounds like a "hisssss" as blood squirts backward through a defective valve. Some people are born with murmurs, while others have valves damaged by infection (such as rheumatic fever). Severe murmurs can reduce blood flow to the point that it causes death. However, most cases of heart murmur are not serious, and those that are can be corrected by replacing the damaged valves with artificial ones or with valves taken from an organ donor (human or other animal, usually a pig).

☑ **CHECKPOINT**

1. What kind of blood vessels carry blood away from the heart? What kind of vessels return blood to the heart?
2. Which chambers pump blood out of the heart? Which chambers receive blood returning to the heart?

Answers: **1.** *arteries; veins* **2.** *ventricles; atria*

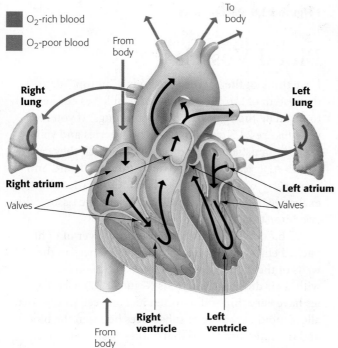

▼ **Figure 23.4 Path of blood flow through the human heart.** The heart contains four chambers, with two atria located above two ventricles. Valves help maintain a one-way flow of blood. Notice that oxygen-poor blood and oxygen-rich blood do not mix.

- ■ O₂-rich blood
- ■ O₂-poor blood

To body

From body

Right lung

Left lung

Right atrium

Left atrium

Valves

Valves

From body

Right ventricle

Left ventricle

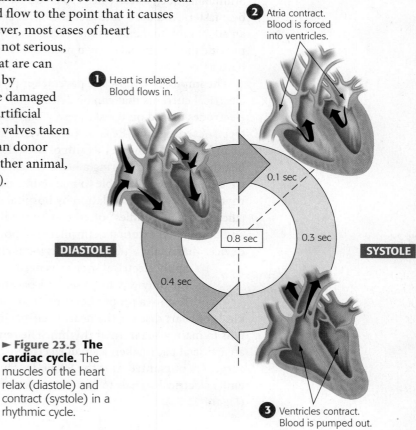

❷ Atria contract. Blood is forced into ventricles.

❶ Heart is relaxed. Blood flows in.

0.1 sec

0.8 sec

0.3 sec

DIASTOLE

SYSTOLE

0.4 sec

► **Figure 23.5 The cardiac cycle.** The muscles of the heart relax (diastole) and contract (systole) in a rhythmic cycle.

❸ Ventricles contract. Blood is pumped out.

The Pacemaker and the Control of Heart Rate

All the muscle cells in your heart beat in unison under the direction of a conductor called the **pacemaker**, or **SA (sinoatrial) node** (Figure 23.6a). (Here we are referring to the body's natural pacemaker; we will discuss artificial pacemakers shortly.) **1** The pacemaker is made up of specialized muscle tissue in the wall of the right atrium that generates electrical impulses. **2** Impulses from the pacemaker spread quickly through the walls of both atria, prompting the atria to contract at the same time. The impulses then pass to a relay point called the **AV (atrioventricular) node** that delays the signals by about 0.1 second. This delay allows the atria to empty completely before the impulses are passed to the ventricles. **3** Once the impulses reach the ventricles, the ventricles contract strongly, driving the blood out of the heart.

A variety of cues influence the signals sent by the pacemaker. For example, epinephrine (also called adrenaline), the "fight-or-flight" hormone released during times of stress, increases heart rate (see Chapter 25). Adrenaline is often injected by paramedics to help restart a stopped heart. Stimulants, such as caffeine, also make the heart beat faster. And heart rate increases with exercise, an adaptation that enables the circulatory system to provide the additional oxygen needed by muscles hard at work.

The impulses sent by the pacemaker produce electrical currents that can be detected by electrodes placed on the skin and recorded as an **electrocardiogram** (**ECG** or **EKG**). Careful reading of an EKG can provide a wealth of data about the health of the heart. During a heart attack, the heart's pacemaker is often unable to maintain a normal rhythm. Electrical stimulation by hospital defibrillators (the electrical "paddles" often seen in medical dramas) and automated external defibrillators—portable devices that analyze the heart's electrical rhythm and apply electrical shocks as needed—may be the only way to "reset" the pacemaker and restore a proper heart rhythm. In certain kinds of heart disease, the heart's self-pacing system fails to maintain a normal rhythm. The remedy is an artificial pacemaker, a small electronic device surgically implanted near the SA node. This device emits electrical signals to maintain normal heart beats (Figure 23.6b).

How does a defibrillator work?

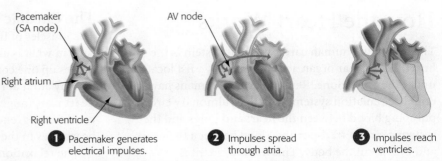

Pacemaker (SA node)   AV node

Right atrium

Right ventricle

1 Pacemaker generates electrical impulses.   **2** Impulses spread through atria.   **3** Impulses reach ventricles.

(a) The heart's natural pacemaker. The SA (sinoatrial) node is located within the muscle tissue in the wall of the right atrium. The yellow represents how far the electrical signals have spread.

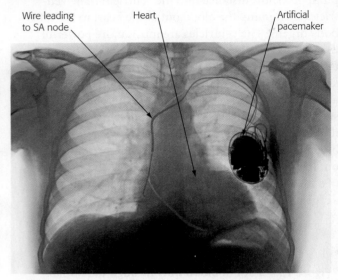

Wire leading to SA node   Heart   Artificial pacemaker

(b) Artificial pacemaker. A small electronic device surgically implanted into cardiac muscle or (as shown here) the chest cavity and connected to the SA node by a wire can help maintain the proper electrical rhythms of a defective heart.

▲ Figure 23.6 **Pacemakers.**

Blood Vessels

If we think of the heart as the body's "pump," then the system of arteries, veins, and capillaries connected to it can be thought of as the "plumbing." If you review Figure 23.3, you'll notice that arteries and veins are distinguished by the direction in which they carry blood: Arteries carry blood *away from* the heart, and veins carry blood *toward* the heart. Capillaries allow for exchange between the bloodstream and the tissue cells (via interstitial fluid).

All blood vessels are lined by a thin layer of tightly packed epithelial cells. Structural differences in the walls of the different kinds of blood vessels correlate with their different functions (Figure 23.7). Capillaries have very thin walls—often just one cell thick—that allow rapid exchange of substances between the blood and the interstitial fluid that bathes tissue cells. The smallest capillaries are so small that blood cells must pass through them single file. The walls of arteries and veins have two additional, thicker layers. An outer layer of elastic connective tissue allows the vessels to stretch and recoil. Between this layer and the epithelial cells is a middle layer of smooth muscle. By constricting or relaxing in response to signals from the brain, smooth muscle can narrow or widen the blood vessels, thereby regulating blood flow. Certain blood pressure medications work by blocking the chemicals involved in this system. This action widens the vessels, lowers blood pressure, and reduces the risk of heart attack and stroke. Veins convey blood back to the heart at low velocity and pressure after the blood has passed through capillary beds. Veins (but not arteries) also have one-way valves that prevent backflow, ensuring that blood always moves toward the heart. ☑

Blood Flow through Arteries

The force that blood exerts against the walls of your blood vessels is called **blood pressure**. Created by the pumping of the heart, blood pressure pushes blood from the heart through the arteries and arterioles to the capillary beds. When the ventricles contract during systole, blood is forced into the arteries faster than it can flow into the arterioles. This stretches the elastic walls of the arteries. You can feel this rhythmic stretching of your arteries when you take your **pulse**. The elastic walls of the arteries snap back during diastole, maintaining enough pressure on the remaining blood to sustain a constant flow into arterioles and capillaries. Thus, blood pressure is recorded as two numbers, such as 120/80 ("120 over 80"). The first number is blood pressure during systole (in millimeters of mercury, a standard pressure unit); the second number is the blood pressure that remains in the arteries during diastole.

Normal blood pressure falls within a range of values, but optimal blood pressure for adults is below 120 systolic and below 80 diastolic (as measured on the upper arm). Lower values are generally considered better, although very low blood pressure may lead to light-headedness and fainting. Blood pressure higher than normal may indicate a serious cardiovascular disorder.

High blood pressure, or **hypertension**, is persistent systolic blood pressure higher than 140 and/or diastolic blood pressure higher than 90. Hypertension affects approximately one-quarter of the adult population in the United States. It is sometimes called a "silent killer" because it often displays no outward symptoms for years while increasing the risks of heart disease, a heart attack, or a stroke (death of brain tissue due to lack of oxygen). To control hypertension, you can eat a heart-healthy diet, avoid smoking and excess alcohol (more than two

▼ Figure 23.7 **The structure of blood vessels.** Arteries branch into smaller vessels called arterioles, which in turn branch into capillaries. Chemical exchange between blood and interstitial fluid occurs across the thin walls of the capillaries. The capillaries converge into venules, which deliver blood to veins. All of these vessels are lined by a thin, smooth epithelium. Arteries and veins have additional layers of smooth muscle and connective tissue.

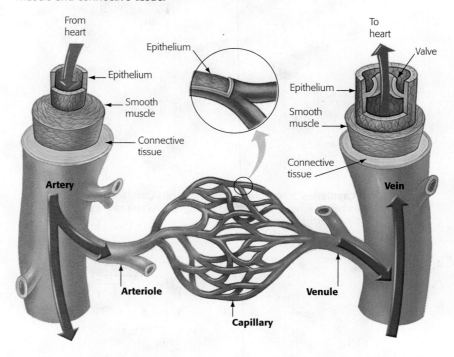

drinks per day), exercise regularly (at least 30 minutes of moderate activity on most days), and maintain a healthy weight. If lifestyle changes don't work, there are several medications that can help lower blood pressure.

Blood Flow through Capillary Beds

Muscles control the flow of blood into capillary beds, and only about 5–10% of your capillaries have a steady flow of blood running through them at any given time. Blood flows continuously through capillaries in your most vital organs, such as the brain, heart, kidneys, and liver. In many other sites, the blood supply varies as blood is diverted from one part of the body to another, depending on need. After a meal, for instance, blood flow to the digestive tract increases. During strenuous exercise, blood is shunted away from the digestive system and supplied more generously to the skeletal muscles and skin. This is one reason why heavy exercise right after eating may cause indigestion or muscle cramping (and why you shouldn't swim too soon after eating—just like mom always said).

The walls of capillaries are thin and leaky. Consequently, as blood enters a capillary at the arterial end, blood pressure pushes fluid rich in O_2, nutrients, and other substances needed by the surrounding cells out of

☑ CHECKPOINT

How are capillary walls an example of form fitting function?

Answer: The thinness of capillary walls helps the exchange of substances with cells.

▼ **Figure 23.8 Chemical exchange between the blood and tissue cells.**

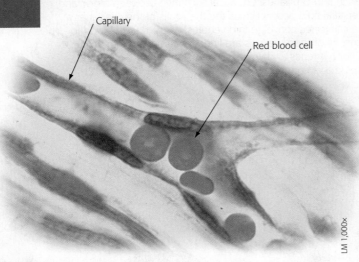

Capillary

Red blood cell

LM 1,000x

(a) Capillaries. Blood flowing through the circulatory system eventually reaches capillaries, the small vessels where exchange with cells actually takes place.

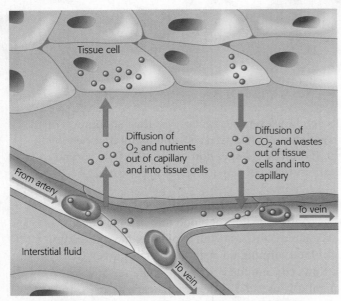

Tissue cell

Diffusion of O_2 and nutrients out of capillary and into tissue cells

Diffusion of CO_2 and wastes out of tissue cells and into capillary

From artery

To vein

Interstitial fluid

To vein

(b) Chemical exchange. Within the capillary beds, there is local exchange of molecules between the blood and interstitial fluid, which bathes the cells of tissues.

CHECKPOINT

List the three major types of blood vessels in order of the pressure of blood within them, from highest pressure to lowest.

Answer: arteries, capillaries, veins

the capillary and into the interstitial fluid (**Figure 23.8**). These molecules then diffuse from the interstitial fluid into nearby tissue cells. Blood cells and other large components usually remain in the blood because they are too large to pass through the capillary walls. At the venous end of the capillary, CO_2 and other wastes diffuse from tissue cells, through the interstitial fluid, and into the capillary bloodstream. This local chemical exchange—between the blood and tissue cells within capillary beds—is the most important function of the circulatory system.

Blood Return through Veins

After chemicals are exchanged between the blood and body cells, blood flows from the capillaries into small venules, then into larger veins, and finally to the inferior and superior venae cavae, the two large blood vessels that flow into the heart. By the time blood enters the veins, the pressure originating from the heart has dropped to near zero. The blood still moves through veins, even against the force of gravity, because veins are sandwiched between skeletal muscles (**Figure 23.9**). As these muscles contract (when you walk, for example), they squeeze the blood along.

You may witness firsthand the importance of muscle contraction in conveying blood through your veins if you stand still for too long. After a while without contracting your muscles, you will start to become weak and dizzy and may even faint because gravity prevents blood from returning to your heart in sufficient amounts to supply your brain with oxygen.

Over time, leg veins may stretch and enlarge and the valves within them weaken. As a result, veins just under the skin can become visibly swollen, a condition called varicose veins. Besides being unsightly, varicose veins may cause serious problems, such as cramping, blood clots, and open breaks in the skin. ☑

▼ **Figure 23.9 Blood flow in a vein.** The contraction of muscles surrounding veins squeezes blood toward the heart. Flaps of tissue in the veins act as one-way valves, preventing backflow.

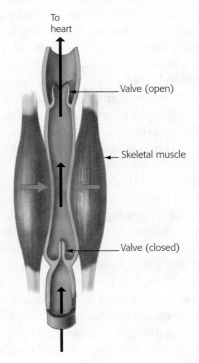

To heart

Valve (open)

Skeletal muscle

Valve (closed)

Blood

Now that we have examined the structures and functions of the heart and blood vessels, let's focus on the composition of blood itself (Figure 23.10). The circulatory system of an adult human has about 5 L (11 pints) of blood. Just over half this volume consists of a yellowish liquid called **plasma**. Plasma is about 90% water. The other 10% of plasma is made up of dissolved salts, proteins, and various other molecules being transported by the blood, such as nutrients, wastes, and hormones. Suspended within the plasma are three types of cellular elements: red blood cells, white blood cells, and platelets. Let's examine each of them in turn.

If you donate a pint of blood, how much do you have left?

Red Blood Cells and Oxygen Transport

Red blood cells, also called **erythrocytes**, are by far the most numerous type of blood cell. There are about 25 trillion of these cells in the average person's bloodstream. Carbohydrate-containing molecules on the surface of red blood cells determine a person's blood type, such as A, B, AB, or O (see Figure 9.20).

Each red blood cell contains approximately 250 million molecules of **hemoglobin**, an iron-containing protein that transports oxygen. As red blood cells pass through the capillary beds of your lungs, oxygen diffuses into the red blood cells and binds to the hemoglobin. This process is reversed in the capillaries of the systemic circuit, where the hemoglobin unloads its cargo of oxygen to the body's cells.

Human red blood cells are shaped like disks with indentations in the middle, increasing the surface area available for gas exchange (see Figure 23.10). In addition to their shape, the red blood cells of mammals have another feature that enhances their oxygen-carrying capacity: They lack nuclei and other organelles, leaving more room to carry hemoglobin. Red blood cells are also very small relative to other cells. Therefore, a population of red blood cells has a greater total surface area for gas exchange than the same volume of larger cells.

Adequate amounts of hemoglobin and red blood cells are essential to the normal functioning of the body. **Anemia** is a condition in which there is an abnormally low amount of hemoglobin or a low number of red blood cells. An anemic person feels constantly tired and run-down because the body cells do not get enough oxygen. Anemia can result from a variety of factors, including excessive blood loss, vitamin or mineral deficiencies, and certain cancers. A mutation in the gene for hemoglobin may result in sickle-cell disease, another cause of anemia (see Chapter 9).

The production of red blood cells in the bone marrow is controlled by a feedback system that monitors the amount of oxygen reaching tissues via the blood. If the tissues are not receiving enough oxygen, the kidneys produce a hormone called erythropoietin (EPO) that boosts the bone marrow's production of oxygen-carrying red blood cells. Doctors prescribe synthetic EPO to relieve the symptoms of anemia.

Because additional red blood cells boost the functions of the circulatory and respiratory systems, EPO increases athletic stamina, potentially offering a huge advantage in long athletic competitions. Thus, some endurance athletes have abused synthetic EPO in an attempt to gain an artificial advantage. EPO abuse, one

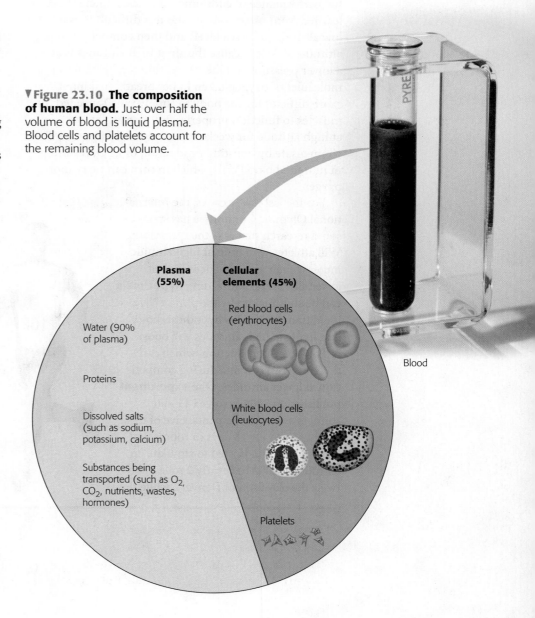

▼Figure 23.10 **The composition of human blood.** Just over half the volume of blood is liquid plasma. Blood cells and platelets account for the remaining blood volume.

Plasma (55%)

Cellular elements (45%)

Water (90% of plasma)

Proteins

Dissolved salts (such as sodium, potassium, calcium)

Substances being transported (such as O_2, CO_2, nutrients, wastes, hormones)

Red blood cells (erythrocytes)

White blood cells (leukocytes)

Platelets

Blood

type of "blood doping," is difficult to detect because it is a hormone produced naturally by the body and because synthetic EPO is rapidly cleared from the bloodstream. One way that athletic commissions test for cheaters is by measuring the percentage of red blood cells in the blood volume. A value of more than 50% is usually grounds for disqualification. EPO is banned not only because it confers an unfair advantage but also because it is dangerous: It has been blamed for the deaths of dozens of professional athletes. Fortunately, there are other, healthier ways to achieve an increase in performance, as we'll see next.

Athletic Endurance THE PROCESS OF SCIENCE

Live High, Train Low?

Exercise physiologists have known for years that properly designed training regimens can vastly improve the performance of endurance athletes. Athletes have learned from **observation** that it is difficult to train at low altitude (near sea level) and then compete at high altitude. This is because the air at high altitudes is at a lower pressure and therefore "thinner," with fewer molecules of oxygen taken in per breath, making it more difficult for the body to supply the O_2 needed for muscles to function properly. But if an athlete stays at high altitude for weeks or months, the kidneys will compensate by boosting production of EPO, resulting in more red blood cells, which in turn can carry more oxygen.

For the last few decades, the International Olympic Committee has sponsored research that asks the **question**: Will athletes who train at high altitude increase their performance when at lower altitudes? One leading **hypothesis** can be summed up by the phrase "live high, train low." This hypothesis holds that living at high altitudes will boost red blood cell production, which can then improve stamina during competition at lower altitudes. One **experiment** published in 2006 involved 11 elite runners as test participants. Five of these athletes lived for 18 days in rooms that were gradually adjusted to simulate an altitude of 3,000 m (nearly 2 miles, about twice the elevation of Denver), while the

other six athletes lived at 1,200 m. All the athletes trained at 1,200 m.

At the start of the study (day 0), the **results** of endurance tests showed that both groups were similar in their aerobic capacity, a measure of the body's ability to take in and use oxygen (**Figure 23.11**, first pair of bars). But by the end of the training regimen (day 18), the "live high, train low" group had a higher aerobic capacity (middle pair of bars) that gradually fell over two weeks (day 33, third pair of bars). These results, as well as those from many other similar studies, are providing a scientific basis for new training regimens aimed to improve the performance of today's endurance athletes.

▼ **Figure 23.11 Live High, Train Low.** The results of this study suggest that living at high altitude while training at low altitude can improve athletic performance, but the effect fades.

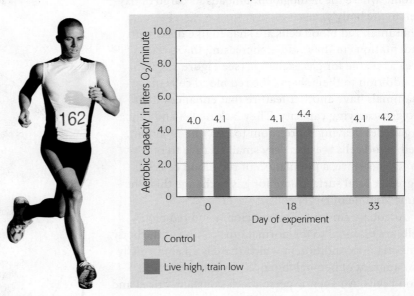

White Blood Cells and Defense

Red blood cells are just one of the cellular components of blood (**Figure 23.12**). As a group, **white blood cells**, or **leukocytes**, fight infections. White blood cells are larger than red blood cells and they lack hemoglobin but contain nuclei and all other organelles. There are about 700 times fewer white blood cells than red blood cells, although their numbers temporarily increase when the body is combating an infection.

Platelets and Blood Clotting

Although you get cuts and scrapes, you do not bleed to death because your blood contains two components that help form clots: platelets and fibrinogen. **Platelets** are bits of membrane-wrapped cytoplasm pinched off from larger cells in the bone marrow. Clotting begins when the tissue lining a blood vessel is damaged. Almost immediately, platelets adhere to the damaged tissue to form a sticky cluster that seals minor breaks. Platelets also release clotting factors, molecules that convert **fibrinogen**, a protein found in the plasma, to a threadlike protein called **fibrin**. Molecules of fibrin form a dense network to create a patch (see the inset in Figure 23.12). On the skin, such clots are called scabs.

The clotting mechanism is so important that any defect in it can be life-threatening. In the disease hemophilia, a genetic mutation in a gene for a clotting factor results in excessive, sometimes fatal bleeding. Too much clotting can also be fatal. An embolus is a blood clot that forms within a blood vessel but then dislodges from its point of origin and travels in the blood. If an embolus lodges in an artery of the heart and is large enough to block it, a heart attack occurs. Similarly, an embolus in the head can cause a stroke. Aspirin and heparin are anticoagulant drugs that prevent undesirable clotting in patients at risk for an embolus. ☑

Stem Cells and the Treatment of Leukemia

The red marrow inside some of your bones contains stem cells that differentiate into red and white blood cells as well as into the cells that produce platelets. (Recall from Chapter 11 that stem cells have the potential to differentiate into other types of cells.) After forming in the early embryo, these stem cells continually reproduce themselves and create all the blood cells needed throughout life. Bone marrow stem cells show great promise for the treatment of disease, particularly leukemia.

Leukemia is cancer of the white blood cells (leukocytes). Because cancerous cells grow uncontrollably, a person with leukemia has an unusually high number of white blood cells, most of which are defective. The overabundant cells crowd out the normal bone marrow cells that produce red blood cells and platelets, causing severe anemia and impaired clotting.

Some cases of leukemia do not respond to standard cancer treatments—radiation and chemotherapy. An alternative treatment involves completely destroying cancerous bone marrow and replacing it with healthy bone marrow. Marrow from the patient is harvested, processed to remove as many cancerous cells as possible, and then reinjected. Alternatively, a matching donor, often a sibling, may provide marrow.

☑ **CHECKPOINT**

Which blood cells carry oxygen? Which provide immunity? What cellular element is needed for clotting?

Answers: red blood cells (erythrocytes); white blood cells (leukocytes); platelets

---

CELLULAR COMPONENTS OF BLOOD

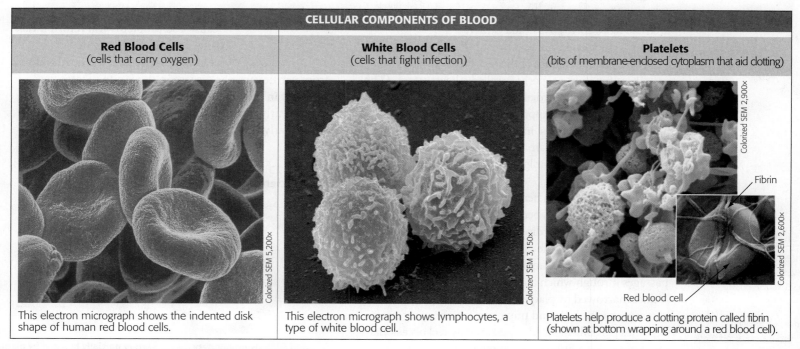

Red Blood Cells
(cells that carry oxygen)

Colorized SEM 5,200x

This electron micrograph shows the indented disk shape of human red blood cells.

White Blood Cells
(cells that fight infection)

Colorized SEM 3,150x

This electron micrograph shows lymphocytes, a type of white blood cell.

Platelets
(bits of membrane-enclosed cytoplasm that aid clotting)

Colorized SEM 2,900x

Colorized SEM 2,600x

Fibrin

Red blood cell

Platelets help produce a clotting protein called fibrin (shown at bottom wrapping around a red blood cell).

▲ **Figure 23.12 The three cellular components of blood.**

Cardiovascular Disease

The circulatory system performs several homeostatic functions that help maintain relatively constant internal conditions. First, by exchanging nutrients and wastes with the interstitial fluid, the circulatory system helps control the chemical balance of the fluid that surrounds cells. Second, the circulatory system helps control the composition of the blood by continuously moving it through organs, such as the lungs, liver, and kidneys, that regulate the blood's contents. The circulatory system is also involved in the body's temperature regulation, hormone distribution, and defense against foreign invaders—all topics that are discussed in other chapters.

What happens when the circulatory system cannot perform its normal functions? **Cardiovascular disease**, diseases of the heart and blood vessels, accounts for 40% of all deaths in the United States, killing more than 1 million people each year. Like all of your cells, your heart muscle cells require oxygen-rich blood to survive. When blood exits the heart, several **coronary arteries** (shown in dark red in **Figure 23.13**) immediately branch off the aorta to feed the heart muscle. If one or more of these blood vessels become blocked, heart muscle cells quickly die from lack of O_2 (gray area in Figure 23.13). As noted earlier,

What happens during a myocardial infarction?

such an event, and the subsequent failure of the heart to function properly, is called a heart attack. (The medical term is myocardial infarction, meaning "death of heart muscle tissue.") Approximately one-third of heart attack victims die almost immediately. For those who survive, the ability of the damaged heart to pump blood may be seriously impaired for life because heart muscle cannot be replaced or repaired.

The suddenness of a heart attack belies the fact that the arteries of most victims became impaired gradually by a chronic cardiovascular disease called **atherosclerosis**. During the course of the disease, fatty deposits called plaque develop in the inner walls of arteries, clogging the passages through which blood can flow **(Figure 23.14)**. Vessels narrowed by plaque increase blood pressure and can more easily form and trap clots. If a coronary artery becomes partially blocked, a person may feel occasional chest pain, a condition called angina.

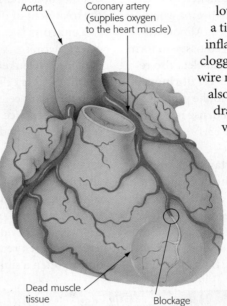

▼ **Figure 23.13 Blockage of a coronary artery, resulting in a heart attack.** If one or more coronary arteries become blocked, the heart muscle cells that they feed will die from lack of oxygen. Such an event, called a heart attack, can lead to permanent damage of the heart muscle.

Aorta

Coronary artery (supplies oxygen to the heart muscle)

Dead muscle tissue

Blockage

To some extent, the tendency to develop cardiovascular disease is inherited. However, three everyday behaviors significantly impact the risk of cardiovascular disease and heart attack. Smoking doubles the risk of heart attack and increases the severity if one does occur. Regular exercise (particularly "cardio" or "aerobic" workouts) can cut the risk of heart disease in half. Eating a heart-healthy diet, low in cholesterol, trans fats, and saturated fats (see Chapter 3) and high in fruits, vegetables, and whole grains can reduce the risk of developing atherosclerosis.

If a person already has cardiovascular disease, there are treatments available. Certain drugs can lower cholesterol. Angioplasty (inserting a tiny catheter with a balloon that is inflated to compress plaque and widen clogged coronary arteries) and stents (small wire mesh tubes that prop open arteries) can also help. Bypass surgery is a much more drastic remedy. In this procedure, blood vessels removed from a patient's legs are sewn onto the heart to shunt blood around clogged coronary arteries. In an even more drastic measure, a defective heart can be replaced by a transplant or even with an artificial heart (although no one has survived long with an artificial heart). Unfortunately, surgery of any kind only treats the disease symptoms, not the underlying causes, so problems will return if risk factors are not minimized.

On the bright side, the death rate from cardiovascular disease in the United States has been cut in half during the past 50 years. Health education, early diagnosis, and reduction of risk factors, particularly smoking, are mostly responsible. ☑

▼ **Figure 23.14 A normal artery and an artery showing atherosclerosis.**

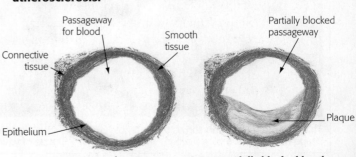

Passageway for blood

Smooth tissue

Partially blocked passageway

Connective tissue

Epithelium

Plaque

Normal artery

Artery partially blocked by plaque

☑ **CHECKPOINT**

Name three things you can do to lower your risk of cardiovascular disease.

Answer: eat a heart-healthy diet, exercise regularly, and avoid smoking

Unifying Concepts of Animal Respiration

Your survival depends on close cooperation between the circulatory and respiratory systems. The circulatory system transports gases and other substances to and from body cells. Recall that within all cells, the process of cellular respiration (the topic of Chapter 6) uses oxygen and glucose to produce water, carbon dioxide, and energy in the form of ATP. All working cells therefore require a steady supply of O_2 from the environment and must continuously dispose of CO_2:

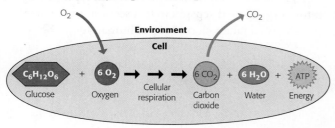

The **respiratory system** consists of several organs that facilitate exchange of O_2 and CO_2 between cells and the environment. (Note that in the context of a whole organism, the word *respiratory* refers to the process of breathing, not to cellular respiration.) ☑

The Structure and Function of Respiratory Surfaces

Earth's main reservoir of oxygen is the atmosphere, which is about 21% O_2. Terrestrial animals access this oxygen by breathing air. Oceans, lakes, and other bodies of water also contain O_2 in the form of dissolved gas, but it makes up only 3–5% of that environment. Many aquatic animals obtain oxygen by passing water over their gills. The part of an animal where O_2 from the environment diffuses into living cells and CO_2 diffuses out to the surrounding environment is called the **respiratory surface**. The respiratory surface is usually covered with a single layer of living cells that is thin enough and moist enough to allow rapid diffusion between the body and the environment. It must be large enough to take up O_2 for every cell in the body.

Within the animal kingdom, a variety of respiratory surfaces have evolved. For some animals, such as sponges and flatworms, the plasma membrane of every cell in the body is close enough to the outside environment for gases to diffuse in and out. In many animals, however, the bulk of the body does not have direct access to the outer environment, and the respiratory surface is the place where the environment and the blood meet. The blood then transports gases to and from the rest of the body.

Some animals use their entire outer skin as a respiratory surface. An earthworm, for example, has moist skin, and gases diffuse across its whole body surface. This results in an exchange of O_2 and CO_2 between the environment and a dense net of capillaries just below the earthworm's skin **(Figure 23.15a)**. Earthworms and other skin-breathers (such as frogs) must live in wet environments because their entire body surface must stay moist for this exchange to occur. For most animals, however, the outer body surface is either impermeable to gases or lacks sufficient area to exchange gases for the whole body. In such animals, specialized regions of the body have extensively folded or branched surfaces that provide a large surface area for gas exchange.

Gills are found in most aquatic animals, such as lobsters, which are invertebrates, and fishes, which are vertebrates. The feathery gills located on either side of a fish's head have a respiratory surface area much greater than the rest of the body surface. A fish obtains oxygen by continuously pumping water over its gills. As water passes over the respiratory surface of the gills, gases diffuse between the water and the blood. The blood then carries oxygen to the rest of the body **(Figure 23.15b)**. Gills—especially those of large, active fishes such as tuna—must be very efficient to obtain enough oxygen from water. Indeed, some aquatic animals can remove more than 80% of the oxygen from the water moving over their gills. In comparison, human lungs extract only about 25% of the oxygen in air.

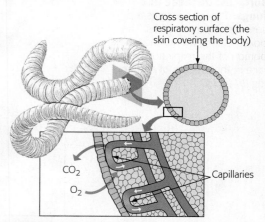

Cross section of respiratory surface (the skin covering the body)

CO_2

O_2

Capillaries

(a) Skin. Some small animals, such as earthworms, use their entire moist outer skin as a respiratory organ.

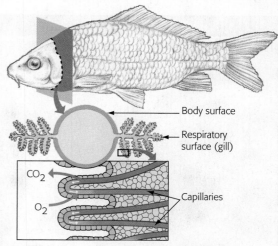

Body surface

Respiratory surface (gill)

CO_2

O_2

Capillaries

(b) Gills. Fishes and many other aquatic animals have gills, feathery respiratory surfaces that extend into the surrounding water.

► **Figure 23.15 Respiratory surfaces: skin and gills.** The yellow areas represent respiratory surfaces. The boxed enlargements show a portion of the respiratory surface in the process of exchanging O_2 and CO_2.

507

In most land-dwelling animals, the respiratory surfaces are folded into the body rather than extending from it. The infolded surfaces are open to the air only through narrow tubes. This anatomical arrangement means that only those respiratory cells needed for gas exchange must be kept moist, rather than the entire body surface (as in earthworms or frogs). The two types of respiratory structures seen in land-dwelling animals are tracheal systems and lungs.

Insects breathe using a **tracheal system**, an extensive network of branching internal tubes called tracheae (**Figure 23.16a**). Tracheae begin near the body's surface and branch down to narrower tubes that extend to nearly every cell. Gas exchange with cells occurs via diffusion across the moist epithelium that lines the tips of the tubes. Because almost every body cell is near the respiratory surface, gas exchange in insects requires no assistance from the circulatory system.

Lungs are the most common respiratory surface among snails, some spiders, and terrestrial vertebrates such as amphibians, birds and other reptiles, and mammals. In contrast to tracheae, which branch throughout an insect's body, **lungs** are localized organs lined with moist epithelium (**Figure 23.16b**). Gases are carried between the lungs and the body cells by the circulatory system.

Figure 23.17 summarizes the different types of respiratory organs we discussed in this section. In the next section, we'll take a closer look at human lungs. ☑

► **Figure 23.16 Respiratory surfaces: tracheae and lungs.** The yellow areas represent respiratory surfaces. The boxed enlargements show a portion of the respiratory surface in the process of exchanging O_2 and CO_2.

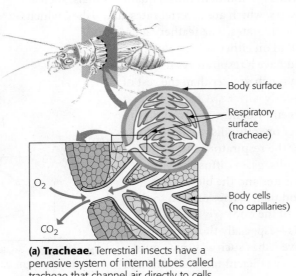

(a) Tracheae. Terrestrial insects have a pervasive system of internal tubes called tracheae that channel air directly to cells.

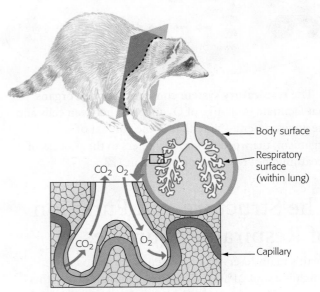

(b) Lungs. Most terrestrial vertebrates exchange gases across the thin lining of lungs, internal organs with a rich blood supply.

▼**Figure 23.17 Types of respiratory organs.**

RESPIRATORY ORGANS			
Skin (entire body surface)	**Gills** (extensions of the body surface)	**Tracheae** (branching internal tubes)	**Lungs** (localized internal organs)
Moist skin of a leech	Gills of a sea slug	Tracheae of a silk moth caterpillar	Model of a pair of human lungs

The Human Respiratory System

Figure 23.18 provides an overview of three phases of gas exchange in humans. **①** The first step of gas exchange is **breathing**, the ventilation of the lungs by alternate inhalation and exhalation. When an animal with lungs breathes, a large, moist internal surface is exposed to air. Oxygen diffuses across the cells lining the lungs and into the surrounding blood vessels. Simultaneously, CO_2 passes out of the blood vessels, into the lungs, and is exhaled. Most land animals require a lot of oxygen. The inner tubes of the lungs are extensively branched, providing a large respiratory surface. **②** The second step in gas exchange is the transport of O_2 from the lungs to the rest of the body via the circulatory system. The blood also carries CO_2 from the tissues back to the lungs. **③** In the final step of gas exchange, O_2 diffuses from red blood cells into body cells, which release CO_2 into the blood. The delivered O_2 is used by the body cells to obtain energy from food via the process of cellular respiration. This same process produces CO_2 as a waste product that cells pass to the blood. The circulatory system transports the CO_2 back to the lungs, where it is exhaled. **☑**

☑ CHECKPOINT

Which type of cellular transport is responsible for moving respiratory gases between the circulatory system and the rest of the body?

Answer: diffusion

▼ **Figure 23.18 The three phases of gas exchange.**

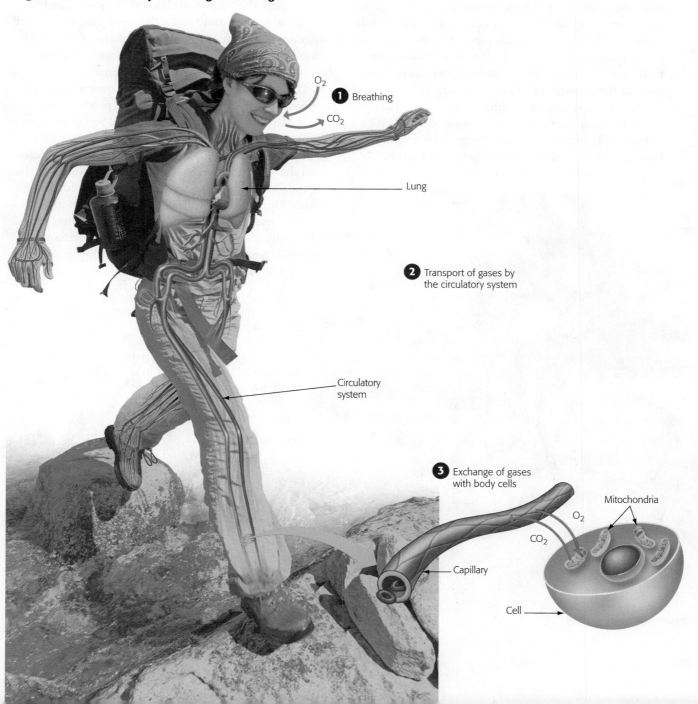

① Breathing — O_2 / CO_2

Lung

② Transport of gases by the circulatory system

Circulatory system

③ Exchange of gases with body cells

Mitochondria

O_2

CO_2

Capillary

Cell

The Structure and Function of the Human Respiratory System

Figure 23.19a shows the human respiratory system. Our lungs are located in the chest cavity, protected by the rib cage and bordered along the bottom by the **diaphragm**, a sheet of muscle. Let's get an overview of the respiratory system by following the flow of air into the lungs.

Air enters the respiratory system through the nostrils and mouth. In the nasal cavity, the air is filtered by hairs and mucus, warmed, humidified, and sampled by smell receptors. The air passes to the **pharynx**, where the digestive and respiratory systems meet. If a piece of food lodges in your pharynx, blocking passage of air to your lungs, you can choke and quickly die. Learning the Heimlich maneuver (quick thrusts to the diaphragm to compress the lungs and force air upward through the trachea, dislodging any stuck objects) may allow you to save the life of someone who is choking.

From the pharynx, air is inhaled into the **larynx** (voice box) and then into the **trachea** (windpipe). The trachea forks into two **bronchi** (singular, *bronchus*), one leading to each lung. Within the lungs, each bronchus

branches repeatedly into finer and finer tubes called **bronchioles**. The system of branching tubes looks like an inverted tree, with the trachea as the trunk and the bronchioles as the smallest branches. Bronchitis is an illness in which these small tubes become inflamed.

The bronchioles dead-end in grapelike clusters of air sacs called **alveoli** (singular, *alveolus*) (**Figure 23.19b**). Each of your lungs contains millions of these tiny sacs. The inner surface of each alveolus is lined with a layer of epithelial cells, where the exchange of gases actually takes place. O_2 enters the bloodstream by diffusing from the air into a web of blood capillaries that surrounds each alveolus. CO_2 diffuses from the blood in the capillaries into the alveoli. The CO_2 in the alveoli is then exhaled through the bronchioles to the bronchus, up through the trachea, and out of the body. The tiny alveoli are delicate and easily damaged, and after age 20 they are not replaced. Destruction of alveoli (usually by smoking, but also by involuntary exposure to air pollution) causes the lung disease emphysema.

During exhalation, outgoing air moves over a pair of **vocal cords** within the larynx. You produce vocal sounds by flexing muscles in the voice box as air rushes by, stretching the vocal cords and making them vibrate. You make high-pitched sounds by tensing the muscles and shortening the vocal cords; you make lower-pitched sounds by reducing the tension and lengthening the cords. During puberty, the voice box of males grows rapidly, resulting in a deeper voice. During their period of growth, pubescent boys often have trouble controlling their lengthening vocal cords, resulting in a "breaking" voice. ☑

☑ CHECKPOINT

Put the following parts of the human respiratory system in the order that an inhaled breath would encounter them: bronchi, larynx, nasal cavity, alveoli, pharynx, bronchioles, trachea.

Answer: nasal cavity → pharynx → larynx → trachea → bronchi → bronchioles → alveoli

▶ **Figure 23.19 The human respiratory system.**

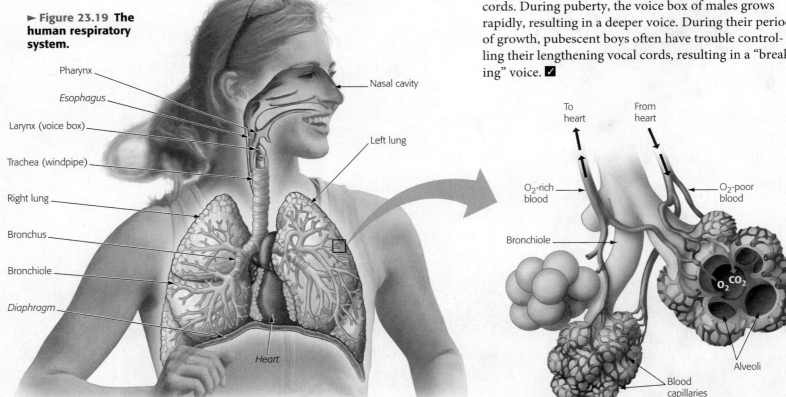

Pharynx
Esophagus
Larynx (voice box)
Trachea (windpipe)
Right lung
Bronchus
Bronchiole
Diaphragm
Nasal cavity
Left lung
Heart

(a) Overview of the human respiratory system

To heart
From heart
O_2-rich blood
O_2-poor blood
Bronchiole
O_2 CO_2
Alveoli
Blood capillaries

(b) The structure of alveoli. Capillaries surround air sacs called alveoli. These are the sites of gas exchange in the lungs.

Taking a Breath

Figure 23.20 shows the changes that occur during breathing, the alternate inhaling and exhaling of air. If you place your hands on your rib cage and inhale, you can feel your ribs move upward and spread out as muscles between them contract. Meanwhile, your diaphragm moves downward, expanding the chest cavity. All of this increases the volume of the lungs, dropping the air pressure in the lungs to below the air pressure of the atmosphere. The result is that air rushes in through the mouth and nostrils from an area of higher pressure to an area of lower pressure, filling the lungs. Although it may seem that you actively suck in air when you inhale, air actually moves into your lungs passively after the air pressure in them drops. This type of ventilation is called **negative pressure breathing**. (In contrast, amphibians use muscles in the mouth and throat to push air into their lungs, a process called positive pressure breathing.)

During exhalation, the rib and diaphragm muscles relax, decreasing the volume of the chest cavity. This decreased volume increases the air pressure inside the lungs, forcing air to rush out of the respiratory system. Movement of the diaphragm is vital to normal breathing. That is why a punch to the diaphragm can "knock the wind out of you." It shocks the diaphragm muscle, prevents movement of the chest cavity, and stops you from taking a normal breath. Other times, sudden involuntary contractions of the diaphragm force air through the voice box, causing hiccups.

You can consciously speed up or slow down your breathing. You can even hold your breath (although,

Why does a blow to the midsection knock the wind out of you?

despite the claims of angry children, you would pass out and return to normal breathing before you turned blue). Usually, however, you aren't aware of breathing; you certainly aren't aware of it when you're asleep. What, then, controls your breathing?

Most of the time, nerves from breathing control centers in the brainstem send signals that maintain a respiratory rate of 10–14 inhalations per minute. This rate can vary, however. **Figure 23.21** highlights one respiratory control system. **1** Levels of CO_2 in the blood affect breathing rate. When you exercise, for example, cellular respiration kicks into high gear, producing more ATP for your muscles and raising the amount of CO_2 in the blood. **2** When the brain senses the higher CO_2 level, **3** breathing control centers increase the breathing rate and depth. As a result, more CO_2 is eliminated in the exhaled air and more O_2 is provided to muscles.

You can become dizzy by hyperventilating—taking excessively rapid, deep breaths. This rapid breathing purges the blood of so much CO_2 that the control centers temporarily slow the signals being sent the diaphragm and rib muscles. Changes in blood chemistry cause arterioles in the brain to constrict, decreasing the brain's blood supply and causing dizziness. Slow breathing continues until the CO_2 level increases enough to switch the breathing control centers back to their normal function. ☑

▼ **Figure 23.21** **Control centers in the brain that regulate breathing.**

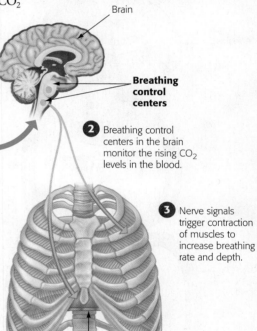

Brain

1 CO_2 levels in the blood rise as a result of exercise.

Breathing control centers

2 Breathing control centers in the brain monitor the rising CO_2 levels in the blood.

3 Nerve signals trigger contraction of muscles to increase breathing rate and depth.

Rib muscles   Diaphragm

▼ **Figure 23.20** **How a human breathes.**

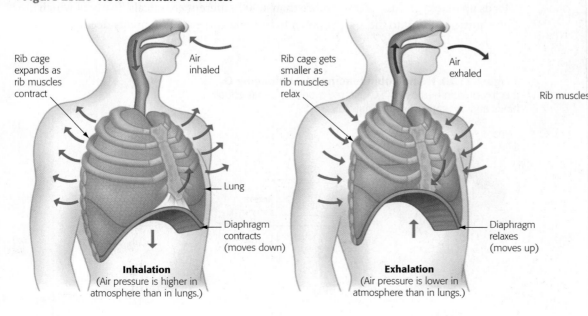

Rib cage expands as rib muscles contract

Air inhaled

Lung

Diaphragm contracts (moves down)

Inhalation
(Air pressure is higher in atmosphere than in lungs.)

Rib cage gets smaller as rib muscles relax

Air exhaled

Diaphragm relaxes (moves up)

Exhalation
(Air pressure is lower in atmosphere than in lungs.)

☑ CHECKPOINT

Why should a hyperventilating person breathe into a paper bag?

Answer: Breathing into a paper bag causes the person to inhale CO_2 back into their lungs. This helps increase the level of CO_2 in the blood, allowing the breathing control centers to function normally.

The Role of Hemoglobin in Gas Transport

The human respiratory system takes O_2 into the body and expels CO_2, but it relies on the circulatory system to shuttle these gases between the lungs and the body's cells (**Figure 23.22**). In the lungs, O_2 diffuses from air spaces inside the alveoli into capillaries surrounding the alveoli. Oxygen moves out of the air and into the blood because air is richer in O_2. At the same time, CO_2 diffuses along its own gradient, from the blood out to the air in the lungs.

But there is a problem with this simple scheme: Oxygen does not readily dissolve in blood, so oxygen will not tend to move from the air into the blood on its own. This problem is solved by the fact that most of the O_2 in blood is carried by hemoglobin molecules within red blood cells (**Figure 23.23**). Each molecule of hemoglobin consists of four polypeptide chains. Attached to each polypeptide is a chemical group called a heme ( ), at the center of which is an atom of iron (shown in black). Each iron atom can hold one O_2 molecule, so one molecule of hemoglobin can carry a maximum of four molecules of O_2. Each red blood cell has about 250 million molecules of hemoglobin, so one tiny cell can carry 1 billion O_2 molecules. Hemoglobin loads up on oxygen in the lungs, carries it to the

body's cells, and unloads it. When hemoglobin binds oxygen, it changes the color of blood to a bright cherry red. Oxygen-poor blood is a dark maroon that appears blue through the skin. This is why a person who has stopped breathing—such as a drowning victim—turns blue.

Because iron (one atom per heme group) is so important in the structure of hemoglobin, a shortage of iron causes less hemoglobin to be produced by the body. In fact, iron deficiency is the most common cause of anemia (a condition in which the blood is deficient in red blood cells). Women are more likely to develop iron deficiency than men because of blood lost during menstruation. Pregnant women can benefit from iron supplements to support the developing fetus.

Besides binding O_2, hemoglobin can bind carbon monoxide (CO), a colorless, odorless gas. In fact, CO binds to hemoglobin even more tightly than O_2 does. Breathing CO can therefore interfere with the delivery of O_2 to body cells. Because CO also interferes with cellular respiration, it can cause rapid death. Sitting in an idling car in an enclosed space, like a garage, can be fatal because CO is emitted as an air pollutant in the exhaust from gasoline-powered engines. And despite its potentially deadly effects, millions of Americans willingly inhale CO in the form of cigarette smoke.

How Smoking Affects the Lungs

Every breath you take exposes your respiratory tissues to potentially damaging chemicals. One of the worst sources of air pollution is tobacco smoke. The visible smoke from burning tobacco is mostly microscopic particles of carbon. Sticking to the carbon particles are more than 4,000 different chemicals, many of which are known to be toxic and even potentially deadly.

▼**Figure 23.22 Gas transport and exchange in the body.** O_2-rich blood is sent from the lungs to capillaries in other body tissues via the heart. O_2 enters body tissue cells and CO_2 leaves, entering the blood. The O_2-poor blood is circulated back to the heart, then to the lungs.

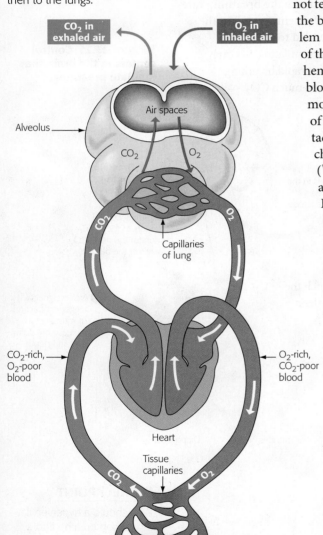

CO$_2$ in exhaled air

O$_2$ in inhaled air

Air spaces

Alveolus

CO$_2$ O$_2$

Capillaries of lung

CO$_2$-rich, O_2-poor blood

O_2-rich, CO$_2$-poor blood

Heart

Tissue capillaries

CO$_2$ Interstitial fluid   O$_2$

Tissue cells throughout body

▼**Figure 23.23 Hemoglobin loading and unloading O₂.** It is the protein hemoglobin within red blood cells that actually binds and transports oxygen molecules.

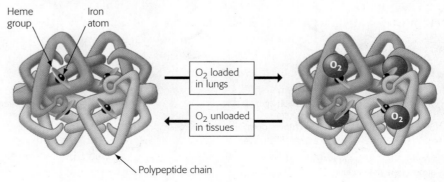

Heme group   Iron atom

O_2 loaded in lungs

O_2 unloaded in tissues

Polypeptide chain

The epithelial tissue lining our respiratory system is extremely delicate. Its main protection is the mucus covering the cells and the beating hairlike cilia that sweep dirt particles and microorganisms off their surfaces (see Figure 4.22c). Tobacco smoke damages the cells that line the bronchi and trachea, destroying their cilia. This interferes with the normal cleansing mechanism of the respiratory system, allowing more toxin-laden smoke particles to reach and damage the lungs' delicate alveoli. Frequent coughing—common in heavy smokers—is the respiratory system's attempt to replace the action of the dead cilia.

The health statistics associated with smoking are staggering. Every year, smoking kills about 440,000 Americans, more than all the deaths caused by accidents, alcohol and drug abuse, HIV, and murders *combined*. One in two American smokers will die from their habit. On average, adults who smoke cigarettes die 13 to 14 years earlier than nonsmokers. Smokers account for 90% of all cases of lung cancer, one of the deadliest forms of cancer: Only 15% of people diagnosed with lung cancer survive five years, and lung cancer kills more Americans than any other form of cancer by a wide margin. **Figure 23.24a** shows a cutaway view of a pair of healthy human lungs (and heart). In contrast,

Figure 23.24b shows the lungs of a smoker, turned black from the long-term buildup of smoke particles.

There is no lifestyle choice that can have a more positive impact on your long-term health (and the health of the people you live with) than not smoking. After quitting, it takes about 15 years for a former smoker's risk to even out with that of a nonsmoker, so not starting is clearly the best option. Unfortunately, even nonsmokers may be affected by tobacco, as studies have found that secondhand cigarette smoke is also a substantial health hazard, particularly to young children. ☑

▼ **Figure 23.24** **Healthy versus cancerous lungs.**

(a) Healthy lung (nonsmoker)   **(b) Cancerous lung (smoker)**

☑ **CHECKPOINT**
How does smoking damage the lungs?

Answer: Smoking damages the epithelial tissue that lines the respiratory system, preventing pollutants from being removed. These pollutants can then damage the delicate alveoli of the lungs where gas exchange occurs.

Athletic Endurance EVOLUTION CONNECTION

Evolving Endurance

In this chapter, we've used the topic of athletic endurance to illustrate the importance of the circulatory and respiratory systems. We've seen how conditioning and even cheating can be used to boost athletic performance by improving the ability of these systems to deliver oxygen to muscles. But as it turns out, not everyone needs conditioning to boost their stamina: Some people are born that way.

Tibet, a plateau region of Asia within the Himalayan mountain range, is the highest region on Earth, with an average elevation of 16,000 feet—nearly 3 miles high! Many Tibetans live and work at altitudes above 13,000 feet, where the amount of oxygen that reaches the blood is 40% less than at sea level **(Figure 23.25)**. Without extensive conditioning, such altitudes render most people sick or even unconscious. Many Tibetans work as mountain guides yet rarely experience "mountain sickness." How have the Tibetan people come to be so tolerant of their surroundings?

A 2010 study by a team of Chinese biologists demonstrated that over the last several thousand years, Tibetans have evolved the ability to thrive at high altitude. By comparing the genomes of 50 Tibetans with the genomes of 40 nearby low-dwelling Chinese, the researchers found at least 30 genes that differed between the two populations. In each case, one version of the gene that is rare among the low-dwelling Chinese group had evolved to become common among Tibetans. Many of these genes are ones already known to contribute to the functioning of the circulatory and respiratory systems. Furthermore, the scientists conducting this study were able to identify the mechanism of natural selection: At high altitude, people who lack such gene mutations have three times the infant mortality rate of people who harbor the mutations. Thus, there is a clear survival and reproductive advantage for those Tibetans who inherit the mutant genes. The Tibetan ability to work and thrive atop the Himalayans can be understood as both a testament to their inborn endurance and another manifestation of biology's unifying theme of evolution.

▲ **Figure 23.25** **A Tibetan mountaineer.** Tibetans are renowned for their ability to live and work at high altitudes.

Chapter Review

SUMMARY OF KEY CONCEPTS

Go to **www.masteringbiology.com** for homework assignments, practice quizzes, Pearson eText, and more.

Unifying Concepts of Animal Circulation

The circulatory system facilitates the exchange of materials and energy between the cells of an organism and its environment.

Open and Closed Circulatory Systems

In an open circulatory system, circulating fluid is pumped through open-ended tubes and circulates freely among cells. In a closed circulatory system, the circulating fluid (blood) is confined within tubes.

The Human Cardiovascular System

The Path of Blood

Trace the path of blood in this figure, noting where blood is oxygen-poor and where it is oxygen-rich.

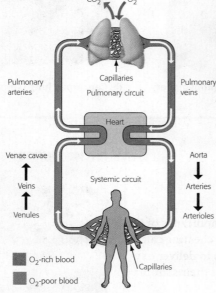

How the Heart Works

Review the structure of the heart by tracing the flow of blood in this diagram.

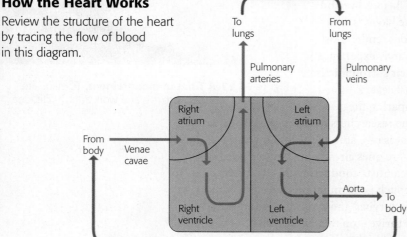

The cardiac cycle is composed of two phases: systole (contraction) and diastole (relaxation). The pacemaker, which sets the tempo of the heartbeat, generates electrical impulses that stimulate the atria and ventricles to contract.

Blood Vessels

Muscular arteries carry blood away from the heart. Exchange between the blood and interstitial fluid occurs across the thin walls of capillaries. Valves in the veins and contractions of surrounding skeletal muscle keep blood moving back to the heart.

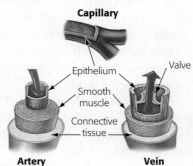

Blood

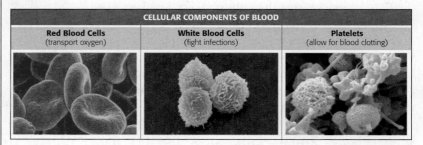

New blood cells are continually formed from stem cells found in red bone marrow.

Cardiovascular Disease

Diseases of the heart and blood vessels—including heart attack and stroke—kill more Americans than any other type of disease. Atherosclerosis is the buildup of fatty substances in the inner walls of arteries.

Unifying Concepts of Animal Respiration

The respiratory system facilitates gas exchange.

The Structure and Function of Respiratory Surfaces

Various respiratory surfaces have evolved in animals. The respiratory surface is the part of the body where gas exchange takes place. This can include the entire body surface, gills, tracheae, or lungs.

The Human Respiratory System

The Structure and Function of the Human Respiratory System

When you take a breath, air moves sequentially from the

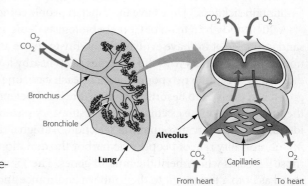

nostrils and/or mouth to the pharynx, larynx, trachea, bronchi (which enter the lungs), bronchioles, and finally the alveoli (the actual respiratory surfaces).

Taking a Breath

During inhalation, the chest cavity expands and air pressure in the lungs decreases, causing air to rush into the lungs. During exhalation, air pressure in the lungs increases and air moves out of the lungs. Breathing rate is set by breathing control centers in the brain, which in turn are influenced by CO_2 concentrations in the blood.

The Role of Hemoglobin in Gas Transport

After O_2 enters the lungs, it binds to hemoglobin in red blood cells and is transported to body tissue cells by the circulatory system.

How Smoking Affects the Lungs

Tobacco smoke damages the respiratory surfaces of the lungs, impairing alveolar function and causing multiple health problems.

SELF-QUIZ

1. What is the difference between an open circulatory system and a closed circulatory system?

2. Why is the following statement false? "All arteries carry oxygen-rich blood, while all veins carry oxygen-poor blood."

3. Match each chamber of the heart with its function.
   a. left atrium
   b. right atrium
   c. left ventricle
   d. right ventricle
   1. receives blood from the body via the venae cavae
   2. sends blood to the lungs via the pulmonary arteries
   3. receives blood from the lungs via the pulmonary veins
   4. sends blood to the body via the aorta

4. Some babies are born with a small hole in the wall of muscle that separates the left and right ventricles. How does this affect the oxygen content of the blood pumped out of the heart in the systemic circuit?

5. People who do not get enough iron in their diet run the risk of developing _____.

6. Match each element of the blood with its main function.
   a. plasma
   b. platelets
   c. red blood cells
   d. white blood cells
   1. transporting O_2
   2. fighting infections
   3. carrying dissolved elements
   4. aiding in clotting

7. A heart-healthy diet can significantly reduce your risk of cardiovascular disease. Name three foods that should be eaten in abundance for a heart-healthy diet, and name three dietary components that should be limited.

8. What is the main difference between the respiratory organs of fishes and humans in terms of where they are located in the body?

9. The respiratory surface of vertebrate lungs consists of tiny sacs within the lungs called _____.

10. During inhalation, when the diaphragm contracts and the ribs spread apart, air pressure inside the lungs
    a. increases.
    b. decreases.
    c. decreases, then increases.
    d. is unchanged.

11. Why is carbon monoxide deadly?
    a. It binds to hemoglobin in white blood cells in place of O_2.
    b. It binds to hemoglobin in red blood cells in place of O_2.
    c. It binds to hemoglobin in red blood cells in place of CO_2.
    d. It binds to hemoglobin in white blood cells in place of CO_2.

Answers to these questions can be found in Appendix: Self-Quiz Answers.

THE PROCESS OF SCIENCE

12. Mammals have a four-chambered heart, with two ventricles and two atria. So do birds, alligators, and crocodiles, but other living reptiles have a three-chambered heart, with just one ventricle. Paleontologists debate whether dinosaurs had a three-chambered or a four-chambered heart. Long-necked sauropod dinosaurs could have had unusual circulatory demands because their head may have been raised far above the heart. The farther the head is above the heart, the greater the systolic pressure needs to be for blood to reach the brain. For example, the long-necked dinosaur *Brachiosaurus* may have carried its head as much as 6 m (20 feet) above its heart. It is estimated that such an anatomy demanded a systolic blood pressure of 500 mm of mercury for blood to reach the brain! Some paleontologists consider this evidence that dinosaurs had a four-chambered heart that supported a dual circulatory system similar to that of birds and mammals, rather than the three-chambered heart of most nonbird reptiles. Can you explain why?

13. During a college swim meet, John told his friends that before a race he likes to "charge up" on oxygen by hyperventilating so he can hold his breath longer. Although John is correct that this will allow him to hold his breath longer, it is not for the reason that he gave. How is he mistaken? Why is this use of hyperventilation actually very dangerous?

BIOLOGY AND SOCIETY

14. Several years ago, a 19-year-old woman received a bone marrow transplant from her 1-year-old sister. The woman was suffering from a form of leukemia and was almost certain to die without a transplant. The woman's parents decided to have another child in a final attempt to provide their daughter with a matching donor. Although the ethics of the parents' decision were criticized, doctors reported that this situation is not uncommon. In your opinion, is it acceptable to have a child to provide tissue or an organ? Why or why not?

15. Many endurance sports—such as the Tour de France bicycle race—have been wracked by blood doping scandals in recent years. Should all forms of artificial red blood cell boosting be banned? What punishment do you think is appropriate for an athlete caught cheating in this way? Should athletes have the right to train however they please, even if it involves artificial therapies?

24 The Body's Defenses

Fighting a killer. Activists in South Africa march in support of AIDS research.

HIV and AIDS BIOLOGY AND SOCIETY

The Elusive Search for an AIDS Vaccine

One of the greatest medical advances of the 1900s was the development of vaccines against deadly viral diseases. A vaccine contains a harmless version or piece of a disease-causing microbe. Once it has been injected, the vaccine can prime the body's defenses so they are ready to mount a vigorous attack if the actual virus is ever encountered. Because there are few antiviral drugs, vaccines are the only medical weapons that can be deployed against many harmful viruses.

One important target of vaccine research is HIV, the human immunodeficiency virus, which causes AIDS (acquired immunodeficiency syndrome). HIV is deadly because it destroys the defenses of its host, leaving the body unable to fight most invaders. In other words, HIV's treacherous means of action wipes out the very body defenses that would normally offer protection.

Despite decades of effort by the world's scientists, an effective AIDS vaccine has never been found. This is not for lack of trying. In an early trial, participants were injected with a virus that infects pet birds, modified to carry three HIV genes. This trial was halted when data showed that the vaccine offered no benefit in helping to prevent infection by the real AIDS virus. Another set of trials used a vaccine made from a modified form of a protein found on the surface of HIV. These studies were also unsuccessful. Researchers were quite surprised, then, by the results of a recent AIDS vaccine study that followed 16,000 volunteers from Thailand over six years. This trial used the two vaccines that had previously been shown to fail. But for reasons no one understands, the *combination* of both of these vaccines offered some protection. Although the difference between the control and experimental groups was so small as to be barely measurable, these results offered the first hint of success after 20 years of effort. When it comes to understanding how to vaccinate against AIDS, we appear to be no closer today than we were decades ago.

AIDS kills by disabling the body's defenses. And vaccines work by stimulating those same defenses. The ongoing battle with HIV is just one illustration of how important your built-in system of defenses is to maintaining your health. This chapter examines how these defenses work to protect your body. We'll also look at how knowledge of this system has been applied to improve human health, what happens when the body's protective system malfunctions, and the continuing struggle against AIDS.

Innate Defenses

Nearly everything in the environment—including most of what you touch or taste and even the air you breathe—teems with microbes, some of which can make you sick. Yet you do not constantly become ill, thanks to your **immune system**, your body's system of defenses against infectious disease.

The human body has three cooperative lines of defense that protect you against the constant barrage of **pathogens**, disease-causing viruses and microorganisms (**Figure 24.1**). The first line of defense is external—barriers that prevent pathogens from getting deep inside the body. If that line fails, some internal protections stand ready as a second line of defense. These first two lines of defense are **innate defenses**—that is, they are always deployed and at the ready. Later in the chapter, we'll discuss the third line of defense, the **adaptive defenses** (also known as acquired defenses), which are internal defenses that must be activated by exposure to specific invaders. While nearly all animals have innate defenses, only vertebrates have adaptive defenses. Throughout this chapter, we'll focus on the innate and adaptive defenses of humans.

CHECKPOINT

What makes the body's first two lines of defense "innate"?

Answer: These defenses are at full strength before an invader is ever encountered.

External Innate Defenses

For a foreign substance to get inside the body, it must first get by the body's external barriers. These barriers form an important protective front line because they *prevent* infection, as opposed to the body's other defenses, which act only *after* infection has occurred.

Some barriers block or filter out microbes. Intact skin forms a tough outer layer that most bacteria and viruses cannot penetrate. Nostril hairs filter many particles from the incoming air. Wax in the ear canal traps particles before they can get deep inside. Organ systems that are open to the external environment (such as the respiratory and reproductive systems) are lined with mucous membranes that secrete mucus, a sticky fluid that traps bacteria, dust, and other particles. Beating cilia extending from cells of the respiratory tract sweep mucus with the trapped particles outward until it is swallowed or expelled by sneezing, coughing, or blowing the nose.

External barriers also include chemical defenses in the form of antimicrobial secretions. Sweat, saliva, and tears contain enzymes that disrupt bacterial cell walls. Glands produce oils and acids that make the skin inhospitable to many microbes. Concentrated stomach acid kills most of the bacteria we swallow before they can enter the bloodstream. ☑

▼ **Figure 24.1 Overview of the body's defenses.** Note that the lymphatic system is involved in both innate and adaptive defenses.

THE BODY'S DEFENSES	
Innate Defenses (always deployed)	**Adaptive Defenses** (activated by exposure to specific pathogens)

External innate defenses
- Skin
- Secretions
- Mucous membranes

Cilia

Mucus-producing cells

Colorized SEM 3,300×

Internal innate defenses
- Phagocytic cells

Invading microbe

Phagocytic cell

- Natural killer cells
- Defensive proteins
- Inflammatory response

Adaptive Defenses
- Lymphocytes

B cell

T cell

- Antibodies

The Lymphatic System (involved in internal innate defenses and adaptive defenses)

Lymph node

518

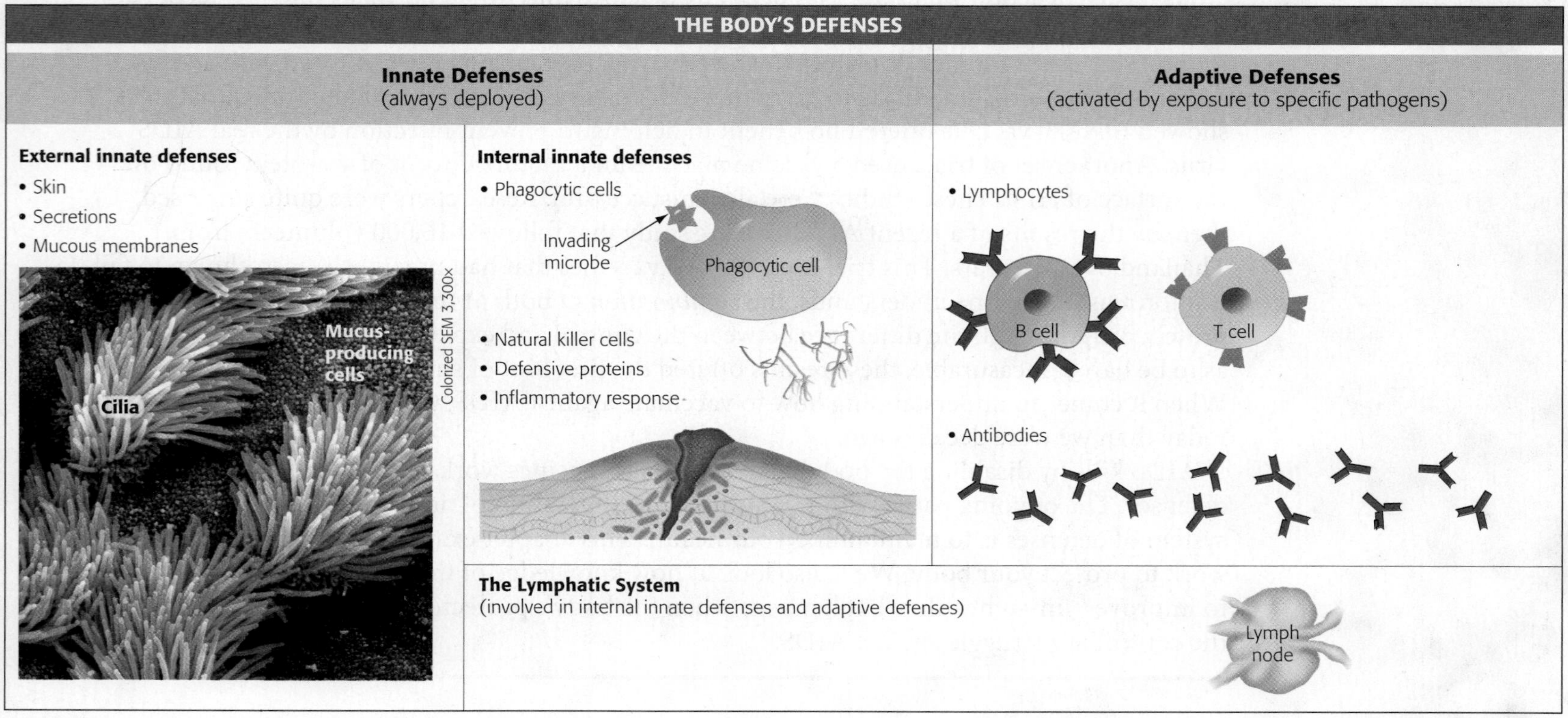

Internal Innate Defenses

When an invader breaches the body's external barriers, it is no longer an outsider. To fight pathogens within the body, the animal's immune system must first detect foreign particles and cells. In other words, an immune system must be able to distinguish nonself from self. This is accomplished by a second line of innate defenses that consists of white blood cells and defensive proteins (**Figure 24.2**).

Two types of white blood cells contribute to your internal innate defenses: phagocytic cells and natural killer cells. **Phagocytic cells** engulf foreign cells or molecules and debris from dead cells by phagocytosis, or "cellular eating" (see Figure 5.18). **Natural killer (NK) cells** can often recognize virus-infected or cancerous body cells. When contact is made, the NK cells release chemicals that kill the diseased cells.

The defensive proteins that aid in internal innate defense include **interferons**, which are produced by body cells that have been infected by viruses (**Figure 24.3**). Virus-infected cells ❶ make and release interferons that ❷ bind to plasma membrane receptors on nearby uninfected cells. This binding stimulates the healthy cells to ❸ produce proteins that inhibit viral reproduction. Because of their strong antiviral properties, injected interferons are sometimes used to treat some viral diseases, such as hepatitis and genital warts. **Complement proteins** attack pathogens directly. Some coat the surfaces of microbes, making them easier for phagocytic cells to engulf. Others cut lethal holes in microbial membranes, causing the invading cells to burst (lyse). Still other proteins help trigger the inflammatory response, our next topic. ☑

▼ **Figure 24.2 The body's second line of defense.** When the external barriers fail, a set of internal innate defenses stands ready as the body's next line of protection.

INTERNAL INNATE DEFENSES			
White Blood Cells		**Defensive Proteins**	
Phagocytic cells (engulf foreign cells or substances)	**Natural killer cells** (destroy infected and cancerous body cells)	**Interferons** (protect body cells against viral infection)	**Complement proteins** (cause invading microbial cells to lyse)

► **Figure 24.3 The action of interferon.** When a virus infects a body cell, the cell produces and releases interferon molecules that bind to receptors on healthy cells, stimulating them to produce antiviral proteins that inhibit the growth of other viruses.

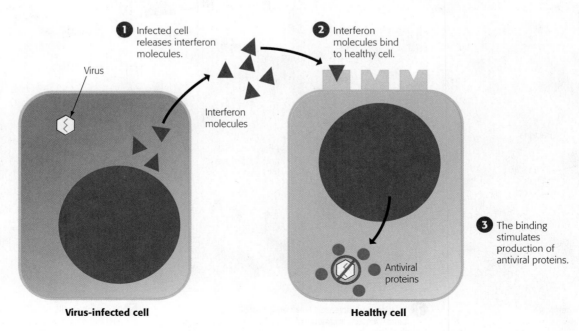

❶ Infected cell releases interferon molecules.

❷ Interferon molecules bind to healthy cell.

Virus

Interferon molecules

❸ The binding stimulates production of antiviral proteins.

Antiviral proteins

Virus-infected cell

Healthy cell

519

The Inflammatory Response

What happens if you get a splinter in your finger and don't take care of it? The next day, the finger is often red, swollen, painful, and warm to the touch. These are signs of the **inflammatory response** to injury and infection, another example of an internal innate defense in action **(Figure 24.4)**. When tissue becomes damaged (from cuts, scratches, bug bites, or burns, for example), ❶ the injured cells release chemicals that trigger various innate defenses. One such chemical signal, **histamine**, ❷ causes nearby blood vessels to dilate (widen) and leak fluid into the wounded tissue, causing it to swell. The swelling helps the tissue to heal by diluting toxins, bringing extra oxygen, and delivering platelets and clotting proteins that promote scabbing. The chemical signals also attract phagocytic cells. ❸ These cells engulf bacteria and the remains of body cells killed by bacteria or by the physical injury. The pus that often fills an infected injury consists of phagocytic cells, fluid that leaked from capillaries, and other tissue debris.

Why does pus form around a healing cut?

Damaged cells also release chemical signals that increase blood flow to the damaged area, causing the wound to turn red and warm. (The word *inflammation* means "setting on fire.") In response to severe tissue damage or infection, damaged cells may release other chemicals that travel through the bloodstream to the brain, where they stimulate a fever that may discourage bacterial growth.

Anti-inflammatory drugs such as aspirin and ibuprofen dampen the normal inflammatory response and help reduce swelling and fever. Aspirin, for example, inhibits dilation of blood vessels, which reduces swelling. This is an example of treating the symptoms of an illness (for example, swelling) without addressing the underlying cause (which is the injury or infection).

All the defenses you've learned about so far are called innate because they're ready "off the rack"; that is, innate defenses are already deployed in the body and at the ready without any preparation. Soon you'll learn about the body's adaptive defenses—ones that are "custom-tailored" to specific invaders. But first let's look at a system that contributes to both innate and adaptive defenses: the lymphatic system. ☑

The Lymphatic System

The **lymphatic system** consists of a branching network of vessels, numerous **lymph nodes** (little round organs packed with white blood cells), and several other organs **(Figure 24.5)**. The lymphatic vessels carry fluid called **lymph**, which is similar to the interstitial fluid surrounding body cells. The two main functions of the lymphatic system are to return tissue fluid to the circulatory system and to fight infection.

☑ CHECKPOINT

Name the signs of the inflammatory response.

Answer: swelling, redness, warmth, pain, and sometimes fever

▼ **Figure 24.4 The inflammatory response.** Whenever tissue is damaged, the body responds with a coordinated set of internal innate defenses called the inflammatory response.

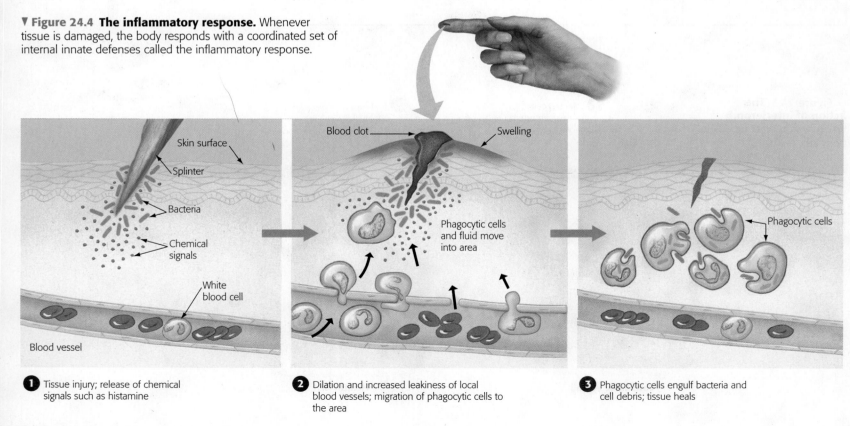

❶ Tissue injury; release of chemical signals such as histamine

❷ Dilation and increased leakiness of local blood vessels; migration of phagocytic cells to the area

❸ Phagocytic cells engulf bacteria and cell debris; tissue heals

A small amount of the fluid that enters the tissue spaces from the blood in a capillary bed does not reenter the blood capillaries. Instead, it flows into lymphatic capillaries that are intermingled with blood capillaries. Now called lymph, this fluid drains from the lymphatic capillaries into larger and larger lymphatic vessels. Eventually, the fluid reenters the circulatory system through two large lymphatic vessels that fuse with veins near the shoulders.

When your body is fighting an infection, the lymphatic system is the main battleground. Lymph nodes fill with huge numbers of white blood cells, causing the tender "swollen glands" in your neck and armpits that your doctor feels for as a likely sign of infection. Because lymphatic vessels penetrate nearly every tissue, lymph can pick up microbes from infection sites just about anywhere in the body and deliver them to the lymphatic nodes and other organs. As the lymph passes through the lymphatic tissue, phagocytic cells engulf invaders. Lymph also carries white blood cells involved in the adaptive defenses, which we'll discuss next. ☑

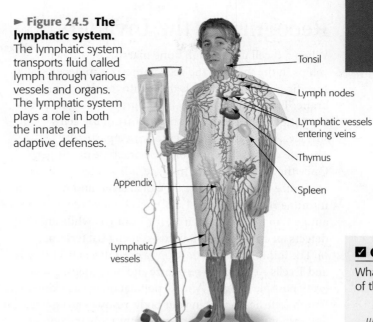

► Figure 24.5 **The lymphatic system.** The lymphatic system transports fluid called lymph through various vessels and organs. The lymphatic system plays a role in both the innate and adaptive defenses.

Tonsil

Lymph nodes

Lymphatic vessels entering veins

Thymus

Spleen

Appendix

Lymphatic vessels

☑ **CHECKPOINT**

What are the two functions of the lymphatic system?

Answer: to collect fluid that leaks from blood capillaries within tissues and to help protect the body from foreign cells and molecules

Adaptive Defenses

When the innate defenses fail to ward off a pathogen, the adaptive defenses provide a third line of defense (see Figure 24.1). This third line is called *adaptive* because it is activated only after exposure to specific pathogens. Adaptive defenses depend on white blood cells called **lymphocytes** that recognize and respond to specific invading pathogens. There are two types of lymphocytes: B cells and T cells. Like all blood cells, lymphocytes originate from stem cells in the bone marrow **(Figure 24.6)**. Some immature lymphocytes continue developing in the bone marrow; these become specialized as **B cells**. Other immature lymphocytes migrate via the blood to the thymus, a gland in the chest, where they become specialized as **T cells**. Both B cells and T cells eventually make their way to the lymph nodes and other lymphatic organs. Over 2 trillion lymphocytes are spread throughout the bloodstream and lymphatic system, making possible an elaborately coordinated response to infection.

Whereas the innate defenses are always ready to fight a variety of infections, lymphocytes must be primed by exposure to a foreign molecule. Any molecule that elicits a response from a lymphocyte is called an **antigen**. Most antigens are molecules on the surfaces of viruses or foreign cells, such as cells of bacteria or parasitic worms. Antigens can also be molecules from mold spores, pollen, and house dust, as well as molecules on

cell surfaces of transplanted tissue. We'll look at how lymphocytes recognize antigens and then explore how they respond to these invaders. ☑

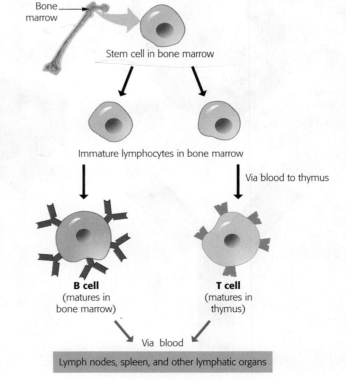

Bone marrow

Stem cell in bone marrow

Immature lymphocytes in bone marrow

Via blood to thymus

B cell (matures in bone marrow)

T cell (matures in thymus)

Via blood

Lymph nodes, spleen, and other lymphatic organs

◄ Figure 24.6 **The development of lymphocytes.** All lymphocytes arise in the bone marrow, but they mature in different locations: B cells in the bone marrow and T cells in the thymus. Once mature, lymphocytes are released into the blood and lymphatic system.

☑ **CHECKPOINT**

1. What are the two main types of lymphocytes?
2. What is an antigen? Name some examples.

Answers: 1. B cells and T cells 2. An antigen is a molecule that elicits a response from a lymphocyte. Examples include pollen, dust, and proteins on the surfaces of microorganisms.

Recognizing the Invaders

When a B cell develops in bone marrow or a T cell develops in the thymus, the cell synthesizes molecules of a specific protein and builds them into its plasma membrane. These protein molecules (purple in Figure 24.6) are antigen receptors that stick out from the cell's surface. All the antigen receptors on a particular lymphocyte can bind to only one specific type of antigen. Once these receptors are in place, a B cell or T cell can recognize a single specific type of antigen and mount an immune response against it. One cell may recognize an antigen on the mumps virus, for instance, while another detects an antigen on a tetanus-causing bacterium.

The immune system develops a great diversity of B cells and T cells—enough to recognize and bind to just about every possible antigen. A small population of each kind of lymphocyte lies in wait in your body, ready to recognize and respond to a specific antigen. Only a tiny fraction of the lymphocytes will ever be used, but they are all available if needed. It is as if the immune system maintains a huge standing army of soldiers, each made to recognize one particular kind of invader. The majority of soldiers never encounter their target and remain idle. But when an invader does appear, chances are good that some lymphocytes will recognize it, bind to it, and call in reinforcements.

After binding to an antigen, a B cell can give rise to short-lived cells that secrete receptor-like molecules that circulate in the blood and lymph. Such a secreted molecule is called an **antibody** and is specific for that same antigen (**Figure 24.7**). Each antibody molecule consists of four polypeptide chains joined together to form a Y shape. The tip of each arm of an antibody forms an antigen-binding site, a region responsible for recognizing and binding to the antigen. An antigen-binding site and the antigen it binds have complementary shapes, like an enzyme and substrate or a lock and key. A huge variety in the shapes of the binding sites of different antibodies enables the immune system to react to any kind of antigen. The main role of an antibody is to mark an antigen by combining with it to form an antigen-antibody complex. As you'll see later, such binding triggers responses that help destroy the invader.

Because of their ability to tag specific molecules or cells, antibodies are widely used in laboratory research, in clinical diagnosis, and in the treatment of disease. Using cell cultures, researchers can artificially produce large quantities of antibodies, which have many uses. Some are used to treat disorders of the immune system, such as transplant rejection and autoimmune diseases, particularly rheumatoid arthritis. Herceptin, a genetically engineered antibody, is used to treat certain cases of aggressive breast cancer. A common type of home pregnancy test uses antibodies to detect a hormone called human chorionic gonadotropin (HCG), present in the urine of pregnant women. When a testing strip is dipped into urine, antibodies on the strip bind to any HCG that is present, causing the strip to change color. And antibodies are one of the keys to diagnosing HIV infection, as you'll see next. ✔

☑ **CHECKPOINT**

What are antibodies? What is their role in the adaptive immune response?

Answer: receptor proteins secreted by short-lived B cells; to mark an antigen by binding to it

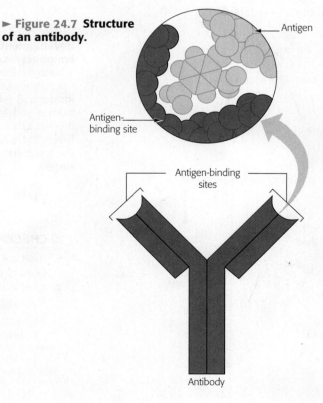

► **Figure 24.7 Structure of an antibody.**

Antigen

Antigen-binding site

Antigen-binding sites

Antibody

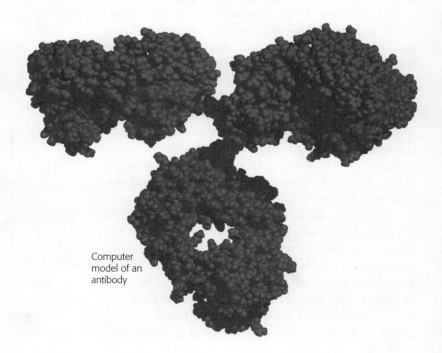

Computer model of an antibody

How Was HIV First Linked to AIDS?

The disease now called AIDS was first recognized by doctors in 1981. **Observation** of the spread of AIDS among sexual partners, intravenous drug users, and blood transplant recipients strongly suggested that some infectious agent caused the disease (rather than, say, an environmental poison). But the key **question**—What pathogen causes AIDS?—remained unanswered for three years after AIDS was first described.

In 1984, a group of researchers led by Robert Gallo, of the U.S. National Cancer Institute, announced a major breakthrough. Their work began with the **hypothesis** that AIDS was caused by a new virus discovered by French biologist Luc Montagnier (who received a 2008 Nobel Prize for his discovery). This hypothesis led to the **prediction** that the blood of people with AIDS would contain antibodies to this new virus.

Their **experiment**, summarized in **Figure 24.8**, used one kind of antibody to test for another. First, blood samples were taken from people with AIDS and from negative controls (people with no behaviors known to be associated with HIV). Next, the blood was added to the well (indentation) of a laboratory dish that had

① fragments from the suspected virus stuck to the bottom. ② If the test subject's blood had antibodies to the virus, they would ③ bind to the virus, forming an antibody-virus complex that was fixed to the dish. ④ Finally, another kind of antibody, one that binds to any human antibody, was added along with an enzyme that ⑤ would react with the complex to produce a color. The dishes were washed, so any remaining color could only indicate antibodies that had bound to the virus (which was attached to the dish so it wouldn't wash away). Their **results** showed that almost every patient with AIDS had antibodies to the new virus, whereas none of the control people did. In a series of classic papers published in 1984, Gallo combined these results with other evidence to prove that the new virus, now called HIV, causes AIDS.

▼ **Figure 24.8 HIV blood test.** The test described here is still used today as a diagnostic tool to test people for HIV infection. (The molecules shown in this figure are not to scale; they are actually much smaller than the wells.)

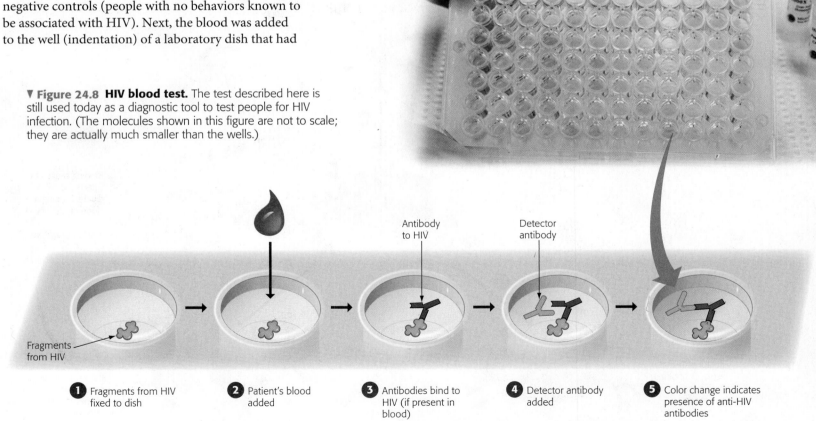

Fragments from HIV

| ① Fragments from HIV fixed to dish | ② Patient's blood added | ③ Antibodies bind to HIV (if present in blood) | ④ Detector antibody added | ⑤ Color change indicates presence of anti-HIV antibodies |

Responding to the Invaders

Now that you know how lymphocytes recognize antigens, we'll look at how they fight these intruders. B cells and T cells have distinct responses, but they carry out a coordinated attack along with the innate defenses.

Clonal Selection: Multiplying Lymphocytes

Recall that the immune system maintains a vast collection of different kinds of white blood cells. With so many kinds of B cells and T cells, how does the body marshal enough of the right kind of lymphocyte to fight a specific invading antigen? The key is a process called **clonal selection**. The concept is simple. At first, an antigen activates only a tiny number of lymphocytes with receptors specific to that antigen. These "selected" cells then proliferate, forming a clone of cells (a population of genetically identical B cells or T cells) that are specific for the stimulating antigen.

Figure 24.9 illustrates how clonal selection of lymphocytes works, using B cells as an example; a similar mechanism activates clonal selection for T cells. The top row

shows three different B cells, each with its own specific type of antigen receptor embedded in its surface. ❶ Once an antigen enters the body, it binds with a B cell that has complementary receptors. Other lymphocytes without the appropriate binding sites are not affected. ❷ The binding activates the cell—it grows, divides, and develops further. This produces clones of cells specialized for defending against the very antigen that triggered the response. ❸ Some of the newly produced cells are short-lived cells that have an immediate effect against the antigen and are therefore called **effector cells**. In the case of B cells, the effector cells secrete huge quantities of antibodies into the blood and lymph—as many as 2,000 copies per second. These antibodies bind to the invading antigen and, as you'll see later, contribute to its destruction or block its harmful effects.

The first response to exposure of lymphocytes to an antigen, called the **primary immune response**, takes several days to produce effector cells via clonal selection. The antibodies produced by effector B cells reach their peak levels about two weeks after first exposure and then start to decline. Each effector cell lives only four or five days, and the primary immune response subsides as the effector cells die out. ❹ Clonal selection also produces memory cells, which we'll discuss next.

▼ **Figure 24.9 Clonal selection.** In this example of clonal selection, an antigen "selects" a B cell that binds to it and causes the cell's proliferation. A similar kind of clonal selection operates on T cells.

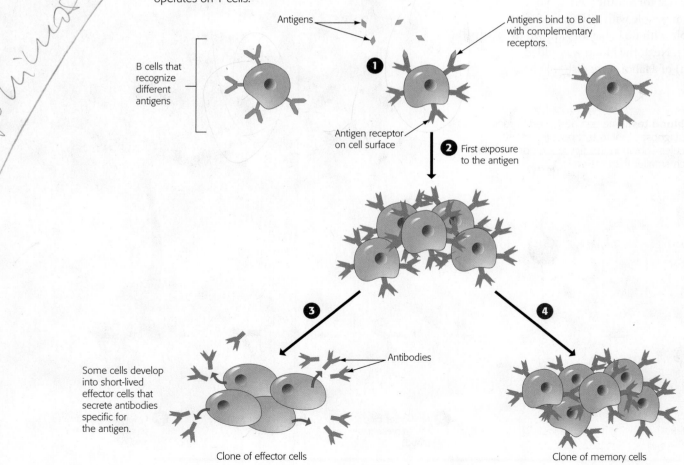

Antigens

B cells that recognize different antigens

Antigens bind to B cell with complementary receptors.

❶

Antigen receptor on cell surface

❷ First exposure to the antigen

Binding causes the selected B cell to divide, forming a clone of identical cells with the same antigen receptors.

❸

❹

Antibodies

Some cells develop into short-lived effector cells that secrete antibodies specific for the antigen.

Clone of effector cells

Some cells develop into long-lived memory cells. If later exposed to the same antigen, they produce larger clones of memory and effector cells.

Clone of memory cells

Immunological Memory

Figure 24.9 shows that clonal selection produces both effector cells and memory cells. **Memory cells** are long-lived cells that respond to subsequent exposures to the antigen by giving rise to effector cells and more memory cells. Thus, clonal selection produces not only cells that will fight the first exposure to an antigen (effector cells) but also cells that will respond to future exposures (memory cells).

What's in all those shots that you were given as a young child?

In contrast to short-lived effector cells, memory cells can last decades in the lymph nodes, poised to be activated by a second exposure to the antigen. When the antigen is encountered again, the memory cells that bind to it initiate a faster and stronger response called the **secondary immune response**. The activated memory cells multiply quickly, producing a large new clone of lymphocytes. In the case of B cells, the new clone produces antibodies that are often more effective than those produced during the primary immune response.

Thus, with adaptive defenses, unlike innate defenses, exposure to a particular foreign molecule enhances future responses to that same molecule. For example, if a person gets chicken pox or receives the chicken pox vaccine, memory cells are formed that have receptors against molecules on the virus that causes this disease. If the virus enters the body again, the memory cells react quickly, giving rise to effector cells that usually destroy the virus before symptoms appear. One early observation of the effect of the immune system's remarkable "memory" is in the writings of the Greek historian Thucydides, almost 2,400 years ago. He noted that survivors of the plague could safely care for people who were sick or dying of that disease, "for the same man was never attacked twice—never at least fatally."

Vaccination

Immunity is obtained after an infection, but it can also be achieved artificially by **vaccination** (also called immunization). As discussed in the Biology and Society section, the immune system can be confronted with a **vaccine** composed of a harmless version of a disease-causing microbe or one of its parts. The vaccine stimulates the immune system to mount defenses against these harmless antigens. These defenses will also be effective against the actual pathogen because it has similar antigens. When a person has been successfully vaccinated, the immune system responds quickly if exposed to the pathogen. Such protection may last for life.

In the United States, most children receive a series of shots starting soon after birth **(Figure 24.10)**. The shots include vaccinations against diphtheria/pertussis/tetanus (DPT, or "diptet"), polio, hepatitis, chicken pox, and measles/mumps/rubella (MMR). In the United States, widespread childhood vaccination has virtually eliminated several of these diseases, including polio and mumps. As noted in the Biology and Society section, researchers are trying to develop an HIV vaccine, although success remains elusive (for reasons to be discussed in the Evolution Connection section). One of the major triumphs of modern vaccination involves smallpox, a potentially fatal viral infection that affected over 50 million people a year worldwide in the 1950s. A massive vaccination effort has been so effective that in 1977 the World Health Organization of the United Nations declared smallpox to be completely eradicated. Since 2001, however, the U.S. government has stockpiled millions of doses of smallpox vaccine and has vaccinated high-risk military and health-care workers in case the smallpox virus is used in a bioterrorist attack.

So far, you've seen that the binding of foreign antigens triggers lymphocytes of the immune system to multiply, producing clones of effector cells and memory cells. Next we'll look at how the effector cells disable or destroy the intruders. ✔

✔ CHECKPOINT

Given that there are so many possible pathogens that can invade your body, how does your immune system produce enough of the right cells to fight off a major infection?

Answer: The process of clonal selection causes those few cells with receptors that are complementary to the antigens of the infectious agent to selectively multiply.

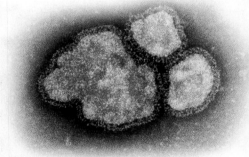

▼ **Figure 24.10 Vaccinating a child against the measles virus (inset).**

Colorized SEM 144,000×

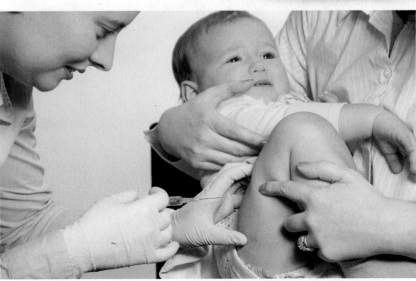

B Cells and the Humoral Immune Response

The secretion of free-floating antibodies into the blood and lymph by B cells is called the **humoral immune response**. (The word *humoral* comes from *humors*, an old term for blood and other body fluids.) This response defends primarily against bacteria and viruses that are circulating in body fluids. Sometimes the binding of antibodies neutralizes antigens by physically blocking them. For example, the attachment of antibodies to viral surface proteins may inhibit the virus from entering body cells. Other times, the binding to viruses or foreign cells causes the formation of clumps of pathogens that are easily captured by circulating phagocytic cells. Additionally, the antigen-antibody complex may activate complement proteins that destroy the antigen-carrying cells.

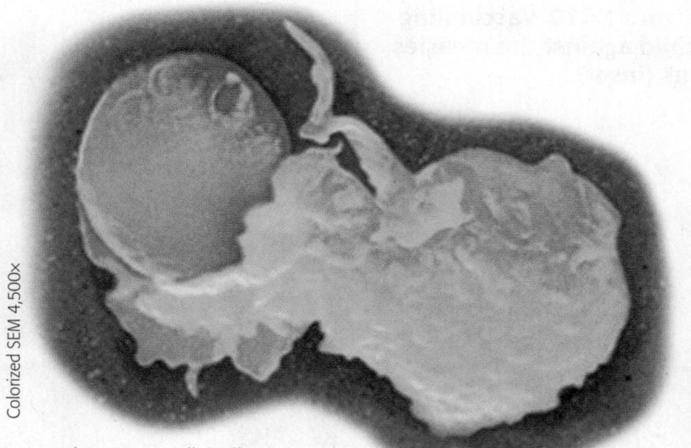

T Cells and the Cell-Mediated Immune Response

Whereas the humoral immune response involves antibodies secreted by effector B cells into the blood and lymph, effector T cells respond directly to antigens that have already entered body cells. Because this response is carried out directly by cells rather than by antibodies, it is called the **cell-mediated immune response**. It involves two main kinds of T cells: helper T cells and cytotoxic T cells.

Helper T cells bind to other white blood cells that have previously encountered an antigen. In the example in **Figure 24.11**, ❶ a phagocytic cell engulfs a microbe and breaks it into fragments, each of which is a foreign antigen (*nonself* molecule). Protein molecules belonging to the phagocytic cell, which are referred to as *self* proteins because they belong to the body itself, ❷ bind to the foreign antigens and ❸ display them on the cell's outer surface. ❹ Receptors embedded in the helper T cell's plasma membrane recognize and bind to the combination of self protein and nonself molecule displayed on the phagocytic cell.

▼ **Figure 24.11 Interaction of a phagocytic cell and a helper T cell.**

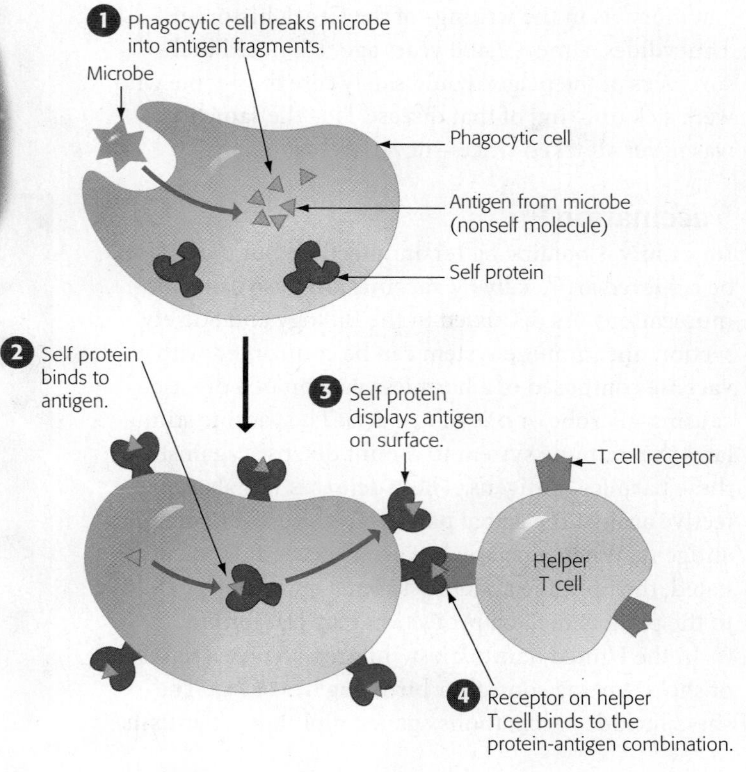

Colorized SEM 4,500×

Phagocytic cell (yellow) engulfing a foreign cell

❶ Phagocytic cell breaks microbe into antigen fragments.

Microbe

Phagocytic cell

Antigen from microbe (nonself molecule)

Self protein

❷ Self protein binds to antigen.

❸ Self protein displays antigen on surface.

T cell receptor

Helper T cell

❹ Receptor on helper T cell binds to the protein-antigen combination.

▼ **Figure 24.12 The roles of an activated helper T cell.** Activated helper T cells promote both the cell-mediated immune response (via cytotoxic T cells) and the humoral immune response (via B cells).

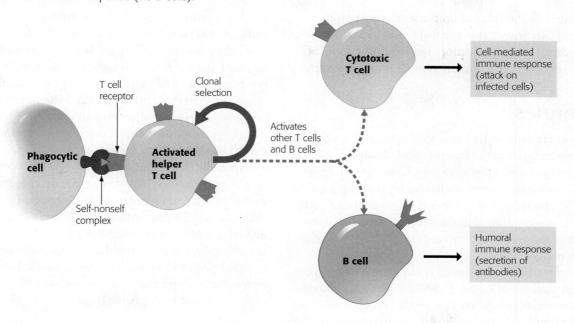

The binding of a T cell receptor to the self-nonself combination activates the helper T cell (**Figure 24.12**). An activated helper T cell responds in several ways. It grows and divides, producing more activated helper T cells, as well as memory T cells (not shown in figure). In addition, it stimulates the activity of cytotoxic T cells and helps activate B cells, thus engaging the humoral immune response as well. Given its central role in so many aspects of immunity, it is not surprising that an HIV infection—which destroys helper T cells specifically—has such devastating consequences.

Cytotoxic T cells are the only T cells that actually kill infected cells. They identify infected body cells in the same way that helper T cells identify their targets: through binding of a receptor to a self-nonself complex. As shown in **Figure 24.13**, ❶ a cytotoxic T cell binds to an infected cell. The binding activates the T cell. ❷ The activated cell synthesizes and discharges several proteins, including one called perforin that makes holes in the infected cell's plasma membrane. ❸ Other T cell proteins enter the infected cell through the newly created hole and trigger a process that results in ❹ death of the cell by lysis (bursting). ☑

▼ **Figure 24.13 How a cytotoxic T cell kills an infected cell.**

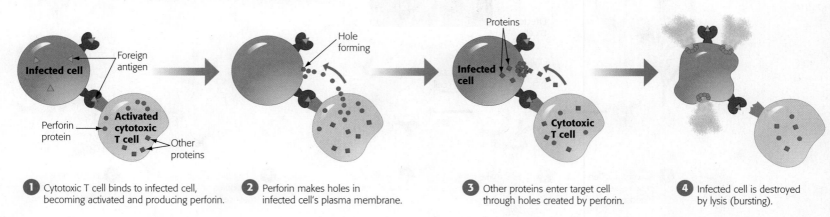

❶ Cytotoxic T cell binds to infected cell, becoming activated and producing perforin.

❷ Perforin makes holes in infected cell's plasma membrane.

❸ Other proteins enter target cell through holes created by perforin.

❹ Infected cell is destroyed by lysis (bursting).

Immune Disorders

If the intricate interplay of immune cells goes awry, problems can arise that range from mild irritations to deadly diseases. In this section, we'll examine some of the consequences of a malfunctioning immune system.

Allergies

Allergies are exaggerated sensitivities to otherwise harmless antigens in the environment. Antigens that cause allergies are called **allergens**. Common allergens include protein molecules on pollen grains, on the feces of tiny mites that live in house dust, and in animal dander (shed skin cells). Allergic reactions typically occur very rapidly in response to tiny amounts of an allergen.

If someone is allergic to dust, what are they really allergic to?

The symptoms of an allergy result from a two-stage reaction outlined in **Figure 24.14**. The first stage, called sensitization, occurs when a person is first exposed to an allergen—pollen, for example. **1** An allergen enters the bloodstream. There it binds to B cells with complementary receptors, tagging them for clonal selection (as in Figure 24.9). **2** The B cells then proliferate and secrete large amounts of antibodies to that allergen. **3** Some of these antibodies attach to receptor proteins on the surfaces of mast cells, body cells that produce histamine and other chemicals that trigger the inflammatory response.

Allergy symptoms do not arise until the second stage, which begins when the same allergen enters the body and **4** binds to the antibodies on the mast cells. In response to this binding, **5** the mast cells release

histamine, which triggers allergy symptoms. Histamine causes blood vessels to dilate and leak fluid, causing nasal irritation, itchy skin, and tears. Because allergens usually enter the body through the nose and throat, symptoms are often most prominent there. Antihistamines are drugs that interfere with histamine's action and give temporary relief from an allergy.

Allergic reactions range from seasonal nuisances to severe, life-threatening responses. Anaphylactic shock is an especially dangerous type of allergic reaction. Some people are extremely sensitive to certain allergens, such as the venom from a bee sting or allergens in peanuts or shellfish. Any contact with these allergens causes a sudden release of inflammatory chemicals. Blood vessels dilate abruptly, causing a rapid and potentially fatal drop in blood pressure, a condition called shock. Fortunately, anaphylactic shock can be counteracted with injections of the hormone epinephrine **(Figure 24.15)**. ☑

▼ **Figure 24.15 Single-use epinephrine syringes.** People who know they have severe allergies can carry single-use syringes that contain the hormone epinephrine (also called adrenaline). An injection can quickly stop a life-threatening allergic reaction.

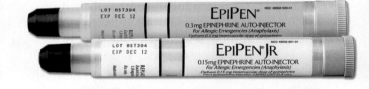

► **Figure 24.14 How allergies develop.** The first exposure to an allergen causes sensitization. Subsequent exposures to the same allergen produce allergy symptoms.

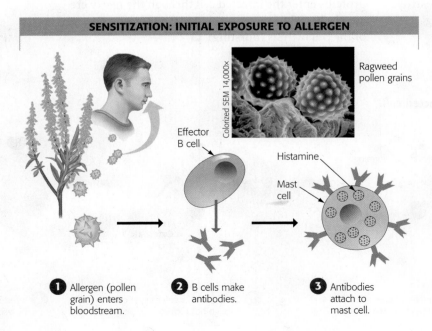

SENSITIZATION: INITIAL EXPOSURE TO ALLERGEN

Colorized SEM 14,000×

Ragweed pollen grains

Effector B cell

Histamine

Mast cell

1 Allergen (pollen grain) enters bloodstream.

2 B cells make antibodies.

3 Antibodies attach to mast cell.

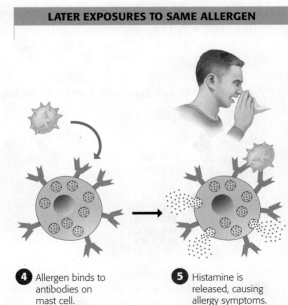

LATER EXPOSURES TO SAME ALLERGEN

4 Allergen binds to antibodies on mast cell.

5 Histamine is released, causing allergy symptoms.

Autoimmune Diseases

The immune system's ability to distinguish self from nonself enables it to battle foreign invaders without harming healthy body cells. Self proteins on the surfaces of cells are the key to this ability. Each person's cells have a particular collection of self proteins that mark body cells as "off-limits" to attacks from the immune system. Because every person has a unique set of self proteins, the immune system can distinguish the body's cells from those of other people and from microbes.

The immune system's ability to recognize and attack foreign antigens does not always work in our favor. For example, when a person receives an organ transplant, the immune system recognizes the donor's cells as foreign and attacks them. To minimize rejection, doctors look for a donor with self proteins matching the recipient's as closely as possible (often a close relative) and use drugs to suppress the immune response. Such drugs greatly reduce the risk of rejection but increase the risk of infections and must often be administered for life.

Autoimmune diseases result when the immune system improperly turns against the body's own molecules. In systemic lupus erythematosus (lupus), B cells make antibodies against many sorts of self molecules, even proteins and DNA released by the normal breakdown of body cells. Rheumatoid arthritis is an autoimmune disease that leads to damage and painful inflammation of the cartilage and bones of joints **(Figure 24.16)**. In type 1 (insulin-dependent) diabetes, the insulin-producing cells of the pancreas are the targets of cytotoxic T cells. In multiple sclerosis (MS), T cells wrongly attack proteins in neurons (see Figure 27.2), often causing progressive muscle paralysis. Recent research suggests that Crohn's disease, a chronic inflammation of the digestive tract, may be caused by an autoimmune reaction against bacteria that normally inhabit the intestinal tract.

Immunodeficiency Diseases

In contrast to autoimmune diseases are a variety of defects called **immunodeficiency diseases**. Immunodeficient people lack one or more of the components of the immune system and are therefore susceptible to infections that would not ordinarily cause a problem. In the rare genetic disease called severe combined immunodeficiency (SCID), both B cells and T cells are absent or inactive. People with SCID are extremely vulnerable to even minor infections, forcing them to live behind protective barriers (providing inspiration for various "bubble boy" stories in the popular media) or to receive bone marrow transplants.

Why might someone have to live in a sterile "bubble"?

Immunodeficiency is not always an inborn condition; it may be acquired later in life. For instance, Hodgkin's disease, a type of cancer that affects lymphocytes, can depress the immune system. Radiation therapy and drug treatments used against many cancers can have the same effect. Next we will look at the most dreaded acquired immunodeficiency disease of our time: AIDS. ☑

☑ CHECKPOINT

1. What is an autoimmune disease?
2. What is an immunodeficiency disease?

Answers: 1. a disease in which cells of the immune system attack certain of the body's own cells as foreign 2. a disease in which one or more parts of the immune system are defective, resulting in an inability to fight infections

---

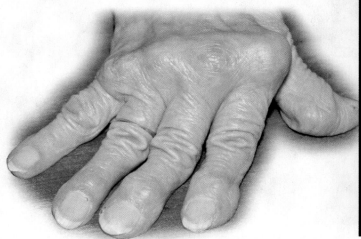

▼ **Figure 24.16 Rheumatoid arthritis.** The hands in this photo and X-ray are from a person with rheumatoid arthritis, an autoimmune disease in which the cartilage and bones of joints become damaged, resulting in malformation of the hands.

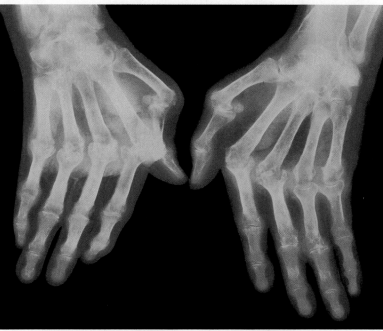

AIDS

Since the epidemic was first recognized in 1981, AIDS (acquired immunodeficiency syndrome) has killed more than 30 million people worldwide, and more than 33 million people are currently living with the AIDS virus, HIV. In 2009, 6 million people were newly infected with HIV, and nearly 2 million died, including over 300,000 children under the age of 15. The vast majority of HIV infections and AIDS deaths occur in sub-Saharan Africa and southeastern Asia.

HIV is deadly because it destroys the immune system, leaving the body defenseless against most invaders. HIV can infect a variety of cells, but it most often attacks helper T cells—the cells that activate other T cells and B cells (see Figure 24.12). As HIV depletes the body of helper T cells, both the cell-mediated and humoral immune responses are severely impaired. Death usually results not from HIV itself but from another infectious agent or from cancer. The name AIDS refers to the fact that the disease is *acquired* through an infection that results in severe *immunodeficiency* due to a lack of helper T cells and presents as a *syndrome*, a combination of symptoms. (See Figure 10.32 to review the course of cell infection by HIV.)

Education is the best weapon against the spread of AIDS. Safe sex behaviors, such as reducing promiscuity and using condoms, can save many lives. (Chapter 26 includes further discussion of AIDS prevention.)

HIV and AIDS EVOLUTION CONNECTION

HIV Evolution

Throughout this chapter, we have returned to the topic of HIV and AIDS as a way to highlight the importance of the immune system. To understand why HIV is so harmful, we need to keep in mind biology's unifying theme of evolution. As HIV reproduces, frequent mutations generate new strains of the virus. In fact, HIV has one of the fastest rates of mutation of any pathogen ever studied. This startling fact has led researchers to view evolution of drug-resistant HIV strains as the main obstacle to eradicating AIDS.

At one time, there was great hope that a "cocktail" of three anti-AIDS drugs, each of which attacks a different part of the HIV life cycle, could completely eliminate the virus in an infected person (Figure 24.17). It was hoped that virus strains resistant to one drug would be defeated by another. Such hope greatly underestimated the ability of HIV to evolve. Although people with access to such drugs do survive much longer and have a greatly improved quality of life, drug resistance to even multidrug treatments has evolved in some HIV strains. Thus, the virus is usually not eliminated from a patient's immune system. Although current HIV treatment prolongs the life of HIV-positive people, it is not a cure for AIDS.

Disturbingly, drug-resistant HIV strains are now being found in newly infected patients. This demonstrates that HIV is adapting through natural selection to a changing environment—one in which drug treatments are widely available. In other words, the presence of anti-AIDS drugs in the environment has favored the spread of drug-resistant strains. For now, the battle continues, with medical science on one side and the constantly evolving HIV on the other.

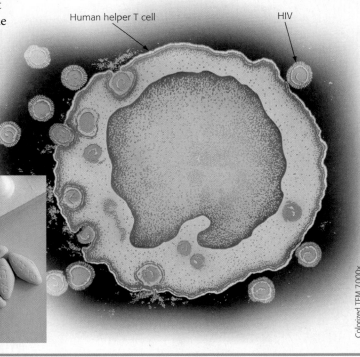

Human helper T cell

HIV

Colorized TEM 7,000x

▶ **Figure 24.17 Anti-AIDS drugs.** A three-drug cocktail can help slow, but usually not eliminate, infection by HIV (virus particles shown on the T cell at right).

Chapter Review

SUMMARY OF KEY CONCEPTS

(MB) Go to **www.masteringbiology.com** for homework assignments, practice quizzes, Pearson eText, and more.

Innate Defenses

The human body contains two lines of defense (external barriers and internal defenses) that are innate, fully ready to respond before an invader has been encountered.

INNATE DEFENSES			
External	**Internal**		
• Skin • Mucous membranes • Secretions	White blood cells	Defensive proteins	The inflammatory response
	• Phagocytic cells • Natural killer cells	• Interferons • Complement proteins	• Involves chemical signals and phagocytic cells

The Lymphatic System

The lymphatic system is a network of lymphatic vessels and organs involved in both innate and adaptive defenses. The vessels collect fluid from body tissues and return it to the blood. The lymphatic organs, including the lymph nodes, are packed with white blood cells that fight infections.

Adaptive Defenses

The adaptive defenses consist of a large collection of lymphocytes, white blood cells that respond to specific invaders. Antigens are molecules that elicit responses from lymphocytes.

Recognizing the Invaders

Two kinds of lymphocytes carry out the adaptive immune response to specific invaders carrying nonself molecules.

LYMPHOCYTES (Immune system contains millions of different kinds.)	
B cells (humoral immune response)	**T cells** (cell-mediated immune response)
• Secrete antibodies, which mark invaders	• Attack infected cells • Help activate B cells

Antigen receptors recognize one specific kind of antigen.

Antibodies recognize antigens through specific binding, which can trigger destruction of the antigen-bearing molecule or cell by several mechanisms. An antibody molecule has four polypeptide chains arranged in a Y shape, with the antigen-binding sites at the tips of the arms of the Y.

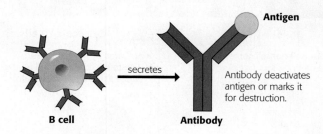

Antibody deactivates antigen or marks it for destruction.

Responding to the Invaders

When an antigen enters the body, it activates only lymphocytes with complementary receptors, a process called clonal selection.

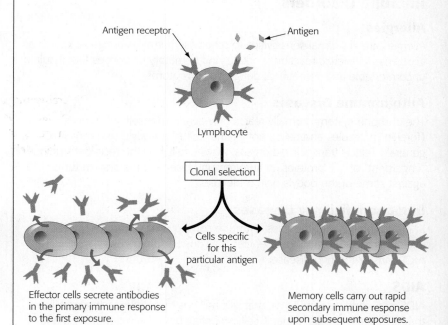

Effector cells secrete antibodies in the primary immune response to the first exposure.

Memory cells carry out rapid secondary immune response upon subsequent exposures.

The immune system reacts to antigens and "remembers" an invader. Helper T cells and cytotoxic T cells are the main effector cells in the cell-mediated immune response. Helper T cells also stimulate the humoral immune response, the release of antibodies into body fluids (blood and lymph) by effector B cells. The cell-mediated immune response typically involves a phagocytic cell displaying a foreign antigen (a nonself molecule) and one of the body's own self proteins to a helper T cell. The helper T cell's receptors

531

recognize the self-nonself complexes, and the interaction activates the helper T cell. In turn, the helper T cell can activate cytotoxic T cells with the same receptors (and can stimulate B cell activation as well). Cytotoxic T cells bind to and destroy infected body cells displaying both self proteins and foreign antigens.

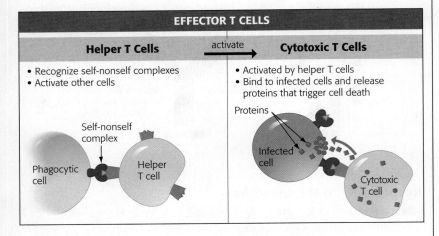

Immune Disorders

Allergies

Allergies are abnormal sensitivities to otherwise harmless antigens, known as allergens. An allergic reaction produces inflammatory responses that result in uncomfortable and sometimes dangerous symptoms.

Autoimmune Diseases

The immune system normally reacts only against nonself substances (foreign molecules and cells), not against self (the body's own molecules). It generally rejects transplanted organs, whose cells lack the recipient's unique "fingerprint" of self proteins. In autoimmune diseases, the system turns against some of the body's own molecules.

Immunodeficiency Diseases

In immunodeficiency diseases, immune components are lacking, and infections recur. Immunodeficiencies may arise through inborn genetic mutations or through disease.

AIDS

AIDS is a worldwide epidemic that kills millions of people each year. HIV, the AIDS virus, attacks helper T cells, crippling both the cell-mediated and humoral immune responses. Practicing safer sex could save many lives.

SELF-QUIZ

1. Molecules that elicit a response from lymphocytes are called _____. Proteins secreted by the immune system that bind to these molecules are called_____.

2. Classify each of the following components of the immune system as being an innate defense or adaptive defense.
   a. natural killer cells
   b. complement proteins
   c. antibodies
   d. inflammation
   e. interferons
   f. cytotoxic T cells
   g. helper T cells

3. Which of the following best describes the difference in the way B cells and T cells deal with invaders?
   a. B cells provide permanent immunity; T cells provide temporary immunity.
   b. B cells send out antibodies that bind to invaders; T cells directly engage the invaders.
   c. T cells handle the primary immune response; B cells handle the secondary immune response.
   d. B cells are responsible for the cell-mediated immune response; T cells are responsible for the humoral immune response.

4. What makes a secondary immune response faster than a primary immune response?

5. Match each type of defensive cell with its function or description.
   a. lymphocyte   1. attacks infected body cells
   b. cytotoxic T cell 2. carries out the humoral immune response
   c. helper T cell   3. white blood cell that engulfs cells or molecules
   d. phagocytic cell   4. general name for B or T cell
   e. B cell   5. initiates the secondary immune response
   f. memory cell   6. cell most commonly attacked by HIV

6. Explain how each of the following characteristics of the inflammatory response helps protect the body: swelling, pain, and fever.

7. Why is AIDS deadlier than most other viral diseases?

8. A baby has been born with an immunodeficiency disease. In trying to diagnose the problem, physicians discover that the child is not producing any antibodies. It is most likely that this child is missing what kind of cells?

9. How does the autoimmune disorder lupus affect the immune system?

10. Once vaccinated, you have had a primary exposure to specific antigens. If you ever encounter these antigens again, your body will mount a rapid immune response. The cells that account for this rapid secondary response are called _____. The process that produces these long-lived cells is called _____.

Answers to these questions can be found in Appendix: Self-Quiz Answers.

THE PROCESS OF SCIENCE

11. Most biologists believe that the immune system's defense against infections largely rests on its ability to distinguish self molecules from nonself molecules. This concept seems central to our understanding of immune function. However, like all scientific ideas, it is not beyond question. Several immunologists have developed an alternative hypothesis: that the immune system's effectiveness rests mostly on its ability to recognize damage to body tissues caused by the invaders, not on its ability to recognize nonself. If you were going to test the "damage" hypothesis, what might you look for? Which type of cell would you expect to be directly affected by damaged tissues? Why? Some proponents argue that the "damage" hypothesis makes more sense from an evolutionary perspective, claiming that it is more advantageous for an organism's defense system to respond to tissue damage than to the mere presence of a foreign microbe. Do you agree? Why or why not?

12. The graph below depicts the concentration of two antibodies from a patient's blood: The red line graphs antibody X (produced in response to antigen X), and the black line graphs antibody Y (produced in response to antigen Y). Using your knowledge of clonal selection, explain why these curves have the shapes they do.

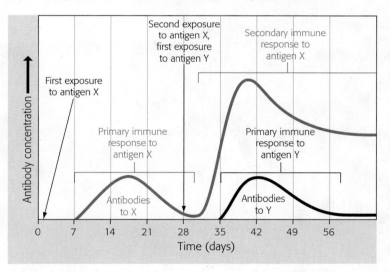

BIOLOGY AND SOCIETY

13. Organ donation saves many lives each year. Even though some transplanted organs are derived from living donors, the majority come from patients who die but still have healthy organs that can help a transplant recipient whose cell surfaces have similar sets of proteins. Potential organ donors can fill out an organ donation card to specify their wishes. If the donor is in critical condition and dying, the donor's family is usually consulted to discuss the donation process. Generally, the next of kin must approve before donation can occur, regardless of whether the patient has completed a donor card. In some cases, the donor's wishes are overridden by a family member. Do you think that family members should be able to deny the stated intentions of the potential donor? Why or why not? Have you signed up to be an organ donor? Why or why not?

25 Hormones

Symbols of the "Steroids Era." Sammy Sosa (left) and Mark McGwire (right) smashed home run records in 1998, but their accomplishments were tainted by revelations that they used performance-enhancing steroids.

 Steroid Abuse BIOLOGY AND SOCIETY

Sluggers and Steroids

For baseball fans, it was one of the greatest seasons ever. Throughout the spring, summer, and fall of 1998, Mark McGwire, of the St. Louis Cardinals, and Sammy Sosa, of the Chicago Cubs, battled each other to break Roger Maris's 37-year record of 61 home runs in a season. Sosa jumped out to a quick lead with an astonishing 20 home runs in the month of June, one of the greatest offensive outbursts in baseball history. On September 8, McGwire became the first player ever to hit 62 home runs in a season. A few weeks later, Sosa became the first player to hit 65. When the dust settled, McGwire triumphed, logging in an astonishing 70 home runs over the season. Sosa finished with 66, the second highest total ever. Baseball fans reveled in the magic of one of the greatest displays of raw talent ever to grace the diamond.

Or did they? Rumors began to swirl that McGwire and Sosa (as well as many other major leaguers) had artificial help. In 2010, McGwire admitted that he used performance-enhancing steroids over the course of his playing career, including the famous 1998 season. Steroids are hormones, chemical signals that help regulate the body. Although everyone's body naturally produces steroid hormones, some athletes abuse anabolic steroids, synthetic hormones that mimic the male sex hormone testosterone. Taken in large doses, anabolic steroids can increase muscle mass, which can bring greater power to a batter's swing. What about Sosa? It has been widely reported that he failed a test for performance-enhancing drugs in 2003, a claim he does not deny. McGwire and Sosa thus join other all-stars of that era, including Raphael Palmeiro, Jose Canseco, and Alex Rodriguez, all of whom have admitted, or been caught, using banned steroids. McGwire and Sosa's historic race for the home run record is thus viewed by many as yet another chapter in baseball's shameful "steroids era." McGwire has since lamented, "I wish I had never touched steroids. It was foolish and it was a mistake."

How do steroids affect those who use them? In this chapter, we explore this question by focusing on hormones and the way they maintain homeostasis within the human body. We begin with an overview of how hormones work in all vertebrates and then turn to the major components of the human endocrine system. Along the way, we'll consider many examples of the effects of hormonal imbalance. We'll also further discuss how some people abuse hormones—both natural and artificial—in pursuit of an athletic advantage.

Hormones: An Overview

Hormones are chemical signals produced by most plants (see Table 29.1) and animals. Animal hormones are carried by the circulatory system (usually in the blood) to other parts of the body, where they may communicate regulatory messages. Hormones are made and secreted mainly by organs called **endocrine glands**. Collectively, all hormone-secreting cells make up the **endocrine system**, the body's main system for internal chemical regulation.

The top-right diagram in **Figure 25.1** shows the release of hormone molecules from membrane-enclosed sacs in an endocrine cell. The circulatory system carries hormones throughout the body, but a hormone can only bind to a **target cell** with receptors for that specific hormone (bottom-right diagram). Imagine many keys floating in your bloodstream; each key can only affect those cells with a matching lock. Because hormones reach all parts of the body, the endocrine system is especially important in controlling whole-body activities. For example, hormones govern our metabolic rate, growth (including muscle development, the

target of steroid abuse), maturation, and reproduction. In many cases, a tiny amount of a hormone influences the activities of an enormous number of target cells in a variety of organs. Hormones trigger changes in target cells in different ways, depending on whether the hormone is water-soluble or lipid-soluble: Water-soluble hormones trigger responses without entering the cell, whereas lipid-soluble hormones trigger responses after entering the cell.

Water-soluble hormones cannot pass through the oily interior of the phospholipid bilayer of the plasma membrane, but they can bring about cellular changes without entering their target cells **(Figure 25.2)**. To start, ❶ a water-soluble hormone (●) binds to a specific receptor protein (⬭) in the plasma membrane of the target cell. The binding activates the receptor protein, which ❷ initiates a signal transduction pathway: a series of changes to molecules that converts a chemical message from outside the cell to a specific response inside the cell. ❸ The final relay molecule (○) activates a protein that either carries out a response in the

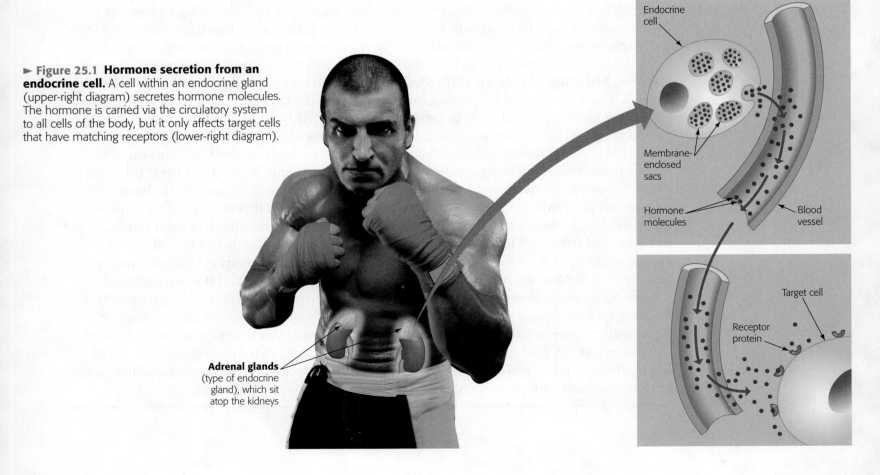

▶ **Figure 25.1 Hormone secretion from an endocrine cell.** A cell within an endocrine gland (upper-right diagram) secretes hormone molecules. The hormone is carried via the circulatory system to all cells of the body, but it only affects target cells that have matching receptors (lower-right diagram).

Adrenal glands (type of endocrine gland), which sit atop the kidneys

Endocrine cell

Membrane-enclosed sacs

Hormone molecules

Blood vessel

Target cell

Receptor protein

cytoplasm (such as activating an enzyme) or affects gene regulation in the nucleus (such as turning on or off genes). This is a bit like the game of "telephone," with a message passed from one person to the next—but this message is (hopefully) received exactly as sent!

Water-soluble hormones that bind to plasma membrane receptors come in three varieties, all derived from amino acids: amine hormones, which are modified versions of single amino acids; peptide hormones, which are short chains of 3–30 amino acids; and protein hormones, made of polypeptides. An example of a protein hormone is erythropoietin (EPO), which regulates the production of red blood cells. Some athletes abuse EPO as a performance-enhancing drug because it increases their capacity for endurance.

How can hormone abuse lead to blood doping?

In contrast, lipid-soluble hormones pass through the phospholipid bilayer and trigger responses by binding to receptors inside the target cell. Steroid hormones—including natural ones such as the sex hormones (testosterone, estrogen, and progesterone) as well as artificial anabolic steroids—work in this manner. As shown in **Figure 25.3**, ① a lipid-soluble hormone (▼) enters a cell by diffusing through the plasma membrane. If the cell is a target cell, the hormone ② binds to a receptor protein (◖) in the cytoplasm or nucleus. Rather than triggering a signal transduction pathway, the receptor itself carries the hormone's signal. ③ The hormone-receptor complex attaches to specific sites on the cell's DNA in the nucleus. ④ The binding to DNA turns specific genes on or off.

We've now completed an overview of how hormones work. The principles presented so far apply to all vertebrates (as well as many invertebrates). In the next section, we'll take a closer look at the endocrine system of one particular vertebrate: humans. ☑

☑ **CHECKPOINT**

1. Why are hormones particularly useful in carrying signals that affect many different organs?
2. What is the difference in the way that lipid-soluble and water-soluble hormones interact with their target cells?

Answers: **1.** they are transported in the blood to all parts of the body **2.** Lipid-soluble hormones bind to receptors inside the cell, whereas water-soluble hormones bind to receptors in the plasma membrane.

▼ Figure 25.2 **A hormone that binds to a plasma membrane receptor.** Hormones that are water-soluble cannot cross the phospholipid bilayer but can bind to membrane receptors outside target cells and activate a signal transduction pathway.

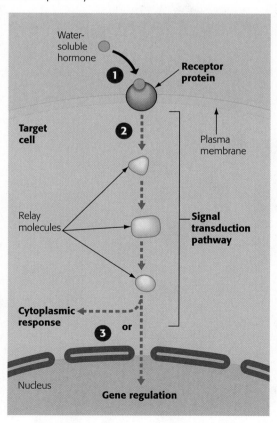

▼ Figure 25.3 **A hormone that binds to an intracellular receptor.** Hormones that are lipid-soluble can cross the phospholipid bilayer and bind to receptors inside target cells. Steroid hormones and other lipid-soluble hormones affect the cell by turning specific genes on and off.

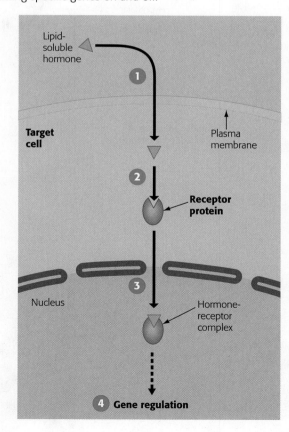

The Human Endocrine System

The human endocrine system consists of about a dozen major glands. Some of these, such as the thyroid and pituitary glands, are endocrine specialists; that is, their primary function is to secrete hormones into the blood. Several other glands have both endocrine and nonendocrine functions. The pancreas, for example, secretes hormones that influence the level of glucose in the blood and also secretes digestive enzymes into the intestine. Other organs are primarily nonendocrine but have some cells that secrete hormones. For example, the stomach is primarily a digestive organ but also releases ghrelin (the "hunger hormone"), which travels to the brain and stimulates appetite. (As you can imagine, ghrelin is the target of weight loss research, but so far no treatments that interact with it have been developed.)

Can a hormone make you hungry?

Figure 25.4 shows the locations of the major human endocrine glands discussed in this chapter. Table 25.1 summarizes the actions of the main hormones they produce. The table provides an overview of the human endocrine system, and you may wish to refer to it as you read along through the chapter as we focus on the individual glands and their hormones.

Hormones have a wide range of targets. Some hormones, like the sex hormones, affect most of the tissues of the body. Others, such as glucagon from the pancreas, have only a few kinds of target cells (in this case, liver and fat cells). In some cases, a hormone elicits different responses in different target cells, depending on the type of cell and its signal transduction pathway.

The rest of this section focuses on the major glands of the human endocrine system. For each gland, you'll learn about the hormones it secretes and how these chemicals help the body maintain homeostasis. Keep in mind that this chapter only covers the major endocrine glands and their hormones; there are other hormone-secreting structures—the heart and liver, for example—and dozens of other hormones that we will not discuss. ☑

☑ CHECKPOINT

According to Table 25.1, which endocrine glands secrete steroid hormones?

Answer: just the adrenal glands (specifically the adrenal cortex) and the gonads

▶ **Figure 25.4 The major endocrine glands in humans.** This figure shows only the major endocrine organs discussed in the text. Several other organs that also have endocrine functions are not shown.

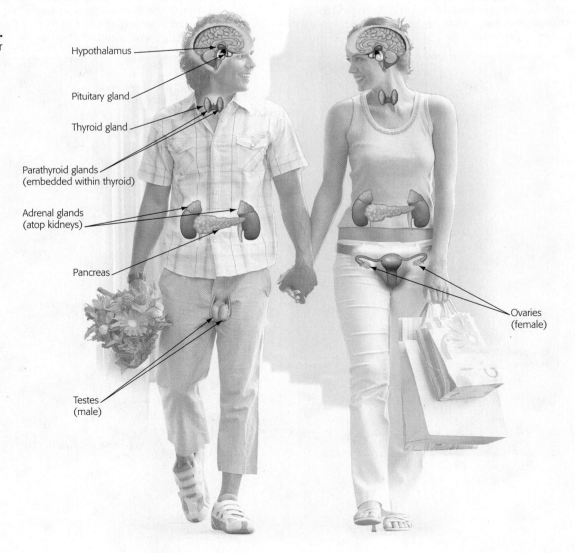

Hypothalamus

Pituitary gland

Thyroid gland

Parathyroid glands
(embedded within thyroid)

Adrenal glands
(atop kidneys)

Pancreas

Testes
(male)

Ovaries
(female)

Table 25.1	Major Human Endocrine Glands and Some of Their Hormones				
Gland	**Hormone**	**Chemical Class**	**Representative Actions**	**Regulated By**	
Hypothalamus 	Hormones released by the posterior pituitary and hormones that regulate the anterior pituitary (see below)				
Pituitary gland Posterior pituitary (releases hormones made by hypothalamus) 	Oxytocin (see Chapter 26)	Peptide	Stimulates contraction of uterus and mammary gland cells	Nervous system	
	Antidiuretic hormone (ADH)	Peptide	Promotes retention of water by kidneys	Water/salt balance	
Anterior pituitary 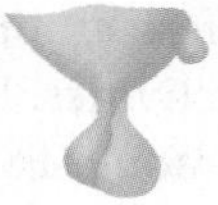	Follicle-stimulating hormone (FSH)	Protein	Stimulates production of ova and sperm	Hypothalamic hormones	
	Luteinizing hormone (LH)	Protein	Stimulates ovaries and testes	Hypothalamic hormones	
	Human growth hormone (HGH)	Protein	Stimulates growth (especially bones) and metabolic functions	Hypothalamic hormones	
	Prolactin (PRL; see Chapter 26)	Protein	Stimulates milk production	Hypothalamic hormones	
	Thyroid-stimulating hormone (TSH)	Protein	Stimulates thyroid gland	Thyroxine in blood; hypothalamic hormones	
	Adrenocorticotropic hormone (ACTH)	Peptide	Stimulates adrenal cortex to secrete glucocorticoids	Glucocorticoids; hypothalamic hormones	
	Endorphins	Peptides	Mask pain	Brain	
Thyroid gland 	Triiodothyronine (T_3) and thyroxine (T_4)	Amines	Stimulate and maintain metabolic processes	TSH	
	Calcitonin	Peptide	Lowers blood calcium level	Calcium in blood	
Parathyroid glands 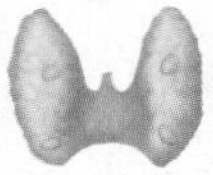	Parathyroid hormone (PTH)	Peptide	Raises blood calcium level	Calcium in blood	
Pancreas 	Insulin	Protein	Lowers blood glucose level	Glucose in blood	
	Glucagon	Protein	Raises blood glucose level	Glucose in blood	
Adrenal glands Adrenal medulla 	Epinephrine (adrenaline) and norepinephrine (noradrenaline)	Amines	Raise blood glucose level; increase metabolic activities; constrict certain blood vessels	Nervous system	
Adrenal cortex 	Glucocorticoids	Steroids	Raise blood glucose level	ACTH	
Gonads Testes 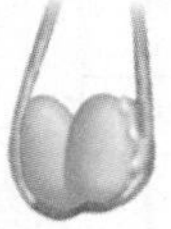	Androgens (testosterone)	Steroids	Support sperm formation; promote development and maintenance of male secondary sex characteristics	FSH and LH	
Ovaries 	Estrogens	Steroids	Stimulate uterine lining growth; promote development and maintenance of female secondary sex characteristics	FSH and LH	
	Progestins	Steroids	Promote uterine lining growth	FSH and LH	

The Hypothalamus and Pituitary Gland

The **hypothalamus** is a gland that acts as the main control center of the endocrine system (**Figure 25.5**). As part of the brain, the hypothalamus receives information from nerves about the internal condition of the body and about the external environment. It then responds by sending out appropriate nervous or endocrine signals. These signals directly control the **pituitary gland**, a pea-sized structure that hangs down from the hypothalamus. In response to signals from the hypothalamus, the pituitary secretes hormones that influence numerous body functions. The hypothalamus thus exerts master control over the endocrine system by using the pituitary to relay directives to other glands.

As Figure 25.5 shows, the pituitary gland consists of two distinct parts: a posterior lobe and an anterior lobe, both tucked in a pocket of skull bone just under the hypothalamus. The **posterior pituitary** is actually an extension of the hypothalamus that stores and secretes hormones made in the hypothalamus. In contrast, the **anterior pituitary** synthesizes and secretes its own hormones directly into the blood. The hypothalamus exerts control over the anterior pituitary by secreting two kinds of hormones into short blood vessels (not illustrated) that connect the two glands: releasing hormones and inhibiting hormones. Releasing hormones stimulate the anterior pituitary to secrete specific hormones, whereas inhibiting hormones induce the anterior pituitary to stop secreting specific hormones.

Why do caffeinated drinks tend to cause dehydration?

Figure 25.6 shows how the hypothalamus operates through the posterior pituitary to direct the activity of the kidneys. The hypothalamus makes antidiuretic hormone (ADH) (▲), which is stored and released by the posterior pituitary. ADH helps kidney cells reabsorb water, preventing dehydration by decreasing urine volume when the body needs to retain water (see Chapter 21). When the body has too much water, the hypothalamus slows the release of ADH from the pituitary. Some drugs, such as caffeine and alcohol, act as a diuretic by inhibiting the release of ADH, which in turn increases the output of urine. This can lead to dehydration.

In response to releasing hormones secreted by the hypothalamus, the anterior pituitary synthesizes and releases many different hormones that influence a broad range of body activities. For example, it releases follicle-stimulating hormone (FSH) and luteinizing hormone (LH), which help regulate the menstrual cycle (as you'll see in Chapter 26).

▼ **Figure 25.6 ADH and osmoregulation.** The hypothalamus regulates water homeostasis by synthesizing ADH. Molecules of this hormone travel via long cellular extensions (gray) to the posterior pituitary, where they are released into the blood. Eventually, the ADH reaches target cells in the kidneys.

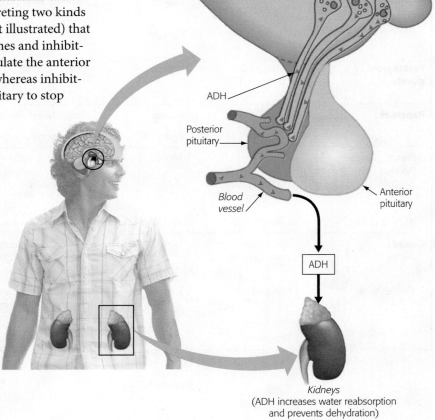

Hypothalamus

ADH

Posterior pituitary

Blood vessel

Anterior pituitary

ADH

Kidneys
(ADH increases water reabsorption and prevents dehydration)

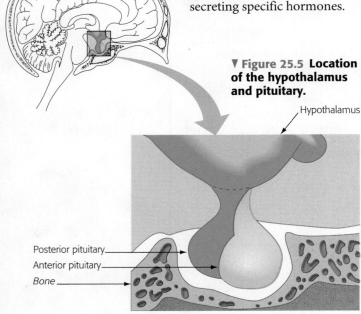

Brain

▼ **Figure 25.5 Location of the hypothalamus and pituitary.**

Hypothalamus

Posterior pituitary

Anterior pituitary

Bone

No pituitary secretion has a broader effect than the protein called **human growth hormone (HGH)**. Overproduction of HGH in adults results in acromegaly, characterized by enlarged bones in the hands, feet, and face (**Figure 25.7a**). During childhood and adolescence, high levels of HGH promote the development and enlargement of all parts of the body. If too much HGH is produced in a very young person, usually because of a pituitary tumor,

gigantism can result (**Figure 25.7b**). In contrast, too little HGH during childhood can lead to dwarfism (**Figure 25.7c**). Administering HGH to children with HGH deficiency can prevent dwarfism. HGH was originally extracted in only minute quantities from the pituitary glands of cadavers, but is now produced in large quantities by genetically engineered bacteria (see Chapter 12). With the increased availability of HGH, some athletes have misused the drug in order to bulk up their muscles. Such abuse is extremely dangerous and can lead to disfigurement, heart failure, and cancer. Consequently, the use of HGH is banned by nearly every athletic governing body.

The **endorphins**, another kind of anterior pituitary hormone, are the body's natural painkillers; they mask the perception of pain. Some researchers speculate that the so-called runner's high results partly from the release of endorphins when stress and pain in the body reach critical levels. The release of endorphins may also produce pleasant feelings during such diverse activities as meditation, acupuncture treatments, and even eating very spicy foods. ✔

✔ CHECKPOINT

Which gland is the primary control center for the entire endocrine system? Which gland is directly controlled by this master gland?

Answer: the hypothalamus; the pituitary

▼ Figure 25.7 **Pituitary growth hormone disorders.**

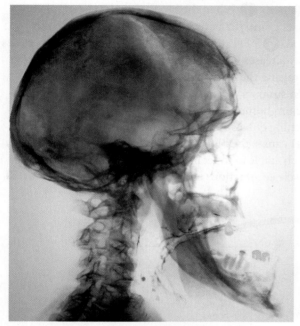

(a) Overproduction of HGH during adulthood. Overproduction of HGH later in life causes acromegaly. The most common symptom of this disease is enlargement of the hands and face, as seen here in this X-ray.

The Thyroid and Parathyroid Glands

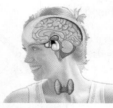

Your **thyroid gland** is in your neck, just under your larynx (voice box). The thyroid produces hormones (thyroxine and triiodothyronine) that increase oxygen consumption and metabolic rate in all the cells of your body. These thyroid hormones also play crucial roles in development and maturation, particularly of the bone and nerve cells. Insufficient levels of the thyroid hormones in the blood (hypothyroidism) or excess levels (hyperthyroidism) can result in serious metabolic disorders. Fortunately, thyroid disorders can be treated easily.

Hypothyroidism (too little thyroid hormones) can result from dietary deficiencies or from a defective thyroid gland. To produce thyroxine and triiodothyronine, the thyroid requires the element iodine. If too little iodine is available, insufficient quantities of these thyroid hormones are produced. This underproduction interrupts feedback loops that control thyroid activity, causing overstimulation and swelling of the thyroid gland. A type of dietary hypothyroidism called goiter has been reduced in many industrialized nations by the incorporation of iodine into table salt (see Figure 2.3). Unfortunately, goiter still affects many people in less industrialized nations.

(b) Overproduction of HGH during development. Yao Defeng's extreme size (7 feet 9 inches) is due to a benign brain tumor that results in excess growth hormone.

(c) Underproduction of HGH during development. The body of actor Peter Dinklage, like those of other dwarfs, produced low amounts of GH during childhood.

A common form of hyperthyroidism (overproduction of thyroid hormones) is Graves' disease, characterized by overheating, profuse sweating, high blood pressure, and protruding eyeballs. One treatment takes advantage of the fact that the thyroid accumulates iodine: Patients drink a solution containing a small dose of radioactive iodine, which kills off just enough cells to reduce thyroid output and relieve symptoms.

Why would someone purposefully drink radioactive iodine?

Embedded within the thyroid are four disk-shaped **parathyroid glands**. The thyroid and parathyroid glands function in calcium homeostasis, keeping the concentration of calcium ions (Ca^{2+}) in the blood within a narrow range. An appropriate level of calcium in the blood and interstitial fluid is essential for many of your body's functions. Without calcium, nerve signals cannot be transmitted from cell to cell, your muscles cannot function properly, your blood cannot clot, and your cells cannot transport molecules across their membranes. **Calcitonin** from the thyroid and **parathyroid hormone (PTH)** from the parathyroids regulate the blood calcium level. They are said to be **antagonistic hormones** because they have opposite effects: Calcitonin lowers the calcium level in the blood, whereas PTH raises it.

As **Figure 25.8** indicates, calcitonin and PTH operate by means of feedback systems that keep the calcium level near the homeostatic set point. ❶ A rise in the blood Ca^{2+} level above the homeostatic set point induces the thyroid gland to secrete calcitonin. ❷ Calcitonin, in turn, has two main effects: It causes more Ca^{2+} to be deposited in the bones, and it makes the kidneys reabsorb less Ca^{2+} as they form urine. ❸ The result is a lower Ca^{2+} level in the blood. ❹ When the blood Ca^{2+} level drops below the set point, the parathyroids release PTH into the blood. ❺ PTH stimulates the release of Ca^{2+} from bones and increases Ca^{2+} uptake by the kidneys and intestines, ❻ raising the calcium level.

In summary, a sensitive balancing system maintains calcium homeostasis. Failure of the system can have far-reaching effects in the body. For example, a shortage of PTH causes the blood calcium level to drop dramatically, which can lead to tetany, a condition of uncontrollable muscle contractions and potentially fatal convulsions. ✔

▶ **Figure 25.8 Calcium homeostasis.** This diagram traces the regulation of blood calcium level by calcitonin and PTH, which act antagonistically. Note that bones, in addition to supporting the body, act as a calcium bank, storing and releasing calcium as needed.

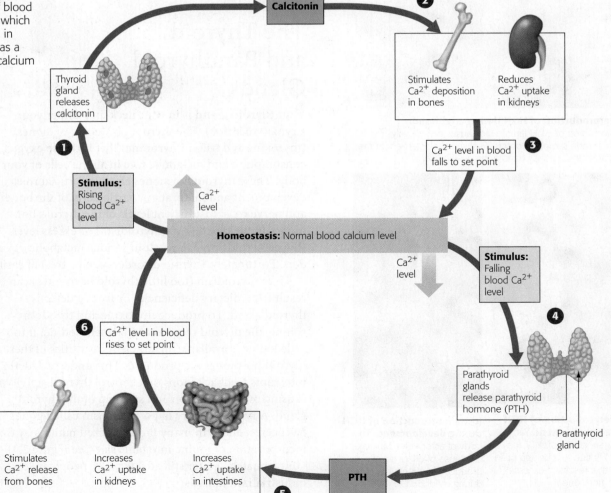

Calcitonin

❷ Stimulates Ca^{2+} deposition in bones — Reduces Ca^{2+} uptake in kidneys

❸ Ca^{2+} level in blood falls to set point

Thyroid gland releases calcitonin

❶

Stimulus: Rising blood Ca^{2+} level

Ca^{2+} level

Homeostasis: Normal blood calcium level

Ca^{2+} level

Stimulus: Falling blood Ca^{2+} level

❹

Parathyroid glands release parathyroid hormone (PTH)

Parathyroid gland

❻ Ca^{2+} level in blood rises to set point

Stimulates Ca^{2+} release from bones — Increases Ca^{2+} uptake in kidneys — Increases Ca^{2+} uptake in intestines

❺ **PTH**

✔ CHECKPOINT

Both calcitonin (from the thyroid) and parathyroid hormone (from the parathyroids) regulate blood calcium level. Why are these two hormones said to be antagonistic?

Answer: These two hormones have opposite effects: Calcitonin lowers blood calcium level, whereas PTH raises it.

The Pancreas

The **pancreas** produces two hormones that play important roles in managing the body's energy supplies. One of the hormones is **insulin**, a protein hormone produced by clusters of specialized pancreatic cells called islet cells. Other islet cells secrete another protein hormone, called **glucagon**. Insulin and glucagon help maintain a homeostatic balance between the amount of glucose available in the blood and the amount of glucose stored as the polymer glycogen in body cells.

As shown in **Figure 25.9**, insulin and glucagon are antagonistic hormones, countering each other in a feedback circuit that precisely manages the level of glucose in the blood. By negative feedback, the concentration of glucose in the blood determines the relative amounts of insulin and glucagon secreted by islet cells. ❶ Rising glucose concentration in the blood—as happens shortly after you eat a carbohydrate-rich meal, for example—stimulates the pancreas to secrete more insulin into the blood. ❷ Body cells take up more glucose from the blood, while liver and skeletal muscle cells take up glucose and use it to make glycogen, which they store. ❸ As a result, the blood glucose level falls to the set point, and the cells of the pancreas lose their stimulus to secrete insulin.

❹ When the blood glucose level dips below the set point, as it may between meals, pancreatic cells respond by secreting more glucagon. ❺ Glucagon is a fuel mobilizer, making liver cells break glycogen down into glucose and release it into the blood. ❻ Then, when the blood glucose level returns to the set point, the pancreas slows its secretion of glucagon.

► **Figure 25.9**
Glucose homeostasis. This diagram traces the regulation of blood glucose level by insulin and glucagon, two antagonistic hormones released by the pancreas.

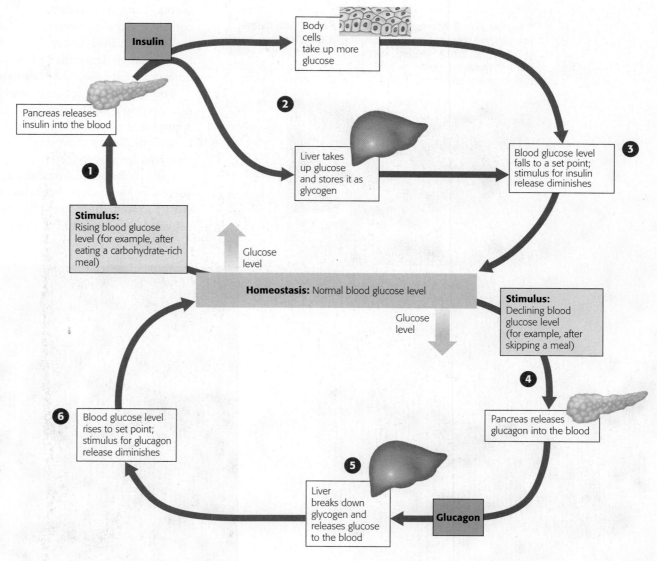

Diabetes mellitus is a serious hormonal disease that affects about 8% of Americans—24 million people—and 6 million of them don't even know they are ill. In diabetes, body cells are unable to absorb glucose from the blood, either because there is not enough insulin in the blood (as in type 1, or insulin-dependent, diabetes) or because the target cells do not respond normally to the insulin in the blood (as in type 2, or non-insulin-dependent, diabetes). A third type of diabetes, called gestational diabetes, can affect any pregnant woman, even one who has never shown symptoms of diabetes before.

In a person with diabetes, cells cannot obtain enough glucose from the blood, even though there is plenty. Starved for fuel, cells are forced to burn the body's supply of fats and proteins. Meanwhile, the digestive system continues to absorb glucose from the diet, causing the glucose concentration in the blood to become dangerously high.

There are treatments for diabetes but no cure. Type 1 patients require regular injections of insulin, usually obtained from genetically modified bacteria (**Figure 25.10**).

Of those Americans who have diabetes, more than 90% have type 2. This form is almost always associated with being overweight and underactive, although whether obesity causes diabetes (and if so, how) remains unknown. Type 2 diabetes can often be managed by controlling sugar intake and by exercising and dieting to reduce weight. However, every year some 300,000 Americans die from diabetes or its complications, which include severe dehydration, cardiovascular and kidney disease, and nerve damage. ☑

The Adrenal Glands

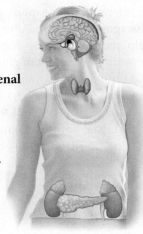

The human body has two **adrenal glands**, one sitting atop each kidney. Each adrenal gland is actually two glands in one: a central portion called the **adrenal medulla** and an outer portion called the **adrenal cortex**. Though the cells they contain and the hormones they produce are different, both the adrenal medulla and the adrenal cortex secrete hormones that enable the body to respond to stress.

You've probably felt your heart beat faster and your skin develop goose bumps when you've sensed danger or approached a stressful situation. Positive emotions, such as extreme pleasure, can produce the same effects. These reactions are triggered by two "fight-or-flight" hormones secreted by the adrenal medulla: **epinephrine** (also called adrenaline) and **norepinephrine**. These two hormones ensure a rapid, short-term response to stress that can be activated in seconds and last for minutes or hours.

▼ **Figure 25.10 Managing diabetes.** People with diabetes use glucose meters (top) to measure the amount of glucose in the blood. When needed, injections of insulin (left) can be self-administered. Some people use a glucose pump (right) to both monitor and inject insulin.

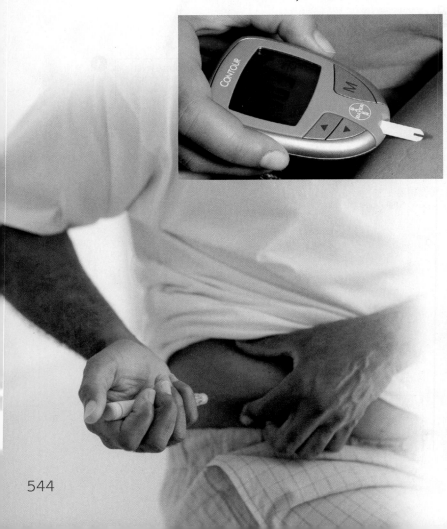

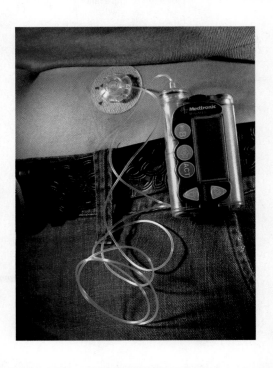

Stressful stimuli, whether negative or positive, activate nerve cells in the hypothalamus. As indicated in the left half of **Figure 25.11**, these cells ❶ send signals that stimulate the adrenal medulla to ❷ secrete epinephrine and norepinephrine (•) into the blood. Epinephrine and norepinephrine both contribute to the short-term stress response by stimulating liver cells to release glucose, making more fuel available for cellular work. They also prepare the body for action by raising blood pressure, breathing rate, heart rate, and metabolic rate. In addition, epinephrine and norepinephrine change blood flow patterns to shuttle blood to where it is most needed: Blood vessels in the brain and skeletal muscles are widened, increasing alertness and the muscles' ability to react to stress, while blood vessels elsewhere are narrowed, reducing activities (such as digestion) that are not immediately involved in the stress response. The short-term stress response occurs and subsides rapidly.

In contrast to epinephrine and norepinephrine (secreted by the adrenal medulla), hormones secreted by the adrenal cortex can provide a slower, longer-lasting response to stress that can last for hours or days. As the right half of Figure 25.11 indicates, the hypothalamus ❸ secretes a releasing hormone (•) that stimulates the pituitary to ❹ secrete a hormone called ACTH (adrenocorticotropic hormone) (•). In turn, ACTH stimulates cells of the adrenal cortex to ❺ synthesize and secrete a family of steroid hormones called **corticosteroids** (•), which include the glucocorticoids. The **glucocorticoids** help promote the synthesis of glucose from noncarbohydrates, such as proteins and fats.

Very high levels of glucocorticoids in the blood can suppress the body's defense system, including the inflammatory response that occurs at infection sites (see Figure 24.4). For this reason, physicians may use glucocorticoids to treat excess inflammation. Cortisone, for example, can be used to treat arthritis. Some professional athletes, such as baseball and football players, often receive cortisone injections into injured joints. With this treatment, the pain usually subsides, but its underlying cause remains. Masking the pain covers up the pain's message—that tissue is damaged and may get worse if not allowed to heal. If an athlete exercises an injured joint before the tissue has recovered, the added stress can cause more serious and longer-lasting damage. ☑

Why might an athlete receive cortisone injections into an injured joint?

☑ CHECKPOINT

Which hormones regulate the short-term stress response? What family of hormones regulates the long-term stress response?

Answer: epinephrine and norepinephrine; corticosteroids

► Figure 25.11 **How the adrenal glands control our response to stress.** Stressful stimuli activate nerve cells in the hypothalamus. In the short-term response to stress, these signals are relayed to the adrenal glands. The long-term stress response is initiated when the hypothalamus sends hormonal signals to the adrenal glands via the pituitary.

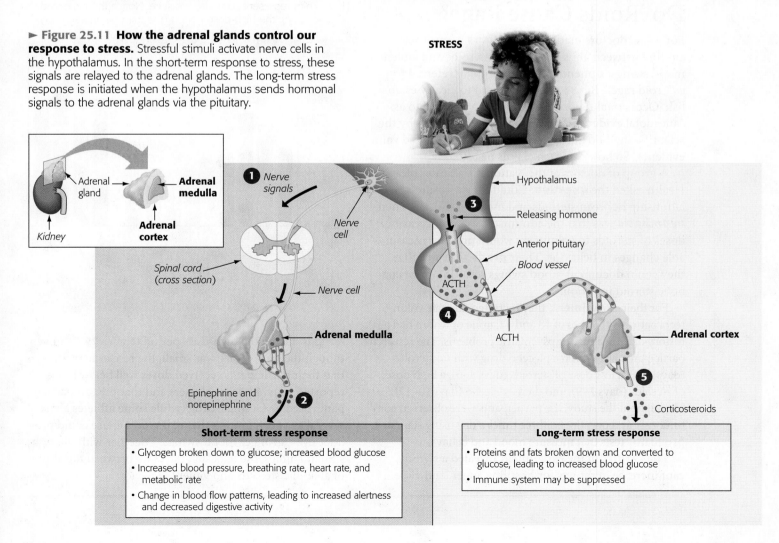

STRESS

The Gonads

Sex hormones are steroid hormones that affect growth and development and regulate reproductive cycles and sexual behavior. Under the direction of the hypothalamus and pituitary gland, the **gonads**, or sex glands (ovaries in the female and testes in the male), secrete sex hormones in addition to producing gametes (sperm and egg).

The gonads of humans produce three major categories of sex hormones: androgens, estrogens, and progestins. Both men and women have all three. In women, estrogens are found in higher concentrations than androgens. **Estrogens** maintain the female reproductive system and promote the development of such female features as breasts and wider hips. **Progestins**, such as progesterone, are primarily involved in preparing the uterus to support a developing embryo.

Men have a high ratio of androgens to estrogens. **Androgens**, mainly testosterone, stimulate the development and maintenance of the male reproductive system. Androgens produced by male embryos during the 7th week of development stimulate the embryo to develop into a male rather than a female. During puberty, a high concentration of testosterone triggers the development of male characteristics, such as a lower-pitched voice, facial hair, and large skeletal muscles.

Anabolic steroids are artificial hormones that mimic the structure and function of testosterone and can therefore allow a person to build muscle quickly. Some athletes abuse "designer steroids"—anabolic steroids specifically designed to elude drug tests. What effects might steroid abuse have? We explore that question next. ☑

Steroid Abuse THE PROCESS OF SCIENCE

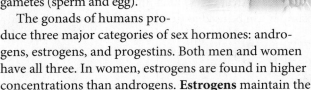

Do 'Roids Cause Rage?

For years, doctors made **observations** of an apparent link between abuse of anabolic steroids and violent mood swings, a phenomenon commonly referred to as "'roid rage." But such a link is hard to clearly establish. Occasional reports (a type of data referred to as "anecdotal evidence") are not subject to analysis by the scientific method and therefore are not considered valid evidence. So how can such claims be tested?

A group of doctors at the National Institutes of Health asked the **question**: Could they measure a relationship between steroids and mood in the lab? Their **hypothesis** was that the administration of increasing doses of steroids to volunteers would produce measurable changes in behavior. Their **prediction** was that they could document mood swings resulting from anabolic steroid injection.

For their **experiment**, they recruited 20 male volunteers between the ages of 18 and 42, none of whom had a history of drug abuse or psychiatric problems. The research participants were given a placebo drug with no steroids (days 1–3), a low dose of steroids (days 4–6), a high dose of steroids (days 7–9), and then a placebo (days 10–12). Throughout the study, the participants were observed continuously and questioned three times a day using standard psychiatric tests that measure mood and behavior.

The **results** of the experiment revealed a significant increase in ratings for hostility, anger, and violent

▼ **Figure 25.12 The mood-altering effects of anabolic steroids.** Each set of bars represents one measure of mood. Each color represents one dosage state. Notice the increased scores during the high-dose period (the third bar in each set).

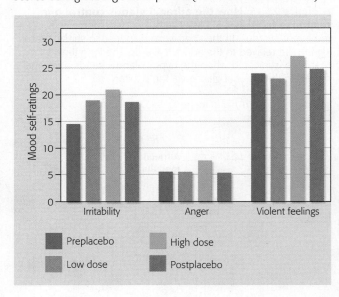

feelings during the high-dose period (**Figure 25.12**). Even though the sample size was small, the researchers noted that their participants received doses well below levels reported taken by some abusers and that the test participants used just a single drug (while some athletes abuse several at once), hinting that real-world abuse could produce even stronger mood swings. Together with many similar studies, the data suggest a link between the abuse of anabolic steroids and violent behavior.

Steroid Abuse EVOLUTION CONNECTION

Steroids and Male Aggression

Among human males, the primary role of testosterone and other androgens is to promote the development and maintenance of male reproductive anatomy and secondary sexual characteristics (such as facial hair). Androgens play a similar role—promoting uniquely male characteristics—in many species. In fact, research has established that the process of sex determination by androgens occurs in a highly similar manner in all vertebrates, suggesting that androgens had this role early in evolution.

Androgens have been shown to produce a wide variety of effects in different species. In many vertebrates, they are responsible for male vocalizations, such as the territorial songs of birds and the mating calls of frogs. As we have discussed, androgens are connected with aggressive behavior—and not just in people. For example, researchers have measured androgens in a type of cichlid fish called the Mozambique tilapia, a native of eastern Africa found in many home aquariums. Researchers have found elevated

androgen levels in males engaged in territorial battles; the victor tends to be the one with the higher level. And in male elephant seals, androgens promote the development of bodies weighing more than 2 tons and aggressive behavior toward other males. These males fight by slamming their bodies against each other **(Figure 25.13)**. After a fight, one male will have established dominance over the other, earning the right to mate with many females, an obvious advantage in terms of Darwinian fitness. Thus, the idea that steroid abuse can lead to aggressive behavior may have an evolutionary basis.

The roles that androgens play among vertebrates illustrate two central aspects of life that result from Darwinian evolution: unity (a consistent effect on the development of the male gonads) and diversity (the variety of secondary effects). The universal nature of gonad development is a strong indication that androgen regulation was an early evolutionary adaptation among vertebrates. But over millions of years of evolution, the specific effects of androgens changed in response to varied environments.

▶ **Figure 25.13 Male elephant seals battling for dominance.**

Chapter Review

SUMMARY OF KEY CONCEPTS

 Go to **www.masteringbiology.com** for homework assignments, practice quizzes, Pearson eText, and more.

Hormones: An Overview

Hormones are chemical signals carried by the circulatory system that communicate regulatory messages throughout the body. The endocrine system consists of a collection of hormone-secreting cells and is the body's main system for internal chemical regulation, particularly of whole-body activities such as growth, reproduction, and control of metabolic rate. Endocrine glands are the primary sites of hormone production and secretion. Changes in target cells are triggered either indirectly by water-soluble hormones or directly by lipid-soluble hormones.

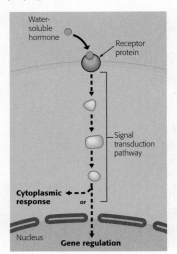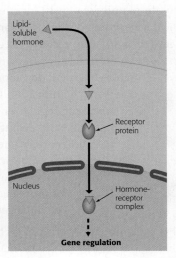

The Human Endocrine System

The human endocrine system consists of about a dozen glands that secrete several dozen hormones. These glands and hormones, such as those summarized in Figure 25.4 and Table 25.1, vary widely in their functions, means of regulation, and targets.

The Hypothalamus and Pituitary Gland

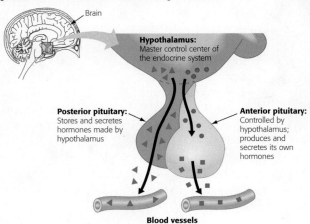

The Thyroid and Parathyroid Glands

Hormones from the thyroid gland regulate an animal's development and metabolism. Too little thyroid hormone in the blood (hypothyroidism) or too much (hyperthyroidism) can lead to metabolic disorders. Blood calcium level is regulated by antagonistic hormones.

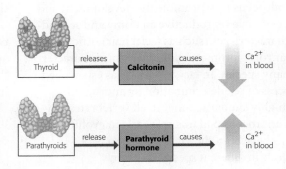

The Pancreas

The pancreas secretes two antagonistic hormones, insulin and glucagon, that control the level of glucose in the blood. Insulin signals cells to take up glucose and the liver to store glucose. Glucagon causes the liver to release stored glucose into the blood. Diabetes mellitus results from a lack of insulin (type 1 diabetes) or a failure of cells to respond to it (type 2 diabetes).

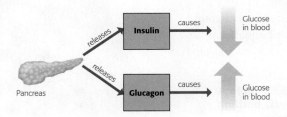

The Adrenal Glands

Hormones from the adrenal glands help maintain homeostasis when the body is stressed. Nerve signals from the hypothalamus stimulate the adrenal medulla to secrete epinephrine and norepinephrine, which quickly trigger the fight-or-flight response. ACTH from the anterior pituitary causes the adrenal cortex to secrete corticosteroids. Corticosteroids include glucocorticoids, which promote the synthesis of glucose. Glucocorticoids, such as cortisone, relieve inflammation and pain, but they can mask injury and suppress immunity.

The Gonads

Estrogens, progestins, and androgens are steroid sex hormones produced by the ovaries in females and the testes in males. Estrogens and progestins stimulate the development of female characteristics and maintain the female reproductive system. Androgens, such as testosterone, trigger the development of male characteristics. The secretion of sex hormones is controlled by the hypothalamus and pituitary gland.

SELF-QUIZ

1. Which of the following is *not* true concerning homeostasis?
   a. It is the maintenance of constant internal conditions.
   b. It involves the regulation of body conditions, such as calcium and glucose levels.
   c. It usually prevents major fluctuations in body conditions.
   d. Its maintenance is solely the responsibility of the endocrine system.

2. Unlike most water-soluble hormones, lipid-soluble hormones
   a. usually do not enter target cells.
   b. bind to receptors in the cytoplasm or nucleus of target cells.
   c. cause a cellular response.
   d. are made of amino acids.

3. Explain how the same hormone can have different effects on two different target cells and no effect on a third type of cell.

4. Which of the following controls the activity of all the others?
   a. thyroid gland
   b. hypothalamus
   c. pituitary gland
   d. adrenal cortex

5. Why does the consumption of alcohol lead to frequent urination?

6. A patient comes to a local health clinic with a large swelling in the neck that appears to be goiter. As the physician is taking the patient's history, the patient mentions not having used iodized salt. The patient is overweight and has a slow metabolism. Does this patient have hyperthyroidism or hypothyroidism? How is this problem related to the lack of iodine in the diet?

7. The pancreas increases its output of insulin in response to
   a. an increase in body temperature.
   b. a decrease in blood glucose.
   c. a hormone secreted by the anterior pituitary.
   d. an increase in blood glucose.

8. Your roommate has just been diagnosed as hyperglycemic, which means having an unusually high blood glucose level. Which of the following could be characteristic of this disorder?
   a. Too much insulin is produced after a high-sugar snack.
   b. The hormone glucagon is underactive.
   c. The receptors on cells do not respond to insulin.
   d. any of the above

9. What problems might an athlete have as a result of chronic use of glucocorticoids to manage pain?

10. Testosterone belongs to a class of sex hormones called
    _____.

11. For each of the following situations, name the hormone that is most likely responsible for the effect described.
    a. While running a marathon, athletes often report that they sense a lot of pain early on. The more they exert themselves, the less pain they report sensing. The hormones involved are _____.
    b. A 9-year-old child has been diagnosed with pituitary dwarfism. The hormone that is lacking is _____.
    c. As part of her treatment for ovarian cancer, a 30-year-old female has both ovaries removed. She begins to notice changes in her skin and breast tissue. These changes are caused by a lack of _____.

Answers to these questions can be found in Appendix: Self-Quiz Answers.

THE PROCESS OF SCIENCE

12. Mice from a genetically modified strain remain healthy as long as they are fed regularly and not allowed to exercise. After they eat, their blood glucose level rises slightly and then declines to a homeostatic level. However, if these mice fast or exercise at all, their blood glucose drops dangerously. Which hypothesis best explains their problem? Explain your choice.
    a. The mice have insulin-dependent diabetes.
    b. The mice lack insulin receptors on their cells.
    c. The mice lack glucagon receptors on their cells.
    d. The mice cannot synthesize glycogen from glucose.

BIOLOGY AND SOCIETY

13. A low rate of secretion of human growth hormone (HGH) causes pituitary dwarfism. Human growth hormone made using recombinant DNA technology enables children who suffer from pituitary dwarfism to grow normally and reach a stature within the normal range. So far, no long-term side effects from HGH used in this way are known. With HGH readily available and relatively inexpensive, some parents who believe that their normal children are not growing fast enough want to use HGH to make them grow faster and taller. Are there reasons to hesitate in treating a normal child with HGH, or are the potential benefits worth the risk? There is some evidence that HGH injected into older adults may delay or even reverse some of the effects of aging. Should HGH be freely available for any adult who wants to use it for that purpose?

14. Type 2 diabetes is becoming increasingly common in the United States. The primary risk factor for type 2 diabetes is a history of obesity. Statistics show that children are becoming obese at an alarmingly high rate, and this correlates with increased rates of type 2 diabetes. When young children become overweight, the problem is usually blamed on nutrition and exercise choices made by the parents. Why do you think today's parents have a harder time feeding their children nutritious meals and providing an exercise program than did parents of previous generations? What can be done to solve this problem? Recently, several families have filed legal action against a fast-food restaurant chain, claiming that their children are obese because they ate there frequently. These parents claim that the restaurant chain is liable because it made the parents think that the food was healthy and would not contribute to obesity. Do you believe that these parents have a case? Explain your response.

26 Reproduction and Development

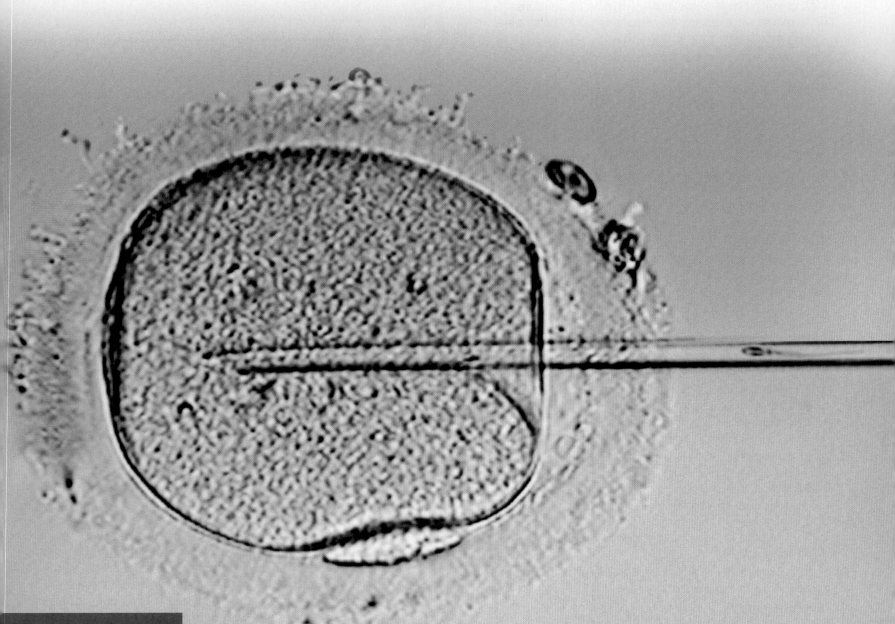

Fertilization in a test tube.
This micrograph shows a technician injecting donor sperm (visible inside the thin glass needle) into a woman's egg.

High-Tech Babies BIOLOGY AND SOCIETY

Life after Death

Throughout their 18-year marriage, Gary and Francia P. always wanted children. But after multiple miscarriages, the couple came to accept that they were infertile, unable to bear children naturally. Seeking help, they visited a fertility clinic, hoping to use reproductive technologies to fulfill their dream of starting a family.

Two weeks later, Gary died suddenly of a heart attack. At the hospital, six hours after his death, Francia requested that a sample of Gary's sperm be removed. Months later, Francia returned to the fertility clinic. The sample obtained from her husband's body provided just enough sperm for one shot at producing a child. Her eggs were surgically removed and combined with Gary's sperm. The resulting embryos were implanted into Francia's uterus, and one grew into a baby son, Jacob, born about one year after his father's death.

Because of his career as a captain in the Newark, New Jersey, police department, Gary's family was entitled to pension benefits that were tied to the size of his family. After Jacob's birth, Francia applied to the pension board for an increase in her widow's benefits. Should Francia be entitled to this increase? The pension board did not think so, ruling that a child born more than a year after a parent's death is not entitled to benefits from that parent.

Francia appealed in court. There were several previous cases where the courts determined that children born to women who used a deceased husband's sperm had full rights as heirs, but these cases involved men who had donated their sperm before death. Because New Jersey does not have laws governing the rights of children born from sperm obtained after death, Francia's case entered new legal territory. As of late 2011, the outcome was still undetermined.

This case illustrates two important points. First, modern technologies allow us to circumvent the natural course of reproduction in many ways. Second, society's laws have not yet caught up to these new technologies. It is up to all of us to decide what is right in such circumstances. To quote the U.S. Court of Appeals in Philadelphia from a related case, "[We] cannot help but observe that this is, indeed, a new world."

In this chapter, we explore the anatomy and physiology of animal reproduction, paying particular attention to the reproductive structures of humans and how human babies develop from a single cell. Along the way, we'll also consider how modern health practices and technologies circumvent the natural process of sexual reproduction.

Unifying Concepts of Animal Reproduction

Although every individual animal has a relatively short life span, species last much longer because of **reproduction**, the creation of new individuals from existing ones. Animals reproduce in a great variety of ways, but there are two principal modes: asexual reproduction and sexual reproduction.

Asexual Reproduction

Asexual reproduction (reproduction without sex) is the creation of offspring that are genetically identical to a lone parent. Several types of asexual reproduction can be found among animals. Many invertebrates reproduce asexually by **budding**, the outgrowth and eventual splitting off of a new individual from a parent. Hydras, relatives of jellies, reproduce this way **(Figure 26.1)**. The sea anemone shown in **Figure 26.2** is undergoing **fission**, the separation of a parent into two or more offspring of about equal size. Another type of asexual reproduction involves fragmentation, the breaking of the body into several pieces, followed by regeneration, the regrowth of lost body parts. Some organisms have remarkable powers of regeneration. In certain species of sea stars, for example, an arm plus a bit of the central body that has split off can give rise to a new sea star (see Figure 8.1). In some species of sea sponges, if a single sponge is pushed through a wire mesh, each of the resulting clumps of cells can regrow into a new sponge. (These are examples of asexual reproduction as it occurs in nature. Other species have been the target of *artificial* asexual reproduction; see the discussion of cloning in Chapter 11.)

In nature, asexual reproduction has several potential advantages. Because it eliminates the need to find a mate, asexual reproduction allows the individual members of a species to perpetuate themselves even if they are isolated from one another. Asexual reproduction also allows organisms to multiply quickly, without spending time or energy producing sperm and eggs. If an individual is very well suited to its environment, asexual reproduction allows it to reproduce rapidly and exploit available resources.

A potential disadvantage of asexual reproduction is that it produces genetically uniform populations. Genetically similar individuals may thrive in a particular environment. But if the environment changes and becomes less favorable to survival (as a result of some natural disaster, say, or a new predator or pathogen), then all individuals may be affected equally, and the entire population may die out. ☑

▼ Figure 26.1 **Asexual reproduction via budding in a hydra.**

Bud

▼ Figure 26.2 **Asexual reproduction via fission in a sea anemone.**

Sexual Reproduction

You know that you have a mix of traits from your mother and father. But you also have a genome distinct from every other human (unless you have an identical twin). You are the product of **sexual reproduction**, creation of offspring by the fusion of two haploid sex cells called **gametes** to form a diploid **zygote**. The male gamete is the **sperm**, and the female gamete is the **egg**. The zygote and the new individual it develops into contain a unique combination of genes carried from the parents via the egg and sperm.

Can you name a multisex animal?

Unlike asexual reproduction, sexual reproduction increases genetic variability among offspring as a result of the huge variety of gametes produced by meiosis (see Chapter 8). Variation is the raw material of evolution by natural selection. When an environment changes, there is a better chance that some of the varying offspring will survive and reproduce than if all the offspring are genetically very similar.

Some animals can reproduce both asexually and sexually, benefiting from both modes. In **Figure 26.3**, you can see two sea anemones of the same species. The one on the left is reproducing asexually (via fission), while the one on the right is releasing eggs. Why would such dual reproductive capabilities be advantageous to an animal? Some animals reproduce asexually when food is ample and conditions are favorable. But when conditions change (becoming colder or drier, for example), these animals switch to sexual reproduction, producing a generation of genetically varied individuals with better potential to adapt to the changing conditions.

Most animals are of a single sex, either male or female. But in some species, each individual is a **hermaphrodite**, meaning that it has both male and female reproductive systems. Some hermaphrodites (such as tapeworms, which can live as parasites in the human intestine) can fertilize their own eggs. Other species require a partner. For example, when earthworms mate, each individual donates and receives sperm.

The mechanics of fertilization play an important part in sexual reproduction. Many aquatic animals use external fertilization, in which the parents discharge their gametes into the water, where fertilization occurs **(Figure 26.4)**. The female and male don't necessarily have to touch to mate. In contrast, nearly all terrestrial animals reproduce when sperm are deposited by a male within the female's body. In the next section, we'll examine the reproductive anatomy that allows one particular terrestrial animal—namely, humans—to achieve sexual reproduction. ✓

✓ CHECKPOINT

What is the most important difference in the genetic makeup of the offspring resulting from sexual versus asexual reproduction?

Answer: Asexual reproduction produces genetically identical offspring, whereas sexual reproduction produces genetically diverse offspring.

▼ **Figure 26.3 Asexual (left) and sexual (right) reproduction in a starlet sea anemone.**

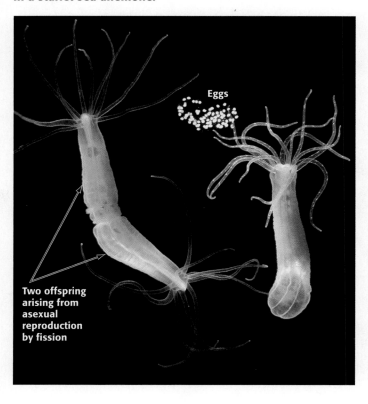

Eggs

Two offspring arising from asexual reproduction by fission

▼ **Figure 26.4 External fertilization in frogs.** Frogs release eggs and sperm (too small to be seen) into the water, where fertilization takes place. The embrace between the two frogs is a mating ritual that coordinates the simultaneous release of gametes.

Egg

Human Reproduction

Although we tend to focus on the differences between human male and female reproductive systems, there are some important similarities. Both sexes have a pair of **gonads**, the organs that produce gametes. And both sexes have ducts that store and deliver the gametes as well as structures that allow mating. We'll now examine the anatomical features of human reproduction, beginning with the male anatomy.

Male Reproductive Anatomy

Figure 26.5 presents a side view and a front view of the male reproductive system. The **penis** contains erectile tissue (shown in blue in the figures) that can fill with blood and cause an erection during sexual arousal. The penis consists of a shaft that supports a highly sensitive glans (head). A **prepuce**, or foreskin, covers the glans. The foreskin may be surgically removed, a procedure known as circumcision.

The **testes** (singular, *testis*), the male gonads, are located outside the abdominal cavity in a sac called the **scrotum**. A testis and a scrotum together are called a **testicle**. Sperm do not develop best at body temperature. By keeping the sperm-forming cells away from the

body, the scrotum keeps them cool enough to develop normally. In cold conditions, muscles around the scrotum contract, pulling the testes toward the body, maintaining the proper temperature.

From puberty into old age, the testes produce hundreds of millions of sperm each day. From the testes, sperm pass into a coiled tube called the epididymis. During **ejaculation**—expulsion of sperm-containing fluid from the penis—the sperm leave the epididymis and travel through a duct called the **vas deferens** (the target of a vasectomy). The **seminal vesicles** and **prostate gland** add fluid that nourishes the sperm and provides protection from the natural acidity of the vagina. The prostate gland is the source of some of the most common medical problems in men over 40, and prostate cancer is the second most commonly diagnosed cancer in the United States. Each vas deferens, one from each of the two testes, empties into the **urethra**. The urethra conveys, at different times, both sperm and urine out through the penis.

Ejaculation, caused by the contraction of muscles along the sperm ducts, releases about 5 mL (1 teaspoonful) of **semen**. Only 5% of semen consists of sperm (typically 200–500 million of them); the remaining 95% of semen is fluid secreted by the various glands. ☑

▼ **Figure 26.5 The male reproductive system.** The color blue highlights erectile tissue. Some nonreproductive structures are also labeled (in italics) to help keep you oriented.

Side view

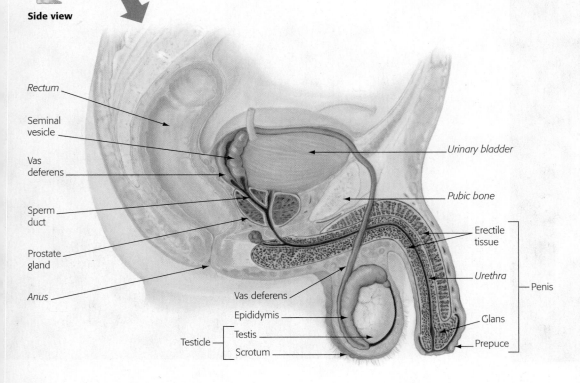

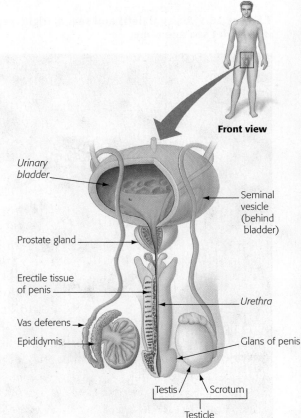

Front view

Female Reproductive Anatomy

Two views of the female reproductive system are shown in **Figure 26.6**. The outer features of the female reproductive anatomy are collectively called the **vulva**. The **vagina**, or birth canal, opens to the outside just behind the opening of the urethra, the tube through which urine is excreted. An outer pair of thick, fatty ridges, the **labia majora**, protects the entire genital region, and a pair of inner skin folds, the **labia minora**, borders the openings. A thin membrane called the **hymen** partly covers the vaginal opening until sexual intercourse or other vigorous physical activity ruptures it. The **clitoris** is an organ that engorges with blood and becomes erect during sexual arousal. It consists of a short shaft supporting a rounded glans, or head, covered by a small hood of skin called the prepuce. The clitoris has an enormous number of nerve endings and is very sensitive to touch.

The **ovaries** are the site of gamete production—the gonads—in human females. A woman's ovaries are each about an inch long and have a bumpy surface. The bumps are **follicles**, each consisting of a single developing egg cell surrounded by cells that nourish and protect it. The follicles also produce estrogen, the female sex hormone (see Chapter 25).

A female is born with over a million follicles, but only several hundred will release egg cells during her reproductive years. Starting at puberty and continuing until menopause (the end of fertility, which usually occurs during middle age), one follicle (or rarely two or more) matures and releases its egg cell about every 28 days. An immature egg cell is ejected from the follicle in the process of **ovulation**. After ovulation, what remains of the follicle grows to form a solid mass called the **corpus luteum**, which secretes hormones during the reproductive cycle (as you'll see later in the chapter). The released egg enters an **oviduct** (also called a fallopian tube), where cilia sweep it toward the uterus. If sperm are present, fertilization may take place in the upper part of the oviduct. If the released egg is not fertilized, it is shed during menstruation, and a new follicle matures during the next cycle.

The **uterus** (also called the womb) is the actual site of pregnancy. The uterus is about the size and shape of an upside-down pear, but can grow to several times that size during pregnancy. The uterus has a thick muscular wall lined with a blood-rich layer of tissue called the **endometrium**. An embryo implants in the endometrium and grows there. The term **embryo** is used for the stage in development from the first division of the zygote until body structures begin to appear, about the 9th week. From the 9th week until birth, a developing human is called a **fetus**.

The narrow neck at the bottom of the uterus is the **cervix**. It is recommended that a woman have a yearly Pap test in which cells are removed from around the cervix and examined under a microscope for signs of cervical cancer. Regular Pap smears greatly increase the chances of detecting cervical cancer early and therefore treating it successfully. The cervix opens into the vagina. During intercourse, the vagina serves as a repository for sperm. ☑

▼ **Figure 26.6 The female reproductive system.** The color blue highlights erectile tissue. Some nonreproductive structures are also labeled (in italics) to help keep you oriented.

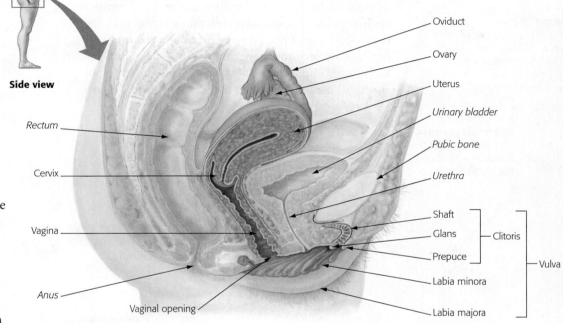

Side view

- Rectum
- Cervix
- Vagina
- *Anus*
- Vaginal opening
- Oviduct
- Ovary
- Uterus
- *Urinary bladder*
- *Pubic bone*
- *Urethra*
- Shaft
- Glans — Clitoris
- Prepuce
- Labia minora — Vulva
- Labia majora

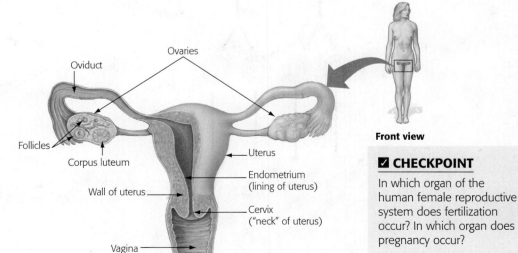

Front view

- Oviduct
- Ovaries
- Follicles
- Corpus luteum
- Wall of uterus
- Vagina
- Uterus
- Endometrium (lining of uterus)
- Cervix ("neck" of uterus)

☑ CHECKPOINT

In which organ of the human female reproductive system does fertilization occur? In which organ does pregnancy occur?

Answer: the oviduct; the uterus

555

Gametogenesis

The production of gametes is called **gametogenesis**. Human gametes—sperm and egg—are haploid cells with 23 chromosomes that develop by meiosis from diploid cells with 46 chromosomes. (You may find it helpful to review the discussion of meiosis in Chapter 8, particularly Figures 8.13–8.15.) There are significant differences in gametogenesis between human males and females, so we'll examine the processes separately.

Spermatogenesis

The formation of sperm cells is called **spermatogenesis (Figure 26.7)**. Sperm cells develop inside the testes in coiled tubes called the **seminiferous tubules**. Cells near the outer walls of the tubules multiply constantly by mitosis. Each day, about 3 million of them differentiate into **primary spermatocytes**, the cells that undergo meiosis. Meiosis I of a primary spermatocyte produces two haploid **secondary spermatocytes**. Then meiosis II forms four cells, each with the haploid number of chromosomes. A sperm cell that develops from one of

these haploid cells is gradually pushed toward the center of the seminiferous tubule. From there, it passes into the epididymis, where it matures, becomes motile, and is stored until ejaculation. Because the pre-sperm cells continuously replenish themselves, there is a never-ending supply of spermatocytes, allowing males to produce sperm throughout their adult lives.

Oogenesis

Figure 26.8 summarizes **oogenesis**, the development of mature egg cells, also called ova (singular, *ovum*). At birth, each ovary contains many thousands of follicles. Each follicle contains a single dormant **primary oocyte**, a diploid cell that has paused its cell cycle in prophase of meiosis I.

► **Figure 26.7**
Spermatogenesis.
This process takes about 65–75 days in the human male.

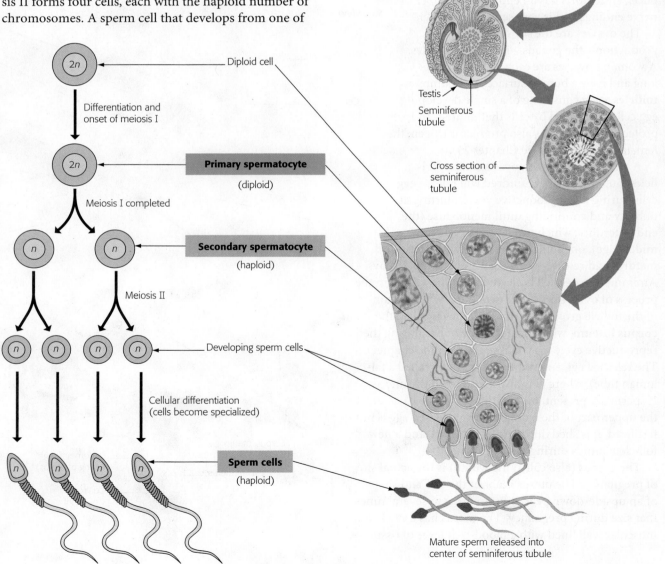

A primary oocyte can be triggered to develop further by the hormone FSH (follicle-stimulating hormone). After puberty and until menopause, about every 28 days, FSH from the pituitary gland stimulates one of the dormant follicles to develop. The follicle enlarges, and the primary oocyte within it completes meiosis I and begins meiosis II. The division of the cytoplasm in meiosis I is unequal, with a single **secondary oocyte** receiving almost all of it. The smaller of the two daughter cells, called the first polar body, receives almost no cytoplasm.

About the time the secondary oocyte forms, the pituitary gland secretes LH (luteinizing hormone), which triggers ovulation. The ripening follicle bursts, releasing its secondary oocyte from the ovary. The ruptured follicle then develops into a corpus luteum. The secondary oocyte enters the oviduct, and if a sperm cell fuses with it, the secondary oocyte completes meiosis II. Meiosis II is also unequal, yielding a small polar body and the mature egg (ovum). The chromosomes of the egg can then fuse with the chromosomes of the sperm cell, producing a diploid zygote. The polar bodies, which are quite small because they received almost no cytoplasm, degenerate. The zygote thus acquires nearly all the cytoplasm and the bulk of the nutrients and organelles contained in the original cell.

Both oogenesis and spermatogenesis produce haploid gametes, but there are several important differences between the two processes. One obvious difference is location: testes in the male and ovaries in the female. Furthermore, human males create new sperm every day from puberty through old age. Human females, on the other hand, create primary oocytes only during their fetal development. Another difference is that four gametes result from each diploid parent cell during spermatogenesis, whereas oogenesis results in only one gamete from each parent cell. Moreover, there are significant differences in the cells produced by meiosis: Sperm are small and motile and contain relatively few nutrients; eggs are large, nonmotile, and well stocked with nutrients and organelles. Finally, oogenesis cannot be completed without stimulation from a sperm cell, whereas spermatogenesis is completed before the sperm leave the testis. ☑

▼ **Figure 26.8 Oogenesis and development of an ovarian follicle.** Notice that oogenesis starts before birth, but the final ovum does not form until fertilization.

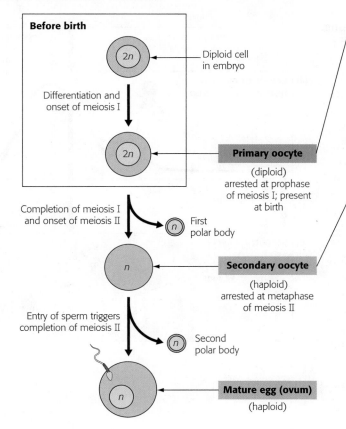

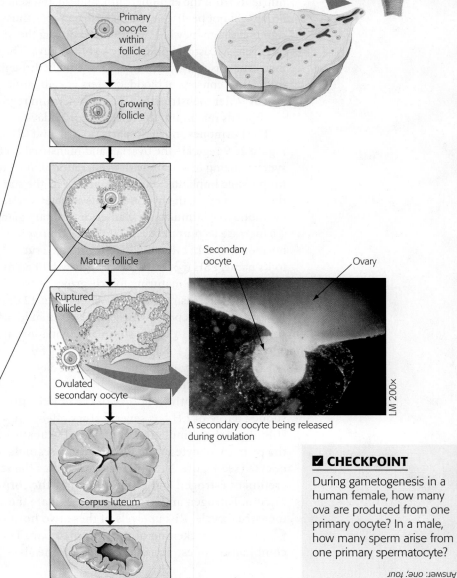

A secondary oocyte being released during ovulation

☑ CHECKPOINT

During gametogenesis in a human female, how many ova are produced from one primary oocyte? In a male, how many sperm arise from one primary spermatocyte?

Answer: one; four

557

The Female Reproductive Cycle

Human females have a **reproductive cycle**, a recurring series of events that produces gametes, makes them available for fertilization, and prepares the body for pregnancy (**Figure 26.9**). The reproductive cycle repeats every 28 days, on average, but cycles from 20 to 40 days are not uncommon. The reproductive cycle is actually two cycles in one. The **ovarian cycle** (see Figure 26.9c) controls the growth and release of an egg. During the **menstrual cycle** (see Figure 26.9e), the uterus is prepared for possible implantation of an embryo. Hormonal messages coordinate the two cycles.

By convention, the first day of a woman's "period" is designated day 1 of the menstrual cycle. **Menstruation** is uterine bleeding caused by the breakdown of the endometrium, the blood-rich inner lining of the uterus. If an embryo implants in the uterine wall, it will obtain nutrients from the endometrium, and the thickened lining will not be discharged. Menstruation is thus a sign that pregnancy has not occurred during the previous cycle. Menstruation usually lasts 3–5 days. The menstrual discharge, which leaves the body through the vagina, consists of blood, clusters of cells, and mucus. After menstruation, the endometrium regrows, reaching its maximum thickness in 20–25 days.

The hormones shown in parts (a), (b), and (d) of Figure 26.9 regulate the ovarian and menstrual cycles, synchronizing ovulation with preparation of the uterus for possible implantation of an embryo. At the start of the ovarian cycle, the hypothalamus secretes a releasing hormone that stimulates the anterior pituitary gland to ❶ increase its output of FSH (follicle-stimulating hormone) and LH (luteinizing hormone). True to its name, FSH ❷ stimulates the growth of an ovarian follicle. As the maturing follicle grows, it secretes estrogen in increasing amounts. After about 12 days, ❸ estrogen levels peak, which causes ❹ a sudden surge of FSH and LH. This stimulates ovulation, and ❺ the developing follicle within the ovary bursts and releases its egg. Ovulation takes place on day 14 of the typical 28-day cycle.

Besides promoting rupture of the follicle, the sudden surge of LH has several other effects. It stimulates the completion of meiosis I, transforming the primary oocyte in the follicle into a secondary oocyte (see Figure 26.8). LH also promotes the secretion of estrogen and progesterone by the corpus luteum. Estrogen and progesterone regulate the menstrual cycle. Rising levels of these two hormones ❻ promote thickening of the endometrium. The combination of estrogen and progesterone also

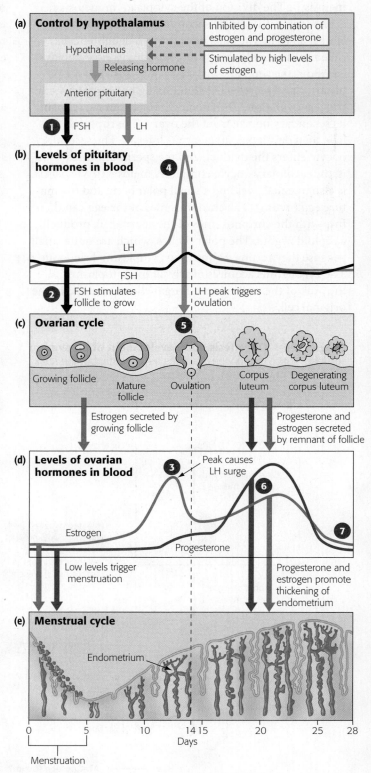

▼ **Figure 26.9 The reproductive cycle of the human female.** This figure shows how (c) the ovarian cycle and (e) the menstrual cycle are regulated by changing hormonal levels, represented in parts (a), (b), and (d). The time scale at the bottom of the figure applies to parts (b)–(e).

(a) Control by hypothalamus

Inhibited by combination of estrogen and progesterone

Stimulated by high levels of estrogen

Hypothalamus

Releasing hormone

Anterior pituitary

❶ FSH   LH

(b) Levels of pituitary hormones in blood

❹

LH

FSH

❷ FSH stimulates follicle to grow

LH peak triggers ovulation

(c) Ovarian cycle ❺

Growing follicle   Mature follicle   Ovulation   Corpus luteum   Degenerating corpus luteum

Estrogen secreted by growing follicle

Progesterone and estrogen secreted by remnant of follicle

(d) Levels of ovarian hormones in blood

❸   Peak causes LH surge

❻

Estrogen

Progesterone

❼

Low levels trigger menstruation

Progesterone and estrogen promote thickening of endometrium

(e) Menstrual cycle

Endometrium

0   5   10   14 15   20   25   28
Days

Menstruation

inhibits further secretion of FSH and LH, ensuring that a second follicle does not mature during this cycle. Further degeneration of the corpus luteum causes the levels of estrogen and progesterone to fall off. Once these hormones **7** fall below a critical level, the endometrium begins to shed, starting menstruation on day 1 of the next cycle. Now that estrogen and progesterone are no longer there to inhibit it, the pituitary secretes FSH and LH, and a new cycle begins.

The description of the reproductive cycle in this section assumes that fertilization has not occurred. If it does, the embryo implants into the endometrium and secretes a hormone called HCG (human chorionic gonadotropin). HCG maintains the corpus luteum, which continues to secrete progesterone and estrogen, keeping the endometrium intact. As you will see later, some forms of contraception work by mimicking the high levels of hormones that occur during pregnancy. Most home pregnancy tests work by detecting HCG in the urine. In males, HCG boosts testosterone production, so its use is banned by many sports organizations. In 2009, baseball slugger Manny Ramirez was suspended from baseball for 50 games after testing positive for HCG. ✅

✅ **CHECKPOINT**
What hormonal changes trigger the start of menstruation?

Answer: decreasing levels of estrogen and progesterone

Reproductive Health

Now that you've read about the anatomy and physiology of the human reproductive system, you can apply this knowledge to two issues of reproductive health: contraception and the transmission of disease.

Contraception

Contraception is the deliberate prevention of pregnancy. There are many forms of contraception that interfere with different steps in the process of becoming pregnant. **Table 26.1** lists the most common methods of birth control and their failure rates when used correctly and when used typically. Note that these two rates are often quite different, emphasizing the importance of learning to use contraception correctly.

Complete abstinence (avoiding intercourse) is the only totally effective method of contraception, but other methods are effective to varying degrees. Sterilization, surgery that prevents sperm from reaching an egg, is very reliable. A woman may have a **tubal ligation** (have her "tubes tied"). In this procedure, a doctor removes a short section from each oviduct, often tying (ligating) the remaining ends and thereby blocking the route of sperm to egg. A man may have a **vasectomy**, in which a doctor cuts a section out of each vas deferens to prevent sperm from reaching the urethra. Both forms of sterilization are free from side effects and relatively safe. They are meant to be permanent but can sometimes be surgically reversed. Although such reversals are becoming increasingly successful, they carry some risk of damaging the ducts.

The effectiveness of other methods of contraception depends on how they are used. Temporary abstinence, also called the **rhythm method** or **natural family planning**, depends on refraining from intercourse during the days around ovulation, when fertilization is most likely. In theory, the time of ovulation can be determined by monitoring changes in body temperature and the composition of cervical mucus, but careful monitoring and record keeping are required. Additionally, the length of the reproductive

What forms of contraception are most reliable?

Table 26.1	Contraceptive Methods	
Pregnancies per 100 Women per Year		
Method	**Used Correctly**	**Typically**
None		85
Birth control pill	0.1	5
Vasectomy	0.1	0.15
Tubal ligation	0.2	0.5
Rhythm method	1–9	20
Withdrawal	4	19
Condom (male)	3	14
Diaphragm and spermicide	6	20
Spermicide alone	6	26

cycle can vary from month to month, and sperm can survive for 3–5 days within the female reproductive tract, making natural family planning among the most unreliable methods of contraception in actual practice. Withdrawal of the penis from the vagina before ejaculation is also ineffective, because sperm may exit the penis before climax.

If used correctly, barrier methods can be quite effective at physically preventing the union of sperm and egg. **Condoms** are sheaths, usually made of latex, that fit over the penis or within the vagina. A **diaphragm** is a dome-shaped rubber cap that covers the cervix. It requires a doctor's visit for proper fitting. To be more effective, barrier devices (including condoms) can be used in combination with **spermicides**, sperm-killing chemicals in the form of a jelly, cream, or foam; spermicides used alone are not reliable.

Some of the most effective methods of contraception prevent the release of gametes. Oral contraceptives, or **birth control pills**, come in several different forms that contain varying formulations of a synthetic estrogen and/or a synthetic progesterone. Steady intake of these hormones simulates their constant levels during pregnancy. In response to being "fooled" that pregnancy has occurred, the hypothalamus fails to send the signals that start development of an ovarian follicle. Ovulation ceases, preventing pregnancy. In addition to pills, various combinations of these hormones are also available as a shot (Depo-Provera), a ring inserted into the vagina, or a skin patch **(Figure 26.10)**. Some of

these contraceptives maintain hormone levels for up to 3 months, so a user will have only four periods a year. Currently, there is no chemical contraceptive available that can prevent the production or release of sperm.

Certain drugs can prevent fertilization or implantation even after intercourse has occurred. Birth control pills can be prescribed in high doses for emergency contraception, also called **morning-after pills (MAPs)**. If taken within 3 days of intercourse, morning-after pills are about 75% effective at preventing pregnancy. Such treatments should only be used in emergency situations because they have significant side effects. In 2006, the Food and Drug Administration approved the sale of morning-after pills (the "Plan B" brand) without a prescription. If pregnancy has occurred, the drug RU-486 (mifepristone) can induce an abortion, the termination of a pregnancy in process. RU-486 must be taken within the first 7 weeks of pregnancy and requires a doctor's prescription and several visits to a medical facility.

Responsible sex involves more than preventing unwanted pregnancies. It also involves preventing the spread of sexually transmitted diseases, the focus of the next section. ✔

Sexually Transmitted Diseases

Sexually transmitted diseases (STDs) are contagious diseases spread by sexual contact. **Table 26.2** lists the STDs most common in the United States, organized by the type of infectious agent. Notice that bacteria, viruses, protists, and fungi can all cause STDs.

The most common bacterial STD (with nearly a million new cases reported annually in the United States and over 90 million worldwide) is **chlamydia**. In fact, chlamydia and gonorrhea are the two most frequently reported infectious diseases in the United States. Chlamydia poses a public health challenge because it is frequently "silent"—often producing no visible symptoms. The primary symptoms are genital discharge and a burning sensation during urination, but half of infected men and three-quarters of infected women do not notice any symptoms. Long-term complications are rare among men, but up to 40% of infected women develop pelvic inflammatory disease (PID). The inflammation associated with PID may block the oviducts or scar the uterus, causing infertility. Fortunately, chlamydia can be easily treated with a single dose of an antibiotic. But early screening is required to catch the disease before any scarring occurs. Sexually active women are encouraged to be screened for chlamydia and other STDs annually.

In contrast to bacterial STDs, viral STDs are not curable. They can be controlled by medications, but

▼ Figure 26.10 **A contraceptive skin patch containing birth control hormones.**

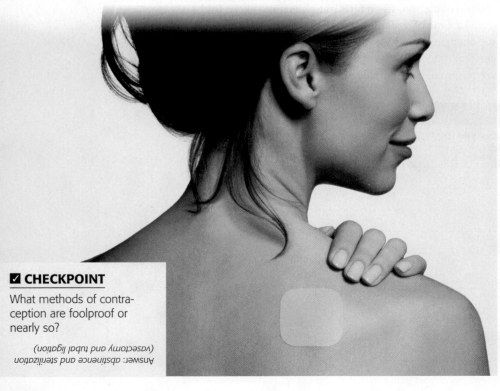

✔ **CHECKPOINT**

What methods of contraception are foolproof or nearly so?

Answer: abstinence and sterilization (vasectomy and tubal ligation)

symptoms and the ability to infect others remain a possibility throughout a person's lifetime. One in five Americans is infected with **genital herpes**, caused by the herpes simplex virus type 2, a variant of the virus that causes cold sores. Most outbreaks heal within a few weeks, but the virus lies dormant within nearby nerve cells. Months or years later, it can reemerge, causing fresh sores that allow the virus to be spread to sexual partners. Abstinence during outbreaks, the use of condoms, and the use of antiviral medications that minimize symptoms can reduce the spread of herpes. But there is no cure, so infection lasts a lifetime.

Which STDs last a lifetime?

AIDS, caused by HIV (discussed in Chapters 10 and 24), poses one of the greatest health challenges in the world today, particularly among the developing nations of Africa and Asia. But even within the United States, there are 56,000 new infections each year, one-third of which result from heterosexual contact.

Another sexually transmitted virus is the human papillomavirus (HPV). There are many known strains of HPV, some of which cause genital warts. Furthermore, HPV infection causes nearly all cases of cervical cancer. A vaccine against HPV is available, but it is only effective before infection. Therefore, it is recommended that a woman be vaccinated (a series of three shots) before she becomes sexually active.

Anyone who is sexually active should have regular medical exams, be tested for STDs, and seek immediate help if any suspicious symptoms appear—even if they are mild. STDs are most prevalent among teenagers and young adults; nearly two-thirds of infections occur among people under 25. The best way to avoid the spread of STDs is, of course, abstinence. Alternatively, latex condoms provide the best protection for "safe sex." ☑

☑ CHECKPOINT

What is the most important difference between STDs caused by viruses and STDs caused by bacteria in terms of their treatment?

Answer: Bacterial STDs can be cured with antibiotics; viral STDs are permanent.

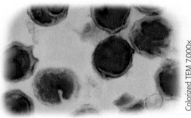

Chlamydia trachomatis

Colorized TEM 7,000x

Neisseria gonorrhoeae

Colorized TEM 17,000x

Treponema pallidum

Colorized SEM 4,000x

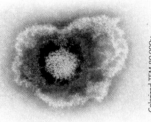

Herpes simplex virus

Colorized TEM 80,000x

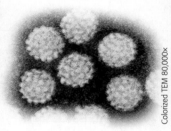

Papillomaviruses

Colorized TEM 80,000x

Trichomonas vaginalis

Colorized SEM 2,200x

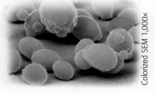

Candida albicans

Colorized SEM 1,000x

Table 26.2	STDs Common in the United States		
Disease	**Microbial Agent**	**Major Symptoms and Effects**	**Treatment**
Bacterial			
Chlamydial infections	*Chlamydia trachomatis*	Genital discharge, itching, and/or painful urination; often no symptoms in women; pelvic inflammatory disease (PID)	Antibiotics
Gonorrhea	*Neisseria gonorrhoeae*	Genital discharge; painful urination; sometimes no symptoms in women; PID	Antibiotics
Syphilis	*Treponema pallidum*	Ulcer (chancre) on genitalia in early stages; spreads throughout body and can be fatal if not treated	Antibiotics can cure in early stages
Viral			
Genital herpes	Herpes simplex virus type 2, occasionally type 1	Recurring symptoms: small blisters on genitalia, painful urination, skin inflammation; linked to cervical cancer, miscarriage, birth defects	The drug valacyclovir can prevent recurrences
Genital warts	Human papillomaviruses (HPV), multiple types	Painless growths on genitalia; HPV can cause cervical cancer	Removal by freezing, vaccine
AIDS and HIV infection	HIV	See Chapter 24	Combination of drugs
Protistan			
Trichomoniasis	*Trichomonas vaginalis*	Vaginal irritation, itching, and discharge; usually no symptoms in men	Antiprotist drugs
Fungal			
Candidiasis (yeast infections)	*Candida albicans*	Similar to symptoms of trichomoniasis; frequently acquired nonsexually	Antifungal drugs

Human Development

Embryonic development begins with **fertilization**, or conception, the union of a sperm and egg to form a zygote. In this section, we will examine the process of fertilization and the subsequent development of a human.

Fertilization

Sexual intercourse releases hundreds of millions of sperm into the vagina, but only a few thousand sperm survive the several-hour trip to the egg in the oviduct. Of these sperm, only a single one can enter and fertilize the egg. All the other millions of sperm die.

Repeating a theme we've seen again and again during our exploration of anatomy, the shape of sperm is related to what they do (form fits function). A mature human sperm has a streamlined shape that enables it to swim through fluids in the vagina, uterus, and oviduct (**Figure 26.11**). The sperm's head contains a haploid nucleus and is tipped with a membrane-enclosed sac called the acrosome. The middle of the sperm contains mitochondria that use high-energy nutrients from the semen, especially the sugar fructose, to fuel movement of the flagellum.

▼ Figure 26.11 A human sperm cell.

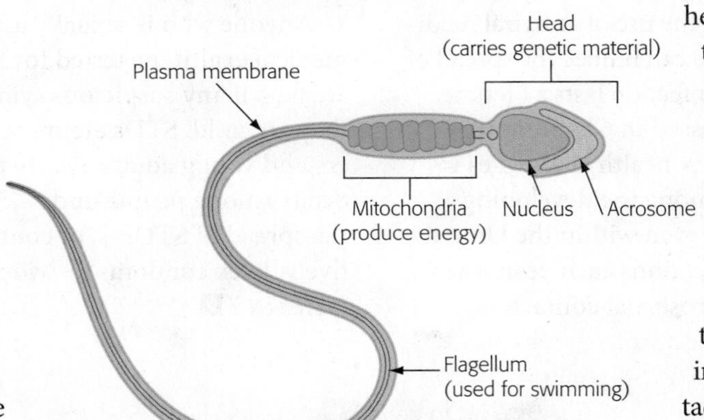

Figure 26.12 traces one sperm through the events of fertilization. The sperm ❶ approaches and then ❷ contacts the jelly coat (red) that surrounds the egg. The acrosome in the sperm's head releases a cloud of enzymes that digest a hole in the jelly. This hole allows the sperm head to ❸ fuse its plasma membrane with that of the egg. Fusion of the two membranes makes it possible for the sperm nucleus to ❹ enter the cytoplasm of the egg. Fusion also triggers completion of meiosis II in the egg. Furthermore, contact of sperm with egg triggers a change in the egg's plasma membrane that makes it impenetrable to other sperm cells. This blockage of other sperm ensures that the zygote that is forming contains only the diploid number of chromosomes. The chromosomes of the egg and sperm nuclei ❺ are eventually enclosed in a single diploid nucleus. In the diploid zygote, the egg's metabolic machinery awakens from dormancy and gears up in preparation for the enormous growth and development that will soon follow. ☑

☑ CHECKPOINT

What is the function of a sperm's acrosome?

Answer: It releases enzymes that dissolve the outer layer of the egg, allowing the sperm to penetrate.

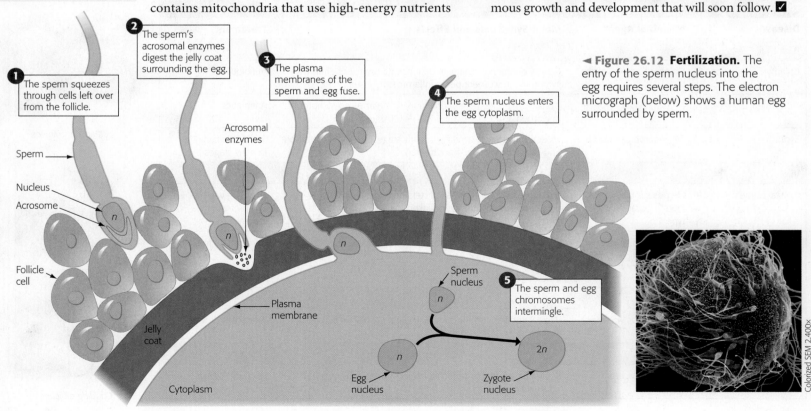

◄ **Figure 26.12 Fertilization.** The entry of the sperm nucleus into the egg requires several steps. The electron micrograph (below) shows a human egg surrounded by sperm.

Basic Concepts of Embryonic Development

A single-celled human zygote formed by fertilization is smaller than the period at the end of this sentence. From this humble start, the zygote develops into a full-fledged organism with trillions of cells organized into complex tissues and organs. Clearly, this process requires an astonishing amount of cell division and specialization. The key to development in all organisms is that each stage takes place in a highly organized fashion.

How are twins formed?

Development begins with **cleavage**, a series of rapid cell divisions that produces a multicellular ball. After the zygote divides for the first time, about 36 hours after fertilization, it is called an embryo. Rarely, and apparently at random, the two cells of the early embryo separate from each other. When this separation happens, each cell may "reset" and act as a zygote; the result is the development of identical (monozygotic) twins. (Nonidentical, or dizygotic, twins result from a completely different mechanism: Two separate eggs fuse with two separate sperm to produce two genetically unique zygotes that develop at the same time.)

During cleavage, DNA replication, mitosis, and cytokinesis occur rapidly, but the total amount of cytoplasm remains unchanged. As a result, the overall size of the embryo does not change; instead, each cell division partitions the embryo into twice as many smaller cells, each with its own nucleus **(Figure 26.13)**. Cleavage continues as the embryo moves down the oviduct toward the uterus. A central cavity begins to form in the embryo. About 6–7 days after fertilization, the embryo has reached the uterus as a fluid-filled hollow ball of about 100 cells called a blastocyst. Protruding into the central cavity on one side of the human blastocyst is a small clump of cells called the inner cell mass, which will eventually form the fetus. Occasionally, an embryo does not travel down the oviduct to the uterus. The result is an ectopic pregnancy, one in which the embryo develops in the wrong location. Ectopic pregnancies are invariably fatal to the embryo and can be dangerous to the mother, requiring immediate medical attention.

The second stage of development, under way by 9 days after conception, is **gastrulation** (see the bottom of Figure 26.13). The cells of the early embryo begin an organized migration that produces the **gastrula**, an embryo with three main layers. The three layers produced in gastrulation are embryonic tissues called ectoderm, endoderm, and mesoderm. The ectoderm eventually develops into the nervous system and outer layer of skin (epidermis). The endoderm becomes the innermost lining of the digestive system and organs such as the liver, pancreas, and thyroid. The mesoderm gives rise to most other organs and tissues, such as the heart, kidneys, and muscles.

At this stage, various cellular changes contribute to the formation of embryonic structures. All developmental processes depend on chemical signals passed between neighboring cells and cell layers, telling embryonic cells precisely what to do and when. The mechanism by which one group of cells influences the development of an adjacent group of cells is called **induction**. Its effect is to switch on a set of genes whose expression makes the receiving cells differentiate into a specific cell or tissue type. For example, inductive signals can cause cells to change shape or to migrate from one location to another within the developing embryo. Another key

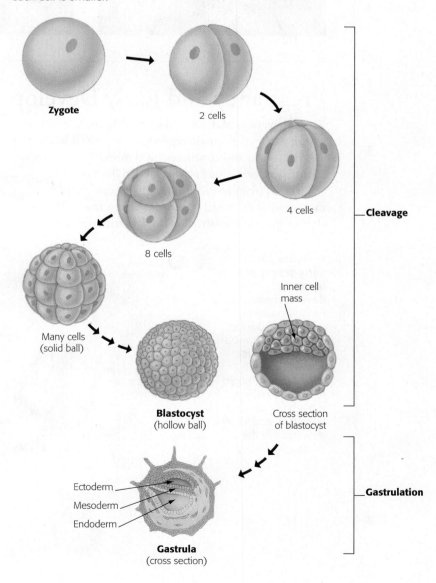

▼ **Figure 26.13 Early development of an embryo.** Notice that each round of division during cleavage does not change the total size of the embryo. Instead, there are more cells, and each cell is smaller.

Zygote

2 cells

4 cells

8 cells

Many cells (solid ball)

Inner cell mass

Blastocyst (hollow ball)

Cross section of blastocyst

Cleavage

Ectoderm

Mesoderm

Endoderm

Gastrula (cross section)

Gastrulation

developmental process is **programmed cell death**, which kills selected cells. For example, some genes encode proteins that kill certain cells in developing human hands and feet, separating the fingers and toes (**Figure 26.14**).

During the course of embryonic development, a sequence of chemical signals between cells leads to increasingly greater specialization as organs begin to take shape. The importance of these processes is underscored by birth defects that result from improper signaling. Spina bifida is a condition that results from the failure of a tube of ectoderm cells to properly close and form the spine during the first month of fetal development. Infants born with spina bifida often have permanent nerve damage that results in paralysis of the lower limbs. ☑

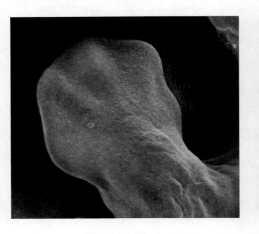 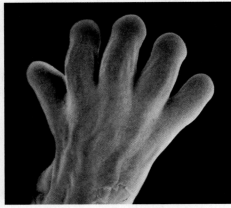

◄ **Figure 26.14**
Programmed cell death in a developing human hand. Proteins produced during human development destroy cells in the early hand (left), creating the spaces between fingers (right).

Pregnancy and Early Development

Pregnancy, or **gestation**, is the carrying of developing young within the female reproductive tract. It begins at fertilization and continues until birth. In humans, gestation lasts about 266 days (38 weeks) from fertilization, but is usually measured as 40 weeks (9 months) from the start of the last menstrual cycle. Other mammals have much shorter or longer gestation periods (3 weeks in mice, 22 months in elephants).

What animal stays pregnant for nearly two years?

The early stages in human development are summarized in **Figure 26.15**. Fertilization and cleavage take place in the oviduct. About a week after conception, the embryo reaches the uterus and implants itself into the

► **Figure 26.15**
Early stages of human development.
Fertilization takes place in the oviduct. As the zygote travels down the oviduct, cleavage starts. By the time the embryo reaches the uterus, it has become a blastocyst, and it implants into the endometrial lining.

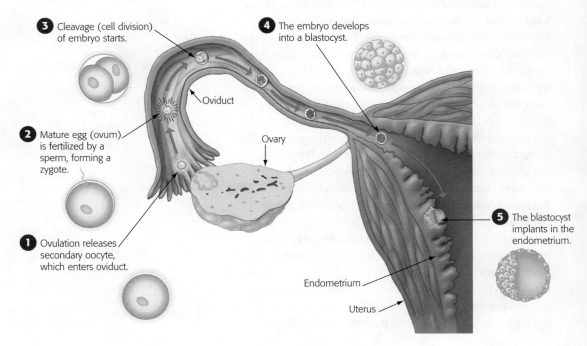

3 Cleavage (cell division) of embryo starts.

4 The embryo develops into a blastocyst.

Oviduct

2 Mature egg (ovum) is fertilized by a sperm, forming a zygote.

Ovary

1 Ovulation releases secondary oocyte, which enters oviduct.

5 The blastocyst implants in the endometrium.

Endometrium

Uterus

endometrium. By this time, the embryo has become a blastocyst, with a central fluid-filled cavity and an inner cell mass (**Figure 26.16a**). These early embryonic cells are **stem cells**, with the potential to give rise to every type of cell in the body. (As discussed in Chapter 11, embryonic stem cells have great potential as medical tools.) The outer cell layer, called the **trophoblast** (**Figure 26.16b**), becomes part of the **placenta**, the organ that provides nourishment and oxygen to the embryo and helps dispose of its wastes.

Figure 26.16c shows the embryo about a month after conception. Besides the growing embryo, there are now several pieces of life-support equipment: the amnion, the yolk sac, the allantois, and the chorion. The amnion is a fluid-filled sac that encloses and protects the embryo. The amnion usually breaks just before childbirth, and the amniotic fluid leaves the mother's body through her vagina. Many anxious couples are startled when her "water breaks," and take this as a sign to get to the hospital. The yolk sac produces the embryo's first blood cells and its first gamete-forming cells in the gonads. The allantois forms part of the **umbilical cord**—the lifeline between the embryo and the placenta. The outermost membrane, the **chorion**, becomes part of the placenta.

The placenta develops **chorionic villi**, finger-like outgrowths containing embryonic blood vessels. These blood vessels are closely associated with blood vessels of the mother's endometrium. The chorionic villi absorb nutrients and oxygen from the mother's blood via diffusion and pass these substances to the embryo. The villi also diffuse wastes from the embryo to the mother's bloodstream. Although substances can pass back and forth via diffusion, the fetus has its own blood supply that does not mix with the mother's. As discussed in Chapter 9, a small sample of chorionic villus tissue can be removed for prenatal genetic testing.

The placenta provides for other needs of the embryo as well. For example, it allows protective antibodies to pass from the mother to the fetus. However, chemicals in tobacco smoke, alcohol, and other drugs can also cross the placenta, and these harmful substances can cause developmental abnormalities and raise the chances of miscarriage. Additionally, viruses—the German measles virus and HIV, for example—can cross the placenta and cause disease. ✓

▼ **Figure 26.16 A human embryo: the first month.**

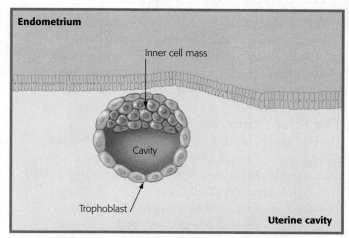

(a) Day 6: Before implantation. By 6 days after conception, the embryo has developed into a blastocyst.

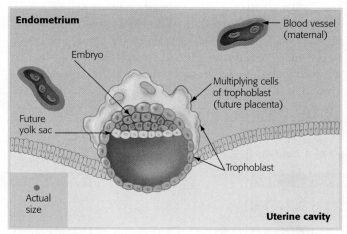

(b) Day 10: Implantation under way. After implantation, the inner cell mass of embryonic stem cells will develop into the fetus. The outer layer of trophoblast cells will become the embryo's contribution to the placenta.

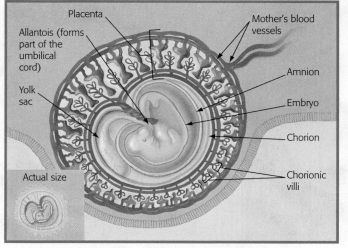

(c) Day 31: The embryo and its life-support equipment

January					
			0	Conception	
	Day 6		Day 10		
			Day 31		

✓ CHECKPOINT

Why should a woman who is trying to get pregnant avoid drugs such as alcohol and nicotine?

Answer: Drugs can pass to the developing embryo from the mother's bloodstream and affect it before the mother even knows she is pregnant.

The Stages of Pregnancy

In this section, we use the series of photographs in **Figure 26.17** to illustrate the rest of human development as it takes place in the uterus. For convenience, we divide pregnancy (the period from conception to birth) into three **trimesters** of about 3 months each.

The First Trimester

The first photograph in Figure 26.17 shows a human embryo about 5 weeks after fertilization. In that brief time, a single cell has developed into a highly organized multicellular embryo about 7 mm (0.28 inch) long. Its brain and spinal cord have begun to take shape. It also has four stumpy limb buds, a short tail, and primitive gill-like structures. Overall, a month-old human embryo looks pretty much like a month-old embryo of any other vertebrate species (see Figure 13.10).

When did you have structures similar to gills and a tail?

The next photograph shows a developing human, now called a fetus, about 9 weeks after fertilization. The large pinkish structure on the left is the placenta, which is attached to the fetus by the umbilical cord. The clear sac around the fetus is the amnion. The fetus is about 5.5 cm (2.2 inches) long and has all of its organs and major body parts, including muscles and the bones of the back and ribs. The limb buds have become tiny arms and legs with fingers and toes. By the end of the first trimester, the fetus looks like a miniature human being, albeit one with an oversized head. By this time, the sex of the fetus can be determined by an ultrasound exam **(Figure 26.18)**.

The Second Trimester

The main developmental changes during the second and third trimesters involve an increase in size and general refinement of the human features—nothing as dramatic as the changes of the first trimester. A 14-week-old fetus is about 6 cm (2.4 inches) long.

At 20 weeks, well into the second trimester, the fetus is about 19 cm (7.6 inches) long, weighs about half a kilogram (1 pound), and has the face of an infant, complete with eyebrows and eyelashes. Its arms, legs, fingers, and toes have lengthened. It also has fingernails and toenails and is covered with fine hair. By this time, the fetal heartbeat is detectable with a stethoscope, and the mother can usually feel the fetus moving. Because of the limited space in the uterus, the fetus flexes forward into the so-called fetal position, with its head tucked against

▼ Figure 26.17 **The development of a human.**

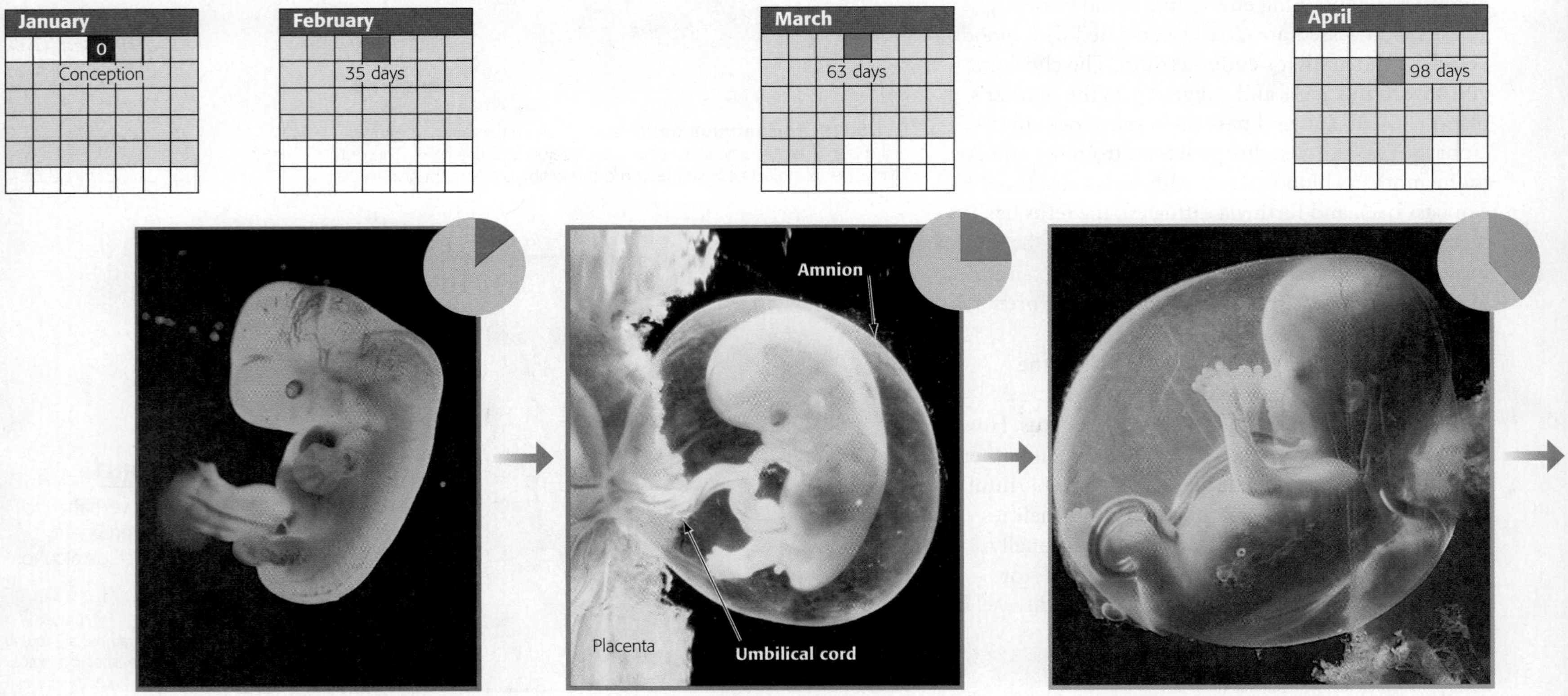

5 weeks (35 days)   **9 weeks** (63 days)   **14 weeks** (98 days)

its knees. By the end of the second trimester, the fetus's eyes are open, its teeth are forming, and its bones have begun to harden.

The Third Trimester

The third trimester is a time of rapid growth as the fetus gains the strength it will need to survive outside the protective environment of the uterus. Babies born prematurely—as early as 24 weeks—may survive, but they require special medical care after birth. During the third trimester, the fetus's circulatory and respiratory systems undergo changes that will allow the switch to air breathing. The fetus begins to gain the ability to maintain its own temperature, and its muscles thicken. It also loses much of its fine body hair, except on its head. The fetus usually rotates so that its head points down toward the cervix, and it becomes less active as it fills the space in the uterus. As the fetus grows and the uterus expands around it, the mother's abdominal organs may be squeezed, causing frequent urination, digestive troubles, and backaches. At birth, babies average about 50 cm (20 inches) in length and weigh 3–4 kg (6–8 pounds). ✓

▼ **Figure 26.18 Ultrasound imaging.** An ultrasound image is produced when high-frequency sounds from an ultrasound scanner held against a pregnant woman's abdomen bounce off the fetus. The inset image shows a fetus in the uterus at about 18 weeks.

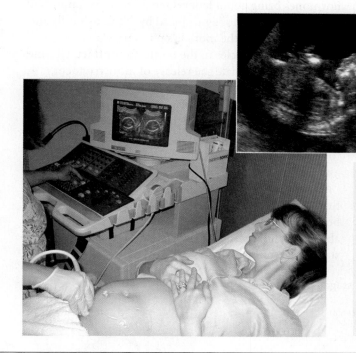

✓ CHECKPOINT

As a human develops in the uterus, why are the first-trimester changes considered the most dramatic?

Answer: The development proceeds from a single-celled zygote to a miniature human. Subsequent changes are mainly growth and refinement of the structures developed during the first trimester.

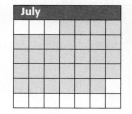
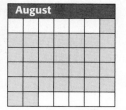

May   140 days   June   July   August   September   October   280 days

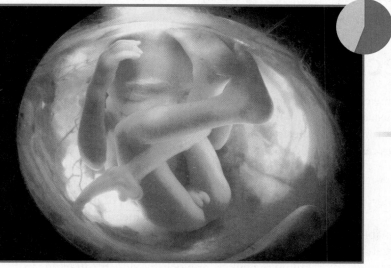

20 weeks (140 days)

At birth (280 days)

567

Childbirth

The birth of a child is brought about by **labor**, a series of strong, rhythmic contractions of the uterus. Several hormones bring about labor. One of the most important is oxytocin, a hormone produced by the fetus's cells and, late in pregnancy, the mother's pituitary gland. Oxytocin stimulates muscles in the uterus to contract. Uterine contractions stimulate the release of more oxytocin, which in turn increases the contractions—an example of positive-feedback control. The result is climactic—the intense muscle contractions that propel a baby from the womb. If a mother is overdue, or if labor has continued for a long time, a doctor may inject oxytocin to promote a more rapid birth.

Figure 26.19 shows the three stages of labor. **1** The first stage, dilation, is the time from the onset of labor until the cervix dilates, or opens, to a width of about 10 cm (about 4 inches). Dilation is the longest stage of labor, typically lasting 6–12 hours, sometimes considerably longer. **2** The period from full dilation of the cervix to delivery of the infant is called the expulsion stage. Strong uterine contractions, lasting about 1 minute each, occur every 2–3 minutes, and the mother feels an increasing urge to push with her abdominal muscles. Within a period of 20 minutes to an hour or so, the infant is forced down and out of the uterus and vagina. After the baby is born, the umbilical cord is clamped and cut. The stump of the cord remains for several weeks, then shrivels and falls off, leaving the belly button. **3** The final stage is the delivery of the placenta ("afterbirth"), usually within 15 minutes after the birth of the baby.

Hormones continue to be important after birth. Decreasing levels of progesterone and estrogen allow the uterus to start returning to its prepregnancy state. The pituitary hormone prolactin promotes milk production (called lactation) by the mammary glands. At first, a yellowish antibody-rich fluid called colostrum is secreted. After 2–3 days, normal milk production begins. ✔

✔ CHECKPOINT

The onset of labor is marked by the dilation of the
_____.

Answer: cervix

▼ **Figure 26.19 The three stages of labor.**

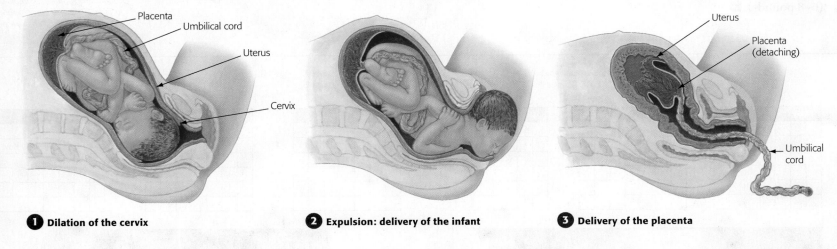

1 Dilation of the cervix   **2** Expulsion: delivery of the infant   **3** Delivery of the placenta

---

Reproductive Technologies

In previous sections, we examined the normal means of human sexual reproduction. Many couples, however, are unable to conceive children because of one or more abnormalities. Today, reproductive technologies can solve many of these problems.

Infertility

About 15% of couples who want children are unable to conceive, even after a year of regular, unprotected sex. Such a condition is called **infertility**, and it can have many causes.

In most cases, infertility can be traced to problems with the man. His testes may not produce enough sperm (a "low sperm count"), or the sperm may not be vigorous enough to reach an egg. In other cases, infertility is caused by **impotence**, also called erectile dysfunction, the inability to maintain an erection. Temporary impotence can result from alcohol or drug use or from psychological problems. Permanent impotence can result from nervous system or circulatory problems.

Female infertility can result from a lack of eggs, a failure to ovulate, or blocked oviducts (often due to scarring resulting from a sexually transmitted disease).

Other women are able to conceive but cannot support a growing embryo in the uterus. The resulting multiple miscarriages can take a heavy emotional toll.

There are reproductive technologies that can help many cases of infertility. For a low sperm count, there is often a simple solution. Underproduction of sperm is frequently caused by a man's scrotum being too warm, so a switch of underwear from briefs (which hold the scrotum close to the body) to boxers may help. If that doesn't work, sperm can be collected, concentrated, and then injected into the woman's uterus via the vagina. Drug therapies (such as Viagra) and penile implants can treat impotence. If a man produces no functioning sperm, the couple may elect to use another man's sperm from a sperm bank.

If a woman has normal eggs that are not being released properly, hormone injections can induce ovulation; such treatments frequently result in multiple pregnancies (twins, triplets, or more). If a woman has no eggs of her own, they can be obtained from a donor for fertilization and injection into the uterus. Although sperm can be collected without any danger to the donor, the collection of eggs is a surgical procedure that involves pain and risk for the donating woman. For this reason, egg "donors" are typically paid for their time and discomfort.

If a woman cannot maintain pregnancy, she and her partner may enter into a legal contract with a surrogate mother who agrees to carry the couple's child to birth. This method has worked for many couples, but serious ethical and legal problems can arise if a surrogate mother changes her mind and wants to keep the baby she has carried. A number of states have laws restricting surrogate motherhood. ✔

In Vitro Fertilization

A procedure performed in vitro ("in glass") happens under artificial laboratory conditions rather than within the living body (in vivo). **In vitro fertilization (IVF)**—sometimes called the creation of a "test-tube baby"—begins with the administration of drugs that promote the development of multiple eggs (instead of the one egg that typically occurs during each ovulation). The eggs are surgically removed and then fertilized with sperm in a petri dish **(Figure 26.20)**, allowed to develop for several days, and then injected into a woman's uterus. There, one or more embryos may successfully implant and continue development. The sperm and eggs, as well as the embryos created, can be used immediately or frozen for later use.

☑ **CHECKPOINT**
What is the difference between infertility and impotence?

Answer: Infertility is the inability to produce offspring; impotence is the inability to maintain an erection.

▼ **Figure 26.20 In vitro fertilization.**

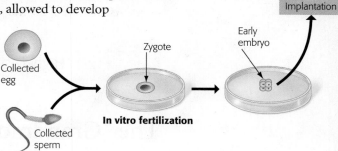

Collected egg

Zygote

Early embryo

Implantation

Collected sperm

In vitro fertilization

High-Tech Babies THE PROCESS OF SCIENCE

Can Viable Embryos Be Identified?

In vitro fertilization typically involves the creation of many embryos. Because the procedure is so expensive, it would be helpful to identify those embryos with the greatest chance of success.

To address this need, some European researchers started with the **observation** that cells can be removed from the outer layer of a preimplantation blastocyst without harming the embryo. The researchers formed the **hypothesis** that analyzing the gene activity within such cells could provide useful information about the chances of a successful pregnancy from the embryo. Their **prediction** was that gene expression would differ between successful and unsuccessful embryos.

Their **experiment** involved a combination of several procedures that you have learned about in previous chapters. The participants were 48 patients who produced 153 blastocysts after undergoing IVF. On the 5th day after fertilization, the researchers collected cells from each embryo **(Figure 26.21)**. After the embryos were transferred into the mothers, 37 of them resulted in healthy births. DNA samples from each baby were matched to the blastocyst cells using DNA profiling (see Chapter 12), allowing researchers to determine which embryos led to successful pregnancies and which did not. The embryonic cells were then screened using DNA microarrays (see Chapter 11) to reveal which genes were turned on and off in each embryo. Their **results** identified a large number of differences in gene expression between embryos that were destined for success and those that were not. In particular, genes for cell-to-cell communication and the ability of cells to stick together were more active in the successful embryos. Fertility researchers hope that these results will lead to tests that can identify the embryos most likely to result in pregnancy, reducing the need to implant multiple embryos and therefore reducing the likelihood of multiple pregnancy and the risks involved.

▼ **Figure 26.21 A 5-day-old human embryo.**

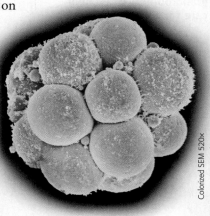

Colorized SEM 520x

The Ethics of IVF

Recent research has shown that IVF babies have a slightly greater risk of birth defects than babies born from natural conception. Despite such risks and the high cost (around $10,000 for each attempt, whether it succeeds or not), IVF is now routinely performed at medical centers throughout the world and results in the birth of thousands of babies each year.

One major difference between natural and artificial fertilization is that technology offers choices that nature does not. For example, sperm can be sorted based on whether they contain an X or Y chromosome, increasing the likelihood of creating a zygote of a particular sex. Furthermore, as discussed in the Process of Science section, cells can be harmlessly removed from early embryos; they can then be tested for disease-causing (or other) genes. As analysis of the human genome progresses, the potential to screen for diseases and physical traits increases. Parents may thus have a lot of information they can use in choosing which embryos to implant.

The concept of parenthood has been greatly complicated by modern reproductive technologies. Mix-ups in fertility clinics have resulted in the implantation of embryos into the wrong women. When this happens, who has what rights? Divorcing couples have sued each other for custody of frozen embryos. An infertile couple could purchase eggs from a woman, sperm from a man, and then hire a surrogate to carry the baby. Who, then, are the baby's true parents? Each new reproductive technology raises moral and legal questions. Many of these have not yet been addressed, much less resolved, by society. All of us need to understand the science behind these complex issues so that we can make informed decisions as citizens and potential parents. ✓

✓ **CHECKPOINT**

Explain how up to five people can be involved in creating one baby.

Answer: A couple can hire a surrogate mother to carry an embryo created with gametes from a sperm donor and an egg donor.

High-Tech Babies EVOLUTION CONNECTION

The "Grandmother Hypothesis"

In this chapter, you have read how reproductive technologies can allow infertile couples to have babies. In recent years, technology has also made it possible for women to become pregnant after menopause, the cessation of ovulation and menstruation caused by changes in hormone levels. Menopause occurs around age 50, but in vitro fertilization has enabled some postmenopausal women to bear children up to age 70.

Given such efforts to artificially extend a woman's childbearing years, it may seem that menopause is an evolutionary disadvantage. Indeed, in most species, females retain their reproductive capacity throughout life. If evolutionary fitness is measured by the number of surviving, fertile offspring, why does menopause occur in humans? Evolutionary biologists have formed several intriguing hypotheses.

As discussed in Chapter 17, a larger brain is one of the hallmarks of human evolution. The development of a large brain requires significant time and nutrients. Humans, unlike almost every other species, continue to depend on their mothers to provide food and care for many years after weaning. Natural selection may thus have favored reproductive adaptations that promote extended maternal care. Human mothers may bear fewer children than some other animals, but each one receives a significant investment of resources and therefore has an increased chance of survival.

Some researchers speculate that menopause actually increases a woman's evolutionary fitness in the long run. Perhaps losing the ability to become pregnant allows a woman to focus her energy on caring for the children she has, rather than producing more that might not survive. Furthermore, women who can no longer bear children themselves can contribute by helping to raise their grandchildren (Figure 26.22). Because a woman shares one-half of her genes with each of her children and one-quarter of her genes with each grandchild, helping to raise two grandchildren can help perpetuate as many genes to future generations as bearing one more child. Thus, even though menopause may cause a woman to have fewer children, this "grandmother hypothesis" suggests that it may actually increase the number of closely related children who will themselves reach maturity, ensuring the continuation of the postmenopausal grandmother's genes. Viewed this way, the unusual reproductive life cycle of human females is another example of biology's unifying theme of evolution.

▼ **Figure 26.22 Human grandmothers often help care for young children.**

Chapter Review

SUMMARY OF KEY CONCEPTS

(MB) Go to **www.masteringbiology.com** for homework assignments, practice quizzes, Pearson eText, and more.

Unifying Concepts of Animal Reproduction

Asexual Reproduction

In asexual reproduction, one parent produces genetically identical offspring by budding, fission, or fragmentation followed by regeneration. Asexual reproduction enables a single individual to produce many offspring rapidly, but the resulting genetically identical population may be less able to survive environmental changes.

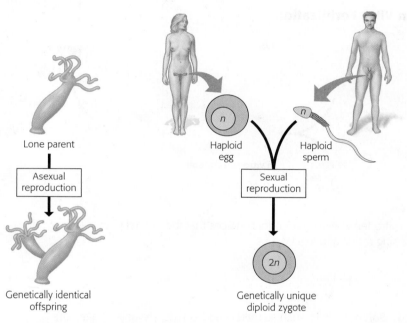

Sexual Reproduction

Sexual reproduction increases the variation among offspring, which may enhance reproductive success in changing environments.

Human Reproduction

Male Reproductive Anatomy

The human reproductive system consists of a pair of gonads, ducts that carry gametes, and structures for sexual intercourse. Located in an external sac called the scrotum, a man's gonads (the testes) produce sperm, which are expelled through ducts during ejaculation. Several glands contribute to the formation of fluid that carries, nourishes, and protects sperm. This fluid and the sperm constitute semen.

Female Reproductive Anatomy

A woman's gonads (her ovaries) contain follicles that nurture eggs and produce sex hormones. Oviducts convey eggs to the uterus, where a fertilized egg develops into a fetus. The uterus opens into the vagina, which receives the penis during intercourse and forms the birth canal.

Gametogenesis

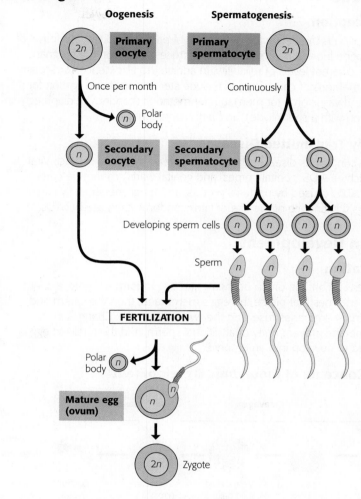

The Female Reproductive Cycle

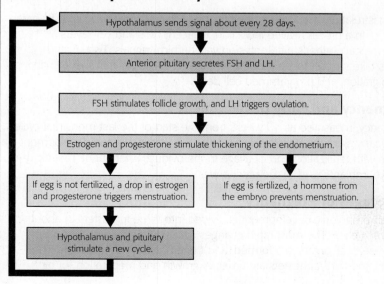

Reproductive Health

Contraception

Contraception is the deliberate prevention of pregnancy. Different forms of contraception block different steps in the process of becoming pregnant and have different levels of reliability. In addition to abstinence, particularly effective methods of contraception include sterilization (tubal ligation for women and vasectomy for men), barrier methods (condom or diaphragm in conjunction with a spermicide), and birth control pills.

Sexually Transmitted Diseases

STDs are contagious diseases that can be spread by sexual contact. Viral STDs (such as AIDS, genital herpes, and genital warts) cannot be cured, whereas STDs caused by bacteria, protists, and fungi are generally curable with drugs. Abstinence or the use of latex condoms can prevent STDs.

Human Development

Fertilization

During fertilization, the union of sperm and egg to form a zygote, a sperm releases enzymes that pierce the egg's membrane; then the sperm and egg plasma membranes fuse, and the two nuclei unite. Changes in the egg membrane prevent entry of additional sperm, and the fertilized egg is stimulated to develop into an embryo.

Basic Concepts of Embryonic Development

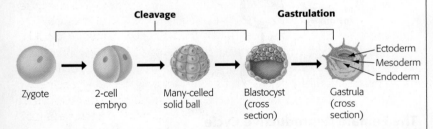

After gastrulation, the three embryonic tissue layers give rise to specific organ systems. In a process called induction, adjacent cells and cell layers influence each other's differentiation via chemical signals. Tissues and organs take shape in a developing embryo as a result of cell shape changes, cell migration, and programmed cell death.

Pregnancy and Early Development

Pregnancy, measured as 40 weeks from the start of the last menstrual cycle, is the carrying of the developing young in the uterus. Human development begins with fertilization and cleavage in the oviduct. After about 1 week, the embryo implants itself in the uterine wall.

The Stages of Pregnancy

Human embryonic development is divided into three trimesters of about 3 months each. The most rapid changes occur during the first trimester. By 9 weeks, all organs are formed, and the embryo is called a fetus. The second and third trimesters are times of growth and preparation for birth.

Childbirth

Hormonal changes induce birth. The cervix dilates, the baby is expelled by strong muscular contractions, and the placenta follows. Prolactin then stimulates milk production.

Reproductive Technologies

Infertility

Infertility, the inability to have children after one year of trying, is most often due to problems in the man, such as underproduction of sperm. Female infertility can arise from a lack of eggs or a failure to ovulate. Technologies can help treat many forms of infertility.

In Vitro Fertilization

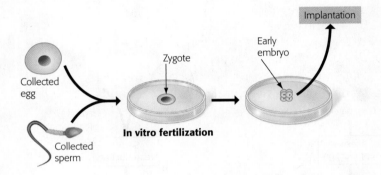

In vitro fertilization

In vitro fertilization (IVF) offers choices that the natural pathway does not, raising moral and legal issues.

SELF-QUIZ

1. Some animals, such as rotifers and aphids, are able to alternate between sexual and asexual reproduction. Under what conditions might it be advantageous to reproduce asexually? Sexually?

2. A fertility specialist determines that a patient is producing a normal amount of sperm but the semen does not contain enough of the fluids needed to nourish the sperm. Which structures are most likely responsible for this problem?

3. Match each reproductive structure with its description:
   a. uterus   1. female gonad
   b. vas deferens   2. site of spermatogenesis
   c. oviduct   3. site of fertilization
   d. ovary   4. site of gestation
   e. endometrium   5. lining of uterus
   f. testis   6. sperm duct

4. A woman has had several miscarriages. Her doctor suspects that a hormonal insufficiency has been causing the lining of the uterus to break down as it does during menstruation, terminating her pregnancies. Treatment with which of the following might help her remain pregnant?
   a. oxytocin
   b. HCG
   c. follicle-stimulating hormone
   d. prolactin

5. Why is it important that the hormones FSH and LH are inhibited after ovulation has occurred in the female cycle? Which female hormones inhibit FSH and LH?

6. What advantage do abstinence and condoms have over other forms of contraception?

7. How does a zygote differ from a mature egg (ovum)?
   a. A zygote has more chromosomes.
   b. A zygote is smaller.
   c. A zygote consists of more than one cell.
   d. A zygote is much larger.

8. If a baby is born missing the outer layer of skin, which of the following layers would have been the most likely site of damage in the embryo?
   a. endoderm
   b. mesoderm
   c. ectoderm
   d. stem cells

9. In an embryo, nerve cells grow out from the spinal cord and form connections with the muscles they will eventually control. What mechanism described in this chapter might explain how these cells "know" where to go and which cells to connect with?

10. A pregnant woman is two weeks past her due date, and the doctor decides to induce her labor. The natural hormone that would be needed is _____.

11. The procedure that creates a "test-tube baby" is _____. What does this term literally mean?

Answers to these questions can be found in Appendix: Self-Quiz Answers.

THE PROCESS OF SCIENCE

12. A typical egg cell survives about 24 hours, but some may survive up to 48 hours. A typical sperm survives 48 hours, but some may live up to 5 days. Assume that a female ovulates on day 14 of her cycle. How many days prior to ovulation and after ovulation is there a chance for pregnancy to occur? What is the total fertility window for this female?

13. A physician is trying to determine the cause of a male patient's infertility. Based on what you know about the male reproductive system, what would be the most logical things to test for?

BIOLOGY AND SOCIETY

14. New technology enables doctors to save a small percentage of babies born 16 weeks prematurely. A baby born this early weighs just over 1 pound and faces months in an intensive-care nursery. The cost for care may be hundreds of thousands of dollars per infant. Some people wonder whether such a huge technological and personnel investment should be devoted to such a small number of babies. They feel that limited resources might be better directed at providing prenatal care that could prevent many premature births. What do you think? In what ways should cost influence medical decisions?

15. Some infertile couples hire a surrogate mother to have their biological child. When couples enter into an agreement with a surrogate mother, all parties sign a contract. But there have been cases where a surrogate mother signed a contract but then decided not to give up the baby to the couple who hired her. Do you think a surrogate mother should have the right to change her mind and keep the baby, even though it is not genetically hers? In some cases, the surrogate will also donate her eggs to be fertilized by the male's sperm, making the baby genetically hers. Should she have a right to change her mind after she has signed a contract and the baby is born? How should judges decide these cases? Can you suggest any laws or regulations for such situations?

16. When a couple uses in vitro fertilization to produce a baby, they are faced with some novel choices. Typically, more embryos are produced than will be used during any one procedure. Thus, a subset of prepared embryos has to be chosen for implantation. How should parents decide which embryos to use? Should they have the right to choose embryos based on the presence or absence of disease-causing genes? What about the sex of the embryo? Should parents be able to choose embryos for implantation based on any criteria? How would you distinguish acceptable criteria from unacceptable ones? Do you think such options should be legislated?

27 Nervous, Sensory, and Locomotor Systems

Feeling the waves.
Migrating elephants may use long-distance seismic waves to communicate with other members of the herd.

Extrahuman Senses BIOLOGY AND SOCIETY

The Seismic Sense of Elephants

We humans have keen senses, but many animals perceive the world in ways we cannot. For example, some bats use echolocation, emitting ultrasonic waves (high-pitched sounds above the range of human hearing) and then navigating by measuring their echoes. Many fishes detect prey by electroreception, detecting changes in the electric fields they produce using organs in their tails. Many animals—including birds, fishes, turtles, and bees—navigate using magnetoreception, the ability to detect Earth's magnetic field.

In the mid-1980s, wildlife biologists discovered that elephants, the largest land animals on Earth, can communicate using low-rumbling infrasounds, sounds too low to be heard by human ears. Under ideal conditions, such sounds can travel for 5 miles through the air, allowing elephants to communicate over long distances. While studying elephants, scientists also began to notice an unusual behavior: A group of elephants—in unison and for no apparent reason—will often freeze, lifting one foot in the air and laying their trunk along the ground. Applying sensitive listening equipment (like the instruments used to detect earthquakes), wildlife researchers discovered that the elephants are responding to a sense that humans lack: the ability to detect seismic waves, which are low-frequency vibrations in the ground.

Recent research has suggested that elephants can detect seismic waves using specialized pressure-sensing nerve endings in their feet and trunk. Such abilities may be an evolutionary adaptation that allows elephants to migrate, meet, and mate over great distances of the African savannah. Perhaps the elephants are sending specific signals to each other; after all, a typical elephant weighs 6 tons or more, so a purposeful foot stomp can produce a sizable ground wave. Or maybe the seismic activity is merely a by-product of elephant activities such as running or trumpeting. Research into the senses of these remarkable creatures remains an active and fascinating area of biology.

Although as a human you lack the animal senses described here, you are able to perceive the world and to process your perceptions. You accomplish this using your brain, which is the hub of an intricate network of structures that detect, integrate, and respond to stimuli from the environment. By examining the structure and function of the nervous, sensory, and motor systems, we will explore how stimuli are translated into responses within the body. Let's begin by focusing on the processing center, the nervous system.

An Overview of Animal Nervous Systems

The **nervous system** forms a communication and coordination network throughout an animal's body. Nervous systems are the most intricately organized data processing systems on Earth. Your brain, for instance, contains an estimated 100 billion **neurons**, nerve cells that carry electrical signals from one part of the body to another. Each neuron may communicate with thousands of others, forming networks that enable us to move, perceive our surroundings, learn, and remember. In this section, we'll focus on features that are common to the nervous systems of all animals.

Organization of Nervous Systems

The nervous systems of most animals have two main anatomical divisions. The **central nervous system (CNS)** consists of the brain and, in vertebrates, the spinal cord. The **peripheral nervous system (PNS)** is made up mostly of nerves that carry signals into and out of the CNS. A **nerve** is a communication line made from cable-like bundles of neuron fibers tightly wrapped in connective tissue.

Figure 27.1 highlights the three interconnected functions of the nervous system and the three types of neurons that carry out these functions. **Sensory input** is the process of sending signals from sensory receptors, such as light-detecting cells

of the eyes, to the CNS. **Sensory neurons** in the PNS (shown in blue) convey this information. **Integration** is the analysis and interpretation of sensory signals and the formulation of appropriate responses. **Interneurons** (green), located entirely within the CNS, perform integration. **Motor output** is the process of sending signals from the integration centers to **effector cells**, such as muscle cells, that perform the body's responses (moving a leg in this example). Motor output is performed by **motor neurons** in the PNS (purple). ☑

▼ **Figure 27.1 Organization of a nervous system.** This figure shows only one neuron of each functional type, but body activity actually involves many. A simplified version of this figure will keep you oriented throughout the chapter.

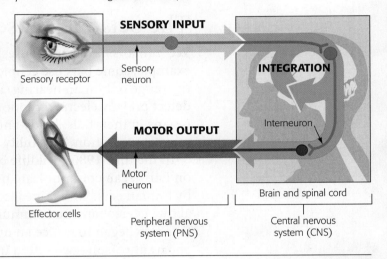

Neurons

The three types of neurons just described vary widely in shape, but most of them share some common features. **Figure 27.2** depicts a motor neuron, like those that carry signals from your spinal cord to your skeletal muscles. A motor neuron has a large **cell body** housing the nucleus and other organelles. Two types of extensions project from the cell body. Numerous **dendrites** are often short and highly branched. Dendrites *receive* incoming messages from other neurons and convey this information toward the cell body.

The other type of extension, a single long fiber called an **axon**, *transmits* signals toward another neuron or toward an effector cell. Some axons, such as the ones that reach from your spinal cord to muscle cells in your feet, can be over a meter long.

Neurons make up only part of a nervous system. Outnumbering neurons by as many as 50 to 1 are **supporting cells** that protect, insulate, and reinforce the neurons. In many vertebrates, axons that convey signals rapidly are enclosed along most of their length by an insulating material called the **myelin sheath**. The myelin sheath is a chain of bead-like supporting cells. The myelin sheath helps speed electrical transmission

◄ **Figure 27.2 Structure of a motor neuron.** This diagram shows a motor neuron. The flow of the electrical signal through a neuron follows this path: dendrite → cell body → axon.

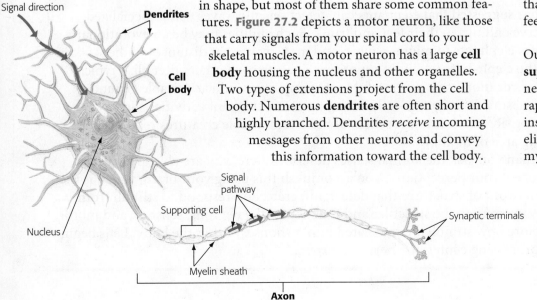

along an axon. In the human nervous system, signals can travel along a myelinated axon about 150 m/sec (over 330 mph!), which means that a command from your brain can make your fingers move in just a few milliseconds.

The debilitating autoimmune disease multiple sclerosis (MS) leads to a gradual destruction of the myelin sheath by the individual's own immune system. This causes a progressive loss of the ability to send signals and control muscles. MS has no cure, but drugs that suppress the immune system can relieve symptoms and slow its progress.

What causes multiple sclerosis?

Returning to Figure 27.2, notice that the axon ends in a cluster of branches. A typical axon has hundreds or thousands of these branches, each with a synaptic terminal at the very end. As we will see later, each **synaptic terminal** relays signals to another neuron or to an effector cell such as a muscle cell. With the basic structure of a neuron in mind, let's take a closer look at how neurons convey signals. ✔

Sending a Signal through a Neuron

To understand nerve signals, we must first study a resting neuron, one that is not transmitting a signal. A resting neuron has potential energy that can be put to work to send nerve signals from one part of the body to another. This potential energy exists in the form of an electrical charge difference across the neuron's plasma membrane. The inside of the cell is negatively charged relative to the outside. Because opposite charges tend to move toward each other, the membrane stores energy by holding opposite charges apart, much like a battery. This difference in charge (voltage) that exists across the plasma membrane of a resting neuron is called the **resting potential**.

The resting potential is caused by the presence of differently charged ions (primarily Na^+ and K^+) on either side of the membrane. What keeps the ions apart? As mentioned in Chapter 5, the hydrophobic interior of the membrane's phospholipid bilayer doesn't let ions pass through. However, the membrane has protein channels and pumps that can allow positive ions across. By carefully controlling the passage of these ions, a neuron can tap into the energy stored in the resting potential.

The Action Potential

Turning on a flashlight uses the potential energy stored in a battery to create light. In a similar way, stimulating a neuron's plasma membrane can trigger the use of the membrane's potential energy to generate an electrical nerve signal. A **stimulus** is any factor that causes a nerve signal to be generated. Examples of stimuli include light, sound, touching a hot surface, or a chemical signal from another neuron. A stimulus of sufficient strength can trigger an **action potential**, a nerve signal that carries information along a neuron. The signal is actually a self-propagating change in the voltage across the plasma membrane.

Figure 27.3 shows the series of events involved in generating an action potential. As you'll see, two different sets of ion channels are involved in this process. ❶ At first, the membrane is at its resting potential, positively charged outside and negatively charged inside. ❷ A stimulus triggers the opening of a few of the first set of ion channels in the membrane (represented by the blue arrows), allowing a few positive ions to enter the neuron. This tiny change makes the inside surface of the membrane slightly less negative than before. If the stimulus is strong enough, a sufficient number of channels open to reach the **threshold**, the minimum change in a membrane's voltage that must occur to trigger the action potential. ❸ Once threshold is reached, more of these channels open and more positive ions rapidly rush in. As a result, the interior of this region of the cell becomes positively charged with respect to the outside. ❹ This electrical change triggers the closing of the first set of channels. Meanwhile, a second set of channels opens (green arrows), allowing other positive ions to diffuse rapidly out and returning the membrane to its resting potential. Within a living neuron, this whole process takes just a few milliseconds, meaning a neuron can produce hundreds of nerve signals in a second.

☑ **CHECKPOINT**

Arrange the following parts of a neuron in the sequence that a signal would pass through them: axon, cell body, dendrite, synaptic terminal. For each part, indicate whether one or many are found in a typical neuron.

Answer: many dendrites → one cell body → one axon → many synaptic terminals

▼ Figure 27.3 **Generation of an action potential.**

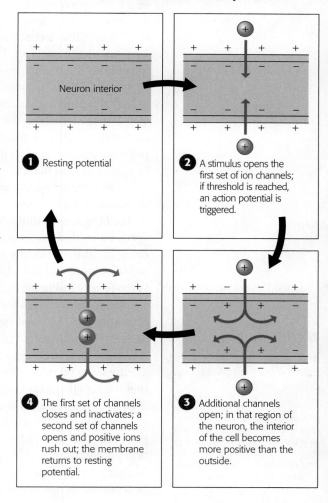

❶ Resting potential

❷ A stimulus opens the first set of ion channels; if threshold is reached, an action potential is triggered.

❸ Additional channels open; in that region of the neuron, the interior of the cell becomes more positive than the outside.

❹ The first set of channels closes and inactivates; a second set of channels opens and positive ions rush out; the membrane returns to resting potential.

Propagation of the Signal

An action potential is a localized electrical event—a rapid change from the resting potential at a specific place along the neuron. A nerve signal starts out as an action potential generated near the cell body of the neuron. To function as a long-distance signal, this local event must be passed along the neuron. This process is like tipping the first of a row of standing dominoes: The first domino does not travel along the row, but its fall is relayed to the end of the row, one domino at a time.

Figure 27.4 shows the changes that occur in part of an axon as a nerve signal passes from left to right. Let's start by focusing only on the axon region at the far left in each panel. ❶ When this region of the axon (blue) has its first set of channels open, positive ions diffuse inward (blue arrows), and an action potential is generated. ❷ That same region then opens the second set of channels, allowing other positive ions to diffuse out of the axon (green arrows) while closing the first set of channels that allow ions in. ❸ A short time later, we would see no action potential at this (far left) spot because the membrane here has restored itself and returned to its resting potential.

Now let's see how these events lead to the "domino effect" of a nerve signal. In step 1 of the figure, the blue arrows pointing sideways within the axon indicate local spreading of the electrical changes caused by the positive ions entering the neuron. These changes trigger the opening of the first set of channels in the membrane just to the right of the action potential. As a result, a second action potential is generated, as indicated by the blue region in step 2. In the same way, a third action potential is generated in step 3. At each point along the neuron, the action potential triggers changes in the adjacent region that result in propagation of the action potential along the neuron.

So why are action potentials propagated in only one direction along the axon (left to right in the figure)? As the blue arrows indicate, local electrical changes do spread in both directions in the axon. However, these changes cannot open the first set of channels and generate an action potential when these channels are inactivated (step 4 in Figure 27.3). Thus, an action potential cannot be generated in the regions where the second set of channels is open and positive charge is leaving the axon (green in Figure 27.4).

Action potentials are all-or-none events; that is, they are the same no matter how strong or weak the stimulus that triggers them (as long as threshold is reached). This is like pulling a trigger: It doesn't matter how gently or roughly you pull the trigger, once it reaches a certain point, the gun is fired just the same. How, then, do action potentials relay different intensities of information? Such information can be achieved by sending more action potentials in a given amount of time. For example,

in the neurons connecting your ears to your brain, loud sounds generate more action potentials per second than quiet sounds. Once your CNS receives information in the form of action potentials, it can process the information and formulate a response to it. ☑

▼ **Figure 27.4 Propagation of an action potential along an axon.**

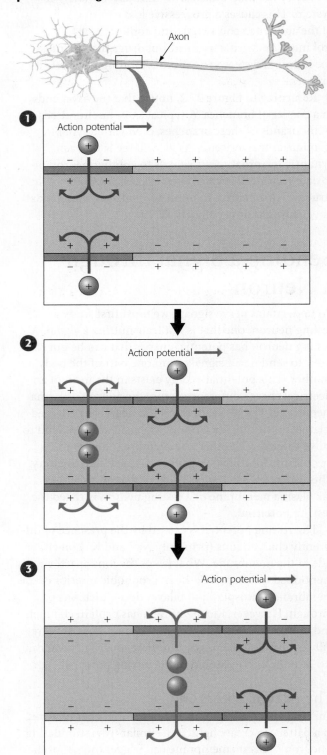

☑ CHECKPOINT

In what way is an action potential an example of positive feedback?

Answer: Positive feedback occurs when the result of a process further stimulates that process. The opening of channels caused by stimulation of the neuron changes the membrane potential, and this change causes more channels to open.

Passing a Signal from a Neuron to a Receiving Cell

If an action potential travels in one direction along a neuron, what happens when the signal arrives at the end of the neuron? To continue conveying information, the signal must be passed to another cell. This occurs at a **synapse**, or relay point, between a neuron and a receiving cell. The receiving cell can be another neuron or an effector cell such as a muscle cell or endocrine cell.

Synapses come in two varieties: electrical and chemical. In an electrical synapse, electric current passes directly from one neuron to the next. In the human body, electrical synapses are found in the heart and digestive tract, where they help maintain steady, rhythmic muscle contractions. Chemical synapses are prevalent in most other organs, including skeletal muscles, and in the central nervous system.

Chemical synapses have a narrow gap, called the **synaptic cleft**, separating the synaptic terminal of the sending neuron from the receiving cell **(Figure 27.5)**. When the action potential (an electrical signal) reaches the end of the sending neuron, it is converted to a chemical signal consisting of molecules of neurotransmitter. A **neurotransmitter** is a chemical that carries information from a nerve cell to another cell that will react, such as another nerve cell or an effector cell. Once a neurotransmitter conveys a chemical signal from the sending neuron, an action potential may then be generated in the receiving cell.

Let's follow the events that occur at a synapse between two neurons in Figure 27.5. ❶ An action potential (red arrow) arrives at the synaptic terminal. ❷ The action potential causes vesicles filled with neurotransmitter ( ) to fuse with the plasma membrane of the sending neuron. ❸ The fused vesicles release their neurotransmitter molecules into the synaptic cleft. ❹ The released neurotransmitter molecules diffuse across the cleft and bind to complementary receptors on ion channel proteins in the receiving neuron's plasma membrane. ❺ The binding of neurotransmitter to receptors opens the ion channels. With the channels open, ions can diffuse into or out of the receiving neuron. In many cases, this triggers a new action potential; in other cases, a neurotransmitter inhibits the generation of an action potential. ❻ The neurotransmitter is broken down or transported back to the sending neuron, causing the ion channels in the receiving cell's plasma membrane to close. Step 6 ensures that the neurotransmitter's effect on the receiving neuron is brief and precise.

▼ **Figure 27.5 Neuron communication at a synaptic cleft.**

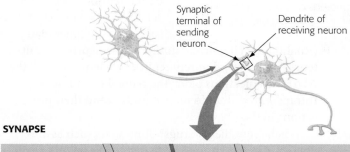

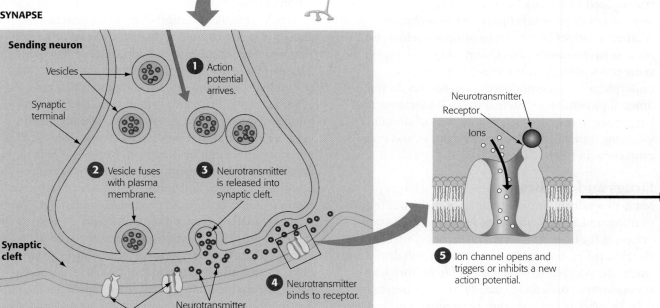

SYNAPSE

Sending neuron

Vesicles

Synaptic terminal

❶ Action potential arrives.

❷ Vesicle fuses with plasma membrane.

❸ Neurotransmitter is released into synaptic cleft.

Synaptic cleft

❹ Neurotransmitter binds to receptor.

Receiving neuron — Ion channels — Neurotransmitter molecules

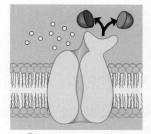

Neurotransmitter
Receptor
Ions

❺ Ion channel opens and triggers or inhibits a new action potential.

❻ Ion channel closes. Neurotransmitter is broken down and released.

☑ CHECKPOINT

How does the structure of a synapse ensure that signals pass only in one direction, from a sending neuron to a receiving cell?

Answer: At the synapse, only the sending neuron releases a neurotransmitter, and only the receiving cell has receptors to receive the neurotransmitter.

Chemical synapses can process extremely complex information. A neuron may receive input from hundreds of other neurons via thousands of synaptic terminals (**Figure 27.6**). The inputs can be highly varied because each sending neuron may secrete a different quantity or kind of neurotransmitter. These factors account for the nervous system's ability to process huge amounts of complex stimuli and formulate appropriate responses. ☑

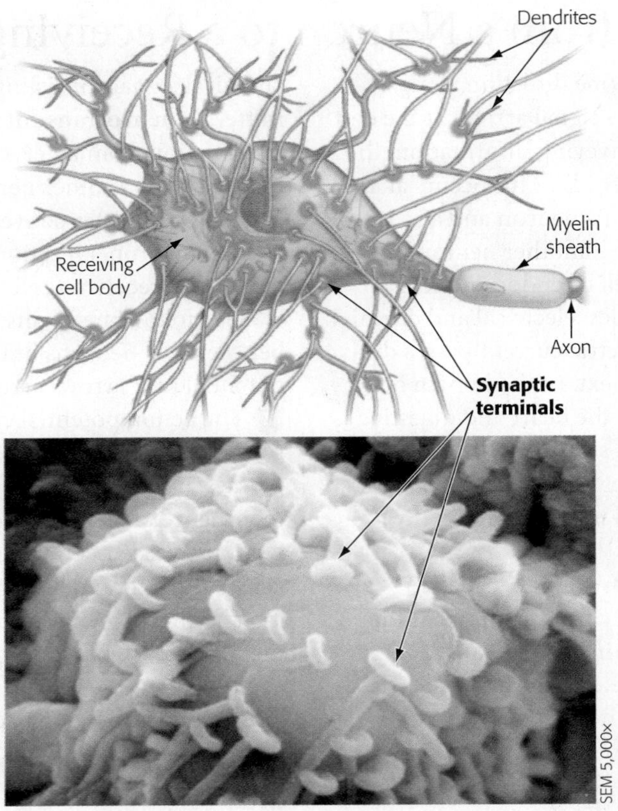

▲ **Figure 27.6 A neuron's multiple synaptic inputs.** As shown in this drawing and micrograph, a single neuron may receive signals from hundreds of other neurons via thousands of synaptic terminals (shown in orange).

Neurotransmitters

A variety of small molecules can act as neurotransmitters, including amines and peptides. The amines are neurotransmitters derived from amino acids. Examples include serotonin, dopamine, epinephrine, and norepinephrine. Serotonin and dopamine affect sleep, mood, attention, and learning. Imbalances of amines are associated with various disorders. For example, reduced levels of norepinephrine and serotonin have been linked to some types of depression. The degenerative illness Parkinson's disease is associated with a lack of dopamine in the brain, and an excess of dopamine is linked to schizophrenia.

Many peptides (short chains of amino acids) also serve as neurotransmitters. One class of such peptides is the endorphins, which also act as hormones. Endorphins decrease our perception of pain during times of physical or emotional stress. Endorphins may be released in response to a wide variety of stimuli, including traumatic injury, muscle fatigue, and even eating certain foods like chocolate.

Drugs and the Brain

Many drugs, including common ones such as caffeine, nicotine, and alcohol, affect the actions of neurotransmitters at the brain's trillions of synapses. Caffeine, found in coffee, tea, chocolate, and many soft drinks and energy drinks, counters the effects of inhibitory neurotransmitters, ones that normally suppress nerve signals. This is why caffeine tends to stimulate you and keep you awake. Nicotine acts as a stimulant by binding to and activating receptors for a neurotransmitter called acetylcholine. Alcohol is a strong depressant; its precise effect on the nervous system is not yet known, but it seems to increase the effects of another inhibitory neurotransmitter.

Many prescription drugs used to treat psychological disorders alter the effects of neurotransmitters. Tranquilizers such as diazepam (Valium) and alprazolam (Xanax) activate the receptors for an inhibitory neurotransmitter. In other cases, a drug may physically block a receptor, preventing a neurotransmitter from binding, thereby reducing its effect. For instance, some drugs used to treat schizophrenia block dopamine receptors. Some drugs used to treat attention deficit hyperactivity disorder (ADHD), such as methylphenidate (Ritalin), are chemically similar to the neurotransmitters dopamine and norepinephrine. Scientists think that ADHD medications block the reuptake of these neurotransmitters, but do not yet understand their precise actions in the brain.

What about illegal drugs? Stimulants such as amphetamines and cocaine increase the release and availability of norepinephrine and dopamine at synapses. Abuse of these drugs can therefore produce symptoms resembling schizophrenia. LSD and mescaline may produce their hallucinatory effects by activating serotonin and dopamine receptors. The active ingredient in marijuana binds to brain receptors normally used by other neurotransmitters that seem to play a role in pain, depression, appetite, memory, and fertility. Opiates—morphine, codeine, and heroin—bind to endorphin receptors, reducing pain and producing euphoria. Opiates are thus usually prescribed to relieve pain.

While the drugs mentioned here have the ability to increase alertness and a sense of well-being or to reduce physical and emotional pain, they also have the potential to disrupt the brain's finely tuned neural pathways, altering the chemical balances that are the product of millions of years of evolution. ☑

☑ CHECKPOINT

What determines whether a neuron is affected by a specific neurotransmitter?

Answer: To be affected by a particular neurotransmitter, a neuron must have specific receptors for that neurotransmitter in its membrane.

The Human Nervous System: A Closer Look

To this point, we have concentrated on cellular mechanisms that are fundamental to nearly all animal nervous systems. Although there is remarkable uniformity throughout the animal kingdom in the way nerve cells function, there is great variety in how nervous systems as a whole are organized. For the rest of this chapter, we'll focus on vertebrates, with particular emphasis on human systems.

Vertebrate nervous systems are diverse in both structure and level of sophistication—the brains of dolphins and humans are much more complex than the brains of frogs and fishes, for instance. However, some features are common to the nervous systems of all vertebrates. All have a nervous system that is concentrated at the head end, and all have a central nervous system (CNS) distinct from a peripheral nervous system (PNS) **(Figure 27.7)**.

The Central Nervous System

INTEGRATION

The vertebrate central nervous system integrates information coming from the senses and transmits signals that produce responses. In all vertebrates, the brain and spinal cord make up the CNS. The **spinal cord**, a jellylike bundle of nerve fibers, lies inside the spine. The spinal cord acts as the central communication conduit between the brain and the rest of the body. Millions of nerve fibers within the cord carry motor information from the brain to the muscles, while other fibers convey sensory information (such as touch, pain, and body position) from the body to the brain. The spinal cord acts like a telephone cable jam-packed with wires, each of which carries messages between the central hub and relay centers for outlying areas. In humans, the spinal cord is well protected by the bony spinal column. However, a traumatic blow to the spinal column can crush the delicate nerve bundles and prevent signals from passing. The result may be a debilitating injury. Such trauma along the back can cause paraplegia—paralysis of the lower half of the body. Trauma higher up on the spinal column can cause quadriplegia—paralysis from the neck down. Such injuries may be permanent because the nerves of the spinal cord, unlike many other body tissues, cannot be repaired.

Why can't paralysis be cured?

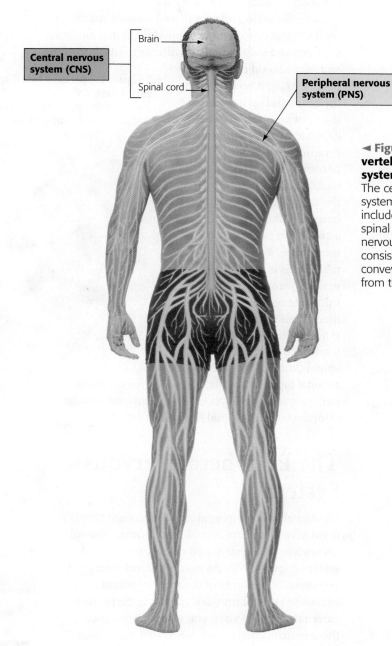

Brain

Central nervous system (CNS)

Spinal cord

Peripheral nervous system (PNS)

◄ **Figure 27.7 A vertebrate nervous system (back view).** The central nervous system (CNS) of humans includes the brain and the spinal cord. The peripheral nervous system (PNS) consists of nerves that convey information to and from the CNS.

The master control center of the nervous system, the **brain**, includes homeostatic centers that keep the body functioning smoothly, sensory centers that integrate data from the sense organs, and (in humans, at least) centers of emotions and intellect. The brain also sends out motor commands to muscles.

Both the brain and spinal cord contain spaces filled with a liquid called **cerebrospinal fluid** that cushions the CNS and helps supply it with nutrients, hormones, and white blood cells **(Figure 27.8)**. Also protecting the brain and spinal cord are layers of connective tissue called **meninges**. If the cerebrospinal fluid becomes infected by bacteria or viruses, the meninges may become inflamed, a condition called meningitis. Viral meningitis is generally not harmful, while bacterial meningitis can be serious if not treated with antibiotics. Infection of the cerebrospinal fluid can be detected by a spinal tap, a procedure that involves inserting a narrow needle through the spinal column to collect a sample of cerebrospinal fluid. ☑

▼ Figure 27.8 **Fluid-filled spaces of the vertebrate CNS.** Spaces in the brain and spinal cord are filled with cerebrospinal fluid, which helps to cushion and supply nutrients to the CNS.

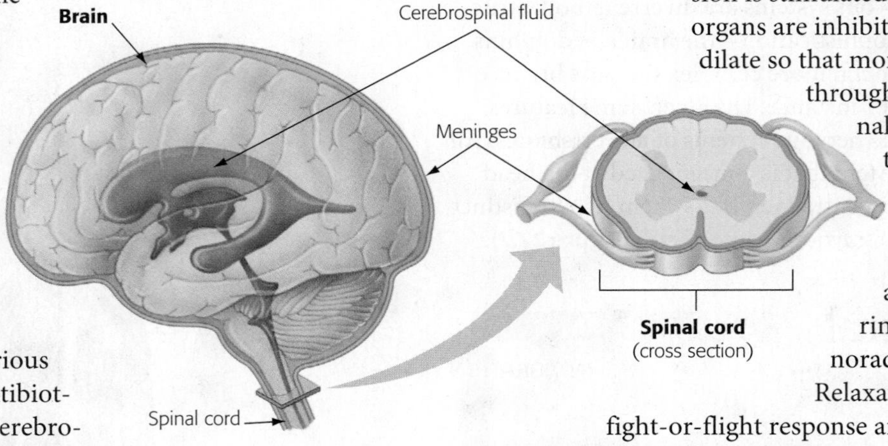

Brain · Cerebrospinal fluid · Meninges · Spinal cord · Spinal cord (cross section)

The Peripheral Nervous System

The vertebrate peripheral nervous system (PNS) is divided into two functional components: the voluntary nervous system and the autonomic nervous system **(Figure 27.9)**. As part of the voluntary nervous system, neurons of the **motor system** carry signals to skeletal muscles, mainly in response to external stimuli. When you walk, for instance, these neurons carry commands that make your legs move. The control of skeletal muscles is usually voluntary, as when you walk, but can also be involuntary, as in the knee-jerk reflex.

The **autonomic nervous system** regulates the internal environment by controlling smooth and cardiac muscles and the organs and glands of the digestive, cardiovascular, excretory, and endocrine systems. This control is generally involuntary. The autonomic nervous system contains two sets of

neurons with opposing effects on most body organs. One set, called the **parasympathetic division**, primes the body for activities that gain and conserve energy for the body ("rest and digest"). These effects include stimulating the digestive organs, decreasing the heart rate, and narrowing the bronchi, which correlates with a decreased breathing rate. The other set of neurons in the autonomic nervous system, the **sympathetic division**, tends to have the opposite effect, preparing the body for intense, energy-consuming activities, such as fighting, fleeing, or competing in a strenuous game ("fight or flight"). When this division is stimulated, the digestive organs are inhibited, the bronchi dilate so that more air can pass through, and the adrenal glands secrete the hormones epinephrine (also called adrenaline) and norepinephrine (also called noradrenaline). Relaxation and the fight-or-flight response are opposite extremes. Your body usually operates somewhere in between, with most of your organs receiving both sympathetic and parasympathetic signals. The opposing signals adjust an organ's activity to a suitable level.

As carriers of command signals, the motor neurons of the parasympathetic and sympathetic systems constitute lower levels of the nervous system's hierarchy. In the next section, we'll take a closer look at the highest level of the hierarchy, the brain. ☑

▼ Figure 27.9 **Functional divisions of the vertebrate PNS.**

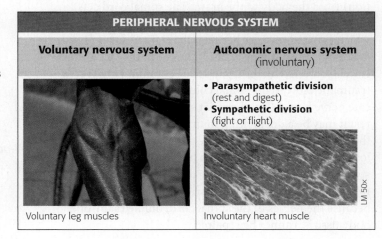

PERIPHERAL NERVOUS SYSTEM	
Voluntary nervous system	**Autonomic nervous system** (involuntary)
	• **Parasympathetic division** (rest and digest) • **Sympathetic division** (fight or flight)
Voluntary leg muscles	Involuntary heart muscle

LM 50x

The Human Brain

Composed of up to 100 billion intricately organized neurons, with a much larger number of supporting cells, the human brain is more powerful than the most sophisticated computer. The brain is divided structurally into three regions: the hindbrain, the midbrain, and the forebrain (**Figure 27.10** and **Table 27.1**).

Two sections of the hindbrain (blue in Figure 27.10), the **medulla oblongata** and the pons, and the midbrain (purple) make up a functional unit called the **brainstem**. All of the sensory and motor neurons carrying information to and from other brain regions pass through the brainstem. The brainstem serves as a sensory filter, selecting which information to pass on. It also regulates sleep and arousal and helps coordinate body movements, such as walking. Table 27.1 lists some of the other functions of the medulla oblongata, pons, and midbrain.

Also part of the hindbrain, the **cerebellum** (light blue in the figure) is a planning center for body movements. The cerebellum receives sensory information about the position of limbs and the length of muscles, as well as information from the auditory and visual systems. It also receives input from the motor pathways, telling it which motor actions are being carried out. The cerebellum uses this information to provide coordination of movement and balance. When you step off a curb, for instance, your cerebellum evaluates your body position and relays a plan for your next movements.

The most sophisticated integrating centers are found in the forebrain (orange and yellow in Figure 27.10); they are the thalamus, the hypothalamus, and the cerebrum. The thalamus contains most of the cell bodies of neurons that relay information to the cerebral cortex, the most extensive portion of the cerebrum. The thalamus first sorts data into categories (all the touch signals from a hand, for instance). It also suppresses some signals and enhances others. The thalamus then sends the sorted information on to the appropriate brain centers for further interpretation and integration.

In Chapter 25, we saw that the hypothalamus controls the pituitary gland and the secretion of many hormones (see Figures 25.5 and 25.6). The **hypothalamus** also regulates body temperature, blood pressure, hunger, thirst, the sex drive, and the fight-or-flight response, and it helps us experience emotions, such as rage and pleasure. A "pleasure center" in the hypothalamus could also be called an addiction center, for it is strongly affected by certain addictive drugs, such as amphetamines and cocaine. Another part of the hypothalamus functions as an internal timekeeper, our biological clock. Receiving visual input from the eyes, the clock maintains our daily biological rhythms, such as cycles of sleepiness and hunger. ✓

✓ CHECKPOINT

Which brain structure— the cerebellum or the cerebrum—contains sophisticated thinking centers?

Answer: the cerebrum

▼ **Figure 27.10 The main parts of the human brain.**

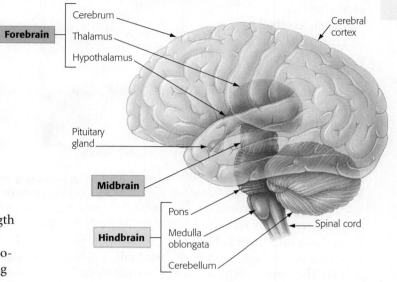

Table 27.1	Structure and Function of the Human Brain
Brain Structure	**Major Functions**
Brainstem	Conducts data to and from other brain centers; helps maintain homeostasis; coordinates body movement
Medulla oblongata	Controls breathing, circulation, swallowing, digestion
Pons	Controls breathing
Midbrain	Receives and integrates auditory data; coordinates visual reflexes; sends sensory data to higher brain centers
Cerebellum	Coordinates body movement; learns and remembers motor responses
Thalamus	Serves as input center for sensory data going to the cerebrum and as output center for motor responses leaving the cerebrum; sorts data
Hypothalamus	Serves as homeostatic control center; controls pituitary gland; acts as biological clock
Cerebrum	Performs sophisticated integration; involved in memory, learning, speech, emotions; formulates complex behavioral responses

The Cerebral Cortex

The **cerebrum**, the largest and most complex part of our brain, consists of right and left cerebral hemispheres **(Figure 27.11)**. A thick band of nerve fibers called the **corpus callosum** connects the cerebral hemispheres, enabling them to process information together.

The **cerebral cortex** is a highly folded layer of tissue that forms the surface of the cerebrum (see Figure 27.10). Although less than 5 mm (0.2 inch) thick (thinner than a pencil), the human cerebral cortex accounts for over 80% of the total brain mass. It contains some 10 billion neurons and hundreds of billions of synapses. Its intricate neural circuitry helps produce our most distinctive human traits: reasoning and mathematical abilities, language skills, imagination, artistic talent, and personality traits. Assembling information it receives from our eyes, ears, nose, taste buds, and touch sensors, the cortex creates our sensory perceptions—what we are actually aware of when we see, hear, smell, taste, or touch. The cerebral cortex also regulates our voluntary movements.

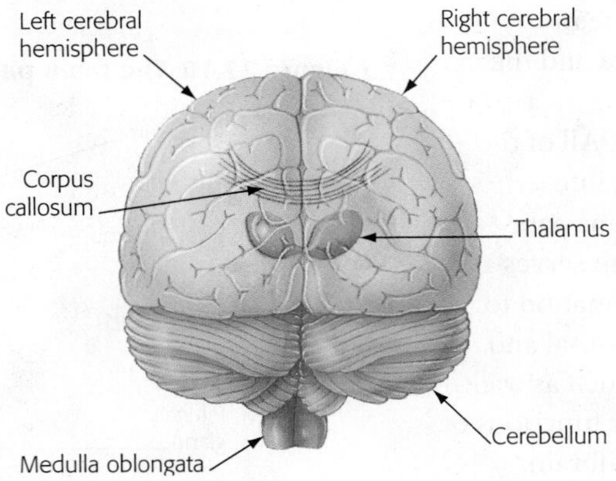

Like the rest of the cerebrum, the cerebral cortex is divided into right and left sides, connected by the corpus callosum. Because the nerve fibers from the cerebral cortex cross in the medulla oblongata, each hemisphere (right and left) receives information from and controls the movement of the opposite side of the body.

Each side of the cerebral cortex has four lobes, each named for a nearby skull bone: the frontal, parietal, temporal, and occipital lobes (represented by different colors in **Figure 27.12**). Researchers have identified a number of functional areas within each lobe. One region of the frontal lobe, for example, called the motor cortex, functions mainly in sending commands to skeletal muscles. The cerebral cortex also has centers that receive and begin processing sensory information such as taste, vision, hearing, and smell.

Making up most of our cerebral cortex are various **association areas**. These are the sites of higher mental activities—roughly, what we call thinking. A large association area in the frontal lobe uses varied inputs from many other areas of the brain to evaluate consequences, make considered judgments, and plan for the future. Language results from some extremely complex interactions among several association areas. For instance, the parietal lobe has association areas for reading and speech. These areas receive visual information (the appearance of words on a page) from the vision centers. Then, if the words are to be spoken aloud, the information is arranged into speech patterns and passed to a speech center in the frontal lobe, which signals the motor cortex to move the tongue, lips, and other muscles to form words.

You may have heard people say that they are "left-brained" or "right-brained." In a phenomenon known as lateralization, areas in the two hemispheres become specialized for different functions.

▲ **Figure 27.11** **A rear view of the brain.** The large cerebrum (yellow) consists of left and right cerebral hemispheres connected by a thick band of nerves called the corpus callosum.

▼ **Figure 27.12** **Functional areas of the cerebrum's left hemisphere.** This figure identifies the main functional areas in the brain's left cerebral hemisphere, which is divided into four lobes.

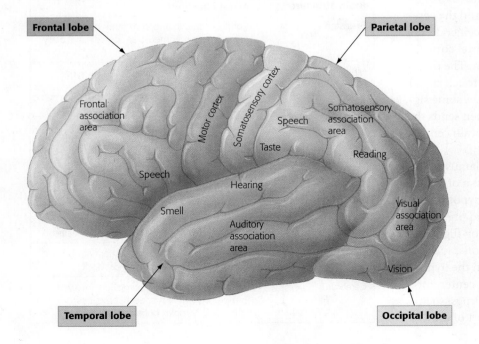

Frontal lobe

Parietal lobe

Frontal association area

Motor cortex

Somatosensory cortex

Speech

Somatosensory association area

Taste

Reading

Speech

Hearing

Smell

Visual association area

Auditory association area

Vision

Temporal lobe

Occipital lobe

In most people, the left hemisphere becomes most adept at language, logic, and mathematical operations. The right hemisphere is stronger at spatial relations, pattern and face recognition, and nonverbal thinking. In about 10% of us, however, the roles of the left and right hemispheres are reversed or the roles are more alike.

Brain Trauma

Interestingly, evidence from brain surgery patients indicates that patterns of lateralization are not fixed. One of the most radical surgical alterations of the brain is hemispherectomy—the removal of almost one-half of the brain (**Figure 27.13**). This procedure is performed to alleviate severe seizure disorders that originate from one of the hemispheres as a result of illness, abnormal development, or stroke. Incredibly, with just half a brain, hemispherectomy patients recover quickly, often leaving the hospital within a few weeks. Although the side of the body opposite the surgery always has partial paralysis, hemispherectomy patients have undiminished intellectual capacities. Higher brain functions that previously originated from the missing half of the brain begin to be controlled by the opposite side. Recovery after hemispherectomy is a striking example of the brain's remarkable ability to adapt.

Can a person survive with just half a brain?

Neurologists sometimes gain insight into how the brain works from people who have suffered brain trauma. The first well-publicized case of this type involved a man named Phineas Gage. In 1848, while working in Vermont as a railroad construction foreman, Gage accidentally exploded a dynamite charge that propelled a 3-foot-long spike through his head. The 13-pound steel rod entered his left cheek and traveled upward behind his left eye and out the top of his skull, landing several yards away. Incredibly, Gage walked away from the accident and appeared to be able to think normally. However, his associates soon noticed drastic changes in his personality, with a new propensity for meanness and vulgarity and an inability to control his behavior. Gage's doctor observed these changes as well but was unable to explain them, given the limited knowledge of the brain at that time. Luckily, the doctor preserved Gage's skull and the spike, allowing a group of researchers in 1994 to produce a computer model of the injury (**Figure 27.14**). The modern analysis offered an explanation for Gage's bizarre behavior: The rod had pierced both frontal lobes of his brain. People with these sorts of injuries often exhibit irrational decision making and difficulty processing emotions. The link between the frontal lobes and personality continues to be an active area of research. ☑

☑ **CHECKPOINT**

The largest and most sophistical part of your brain is the _____. It is divided into two hemispheres connected by the _____. Its surface, called the _____, accounts for most of your brain's mass and is responsible for most distinctively human traits such as language.

Answer: cerebrum; corpus callosum; cerebral cortex

▼ **Figure 27.13 Hemispherectomy.** This top-down X-ray view shows the skull and brain of a hemispherectomy patient after surgery.

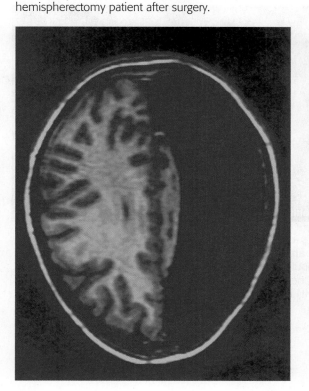

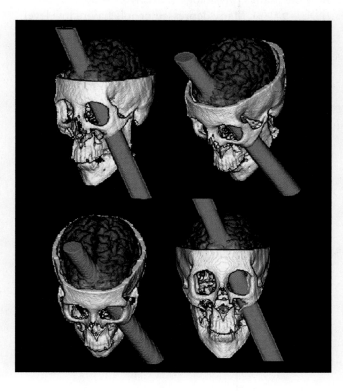

◄ **Figure 27.14 Phineas Gage's accident.** A 1994 computer simulation of an 1848 injury to railroad worker Phineas Gage suggested that the spike that passed through his skull (shown as a red cylinder in the figure) might have damaged both frontal lobes of his brain. Such an injury could account for Gage's personality changes after the accident.

Neurological Disorders

In addition to trauma, various neurological disorders (diseases of the nervous system) can also affect brain function. Nearly 20 million American adults, about two-thirds of them women, are affected by depression. Two broad forms of depressive illness have been identified: major depression and bipolar disorder. People with **major depression** may experience persistent sadness, loss of interest in pleasurable activities, changes in body weight and sleep patterns, loss of energy, and suicidal thoughts. While all of us feel sad from time to time, major depression is extreme and more persistent, leaving the sufferer unable to live a normal life. If left untreated, symptoms may become more frequent and severe over time.

Bipolar disorder, or manic-depressive disorder, involves extreme mood swings. The manic phase is characterized by high self-esteem, increased energy, a flood of thoughts and ideas, and extreme talkativeness, as well as behaviors that often court disaster, such as increased risk taking, promiscuity, and reckless spending. In its milder forms, this phase is sometimes associated with great creativity, and some well-known musicians, artists, and literary figures with bipolar disorder (including Beethoven, Van Gogh, and Hemingway) have had periods of intense output during their manic phases. The depressive phase is marked by sleep disturbances, feelings of worthlessness, and decreased ability to experience interest and pleasure.

In recent years, researchers have begun to examine how the brain's physiology is involved in depression **(Figure 27.15)**. Many depressed people have a low level of serotonin. For this reason, serotonin is the target of the most commonly prescribed class of antidepressant medications, the selective serotonin reuptake inhibitors (SSRIs), including fluoxetine (Prozac), paroxetine (Paxil), and sertraline (Zoloft). These drugs block the reuptake of neurotransmitter at synapses (see step 6 in Figure 27.5), increasing the amount of time that serotonin is available to stimulate neurons in the brain.

How do antidepressant medications work?

Alzheimer's disease is a form of mental deterioration, or dementia, characterized by confusion, memory loss, and a variety of other symptoms. Its incidence is usually age related, rising from about 10% at age 65 to about 35% at age 85. The disease is progressive; patients gradually become less able to function and eventually need to be dressed, bathed, and fed by others. There are also personality changes, almost always for the worse. Patients often lose their ability to recognize people, even family members, and may treat them with suspicion and hostility. At present, a firm diagnosis of Alzheimer's disease is difficult to make while the patient is alive because it is one of several forms of dementia.

Unraveling how networks of neurons in the brain produce thoughts and emotions, store and retrieve memories, and control the body's internal environment is one of the most challenging and engaging aspects of modern biology. In the next section, we'll examine how the brain receives information from the environment via the sense organs. ☑

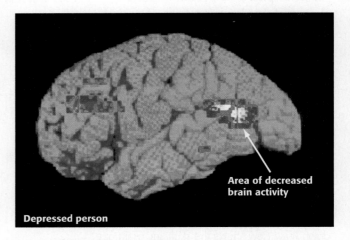

Depressed person

Area of decreased brain activity

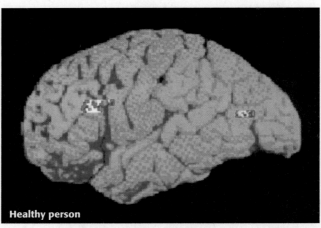

Healthy person

▲ Figure 27.15 **Brain activity in a depressed person and a healthy person.** The purple and pink colors in these computer images indicate areas of low brain activity. Notice that the brain of the depressed person shows decreased activity in certain areas of the brain.

The Senses

In this section, we'll focus on the human body's sensory structures. To begin, we'll examine how these structures gather information and pass it on to the central nervous system (CNS). After that, we'll take a closer look at two of the human senses, vision and hearing.

Sensory Input

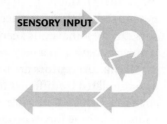

Sensory input is the process of using receptors to sense the environment and send information about it to the CNS to be integrated and acted upon. Sensory receptors, such as the sensory cells in your eyes or the taste buds of your tongue, are tuned to the condition of both the external world and internal organs. Sensory receptors detect stimuli such as chemicals, light, sounds, cold, heat, and touch. The sensory receptors in your eyes, for instance, detect light energy; those in your taste buds detect chemicals dissolved in saliva. The sensory receptor's job is completed when it sends information to the CNS by triggering action potentials.

What exactly do we mean when we say that a sensory receptor detects a stimulus? In stimulus detection, the receptor cell converts one type of signal (the stimulus) to an electrical signal. This conversion of the signal, called **sensory transduction**, occurs as a change in the membrane potential of the receptor cell.

Sensory Transduction

As an example of sensory transduction, **Figure 27.16** shows sensory receptors in a taste bud detecting sugar molecules. ❶ When the sugar molecules (🔵) first come into contact with the taste bud, they bind to membrane receptors of the sensory receptor cells. ❷ This binding triggers a signal transduction pathway that ❸ causes some ion channels in the membrane to close and others to open. Changes in the flow of ions (⊕) alter the membrane potential. This change in membrane potential is called the **receptor potential**. In contrast to action potentials, which are all-or-none phenomena, receptor potentials vary in intensity; the stronger the stimulus, the stronger the receptor potential.

Once a receptor cell converts a stimulus to a receptor potential, this potential usually results in signals being sent to the CNS. In Figure 27.16, ❹ each receptor cell forms a synapse with a sensory neuron. When there are enough sugar molecules, a strong receptor potential is triggered. This receptor potential makes the receptor cell release enough neurotransmitter (🔵) to increase the rate of action potential generation in the sensory neuron. The brain interprets the intensity of the stimulus from the rate at which it receives action potentials. It gains additional information about stimulus intensity by keeping track of how many sensory neurons it receives signals from.

There is an important qualification to what we have just said about stimulus intensity. Have you ever noticed how an odor that is strong at first seems to fade with time, even when you know the smell is still there? Or how the water in a pool is shockingly cold when you first jump in, but then you get used to it? This effect is called **sensory adaptation**, the tendency of some sensory receptors to become less sensitive when they are stimulated

▼ **Figure 27.16 Sensory transduction in a human taste bud.**

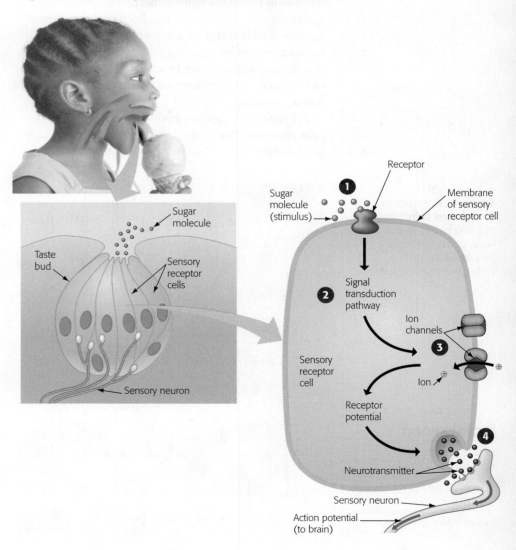

repeatedly. When receptors become less sensitive, they trigger fewer action potentials, causing the brain to receive fewer stimuli. Sensory adaptation keeps the body from continuously reacting to normal background stimuli. Without it, our nervous system would become overloaded with useless information.

Types of Sensory Receptors

Based on the type of signals to which they respond, we can group sensory receptors into five general categories: pain receptors, thermoreceptors (sensors for heat and cold), mechanoreceptors (sensors for touch, pressure, motion, and sound), chemoreceptors (sensors for chemicals), and electromagnetic receptors (sensors for energy such as light and electricity). These five types of receptors work in various combinations to produce the five human senses.

Figure 27.17, showing a section of human skin, reveals why the surface of our body is sensitive to such a variety of stimuli. Our skin contains pain receptors (labeled in red in the figure), thermoreceptors (blue), and mechanoreceptors (green). Each of these receptors is a modified dendrite of a sensory neuron. Each receptor is capable of recognizing a stimulus and responding to it by sending an action potential to the CNS. In other words, each receptor serves as both a receptor cell and a sensory neuron.

All parts of the human body except the brain have pain receptors. Pain is important because it often indicates danger and usually makes an animal withdraw to

safety. Pain can also make us aware of injury or disease. **Pain receptors** may respond to excessive heat or pressure or to chemicals released from damaged or inflamed tissues. Prostaglandins are local regulators that increase pain by sensitizing pain receptors. Aspirin and ibuprofen reduce pain by inhibiting prostaglandin synthesis.

Thermoreceptors in the skin detect either heat or cold. Other temperature sensors located deep in the body monitor the temperature of the blood. The body's major thermostat is the hypothalamus. Receiving action potentials both from surface sensors and from deep sensors, the hypothalamus keeps a mammal's or bird's body temperature within a narrow range (see Figure 21.14).

Mechanoreceptors are highly diverse. Different types are stimulated by different forms of mechanical energy, such as touch and pressure, stretching, motion, and sound. All these forces produce their effects by bending or stretching the plasma membrane of a receptor cell. When the membrane changes shape, it becomes more permeable to positive ions, and the mechanical energy of the stimulus is transduced into a receptor potential. One example of a mechanoreceptor is the touch receptor at the base of a cat's whisker. These receptors are extremely sensitive and enable the animal to detect objects by touch in the dark. The elephants you learned about in the Biology and Society section provide another example; they detect seismic waves through mechanoreceptors in their feet and trunk.

Chemoreceptors include the sensory cells in your nose and taste buds, which are attuned to chemicals in the external environment, as well as some internal receptors that detect chemicals in your body's internal environment. Internal chemoreceptors include sensors in your arteries that monitor your blood, with some sensors detecting changes in pH and others detecting changes in O_2 concentration. In all types of chemoreceptors, a receptor cell develops receptor potentials in response to chemicals dissolved in fluid such as blood or saliva.

Electromagnetic receptors are sensitive to energy of various wavelengths, which takes such forms as magnetism and light. For example, **photoreceptors** detect the electromagnetic energy of light. In the next section, we'll focus on one specific organ that uses photoreceptors: the human eye. ☑

Vision

The human eye is a remarkable sense organ, able to detect a multitude of colors, form images of objects both near and far, and respond to minute amounts of light energy. In this section, you'll learn about the structure of the human eye and how it processes images. You'll also learn why vision problems occur and how they can be corrected.

▶ **Figure 27.17**
Sensory receptors in the human skin. Your skin is sensitive to a wide variety of stimuli because it contains a wide variety of receptors.

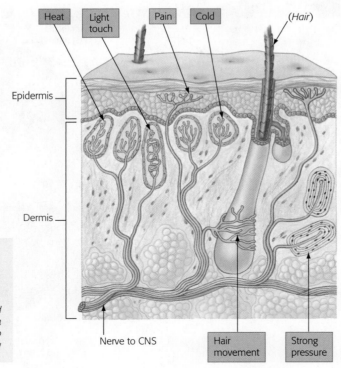

Heat | Light touch | Pain | Cold | (Hair)

Epidermis

Dermis

Nerve to CNS | Hair movement | Strong pressure

Structure of the Human Eye

The outer surface of the human eyeball is a tough, whitish layer of connective tissue called the **sclera (Figure 27.18)**. At the front of the eye, the sclera becomes the transparent **cornea**. The sclera surrounds a pigmented layer called the choroid. At the front of the eye, the choroid forms the **iris**, which gives the eye its color. The opening in the center of the iris is called the **pupil**. Behind the pupil is the disklike **lens**, which is held in position by ligaments. At the back of the eyeball is the **retina**, a layer of tissue just inside the choroid that contains photoreceptor cells. The **optic nerve** connects the retina with the brain. There are no photoreceptor cells in the part of the retina where the optic nerve passes through the back of the eye. We cannot detect light that is focused on this "blind spot," but having two eyes with overlapping fields of view enables us to perceive uninterrupted images.

Two fluid-filled chambers make up the bulk of the eye. The large chamber behind the lens is filled with jellylike **vitreous humor**. The much smaller chamber in front of the lens contains a thinner fluid called the **aqueous humor**. The humors help maintain the shape of the eyeball. In addition, the aqueous humor supplies nutrients and oxygen to the lens, iris, and cornea and carries off wastes. Blockage of the ducts that drain this fluid can cause glaucoma, increased pressure inside the eye that may lead to blindness. If diagnosed early, glaucoma can be treated with medications that increase the circulation of the aqueous humor.

A thin mucous membrane called the conjunctiva helps keep the outside of the eye moist. The conjunctiva lines the inner surface of the eyelids and folds back over the white of the eye (but not the cornea). An infection or allergic reaction may cause inflammation of the conjuctiva, a condition called conjunctivitis or "pink eye." Bacterial conjuctivitis usually clears up with antibiotic eyedrops. Viral conjunctivitis usually clears up on its own, although it is very contagious, especially among young children.

A gland above the eye secretes tears, a dilute salt solution that is spread across the eyeball by blinking and that drains into ducts leading into the nasal cavities. This fluid cleanses and moistens the eye surface. Excess secretion, in response to eye irritation or strong emotions, causes tears to spill over the eyelid and fill the nasal cavities, producing a runny nose.

Function of the Human Eye

The cornea lets light into the eye and also helps focus light. The muscles of the iris regulate the size of the pupil, controlling the amount of light that enters. After going through the pupil, light passes through the lens. The lens focuses light onto the retina by bending light rays. Focusing is accomplished through a change in the shape of the lens (**Figure 27.19**). The thicker the lens, the more sharply it bends light. The shape of the lens is controlled by the muscles attached to the choroid. When the eye focuses on a nearby object, these muscles contract, pulling the choroid layer of the eye inward toward the pupil. This makes the ligaments that suspend the lens slacken. With this reduced tension, the elastic lens becomes thicker and rounder. When the eye focuses on a distant object, the muscles controlling the lens relax, putting tension on the ligaments and flattening the lens. ☑

☑ **CHECKPOINT**

Arrange the following eye parts into the correct sequence encountered by photons of light traveling into the eye: pupil, retina, cornea, lens, vitreous humor, aqueous humor.

Answer: cornea → aqueous humor → pupil → lens → vitreous humor → retina

▼ Figure 27.18 **The human eye.**

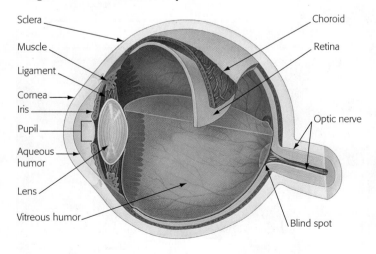

Sclera, Muscle, Ligament, Cornea, Iris, Pupil, Aqueous humor, Lens, Vitreous humor, Choroid, Retina, Optic nerve, Blind spot

► Figure 27.19 **How the lens of the eye focuses light.** When viewing a nearby object (top), the lens becomes thicker and rounder and focuses the image on the retina. When viewing a distant object (bottom), the lens becomes flattened, and the image is again focused on the retina.

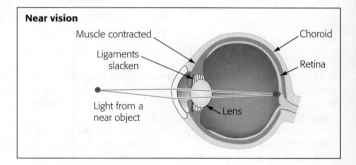

Near vision

Muscle contracted, Ligaments slacken, Light from a near object, Choroid, Retina, Lens

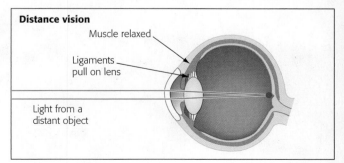

Distance vision

Muscle relaxed, Ligaments pull on lens, Light from a distant object

Photoreceptors

The human retina contains two types of photoreceptors named for their shapes (**Figure 27.20**). **Rods** are extremely sensitive to light and enable us to see in dim light, though only in shades of gray. **Cones** are stimulated by bright light and can distinguish color, but they contribute little to night vision.

In humans, rods are found in greatest density at the outer edges of the retina and are completely absent from the center. In contrast, the retina's center of focus contains a high concentration of cones (**Figure 27.21**). If you look directly at a dim star in the night sky, the star is hard to see. Looking just to the side, however, makes your lens focus the starlight onto the parts of the retina with the most rods, and you can see the star. By contrast, you achieve your sharpest day vision by looking straight at the object of interest. Some birds, such as hawks, have ten times more cones than we do, enabling them to spot small prey from high altitudes.

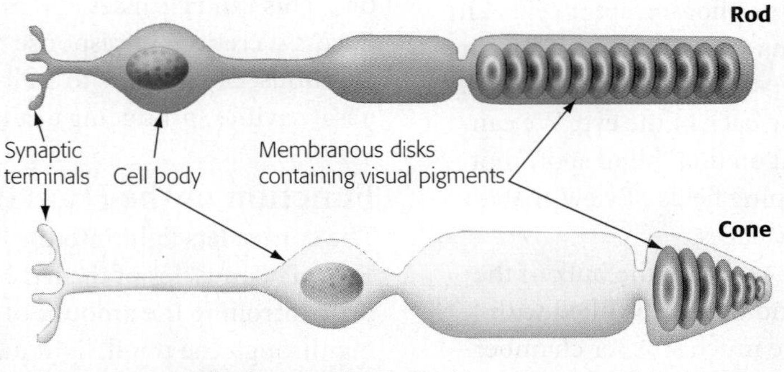

▲ **Figure 27.20 Photoreceptor cells.** Your eyes contain many more rods than cones.

How do rods and cones detect light? As Figure 27.20 shows, each rod and cone includes an array of disks containing light-absorbing visual pigments. Rods contain a visual pigment called rhodopsin, which can absorb dim light. (Rhodopsin is derived from vitamin A, which is why vitamin A deficiency can cause poor night vision; it's also why eating carrots, which are rich in a chemical called beta-carotene that the body converts to vitamin A, helps prevent vision loss.) Cones contain visual pigments called photopsins, which absorb colored, bright light. We have three types of cones, each containing a different type of photopsin. These cells are called blue cones, green cones, and red cones, referring to the colors absorbed best by their photopsin. We can perceive a great number of colors because the light from each particular color triggers a unique pattern of stimulation among the three types of cones. Colorblindness results from a deficiency in one or more types of cones.

Like all receptor cells, rods and cones convert a stimulus to an electrical signal (see Figure 27.21). When rhodopsin and photopsin absorb light, they change chemically, and the change alters the permeability of the cell's membrane. The resulting receptor potentials trigger a complex integration process that begins in the retina. Other retinal neurons start to integrate the receptor potentials and in doing so produce action potentials. These action potentials travel along the optic nerve, carrying the partly integrated information into the brain. Three-dimensional perceptions (what we actually see) result from further integration in several processing centers of the cerebral cortex. ☑

☑ CHECKPOINT

Explain why our night vision is mostly in shades of gray rather than in color.

Answer: Rods are more sensitive than cones to dim light, and thus the low light intensity at night stimulates far more rods than color-sensing cones.

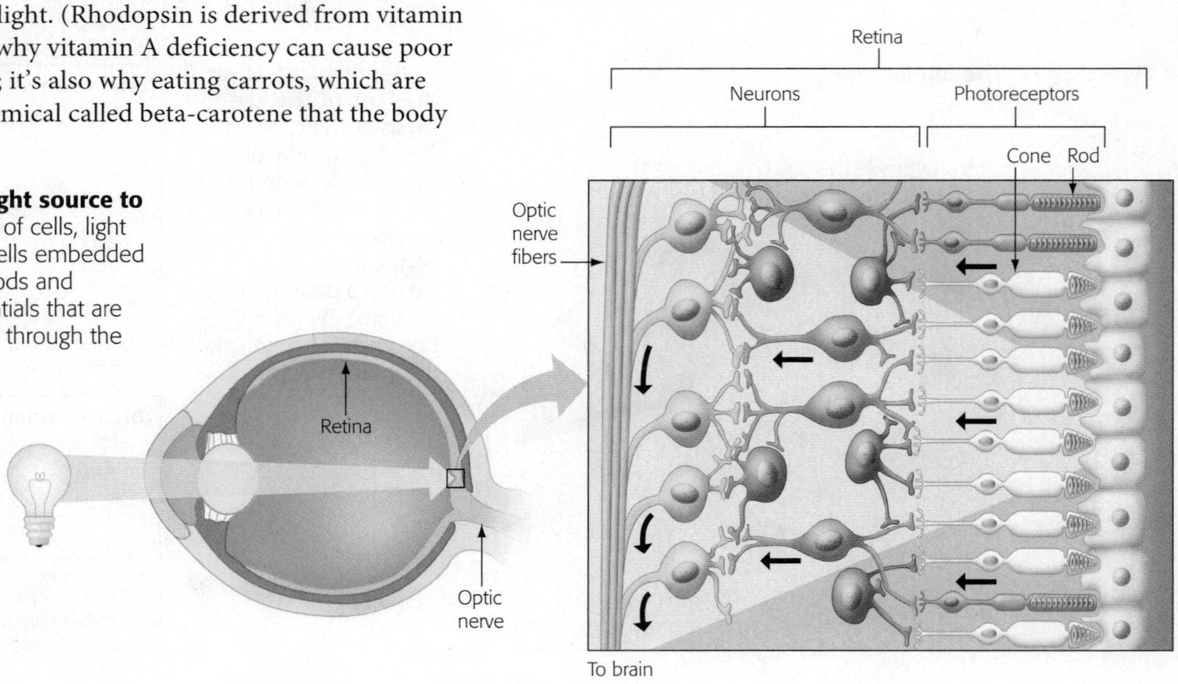

► **Figure 27.21 The vision pathway from light source to optic nerve.** After passing through many layers of cells, light entering the human eye strikes photoreceptor cells embedded in the back of the retina. Once stimulated, the rods and cones convert the light energy to receptor potentials that are integrated by other neurons and communicated through the optic nerve as action potentials to the brain.

Vision Problems and Corrections

When you have your vision tested, you view a chart that shows how various letters of the alphabet would look at various distances. You are asked to read different rows of letters using one eye at a time. If you can read the row that is sized for legibility at a distance of 20 feet with each of your eyes, you have normal (20/20) vision in each eye. Suppose you find out that you have 20/10 vision. This is better than normal; you can read letters from a distance of 20 feet that a person with 20/20 vision can only read at 10 feet. However, someone with 20/50 vision has worse than normal vision. He or she must stand at a distance of 20 feet to read what a person with normal vision can read at 50 feet.

Three of the most common visual problems are near-sightedness, farsightedness, and astigmatism. All three are focusing problems, easily corrected with artificial lenses. People with **nearsightedness** cannot focus well on distant objects, although they can see well at short distances (the condition is named for the type of vision that is *unimpaired*). A nearsighted eyeball **(Figure 27.22a)** is longer than normal. The lens cannot flatten enough to compensate, and it focuses distant objects in front of the retina instead of on it. Nearsightedness (also known as myopia)

How does LASIK surgery work?

is corrected by glasses or contact lenses that are thinner in the middle than at the outside edge. The corrective lenses make the light rays from distant objects diverge slightly as they enter the eye. The image formed by the lens in the eye is then focused at the correct point.

Farsightedness (also known as hyperopia) occurs when the eyeball is shorter than normal, causing the lens to focus images behind the retina **(Figure 27.22b)**. Farsighted people see distant objects normally, but they can't focus on close objects. Corrective lenses that are thicker in the middle than at the outside edge compensate for farsightedness by making light rays from nearby objects converge slightly before they enter the eye.

Astigmatism is blurred vision caused by a misshapen lens or cornea. Any such distortion makes light rays converge unevenly and not focus at any one point on the retina. Lenses that correct astigmatism are asymmetrical in a way that compensates for the asymmetry in the eye.

Surgical procedures are an option for treating vision disorders. In laser-assisted in situ keratomileusis (LASIK), a laser is used to reshape the cornea and change its focusing ability. More than 1 million LASIK procedures are performed each year to correct a variety of vision problems. ☑

THE SENSES

☑ CHECKPOINT

A person who requires reading glasses has a case of _____.

Answer: farsightedness (hyperopia)

▶ **Figure 27.22 A nearsighted eye and a farsighted eye.** Corrective lenses help vision problems by focusing the image exactly on the retina.

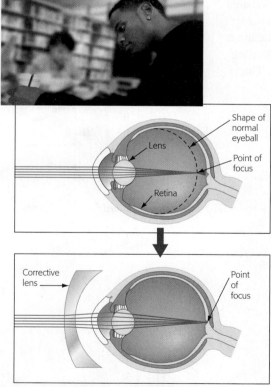

(a) A nearsighted eye (eyeball too long).
Nearsightedness is corrected by lenses that are thinner toward the middle.

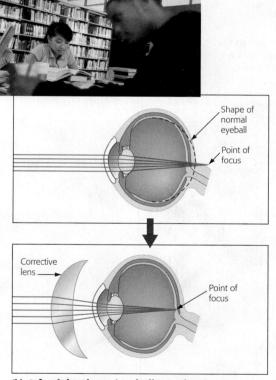

(b) A farsighted eye (eyeball too short).
Farsightedness is corrected by lenses that are thicker in the middle.

Hearing

Although the human ear is less sensitive than that of many other animals, it is capable of hearing a great range of auditory signals. In this section, we'll examine the structure and function of the human ear.

Structure of the Human Ear

The ear is composed of three regions: the outer ear, the middle ear, and the inner ear **(Figure 27.23a)**. The **outer ear** consists of the flap-like **pinna**—the bendable structure we commonly refer to as our "ear"—and the **auditory canal**. A sheet of tissue called the **eardrum** separates the outer ear from the middle ear. Both the outer ear and middle ear are common sites of childhood infections (called swimmer's ear and otitis media, respectively).

The **middle ear** contains three small bones **(Figure 27.23b)**: the hammer (more formally, the malleus), the anvil (incus), and the stirrup (stapes). (Interestingly, the hammer bone of elephants is unusually large, perhaps giving it greater ability to amplify subtle seismic vibrations.) The stirrup is connected to the inner ear through an opening in the skull bone. The **Eustachian tube** conducts air between the middle ear and the back of the throat, allowing air pressure to stay equal on either side of the eardrum. This tube is what enables you to move air in or out to equalize pressure ("pop" your ears) when changing altitude rapidly in an airplane or diving underwater.

The **inner ear** consists of fluid-filled channels in the bones of the skull. One of the channels, the **cochlea**, is a long, coiled tube. Our actual hearing organ, the organ of Corti, is located within a fluid-filled canal inside the cochlea **(Figure 27.24)**. The organ of Corti consists of an array of hair cells embedded in a structure called the basilar membrane. The hair cells are the receptor cells of the ear. Notice that they project into the fluid and that the tips of most are in contact with the overlying jelly-like membrane. Sensory neurons at the base of the hair cells connect to the auditory nerve, which connects in turn to the brain.

▼ **Figure 27.23 An overview of the human ear.**

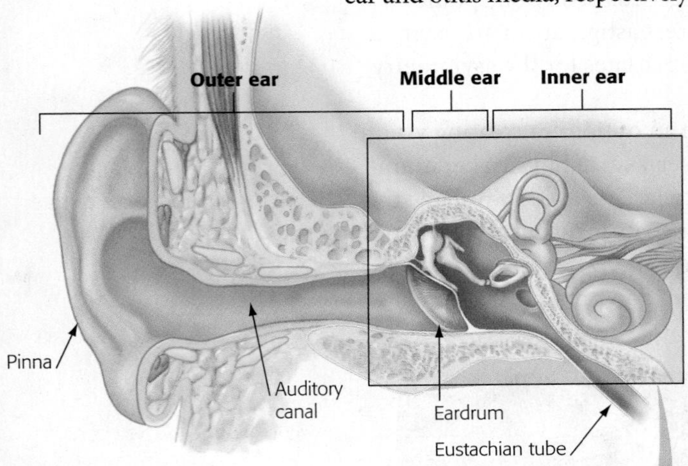

(a) Ear structure. The human ear is divided into three regions: the outer, middle, and inner ears.

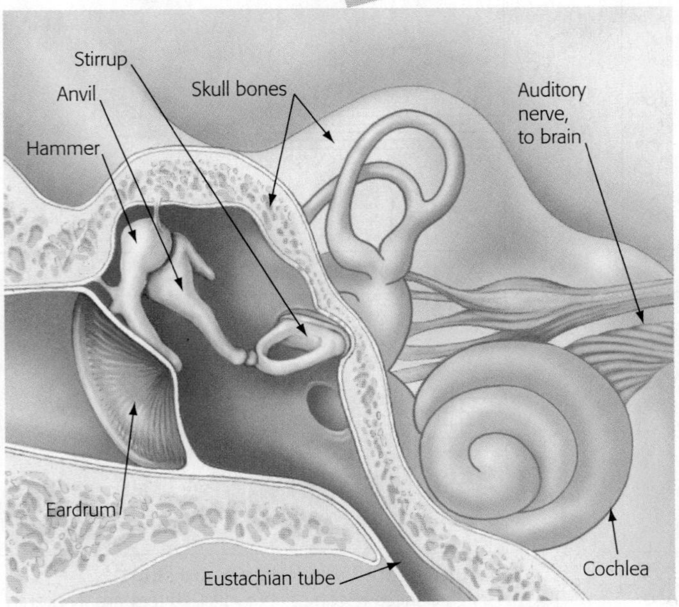

Outer ear

Middle ear Inner ear

Pinna

Auditory canal

Eardrum

Eustachian tube

Stirrup

Anvil

Hammer

Skull bones

Auditory nerve, to brain

Eardrum

Eustachian tube

Cochlea

(b) The middle and inner ears. The bones of the middle ear are connected to the fluid-filled channels of the cochlea in the inner ear.

▼ **Figure 27.24 The organ of Corti.** The organ of Corti is located within a fluid-filled canal inside the cochlea. Receptor cells (hair cells) connect to sensory neurons, which in turn connect to the auditory nerve and the brain.

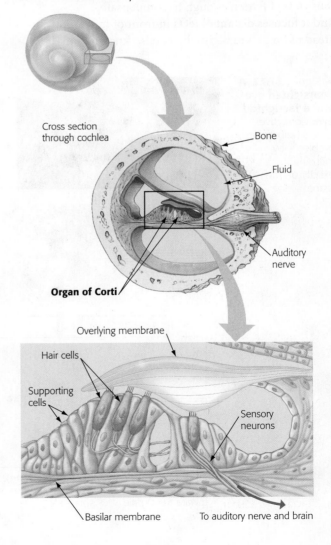

Cross section through cochlea

Bone

Fluid

Auditory nerve

Organ of Corti

Overlying membrane

Hair cells

Supporting cells

Sensory neurons

Basilar membrane

To auditory nerve and brain

Function of the Human Ear

Now let's see how the parts of the ear function in hearing. As indicated in **Figure 27.25**, a vibrating object such as a plucked guitar string creates sound waves in the surrounding air, represented by the up-and-down waves in the figure. The pinna and the auditory canal collect these waves and channel them to the eardrum. The waves make your eardrum vibrate with the same frequency as the sound. (Frequency is the number of vibrations per second.) From the eardrum, the vibrations are concentrated as they pass through the hammer, anvil, and stirrup in the middle ear. The stirrup transmits the vibrations to the inner ear, producing pressure waves in the fluid within the cochlea.

As a pressure wave passes through the cochlea, it makes the basilar membrane vibrate. Vibration of the basilar membrane makes the hairlike projections on the hair cells alternately brush against and draw away from the overlying membrane. When a hair cell's projections are bent, ion channels in its plasma membrane open, and positive ions enter the cell. As a result, the hair cell develops a receptor potential and releases neurotransmitter molecules at its synapse with a sensory neuron. In turn, the sensory neuron sends action potentials through the auditory nerve to the brain.

How is the volume of a sound determined? The higher the volume (loudness) of sound, the greater the amplitude (height) of the pressure wave it generates. In the ear, the greater the amplitude, the more vigorous the vibrations of fluid in the cochlea, the more pronounced the bending of the hair cells, and the more action potentials generated in the sensory neurons.

▼ **Figure 27.25 The route of sound waves through the ear.** This figure traces the path of a sound stimulus as it passes from the environment to the brain.

Outer ear			Middle ear	Inner ear
Pinna	Auditory canal	Ear-drum	Hammer, anvil, stirrup	Cochlea

Pressure

One vibration
Amplitude
Concentration in middle ear
Organ of Corti stimulated
Time

Hearing Problems

Deafness, the loss of hearing, can be caused by the inability to conduct sounds, resulting from middle-ear infections, a ruptured eardrum, or stiffening of the middle-ear bones (a common age-related problem). Deafness can also result from damage to receptor cells or neurons. Because few parts of our anatomy are more delicate than the organ of Corti, deafness is often progressive and permanent. In recent years, however, many deaf people have received cochlear implants, electronic devices that convert sounds to electrical impulses that stimulate the auditory nerve directly.

Frequent or prolonged exposure to very loud sounds can damage or destroy the hair cells of the inner ear. For example, you may have noticed that a few hours in a very loud environment leaves you with ringing or buzzing sounds in your ears, a condition called tinnitus. Ear plugs can provide protection. ☑

Locomotor Systems

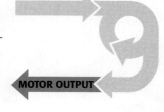

So far, we've seen how the body senses the environment via sensory receptors and integrates this information within the central nervous system. In this section, we'll consider how the body couples stimulus to locomotor response (movement), thereby completing the neural circuit.

Movement is one of the most distinctive features of animals. Whether an animal walks or runs on two, four, or six legs or more, swims, crawls, flies, or sits in one place and only moves its mouthparts, an interplay of organ systems is responsible for its movement. The nervous system plays a key role in issuing commands to the muscular system. The muscular system exerts the force that actually makes an animal or its parts move. But the force exerted by muscles produces movement only when it is applied against a firm structure. In vertebrates, this structure is the skeletal system. In this section, we focus on the human skeleton and muscles and the movement their interactions produce.

MOTOR OUTPUT

The Skeletal System

The **skeletal system** provides anchoring, support, and protection. Most land animals would sag from their own weight if they had no skeleton to support them. Skeletons also protect an animal's soft organs. For example, your ribs form a cage around your heart and lungs. In this section, we'll discuss the human skeleton: its organization, its structure, and some of the problems that may arise with it.

Organization of the Human Skeleton

Humans, like all vertebrates, have an **endoskeleton**—hard supporting elements situated among soft tissues. The human endoskeleton is a combination of cartilage and the 206 bones that make up the skeletal system **(Figure 27.26)**; the cartilage provides flexibility in certain areas.

The human skeleton is organized into two basic units: the axial skeleton and the appendicular skeleton. The **axial skeleton** supports the axis, or trunk, of the body and includes the skull, enclosing and protecting the brain; the vertebrae of the spinal column, enclosing the spinal cord; and the ribs. The appendicular skeleton is made up of the bones of the limbs, shoulders, and pelvis.

The bones of the skeleton are held together at movable joints by strong fibrous tissues called **ligaments**. Much of the versatility of our skeleton comes from three types of movable joints **(Figure 27.27)**. Humans have **ball-and-socket joints** in the shoulder and the hip. These joints enable us to rotate our arms and legs and move them in several planes. In the elbow, a **hinge joint** permits movement in a single plane. A **pivot joint** enables us to rotate the forearm at the elbow. ☑

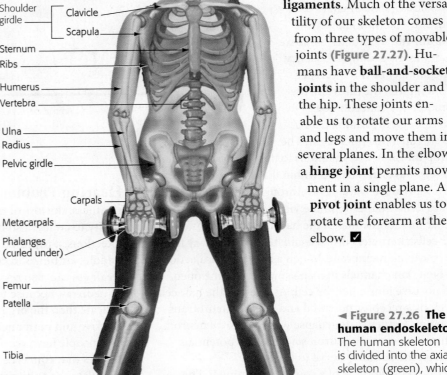

Skull
Shoulder girdle
Clavicle
Scapula
Sternum
Ribs
Humerus
Vertebra
Ulna
Radius
Pelvic girdle
Carpals
Metacarpals
Phalanges (curled under)
Femur
Patella
Tibia
Fibula
Tarsals
Metatarsals
Phalanges

◄ **Figure 27.26 The human endoskeleton.** The human skeleton is divided into the axial skeleton (green), which supports the trunk, and the appendicular skeleton (gold), which supports the limbs. Cartilage (blue) provides flexibility at various points.

▼ **Figure 27.27 Three kinds of joints.**

JOINTS		
Ball-and-socket (example: shoulder)	**Hinge** (example: elbow flexing)	**Pivot** (example: elbow rotation)
Head of humerus Scapula	Humerus Ulna	Ulna — Radius

The Structure of Bones

Although they may appear dry and dead, bones are complex organs consisting of several kinds of living tissues. You can get a sense of some of a bone's complexity from the cutaway view of the human humerus (the upper arm bone) shown in **Figure 27.28**. A sheet of fibrous connective tissue, shown in pink (most visible in the enlargement on the lower right), covers most of the outside surface. This tissue can form new bone during normal growth or in the event of a fracture. At either end of the bone is a thin sheet of cartilage (blue), also living tissue, that cushions joints, protecting the ends of bones as they move against each other. The bone itself contains cells that secrete a surrounding material, or matrix (see Figure 21.4f). Like all living tissues, bone tissues require servicing. Blood vessels course through channels in the bone, transporting nutrients and regulatory hormones to its cells and waste materials from them.

Notice that the shaft of the long bone shown in Figure 27.28 surrounds a central cavity. The central cavity contains yellow bone marrow, which is mostly stored fat brought into the bone by the blood. The ends of the bone have cavities that contain red bone marrow (not shown in the figure), a specialized tissue that produces blood cells (see Chapter 23).

▼ Figure 27.28 **The structure of an arm bone.**

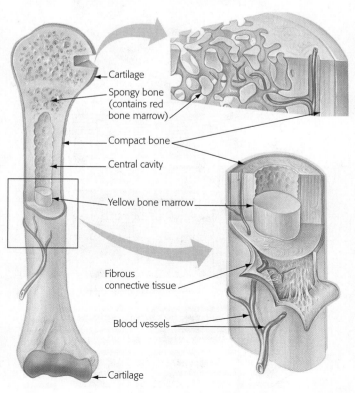

- Cartilage
- Spongy bone (contains red bone marrow)
- Compact bone
- Central cavity
- Yellow bone marrow
- Fibrous connective tissue
- Blood vessels
- Cartilage

Skeletal Diseases and Injuries

Your skeleton is quite strong and provides you with reliable support, but it is susceptible to disease and injury. **Arthritis**—inflammation of the joints—affects one out of every seven people in the United States. The most common form of arthritis occurs as a result of aging: The joints become stiff and sore and often swell as the cartilage between the bones wears down. Sometimes the bones thicken at the joints, producing crunching noises when they rub together and restricting movement. This form of arthritis is irreversible but not crippling in most cases, and moderate exercise, rest, and over-the-counter pain medications usually relieve most symptoms.

Rheumatoid arthritis is a debilitating autoimmune disease. The joints become highly inflamed, and their tissues may be destroyed by the body's immune system (see Figure 24.16). Rheumatoid arthritis usually begins between ages 40 and 50 and affects more women than men. Anti-inflammatory drugs relieve symptoms, but there is no cure.

Osteoporosis is another serious bone disorder. It is most common in women after menopause: Estrogen contributes to normal bone maintenance, and with lowered production of the hormone, bones may become thinner, more porous, and more easily broken. Insufficient exercise, smoking, diabetes mellitus, and an inadequate intake of protein and calcium may also contribute to the disease. Treatments include calcium and vitamin supplements, hormone replacement therapy, and drugs that slow bone loss or increase bone formation. Prevention of osteoporosis begins with sufficient calcium intake while bones are still increasing in density (up until about age 35). Weight-bearing exercise (walking, jogging, lifting weights) builds bone mass and is beneficial throughout life.

Bones are rigid but not inflexible; they will bend in response to external forces. However, as many of us know from personal experience, the skeletal system has its limits. If a force is applied that exceeds a bone's capacity to bend, the result is a broken bone, or fracture. The average American will break two bones during his or her lifetime, most commonly the forearm or, for people over 75, the hip.

Treatment of a fracture involves two steps: putting the bone back into its natural shape and then immobilizing it until the body's natural bone-building cells can repair the fracture. A splint or a cast is usually sufficient to protect the area, prevent movement, and promote healing. In more severe cases, a fracture can only be repaired surgically by inserting plates, rods, and/or screws that hold the broken pieces together (**Figure 27.29**). ☑

▼ **Figure 27.29 Broken bones.** These X-rays show the same set of fractured leg bones (tibia and fibula) before (left) and after they have been held together with screws and a plate (right).

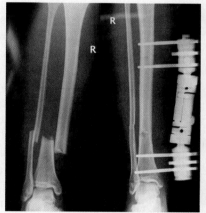

☑ CHECKPOINT

What two things can a young person do to help prevent osteoporosis?

Answer: ingest plenty of calcium and engage in weight-bearing exercise regularly

The Muscular System

Now that you've learned about the skeletal system, we can focus on the **muscular system**, which is made up of all the skeletal muscles in the body. **Skeletal muscles** are attached to the skeleton and produce body movement by interacting with it. **Figure 27.30** illustrates how muscles interact with bones to raise and lower the human forearm. As shown in the figure, strong fibrous tissue called **tendons** connects muscles to bones. For instance, one end of the triceps muscle is attached by tendons to bones of the shoulder. The other end is attached by a tendon to one of the bones in the forearm.

The ability to move the forearm in opposite directions requires that two muscles work as an antagonistic pair—that is, the two muscles must perform opposite tasks.

Why can't you flex your biceps and your triceps simultaneously?

For example, contraction of the biceps muscle shortens the muscle and pulls up the forearm. The triceps muscle is the biceps's antagonist; contraction of the triceps pulls the forearm down. Notice in Figure 27.30 that when one muscle is contracted, the antagonistic (opposite) muscle is relaxed.

The Cellular Basis of Muscle Contraction

Skeletal muscle is made up of a hierarchy of smaller and smaller parallel strands. As shown at the top of **Figure 27.31**, a muscle consists of bundles of parallel muscle fibers. Each muscle fiber is a single, long cell with many nuclei. In the middle of the figure, notice that each muscle fiber is itself a bundle of smaller **myofibrils**. Skeletal muscle is also called striated (striped) muscle because the myofibrils exhibit alternating light and dark bands when viewed with a microscope. A myofibril consists of repeating units called **sarcomeres**. Structurally, a sarcomere is the region between two dark, narrow lines in the myofibril. Functionally, the sarcomere is the contractile apparatus in a myofibril—the muscle fiber's fundamental unit of action.

The micrograph and the diagram below it at the bottom of Figure 27.31 reveal the structure of a sarcomere

in more detail. A myofibril is composed of regular arrangements of two kinds of filaments: **thin filaments** made primarily from the protein actin (blue in the diagram) and **thick filaments** made from the protein myosin (red).

A sarcomere contracts (shortens) when its thin filaments slide past its thick filaments. The model describing this process is known as the sliding-filament model of muscle contraction. **Figure 27.32**, a simplified

▼ **Figure 27.31 The contractile apparatus of skeletal muscle.**

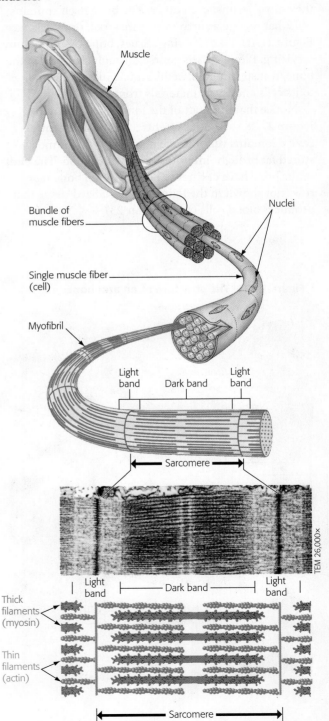

▼ **Figure 27.30**
Antagonistic action of muscles in the human arm. Many movements are produced through the action of two opposing muscles. In this example, contraction of the biceps muscle raises the forearm, while contraction of the triceps muscle lowers the forearm.

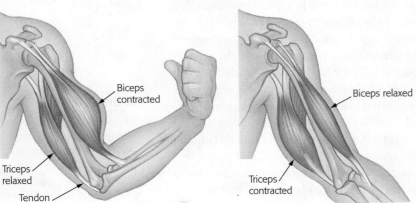

▼ **Figure 27.32 The sliding-filament model of muscle contraction.** Notice that the lengths of the thick and thin filaments do not change; the two types of filaments merely slide past each other to overlap.

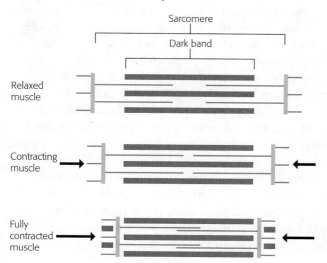

▼ **Figure 27.33 The mechanism of filament sliding.** Though we show only one myosin head in this figure, a typical thick filament has about 350 heads, each of which can bind and unbind to a thin filament about five times per second.

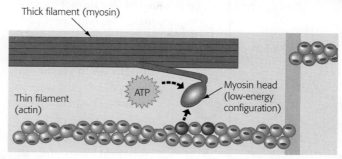

1 ATP binds to a myosin head, which is then released from an actin filament.

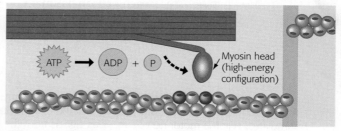

2 The breakdown of ATP cocks the myosin head.

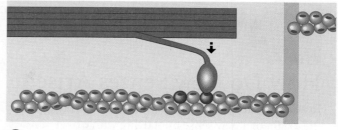

3 The myosin head attaches to an actin binding site.

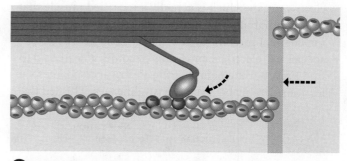

4 The power stroke slides the actin (thin) filament toward the center of the sarcomere.

5 As long as ATP is available, the process can be repeated until the muscle is fully contracted.

diagram of this model, shows a sarcomere in a relaxed muscle, a contracting muscle, and a fully contracted muscle. Notice in the contracting sarcomere that the thin filaments (blue) have moved toward the middle of the sarcomere. When the muscle is fully contracted, the thin filaments overlap in the middle of the sarcomere. Contraction only shortens the sarcomere; it does not change the lengths of the thick and thin filaments. A muscle can shorten to about one-third of its resting length when all of its sarcomeres are contracted.

What makes the thin filaments slide? The key event is the binding between parts (called heads) of the myosin molecules in the thick filaments and specific sites on actin molecules in the thin filaments. The process of contraction requires energy, provided by ATP.

Figure 27.33 indicates how sliding is thought to work. **1** ATP binds to a myosin head ( ), causing the head to detach from a binding site on actin ( ). **2** The myosin head gains energy from the breakdown of ATP and changes position. In this high-energy position, the myosin head is cocked like a pistol ready to fire (actually, ready to bind with another site on the actin molecule). **3** The energized myosin head binds to an exposed binding site on actin. **4** The molecular event that actually causes sliding is called the power stroke. The myosin head bends back to its low-energy position, pulling the thin filament toward the center of the sarcomere. **5** After the power stroke, the whole process repeats: More ATP binds, the myosin head attaches to the next binding site along the thin filament and slides it forward, and so on. As long as sufficient ATP is present, the process continues until the muscle is fully contracted or until the signal to contract stops. ✔

✓ CHECKPOINT

What protein is most abundant in a thin filament of a myofibril? In a thick filament?

Answer: actin; myosin

Motor Neurons: Control of Muscle Contraction

The sarcomeres of a muscle fiber do not contract on their own. They must be stimulated to contract by motor neurons, which are part of the central nervous system. Responding to a signal sent from the brain via the spinal cord, a motor neuron releases a neurotransmitter, which causes the muscle fiber to contract. A typical motor neuron can stimulate more than one muscle fiber because each neuron has many branches. In the example shown in **Figure 27.34**,

you can see two orange **motor units**, each consisting of a neuron and all the muscle fibers it controls (two or three, in this case).

The organization of individual neurons and muscle cells into motor units is the key to the action of whole muscles. Each motor neuron may serve just one or up to several hundred fibers scattered throughout a muscle. Stimulation of the muscle by a single motor neuron produces only a weak contraction. More forceful contractions result when additional motor units are activated. Thus, depending on how many motor units your brain commands to contract, you can apply a small amount of force to lift a fork or considerably more to lift a barbell. In muscles requiring precise control, such as those controlling eye movements, a motor neuron may control only one fiber. And, as you'll see next, anatomical structures similar to those you have been learning about play an important role in a nonhuman sense.

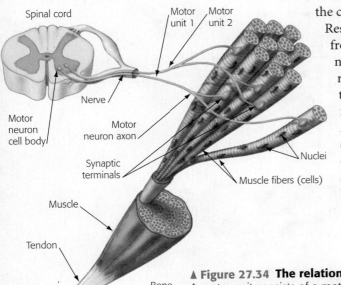

Spinal cord
Motor unit 1
Motor unit 2
Nerve
Motor neuron cell body
Motor neuron axon
Synaptic terminals
Nuclei
Muscle fibers (cells)
Muscle
Tendon
Bone

▲ **Figure 27.34 The relationship between motor neurons and muscle fibers.** A motor unit consists of a motor neuron and the one or more muscle fibers that it stimulates. When a motor neuron receives signals from the CNS, it passes them via synaptic terminals to the muscle fibers, causing the fibers to contract.

Extrahuman Senses THE PROCESS OF SCIENCE

How Do New Senses Arise?

Researchers from the University of Texas investigated the origin of a new sense by starting with **observations** about two species of electric fish, one from Africa and one from South America. These fishes can activate an electric organ, which is actually a modified muscle that has lost its ability to contract and instead uses special ion channel proteins to generate electric fields. Both species use electrical emissions to communicate and to find prey, but the nature of the electrical discharges varies considerably between the two lineages. This led the

researchers to **question** whether different ion channel proteins had evolved in the two electric species.

The researchers formed the **hypothesis** that the ion channel genes of the two electric species had mutated in unique ways. In their **experiment**, they determined the DNA sequence of the gene in the two electric fishes and one closely related but nonelectric South American fish. **Figure 27.35** summarizes their **results**. In the common ancestor of all three of these species, a single ion channel gene had duplicated, and the gene copies later mutated into two forms, referred to as *a* and *b*. In the nonelectric fish, both of these genes function in muscles, much as they do in many other vertebrates. In the two species of electric fish, however, gene *a* had mutated into forms that allow the fishes to produce a current in the electric organ. Slight differences in how gene *a* mutated account for the differences in how each species generates electrical signals. Gene *b*, however, functions in the muscles of the electric fishes as it does in nonelectric fishes. This work demonstrates how a new sense can arise from an old one by gene duplication followed by mutation and natural selection.

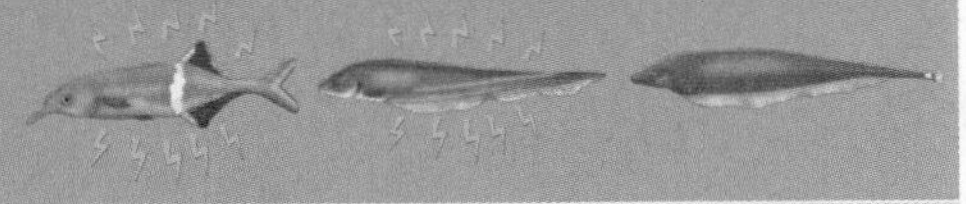

► **Figure 27.35 Duplication of the gene for a muscle ion channel protein led to an electric organ.** In two species of electric fish, the gene for a muscle ion channel protein duplicated and then mutated, producing genes *a* and *b*; gene *a* functions in the electric organ, while gene *b* functions in muscle. In a nonelectric fish species, both genes function in muscle.

Location of gene function	African species Electric fish	South American species	
		Electric fish	Nonelectric fish
Muscle	Gene *b*	*b*	*a* and *b*
Electric organ	Gene *a* (mutation 1)	*a* (mutation 2)	none

Stimulus and Response: Putting It All Together

The forward soars into the air, ready to receive a pass from his teammate and slam it home in an alley-oop **(Figure 27.36)**. Besides enjoying a great play, we can now appreciate these events in terms of sensory input, nervous system integration, and locomotor response.

The forward obtains information about the path of the ball from his sensory structures. Photoreceptors in his eyes track the ball in flight. Sensory neurons convey this information to his brain as a series of action potentials. Within his brain, information about the angle and speed of the ball is integrated. In response, motor neurons signal multiple muscles to perform very specific actions. He jumps upward, twists his body, extends his arms, turns his wrist joints, and flexes his hand muscles. When mechanoreceptors in his hand detect the impact of the ball, this information is communicated and integrated, resulting in signals that move his hand muscles against his finger bones, squeezing his fingers and capturing the ball. His eyes then provide the visual information needed to turn and slam the ball home. The fans see a spectacular play by a talented athlete. But underlying it all is the nervous system directing muscles to respond to information that sensory receptors have gathered about the environment.

We have now completed the unit on animal structure and function. Our overriding theme has been that the evolution of new structures allows adaptations for new functions; that is, the structural adaptations of a cell, tissue, organ, or organ system determine the job it can perform. We'll see the structure-function theme emerge again in the context of adaptations to the environment when we take up the study of plants in the next unit.

► Figure 27.36 **The nervous, sensory, and locomotor systems in action.**

Extrahuman Senses EVOLUTION CONNECTION

Seeing UV

In the Biology and Society section and elsewhere in this chapter, you have read about senses possessed by some animals but not people. Natural selection can foster new adaptations that arise from mutations in genes that control existing adaptations. You have read about one example—which led to the evolution of electroreception in some fishes—in the Process of Science section. This principle is also clearly evident in the evolution of another nonhuman sense: ultraviolet vision.

Many birds can see beyond what we humans can see **(Figure 27.37)**. Ultraviolet (UV) vision—the ability to see light of wavelengths shorter than those in our visual spectrum (see Figure 7.4)—is believed to be important in social communication and food gathering. As you learned in this chapter, visual information is transmitted to the brain after pigment molecules in the eye absorb light. Researchers studying vision in birds found that a single amino acid change in the pigment protein rhodopsin converted it to a UV-detecting form. This is yet another example of a large change—an important extension of a sense—that can be traced to a small change: a single mutation. In nature, if a mutation such as this one confers a survival advantage (the ability to more easily locate food, for example), then natural selection would tend to favor individuals with the mutation. Over time, the new adaptation would eventually become the norm.

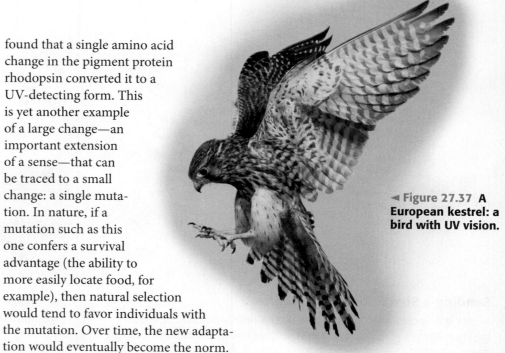

◄ Figure 27.37 **A European kestrel: a bird with UV vision.**

Chapter Review

SUMMARY OF KEY CONCEPTS

Go to **www.masteringbiology.com** for homework assignments, practice quizzes, Pearson eText, and more.

An Overview of Animal Nervous Systems

The nervous system is a communication and coordination network composed of neurons, specialized nerve cells capable of carrying signals throughout the body.

Organization of Nervous Systems

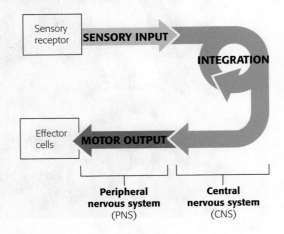

Neurons

Neurons are the functional units of the nervous system.

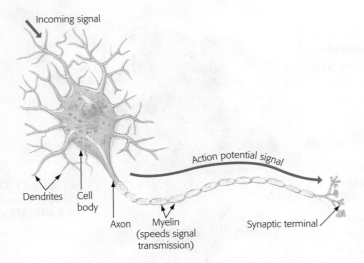

Sending a Signal through a Neuron

At rest, a neuron's plasma membrane has a resting potential caused by the membrane's ability to maintain a positive charge on its outer surface opposing a negative charge on its inner surface. A stimulus alters a portion of the membrane, allowing ions to enter and exit the neuron and creating an action potential. Action potentials are self-propagated in a one-way chain reaction along a neuron. An action potential is an all-or-none event; its size is not affected by differences in stimulus strength. The frequency of action potentials does change with the strength of the stimulus.

Passing a Signal from a Neuron to a Receiving Cell

Signals are transmitted beyond an individual neuron at relay points called synapses. In an electrical synapse, electric current passes directly from one neuron to the next. At chemical synapses, the sending cell secretes a chemical signal, a neurotransmitter, which crosses the synaptic cleft (a gap between the cells) and binds to a specific receptor on the surface of the receiving cell. A cell may receive different signals from many neurons. A wide variety of small molecules can act as neurotransmitters. Many drugs act at synapses by increasing or decreasing the normal effect of neurotransmitters.

The Human Nervous System: A Closer Look

The Central Nervous System and the Peripheral Nervous System

NERVOUS SYSTEM			
Central Nervous System (CNS)		**Peripheral Nervous System** (PNS)	
Brain	Spinal cord: nerve bundle that communicates with body	Voluntary nervous system: voluntary control over muscles	Autonomic nervous system: involuntary control over organs • Parasympathetic division: rest and digest • Sympathetic division: fight or flight

The Human Brain

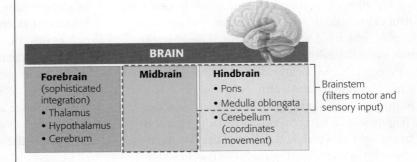

The forebrain's cerebrum, divided into right and left hemispheres, is the largest and most complex part of the brain. In particular, the surface of the cerebrum, the cerebral cortex, is responsible for many of the most distinctive human traits. The right and left cerebral hemispheres specialize in different mental tasks.

The Senses

Sensory Input

The process of sensory transduction:

The strength of the stimulus alters the rate of action potential transmission. Some sensory neurons tend to become less sensitive when stimulated repeatedly, a phenomenon known as sensory adaptation. Pain receptors sense stimuli that may indicate tissue damage; thermoreceptors detect heat or cold; mechanoreceptors respond to mechanical energy (such as touch, pressure, or sound); chemoreceptors respond to chemicals in the external environment or body fluids; and electromagnetic receptors respond to electricity, magnetism, or light (photoreceptors).

Vision

In the human eye, the cornea and lens focus light on the retina. The human lens changes shape to bring objects at different distances into sharp focus. The retina contains two types of photoreceptor cells called rods and cones. Rods contain the visual pigment rhodopsin and function in dim light. Cones contain photopsin, which enables us to see color in full light. Nearsightedness, farsightedness, and astigmatism result from focusing problems in the lens. Corrective lenses bend the light rays to compensate.

Hearing

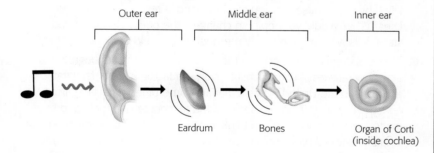

The waves generated in the cochlear fluid move hair cells (mechanoreceptors) of the organ of Corti against an overlying membrane. Bending of the hair cells triggers receptor potentials, sending nerve signals to the brain. Deafness can be caused by infections, injury, or overexposure to loud noises.

Locomotor Systems

Movement is one of the most distinctive features of animals. In the process of locomotor output, the nervous system issues commands to the muscular system, and the muscular system exerts force against the skeleton.

The Skeletal System

The skeletal system functions in support, movement, and the protection of internal organs. The human endoskeleton is composed of cartilage and bone. Movable joints provide flexibility. A bone is a living organ containing several kinds of tissues. It is covered with a connective tissue membrane. Cartilage at the ends of the bone cushions the joints. The human skeleton is versatile, but it is also subject to problems, such as arthritis and osteoporosis. Broken bones can be realigned and immobilized, usually by splints or casts; bone cells then build new bone and repair the break.

The Muscular System

Skeletal muscles pull on bones to produce movements. Antagonistic pairs of muscles produce opposite movements. Each skeletal muscle cell, or fiber, contains bundles of myofibrils, which in striated muscle exhibit alternating light and dark bands. Each myofibril contains bundles of overlapping thick (myosin) and thin (actin) protein filaments. Repeating units of thick and thin filaments, called sarcomeres, are the muscle fiber's contractile units. The sliding-filament model explains the molecular process of muscle contraction. Using ATP, the myosin heads of the thick filaments attach to binding sites on the actin molecules and pull the thin filaments toward the center of the sarcomere. Motor neurons carry action potentials that initiate muscle contraction. A neuron can branch to contact a number of muscle fibers; the neuron and the muscle fibers it controls constitute a motor unit. The strength of a muscle contraction depends on the number of motor units activated.

Stimulus and Response: Putting It All Together

An animal's nervous system connects sensations derived from environmental stimuli to responses carried out by its muscles.

SELF-QUIZ

1. The large, central hub of a neuron, called the _____, contains the nucleus and organelles. Short, numerous fibers called _____ receive incoming messages, while a single long fiber called a(an) _____ conducts signals toward other cells. A neuron ends in many branches, each with a bulb-like _____ that contains neurotransmitters, which can be used to communicate signals to other neurons.

2. What is the function of the myelin sheath?

3. Your nervous system can be divided into two broad subsystems, the _____ and the _____. One of these is made up of nerves that conduct signals to and from the other structures. The other consists of the _____ and _____.

4. The central nervous system is protected by _____, a liquid that cushions it and supplies it with nutrients, and layers of protective tissue called the _____.

5. While driving down the interstate at rush hour, you get cut off by an 18-wheeler and have to slam on the brakes. In addition to a major case of road rage, you also develop a rapid heart rate and a rapid breathing rate. What's causing this increase? Your answer should indicate the branch of the nervous system involved.

6. A victim of a severe head injury can live for years in a nonresponsive state in which the cerebral cortex is not functioning but the person is still alive and performing metabolic functions. Based on your knowledge of brain structure and function, how can this be possible? Make sure your answer indicates which brain structures might be keeping the person alive.

7. How is an action potential different from a receptor potential?

8. For each of the following senses in humans, identify the type of receptor: seeing, tasting, hearing, smelling.

9. Mr. Johnson is becoming slightly deaf. To test his hearing, his doctor holds a vibrating tuning fork tightly against the back of Mr. Johnson's skull. This sends vibrations through the bones of the skull, setting the fluid in the cochlea in motion. Mr. Johnson can hear the tuning fork this way, but not when it is held away from his skull a few inches from his ear. Where is Mr. Johnson's hearing problem located? (Explain your answer.)
   a. in the auditory nerve leading to the brain
   b. in the hair cells in the cochlea
   c. in the bones of the middle ear
   d. in the fluid of the cochlea

10. A human's soft internal organs are protected by the _____ skeleton, while the bones of the limbs make up the _____ skeleton.

11. Arm and leg muscles are arranged in antagonistic pairs. How does this affect their functioning?
   a. It provides a backup if one of the muscles is injured.
   b. One muscle of the pair pushes while the other pulls.
   c. A single neuron controls both of them.
   d. It allows the muscles to produce opposing movements.

12. Muscle A and muscle B are the same size, but muscle A is capable of much finer control than muscle B. Which of the following is likely to be true of muscle A? (Explain your answer.)
   a. It is controlled by more neurons than muscle B.
   b. It contains fewer motor units than muscle B.
   c. It is controlled by fewer neurons than muscle B.
   d. Each of its motor units consists of more cells than the motor units of muscle B.

Answers to these questions can be found in Appendix: Self-Quiz Answers.

THE PROCESS OF SCIENCE

13. Much of what we know about brain function has come from rare individuals whose brains were altered as the result of surgery, accidents, or disease. Suppose a patient has brain surgery on the cerebral cortex, and immediately following the surgery, she appears normal. As she recovers over the next few days, she experiences some unusual things, such as being unable to name objects while looking at them with one eye covered. Her sensory perception seems normal except for when she tries to integrate information. What brain structure might have been damaged during the surgery that would account for these symptoms? Justify your answer.

14. Sensory organs tend to come in pairs. We have two eyes and two ears. Similarly, a planarian worm has two eyecups, a rattlesnake has two infrared receptors, and a butterfly has two antennae. Propose a testable hypothesis that could explain the advantage of having two eyes or ears instead of one.

BIOLOGY AND SOCIETY

15. Brain injuries tend to be so severe because most neurons will not be regenerated once they have been damaged. The use of embryonic stem cells (see Chapter 11) has been proposed as a potential solution to many neurological diseases. Stem cells could be placed into the brain of a person with Alzheimer's or Parkinson's disease. Theoretically, those cells could differentiate into neurons, replacing those that had been killed by the disease. Do you favor or oppose research along these lines? Why? Would your opinion change if the person to be treated with stem cells were a close family member who would die if not treated?

16. Alcohol's depressant effects on the nervous system cloud judgment and slow reflexes. Alcohol consumption is a factor in many fatal traffic accidents in the United States. What are some other impacts of alcohol abuse on society? What are some of the responses of people and society to alcohol abuse? Do you think that alcohol abuse is primarily an individual or societal problem? Do you think our responses to alcohol abuse are appropriate and proportional to the seriousness of the problem?

17. Have you ever felt your ears ringing after listening to music with the volume turned high or attending a loud rock concert? Are you worried that excessively loud music could permanently impair your hearing? Do you think that people are aware of the possible danger of prolonged exposure to loud music? Should anything be done to warn or protect them? If so, what action would you suggest? What effect might warnings have?

Unit 6
Plant Structure and Function

Chapter 28: **The Life of a Flowering Plant**

Chapter Thread: **Agriculture and People**

Chapter 29: **The Working Plant**

Chapter Thread: **The Interdependence of Organisms**

28 The Life of a Flowering Plant

Roasted coffee beans. People have been cultivating, drying, roasting, and drinking coffee for hundreds of years.

Agriculture and People BIOLOGY AND SOCIETY

The Buzz on Coffee Plants

From the dawn of civilization to the frontiers of genetic engineering, human progress has always depended on expanding our use of plants—for food, fuel, clothing, and countless other trappings of modern life. To frame our relationship with plants, think about a particular crop, one that may help get you through a long day of classes: coffee. Today, coffee is one of the most important agricultural products in the world. Americans drink more than $10 billion worth of coffee annually, a startling average of 22 gallons of coffee per American per year.

Ground coffee is made from the seeds of plants belonging to several species in the genus *Coffea*. Historians believe that coffee was discovered in Ethiopia during the 1200s. Locals may have noticed that the plants provided an energizing effect on animals that ate its fruit. African farmers eventually learned to roast, grind, and filter the coffee beans in water. From central Africa, coffee cultivation and consumption spread to the Middle East. By the 1600s, coffee houses had appeared throughout Europe. And by the 1700s, coffee plants imported to the Americas were an important crop. Today, coffee is grown in at least 50 tropical countries around the world. A small but growing percentage of commercial coffee is "Fair Trade Certified." To receive such a designation, farmers agree to provide humane working conditions for their employees and to abide by agricultural practices that promote a healthy and sustainable environment. In exchange, the farmers are guaranteed a fair price for their crop.

Clearly, we have benefited from our agricultural relationship with coffee. But ask yourself this: What is the basis of coffee's popularity? No doubt we love the jolt we get from the caffeine, which is produced in coffee seeds and stimulates the nervous system. It is believed that caffeine acts as a toxin to many herbivores (plant-eaters) and therefore serves as a form of self-defense for the plant. Your morning buzz may therefore be a by-product of an evolutionary adaptation that helps protect the coffee plant from being eaten by pests.

Plants are vital to the well-being of not just humans but the entire biosphere. Above and below the ground, plants provide shelter, food, and breeding areas for animals, fungi, and microorganisms. Because angiosperms—the flowering plants—make up more than 90% of the plant kingdom, we concentrate on them in this unit. (If you'd like to learn about other groups of plants—such as mosses, ferns, and cone-bearing gymnosperms—see Chapter 16.) In this chapter, we begin by examining angiosperm structure, first at the level of the whole plant and then at the microscopic level of tissues and cells. Then we'll see how plant structures function in growth and reproduction.

The Structure and Function of a Flowering Plant

Coffee plant

Angiosperms have dominated the land for more than 100 million years, and about 250,000 species of flowering plants exist today. Most of our foods come from 100 or so species of domesticated flowering plants. Among these foods are roots, such as beets and carrots; the fruits of trees and vines, such as apples, nuts, berries, and squashes; the fruits and seeds of legumes, such as peas, peanuts, and beans; and grains, the fruits of grasses such as wheat, rice, and corn. (Notice that the term *coffee bean* is not strictly correct, because the coffee plant is not a legume; it is coffee seeds that we roast and consume.)

Monocots and Dicots

On the basis of several structural differences, botanists (biologists who study plants) have traditionally classified angiosperms into two groups: monocots and dicots **(Table 28.1)**. The names of the groups refer to embryonic structures called **cotyledons** (also called seed leaves), the first leaves to emerge from a growing seedling. A **monocot** embryo has one seed leaf; a **dicot** embryo has two seed leaves. The largest group of dicots is the **eudicots** (which translates to "true" dicots). In this chapter, we will focus on monocots and eudicots.

Monocots include orchids, palms, and lilies, as well as grains and other grasses. Most monocots have leaves with parallel veins. Monocot stems have vascular tissues (internal tissues that transport water and nutrients) organized into bundles that are arranged in a scattered pattern. The flowers of most monocots have petals and parts in multiples of three. Monocot roots form a fibrous system—a mat of threads—that spreads out just below the soil surface. With most of their roots in the top few centimeters of soil, monocots, especially grasses, make excellent ground covers and can help reduce soil erosion.

Most flowering plants are eudicots, including many food crops (such as nearly all of our fruits and vegetables), the majority of ornamental plants, and most shrubs and trees (except for the gymnosperms). Coffee, for example, grows as a eudicot shrub. Eudicot leaves have a multibranched network of veins, and eudicot stems have vascular bundles arranged in a ring. Eudicot flowers usually have petals and floral parts in multiples of four or five. The large, main root of a eudicot, known as a taproot, goes deep into the soil, as you know if you've ever tried to pull up a dandelion.

As we saw in the preceding unit on animals, a close look at a structure often reveals its function. Conversely, function provides insight into the "logic" of a structure. In the sections that follow, we'll take a detailed look at the correlation between plant structure and function. ☑

☑ **CHECKPOINT**

How do the terms *monocot* and *eudicot* relate to an anatomical difference between these two groups of plants?

Answer: A monocot embryo has a single (mono- means "one") cotyledon (seed leaf), and a eudicot embryo has two (di- means "two").

Table 28.1	Comparing Monocots and Eudicots				
	Seed Leaves	**Leaf Veins**	**Stems**	**Flowers**	**Roots**
Monocots	One cotyledon	Veins usually parallel	Vascular bundles in scattered arrangement	Floral parts usually in multiples of three	Fibrous root system
Eudicots	Two cotyledons	Veins usually branched	Vascular bundles arranged in ring	Floral parts usually in multiples of four or five	Taproot usually present

Plant Organs: Roots, Stems, and Leaves

Plants, just like most animals, have organs made up of different tissues, and these tissues in turn are made up of one or more types of cells. An **organ** consists of several types of tissues that together carry out a particular function.

Plants (along with fungi) first occupied land around 475 million years ago (see Chapter 16). Among the evolutionary adaptations that made it possible for plants to thrive on land were structures for absorbing water and minerals from the soil; a large light-collecting surface; the ability to take in carbon dioxide from the air for photosynthesis; and adaptations for surviving dry conditions. In a land plant, the roots (the belowground structures) and the shoots (the aboveground structures, including stems, leaves, and flowers) perform all these vital functions **(Figure 28.1)**. Neither roots nor shoots can survive without the other. Lacking chloroplasts and living in the dark, the roots would starve without sugar and other organic nutrients transported from photosynthetic stems and leaves. Conversely, stems and leaves depend on the water and minerals absorbed by roots.

Roots

A plant's **roots** anchor it in the soil, absorb and transport minerals and water, and store food. All of a plant's roots make up its **root system**. The fibrous root system of a monocot provides broad exposure to soil water and minerals as well as firm anchorage. In contrast, the eudicot taproot is vertical, with many small secondary roots growing outward. Near the root tips of both monocots and eudicots are tiny projections called **root hairs** that greatly increase the root surface area, providing an extensive outer layer for absorption of water and minerals (Figure 28.1, far right). Each root hair is an outgrowth of a cell on the surface of the root. It is difficult to move an established plant without injuring it because such transplantation often damages the plant's delicate root hairs.

Large taproots, such as those found in carrots, turnips, sugar beets, and sweet potatoes, store food in the form of carbohydrates such as starch **(Figure 28.2a)**. The plants use these stored sugars during periods of active growth and when they are producing flowers and fruit. Other types of modified roots include buttress roots, aerial roots that look like the supporting beams of buildings and support the tall trunks of the trees that produce them **(Figure 28.2b)**.

▼ **Figure 28.1** **The structure of a flowering plant.**

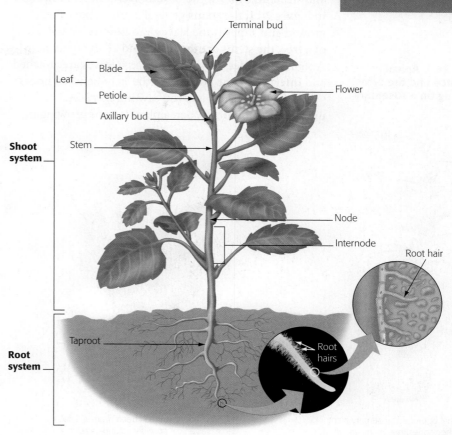

▼ **Figure 28.2** **Modified roots.**

(a) The root of a sugar beet stores carbohydrates.

(b) The buttress roots of this Indonesian Paldoa tree help support the trunk.

Stems

The **shoot system** of a plant is made up of stems, leaves, and structures for reproduction (flowers). As indicated in Figure 28.1, the **stems** generally grow above the ground and support the leaves and flowers. In the case of a tree, the stems are the trunk and all the branches. A stem has **nodes**, the points at which leaves are attached, and **internodes**, the portions of the stem between nodes.

The two types of buds you saw in Figure 28.1 are undeveloped shoots. When a plant stem is growing in length, the **terminal bud**, at the tip of the stem, has developing leaves and a compact series of nodes and internodes. The **axillary buds**, one in each of the crooks formed by a leaf and the stem, are usually dormant. In many plants, the terminal bud produces hormones that inhibit growth of the axillary buds, a phenomenon called **apical dominance**. By concentrating the plant's resources on growing taller, apical dominance is an evolutionary adaptation that increases the plant's exposure to light. Branching is also important for increasing the exposure of the shoot system to the environment, and under certain conditions, the axillary buds begin growing and developing into branches. As any home gardener knows, removing the terminal bud by pruning a fruit tree or "pinching back" a houseplant will make the plant bushier **(Figure 28.3)**.

Stems can take many forms. Strawberry plants have horizontal stems, or runners, that grow along the ground surface. A runner is a means of asexual reproduction; as shown in **Figure 28.4a**, a new plant can emerge from it. This is why strawberries, if left unchecked, can rapidly fill your garden. If you dig up an iris or ginger plant, you'll see a different stem modification; the large, brownish, rootlike structures near the soil surface are actually horizontal underground stems called **rhizomes (Figure 28.4b)**. Rhizomes store food, and because they have buds, they can also form new plants. About every three years, gardeners can dig up iris rhizomes, split them, and plant the partial rhizomes to get multiple identical plants. A potato plant has rhizomes ending in enlarged structures called **tubers** (the potatoes we eat), where food is stored in the form of starch **(Figure 28.4c)**. The "eyes" of a potato are axillary buds, which can grow into new plants, allowing potatoes to be easily propagated.

▼**Figure 28.3 Apical dominance and the effect of pruning on a rosemary plant.**

Terminal bud

The terminal bud of this rosemary plant produces hormones that inhibit growth of the axillary buds, an effect called apical dominance. The result is a tall, thin plant.

Terminal bud removed

This rosemary plant has been pruned, which decreases apical dominance and increases branching and leaf production. The result is an increase in the useful yield of leaves.

▼**Figure 28.4 Modified stems.**

Runner

(a) Strawberry plants

Rhizome

Root

(b) Ginger plant

Taproot

Rhizome

Tuber at end of rhizome

(c) Potato plant

Leaves

Leaves are the primary sites of photosynthesis in most plants, although many plants also have green, photosynthetic stems. A leaf consists of a flattened **blade** and a stalk, or **petiole**, which joins the leaf to the stem (see Figure 28.1).

Plant leaves are highly varied. Leaves can be either simple or compound; some plants even have doubly compound leaves. **Figure 28.5** displays one example of each leaf type, but keep in mind that leaves come in a great variety of sizes and shapes. Grasses and most other monocots have long leaves without petioles. Some eudicots have enormous petioles that contain a lot of water and stored food, such as the edible stalks of celery. A modified leaf called a tendril can help plants such as sweet peas or grapes climb up their supports **(Figure 28.6a)**. And the spines of the cactus **(Figure 28.6b)** are modified leaf parts that may protect the plant from predatory animals. In many cactus species, the main photosynthetic organ is the large green stem, which also stores water.

So far, we have examined plants as we see them with the unaided eye. In the next section, we begin to dissect a plant and explore its microscopic organization. ☑

▼**Figure 28.5 Arrangement of leaves.** You can distinguish simple leaves from compound leaves by looking for axillary buds: Each leaf has only one axillary bud, where the petiole attaches to the stem; leaflets of compound leaves do not have axillary buds.

LEAF ARRANGEMENT		
Simple	**Compound**	**Doubly Compound**
Petiole — Axillary bud	Petiole — Axillary bud	Leaflet — Petiole — Axillary bud
A single individual blade	One blade consisting of many leaflets (which themselves lack axillary buds)	Each leaflet divided into smaller leaflets

▼**Figure 28.6 Modified leaves.**

(a) Tendrils of a gourd plant

Tendril

(b) Spines of a cactus

☑ **CHECKPOINT**

Name the organ you are eating when you eat each of the following foods: celery stalk, lettuce, carrot, potato, turnip.

Answer: stem, leaf, root, stem, root

Plant Tissues and Tissue Systems

As in animals, the organs of plants contain tissues. Each **tissue** is a group of cells that together perform a specialized function. For example, vascular tissue called **xylem** conveys water and dissolved minerals upward from the roots to the stems and leaves, while **phloem** tissue transports sugars from leaves or storage tissues to other parts of the plant.

A **tissue system** consists of one or more tissues organized into a functional unit within a plant. Each plant organ—root, stem, or leaf—is made up of three tissue systems: the dermal, vascular, and ground tissue systems. Each tissue system is continuous throughout the entire plant body, but the systems are arranged differently in leaves, stems, and roots (Figure 28.7).

The **dermal tissue system** (brown in the figure) forms an outer protective covering. Like our own skin, it forms a first line of defense against physical damage and infectious organisms. On leaves and on most stems, dermal cells secrete a waxy coating called the **cuticle**, which helps prevent water loss. The **vascular tissue system** (purple) provides support and long-distance transport throughout the plant; xylem and phloem are part of this system. The **ground tissue system** (yellow) accounts for most of the bulk of a plant; it has diverse functions, including photosynthesis, storage, and support.

Figure 28.8, a cross section of a eudicot root, illustrates the three tissue systems. The epidermis (the outer layer of the dermal tissue system) is a single layer of tightly packed cells covering the entire root. Water and minerals enter the plant from the soil through these cells. Some of the young epidermal cells grow outward and form root hairs. In the center of the root, the vascular tissue system forms a cylinder, with xylem cells radiating from the center like the spokes of a wheel and phloem cells filling in the wedges between the spokes. The ground tissue system of the root forms the **cortex**, where cells store food and take up water and minerals. The innermost layer of cortex is the **endodermis**, a thin cylinder one cell thick. The endodermis is a selective barrier that regulates the passage of substances between the cortex and the vascular tissue.

All plant stems have vascular tissue systems arranged in numerous vascular bundles. The location and arrangement of these bundles differ between monocots and eudicots (see Figure 28.7). In eudicots, another part of the ground tissue system, known as the **pith**, fills the center of the stem and is often important in food storage.

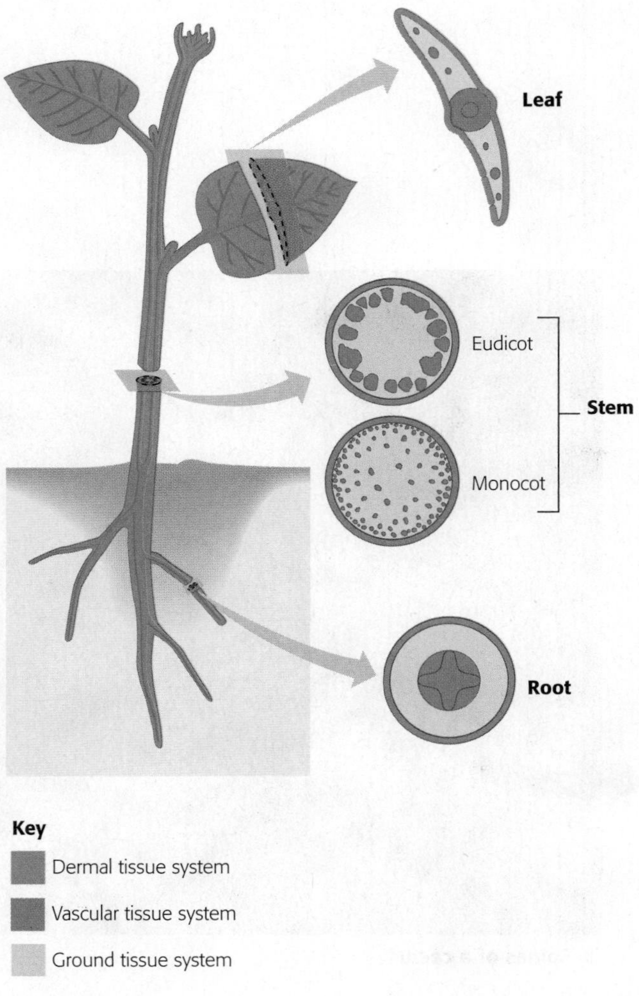

► **Figure 28.7 The three tissue systems of a plant.** The roots, stems, and leaves of a plant are made from three tissue systems (the dermal tissue system, vascular tissue system, and ground tissue system) that are continuous throughout the plant body.

Leaf

Eudicot

Stem

Monocot

Root

Key

■ Dermal tissue system

■ Vascular tissue system

■ Ground tissue system

▼ **Figure 28.8 Tissue systems in a eudicot root.** This colored micrograph is a cross section of a young buttercup root. You can see the single-layered epidermis, the cylindrical vascular tissue system with xylem and phloem, and the ground tissue system that makes up the bulk of the root.

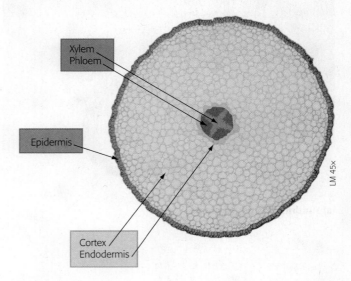

Xylem
Phloem
Epidermis
Cortex
Endodermis
LM 45x

Figure 28.9 illustrates the arrangement of the three tissue systems found in a typical eudicot leaf. The epidermis contains **stomata** (singular, *stoma*), which are tiny pores between two specialized cells called guard cells. The **guard cells** regulate the opening and closing of stomata (see Figure 29.10), allowing gas exchange between the surrounding air and photosynthetic cells inside the leaf.

The main site of photosynthesis is the **mesophyll**, which is the ground tissue system of a leaf. Mesophyll consists mainly of photosynthetic cells containing chloroplasts (green in Figure 28.9).

The leaf's vascular tissue system is made up of a network of veins. As you can see in Figure 28.9, each vein is a vascular bundle composed of xylem and phloem. The veins are in close contact with the leaf's photosynthetic tissues. This ensures that those tissues are supplied with water and minerals from the soil and that sugars made in the leaves are transported throughout the plant. ☑

What structures allow a plant to "breathe"?

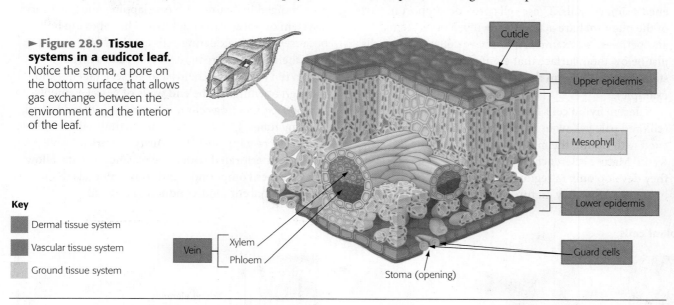

► Figure 28.9 **Tissue systems in a eudicot leaf.** Notice the stoma, a pore on the bottom surface that allows gas exchange between the environment and the interior of the leaf.

Key
- Dermal tissue system
- Vascular tissue system
- Ground tissue system

Cuticle
Upper epidermis
Mesophyll
Lower epidermis
Guard cells
Vein — Xylem / Phloem
Stoma (opening)

Plant Cells

So far, we have examined plant structure at the level of organs and tissues. Now we'll zoom in even closer to examine cells.

In addition to features shared with other eukaryotic cells (see Figure 4.5), most plant cells have three unique structures, as shown in **Figure 28.10**: **chloroplasts**, the sites of photosynthesis; a large **central vacuole** containing fluid that helps maintain the cell's firmness (also referred to as turgor); and a protective **cell wall** that surrounds the plasma membrane.

Plant cell walls consist largely of the structural carbohydrate cellulose. Some plant cells, especially those that provide structural support, have a two-layered cell wall; a primary cell wall grows first, and then a thicker, more rigid secondary cell wall is deposited between the plasma membrane and the primary wall. Plasmodesmata are open channels in adjacent cell walls through which cytoplasm and various substances can flow from cell to cell.

▼ Figure 28.10 **The structure of a plant cell.** The colored boxes highlight the unique features of plant cells. The enlargement shows two adjoining cells.

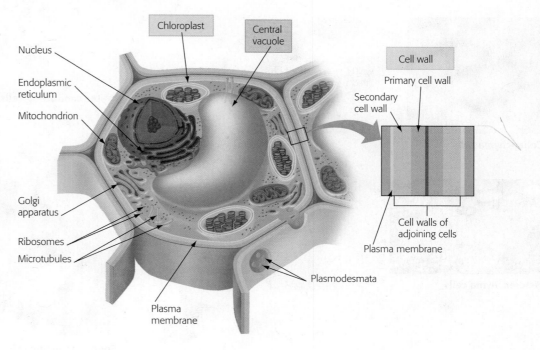

Chloroplast
Central vacuole
Nucleus
Endoplasmic reticulum
Mitochondrion
Golgi apparatus
Ribosomes
Microtubules
Plasma membrane
Cell wall
Primary cell wall
Secondary cell wall
Cell walls of adjoining cells
Plasma membrane
Plasmodesmata

611

Figure 28.11 presents an overview of plant cell types. **Parenchyma cells** are the most abundant type of cell in most plants. They have only primary (often thin) walls. Parenchyma cells perform a variety of functions, including food storage and photosynthesis. Most parenchyma cells can divide and differentiate (become specialized in their structure and function; see Chapter 11) into other types of plant cells, which they may do during repair of an injury.

Collenchyma cells resemble parenchyma cells in lacking secondary walls, but they have unevenly thickened primary walls. These cells provide support in parts of the plant that are actively growing. Young stems and petioles, for example, often have collenchyma cells just below their surface that elongate with the growing stem (these cells form the "strings" of a celery stalk, for example).

Sclerenchyma cells have thick secondary cell walls (colored pale yellow in Figure 28.11) usually strengthened with **lignin**, the main chemical component of wood. Mature sclerenchyma cells cannot elongate, and they develop only in regions that have stopped growing in length. After they mature, most sclerenchyma cells

die, and the rigid cell walls of these dead cells form a "skeleton" that supports the plant much as steel beams do in a building. Sclerenchyma cells make up some commercially important plant products, such as the highly versatile hemp fiber used to make rope and clothing.

Angiosperms have two types of water-conducting cells: tracheids and vessel elements. Both have rigid, lignin-containing secondary cell walls. **Tracheids** are long, thin cells with tapered ends; **vessel elements** are wider, shorter, and less tapered. Water-conducting cells are arranged in chains with overlapping ends that form a system of water-carrying tubes. The tubes are hollow because water-conducting cells are dead when mature; only their cell walls remain. Water passes through pits in the walls of tracheids and vessel elements and through openings in the end walls of vessel elements.

Food-conducting cells are also arranged end to end, forming tubes. Unlike water-conducting cells, however, these cells remain alive at maturity. Their end walls, which are perforated with large plasmodesmata, allow sugars, other compounds, and some minerals to move between adjacent food-conducting cells. ☑

▼ **Figure 28.11 Types of plant cells.**

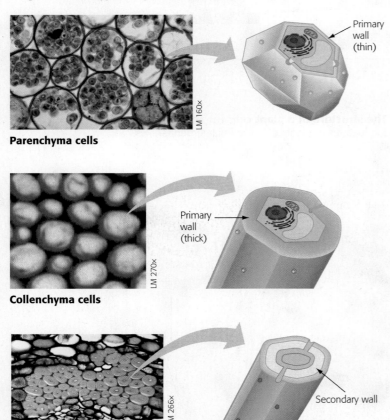

Parenchyma cells

Collenchyma cells

Sclerenchyma cells

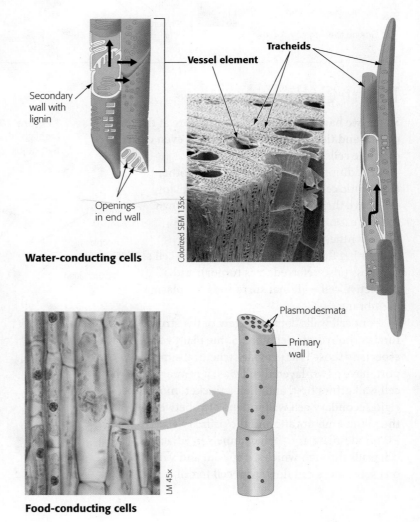

Water-conducting cells

Food-conducting cells

Plant Growth

The growth of a plant differs from that of an animal in a fundamental way. Most animals are characterized by **determinate growth**; that is, they cease growing after reaching a certain size. Most species of plants, in contrast, continue to grow for as long as they live, a condition known as **indeterminate growth**.

Indeterminate growth does not mean that plants are immortal. In fact, different types of plants have very different life spans **(Figure 28.12)**. Plants called **annuals** emerge from seed, mature, reproduce, and die in a single year or growing season. Our most important food crops—wheat, corn, and rice, for example—are annuals. **Biennials** live for two years; flowering and seed production usually occur during the second year. Carrots are biennials, but we usually harvest them in their first year and so miss seeing their flowers. Plants that live and reproduce for many years, including trees, shrubs (such as the coffee plant), and some grasses, are known as **perennials**. Some perennials have life spans well beyond the longest-lived animals; for example, some bristlecone pines have been alive for more than 4,500 years.

Primary Growth: Lengthening

Growth in all plants is made possible by tissues called meristems. A **meristem** consists of undifferentiated (unspecialized) cells that divide when conditions permit, generating new cells and tissues. Meristems at the tips

of roots and in the buds of shoots are **apical meristems**. Cell division in apical meristems produces new cells that enable a plant to grow in length, a process called **primary growth** **(Figure 28.13)**. Tissues produced by primary growth are called primary tissues.

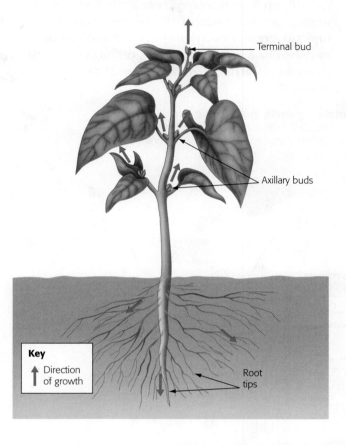

Terminal bud

Axillary buds

Key

↑ Direction of growth

Root tips

◄ **Figure 28.13 Primary growth at apical meristems.** Meristems are tissues responsible for growth in all plants. The apical meristems are located at the root tips and in the buds of shoots.

▼ Figure 28.12 **Plants with varying life spans.**

PLANT LIFE SPANS		
Annuals (live for just one growing season)	**Biennials** (live for two growing seasons)	**Perennials** (live for many growing seasons)
Rice	Wild chervil (also called cow parsley)	Coffee plants

☑ **CHECKPOINT**

What two basic cellular
mechanisms account for
primary growth?

*Answer: cell division and cell
lengthening*

Figure 28.14 shows a slice through a growing onion root. Primary growth enables roots to push through the soil. (A very similar process results in the upward growth of shoots.) At the tip of the root is the **root cap**, a thimble-like cone of cells that protects the delicate, actively dividing cells of the apical meristem. The root's apical meristem (marked with the orange oval in the art and circled in the micrograph) replaces cells of the root cap that are scraped away by the soil (downward arrow) and produces cells for primary growth (upward arrow). Primary growth is achieved not only by cell division but also by the lengthening of cells just above the apical meristem (see Figure 28.14, center).

These cells can undergo a tenfold increase in length, mainly by taking up water. Elongation of these cells is what actually forces a root down through the soil. The elongating cells begin to differentiate, forming primary tissues that develop into the epidermis, cortex, and vascular tissue (see Figure 28.14, top). Cells of this last type eventually differentiate into vascular tissues called primary xylem and primary phloem. ☑

Secondary Growth: Thickening

In addition to lengthwise primary growth, the stems and roots of many plant species also thicken by a process called **secondary growth** (Figure 28.15). Such thickening is most evident in the woody plants—trees, shrubs, and vines—whose stems last from year to year and consist mainly of thick layers of mature, mostly dead xylem tissue, called **wood**. Tissues produced by secondary growth are called secondary tissues.

Secondary growth involves cell division in two meristems we have not yet discussed: the vascular cambium and the cork cambium. The **vascular cambium** (blue-green in **Figure 28.16**) is a cylinder of actively dividing cells between the primary xylem and primary phloem, as you can see in the pie-shaped section at the left of the figure. Secondary growth (red arrows) adds cells on either side of the vascular cambium.

The middle and right drawings in Figure 28.16 show the results of secondary growth. In the middle drawing, the vascular cambium has given rise to two new tissues: secondary phloem to its exterior and secondary xylem to its interior. Yearly production of a new layer of secondary xylem accounts for most of the growth in thickness of a perennial plant.

▼**Figure 28.14 Close-up of primary growth in a root tip.** Primary growth is achieved through two mechanisms. Cells within the apical meristem actively divide. In addition, cells behind the apical meristem elongate up to tenfold.

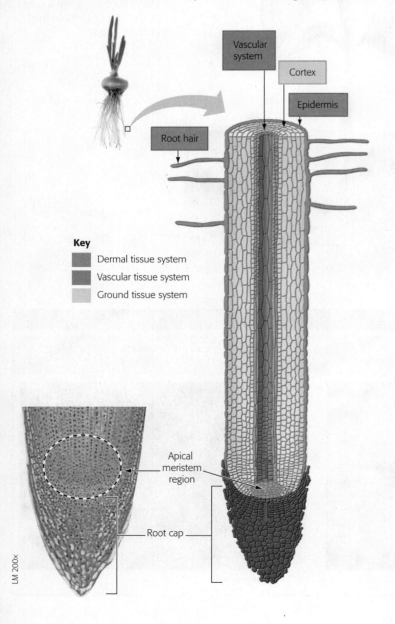

Vascular system

Cortex

Epidermis

Root hair

Key
- Dermal tissue system
- Vascular tissue system
- Ground tissue system

Apical meristem region

Root cap

LM 200×

▼**Figure 28.15 Secondary growth.** Trees (such as these live oaks) thicken from year to year due to secondary growth.

▼ **Figure 28.16 Secondary growth of a woody stem.** The branches of most woody plants are made up of tissues of varying ages, with the youngest regions near the tip and the older regions nearer the trunk. The cross section at the left shows a region of the stem that is just beginning secondary growth. The middle and right cross sections show progressively older regions.

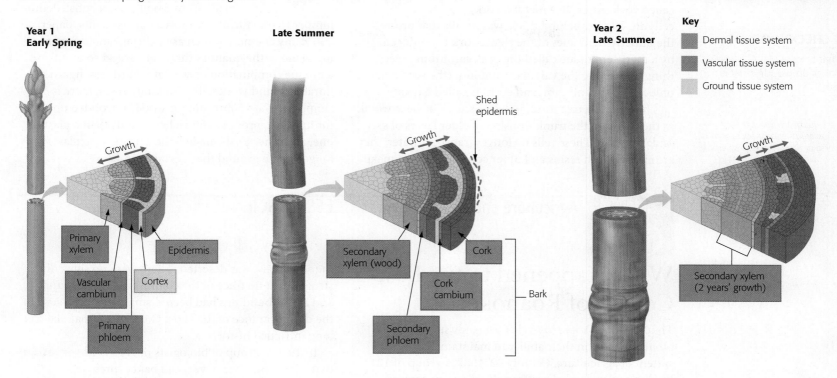

Key
Dermal tissue system
Vascular tissue system
Ground tissue system

Year 1 Early Spring

Growth

Primary xylem

Epidermis

Vascular cambium

Cortex

Primary phloem

Late Summer

Growth

Shed epidermis

Secondary xylem (wood)

Cork

Cork cambium

Secondary phloem

Bark

Year 2 Late Summer

Growth

Secondary xylem (2 years' growth)

Annual growth rings result from the layering of secondary xylem **(Figure 28.17)**. The layers are visible as rings because of uneven activity of the vascular cambium during the year. In woody plants that live in temperate regions, such as most of the United States, the vascular cambium becomes dormant each year during winter, and secondary growth is interrupted. When secondary growth resumes in the spring, a cylinder of early wood forms. Made up of the first new xylem cells to develop, early wood cells are usually larger in diameter and have thinner walls than those produced later in summer. The boundary between the large cells of early wood and the smaller cells of the late wood produced during the previous growing season is usually a distinct ring visible in cross sections of tree trunks and roots. As you've probably heard, a tree's age can be estimated by counting its annual rings. The rings may have varying thicknesses, reflecting the amount of seasonal growth in different years and therefore climate conditions. In fact, the pattern of growth rings in older trees is one source of evidence for recent global climate change. As we'll see in the Process of Science section, tree ring data can even provide insight into subjects outside the bounds of science.

▼ **Figure 28.17 Anatomy of a tree trunk.** On the left, you see a cross section of a locust trunk, with several decades of growth rings visible. On the right, the various layers of a mature trunk are separated for easier viewing.

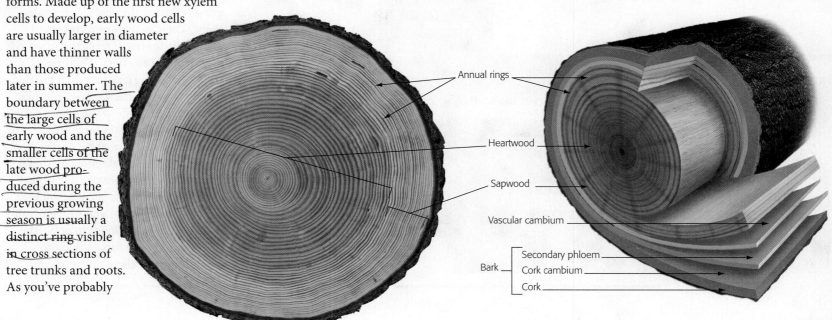

Annual rings

Heartwood

Sapwood

Vascular cambium

Bark {
Secondary phloem
Cork cambium
Cork

The epidermis and cortex make up the young stem's external covering (see Figure 28.16). When secondary growth begins, the epidermis is shed and is replaced with a new outer layer called **cork**. After they mature, cork cells die, leaving behind thick, waxy walls that protect the underlying tissues of the stem. Cork is produced by a meristem tissue called the **cork cambium**. Everything external to the vascular cambium (the secondary phloem, cork cambium, and cork) is called **bark**.

Why are baseball bats usually made from heartwood?

The bulk of a tree trunk is dead tissue. The heartwood, in the center of the trunk, consists of older layers of secondary xylem. These cells no longer transport water; they are clogged with resins and other compounds that make the heartwood very dense and resistant to rotting. The lighter-colored sapwood consists of younger secondary xylem that does conduct water.

Thousands of useful products are made from wood—from construction lumber to fine furniture, musical instruments, paper, and many chemicals, such as artificial vanilla flavoring. Among the qualities that make wood so useful are a unique combination of strength, hardness, lightness, durability, and workability. In many cases, there is simply no good substitute for wood. A wooden oboe, for instance, produces far richer sounds than a plastic one, and fence posts made of heartwood often last much longer in the ground than metal ones. ✔

✔ CHECKPOINT

What type of plant tissue makes up wood? What is bark?

Answer: secondary xylem; all tissues exterior to the vascular cambium: secondary phloem, cork cambium, and cork

---

Agriculture and People   THE PROCESS OF SCIENCE

What Happened to the Lost Colony of Roanoke?

The ability of people to settle new lands successfully often depends on their ability to maintain a healthy system of agriculture. On July 22, 1587, a group of 121 English settlers landed on Roanoke Island, in present-day North Carolina **(Figure 28.18)**. Their supply ship returned to England later that year, leaving 115 colonists behind. When the next ship returned three years later, the settlement was deserted. There were no signs of struggle, yet no trace of the colonists could be found, and all the buildings had been dismantled. The cause of the disappearance of the "Lost Colony" of Roanoke has long intrigued historians.

In 1998, a group of biologists made the **observation** that a large number of very old bald cypress trees (*Taxodinum distichum*) around Roanoke Island could provide a reliable record of the climate over the past 800 years. This led them to **question** whether the tree ring data could provide insight into the colony's mysterious disappearance. Their **hypothesis** was that the loss of the colony corresponded to a period of drought, leading to the **prediction** that the tree ring data would show abnormal growth during the years after settlement. Their **experiment** involved analyzing dozens of trees that covered the period 1185–1984. Their **results** showed that the colonists had the bad luck to arrive at the start of the worst three-year drought in the southeastern United States in 800 years. Indeed, the year they settled was the driest year on record. These data indicate that it is not necessary to invoke a conflict to explain the disappearance of the Lost Colony; the drought and the resulting inability of the colonists to cultivate plants could have forced them to abandon the settlement.

▶ **Figure 28.18 The Lost Colony of Roanoke.** Notice the very narrow growth rings corresponding to the years 1587–1590.

The Life Cycle of a Flowering Plant

The life cycle of an organism is the sequence of stages from the adults of one generation to the adults of the next. In completing the life cycle, many flowering plants can reproduce both asexually and sexually, and both modes have played an important role in the evolutionary adaptation of plant populations to their environments. **Figure 28.19** shows three examples of **asexual reproduction**, the creation of offspring derived from a single parent without fertilization. Through asexual reproduction, a single plant can produce many offspring quickly and efficiently. This ability of plants is useful in agriculture because it allows farmers to grow a large crop of identical plants from a parent with desirable traits. For example, because navel oranges lack seeds, they can only be propagated asexually; every navel orange tree growing today is a clone of a single tree discovered in Brazil around 1820. As in animals, **sexual reproduction** in plants involves **fertilization**, the union of gametes from two parents to produce genetically distinct offspring. This section discusses the sexual life cycle of flowering plants, starting with a look at the flower.

▼Figure 28.19 **Asexual reproduction in plants.**

Garlic. This garlic bulb is actually an underground stem that functions in storage. A single large bulb fragments into several cloves. Each clove can give rise to a separate plant.

Holly trees. Each of the small trees is a sprout from the roots of a single holly tree. Eventually, one or more of these root sprouts may take the place of its parent.

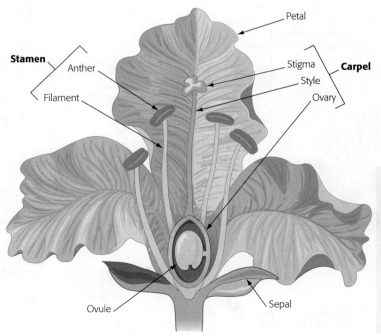

Creosote bushes. This ring of plants is a clone of creosote bushes growing in the Mojave Desert in southern California. All these bushes came from generations of asexual reproduction by roots. This clone apparently began with a single plant that germinated from a seed about 12,000 years ago. The original plant probably occupied the center of the ring.

The Flower

In angiosperms, the structure specific to sexual reproduction is the **flower**. The main parts of a flower—the sepals, petals, stamens, and carpels—are modified leaves (**Figure 28.20**; also see Figure 28.1). The **sepals** enclose and protect the flower bud. The **petals** are often colorful and fragrant, which may serve to advertise the flower to insects and other pollinators.

The flower's reproductive organs are the stamens and carpel. A **stamen** consists of a stalk (filament) tipped by an **anther**. Within the anther are sacs where meiosis occurs and pollen grains develop. Pollen grains house the cells that develop into sperm. A **carpel** has a long slender neck (the style) with a sticky stigma at its tip. The **stigma** is the landing platform for pollen grains. The base of the carpel is the **ovary**. Within the ovary are reproductive structures called **ovules**, each containing one developing egg and the cells that support it. The term pistil is sometimes used to refer to a single carpel or a group of fused carpels. ✓

◄ Figure 28.20 **The structure of a flower.** The flower is the structure used by angiosperms for sexual reproduction.

Stamen
Anther
Filament

Petal
Stigma **Carpel**
Style
Ovary

Ovule
Sepal

✓ CHECKPOINT

Pollen develops within the _____ of sperm-producing organs called stamens. Ovules develop within the ovaries of egg-producing organs called _____.

Answer: anthers; carpels

617

Overview of the Flowering Plant Life Cycle

The life cycle of a sexually reproducing angiosperm is shown in **Figure 28.21**. After fertilization, the ovule of a flower matures into a seed containing the embryo.

▼ **Figure 28.21 The life cycle of an angiosperm.**

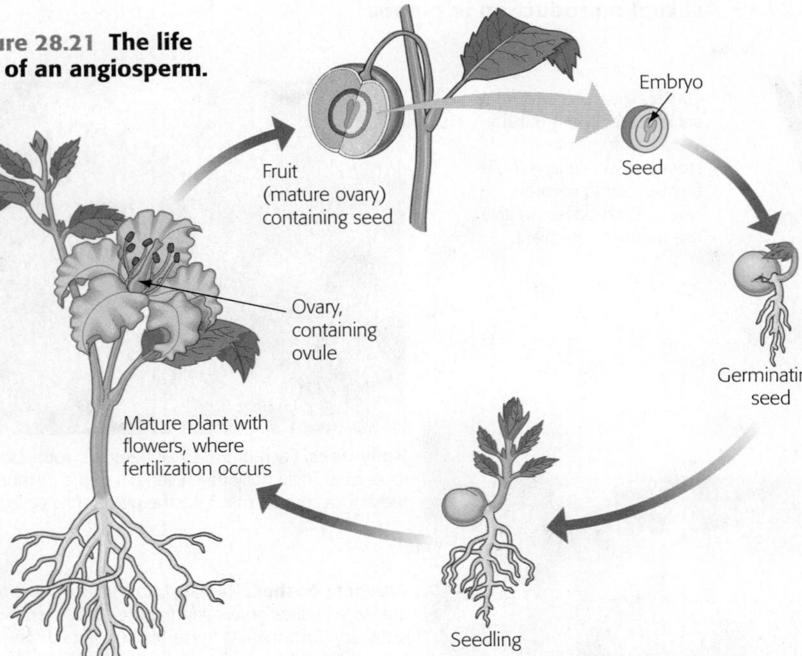

Meanwhile, the ovary develops into a fruit, which protects the seed and aids in dispersing it. Completing the life cycle, the seed **germinates** (begins to grow), the embryo develops into a seedling, and the seedling grows into a mature plant.

Let's look a bit closer at this process from a genetic point of view. The life cycles of all plants include a haploid generation (when each cell has a single set of chromosomes, abbreviated *n*) and a diploid generation (having two sets of chromosomes, abbreviated 2*n*; see Figure 16.10). The roots, stems, leaves, and most of the reproductive structures of angiosperms are diploid. The diploid plant body, called a **sporophyte**, produces the anthers and ovules in which cells undergo meiosis to produce haploid cells called spores. Each spore then divides via mitosis and becomes a multicellular **gametophyte**, the plant's haploid generation. The gametophyte produces gametes by mitosis. Fertilization occurs when the male and female gametes (sperm and egg, respectively) unite, producing a diploid zygote. The life cycle is completed when the zygote divides by mitosis and develops into a new sporophyte. In the rest of this section, we'll examine each stage in the angiosperm sexual life cycle in more detail.

Embryo
Seed
Fruit (mature ovary) containing seed
Germinating seed
Ovary, containing ovule
Mature plant with flowers, where fertilization occurs
Seedling

Pollination and Fertilization

▼ **Figure 28.22**
Development of gametophytes in an angiosperm. The male gametophyte (pollen grain) develops within the anther (top). The female gametophyte (embryo sac) develops within the ovule (bottom). In most species, the ovary of a flower contains several ovules, but only one is shown here.

Fertilization requires gametes, which are produced by gametophytes. The male gametophyte is the **pollen grain**, which is essential for pollination and produces sperm. The female gametophyte is a multicellular structure called the **embryo sac**, which produces the egg. As shown at the top of **Figure 28.22**, ❶ cells within a flower's anthers ❷ undergo meiosis to form four haploid spores. ❸ Each spore then divides by mitosis into two haploid cells. A thick wall forms around these cells, and the resulting pollen grain is ready for release from the anther.

Moving to the bottom of the figure, we see that ❶ within an ovule, a central cell enlarges and ❷ undergoes meiosis, producing four haploid spores. Three of the spores usually degenerate, but the surviving one enlarges and ❸ divides by mitosis, producing the embryo sac. The sac contains a large central cell with two haploid nuclei. One of its other cells is the haploid egg, ready to be fertilized.

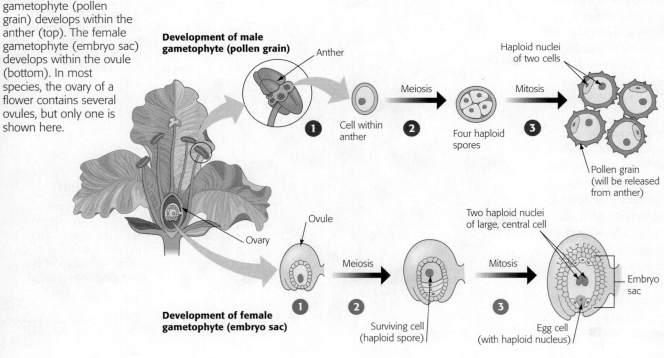

Development of male gametophyte (pollen grain)

Anther
❶ Cell within anther
Meiosis
❷ Four haploid spores
Mitosis
❸ Haploid nuclei of two cells
Pollen grain (will be released from anther)

Ovary

Ovule
Development of female gametophyte (embryo sac)
❶
Meiosis
❷ Surviving cell (haploid spore)
Mitosis
❸
Two haploid nuclei of large, central cell
Embryo sac
Egg cell (with haploid nucleus)

How does fertilization occur? As shown in **Figure 28.23**, the first step is ❶ **pollination**, the delivery of pollen grains from anther to stigma. Many angiosperms are dependent on insects, birds, or other animals to transfer their pollen (a fact we will discuss further in the Evolution Connection section). But the pollen of some plants, such as grasses, is wind-borne—as anyone with pollen allergies knows! ❷ After pollination, the pollen grain germinates on the stigma. It divides by mitosis, forming ❸ two haploid sperm that travel to the ovule through a pollen tube. ❹ One sperm fertilizes the egg, forming the diploid zygote. The other sperm contributes its haploid nucleus to the large diploid central cell of the embryo sac. This cell, now with a triploid (3n) nucleus, will give rise to a food-storing tissue called **endosperm**. The formation of both a zygote and a fertilized central cell with a triploid nucleus is called **double fertilization**. This occurs only in plants, mainly in angiosperms. ✓

▼**Figure 28.23 Pollination and double fertilization.**

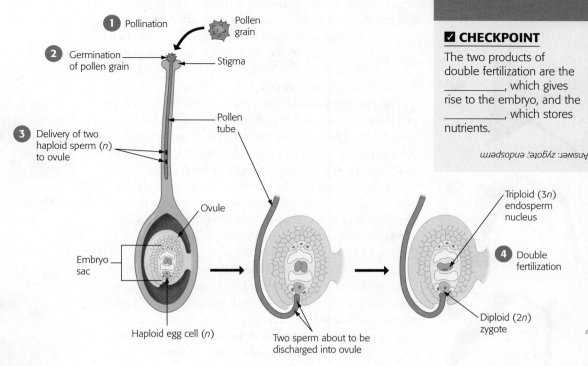

❶ Pollination
Pollen grain
❷ Germination of pollen grain
Stigma
Pollen tube
❸ Delivery of two haploid sperm (n) to ovule
Ovule
Embryo sac
Haploid egg cell (n)
Two sperm about to be discharged into ovule
Triploid (3n) endosperm nucleus
❹ Double fertilization
Diploid (2n) zygote

☑ **CHECKPOINT**

The two products of double fertilization are the _____, which gives rise to the embryo, and the _____, which stores nutrients.

Answer: zygote; endosperm

Seed Formation

After fertilization, the ovule, containing the zygote and the triploid central cell, begins developing into a seed **(Figure 28.24)**. The zygote divides via mitosis into a ball of cells that becomes the embryo. Meanwhile, the triploid cell divides and develops into the endosperm. As cotyledons develop, they absorb nutrients from the endosperm. The result of embryonic development in the ovule is a mature seed (see Figure 28.24, bottom). A **seed** is a plant embryo and endosperm packaged within a tough protective covering called a **seed coat**. (When you grind coffee, you can't see the embryo contained within the coffee bean—which is actually a seed—because it was destroyed by the drying and roasting process.)

At this point, the embryo stops developing and the seed becomes dormant; growth and development are suspended until the seed germinates. Seed dormancy is an important evolutionary adaptation. It allows time for seed dispersal and increases the chance that a new generation of plants will begin growing only when environmental conditions, such as temperature and moisture, favor survival. ✓

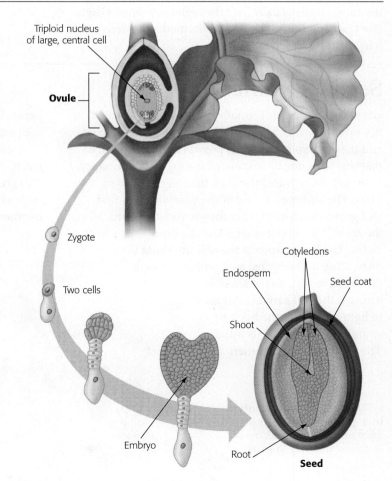

Triploid nucleus of large, central cell
Ovule
Zygote
Two cells
Embryo
Endosperm
Shoot
Cotyledons
Seed coat
Root
Seed

◀**Figure 28.24 Development of a seed.** The plant in this drawing is a eudicot; a monocot would have only one cotyledon.

☑ **CHECKPOINT**

Of these human structures—sperm, egg, ovary, embryo—which one is analogous to a plant seed?

Answer: embryo (a seed contains a plant embryo suspended during growth)

Fruit Formation

Have you eaten a plant ovary today?

Fruit, among the most distinctive features of angiosperms, develop at the same time seeds do. A **fruit** is a mature ovary that acts as a vessel, housing and protecting seeds and helping disperse them from the parent plant. A corn kernel is a fruit, as is a peach, tomato, or pea pod.

The photographs in **Figure 28.25** illustrate the changes in a pea plant that lead to pod formation. ❶ Soon after pollination, ❷ the flower drops its petals and the ovary starts growing. The ovary expands tremendously, and its wall thickens, ❸ forming the pod, or fruit, which holds the seeds. Peas are usually harvested at this stage. If the pods are allowed to develop further, they become dry and brownish and will split open, releasing the dried seeds.

Mature fruits can be either fleshy or dry **(Figure 28.26)**. Oranges, apricots, and grapes are examples of fleshy fruits, in which the wall of the ovary becomes soft during ripening. Dry fruits include beans, nuts, and grains. The dry, wind-dispersed fruits of cereal grains—such as wheat, rice, and barley—are harvested while on the plant and serve as major staple foods for people. Edible fruits are usually nutritious, sweet tasting, and vividly colored, advertising their ripeness. When an animal eats the fruit, it digests the fruit's fleshy part, but the tough seeds usually pass through the animal's digestive tract and are left behind unharmed, complete with a handy supply of fertilizer.

▲ **Figure 28.25**
Development of a pea pod (fruit).

▼ Figure 28.26 **A variety of fruits.**

Fleshy fruits

Dry fruits

Seed Germination

Germination of a seed usually begins when the seed takes up water. The hydrated seed expands, bursting its coat, and the embryo resumes the growth and development that was temporarily suspended during seed dormancy.

Figure 28.27 traces the germination of a garden bean. The embryonic root of the bean emerges first and grows downward from the germinating seed. Next, the embryonic shoot emerges, and a hook forms near its tip. The hook protects the delicate shoot tip by holding it downward as it pushes through the abrasive soil. As the shoot breaks through the soil surface, exposure to light stimulates the hook to straighten, and the tip is lifted. The first foliage leaves then expand from the shoot tip and begin making food for the plant by photosynthesis.

A germinating seed is fragile. In the wild, only a small fraction of seedlings endure long enough to reproduce. The great numbers of seeds produced by most plants compensate for the odds against each seedling, increasing the chances of reproductive success. ✓

✓ **CHECKPOINT**

Is the garden bean shown in Figure 28.27 a monocot or a eudicot?

Answer: It's a eudicot. (You can tell because it has two cotyledon leaves.)

► **Figure 28.27 Germination in a garden bean.** After a seed takes up water, it bursts out of its coat and begins to grow.

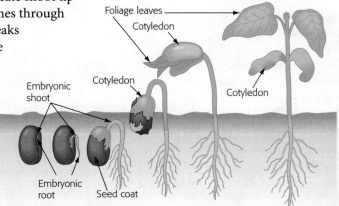

Foliage leaves
Cotyledon
Embryonic shoot
Cotyledon
Cotyledon
Embryonic root
Seed coat

Agriculture and People EVOLUTION CONNECTION

The Problem of the Disappearing Bees

Throughout this chapter, we've discussed how flowering plants and land animals have had mutually beneficial relationships throughout their evolutionary history. You've learned that most angiosperms depend on insects, birds, or mammals for pollination and seed dispersal. And most land animals depend on angiosperms for food and shelter. Such mutual dependencies tend to improve the reproductive success of both the plants and the animals and are thus favored by natural selection.

The flowers of many angiosperms attract pollinators that rely entirely on the flowers' nectar (a sugary fluid) and pollen for food. Evolutionary adaptations for advertising the presence of nectar include flower color and fragrance, which are keyed to pollinators' senses of sight and smell. For example, many flowers pollinated by birds are red or pink, colors to which bird eyes are especially sensitive. Flowers may also have markings that attract pollinators, leading them past pollen-bearing organs on their way to gathering nectar (Figure 28.28). For example, flowers pollinated by bees often have markings that reflect ultraviolet light. Such markings are invisible to us, but vivid to bees. Many other animals—including hummingbirds, butterflies, and fruit bats—have similar relationships with other flower species. To a large extent, flowering plants are as diverse and successful as they are today because of their close connections with animals.

The importance of such interactions has been underscored by concern over colony collapse disorder. In late 2006, U.S. beekeepers noticed a sudden and drastic die-off in their bee colonies. The next year, similar problems were reported in Europe. Agricultural scientists fear that a shortage of bees could have devastating consequences on many food staples that require bees for pollination, such as almonds, berries, and fruits. Bees pollinate $15 billion worth of crops each year, and an estimated one-third of our food supply relies on bees. The cause of the die-off has not yet been explained, although several biological agents—such as mites or their pathogens—have been implicated. This much is certain: Colony collapse disorder is yet another reminder of how much we all depend on plants for our survival.

▼ Figure 28.28 **A busy bee.**

Chapter Review

SUMMARY OF KEY CONCEPTS

Go to **www.masteringbiology.com** for homework assignments, practice quizzes, Pearson eText, and more.

The Structure and Function of a Flowering Plant

Flowering plants, or angiosperms, account for nearly 90% of the plant kingdom.

Monocots and Dicots

Angiosperms can be grouped into two categories based on the number of cotyledons (seed leaves) found in the embryo and other structural differences. Most dicots are eudicots.

Plant Structures					
	Seed leaves	**Leaf veins**	**Vascular bundles**	**Floral parts**	**Roots**
Monocots	One cotyledon	Parallel	Scattered	Multiples of three	Fibrous
Eudicots	Two cotyledons	Branched	Ring	Multiples of four or five	Taproot

Plant Organs: Roots, Stems, and Leaves

A plant body consists of a root system and a shoot system, each dependent on the other.

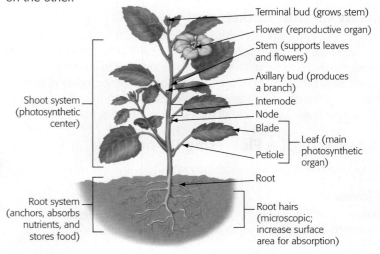

Terminal bud (grows stem)
Flower (reproductive organ)
Stem (supports leaves and flowers)
Axillary bud (produces a branch)
Internode
Node
Blade
Leaf (main photosynthetic organ)
Petiole
Root
Shoot system (photosynthetic center)
Root system (anchors, absorbs nutrients, and stores food)
Root hairs (microscopic; increase surface area for absorption)

621

A growing shoot often lengthens only at the terminal bud; its axillary buds are dormant. This condition is called apical dominance and allows the plant to grow tall quickly.

Plant Tissues and Tissue Systems

Roots, stems, and leaves are made up of tissues organized into three tissue systems: the dermal tissue system, the vascular tissue system, and the ground tissue system.

The Three Tissues of Plant Organs		
Dermal Tissue System	**Vascular Tissue System**	**Ground Tissue System**
• Functions in protection • Includes the epidermis, an outer layer that covers and protects the plant • Stomata (each surrounded by two guard cells): pores that regulate gas exchange between the cells of the leaf and the environment	• Functions in support and transport • Xylem: transports water and dissolved minerals • Phloem: transports sugars	• Functions mainly in storage • Includes leaf mesophyll, where most photosynthesis occurs

Plant Cells

Plant cells are distinguished by the presence of chloroplasts, a large central vacuole, and cell walls. There are several types of plant cells: parenchyma cells, collenchyma cells, sclerenchyma cells, water-conducting cells (tracheids and vessel elements), and food-conducting cells.

Plant Growth

Most plants display indeterminate growth, growing as long as they are alive. Some plants grow, reproduce, and die in one year (annuals); some live for two years (biennials); and some live for many years (perennials).

Primary Growth: Lengthening

Plant growth originates in meristems, areas of undifferentiated, dividing cells. Apical meristems are located at the tips of roots and in the terminal and axillary buds of shoots. These meristems initiate lengthwise growth by producing new cells. A root or shoot lengthens further as the new cells elongate. This cell division and elongation is called primary growth. The new cells eventually differentiate into specialized tissues.

Secondary Growth: Thickening

An increase in a plant's girth, called secondary growth, arises from cell division in a cylindrical meristem called the vascular cambium. The vascular cambium produces layers of secondary xylem, or wood, next to its inner surface. Outside the vascular cambium is bark, which consists of secondary phloem, a meristem called the cork cambium, and cork cells produced by the cork cambium. The outer layers of bark are sloughed off as the plant thickens.

The Life Cycle of a Flowering Plant

Many flowering plants can reproduce both asexually and sexually.

The Flower

In angiosperms, the flower is the structure specific to sexual reproduction. The stamen contains the anther, in which pollen grains are produced. The carpel contains the stigma, which receives pollen, and the ovary, which contains the ovule.

Overview of the Flowering Plant Life Cycle

The plant life cycle alternates between diploid ($2n$) and haploid (n) generations. The spores in the anthers give rise to male gametophytes, or pollen grains, each of which produces two sperm. A spore in an ovule produces the female gametophyte, called an embryo sac. Each embryo sac contains an egg cell.

Pollination and Fertilization

After pollen lands on the stigma (pollination), the sperm pass down the stigma into the ovule. One sperm combines with the egg and the other combines with a second, diploid cell. This process, called double fertilization, is unique to plants.

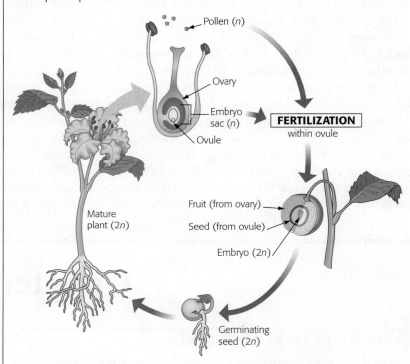

Seed Formation

After fertilization, the ovule becomes a seed, and the fertilized egg within it divides to become an embryo. The other fertilized cell (now triploid) develops into the endosperm, which stores food for the embryo. A tough seed coat protects the embryo and endosperm. The embryo develops cotyledons (seed leaves), which absorb food from the endosperm.

Fruit Formation

While the ovule becomes a seed, the ovary develops into a fruit, which helps protect and disperse the seeds.

Seed Germination

A seed starts to germinate when it takes up water, expands, and bursts its seed coat. The embryo resumes growth, an embryonic root emerges, and a shoot pushes upward and expands its leaves.

SELF-QUIZ

1. While walking in the woods, you encounter an unfamiliar flowering plant. Which of the following plant features would help you determine whether that plant is a monocot or a eudicot? (Choose all that are appropriate.)
   a. size of the plant
   b. number of seed leaves
   c. shape of its root system
   d. number of petals in its flowers
   e. arrangement of vascular bundles in its stem
   f. whether or not it produces seed-bearing cones

2. Your friend plants a new herb (which is a eudicot and a perennial). During the first year, she allows the plants to grow naturally. Her plants grow tall and relatively spindly during the growing season, and when it comes time to harvest, she doesn't have a large yield. What phenomenon is responsible for her poor yield? What could your friend do to increase her yield next year?

3. A pea pod is formed from a(n) _____. A pea inside the pod is formed from a(n) _____.

4. Match each flower structure with its function.
   a. pollen grain
   b. ovule
   c. anther
   d. ovary
   e. sepal
   f. petal

   1. attracts pollinators
   2. develops into seed
   3. protects an unopened flower
   4. produces sperm
   5. produces pollen
   6. contains ovules

5. Many plant species can reproduce both sexually and asexually. Which mode of reproduction would generally be more advantageous in a location where the composition of the soil is changing rapidly? Why?

6. What part of a plant are you eating when you consume each of the following?
   a. tomato
   b. apple
   c. spinach
   d. sweet potato
   e. black bean

7. In the angiosperm life cycle, which of the following processes is directly dependent on meiosis?
   a. production of gametophytes
   b. production of gametes
   c. production of spores
   d. all of the above

8. In angiosperms, each pollen grain produces two sperm. What do these sperm do?
   a. Each one fertilizes a separate egg cell.
   b. One fertilizes an egg, and the other fertilizes the fruit.
   c. One fertilizes an egg, and the other is kept in reserve.
   d. Both fertilize a single egg cell.
   e. One fertilizes an egg, and the other fertilizes a cell that develops into stored food.

9. Which of the following is closest to the center of a woody stem? Which is farthest from the center?
   a. cork cambium
   b. primary xylem
   c. primary phloem
   d. secondary xylem
   e. secondary phloem

10. A gardener is concerned that his perennial plants are not growing well. He notes that the stems on his plants are not thickening adequately over the years. This suggests reduced activity of which plant tissue?

Answers to these questions can be found in Appendix: Self-Quiz Answers.

THE PROCESS OF SCIENCE

11. During a recent ice storm, many old trees were snapped by the weight of the ice. A botanist in the area would like to analyze the remains of the trees and determine how old they really were. Describe a procedure that could be used to determine the approximate age of the trees. Explain the basis of this method in terms of plant tissue growth.

12. Plants can alter the shape of their guard cells, thereby regulating the size of the stomata on their leaves. Stomata must be open to allow entrance of carbon dioxide, which is necessary for photosynthesis. During the summer, the stomata are often closed around noon, when the most sunlight is likely to reach the plant. Propose an explanation for why it may be advantageous for stomata to be closed when conditions seem optimal for photosynthesis. How could you test your hypothesis?

BIOLOGY AND SOCIETY

13. Tropical forests contain a wealth of plants that are potential new sources of food, medicine, and other useful products. As a result of growing populations and debt, however, many tropical forests in less industrialized countries are being cut for lumber and farmland, and many species are disappearing. More industrialized countries are pressuring the tropical countries to protect the forests before even more species are lost. Many people in the less industrialized nations see little incentive to preserve the forests only to have corporations from more industrialized countries profit from their products. Is there a way to preserve the tropical forests so that both the less industrialized and more industrialized nations will benefit from their abundance?

14. Cloning is a fiercely debated topic in our country. Most of the ethical debates concerning cloning center on the cloning of animals. There is not much talk about the cloning of plants. Do you have the same opinion about cloning plants and animals? Why or why not? Do you think that they should be similarly regulated? What unique problems might each present?

29 The Working Plant

Cleansing plants. This photo, taken about four months after the 2011 tsunami in northeastern Japan, shows sunflowers used to treat radioactive contamination.

The Interdependence of Organisms BIOLOGY AND SOCIETY

Planting Hope in the Wake of Disaster

On March 11, 2011, a magnitude 9.0 earthquake originating beneath the Pacific Ocean produced a 100-foot tsunami that swept 6 miles into northeastern Japan. One of the five strongest earthquakes ever recorded, the disaster had far-reaching consequences, killing more than 15,000 people and damaging or destroying at least 125,000 buildings. After the surge of ocean water from the tsunami flooded the Fukushima Nuclear Power Plant, the resulting loss of power and failure of the backup cooling systems led to a reactor core meltdown. Fukushima joined the 1986 Chernobyl disaster in Ukraine as one of the worst nuclear accidents the world has ever seen.

The cleanup effort in Japan will take decades. In addition to bulldozers and wrecking crews, help is coming from a natural source: plants. The use of plants to help clean up polluted soil and groundwater is called phytoremediation. Phytoremediation is one type of bioremediation, the use of living organisms to detoxify polluted sites. Plants can efficiently move minerals and other compounds from the soil into the plant body. Usually, the absorbed compounds are nutrients that help the plant grow. But many species of plants are capable of absorbing large amounts of radioactive isotopes and heavy metals. Efforts are under way to plant millions of sunflowers in the Fukushima Prefecture to help restore the area. A similar effort continues today in New Orleans as a way to detoxify soil that was contaminated in the aftermath of Hurricane Katrina, which devastated the region in 2005.

Because crews cleaning up after such disasters have only to remove a few cubic meters of plant material rather than the thousands of cubic meters of soil that are actually contaminated, phytoremediation can be a cost-effective and efficient process. An added benefit: Using plants to clean the soil can detoxify an area without dramatically disturbing the landscape. And sunflowers—such as those shown on the left that were photographed near Natori, Japan—provide an uplifting message to the community, bringing beauty and life back to an area weary with grief and loss.

By using plants to clean up toxic wastes, we are benefiting from millions of years of plant evolution. Although plants are unable to move about in search of food, they have evolved an amazing ability to pull water and nutrients out of the soil and air. In this chapter, we'll see how plants obtain essential nutrients and how they transport them throughout their roots, stems, and leaves. Then we'll examine other aspects of the life of a working plant, including the crucial roles played by hormones and how certain plant activities are affected by stimuli from the environment. Throughout the discussion, we'll explore the theme of how different forms of life—such as plants and animals—depend on each other for survival within Earth's biosphere.

How Plants Acquire and Transport Nutrients

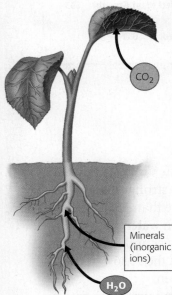

▼ Figure 29.1 The uptake of nutrients by a plant. A plant absorbs the CO_2 it needs from the air and minerals and H_2O from the soil.

CO₂

Minerals (inorganic ions)

H₂O

Watch a plant grow from a tiny seed and you can't help wondering where all the mass comes from. About 96% of a plant's dry weight is organic (carbon-containing) material synthesized from inorganic nutrients extracted from the surroundings. Plants obtain carbon dioxide (CO_2) from the air and water (H_2O) and **minerals** (inorganic ions) from the soil **(Figure 29.1)**. From the CO_2 and H_2O, plants produce sugars via photosynthesis. These sugars, combined with minerals, are used to construct all the other organic materials a plant needs **(Figure 29.2)**. Plants, like people, require a balanced diet. So let's start by discussing plant nutrition.

▼ Figure 29.2 A banyan tree is a giant product of photosynthesis. Plants use sugars created by photosynthesis to produce all the organic materials they need. The giant trunk and long branches of this tree consist largely of molecules derived from sugars.

Plant Nutrition

A chemical element is considered an **essential element** if a plant must obtain it from its environment to complete its life cycle. Seventeen elements are essential to all plants, and a few others are essential to certain types of plants. Of the 17 essential elements, 9 are called **macronutrients** because plants require relatively large amounts of them. Elements that plants need in extremely small amounts are called **micronutrients**.

Macronutrients

Six of the nine macronutrients—carbon, oxygen, hydrogen, nitrogen, sulfur, and phosphorus—make up almost 98% of a plant's dry weight. The other three macronutrients—calcium, potassium, and magnesium—make up another 1.5%.

What does a plant do with macronutrients? Carbon, oxygen, and hydrogen are the basic ingredients of a plant's organic compounds. Nitrogen is a component of all nucleic acids and proteins, as well as ATP, chlorophyll

(the key light-absorbing molecule in plants), and many plant hormones. Sulfur is a component of most proteins. Phosphorus is a major component of nucleic acids, phospholipids, and ATP. The other macronutrients, although present in smaller amounts, play similarly important roles. For example, magnesium is an essential component of chlorophyll.

Micronutrients

Eight micronutrients make up the remaining 0.5% of a plant's dry weight and are required by all plants. The eight micronutrients are iron, chlorine, copper, manganese, zinc, molybdenum, boron, and nickel. A plant recycles the atoms of micronutrients over and over, so it needs them in only minute quantities. Yet a deficiency of any micronutrient can kill a plant.

Fertilizers

The quality of soil, especially the availability of nutrients, affects the health of plants and, for plants we consume, the quality of our own nutrition ("You are what you eat!"). Nitrogen shortage is the most common nutritional problem for plants **(Figure 29.3)**. Nitrogen-deficient crop plants may produce grain, but the grain will have a lower nutritional value, and its nutrient deficiencies will be passed on to livestock or human consumers.

Fertilizers are compounds given to plants via the soil to promote the plants' growth. There are two basic types of fertilizers: inorganic and organic. Inorganic fertilizers contain simple inorganic minerals, such as mined limestone (rich in calcium) or phosphate rock. Inorganic fertilizers come in a wide variety of formulations, but most emphasize the "N-P-K ratio," the relative amounts of the three nutrients most often deficient in depleted soils: nitrogen (N), phosphorus (P), and potassium (K). An all-purpose fertilizer, for example, might be "5-5-5," with 5% of each of these vital nutrients.

Organic fertilizers are composed of chemically complex organic matter such as **compost**, a soil-like mixture of decomposed organic matter. Many gardeners maintain a free-standing compost pile or an enclosed compost bin to which they add leaves, grass clippings, yard waste, and kitchen scraps (avoiding meat, fat, and bones). Over time, the vegetable matter is broken down by microbes, fungi, and animals **(Figure 29.4)**. Occasional turning and watering speeds the process. The compost, which is highly valued by gardeners for its nutrient-rich composition, can be applied to outdoor gardens or indoor pots.

Compost and other organic fertilizers are a key to **organic farming**. Organic farmers follow guidelines that promote sustainable agriculture—a system of farming that protects biological diversity, maintains and replenishes soil quality (as by crop rotation), manages pests with no (or few) synthetic pesticides, avoids genetically modified organisms, conserves water, and uses no (or few) synthetic fertilizers. In the United States, organic farming is one of the fastest-growing segments of agriculture, but organic farms still account for fewer than 1% of total agricultural acreage. ☑

▶ **Figure 29.3 The effect of nitrogen shortage.** These images contrast a normal buckwheat plant (left) with one that was grown in nitrogen-poor conditions (right). Nitrogen-deficient plants can be diagnosed by stunted growth and leaves that turn yellow starting at the tips.

▼ **Figure 29.4 Compost.** Steam is produced by the metabolic activity of naturally occurring organisms that break down the organic matter of rotting vegetation.

☑ CHECKPOINT

What inorganic nutrients do plants acquire from the air? What nutrients do plants extract from the soil?

Answer: carbon dioxide; water and minerals (inorganic ions)

627

▼ Figure 29.5 Root hairs that enable efficient absorption. The root hairs of a plant, clearly visible in this photograph of a radish seedling, are extensions of epidermal cells on the outer surface of the root.

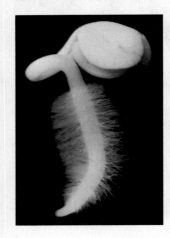

From the Soil into the Roots

Plant roots have a remarkable capacity for absorbing water and essential nutrients from soil because of their root hairs, extensions of epidermal cells that dramatically increase the surface area available for absorption **(Figure 29.5)**. For example, the root hairs of a single sunflower plant, if laid end to end, could stretch many miles, providing a huge surface area in contact with nutrient-containing soil.

All substances that enter a plant root are dissolved in water. To be transported, water and solutes must move from the soil through the epidermis and cortex of the root, then into the water-conducting xylem tissue in the root's central cylinder (see Figure 28.8). To reach the xylem, the solution must pass through the plasma membranes of root cells. Because these membranes are selectively permeable, only certain solutes reach the xylem. This selectivity helps regulate the mineral composition of a plant's vascular system.

Many plants gain significant surface area for absorption through symbiotic associations with fungi. Together, the plant's roots and the associated fungus form a mutually beneficial (mutualistic) structure called a **mycorrhiza** (plural, *mycorrhizae*) **(Figure 29.6)**. Fungal filaments around the roots absorb water and minerals much more rapidly than can the roots alone. Some of the water and minerals taken up by the fungus are transferred to the plant, and the plant's photosynthetic products nourish the fungus.

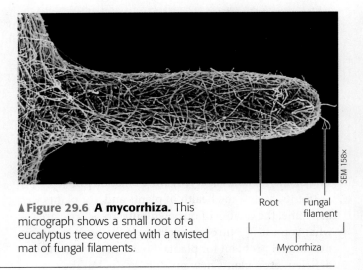

▲ **Figure 29.6 A mycorrhiza.** This micrograph shows a small root of a eucalyptus tree covered with a twisted mat of fungal filaments.

SEM 158×

Root   Fungal filament

Mycorrhiza

The Role of Bacteria in Nitrogen Nutrition

Air penetrates the soil around roots, but plants cannot use the form of nitrogen found in air—gaseous N_2. For plants to absorb nitrogen from the soil, N_2 must first be converted to ammonium (NH_4^+) or nitrate (NO_3^-). Most plants rely on bacteria for these conversions.

In what way do farmers depend on bacteria?

Soil Bacteria and Nitrogen

Figure 29.7 shows three types of soil bacteria that play essential roles in supplying plants with nitrogen. One type, called nitrogen-fixing bacteria (), converts atmospheric N_2 to ammonium, a process called **nitrogen fixation**. A second type, called ammonifying bacteria (), adds to the soil's supply of ammonium by decomposing organic matter. A third type of soil bacteria, called nitrifying bacteria (), converts soil ammonium to nitrate.

Plants take up most of their nitrogen in this form. They then convert nitrate back to ammonium, which plants can incorporate into proteins and other nitrogen-containing organic molecules. Although we often think of bacteria as troublesome (particularly when they infect us), it is important to note that our lives utterly depend on bacteria: Without bacteria, our crop plants could not obtain sufficient nitrogen, and we would be unable to feed ourselves.

▼ Figure 29.7 The role of bacteria in supplying nitrogen to plants.

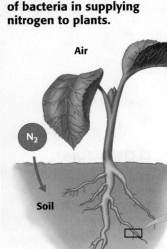

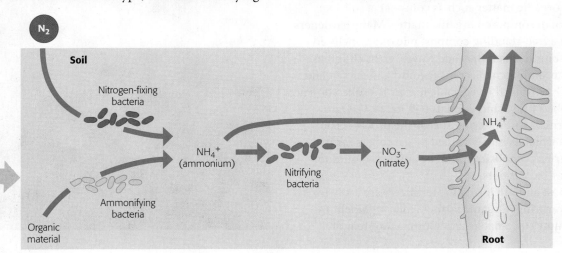

Air

N_2

Soil

Soil

N_2

Nitrogen-fixing bacteria

NH_4^+ (ammonium)

Nitrifying bacteria

NO_3^- (nitrate)

NH_4^+

Ammonifying bacteria

Organic material

Root

Root Nodule Bacteria and Nitrogen

Some plant families, including legumes—peas, beans, peanuts, and many other plants that produce their seeds in pods—have their own built-in source of ammonium: nitrogen-fixing bacteria that live in swellings called root nodules **(Figure 29.8)**. Within these nodules, plant cells have been "infected" by nitrogen-fixing bacteria that reside inside cytoplasmic vesicles. The symbiotic relationship between a plant and its nitrogen-fixing bacteria is mutually beneficial ("You scratch my back, I'll scratch yours"). The bacteria have enzymes that help convert atmospheric N_2 to ammonium (NH_4^+), a form readily used by the plant; the plant, in turn, provides the bacteria with other nutrients. When conditions are favorable, root nodule bacteria fix so much nitrogen that the nodules secrete excess ammonia, which improves the soil. This is one reason farmers practice crop rotation, one year planting a nonlegume such as corn and the next year planting a legume such as soybeans. The legume crops may be plowed under to decompose into "green manure," reducing the need for fertilizer. ☑

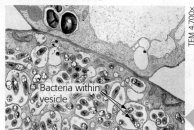
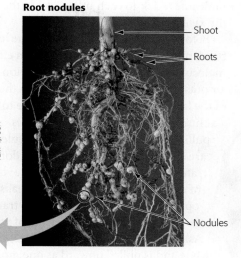

▶ **Figure 29.8 Root nodules that contain nitrogen-fixing bacteria.** Legumes, such as the soybean plant, have root nodules that contain nitrogen-fixing bacteria.

Root nodule bacteria

Bacteria within vesicle

TEM 4,700×

Root nodules

Shoot

Roots

Nodules

☑ CHECKPOINT

Why might a pollutant that kills soil bacteria result in nitrogen deficiency in plants?

Answer: because certain soil bacteria make nitrogen available to plants in forms they can use

The Transport of Water

As a plant grows upward toward sunlight, it needs an increasing supply of resources from the soil. Imagine hauling a 5-gallon bucket of water up five flights of stairs every 20 minutes, all day long. To thrive, a typical tree must transport that quantity of water from its roots to the rest of the plant.

As discussed in Chapter 28, mature water-conducting cells of the xylem are arranged end to end to form very thin vertical tubes (see Figure 28.11). A solution of water and inorganic nutrients, called **xylem sap**, flows through these tubes all the way from a plant's roots to the tips of its leaves. Let's look at how this sap is moved through the body of the plant.

The Ascent of Xylem Sap

What force moves xylem sap up against the downward pull of gravity? For the most part, xylem sap is pulled upward by **transpiration**, the loss of water from the leaves of a plant by evaporation **(Figure 29.9)**. Most transpiration occurs through the stomata of leaves. The stomata open into air spaces, which are filled with water molecules that have evaporated from the surrounding mesophyll cells. ❶ Water vapor diffuses out of the stomata because the surrounding air is usually drier than the inside of the leaf.

Transpiration can pull xylem sap up a tree because of two special properties of water: cohesion and adhesion. **Adhesion** is the sticking together of molecules of different kinds. ❷ Water molecules tend to adhere to cellulose molecules in the walls of xylem cells. **Cohesion** is the sticking

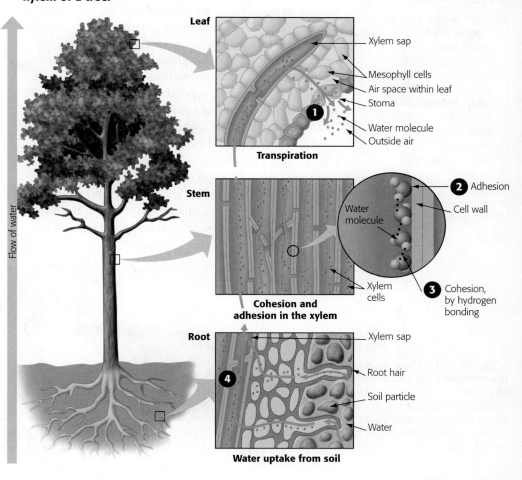

▼ **Figure 29.9 How transpiration pulls water up the xylem of a tree.**

Flow of water

Leaf

Xylem sap
Mesophyll cells
Air space within leaf
Stoma
Water molecule
Outside air

❶ **Transpiration**

Stem

Water molecule

❷ Adhesion
Cell wall

❸ Cohesion, by hydrogen bonding

Xylem cells

Cohesion and adhesion in the xylem

Root

Xylem sap

Root hair

Soil particle

Water

❹

Water uptake from soil

together of molecules of the same kind. ❸ In the case of water, hydrogen bonds make the H₂O molecules stick to one another (see Figure 2.9). ❹ Together, adhesion and cohesion create a continuous string of water molecules running from the roots to the leaves. These molecules stick to each other and to the inside walls of the xylem tubes.

Before a water molecule can exit the leaf, it must break off from the top of the string. In effect, the water molecule is pulled off by a concentration gradient: The air outside the leaf is much drier than the moist interior of the leaf, causing the water molecule to diffuse outward. Cohesion resists this pulling force (because water molecules are attracted to each other and so don't want to separate) but is not strong enough to overcome the force of evaporation. The molecule breaks off, and the opposing forces of cohesion and transpiration put tension on the rest of the string of water molecules. As long as transpiration continues, the string is kept tense and is pulled upward as one molecule exits the leaf and the one behind it is tugged up into its place.

Water molecules are thus pulled upward by this string, one at a time. Biologists call this explanation for the ascent of xylem sap the **transpiration-cohesion-tension mechanism**. Transpiration exerts a pull on a tense, unbroken string of water molecules that is held together by cohesion and helped upward by adhesion.

Note that the transport of xylem sap requires no energy expenditure by the plant; a plant has no muscles for pumping. Physical properties—cohesion, adhesion, and the evaporating effect of the sun—move water and dissolved minerals from a plant's roots to its shoots. Transpiration is thus a highly efficient means of moving a lot of water upward through the body of a plant.

You have probably tasted xylem sap moved via transpiration yourself. When maple trees resume growth in the spring after a leafless winter, starch that was produced the previous summer and stored in the roots is converted to sugar, which is transported upward in the xylem sap via transpiration to nourish the developing leaf buds. This sap can be harvested in buckets and boiled to concentrate the sugar. It takes about 50 gallons of sap to make one gallon of maple syrup.

The Regulation of Transpiration by Stomata

Although necessary to distribute water, transpiration also works against plants because it can result in the loss of an astonishing amount of water. Transpiration is usually greatest on days that are sunny, warm, dry, and windy, because these weather conditions increase evaporation. An average-sized maple tree (about 20 m high) can lose more than 200 L of water per hour during a summer day. As long as water moves up from the soil fast enough to replace the lost water, this presents no problem. But if the soil dries out and transpiration exceeds the delivery of water, the leaves will wilt. Unless the soil and leaves are rehydrated, the plant will eventually die.

Why are plants more likely to wilt on windy days?

The leaf stomata, which can open and close, are evolutionary adaptations that help plants adjust their transpiration rates to changing environmental conditions. In many plants, stomata are open during the day, which allows CO₂ to enter the leaf from the atmosphere and thus keep photosynthesis going when sunlight is available. However, the plant also loses water through transpiration. At night, when there is no light for photosynthesis and therefore no need for CO₂, many plants close their stomata, saving water. Stomata may also close during the day if a plant is losing water too fast. The opening and closing of stomata is controlled by the changing shape of the two guard cells flanking each stoma **(Figure 29.10)**. ☑

The Transport of Sugars

A plant's survival depends not only on the transport of water and minerals absorbed from the soil but also on the transport of the sugars it makes by photosynthesis. This is the main function of phloem.

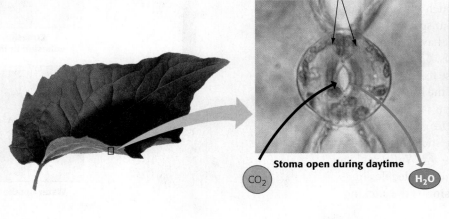
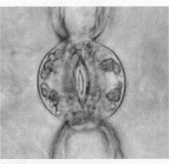

Guard cells

Stoma open during daytime   **Stoma closed at night**

CO₂   H₂O

► **Figure 29.10 How stomata control transpiration via guard cells.** A pair of guard cells (each the shape of a half-circle) surrounding a stoma can change shape in response to environmental signals, regulating the rate of transpiration and CO₂ uptake.

Phloem consists of living food-conducting cells arranged end to end into long tubes. Through perforations in the end walls of these cells, sugary liquid called **phloem sap** moves freely from one cell to the next (Figure 29.11). Phloem sap contains inorganic ions, amino acids, and hormones in transit from one part of the plant to another, but its main solute is usually the disaccharide sugar sucrose (table sugar).

In contrast to xylem sap, which only flows upward from the roots, phloem sap moves throughout the plant in various directions. A location in a plant where sugar is being produced (either by photosynthesis or by the breakdown of stored starch) is called a **sugar source**. A receiving location in the plant, where the sugar will be stored or consumed, is called a **sugar sink**. Sugar moves within food-conducting tubes of phloem from a source, such as a leaf, to a sink, such as a root or a fruit.

What causes phloem sap to flow from a source to a sink? Figure 29.12 uses a beet plant to illustrate a widely accepted model called the **pressure-flow mechanism**. At the sugar source (the beet leaves), ❶ sugar is loaded from a photosynthetic cell into a phloem tube via active transport. Sugar loading at the source end raises the solute (sugar) concentration inside the phloem tube. ❷ The high solute concentration draws water into the tube by osmosis, usually from the xylem. The flow of water from the xylem into the phloem raises the water pressure at the source end of the phloem tube.

At the sugar sink (the beet root), both sugar and water leave the phloem tube. ❸ As sugar leaves the phloem, lowering the sugar concentration at the sink end, ❹ water moves by osmosis back into the xylem. The exit of water lowers the water pressure in the tube.

The building of water pressure at the source end of the phloem tube and the reduction of water pressure at the sink end cause phloem sap to flow from source to sink. This pressure-flow mechanism explains why phloem sap always flows from a sugar source to a sugar sink, regardless of their locations in the plant.

We now have a broad picture of how a plant absorbs substances from the soil and transports materials from one part of its body to another: Water and inorganic ions enter from the soil and are pulled upward through xylem by transpiration. Carbon dioxide enters leaves through the stomata and is incorporated into sugars, which are distributed by phloem. Pressure flow drives the phloem sap from leaves and storage sites to other parts of the plant, where the sugars are used or stored. In the next section, we'll consider various ways that a working plant uses these resources. ☑

☑ CHECKPOINT

In the pressure-flow mechanism, phloem sap always flows from a _____ to a _____.

Answer: sugar source; sugar sink

▼ Figure 29.11 **Food-conducting cells of phloem.** The main function of phloem is to transport sugars through living food-conducting cells arranged into tubes. Phloem sap moves through openings between the cells.

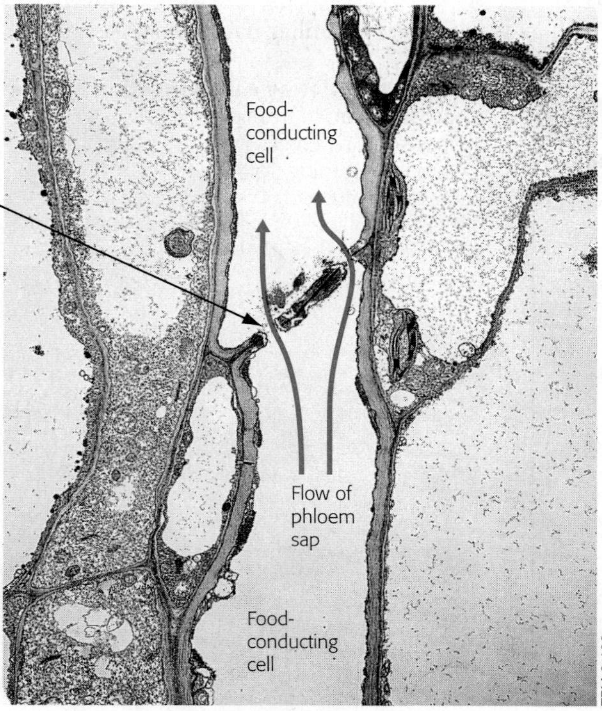

Opening between cells

Food-conducting cell

Flow of phloem sap

Food-conducting cell

TEM 2,400x

▼ Figure 29.12 **Pressure flow in plant phloem.** The red dots in the phloem tube represent sugar molecules; notice that a concentration gradient decreasing from top to bottom creates a pressure flow (wide red arrow). The wide blue arrow represents a parallel gradient of water pressure due to transpiration in the xylem sap; water pressure decreases from bottom to top. Xylem tubes transport the water back from sink to source.

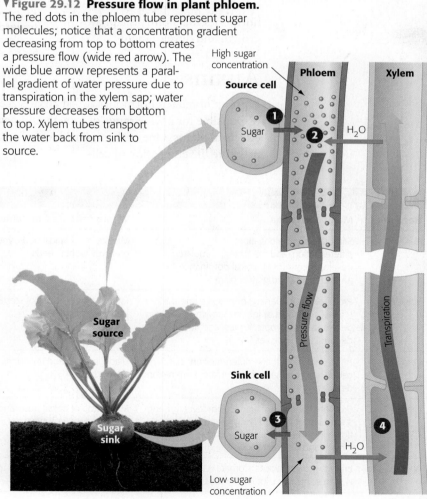

High sugar concentration

Phloem

Xylem

Source cell

Sugar

❶

❷

H_2O

Sugar source

Sugar sink

Pressure flow

Transpiration

Sink cell

Sugar

❸

❹

H_2O

Low sugar concentration

Plant Hormones

A **hormone** is a chemical signal produced in one part of an organism and transported to other parts, where it acts on target cells to change their functioning (see Chapter 25). Plants produce hormones in very small amounts, but even a tiny amount of any of these chemicals can have profound effects on growth and development. As they do in people, hormones in plants control growth and development by affecting the division, elongation, and differentiation of cells.

Plant biologists have identified five major types of plant hormones, which are listed in **Table 29.1**. Each type of hormone can produce a variety of effects, depending on the species and developmental stage of the plant as well as the hormone's concentration and site of action. In most situations, a plant hormone does not act alone. Instead, it is the relative concentration of two or more hormones that controls a plant's growth and development.

▲ **Figure 29.13 Sunflowers growing toward light.** Phototropism guides growing plants toward the sunlight needed for photosynthesis.

Auxins

A group of related hormones called **auxins** are responsible for a wide range of growth and development effects in plants. One of the main effects of auxins is to promote the elongation of cells.

Phototropism and Cell Elongation

Phototropism is the directional growth of a plant shoot in response to light. For example, a sunflower will rotate its flower and grow toward sunlight **(Figure 29.13)**. And houseplants on a windowsill will tend to grow toward the sunlight in the window. Phototropism directs both growing seedlings and the shoots of mature plants toward the sunlight they use for photosynthesis.

How does a plant grow in a particular direction? Microscopic observations of growing plants reveal the cellular mechanism that underlies phototropism **(Figure 29.14)**. Cells on the side of a stem that gets the least amount of light are larger—actually, they have elongated faster—than those on the brighter side, causing the shoot to bend toward the light. If a seedling is illuminated uniformly from all sides or if it is kept in the dark, the cells all elongate at a similar rate and the seedling grows straight upward.

What causes plant cells on the dark side of a shoot to grow faster than those on the bright side? Our present understanding of this phenomenon emerged from a series of classic experiments conducted by two scientists with a very familiar name, as we see next.

Table 29.1	Major Types of Plant Hormones	
Hormone	**Major Functions**	**Where Produced or Found in Plant**
Auxins	Stimulate stem elongation; affect root growth, differentiation, and branching; stimulate development of fruit, apical dominance, phototropism, and gravitropism	Meristems of apical buds, young leaves, embryos within seeds
Ethylene	Promotes fruit ripening; opposes some auxin effects; promotes or inhibits growth and development of roots, leaves, and flowers, depending on species	Ripening fruit, nodes of stems, aging leaves and flowers
Cytokinins	Affect root growth and differentiation; stimulate cell division and growth; stimulate germination; delay aging	Made in roots and transported to other organs
Gibberellins	Promote seed germination, bud development, stem elongation, and leaf growth; stimulate flowering and fruit development; affect root growth and differentiation	Meristems of apical buds and roots, young leaves, embryos
Abscisic acid	Inhibits growth; closes stomata when water is scarce; helps maintain dormancy	Leaves, stems, roots, green fruit

▼ **Figure 29.14 How cell elongation causes phototropism.** In this figure, a grass seedling curves toward light coming from one side because of the faster elongation of cells on the shaded side.

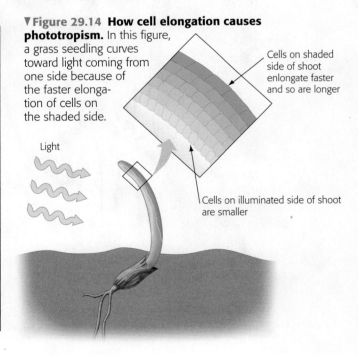

Cells on shaded side of shoot enlongate faster and so are longer

Light

Cells on illuminated side of shoot are smaller

Do Chemical Signals Affect Plant Growth?

In the late 1800s, Charles Darwin and his son Francis performed some of the earliest experiments on phototropism **(Figure 29.15)**. They began with the **observation** that grass seedlings bent toward light only if the tips of their shoots were present. This led them to **question** whether the tips of the seedlings produced some kind of chemical growth signal. Their **hypothesis** was that the plant tips sensed light and produced a growth signal in response. They made a **prediction**: Removing a shoot tip or blocking its access to light would prevent phototropism. Several of their **experiments** are summarized in Figure 29.15.

The Darwins' **results** showed that removing the tip of a grass shoot did prevent growth toward light. The shoot also remained straight when they placed an opaque cap on its tip. However, the shoot curved normally when they placed a transparent cap on its tip or an opaque shield around its base. The Darwins concluded that the tip of the shoot was responsible for sensing light. They also recognized that the growth response, the bending of the shoot, occurred below the tip. Therefore, they speculated that some unknown growth signal was transmitted downward from the tip to the growing region of the shoot.

Building on the Darwins' results, botanists have since discovered the mechanisms of many other plant hormones. This understanding is one of the cornerstones of modern agriculture, allowing people to control the growth of plants in a variety of ways.

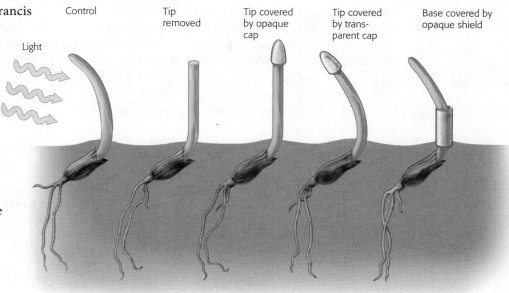

▲ **Figure 29.15 The Darwins' classic experiments on phototropism.** This figure summarizes experiments conducted by Charles Darwin and his son Francis. Together, these results suggested that a substance produced by the tip of a seedling controls phototropism.

The Action of Auxins

The hormones responsible for the phototropism observed by the Darwins are auxins produced by the apical meristem at the tip of a shoot. Illuminating one side of a shoot results in a concentration of auxin in the cells on the dark side. This uneven distribution of auxins makes cells on the dark side elongate, causing the shoot to bend.

Auxins promote cell elongation in stems only when they are present within a certain concentration range. Interestingly, this same concentration range inhibits cell elongation in roots. Above this range, auxins inhibit cell elongation in stems; and below this range, they cause root cells to elongate. This complex set of effects reinforces two points: (1) The same hormone may have different effects at different concentrations in the same target cell, and (2) a particular concentration of a hormone may have different effects on different target cells.

In addition to causing stems and roots to lengthen, auxins promote growth in stem diameter. Furthermore, auxins made in developing seeds promote the growth of fruit. Farmers sometimes produce seedless tomatoes, cucumbers, and eggplants by spraying unpollinated plants with synthetic auxins.

The discovery of plant hormones has produced many advances in agriculture. The use of synthetic plant hormones allows more food to be produced at lower cost. For example, one of the most widely used herbicides, or weed killers, is a synthetic auxin that disrupts the normal balance of hormones that regulate plant growth. Because dicots are more sensitive than monocots to this herbicide, it can be used to selectively remove dandelions and other unwanted broadleaf dicot weeds from a monocot lawn or field of grain. By applying herbicides to cropland, a farmer can reduce the amount of plowing required to control weeds, thus reducing soil erosion, fuel consumption, and labor costs.

At the same time, there is growing concern that the heavy use of artificial chemicals in food production may pose environmental and health hazards. Also, many consumers are concerned that foods produced using artificial hormones may not be as tasty or nutritious as those raised naturally. This highlights an important question about modern agricultural techniques: Should we continue to produce cheap, plentiful food using artificial chemicals and tolerate the potential problems; or should we put more of our agricultural effort into organic farming, recognizing that foods may be less plentiful and more expensive as a result? This is something you need to consider as you make choices about the foods you buy and eat. ✓

Ethylene

Ethylene is a hormone, released as a gas, that triggers a variety of aging responses in plants, including fruit ripening and dropping of leaves.

Fruit Ripening

A burst of ethylene production in a fruit triggers its ripening. Because ethylene is a gas, the signal to ripen spreads from fruit to fruit: One bad apple really can spoil the bunch! You can make fruit ripen faster if you store it with already ripened fruit in a bag so that the ethylene gas accumulates **(Figure 29.16)**. On a commercial scale, many kinds of fruit—tomatoes, for instance—are often picked green and then partially ripened in huge storage bins into which ethylene gas is piped. In other cases, growers take measures to retard the ripening action of natural ethylene. Stored apples are often flushed with CO_2, which inhibits the action of ethylene. In this way, apples picked in autumn can be stored for sale the following summer.

Why can one bad peach spoil a whole bowlful?

Leaf Drop

The loss of leaves in autumn is affected by ethylene. Leaf drop is triggered by environmental stimuli, including the shortening days of autumn and cooler temperatures. These stimuli cause a change in the balance of ethylene and auxins that weakens the cell walls in a layer of cells at the base of the leaf stalk. The weight of the leaf, often assisted by wind, causes this layer to split, releasing the leaf. ✓

Cytokinins

Cytokinins are a group of closely related hormones that act as growth regulators. These regulators promote cell division, or cytokinesis. Cytokinins are produced in

▼ **Figure 29.16 The effect of ethylene on the ripening of bananas.** Two unripe bananas were stored for the same amount of time in bags. The banana on top was stored alone; the bottom banana was stored with an ethylene-releasing peach.

Banana alone

Banana plus ethylene-releasing peach

actively growing tissues, particularly in roots, embryos, and fruits.

Cytokinins stimulate the growth of axillary buds, making a plant grow more branches and become bushy. Christmas tree growers sometimes use cytokinins to produce attractive branching. Cytokinins entering the shoot system from the roots counter the inhibitory effects of auxins coming down from the terminal buds. The complex growth patterns of most plants probably result from the relative concentrations of auxins and cytokinins.

Gibberellins

Gibberellins are another group of growth-regulating hormones. Roots and young leaves are major sites of gibberellin production. One of the main effects of gibberellins is to stimulate cell elongation and cell division in stems and leaves. This action generally enhances that of auxins. Also in combination with auxins, gibberellins can influence fruit development, and gibberellin-auxin sprays can make apples, currants, and eggplants develop without pollination and seed production. Gibberellins are used commercially to make seedless grapes grow larger and farther apart in a cluster, the benefits of which are evident in **Figure 29.17**.

Gibberellins are also important in seed germination in many plants. Many seeds that require special environmental conditions to germinate, such as exposure to light or cold, will germinate when sprayed with gibberellins. In nature, gibberellins in seeds are probably the link between environmental cues and the metabolic processes that reactivate growth of the embryo after a period of dormancy. For example, when water becomes available to a grass seed, it causes the embryo in the seed to release gibberellins, which promote germination by mobilizing nutrients stored in the seed.

Abscisic Acid

Unlike the growth-stimulating hormones we have studied so far, **abscisic acid** *slows* growth. One of the times in a plant's life when it is advantageous to suspend growth is at the onset of seed dormancy (inactivity of the seed). Seed dormancy is an evolutionary adaptation that ensures that a seed will germinate only when there are appropriate conditions of light, temperature, and moisture.

Many types of dormant seeds will germinate only when abscisic acid is removed or inactivated in some way. The seeds of some plants—such as the perennials rosemary and rhubarb—require prolonged exposure to cold during the winter to inactivate abscisic acid and trigger seed germination in the spring. The seeds of some desert plants remain dormant for years (even decades) until a sufficient downpour washes out the abscisic acid, allowing them to germinate when water is available for plant growth **(Figure 29.18)**. For many plants, the ratio of abscisic acid (which inhibits seed germination) to gibberellins (which promote seed germination) determines whether the seed will remain dormant or germinate. ☑

▼ **Figure 29.17 The effect of gibberellins on grapes.** The right cluster of grapes shows the effect of gibberellin treatment: larger grapes farther apart in the cluster.

Untreated

Treated with gibberellins

▼ **Figure 29.18 The effect of abscisic acid removal on seed dormancy.** These wildflowers grew in the Organ Pipe Cactus National Monument, in Arizona, just after a hard rain washed abscisic acid out of the seeds, allowing them to germinate.

☑ CHECKPOINT

Which two hormones regulate seed dormancy and germination? What are their opposing effects?

Answer: Abscisic acid maintains seed dormancy; gibberellins promote germination.

Response to Stimuli

In this section, we'll consider how a plant responds to physical stimuli from the environment—including light, touch, and gravity.

Tropisms

Tropisms are directed growth responses that cause parts of a plant to grow toward or away from a stimulus **(Figure 29.19)**. Phototropism, as you saw in Figure 29.13, is a particularly important example, but there are other directed growth responses. For example, **thigmotropism** is a response to touch, as when a pea tendril (which is actually a modified leaf) contacts a string or wire and coils around it for support. The tendril in the center photo in Figure 29.19 grew straight until it touched the support. Contact then stimulated the cells to grow at different rates on opposite sides of the tendril (slower in the contact area), making the tendril coil around the wire.

Gravitropism is the directional growth of a plant organ in response to gravity: Shoots grow upward and roots grow downward, regardless of the orientation of the seed. Auxins play an important role in gravitropism. The seedling shown on the right in Figure 29.19 responded to gravity by redistributing auxins to the lower side of its horizontally growing root. A high concentration of auxins inhibits the growth of root cells. As growth of the lower side of the root was slowed, cells on the upper side continued to elongate normally, and the root curved downward.

Why don't you have to worry about planting seeds upside down?

Photoperiod

In addition to providing energy for photosynthesis and directing growth, light helps regulate a plant's life cycle. Flowering, seed germination, and the onset and ending of dormancy are stages in plant development that usually occur at specific times of the year. The environmental stimulus that plants most often use to detect the time of year is called **photoperiod**, the relative lengths of day and night.

Plants whose flowering is triggered by photoperiod fall into two groups: long-night plants and short-night plants **(Figure 29.20)**. (Historically, botanists erroneously referred to these plants as short- and long-day plants; we now know that it is night length, not day length, that affects a plant's flowering.) Long-night plants, such as chrysanthemum and poinsettia, generally flower in fall or winter, when nights lengthen. Short-night plants, such as lettuce, iris, and many grains, usually flower in spring or summer, when nights are briefer. Some plants, such as dandelions, are night-neutral; their flowering is unaffected by photoperiod. Florists apply knowledge of the photoperiod of particular plants to bring us flowers out of season. The blooming of chrysanthemums, for instance, can be stalled until spring by interrupting each long night with a flash of light, thus turning one long night into two short nights. ☑

☑ CHECKPOINT

1. A common houseplant called the "sensitive plant" (*Mimosa pudica*) has leaves that curl when touched. This is an example of what kind of growth response?
2. A particular long-night plant won't flower in the spring. You try to induce flowering by using a short, dark interruption to split a long-day period of spring into two short-day periods. What result do you predict?

Answers: **1.** *thigmotropism* **2.** *The plants still won't flower, because it is actually night length, not day length, that controls flowering.*

▼**Figure 29.19 Tropisms.**

TROPISMS
(directed growth responses)

Phototropism

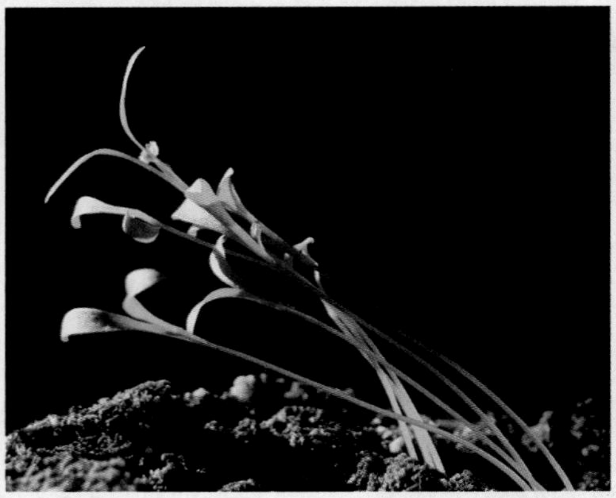

These seedlings bending toward the light are young cilantro plants (a common herb).

Thigmotropism

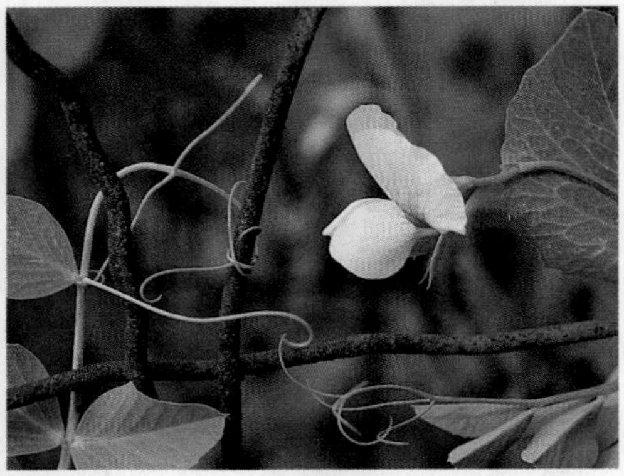

Thigmotropism, growth in response to touch, allows vining plants to wrap around support structures. In this photo, the tendril of a pea plant coils around a wire fence.

Gravitropism

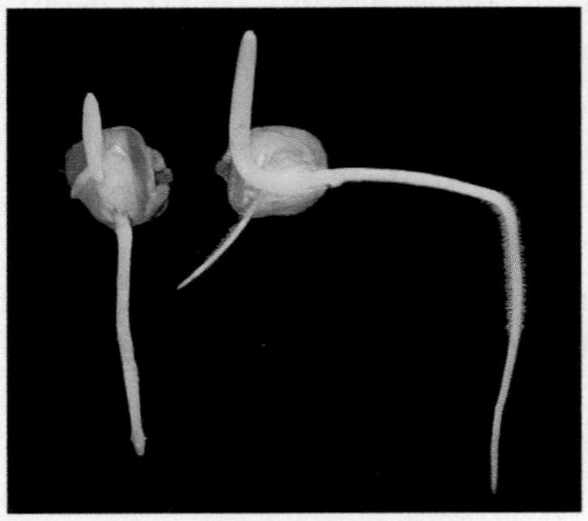

These seedlings were both germinated in the dark. The one on the left was left alone. The one on the right was turned on its side two days after germination so that the shoot and root were horizontal. When this photo was taken, the shoot had turned back upward and the root had turned down.

▼Figure 29.20 **Photoperiod and flowering.** Photoperiod, the relative lengths of day and night, can trigger flowering.

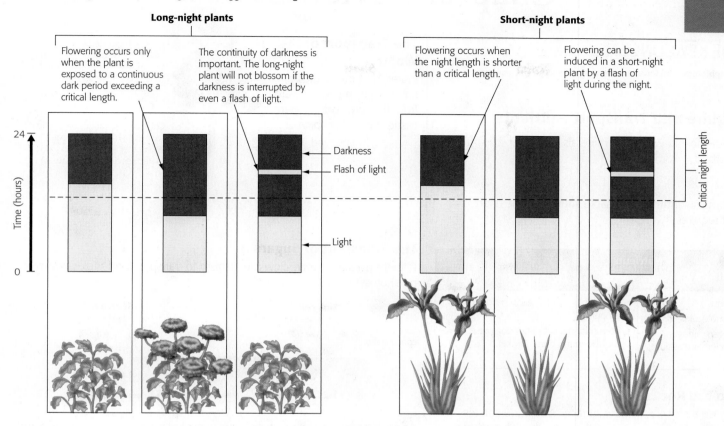

Long-night plants

Flowering occurs only when the plant is exposed to a continuous dark period exceeding a critical length.

The continuity of darkness is important. The long-night plant will not blossom if the darkness is interrupted by even a flash of light.

Short-night plants

Flowering occurs when the night length is shorter than a critical length.

Flowering can be induced in a short-night plant by a flash of light during the night.

Time (hours)

24

0

Darkness

Flash of light

Light

Critical night length

The Interdependence of Organisms EVOLUTION CONNECTION

Plants, Mantises, and People

As you learned in the last chapter, most flowering plants depend on insects or other animals for pollination and seed dispersal. In this chapter, you saw that plants rely on organisms from two other kingdoms to help acquire nutrients: soil bacteria and the fungi of mycorrhizae. Indeed, the mycorrhizal connection may have altered the entire course of evolution by helping make possible the colonization of land. Today, nearly all land animals depend on plants (or animals that eat plants) for food.

Both the cover of this book and **Figure 29.21** show an African mega mantis (*Plistospilota guineensis*), a particularly striking member of the order Mantodea, a group of insects commonly called praying mantises. This species is found in western Africa, where its members occupy warm, damp, shrubby terrain. Like most mantises, the mega mantis is predatory: It lies in wait to ambush prey (such as flies, moths, crickets, and cockroaches) that strays near it, grasping its meal with its spiked legs.

In turn, mantises are themselves prey for spiders, frogs, birds, and even monkeys. When threatened, a mega mantis will sometimes spread its limbs and wings to appear bigger and more threatening.

Thus, we close this chapter—and this book—illustrating one of biology's overarching themes: the interrelatedness of organisms. Animals depend on other animals and plants, which in turn depend on animals, fungi, and protists. And all eukaryotic life depends on prokaryotes. This interdependency reminds us that it is impossible to separate ourselves from all of the living creatures that share the biosphere. We hope that *Campbell Essential Biology with Physiology* has given you a new appreciation of your place in the living world.

▼Figure 29.21 **The interdependence of organisms.** This African mega mantis (*Plistospilota guineensis*) depends on protists, plants, and animals for food and is itself eaten by other animals. These relationships emphasize the interrelatedness of all life on Earth.

Chapter Review

SUMMARY OF KEY CONCEPTS

(MB) Go to **www.masteringbiology.com** for homework assignments, practice quizzes, Pearson eText, and more.

How Plants Acquire and Transport Nutrients

As a plant grows, its roots absorb water and minerals (inorganic ions) from the soil. Its leaves absorb CO_2 from the air.

Plant Nutrition

A plant must obtain from its surroundings usable sources of the chemical elements (nutrients) it requires.

Nutrients	
Macronutrients	**Micronutrients**
• Needed in large amounts • Used to build organic molecules • Carbon, oxygen, hydrogen, nitrogen, sulfur, phosphorus, calcium, potassium, magnesium	• Reusuable, so needed in much smaller amounts • Iron, chlorine, copper, manganese, zinc, molybdenum, boron, nickel

From the Soil into the Roots

Root hairs greatly increase a root's absorbing surface. Water and solutes move through the root's epidermis and cortex, then into the xylem (water-conducting tissue) for transport upward. Relationships with other organisms help plants obtain nutrients. Many plants form mycorrhizae, mutually beneficial associations with fungi. A network of fungal threads increases a plant's absorption of nutrients, and the fungus receives nutrients from the plant.

The Role of Bacteria in Nitrogen Nutrition

Most plants depend on bacteria to convert nitrogen to a form usable by the plant.

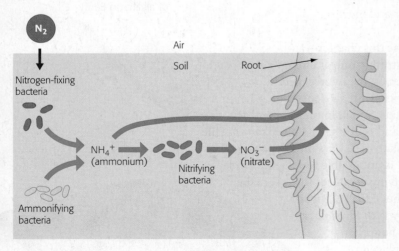

Legumes and certain other plants have nodules in their roots that house vesicles filled with nitrogen-fixing bacteria.

The Transport of Water

Water (and the solutes dissolved in it) moves upward from the roots within xylem tissue due to transpiration.

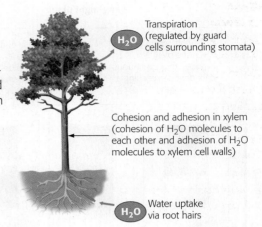

Transpiration (regulated by guard cells surrounding stomata)

Cohesion and adhesion in xylem (cohesion of H_2O molecules to each other and adhesion of H_2O molecules to xylem cell walls)

Water uptake via root hairs

The Transport of Sugars

Phloem uses a pressure-flow mechanism to transport food molecules made by photosynthesis.

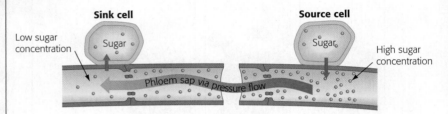

An increase in sugar concentration and water pressure at the sugar source and a decrease at the sugar sink cause phloem sap to flow from source to sink.

Plant Hormones

Hormones coordinate the internal activities of plants.

Auxins

Phototropism, directional growth in response to light, results from faster cell growth on the shaded side of the shoot than on the lighted side. This effect is regulated by auxins, a class of hormones. Plants produce auxins in the apical meristems at the tips of shoots. At different concentrations, auxins stimulate or inhibit the elongation of shoots and roots.

Ethylene

As a fruit ages, it gives off ethylene gas, which hastens ripening. A changing ratio of auxins to ethylene, triggered mainly by longer nights, causes the loss of leaves from certain trees.

Cytokinins

Cytokinins, produced by growing roots, embryos, and fruits, are hormones that promote cell division. The ratio of auxins to cytokinins helps coordinate the growth of roots and shoots.

Gibberellins

Gibberellins stimulate the elongation of stems and leaves and the development of fruits. Gibberellins released from embryos function in some of the early events of seed germination. Auxins and gibberellins are used in agriculture to produce seedless fruits.

Abscisic Acid

Abscisic acid inhibits the germination of seeds. The ratio of abscisic acid to gibberellins often determines whether a seed will remain dormant or germinate. Seeds of many plants remain dormant until their abscisic acid is inactivated or washed away.

Response to Stimuli

Tropisms

Tropisms are growth responses that make a plant grow toward or away from a stimulus. Important tropisms include phototropism, thigmotropism (a response to touch), and gravitropism (a response to gravity).

Photoperiod

Plants mark the seasons by measuring photoperiod, the relative lengths of night and day. The timing of flowering is one of the seasonal responses to photoperiod. Long-night plants flower when nights exceed a certain critical length; short-night plants flower when nights are shorter than a critical length.

SELF-QUIZ

1. Certain fungi cause diseases in plants. There are a variety of antifungal sprays that can be used to control this problem. Some gardeners constantly spray their plants with fungicides, even when no signs of disease are evident. How might this be disadvantageous to the plant?

2. Which of the following activities of soil bacteria does not contribute to creating usable nitrogen for plant use?
   a. the fixation of atmospheric nitrogen
   b. the conversion of ammonium to nitrate
   c. the assembly of amino acids into proteins
   d. the generation of ammonium from proteins in dead leaves

3. Plants transport two types of sap. _____ sap, a solution of mostly water and sucrose, is transported from sites of sugar production to other parts of the plant. _____ sap, a solution of mostly water and inorganic ions, is transported from the roots to the rest of the plant body.

4. Contrast cohesion and adhesion, and describe the role of each in the ascent of xylem sap.

5. Auxins cause a shoot to bend toward light by
   a. causing cells to shrink on the dark side of the shoot.
   b. stimulating growth on the dark side of the shoot.
   c. causing cells to shrink on the lighted side of the shoot.
   d. stimulating growth on the lighted side of the shoot.

6. The status of axillary buds—dormant or growing—depends on the relative concentrations of _____ moving down from the shoot tip and _____ moving up from the roots.

7. Why do many plants become bushier if you pinch off their terminal buds?

8. Match each of the following hormones to its primary role in a plant.
   a. auxins
   b. ethylene
   c. cytokinins
   d. gibberellins
   e. abscisic acid

   1. at different concentrations, stimulate or inhibit the elongation of shoots and roots
   2. produced by roots, promote cell division
   3. inhibits seed germination
   4. hastens fruit ripening
   5. promote fruit development

9. Match each of the following terms to its meaning.
   a. gravitropism
   b. photoperiod
   c. phototropism
   d. thigmotropism

   1. growth response to light
   2. growth response to touch
   3. relative lengths of night and day
   4. growth response to gravity

10. Jon just started a new job as night watchman at a plant nursery. His boss told him to stay out of a room where chrysanthemums (which are long-night plants) were about to flower. Around midnight, looking for the rest room, Jon accidentally opened the door to the chrysanthemum room and turned on the lights for a moment. How might this affect the chrysanthemums?

Answers to these questions can be found in Appendix: Self-Quiz Answers.

THE PROCESS OF SCIENCE

11. In some situations, the application of nitrogen fertilizer to crops has to be increased each year because the fertilizer decreases the rate of nitrogen fixation in the soil. Propose a hypothesis to explain this phenomenon. Describe a test for your hypothesis. What results would you expect from your test?

BIOLOGY AND SOCIETY

12. Agriculture is by far the biggest user of water in arid western states, including Colorado, Arizona, and California. The populations of these states are growing, and there is an ongoing conflict between cities and farm regions over water. To ensure water supplies for urban growth, cities are purchasing water rights from farmers. This is often the least expensive way for a city to obtain more water, and some farmers can make more money selling water than growing crops. Discuss the possible consequences of this trend. Is this the best way to allocate water for all concerned? Why or why not?

13. Imagine the following scenario: A plant scientist has developed a synthetic chemical that mimics the effects of a plant hormone. The chemical can be sprayed on apples before harvest to prevent flaking of the natural wax that is formed on the skin. This makes the apples shinier and gives them a deeper color. What kinds of questions do you think should be answered before farmers start using this chemical on apples? How might the scientist go about finding answers to these questions?

Appendix A Metric Conversion Table

MEASUREMENT	UNIT AND ABBREVIATION	METRIC EQUIVALENT	APPROXIMATE METRIC-TO-ENGLISH CONVERSION FACTOR	APPROXIMATE ENGLISH-TO-METRIC CONVERSION FACTOR
Length	1 kilometer (km)	= 1,000 (10^3) meters	1 km = 0.6 mile	1 mile = 1.6 km
	1 meter (m)	= 100 (10^2) centimeters	1 m = 1.1 yards	1 yard = 0.9 m
		= 1,000 millimeters	1 m = 3.3 feet	1 foot = 0.3 m
			1 m = 39.4 inches	
	1 centimeter (cm)	= 0.01(10^{-2}) meter	1 cm = 0.4 inch	1 foot = 30.5 cm
				1 inch = 2.5 cm
	1 millimeter (mm)	= 0.001 (10^{-3}) meter	1 mm = 0.04 inch	
	1 micrometer (μm)	= 10^{-6} meter (10^{-3} mm)		
	1 nanometer (nm)	= 10^{-9} meter (10^{-3} μm)		
	1 angstrom (Å)	= 10^{-10} meter (10^{-4} μm)		
Area	1 hectare (ha)	= 10,000 square meters	1 ha = 2.5 acres	1 acre = 0.4 ha
	1 square meter (m²)	= 10,000 square centimeters	1 m² = 1.2 square yards	1 square yard = 0.8 m²
			1 m² = 10.8 square feet	1 square foot = 0.09 m²
	1 square centimeter (cm²)	= 100 square millimeters	1 cm² = 0.16 square inch	1 square inch = 6.5 cm²
Mass	1 metric ton (t)	= 1,000 kilograms	1 t = 1.1 tons	1 ton = 0.91 t
	1 kilogram (kg)	= 1,000 grams	1 kg = 2.2 pounds	1 pound = 0.45 kg
	1 gram (g)	= 1,000 milligrams	1 g = 0.04 ounce	1 ounce = 28.35 g
			1 g = 15.4 grains	
	1 milligram (mg)	= 10^{-3} gram	1 mg = 0.02 grain	
	1 microgram (μg)	= 10^{-6} gram		
Volume *(solids)*	1 cubic meter (m³)	= 1,000,000 cubic centimeters	1 m³ = 1.3 cubic yards	1 cubic yard = 0.8 m³
			1 m³ = 35.3 cubic feet	1 cubic foot = 0.03 m³
	1 cubic centimeter (cm³ or cc)	= 10^{-6} cubic meter	1 cm³ = 0.06 cubic inch	1 cubic inch = 16.4 cm³
	1 cubic millimeter (mm³)	= 10^{-9} cubic meter (10^{-3} cubic centimeter)		
Volume *(liquids and gases)*	1 kiloliter (kL or kl)	= 1,000 liters	1 kL = 264.2 gallons	1 gallon = 3.79 L
	1 liter (L)	= 1,000 millimeters	1 L = 0.26 gallon	1 quart = 0.95 L
			1 L = 1.06 quarts	
	1 milliliter (mL or ml)	= 10^{-3} liter	1 mL = 0.03 fluid ounce	1 quart = 946 mL
		= 1 cubic centimeter	1 mL = approx. ¼ teaspoon	1 pint = 473 mL
			1 mL = approx. 15–16 drops	1 fluid ounce = 29.6 mL
				1 teaspoon = approx. 5 mL
	1 microliter (μl or μL)	= 10^{-6} liter (10^{-3} milliliters)		
Time	1 second (s)	= $\frac{1}{60}$ minute		
	1 millisecond (ms)	= 10^{-3} second		
Temperature	Degrees Celsius (°C)		$°F = \frac{9}{5}°C + 32$	$°C = \frac{5}{9}(°F - 32)$

Appendix B The Periodic Table

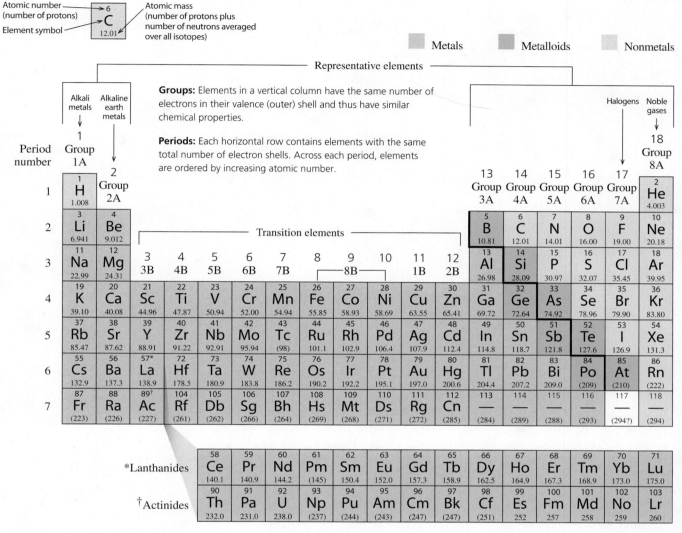

Atomic number
(number of protons)

Element symbol

Atomic mass
(number of protons plus
number of neutrons averaged
over all isotopes)

6
C
12.01

☐ Metals ☐ Metalloids ☐ Nonmetals

Representative elements

Groups: Elements in a vertical column have the same number of electrons in their valence (outer) shell and thus have similar chemical properties.

Periods: Each horizontal row contains elements with the same total number of electron shells. Across each period, elements are ordered by increasing atomic number.

Alkali metals | Alkaline earth metals

Halogens Noble gases

Transition elements

NAME (SYMBOL)	ATOMIC NUMBER	NAME (SYMBOL)	ATOMIC NUMBER	NAME (SYMBOL)	ATOMIC NUMBER	NAME (SYMBOL)	ATOMIC NUMBER	NAME (SYMBOL)	ATOMIC NUMBER
Actinium (Ac)	89	Copernicium (Cn)	112	Iridium (Ir)	77	Palladium (Pd)	46	Sodium (Na)	11
Aluminum (Al)	13	Copper (Cu)	29	Iron (Fe)	26	Phosphorus (P)	15	Strontium (Sr)	38
Americium (Am)	95	Curium (Cm)	96	Krypton (Kr)	36	Platinum (Pt)	78	Sulfur (S)	16
Antimony (Sb)	51	Darmstadtium (Ds)	110	Lanthanum (La)	57	Plutonium (Pu)	94	Tantalum (Ta)	73
Argon (Ar)	18	Dubnium (Db)	105	Lawrencium (Lr)	103	Polonium (Po)	84	Technetium (Tc)	43
Arsenic (As)	33	Dysprosium (Dy)	66	Lead (Pb)	82	Potassium (K)	19	Tellurium (Te)	52
Astatine (At)	85	Einsteinium (Es)	99	Lithium (Li)	3	Praseodymium (Pr)	59	Terbium (Tb)	65
Barium (Ba)	56	Erbium (Er)	68	Lutetium (Lu)	71	Promethium (Pm)	61	Thallium (Tl)	81
Berkelium (Bk)	97	Europium (Eu)	63	Magnesium (Mg)	12	Protactinium (Pa)	91	Thorium (Th)	90
Beryllium (Be)	4	Fermium (Fm)	100	Manganese (Mn)	25	Radium (Ra)	88	Thulium (Tm)	69
Bismuth (Bi)	83	Fluorine (F)	9	Meitnerium (Mt)	109	Radon (Rn)	86	Tin (Sn)	50
Bohrium (Bh)	107	Francium (Fr)	87	Mendelevium (Md)	101	Rhenium (Re)	75	Titanium (Ti)	22
Boron (B)	5	Gadolinium (Gd)	64	Mercury (Hg)	80	Rhodium (Rh)	45	Tungsten (W)	74
Bromine (Br)	35	Gallium (Ga)	31	Molybdenum (Mo)	42	Roentgenium (Rg)	111	Uranium (U)	92
Cadmium (Cd)	48	Germanium (Ge)	32	Neodymium (Nd)	60	Rubidium (Rb)	37	Vanadium (V)	23
Calcium (Ca)	20	Gold (Au)	79	Neon (Ne)	10	Ruthenium (Ru)	44	Xenon (Xe)	54
Californium (Cf)	98	Hafnium (Hf)	72	Neptunium (Np)	93	Rutherfordium (Rf)	104	Ytterbium (Yb)	70
Carbon (C)	6	Hassium (Hs)	108	Nickel (Ni)	28	Samarium (Sm)	62	Yttrium (Y)	39
Cerium (Ce)	58	Helium (He)	2	Niobium (Nb)	41	Scandium (Sc)	21	Zinc (Zn)	30
Cesium (Cs)	55	Holmium (Ho)	67	Nitrogen (N)	7	Seaborgium (Sg)	106	Zirconium (Zr)	40
Chlorine (Cl)	17	Hydrogen (H)	1	Nobelium (No)	102	Selenium (Se)	34		
Chromium (Cr)	24	Indium (In)	49	Osmium (Os)	76	Silicon (Si)	14		
Cobalt (Co)	27	Iodine (I)	53	Oxygen (O)	8	Silver (Ag)	47		

Appendix C Credits

PHOTO CREDITS

FRONT MATTER: p. i, iv left Igor Siwanowicz/Fame Pictures, Inc.; **iv right**; Ellen McKnight/Alamy; **p. v** NIBSC/Photo Researchers, Inc.; **p. vi left** Dr. Torsten Wittmann/Photo Researchers, Inc.; **vi right** Flirt/SuperStock; **vii left** All Canada Photos/SuperStock; **vii right** NHPA/SuperStock; **p. viii left** Adrian Sherratt/Alamy; **viii right** DASFA/ZJAH WENN Photos/Newscom; **p. ix left** OREDUN ANIMAL HEALTH LTD/Photo Researchers, Inc.; **ix right** Science Photo Library/Alamy; **p. xi** Beawiharta Beawiharta/REUTERS; **p. xii left** Steven Kazlowski/Photolibrary; **xii right** Richard Carey/Alamy; **p. xiii left** JAMES P. BLAIR/National Geographic Stock; **xiii right** GmbH & Co. KG/Alamy Images; **p. xiv left** Maridav/iStockphoto; **xiv right** Steve Lovegrove/iStockphoto; **p. xv** AJPhoto/Photo Researchers; **p. xvi left** Kitch Bain/AGE Fotostock; **xvi right** marco mayer/Shutterstock.com; **p. xvii** YOSHIKAZU TSUNO/AFP/Getty Images/Newscom.

UNIT OPENERS: Unit 1 left Dr. Torsten Wittmann/Photo Researchers, Inc. **Unit 1 top left** imagebroker.net/SuperStock; **Unit 1 top right** Bon Appetit/Alamy; **Unit 1 middle left** NIBSC/Photo Researchers, Inc.; **Unit 1 middle right** Dr. Torsten Wittmann/Photo Researchers, Inc.; **Unit 1 bottom left** Flirt/SuperStock; **Unit 1 bottom right** All Canada Photos/SuperStock; **Unit 2 left** Eye of Science/Photo Researchers, Inc.; **Unit 2 top left** NHPA/SuperStock; **Unit 2 top right** Adrian Sherratt/Alamy; **Unit 2 middle left** DASFA/ZJAH WENN Photos/Newscom; **Unit 2 middle right** OREDUN ANIMAL HEALTH LTD/Photo Researchers, Inc.; **Unit 2 bottom** Science Photo Library/Alamy; **Unit 3 left** Alex Mustard/Nature Picture Library; **Unit 3 top left** Ton Koene/Photolibrary; **Unit 3 top right** Tier und Naturfotografie/SuperStock; **Unit 3 middle left** Frans Lanting Studio/Alamy; **Unit 3 middle right** FILIPPO MONTEFORTE/AFP/Getty Images/Newscom; **Unit 3 bottom** Beawiharta Beawiharta/REUTERS; **Unit 4 left** Markus Varesvuo/Nature Picture Library; **Unit 4 top left** Steven Kazlowski/Photolibrary; **Unit 4 top right** Richard Carey/Alamy; **Unit 4 bottom** JAMES P. BLAIR/National Geographic Stock; **Unit 5 left** Exactostock/SuperStock; **Unit 5 top left** GmbH & Co. KG/Alamy Images; **Unit 5 top right** Maridav/iStockphoto; **Unit 5 middle left** Steve Lovegrove/iStockphoto; **Unit 5 middle right** RODGER BOSCH/AFP/Getty Images/Newscom; **Unit 5 bottom left** UPI Photo Service/Newscom; **Unit 5 bottom middle** AJPhoto/Photo Researchers; **Unit 5 bottom right** Kitch Bain/AGE Fotostock; **Unit 6 left** Dave Zubraski/AGE Fotostock; **Unit 6 top left** marco mayer/Shutterstock.com; **Unit 6 top right** YOSHIKAZU TSUNO/AFP/Getty Images/Newscom.

CHAPTER 1: Chapter opening photo Ellen McKnight/Alamy; **p. 3, 15, 18** Ellen McKnight/Alamy; **1.1a** Nikreates/Alamy; **1.1b** P. Narayan/The Image Bank/AGE Fotostock; **1.1c** Near and Far Photography/Shutterstock; **1.1d** Michael Lander/NordicPhotos/AGE Fotostock; **1.1e** Kim Taylor and Jane Burton/DK Images; **1.1f** Steve Bloom Images/Alamy; **1.1g** Mark Taylor/Nature Picture Library; **1.2 top left to bottom left** Goddard Space Flight Center/NASA;

Pete Oxford/Nature Picture Library; Dave G. Houser/Alamy; Manfred Kage/Peter Arnold Inc./Photolibrary; **1.3** Christopher Elwell/Shutterstock.com; **1.4 left** S. C. Holt/Biological Photo Service; **1.4 right** Steve Gschmeissner/Photo Researchers; **1.6** KK/AP Images; **1.7** Daniela Dirscherl/AGE Fotostock America Inc.; **1.8 top to bottom** Eye of Science/Photo Researchers, Inc.; Eye of Science/Photo Researchers, Inc.; Neil Fletcher/DK Images; Malcom Coulson/DK Images; Stockbyte/Getty Images; D. P. Wilson/Photo Researchers; **1.9** Richard T. Nowitz/Photo Researchers, Inc.; **1.11 clockwise from top left** Mike Hayward/Alamy; American Museum of Natural History; Michael Nolan/SpecialistStock; **1.13a from left to right** Simon Krzi/iStockphoto; Paul Rapson/Alamy; Foodcollection.com/Alamy; Suzannah Skelton/iStockphoto; iStockphoto; iStockphoto; **1.13b left** Eric Baccega/Nature Picture Library; **1.13b right** Erik Lam/Shutterstock.com; **1.14 left** Michael Nichols/National Geographic Image Collection; **1.14 right** Tim Ridley/DK Images; **1.15** Adrian Sherratt/Alamy; **1.16** ancroft/Shutterstock.com; **1.17** Jim Newcomb; **1.18** Scott Strazzante/MCT/Newscom; **1.19 bottom** Massachusetts Department of Public Health; **1.19 top** Eye of Science/Photo Researchers, Inc.

CHAPTER 2: Chapter opening photo imagebroker.net/SuperStock; **p. 23, 31, 33.1** imagebroker.net/SuperStock; **2.1** Clive Streeter/DK Images; **2.3 woman left** Ivan Polunin/Bruce Coleman/Photoshot Holdings Ltd; **montage clockwise from bottom left** Lukasz Panek/iStockphoto; Enrico Fianchini/iStockphoto; Howard Shooter/Dorling Kindersley; Alessio Cola/Shutterstock.com; **2.5** Will & Deni McIntyre/Photo Researchers; **2.10** Sylvain Cordier/Photolibrary, Inc.; **2.11 left** Stephen Alvarez/National Geographic Image Collection; **2.11 right** Andrew Syred/Photo Researchers; **2.12** Dietmar Nill/Photolibrary, Inc.; **2.13** Joe Fox/Alamy; **2.14** iStockphoto; **2.15** Kristin Piljay; **p. 31** Blend Images/SuperStock; **2.17 top to bottom** Beth Van Trees/Shutterstock.com; Monika Wisniewska/iStockphoto; VR Photos/Shutterstock.com; terekhov igor/Shutterstock.com; Jakub Semeniuk/iStockphoto; **2.18** J M Hall Spencer; **2.19 left** NASA Earth Observing System; **2.19 right** NASA.

CHAPTER 3: Chapter opening photo Bon Appetit/Alamy; **p. 37, 51** Bon Appetit/Alamy; **3.3 left** James M. Phelps, Jr./Shutterstock.com; **3.3 right** Dorling Kindersley; **3.5** Irochka/Fotolia; **3.7** Bon Appetit/Alamy; **3.8 bottom** Kristin Piljay; **3.8 top** Sandra Caldwell/iStockphoto.com; **3.9 top left** Dougal Waters/Getty Images; **3.9 top right** Biophoto Associates/Photo Researchers, Inc.; **3.9 middle right** Dr. Lloyd M. Beidler; **3.9 bottom** Biophoto Associates/Photo Researchers, Inc.; **3.10** Martyn F. Chillmaid/SPL/Photo Researchers, Inc.; **3.12 left box from top left to bottom right** Hannamariah/Shutterstock.com; Joe Potato Photo/iStockphoto.com; Valentin Mosichev/Shutterstock; Thomas M. Perkins/Shutterstock; **3.12 right box from bottom left to bottom right** Multiart/Shutterstock; Dorling Kindersley; Juanmonino/iStockphoto.com; Oleksandr Staroseltsev/iStockphoto.com; Robyn Mackenzie/Shutterstock.com; vladm/Shutterstock.com; **3.13 left** EcoPrint/Shutterstock.com; **3.13 right** Stockbyte/

Getty Images; **3.14 left** Pool Getty Images/AP Images; **3.14 right** New York Daily News/WENN/Newscom; **3.15 left to right** Glow Images/Alamy; Dorling Kindersley; Dave King/Dorling Kindersley; Harry Taylor/Dorling Kindersley; kolvenbach/Alamy; Steve Gschmeissner/SPL/Photo Researchers, Inc.; Kristin Piljay; **3.19** Ingram Publishing/Photolibrary, Inc.; **3.28** SuperStock/Photolibrary, Inc.

CHAPTER 4: Chapter opening photo main NIBSC/Photo Researchers, Inc.; **left inset** Leonard Lessin/Photo Researchers, Inc.; **right inset** Dr. Tim Evans/Photo Researchers, Inc.; **p. 55, 61, 71** NIBSC/Photo Researchers, Inc.; **4.1 left to right** M.I. Walker/Photo Researchers, Inc.; SPL/Photo Researchers, Inc.; Educational Images LTD/Custom Medical Stock Photo; **4.2** Exactostock/SuperStock; **4.4** NIBSC/SPL/Photo Researchers, Inc.; **4.7** CDC/SPL/Photo Researchers, Inc.; **4.8 left** The Rockefeller University Press; **4.8 right** Richard Rodewald/Biological Photo Service; **4.10** Hybrid Medical Animation/Photo Researchers; **4.11** D. W. Fawcett/Photo Researchers, Inc.; **4.13** Barry King/Biological Photo Service; **4.15** SPL/Photo Researchers, Inc.; **4.16** Daniel S. Friend; **4.17a** Michael Abbey/Photo Researchers, Inc.; **4.17b** Dr. Jeremy Burgess/Photo Researchers, Inc.; **4.18** Garry Cole/Biological Photo Service; **4.19** Courtesy of W.P. Wergin and E.H. Newcomb, University of Wisconsin/BPS; **4.20** Daniel S. Friend; **4.21a** Dr. Torsten Wittmann/Photo Researchers, Inc.; **4.21b** Dr. D. J. Patterson/SPL/Photo Researchers, Inc.; **4.22a** Exactostock/SuperStock; **4.22b** Steve Gschmeissner/SPL/Photo Researchers, Inc.; **4.22c** Charles Daghlian/Photo Researchers, Inc.; **4.23 bottom** Centers for Disease Control and Prevention (CDC); **4.23 top** The Advertising Archives.

CHAPTER 5: Chapter opening photo Dr. Torsten Wittmann/Photo Researchers, Inc.; **p. 75, 81, 87** Dr. Torsten Wittmann/Photo Researchers, Inc.; **5.1** Thinkstock; **5.3a** Dave King/Dorling Kindersley; **5.3b** blickwinkel/Alamy; **5.8** The Protein Data Bank/RCSB; **5.15** David Cook/blueshiftstudios/Alamy; **5.19** Fuse/Getty Images; **5.20** Peter B. Armstrong.

CHAPTER 6: Flirt/SuperStock; **p. 91, 102, 103** Flirt/SuperStock; **6.1** Westend61/SuperStock; **6.2 left to right** Elena Elisseeva/iStockphoto.com; Eric Isselée/Shutterstock.com; Ultrashock/Shutterstock.com; **6.3** Belinda Images/SuperStock; **6.14** Chris Mole/Shutterstock.com; **6.16 left** stanislaff/iStockphoto.com; **6.16 right** stocksnapp/Shutterstock.com; **6.17** José Carlos Pires Pereira/iStockphoto.com.

CHAPTER 7: Chapter opening photo All Canada Photos/SuperStock; **p. 107, 111, 115** All Canada Photos/SuperStock; **7.1 left to right** Dorling Kindersley; Jeff Rotman/Nature Picture Library; Susan M. Barns, Ph.D.; **7.2 top to bottom** John Fielding/Dorling Kindersley; John Durham/Photo Researchers, Inc.; E.H. Newcomb & W.P. Wergin/Biological Photo Service; **7.5** Jamie Grill/Dorling Kindersley; **7.7** Corbis/SuperStock; **7.8** LQ/Alamy; **7.14 left** Dinodia/Pixtal/agefotostock.com; **7.14 right** ImageDJ/Jupiter Images.

CHAPTER 8: Chapter opening photo NHPA/SuperStock; **p. 121, 137, 140** NHPA/SuperStock; **8.1 left to right** Dr. Torsten Wittmann/Photo Researchers, Inc.; Dr. Yorgos

Nikas/Photo Researchers, Inc.; Biophoto Associates/Photo Researchers, Inc.; Roger Steene/Image Quest Marine; Eric J. Simon; **8.2 top to bottom** Eric Isselée/Shutterstock.com; Christian Musat/Shutterstock.com; Edyta Pawlowska/iStockphoto.com; Eric Isselée/Shutterstock.com; Milton H. Gallardo; **8.3** Ed Reschke/Photolibrary/Getty Images; **8.4 top** A.L. Olins/Biological Photo Service; **8.4 bottom** Biophoto Associates/Photo Researchers, Inc.; **8.7** Conly L. Rieder, Ph.D.; **8.8a** Don W. Fawcett/Photo Researchers, Inc.; **8.8b** Kent Wood/Photo Researchers, Inc.; **8.10** Big Cheese Photo/SuperStock; **8.11** Science Source/CNRI/SPL/Photo Researchers, Inc.; **8.12** iofoto/Shutterstock.com; **8.14** Ed Reschke/Peter Arnold, Inc./Photolibrary; **8.17** David M. Phillips/Photo Researchers, Inc.; **8.19** Dr. David Mark Welch; **8.22 bottom** SPL/Photo Researchers, Inc.; **8.22 top** Lauren Shear/Photo Researchers, Inc.; **8.24** David Hosking/FLPA; **p. 143** ARS/Agricultural Research Service/USDA.

CHAPTER 9: Chapter opening photo Adrian Sherratt/Alamy; **p. 145, 157, 167** Adrian Sherratt/Alamy; **9.1** Science Source/Photo Researchers; **9.4** Patrick Lynch/Alamy; **9.5** James King-Holmes/Photo Researchers, Inc.; **9.8** Martin Shields/Photo Researchers, Inc.; **9.9 left to right** Tracy Morgan/Dorling Kindersley; Tracy Morgan/Dorling Kindersley; Eric Isselée/Shutterstock.com; Andrew Johnson/iStockphoto.com; **9.10 left** Tracy Morgan/Dorling Kindersley; **9.10 right** Eric Isselée/Shutterstock.com; **9.12 top left to right** James Woodson /Getty Images; ostill/Shutterstock.com; Jose Luis Pelaez, Inc./Blend Images/Getty Images; **9.12 bottom left to right** John Evans/iStockphoto.com; Image Source/Getty Images; Blend Images/Shutterstock.com; **9.13 left to right** Comstock Images; Blend Images/Shutterstock.com; Jose Luis Pelaez, Inc./Blend Images/Getty Images; **9.15** Michael Ciesielski Photography; **9.16** Will Binns, Pacificcoastnews/Newscom; **9.17 left** J-L. Klein & M-L. Hubert/Photolibrary, Inc.; **9.17 right** Vasiliy Khimenko/Shutterstock.com; **9.20** Mauro Fermariello/Photo Researchers, Inc.; **9.21 left** Oliver Meckes & Nicole Ottawa/Photo Researchers, Inc.; **9.21 right** Eye of Science/Photo Researchers, Inc.; **9.23** Eric J. Simon; **9.29 top left to right** iStockphoto.com; Yuri Arcurs/iStockphoto.com; Andrew Syred/Photo Researchers, Inc.; **9.29 bottom left to right** Dave King/Dorling Kindersley; Jo Foord/Dorling Kindersley; **9.32** Archive Pics/Alamy; **9.33 top left to bottom right** Jerry Young/Dorling Kindersley; Nikolay Titov/iStockphoto.com; Dave King/Dorling Kindersley; Dave King/Dorling Kindersley; Tracy Morgan/Dorling Kindersley; Dave King/Dorling Kindersley; Jerry Young/Dorling Kindersley; Dave King/Dorling Kindersley; Dave King/Dorling Kindersley; Tracy Morgan/Dorling Kindersley; Le Loft 1911/Shutterstock.com; **p. 167** Eric Simon; **p. 169 left** iStockphoto.com; **p. 169 right** Yuri Arcurs/iStockphoto.com; **p. 171** USDA/APHIS Animal And Plant Health Inspection Service.

CHAPTER 10: Chapter opening photo DASFA/ZJAH WENN Photos/Newscom; **p. 173, 192, 194** DASFA/ZJAH WENN Photos/Newscom; **10.3 left** Barrington Brown/Photo Researchers, Inc.; **10.3 top right** Courtesy of the Library of Congress; **10.3 bottom right** Cold Spring Harbor Laboratory Archives; **10.9** Woodfall Wild Images/Photoshot Holdings Ltd.; **10.12** Masaru Okabe; **10.23** Dennis Frates/Alamy; **10.24** MIXA/Alamy; **10.25** Oliver Meckes/Photo Researchers, Inc.; **10.26** Russell Kightley/SPL/Photo Researchers, Inc.; **10.27** N. Thomas/Photo Researchers, Inc.; **10.29** Hazel Appleton, Centre for Infections/Health Protection Agency/SPL/Photo Researchers, Inc.; **10.30** Jeff Zelevansky/Reuters; **10.32** NIBSC/Science Photo Library/Photo Researchers, Inc.; **10.33** Will & Deni McIntyre/SPL/Photo Researchers, Inc.; **10.34** Sinclair Stammers/Photo Researchers, Inc.; **10.35** CHINE NOUVELLE/SIPA/Newscom.

CHAPTER 11: Chapter opening photo OREDUN ANIMAL HEALTH LTD/Photo Researchers, Inc.; **p. 199, 212, 215** OREDUN ANIMAL HEALTH LTD/Photo Researchers, Inc.; **11.1 left to right** Steve Gschmeissner/Photo Researchers, Inc.; Science Photo Library/Alamy; Ed Reschke/Photolibrary; **11.4** Patrick A. Krost/istockphoto; **11.9** F. Rudolf Turner; **11.11** American Association for the Advancement of Science; **11.12** Videowokart/Shutterstock.com; **11.13** Courtesy of the Roslin Institute, Edinburgh; **11.14a** Pat Sullivan/AP Images; **11.14b** University of Missouri; **11.14c left to right** Pasqualino Loi; Robert Lanza; Robert Lanza; Lee Jae Woon/Reuters; **11.16 left** Cord Blood Registry; **11.16 right** Craig Hammell; **11.19 left** Blend Images/Alamy; **11.19 right** Simon Fraser/Royal Victoria Infirmary, Newcastle upon Tyne/Photo Researchers, Inc.; **11.20** GeoM/Shutterstock.com; **11.22** Chris Bjornberg/Photo Researchers, Inc.; **11.23** CNRI/Photo Researchers.

CHAPTER 12: Chapter opening photo Science Photo Library/Alamy; **p. 219, 233, 237** Science Photo Library/Alamy; **12.1** AP Images; **12.2** Copyright Eli Lilly and Company. Used with permission; **12.3** Volker Steger/SPL/Photo Researchers, Inc.; **12.4 left** USDA; **12.4 right** Christopher and Sally Gable/Dorling Kindersley; **12.5** International Rice Research Institute; **12.6** DNX/Peter Arnold, Inc./Photolibrary; **12.7 inset** Prof. S. Cohen/Photo Researchers, Inc.; **12.7** Huntington Potter, University of South Florida College of Medicine; **12.12** Hank Morgan/SPL/Photo Researchers, Inc.; **12.14 left** Michael Stephens/AP Images; **12.14 right** Kim Sayer/Dorling Kindersley; **12.15** Applied Biosystems; **12.20** CHUCK KENNEDY KRT/Newscom; **12.21 bottom** Scott Camazine/Photo Researchers, Inc.; **12.21 top** Newscom; **12.22 bottom** David Parker/Science Photo Library/Photo Researchers, Inc.; **12.22 top** Edyta Pawlowska/Shutterstock.com; **12.24** Phil Date/Shutterstock.com; **12.25** ER Productions/BrandX/Corbis Images; **12.26** AFP/Getty Images; **12.27** 23andMe, Inc.

CHAPTER 13: Ton Koene/Photolibrary; **p. 243, 254, 265** Ton Koene/Photolibrary; **13.1a** Curtis Strauss/Photolibrary; **13.1b** Barbara Jablonska/Shutterstock.com; **13.1c** Edward S. Ross, California Academy of Sciences; **13.2** Cambridge University Library; **13.3a** Chris Pole/Shutterstock.com; **13.3b** Sabena Jane Blackbird/Alamy; **13.4 left** George Richmond/Photo Researchers, Inc.; **13.4 right** Classic Image/Alamy; **13.5 left** Cathleen A. Clapper/Shutterstock.com; **13.5 right** David B. Fleetham/Photolibrary; **13.6** Corbis Images; **13.7** Dr. Philip D. Gingerich; **13.8 top left** Kim Taylor and Jane Burton/Dorling Kindersley; **13.8 center** Planetary Visions Ltd./Photo Researchers; **13.8 top right** Bill Ling/Dorling Kindersley; **13.8 bottom left** Geoff Dann/Dorling Kindersley; **13.8 bottom right** Rob Reichenfeld/Dorling Kindersley; **13.10 left** Dr. Keith Wheeler/Photo Researchers; **13.10 right** Scanpix Sweden AB; **13.12a** Tui DeRoy/Photoshot Holdings Ltd.; **13.12b** NHPA/SuperStock; **13.12c** Tui DeRoy/Photoshot Holdings Ltd.; **13.13** Alain Barrère/Photo Researchers, Inc.; **13.14** Laura Jesse; **13.16** American Association for the Advancement of Science; **13.18a** Photo Alto/Getty Images; **13.18b** NASA Images; **13.19** Edmund D. Brodie III; **13.20** Andy Levin/Photo Researchers, Inc.; **13.22** Anne Dowie; **13.25** Steve Bloom Images/Alamy; **13.26** Hulton-Deutsch Collection/Corbis; **13.27** Natural Visions/Alamy Images; **13.28** Rinusbaak/Dreamstime.com; **13.30a** Reinhard/ARCO/Nature Picture Library; **13.30b** John Cancalosi/AGE Fotostock.com; **13.31** Bill Longcore/Photo Researchers, Inc.

CHAPTER 14: Chapter opening photo Tier und Naturfotografie/SuperStock; **p. 269, 284, 289** Tier und Naturfotografie/SuperStock; **14.1** Papilio/Alamy; **14.2 Clockwise from far left** Bill Draker/Rolfnp/Alamy; David Kjaer/Nature Picture Library; Comstock; www.photos.com/Jupiter Images; Phil Date/Shutterstock.com; Robert Kneschke/iStockphoto.com; Comstock Images; Comstock Images; **14.4 p. 272 left to right** USDA/APHIS Animal And Plant Health Inspection Service; Brian Kentosh; Joe McDonald/Photoshot Holdings, Ltd.; Moses Michelsohn; **14.4 p. 273 left to right** J & C Sohns/Tier und Naturfotografie Collection/AGE Fotostock; Takahiro Asami; Richard Herrmann/Photolibrary; **14.5 left** Charles W. Brown; **14.5 center top to bottom** dogist/Shutterstock.com; Dorling Kindersley; Alistair Duncan/Dorling Kindersley; **14.5 right** Kazutoshi Okuno; **14.7** Corbis Images; **14.7 top left inset** John Shaw/Photoshot Holdings Ltd.; **14.7 top right inset** Michael Fogden/Photoshot Holdings Ltd.; **14.9** Zeljko Radojko/Shutterstock.com; **14.11** Chip Clark; **14.12** Jane Burton/Photoshot Holdings, Ltd.; **14.13 top** Michel Gunther/Photolibrary; **14.13 bottom** Hemera Technologies/Getty Images/AbleStock.com/JupiterImages; **14.14 top left** Francois Gohier/Photo Researchers, Inc.; **14.14 top right** George Gerster/Photo Researchers, Inc.; **14.14 center** Francois Gohier/Photo Researchers, Inc.; **14.14 bottom left** Pixtal/Superstock; **14.14 bottom right** Francis Latrielle/Mammuthus/Vostok; **14.16** ZUMA Press/Newscom; **14.18 right** Mark Pilkington/Geological Survey of Canada/SPL/Photo Researchers, Inc.; **14.19 top** Philip Dowell/Dorling Kindersley; **14.19 center left** Dave King/Dorling Kindersley; **14.19 center right** Dave King/Dorling Kindersley; **14.19 bottom** Philip Dowell/Dorling Kindersley; **14.20** Jeremy Woodhouse/Photolibrary; **14.22** Manfred Cage/Getty/Photolibrary; **14.26** Arco Images GmbH/Alamy.

CHAPTER 15: Chapter opening photo Frog 974/Fotolia; **p. 293, 297, 311** Frog 974/Fotolia; **15.3** National Museum of Natural History, Smithsonian Institution; **15.6.** George Luther; **15.7 left** Hemera Technologies/Jupiterimages; **15.7 right** Dr. Tony Brain and David Parker/Science Photo Library/Photo Researchers, Inc.; **15.8 left to right** Scimat/SPL/Photo Researchers, Inc.; NIAID/CDC/Photo Researchers, Inc.;

CNRI/SPL/Photo Researchers, Inc.; **15.9a** David M. Phillips/Science Source/Photo Researchers, Inc.; **15.9b** Susan M. Barns, Ph.D.; **15.9c** Heide Schulz/Max-Planck Institut Fur Marine Mikrobiologie; **15.10** Science Photo Library/Photolibrary; **15.11** H.S. Pankratz, T.C. Beaman/ BPS; **15.12 top left** Martin Shields/Photo Researchers, Inc.; **15.12 top right** Alfred Pasieka/Photo Researchers, Inc.; **15.12 bottom left** Pasieka/SPL/Photo Researchers, Inc.; **15.12 bottom right** Westend61/SuperStock; **15.13a** Helen E. Carr/BiologicalPhoto Service; **15.13b** Russell Burden/Photolibrary; **15.14.** Dr. Tony Brain/Science Photo Library/Photo Researchers, Inc.; **15.15 bottom left to right** Centers for Disease Control and Prevention (CDC); Scott Camazine/Photo Researchers, Inc.; David M. Phillips/Photo Researchers, Inc.; **15.15 top** Stefan Sollfors/ Alamy; **15.16** Centers for Disease Control and Prevention (CDC); **15.18** ExxonMobil Corporation; **15.20a** Carol Buchanan/AGEFotostock.com; **15.20b** Oliver Meckes/ Photo Researchers, Inc.; **15.20c** blickwinkel/Alamy; **15.21** M. I. Walker/Photo Researchers, Inc.; **15.22 p. 308 left to right** Eye of Science/Photo Researchers, Inc.; David M. Phillips/Photo Researchers, Inc.; Biophoto Associates/ Photo Researchers, Inc.; **15.22 p. 309 left to right** Manfred Kage/Getty/Photolibrary; **15.22** Dr. Masamichi Aikawa; Michael Abbey/Photo Researchers, Inc.; **15.23** The Hidden Forest, www.hiddenforest.co.nz; **15.24 left** Courtesy of Matt Springer, Stanford University; **15.24 right top to bottom** Courtesy of Robert Kay, MRC Cambridge; Courtesy of Robert Kay, MRC Cambridge; **15.25a** Biophoto Associates/ Photo Researchers, Inc.; **15.25b** Kent Wood/Photo Researchers, Inc.; **15.25c** Microfield Scientific Ltd/SPL/ Photo Researchers, Inc.; **15.25d** Manfred Kage/Photolibrary; **15.26 left to right** Marevision/AGEFotostock .com; Marevision/AGEFotostock.com; David Hall/Photo Researchers, Inc.

CHAPTER 16: Chapter opening photo FILIPPO MONTEFORTE/AFP/Getty Images/Newscom; **p. 315, 331, 332** FILIPPO MONTEFORTE/AFP/Getty Images/ Newscom; **16.2** Dr. Jeremy Burgess/SPL/Photo Researchers, Inc.; **16.3** Dorling Kindersley; **16.4** Graham Kent; **16.5 left** Bob Gibbons/Alamy Images; **16.5 right** Linda Graham, University of Wisconsin-Madison; **16.7 left to right** Photolibrary; James Randklev/Getty Images/Photolibrary; V.J. Matthew/Shutterstock.com; Dale Wagler/Shutterstock. com; **16.8** Duncan Shaw/SPL/Photo Researchers, Inc.; **16.9** John Serrao/Photo Researchers, Inc.; **16.11 bottom left inset** Ed Reschke/Getty Images/Photolibrary; **16.11 bottom right inset** Kim Taylor and Jane Burton/ Dorling Kindersley; **16.11 top right inset** Biophoto Associates/ Photo Researchers, Inc.; **16.11 main** Photolibrary; **16.12** The Field Museum, Neg#CSGE075400c, Chicago; **16.13** Danilo Donadoni/AGE Fotostock; **16.15 left to right** Stephen P. Parker/Photo Researchers, Inc.; Morales/AGEFotostock .com; Gunter Marx/Alamy; **16.16** Gene Cox/Photo Researchers, Inc.; **16.18 left to right** Smart-foto/ Shutterstock.com; Tyler Boyes/Shutterstock.com; Christopher Marin/Shutterstock.com; Howard Rice/ Dorling Kindersley; **16.20 left** Jean Dickey; **16.20 top right** Scott Camazine/Photo Researchers, Inc.; **16.20 bottom right** Juniors Bildarchiv/Alamy; **16.21** Martin

Wendler/Photo Researchers, Inc.; **Table 16.1 top to bottom** Dorling Kindersley; Jon Rasmussen/iStockphoto. com; Ben Mcleish/iStockphoto.com; Radu Razvan/ Shutterstock.com; Dorling Kindersley, Courtesy of the Natural History Museum, London; Greg Vaughn/Getty Images/Photolibrary; National Tropical Botanical Garden; Alle/Shutterstock.com; **16.22 left** Marc Anderson/Alamy; **16.22 top center** Stan Rohrer/Alamy; **16.22 bottom center** Elizabeth Peardon/iStockphoto.com; **16.22 inset** VEM/ Photo Researchers, Inc.; **16.22 top right** J. Forsdyke/Gene Cox/Science Photo Library/Photo Researchers, Inc.; **16.22 bottom right** G.L. Barron & N. Allin/Biological Photo Service; **16.23 bottom** blickwinkel/Alamy; **16.23 top** Jupiter Images; **16.24a** Bedrich Grunzweig/Photo Researchers, Inc.; **16.24b** Nigel Cattlin/Photo Researchers, Inc.; **16.25** North Wind/North Wind Picture Archives; **16.26 top left** Ed Reschke/Photolibrary; **16.26 bottom left** imagebroker. net/SuperStock; **16.26 right** Will Heap, Dorling Kindersley; **16.27** Christine Case/Skyline College; **16.28 left** Jean Dickey; **16.28 right** Eye of Science/Photo Researchers, Inc.

CHAPTER 17: Chapter opening photo Beawiharta Beawiharta/REUTERS; **p. 337, 365, 367** Beawiharta Beawiharta/REUTERS; **17.1** Gunter Ziesler/Getty Images/ Photolibrary; **17.2** Georgette Douwman/Nature Picture Library; **17.4 left** South Australian Museum; **17.4 right** Museum of Paleontology; **17.5 left** Publiphoto/Photo Researchers, Inc.; **17.5 right** Chip Clark; **17.9** James D. Watt/Image Quest Marine; **17.10 top left to right** Sue Daly/ Nature Picture Library; Michael Klenetsky/Shutterstock. com; Kim Taylor/Nature Picture Library; **17.10 bottom** Jordi Chias/Image Quest Marine; **17.13 top left** Georgette Douwma/Nature Picture Library; **17.13 top** Georgette Douwma/Nature Picture Library; **bottom left** Jez Tryner/ Image Quest Marine; **center left to right** Harold W. Pratt/ Biological Photo Service; Marevision/AGEFotostock. com; Daniela Dirscherl/Photolibrary; **17.14 top** David Scharf/Photolibrary; **17.14 bottom left to right** Geoff Brightling/Dorling Kindersley; **17.14** Eye of Science/Photo Researchers, Inc.; **17.15 left to right** Photoshot/NHPA Limited; Carol Buchanan/Getty Images/Photolibrary; Wildlife/Getty Images/Photolibrary; **p. 346** Astrid & Hanns-Frieder Michler/Photo Researchers, Inc.; **17.17a** Steve Gschmeissner/Photo Researchers, Inc.; **17.17b** Eye of Science/Photo Researchers, Inc.; **17.17c** David Scharf/Photo Researchers, Inc.; **17.18 top to bottom** Callan Morgan/ Getty Images/Photolibrary; Maximilian Weinzierl/Alamy Images; George Grall/National Geographic; ephotocorp/ Alamy Images; **17.19** Dave King/Dorling Kindersley; **17.20 top left to right** Herbert Hopfensperger/AGEFotostock. com; Dorling Kindersley; Andrew Syred/Photo Researchers, Inc.; **17.20 bottom left to right** Callan Morgan/Getty Images/Photolibrary; Larry West/Photo Researchers, Inc.; **17.21 top** Dave King/Dorling Kindersley; **17.21 center left to right** Maximilian Weinzierl/Alamy; Tom McHugh/Photo Researchers, Inc.; Nature's Images/Photo Researchers, Inc.; **17.21 bottom left to right** Dietmar Nill/naturepl.com; Nancy Sefton/SPL/Photo Researchers, Inc.; **17.22 left** George Grall/National Geographic; **17.22 right** Tom McHugh/ Photo Researchers, Inc.; **17.23** Radius Images/Alamy; **17.24 clockwise from top right** D & S Tollerton/Photolibrary;

Cordier-Huguet/agefotostock.com; Chris Mattison/ Photolibrary; Jean Dickey; ephotocorp/Alamy; Joël Héras/ Photolibrary; Kerstin Hinze/Photolibrary; Stuart Wilson/ Photo Researchers, Inc.; **17.25 top** First Light/Alamy; **17.25 bottom** Keith Dannemiller/Alamy; **17.26 top left** Roger Steene/Image Quest Marine; **17.26 inset** Andrew J. Martinez/Photo Researchers, Inc.; **17.26 top right** Jose B. Ruiz/Nature Picture Library; **17.26 bottom left to right** tbkmedia.de/Alamy; Image Quest Marine; Roger Steene/Image Quest Marine; **17.27** Colin Keates/Dorling Kindersley; **17.29 left** Oxford Scientific/Photolibrary; **17.29 right** Roger Steene/Image Quest Marine; **17.31a** Tom McHugh/Photo Researchers, Inc.; **17.31b** F. Hecker/ AGE Fotostock; **17.31b inset** A. Hartl/AGE Fotostock; **17.31c** George Grall/National Geographic; **17.31d** Christian Vinces/Shutterstock.com; **17.32a top** Gary Meszaros/Photo Researchers, Inc.; **17.32a bottom** Bill Brooks/Alamy; **17.32b left** Tom McHugh/Photo Researchers, Inc.; **17.32b right** Jack Goldfarb/agefotostock.com; **17.34 p. 358 left to right** Sylvain Cordier/Photolibrary, Inc.; © Universal Images Group Limited/Alamy; LYNN M. STONE/naturepl.com; **17.34 p. 359 left to right** Jerry Young/Dorling Kindersley; DLILL/Corbis Images; Miguel Periera/Dorling Kindersley; Adam Jones/Digital Vision/Getty Images; **17.36 left to right** Jean Phillipe Varin/Jacana/Photo Researchers, Inc.; Martin Rugner/Photolibrary; Barry Lewis/Alamy; **17.38 Clockwise from top left** Creative Studio Heinemann/Photolibrary; Siegfried Grassegger/Getty Images/Photolibrary; Arco Images GmbH/Alamy; Juan Carlos Munoz/agefotostock. com; Anup Shah/Nature Picture Library; John Kelly/Getty Images; Anup Shah/Nature Picture Library; Colette3/ Shutterstock; P. Wegner/Arco Images/Getty Images/ Photolibrary; **17.40b** John Reader/SPL/Photo Researchers, Inc.; **17.41** Rosino, http://www.flickr.com/people/rosino; **17.42** Photo Researchers, Inc.; **17.44** Hemis.fr/SuperStock; **17.45** Kablonk/SuperStock; **17.46** Stefan Espenhahn/AGE Fotostock America, Inc.

CHAPTER 18: Chapter opening photo Steven Kazlowski/ Photolibrary; **p. 373, 396, 399** Steven Kazlowski/ Photolibrary; **18.1** Philippe Psaila/Photo Researchers, Inc.; **18.2** JAY DIRECTO/AFP/GETTY IMAGES/Newscom; **18.3a** Barry Mansell/Nature Picture Library; **18.3b** Sue Flood/Alamy; **18.3c** Junior Bildarchiv/agefotostock.com; **18.3d** Jeremy Woodhouse/Getty Images; **18.4** David Wall/Alamy; **18.5** NASA Earth Observing System; **18.6 left** Verena Tunnicliffe, University of Victoria; **18.6 right** Woods Hole Oceanographic Institution; **18.7** John Cancalosi/Photolibrary; **18.8a** Picture Hooked/Malcolm Schuyl/Alamy; **18.8b** age fotostock/SuperStock; **18.9** Antti Leinonen/Johners; **18.11 left** Daniel Cox/Getty Images/ Photolibrary; **18.11 right** J & C Sohns/agefotostock.com; **18.12** Ed Reschke/Photolibrary; **18.13** Robert Stainforth/ Alamy; **18.14** Worldsat International Inc./SPL /Photo Researchers, Inc. **18.16** Ishbukar Yalilfatar/Shutterstock. com; **18.17** Kevin Schafer/Alamy; **18.18** Jean Dickey; **18.20** Getty Images; **18.21** Spring Images/Alamy; **18.22** George McCarthy/naturepl.com; **18.29** age fotostock/ SuperStock; **18.30** Eric Isselée/Shutterstock.com; **18.31** Juan Carlos Munoz/agefotostock.com; **18.32** The California Chaparral Institute; **18.33** All Canada Photos/SuperStock;

18.34 Visions of America, LLC/Alamy; 18.35 Jorma Luhta/Nature Picture Library; 18.36 PAUL NICKLEN/National Geographic Stock; 18.37 Gordon Wiltsie/National Geographic Image Collection; 18.39 UNEP/GRID - Sioux Falls (DEWA); 18.40 JUAN PABLO MOREIRAS/FFI/Photolibrary; 18.41a, b UNEP/GRID - Sioux Falls (DEWA); 18.42 Jim West/Alamy; 18.43 Kamira/Shutterstock.com; 18.47 Chris Martin Bahr/Photo Researchers, Inc.; 18.48 Mike Meadows/AP Photos; 18.49 Drake Fleege/Alamy; 18.50 University of North Carolina; 18.51 Chris Cheadle/Getty Images/Photolibrary.com; 18.52a William E. Bradshaw; 18.52b Steven Kazlowski/naturepl.com.

CHAPTER 19: Chapter opening photo Richard Carey/Alamy; **p. 403, 415, 421** Richard Carey/Alamy; **19.1** Frans Lanting/National Geographic Stock; **19.2** Wave Royalty Free/Alamy; **19.3** WorldFoto/Alamy; **19.4 left to right** Yuri Arcurs/Shutterstock.com; Jane Burton/Dorling Kindersley; Roger Phillips/Dorling Kindersley; **p. 407 left** Achim Prill/Shutterstock.com; **p. 407 right** Anke van Wyk/Shutterstock.com; **19.5** Joshua Lewis/Shutterstock.com; **19.6** Tom Vezo/naturepl.com; **19.7 left** Joshua Lewis/Shutterstock.com; **19.7 right** WizData/Shutterstock.com; **19.8a** Marcin Perkowski/Shutterstock.com; **19.8b** Nigel Cattlin/Alamy; **19.9** Design Pics/SuperStock; **19.10** Meul/ARCO/Nature Picture Library; **19.11** Alan Carey/Photo Researchers, Inc.; **19.12 left to right** Rob Curtis/The Early Birder; USDA Forest Service; Gilbert S. Grant/Photo Researchers, Inc.; **19.13** Dan Burton/Nature Picture Library; **19.14** Ed Reschke/Photolibrary; **19.15** ZUMA Press/Newscom; **19.16** CHRIS JOHNS/National Geographic Stock; **19.17** David R. Frazier Photolibrary, Inc./Alamy; **19.18** Science Photo Library/Alamy; **19.19** Nigel Cattlin/Alamy; **19.20** Claudius Thiriet/Photolibrary; **19.24** Peter Menzel Photography; **19.26** franzfoto.com/Alamy.

CHAPTER 20: Chapter opening photo JAMES P. BLAIR/National Geographic Stock; **p. 425, 446, 448** JAMES P. BLAIR/National Geographic Stock; **20.1** James King-Holmes/Photo Researchers, Inc.; **20.2 left** Mark Carwardine/Getty Images/Photolibrary; **20.2 right** Michael Fogden/Photolibrary; **20.3** Andre Seale/AGE Fotostock; **20.4** American Folklife Center, Library of Congress; **20.5** Gerald Herbert/AP Photo; **20.6** Richard D. Estes/Photo Researchers, Inc.; **20.7a** Jim Zipp/Photo Researchers, Inc.; **20.7b** All Canada Photos/SuperStock; **20.8 bottom** M. I. Walker/SPL/Photo Researchers, Inc.; **20.8 top** M. I. Walker/Photo Researchers, Inc.; **20.9** Jurgen Freund/Nature Picture Library; **20.10** Eric Lemar/Shutterstock.com; **20.11** ARCO/P. Wegner/AGE Fotostock America, Inc.; **p. 430** Jean Dickey; **20.12 left** Steve Kaufman/Photolibrary; **20.12 right** Barry Mansell/Nature Picture Library; **20.13 left** Dante Fenolio/Photo Researchers, Inc.; **20.13 right** Peter J. Mayne; **20.14 top left** Bildagentur-Online/TH Photo/SPL/Photo Researchers, Inc.; **20.14 top right** Luca Invernizzi Tettoni/Getty Images/Photolibrary; **20.14 bottom** ImageState/Alamy; **20.16** Jim West/Photolibrary; **20.21** Visual&Written SL/Alamy; **20.22** Todd Sieling/Corvus Consulting; **20.23** Frans Lanting Studio/Alamy; **20.24** Jeff & Alexa Henry/Photolibrary; **20.30** Wing-Chi Poon; **20.35** Michael Marten/SPL/Photo Researchers, Inc.; **20.36 top** NASA/Goddard Space Flight Center; **20.36 bottom left and right** NASA/Goddard Space Flight Center; **20.38 bottom** James P. Blair/NGS Image Collection; **20.38 top** Lee Foster/Alamy; **20.39** Joel Sartore/National Geographic; **20.40** R. O. Bierregaard, Jr., Biology Department, University of North Carolina, Charlotte; **20.41** United States Department of Agriculture; **20.42** Photo provided by Kissimmee Division staff, South Florida Water Management District (WPB); **20.43** Frans Lanting/National Geographic Stock; **20.44 left** WaterFrame/Alamy; **20.44 top right** Chad Ehlers/Photolibrary; **20.44 bottom left** Beanstock Images/Photolibrary; **20.44 bottom right** Image Source/Corbis Images; **p. 450 Biodiversity table left to right** James King-Holmes/Photo Researchers; Michael Fogden/Photolibrary; Andre Seale/AGE Fotostock; **p. 450 Interactions table left top to bottom** EOC.Jim Zipp/Photo Researchers, Inc.; All Canada Photos/SuperStock; Jurgen Freund/Nature Picture Library; **p. 450 Interactions table right top to bottom** Outdoor-Archiv/Alamy; Scott Camazine/Alamy; Renaud Visage/Getty Images.

CHAPTER 21: Chapter opening photo GmbH & Co. KG/Alamy Images; **p. 455, 468, 471** GmbH & Co. KG/Alamy Images; **21.1** Andy Crawford/Dorling Kindersley; **21.2a** Segey Nastenko/iStockphoto; **21.2b** Janice Sheldon; **21.2c** Thomas Deerinck, NCMIR/Photo Researchers, Inc.; **21.3** Blend Images/Alamy; **21.4a** Nina Zanetti; **21.4b** Nina Zanetti; **21.4c** Dr. Gopal Murti/SPL/Photo Researchers, Inc.; **21.4d** Biophoto Associates/Photo Researchers, Inc.; **21.4e** Chuck Brown/Photo Researchers, Inc.; **21.4f** Nina Zanetti; **21.4 left** Mike Kemp/Getty Images; **21.5a** Nina Zanetti; **21.5b** Manfred Kage/Getty Images/Photolibrary; **21.5c** Michael Abbey/Photo Researchers, Inc.; **21.5 middle** Blend Images/Alamy; **21.6 left** James Cavallini/Photo Researchers, Inc.; **21.6 right** John Davis/Dorling Kindersley; **21.7** Blend Images/Alamy; **21.8 p. 462 top left** Phil Date Photography/iStockphoto.com; **21.8 p. 462 top right** Douglas Pulsipher/Alamy; **21.8 p. 462 center** Sean Justice/Getty Images; **21.8 p. 462 bottom left** Andy Crawford/Dorling Kindersley; **21.8 p. 462 bottom right** Tim Tadder/Corbis; **21.8 p. 463 top left** Image100/Corbis; **21.8 p. 463 top right** Photodisc/Getty Images; **21.8 p. 463 bottom left to right** Goodshoot/Corbis; bonniej/iStockphoto.com; moodboard/Corbis; **21.9** James W. Evarts/Photo Researchers, Inc.; **21.10** SPL/Photo Researchers, Inc.; **21.12** Jane Burton/Dorling Kindersley; **21.16** Good Olga/iStockphoto.com; **21.17** Tim Tadder/Corbis Images; **21.20 top left** Goinyk Volodymyr/Dreamstime; **21.20 bottom left** vario images GmbH & Co.KG/Alamy; **21.20 middle** Vendla Stockdale/Shutterstock.com; **21.20 right** Regien Paassen/Shutterstock.com; **p. 472** Andy Crawford/Dorling Kindersley.

CHAPTER 22: Chapter opening photo Maridav/iStockphoto; **p. 475, 490, 491** Maridav/iStockphoto; **22.1 left to right** Arco Images GmbH/Alamy; Bence Mate/Nature Picture Library; Reggie Casagrande/Jupiter Images; **22.2** Corbis; **22.5** GeoM/Shutterstock; **22.17 top left** Lindsay Noechel/Shutterstock; **22.17 top right** Roger Phillips/DK Images; **22.17 bottom left to right** DK Images; DK Images; David Murray and Jules Selmes/DK Images; **p. 487** rebvt/Shutterstock.com; **22.18** Kristin Piljay; **22.19** Hartmut Schwarzbach/Argus/Photolibrary; **22.21** Jackson Laboratory; **22.23** Stuart Gregory/Getty Images.

CHAPTER 23: Chapter opening photo Steve Lovegrove/iStockphoto; **p. 495, 504, 513** Steve Lovegrove/iStockphoto; **23.6b** Gustoimages/Photo Researchers; **23.8a** Scanpix Sweden AB; **23.10** Martyn F. Chillmaid/Photo Researchers; **23.11** Corbis/Photolibrary; **23.12 left to right** Susumu Nishinaga/Photo Researchers, Inc.; SPL/Photo Researchers, Inc.; Scimat/Photo Researchers; **23.12 right inset** The Gillette Co.; **23.14 left** Biophoto Associates/Photo Researchers, Inc.; **23.14 right** Biophoto Associates/Photo Researchers, Inc.; **23.17 left to right** ARCO/H Reinhard/AGE Fotostock; Matthew Oldfield, ScubaZoo/Photo Researchers; Dr. Keith Wheeler/Photo Researchers; Cordelia Molloy/Photo Researchers; **23.18** imagebroker.net/SuperStock; **23.19a** Douglas Pulsipher/Alamy; **23.24a** Creative Digital Visions; **23.24b** Medical-on-Line/Alamy; **23.25** Pep Roig/Alamy; **p. 514 Blood table left to right** Susumu Nishinaga/Photo Researchers, Inc.; SPL/Photo Researchers, Inc.; The Gillette Co.

CHAPTER 24: Chapter opening photo RODGER BOSCH/AFP/Getty Images/Newscom; **p. 517, 523, 530** RODGER BOSCH/AFP/Getty Images/Newscom; **24.1** Charles Daghlian/Photo Researchers, Inc.; **24.4.** Getty Images; **24.5** bonniej/iStockphoto.com; **24.8** Hank Morgan/Photo Researchers, Inc.; **24.10 bottom** Samuel Ashfield/Photo Researchers, Inc.; **24.10 top** Hazel Appleton, Health Protection Agency Centre for Infections/Photo Researchers, Inc.; **24.11** Biology Media/Science Source/Photo Researchers; **24.14** Ralph C. Eagle Jr./Photo Researchers, Inc.; **24.15** Dey L. P. Pharmaceuticals; **24.16 left** SPL/Photo Researchers; **24.16 right** Salisbury District Hospital/Photo Researchers; **24.17 left** Philippe Garo/Photo Researchers; **24.17 right** Chris Bjornberg/Photo Researchers.

CHAPTER 25: Chapter opening photo UPI Photo Service/Newscom; **p. 535, 546, 547** UPI Photo Service/Newscom; **25.1** Milos_Kula/iStockphoto; **25.4** Image100/Corbis; **25.6** Image100/Corbis; **25.7a** Zephyr/Photo Researchers, Inc.; **25.7b** AP Wide World Photos; **25.7c** Peter Kramer/AP Wide World Photos; **p. 451** David P. Smith/Shutterstock; **25.10 inset** Edward Kinsman/Photo Researchers; **25.10 left** Ian Hooton/Photo Researchers; **25.10 right** ZUMA Press/Newscom; **25.11** Image Source/Corbis; **25.13** Bob Evans/Photolibrary; **p. 540, 541, 543, 544, 546** Image100/Corbis.

CHAPTER 26: Chapter opening photo AJPhoto/Photo Researchers; **p. 551, 569, 570** AJPhoto/Photo Researchers; **26.1** Oxford Scientific/Photolibrary; **26.2** Mary Jo Adams; **26.3** Adam Reitzel, John R. Finnerty, Boston University; **26.4** Alessandra Sarti/Alamy; **26.8** C. Edelman/La Vilette/Petit Format/Photo Researchers; **26.10** Reuters NewMedia Inc.; **Table 26.2 clockwise from top left** David M. Phillips/Photo Researchers, Inc.; Kwangshin Kim/Photo Researchers; Chris Bjornberg/Science Photo Library/Photo Researchers; Hazel Appleton, Centre for Infections/Health Protection Agency/Photo Researchers; Dr. Linda Stannard, Uct/Photo Researchers; Photo Researchers; Eye of Science/Photo Researchers, Inc.; **26.12** David M. Phillips/Photo Researchers; **26.14 left** David Barlow Photographer;

26.14 right David Barlow/BBC Photo Library; 26.17 p. 566 Scanpix Sweden AB; 26.17 p. 567 left Scanpix Sweden AB; 26.17 p. 567 right Eric J. Simon; 26.18 Eric J. Simon; 26.18 Trevor Smith/Alamy; 26.21 Dr. Yorgos Nikas/Photo Researchers; 26.22 Design Pics Inc./Alamy.

CHAPTER 27: Chapter opening photo Kitch Bain/AGE Fotostock; p. 575, 598, 599 Kitch Bain/AGE Fotostock; 27.6 Edwin R. Lewis, Professor Emeritus; 27.7 John Davis/ Dorling Kindersley; 27.9 left 66North/iStockphoto; 27.9 right Pasieka/SPL/Photo Researchers, Inc.; 27.13 Johns Hopkins University; 27.14 The Dornsife Neuroscience Imaging Center; 27.15 WDCN/Univ. College London/ SPL/Photo Researchers; 27.16 Liaison/Getty Images; 27.22 Corbis; 27.25 Getty Images; 27.26 Phil Date Photography/ iStockphoto; 27.29 Jochen Tack/Alamy; 27.31 Professor Clara Franzini-Armstrong; 27.36 Danny Moloshok/AP Images; 27.37 Frank Greenaway/DK Images.

CHAPTER 28: Chapter opening photo marco mayer/ Shutterstock.com; p. 605, 616, 621 marco mayer/ Shutterstock.com; 28.1 Adam Hart-Davis/Photo Researchers, Inc.; page 606 Eric J. Simon; 28.2a Nigel Cattlin/Alamy; 28.2b Michael Fogden/Photolibrary; 28.3 left Smit/Shutterstock; 28.3 right bluemagenta/Alamy; 28.4a NHPA/SuperStock; 28.4b Donald Gregory Clever; 28.4c Datacraft/AGE Fotostock; 28.6a Yogesh S. More/AGE Fotostock; 28.6b PIXTAL/AGE Fotostock; 28.11 left top to bottom Ed Reschke/Photolibrary; Graham Kent; Graham Kent; 28.11 right top Andrew Syred/Photo Researchers; 28.11 right bottom Biophoto Associates/Photo Researchers; 28.12 left to right Jtb/Photolibrary; Andrew Lawson/DK Images; Terry Smith Images/Alamy; 28.14 Biology Pics/ Photo Researchers, Inc.; 28.15 Ray Hendley/AGE Fotostock; 28.17 Don Mason/Corbis; 28.18 Courtesy of David W. Stahle, Tree-Ring Laboratory, University of Arkansas; 28.19 bottom Dan Suzio/SPL/Photo Researchers; 28.19 top teft Tim Hill/Alamy; 28.19 top right Duncan Smith/Photo Researchers; 28.25 Walter H. Hodge/Photolibrary; 28.26 bottom Ewa Walicka/Shutterstock.com; 28.26 top ILYA GENKIN/Shutterstock.com; 28.27 Nigel Cattlin/Alamy; 28.28 Volodymyr Pylypchuk/Shutterstock.com.

CHAPTER 29: Chapter opening photo YOSHIKAZU TSUNO/AFP/Getty Images/Newscom; p. 625, 633, 637 YOSHIKAZU TSUNO/AFP/Getty Images/Newscom; 29.2 Eric J. Simon; 29.3 Educational Images LTD/Custom Medical Stock Photo/Newscom; 29.4 Paul Rapson/SPL/ Photo Researchers; 29.5 Brian Capon; 29.6 R. L. Peterson/ Biological Photo Service; 29.8 left David M. Dennis/ Photolibrary; 29.8 right E. H. Newcomb and S. R. Tandon/ Biological Photo Service; p. 606 Daniel Wiedemann/ Shutterstock.com; 29.10 left to right Frank Greenaway/ DK Images; Jeremy Bur/Photo Researchers; Jeremy Bur/ Photo Researchers; 29.11 Professor Ray F. Evert; 29.12 Lezh/ iStockphoto; 29.13 Dmitry Baevskiy/Dreamstime; 29.16 Kristin Piljay/Pearson Education/Pearson Science; 29.17 Fred Jensen; 29.18 Don Paulson Photography/Purestock/ SuperStock; 29.19 left to right Maryann Frazier/SPL/Photo Researchers; Scott Camazine/Photo Researchers; Michael Evans; 29.21 Igor Siwanowicz/Fame Pictures, Inc.

ILLUSTRATION AND TEXT CREDITS

CHAPTER 5: 5.3: Data from S. E. Gebhardt and R. G. Thomas, *Nutritive Values of Foods* (USDA, 2002); S. A. Plowman and D. L. Smith, *Exercise Physiology for Health, Fitness, and Performance,* 2nd ed. Copyright © 2003 Pearson Education, Inc. publishing as Pearson Benjamin Cummings.

CHAPTER 6: 6.5: Copyright © 2002 from *Molecular Biology of the Cell,* 4th ed. by Bruce Alberts et al., fig. 2.69, p. 92. Garland Science/Taylor & Francis Books, Inc. Reproduced by permission of Garland Science/Taylor & Francis LLC.

CHAPTER 7: 7.12: Adapted from Richard and David Walker, *Energy, Plants and Man,* fig. 4.1, p. 69. Oxygraphics. Copyright © Richard Walker. Used courtesy of Richard Walker, http://www.oxygraphics.co.uk.

CHAPTER 10: Page 194: Text quotation by Joshua Lederberg, from Barbara J. Culliton, "Emerging Viruses, Emerging Threat," *Science, 247,* p. 279, 1/19/1990. Copyright © 1990 American Association for the Advancement of Science.

CHAPTER 11: Table 11.1: Data from the American Cancer Society website, "Cancer Facts & Figures 2008" at http:// www.cancer.org/docroot/STT/stt_0.asp; 11.10: Adapted from an illustration by William McGinnis in Peter Radetsky, "The homeobox: Something very precious that we share with flies, from egg to adult." Bethesda, MD: Howard Hughes Medical Institute, 1992, p. 92. Reprinted by permission of William McGinnis.

CHAPTER 13: 13.16: Data for graph from K. V. Young et al., "How the horned lizards got its horns," in *Science, 304,* 4/2/2004, p. 65. American Association for the Advancement of Science; 13.31: Adapted from A. C. Allison, "Abnormal Hemoglobins and Erythrovute Enzyme-Deficiency Traits," in *Genetic Variation in Human Populations,* by G. A. Harrison, ed. (Oxford: Elsevier Science, 1961).

CHAPTER 15: 15.17: Adapted from G. J. Tortora, B. R. Funke, and C. L. Case, *Microbiology: An Introduction,* 9th ed. Copyright © 2007 Pearson Education, Inc., publishing as Pearson Benjamin Cummings. Reprinted and electronically reproduced by permission of Pearson Education, Inc., Upper Saddle River, New Jersey.

CHAPTER 17: 17.38: Drawn from photos of fossils: *A. ramidus* adapted from www.age-of-the-sage.org/ evolution/ardi_fossilized_skeleton.htm. *H. neanderthalensis* adapted from *The Human Evolution Coloring Book.* *P. boisei* drawn from a photo by David Bill; 17.43: Migration of modern H. sapiens, illustration by Bob Crimi from *Nature Genetics.* Authors L. Luca Cavalli-Sforza and M. W. Feldman. 2003. The application of molecular genetic approaches to the study of human evolution. Vol. 33: 266–275, fig. 3, copyright 2003. Reprinted by permission of Bob Crimi.

CHAPTER 18: 18.25: From J. H. Withgott and S. R. Brennan, *Environment: The Science Behind the Stories,* 3rd ed., fig, 6.30, p 169. Copyright © 2008 Pearson Education, Inc., Prentice Hall. Reprinted and electronically reproduced by permission of Pearson Education, Inc., Upper Saddle River, New Jersey; 18.44: From "Global Temperature Change," J. Hansen et al., *PNAS,* Sept. 26, 2006, Vol. 103, No. 39, Fig. 1B. Copyright 2006 National Academy of Sciences, U.S.A. Reprinted with permission; 18.45: Adapted from *Climate Change 2007: The Physical Science Basis.* Working Group I Contribution to the Fourth Assessment Report of the Intergovernmental Panel on Climate Change, FAQ 2.1, Fig. 1. Cambridge University Press. Reprinted by permission of IPCC, c/o World Meteorological Organization.

CHAPTER 19: 19.13: Data from Fisheries and Oceans, Canada, 1999; 19.21: Data from United Nations, the World at Six Billion, 2007; 19.22 and 19.23: Data from U. S. Census Bureau International Data Base; 19.25: From *The Ecological Footprint Atlas 2009* by B. Ewing et al., p. 31, Map 2. © 2009 Global Footprint Network. All rights reserved. Used by permission; Table 19.1: Data from Centers for Disease Control and Prevention website, "United States Life Tables, 2003," *National Vital Statistics Report,* vol. 50, no. 14, April 19, 2006. www.cdc.gov; Table 19.3: Data from Population Reference Bureau, 2008, www.prb.org.

CHAPTER 20: 20.42: Map by Patterson Clark, June 23, 2002. Copyright (c) 2002, The Washington Post. All rights reserved. Used by permission and protected by the Copyright Laws of the United States. The printing, copying, redistribution, or retransmission of the Material without express written permission is prohibited.

CHAPTER 21: 21.15: Adapted from fig. 2 in V. H. Hutchison et al. Thermoregulation in a brooding female Indian python, Python molurus bivittatus. *Science* 151: 694-695, fig. 2. Copyright © 1966. Reprinted with permission from AAAS.

CHAPTER 22: 22.20: Data adapted from *Clinical Guidelines on the Identification, Evaluation, and Treatment of Overweight and Obesity in Adults: The Evidence Report.* Data found at the National Heart, Lung, and Blood Institute: http://www.nhlbi.nih.gov/guidelines/obesity/bmi_tbl.htm; Table 22.1: Data from S. E. Gebhardt and R. G. Thomas, *Nutritive Values of Foods* (USDA, 2002); S. A. Plowman and D. L. Smith, *Exercise Physiology for Health, Fitness, and Performance,* 2nd ed. Copyright © 2003 Pearson Education, Inc. publishing as Benjamin Cummings.

CHAPTER 23: 23.23: Illustration of hemoglobin structure by Irving Geis. Image from Irving Geis Collection, HHMI. Rights owned by Howard Hughes Medical Institute (HHMI). Not to be reproduced without permission.

CHAPTER 26: Table 26.1: Data from R. Hatcher et al., *Contraceptive Technology: 1990—1992,* p. 134 (New York: Irvington, 1990).

CHAPTER 27: 27.5: Adapted from W. M. Becker and D. W. Deamer, *The World of the Cell,* 2e. fig. 20.16. Copyright © 1991 Pearson Education, Inc., publishing as Pearson Benjamin Cummings. Reprinted and electronically reproduced by permission of Pearson Education, Inc., Upper Saddle River, New Jersey.

Appendix D Self-Quiz Answers

CHAPTER 1

1. b (some living organisms are single-celled)
2. atom, molecule, cell, tissue, organ, organism, population, ecosystem, biosphere; the cell
3. Photosynthesis cycles nutrients by converting the carbon in carbon dioxide to sugar, which is then consumed by other organisms. Additionally, the oxygen in water is released as oxygen gas. Photosynthesis contributes to energy flow by converting sunlight to chemical energy, which is then also consumed by other organisms, and by producing heat.
4. a4, b1, c3, d2.
5. On average, those individuals with heritable traits best suited to the local environment produce the greatest number of offspring that survive and reproduce. This increases the frequency of those traits in the population over time. The result is the accumulation of evolutionary adaptations.
6. Without a control group, you don't know if the experimental outcome is due to the variable you are trying to test or to some other variable.
7. d
8. c
9. Evolution
10. a3, b2, c1, d4

CHAPTER 2

1. electrons; neutrons; protons
2. Nitrogen-14 has an atomic number of 7 and a mass number of 14. The radioactive isotope, nitrogen-16, has an atomic number of 7 and a mass number of 16.
3. Organisms incorporate radioactive isotopes of an element into their molecules just as they do the nonradioactive isotopes, and researchers can detect the presence of the radioactive isotopes.
4. two
5. Each carbon atom has only three covalent bonds instead of the required four.
6. The positively charged hydrogen regions would repel each other.
7. d
8. a

9. The positive and negative poles cause adjacent water molecules to become attracted to each other, forming hydrogen bonds. The properties of water such as cohesion, temperature regulation, and water's ability to act as a solvent all arise from this atomic stickiness.
10. The cola is an aqueous solution, with water as the solvent, sugar as the main solute, and the CO_2 making the solution acidic.

CHAPTER 3

1.
$$\begin{array}{ccc} H & & H \\ & C = C & \\ H & & H \end{array}$$

2. dehydration; water; hydrolysis
3. b
4. fatty acid; glycerol
5. b
6. c
7. d
8. Hydrophobic amino acids are most likely to be found within the interior of a protein, far from the watery environment.
9. a
10. starch (or glycogen or cellulose); nucleic acid
11. Both DNA and RNA are polynucleotides; both have the same phosphate group along the backbone; and both use A, C, and G bases. But DNA uses T while RNA uses U as a base; the sugar differs between them; and DNA is usually double-stranded, while RNA is usually single-stranded.
12. Structurally, a gene is a long stretch of DNA. Functionally, a gene contains the information needed to produce a protein.

CHAPTER 4

1. d
2. about 0.075 mm, which equals 75 μm
3. b
4. A membrane is fluid because its components are not locked into place. A membrane is mosaic because it contains a variety of embedded proteins.
5. endomembrane system
6. smooth ER; rough ER
7. rough ER, Golgi apparatus, plasma membrane

8. Both organelles use membranes to organize enzymes and both provide energy to the cell. But chloroplasts use pigments to capture energy from sunlight in photosynthesis, whereas mitochondria release energy from glucose using oxygen in cellular respiration. Chloroplasts are only in photosynthetic plants and protists, whereas mitochondria are in almost all eukaryotic cells.
9. a3, b1, c5, d2, e4
10. nucleus, nuclear pores, ribosomes, rough ER, Golgi apparatus
11. Both are motile appendages that extend from the surface of a cell and help in movement. Cells with flagella typically have one long flagellum that propels the cell in a whiplike motion; cilia are usually shorter, more numerous, and beat together.

CHAPTER 5

1. You convert the chemical energy from food to the kinetic energy of your upward climb. At the top of the stairs, some of the energy has been stored as potential energy because of your higher elevation. The rest has been converted to heat.
2. Energy; entropy
3. 10,000 g (or 10 kg); remember that 1 Calorie on a food label equals 1,000 calories of heat energy.
4. The three phosphate groups store chemical energy, a form of potential energy. The release of a phosphate group makes some of this potential energy available to cells to perform work.
5. Hydrolases are enzymes that participate in hydrolysis reactions, breaking down large molecules into the smaller molecules that make them up.
6. An inhibitor's binding to another site on the enzyme can cause the enzyme's active site to change shape.
7. b
8. a
9. *Hypertonic* and *hypotonic* are relative terms. A solution that is hypertonic to tap water could be hypotonic to seawater. In using these terms, you must provide a comparison, as in "The solution is hypertonic to the cell's cytoplasm."

10. Passive transport moves atoms or molecules along their concentration gradient (from higher to lower concentration), while active transport moves them against their concentration gradient.
11. b
12. signal transduction pathway

CHAPTER 6

1. d
2. Plants produce organic molecules by photosynthesis. Consumers must acquire organic material by consuming it rather than making it.
3. In breathing, your lungs exchange CO_2 and O_2 between your body and the atmosphere. In cellular respiration, your cells consume the O_2 in extracting energy from food and release CO_2 as a waste product.
4. the electron transport chain
5. glucose; NAD^+
6. O_2
7. The majority of the energy provided by cellular respiration is generated during the electron transport chain. Shutting down that pathway will deprive cells of energy very quickly.
8. b
9. Glycolysis
10. b
11. Because fermentation supplies only 2 ATP per glucose molecule compared with about 32 from cellular respiration, the yeast will have to consume 19 times as much glucose to produce the same amount of ATP.

CHAPTER 7

1. thylakoids; stroma
2. The Calvin cycle, which consumes the NADPH and ATP, occurs in the stroma.
3. inputs: a, d, e; outputs: b, c
4. Green light is reflected by chlorophyll, not absorbed, and therefore cannot drive photosynthesis.
5. H_2O
6. c
7. The reactions of the Calvin cycle require the outputs of the light reactions (ATP and NADPH).
8. In hot, dry environments, most plants close their stomata, which saves water but decreases the amount of CO_2 available inside the leaves.

9. C_4 and CAM plants can close their stomata and save water without shutting down photosynthesis.
10. c

CHAPTER 8

1. c
2. They have identical genes (DNA).
3. They are in the form of very long, thin strands.
4. b
5. prophase and telophase
6. a. 1,1; b. 1, 2; c. 2, 4; d. $2n$, n; e. individually, by homologous pair; f. identical, unique; g. repair, growth, asexual reproduction; gamete formation
7. c
8. 39
9. Prophase II or metaphase II; it cannot be during meiosis I because then you would see an even number of chromosomes; it cannot be during a later stage of meiosis II because then you would see the sister chromatids separated.
10. benign; malignant
11. 16 ($2n = 8$, so $n = 4$ and $2^n = 2^4 = 16$)
12. Nondisjunction would create just as many gametes with an extra copy of chromosome 3 or 16, but extra copies of chromosome 3 or 16 are probably fatal.

CHAPTER 9

1. genotype; phenotype
2. Statement **a.** is the law of independent assortment; statement **b.** is the law of segregation.
3. c
4. c
5. d
6. d
7. d
8. $\frac{1}{4}$ ($\frac{1}{2}$ chance the child will be male times $\frac{1}{2}$ chance that he will inherit the X carrying the disease allele)
9. The two parental-type gametes, *WS* and *ws*, are produced through meiosis. The process of recombination (due to crossing over) can produce two kinds of recombinant gametes, *Ws* and *wS*.
10. Height appears to result from polygenic inheritance, like human skin color. See Figure 9.22.
11. The brown allele appears to be dominant, the white allele recessive.

The brown parent appears to be homozygous dominant, *BB*, and the white mouse is homozygous recessive, *bb*. The F_1 mice are all heterozygous, *Bb*. If two of the F_1 mice are mated, $\frac{3}{4}$ of the F_2 mice will be brown.

12. The best way to find out whether a brown F_2 mouse is homozygous dominant or heterozygous is to do a testcross: Mate the brown mouse with a white mouse. If the brown mouse is homozygous, all the offspring will be brown. If the brown mouse is heterozygous, you would expect half the offspring to be brown and half to be white.
13. Freckles are dominant, so Tim and Jan must both be heterozygous. There is a $\frac{3}{4}$ chance that they will produce a child with freckles, a $\frac{1}{4}$ chance that they will produce a child without freckles. The probability that the next two children will have freckles is $\frac{3}{4} \times \frac{3}{4} = \frac{9}{16}$.
14. According to the odds, half their children will be heterozygous and have elevated cholesterol levels. There is a $\frac{1}{4}$ chance that their next child will be homozygous, *hh*, and have an extremely high cholesterol level, like Katerina.
15. The bristle-shape alleles are sex-linked, carried on the X chromosome. Normal bristles is dominant (F) and forked is recessive (f). The genotype of the female parent is $X^f X^f$. The genotype of the male parent is $X^F Y$. Their female offspring are $X^F X^f$; their male offspring are $X^f Y$.
16. The mother is a heterozygous carrier, and the father is normal. See Figure 9.32 for a pedigree. $\frac{1}{4}$ of their children will be boys suffering from hemophilia; $\frac{1}{4}$ will be female carriers.
17. For a woman to be colorblind, she must inherit X chromosomes bearing the colorblindness allele from both parents. Her father has only one X chromosome, which he passes on to all his daughters, so he must be colorblind. A male only needs to inherit the colorblindness allele from a carrier mother; both his parents are usually phenotypically normal.

CHAPTER 10

1. polynucleotides; nucleotides; sugar (deoxyribose); phosphate; nitrogenous base
2. b
3. Each daughter DNA molecule will have half the radioactivity of the parent molecule, since one polynucleotide from the original parental DNA molecule winds up in each daughter DNA molecule.
4. CAU; GUA; histidine (His)
5. A gene is the polynucleotide sequence with information for making one polypeptide. Each codon—a triplet of bases in DNA or RNA—codes for one amino acid. Transcription occurs when RNA polymerase produces mRNA using one strand of DNA as a template. A ribosome is the site of translation, or polypeptide synthesis, and tRNA molecules serve as interpreters of the genetic code. Each tRNA molecule has an amino acid attached at one end and a three-base anticodon at the other end. Beginning at the start codon, mRNA moves relative to the ribosome a codon at a time. A tRNA with a complementary anticodon pairs with each codon, adding its amino acid to the polypeptide chain. The amino acids are linked by peptide bonds. Translation stops at a stop codon, and the finished polypeptide is released. The polypeptide folds to form a functional protein, sometimes in combination with other polypeptides.
6. a3, b3, c1, d2, e2 and 3
7. d
8. d
9. The genetic material of these viruses is RNA, which is replicated inside the infected cell by special enzymes encoded by the virus. The viral genome (or its complement) serves as mRNA for the synthesis of viral proteins.
10. reverse transcriptase
11. The process of reverse transcription occurs only in infections by RNA-containing retroviruses like HIV. Cells do not require reverse transcriptase (their RNA molecules do not undergo reverse transcription), so reverse

transcriptase can be knocked out without harming the human host.

CHAPTER 11

1. c
2. operon
3. b
4. a
5. DNA polymerase and other proteins required for transcription do not have access to tightly packed DNA.
6. the ability of these cells to produce entire organisms through cloning
7. nuclear transplantation
8. which genes are active in a particular sample of cells
9. b
10. embryonic tissue (ES cells), umbilical cord blood, and bone marrow (adult stem cells)
11. Proto-oncogenes are normal genes involved in the control of the cell cycle. Mutation or viruses can cause them to be converted to oncogenes, or cancer-causing genes. Proto-oncogenes are necessary for normal control of cell division.
12. Master control genes, called homeotic genes, regulate many other genes during development.

CHAPTER 12

1. c, d, b, a
2. because it does not contain introns
3. vector
4. Such an enzyme creates DNA fragments with "sticky ends," single-stranded regions whose unpaired bases can hydrogen-bond to the complementary sticky ends of other fragments created by the same enzyme.
5. PCR
6. Different people tend to have different numbers of repeats at each STR site. DNA fragments prepared from the STR sites of different people will thus have different lengths, causing them to migrate to different locations on a gel.
7. a
8. b
9. Chop the genome into fragments using restriction enzymes, clone and sequence each fragment, and reassemble the short sequences into

a continuous sequence for every chromosome.

10. c, b, a, d

CHAPTER 13

1. c
2. Lyell and other geologists presented evidence for the gradual change of geologic features over millions of years. Darwin applied this idea to suggest that species evolve through the slow accumulation of small changes over long periods of time.
3. *Bb*: 0.42; *BB*: 0.49; *bb*: 0.09
4. The fitness of an individual (or of a particular genotype) is measured by the relative number of alleles that it contributes to the gene pool of the next generation compared with the contribution of others. Thus the number of fertile offspring produced determines an individual's fitness.
5. e
6. c
7. Both effects result in populations small enough for significant sampling error in the gene pool for the first few generations. A bottleneck event reduces the size of an existing population in a given location. The founder effect occurs when a new, small population colonizes a new territory.
8. stabilizing selection
9. b, c, d
10. the prevalence of malaria

CHAPTER 14

1. Microevolution is a change in the gene pool of a population, often associated with adaptation. Speciation is an evolutionary process in which one species splits into two or more species. Macroevolution is evolutionary change above the species level, including the origin of evolutionary novelty and new taxonomic groups and the impact of mass extinctions on the diversity of life and its subsequent recovery. Macroevolution is marked by major changes in the history of life, including the origin of new species, and these changes are often noticeable enough to be evident in the fossil record.
2. b

3. prezygotic: a, b, c, e; postzygotic: d
4. because a small gene pool is more likely to be changed substantially by genetic drift and natural selection
5. exaptations
6. d
7. d
8. species, genus, family, order, class, phylum, kingdom, domain
9. 2.6
10. Archaea and Bacteria

CHAPTER 15

1. g, d, f, c, b, a, e
2. d, c, a, b, e
3. DNA polymerase is a protein, which must be transcribed from a gene. But a DNA gene requires DNA polymerase to be replicated. This creates a paradox about which came first—DNA or protein. But RNA can act as both an information storage molecule and an enzyme, suggesting that dual-role RNA may have preceded both DNA and proteins.
4. Exotoxins are poisons secreted by pathogenic bacteria; endotoxins are components of the outer membrane of pathogenic bacteria.
5. Autotrophs make their own organic compounds from CO_2, while heterotrophs must obtain at least one type of organic compound from another organism.
6. They can form endospores.
7. Both you and a mushroom are chemoheterotrophs.
8. because the first eukaryotes were protists, and these ancient protists were ancestral to all other eukaryotes, including plants, fungi, animals, and modern protists
9. c
10. b

CHAPTER 16

1. cuticle
2. flowers
3. a. sporophyte b. cones; angiosperms c. fruit
4. b
5. b
6. a fern
7. Because the plants do not lose their leaves during autumn and winter, the leaves are already fully developed for photosynthesis when the short growing season begins in spring.
8. vascular plant

9. a
10. a ripened ovary of a flower that protects and aids in the dispersal of seeds contained in the fruit
11. algae; fungi
12. A fungus digests its food externally by secreting digestive juices into the food and then absorbing the small nutrients that result from digestion. In contrast, humans and most other animals ingest relatively large pieces of food and digest the food within their bodies.

CHAPTER 17

1. c
2. coelom; pseudocoelom
3. arthropod
4. amphipod
5. b
6. Chordata; notochord; cartilage disks between your vertebrae
7. bipedalism
8. a
9. *Australopithecus* species, *Homo habilis*, *Homo erectus*, *Homo sapiens*
10. a4, b5, c1, d2, e3

CHAPTER 18

1. organismal ecology, population ecology, community ecology, ecosystem ecology
2. light, water temperature, chemicals added
3. physiological; behavioral
4. d
5. a. desert; b. grassland; c. tropical rain forest; d. temperate broadleaf forest; e. coniferous forest; f. tundra
6. chaparral
7. permafrost, very cold winters, and high winds
8. agriculture
9. Carbon dioxide and other gases in the atmosphere absorb heat energy radiating from Earth and reflect it back toward Earth. This is called the greenhouse effect. As the carbon dioxide concentration in the atmosphere increases, more heat is retained, causing global warming.
10. c
11. populations of organisms that have high genetic variability and short life spans

CHAPTER 19

1. the number of people and the land area in which they live

2. III; I
3. O; O; E; O; E
4. a. The *x*-axis is time; the *y*-axis is the number of individuals; the red curve represents exponential growth; the blue curve represents logistic growth.
   b. carrying capacity
   c. In exponential growth, the population growth rate continues to increase as long as the population size increases. In logistic growth, the population grows fastest when it is about ½ the carrying capacity.
   d. exponential growth curve, though the worldwide growth rate is slowing
5. d
6. opportunistic
7. c
8. The large population segment, the baby boomers, are currently in the workforce and are in their peak earning years.
9. d

CHAPTER 20

1. habitat destruction
2. d
3. c
4. a2, b5, c5, d3 or d4, e1
5. because the pesticides become concentrated in their prey
6. succession
7. Only 10% of the energy trapped by photosynthesis is turned into biomass by the plant, and only 10% of that energy is turned into the meat of a grazing animal. Therefore, eating grain-fed beef obtains only about 1% of the energy captured by photosynthesis.
8. Many nutrients come from the soil, but carbon comes from the air.
9. landscape
10. b

CHAPTER 21

1. atom, molecule, organelle, cell, tissue, organ, organ system, organism
2. A very thin or flat organism may have all of its body cells in contact with the environment and therefore would not need a circulatory system. In contrast, a thicker organism will require a circulatory system to transport substances to all body cells.
3. c

4. interstitial fluid
5. positive; negative
6. Endotherms get most of their body heat from metabolic processes, whereas ectotherms get most of their body heat from the environment.
7. osmoregulator; osmoconformer
8. d
9. b
10. Most of the water is reabsorbed into the blood; the rest is excreted in the urine.

CHAPTER 22

1. Large food items could not be digested; it would be difficult to eliminate wastes; and it would be difficult to nourish the many cells that compose a large animal.
2. Yes, absorption is the uptake of nutrients into body cells. Without it, you would never gain any calories (or nutritional value) from your food.
3. Digestion; absorption
4. because peristalsis pushes the food along
5. proteins; pepsin
6. bacteria (specifically, *Helicobacter pylori*); by using antibiotics and bismuth
7. d
8. The antibiotics kill the bacteria that synthesize vitamin K in the colon.
9. b
10. because cellular respiration requires oxygen to break down food
11. Many plant proteins are incomplete, meaning that they lack certain essential amino acids. Animal products tend to have complete proteins that contain all the essential amino acids. Vegetarians must therefore eat a variety of plant products to receive all the essential amino acids.
12. a (Overdoses of fat-soluble vitamins can be dangerous because the body cannot rid itself of them quickly.)

CHAPTER 23

1. In an open circulatory system, vessels have open ends and the circulating fluid flows directly around the body cells. In a closed circulatory system, the circulating fluid stays within a closed system of vessels.
2. Arteries carry oxygen-rich blood to the body, but they carry oxygen-

poor blood to the lungs. Veins carry oxygen-poor blood from the body to the heart, but they carry oxygen-rich blood from the lungs to the heart. Arteries are defined as vessels that carry blood away from the heart; veins carry blood to the heart.
3. a3, b1, c4, d2
4. Oxygen levels are reduced, as oxygen-depleted blood mixes with oxygen-rich blood.
5. anemia
6. a3, b4, c1, d2
7. fruits, vegetables, and whole grains; cholesterol, saturated fats, and trans fats
8. Gills (the respiratory organ of fishes) extend outward from the body into the surrounding environment, whereas lungs (the respiratory organ of humans) are internal.
9. alveoli
10. b
11. b

CHAPTER 24

1. antigens; antibodies
2. innate: a, b, d, e; adaptive: c, f, g
3. b
4. It takes several days for a clone of effector cells to be formed during the primary response. In a secondary response, memory cells can respond more quickly.
5. a4, b1, c6, d3, e2, f5
6. Swelling dilutes toxins, delivers more oxygen, promotes scabbing; pain changes behavior to discourage further damage; fever may inhibit bacterial growth.
7. HIV destroys helper T cells, thereby impairing both the cell-mediated and the humoral immune response.
8. B cells
9. In a person with lupus, the immune system makes antibodies against the person's own (self) molecules.
10. memory cells; clonal selection

CHAPTER 25

1. d
2. b
3. The first two cells could have membrane receptors for that hormone, but they might trigger different signal transduction pathways. The third cell could lack membrane receptors for that particular hormone.
4. b

5. Alcohol slows the release of antidiuretic hormone (ADH) from the pituitary. Decreased levels of ADH result in decreased levels of water reabsorption by the kidneys, increasing urine output.
6. The patient has hypothyroidism. The thyroid cannot produce its metabolism-regulating hormones without iodine.
7. d
8. c
9. At high levels, glucocorticoids suppress the immune system. Although this is good for relieving pain and inflammation, the immune system can no longer respond appropriately to threats such as infection. Additionally, glucocorticoids may mask pain, leading to behaviors that aggravate the injury.
10. androgens
11. a. endorphins b. human growth hormone (HGH) c. estrogens

CHAPTER 26

1. Asexual reproduction is favorable in a stable environment with many resources. Sexual reproduction may enhance success in a changing environment by producing genetically variable offspring.
2. the seminal vesicles and/or the prostate
3. a4, b6, c3, d1, e5, f2
4. b
5. Inhibiting FSH and LH after ovulation ensures that another egg will not be released during this cycle. Estrogen and progesterone inhibit FSH and LH.
6. They also help prevent the spread of sexually transmitted diseases.
7. a
8. c
9. The nerve cells may follow chemical trails to the muscle cells (induction).
10. oxytocin
11. in vitro fertilization; fertilization "in glass"

CHAPTER 27

1. cell body; dendrites; axon; synaptic terminal
2. It speeds up conduction of signals along an axon.
3. central nervous system; peripheral nervous system; brain; spinal cord

4. cerebrospinal fluid; meninges
5. activation of the sympathetic branch of the peripheral nervous system
6. The cerebral cortex deals with sensory information, while structures in the brainstem maintain vital functions. If a person suffers a severe head injury, the cerebral cortex may be damaged while the brainstem is still able to function, leaving the person unresponsive but alive.
7. An action potential (used by neurons) is an all-or-none situation; it doesn't vary in intensity. A receptor potential (used by sensory receptor cells) conveys information about the strength of the stimulus.
8. photoreceptor, chemoreceptor, mechanoreceptor, chemoreceptor
9. c (He can hear the tuning fork against his skull, so the cochlea, nerve, and brain are all functioning properly. Apparently, sounds are not being transmitted to the cochlea; therefore, the bones of the middle ear are the problem.)
10. axial; appendicular
11. d
12. a (Each neuron controls a smaller number of muscle fibers.)

CHAPTER 28

1. b, c, d, e
2. When most plants grow naturally, they exhibit apical dominance, which inhibits the outgrowth of the axillary buds. If your friend were to pinch back the terminal buds, there would be increased growth from the axillary buds. This would result in more branches and leaves, which would increase next year's yield.
3. ovary; ovule
4. a4, b2, c5, d6, e3, f1
5. sexual, because it generates genetic variation among the offspring, enhancing the potential for adaptation to a changing environment
6. a. fruit (ripened ovary); b. fruit; c. leaf; d. root; e. fruit
7. c
8. e
9. b; a
10. vascular cambium

CHAPTER 29

1. Excessive amounts of fungicides could destroy mycorrhizae,

symbiotic associations of fungi and plant root hairs. The fungal filaments provide lots of surface area for absorption of water and nutrients. Destroying the mycorrhizae could cause a water or nutrient deficiency in the plant.
2. c
3. Phloem; Xylem

4. Cohesion is the sticking together of identical molecules—water molecules in the case of xylem sap. Adhesion is the sticking together of different kinds of molecules, as in the adhesion of water to the cellulose of xylem walls. Cohesion enables transpiration to pull xylem sap up without the water in the vessels separating; adhesion helps

to support the sap against the downward pull of gravity.
5. b
6. auxins; cytokinins
7. The terminal bud produces auxins, which counter the effects of cytokinins from the roots and inhibit the growth of axillary buds. If the terminal bud is removed, the cytokinins predominate, and

branching occurs at the axillary buds.
8. a1; b4; c2; d5; e3
9. a4; b3; c1; d2
10. The room lights will inhibit flowering in the chrysanthemums.

Glossary

GLOSSARY

A

abiotic factor (*ā'bī-ot'-ik*)
A nonliving component of an ecosystem, such as air, water, light, minerals, or temperature.

abiotic reservoir
The part of an ecosystem where a chemical, such as carbon or nitrogen, accumulates or is stockpiled outside of living organisms.

ABO blood groups
Genetically determined classes of human blood that are based on the presence or absence of carbohydrates A and B on the surface of red blood cells. The ABO blood group phenotypes, also called blood types, are A, B, AB, and O.

abscisic acid (*ab-sis'-ik*)
A plant hormone that inhibits cell division and promotes dormancy. Abscisic acid interacts with gibberellins in regulating seed germination.

absorption
The uptake of small nutrient molecules by an organism's own body. In animals, absorption is the third main stage of food processing, following digestion; in fungi, it is acquisition of nutrients from the surrounding medium.

acclimation (*ak-li-mā-shun*)
Physiological adjustment that occurs gradually, though still reversibly, in response to an environmental change.

achondroplasia (*uh-kon'-druh-plā'-zhuh*)
A form of human dwarfism caused by a single dominant allele. The homozygous condition is lethal.

acid
A substance that increases the hydrogen ion (H⁺) concentration in a solution.

action potential
A self-propagating change in the voltage across the plasma membrane of a neuron; a nerve signal.

activation energy
The amount of energy that reactants must absorb before a chemical reaction will start.

activator
A protein that switches on a gene or group of genes by binding to DNA.

active site
The part of an enzyme molecule where a substrate molecule attaches (by means of weak chemical bonds); typically, a pocket or groove on the enzyme's surface.

active transport
The movement of a substance across a biological membrane against its concentration gradient, aided by specific transport proteins and requiring the input of energy (often as ATP).

adaptive defense
An immune system defense that is found only in vertebrates and that must be activated by exposure to a specific invader.

adenine (A) (*ad'-uh-nēn*)
A double-ring nitrogenous base found in DNA and RNA.

adhesion
The attraction between different kinds of molecules.

adipose tissue
A type of connective tissue in which the cells contain fat.

ADP
Adenosine diphosphate (*a-den'-ō-sēn dī-fos'-fāt*)
A molecule composed of adenosine and two phosphate groups. The molecule ATP is made by combining a molecule of ADP with a third phosphate in an energy-consuming reaction.

adrenal cortex (*uh-drē'-nul*)
The outer portion of an adrenal gland, controlled by ACTH from the anterior pituitary; secretes hormones called glucocorticoids.

adrenal gland
One of a pair of endocrine glands, located atop each kidney in mammals, composed of an outer cortex and a central medulla.

adrenal medulla (*uh-drē'-nul muh-dul'-uh*)
The central portion of an adrenal gland, controlled by nerve signals; secretes the fight-or-flight hormones epinephrine and norepinephrine.

adult stem cell
A cell present in adult tissues that generates replacements for nondividing differentiated cells.

aerobic (*ār-ō'-bik*)
Containing or requiring molecular oxygen (O₂).

age structure
The relative number of individuals of each age in a population.

AIDS
Acquired immunodeficiency syndrome; the late stages of HIV infection, characterized by a reduced number of T cells; usually results in death caused by opportunistic infections.

alga (*al'-guh*)
(plural, **algae**) An informal term that describes a great variety of protists, most of which are unicellular or colonial photosynthetic autotrophs with chloroplasts. Heterotrophic and multicellular protists closely related to unicellular autotrophs are also regarded as algae.

alimentary canal (*al'-uh-men'-tuh-rē*)
A digestive tube running between a mouth and an anus; also called a digestive tract.

allele (*uh-lē'-ul*)
An alternative version of a gene.

allergen (*al'-er-jen*)
An otherwise harmless antigen that causes an allergic reaction.

allergy
An exaggerated sensitivity to an antigen. Symptoms are triggered by histamines released from mast cells.

allopatric speciation
The formation of a new species in populations that are geographically isolated from one another. *See also* sympatric speciation.

alternation of generations
A life cycle in which there is both a multicellular diploid form, the sporophyte, and a multicellular haploid form, the gametophyte; a characteristic of plants and multicellular green algae.

alternative RNA splicing
A type of regulation at the RNA-processing level in which different mRNA molecules are produced from the same primary transcript, depending on which RNA segments are treated as exons and which as introns.

alveolus (*al-vē'-oh-lus*)
(plural, **alveoli**) One of millions of tiny sacs within the vertebrate lungs where gas exchange occurs.

Alzheimer's disease
A form of mental deterioration, or dementia, characterized by confusion and memory loss.

amino acid (*uh-mēn'-ō*)
An organic molecule containing a carboxyl group, an amino group, a hydrogen atom, and a variable side group (also called a radical group or R group); serves as the monomer of proteins.

amniote
Member of a clade of tetrapods that has an amniotic egg containing specialized membranes that protect the embryo. Amniotes include mammals and reptiles (including birds).

amniotic egg (*am'-nē-ot'-ik*)
A shelled egg in which an embryo develops within a fluid-filled amniotic sac and is nourished by yolk. Produced by reptiles (including birds) and egg-laying mammals, it enables them to complete their life cycles on dry land.

amoeba (*uh-mē'-buh*)
A general term for a protozoan (animal-like protist) characterized by great structural flexibility and the presence of pseudopodia.

amphibian
Member of a class of vertebrate animals that includes frogs and salamanders.

anaerobic (*an'-ār-ō'-bik*)
Lacking or not requiring molecular oxygen (O₂).

analogy
The similarity between two species that is due to convergent evolution rather than to descent from a common ancestor with the same trait.

anaphase
The third stage of mitosis, beginning when sister chromatids separate from each other and ending when a complete set of daughter chromosomes has arrived at each of the two poles of the cell.

anatomy
The study of the structure of an organism and its parts.

G-1

androgen (an'-drō-jen)
A sex hormone secreted by the gonads that promotes the development and maintenance of the male reproductive system and male body features.

anemia (uh-nē'-me-ah)
A condition in which an abnormally low amount of hemoglobin or a low number of red blood cells results in the body cells not receiving enough oxygen.

angiosperm (an'-jē-ō-sperm)
A flowering plant, which forms seeds inside a protective chamber called an ovary.

animal
A eukaryotic, multicellular, heterotrophic organism that obtains nutrients by ingestion.

annelid (an'-uh-lid)
A segmented worm. Annelids include earthworms, polychaetes, and leeches.

annual
A plant that completes its life cycle in a single year or growing season.

anorexia nervosa
An eating disorder that results in self-starvation due to an intense fear of gaining weight, even when the person is underweight.

antagonistic hormones
Two hormones that have opposite effects.

anterior pituitary (puh-tū'-uh-tār-ē)
An endocrine gland, adjacent to the hypothalamus and the posterior pituitary, that synthesizes and secretes several hormones, including some that control the activity of other endocrine glands.

anther
A sac in which pollen grains develop, located at the tip of a flower's stamen.

anthropoid (an'-thruh-poyd)
Member of a primate group made up of the apes (gibbons, orangutans, gorillas, chimpanzees, and bonobos), monkeys, and humans.

antibody (an'-tih-bod'-ē)
A protein that is secreted by a B cell and attaches to a specific kind of antigen, helping counter its effects.

anticodon (an'-tī-kō'-don)
On a tRNA molecule, a specific sequence of three nucleotides that is complementary to a codon triplet on mRNA.

antigen (an'-tuh-jen)
Any molecule that elicits a response from a lymphocyte.

anus
The digestive system opening through which undigested materials are expelled.

aphotic zone (ā-fō'-tik)
The region of an aquatic ecosystem beneath the photic zone, where light levels are too low for photosynthesis to take place.

apical dominance (ā'-pik-ul)
In a plant, the hormonal inhibition of axillary buds by a terminal bud.

apical meristem (ā'-pik-ul mer'-uh-stem)
A meristem at the tip of a plant root or in the terminal or axillary bud of a shoot.

apicomplexan (ap'-ē-kom-pleks'-un)
A type of parasitic protozoan (animal-like protist). Some apicomplexans cause serious human disease.

appendicular skeleton (ap'-en-dik'-yū-ler)
Components of the skeletal system that support the arms and legs of a land vertebrate; bones of the limbs, shoulders, and pelvis. *See also* axial skeleton.

appendix (uh-pen'-dix)
A small, finger-like extension near the union of the small and large intestines.

aqueous humor (ā'-kwē-us hyū'-mer)
A liquid in the space between the lens and cornea in the vertebrate eye that helps maintain the shape of the eye, supplies nutrients and oxygen to its tissues, and disposes of its wastes.

aqueous solution (ā'-kwē-us)
A solution in which water is the solvent.

arachnid
Member of a major arthropod group that includes spiders, scorpions, ticks, and mites.

Archaea (ar-kē'-uh)
One of two prokaryotic domains of life, the other being Bacteria.

archaean (ar-kē'-uhn)
(plural, **archaea**) An organism that is a member of the domain Archaea.

arteriole (ar-tar'-ē-ōl)
A small vessel that conveys blood between an artery and a capillary bed.

artery
A vessel that carries blood away from the heart to other parts of the body.

arthritis (ar-thrī'-tis)
A skeletal disorder characterized by inflamed joints and deterioration of the cartilage between bones.

arthropod (ar'-thruh-pod)
Member of the most diverse phylum in the animal kingdom; includes the horseshoe crab, arachnids (for example, spiders, ticks, scorpions, and mites), crustaceans (for example, crayfish, lobsters, crabs, and barnacles), millipedes, centipedes, and insects. Arthropods are characterized by a chitinous exoskeleton, molting, jointed appendages, and a body formed of distinct groups of segments.

asexual reproduction
The creation of genetically identical offspring by a single parent, without the participation of gametes (sperm and egg).

association areas
Areas of the cerbral cortex where different types of incoming sensory information are integrated.

astigmatism (uh-stig'-muh-tizm)
Blurred vision caused by a misshapen lens or cornea.

atherosclerosis (ath'-uh-rō'-skluh-rō'-sis)
A cardiovascular disease in which a buildup of fatty deposits called plaques develop on the inner walls of the arteries, narrowing the passageways through which blood can flow.

atom
The smallest unit of matter that retains the properties of an element.

atomic number
The number of protons in each atom of a particular element.

ATP Adenosine triphosphate (a-den'-ō-sēn trī-fos'-fāt)
A molecule composed of adenosine and three phosphate groups; the main energy source for cells. A molecule of ATP can be broken down to a molecule of ADP (adenosine diphosophate) and a free phosphate; this reaction releases energy that can be used for cellular work.

ATP synthase
A protein cluster, found in a cellular membrane (including the inner membrane of mitochondria, the thylakoid membrane of chloroplasts, and the plasma membrane of prokaryotes), that uses the energy of a hydrogen ion concentration gradient to make ATP from ADP. An ATP synthase provides a port through which hydrogen ions (H^+) diffuse.

atrium (ā'-trē-um)
(plural, **atria**) A heart chamber that receives blood from the body or lungs via veins.

auditory canal
The part of the outer ear that channels sound waves from the pinna, or outer body surface, to the eardrum.

autoimmune disease
An immunological disorder in which the immune system improperly attacks the body's own molecules.

autonomic nervous system (ot'-ō-nom'-ik)
A component of the peripheral nervous system of vertebrates that regulates the internal environment. The autonomic nervous system is made up of the sympathetic and parasympathetic subdivisions. The autonomic nervous system is primarily under involuntary control.

autosome
A chromosome not directly involved in determining the sex of an organism; in mammals, for example, any chromosome other than X or Y.

autotroph (ot'-ō-trōf)
An organism that makes its own food from inorganic ingredients, thereby sustaining itself without eating other organisms or their molecules. Plants, algae, and photosynthetic bacteria are autotrophs.

auxin (ok'-sin)
Any of a group of plant hormones whose chief effect is to promote the growth and development of shoots.

AV (atrioventricular) node
A region of muscle tissue between the heart's right atrium and right ventricle. It generates electrical impulses that primarily cause the ventricles to contract.

axial skeleton (ak'-sē-ul)
Components of the skeletal system that support the central trunk of the body; the skull, backbone, and rib cage in a vertebrate. *See also* appendicular skeleton.

axillary bud (ak'-sil-ār-ē)
An embryonic shoot present in the angle formed by a leaf and stem.

axon (ak'-son)
A neuron fiber that extends from the cell body and conducts signals to another neuron or to an effector cell.

B

B cell
A type of lymphocyte that matures in the bone marrow and later produces antibodies; responsible for the humoral immune response. *See also* T cell.

bacillus (buh-sil'-us)
(plural, **bacilli**) A rod-shaped prokaryotic cell.

Bacteria
One of two prokaryotic domains of life, the other being Archaea.

bacteriophage (bak-tēr'-ē-ō-fāj)
A virus that infects bacteria; also called a phage.

bacterium
(plural, **bacteria**) An organism that is a member of the domain Bacteria.

ball-and-socket joint
A joint that allows rotation and movement in several planes. Examples in humans are the shoulder and hip joints.

bark
All the tissues external to the vascular cambium in a plant with secondary growth. Bark is made up of secondary phloem, cork cambium, and cork.

basal metabolic rate (BMR)
The number of kilocalories a resting animal requires to fuel its essential body processes for a given time.

base
A substance that decreases the hydrogen ion (H⁺) concentration in a solution.

benign tumor
An abnormal mass of cells that remains at its original site in the body.

benthic realm
A seafloor or the bottom of a freshwater lake, pond, river, or stream. The benthic realm is occupied by communities of organisms known as benthos.

biennial
A plant that completes its life cycle in two years.

bilateral symmetry
An arrangement of body parts such that an organism can be divided equally by a single cut passing longitudinally through it. A bilaterally symmetric organism has mirror-image right and left sides.

bile
A solution of salts secreted by the liver that emulsifies fats and aids in their digestion.

binary fission
A means of asexual reproduction in which a parent organism, often a single cell, divides into two individuals of about equal size.

binomial
A two-part Latinized name of a species; for example, *Homo sapiens*.

biodiversity
The variety of living things; includes genetic diversity, species diversity, and ecosystem diversity.

biodiversity hot spot
A small geographic area that contains a large number of threatened or endangered species and an exceptional concentration of endemic species (those found nowhere else).

biofilm
A surface-coating cooperative colony of prokaryotes.

biogenesis
The principle that all life arises by the reproduction of preexisting life.

biogeochemical cycle
Any of the various chemical circuits occurring in an ecosystem, involving both biotic and abiotic components of the ecosystem.

biogeography
The study of the geographic distribution of species.

biological control
The intentional release of a natural enemy to attack a pest population.

biological magnification
The accumulation of persistent chemicals in the living tissues of consumers in food chains.

biological species concept
The definition of a species as a population or group of populations whose members have the potential in nature to interbreed and produce fertile offspring.

biology
The scientific study of life.

biomass
The amount, or mass, of living organic material in an ecosystem.

biome (bī'-ōm)
A major terrestrial or aquatic life zone, characterized by vegetation type in terrestrial biomes and the physical environment in aquatic biomes.

biophilia
The human desire to affiliate with other life in its many forms.

bioremediation
The use of living organisms to detoxify and restore polluted and degraded ecosystems.

biosphere
The global ecosystem; the entire portion of Earth inhabited by life; all of life and where it lives.

biotechnology
The manipulation of living organisms to perform useful tasks. Today, biotechnology often involves DNA technology.

biotic factor (bī-ot'-ik)
A living component of a biological community; any organism that is part of an individual's environment.

bipolar disorder
Depressive mental illness characterized by extreme mood swings; also called manic-depressive disorder.

bird
Member of a group of reptiles with feathers and adaptations for flight.

birth control pill
A chemical contraceptive that inhibits ovulation, retards follicular development, or alters a woman's cervical mucus to prevent sperm from entering the uterus.

bivalve
Member of a group of molluscs that includes clams, mussels, scallops, and oysters.

blade
The flattened portion of a typical leaf.

blastula (blas'-tyū-luh)
An embryonic stage that marks the end of cleavage during animal development; a hollow ball of cells in many species.

blood
A type of connective tissue with a fluid matrix called plasma in which blood cells are suspended.

blood pressure
The force that blood exerts against the walls of the blood vessels.

body cavity
A fluid-filled space separating the digestive tract from the outer body wall.

body mass index (BMI)
A ratio of weight to height used as a measure of obesity.

body segmentation
Subdivision of an animal's body into a series of repeated parts called segments.

bone
A type of connective tissue consisting of living cells held in a rigid matrix of collagen fibers embedded in calcium salts.

bony fish
A fish that has a stiff skeleton reinforced by calcium salts.

bottleneck effect
Genetic drift resulting from a drastic reduction in population size.

brain
The master control center of the central nervous system, which is involved in regulating and controlling body activity and interpreting information from the senses.

brainstem
A functional unit of the vertebrate brain, composed of the midbrain, medulla oblongata, and pons; serves mainly as a sensory filter, selecting which information reaches higher brain centers.

breathing
The ventilation of the lungs by alternate inhalation and exhalation, supplying a lung or gill with O₂-rich air or water and expelling CO₂-rich air or water.

bronchiole (brong'-kē-ōl)
A thin breathing tube that branches from a bronchus within a lung.

bronchus (*brong'-kus*)
(plural, **bronchi**) One of a pair of breathing tubes that branch from the trachea into the lungs.

bryophyte (*brī'-uh-fīt*)
A type of plant that lacks xylem and phloem; a nonvascular plant. Bryophytes include mosses and their close relatives.

budding
A means of asexual reproduction in which a new individual splits off after developing from an outgrowth of a parent.

buffer
A chemical substance that resists changes in pH by accepting hydrogen ions from or donating hydrogen ions to solutions.

bulimia
An eating disorder characterized by episodic binge eating followed by purging through induced vomiting, abuse of laxatives, or excessive exercise.

C

C₃ plant
A plant that used the Calvin cycle for the initial steps that incorporate CO_2 into organic material, forming a three-carbon compound as the first stable intermediate.

C₄ plant
A plant that prefaces the Calvin cycle with reactions that incorporate CO_2 into four-carbon compounds, the end product of which supplies CO_2 for the Calvin cycle.

calcitonin (*kal'-sih-tōn'-in*)
A peptide hormone, secreted by the thyroid gland, that lowers blood calcium level.

calorie
The amount of energy that raises the temperature of 1 g of water by 1°C.

Calvin cycle
The second of two stages of photosynthesis; a cyclic series of chemical reactions that occur in the stroma of a chloroplast, using the carbon in CO_2 and the ATP and NADPH produced by the light reactions to make the energy-rich sugar molecule G3P, which is later used to produce glucose.

CAM plant
A plant that uses the following adaptation for photosynthesis in arid conditions: Carbon dioxide entering open stomata during the night is converted to organic compounds, which release CO_2 for the Calvin cycle during the day, when stomata are closed.

cancer
A malignant growth or tumor caused by abnormal and uncontrolled cell division.

cap
Extra nucleotides added to the beginning of an RNA transcript in the nucleus of a eukaryotic cell.

capillary (*kap'-il-ar-ē*)
A microscopic blood vessel that conveys blood between an artery and a vein or between an arteriole and a venule; enables the exchange of nutrients and dissolved gases between the blood and interstitial fluid.

carbohydrate (*kar'-bō-hī'-drāt*)
A biological molecule consisting of a simple sugar (a monosaccharide), two monosaccharides joined into a double sugar (a disaccharide), or a chain of monosaccharides (a polysaccharide).

carbon fixation
The initial incorporation of carbon from CO_2 into organic compounds by autotrophic organisms such as photosynthetic plants, algae, or bacteria.

carbon footprint
The amount of greenhouse gas emitted as a result of the actions of a person, nation, or other entity.

carcinogen (*kar-sin'-uh-jin*)
A cancer-causing agent, either high-energy radiation (such as X-rays or UV light) or a chemical.

cardiac cycle (*kar'-dē-ak*)
The alternating contractions and relaxations of the heart.

cardiac muscle
Striated muscle that forms the contractile tissue of the heart.

cardiovascular disease
(*kar'-dē-ō-vas'-kyū-ler*)
A set of diseases of the heart and blood vessels.

cardiovascular system
A closed circulatory system, found in vertebrates, with a heart and a branching network of arteries, capillaries, and veins.

carnivore
An animal that mainly eats other animals. *See also* herbivore; omnivore.

carpel (*kar'-pul*)
The egg-producing part of a flower, consisting of a stalk with an ovary at the base and a stigma, which traps pollen, at the tip.

carrier
An individual who is heterozygous for a recessively inherited disorder and who therefore does not show symptoms of that disorder.

carrying capacity
The maximum population size that a particular environment can sustain.

cartilage (*kar'-ti-lij*)
A type of connective tissue consisting of living cells embedded in a rubbery matrix with collagen fibers.

cartilaginous fish (*kar-ti-laj'-uh-nus*)
A fish that has a flexible skeleton made of cartilage.

cell body
The part of a cell, such as a neuron, that houses the nucleus and other organelles.

cell cycle
An ordered sequence of events (including interphase and the mitotic phase) that extends from the time a eukaryotic cell is first formed from a dividing parent cell until its own division into two cells.

cell cycle control system
A cyclically operating set of proteins that triggers and coordinates events in the eukaryotic cell cycle.

cell division
The reproduction of a cell.

cell junction
A structure that connects animal cells to one another in a tissue.

cell plate
A membranous disk that forms across the midline of a dividing plant cell. During cytokinesis, the cell plate grows outward, accumulating more cell wall material and eventually fusing into a new cell wall.

cell theory
The theory that all living things are composed of cells and that all cells come from other cells.

cell wall
A protective layer external to the plasma membrane in plant cells, bacteria, fungi, and some protists; protects the cell and helps maintain its shape.

cell-mediated immune response
The type of adaptive immune response that involves T cells, lymphocytes that fight body cells infected with pathogens. *See also* humoral immune response.

cellular differentiation
Specialization in the structure and function of cells that occurs during the development of an organism; results from selective activation and deactivation of the cells' genes.

cellular respiration
The aerobic harvesting of energy from food molecules; the energy-releasing chemical breakdown of food molecules, such as glucose, and the storage of potential energy in a form that cells can use to perform work; involves glycolysis, the citric acid cycle, the electron transport chain, and chemiosmosis.

cellular slime mold
A type of protist that has unicellular amoeboid cells and a multicellular reproductive body in its life cycle.

cellulose (*sel'-yū-lōs*)
A large polysaccharide composed of many glucose monomers linked into cable-like fibrils that provide structural support in plant cell walls. Because cellulose cannot be digested by animals, it acts as fiber, or roughage, in the diet.

centipede
A carnivorous terrestrial arthropod that has one pair of long legs for each of its numerous body segments, with the front pair modified as poison claws.

central nervous system (CNS)
The integration and command center of the nervous system; the brain and, in vertebrates, the spinal cord.

central vacuole (*vak'-yū-ōl*)
A membrane-enclosed sac occupying most of the interior of a mature plant cell, having diverse roles in reproduction, growth, and development.

centromere (sen'-trō-mer)
The region of a chromosome where two sister chromatids are joined and where spindle microtubules attach during mitosis and meiosis. The centromere divides at the onset of anaphase during mitosis and anaphase II of meiosis.

centrosome (sen'-trō-sōm)
Material in the cytoplasm of a eukaryotic cell that gives rise to microtubules; important in mitosis and meiosis; functions as a microtubule-organizing center.

cephalopod
Member of a group of molluscs that includes squids and octopuses.

cerebellum (sār'-ruh-bel'-um)
Part of the vertebrate hindbrain; mainly a planning center that interacts closely with the cerebrum in coordinating body movement.

cerebral cortex (suh-rē'-brul kor'-teks)
A highly folded layer of tissue that forms the surface of the cerebrum. In humans, it contains integrating centers for higher brain functions, such as reasoning, speech, language, and imagination.

cerebrospinal fluid
(suh-rē'-brō-spī'-nul)
Fluid that surrounds, cushions, and nourishes the brain and spinal cord and protects them from infection.

cerebrum (suh-rē'-brum)
The largest, most sophisticated, and most dominant part of the vertebrate forebrain, made up of right and left cerebral hemispheres. The cerebrum contains the cerebral cortex.

cervix (ser'-viks)
The narrow neck at the bottom of the uterus, which opens into the vagina.

chaparral (shap-uh-ral')
A terrestrial biome limited to coastal regions where cold ocean currents circulate offshore, creating mild, rainy winters and long, hot, dry summers; also known as the Mediterranean biome. Chaparral vegetation is adapted to fire.

character
A heritable feature that varies among individuals within a population, such as flower color in pea plants.

charophyte (kār'-uh-fīt')
A member of the green algal group that shares features with land plants. Charophytes are considered the closest relatives of land plants; modern charophytes and modern plants likely evolved from a common ancestor.

chemical bond
An attraction between two atoms resulting from a sharing of outer-shell electrons or the presence of opposite charges on the atoms. The bonded atoms gain complete outer electron shells.

chemical cycling
The use and reuse of chemical elements such as carbon within an ecosystem.

chemical energy
Energy stored in the chemical bonds of molecules; a form of potential energy.

chemical reaction
A process leading to chemical changes in matter, involving the making and/or breaking of chemical bonds.

chemoreceptor (kē'-mō-rē-sep'-ter)
A sensory receptor that detects chemical changes within the body or a specific kind of chemical in the external environment; chemoreceptors are involved in our senses of taste and smell.

chemotherapy (kē'-mo-ther'-uh-pē)
Treatment for cancer in which drugs are administered to disrupt cell division of the cancer cells.

chiasma (kī-az'-muh)
(plural, **chiasmata**) The microscopically visible site where crossing over has occurred between chromatids of homologous chromosomes during prophase I of meiosis.

chlamydia
A common sexually transmitted disease caused by a bacterial infection. Its primary symptoms are genital discharge and burning during urination. It is easily treatable with antibiotics.

chlorophyll (klor'-ō-fil)
A light-absorbing pigment in chloroplasts that plays a central role in converting solar energy to chemical energy.

chlorophyll a (klor'-ō-fil ā)
A green pigment in chloroplasts that participates directly in the light reactions.

chloroplast (klō'-rō-plast)
An organelle found in plants and photosynthetic protists. Enclosed by two concentric membranes, a chloroplast absorbs sunlight and uses it to power the synthesis of organic food molecules (sugars).

chordate (kor'-dāt)
An animal that at some point during its development has a dorsal, hollow nerve cord, a notochord, pharyngeal slits, and a post-anal tail. Chordates include lancelets, tunicates, and vertebrates.

chorion (kor'-ē-on)
In animals, the outermost membrane protecting an embryo. In mammals, the chorion becomes part of the placenta.

chorionic villus (kor'-ē-on'-ik vil'-us)
(plural, **villi**) An outgrowth of the chorion, containing embryonic blood vessels. As part of the placenta, chorionic villi absorb nutrients and oxygen from the mother's bloodstream and pass wastes into the mother's bloodstream.

chromatin (krō'-muh-tin)
The combination of DNA and proteins that constitutes chromosomes; often used to refer to the diffuse, very extended form taken by the chromosomes when a eukaryotic cell is not dividing.

chromosome (krō'-muh-sōm)
A gene-carrying structure found in the nucleus of a eukaryotic cell and most visible during mitosis and meiosis; also, the main gene-carrying structure of a prokaryotic cell. Each chromosome consists of one very long threadlike DNA molecule and associated proteins. See also chromatin.

chromosome theory of inheritance
A basic principle in biology stating that genes are located on chromosomes and that the behavior of chromosomes during meiosis accounts for inheritance patterns.

chyme (kīm)
A mixture of recently swallowed food and gastric juice.

ciliate (sil'-ē-it)
A type of protozoan (animal-like protist) that moves and feeds by means of cilia.

cilium (sil'-ē-um)
(plural, **cilia**) A short appendage that propels some protists through the water and moves fluids across the surface of many tissue cells in animals.

circulatory system
The organ system that transports materials such as nutrients, O_2, and hormones to body cells and transports CO_2 and other wastes from body cells.

citric acid cycle
The metabolic cycle that is fueled by acetyl CoA formed after glycolysis in cellular respiration. Chemical reactions in the cycle complete the metabolic breakdown of glucose molecules to carbon dioxide. The cycle occurs in the matrix of mitochondria and supplies most of the NADH molecules that carry energy to the electron transport chains. Also referred to as the Krebs cycle.

clade
An ancestral species and all its descendants—a distinctive branch in the tree of life.

cladistics (kluh-dis'-tiks)
The study of evolutionary history; specifically, an approach to systematics in which organisms are grouped by common ancestry.

class
In classification, the taxonomic category above order.

cleavage (klē-vij)
(1) Cytokinesis in animal cells and in some protists, characterized by pinching in of the plasma membrane. (2) In animal development, the succession of rapid cell divisions without cell growth, converting the animal zygote to a ball of cells.

cleavage furrow
The first sign of cytokinesis during cell division in an animal cell; a shallow groove in the cell surface near the old metaphase plate.

clitoris (klit'-uh-ris)
An organ in the female that engorges with blood and becomes erect during sexual arousal.

clonal selection (klōn'-ul)
The production of a population of genetically identical lymphocytes (white blood cells) that recognize

and attack the specific antigen that stimulated their proliferation. Clonal selection is the mechanism that underlies the immune system's specificity and memory of antigens.

clone
As a verb, to produce genetically identical copies of a cell, organism, or DNA molecule. As a noun, the collection of cells, organisms, or molecules resulting from cloning; also (colloquially), a single organism that is genetically identical to another because it arose from the cloning of a somatic cell.

closed circulatory system
A circulatory system in which blood is confined to vessels and is kept separate from the interstitial fluid.

cnidarian (nī-dār'-ē-an)
An animal characterized by cnidocytes, radial symmetry, a gastrovascular cavity, and a polyp or medusa body form. Cnidarians includes hydras, jellies, sea anemones, and corals.

coccus (kok'-us)
(plural, **cocci**) A spherical prokaryotic cell.

cochlea (kok'-lē-uh)
A coiled tube in the inner ear that contains the hearing organ, the organ of Corti.

codominant
Expressing two different alleles of a gene in a heterozygote.

codon (kō'-don)
A three-nucleotide sequence in mRNA that specifies a particular amino acid or polypeptide termination signal; the basic unit of the genetic code.

coelom (sē'-lōm)
A body cavity completely lined by tissue derived from mesoderm.

cohesion (kō-hē'-zhun)
The attraction between molecules of the same kind.

collenchyma cell (kuh-leng'-kuh-muh)
In plants, a type of cell with a thick primary wall and no secondary wall, functioning mainly in supporting growing parts.

colon (kō'-lun)
Most of the length of the large intestine, the tubular portion of the vertebrate alimentary canal between the small intestine and the rectum;

functions mainly in water absorption and the formation of feces.

community
All the organisms inhabiting and potentially interacting in a particular area; an assemblage of populations of different species.

community ecology
The study of how interactions between species affect community structure and organization.

comparative anatomy
The comparison of body structures in different species.

competitive exclusion principle
The concept that populations of two species cannot coexist in a community if their niches are nearly identical. Using resources more efficiently and having a reproductive advantage, one of the populations will eventually outcompete and eliminate the other.

complement protein
A defensive blood protein that attacks pathogens directly as part of an innate internal defense. Complement proteins can enhance phagocytosis and cut holes in microbial membranes, causing the cells to burst.

complementary DNA (cDNA)
A DNA molecule made in vitro using mRNA as a template and the enzyme reverse transcriptase. A cDNA molecule therefore corresponds to a gene but lacks the introns present in the DNA of the genome.

complete digestive tract
A digestive tube with two openings, a mouth and an anus.

compost
A soil-like mixture of decomposed organic matter used to fertilize plants.

compound
A substance containing two or more elements in a fixed ratio; for example, table salt (NaCl) consists of one atom of the element sodium (Na) for every atom of chlorine (Cl).

concentration gradient
An increase or decrease in the density of a chemical substance within a given region. Cells often maintain concentration gradients of hydrogen ions across their membranes. When a gradient exists,

the ions or other chemical substances involved tend to move from where they are more concentrated to where they are less concentrated.

condom
A flexible sheath, usually made of thin rubber or latex, designed to cover the penis during sexual intercourse for contraceptive purposes or as a means of preventing sexually transmitted diseases.

cone
(1) In vertebrates, a photoreceptor cell in the retina, stimulated by bright light and enabling color vision. (2) In conifers, a reproductive structure bearing pollen or ovules.

conifer (kon'-uh-fer)
A gymnosperm, or naked-seed plant, most of which produce cones.

coniferous forest (kō-nif'-rus)
A terrestrial biome characterized by conifers, cone-bearing evergreen trees.

connective tissue
Tissue consisting of cells held in an abundant extracellular matrix.

conservation biology
A goal-oriented science that seeks to understand and counter the loss of biodiversity.

conservation of energy
The principle that energy can neither be created nor destroyed.

consumer
An organism that obtains its food by eating plants or by eating animals that have eaten plants.

contraception
The deliberate prevention of pregnancy.

controlled experiment
A component of the process of science whereby a scientist carries out two parallel tests, an experimental test and a control test. The experimental test differs from the control by one factor, the variable.

convergent evolution
The evolution of similar features in different evolutionary lineages, which can result from living in very similar environments.

coral reef
Tropical marine biome characterized by hard skeletal structures secreted primarily by the resident cnidarians.

cork
The outermost protective layer of a plant's bark, produced by the cork cambium.

cork cambium
Meristem tissue that produces cork cells during secondary growth of a plant.

cornea (kor'-nē-uh)
The transparent front portion of the sclera that admits light into the vertebrate eye.

coronary artery (kor'-uh-nār-ē)
A large blood vessel that conveys blood from the aorta to the tissues of the heart.

corpus callosum (kor'-pus kuh-lō'-sum)
A thick band of nerve fibers that connects the right and left cerebral hemispheres, enabling them to process information together.

corpus luteum (kor'-pus lū'-tē-um)
A small body of endocrine tissue that develops from an ovarian follicle after ovulation. The corpus luteum secretes progesterone and estrogen during pregnancy.

cortex
In plants, the ground tissue system of a root, which stores food and absorbs water and minerals that have passed through the epidermis. See also adrenal cortex; cerebral cortex.

corticosteroid
One of a family of steroid hormones, including glucocorticoids, synthesized and secreted by the adrenal cortex.

cotyledon (kot'-uh-lē'-don)
The first leaf that appears on an embryo of a flowering plant; a seed leaf. Monocot embryos have one cotyledon; dicot embryos have two.

covalent bond (kō-vā'-lent)
An attraction between atoms that share one or more pairs of outer-shell electrons.

crista (kris'-tuh)
(plural, **cristae**) A fold of the inner membrane of a mitochondrion. Enzyme molecules embedded in cristae make ATP.

cross
The cross-fertilization of two different varieties of an organism or of two different species; also called hybridization.

crossing over
The exchange of segments between chromatids of homologous chromosomes during prophase I of meiosis.

crustacean
Member of a major arthropod group that includes lobsters, crayfish, crabs, shrimps, and barnacles.

cryptic coloration
Adaptive coloration that makes an organism difficult to spot against its background.

culture
The accumulated knowledge, customs, beliefs, arts, and other human products that are socially transmitted over the generations.

cuticle (kyū'-tuh-kul)
(1) In animals, a tough, nonliving outer layer of the skin. (2) In plants, a waxy coating on the surface of stems and leaves that helps retain water.

cystic fibrosis (sis'-tik fī-brō'-sis)
A genetic disease that occurs in people with two copies of a certain recessive allele; characterized by an excessive secretion of mucus and consequent vulnerability to infection; fatal if untreated.

cytokinesis (sī'-tō-kuh-nē'-sis)
The division of the cytoplasm to form two separate daughter cells. Cytokinesis usually occurs during telophase of mitosis, and the two processes (mitosis and cytokinesis) make up the mitotic (M) phase of the cell cycle.

cytokinin (sī'-tō-kī'-nin)
Any of a family of plant hormones that promote cell division, retard aging in flowers and fruits, and may counter the effects of auxins in regulating plant growth and development.

cytoplasm (sī'-tō-plaz'-um)
Everything inside a eukaryotic cell between the plasma membrane and the nucleus; consists of a semifluid medium and organelles; can also refer to the interior of a prokaryotic cell.

cytosine (C) (sī'-tuh-sēn)
A single-ring nitrogenous base found in DNA and RNA.

cytoskeleton
A meshwork of fine fibers in the cytoplasm of a eukaryotic cell; includes microfilaments, intermediate filaments, and microtubules.

cytosol (sī'-tuh-sol)
The fluid part of the cytoplasm, in which organelles are suspended.

cytotoxic T cell (sī'-tō-tok'-sik)
A type of lymphocyte that directly attacks body cells infected by pathogens.

D

decomposer
An organism that secretes enzymes that digest molecules in organic material and convert them to inorganic form.

dehydration (dē-hī-drā'-shun)
A chemical process in which a polymer forms when monomers are linked by the removal of water molecules. One molecule of water is removed for each pair of monomers linked. A dehydration reaction is essentially the reverse of a hydrolysis reaction.

denaturation (dē-nā'-chuh-rā'-shun)
A process in which a protein unravels, losing its specific conformation and hence its function; can be caused by changes in pH or salt concentration or by high temperature; also refers to the separation of the two strands of the DNA double helix, caused by similar factors.

dendrite (den'-drīt)
A short, branched neuron fiber that receives signals and conveys them from its tip inward, toward the rest of the neuron.

density-dependent factor
A limiting factor whose effects intensify with increasing population density.

density-independent factor
A limiting factor whose occurrence and effects are not related to population density.

dermal tissue system
In plants, the tissue system that forms an outer protective covering.

desert
A terrestrial biome characterized by low and unpredictable rainfall (less than 30 cm per year).

determinate growth
Termination of growth after reaching a certain size, as in most animals. *See also* indeterminate growth.

detritivore (di-trī'-tuh-vor)
An organism that consumes dead organic matter (detritus).

detritus (di-trī'-tus)
Dead organic matter.

diabetes mellitus (dī-uh-bē'-tis mel'-uh-tus)
A human hormonal disease in which body cells cannot absorb enough glucose from the blood and become energy starved. Body fats and proteins are then consumed for their energy. Insulin-dependent diabetes results when the pancreas does not produce insulin. Non-insulin-dependent diabetes results when body cells fail to respond to insulin. A third type of diabetes, called gestational diabetes, can affect any pregnant woman, even one who has never shown symptoms of diabetes before.

dialysis (dī-al'-uh-sis)
Separation and disposal of metabolic wastes from the blood by mechanical means; an artificial method of performing the functions of the kidneys.

diaphragm (dī'-uh-fram)
(1) The sheet of muscle separating the chest cavity from the abdominal cavity in mammals. Its contraction expands the chest cavity, and its relaxation reduces it. (2) A dome-shaped rubber cap that covers a woman's cervix, serving as a barrier method of contraception.

diastole (dī-as'-tuh-lē)
The stage of the cardiac cycle in which the heart muscle is relaxed, allowing the chambers to fill with blood. *See also* systole.

diatom (dī'-uh-tom)
A unicellular photosynthetic alga with a unique glassy cell wall containing silica.

dicot (dī'-kot)
A flowering plant whose embryos have two seed leaves, or cotyledons.

diffusion
The spontaneous movement of particles of any kind down a concentration gradient; that is, movement of particles from where they are more concentrated to where they are less concentrated.

digestion
The mechanical and chemical breakdown of food into molecules small enough for the body to absorb; the second stage of food processing, following ingestion.

digestive tract
A digestive compartment with two openings: a mouth for the entrance of food and an anus for the exit of undigested wastes. Most animals, including humans, have a digestive tract, more commonly called an alimentary canal.

dihybrid cross (dī'-hī'-brid)
A mating of individuals differing at two genetic loci.

dinoflagellate (dī'-nō-flaj'-uh-let)
A unicellular photosynthetic alga with two flagella situated in perpendicular grooves in cellulose plates covering the cell.

diploid (dip'-loid)
Containing two sets of chromosomes (pairs of homologous chromosomes) in each cell, one set inherited from each parent; referring to a 2n cell.

directional selection
Natural selection that acts in favor of the individuals at one end of a phenotypic range.

disaccharide (dī-sak'-uh-rīd)
A sugar molecule consisting of two monosaccharides linked by a dehydration reaction.

discovery science
The process of scientific inquiry that focuses on using observations to describe nature. *See also* hypothesis-driven science.

disruptive selection
Natural selection that favors extreme over intermediate phenotypes.

disturbance
In an ecological sense, a force that damages a biological community, at least temporarily, by destroying organisms and altering the availability of resources needed by organisms in the community. Disturbances such as fires and storms play a pivotal role in structuring many biological communities.

DNA Deoxyribonucleic acid (*dē-ok'-si-rī'-bō-nū-klā'-ik*)
The genetic material that organisms inherit from their parents; a double-stranded helical macromolecule consisting of nucleotide monomers with deoxyribose sugar, a phosphate group, and the nitrogenous bases adenine (A), cytosine (C), guanine (G), and thymine (T). *See also* gene.

DNA ligase (*lī'-gās*)
An enzyme, essential for DNA replication, that catalyzes the covalent bonding of adjacent DNA nucleotides; used in genetic engineering to paste a specific piece of DNA containing a gene of interest into a bacterial plasmid or other vector.

DNA microarray
A glass slide containing thousands of different kinds of single-stranded DNA fragments arranged in an array (grid). Tiny amounts of DNA fragments, representing different genes, are attached to the glass slide. These fragments are tested for hybridization with various samples of cDNA molecules, thereby measuring the expression of thousands of genes at one time.

DNA polymerase (*puh-lim'-er-ās*)
An enzyme that assembles DNA nucleotides into polynucleotides using a preexisting strand of DNA as a template.

DNA profiling
A procedure that analyzes an individual's unique collection of genetic markers using PCR and gel electrophoresis. DNA profiling can be used to determine whether two samples of genetic material were derived from the same individual.

DNA technology
Methods used to study or manipulate genetic material.

domain
A taxonomic category above the kingdom level. The three domains of life are Archaea, Bacteria, and Eukarya.

dominant allele
In a heterozygote, the allele that determines the phenotype with respect to a particular gene.

dorsal, hollow nerve cord
One of the four hallmarks of chordates; the chordate brain and spinal cord.

double circulation system
A circulation scheme with separate pulmonary and systemic circuits.

double fertilization
In flowering plants, the formation of both a zygote and a cell with a triploid nucleus, which develops into the endosperm.

double helix
The form assumed by DNA in living cells, referring to its two adjacent polynucleotide strands wound into a spiral shape.

Down syndrome
A human genetic disorder resulting from a condition called trisomy 21, the presence of an extra chromosome 21; characterized by heart and respiratory defects and varying degrees of mental retardation.

duodenum (*dū-ō-dē'-num*)
The first portion of the vertebrate small intestine after the stomach, where chyme from the stomach is mixed with bile and digestive enzymes.

E

eardrum
A sheet of connective tissue separating the outer ear from the middle ear. The eardrum vibrates when stimulated by sound waves and passes the vibrations to the middle ear.

earthworm
A type of annelid, or segmented worm, that extracts nutrients from soil.

echinoderm (*ih-kī'-nuh-derm*)
Member of a group of slow-moving or stationary marine animals characterized by a rough or spiny skin, a water vascular system, typically an endoskeleton, and radial symmetry in adults. Echinoderms include sea stars, sea urchins, and sand dollars.

ecological footprint
An estimate of the amount of land required to provide the raw materials an individual or a population consumes, including food, fuel, water, housing, and waste disposal.

ecological niche
The sum of a species' use of the biotic and abiotic resources in its environment.

ecological succession
The process of biological community change resulting from disturbance; transition in the species composition of a biological community, often following a flood, fire, or volcanic eruption. *See also* primary succession; secondary succession.

ecology
The scientific study of the interactions between organisms and their environments.

ecosystem (*ē'-kō-sis-tem*)
All the organisms in a given area, along with the nonliving (abiotic) factors with which they interact; a biological community and its physical environment.

ecosystem ecology
The study of energy flow and the cycling of chemicals among the various biotic and abiotic factors in an ecosystem.

ecosystem services
Functions performed by an ecosystem that directly or indirectly benefit people.

ectotherm (*ek'-tō-therm*)
An animal that warms itself mainly by absorbing heat from its surroundings.

effector cell
A short-lived lymphocyte that has an immediate effect against a specific pathogen; a cell capable of carrying out some action in response to a command from the nervous system.

egg
A female gamete.

ejaculation (*ih-jak'-yū-lā'-shun*)
The expulsion of sperm-containing fluid (semen) from the penis.

electrocardiogram (ECG or EKG)
A record of the electrical impulses that travel through heart muscle during the cardiac cycle.

electromagnetic receptor
A sensory receptor that detects energy of different wavelengths, such as magnetism and light.

electromagnetic spectrum
The full range of radiation, from the very short wavelengths of gamma rays to the very long wavelengths of radio signals.

electron
A subatomic particle with a single unit of negative electrical charge.

One or more electrons move around the nucleus of an atom.

electron microscope (EM)
An instrument that focuses an electron beam through or onto the surface of a specimen. An electron microscope achieves a thousandfold greater resolving power than a light microscope; the most powerful EM can distinguish objects as small as 0.2 nm (2×10^{-10} m).

electron transport
A redox (oxidation-reduction) reaction in which one or more electrons are transferred to carrier molecules. A series of such reactions, called an electron transport chain, can release the energy stored in high-energy molecules such as glucose. *See also* electron transport chain.

electron transport chain
A series of electron carrier molecules that shuttle electrons during the redox reactions that release energy used to make ATP; located in the inner membrane of mitochondria, the thylakoid membrane of chloroplasts, and the plasma membrane of prokaryotes.

element
A substance that cannot be broken down into other substances by chemical means. Scientists recognize 92 chemical elements occurring in nature.

elimination
The passing of undigested material out of the digestive compartment; the fourth stage of food processing, following absorption.

embryo (*em'-brē-ō*)
A developing stage of a multicellular organism. In humans, the stage in the development of offspring from the first division of the zygote until body structures begin to appear, about the 9th week of pregnancy.

embryo sac
The female gametophyte contained in the ovule of a flowering plant.

embryonic stem cell (ES cell)
Any of the cells in the early animal embryo that differentiate during development to give rise to all the kinds of specialized cells in the body.

emerging virus
A virus that has appeared suddenly or has recently come to the attention of medical scientists.

endangered species
As defined in the U.S. Endangered Species Act, a species that is in danger of extinction throughout all or a significant portion of its range.

endemic species
A species whose distribution is limited to a specific geographic area.

endocrine gland (en'-dō-krin)
A gland that synthesizes hormone molecules and secretes them directly into the bloodstream.

endocrine system
The body's main system for internal chemical regulation, consisting of all hormone-secreting cells; cooperates with the nervous system in regulating body functions and maintaining homeostasis.

endocytosis (en'-dō-sī-tō'-sis)
The movement of materials from the external environment into the cytoplasm of a cell via vesicles or vacuoles.

endodermis
The innermost layer (a one-cell-thick cylinder) of the cortex of a plant root. The endodermis forms a selective barrier, determining which substances pass from the cortex into the vascular tissue.

endomembrane system
A network of organelles that partitions the cytoplasm of eukaryotic cells into functional compartments. Some of the organelles are structurally connected to each other, whereas others are structurally separate but functionally connected by the traffic of vesicles among them.

endometrium (en'-dō-mē'-trē-um)
The inner lining of the uterus in mammals, richly supplied with blood vessels that provide the maternal part of the placenta and nourish the developing embryo.

endoplasmic reticulum (ER) (reh-tik'-yuh-lum)
An extensive membranous network in a eukaryotic cell, continuous with the outer nuclear membrane and composed of ribosome-studded (rough) and ribosome-free (smooth) regions. *See also* rough ER; smooth ER.

endorphin (en-dōr'-fin)
A pain-inhibiting hormone produced by the anterior pituitary; also serves as a neurotransmitter.

endoskeleton
A hard interior skeleton located within the soft tissues of an animal; found in all vertebrates and a few invertebrates (such as echinoderms).

endosperm
In flowering plants, a nutrient-rich mass formed by the union of a sperm cell with the diploid central cell of the embryo sac during double fertilization; provides nourishment to the developing embryo in the seed.

endospore
A thick-coated, protective cell produced within a prokaryotic cell exposed to harsh conditions.

endosymbiosis (en'-dō-sim-bē-ō'-sis)
Symbiotic relationship in which one species resides within another species. The mitochondria and chloroplasts of eukaryotic cells probably evolved from symbiotic associations between small prokaryotic cells living inside larger ones.

endotherm
An animal that derives most of its body heat from its own metabolism.

endotoxin
A poisonous component of the outer membrane of certain bacteria.

energy
The capacity to cause change, or to move matter in a direction it would not move if left alone.

energy flow
The passage of energy through the components of an ecosystem.

enhancer
A eukaryotic DNA sequence that helps stimulate the transcription of a gene at some distance from it. An enhancer functions by means of a transcription factor called an activator, which binds to it and then to the rest of the transcription apparatus. *See also* silencer.

entropy (en'-truh-pē)
A measure of disorder, or randomness. One form of disorder is heat, which is random molecular motion.

enzyme (en'-zīm)
A protein that serves as a biological catalyst, changing the rate of a chemical reaction without itself being changed in the process.

enzyme inhibitor
A chemical that interferes with an enzyme's activity by changing the enzyme's shape, either by plugging up the active site or by binding to another site on the enzyme.

epinephrine (ep'-uh-nef'-rin)
An amine hormone (also called adrenaline) that is secreted by the adrenal medulla and that prepares body organs for "fight or flight"; also serves as a neurotransmitter.

epithelial tissue (ep'-uh-thē'-lē-ul)
A sheet of tightly packed cells lining organs and cavities; also called epithelium.

epithelium
(plural, **epithelia**) *See* epithelial tissue.

equilibrial life history (ē-kwi-lib'-rē-ul)
The pattern of reaching sexual maturity slowly and producing few offspring but caring for the young; often seen in long-lived, large-bodied species.

erythrocyte (ih-rith'-ruh-sīt)
See red blood cell.

esophagus (ih-sof'-uh-gus)
The channel through which food passes in a digestive tube, connecting the pharynx to the stomach.

essential amino acid
Any amino acid that an animal cannot synthesize itself and must obtain from food. Eight amino acids are essential for the human adult.

essential element
In plants, a chemical element required for the plant to complete its life cycle (to grow from a seed and produce another generation of seeds).

essential fatty acid
An unsaturated fatty acid that animals need but cannot make.

essential nutrient
A substance that an organism must absorb in preassembled form because it cannot synthesize the nutrient from any other material. Humans require vitamins, minerals, essential amino acids, and essential fatty acids.

estrogen (es'-trō-jen)
One of several chemically similar sex hormones secreted by the gonads. Estrogen maintains the female reproductive system and promotes the development of female body features.

estuary (es'-chuh-wār-ē)
The area where a freshwater stream or river merges with seawater.

ethylene
A gas that functions as a hormone in plants, triggering aging responses such as fruit ripening and leaf drop.

eudicot (yū-dī'-kot)
Member of a group consisting of the vast majority of flowering plants that have two cotyledons (embryonic seed leaves).

Eukarya (yū-kār'-yuh)
The domain of eukaryotes, organisms made up of eukaryotic cells; includes all of the protists, plants, fungi, and animals.

eukaryote (yū-kār'-ē-ōt)
An organism characterized by eukaryotic cells. *See also* eukaryotic cell.

eukaryotic cell (yū-kār-ē-ot'-ik)
A type of cell that has a membrane-enclosed nucleus and other membrane-enclosed organelles. All organisms except bacteria and archaea are composed of eukaryotic cells.

Eustachian tube (yū-stā'-shun)
An air passage between the middle ear and throat that equalizes air pressure on either side of the eardrum.

eutherian (yū-thēr'-ē-un)
See placental mammal.

evaporative cooling
A property of water whereby a body becomes cooler as water evaporates from it.

evo-devo
Evolutionary developmental biology, which studies the evolution of developmental processes in multicellular organisms.

evolution
Descent with modification; genetic change in a population or species over generations; the heritable changes that have produced Earth's diversity of organisms.

evolutionary adaptation
A population's increase in the frequency of traits suited to the environment.

evolutionary tree
A branching diagram that reflects a hypothesis about evolutionary relationships between groups of organisms.

excretion (ek-skrē'-shun)
The disposal of nitrogen-containing metabolic wastes.

exocytosis (ek'-sō-sī-tō'-sis)
The movement of materials out of the cytoplasm of a cell via membranous vesicles or vacuoles.

exon (ek'-son)
In eukaryotes, a coding portion of a gene. See also intron.

exoskeleton
A hard, external skeleton that protects an animal and provides points of attachment for muscles.

exotoxin
A poisonous protein secreted by certain bacteria.

exponential population growth
A model that describes the expansion of a population in an ideal, unlimited environment.

extracellular matrix
The meshwork that surrounds animal cells, consisting of a web of protein and polysaccharide fibers embedded in a liquid, jelly, or solid.

F

F$_1$ generation
The offspring of two parental (P generation) individuals. F$_1$ stands for first filial.

F$_2$ generation
The offspring of the F$_1$ generation. F$_2$ stands for second filial.

facilitated diffusion
The passage of a substance across a biological membrane down its concentration gradient, aided by specific transport proteins.

family
In classification, the taxonomic category above genus.

farsightedness
An inability to focus on close objects; occurs when the eyeball is shorter

than normal and the focal point of the lens is behind the retina; also called hyperopia.

fat
A large lipid molecule made from an alcohol called glycerol and three fatty acids; a triglyceride. Most fats function as energy-storage molecules.

feces
The wastes of the digestive tube.

fermentation
The anaerobic harvest of food by some cells.

fern
Any of a group of seedless vascular plants.

fertilization
The union of a haploid sperm cell with a haploid egg cell, producing a zygote.

fertilizer
A compound applied to the soil to promote plant growth.

fetus (fē'-tus)
A developing human from the 9th week of pregnancy until birth. The fetus has all the major structures of an adult.

fever
An abnormally high internal body temperature, usually the result of an infection.

fibrin (fī'-brin)
The activated form of the blood-clotting protein fibrinogen, which aggregates into threads that form the fabric of a blood clot.

fibrinogen (fī-brin'-uh-jen)
The plasma protein that is activated to form a clot when a blood vessel is injured.

fibrous connective tissue
A dense tissue with large numbers of collagen fibers organized into parallel bundles. This is the dominant tissue in tendons and ligaments.

filtrate
Fluid extracted by the excretory system from the blood or body cavity. The excretory system produces urine from the filtrate after extracting valuable solutes from it and concentrating it.

filtration
In the vertebrate kidney, the extraction of water and small solutes, including metabolic wastes, from the blood by the nephrons.

fission
A means of asexual reproduction whereby a parent separates into two or more genetically identical individuals of about equal size.

flagellate (flaj'-uh-lit)
A protozoan (animal-like protist) that moves by means of one or more flagella.

flagellum (fluh-jel'-um)
(plural, **flagella**) A long appendage that propels protists through the water and moves fluids across the surface of many tissue cells in animals. A cell may have one or more flagella.

flatworm
A bilateral animal with a thin, flat body form, a gastrovascular cavity with a single opening, and no body cavity. Flatworms include planarians, flukes, and tapeworms.

flower
In an angiosperm, a short stem with four sets of modified leaves, bearing structures that function in sexual reproduction.

fluid mosaic
A description of membrane structure, depicting a cellular membrane as a mosaic of diverse protein molecules embedded in a fluid bilayer of phospholipid molecules.

follicle (fol'-uh-kul)
A cluster of cells surrounding, protecting, and nourishing a developing egg cell in the ovary. The follicle also secretes estrogen.

food chain
The sequence of food transfers between the trophic levels of a community, beginning with the producers.

food web
A network of interconnecting food chains.

foram
A marine protozoan (animal-like protist) that secretes a shell and extends pseudopodia through pores in its shell.

forensics
The scientific analysis of evidence for crime scene investigations and other legal proceedings.

fossil
A preserved imprint or remains of an organism that lived in the past.

fossil fuel
An energy deposit formed from the fossilized remains of long-dead plants and animals.

fossil record
The ordered sequence of fossils as they appear in the rock layers, marking the passing of geologic time.

founder effect
The genetic drift resulting from the establishment of a small, new population whose gene pool differs from that of the parent population.

fruit
A ripened, thickened ovary of a flower, which protects dormant seeds and aids in their dispersal.

functional group
A group of atoms that form the chemically reactive part of an organic molecule. A particular functional group usually behaves similarly in different chemical reactions.

fungus
(plural, **fungi**) A chemo-heterotrophic eukaryote that digests its food externally and absorbs the resulting small nutrient molecules. Most fungi consist of a netlike mass of filaments called hyphae. Molds, mushrooms, and yeasts are examples of fungi.

G

gallbladder
An organ that stores bile and releases it as needed into the small intestine.

gametangium (gam'-uh-tan'-jē-um)
(plural, **gametangia**) A reproductive organ that houses and protects the gametes of a plant.

gamete (gam'-ēt)
A sex cell; a haploid egg or sperm. The union of two gametes of opposite sex (fertilization) produces a zygote.

gametogenesis
The creation of gametes within the gonads.

gametophyte (guh-mē'-tō-fīt)
The multicellular haploid form in the life cycle of organisms undergoing alternation of generations; results from a union of spores and mitotically produces haploid

gametes that unite and grow into the sporophyte generation.

gastric juice
The collection of fluids secreted by the epithelium lining the stomach.

gastropod
Member of the largest group of molluscs, including snails and slugs.

gastrovascular cavity
A digestive compartment with a single opening that serves as both the entrance for food and the exit for undigested wastes; may also function in circulation, body support, and gas exchange. Jellies and hydras are examples of animals with a gastrovascular cavity.

gastrula (*gas'-trū-luh*)
The embryonic stage resulting from gastrulation in animal development. Most animals have a gastrula made up of three layers of cells: ectoderm, endoderm, and mesoderm.

gastrulation (*gas'-trū-lā'-shun*)
The phase of embryonic development that transforms the blastula (blastocyst in mammals) into a gastrula. Gastrulation adds more cells to the embryo and sorts the cells into distinct cell layers.

gel electrophoresis (*jel' e-lek'-trō-fōr-ē'-sis*)
A technique for sorting macromolecules. A mixture of molecules is placed on a gel between a positively charged electrode and a negatively charged one; negative charges on the molecules are attracted to the positive electrode, and the molecules migrate toward that electrode. The molecules separate in the gel according to their rates of migration.

gene
A unit of inheritance in DNA (or RNA, in some viruses) consisting of a specific nucleotide sequence that programs the amino acid sequence of a polypeptide. Most of the genes of a eukaryote are located in its chromosomal DNA; a few are carried by the DNA of mitochondria and chloroplasts.

gene cloning
The production of multiple copies of a gene.

gene expression
The process whereby genetic information flows from genes to proteins; the flow of genetic information from the genotype to the phenotype: DNA → RNA → protein.

gene flow
The gain or loss of alleles from a population by the movement of individuals or gametes into or out of the population.

gene pool
All the genes in a population at any one time.

gene regulation
The turning on and off of specific genes within a living organism.

genetic code
The set of rules giving the correspondence between nucleotide triplets (codons) in mRNA and amino acids in protein.

genetic drift
A change in the gene pool of a population due to chance.

genetic engineering
The direct manipulation of genes for practical purposes.

genetic recombination
The production of offspring with gene combinations that differ from that found in either parent.

genetically modified (GM) organism
An organism that has acquired one or more genes by artificial means. If the gene is from another organism, typically of another species, the recombinant organism is also known as a transgenic organism.

genetics
The scientific study of heredity (inheritance).

genital herpes
A common sexually transmitted disease caused by a virus. The primary symptom is sores on the genitalia. Although outbreaks can be controlled with medication, genital herpes is incurable.

genomic library (*juh-nō'-mik*)
The entire collection of DNA segments from an organism's genome. Each segment is usually carried by a plasmid or phage.

genomics
The study of whole sets of genes and their interactions.

genotype (*jē'-nō-tīp*)
The genetic makeup of an organism.

genus (*jē'-nus*)
(plural, **genera**) In classification, the taxonomic category above species; the first part of a species' binomial; for example, *Homo*.

geologic time scale
A time scale established by geologists that reflects a consistent sequence of geologic periods, grouped into four divisions: Precambrian, Paleozoic, Mesozoic, and Cenozoic.

germinate
To initiate growth, as in a plant seed.

gestation (*jes-tā'-shun*)
Pregnancy; the state of carrying developing young within the female reproductive tract.

gibberellin (*jib'-uh-rel'-in*)
Any of a family of plant hormones that trigger the germination of seeds and interact with auxins in regulating growth and fruit development.

gill
An extension of the body surface of an aquatic animal, specialized for gas exchange and/or suspension feeding.

glucagon (*glū'-kuh-gon*)
A protein hormone, secreted by islet cells in the pancreas, that raises the level of glucose in the blood.

glucocorticoid (*glū'-kuh-kor'-tih-koyd*)
A corticosteroid hormone, secreted by the adrenal cortex, that increases the blood glucose level and helps maintain the body's response to long-term stress.

glycogen (*glī'-kō-jen*)
A complex, extensively branched polysaccharide made up of many glucose monomers; serves as an energy-storage molecule in liver and muscle cells.

glycolysis (*glī-kol'-uh-sis*)
The multistep chemical breakdown of a molecule of glucose into two molecules of pyruvic acid; the first stage of cellular respiration in all organisms; occurs in the cytoplasmic fluid.

Golgi apparatus (*gol'-jē*)
An organelle in eukaryotic cells consisting of stacks of membranous sacs that modify, store, and ship products of the endoplasmic reticulum.

gonad
An animal sex organ that produces gametes; an ovary or a testis.

granum (*gran'-um*)
(plural, **grana**) A stack of hollow disks formed of thylakoid membrane in a chloroplast. Grana are the sites where light energy is trapped by chlorophyll and converted to chemical energy during the light reactions of photosynthesis.

gravitropism (*grav'-uh-trō'-pizm*)
A plant's directional growth in response to gravity.

green alga
One of a group of photosynthetic protists that includes unicellular, colonial, and multicellular species. Green algae are the photosynthetic protists most closely related to plants.

greenhouse effect
The warming of the atmosphere caused by CO_2, CH_4, and other gases that absorb heat radiation and slow its escape from Earth's surface.

greenhouse gas
Any of the gases in the atmosphere that absorb heat radiation, including CO_2, methane, water vapor, and synthetic chlorofluorocarbons.

ground tissue system
A tissue that makes up the bulk of a plant, filling the space between the epidermis and the vascular tissue system. The ground tissue system fulfills a variety of functions, including storage, photosynthesis, and support.

growth factor
A protein secreted by certain body cells that stimulates other cells to divide.

guanine (G) (*gwa'-nēn*)
A double-ring nitrogenous base found in DNA and RNA.

guard cell
A specialized epidermal cell in plants that regulates the size of a stoma, allowing gas exchange between the surrounding air and the photosynthetic cells in the leaf.

gymnosperm (*jim'-nō-sperm*)
A naked-seed plant. Its seed is said to be naked because it is not enclosed in an ovary.

H

habitat
A place where an organism lives; a specific environment in which an organism lives.

haploid
Containing a single set of chromosomes; referring to an *n* cell.

Hardy-Weinberg equilibrium
The condition describing a nonevolving population (one that is in genetic equilibrium).

heart
(1) The chambered muscular organ in vertebrates that pumps blood received from the veins into the arteries, thereby maintaining the flow of blood through the entire circulatory system. (2) A similarly functioning structure in invertebrates.

heart attack
Damage or death of heart muscle tissue and the resulting failure of the heart to deliver enough blood to the body.

heart murmur
A hissing sound emitted by an abnormal heart, usually caused by a defective heart valve.

heart rate
The number of heartbeats per minute.

heat
The amount of kinetic energy contained in the movement of the atoms and molecules in a body of matter. Heat is energy in its most random form.

helper T cell
A type of lymphocyte that helps activate other T cells and helps stimulate B cells to produce antibodies.

hemoglobin (*hē'-muh-glō-bin*)
An iron-containing protein in red blood cells that reversibly binds O_2 and transports it to body tissues.

hemophilia (*hē'-muh-fil'-ē-uh*)
A human genetic disease caused by a sex-linked recessive allele and characterized by excessive bleeding following injury.

herbivore
An animal that eats mainly plants, algae, or phytoplankton. *See also* carnivore; omnivore.

herbivory
The consumption of plant parts or algae by an animal.

heredity
The transmission of traits from one generation to the next.

hermaphrodite (*her-maf'-rō-dīt*)
An individual that has both female and male reproductive systems, producing both sperm and eggs.

heterotroph (*het'-er-ō-trōf*)
An organism that cannot make its own organic food molecules from inorganic ingredients and must obtain them by consuming other organisms or their organic products; a consumer or a decomposer in a food chain.

heterozygous (*het'-er-ō-zī'-gus*)
Having two different alleles for a given gene.

hinge joint
A joint that allows movement in only one plane. In humans, examples include the elbow and knee.

histamine (*his'-tuh-mēn*)
A chemical alarm signal released by injured cells that causes blood vessels to dilate during an inflammatory response.

histone (*his'-tōn*)
A small protein molecule associated with DNA and important in DNA packing in the eukaryotic chromosome.

HIV
Human immunodeficiency virus; the retrovirus that attacks the human immune system and causes AIDS.

homeostasis (*hō'-mē-ō-stā'-sis*)
The steady state of body functioning; the tendency to maintain relatively constant conditions in the internal environment even when the external environment changes.

homeotic gene (*hō'-mē-ot'-ik*)
A master control gene that determines the identity of a body structure of a developing organism, presumably by controlling the developmental fate of groups of cells. (In plants, such genes are called organ identity genes).

hominin (*hah'-mi-nin*)
Any anthropoid on the human branch of the evolutionary tree, more closely related to humans than to chimpanzees.

homologous chromosomes (*hō-mol'-uh-gus*)
The two chromosomes that make up a matched pair in a diploid cell. Homologous chromosomes are of the same length, centromere position, and staining pattern and possess genes for the same characteristics at corresponding loci. One homologous chromosome is inherited from the organism's father, the other from the mother.

homology (*hō-mol'-uh-jē*)
Anatomical similarity due to common ancestry.

homozygous (*hō'-mō-zī'-gus*)
Having two identical alleles for a given gene.

hormone
In multicellular organisms, a regulatory chemical that travels in body fluids from its production site to other sites, where target cells respond to the regulatory signal.

host
An organism that is exploited by a parasite or pathogen.

human gene therapy
A recombinant DNA procedure intended to treat disease by altering an afflicted person's genes.

Human Genome Project
An international collaborative effort that sequenced the DNA of the entire human genome.

human growth hormone (HGH)
A protein hormone, secreted by the anterior pituitary, that promotes development and growth and stimulates metabolism.

humoral immune response
The type of adaptive immune response that involves secretion of antibodies into the blood and lymph by effector B cells. These antibodies fight bacteria and viruses in body fluids. *See also* cell-mediated immune response.

Huntington's disease
A human genetic disease caused by a dominant allele; characterized by uncontrollable body movements and degeneration of the nervous system; usually fatal 10 to 20 years after the onset of symptoms.

hybrid
The offspring of parents of two different species or of two different varieties of one species; the offspring of two parents that differ in one or more inherited traits; an individual that is heterozygous for one or more pairs of genes.

hydrocarbon
A chemical compound composed only of the elements carbon and hydrogen.

hydrogen bond
A type of weak chemical bond formed when a partially positive hydrogen atom from one polar molecule is attracted to the partially negative atom in another molecule (or in another part of the same molecule).

hydrogenation
The process of converting unsaturated fats to saturated fats by adding hydrogen.

hydrolysis (*hī-drol'-uh-sis*)
A chemical process in which macromolecules are broken down by the chemical addition of water molecules to the bonds linking their monomers; an essential part of digestion. A hydrolysis reaction is the opposite of a dehydration reaction.

hydrophilic (*hī'-drō-fil'-ik*)
"Water-loving"; pertaining to polar, or charged, molecules (or parts of molecules), which are soluble in water.

hydrophobic (*hī'-drō-fō'-bik*)
"Water-fearing"; pertaining to nonpolar molecules (or parts of molecules), which do not dissolve in water.

hymen
A thin membrane that partly covers the vaginal opening in the human female and is ruptured by sexual intercourse or other vigorous activity.

hypercholesterolemia (*hī'-per-kō-les'-tur-ah-lēm'-ē-uh*)
An inherited human disease characterized by an excessively high level of cholesterol in the blood.

hypertension
Abnormally high blood pressure consisting of a persistent systolic blood pressure higher than 140 and/or diastolic blood pressure higher than 90. This condition can lead to a variety of serious cardiovascular disorders.

hypertonic

In comparing two solutions, referring to the one with the greater concentration of solutes.

hypha (*hī'-fuh*)

(plural, **hyphae**) One of many filaments making up the body of a fungus.

hypothalamus (*hī'-pō-thal'-uh-mus*)

The main control center of the endocrine system, located in the vertebrate forebrain. The hypothalamus functions in maintaining homeostasis, especially in coordinating the endocrine and nervous systems. It synthesizes hormones secreted by the posterior pituitary and regulates the secretion of hormones by the anterior pituitary.

hypothesis (*hī-poth'-uh-sis*)

(plural, **hypotheses**) A tentative explanation that a scientist proposes for a specific phenomenon that has been observed.

hypothesis-driven science

The process of scientific inquiry that uses the steps of the scientific method to answer questions about nature. *See also* discovery science; scientific method.

hypotonic

In comparing two solutions, referring to the one with the lower concentration of solutes.

I

immune system

The body's system of defenses against infectious disease.

immunodeficiency disease

An immunological disorder in which the body lacks one or more components of the immune system, making a person susceptible to infectious agents that would not ordinarily cause a problem.

impotence

The inability to maintain an erection; also called erectile dysfunction.

in vitro fertilization (IVF) (*vē'-tro*)

Uniting sperm and egg in a laboratory container, followed by the placement of a resulting early embryo into the mother's uterus.

inbreeding

The mating of close relatives.

incomplete dominance

A type of inheritance in which the phenotype of a heterozygote (*Aa*) is intermediate between the phenotypes of the two types of homozygotes (*AA* and *aa*).

indeterminate growth

Growth that continues throughout life, as in most plants. *See also* determinate growth.

induced fit

The interaction between a substrate molecule and the active site of an enzyme, which changes shape slightly to embrace the substrate and catalyze the reaction.

induction

During embryonic development, the influence of one group of cells on an adjacent group of cells.

infertility

The inability to conceive after one year of regular, unprotected sexual intercourse.

inflammatory response

An example of internal innate defense involving the release of histamine and other chemical alarm signals, which trigger increased blood flow, a local increase in white blood cells, and fluid leakage from the blood. The results include redness, heat, and swelling in the affected tissues.

ingestion

The act of eating; the first stage of food processing.

innate defense

An immune system defense that is always present in its final form and ready to act.

inner ear

One of three main regions of the human ear; includes the cochlea, which contains the organ of Corti, the hearing organ.

insect

An arthropod that usually has three body segments (head, thorax, and abdomen), three pairs of legs, and one or two pairs of wings.

insulin

A protein hormone, secreted by islet cells in the pancreas, that lowers the level of glucose in the blood.

integration

The interpretation of sensory signals and the formulation of responses within the central nervous system.

interferon (*in'-ter-fēr'-on*)

A defensive protein that is produced by virus-infected cells and that helps other cells resist viruses as part of internal innate defense.

interneuron (*in'-ter-nūr'-on*)

A nerve cell, entirely within the central nervous system, that integrates sensory signals and may relay command signals to motor neurons.

internode

The portion of a plant stem between two nodes.

interphase

The phase in the eukaryotic cell cycle when the cell is not actually dividing. During interphase, cellular metabolic activity is high, chromosomes and organelles are duplicated, and cell size may increase. Interphase accounts for 90% of the cell cycle. *See also* mitosis.

interspecific competition

Competition between populations of two or more species that require similar limited resources.

interspecific interaction

Any interaction between members of different species.

interstitial fluid (*in'-ter-stish'-ul*)

An aqueous solution that surrounds body cells and through which materials pass back and forth between the blood and the body tissues.

intertidal zone (*in'-ter-tīd'-ul*)

A shallow zone where the waters of an estuary or ocean meet land.

intraspecific competition

Competition between individuals of the same species for the same limited resources.

intron (*in'-tron*)

In eukaryotes, a nonexpressed (noncoding) portion of a gene that is excised from the RNA transcript. *See also* exon.

invasive species

A non-native species that has spread far beyond the original point of introduction and causes environmental or economic damage by colonizing and dominating suitable habitats.

invertebrate

An animal that does not have a backbone.

ion (*ī'-on*)

An atom or molecule that has gained or lost one or more electrons, thus acquiring an electrical charge.

ionic bond (*ī-on'-ik*)

An attraction between two ions with opposite electrical charges. The electrical attraction of the opposite charges holds the ions together.

iris

The colored part of the vertebrate eye, formed by the anterior portion of the pigmented layer called the choroid.

isomer (*ī'-sō-mer*)

One of two or more molecules with the same molecular formula but different structures and thus different properties.

isotonic (*ī-sō-ton'-ik*)

Having the same solute concentration as another solution.

isotope (*ī'-sō-tōp*)

A variant form of an atom. Isotopes of an element have the same number of protons and electrons but different numbers of neutrons.

K

karyotype (*kār'-ē-ō-tīp*)

A display of micrographs of the metaphase chromosomes of a cell, arranged by size and centromere position.

keystone species

A species whose impact on its community is much larger than its biomass or abundance indicates.

kilocalorie (kcal)

A quantity of heat equal to 1,000 calories. Used to measure the energy content of food, it is usually called a "Calorie."

kinetic energy (*kuh-net'-ik*)

Energy of motion. Moving matter performs work by transferring its motion to other matter, such as leg muscles pushing bicycle pedals.

kingdom

In classification, the broad taxonomic category above phylum.

L

labia majora (*lā'-bē-uh muh-jor'-uh*)
A pair of outer thickened folds of skin that protect the female genital region.

labia minora (*lā'-bē-uh mi-nor'-uh*)
A pair of inner folds of skin bordering and protecting the female genital region.

labor
A series of strong, rhythmic uterine contractions that expels a baby out of the uterus and vagina during childbirth.

lancelet
One of a group of bladelike invertebrate chordates.

landscape
A regional assemblage of interacting ecosystems.

landscape ecology
The application of ecological principles to the study of land-use patterns; the scientific study of the biodiversity of interacting ecosystems.

large intestine
The tubular portion of the vertebrate alimentary canal between the small intestine and the anus. *See also* colon.

larynx (*lār'-inks*)
The voice box, containing the vocal cords.

lateral line system
A row of sensory organs along each side of a fish's body. Sensitive to changes in water pressure, it enables a fish to detect minor vibrations in the water.

law of independent assortment
A general rule of inheritance, first proposed by Gregor Mendel, that states that when gametes form during meiosis, each pair of alleles for a particular character segregate (separate) independently of each other pair.

law of segregation
A general rule of inheritance, first proposed by Gregor Mendel, that states that the two alleles in a pair segregate (separate) into different gametes during meiosis.

leaf
The main site of photosynthesis in a plant; consists of a flattened blade and a stalk (petiole) that joins the leaf to the stem.

leech
A type of annelid, or segmented worm, that typically lives in fresh water.

lens
The disklike structure in an eye that focuses light rays onto the retina.

leukemia (*lū-kē'-mē-ah*)
Cancer of the white blood cells (leukocytes), characterized by excessive production of these cells, resulting in an abnormally high number in the blood.

leukocyte (*lū'-kō-sīt*)
See white blood cell.

lichen (*lī'-ken*)
A mutually beneficial symbiotic association between a fungus and an alga or between a fungus and a cyanobacterium.

life
The set of common characteristics that distinguish living organisms from non-living matter, including such properties and processes as order, regulation, growth and development, energy utilization, response to the environment, reproduction, and the capacity to evolve over time.

life cycle
The entire sequence of stages in the life of an organism, from the adults of one generation to the adults of the next.

life history
The traits that affect an organism's schedule of reproduction and survival.

life table
A listing of survivals and deaths in a population in a particular time period and predictions of how long, on average, an individual of a given age will live.

ligament
A type of fibrous connective tissue that joins bones together at joints.

light microscope (LM)
An optical instrument with lenses that refract (bend) visible light to magnify images and project them into a viewer's eye or onto photographic film.

light reactions
The first of two stages in photosynthesis, the steps in which solar energy is absorbed and converted to chemical energy in the form of ATP and NADPH. The light reactions power the sugar-producing Calvin cycle but produce no sugar themselves.

lignin (*lig'-nin*)
A chemical that hardens the cell walls of plants. Lignin makes up most of what we call wood.

limiting factor
An environmental factor that restricts the number of individuals that can occupy a particular habitat, thus holding population growth in check.

linkage map
A map of a chromosome showing the relative positions of genes.

linked genes
Genes located close enough together on a chromosome that they are usually inherited together.

lipid
An organic compound consisting mainly of carbon and hydrogen atoms linked by nonpolar convalent bonds and therefore mostly hydrophobic and insoluble in water. Lipids include fats, waxes, phospholipids, and steroids.

liver
The largest organ in the vertebrate body. The liver performs diverse functions, such as producing bile, preparing nitrogenous wastes for disposal, and detoxifying poisonous chemicals in the blood.

lobe-finned fish
A bony fish with strong, muscular fins supported by bones.

locus
(plural, **loci**) The particular site where a gene is found on a chromosome. Homologous chromosomes have corresponding gene loci.

logistic population growth
A model that describes population growth that decreases as population size approaches carrying capacity.

loose connective tissue
The most widespread connective tissue in the vertebrate body. It binds epithelia to underlying tissues and functions as packing material, holding organs in place.

lung
An internal sac, lined with moist epithelium, where gases are exchanged between inhaled air and the blood.

lymph
A fluid similar to interstitial fluid that circulates in the lymphatic system.

lymph node
A small organ that is located along a lymph vessel and that filters lymph.

lymphatic system (*lim-fat'-ik*)
The organ system through which lymph circulates; includes lymph vessels, lymph nodes, and several other organs. The lymphatic system helps remove toxins and pathogens from the blood and interstitial fluid and returns fluid and solutes from the interstitial fluid to the circulatory system.

lymphocyte (*lim'-fuh-sīt*)
A type of white blood cell that carries out adaptive defenses—recognizing and responding to specific invading pathogens. There are two types of lymphocytes: B cells and T cells. *See also* B cell; T cell.

lysogenic cycle (*lī-sō-jen'-ik*)
A bacteriophage reproductive cycle in which the viral genome is incorporated into the bacterial host chromosome as a prophage. New phages are not produced, and the host cell is not killed or lysed unless the viral genome leaves the host chromosome.

lysosome (*lī'-sō-sōm*)
A digestive organelle in eukaryotic cells; contains enzymes that digest the cell's food and wastes.

lytic cycle (*lit'-ik*)
A viral reproductive cycle resulting in the release of new viruses by lysis (breaking open) of the host cell.

M

macroevolution
Evolutionary change above the species level, including the origin of evolutionary novelty and new taxonomic groups and the impact of mass extinctions on the diversity of life and its subsequent recovery.

macromolecule

A giant molecule formed by joining smaller molecules. Examples of macromolecules include proteins, polysaccharides, and nucleic acids.

macronutrient

A chemical element that an organism must obtain in relatively large amounts. *See also* micronutrient.

magnification

An increase in the apparent size of an object.

major depression

Depressive mental illness characterized by persistent sadness and loss of interest in pleasurable activities.

malignant tumor

An abnormal tissue mass that spreads into neighboring tissue and to other parts of the body; a cancerous tumor.

malnutrition

The absence of one or more essential nutrients from the diet.

mammal

Member of a class of endothermic amniotes that possesses mammary glands and hair.

mantle

In molluscs, the outgrowth of the body surface that drapes over the animal. The mantle produces the shell and forms the mantle cavity.

marsupial (*mar-sū´-pē-ul*)

A pouched mammal, such as a kangaroo, opossum, or koala. Marsupials give birth to embryonic offspring that complete development while housed in a pouch and attached to nipples on the mother's abdomen.

mass

A measure of the amount of material in an object.

mass number

The sum of the number of protons and neutrons in an atom's nucleus.

matrix

The thick fluid contained within the inner membrane of the mitochondrion.

matter

Anything that occupies space and has mass.

mechanoreceptor (*mek´-uh-nō-ri-sep´-ter*)

A sensory receptor that detects physical changes in the environment, associated with pressure, touch, stretch, motion, and sound.

medulla oblongata (*meh-duh´-luh ob´-long-got´-uh*)

Part of the vertebrate hindbrain continuous with the spinal cord; passes data between the spinal cord and forebrain and controls autonomic, homeostatic functions, including breathing, heart rate, swallowing, and digestion.

medusa (*med-ū´-suh*)

(plural, **medusae**) One of two types of cnidarian body forms; a floating, umbrella-like body form; also called a jelly.

meiosis (*mī-ō´-sis*)

In a sexually reproducing organism, the process of cell division that produces haploid gametes from diploid cells within the reproductive organs.

memory cell

A long-lived lymphocyte that responds to subsequent exposures to a specific pathogen. A memory cell is formed during the primary immune response and is activated by exposure to the same antigen that triggered its formation. When activated, a memory cell forms large clones of effector cells and memory cells that mount the secondary immune response.

meninges (*muh-nin´-jēz*)

Layers of connective tissue that enwrap and protect the brain and spinal cord.

menstrual cycle (*men´-strū-ul*)

The hormonally synchronized cyclic buildup and breakdown of the endometrium in some primates, including humans.

menstruation (*men´-strū-ā´-shun*)

Uterine bleeding resulting from the breakdown of the endometrium during a menstrual cycle.

meristem (*mār´-eh-stem*)

Plant tissue consisting of undifferentiated cells that divide and generate new cells and tissues.

mesophyll (*mes´-ō-fil*)

The green tissue in the interior of a leaf; a leaf's ground tissue system, the main site of photosynthesis.

messenger RNA (mRNA)

The type of ribonucleic acid that encodes genetic information from DNA and conveys it to ribosomes, where the information is translated into amino acid sequences.

metabolic rate

Energy expended by the body per unit time.

metabolism (*muh-tab´-uh-liz-um*)

The total of all the chemical reactions in an organism.

metamorphosis (*met´-uh-mōr´-fuh-sis*)

The transformation of a larva into an adult.

metaphase (*met´-eh-fāz*)

The second stage of mitosis. During metaphase, the centromeres of all the cell's duplicated chromosomes are lined up on an imaginary plate equidistant between the poles of the mitotic spindle.

metastasis (*muh-tas´-tuh-sis*)

The spread of cancer cells beyond their original site.

microevolution

A change in a population's gene pool over a succession of generations; evolutionary changes in species over relatively brief periods of geologic time.

micronutrient

A chemical element that an organism needs in very small amounts. *See also* macronutrient.

microtubule

The thickest of the three main kinds of fibers making up the cytoskeleton of a eukaryotic cell; a straight, hollow tube made of globular proteins called tubulins. Microtubules form the basis of the structure and movement of cilia and flagella.

middle ear

One of three main regions of the human ear; a chamber containing three small bones (the hammer, anvil, and stirrup) that convey vibrations from the eardrum to the inner ear.

millipede

A terrestrial arthropod that has two pairs of short legs for each of its numerous body segments and that eats decaying plant matter.

mineral

In nutrition, an inorganic chemical element (other than carbon, hydrogen, oxygen, or nitrogen) that an organism requires for proper body functioning.

mitochondrion (*mī´-tō-kon´-drē-on*)

(plural, **mitochondria**) An organelle in eukaryotic cells where cellular respiration occurs. Enclosed by two concentric membranes, it is where most of the cell's ATP is made.

mitosis (*mī´-tō-sis*)

The division of a single nucleus into two genetically identical daughter nuclei. Mitosis and cytokinesis make up the mitotic (M) phase of the cell cycle.

mitotic (M) phase

The phase of the cell cycle when mitosis divides the nucleus and distributes its chromosomes to the daughter nuclei and cytokinesis divides the cytoplasm, producing two daughter cells.

mitotic spindle

A spindle-shaped structure formed of microtubules and associated proteins that is involved in the movement of chromosomes during mitosis and meiosis. (A spindle is shaped roughly like a football.)

modern synthesis

A comprehensive theory of evolution that incorporates genetics and includes most of Darwin's ideas, focusing on populations as the fundamental units of evolution.

molecular biology

The study of the molecular basis of heredity; molecular genetics.

molecule

A group of two or more atoms held together by covalent bonds.

mollusc (*mol´-lusk*)

A soft-bodied animal characterized by a muscular foot, mantle, mantle cavity, and radula. Molluscs include gastropods (snails and slugs), bivalves (clams, oysters, and scallops), and cephalopods (squids and octopuses).

monocot (*mon´-uh-kot*)

A flowering plant whose embryos have a single seed leaf, or cotyledon.

monohybrid cross

A mating of individuals differing at one genetic locus.

monomer (*mon´-uh-mer*)

A chemical subunit that serves as a building block of a polymer.

monosaccharide (*mon´-uh-sak´-uh-rīd*)

The smallest kind of sugar molecule; a single-unit sugar; also known as a simple sugar. Monosaccharides are the building blocks of more complex sugars and polysaccharides.

monotreme (*mon'-uh-trēm*)
An egg-laying mammal, such as the duck-billed platypus.

morning-after pill (MAP)
A birth control pill taken within three days of unprotected intercourse to prevent fertilization or implantation.

moss
Any of a group of seedless nonvascular plants.

motor neuron
A nerve cell that conveys command signals from the central nervous system to effector cells, such as muscle cells or gland cells.

motor output
The conduction of signals from the central nervous system to effector cells.

motor system
A component of the peripheral nervous system of vertebrates composed of neurons that carry signals to skeletal muscles, mainly in response to external stimuli. The motor system is primarily under voluntary control.

motor unit
A motor neuron and all the muscle fibers it controls.

mouth
See oral cavity.

movement corridor
A series of small clumps or a narrow strip of quality habitat (usable by organisms) that connects otherwise isolated patches of quality habitat.

muscle tissue
Tissue consisting of long muscle cells that are capable of contracting when stimulated by nerve impulses. *See also* skeletal muscle; cardiac muscle; smooth muscle.

muscular system
All the skeletal muscles in the body. (Cardiac muscle and smooth muscle are components of other organ systems.)

mutagen (*myū'-tuh-jen*)
A chemical or physical agent that interacts with DNA and causes a mutation.

mutation
A change in the nucleotide sequence of DNA; a major source of genetic diversity.

mutualism
An interspecific interaction in which both partners benefit.

mycelium (*mī-sē'-lē-um*)
(plural, **mycelia**) The densely branched network of hyphae in a fungus.

mycorrhiza (*mī'-kō-rī'-zuh*)
(plural, **mycorrhizae**) A mutually beneficial symbiotic association of a plant root and fungus.

myelin sheath (*mī'-uh-lin*)
A chain of bead-like supporting cells that insulate the axon of a nerve cell in vertebrates. This insulation helps to speed electrical transmission along the axon.

myofibril (*mī'-ō-fī'-bril*)
A contractile unit in a muscle cell (fiber) made up of many arcomeres. Longitudinal bundles of myofibrils make up a muscle fiber.

N

NADH
An electron carrier (a molecule that carries electrons) involved in cellular respiration and photosynthesis. NADH carries electrons from glucose and other fuel molecules and deposits them at the top of an electron transport chain. NADH is generated during glycolysis and the citric acid cycle.

NADPH
An electron carrier (a molecule that carries electrons) involved in photosynthesis. Light drives electrons from chlorophyll to NADP$^+$, forming NADPH, which provides the high-energy electrons for the reduction of carbon dioxide to sugar in the Calvin cycle.

natural family planning
See rhythm method.

natural killer (NK) cell
A white blood cell that attacks cancer cells and infected body cells as part of internal innate defense.

natural selection
A process in which organisms with certain inherited characteristics are more likely to survive and reproduce than are organisms with other characteristics; unequal reproductive success.

nearsightedness
An inability to focus on distant objects; occurs when the eyeball is longer than normal and the lens focuses distant objects in front of the retina; also called myopia.

negative feedback
A control mechanism in which a chemical reaction, metabolic pathway, or hormone-secreting gland is inhibited by the products of the reaction, pathway, or gland. As the concentration of the products builds up, the product molecules themselves inhibit the process that produced them.

negative pressure breathing
A breathing system in which lower air pressure in the lungs causes air to enter the lungs.

nematode (*nem'-uh-tōd*)
An animal characterized by a pseudocoelom, a cylindrical, wormlike body form, and a complete digestive tract; also called a roundworm.

nephron
The tubular excretory unit and associated blood vessels of the vertebrate kidney. The nephron extracts filtrate from the blood and refines it into urine.

nerve
A communication line made up of cable-like bundles of neuron fibers (axons and dendrites) tightly wrapped in connective tissue.

nervous system
The organ system that forms a communication and coordination network throughout an animal's body.

nervous tissue
Tissue made up of neurons and supportive cells.

neuron (*nūr'-on*)
A nerve cell; the fundamental structural and functional unit of the nervous system, specialized for carrying signals from one location in the body to another.

neurotransmitter
A chemical messenger that carries information from a transmitting neuron to a receiving cell, either another neuron or an effector cell.

neutron
An electrically neutral particle (a particle having no electrical charge), found in the nucleus of an atom.

nitrogen fixation
The conversion of atmospheric nitrogen (N_2) to nitrogen compounds (NH_4, NO_3) that plants can absorb and use.

node
The point of attachment of a leaf on a stem.

nondisjunction
An accident of meiosis or mitosis in which a pair of homologous chromosomes or a pair of sister chromatids fail to separate at anaphase.

norepinephrine (*nor'-ep-uh-nef'-rin*)
An amine hormone (also called noradrenaline) that is secreted by the adrenal medulla and that prepares body organs for "fight or flight"; also serves as a neurotransmitter.

notochord (*nō'-tuh-kord*)
A flexible, cartilage-like, longitudinal rod located between the digestive tract and nerve cord in chordate animals, present only in embryos in many species.

nuclear envelope
A double membrane, perforated with pores, that encloses the nucleus and separates it from the rest of the eukaryotic cell.

nuclear transplantation
A technique in which the nucleus of one cell is placed into another cell that already has a nucleus or in which the nucleus has been previously destroyed. The cell is then stimulated to grow, producing an embryo that is a genetic copy of the nucleus donor.

nucleic acid (*nū-klā'-ik*)
A polymer consisting of many nucleotide monomers; serves as a blueprint for proteins and, through the actions of proteins, for all cellular structures and activities. The two types of nucleic acids are DNA and RNA.

nucleic acid probe (*nū-klā'-ik*)
In DNA technology, a labeled single-stranded nucleic acid molecule used to find a specific gene or other nucleotide sequence within a mass of

DNA. The probe hydrogen-bonds to the complementary sequence in the targeted DNA.

nucleoid
A non–membrane-enclosed region in a prokaryotic cell where the DNA is concentrated.

nucleolus (nū-klē'-ō-lus)
A structure within the nucleus of a eukaryotic cell where ribosomal RNA is made and assembled with proteins to make ribosomal subunits; consists of parts of the chromatin DNA, RNA transcribed from the DNA, and proteins imported from the cytoplasm.

nucleosome (nū'-klē-ō-sōm)
The bead-like unit of DNA packing in a eukaryotic cell; consists of DNA wound around a protein core made up of eight histone molecules.

nucleotide (nū'-klē-ō-tīd)
An organic monomer consisting of a five-carbon sugar covalently bonded to a nitrogenous base and a phosphate group. Nucleotides are the building blocks of nucleic acids.

nucleus
(plural, **nuclei**) (1) An atom's central core, containing protons and neutrons. (2) The genetic control center of a eukaryotic cell.

O

obesity
An excessively high body mass index, a ratio of weight to height.

omnivore
An animal that eats both plants and animals. *See also* carnivore; herbivore.

oncogene (on'-kō-jēn)
A cancer-causing gene; usually contributes to malignancy by abnormally enhancing the amount or activity of a growth factor made by the cell.

oogenesis (ō'-uh-jen'-uh-sis)
The formation of egg cells within the ovaries.

open circulatory system
A circulatory system in which the circulating fluid is pumped through open-ended vessels and out among the body cells. In an animal with an open circulatory system, the circulating fluid and interstitial fluid are the same.

open system
Any system that exchanges chemicals and energy with its surroundings. All organisms are open systems.

operator
In prokaryotic DNA, a sequence of nucleotides near the start of an operon to which an active repressor can attach. The binding of repressor prevents RNA polymerase from attaching to the promoter and transcribing the genes of the operon.

operculum (ō-per'-kyū-lum)
(plural, **opercula**) A protective flap on each side of a bony fish's head that covers a chamber housing the gills.

operon (op'-er-on)
A unit of genetic regulation common in prokaryotes; a cluster of genes with related functions, along with the promoter and operator that control their transcription.

opportunistic life history
The pattern of reproducing when young and producing many offspring that receive little or no parental care; often seen in short-lived, small-bodied species.

optic nerve
A nerve that arises from the retina in each eye and carries visual information to the brain.

oral cavity
An opening through which food is taken into an animal's body; also known as the mouth.

order
In classification, the taxonomic category above family.

organ
A structure consisting of two or more tissues that coordinate to perform specific functions.

organ system
A group of organs that work together in performing vital body functions.

organelle (ōr-guh-nel')
A membrane-enclosed structure with a specialized function within a eukaryotic cell.

organic compound
A chemical compound containing the element carbon and usually synthesized by cells.

organic farming
A method of farming intended to promote environmental sustainability through such practices as crop rotation, water conservation, and avoidance of synthetic fertilizers, pesticides, and genetically modified organisms.

organism
An individual living thing, such as a bacterium, fungus, protist, plant, or animal.

organismal ecology
The study of the evolutionary adaptations that enable individual organisms to meet the challenges posed by their abiotic environments.

osmoconformer (oz'-mō-con-form'-er)
An organism whose body fluids have a solute concentration equal to that of its surroundings. Osmoconformers do not have a net gain or loss of water by osmosis.

osmoregulation
The control of the gain or loss of water and dissolved solutes in an organism.

osmoregulator
An organism whose body fluids have a solute concentration different from that of its environment and that must use energy in controlling water loss or gain.

osmosis (oz-mō'-sis)
The diffusion of water across a selectively permeable membrane.

osteoporosis (os'-tē-ō-puh-rō'-sis)
A skeletal disorder characterized by thinning, porous, and easily broken bones. Osteoporosis is common among women after menopause and is often related to low estrogen levels.

outer ear
One of three main regions of the ear in humans and some other animals. The outer ear is made up of the auditory canal and the pinna.

ovarian cycle (ō-vār'-ē-un)
Hormonally synchronized cyclic events in the mammalian ovary, culminating in ovulation.

ovary
(1) In animals, the female gonad, which produces egg cells and reproductive hormones. (2) In flowering plants, the base of a carpel in which the egg-containing ovules develop.

oviduct (ō'-vuh-dukt)
The tube that conveys egg cells away from an ovary; also called a fallopian tube.

ovulation (ah'-vyū-lā'-shun)
The release of an egg cell from an ovarian follicle.

ovule (ō'-vyūl)
In a seed plant, a reproductive structure that contains the female gametophyte and the developing egg. An ovule develops into a seed.

oxidation
The loss of electrons from a substance involved in a redox reaction; always accompanies reduction.

P

P generation
The parent individuals from which offspring are derived in studies of inheritance. P stands for parental.

pacemaker
The SA (sinoatrial) node; a region of cardiac muscle that maintains the heart's pumping rhythm (heartbeat) by setting the rate at which the heart contracts.

paedomorphosis (pē'-duh-mōr'-fuh-sis)
The retention in the adult of features that were juvenile in ancestral species.

pain receptor
A sensory receptor that detects painful stimuli.

pancreas (pan'-krē-us)
A gland with dual functions: The nonendocrine portion secretes digestive enzymes and an alkaline solution into the small intestine via a duct; the endocrine portion secretes the hormones insulin and glucagon into the blood.

parasite
An organism that lives in or on another organism (the host) from which it obtains nourishment; an organism that benefits at the expense of another organism, which is harmed in the process.

parasympathetic division
One of two sets of neurons in the autonomic nervous system; generally promotes body activities that gain and conserve energy ("rest

and digest"). *See also* sympathetic division.

parathyroid gland (*pār'-uh-thī'-royd*) One of four endocrine glands embedded in the surface of the thyroid gland that secrete parathyroid hormone; functions in calcium homeostasis.

parathyroid hormone (PTH) A peptide hormone, secreted by the parathyroid glands, that raises blood calcium level.

parenchyma cell (*puh-reng'-kuh-muh*) In plants, an abundant and relatively unspecialized type of cell with a thin primary wall and no secondary wall; functions in photosynthesis, food storage, and aerobic respiration and may differentiate into other cell types.

passive transport The diffusion of a substance across a biological membrane without any input of energy.

pathogen A disease-causing virus or organism.

pedigree A family tree representing the occurrence of heritable traits in parents and offspring across a number of generations.

pelagic realm (*puh-laj'-ik*) The open-water region of an ocean.

penis The structure in male mammals that functions in sexual intercourse.

pepsin An enzyme present in gastric juice that begins the hydrolysis of proteins.

peptide bond The covalent linkage between two amino acid units in a polypeptide, formed by a dehydration reaction between two amino acids.

perennial (*puh-ren'-ē-ul*) A plant that lives for many years.

peripheral nervous system (PNS) The network of nerves carrying signals into and out of the central nervous system.

peristalsis (*par'-uh-stal'-sis*) Rhythmic waves of contraction of smooth muscles. Peristalsis propels food through a digestive tube and also enables many animals, such as earthworms, to crawl.

permafrost Continuously frozen subsoil found in the arctic tundra.

petal A modified leaf of a flowering plant. Petals are the often colorful parts of a flower that advertise it to insects and other pollinators.

petiole (*pet'-ē-ōl*) The stalk of a leaf, which joins the leaf to a node of the stem.

pH scale A measure of the relative acidity of a solution, ranging in value from 0 (most acidic) to 14 (most basic). pH stands for potential hydrogen and refers to the concentration of hydrogen ions (H^+).

phage (*fāj*) *See* bacteriophage.

phagocytic cell (*fag'-ō-si-tik*) A white blood cell that engulfs bacteria, foreign proteins, and the remains of dead body cells as part of internal innate defense.

phagocytosis (*fag'-ō-sī-tō'-sis*) Cellular "eating"; a type of endocytosis whereby a cell engulfs large molecules, other cells, or particles into its cytoplasm.

pharyngeal slit (*fuh-rin'-jē-ul*) A gill structure in the pharynx, found in chordate embryos and some adult chordates.

pharynx (*far'-inks*) The organ in a digestive tract that receives food from the oral cavity; in terrestrial vertebrates, the throat region where the air and food passages cross.

phenotype (*fē'-nō-tīp*) The expressed traits of an organism.

phloem (*flō'-um*) The portion of a plant's vascular system that conveys sugars, nutrients, and hormones throughout a plant. Phloem is made up of live food-conducting cells.

phloem sap The solution of sugars, other nutrients, and hormones conveyed throughout a plant via phloem tissue.

phospholipid (*fos'-fō-lip'-id*) A molecule that is a constituent of the inner bilayer of biological membranes, having a hydrophilic head and a hydrophobic tail.

phospholipid bilayer A double layer of phospholipid molecules (each molecule consisting of a phosphate group bonded to two fatty acids) that is the primary component of all cellular membranes.

photic zone (*fō'-tik*) Shallow water near shore or the upper layer of water away from the shore; region of an aquatic ecosystem where sufficient light is available for photosynthesis.

photon (*fō'-ton*) A fixed quantity of light energy. The shorter the wavelength of light, the greater the energy of a photon.

photoperiod The length of the day relative to the length of the night; an environmental stimulus that plants use to detect the time of year.

photoreceptor A type of electromagnetic receptor that detects light.

photosynthesis (*fō'-tō-sin'-thuh-sis*) The process by which plants, algae, and some bacteria transform light energy to chemical energy stored in the bonds of sugars. This process requires an input of carbon dioxide (CO_2) and water (H_2O) and produces oxygen gas (O_2) as a waste product.

photosystem A light-harvesting unit of a chloroplast's thylakoid membrane; consists of several hundred molecules, a reaction-center chlorophyll, and a primary electron acceptor.

phototropism (*fō'-tō-trō'-pizm*) The directional growth of a plant shoot in response to light.

phylogenetic tree (*fī'-lō-juh-net'-ik*) A branching diagram that represents a hypothesis about evolutionary relationships between organisms.

phylum (*fī'-lum*) (plural, **phyla**) In classification, the taxonomic category above class and below kingdom. Members of a phylum all have a similar general body plan.

physiology (*fi'-zē-ol'-uh-jē*) The study of the function of an organism's structural equipment.

phytoplankton (*fī'-tō-plank'-ton*) Algae and photosynthetic bacteria that drift passively in aquatic environments.

pinna (*pin'-uh*) The flap-like part of the outer ear in humans and some other animals. The pinna collects sound waves and channels them to the auditory canal.

pith Part of the ground tissue system of a eudicot plant. Pith fills the center of a stem and may store food.

pituitary gland (*puh-tū'-uh-tār'-ē*) An endocrine gland at the base of the hypothalamus; consists of a posterior lobe, which stores and releases two hormones produced by the hypothalamus, and an anterior lobe, which produces and secretes many hormones that regulate diverse body functions.

pivot joint A joint that allows precise rotations in multiple planes. An example in humans is the elbow.

placenta (*pluh-sen'-tuh*) In most mammals, the organ that provides nutrients and oxygen to the embryo and helps dispose of its metabolic wastes. The placenta is formed of the embryo's chorion and the mother's endometrial blood vessels.

placental mammal (*pluh-sen'-tul*) Mammal whose young complete their embryonic development in the uterus, nourished via the mother's blood vessels in the placenta; also called a eutherian.

plankton Communities of organisms, mostly microscopic, that drift passively in ponds, lakes, and oceans.

plant A multicellular eukaryote that carries out photosynthesis and has a set of structural and reproductive terrestrial adaptations, including a multicellular, dependent embryo.

plasma The yellowish liquid of the blood in which the blood cells are suspended.

plasma membrane The thin layer of lipids and proteins that sets a cell off from its surroundings and acts as a selective barrier to the passage of ions and molecules into and out of the cell; consists of a phospholipid bilayer in which proteins are embedded.

plasmid
A small ring of self-replicating DNA separate from the chromosome(s). Plasmids are found in prokaryotes and yeasts.

plasmodial slime mold (*plaz-mō'-dē-ul*)
A type of protist named for an amoeboid plasmodial feeding stage in its life cycle.

platelet
A piece of cytoplasm from a large cell in the bone marrow; a blood-clotting element.

pleiotropy (*plī'-uh-trō-pē*)
The control of more than one phenotypic character by a single gene.

polar ice
A terrestrial biome that includes regions of extremely cold temperature and low precipitation located at high latitudes north of the arctic tundra and in Antarctica.

polar molecule
A molecule containing an uneven distribution of charge due to the presence of polar covalent bonds (bonds having opposite charges on opposite ends).

pollen grain
In a seed plant, the male gametophyte that develops within the anther of a stamen. It houses cells that will develop into sperm.

pollination
In seed plants, the delivery, by wind or animals, of pollen from the male parts of a plant to the stigma of a carpel on the female.

polychaete
A type of annelid, or segmented worm, that typically lives on the seafloor.

polygenic inheritance (*pol'-ē-jen'-ik*)
The additive effect of two or more genes on a single phenotypic characteristic.

polymer (*pol'-uh-mer*)
A large molecule consisting of many identical or similar molecular units, called monomers, covalently joined together in a chain.

polymerase chain reaction (PCR) (*puh-lim'-uh-rās*)
A technique used to obtain many copies of a DNA molecule or many copies of part of a DNA molecule. A small amount of DNA mixed with the enzyme DNA polymerase, DNA nucleotides, and a few other ingredients replicates repeatedly in a test tube.

polynucleotide (*pol'-ē-nū'-klē-ō-tīd*)
A polymer made up of many nucleotides covalently bonded together.

polyp (*pol'-ip*)
One of two types of cnidarian body forms; a stationary (sedentary), columnar, hydra-like body.

polypeptide
A chain of amino acids linked by peptide bonds.

polysaccharide (*pol'-ē-sak'-uh-rīd*)
A carbohydrate polymer consisting of many monosaccharides (sugars) linked by covalent bonds.

population
A group of interacting individuals belonging to one species and living in the same geographic area at the same time.

population density
The number of individuals of a species per unit area or volume of the habitat.

population ecology
The study of how members of a population interact with their environment, focusing on factors that influence population density and growth.

population momentum
In a population in which the fertility rate averages two children per female (replacement rate), the continuation of population growth as girls reach their reproductive years.

positive feedback
A control mechanism in which the products of a process stimulate the process that produced them.

post-anal tail
A tail posterior to the anus, found in chordate embryos and most adult chordates.

posterior pituitary
An extension of the hypothalamus composed of nervous tissue that secretes hormones made in the hypothalamus; a temporary storage site for hypothalamic hormones.

postzygotic barrier (*pōst'-zī-got'-ik*)
A reproductive barrier that operates if interspecies mating occurs and forms hybrid zygotes.

potential energy
Stored energy; the energy that an object has due to its location and/or arrangement. Water behind a dam and chemical bonds both possess potential energy.

predation
An interaction between species in which one species, the predator, kills and eats the other, the prey.

prepuce (*prē'-pyūs*)
A fold of skin covering the head of the clitoris or penis.

pressure-flow mechanism
The method by which phloem sap is transported through a plant from a sugar source, where sugars are produced, to a sugar sink, where sugars are used. The mechanism relies on building up water pressure at the source end of the phloem tube and reducing water pressure at the sink end.

prezygotic barrier (*prē'-zī-got'-ik*)
A reproductive barrier that impedes mating between species or hinders fertilization of eggs if members of different species attempt to mate.

primary consumer
An organism that eats only autotrophs; an herbivore.

primary electron acceptor
A molecule in the reaction center of a photosystem that traps the light-excited electron from the reaction-center chlorophyll.

primary growth
Growth in the length of a plant root or shoot produced by an apical meristem.

primary immune response
The initial immune response to an antigen, which includes production of effector cells that respond to the antigen within a few days and also memory cells that will respond to future exposure to the antigen.

primary oocyte (*ō'-uh-sīt*)
A diploid cell, in prophase I of meiosis, that can be hormonally triggered to develop into an ovum.

primary production
The amount of solar energy converted to chemical energy (organic compounds) by autotrophs in an ecosystem during a given time period.

primary spermatocyte (*sper-mat'-eh-sīt'*)
A diploid cell in the testis that undergoes meiosis I.

primary structure
The first level of protein structure; the specific sequence of amino acids making up a polypeptide chain.

primary succession
A type of ecological succession in which a biological community begins in an area without soil. *See also* secondary succession.

primate
Member of the mammalian group that includes lorises, pottos, lemurs, tarsiers, monkeys, apes, and humans.

prion
An infectious form of protein that may multiply by converting related proteins to more prions. Prions cause several related diseases in different animals, including scrapie in sheep, mad cow disease, and Creutzfeldt-Jakob disease in humans.

producer
An organism that makes organic food molecules from carbon dioxide, water, and other inorganic raw materials: a plant, alga, or autotrophic bacterium; the trophic level that supports all others in a food chain or food web.

product
An ending material in a chemical reaction.

progestin (*prō-jes'-tin*)
One of a family of sex hormones, including progesterone, produced by the mammalian ovary. Progestins prepare the uterus for pregnancy.

programmed cell death
The timely death (and disposal of the remains) of certain cells, triggered by certain genes; an essential process in normal development.

prokaryote (*prō-kār'-ē-ōt*)
An organism characterized by prokaryotic cells. *See also* prokaryotic cell.

prokaryotic cell (*prō-kār'-ē-ot'-ik*)
A type of cell lacking a nucleus and other organelles. Prokaryotic cells are found only in the domains Bacteria and Archaea.

promoter
A specific nucleotide sequence in DNA, located at the start of a gene,

that is the binding site for RNA polymerase and the place where transcription begins.

prophage (*prō'-fāj*)
Phage DNA that has inserted into the DNA of a prokaryotic chromosome.

prophase
The first stage of mitosis. During prophase, duplicated chromosomes condense to form structures visible with a light microscope, and the mitotic spindle forms and begins moving the chromosomes toward the center of the cell.

prostate gland (*pros'-tāt*)
A gland in human males that secretes an acid-neutralizing component of semen.

protein
A biological polymer constructed from amino acid monomers.

proteomics
The systematic study of the full protein sets (proteomes) encoded by genomes.

protist (*prō'-tist*)
Any eukaryote that is not a plant, animal, or fungus.

proton
A subatomic particle with a single unit of positive electrical charge, found in the nucleus of an atom.

proto-oncogene (*prō'-tō-on'-kō-jēn*)
A normal gene that can be converted to a cancer-causing gene.

protozoan (*prō'-tō-zō'-un*)
A protist that lives primarily by ingesting food; a heterotrophic, animal-like protist.

provirus
Viral DNA that inserts into a host genome.

pseudocoelom (*sū'-dō-sē'-lōm*)
A body cavity that is not completely lined by tissue derived from mesoderm.

pseudopodium (*sū'-dō-pō'-dē-um*)
(plural, **pseudopodia**) A temporary extension of an amoeboid cell. Pseudopodia function in moving cells and engulfing food.

pulmonary circuit
One of two main blood circuits in terrestrial vertebrates; conveys blood between the heart and the lungs. *See also* systemic circuit.

pulse
The rhythmic stretching of the arteries caused by the pressure of blood forced through the arteries by contractions of the ventricles during systole.

punctuated equilibria
In the fossil record, long periods of little apparent change (equilibria) interrupted (punctuated) by relatively brief periods of sudden change.

Punnett square
A diagram used in the study of inheritance to show the results of random fertilization.

pupil
The opening in the iris that admits light into the interior of the vertebrate eye. Muscles in the iris regulate its size.

pyramid of production
A diagram depicting the cumulative loss of energy with each transfer in a food chain.

Q

quaternary consumer (*kwot'-er-nār-ē*)
An organism that eats tertiary consumers.

R

radial symmetry
An arrangement of the body parts of an organism like pieces of a pie around an imaginary central axis. Any slice passing longitudinally through a radially symmetric organism's central axis divides the organism into mirror-image halves.

radiation therapy
Treatment for cancer in which parts of the body that have cancerous tumors are exposed to high-energy radiation to disrupt cell division of the cancer cells.

radioactive isotope
An isotope whose nucleus decays spontaneously, giving off particles and energy.

radiometric dating
A method for determining the age of fossils and rocks from the

ratio of a radioactive isotope to the nonradioactive isotope(s) of the same element in the sample.

radula (*rad'-yū-luh*)
A file-like organ found in many molluscs, used to scrape up or shred food.

ray-finned fish
A bony fish having fins supported by thin, flexible skeletal rays. All but one living species of bony fishes are ray-fins. *See* lobe-finned fish.

reabsorption
In the vertebrate kidney, the reclaiming of water and valuable solutes from the filtrate.

reactant
A starting material in a chemical reaction.

reaction center
In a photosystem in a chloroplast, the chlorophyll *a* molecule and primary electron acceptor that trigger the light reactions of photosynthesis. The chlorophyll donates an electron excited by light energy to the primary electron acceptor, which passes an electron to an electron transport chain.

receptor potential
The change in membrane potential of a sensory receptor cell that results from sensory transduction.

recessive allele
In heterozygotes, the allele that has no noticeable effect on the phenotype.

recombinant DNA
A DNA molecule carrying genes derived from two or more sources, often from different species.

recombination frequency
With respect to two given genes, the number of recombinant progeny from a mating divided by the total number of progeny. Recombinant progeny carry combinations of alleles different from that seen in either of the parents as a result of independent assortment of chromosomes and crossing over.

rectum
The terminal portion of the large intestine, where the feces are stored until they are eliminated.

red blood cell
A blood cell containing hemoglobin, which transports O_2; also called an erythrocyte.

red-green colorblindness
A common sex-linked human disorder involving several genes on the X chromosome and characterized by a malfunction of light-sensitive cells in the eyes; affects mostly males but also homozygous females.

redox reaction
Short for reduction-oxidation reaction; a chemical reaction in which electrons are lost from one substance (oxidation) and added to another (reduction). Oxidation and reduction always occur together.

reduction
The gain of electrons by a substance involved in a redox reaction; always accompanies oxidation.

regeneration
The regrowth of body parts from pieces of an organism.

relative abundance
The proportional representation of a species in a biological community; one component of species diversity.

relative fitness
The contribution an individual makes to the gene pool of the next generation relative to the contribution of other individuals in the population.

repetitive DNA
Nucleotide sequences that are present in many copies in the DNA of a genome. The repeated sequences may be long or short and may be located next to each other or dispersed in the DNA.

repressor
A protein that blocks the transcription of a gene or operon.

reproduction
The creation of new individuals from existing ones.

reproductive barrier
Anything that prevents individuals of closely related species from interbreeding, even when populations of the two species live together.

reproductive cloning
Using a somatic cell from a multicellular organism to make one or more genetically identical individuals.

reproductive cycle
In females, a recurring series of events that produces gametes, makes

them available for fertilization, and prepares the body for pregnancy.

reptile
Member of the clade of amniotes that includes snakes, lizards, turtles, crocodiles, alligators, birds, and a number of extinct groups (most of the dinosaurs).

resolving power
A measure of the clarity of an image; the ability of an optical instrument to show two objects as separate.

respiratory surface
The part of an animal where gases are exchanged with the environment.

respiratory system
The organ system that functions in exchanging gases with the environment, taking in O_2 and disposing of CO_2.

resting potential
The voltage across the plasma membrane of a resting neuron.

restoration ecology
A field of ecology that develops methods of returning degraded ecosystems to their natural state.

restriction enzyme
A bacterial enzyme that cuts up foreign DNA at one very specific nucleotide sequence, thus protecting bacteria against intruding DNA from phages and other organisms. Restriction enzymes are used in DNA technology to cut DNA molecules in reproducible ways.

restriction fragment
A molecule of DNA produced from a longer DNA molecule cut up by a restriction enzyme; used in genome mapping and other applications.

restriction site
A specific sequence on a DNA strand that is recognized and cut by a restriction enzyme.

retina (ret'-uh-nuh)
The light-sensitive layer in an eye, made up of photoreceptor cells and sensory neurons.

retrovirus
An RNA virus that reproduces by means of a DNA molecule. It reverse-transcribes its RNA into DNA, inserts the DNA into a cellular chromosome, and then transcribes more copies of the RNA from the viral DNA. HIV and a number

of cancer-causing viruses are retroviruses.

reverse transcriptase (tran-skrip'-tās)
An enzyme that catalyzes the synthesis of DNA on an RNA template.

rheumatoid arthritis
An autoimmune disease in which the joints become highly inflamed.

rhizome (rī'-zōm)
A horizontal stem that grows below the ground.

rhythm method
A form of contraception that relies on refraining from sexual intercourse when conception is most likely to occur; also called natural family planning.

ribosomal RNA (rRNA) (rī'-buh-sōm'-ul)
The type of ribonucleic acid that, together with proteins, makes up ribosomes; the most abundant type of RNA.

ribosome (rī'-buh-sōm)
A cellular structure consisting of RNA and protein organized into two subunits and functioning as the site of protein synthesis in the cytoplasm. The ribosomal subunits are constructed in the nucleolus.

RNA
Ribonucleic acid (rī'-bō-nū-klā'-ik) A type of nucleic acid consisting of nucleotide monomers, with a ribose sugar, a phosphate group, and the nitrogenous bases adenine (A), cytosine (C), guanine (G), and uracil (U); usually single-stranded; functions in protein synthesis and as the genome of some viruses.

RNA polymerase (puh-lim'-uh-rās)
An enzyme that links together the growing chain of RNA nucleotides during transcription, using a DNA strand as a template.

RNA splicing
The removal of introns and joining of exons in eukaryotic RNA, forming an mRNA molecule with a continuous coding sequence; occurs before mRNA leaves the nucleus.

rod
A photoreceptor cell in the vertebrate retina, enabling vision in dim light (but only in shades of gray).

root
The underground organ of a plant. Roots anchor the plant in the soil,

absorb and transport minerals and water, and store food.

root cap
A cone of cells at the tip of a plant root that protects the root's apical meristem.

root hair
An outgrowth of an epidermal cell on a root, which increases the root's absorptive surface area.

root system
All of a plant's roots, which anchor it in the soil, absorb and transport minerals and water, and store food.

rough ER (rough endoplasmic reticulum) (reh-tik'-yuh-lum)
A network of interconnected membranous sacs in a eukaryotic cell's cytoplasm. Rough ER membranes are studded with ribosomes that make membrane proteins and secretory proteins. The rough ER constructs membrane from phospholipids and proteins.

roundworm
See nematode.

rule of multiplication
A rule stating that the probability of a compound event is the product of the separate probabilities of the independent events.

S

SA (sinoatrial) node (sī'-nō-ā'-trē-ul)
The pacemaker of the heart, located in the wall of the right atrium. At the base of the wall separating the two atria is another patch of nodal tissue called the atrioventricular (AV) node. See also pacemaker.

salivary gland
A gland associated with the oral cavity that secretes substances that lubricate food and begin the process of chemical digestion.

sarcomere (sar'-kō-mēr)
The fundamental unit of muscle contraction, composed of thin filaments and thick filaments; the region between two narrow, dark lines in the myofibril.

saturated
Pertaining to fats and fatty acids the hydrocarbon chains of which contain the maximum number of hydrogens and therefore have no

double covalent bonds. Because of their straight, flat shape, saturated fats and fatty acids tend to be solid at room temperature.

savanna
A terrestrial biome dominated by grasses and scattered trees. Frequent fires and seasonal drought are significant abiotic factors.

scanning electron microscope (SEM)
A microscope that uses an electron beam to study the surface architecture of a cell or other specimen.

scavenger
An animal that feeds on the carcasses of dead animals.

science
Any method of learning about the natural world that follows the scientific method. See discovery science; hypothesis-driven science.

scientific method
Scientific investigation involving the observation of phenomena, the formulation of a hypothesis concerning the phenomena, experimentation to demonstrate the truth or falseness of the hypothesis, and results that validate or modify the hypothesis.

sclera (sklār'-uh)
A tough, whitish layer of connective tissue forming the outer surface of the vertebrate eye. The cornea is the front part of the sclera.

sclerenchyma cell (skli-reng'-kuh-muh)
In plants, a supportive type of cell with a rigid secondary wall hardened with lignin.

scrotum
A pouch of skin outside the abdomen that houses a testis. The scrotum functions in cooling the sperm, thereby keeping them viable.

seaweed
A large, multicellular marine alga.

secondary consumer
An organism that eats primary consumers.

secondary growth
An increase in a plant's girth, involving cell division in the vascular cambium and cork cambium.

secondary immune response
The immune response elicited by memory cells upon exposure to a previously encountered antigen. The

secondary immune response is more rapid, of greater magnitude, and of longer duration than the primary immune response.

secondary oocyte (ō'-uh-sīt')
A haploid cell that results from meiosis I in oogenesis and that will become an ovum after meiosis II.

secondary spermatocyte (sper-mat'-uh-sīt')
A haploid cell that results from meiosis I in spermatogenesis and that will become a sperm cell after meiosis II.

secondary succession
A type of ecological succession that occurs where a disturbance has destroyed an existing biological community but left the soil intact. *See also* primary succession.

secretion
In the vertebrate kidney, the transport of certain substances, such as some ions and drugs, from the blood into the filtrate.

seed
A plant embryo packaged with a food supply within a protective covering.

seed coat
A tough outer covering of a seed, formed from the outer coat of an ovule. In a flowering plant, it encloses and protects the embryo and endosperm.

semen (sē'-mun)
The sperm-containing fluid that is ejaculated by the male during orgasm.

seminal vesicle (sem'-uh-nul ves'-uh-kul)
A gland in males that secretes a fluid component of semen that lubricates and nourishes sperm.

seminiferous tubule (sem'-uh-nif'-uh-rus)
A coiled sperm-producing tube in a testis.

sensory adaptation
The tendency of some sensory receptors to become less sensitive when they are stimulated repeatedly.

sensory input
The conduction of signals from sensory receptors to integration centers in the central nervous system.

sensory neuron
A nerve cell that receives information from sensory receptors and conveys

signals into the central nervous system.

sensory transduction
The conversion of a stimulus signal to an electrical signal by a sensory receptor cell.

sepal (sē'-pul)
A modified leaf of a flowering plant. A whorl of sepals encloses and protects the flower bud before it opens.

sex chromosome
A chromosome that determines whether an individual is male or female; in mammals, for example, the X or Y chromosome.

sex-linked gene
A gene located on a sex chromosome.

sexual dimorphism
Distinction in appearance based on secondary sexual characteristics, noticeable differences not directly associated with reproduction or survival.

sexual reproduction
The creation of genetically distinct offspring by the fusion of two haploid sex cells (gametes: sperm and egg), forming a diploid zygote.

sexual selection
A form of natural selection in which individuals with certain characteristics are more likely than other individuals to obtain mates.

sexually transmitted disease (STD)
A contagious disease spread by sexual contact.

shoot
The aerial organ of a plant, consisting of stem and leaves. Leaves are the main photosynthetic structures of most plants.

shoot system
All of a plant's stems, leaves, and reproductive structures.

short tandem repeat (STR)
DNA consisting of tandem (in a row) repeats of a short sequence of nucleotides.

sickle-cell disease
A genetic disorder in which the red blood cells have abnormal hemoglobin molecules and take on an abnormal shape.

signal transduction pathway
A series of molecular changes that converts a signal received on a target

cell's surface to a specific response inside the cell.

silencer
A eukaryotic DNA sequence that inhibits the start of gene transcription; may act analogously to an enhancer, binding a repressor.

sister chromatid (krō'-muh-tid)
One of the two identical parts of a duplicated chromosome. While joined, two sister chromatids make up one chromosome; chromatids are eventually separated during mitosis or meiosis II.

skeletal muscle
Striated muscle attached to the skeleton. The contraction of striated muscle produces voluntary movements of the body.

skeletal system
The organ system that provides body support, protects body organs such as the brain, heart, and lungs, and anchors the muscles.

small intestine
The longest section of the alimentary canal. It is the principal site of the enzymatic hydrolysis of food molecules and absorption of nutrients.

smooth ER (smooth endoplasmic reticulum) (reh-tik'-yuh-lum)
A network of interconnected membranous tubules in a eukaryotic cell's cytoplasm. Smooth ER lacks ribosomes. Enzymes embedded in the smooth ER membrane function in the synthesis of certain kinds of molecules, such as lipids.

smooth muscle
Muscle made up of cells without striations, found in the walls of organs such as the digestive tract, urinary bladder, and arteries.

solute (sol'-yūt)
A substance that is dissolved in a liquid (which is called the solvent) to form a solution.

solution
A liquid consisting of a homogeneous mixture of two or more substances: a dissolving agent, the solvent, and a substance that is dissolved, the solute.

solvent
The dissolving agent in a solution. Water is the most versatile known solvent.

somatic cell (sō-mat'-ik)
Any cell in a multicellular organism except a sperm or egg cell or a cell that develops into a sperm or egg; a body cell.

speciation (spē-sē-ā'-shun)
An evolutionary process in which one species splits into two or more species.

species
A group of populations whose members possess similar anatomical characteristics and have the ability to interbreed. *See also* biological species concept.

species diversity
The variety of species that make up a biological community; the number and relative abundance of species in a biological community.

species richness
The total number of different species in a community; one component of species diversity.

sperm
A male gamete.

spermatogenesis (sper-mat'-ō-jen'-uh-sis)
The formation of sperm cells.

spermicide
A sperm-killing chemical, in the form of a cream, jelly, or foam, that works with a barrier device as a method of contraception.

spinal cord
In vertebrates, a jellylike bundle of nerve fibers located within the vertebral column. The spinal cord and the brain together make up the central nervous system.

sponge
An aquatic stationary animal characterized by a highly porous body, choanocytes, and no true tissues.

spontaneous generation
The incorrect notion that life can emerge from nonliving matter.

spore
(1) In plants and algae, a haploid cell that can develop into a multicellular haploid individual, the gametophyte, without fusing with another cell. (2) In fungi, a haploid cell that germinates to produce a mycelium.

sporophyte (spōr'-uh-fīt)
The multicellular diploid form in the life cycle of organisms undergoing alternation of generations; results from

a union of gametes and meiotically produces haploid spores that grow into the gametophyte generation.

stabilizing selection
Natural selection that favors intermediate variants by acting against extreme phenotypes.

stamen (stā'-men)
A pollen-producing part of a flower, consisting of a stalk (filament) and an anther.

starch
A storage polysaccharide found in the roots of plants and certain other cells; a polymer of glucose.

start codon (kō'-don)
On mRNA, the specific three-nucleotide sequence (AUG) to which an initiator tRNA molecule binds, starting translation of genetic information.

stem
That part of a plant's shoot system that generally grows above the ground and supports the leaves and reproductive structures.

stem cell
A relatively unspecialized cell that can give rise to one or more types of specialized cells. *See* embryonic stem cell (ES cell); adult stem cell.

steroid (stir'-oyd)
A type of lipid whose carbon skeleton is in the form of four fused rings: three 6-sided rings and one 5-sided ring. Examples are cholesterol, testosterone, and estrogen.

stigma (stig'-muh)
(plural, **stigmata**) The sticky tip of a flower's carpel that traps pollen.

stimulus
(plural, **stimuli**) In a nervous system, a factor that triggers a nerve signal.

stoma (stō'-muh)
(plural, **stomata**) A pore surrounded by guard cells in the epidermis of a leaf. When stomata are open, CO_2 enters the leaf, and water and O_2 exit. A plant conserves water when its stomata are closed.

stomach
A pouch-like organ in a digestive tube that grinds and churns food and may store it temporarily.

stop codon (kō'-don)
In mRNA, one of three triplets (UAG, UAA, UGA) that signal gene translation to stop.

STR analysis
A method of DNA profiling that compares the lengths of STR sequences at specific sites in the genome.

stroma (strō'-muh)
A thick fluid enclosed by the inner membrane of a chloroplast. Sugars are made in the stroma by the enzymes of the Calvin cycle.

substrate
(1) A specific substance (reactant) on which an enzyme acts. Each enzyme recognizes only the specific substrate of the reaction it catalyzes. (2) A surface in or on which an organism lives.

sugar sink
A plant organ that is a net consumer or storer of sugar. Growing roots, shoot tips, stems, and fruits are sugar sinks supplied by phloem.

sugar source
A plant organ in which sugar is being produced by either photosynthesis or the breakdown of starch. Mature leaves are the primary sugar sources of plants.

sugar-phosphate backbone
The alternating chain of sugar and phosphate to which DNA and RNA nitrogenous bases are attached.

supporting cell
In the nervous system, a cell that protects, insulates, and reinforces a neuron.

survivorship curve
A plot of the number of individuals that are still alive at each age in the maximum life span; one way to represent age-specific mortality.

sustainability
The goal of developing, managing, and conserving Earth's resources in ways that meet the needs of people today without compromising the ability of future generations to meet their needs.

sustainable development
The long-term prosperity of human societies and the ecosystems that support them.

swim bladder
A gas-filled internal sac that helps bony fishes maintain buoyancy.

symbiosis (sim'-bē-ō'-sis)
An interaction between organisms of different species in which one

species, the symbiont, lives in or on another species, the host.

sympathetic division
One of two sets of neurons in the autonomic nervous system; generally prepares the body for energy-consuming activities ("fight or flight"). *See also* parasympathetic division.

sympatric speciation
The formation of a new species in populations that live in the same geographic area. *See also* allopatric speciation.

synapse (sin'-aps)
A junction, or relay point, between two neurons or between a neuron and an effector cell. Electrical and chemical signals are relayed from one cell to another at a synapse.

synaptic cleft (sin-ap'-tik)
A narrow gap separating the synaptic terminal of a transmitting neuron from a receiving neuron or an effector cell.

synaptic terminal
The bulb-like structure at the tip of a transmitting neuron's axon, where signals are sent to another neuron or to an effector cell.

systematics
A discipline of biology that focuses on classifying organisms and determining their evolutionary relationships.

systemic circuit
One of two main blood circuits in terrestrial vertebrates; conveys blood between the heart and the rest of the body. *See also* pulmonary circuit.

systole (sis'-tō-lē)
The contraction stage of the cardiac cycle, when the heart chambers actively pump blood. *See also* diastole.

T

T cell
A type of lymphocyte that matures in the thymus and is responsible for the cell-mediated immune response. *See also* B cell.

taiga (tī'-guh)
The northern coniferous forest, characterized by long, snowy winters and short, wet summers. Taiga

extends across North America and Eurasia, to the southern border of the arctic tundra; it is also found just below alpine tundra on mountainsides in temperate zones.

tail
Extra nucleotides added at the end of an RNA transcript in the nucleus of a eukaryotic cell.

target cell
A cell that responds to a regulatory signal, such as a hormone.

taxonomy
The branch of biology concerned with identifying, naming, and classifying species.

telophase
The fourth and final stage of mitosis, during which daughter nuclei form at the two poles of a cell. Telophase usually occurs together with cytokinesis.

temperate broadleaf forest
A terrestrial biome located throughout midlatitude regions where there is sufficient moisture to support the growth of large, broadleaf deciduous trees.

temperate grassland
A terrestrial biome located in the temperate zone and characterized by low rainfall and nonwoody vegetation. Tree growth is hindered by occasional fires and periodic severe drought.

temperate rain forest
A coniferous forest of coastal North America (from Alaska to Oregon) supported by warm, moist air from the Pacific Ocean.

temperate zones
Latitudes between the tropics and the Arctic Circle in the north and the Antarctic Circle in the south; regions with milder climates than the tropics or polar regions.

temperature
A measure of the intensity of heat, reflecting the average kinetic energy or speed of molecules.

tendon
Fibrous connective tissue connecting a muscle to a bone.

terminal bud
Embryonic tissue at the tip of a shoot, made up of developing leaves and a compact series of nodes and internodes.

terminator
A special sequence of nucleotides in DNA that marks the end of a gene. It signals RNA polymerase to release the newly made RNA molecule, which then departs from the gene.

tertiary consumer (ter'-shē-ār-ē)
An organism that eats secondary consumers.

testcross
The mating between an individual of unknown genotype for a particular character and an individual that is homozygous recessive for that same character.

testicle
A structural component of the male reproductive system consisting of a testis and scrotum.

testis
(plural, **testes**) The male gonad in an animal. The testis produces sperm and, in many species, reproductive hormones.

tetrapod
A vertebrate with four limbs. Tetrapods include mammals, amphibians, and reptiles (including birds).

theory
A widely accepted explanatory idea that is broad in scope and supported by a large body of evidence.

therapeutic cloning
The cloning of human cells by nuclear transplantation for therapeutic purposes, such as the replacement of body cells that have been irreversibly damaged by disease or injury. *See also* nuclear transplantation; reproductive cloning.

thermoreceptor
A sensory receptor that detects heat or cold.

thermoregulation
The maintenance of internal temperature within a range that allows cells to function efficiently.

thick filament
The thicker of the two types of filaments that make up a sarcomere, consisting of the protein myosin.

thigmotropism (thig'-mō-trō'-pizm)
Growth of a plant in response to touch.

thin filament
The thinner of the two types of filaments that make up a sarcomere, consisting of the protein actin.

threatened species
As defined in the U.S. Endangered Species Act, a species that is likely to become endangered in the foreseeable future throughout all or a significant portion of its range.

three-domain system
A system of taxonomic classification based on three basic groups: Bacteria, Archaea, and Eukarya.

threshold
The minimum change in a membrane's voltage that must occur to generate a nerve signal (action potential).

thylakoid (thī'-luh-koyd)
One of a number of disk-shaped membranous sacs inside a chloroplast. Thylakoid membranes contain chlorophyll and the enzymes of the light reactions of photosynthesis. A stack of thylakoids is called a granum.

thymine (T) (thī'-mēn)
A single-ring nitrogenous base found in DNA.

thyroid gland (thī'-royd)
An endocrine gland, located in the neck, that secretes hormones that increase oxygen consumption and metabolic rate and help regulate development and maturation.

tissue
An integrated group of similar cells that performs a specific function within a multicellular organism.

tissue system
An organized collection of plant tissues. The organs of plants (such as roots, stems, and leaves) are formed from the dermal, vascular, and ground tissue systems.

tongue
A muscular organ of the mouth that helps to taste and swallow food.

trace element
An element that is essential for the survival of an organism but is needed in only minute quantities.

trachea (trā'-kē-uh)
(plural, **tracheae**) (1) The windpipe; the portion of the respiratory tube between the larynx and the bronchi. (2) One of many tiny tubes that branch throughout an insect's body, enabling gas exchange between outside air and body cells.

tracheal system
In insects, an extensive network of branching internal tubes called tracheae, used in respiration.

tracheid (trā'-kē-id)
A tapered, porous, water-conducting, supportive cell in plants. Chains of tracheids or vessel elements make up the water-conducting, supportive tubes in xylem.

trait
A variant of a character found within a population, such as purple flowers in pea plants.

trans fats
An unsaturated fatty acid produced by the partial hydrogenation of vegetable oils and present in hardened vegetable oils, most margarines, many commercial baked foods, and many fried foods.

transcription
The synthesis of RNA on a DNA template.

transcription factor
In the eukaryotic cell, a protein that functions in initiating or regulating transcription. Transcription factors bind to DNA or to other proteins that bind to DNA.

transfer RNA (tRNA)
A type of ribonucleic acid that functions as an interpreter in translation. Each tRNA molecule has a specific anticodon, picks up a specific amino acid, and conveys the amino acid to the appropriate codon on mRNA.

transgenic organism
An organism that contains genes from another organism, typically of another species.

translation
The synthesis of a polypeptide using the genetic information encoded in an mRNA molecule. There is a change of "language" from nucleotides to amino acids.

transmission electron microscope (TEM)
A microscope that uses an electron beam to study the internal structure of thinly sectioned specimens.

transpiration
The evaporative loss of water from a plant.

transpiration-cohesion-tension mechanism
The transport mechanism of xylem sap whereby transpiration exerts a pull that is relayed downward along a string of water molecules held together by cohesion and helped upward by adhesion.

transport protein
A membrane protein that helps move substances across a cell membrane.

transport vesicle
A tiny membranous sphere in a cell's cytoplasm carrying molecules produced by the cell. The vesicle buds from the endoplasmic reticulum or Golgi apparatus and eventually fuses with another organelle or the plasma membrane, releasing its contents.

triglyceride (trī-glis'-uh-rīd)
A dietary fat that consists of a molecule of glycerol linked to three molecules of fatty acids.

trimester
In human development, one of three 3-month-long periods of pregnancy.

trisomy 21
See Down syndrome.

trophic structure (trō'-fik)
The feeding relationships among the various species in a community.

trophoblast (trōf'-ō-blast)
In mammalian development, the outer portion of a blastocyst. Cells of the trophoblast secrete enzymes that enable the blastocyst to implant in the endometrium of the mother's uterus.

tropical forest
A terrestrial biome characterized by warm temperatures year-round.

tropics
Region between the Tropic of Cancer and the Tropic of Capricorn; latitudes between 23.5° north and south.

tropism (trō'-pizm)
A growth response that makes a plant grow toward or away from a stimulus.

tubal ligation
A means of sterilization in which a woman's two oviducts (fallopian tubes) are tied closed to prevent eggs from reaching the uterus. A segment of each oviduct is removed.

tuber
An enlargement at the end of a rhizome, in which food is stored.

tubule
A thin tube within the internal structure of the human kidney.

tumor
An abnormal mass of cells that forms within otherwise normal tissue.

tumor-suppressor gene
A gene whose product inhibits cell division, thereby preventing uncontrolled cell growth.

tundra
A terrestrial biome characterized by bitterly cold temperatures. Plant life is limited to dwarf woody shrubs, grasses, mosses, and lichens. Arctic tundra has permanently frozen subsoil (permafrost); alpine tundra, found at high elevations, lacks permafrost.

tunicate
One of a group of stationary invertebrate chordates.

U

umbilical cord
A structure containing arteries and veins that connects a developing embryo to the placenta of the mother.

unsaturated
Pertaining to fats and fatty acids of which hydrocarbon chains lack the maximum number of hydrogen atoms and therefore have one or more double covalent bonds. Because of their bent shape, unsaturated fats and fatty acids tend to stay liquid at room temperature.

uracil (U) (*yū'-ruh-sil*)
A single-ring nitrogenous base found in RNA.

ureter (*yū-rē'-ter* or *yū'-reh-ter*)
A duct that conveys urine from the kidney to the urinary bladder.

urethra (*yū-rē'-thruh*)
A duct that conveys urine from the urinary bladder to outside the body. In the male, the urethra also conveys semen out of the body during ejaculation.

urinary bladder
The pouch where urine is stored before elimination.

urine
Concentrated filtrate produced by the kidneys and excreted via the bladder.

uterus (*yū'-ter-us*)
In the reproductive system of a mammalian female, the organ where the development of young occurs; the womb.

V

vaccination (*vak'-suh-nā'-shun*)
A procedure that presents the immune system with a harmless version of a pathogen, thereby stimulating an adaptive defense when the pathogen itself is encountered.

vaccine (*vak-sēn'*)
A harmless version or piece of a pathogen (a disease-causing virus or organism) used to stimulate a host organism's immune system to mount a long-term defense against the pathogen.

vacuole (*vak'-ū-ōl*)
A membrane-enclosed sac, part of the endomembrane system of a eukaryotic cell, having diverse functions.

vagina (*vuh-jī'-nuh*)
Part of the female reproductive system between the uterus and the outside opening; the birth canal in mammals. The vagina accommodates the male's penis and receives sperm during copulation.

vas deferens (*vas def'-er-enz*)
(plural, **vasa deferentia**) Part of the male reproductive system that conveys sperm away from the testis; the sperm duct; in humans, the tube that conveys sperm between the epididymis and the common duct that leads to the urethra.

vascular cambium
(*vas'-kyū-ler kam'-bē-um*)
In plants, a cylinder of meristem tissue found between the primary xylem and phloem. During secondary growth, the vascular cambium produces secondary xylem and phloem.

vascular tissue
Plant tissue consisting of cells joined into tubes that transport water and nutrients throughout the plant body.

Xylem and phloem make up vascular tissue.

vascular tissue system
A system formed by xylem and phloem throughout a plant, serving as a long-distance transport system for water and nutrients, respectively.

vasectomy (*vuh-sek'-tuh-mē*)
Surgical removal of a section of the two sperm ducts (vasa deferentia) to prevent sperm from reaching the urethra; a means of sterilization in the male.

vector
A piece of DNA, usually a plasmid or a viral genome, that is used to move genes from one cell to another.

vein
(1) In animals, a vessel that returns blood to the heart. (2) In plants, a vascular bundle in a leaf, composed of xylem and phloem.

ventricle (*ven'-truh-kul*)
A heart chamber that pumps blood out of the heart to the body or lungs via arteries.

venule (*ven'-yūl*)
A small vessel that conveys blood between a capillary bed and a vein.

vertebrate (*ver'-tuh-brāt*)
A chordate animal with a backbone. Vertebrates include lampreys, cartilaginous fishes, bony fishes, amphibians, reptiles (including birds), and mammals.

vessel element
A short, open-ended, water-conducting, supportive cell in plants. Chains of vessel elements or tracheids make up the water-conducting, supportive tubes in xylem.

vestigial structure
A structure of marginal, if any, importance to an organism. Vestigial structures are historical remnants of structures that had important functions in ancestors.

virus
A microscopic particle capable of infecting cells of living organisms and inserting its genetic material. Viruses have a very simple structure and are generally not considered to be alive because they do not display all of the characteristics associated with life.

vitamin
An organic nutrient that an organism requires in very small quantities.

Vitamins generally function as coenzymes.

vitreous humor (*vit'-rē-us hyū'-mer*)
A jellylike substance that fills the space behind the lens in the vertebrate eye and helps maintain the shape of the eye.

vocal cord
One of a pair of tissues in the larynx. Air rushing past the tensed vocal cords makes them vibrate, producing sounds.

vulva
The outer features of the female reproductive anatomy.

W

warning coloration
The bright color pattern, often yellow, red, or orange in combination with black, of animals that have effective chemical defenses.

water vascular system
In echinoderms, a radially arranged system of water-filled canals that branch into extensions called tube feet. The system provides movement and circulates water, facilitating gas exchange and waste disposal.

wavelength
The distance between crests of adjacent waves, such as those of the electromagnetic spectrum.

wetland
An ecosystem intermediate between an aquatic ecosystem and a terrestrial ecosystem. Wetland soil is saturated with water permanently or periodically.

white blood cell
A blood cell that functions in defending the body against infections; also called a leukocyte.

whole-genome shotgun method
A method for determining the DNA sequence of an entire genome by cutting it into small fragments, sequencing each fragment, and then placing the fragments in the proper order.

wild-type trait
The trait most commonly found in nature.

wood
Secondary xylem of a plant.

X

X chromosome inactivation
In female mammals, the inactivation of one X chromosome in each somatic cell. Once X inactivation occurs in a given cell (during embryonic development), all descendants of that cell will have the same copy of the X chromosome inactivated.

xylem (*zī'-lum*)
The portion of a plant's vascular system that provides support and conveys water and inorganic nutrients from the roots to the rest of the plant. Xylem consists mainly of vessel elements and/or tracheids, water-conducting cells.

xylem sap
The solution of inorganic nutrients conveyed in xylem tissue from a plant's roots to its shoots.

Z

zooplankton
In aquatic environments, free-floating animals, including many microscopic ones.

zygote (*zī'-gōt*)
The fertilized egg, which is diploid, that results from the union of haploid gametes (sperm and egg) during fertilization.

Index